Problem Solving Steps

1. Define the Problem

2. Develop a Solution

3. Refine the Solution

4. Code

5. Debug and Test

6. Complete the Documentation

7. Maintain the Solution

Program Documentation

Description of the Program

Algorithm Development

Program Listing

Sample Run(s)

Users' Manual

Procedure Syntax

```
PROCEDURE  ProcedureName;

    (*no IMPORT lists allowed in procedures *)

    declarations;
        (* CONSTants, TYPEs, VARiables, PROCEDUREs *)

    BEGIN

      executable statements;

    END ProcedureName;
```

Module Syntax

```
MODULE    ModuleName;
    (* Comments may appear anywhere except within identifier names. *)

    IMPORT lists;

    declarations;
        (* CONSTants, TYPEs, VARiables, PROCEDUREs *)

    BEGIN

      executable statements;

    END ModuleName.
```

Introducing Computer Science with Modula-2

Introducing Computer Science with Modula-2

R. Kenneth Walter
Weber State University

West Publishing Company

St. Paul   New York   Los Angeles   San Francisco

West's Commitment to the Environment

In 1906, West Publishing Company began recycling materials left over from the production of books. This began a tradition of efficient and responsible use of resources. Today, up to 95 percent of our legal books and 70 percent of our college texts are printed on recycled, acid-free stock. West also recycles nearly 22 million pounds of scrap paper annually—the equivalent of 181,717 trees. Since the 1960s, West has devised ways to capture and recycle waste inks, solvents, oils, and vapors created in the printing process. We also recycle plastics of all kinds, wood, glass, corrugated cardboard, and batteries, and have eliminated the use of styrofoam book packaging. We at West are proud of the longevity and the scope of our commitment to our environment.

Prepress, printing, and binding by West Publishing Company.
Designer: John Rokusek/Rokusek Design
Typesetter: Carlisle Communications
Artwork: Carlisle Communications
Cover Image: Katherine Townes

Library of Congress Cataloging in Publication Data

Walter, R. Kenneth.
    Introducing computer science with Modula-2 / R. Kenneth Walter.
      p.   cm.
    Includes index.
    ISBN 0–314–93387–5
    1. Computers.   2. Modula-2 (Computer program language)
3. Structured programming.   I. Title.
QA76.5.W2856   1992
005.13'3 — dc20   92–2529
                                                  CIP ∞

CONTENTS

Preface

Purpose

The major objectives of this book are to introduce, develop, and reinforce well-organized, structured problem solving skills, and to present the Modula-2 language as a powerful problem solving tool.

The book is designed for a CS1 course (and an introduction to CS2). Topics recommended by the Association for Computing Machinery form the content of the book. Modula-2 is the support language of choice, because it is powerful enough to be used for development work; yet its Pascal-like code is more readable than languages like C, and it is easy to learn as a first, structured language.

Students should be familiar with fundamental algebra, but no other prerequisites are assumed. A short Chapter 1 briefly presents computer literacy material for those who need that background. Large numbers of examples and exercises are drawn from everyday experience, business, and technical fields. The instructor may choose those which match students' experience or for a particular emphasis.

Distinctive Features of this Book

The book has some special features, which make it especially valuable for the study of introductory computer science and Modula-2 language.

Spiral Approach

A **flexible, spiral approach** is taken to present important topics. Students start to solve simple problems early with fundamental language concepts; then they learn and expand their inventory of tools as needed.

For example, Chapter 3 introduces top-down design and simple procedures, which students may use to practice good programming structure until they are ready for the formal details of procedures and parameters presented in Chapter 6. Chapter 2 presents the concept of modules, and by Chapter 9 students are creating their own modules. So that it can be used and practiced throughout the remainder of the course, recursion appears with examples and exercises in Chapter 9; however, if desired, the instructor may postpone discussing recursion. Chapters 4 through 7 intentionally handle iteration, giving primary emphasis to the WHILE structure so that students may become proficient with iterative solutions before they need post-test, midtest, and counting tools.

Complete Examples

Examples are kept as short as feasible while still illustrating the pertinent points. However, the length of examples and exercises must grow with the students' expertise in problem solving. Special care has been taken to insure that, with few exceptions, all examples end with complete, executable programs rather than confusing, frustrating segments of code.

Most examples and exercises simulate real-world applications. However, at this introductory level, especially in early chapters, some examples appear in greatly simplified form out of necessity. This allows students to learn and practice elementary concepts without being confused by details which can appear only later in a logical progression of topics.

The goal of the programming style presented in this book is to provide readable code without being unnecessarily wordy. Although more white space within the code would be desirable, it had to be limited in order to produce a finite length text with extensive, complete program examples. Students should be encouraged to write one program statement per line; however, economy of space has dictated sometimes that more than one statement appear on a single line, especially when those statements produce a single line of output or are otherwise logically related. One benefit of this style is that most of the coding examples are displayed in the book on one page or on two pages. Indentations are kept large enough to be easily recognized but small enough to allow several levels of structure to occur within the width of a printed page or an 80-column terminal display.

Emphasis on Formal Problem-Solving Techniques

Six **formal problem-solving steps** form the organization of virtually every example:

1. Define the Problem
2. Develop a Solution
3. Refine the Solution
4. Code
5. Debug and Test
6. Complete the Documentation

If students are to develop good problem solving habits, they must begin to use these techniques, even with the simplest exercises, and practice them repeatedly.

Focus on Problem Solving

Special sections at the end of most chapters discuss additional strategies for effective problem solving and demonstrate the application of these techniques in complete example problems. Some of the topics emphasized in these **Focus on Problem Solving** units include, for example:

Section 2.9   Debugging Techniques
Section 3.6   Stepwise Refinement and Structure Diagrams
Section 6.6   Local Modules
Section 9.5   Extended Practice with Recursion

End-of-Section Questions

There are over **300 questions at the end of chapter sections**, from which instructors can choose. Most of these require short answers, involve tracing through short code, and/or test students' grasp of semantics and syntax.

End-of-Chapter Exercises

The **274 exercises at chapter end** concentrate on using the Modula-2 language to solve problems. Many of these exercises which have lengthy solutions are presented in modular steps and/or contain hints to assist the students in developing software engineering skills. Some are intentionally quite challenging.

About one third of those exercises indicate the name of a file where existing code is found and ask students to modify or complete an example program. All exercises are keyed to the chapter section which discusses the techniques applicable to their solution.

Pseudocode and Charts

More than **200 illustrations** are included to enhance understanding of problems and their solutions. Many of these are structure charts, tables, and program listings which are designed to help students learn good problem solving techniques. Pseudocode is emphasized. However, students are introduced to flowcharts as well. Many software engineers are returning to flowcharts because of their clarity in developing and testing software, and Computer Aided Software Engineering (CASE) tools are making charts easier to produce and maintain.

Bit of Background Notes

To make the study of computer science even more rewarding, forty-seven notes called *A Bit of Background* are carefully placed throughout the book. These notes supplement the technical material with historical, biographical, and other interesting factual asides.

☐ Appendices

Six Appendices are packed with valuable, important resource material.

External Modules

One appendix contains listings of the standard DEFINITION modules which are Modula-2 standards. Another includes both **DEFINITION and IMPLEMENTA-TION modules** for Strings, character-oriented graphics, fixed fomat REAL number display, and a random number generator, as well as procedures for manipulating stacks, queues, and linked lists. These provide a fixed point of reference for discussing topics where various compilers differ in implementation. The treatment of such topics within the book contains reminders that the students' Modula-2 compilers may have modules which handle things differently, and that they should become acquainted with their compiler manuals. Otherwise, the book handles problem solving and the Modula-2 language concepts generically, as much as possible avoiding practices which pertain only to a particular computer or compiler.

Procedures, Functions, and Answers

Three of the Appendices are organized for **quick reference.** They describe Modula-2 features, procedures, and functions. An introduction to binary number and character representations is presented, and answers to one or two exercises from each chapter illustrate possible solutions to some of the problems.

Syntax, Comparison of Modula-2 with Pascal

Although **syntax diagrams** are not used throughout the book, an appendix describes and displays a complete collection of those diagrams for Modula-2. For the benefit of those who wish to make a transition from one language to the other, this appendix also **compares the structure of standard Pascal with Modula-2.**

☐ Content

The book follows a logical order of topics to help the students progress from basic literacy to advanced problem solving using Modula-2 constructs. However, given some constraints, instructors may choose the order and range of topics for courses of different length and emphasis. **A minimal course** should include at least the following material in order:

Chapter 2, Problem Solving (Sections 1–7, 9) introduces problem solving techniques and how to use the computer.

Chapter 3, Variables, Types, and Operations (Sections 1–4) acquaint students with the fundamental features of Modula-2 and helps them start building programs.

Chapter 4, Selection and Iteration (Sections 1–2) introduce simple selection and interaction concepts.

Chapter 5, Character Variables (Sections 1–3) allows students to begin manipulating characters.

Chapter 6, Procedures, Functions, and Parameters (Sections 1–5) provide a solid foundation in procedure management.

Chapter 7, Multiple Selection (Sections 1–3, 5) expands upon selection structures.

Chapter 8, More Iteration Structures (Section 2–4) extends iteration capability.

Chapter 9, Problem Solving Techniques (Section 1) allows students to create and use external modules.

Chapter 10, Arrays (Sections 1–4, 7) introduces array handling and a linear search. The instructor may chose which sorting algorithm(s) to discuss.

Chapter 13, Records (Sections 1–3) acquaints the student with concepts of record handling.

Chapter 16, Pointers and Dynamic Structures (Sections 1–2) introduce pointer concepts and applies pointers to create dynamic stacks. RPN arithmetic could be skipped in a minimal course.

Other topics which may be covered in a different order, if desired, or skipped, depending upon the course emphasis are:

Chapter 1, Computer Fundamentals is intended as an introduction to, but not a comprehensive coverage of, computer literacy topics.

Chapter 3, (Section 5, Redirection of I/O) may be needed early by students on many systems to save and produce hardcopy of test runs.

Chapter 4, (Sections 3–4) covers style, invariants, and debugging techniques.

Chapter 5, (Sections 4–5) applies the Terminal module when I/O is redirected and develops a Tab function.

Chapter 6, (Sections 6–7) introduces local modules, which some instructors emphasize early and others may postpone until much later, and shows how to use drivers and stubs.

Chapter 7, (Section 4) covers decision trees and tables.

Chapter 8, (Sections 5–6) focuses on nested iterations and on deciding which iterative structure to use.

Chapter 9, (Sections 2–5) discusses random numbers and recursion.

Chapter 10, (Sections 5–6) extends array concepts with multidimensions and recursion.

Chapter 11, Data Types, Strings, and Enumeration develops a Strings module, and allows users to define and apply enumeration data types.

Chapter 12, More Graphs, Types, Search, and Sort extends character-oriented graphics and introduces procedure types, the binary search, and the Quicksort.

Chapter 13, (Section 4) extends record handling to include variant parts.

Chapter 14, Data Files extends file handling, using the FileSystem module, and introduces binary and random access files.

Chapter 15, Sets instructs the student in set handling concepts.

Chapter 16, (Sections 3–6) develops a Dynamic data structures module (with stacks, queues, and linked lists) and introduces binary trees and opaque data types.

Chapter 17, SYSTEM, Coroutines, and Special Features prepares students to handle advanced features of Modula-2 and to manage coroutines and processes.

Supplements

An instructor's manual expands upon the outline presented above for alternative approaches, order of topics, and adjustments for quarter length, semester length, or longer courses. It includes answers to questions and exercises and will be accompanied by a diskette containing code for the exercise solutions.

Transparency masters of the figures are available with the instructor's manual.

A diskette, which contains source code for all examples in the book and those exercises with answers in Appendix F, is available to departments who adopt the book. This diskette also contains the source code for the Strings, Graphics, MyMath, Dynamic, RandGen, and FRealOut DEFINITION and IMPLEMENTATION modules from Appendix C.

Acknowledgments

I thank my colleagues in the Computer Science Department at Weber State University (Neil Sorensen, Charles Crittenden, David Wolford, David Hart, Ronald Peterson, Robert Capener, William Hoggan, and Greg Anderson) for testing the manuscript in classes and handling some of my duties while the book was being developed. Special recognition is due to John Gordon, who developed solutions to many of the exercises. I am also indebted to Dean Warren Hill and to Ginger Hauser for absorbing some of my administrative load, to Mary Ellen Jones for encouragement and professional secretarial support, and to hundreds of students who have suffered through versions of the manuscript used in their classes.

The assistance of the following reviewers has been critical in pointing out problems and suggesting improvements to polish the book and make it a valuable resource:

Shoshana Abel, San Francisco State University; Judy Boxler, Vancouver Community College; Lois Brady, California State Polytechnic University, San Luis Obispo; William E. Clark, Texas A & M University; Daniel J. Codespoti, University of South Carolina at Spartanburg; Daniel W. Cooke, University of South Carolina at Spartanburg; Ronald Curtis, State University of New York at Buffalo; Henry A. Etlinger, Rochester Institute of Technology; Rhonda Ficek, Moorhead State University; Robert G. Ford, State University of New York at Plattsburg; John C. Gaffrey, Moorhead State University; Peter H. Greene, Illinois Institute of Technology; James Hearne, Western Washington University; Michael Hennessy, University of Oregon; Reine Hilton, University of Montana; Ralph G. Hollingsworth, Muskingum College; David Hughes, Abilene Christian University; Richard Hunkler, Slippery Rock University of Pennsylvania; Larry Irwin, Ohio University; Peter Isaacson, University of Northern Colorado; Gregory Jones, Utah State University; Abraham Kandel, Florida State University; Hue McCoy, New Mexico State University; Mike Michaelson, Palomar College; Rayno Niemi, Rochester Institute of Technology; Jeff Parker, Sun Microsystems; Pasha A. Rostov, California State Polytechnic University, San Luis Obispo; Paul A. Sand, University of New Hampshire; Ernst Schuegraf, St. Francis Xavier University; Thiab R. Taha, University of Georgia.

I thank Springer-Verlag for permission to use Dr. Wirth's Modula-2 syntax diagrams from *Programming in Modula-2,* Fourth Edition, 1988.

My gratitude is extended to the staff of West Educational Publishing for their help, persistence, and patience, especially the sponsoring editor, Richard Mixter, his assistants Keith Dodson and Melanie Shouse, the production editor Nancy Roth, and the promotion manager Ellen Stanton.

Finally, I dearly appreciate my wife, Zora, for her understanding and support during the long, secluded hours spent on this book.

R. Kenneth Walter
Ogden, Utah

Introducing Computer Science with Modula-2

1

Computer Fundamentals

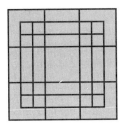

Chapter Outline

The goal of this book is to help you learn to use the computer to solve problems. You will need three sets of tools for this task; namely,

1. logical techniques for developing and managing problem solutions,
2. computer software, and
3. computer hardware.

The concepts and historical development of hardware and software are discussed briefly in this chapter. After that, we move right on into problem-solving methods and the details of using the Modula-2 language to implement your solutions.

In this chapter you will find a very short introduction to some concepts and terminology with which you should be familiar before you proceed. If you know about computers already—either through experience or from an introductory course—you may wish to read the chapter quickly to verify your knowledge and then proceed immediately to Chapter 2. If the information in this chapter sparks your interest, you will want to refer to one of the many computer literacy books on the market to enrich your understanding.

1.1 *Hardware*

Computer **hardware**, by definition, includes those physical entities that occupy space, have weight, or can be touched. Contrast this with **software**, which includes the intangible, but all-important, programs and problem solutions. In order for computer hardware to be useful it must have the minimum components illustrated in Figure 1–1.

The CPU

Numbers, alphabetic characters, and other signals that are entered into a digital computer from an input device (such as a keyboard) are called raw **data**. The **memory** of the computer consists of circuits that store the data as a collection of electronic patterns.

Figure 1–1
Computer Hardware

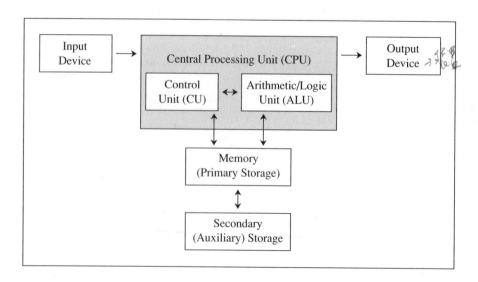

The **central processing unit (CPU)** of the computer takes raw data from memory and processes that data into hopefully useful information, which will either be stored in the computer's memory or transferred to an output device (such as a screen or printer), where it is accessible to the computer user.

Within the CPU, a **control unit (CU)** directs the activities of the computer by handling such operations as fetching signals from memory, which stores signals for use as instructions for performing various activities. Typically, when the control unit fetches an instruction, it stores it in a special memory location called a **register**, from where it can be retrieved quickly and manipulated easily. Then the control unit hands the task of executing the instruction to the **Arithmetic/Logic Unit (ALU)**. For example, to execute a command to Add, the CU could copy data from one location in memory into a special register called an **accumulator**, request the ALU to add data from a second memory location to the accumulator, then copy the sum of the numbers from the accumulator back into memory. The operations for the CU to complete a task constitute a **machine cycle**, and the time required to execute a machine cycle is a measure of the speed of the computer.

Primary Memory

The **primary memory** of a digital computer stores data and program instructions in binary code.

Bits and Bytes

Binary refers to a two-state system in which data are represented by 0s and 1s, called **binary digits or bits.** Bits lend themselves well to electronic systems, which are either ''on'' (often representing a 1) or ''off'' (representing 0). A sequence of 8 bits is typically referred to as a **byte**. The binary representation of even relatively small values extends to many digits, which are difficult for people to read, remember, and record correctly. For humans, numbers are easier to handle if they are short. Therefore, binary digits often are collected into groups of 3 and written in number-base 8, which is called **octal notation.** Other times they may be collected into groups of 4 and written in base 16, which is referred to as **hexadecimal** or **hex notation**. In hex, 6 additional symbols beyond 0 through 9 are needed for representing the numbers 10 through 15, and the letters A through F serve as these symbols. The first 18 binary numbers and their decimal, octal, and hexadecimal equivalents are shown in Figure 1–2.

A computer **word** is the number of bytes the computer can handle in one operation. For example, on a personal computer, the size of a word may be 2 or 4 bytes; on a larger machine, it may be 8 or more bytes. Memory is partitioned logically into areas that accommodate either a byte or a word. Each memory area is assigned an address (beginning with 0 and extending to the maximum number of bytes or words that can be stored). You may ask your computer to perform a memory **dump**; that is, to display a word or a collection of words stored at different addresses in memory. Typically, the computer will convert those words to octal or hex to make them easier for you to read. Thus, a 16-bit word

1 0 1 1 1 0 0 0 0 1 0 1 1 1 1 1 (binary)

would be divided into groups of 4 bits

1 0 1 1   1 0 0 0   0 1 0 1   1 1 1 1

Figure 1–2
Binary Numbers

Binary	Decimal	Octal	Hexidecimal
0 0 000	0	0	0
0 0 001	1	1	1
0 0 010	2	2	2
0 0 011	3	3	3
0 0 100	4	4	4
0 0 101	5	5	5
0 0 110	6	6	6
0 0 111	7	7	7
0 1 000	8	10	8
0 1 001	9	11	9
0 1 010	10	12	A
0 1 011	11	13	B
0 1 100	12	14	C
0 1 101	13	15	D
0 1 110	14	16	E
0 1 111	15	17	F
1 0 000	16	20	10
1 0 001	17	21	11

and the hex equivalent of each group written (from Figure 1–2) to display

B   8   5   F   (hex).

Alternatively, the word could be divided into groups of 3 bits

1   011   100   001   011   111

and the octal equivalent of each group written (from Figure 1–2), to display

1   3   4   1   3   7   (octal).

The decimal equivalent of this number is obtained by adding the powers of 2 represented by each digit, as illustrated in Figure 1–3. You can find more information in Appendix E about converting numbers represented by the decimal, binary, octal, and hexadecimal notation systems.

Note how each digit in a binary number is represented in decimal by 2 raised to its place value, where place values begin with 0. The largest binary number that can be represented by n digits would be n 1s, which in decimal is the sum

$$2^{n-1} + 2^{n-2} + 2^{n-3} + \ldots + 2^2 + 2^1 + 2^0,$$

or $2^n - 1$. For example, with 16 bits, you could represent $2^{16}(= 65,536)$ different binary numbers ranging from 0 to $2^{16} - 1$; that is, from 0 through 65,535.

$2^{10} (= 1024)$ bytes of memory are called a **kilobyte (KB)**. Suppose you wish a register to store the addresses of different bytes of memory. If the register can store 16 bits, for example, you can represent as many as 2^{16} different addresses. That computer would be said to have a capacity of addressing, in its registers,

2^{15}	2^{14}	2^{13}	2^{12}	2^{11}	2^{10}	2^9	2^8	2^7	2^6	2^5	2^4	2^3	2^2	2^1	2^0
32678	16384	8192	4096	2048	1024	512	256	128	64	32	16	8	4	2	1
1	0	1	1	1	0	0	0	0	1	0	1	1	1	1	1

```
1 0 1 1 1 0 0 0 0 1 0 1 1 1 1 (binary)

    =    1  x   32768

       + 0  x   16384

       + 1  x    8192

       + 1  x    4096

       + 1  x    2048

       + 0  x    1024

       + 0  x     512

       + 0  x     256

       + 0  x     128

       + 1  x      64

       + 0  x      32

       + 1  x      16

       + 1  x       8

       + 1  x       4

       + 1  x       2

       + 1  x       1

    = 32768 + 8192 + 4096 + 2048 + 64 + 16 + 8 + 4 + 2 + 1

    = 47199 (decimal)
```

Figure 1–3
Converting Binary to Decimal

$$2^{16} = 2^6 \times 2^{10} = 64 \times 2^{10} = 64(\text{KB})$$

of memory. Since 1024 is roughly 1000, 64 kilobytes is roughly 64,000 bytes, and exactly 64×1024 (= 65,536) bytes. Similarly, 2^{20} bytes (= 1,048,576 bytes) is a **megabyte (MB)** or roughly a million bytes; and 2^{30} bytes (= 1,073,741,824 bytes) is a **gigabyte (GB)** or roughly a thousand million bytes.

Example 1.1.1

a. How many bytes of memory could be directly addressed in a computer where the address registers can hold 24 bits?

b. What is the largest number that can be stored in any word in the computer if the words are only 8 bits long?

Solution

a. If the address register can contain 24 bits, then addresses range from 0 to $2^{24} - 1$. That is, there can be 2^{24} different addresses. $2^{24} = 2^4 \times 2^{20} = 16 \times 2^{20}$. Therefore, there can be 16 megabytes (16 MB $= 16 \times 1,048,576 = 16,777,216$ bytes) of memory.

b. In each computer word there are 8 bits, so numbers can range from 0 to $2^8 - 1$. Therefore, the largest number that could be stored in any word would be $2^8 - 1$ ($= 255$).

Alphanumeric Data

Much data processing is done with alphabetic characters rather than with numbers. For example, storing a person's name and address in the computer requires **alphanumeric** characters; that is, codes that can represent both alphabet letters and numerical digits. Numerous such codes have been developed during the past century. The most common code used for small computers now is the American Standard Code for Information Interchange (ASCII), which is tabulated in Appendix E. In standard ASCII, each character is represented by seven bits, so there are 2^7 ($=$ 128) different characters. The first 32 of these are called **control characters**. They are used to control data transmission and storage operations. Most of the remaining 96 are codes for the characters on your keyboard. Usually, a byte is reserved for storing an ASCII character. Many computers use an "extended" version of ASCII in which the eighth bit in a byte is used as part of the code and doubles the number of possible characters to 2^8 ($=$ 256). Otherwise, the available extra eighth bit is ignored, is used for error checking, or is used to represent graphics or other symbols needed for special situations.

You may encounter other codes, such as Extended Binary Coded Decimal Interchange Code (EBCDIC), which has been used traditionally for IBM mainframe and compatible computers. Tables of these other codes can be found in the respective system manuals.

RAM and ROM

Every computer contains primary memory of two fundamental types: **RAM** and **ROM.** RAM stands for **Random Access Memory** and is usually **volatile**, which means that what is recorded there disappears when the computer's power is turned off. Your programs and data will be stored in RAM while you are using the computer. The size of a computer memory is usually specified in terms of how many bytes of RAM are available to the user.

ROM, the acronym for **Read Only Memory**, contains fundamental instructions that cannot be lost or changed by the casual computer user. These instructions include those necessary for loading anything else into the machine when it is first turned on and any other instructions the manufacturer requires to be permanently accessible. ROM is **nonvolatile**; its contents are not lost when the power goes off.

Actually, most ROM is in the form of PROM (Programmable Read Only Memory), which is programmed permanently using a special computer. EPROM (Erasable Programmable Read Only Memory) is another version of ROM that can be erased with special equipment and then reprogrammed.

Secondary Storage

Because RAM in large quantities is still relatively expensive *and* volatile, it usually is not practical to store your programs and data permanently in primary memory. **Secondary** or **auxiliary storage** devices must be provided for that purpose. Although data have been stored on punched cards, paper tape, drums, and other media in the past, virtually all secondary storage is now done on magnetic tape, magnetic disk, or optical storage media.

Magnetic Disks and Tapes

The surfaces of magnetic tapes and disks are coated with a material that can be magnetized by a write head, and the stored magnetic field can be detected by a read head, much like the read and write heads on an audio or video tape player. Some large-capacity tapes have numerous read/write heads positioned across the width of the tape, which allows the magnetic fields representing an entire byte to be read or written all at once. Such tapes can store data at densities of thousands of **bytes per inch (bpi)** along the tape, and a single tape may store up to hundreds of megabytes. Figure 1–4a illustrates a typical format for data storage on magnetic tape.

On early personal computers, cassette tapes identical to those on which music is recorded were used for secondary storage. Such cassettes are slow and unreliable, however, and they are no longer used. Now there are a variety of high-quality cassettes containing tape on which data are stored at very high densities, and the tape streams past the read/write heads at high speed. Such **streaming tapes** commonly provide a critical **backup** capability; they are used to copy and save data in recoverable form in case the original data on large-capacity disks are accidentally lost or changed.

By nature, tapes are **sequential** storage media; that is, they allow data to be written or read in one sequential stream from beginning to end. Should you desire access to a block of data at the middle of a tape, you must scan all preceding data on the tape to find the block of interest. This is not unacceptable when most of the data is to be accessed at once, such as with a very short file or when reading an entire mailing list; but it is very inconvenient when only one piece of information is to be retrieved from a large file, such as when a single customer's account at a large bank is to be found.

To gain access to a single item of information quickly, a **direct access storage device (DASD)** must be used. The most popular DASD in recent years has been the magnetic disk. A **magnetic hard disk** consists of either a single rigid platter or several platters that spin together on a common spindle. A movable access arm positions the read/write heads over, but not quite touching, the recordable surfaces. Such a configuration is shown in Figure 1–4b. Other disk features shown in the figure are described on page 9.

Disk packs may be removable, as for handling large jobs such as the payroll for a corporation. Such tasks, which can occupy most of the computer's time and resources while they are run, are called **batch jobs**. More often, when many users share a single system's time, the disk packs remain fixed within the system and are

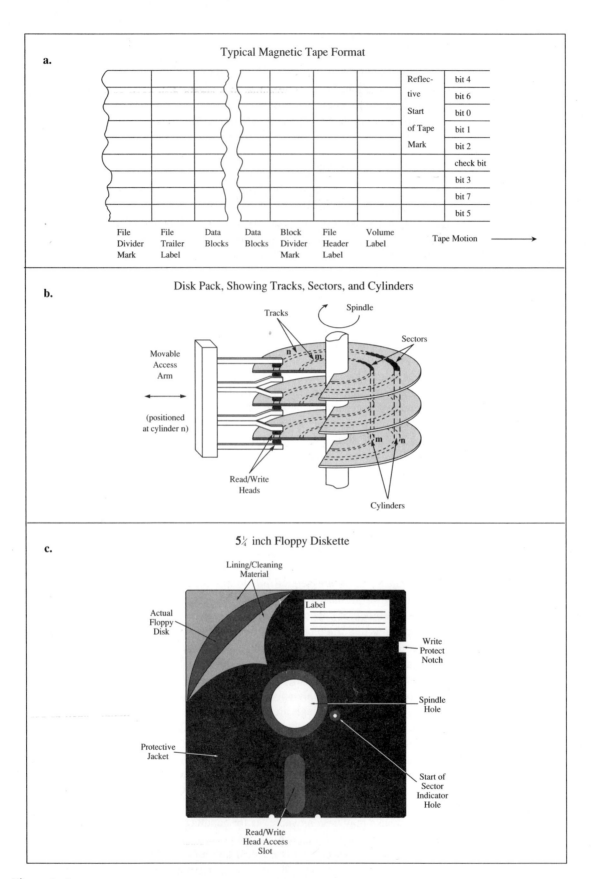

Figure 1–4

Secondary Storage Media **a.** A Typical Magnetic Tape Format **b.** A Disk Pack, Showing Tracks, Sectors, and Cylinders **c.** A $5\frac{1}{4}$-inch Floppy Diskette

not removed. It is for such fixed disks that high-speed backup media, such as streaming tapes, are needed. Capacities of a single disk pack on a large machine may run as high as a few gigabytes.

Removable disks on modern microcomputers often take the form of flexible **floppy diskettes**. Currently, the most popular sizes for these are 5¼ inches and 3½ inches in diameter, and their capacities typically range from 160 kilobytes to 1.5 megabytes or more. Sophisticated flexible disk handling systems, such as the Bernoulli box,* can store up to 100 megabytes on a single removable disk. The construction of a typical floppy diskette is shown in Figure 1–4c.

Optical Storage

Optical media, in which capacities on a single removable diskette a few inches in diameter may be several gigabytes, are becoming increasingly popular. On this medium, data is stored by changing the reflective properties of a surface onto which laser light is directed. A single removable diskette similar or identical to a video compact disk is called a **CD ROM**. Until recently, optical media were limited to nonerasable Write Once, Read Many times (WORM) techniques. They were appropriate for storing encyclopedias, law libraries, permanent archives, and the like. Now, erasable methods allow the user to record, erase, and reuse an optical disk in much the same manner as a very high capacity magnetic disk. Some computers, such as the NeXT† machine, have adopted the CD ROM as their major secondary storage device.

Physical and Logical Data Units

On virtually any type of DASD, the surface is divided into concentric **tracks**, which in turn are subdivided into **sectors**, as illustrated in Figure 1-4b. A **cylinder** of a multiple-platter disk pack is the set of tracks that can be accessed at one position of the access arm. For example, cylinder 5 would consist of every track number 5 in the collection of disks.

When a disk is **formatted** for a particular device, special bit codes are recorded on the disk so that the particular device that uses the disk can find the beginning of each cylinder, track, and sector. At least one track will be reserved for the directory, which stores information about the names of the blocks of data stored on the disk, their track and sector locations, and their size (in bytes or sectors). The minimum distance between tracks, and between bits stored on a track, determines the density of the data and the total capacity of the medium. As technology improves, these distances become smaller, and the capacities become correspondingly greater.

The **physical description** of data storage is in terms of bits, bytes, sectors, tracks, cylinders, and blocks. On the other hand, a **logical description** of data organization is the way people prefer to categorize the data. Logically, the smallest data unit is a single **character**. Characters are combined into **fields**—such as perhaps name, social security number, and age. Related fields are collected into **records.** For example, the record for one student may contain fields describing his or her name, age, address, grade point average, and so on. Finally, related records are combined into data **files**, which, in the student example, might contain the records of all of the students in a particular class. Much more will be said about records and files later in the book.

*Bernoulli box is a registered trademark of IOMEGA Corportion.
†NeXT is a registered trademark of NeXT Computer, Inc.

☐ Input and Output

Devices for providing computer **input and output (I/O)** take many forms.

Secondary Storage

Obviously, secondary storage media may receive data from the computer as well as pass data on to memory. Thus, secondary storage devices act as both input and output peripherals to the computer.

CRT Monitors

The most common input device is the keyboard, with which most users enter data directly into the computer. The most common output device is the display screen, also called a **Cathode Ray Tube (CRT)** or monitor. A combination of keyboard and screen may be called a **Video Display Terminal (VDT).**

The least expensive monitors are **monochrome** (single-color) displays designed to handle only alphanumeric characters. More sophisticated terminals, capable of handling graphics (that is, diagrams, pictures, etc.) begin in the low price range with a monochrome, low-resolution screen. The resolution of a monitor is determined by the number of dots, called picture elements or **pixels**, that can be manipulated by the graphics programs and hardware. As the complexity of graphics terminals increases, hundreds of colors appear on the screen, and the resolution increases from the display of a few hundred addressable pixels wide by a few hundred high, to thousands in each dimension. Of course, as the sophistication of the terminal increases, its price does also and so must the memory capacity, speed, and cost of the graphics hardware within the computer.

Printers

Printers are almost as popular as CRTs for output. Printers are said to produce **hardcopy** of computer output and vary considerably in price and complexity. A **dot matrix** printer produces characters by an array of pins striking a ribbon. The more pins within the print head, the better is the character quality—and the more expensive the printer. Very high speed hardcopy has been produced traditionally by line printers, in which characters on a band, chain, or drum are pushed against a ribbon by hammers to produce an entire line of output at once. These devices were found most often in high-production data processing environments. **Daisy wheel** printers, after which many electronic typewriters have been patterned, print letter-quality characters by means of a hammer striking individual letters that are at the ends of "petals" on a rotatable plastic or metal disk. Dot matrix, daisy wheel, and traditional line printers are called **impact** devices, because the print mechanism actually impacts the paper. These printers are being replaced by quieter, more versatile, nonimpact peripherals.

Ink jet printers, which spray ink at the paper through a matrix of tiny nozzles, are a relatively low cost alternative to impact equipment. Some of these feature multiple sets of nozzles by which many different colors of ink can be sprayed to produce multicolor documents. Laser printers use a beam of light to sensitize a drum, which then attracts the ink toner to the page to form images. Their versatility, speed, and nearly print-shop character quality and graphics make laser printers the best choice for many environments.

Other I/O Devices

Other input and output peripherals expand the computer's versatility. Special terminals in which a wand or reader scans and recognizes optically readable characters or coded bars are seen in most department stores and supermarkets.

A **mouse** is a small boxlike device about 2 inches wide by 4 inches long, with one or more pushbuttons. As the mouse is moved around on the desktop, the cursor or pointer on the screen moves accordingly. Pressing, or "clicking," one of the mouse buttons allows the user to select a menu item pointed to on the screen. The mouse is a user-friendly input device of choice for many computer owners. The joystick and the trackball function much like the mouse and are especially popular for playing video games and entering graphics. **Touch-sensitive** CRT screens allow the user simply to touch the desired menu item on the screen to make a selection.

Speech-recognition and **voice-synthesis** devices allow the computer to accept spoken commands and to issue verbal instructions. Although voice techniques are improving, considerable research and development still are needed to create machines that can recognize everyone's speech without extensive training for the computer and the speaker. At this stage of evolution, computers emulate some people, those who talk better than they listen.

1.2   *The Hardware Generations*

Mechanical computing aids have been available for a long time. The two-thousand-year-old abacus, on which numbers are represented by rows of beads, and the slide rule based upon John Napier's invention of logarithms early in the seventeeth century, were the primary, affordable calculating tools even until the mid 1970s. Blaise Pascal had invented a mechanical calculator by 1643. However, the first recorded design of a "computer" (complete with processor, storage, and I/O components) was Charles Babbage's attempt to create his Difference Engine, in 1822.

Vacuum Tubes

The first generation of electronic digital computer hardware was conceived at Iowa State University in 1937 by Dr. John Atanasoff. He envisioned a vacuum tube machine that would process computations of binary numbers. With graduate student Clifford Berry, Atanasoff completed the Atanasoff–Berry Computer (ABC) in 1939 at a cost of $650. The first commercial vacuum tube computer, the UNIVAC I, was sold to the U.S. Census Bureau in 1951. This now-primitive technology had its problems. Tubes required considerable space and power and generated a lot of heat. Since tubes burned out frequently, computers with large numbers of them had a mean time between failures of only a few hours at best. The apocryphal first **bug** in a computer was literally a dead bug. A moth, attracted to a computer's mechanical relay switch by the heat, is said to have been removed by Grace Hopper in 1947. Since that time, solving problems in hardware or software has been referred to as **debugging**.

Transistors

In the late 1950s the transistor, developed at Bell Laboratories, became the basis of a second generation of electronic computers. Transistors replaced vacuum tubes one

A Bit of Background

Admiral Grace Hopper, USN

Grace Hopper received a Ph.D. degree from Yale University and joined the Naval Reserve in 1943. In her assignment to the Bureau of Ordinance Computation Project at Harvard she programmed the Mark I, the first large-scale, electromechanical, digital computer. Later she applied her outstanding talents in mathematics as senior programmer of the UNIVAC I.

Commodore Hopper became a pioneer in the development of computer languages and served on the Conference of Data System Languages (CODASYL) committee. She helped develop COBOL and is credited with producing the first practical program in that language. In 1959 she invented a COBOL compiler, which allowed programs written in a standardized language to be transported between different computers for the first time.

Admiral Hopper remained a colorful figure in the computing community after her retirement from active duty in the U. S. Navy in August 1986 at the age of 79.

for one, but they were much smaller (about the size of a pencil eraser), drew much less power, were faster, and were considerably more reliable than tubes. Most transistor machines were large mainframes, costing a million dollars or more. Many still were operated in an **open shop** environment, where programmers learned how to operate the computer, as well as how to program it, and then scheduled time to run their own programs.

Integrated Circuits

In the 1960s, a third step toward compact, reliable computer technology was taken when techniques were perfected for placing the equivalent of several transistor circuits on a single **integrated circuit (IC)** chip. By 1965, Digital Equipment Corporation had announced its DEC PDP–8, which was deemed a **minicomputer** because, rather than occupying an entire room, it could sit on top of a large desk. About the same time, IBM unveiled its IC-based mainframes. The push to send a human to the moon before 1970 served to bring about tremendous strides in circuit miniaturization and capability.

VLSI and Microprocessors

In 1971, Intel Corporation introduced the **microprocessor** chip to the market. It was based on **Large-Scale Integration (LSI)** technology, by which more than 15,000 circuit elements could be placed on a single chip smaller than a fingernail. The microprocessor chip contained all of the logic capability of a computer and formed the basis of fourth-generation **microcomputers**. The earliest microcomputer was available in kit form from Altair Corporation in 1974, but by the late 1970s completely assembled machines with keyboard, monitor, and secondary storage were being sold by Apple, Commodore, and Radio Shack. Though it was a relative latecomer to the microcomputer business, IBM set a standard with the introduction of its **personal computer** in the early 1980s. Today, **Very Large Scale Integration (VLSI)** places millions of circuits on a single chip, and recent microcomputers have more computing power and flexibility than could have been dreamed about for the mainframes of the 1960s.

Parallel Processing

The fifth generation of computer hardware is blossoming now with ever more powerful machines developed primarily in the United States and Japan. This gen- eration is characterized by multiple processors—perhaps ultimately hundreds of processor units in one machine— that are capable of handling massive amounts of data in simultaneous operations. These parallel-architecture machines are bringing about another revolution in computer applications.

1.3 *Computer Theory and Software*

Years before the first practical electronic computers were manufactured, a number of theorists devoted their talents to determining what could be done with computing machines and how they should operate. The first person to earn a lasting reputation as a programmer was Ada Augusta Byron, who developed techniques for solving problems with Babbage's Difference Engine in the early 1830s.

Turing Theory

In the 1930s and 1940s, Alan Turing, Alonzo Church, and Emil Post made major contributions to the design of what they envisioned as a "universal algorithm machine," a computer that could solve any problem—in theory at least. They developed the concepts of how such a machine should work and what it could do, and they discovered that there are some types of problems that computers would not be able to solve. Turing's theory of how data should be manipulated in a computing machine provided the basis for modern computer theory, the architecture of com- puters, and the structure of computer languages. These achievements are especially impressive because these men did most of their work on paper before the invention of the electronic computer itself.

Stored Programs

Early general-purpose machines of the 1940s and 1950s were programmed by rewiring the computer. The programmer had to locate contacts to the computer's circuits behind large plugboards and then to connect wires between the appropriate holes on the plugboard to create a program. This process was not only inconvenient; it created a nest of wires, and it was extremely difficult to avoid errors. In 1945, John von Neumann wrote a paper in which he described a technique for writing a sequence of instructions to be stored in memory, along with the data. These instructions, to be executed in order, were called a *computer program*. Though John Mauchly, J. Presper Eckert, and others had contributed to the idea, von Neumann was credited with developing the concept of the stored program, which made modern computing possible.

System Software

Two logical categories of computer programs are system software and application software. **Application software** consists of those programs written to perform particular tasks required by the users. Most of the examples in this book would be called application software. **System software** is the collection of programs that must be readily available to any computer system in order for it to operate at all.

In the early computer environment, the user had to load a few system instructions by hand—using rows of binary switches on a front panel—to prepare the computer to do anything at all. Those initial, hand-entered commands were said to **boot** the computer, an expression derived from "pulling oneself up by the bootstraps." Today the so-called **bootstrap loader** is found in ROM and is a permanent, automatically executed component of the computer's system software. Before the 1960s, if you wanted to use a computer, it was not uncommon to have to borrow from colleagues who regularly used the machine decks of punched cards containing the programs necessary for reading from and writing to the I/O devices that you intended to use. Similarly, you were required to find the code that would translate your application program to the computer's internal machine language so that it could be executed. Typically, most of these **utilities** are now kept on either a hard disk or a floppy diskette and are booted into the computer either automatically when the system is powered up or on command by the user.

Various acronyms are used by different manufacturers for the collection of system utilities called the **operating system**. Often, the system software name ends with *OS* or *DOS* (for Disk Operating System). Additional tasks handled by modern operating systems include memory, I/O, and secondary storage management. Many systems handle very large programs, as well as multiple users concurrently, by dividing programs into pages or segments that are moved between disk and memory as needed. Thus the operating system creates a **virtual memory**, which appears to be as large as necessary to handle any job; and a **time-sharing** environment is produced which gives each users the impression that the computer and peripherals are theirs alone.

Most system operations are **transparent** to the user; that is, they take place internally without user intervention. However, some OS commands are provided intentionally for you to interact directly with the system. The most common of these commands are those that allow the handling of data files on a disk. Some of these are listed in Figure 1–5 by the names with which they are implemented in the popular MS-DOS.*

---

*MS-DOS is a registered trademark of Microsoft Corporation.

This list is intended only to illustrate types of utilities that may be available. Command names are those used in MS-DOS. Consult the operating system manual for your installation to determine the exact form of the commands and the conventions for naming files and directories.

```
DIR
     Displays the directory of all files available.

ERASE OR DELETE FileName(s)
     Erases a specified file or collection of files.

COPY Source Destination
     Makes a copy of the Source file at the Destination.

TYPE FileName
     Displays the content of the specified file to the monitor.

PRINT FileName
     Copies the content of the specified file to the printer.

A:  or   B:  or   C:, etc.
     Changes the currently accessed disk area to the one indicated.
```

Some single-key-initiated operating system commands that may be available:

```
CTRL Break   or   CTRL Z   or   CTRL C
     Forces a permanent halt to the currently executing operation.

CTRL S
     Forces a temporary suspension of the current operation (often used to suspend
     output temporarily).

CTRL P
     Resume the current operation, recovers from CTRL S.
```

Figure 1−5
Type of Operating System Utilities Commonly Accessible to the User

1.4 *Programming Languages*

Techniques of computer programming have developed parallel with the design of computer hardware, known as computer architecture.

Machine Language

If you were to examine the code used to program the earliest computers, or if you managed to have your present machine display instructions in the form in which they actually are executed, you would see a sequence of binary numbers such as this:

```
10101101 000000010000 000000010001
11100000 011011110010 010011000011
10001011 010000101001 010000101010
.  .  .  .
```

These represent **machine language** instructions, the **object code** to which all programs must be translated before the computer can execute them. Every type of computer architecture recognizes a distinct set of machine language instructions. As you can imagine, programming first-generation computers in machine language was tedious and frustrating.

Usually, the leftmost bits in machine language code specify which operation is to be performed. This is called the instruction's **Opcode**. The remaining bits specify the **Operands**, namely the memory addresses upon which the instruction is to operate. If, on a particular machine, the 8-bit opcode 10101101 signified ADD, the sequence 11100000 meant MOVE, and the operands were 12-bit binary addresses, then the first two instructions in the sequence above would be interpreted as shown in Figure 1–6.

Assembly Language

The next obvious step in the development of languages was to write the machine language instructions in terms of mnemonic opcodes and readable addresses, as in

```
ADD    16,   17
MOVE 1778, 1219
```

(Refer to Figure 1-6 here also.) This symbolic form is called **assembly language**; and programs called **assemblers** allow the computer to translate assembly language instructions into corresponding machine language.

High-Level Languages

As faster computers were built and memory capacity grew, it became possible for programmers to solve their problems in **high-level languages**, in which the codes look more like the solutions to the problems. Using high-level languages, programmers do not need to worry about the details of the machine language for their particular computers. The first widely accepted high-level language, FORTRAN, was introduced by IBM in 1954, and updated versions are used today. (*FORTRAN* stands for FORmula TRANslator.) In its latest version, the instructions to perform an addition may look like this:

```
A  =   5.3
B  =  19.2
SUM  = A + B
PRINT  *, SUM
```

A program written in a high-level language such as FORTRAN is called a **source code**. A computer program that translates the source code to machine language is called a **compiler**.

Close on the heels of FORTRAN, numerous other high-level languages emerged, including the COmmon Business Oriented Language (COBOL), a simplified instructional language called BASIC, and languages designed for specific applications, such as APL, PL/I, and Lisp.

As programs became longer and more complex, it became apparent that some techniques and rules would have to be developed for handling sophisticated problems. Otherwise, one person's convoluted code would not be understandable to

Figure 1–6
An Interpretation of
Machine Language
Instructions

```
    Opcode              Operand 1              Operand 2

  1010 1101        0000 0001 0000        0000 0001 0001

    ADD                  16                     17


Add the content of memory location 16 to that of location 17.
```

```
    Opcode              Operand 1              Operand 2

  1110 0000        0110 1111 0010        0100 1100  0011

    MOVE                1778                   1219


Copy the content of memory location  1778  into location  1219.
```

anyone else, and some large programs might never be completely debugged. The techniques of **structured programming** were created in the mid 1960s, motivated in part by the controversial writings of software expert Edsger Dijkstra and developed by C. Bohm, G. Jacopini, and many others who followed. Structured programming means essentially that every program should be written in terms of a few basic structures that can be combined in readable form. These structures are discussed in detail in the next chapter.

A new family of high-level languages has been created that encourage and enforce the use of structured problem-solving concepts. The most popular members of this family are **Pascal** (a good language for introducing structured programming), **Modula-2** (a further development and improvement upon Pascal), **C** (a very powerful, compact language), and **Ada** (a highly structured language adopted by the U.S. Department of Defense and supported in education and industry).

☐ Why Modula-2?

The goal of this book is to help you become a good problem solver using structured techniques. In 1971 Dr. Niklaus Wirth developed a programming language called Pascal, which provided readable, easy-to-use code for systematic, structured problem solving. By 1978 Dr. Wirth had expanded upon Pascal to allow programs to be divided into units, called **modules**, which give the programmer greater power and flexibility while retaining the simplicity and readability of Pascal. The current version of this new language is called Modula-2 and it is the one you will use throughout this book to implement your problem solutions.

☐ Software Engineering

The extension of structured programming to a comprehensive method of solving problems in general is called **software engineering**. Even desktop machines in the new generation of computers address megabytes or gigabytes of memory and operate at speeds orders-of-magnitude faster than older mainframes. At the same time, new languages and **Computer-Aided Software Engineering (CASE)** tools have emerged. These allow you to perform many, many problem-solving tasks— from problem conception, to the diagrams and structures used in design and development, to coding, testing, and documentation—all with the aid of the computer. **Object-Oriented Programming Systems (OOPS)**, aided by software packages called **expert systems**, guide you through problem solutions and permit you to specify your problem in whatever form is most comfortable for you. Many of the details of converting your problem solution into the form required by the computer will soon be handled automatically.

Nevertheless, the ability to solve problems and to convert problem solutions to computer code are fundamental skills for a computer scientist. People who understand software engineering and can design and manipulate CASE tools, OOPS languages, expert systems, and the total computer environment will continue to be in demand by employers and will contribute significantly to the progress of society. Mastering the techniques presented in this book will give you a start in the right direction.

1.5   *Summary*

Each chapter in this book concludes with a summary that lists and reviews the concepts discussed in the chapter. You may wish to read each summary carefully, make sure you understand the terms presented, and reexamine the sections of the chapter that discuss those topics with which you do not feel comfortable.

Hardware   The hardware components of a computer include input, processing, output, memory, and storage devices and media.

CPU, CU, ALU   The central processing unit (CPU) incorporates a control unit (CU) and an arithmetic/logic unit (ALU), which together operate in a cycle to perform processing operations.

Memory   Primary memory RAM and ROM chips store data in bits and bytes, which can be interpreted as binary numbers, alphanumeric character codes, instructions, or other data.

Secondary Storage   Secondary storage allows relatively permanent storage of data on tapes, disks, or optical media. Tapes must be accessed sequentially; disks and optical devices form direct access media.

I/O   Popular input and output (I/O) peripherals include keyboards, monitors, and printers, with a broad range of capability and cost.

Electronic Computers   The development of the electronic computer has progressed from large, unreliable, vacuum-tube-based mainframes of the 1940s to the powerful VLSI-based desktop machines of today.

Computer Theory   Much of the theory of computing was developed by Turing and others before the first electronic digital computers were constructed. However, problem solving theory and software engineering techniques have developed from the use of machine language to the popular procedure-oriented languages of today such as Modula-2. The creation of CASE tools, OOPS languages, and expert systems for the new generation of high-speed computers with large memories continues to push computer scientists into sophisticated techniques for solving the problems of the future.

2

Problem Solving

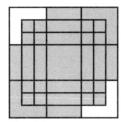

Chapter Outline

In this chapter and those to follow, techniques are developed that will help you use the computer to solve complex problems. You probably could write computer solutions for many of the exercises in this book without paying much attention to a formal problem solving approach. You may even feel that the use of formal techniques is a waste of time for something so simple. Be assured, however, that the effort spent learning to apply appropriate methods to the easier tasks will give you the tools to solve future important, difficult problems that you might not otherwise be able to handle at all.

2.1   *Overview of Problem Solving*

No matter what field of work you choose or what your lifestyle may be, you will have to solve problems. Many of these, such as adding up the change in your pocket, can be solved quickly and easily. Others, such as riding a bicycle, require some practice but soon become automatic. Still others require considerable planning and forethought if the solution is to be appropriate and efficient. For example, sending a satellite into orbit or creating an inventory management system for a computer store are problems for which trial-and-error solutions could prove expensive and disastrous.

The Seven Steps in Solving a Problem

There are seven critical steps in problem solving, namely,

1. **Define the Problem.**   What should the solution of the problem accomplish?
2. **Develop a Solution.**   What output is requested? What data is available for input? What approach should be taken to convert the available input to the desired output?
3. **Refine the Solution.**   Refine your understanding of how to solve the problem. Define the processes necessary to achieve the solution.
4. **Code.**   Write the solution in complete, executable computer code.
5. **Debug and Test.**   Make certain that the program works and produces meaningful results.
6. **Complete the Documentation.**   Collect the problem description, program design, computer code, sample test runs, and users' guide to support those who need to use your solution.
7. **Maintain the Solution.**   Be prepared to keep the code up to date, to make changes when necessary, and to expand or modify the solution so that it will continue to meet users' needs.

In business and industry, the useful lifetime of a solution may extend for years or decades. Computer scientists spend much of their time maintaining those solutions. The examples and exercises in this book are designed to help you develop expertise in the first six of the problem solving steps. You will learn how to maintain solutions in your future study of software engineering.

The solutions to two simple problems are presented in this chapter, with their Modula-2 code, as is a discussion of how to get started on your computer.

2.2   *Define the Problem*

Countless hours have been spent writing computer programs that have never been used because the programmer/analyst did not produce what the user needed. The first step in solving any problem is to determine what information is to be found. Before proceeding to solve a problem on the computer you must be absolutely certain that you understand exactly what the program or system is supposed to accomplish. This is often accomplished through interviews with the prospective users, careful analysis of the task, and production of specification documents.

Example 2.2.1

(Step 1, Define the problem)   Suppose that this mail message appears on the terminal at your desk:

> Write a program that gives the information
> about circles. Complete by tomorrow.
>
> —Management

It would be a major mistake to begin writing a program immediately so as to get it finished on time. Your first step should be to contact "Management" to define exactly what the program should produce. Suppose that you do this and that you learn what they really want is a program that will calculate and print the area of a circle when given the radius. With the problem defined, you may proceed.

Example 2.2.2

(Step 1, Define the problem)   The assigned task is to find selling prices for new items of inventory. First you must define the problem by determining that the cost and percentage markup for each item will be given. Then you are able to write a program that will calculate and print the selling prices.

Question 2.2

A note from your supervisor, Ms. J. Williams, says:

> Solve our payroll deduction problems.
>
> —J. Williams

   a. What should be your first task?
   b. How would you accomplish this task?
   c. How long would you expect this task to take, assuming everyone cooperates?

2.3   *Develop a Solution*

Now that you know what is to be determined, you are ready to develop solutions to the problems. An outline of the step-by-step solution to a problem is called an **algorithm.**

A Bit of Background

Al-Khowarizmi

One of the first great mathematicians was Mohammed ibn Musa al-Khowarizmi, who wrote a treatise in about A.D. 825 called *Ilm al-jabr wa'l muqabalah* ("the science of reduction and calculation"). The word *algorism* or *algorithm* is derived from al-Khowarizmi's name, and our word *algebra* is derived from *al-jabr* in the title of his work.

☐ Determine Output, Input, and Process

The first step in developing a computer algorithm is to decide what the output should be and where it is to appear. Then you determine the source of the input data and what it will look like. After having determined the output requirements and the nature of the input, you can write the steps necessary to process the input and produce the output.

(The asterisk (*) is used in most programming languages to represent multiplication and it will be used in this book during problem development as well.)

Example 2.3.1

(Step 2, Develop a solution)   In the problem to determine the area of a circle, *Output* is the Area, to be printed on the terminal screen. *Input* is the Radius that "Management" has said will be entered by the user at the keyboard. The *process* for finding the Area of a circle when given the Radius is stated by the formula Area = PI * Radius * Radius, where PI equals approximately 3.14159.

Example 2.3.2

(Step 2, Develop a solution)   The problem is to determine selling price (called SellPrice) from cost (called PurchasePrice) and markup (called Markup). *Output* will be a screen display of the values of PurchasePrice, Markup, and SellPrice under an appropriate heading. *Input* will be PurchasePrice and Markup (as a percent of PurchasePrice). Both of these will be entered from the keyboard. The *process* for obtaining the output information, given the input data, is given by the formula

```
SellPrice = PurchasePrice + (Markup * PurchasePrice)
```

Questions 2.3

1. Number these steps toward developing a problem solution in the order in which they normally should be performed (1, 2, 3).
   - _3_ Determine the process for converting input to output.
   - _2_ Determine what input is needed and available.
   - _1_ Determine what output is desired and how it should appear.
2. Assume the task is to determine and report each employee's payroll deductions and then to print the employee paychecks.
   a. What would be the desired outputs, and on which media should they appear?
   b. What input would be needed? Where would it come from?

c. What would be input, process (formula), and output for insurance-premium deductions if those deductions are 2% of the gross pay?

2.4 *Introducing Structures; Refine the Solution*

Now it is time to describe the solution algorithm in more detail and in a form that shows how the computer will be used to solve the problem. The solution at this point will be written in **pseudocode**, a representation of the algorithm in English-like statements. Although the pseudocode steps eventually may look very much like the final computer program, they need not contain the detail required by a programming language. Pseudocode illustrates the **structure** of an algorithm; that is, how the problem is to be solved.

Four fundamental **control structures** constitute the building blocks of a computer program and control how the program executes:

1. Sequence
2. Selection
3. Iteration 重複 (repetition)
4. Invocation

The four control structures will be explained now.

Sequence

Sequence refers to the orderly execution of statements in a program. If the sequence is not logically orderly, programming attempts result in chaos. The pseudocode for sequential execution will be illustrated by refining the solutions for the circle and markup problems.

In pseudocode, the starting and ending points of a task are often denoted by the words *Begin* and *End* and then the name or description of the task. Between *Begin* and *End* the steps for performing the job are written with one logical operation on each line. The indentations of the lines show which steps form a logical unit and which are subsidiary to others, just as in an outline. *Comments* in the pseudocode are statements that provide information to the user—rather than to the computer. In this book these comments are enclosed between the symbols (* and *), as they are in Modula-2.

Example 2.4.1

(Step 3, Refine the solution) The pseudocode for the area of a circle could be written as

```
Begin FindCircleArea
      Print the message "What is the radius?" to the screen
          (*  Double quotes "   " define a message called a string of characters to be printed.  *)
      Accept input of Radius from the keyboard
      Calculate Area = PI * Radius * Radius
          (* The symbol "=" should be read "The value PI * Radius * Radius is calculated and assigned to the Area",
              rather than "equals". *)
      Print the value of Area to the screen
End FindCircleArea
```

Example 2.4.2

(Step 3, Refine the solution)   The pseudocode for the markup problem could look like

```
Begin FindSellingPrice
    Print the message "What is the Purchase Price?"
    Accept input of PurchasePrice from the keyboard
    Print the message "What is the Percentage Markup?"
    Accept input of Markup from the keyboard

    Change Percentage Markup to a fraction
        FractionMarkup = Markup / 100.0
            (* The value of Markup / 100.0 is calculated and assigned to FractionMarkup. *)

    Calculate the Selling Price
        SellPrice = PurchasePrice + (FractionMarkup * PurchasePrice)
            (* The value on the right-hand side is calculated and assigned to SellPrice. *)

    Print the headings
        "Purchase Price      Percent Markup      Selling Price"
    Print the values of PurchasePrice, Markup, and SellPrice
End FindSellingPrice
```

☐ Selection

The **selection** control structure allows you to make a choice between different operations, depending upon some condition. In the circle problem, for example, suppose it is desired to print a warning message if a negative radius is entered. The pseudocode could look like

```
Begin FindCircleArea
    Print the message "What is the radius?" to the screen
    Accept input of Radius from the keyboard

    If Radius < 0 then
                Print "A circle cannot have a negative radius."
    Otherwise
                Calculate Area = PI * Radius * Radius
                Print the value of Area to the screen
End FindCircleArea
```

where Radius < 0 means "Radius is less than 0."

☐ Iteration

Iteration is sometimes referred to as *repetition* or *looping.* It allows the same operation to be performed repeatedly. There needs to be a condition that is tested with every iteration and eventually causes the repetition to stop. Otherwise, an **infinite loop** results, which executes forever or until the program is aborted by some drastic measure such as turning off the computer. Suppose the goal were to determine the areas of many circles of various non-negative radii. Values for Radius are to be entered repeatedly and the corresponding values of Area printed until a negative value is entered for Radius. The pseudocode for this could be

```
Begin FindCircleArea
    Print the messge "What is the radius?"
    Accept input of Radius
```

```
    While Radius >= 0
        Calculate Area = PI * Radius * Radius
            Print the value of Area
            Print the message "What is the next radius?"
            Accept input of Radius
        End While
    End FindCircleArea
```

where Radius $>= 0$ means "Radius is greater than or equal to 0." The statements between While and End While form a loop that executes repeatedly until it is no longer true that Radius has a positive or zero value. Entering the next radius is the step that changes the Radius $>= 0$ condition to cause the loop eventually to stop.

Invocation

If you wish to do many things in a program—each of which is itself a lengthy task—or if you wish to do the same task at many different points in a program, you may use the **invocation** control structure. Suppose, for example, that the tasks are to calculate the Diameter, Circumference, and Area of a circle. Separate subprograms, called **procedures** or functions, could be written to perform each of these tasks individually. If these subprograms were called FindDiameter, FindCircumference, and FindArea, then pseudocode for the program to do all three could appear as

```
Begin DoCircleCalculations
        Print the message "What is the radius?"
        Accept input of Radius
        FindDiameter(Radius, Diameter)
        FindCircumference(Radius, Circumference)
        FindArea(Radius, Area)
        Print the values of Radius, Diameter, Circumference, and Area
End DoCircleCalculations
```

Here the three procedures are called up, *invoked,* ensuring that the values of Radius, Diameter, Circumference, and Area are passed between the procedures and the Circle program, as indicated by the identifiers in parentheses—(Radius, Diameter), (Radius, Circumference), and (Radius, Area). The Modula-2 language is superior to many others in the ease with which it allows the invocation of subprograms, even if they have been written for another program at another time by another person.

GOTO-less Programming

You probably have noticed that no control structure called "GO TO" or "Jump" has been discussed. Machine, assembly, and early high-level languages used such commands to jump back and forth between statements in a program. This made it very difficult to follow the program sequence and created serious problems in creating, reading, correcting, and modifying programs. Although there may be times when you feel it would be simpler to jump to another place in a program, it is possible to avoid the "GO TO" temptation by using Selection, Iteration, and Invocation; and it is virtually always better to do so. For this reason, most versions of Modula-2 do not even have a GO TO or a Jump command. If you are accustomed to using GO TO or other jump commands in another language, you will find the algorithms (for avoiding GO TO) in Figure 2–1 useful. Remember where this figure is, because it may prove valuable later.

Figure 2–1
How to Avoid the
"GO TO"
Temptation

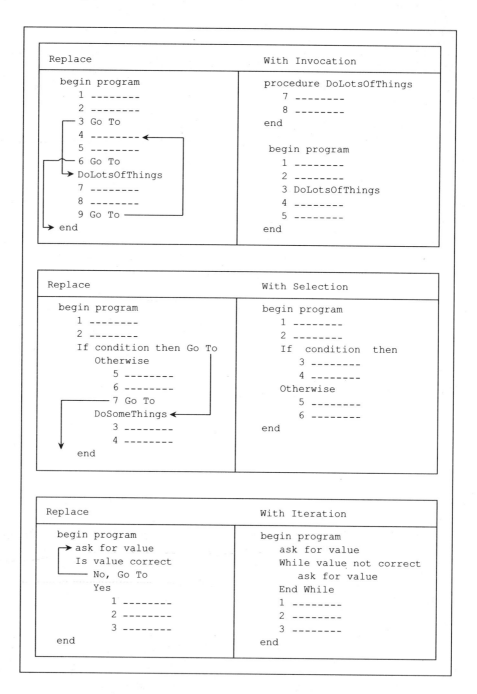

1. Which of the following should generally be avoided in structured programming? Why?
   a. The program executes in order from beginning to end.
   b. The program jumps to another part of the code and then back to where it was.
   c. Loops in the program execute repeatedly until some condition is met.
   d. The program chooses between alternative operations.
2. What is the difference between pseudocode and Modula-2 code?
3. Write pseudocode that outlines the input, process (formula), and output needed to deduct insurance premiums from an employee's pay if the insurance deduction is to be 2% of the gross pay or $25.00, whichever is less.

A Bit of Background

Blaise Pascal

Pascal language is named after Blaise Pascal, a French mathematician and philosopher who lived from 1623 to 1662. He is credited with having invented the first mechanical calculating machine in 1642 at the age of nineteen.

"All our dignity consists then in thought. By it we must elevate ourselves, and not by space and time which we cannot fill. Let us endeavor then to think well; this is the principle of morality." (Pascal's *Pensees*, Number 347)

2.5   *Code*

Once a problem has been refined so that the pseudocode resembles the control structures of the program, it is time to perform the next problem-solving step, namely that of coding the program in a computer language such as Modula-2.

Pascal and Modula-2

In 1971 Dr. Niklaus Wirth announced a new language he had designed and named *Pascal*. Pascal became very popular in the 1970s and early 1980s because of its emphasis on the sequence, selection, iteration, and invocation control structures. It was easy to learn and use as a first programming language. Pascal compilers quickly became available for microcomputers. The College Entrance Examination Board decreed that the Advanced Placement Examination in Computer Science would be based upon Pascal, and most college and university computer science departments adopted the language for their introductory courses. By 1978 Wirth had modified Pascal to a **Modular Language,** which he called *Modula*. This language and the further-refined version, called **Modula-2,** allow programs to be divided into separate ''modules'' that can be imported into other new programs.

Information Hiding, Modularization, and Portability

Important concepts in Modula-2 are information hiding, modularization, and portability. **Modularization** is the feature that allows programmers or users to build programs by invoking subprograms from separate units or modules. They need not know — or even have access to — the details about how those other modules work or how they define the data internally. In fact, this information may be hidden from

---

A Bit of Background

Niklaus Wirth

Niklaus Wirth received an M.S. degree from the University of Quebec in 1962 and the Ph.D. from the University of California at Berkeley in 1963. He then returned to his undergraduate alma mater, the Swiss Federal Institute of Technology, to teach. While serving there as Professor of Computer Science and Chair of the Computer Science Department, he has developed the Pascal, Modula, and Modula-2 languages. These languages have been a major catalyst in the adoption of a disciplined, structured approach to programming.

those who do not need it. When a Modula-2 program is moved from one computer to another computer that has a different operating system and machine language, the program need not be changed; it is **portable.** One just needs to ensure that any machine-dependent modules the program imports will work on the new machine. There are many Modula-2 compilers now available for machines ranging from microcomputers to supercomputers. Though they may vary in some respects, most implementations of the language follow the description of Modula-2 described in Dr. Wirth's book, *Programming in Modula-2* (4th edition, Springer-Verlag, New York, 1988).

Module Syntax

Figure 2–2 shows a very simple Modula-2 program. If you were to execute the program in Figure 2–2a, you would see

```
Hello, World.
Here I am!
```

displayed on the screen.

Programs in Modula-2 begin with a **heading,** namely the word MODULE followed by the name of the program (MODULE SignOn; in Figure 2–2a). The main body of executable statements in the program is enclosed between BEGIN and END statements, and executable commands (to perform specific tasks), such as

```
WriteString('' Hello, World. ''); WriteLn;
WriteString('' Here I am! ''); WriteLn;
```

are separated by semicolons (;) so that the entire code reads like a compound sentence. The final END statement is followed by the module name and a period (.) to indicate the end of the program sentence. Figure 2–2b outlines the general syntax of Modula-2 program MODULEs.

Words, such as MODULE, FROM, IMPORT, BEGIN, END, which are used to define the fundamental features of the language itself, are called *reserved words* and are written in capital letters. (The reserved words for Modula-2 are listed in Appendix A.) Memory space is allocated for constants, data types, variables, and procedures that are to be used during program execution by identifying or "declaring" the names of those parts before the program BEGINs.

White spaces (spaces, tabs, and blank lines) are ignored except in the middle of reserved words and in other identifying names. Therefore, you may place *statements* (virtually anything you write as part of the program) anywhere you wish on a line. This is called *free format* and it makes programs in a language such as Modula-2 much more adaptable and readable than previous languages (such as FORTRAN), which required certain items to be placed within specified columns.

Comments—notes to yourself that are to be ignored by the program—are enclosed between the symbols (*   *) and may be inserted almost anywhere. You are encouraged to use comments, indentation, and spacing freely to make your code readable and understandable. In Modula-2, **case** (capital versus lowercase letters) is critical; for example, *AREA, area,* and *Area* would be interpreted as three different identifiers. This makes typing Modula-2 programs a bit more difficult, but it allows you to be flexible in deciding exactly how you want your code to look.

a.
```
MODULE SignOn;
   (* Prints a sign on message.
      FileName:CH2F2A     Modula-2     RKW     Jan. 1991 *)

FROM InOut IMPORT WriteString, WriteLn;
   (* The commands WriteString (to display a string of characters) and
      WriteLn (to perform a carriage return and line feed) are imported
      from a module called InOut. *)

(* CONSTants, Data TYPEs, VARiables, PROCEDUREs and other items to be
   used in the program would be declared and/or defined here.  This
   program requires no additional definitions. *)

BEGIN
   (* Executable commands are enclosed between BEGIN and END and are
      separated from each other by semicolons. *)

   WriteString("Hello, World."); WriteLn;
   WriteString("Here I am!"); WriteLn;
END SignOn.
```

b.
```
MODULE Name;

   imported items;
      (* modules, procedures, data types, etc. *)

   declarations;
      (* constants, types, variables, procedures, etc. *)

   BEGIN

   executable commands;

   END Name.
```

Figure 2–2
A Simple Program and General Modula-2 Syntax **a.** A Simple Program **b.** Modula-2 Program Module
Syntax (Case Sensitive)

☐ The Assignment Operator

In Modula-2 the **assignment operator** for placing values into memory locations is
written := . The statement *Total := 5.0* should be read "Assign the value 5.0 to
Total," or "The value of Total becomes 5.0," or "The content of memory location
Total is replaced by 5.0." Do not invite confusion by reading it as "Total equals
5.0."

Total := Total + 5.0 is a valid expression that means "The new value of Total
is the old value plus 5.0." A single variable identifier name must appear by itself
to the left of the := assignment operator. To the right you may place an identifier
name or any expression that has an appropriate value. Thus you have

Valid	Invalid
Total := 5.0;	5.0 := Total;
Total := 2.0 * Total;	Total + 3.0 := 7.0;

Each of these invalid expressions is invalid because it assigns a value to a fixed constant or to a calculation, rather than to a memory location with a specific identifier name.

Now you are ready to code the Circle and Markup programs.

Example 2.5.1

(Step 4, Code)   *Area of a Circle — Modula-2*

```
MODULE FindCircleArea;
   (* Finds the area of a circle given the radius
        File Name:CH2A     Modula-2    RKW     Jan. 1991 *)

FROM InOut IMPORT WriteString, WriteLn;
FROM RealInOut IMPORT ReadReal, WriteReal;

CONST  PI = 3.14159;
VAR    Radius, Area : REAL;

BEGIN
   WriteString("What is the radius? ");
    ReadReal(Radius);  WriteLn;

    Area := PI * Radius * Radius;

    WriteString("The area is ");
     WriteReal(Area, 12); WriteLn;
END FindCircleArea.
```

When this Modula-2 program is executed the output will appear as

```
What is the radius? 3.5
The area is   3.8485E+001
```

The area is displayed in exponential format $3.8485E+001$, which means $3.8485 \times 10^1 = 38.485$.

☐ Variables and Procedures

WriteString and WriteLn in the program above are procedures imported from a standard module, called InOut, that comes with every Modula-2 compiler. WriteString prints the string of characters enclosed between double quotes, " ". WriteLn causes a carriage return and line feed; thus the screen cursor moves to the beginning of the next line. ReadReal and WriteReal are imported from standard module RealInOut. ReadReal(Radius) in this program waits for the user to type a real numeric value on the keyboard and then assigns the value to the memory location named by variable Radius.

Write String,

WriteLn

⟹ In Out

FRealOut

Radius is called a **variable,** because its value may change, or vary, in the program. Variables Area and Radius have been declared in the VAR statement to be of type REAL. This means that the contents of memory locations specified by Area and Radius will be interpreted by the program as numbers with decimal points. Note that the assignment operator (:=) is used to assign the result of the calculation PI * Radius * Radius to Area. In contrast, the equal symbol (=) is used to specify that the CONSTant PI is defined to be equal to 3.14159 and will not change.

☐ **FWriteReal, WriteRealFixed, WriteRealFormat** *⟹ Real In Out*

In Example 2.5.1 WriteReal(Area, 12) uses 12 spaces on the screen to display the value of Area. WriteReal displays values in **exponential** form; that is, with one nonzero digit to the left of the decimal point, and an exponential part (E + 001 in this case) specifying by what power of 10 the value is to be multiplied.

Although it is not exactly the same in every implementation, most versions of Modula-2 also have a procedure that allows real values to be printed with a fixed number of decimal places, rather than in exponential form. Called *FWriteReal, WriteRealFixed,* or *WriteRealFormat,* it must be imported from module RealInOut (or some other module, such as SpecialIO). Consult the reference manual that accompanies your Modula-2 compiler to determine which form your version uses. If the manual is unavailable, try all three commands to see which ones give you error messages and which one works. Throughout this book it will be assumed that the correct form is FWriteReal. *If your Modula-2 uses a different form, you will need to replace FWriteReal,* wherever it occurs, with the command recognized by your version.

Appendix C in this book contains an FWriteReal procedure in a module called FRealOut. If you cannot find an equivalent in your Modula-2, you can compile FRealOut as indicated by the comments in the module. Then you would use the import command

```
FROM FRealOut IMPORT FWriteReal;
```

to make FWriteReal available in a program.

To write the value of Area in fixed format to a display field twelve spaces wide, rounded to two digits after the decimal point, change the corresponding commands in the FindCircleArea program to

```
FROM RealInOut IMPORT ReadReal, FWriteReal;
```

or

```
FROM RealInOut IMPORT ReadReal;
FROM FRealOut IMPORT FWriteReal;
```

and

```
FWriteReal(Area, 12,2);
```

Then the output will look like

```
What is the radius? 3.5
The area is   38.48
```

Now examine the code of the markup problem to convince yourself that it uses the procedures just discussed to perform the appropriate tasks.

Example 2.5.2

(Step 4, Code)   *Calculating Selling Price—Modula-2*

```
MODULE FindSellingPrice;
  (* Calculate Selling Price given Purchase Price and Markup
      FileName:CH2B      Modula-2    RKW    Jan. 1991 *)

FROM InOut IMPORT WriteString, WriteLn;
FROM RealInOut IMPORT ReadReal, FWriteReal;

VAR  PurchasePrice, Markup, FractionMarkup, SellPrice : REAL;

BEGIN
   WriteString("What is the Purchase Price? ");
    ReadReal(PurchasePrice); WriteLn;
   WriteString("What is the Percentage Markup? ");
    ReadReal(Markup); WriteLn; WriteLn;

   FractionMarkup := Markup / 100.0;
   SellPrice := PurchasePrice  + (FractionMarkup * PurchasePrice);

   WriteString("Purchase Price   Percent Markup   Selling Price");
    WriteLn;
    FWriteReal(PurchasePrice,14,2); FWriteReal(Markup,17,2);
    FWriteReal(SellPrice,16,2); WriteLn;
END FindSellingPrice.
```

You should convince yourself that when 5.50 and 10.0 are entered from the keyboard the output will look like

```
What is the Purchase Price?   5.50
What is the Percent Markup?   10.0

Purchase Price  Percent Markup  Selling Price
        5.50            10.00            6.05
```

☐ **Comments and Style**

In this book, comments after a program heading usually will be in the form

```
(* Short Description of the Program
     FileName            Language        Author        Date *)
```

where FileName tells where the program can be found and Date is the date of the most recent version. Of course, you may also include any other information you wish in such comments, such as assumptions about what values are legal for input, precautions to take when running the program, and the like.

The usual style of code is that each statement appears on a separate line, except where commands are related intimately, such as writing or reading numbers, strings, and values on the same line. Blank lines may be used to separate logical steps in the program. Indentations also have meaning. In this book a one-space indent indicates that the line is a continuation of the previous line, and indentation by three or more spaces distinguishes statements that are subordinate to others.

You may prefer to use other rules for comments, blank lines, and indentation. The Modula-2 compiler doesn't care what style you use, but developing and following a set of rules similar to those used in this book will enable you and others to understand what you have written.

To maintain the desired length of this book (while still including extensive, complete program examples) it has been necessary to limit blank lines and combine some related statements on one line of code. However, to make your programs easy to read and understand, you should make full use of comments and blank lines and write code with only one statement per line whenever possible.

Implementation 復門. 實施.

Now it is time to discuss how to make your programs work on the computer. Four steps are required to implement any program written in a compiled high-level language such as Modula-2, namely,

1. Editing
2. Compiling
3. Linking
4. Loading and Executing

Editing

A **text file** consists of data stored as a sequence of character codes. An **editor** is a program that allows you to type anything you wish into a text file and save it on a secondary storage medium, such as a disk. Some editors handle one line at a time; to add, change, or delete text, you refer to a specific line by number and edit that line. *Line editors* sometimes are inconvenient to use, but they make efficient use of memory and CPU time. *Full-screen editors* allow you to move the cursor to insert, delete, or change at any point on the screen. Word processors are powerful full-screen editors. Most Modula-2 compilers for small computers are packaged with an editor; on larger machines you will use the general editor for that machine. You need to become familiar with an editor in order to be able to type your program *source code,* which is text that looks like Modula-2.

Stored files must be given names. File-naming conventions vary among computer systems, but often you may specify names with up to 8 characters, followed by a period and an extension of up to 3 characters. Although some systems allow other combinations, to be safe, you should begin the file name *and* the extension with a letter of the alphabet and use only letters and digits. Thus, on many computers

Valid File Name	Invalid File Name
Help.Me2	23SKIDOO.4U
LIFE4ALL.A1	Try@IT?.BEST

If you wished to create and edit a program to a file called The Prog.MOD, for example, you would begin with a command that calls the editor, such as

```
EDIT  TheProg.MOD
```

Compiling

After the editor has been used to enter and save the source code, the program must be **compiled.** Part of every Modula-2 package is the machine-specific compiler program that translates a source-code text file of Modula-2 commands to the machine language for the particular computer on which the commands are to be executed. The manual for your version of the compiler will specify the exact form, but in many cases the compiler will be invoked by a command with a name such as M2COMPILE. So you would type something like

```
M2COMPILE   TheProg.MOD
```

This automatically creates a new file named something like

```
TheProg.OBJ
```

which contains the machine language **object code** of your original program plus information on the items imported by your program.

Linking

Before the program will run, the object code for all the procedures imported and used by the program must be **linked** to the program object code. This creates one large machine-language file of everything the computer needs to know in order to execute the program. A typical link command, with a name such as M2LINK, would be invoked by typing something like

```
M2LINK   TheProg.OBJ
```

The linker operates on the object-code file. It causes the executable machine-language program to be stored in a new file on disk, which probably will be called something like

```
TheProg.REL   or   TheProg.EXE   or   TheProg.COM.
```

If the source code of   TheProg.MOD   were a short program of 300 bytes you may find by examining the disk directory that the compiled object code TheProg.-OBJ contains 1500 bytes or so, and that the linked executable code   TheProg.-EXE   is 15,000 bytes or larger. *A word of caution:* You will want to print the source-code text files to the screen or printer using operating-system commands— often called TYPE, PRINT, or something similar— so that you can see and work with these files. Do NOT, however, try to print the object or executable code files in the same manner, because they are not text files. If you do, at best, you will see un-recognizable characters on the screen or printer as the commands try to interpret binary code as text. Even worse, you may lock up the keyboard, print a ream of paper with one character on each page, or do something equally distasteful when some bytes perform terminal control functions.

Executing

To **execute** the program on most systems, you simply type the name of the executable file, generally without the extension (.REL, .EXE, or .COM). Thus, entering something like

```
TheProg   or   RUN   TheProg
```

causes the executable code to be copied from disk into available memory from where it is executed. Finally, you see the fruits of your labor, namely the output produced by the running program.

On some systems, the commands to compile, link, load, and execute may be combined into one compile-and-go operating-system program so that using a single command such as

```
M2RUN   TheProg.MOD
```

performs all of the steps in order without further user intervention.

Questions 2.5

1. Fill in the blanks in this Modula-2 program:

```
MoDule      HereWeGo;
    (* This program adds 5.0 to WhatToPrint and displays the final value.
       FileName:S2P5Q1    Modula-2    Author    Date  _____

FROM  In Out      IMPORT  WriteString,  WriteLn ;
FROM  Real InOut  IMPORT  WriteReal;

CONST  ADDIT = 5.0;
VAR  WhatToPrint : REAL;

Begin
    WhatToPrint := 3.0;
    WhatToPrint  :  =      WhatToPrint  +  ADDIT;
    WriteString("The final value of WhatToPrint is ");
    Writereal  ; WriteLn;
END  Here we Go.
```

Editing. Compiling. Linking. Executing.

2. List in order the 4 steps you would need to perform in order to implement the program in question 1 on your computer.

3. How would you change the program in question 1 to:
   a. ask the user to enter the initial value of WhatToPrint?
   b. add 7.5 instead of 5.0?
   c. display the result in fixed real-number format with 2 digits after the decimal point, rather than in exponential form?

4. Which of these assignment statements are valid and which are invalid? Show how the invalid ones break the syntax rules.
   a. Taxes := Taxes * 0.35;
   b. Work + Play := 5.0 * Time;
   c. 53.4 := Helpers;
   d. SevenPlusEleven := 7.0 + 11.0;
   e. IWonderWhy + 3.14159 := 18.2 * 3.5;
   f. NewValue := OldValue + Change/2.0;
   g. Gross − Deductions := Net;
   h. 98.6 +OR − ALittle := HumanTemperature;
   i. 3.0 := WhatToPrint;

5. Which of these file names are valid and which are invalid on your computer system? Explain why the invalid ones are not valid.
   a. NOWSTHETIME.FORALL   **f.** WHYNOT.NOW
   b. Program3.DAT   **g.** 2ndProg.92
   c. Two+Two.MOD   **h.** A1.TWO
   d. C2P5Q3.TXT   **i.** Name.T32
   e. C3P0.ROB   **j.** A&B2.T,U

2.6 *Debug and Test*

The larger a program is, the less likely it is to compile and execute perfectly the first time. Programming errors—called **bugs**—seem to be inevitable and they occur in two forms, *syntax errors* and *logical errors*.

不可避免的

Compiler-Detected Errors

Mistakes in coding, such as misspellings, omitting a semicolon, forgetting to use the word BEGIN, and the like, are **syntax errors.** Before you compile the source code, examine it carefully and correct any syntax errors you find. Most compilers will spot many of the syntax errors you missed, try to indicate where an error occurred, and display a message hinting at the nature of the problem. Then you can edit to correct the errors and recompile. Be aware that the compiler may have some difficulty detecting the exact location of the error and its cause. For example, in the following module the compiler probably would point to the position indicated by the caret ($\wedge$):

```
MODULE FirstTry;
FROM InOut IMPORT WriteString, WriteLn;
(* This program prints a message
BEGIN
    WriteString("Hello !"); WriteLn;
END FirstTry.
          ^
```

Then it would display a message something like

```
Error. End of File before End of Module.
```

To find the problem, begin at the error indicator and work backward until you detect a syntax error. In this case the error occurred before BEGIN, where the comment did not get closed with *) after the word *message*. The compiler treated the whole program after (* as one long comment and detected a problem when it ran out of code before recognizing an END command.

Error Cascades

Many times a long list of errors will appear. When this happens you always should look at the first error flagged by the compiler. A single error may cause a **cascade of error messages** that will disappear when you correct the first one. For example, if a declaration were given as

```
VAR Taxes : REAL;
```

instead of the intended

```
VAR TAX : REAL;
```

then the compiler would flag every occurrence of TAX in the program with a message such as

```
Error. Undefined Variable.
```

In fact, sometimes the error cascade occurs because the first error gets the computer so confused that it cannot figure out the rest of the code.

Run-Time Errors

Logical errors are those that are made in the solution to the problem. Often they are not detected until **run time,** when the program is executed. The program may compile, link, and execute perfectly and yet display incorrect answers or do something other than what was expected. This indicates a logical error, and an error in logic can be much more difficult to find than an error in syntax. Generally the process for finding a logical error is to trace through the execution of the program with some sample data, first by hand and then with the computer's help. Some techniques for finding logical errors are illustrated in Section 2.9, Focus on Problem Solving.

☐ Test Data

To catch and correct logical errors it is important to develop a set of *test data* by which to determine whether the program gives correct answers. In fact, an accepted step in formal software development is to plan the test procedures and create meaningful test data before writing the code. This tends to help the person to be more objective about what the program must do, as it essentially circumvents the subconscious temptation after coding to choose test data that he or she is pretty certain will work. The procedures for testing a program should examine every possible situation under which the program will be used. The program should be tested with data in a reasonable range as well as at the limits and in areas where the program should tell the user that the data are invalid. Developing good test procedures and data for sophisticated problems can be more difficult than writing the program code itself.

☐ Backup

It is critical to make and keep **backup** copies of the program at each step of the debugging process. It is easy to delete, change beyond recognition, or lose the current working version by accident. Backup copies allow the recovery of the last stage of the work with a minimum of effort. The final working version of a useful program should be backed-up at least twice. A corollary to Murphy's Law is ''Backup is unimportant if you don't mind having to start all over again.'' The three most fundamental rules of maintaining program and data integrity are

1. backup
 2. Backup
  3. BACKUP

Many organizations keep at least one backup on site, where it can be easily retrieved, and other backup copies at a remote location, where they will be safe in the event of a disaster at the home site.

Questions 2.6

1. If you made a typing error filling in one of the blanks in the program in question 1 at the end of Section 2.5, would the compiler be likely to detect it? What type of error (syntax or logical) would this be?

2. If you place a negative sign ($-$) instead of $+$ in the line

```
WhatToPrint _____ WhatToPrint + ADDIT;
```

in question 1 at the end of Section 2.5, what type of error are you introducing? Whose responsibility would it be to find this error, yours or the compiler's?

3. Suppose that after compiling and executing a program you determine you have the wrong answer because you typed a command

```
Diameter := 4.0 * Radius;
```

instead of

```
Diameter := 2.0 * Radius;
```

What implementation steps would you have to perform to correct the error and have the program execute correctly?

4. When the compiler points out a number of syntax errors in a program, which one should you try to correct first? Why?

5. **a.** What command(s) would you give on your computer system to back-up a file called MYPROG.MOD?

   b. If you had to choose to back-up only one file, would you back-up the program source code or the executable object code? Why?

2.7   *Complete the Documentation*

If you are absolutely certain that your program works perfectly, if you never want to modify it, if you are the only person who will ever use the program and you will use it every day for the rest of your working life so that you never forget how it works or what it does, then you are finished, not only with the program, but probably also as a computer professional.

So much work becomes useless or lost, and so many tasks must be repeated because of inadequate documentation, that it easily could be argued that documenting your work is the most important step in problem solving. You already have created many of the critical documents during the steps of Defining the Problem, Developing and Refining the Solution, Coding, and Debugging and Testing. Now it is time to collect these documents and complete the documentation in a form that is most useful to you and your organization.

Although not everybody classifies them in the same way, there are essentially five important documents for every problem solution:

1. Program Description
2. Algorithm Development and Change Log
3. Well-Commented Program Listing
4. Sample Test Runs
5. Users' Manual

"Putting yourself in the shoes" of a member of a large organization's team that might use your work—anyone from the secretary to the programmer/analysts and management—should help you to make the content and design of the important documentation clear.

Description of the Program

It is common practice for a catalog to be kept containing program descriptions of all the programs available in the organization. Essentially, the **program description** is the final definition of the problem you developed as the first step in the problem-solving process. It should state clearly and succinctly exactly what the program is designed to do. For example, the description of FindSellingPrice might read

> This program calculates and displays on the terminal screen the selling price of an item for which the purchase price and percentage markup have been entered from the keyboard.

☐ Algorithm Development

The **algorithm development** and **change log** are logical outlines of how the program works. These will be in the form of the pseudocode you wrote and/or logic diagrams (which will be discussed later). These records of how you developed the solution algorithm should include a dated log of any significant changes and updated versions of the pseudocode and/or diagrams. These documents are very important, because they will enable you or your successors to maintain and update the program as necessary. No matter how well you understand your solution of the problem now, you almost certainly will not remember the details when you are asked to update the program in the future. Good pseudocode, diagrams, and records of changes will be invaluable.

☐ Printed Program and Sample Runs

Obviously a printed **program listing** containing copious comments is a critical part of the documentation package for any program. It is wise to begin every program with a comment statement that records what the program does, where to find it, in what language it is written, who wrote it, and when. Also, a printout of at least some **sample test runs** should be included to illustrate how the program works.

☐ The Users' Manual

Finally you must write a **users' manual.** If you pretend that you are a secretary who has been asked to run this program, you will understand that the users must know, at least,

1. where to find the program. What is the file name?
2. how you get the program to run. Is it source code, which needs to be compiled, or is it executable code?
3. what is to be entered from the keyboard, in what form, and when. Is there an input file from which data will be read instead of being accepted from the keyboard? Will the output be found on the screen, in a secondary storage file, on the printer, or elsewhere? How should output be interpreted? If the program is well written, input and output instructions probably are printed clearly by the program during execution, and the users' manual may need only to state something like "Answer the questions posed by the program and wait for output to appear on the screen."
4. precautions and pitfalls. For example, the user of the FindSellingPrice program probably should be warned, "Markup should be entered as a positive percentage number; for example, as 25 percent rather than 0.25."

Figure 2–3 illustrates a collection of documents that would comprise good documentation for the Area of a Circle problem.

⊞ 2.8 *Software Engineering*

Prior to the late 1960s, computer programming was considered more of an art than engineering or science. Code often was convoluted, difficult to read and debug, and maintainable only by the original author, if at all. As the magnitude of software tasks grew, it became apparent that techniques needed to be developed to provide for the systematic solution of problems. Since then, considerable effort has been

Program Description   FindCircleArea
    This program calculates and prints to the
screen the area of a circle when the radius of the
circle is entered from the keyboard.

Algorithm Development

                    Pseudocode

Begin FindCircleArea
    Print message "What is the radius?" to screen
    Accept input of r from the keyboard
    Calculate Area = PI * Radius * Radius
    Print the value of Area to the screen
End

Program Listing

```
MODULE FindCircleArea;
   (* Finds the area of a circle given the radius)
       File Name:CH2A     Modula-2     RKW     Jan. 1991 *)

FROM InOut IMPORT WriteString, WriteLn;
FROM RealInOut IMPORT ReadReal, WriteReal;

CONST  PI = 3.14159;
VAR    Radius, Area : REAL;

BEGIN
    WriteString("What is the radius? ");
     ReadReal(Radius); WriteLn;

    Area := PI * Radius * Radius;

    WriteString("The area is ");
     WriteReal(Area, 12); WriteLn;
END FindCircleArea.
```

Sample Runs

```
When R = 3.5
        What is the radius? 3.5
        The area is    3.8484E+001
When R = 82.6
        What is the radius? 82.6
        The area is    2.1434E+004
```

Users' Manual   FindCircleArea

        The Source Code file is named CH2A and is written in
    Modula-2. If the program is to be executed from this file it
    must be compiled with a Modula-2 compiler, linked, loaded, and
    executed. Note: If the user does not know how to compile, link,
    and execute a Modula-2 program, those instructions should be
    included.
        The program asks you for the radius of the circle, which you
    will enter from the keyboard with a decimal point and a fractional
    part if desired. Then the area is printed to the screen in
    exponential form and execution stops.
        Caution: the program does not check for negative radius. If
    you enter a negative radius, the area printed will be that for a
    circle with a positive radius of the same magnitude.

Figure 2–3
Documentation for Area of a Circle

made to establish engineering principles for designing efficient, reliable, maintainable software. The problem-solving techniques and programming structures discussed in this chapter are critical components of this **software engineering** process.

Definition, Development, Maintenance

Software engineering entails three phases:

1. Definition of the problem
2. Development of the solution and refinement of the problem specifications
3. Maintenance of the system

In the definition phase, the focus is on *what* data are to be processed, what the system is to be designed to do, what criteria will be used to determine that the system has been implemented successfully, what the overall requirements of the system should be, and how the solution is to be developed (what processes are to be used). This phase includes the steps of system analysis, planning the project, and the analysis of the requirements. This is what is meant by Defining the Problem.

In the development phase, the software engineer concentrates on *how* the problem is to be solved. This involves developing and refining the solution, designing the software requirements, coding the solution, and testing to discover and correct faults in logic and implementation.

Finally, the maintenance phase is concerned with ongoing correction of problems, revision to meet changing needs, and adding new features. Maintenance is often the major effort, the primary source of revenue, and the longest-lasting of the engineering phases. While development may take days or months, maintenance may continue for years or decades. The better the documentation is, the more efficiently this phase can be performed and the happier the customer will be.

2.9   *Focus on Problem Solving*

In this section the FindCircleArea program is presented in a version containing logical errors. You will learn supplemental-write-command techniques for detecting and correcting those errors.

Suppose that the circle problem had been typed as in this example.

Example 2.9.1

(Step 5, Debug and test)   Area of a Circle — Modula-2, with Logical Errors

```
MODULE FindCircleArea;
   (* Finds the area of a circle given the radius - Contains Logical Errors
      FileName:CH2A2     Modula-2    RKW    Jan. 1991 *)

FROM InOut IMPORT WriteString, WriteLn;
FROM RealInOut IMPORT ReadReal, FWriteReal;

CONST  PI = 3.0;
VAR    Radius, Area : REAL;

BEGIN
   WriteString("What is the radius? ");
   ReadReal(Area);  WriteLn;
```

```
        Area := PI * Radius;

    WriteString("The area is ");
      FWriteReal(Area, 12, 2); WriteLn;
END FindCircleArea.
```

Reasonable test data for the Radius of the circle might be

- a limiting value, 0, in this case
- a value that is easy to follow through by hand, such as 1.0
- acceptable numbers that could be calculated with a calculator, such as 3.5 and 82.6
- at least one invalid radius, such as -3.5

Following through the program by hand for Radius = 0, the question "What is the radius?" is answered with 0. Then Area becomes $\pi * 0 = 3.0 * 0 = 0$. The area for a circle of Radius 0 is indeed 0, so the results seem to be correct; and you might draw the wrong conclusion if this were the only test point chosen. Next run the program with Radius = 1.0. The result is probably still Area = 0.0 or some other strange incorrect value, so now you must determine why.

Supplemental Write Commands

One of the most effective ways to find logical errors is to insert supplemental Write statements into the program to

- echo values of variables immediately after reading them
- print values of variables before and after calculations
- tell the user what point has been reached in the execution of the program

Some systems have built-in debugger programs that trace the values of variables and the program execution for you.

Assuming you are not using a debugger program, insert some extra Write statements into the circle program of Example 2.9.1 to help you find the logical errors, as shown here.

Area of a Circle—Modula-2, with Logical Errors and Debugging Write Statements

```
MODULE FindCircleArea;
    (* Finds the area of a circle given the radius
       Contains Logical Errors and Debugging Write Statements
       FileName:CH2A3      Modula-2    RKW    Jan. 1991 *)

FROM InOut IMPORT WriteString, WriteLn;
FROM RealInOut IMPORT ReadReal, FWriteReal;

CONST  PI = 3.0;
VAR    Radius, Area : REAL;

BEGIN
    WriteString("What is the radius? ");
      ReadReal(Area);  WriteLn;

    Area := PI * Radius;
```

```
(* Supplemental write statements, for debugging only - often placed
   at the left margin, so they can be found easily. *)
WriteString("Radius entered was "); FWriteReal(Radius,6,2); WriteLn;
WriteString("We are about to calculate Area"); WriteLn;
WriteString("PI is "); FWriteReal(PI,12,5); WriteLn;

   WriteString("The area is ");
    FWriteReal(Area, 12, 2); WriteLn;
END FindCircleArea.
```

Now run the program again with Radius = 1.0 and see

```
What is the radius? 1.0
Radius entered was 0.00
We are about  to calculate Area
PI is         3.00000
The area is         0.00
```

This makes it apparent, first, that the Radius has not been read correctly, and you discover that ReadReal(Area) should be ReadReal(Radius). Second, the value of PI is wrong, and CONST PI = 3.0 must be changed to CONST PI = 3.14159. After making these changes you can rerun the program with Radius = 1.0 and see

```
What is the radius? 1.0
Radius entered is 1.0
We are about to calculate Area
PI is      3.14159
The area is        3.14
```

Again the program appears to give the correct answer, since the area of the circle of radius 1.0 is indeed approximately 3.14. However, you still need to try some more test values. The next test value is Radius = 3.5. Executing with this value displays

```
What is the radius? 3.5
Radius entered is 3.50
We are about to calculate Area
PI is      3.14159
The area is        11.00
```

But your calculator will show that the area of a circle with radius 3.5 is approximately 38.48. Everything seems to be all right except the calculation of Area, which you discover should be changed from Area := PI * Radius to Area := PI * Radius * Radius. After making this correction, you run the program again for all of the test values and confirm that the answers are now correct.

The illegal value Radius = −3.5 should return an error message, but instead gives 38.48 for the area. A discussion of how this problem is corrected appears in a later chapter, but a quick-and-dirty fix can be made now by changing the first WriteString command to

```
WriteString(''What is the radius (must be >= 0) ? '');
```

which, at least, will tell the user that the radius should not be negative.

Nested Comments

Now that the logical errors in this program have been corrected, the supplemental write statements can be erased or enclosed within comment brackets, (*   *), in case they are needed later; and you have a working program. In Modula-2, comments may be nested; that is, they may be enclosed within other comments. Thus, for example,

```
(* Here is a comment (* with this nested comment *) *)
```

would be accepted by the compiler.

Questions 2.9

Consider the FindCircleArea program with Logical Errors and Debugging Write Statements in this section.

1. Why wasn't an extra supplemental write statement inserted to display the value of Area to the screen as soon as it had been calculated?
2. Strictly speaking, it would have been better to put the supplemental write statement

```
WriteString("PI is "); FWriteReal(PI,12,5); WriteLn;
```

immediately after BEGIN. Why? Why not put this statement immediately after CONST PI = 3.0; ?
3. Why might you want to put comment symbols around the supplemental write statements after you have found and corrected the errors in the program, rather than deleting the statements? Show how the block of supplemental write statements would look enclosed within comment indicators.

2.10 *Summary*

Seven Problem-Solving Steps Six major steps in problem solving have been examined:

1. Define the problem
2. Develop a solution
3. Refine the solution
4. Code
5. Debug and test
6. Complete the documentation

The seventh step,

7. Maintain the solution

is important, but it extends beyond the range of the material in this book.

Control Structures Pseudocode assists you in the process of Refining the Solution. The four fundamental program control structures are

1. Sequence
2. Selection
3. Iteration
4. Invocation

Modula-2 Syntax Basic syntax of Modula-2 is illustrated in Figure 2–2.

Implementation Editing, compiling, linking, loading, and executing a program are the operations necessary to make your program run in a compiled language such as Modula-2. Modula-2 code was written for two programs and used to illustrate debugging, testing, and documentation.

Software Engineering   The steps in problem solving and documentation of the problem are critical components in the processes of software engineering.

Syntax and Logical Errors   Errors in typing, mistakes in spelling, or problems with the program code itself are called syntax errors; and many can be detected and indicated by the compiler. Errors in logic generally are detected at run time, when the program gives wrong answers or does not operate properly. Supplemental write statements may be valuable in finding and correcting logical errors.

2.11   *Exercises*

Exercises marked with (FileName: _____) indicate those that ask you to use, modify, or extend the text examples. The numbers in square brackets, [ ], indicate the chapter section that contains the material you need for completing the exercise.

1. [2.5] (FileName:CH2A) Implement the FindCircleArea program of Example 2.5.1 on your computer and submit with complete documentation.
2. [2.5] (FileName:CH2B) Implement the FindSellingPrice program of Example 2.5.2 on your computer and submit with complete documentation.

For each problem in Exercises 3 through 6

    a. Write the program description (definition).
    b. Write pseudocode.
    c. Write well-commented program code.
    d. Choose good sample test data, debug, and run.
    e. Submit with complete documentation, including a users' manual.

3. [2.7] Given the Radius of a circle find the Circumference. *Note:* Circumference = 2.0 * PI * Radius.
4. [2.7] Enter two real numbers, *P* and *Q*, from the keyboard and calculate and print to the screen their sum $(P + Q)$, difference $(P - Q)$, product $(P * Q)$, and quotient (P/Q).
5. [2.7] The final grades for your three courses last term were B+ (3.3), A (4.0), and B (3.0). Each course carried the same number of credit hours. What was your average grade point (on 4.0 scale) for the term?
6. [2.7] Enter your first name from the keyboard and print it three times to the screen. *Hint:* Use

```
FROM InOut IMPORT WriteString, ReadString;
CONST MAXNUMOFLETTERS = 20;
VAR MyName : ARRAY [1..MAXNUMOFLETTERS] OF CHAR;
```

Then

```
ReadString(MyName);
```

and

```
WriteString(MyName);
```

For each problem in Exercises 7 through 12 write *only pseudocode,* using the fundamental program control structures as appropriate.

7. [2.4] Selection: Use Heron's formula for calculating the area of a triangle with sides *a*, *b*, and *c*, where $s = (a + b + c)/2$, AreaSquared = $s(s - a)$

$(s - b)(s - c)$, and Area = Square root of AreaSquared. If AreaSquared is positive, calculate and print Area; otherwise, print the message that these three sides do not form a triangle. *Note:* The sqrt function, from Dr. Wirth's module MathLib0, finds the square root. To implement a program from your pseudocode, you would use

```
FROM MathLib0 IMPORT sqrt;
```

and

```
Area :/ sqrt(AreaSquared);
```

8. [2.4] Selection: Ask whether three resistors R1, R2, and R3, are connected in series or in parallel. Calculate and print the equivalent Resistance, where if in series, Resistance = $R1 + R2 + R3$ if in parallel, $1.0/Resistance = (1.0/R1) + (1.0/R2) + (1.0/R3)$

9. [2.4] Iteration: Print a table of Fahrenheit vs. Celsius temperatures for Celsius = 0.0, 5.0, 10.0, 15.0, . . . , 100.0. *Note:* Fahrenheit = $(9.0/5.0) * Celsius + 32.0$.

10. [2.4] Iteration: Find the sum of $(1 * 1) + (2 * 2) + (3 * 3) + . . . + (10 * 10)$.

11. [2.4] Invocation: For the Earth and Mars, ask for the name of the body and the values of two variables called K and Diameter of orbit. Calculate the Speed in miles per hour of a satellite in a circular orbit at Distance (miles) from the center of the Earth and then Mars, where Speed = Square root of $(K/Diameter)$. K has the values 1.2E12 for Earth and 1.3E11 for Mars (where En is exponential notation meaning $* 10^n$). Print the name of the body, the values of K and Diameter, and the orbital Speed for both. Assume that you can import an already written procedure, CalculateOrbit(K, Diameter), which performs the calculation for Speed and returns its value to the program. *Note:* See hints in Exercises 6 and 7 and the DoCircleCalculations pseudocode in Section 2.4.

12. [2.4] Invocation: Assume that you can import previously written procedures called Factorial(x), Combinations(n,r), and Permutations(n,r), which calculate and return to the main program $x!$ (x-factorial), combinations $C(n,r)$ of n things taken r at a time, and permutations $P(n,r)$ of n things taken r at a time, respectively. Ask for n and r and calculate and print $n!$, $r!$, $(n - r)!$, $C(n,r)$, and $P(n,r)$. *Hint:* See DoCircleCalculations pseudocode in Section 2.4.

13. [2.5] Given the side length (Side), the Area of a square is given by Area = Side $*$ Side. Using the Circle program (Example 2.5.1) as a guide, write a program to ask for the length of the side of a square and calculate and print the area of the square. Submit the program listing and a sample run.

14. [2.5] (FileName:CH2B) Modify the FindSellingPrice program (Example 2.5.2) so that it finds the price after a discount. Use the formula

DiscountPrice = OriginalPrice − (FractionDiscount * OriginalPrice).

Print the appropriate questions for input and headings for output. Submit the program listing and a sample run.

15. [2.9] (FileName:CH2B2) This version of the FindSellingPrice program contains syntax errors and logical errors.

```
MODULE FindSellingPrice;
   (* Calculate Selling Price given Purchase Price and Markup
      With Syntax Errors and Logical Errors
      FileName:CH2B2     Modula-2     RKW    Jan. 1991 *)
```

```
FROM InOut IMPORT WriteString, WriteLn;
FROM RealInOut IMPORT ReadReal, FWriteReal;

VAR  PurchasePrice, Markup, FractionMarkup, SellPrice : REAL;

BEGIN
   WriteString("What is the Purchase Price? ");
    ReadReal(PurchasePrice); WriteLine;
   WriteString("What is the Percentage Markup? ");
    ReadReal(FractionMarkup); WriteLine; WriteLine;

   FractionMarkup = Markup / 10.0;
   SellPrice := PurchasePrice  + (FractionMarkup / PurchasePrice);

   WriteString("Purchase Price   Percent Markup   Selling Price");
    WriteLine;
   FWriteReal(PurchasePrice,14,2; FWriteReal(Markup,17,2);
    FWriteReal(PruchasePrice,16,2); WriteLine;
END FindSellingPrice.
```

First, see how many of those errors you can find by tracing through the program by hand. Then use your compiler and editor to find the syntax errors and insert supplemental write statements, as explained in Section 2.9, to find and correct the logical errors. Submit a listing and sample run of your program with the supplemental write statements.

16. [2.9] Use the computer to solve the following problem and submit with complete documentation. Monthly payments (Payment) on a 30-year loan of $62,000 (Principal) at 10% annual interest are $544.11. How much of the first payment is interest (InterestPaid), how much goes toward paying off the principal (PrincipalPaid), and what is the balance due (BalanceDue) after the first payment is made? *Hints:*

```
Monthly Interest Rate = 0.10/12.0;
        Interest Paid = Principal * Monthly Interest Rate
       Principal Paid = Payment - Interest Paid
         Balance Due = Principal - Principal Paid
```

3

Variables, Types, Operations

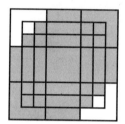

Chapter Outline

A Bit of Background

Transcendental Pi

Pi = 3.14159 26535 89793 23846 26433
83279 50288 41971 69399 . . .

The first recorded reference to the problem of "squaring the circle" is found in the Ahmes Papyrus, from about 1550 B.C. The problem of using only a compass and straightedge to find a square whose area is the same as that of a given circle involves finding the ratio of the circle's circumference to its diameter. That ratio, named π (pi) by William Jones (1706) and Euler (1737), has received considerable attention from Anaxagoras (450 B.C.), Archimedes (225 B.C.), Ptolemy (150), Fibonacci (1220), and other noted scientists

throughout history. Various approximations have been used, such as 3, sqrt(10), 22/7, 355/113, and others. However, German mathematician F. Lindemann proved in 1882 that pi is transcendental; that its value cannot be determined by using a straightedge and compass alone. Thus the door was closed forever to squaring the circle. Using modern computers, the value of pi (whose pattern of digits never terminates and never repeats) can be calculated to millions of decimal places. For most applications, however, 3.14159 is close enough.

In this chapter you will learn how to define constants and variables, to specify what types of values they may contain, and to manipulate them using fundamental operations. Then you will discover and practice top-down design, stepwise refinement, and modularization problem-solving techniques.

3.1 *Constants and Variables*

Recall that the fundamental syntax for a Modula-2 program is

```
MODULE Name;
  import lists;
    (* entities to be imported from external modules *)
  declarations;
    (* constants, types, variables, procedures *)

BEGIN
  executable commands;
END Name.
```

Constants

Names for constants and variables to be used in your program must be declared in the declarations section. The CONST statement and its assignment operator (=) define values that do not change during program execution, such as

```
CONST PI = 3.1416;
```

Possible constant values include the counting (cardinal) numbers, positive and negative integers, decimal values, single characters, lists of characters, and the logical values TRUE and FALSE. The compiler decides which type of quantity a constant represents by the value you assign to it. Some examples of constant declarations are

```
CONST MAXNUMBER = 23:
      LOWTEMPERATURE = -17;
      TAXRATE = 0.05;
      LETTER = 'k';
      MESSAGE = ''Help! I am a computer captive.'';
      ItsOK = FALSE;
```

It is good programming practice to declare a constant, such as CONST TAXRATE = 0.05, and use its name, rather than to insert numbers or values throughout a program. If you should wish to change the program (so that TAXRATE = 0.075, for example), then you only need to change the constant declaration, rather than try to find and change every occurrence of the value throughout your program code. Names of constants need not be capitalized, but they often are, to help you distinguish them from variables.

☐ Variables

Quantities for which the value may change during program execution are called **variables.** Variables are declared using the VAR statement within the program declarations section. Since the computer must be told how much memory space to reserve and how to interpret the bits in that location, a variable definition specifies what kind (or **type**) of quantity the variable represents. For example,

```
VAR Root, Time : REAL;
    NumOfApples : INTEGER;
```

directs the computer to interpret values stored in memory locations named by Root and by Time as REAL numbers with decimal points. Similarly, values stored in the memory location reserved for variable NumOfApples will be interpreted as whole numbers with positive, negative, or zero value.

☐ Identifier Names

The names of variables, constants, and types are called **identifiers.** Some words, such as MODULE, VAR, IMPORT, BEGIN, INTEGER, CONST, and so on, are reserved for standard commands, statements, procedures, and values from which the Modula-2 language is built. These **reserved words,** listed in Appendix A, are written in *uppercase* and may not be used to identify anything else.

For creating your own identifier names, the rules are short and simple:

Rules for Identifiers
1. An identifier must begin with an uppercase or lowercase letter.
2. Use only letters and digits in identifier names.
3. Do not use reserved words.

Some compilers accept certain punctuation or other symbols in identifiers. However, identifying names containing characters other than letters and digits may prevent your program from running on a different computer and thus should be avoided. Under no circumstances should spaces, periods, commas, or semicolons be placed within an identifier name. These characters act as **separators;** they force the computer to interpret what you thought was a single identifier as a list of identifiers.

Figure 3–1
Examples of Valid
and Invalid
User-Defined
Identifiers

Valid Identifiers	Invalid Identifiers
X	Mash 4077
X3	Six+Five
C3PO	MODULE
R2D2	76Trombones
MyName	Tom'sDiner
my2ndName	57Varieties
Start	9TO5
milespergallon	BEGIN

Uppercase and Lowercase Letters

Because Modula-2 distinguishes between uppercase and lowercase letters, *HighLow, HIGHLOW,* and *highlow* would all be different identifiers.

In theory identifiers may be of any length; in practice, however, each computer accepts a maximum number of characters. Beyond this maximum, either you will receive an error message, such as "identifier too long," or the computer will ignore the extra characters. You should give your identifiers meaningful names, such as *TaxBill* or *TimeOut,* rather than *T.* However, since very long identifier names are easy to type incorrectly, you may wish to compromise on a length of a few meaningful characters. Figure 3–1 lists some valid and invalid identifiers.

Questions 3.1

1. **a.** For each of the invalid identifiers in Figure 3–1, state which rule is violated.
   b. Rank the valid identifiers in Figure 3–1 in order, from those most likely to be meaningful to those least likely to indicate their meaning to the user.
2. Determine which of the following are valid and which are not valid identifiers for variables or constants in Modula-2. For those that are not valid, explain why.
   a. TaxesOwed   **e.** 2BOrNot2B   **i.** PlayTicTacToe
   b. HoursOver40   **f.** File Name   **j.** 31Flavors
   c. END   **g.** Button Shoe   **k.** Q
   d. AverageMark   **h.** Seven*Five   **l.** WillHeFinishOrWillHeNot
3. Tell whether it is appropriate to use a CONSTant or a VARiable for each italicized entity below; and give each a meaningful (descriptive), valid identifier name.
   a. A program may be customized to refer repeatedly to the same user by *name.*
   b. The *amount* of each customer's electric bill is calculated to the nearest cent with different input data.
   c. A program *counts* how many times batters strike out.
   d. The program uses a *conversion factor* to change inches to feet.

    e. An alarm sounds when the *minimum temperature* is less than -15 degrees.

    f. A program determines *which character* occurs most often in a sentence entered from the keyboard.

3.2 *Numeric Data Types and Operations*

Every variable is defined in terms of its type and the operations that may be performed upon it. Some variables in the examples so far have been of type REAL, which means that they represent numbers that contain decimal points. Other standard types in Modula-2 include CARDINAL and INTEGER numbers, CHARacter variables, and BOOLEAN (logical) values. REAL, CARDINAL, and INTEGER represent *numeric* variable types, because they define memory locations in which numbers may be stored.

The numeric data types are discussed in this section. Section 3.3 introduces CHAR and BOOLEAN types. In later chapters, you will learn more about these types, as well as about types that define strings (or lists) of characters, sets, records, data files, and pointers. You even will learn how to define and use new **abstract data types.** That is, you will learn to specify what kinds of values may be assigned to a variable and to write procedures for performing the operations you define for that data type.

CARDINAL Type

CARDINAL-type data consist of the counting numbers—that is, positive whole numbers and zero. A CARDINAL value may be preceded by a plus sign ($+$), but it need not be. There are no decimal points in CARDINALs, and no commas are used to separate the digits of a number of any type. Some valid and invalid representations of CARDINAL values are shown at the top of Figure 3–2. (Other parts of Figure 3–2 are discussed in the following subsections.) CARDINAL variables are declared with the CARDINAL-type identifier.

ReadCard, WriteCard, Assignment
In Modula-2, the standard utility procedures ReadCard and WriteCard, imported from the InOut module, allow you to read and write CARDINAL values. For example, the statement

```
VAR Count, HowMany, HowWide : CARDINAL;
```

declares variables Count, HowMany, and HowWide to be of type CARDINAL.

```
ReadCard(Count);
```

accepts input of a CARDINAL value and stores it as the value of variable Count.

```
HowMany := 73;
```

assigns the value 73 to variable HowMany. Then

```
WriteCard(Count, 6);
WriteCard(HowMany, 3);
WriteCard(182, 5);
```

would display the value of Count in an area 6 spaces wide—called a **field**—on the page or the screen. The value of HowMany, 73, would be displayed in a field of width 3, and the value 182 would be presented in a field of width 5.

```
Declaration:   VAR Count, HowMany : CARDINAL;
```

Valid Cardinals	Invalid Cardinals
0	-5
+839	3,267
65432	18.42

```
Range:    MIN(CARDINAL) = 0
          On a system that reserves 16 bits for a cardinal value
          MAX(CARDINAL) = 2¹⁶ - 1  =  65535
```

Range: MIN(CARDINAL) = 0
          On a system that reserves 16 bits for a cardinal value
          MAX(CARDINAL) = $2^{16} - 1$ = 65535

```
Operators:
    Read and Write
          FROM InOut IMPORT   ReadCard, WriteCard;

          ReadCard(CardinalVariableIdentifier);
          WriteCard(CardinalValue, FieldWidth);

    Assignment   ( := )
          CardinalVariableIdentifier := Cardinal Value;

          Examples:  HowMany := 73;   Count := HowMany - 5;
                     HowWide := 2 * (4 - 1);

    Arithmetic
          Operation    Operator    Examples
          Add             +        3 + 87    HowMany + 9    3246 + Count

          Subtract        -        87 - 3    HowMany - 9    3246 - Count

          Multiply        *        87 * 3    HowMany * 9    12 * Count

          Divide         DIV       383 DIV 5    HowMany DIV 9
                         MOD       383 MOD 5    HowMany MOD 9

    Arithmetic Precedence    1. Parenthesized expressions
                             2. *  DIV  MOD  from left to right
                             3. +  -  from left to right
```

Valid Cardinal Expressions	Invalid Cardinal Expressions
5 * 7 + 3	5 / 3
173 * (6 - 4)	12 (4 + 18)
8 + (5 DIV 2)	180 DIV MOD 7
68 * (+ 3)	43 * + 4
(33 MOD 7) DIV 2	18 * (14.3 - 21) DIV 4
3 * (6 + (12 MOD 5 - 1)) + 2	8 * (81 - (4 + 7) - 6

```
Conversion:    To INTEGER        INTEGER(CardinalValue);
                                 VAL (INTEGER, CardinalValue);
               To REAL           FLOAT(CardinalValue);
```

Figure 3–2
CARDINAL Data Type

The syntax of the ReadCard and WriteCard commands is

```
ReadCard( CardinalVariableIdentifier );

WriteCard( CardinalValue, FieldWidth );
```

In ReadCard, the single argument inside the parentheses must be a CARDINAL variable identifier, such as HowMany. In WriteCard, the CardinalValue argument may be a CARDINAL variable identifier, a CARDINAL constant (such as 182), or an expression (such as 7 + 35 or HowMany + 3) that evaluates to a valid CARDINAL value. The rules for constructing valid CARDINAL expressions are discussed in the subsection entitled "CARDINAL Expressions and Operator Precedence."

A FieldWidth argument must be specified in a WriteCard command. Although FieldWidth is usually a constant value, such as 6, it may also be represented by a CARDINAL variable identifier or a valid CARDINAL expression. If the FieldWidth is larger than needed, the extra leftmost spaces in the field will be filled with blanks, and the number is said to be *right-justified* in the field. If the specified FieldWidth is too small, it is ignored, and the default field width becomes the exact number of spaces required to display the value. For example, the following commands should produce the indicated displays.

Command	Display
HowMany := 73;	
HowWide := 2;	
WriteLn;	
WriteCard(12345, 3): WriteLn;	12345
WriteCard(HowMany, 3): WriteLn;	73
WriteCard(HowMany, HowWide + 2); WriteLn;	73
WriteCard(182, 5); WriteLn;	182
WriteCard(7 + 35, 6); WriteLn;	42
WriteCard(HowMany + 3, HowWide); WriteLn;	76

CARDINAL Range

For every variable, there is a limited range of allowable values. That range depends upon how much space the computer reserves for a variable of that type. On most systems, at least 2 bytes (16 bits) are reserved for CARDINAL numbers; and the range of allowable CARDINAL numbers in that 16-bit representation would be from 0 to $2^{16} - 1$ (which is 65535). Built-in functions, MIN and MAX, enable you to determine the smallest and largest CARDINAL values to be allowed on your system. In the case of a 16-bit representation, executing the command WriteCard(MAX(CARDINAL), 6) would display the value 65535.

CARDINAL Operations

A complete data-type definition includes both the kind and range of values allowed for variables of that type, as well as the operations that may be performed upon those values.

Operations allowed on numeric data include add, subtract, multiply, divide, read, write, and assignment of a value to a variable.

Read and Write for CARDINAL values are performed by the ReadCard and WriteCard commands found in the standard InOut module.

Figure 3–3
A Long Division
Problem

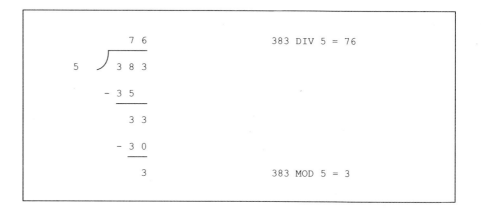

Addition, subtraction, and multiplication of CARDINAL numbers are performed by using the operator symbols +, −, and *, respectively. Be careful not to create error messages, such as ''out of range'' or ''overflow,'' by using these operations to produce results less than 0 or greater than MAX(CARDINAL). Two arithmetic operators may not be juxtaposed as adjacent symbols; that is, expressions such as a * + b are not allowed. Figure 3–2 summarizes CARDINAL Operations and provides some examples.

Division of one CARDINAL value by another requires two operators, namely DIV and MOD. The DIV operation produces the quotient, and MOD produces the remainder. A long division example illustrates the DIV and MOD operations. For example, consider the problem 383 divided by 5, shown in Figure 3–3. In this problem

```
Quotient   383 DIV 5  =  76
Remainder  383 MOD 5  =  3
```

The divisor (the number following DIV or MOD) may not be zero. An attempt to divide by zero results in aborted program execution, with an error message such as ''divide by zero attempted.''

CARDINAL Expressions and Operator Precedence

An arithmetic expression of a given type is formed by applying the valid arithmetic operations to variables or values of that numeric type in order to produce a result of the same type. CARDINAL expressions may be formed by combining CARDINAL values and/or variables with the operators *, DIV, MOD, +, and −. Figure 3–2 shows some valid and invalid CARDINAL expressions. A CARDINAL expression may be assigned to a single CARDINAL variable and may be used wherever a CARDINAL value is allowed.

Following the rules of operator precedence ensure that operations always occur in a predictable order. The rules are

Rules of Precedence for CARDINAL Operations
1. Perform all operations in parentheses first, in order from innermost to outermost parentheses.
2. Perform *, DIV, and MOD operations in order from left to right.
3. Perform + and − operations in order from left to right.
4. When in doubt about how an expression will be evaluated, use parentheses.

Associative operations, where a multiplier precedes a parenthetical expression, require that the multiplication symbol, * , be written explicitly before the parenthesis, as in 6 * (HowMany + 7). Every left parenthesis, (, must be balanced by a corresponding right parenthesis,) . In theory, parentheses may be nested as deeply as you wish in Modula-2. However, nesting parentheses more deeply than a few levels makes expressions difficult to read; and such expressions should be replaced by a sequence of assignments to evaluate and then combine the parts. For example, given the declarations

```
VAR UltimateValue, SubValue1, SubValue2 : CARDINAL;
```

the statement

```
UltimateValue := 3 * (6 + (12 MOD 5 - 1)) + 2;
```

might be easier for people to read and evaluate in the form

```
SubValue1      := 12 MOD 5 - 1;
SubValue2      := 6+SubValue1;
UltimateValue  := 3 * SubValue2 + 2;
```

Now consider a more comprehensive example of the use of CARDINAL variables.

Example 3.2.1

Your organization's computer lab supervisor visits the wholesale warehouse to restock supplies of floppy diskettes. Calculate the total quantity and total cost of disks purchased.

Define the problem   The wholesaler sells disks only in boxes of 12 disks. The supervisor first purchases 5¼″ disks at 27 cents per disk, then 3½″ disks at 65 cents per disk. The program will ask her to enter from the keyboard how many boxes of each she purchases.

Find the total number of disks purchased. Then determine the total cost—first in total cents, then in dollars and cents—of all disks purchased.

Develop a solution   To illustrate CARDINAL operations, the calculations in this problem will be handled exclusively with CARDINAL values, recognizing that the problem could also be solved using REAL values. The total number and total cost (in cents) of each type of disk will be calculated first. Then these totals will be added to obtain the grand total of disks and the grand total cost. DIV and MOD will be used to calculate dollars and cents.

The number of disks per box, cents per dollar, cost per 5-inch disk, and cost per 3-inch disk will be defined as constants.

Refine the solution   *Pseudocode*

```
declare  CONSTants  CENTSPERDOLLAR = 100;  DISKSPERBOX = 12;
                    CENTSPER5INDISK = 27;  CENTSPER3INDISK = 65;

         VARiables  Num5InBoxes, Num3InBoxes,
                    Num5InDisks, Num3InDisks, TotalNumDisks,
                    Cost5In, Cost3In, TotalCostInCents,
                    TotalDollarCost, TotalCentsCost : CARDINAL;
```

```
begin
    calculate numbers of disks and costs
        ask how many boxes of each type of disk were purchased
        Num5InDisks    = DISKSPERBOX * Num5INBoxes
        Num3InDisks    = DISKSPERBOX * Num3InBoxes
        TotalNumDisks = Num5InDisks + Num3InDisks
        Cost5In = Num5InDisks * CENTSPER5INDISK
        Cost3In = Num3InDisks * CENTSPER3INDISK
        TotalCostInCents = Cost5In + Cost3In

        TotalDollarCost = TotalCostInCents DIV CENTSPERDOLLAR
        TotalCentsCost = TotalCostInCents MOD CENTSPERDOLLAR

    display
        TotalNumDisks, TotalDollarCost, TotalCentsCost
end
```

Modula-2 code

```
MODULE  FindDiskCosts;
    (* Find the total number of disks purchased and total costs.
        FileName:CH3A      Modula-2      RKW      Jan. 1991    *)

FROM InOut IMPORT ReadCard, WriteCard, WriteString, WriteLn;

CONST  CENTSPERDOLLAR = 100;  DISKSPERBOX = 12;
        CENTSPER5INDISK = 27;  CENTSPER3INDISK = 65;

VAR  Num5InBoxes, Num3InBoxes, Num5InDisks, Num3InDisks, TotalNumDisks,
        Cost5In, Cost3In,
        TotalCostInCents, TotalDollarCost, TotalCentsCost : CARDINAL;

BEGIN
    WriteString("How many boxes of 5 inch disks purchased? ");
     ReadCard(Num5InBoxes); WriteLn;
    WriteString("How many boxes of 3 inch disks purchased? ");
     ReadCard(Num3InBoxes); WriteLn; WriteLn;

    Num5InDisks := DISKSPERBOX * Num5InBoxes;
    Num3InDisks := DISKSPERBOX * Num3InBoxes;
    TotalNumDisks := Num5InDisks + Num3InDisks;

    Cost5In := Num5InDisks * CENTSPER5INDISK;
    Cost3In := Num3InDisks * CENTSPER3INDISK;
    TotalCostInCents := Cost5In + Cost3In;

    TotalDollarCost := TotalCostInCents DIV CENTSPERDOLLAR;
    TotalCentsCost  := TotalCostInCents MOD CENTSPERDOLLAR;

    WriteString("Total number of disks purchased = ");
     WriteCard(TotalNumDisks,5); WriteLn;
    WriteString("Total cost of disks = ");
     WriteCard(TotalDollarCost,5); WriteString(" dollars and  ");
     WriteCard(TotalCentsCost,2); WriteString(" cents."); WriteLn;
END FindDiskCosts.
```

Debug and test To test this program run it with several different numbers of boxes of disks and check the results with a calculator. If the results are not consistent, a good first step in debugging is to do some **desk checking**—read the code "in person" to make certain all quantities and formulas are correct. Inserting additional WriteCard commands to display such intermediate results as Num5InDisks, Num3InDisks, Cost5In, Cost3In, and TotalCostInCents could be your second debugging step. A sample run with 33 boxes of 5-inch disks and 21 boxes of 3-inch disks should result in this display.

```
How many boxes of 5 inch disks purchased? 33
How many boxes of 3 inch disks purchased? 21

Total number of disks purchased =  648
Total cost of disks =  270 dollars and 72 cents
```

Complete the documentation The problem definition, pseudocode, code, and a sample run should be collected for the final documentation. Add a users' manual, which should state

The Modula-2 source code for this program is in file CH3A. To run the program, compile, link, and execute. Enter the numbers of boxes purchased when requested by the program. The total number of disks purchased and total cost of disks will be displayed to the screen.

CARDINAL Type Conversion and Mixed Mode

You should not mix variables and values of different types in the same expression. For example, do not mix REAL and CARDINAL. Even if a system allows such **mixed-mode calculations,** it is poor programming practice and can lead to unexpected, erroneous results. For this reason Modula-2 makes provisions for converting values from one numeric data type to another.

CARDINAL values may be converted to INTEGER values by using either of two built-in standard functions

```
INTEGER(CardinalValue);
VAL(INTEGER, CardinalValue);
```

Both of these change CardinalValue to a corresponding INTEGER. The INTEGER function does not check CardinalValue to ensure it is in the proper range for an INTEGER. Therefore, using the VAL function, which does perform the range checking, is preferred.

Converting a CARDINAL to REAL is accomplished using the standard function

```
FLOAT(CardinalValue);
```

which converts CardinalValue to a corresponding REAL value.

Functions are subprograms that calculate a value of the appropriate type. The function itself then is considered to have that value. The built-in, standard functions are listed in Appendix A and need not be imported. A function may be used anywhere a value of the appropriate type is used.

Assume, for example, that you have the following declarations,

```
VAR   CountEmUp : CARDINAL;
      RealCount  : REAL;
      IntegerCount : INTEGER;
```

A Bit of Background

Binary ABC

Dr. John V. Atanasoff agonized several years over the design of a computing machine to help his Iowa State University graduate students solve complex equations. He considered building a machine based on binary numbers—the most natural system to use with electromechanical equipment—but he feared people would not use a machine that was not based upon the familiar and comfortable decimal system. Finally, on a cold evening at a roadhouse in Illinois in 1937, he determined that it had to be done the simplest and least expensive way, with binary digits (bits). Over the next two years he and graduate student Clifford Berry built the first electronic digital computer, called the *ABC* (for Atanasoff–Berry Computer), and computer users have been stuck with binary, octal, and hexadecimal ever since.

---

and the assignment command

```
CountEmUp := 463;
```

Now you could perform the conversions

```
RealCount := FLOAT(CountEmUp);
    (* The value of RealCount becomes 463.0 *)
IntegerCount := VAL(INTEGER, CountEmUp);
    (* The value of IntegerCount becomes 463 *)
```

Then RealCount could be used without error in any expression involving REAL values, and IntegerCount could be used in any expression with INTEGER values.

CARDINAL Data in Octal and Hexadecimal

(Optional Material; may be omitted without loss of continuity.)

Modula-2 allows you to enter and display CARDINAL values in decimal, octal, or hexadecimal form. In addition to WriteCard, which displays the decimal value of a CARDINAL number, the standard utility module InOut contains the procedures

```
WriteOct(CardinalVariableIdentifier, FieldWidth)
WriteHex(CardinalVariableIdentifier, FieldWidth)
```

which respectively display the octal and hexadecimal values of a CARDINAL number.

Octal and hexadecimal values may be assigned to CARDINAL variables by appending B or H, respectively, to the numbers. For example, given the declaration

```
VAR Single, Temporary : CARDINAL;
```

you may assign

```
Single := 246B;
    (* Single has the value 246_8 = 166_10 = 0A6_16 *)
Temporary := 0AC3H;
    (* Temporary has the value 0AC3_16 = 2755_10 = 5303_8 *)
    (* A hex number must begin with a digit. Those starting with A
through F must have an initial 0 appended. *)
```

These values then could be displayed in decimal, octal, or hexadecimal notation.

Thus, the following commands would produce the indicated displays

Command	Display
WriteCard(Single, 3); WriteLn;	166
WriteOct(Single, 4); WriteLn;	246
WriteHex(Single, 4); WriteLn;	0A6
WriteCard(Temporary, 5); WriteLn;	2755
WriteOct(Temporary, 5); WriteLn;	5303
WriteHex(Temporary, 5); WriteLn;	0AC3

☐ INTEGER Type

INTEGER-type data consist of positive and negative whole numbers and zero. INTEGERs may be preceded by a positive or a negative sign; if no sign is present, the number is assumed to be positive. There are no decimal points or commas in INTEGERs. Some valid and invalid representations of INTEGERs are shown in Figure 3–4. INTEGER variables are declared with the INTEGER type identifier.

ReadInt, WriteInt

In Modula-2, the standard utility procedures ReadInt and WriteInt, imported from the InOut module, allow you to read and write INTEGER values. For example,

```
VAR Temperature, Whole : INTEGER;
```

declares variables Temperature and Whole to be of type INTEGER.

```
ReadInt(Temperature);
```

accepts input of an INTEGER and stores it as the value of variable Temperature.

```
Whole := -861;
```

assigns the value −861 to variable Whole. Then

```
WriteInt(Temperature, 7);
WriteInt(Whole, 4);
WriteInt(-9876, 6);
```

would display the values of Temperature in a field 7 spaces wide; Whole in a field of width 4; and −9876 in a field of width 6.

The syntax of ReadInt and WriteInt commands is

```
ReadInt(IntegerVariableIdentifier);
WriteInt(IntegerValue, FieldWidth);
```

In ReadInt, the single argument must be an INTEGER variable identifier, such as Whole. In WriteInt, IntegerValue may be an INTEGER variable identifier, an IN-TEGER constant (such as −9876), or a valid INTEGER expression (such as −17 + 33 or Whole − 99).

The FieldWidth argument in the WriteInt command has a CARDINAL value. The FieldWidth should be large enough to encompass the negative sign (−) if the IntegerValue is negative. If the width is larger than needed, the number is right justified in the field. A field width that is too small is ignored and defaults to the necessary width, just as in the WriteCard command.

```
Declaration:         VAR  Temperature, Whole : INTEGER;
```

Valid Integers	Invalid Integers
73	73.
+73	7.3
-73	- .84
-25004	-25.004

Range: On a system that reserves 16 bits for an integer value,
         with the leftmost bit representing a sign,
         MIN(INTEGER) = -2^{15} = $- 32768$
         MAX(INTEGER) = $2^{15} - 1$ = 32767

Operators:
  <u>Read and Write</u>
      FROM InOut IMPORT ReadInt, WriteInt;

        ReadInt (IntegerVariableIdentifier);
        WriteInt(IntegerValue, FieldWidth);

  <u>Assignment</u>   (:=)
      IntegerVariableIdentifier := Integer Value;

        Examples: Temperature := -18;   Whole := Temperature + 3;
               Whole := Whole * (642 - 184);

  <u>Arithmetic</u>

Operation	Operator	<u>Examples</u>		
Add	+	-3 + 87	Temperature + (-22)	Whole + 4
Subtract	-	87 - 3	Temperature - (-8)	4 - Whole
Multiply	*	87 * 3	Temperature * (-2)	-5 * Whole
Divide	DIV	-383 DIV 5	383 DIV (-4)	Whole DIV 9
	MOD	-383 MOD 5	383 MOD (-4)	Whole MOD 9

  <u>Arithmetic Precedence</u>   1. Parenthesized expressions
                        2. * DIV MOD from left to right
                        3. + - from left to right

Valid Integer Expressions	Invalid Integer Expressions
3 - 5 * 7	3 / 5 * 7
-170 * (4 - 9)	17 (3 - 160)
9 - (14 MOD 4)	193 MOD - 7
-193 DIV (-5)	1219 DIV - (6 * 2)
-4 * (-6 + (-2) * (83 MOD (-9)))	-9) * 5 + (6 - (4 * 3))

Conversion: To CARDINAL   CARDINAL(IntegerValue);
                             VAL(CARDINAL, IntegerValue);
           To REAL   FROM MathLib0 IMPORT real;
                         real(IntegerValue);
                    or FLOAT(IntegerValue);

Figure 3–4
INTEGER Data Type

INTEGER Range

In INTEGER representation, the leftmost bit is reserved for a sign, where a leftmost 0 or 1 would represent a positive or negative value, respectively. Therefore, the range of allowable INTEGERs in a 16-bit representation would be from -2^{15}, which is -32768, to $+(2^{15}-1)$, which is $+32767$. (The difference between maximum and minimum values arises because 1111 1111 1111 1111 binary $=$ -32767, while 1000 0000 0000 0000 binary is interpreted as -32768; but 0111 1111 1111 1111 binary $=$ $+32767$, while 0000 0000 0000 0000 binary is interpreted as 0.) MAX and MIN functions allow you to determine the largest and smallest INTEGERs, respectively, allowed on your system. For a 16-bit representation, WriteInt(MIN(INTEGER),12) would display -32768. On some systems, an attempt to use an INTEGER outside the allowable range will produce an "overflow" or "out of range" error message; on other systems the result will be an incorrect INTEGER.

INTEGER Operations

Read and Write operations for INTEGER values are performed with the ReadInt and WriteInt commands, found in the standard InOut module.

Assignment and arithmetic operators for INTEGERS are the same as those for CARDINAL values; namely, := , + , − , *, DIV, and MOD. Because two arithmetic operators may not be juxtaposed, an INTEGER expression such as 3 + − 5 must be written with parentheses, as 3 + (−5). Operator precedence for INTEGER operations is the same as that for CARDINAL operations.

INTEGER Type Conversion

Converting an INTEGER to a CARDINAL value requires one of the standard functions

```
CARDINAL(IntegerValue);   or   VAL(CARDINAL, IntegerValue);
```

where the VAL form is preferred, because it performs range checking to ensure that IntegerValue corresponds to a valid CARDINAL number.

Converting an INTEGER to REAL is accomplished by importing the function "real" from standard module MathLib0, or (in the most recent versions of Modula-2) by using FLOAT. Then, either

```
real(IntegerValue);   or   FLOAT(IntegerValue);
```

represents the REAL number corresponding to IntegerValue.

☐ REAL Type

When you declare REAL values

```
VAR TaxesDue, ReCalc, Time : REAL;
```

the compiler takes care of the details and reserves memory to be used in a manner similar to that illustrated in Figure 3–5.

REAL Precision and Range

All Modula-2 compilers allocate a **mantissa** (a binary fraction form of the number, as shown in Figure 3–5) that gives at least 7-decimal-digit precision, and many

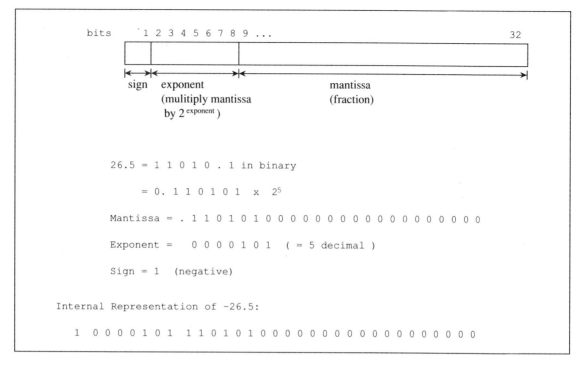

Figure 3–5
A Binary Representation of − 26.5 in a 32-bit Memory Space

compilers allow up to 14-digit accuracy or better. The minimum range will be roughly

$$-1.0E38 \text{ to } -1.0E-38 \quad \text{and} \quad 1.0E-38 \text{ to } 1.0E+38,$$

with **E + n** being computer notation for 10^n. Many compilers allow exponents, n, from − 99 to + 99; and on some systems, allowable exponent size may exceed 300. Because there is no standard function to determine the maximum REAL number, you may wish to consult your compiler manual to determine the precision and range that your system will handle.

ReadReal, WriteReal

The standard utility procedures in Modula-2 for input and output (I/O) of REAL numbers are ReadReal and WriteReal, which must be imported from module RealInOut. A REAL number may contain digits, a positive or negative sign, and a decimal point, but no commas. If the leading sign is omitted, the number is assumed to be positive. REAL numbers always should be expressed with a decimal point; for example,

specify   32.0   instead of   32

Similarly, a leading zero should be appended to the left of a ''bare'' decimal point; that is,

specify   0.234   instead of   .234.

You may express REAL values in **fixed format**, such as

$$12.387$$
$$-624.005$$
$$18.0$$
$$0.234$$

but *not* as $-486,931.7$, because commas are not allowed.

You also may use **exponential form** for REAL number I/O. In this form, the numbers above could appear as

$$1.2387E+01$$
$$-6.24005E+02$$
$$1.8E+01$$
$$2.34E-01$$
$$-4.869317E+05$$

The exponent, following E, must be an INTEGER value. When entering numbers in exponential form, you need not place just one digit before the decimal point, although the WriteReal command does so. For example, you could enter $234.0E-03$ or $23.4E-02$ instead of $2.34E-01$.

Some valid and invalid representations of REAL numbers are shown in Figure 3–6.

The syntax of the ReadReal and WriteReal commands is

```
ReadReal(RealVariableIdentifier);
WriteReal(RealValue, FieldWidth);
```

In ReadReal, the single argument must be a REAL variable identifier, such as ReCalc. In WriteReal, RealValue may be a REAL variable identifier—such as TaxesDue; it may be a REAL constant—expressed either in fixed or in exponential format; or it may be an expression—formed from REAL variable identifiers and/or REAL constant values combined with valid REAL number operators.

If you wish to enter -486931.7 into variable locations ReCalc, you could respond to ReadReal(ReCalc) with -486931.7 or $-4.869317E+05$, or you could assign

```
ReCalc := -486931.7;   or   ReCalc := -4.869317E+05;
```

WriteReal requires a CARDINAL FieldWidth argument, and the RealValue is right-justified within that field width. If the FieldWidth is too small, the display shows the correct value with no leading blanks but with the fractional part rounded to some number of digits determined by the compiler. For example, the following commands should produce the indicated displays.

Command	Display
ReCalc := -4.869317E+05;	
WriteLn;	
WriteReal(ReCalc, 16); WriteLn;	$-4.869317E+005$
WriteReal(ReCalc, 2); WriteLn;	$-4.87E+005$
	(* decimal digits determined by compiler *)

FWriteReal, WriteRealFixed, WriteRealFormat

There is no standard utility function in Modula-2 to display a REAL number in fixed format (with a fixed number of digits after the decimal point). However, a procedure

```
Declaration:       VAR  TaxesDue, ReCalc : REAL;
```

Valid Real Values	Invalid Real Values
32.0	.32
381.65	1,382.872
-0.1486	0.938,264
4.21E+07	84.0E+9822
-863.2E-20	93.45E+21.2

Range and Precision: At least $-1.0E^{+38}$ to $-1.0E^{-38}$ and $1.0E^{-38}$ to $1.0E^{+38}$
and 7 decimal digits of accuracy

Operators:
  <u>Read and Write</u>
       FROM RealInOut IMPORT ReadReal, WriteReal; (* exponential form *)

            ReadReal(RealVariableIdentifier);
            WriteReal(RealValue, FieldWidth);

       FROM RealInOut IMPORT FWriteReal; (* fixed decimal digits form *)

            FWriteReal(RealValue, FieldWidth, DecimalDigits);
               (* FWriteReal may be called WriteRealFixed, WriteRealFormat,
                  etc. The import module may be called SpecialIO, etc. *)

  <u>Assignment</u> (:=)
       RealVariableIdentifier := Real Value;

            Examples: TaxesDue := 75.25; ReCalc := TaxesDue + 5.27E+01;
                      ReCalc := 2.0 * (ReCalc + 4.25);

  <u>Arithmetic</u>

<u>Operation</u>	<u>Operator</u>	<u>Examples</u>	
Add	+	3.0 + (-87.5)	ReCalc + 3.87E+02
Subtract	-	-3.0 - (-87.5)	ReCalc - 387.0
Multiply	*	-3.0 * 2.5E+01	ReCalc * 12.67
Divide	/	3.56 / (-1.49E+03)	13.7 / ReCalc

  <u>Arithmetic Precedence</u>   1. Parenthesized expressions
                            2. * / from left to right
                            3. + - from left to right

Valid Real Expressions	Invalid Real Expressions
43.0 - 5.2 / 7.4	43.0 - 5.2 DIV 7.4
-181.6E-01 * (12.2 - 9.3)	183 (8.2 - 7.1)
98.0 - (83.0 / 16.0)	98.0 * - 16.2
-216.43176 + (-5.7) / 5.3	127.6 / 18 MOD 5
(8.2E+02)*(-5.4+(-2.8))/(19.5*4.25)	7.5 * (4.75 - 3.0 / (1.4 - 2.0)

Conversion: To CARDINAL   TRUNC(RealValue);
            To INTEGER   FROM MathLib0 IMPORT entier:
                            entier(RealValue);

Figure 3–6
REAL Data Type

for that purpose (called FWriteReal, WriteRealFixed, or WriteRealFormat in most implementations) may be found in a nonstandard module such as RealInOut or SpecialIO. FWriteReal, from module RealInOut, is used throughout this book. Check your compiler manual to determine which identifier to use on your system.

Appendix C in this book contains an FWriteReal procedure in a module called FRealOut. If you cannot find an equivalent in your Modula-2, you can compile FRealOut as indicated by the comments in the module. Then you would use the import command

```
FROM FRealOut IMPORT FWriteReal;
```

to make FWriteReal available in a program.

The syntax

```
FWriteReal(RealValue, FieldWidth, DecimalDigits);
```

requires a CARDINAL FieldWidth and a CARDINAL DecimalDigits argument that specifies the number of digits to be displayed after the decimal point. For example,

```
FWriteReal(ReCalc, 15, 4)    displays    -486931.7000
```

with 3 trailing zeros (to fill the 4 decimal places) and with 3 leading blanks (to right-justify the number in the 15-space field). The decimal point and the sign are counted in the total field width. If the field width is too small, it is ignored, and the number is displayed in the minimum field necessary to handle the value rounded to the specified number of decimal places.

REAL Operations

The arithmetic operators for multiplication, addition, and subtraction of REAL values are the same as those for CARDINAL and INTEGER numbers; namely, $*$, $+$, and $-$. However, the division operator is represented by the forward slash ($/$). For example,

$$279.37/18.2 \quad \text{produces the REAL number quotient} \quad 15.35.$$

Attempting to divide by zero aborts the program with a "division by zero" error; and division by a number small enough to produce a quotient outside the allowable REAL number range causes an "overflow" error. No two REAL operators may be juxtaposed. So instead,

$$32.0/-5.4 \quad \text{should be written as} \quad 32.0/(-5.4).$$

The precedence of REAL number operations are given by

Rules of Precedence for REAL Operations
1. parenthesized expressions
2. $*$ and $/$ from left to right
3. $+$ and $-$ from left to right.

REAL Type Conversion

The built-in standard function **TRUNC(RealValue);** converts a positive RealValue to the next-smaller CARDINAL number by dropping the decimal fraction. Similarly, function **entier(RealValue);** imported from standard module MathLib0, converts RealValue to the next-smaller INTEGER value. For example, the following commands produce the indicated results.

Command		Result
TRUNC(183.95)	183	a CARDINAL value
TRUNC(26.24)	26	a CARDINAL value
TRUNC(−18.87)	error	TRUNC cannot convert a negative value.
entier(183.95)	183	an INTEGER value
entier(−18.87)	−19	an INTEGER value
entier(−123.24)	−124	an INTEGER value

The functions for converting between numeric types are summarized in Appendix A.

Now consider an example that involves both REAL and INTEGER operations.

Example 3.2.2

Divide two numbers. Display the INTEGER quotient and remainder and the decimal quotient.

Define the problem The user enters INTEGER dividend and divisor from the keyboard. The long division quotient and remainder will be displayed, as well as the decimal quotient.

Develop a solution The user is asked to enter INTEGER Dividend and Divisor and warned that the Divisor must not be zero. INTEGER division is performed using

Dividend DIV Divisor   and   Dividend MOD Divisor.

Dividend and Divisor then are converted to REAL numbers, RealDividend and RealDivisor, using the utility function real imported from MathLib0. Finally, REAL division RealDividend/RealDivisor is performed.

Refine the solution *Pseudocode*

```
begin divide
   ask for integers Dividend and Divisor
      warn that Divisor must not be zero
   calculate and print quotient; i.e., Dividend DIV Divisor
   calculate and print remainder; i.e., Dividend MOD Divisor
   convert Dividend and Divisor
      to RealDividend and RealDivisor
   calculate and print real quotient;
      i.e. RealDividend / RealDivisor
end
```

Modula-2 code

```
MODULE Divide;
   (* Finds quotient and remainder and real quotient of
      integer dividend and divisor entered from the keyboard.
      FileName:CH3B    Modula-2    RKW    Jan. 1991 *)

FROM InOut IMPORT WriteString, WriteLn, ReadInt, WriteInt;
FROM RealInOut IMPORT FWriteReal;
FROM MathLib0 IMPORT real;
```

```
VAR  Dividend, Divisor, Quotient, Remainder : INTEGER;
     RealDividend, RealDivisor, Answer : REAL;

BEGIN
   WriteString("Enter the INTEGER value of the dividend: ");
    ReadInt(Dividend); WriteLn; WriteLn;
   WriteString("Enter the INTEGER value of the divisor. ");
    WriteString("Divisor must NOT be ZERO: ");
    ReadInt(Divisor); WriteLn; WriteLn;

   Quotient  :=  Dividend DIV Divisor;
   Remainder :=  Dividend MOD Divisor;

   WriteInt(Dividend,5); WriteString(" divided by ");
    WriteInt(Divisor,5);
    WriteString(" is "); WriteInt(Quotient,5);
    WriteString(" with a remainder of "); WriteInt(Remainder,5);
    WriteLn; WriteLn;

   RealDividend := real(Dividend);
   RealDivisor  := real(Divisor);
   Answer  :=  RealDividend / RealDivisor;

   WriteString("         In decimal form this is: ");
    FWriteReal(Answer,12,4); WriteLn;
END Divide.
```

Debug and test Executing the program, entering 23 for the Dividend and 7 for the Divisor, produces the following display:

```
Enter the INTEGER value of the dividend: 23
Enter the INTEGER value of the divisor. Divisor must NOT be ZERO: 7
   23 divided by    7 is    3 with a remainder of    2
      In decimal form this is:    3.2857
```

The program should be tested with positive and negative values for Dividend and Divisor. What happens if any of the numbers exceed the range for INTEGERs on your computer, when the dividend is zero, or when the divisor is zero?

Complete the documentation Collect the problem definition, pseudocode, code, and sample run. Write a users' manual. Remember to warn the user about the pitfalls of division by zero.

☐ Exponentiation

(Optional material; may be omitted without loss of continuity.)

There is no standard operator in Modula-2 to perform **exponentiation** (raise a number to a power). One way to raise any value to a cardinal power (other than zero) is to multiply the value by itself the appropriate number of times. For example, to raise a number x (of any type) to the 5th power, you would perform the multiplication $x * x * x * x * x$, which gives you an exact answer, if the product does not overflow the allowed range of values. Similarly, to raise a number to a negative-integer power, use the rule that $x^{-n} = 1/x^n$, multiply x by itself n times, convert to

REAL, and take the reciprocal of the result. When x is not zero, the value of x^0 is defined as 1.0 and may be handled as a special case.

A straightforward method to raise a value x to a REAL power y is to convert x to REAL, use the functions exp and ln (imported from built-in standard module MathLib0), and apply the formula

$$x^y = \exp(y * \ln(x)).$$

For example, if Base is a CARDINAL variable, then

$$\text{Base}^{1.8} = \exp(1.8 * \ln(\text{FLOAT(Base)})).$$

You may not raise a negative or zero Base to a REAL power using this algorithm.

Questions 3.2

1. State the reasons why each invalid value and invalid expression would not be valid, and give the value of each valid expression in **a.** Figure 3−2, **b.** Figure 3−4, **c.** Figure 3−6.

2. Given the declarations

```
VAR   NumberOnHand, Inventory : CARDINAL;
      PurchasedOrSold : INTEGER;
      AmountDue, CostPerItem : REAL;
```

By inserting the appropriate conversion functions, correct each of the following so that they are valid expressions, without mixed mode.
   a. NumberOnHand := NumberOnHand + PurchasedOrSold;
   b. WriteInt(PurchasedOrSold − Inventory, 10);
   c. AmountDue := CostPerItem * PurchasedOrSold;
   d. WriteReal(Inventory * CostPerItem, 16);
   e. NumberOnHand := AmountDue / CostPerItem;
   f. PurchasedOrSold := AmountDue DIV CostPerItem;

3. **a.** Use the MAX and MIN functions to determine the range of CARDINAL and INTEGER values on your computer.
   b. Determine the range and precision of REAL values for your computer.
   c. What is the name of the procedure used by your compiler to display REAL values with a fixed number of decimal places? From which module is it imported?

4. (Optional) If variables A, B, and C are declared to be CARDINAL, and x is REAL,
   a. what would be displayed by the commands

```
A := 17;
WriteCard(A,2); WriteLn;
WriteOct(A,2); WriteLn;
WriteHex(A,2); WriteLn;
```

   b. what would be displayed by the commands

```
B := 26B;
C := 0A3H;
WriteCard(B,3); WriteLn;
WriteOct(B,3); WriteLn;
WriteHex(B,3); WriteLn;
WriteCard(C,3); WriteLn;
WriteOct(C,3); WriteLn;
WriteHex(C,3); WriteLn;
```

c. what would be displayed by the commands

```
X := 19.7;
C := TRUNC(x);
FWriteReal(x,6,2); WriteLn;
WriteCard(C,3); WriteLn;
WriteOct(C,3); WriteLn;
WriteHex(C,3); WriteLn;
```

5. (Optional) For each Base and Exponent value, show how you would calculate the result *Base^{Exponent}* and determine the value of the result (if it exists).
   a. CARDINAL Base = 5, and CARDINAL Exponent = 3
   b. CARDINAL Base = 5, and REAL Exponent = 2.5
   c. INTEGER Base = 5, and REAL Exponent = 2.5
   d. REAL Base = 2.3, and CARDINAL Exponent = 3
   e. REAL Base = 3.0, and INTEGER Exponent = −3
   f. INTEGER Base = − 5, and CARDINAL Exponent = 3
   g. INTEGER Base = −5, and INTEGER Exponent = −3
   h. INTEGER Base = −5, and REAL Exponent = −2.5

3.3   CHAR and BOOLEAN Data Types

Now consider two standard data types that are not numeric. That is, operations on these types do not include addition, subtraction, multiplication, or division.

CHARacter Type

On most systems, the memory location reserved for a variable of CHAR type is one byte long, sufficient to hold the binary code for one alphanumeric character. Character codes will be discussed in detail in Chapter 5, but for now, it is important to know that virtually any character represented on the keyboard — including punctuation marks and the space bar — may be assigned to a CHAR variable or constant. A CHARacter value consists of exactly one character. A CHARacter constant is enclosed between single quotes (' '). Some representations of CHARacter values are shown in Figure 3–7. Other parts of the figure are discussed in the following subsection.

Read, Write, Assignment of CHARacters
Operations on characters include using the Read and Write commands imported from module InOut, the syntax of which is

```
Read(CharacterVariableIdentifier);
Write(CharacterValue);
```

In the Read command, the argument is a variable identifier defined to be of type CHAR; that is,

```
VAR CharacterVariableIdentifier : CHAR;
```

In the Write command, CharacterValue is a CHARacter constant, a CHARacter-type variable identifier, or an expression that has a valid single CHARacter value. For example, the statement

```
VAR Symbol, Letter, Mark : CHAR;
```

declares variables Symbol, Letter, and Mark to be of type CHARacter.

Figure 3–7
CHARacter Data Type

```
Declaration:        VAR  Symbol, Letter, Mark : CHAR;


Valid Single CHARacter Values    |  Invalid Single CHARacter Values
  'A'                            |   'ABC'
  'q'                            |   **
  '5'   the character '5'        |   71
  '$'                            |   '-5'
  ' '   blank space             |   ' b '    blank b blank


Operations:
  Read and Write
      FROM InOut IMPORT  Read, Write:

          Read(CharacterVariableIdentifier);
          Write(CharacterValue);

  Assignment   ( := )
      CharacterVariableIdentifier := CHARacterValue;

      Examples:      Letter := 'r';
                     Mark   := '8';
```

Read(Symbol) accepts input of a single character and stores it as the value of Symbol. When entering a character from the keyboard in response to Read, only the character itself is entered; that is, to enter *T* press only the T key, not 'T'.

Letter := 'r' assigns the character *r* to variable Letter. For assignment, the character must be enclosed within single quotes.

Then the following commands would produce the indicated displays.

Command	Display
Letter := 'r';	
Mark := '8';	
WriteLn;	
Write(Letter); WriteLn;	r
Write(Mark); WriteLn;	8
Write('Q'); WriteLn;	Q

Read, Write, and assignment are the only standard operations defined for CHARacter variables. In Chapters 5, 10, and 11 you will discover that character codes also may be compared with each other, and you will find specially designed algorithms to perform other operations on CHARacters.

The following code illustrates assignment, Read, and Write upon CHARacter values.

```
MODULE TestCharacters;
   (* Illustrates CHARacter constants, variables, and operations.
      File Name:CH3C    Modula-2   RKW    Jan. 1991  *)

FROM InOut IMPORT Read, Write, WriteString, WriteLn;

CONST  Star = '*' ;    (* Assign * and space as CHAR constants *)
       Blank = ' ' ;
```

```
VAR  NiceSymbol, GoodMark, Letter, Terminator : CHAR ;

BEGIN
    (* Assign value to Letter.  Read values for NiceSymbol and GoodMark. *)
    Letter := 'Q';
    WriteString("Press the nicest key on the keyboard:  ");
     Read(NiceSymbol); Write(NiceSymbol); Read(Terminator); WriteLn;
    WriteString("Now press a key for GoodMark: ");
     Read(GoodMark); Write(GoodMark); Read(Terminator); WriteLn; WriteLn;

    (* Write CHAR constants, declared constants, and variables *)
    Write('H'); Write('e'); Write('l'); Write('p'); Write('!'); WriteLn;

    WriteString("Star Letter Star is  ");
     Write(Star); Write(Letter); Write(Star); WriteLn;
    WriteString("How is this for nice?  ");
     Write(NiceSymbol); Write(NiceSymbol); Write(Blank);
     Write(NiceSymbol); Write(NiceSymbol); WriteLn;
    WriteString("GoodMark is  "); Write(GoodMark); WriteLn;
END TestCharacters.
```

When you run this program, pressing the *&* and *8* keys for NiceSymbol and GoodMark, the screen display is

```
Press the nicest key on the keyboard:  &
Now press a key for Goodmark: 8

Help!
Star Letter Star is  *Q*
How is this for nice?  && &&
GoodMark is  8
```

Terminator represents a CHAR variable that is read and never used. When you Read a character, some systems store that character in a temporary memory location (called a *buffer*) until a key such as Enter is pressed to terminate entry. Then the code for the terminating key gets assigned as a CHARacter itself. If the first Read(Terminator) command is omitted, the program may not even wait for the value of GoodMark, because GoodMark already has been assigned the value of the Enter (or other) key, which was pressed after NiceSymbol was entered.

☐ Array of CHARacters

Constants of type ARRAY OF CHAR have been used in every example so far. ARRAY OF CHAR refers to a **string** (or list) of characters. Thus, when you declare

```
CONST Phrase =  ''2B or not 2B '';
```

and execute the commands

```
WriteString(Phrase); WriteLn;
WriteString(''This is fun!''); WriteLn;
```

you see

```
2B or not 2B
This is fun!
```

Constants consisting of character strings usually are enclosed within double quotes (" "). However, if you wish to include a double quote (") as one of the characters in the string, you should enclose the string itself within single quotes (' ') instead.

Strings are printed with the standard utility procedure WriteString, imported from module InOut. String variables may be declared and used by defining a data TYPE, ARRAY [0..LASTONE] OF CHAR, where the CARDINAL constants within the brackets spell out explicitly that the string variable contains up to LASTONE + 1 characters, numbered left to right from 0 to LASTONE.

Values may be assigned to string variables, or they may be entered via

```
ReadString(StringOfCharacters);
```

which is imported from InOut. When you use ReadString to accept input from the keyboard you may not enter spaces in the string, because this command considers a space character to be an input terminator. Ways of handling this problem are considered in detail in Chapter 5, Section 5.2. Declaration, assignment, ReadString, WriteString, and the use of double and single quotes for CHARacter strings are illustrated in the following program.

```
MODULE TestStrings;
   (* Illustrates ARRAY OF CHAR for String constants & variables
      File Name:CH3D    Modula-2    RKW    Jan. 1991   *)

FROM InOut IMPORT ReadString, WriteString, WriteLn;

CONST  Phrase = "Then she went away.";
       HOWMANYCHARSLESS1 = 79;
TYPE   STRINGOFCHARS = ARRAY [0..HOWMANYCHARSLESS1] OF CHAR;
VAR  Saying1, Saying2, Saying3, FirstName, LastName : STRINGOFCHARS;

BEGIN
   Saying1 := 'She said, "';
   Saying2 := "It's ";
   Saying3 := 'finished!" ';

   WriteString("What is your first name? "); ReadString(FirstName); WriteLn;
    WriteString("What is your last name?  "); ReadString(LastName); WriteLn;
    WriteLn;

   WriteString("Memo to:  "); WriteString(LastName); WriteString(", ");
    WriteString(FirstName); WriteLn;

   WriteString(Saying1); WriteString(Saying2); WriteString(Saying3);
    WriteString(Phrase); WriteLn;
END TestStrings.
```

Observe carefully how the quotes (" ") and apostrophe (') were handled by the program. Although any characters whatsoever may be assigned to a string variable, string constants may not contain both a double quote and a single quote (apostrophe). If the string constant itself is enclosed within double quotes, then the single quote character may be contained therein, and vice versa.

Even though the number of characters allowed in a particular string is defined in the declaration of that string, the WriteString command displays only through the last character entered or assigned.

If your name were *Charles Darwin*, the output produced by the program would be

```
What is your first name? Charles
What is your last name? Darwin

Memo to: Darwin, Charles
She said, "It's finished!" Then she went away.
```

BOOLEAN Type

Still another type of variable is the BOOLEAN or logical type. A variable or constant of type BOOLEAN may be assigned only the value TRUE or the value FALSE or an expression that evaluates to be either true or false. For example, given the declaration

```
VAR  TestItOut : BOOLEAN;
```

you may make assignments

```
TestItOut := TRUE;   (* or FALSE *)
```

and

```
TestItOut := (3 = 5); (* whose value is FALSE *)
```

There are no standard utility procedures to read or write BOOLEAN variables. Standard BOOLEAN operations are limited to assigning values to the variables and testing those values. (In chapter 4, Section 4.1, you will develop your own procedure to display a BOOLEAN value.) Figure 3–8 shows the features of BOOLEAN data type.

Figure 3–8
BOOLEAN Data Type

```
Declaration:           VAR  TestItOut, ItIsRight : BOOLEAN;

Valid BOOLEAN Values          |  Invalid BOOLEAN Values
   TRUE                       |        true
   FALSE                      |        false
                              |        'T'
                              |        F

Operations
   Read and Write
        There are no standard functions to read or
        write BOOLEAN Values.

   Assignment   ( := )
        BooleanVariableIdentifier  := BooleanValue;

           Examples:   TestItOut := FALSE;
                       ItIsRight := (17 > 3);

   Testing   (* see chapters 4 and 7 *)

       IF  BooleanValue  THEN
          executable commands;
       END; (* IF *)
```

Questions 3.3

1. Given the declarations

```
CONST  OneLetter = 'a';  OneChar = 'I';
       NUMCHARSLESS1 = 19;
       Blank = ' ';
TYPE   STR = ARRAY [0..NUMCHARSLESS1] OF CHAR;
VAR    Letter, Character, Initial ; CHAR;
       Sentence, Words ; STR;
```

what would be displayed by each of the following?

a. ```
   Write(OneChar); Write(Blank); Write(OneLetter);
   Write('m'); Write(Blank); Write(Blank);
   Words := ''Happy!'';
   WriteString(Words); WriteLn;
   ```

b. ```
   Words := ''Help,'';
   Sentence := ''m'';
   WriteString(Words); Write(Blank);
   Write(OneChar); WriteString(Sentence);
   WriteString(' caught in a computer.'); WriteLn;
   ```

2. Given the declarations

```
CONST  OK = TRUE;
VAR    TestIt, TorF ; BOOLEAN;
       Num1, Num2 ; CARDINAL;
       RealNum ; REAL;
```

what is the value (TRUE or FALSE) of TestIt after executing each of the following fragments of code?

a. ```
   TorF := FALSE;
   TestIt := TorF;
   ```

b. ```
   TorF := OK;
   TestIt := TorF;
   ```

c. ```
   Num1 := 5;
   RealNum := 7.2;
   Num2 := TRUNC(RealNum);
   TestIt := Num1 > Num2; (* > means ''is greater
                                than'' *)
   ```

d. ```
   RealNum := 18.4;  Num1 := 4;  Num2 := 9;
   TestIT := RealNum >  ( FLOAT(Num1) + FLOAT(Num2) );
   ```

3. Variable Message is declared at the beginning of a program by the statement

```
VAR Message : ARRAY [Start..Stop] OF CHAR;
```

Where and how should Start and Stop be declared?

3.4 *Top–Down Design and Invocation*

Now that you understand some data types and operations, you are prepared to develop new problem solving skills. One of these skills is called top-down design. It will help you create well thought out, logically designed programs. You will use pseudocode and the Sequence control structure to practice top-down design and to examine more features of Modula-2.

☐ **Designing a Solution**

Dividing a problem into smaller, more manageable subproblems is called **top-down design.** If the subproblems still include too many tasks, they may be subdivided further; and the process continues until the complexity of the problem has been reduced to a solvable level. The important first step in top-down design is to *define the problem well*. This includes determining the destination and structure of the output information as well as the content, form, and source of the input data. It is critical to know what the output information should contain, how it should look, and whether it is to appear on the CRT, be printed, or be directed to secondary storage. Then you can determine what input data are needed and whether they will be entered from the keyboard, read from a disk file, or accumulated directly from equipment such as a point-of-sale terminal, timeclock, thermostat, et cetera.

☐ **Pseudocode and Procedures**

After a problem has been divided into manageable parts, each piece may be developed as a separate subprogram called a **procedure,** and the program can be written and tested as a sequential list of procedure invocations. For example, pseudocode for a sales transaction in a department store might appear as follows:

```
begin Sales Transaction
        read product description and number of items from clerk's terminal
        find price from a data file
        calculate cost of item
        display cost of item
        update the store records
            update inventory
            accumulate daily record
                record for clerk
                record for the store
end
```

Each procedure listed here could have its own pseudocode. If each line in the pseudocode represented a subprogram, there could be 9 additional sets of pseudocode for the problem, corresponding to the 9 subprograms. The hierarchy indicated by indentations shows that some procedures, such as ''accumulate daily record,'' invoke other procedures. Also, some procedures, such as ''update inventory,'' may need to be subdivided further in order to become solvable problems themselves.

Importing, Declaring, and Defining
In order to translate source code to machine language, the compiler must know

1. which modules, procedures, functions, and other information to import from elsewhere,
2. the names and values of permanent constants,
3. the names and sizes of memory locations to reserve for all variables, and
4. the code for the procedures that are to be included in the program.

Therefore, at the beginning of a program you IMPORT needed entities from external modules, such as InOut. Then you declare constants, types, variables, and your own procedure definitions. These declarations may occur in any sequence, but most often they appear in the order:

CONSTants
TYPEs

VARiables
PROCEDUREs

In Modula-2, the only rule for the order of declarations is that each entity must be defined before it is used. (There are some exceptions to this rule, such as with recursion and pointers, and they will be treated later as special cases.) Already, you have declared CONSTants and VARiables of a variety of types. In the previous section you even defined a new TYPE for an ARRAY OF CHARacters. You will have the opportunity later to define other new data TYPEs. PROCEDURE declarations will include the complete code for the procedures.

IMPORTing from Modules
The Modula-2 IMPORT command provides a way of accessing procedures, data types, and data that have been collected in a module external to your program. A number of standard modules with procedures, such as WriteString, WriteLn, and others, are included with every Modula-2 compiler. Definitions of these are collected in Appendix B.

One syntax used for the IMPORT command has been shown in the examples so far, namely,

```
FROM NameOfModule IMPORT ListOfProcedures;
```

Another syntax is shown in Section 5.4.

External modules are written in two parts. The first part, called the DEFINITION MODULE, contains declarations of the types, constants, variables, and procedures defined within the module. The second part, called the IMPLEMENTATION MODULE, contains the actual code for each procedure. Usually the DEFINITION MODULE is accessible and readable. The IMPLEMENTATION MODULE may not be made available because you, the programmer, seldom need (or even want) to know *how* the procedure works; your interest is in *what* the procedure does, which is described in the DEFINITION MODULE. This illustrates the principle of **information hiding,** which prevents the programmer and the user from being burdened with the details of how data are defined and how tasks are performed.

If you examine DEFINITION MODULE InOut in Appendix B, you will see some of the procedures you have used to read and write various types of data. The heading for

```
PROCEDURE WriteString(s : ARRAY OF CHAR)
```

for example, shows you that this procedure intends to display the contents of a memory location specified by a variable named *s* (called a **parameter**), which contains an ARRAY OF CHARacters passed to it by your program. On the other hand,

```
PROCEDURE WriteLn
```

need not refer to any parameters, since it always executes the same carriage return and/or line feed commands.

Writing a Procedure
Obviously, not every procedure you need to use will have been written previously and found in a standard module. Therefore, you will need to create subprograms yourself and include the code in the PROCEDUREs declaration part of a program. Procedures and functions will be discussed in detail in Chapter 6, but the following information will allow you to start using good top-down design now.

Table 3-1
Differences between
PROCEDURE and
MODULE Syntax

PROCEDURE (Subprogram) Syntax	MODULE (Program) Syntax
Heading begins with the word PROCEDURE.	Heading begins with the word MODULE.
ListOfParameters follows the ProcedureName.	No ListOfParameters follows the ModuleName.
Final punctuation after END ProcedureName is a semicolon(;).	Final punctuation after END ModuleName is a period(.).
No IMPORT commands are allowed within a procedure.	All IMPORTing must be done through the main module.

Since a PROCEDURE is actually a small program, its code looks like a program module. A simple syntax is

```
PROCEDURE  ProcedureName(ListOfParameters);

   declarations;
    (* constants, variables, etc. *)
   BEGIN

      executable commands;

   END ProcedureName;
```

Comparison of this PROCEDURE syntax with the MODULE syntax in Figure 2-2b shows only four differences that are important now. They are summarized in Table 3-1.

Calling a Procedure; Parameters

A procedure is called and executed from the program by specifying its name and the parameters in the same order as listed in the procedure heading. The ListOfParameters in the calling command and in the procedure heading represents the collection of values that is passed into and/or out of the PROCEDURE by the program.

You may specify that a parameter be passed from the program into the procedure but not back out again. Or you may ask that the value of a parameter be passed back out to the program after the procedure has executed. The first type of parameter is called an **In Only** or Value parameter. It must have a defined value before the procedure is invoked. The second type of parameter is called an **In/Out** or VARiable parameter. Whatever a procedure does to a Value (In Only) parameter happens only inside the procedure; it does not change the original value in the calling program. Changes made to a VARiable parameter are made also in the calling program. An initial value of a VARiable parameter may be, but need not be, defined before the procedure is called.

In the command that calls a procedure, the parameters to be passed are simply listed by name. In the procedure heading, corresponding parameters are listed in the same order by name and data type; and VARiable parameter names are preceded by VAR.

For example, assume a procedure named DoItNow is to receive INTEGER values Num1 and Num2 from the program and will calculate and return to the program the Sum and Difference of the numbers. Then the program command that calls the procedure would look like

```
DoItNow(Num1, Num2, Sum, Difference);
```

The corresponding procedure heading could appear as

```
PROCEDURE  DoItNow(Integer1, Integer2 : INTEGER;
                   VAR  Total, Difference : INTEGER);
```

Notice that the names by which the procedure refers to the parameters may be, but are not required to be, the same as those used in the program. However, the number, order, and data types must match.

Thus, for the procedure and call to DoItNow,

Program Parameter	corresponds to	Procedure Parameter	Parameter Type
Num1	→	Integer1	Value (In Only)
Num2	→	Integer2	Value (In Only)
Sum	↔	Total	VARiable (In/Out)
Difference	↔	Difference	VARiable (In/Out)

where the arrows represent the direction(s) values are passed.

The following example illustrates defining and invoking procedures to implement part of a sales transaction.

Example 3.4.1

Calculate the AmountDue on the sale of a single item.

Define the problem   The program will ask for the CostPerItem, the NumberOfItems purchased, and DiscountRate. Then it will calculate and display TotalCost, TaxDue, and AmountDue.

Develop a solution   The three procedures constituting the program commands will be

1. EnterSalesData, which will ask the user to enter the NumberOfItems purchased and CostPerItem,
2. CalculateCosts, which defines a TAXRATE CONSTant, asks the user for the DiscountRate, and calculates

TotalCost	= NumberOfItems * CostPerItem
TotalCost (discounted)	= TotalCost − (DiscountRate * TotalCost)
TaxDue	= TotalCost * TAXRATE
AmountDue	= TotalCost + TaxDue

3. DisplayCosts, which displays the TotalCost, TaxDue, and AmountDue.

Refine the solution
Pseudocode for Program Module MakeASale

```
begin MakeASale
      EnterSalesData(NumberOfItems, CostPerItem)
      CalculateCosts(NumberOfItems, CostPerItem, TotalCost, TaxDue, AmountDue)
      DisplayCosts(TotalCost, TaxDue, AmountDue)
end MakeASale
```

Pseudocode for Procedure EnterSalesData(HowMany, UnitCost)

```
begin EnterSalesData
        ask how many of this item were purchased, HowMany
        ask what is the cost of each, UnitCost
end EnterSalesData
```

Pseudocode for Procedure CalculateCosts(NumItems, ItemCost, Cost, Taxes, Due)

```
set TAXRATE constant = 0.0625
declare local variable DiscountRate
begin CalculateCosts
        ask what is the discount rate, DiscountRate
        calculate    Cost = NumItems * ItemCost
        calculate    Cost = Cost − (DiscountRate * Cost)
        calculate    Taxes = Cost * TAXRATE
        calculate    Due = Cost + Taxes
end CalculateCosts
```

Pseudocode for DisplayCosts(PurchaseCost, HowMuchTax, AmountDue)

```
begin DisplayCosts
        display    "Purchase    = $" PurchaseCost
        display    "Tax         = $" HowMuchTax
        display    "Amount Due = $" AmountDue
end DisplayCosts
```

Modula-2 code

```modula2
MODULE  MakeASale;
    (* Asks for Number of Items and Cost Per Item.  Defines and invokes
       procedures to Calculate and Display Costs and Taxes.
       FileName:CH3E      Modula-2      RKW      Jan. 1991   *)

FROM InOut IMPORT WriteString, WriteLn, ReadCard;
FROM RealInOut IMPORT ReadReal, FWriteReal;

VAR  CostPerItem, TotalCost, TaxDue, AmountDue : REAL;
     NumberOfItems : CARDINAL;

PROCEDURE  EnterSalesData(VAR HowMany : CARDINAL;   VAR UnitCost : REAL);
    BEGIN
       WriteString("How many of this item were purchased? ");
        ReadCard(HowMany); WriteLn;
       WriteString("What is the cost of each? ");
        ReadReal(UnitCost); WriteLn;
    END EnterSalesData;

PROCEDURE  CalculateCosts(NumItems : CARDINAL;   ItemCost : REAL;
                         VAR Cost, Taxes, Due : REAL);
    CONST  TAXRATE = 0.0625;
    VAR  DiscountRate : REAL;   (* DiscountRate is called a local variable,
                                   for use within this procedure only *)
    BEGIN
       WriteString("What is the discount rate (e.g. enter 0.10 for 10%)? ");
        ReadReal(DiscountRate); WriteLn;
       Cost  := FLOAT(NumItems) * ItemCost;
        Cost := Cost - (DiscountRate * Cost);
```

```
      Taxes := Cost * TAXRATE;
      Due   := Cost + Taxes;
   END CalculateCosts;

PROCEDURE  DisplayCosts(PurchaseCost, HowMuchTax, AmountDue : REAL);
   BEGIN
      WriteString("Purchase    = $"); FWriteReal(PurchaseCost,8,2); WriteLn;
      WriteString("Tax         = $"); FWriteReal(HowMuchTax,8,2); WriteLn;
      WriteString("Amount Due = $"); FWriteReal(AmountDue,8,2); WriteLn;
   END DisplayCosts;


BEGIN  (* Program MakeASale *)
   EnterSalesData(NumberOfItems, CostPerItem); WriteLn;
   CalculateCosts(NumberOfItems, CostPerItem, TotalCost, TaxDue, AmountDue);
    WriteLn;
   DisplayCosts(TotalCost, TaxDue, AmountDue); WriteLn;
END MakeASale.
```

A sample run of this program appears as follows

```
How many of this item were purchased? 3
What is the cost of each? 1.59

What is the discount rate (e.g., enter 0.10 for 10%)?
0.125

Purchase    = $    4.17
Tax         = $    0.26
Amount Due = $    4.43
```

Debug and test You should study this program code carefully. The program module itself contains only three commands—those to call the three procedures. Note carefully how the parameters are passed to and from the procedure, which ones are In Only (Value), and which are In/Out (VARiable). What would happen, for example, if UnitCost in PROCEDURE EnterSalesData had not been declared as a VARiable parameter?

Also note the local CONSTant TAXRATE and local variable DiscountRate in PROCEDURE CalculateCosts. These are defined within the procedure, rather than in the program module, because they are needed only within PROCEDURE CalculateCosts.

Test the program with limiting values of 0 for NumberOfItems, CostPerItem, and DiscountRate, as well as for other reasonable values.

Complete the documentation Collect the problem definition, pseudocode, codes, and sample run. Write a users' manual stating the location of the source code (CH3E) and how to run the program. Should users receive any instructions about restrictions on the value of data to be entered?

Questions 3.4

1. What is a standard module? What is its purpose?
2. Why are programmers and users often allowed to see DEFINITION modules, but not IMPLEMENTATION modules?

3. **a.** What term denotes a value that is passed to a procedure by listing it in the procedure call and in the procedure heading?

   b. Distinguish between an In Only (Value) parameter and an In/Out (VARiable) parameter. How are they represented in PROCEDURE headings?

4. A procedure AreaOfSquare needs to obtain the REAL value of the length of a side of the square from the main program. Show how the procedure heading and a command invoking the procedure should look.

5. A procedure needs to use the WriteCard command from module InOut. How does the procedure gain access to this command?

6. Complete this chart for the parameters of *all three* procedures of the MakeASale program (File:CH3E, Example 3.4.1).

PROCEDURE CalculateCosts

Program Parameter	corresponds to	Procedure Parameter	Parameter Type
NumberOfItems	→	NumItems	Value (In Only)
TotalCost	↔	Cost	VARiable (In/Out)
. . .	. . .	. . .	. . .

7. Explain in your own words what top-down design is.

3.5   *Redirection of I/O*

Until now all input has been entered from the keyboard, and output has been directed to the screen. Some computers allow you to issue operating system commands that **redirect** input and output from and to devices other than the keyboard and screen. The standard InOut module of Modula-2 also contains procedures that allow your program to redirect I/O to receive input data from a previously written file and to send the output to a disk file where it can be stored permanently, copied, sent to a printer, redisplayed on the screen, and so on. (More sophisticated file-handling methods also are available in Modula-2; they are discussed in Chapter 14.)

OpenInput, CloseInput, OpenOutput, CloseOutput

Redirection from a Modula-2 program is accomplished by using four standard utility procedures imported from module InOut. The procedures for redirection are

```
OpenOutput(Extension);
     (* Waits for the user to enter an output file name, opens
        the output file, and closes the default device (normally
        the terminal screen) to output. *)

CloseOutput;
     (* Closes the output file and reopens screen for output. *)

OpenInput(Extension);
     (* Waits for the user to enter an input file name, opens the
        input file, and closes the default device (normally the
        keyboard) for input. *)

CloseInput;
     (* Closes the input file and reopens keyboard for input. *)
```

In some versions of Modula-2, the "Extension" parameter is a default, such as "DAT", which OpenInput and OpenOutput may append to the data file name. In other versions, "Extension" may contain a message that is displayed to prompt the user for a filename when OpenOutput or OpenInput is called. In still other versions, the "Extension" argument is ignored or not even allowed.

In order to use OpenInput, a file must already exist by the given name. This file can be created using an editor or by any other method that puts data into the file. For OpenOutput, if a file does not exist by the name the user specifies, a file by that name will be created and opened. If the named file already exists, then the Open-Output command opens that file and replaces its contents with the newly written material.

Once the OpenInput command is executed, all Read, ReadInt, ReadCard, ReadReal, ReadString and other Read... commands accept input from the file, rather than from the keyboard. This continues until CloseInput occurs. If OpenInput is issued again on the same file, after CloseInput, the first Read... statement begins reading again from the beginning of the file. Once the OpenOutput command is executed, all Write... commands send output to the file, rather than to the terminal screen. This continues until CloseOutput occurs. If OpenOutput is issued again on the same file, after CloseOutput, the first Write... statement begins writing again at the beginning of the file. All previous output to the file is lost, even if the new output is shorter, because an End-of-File mark is placed after the most recently written data, and the computer will not read past the indicated end of file.

Example 3.5.1

Rewrite the MakeASale example (3.4.1) to send output to a file called OUTDATA, while still accepting input from the keyboard.

Define the problem   Before the call to procedure DisplayCosts, an OpenOutput command will redirect output to an output file called OUTDATA. Then the command CloseOutput will be executed before END MakeASale.

Develop a solution   The solution is described earlier in Example 3.4.1. The only addition is to open and close the output file.

Refine the solution   Here is the new pseudocode for MakeASale.

```
begin MakeASale
    EnterSalesData(NumberOfItems, CostPerItem)
    CalculateCosts(NumberOfItems, CostPerItem, TotalCost, TaxDue, AmountDue)
    open the output file
    DisplayCosts(TotalCost, TaxDue, AmountDue)
    close the output file
end MakeASale
```

Modula-2 code

```
MODULE  MakeASale;
    (* Defines and invokes procedures to Calculate and Display Costs
       and Taxes.   OUTPUT REDIRECTED.
       CODE INCOMPLETE.   PROCEDURES MUST BE SUPPLIED FROM FILE CH3E.
       FileName:CH3F2     Modula-2     RKW       Jan. 1991    *)
```

```
(* NOTE IMPORT OF OpenOutput, CloseOutput *)
FROM InOut IMPORT WriteString, WriteLn, ReadCard,
                  OpenOutput, CloseOutput;

FROM RealInOut IMPORT ReadReal, FWriteReal;

VAR  CostPerItem, TotalCost, TaxDue, AmountDue : REAL;
     NumberOfItems : CARDINAL;


(* Define PROCEDURES EnterSalesData, CalculateCosts, DisplayCosts
     here.  See File CH3E,  Example 3.4.1  *)


BEGIN  (* Program MakeASale *)
   EnterSalesData(NumberOfItems, CostPerItem); WriteLn;
   CalculateCosts(NumberOfItems, CostPerItem, TotalCost, TaxDue, AmountDue);
   WriteLn;

   WriteString("Enter the name of the output file: ");
    OpenOutput("DAT");    (* OUTPUT FILE OPENED *)
   DisplayCosts(TotalCost, TaxDue, AmountDue); WriteLn;
   CloseOutput;               (* OUTPUT FILE CLOSED *)

END MakeASale.
```

Observe that the OpenOutput command was not issued until after the sales data was entered, so that the prompt messages to enter data still were directed to the screen and not to the output file. Also a WriteString prompt was issued before the OpenOutput command, so that the user knows what is expected. If you are using a system that allows you to specify a particular disk drive (such as B), you may do that by prefacing the file name with the drive designation (such as B:OUTDATA).

Debug and test   You must insert the three PROCEDURES from Example 3.4.1 (File:CH3E) into the program to have complete, executable code. Debugging a program in which the output has been redirected to a file can be frustrating, because you do not see the output until the program has executed successfully and the output file has been displayed. If the program does not run successfully, you may never get to see the output at all. For debugging purposes it is most convenient to *enclose the commands that redirect the output between comment indicators (*   *).* This includes the WriteString prompts for the file name, the OpenOutput, and the Close-Output commands. Then, when the program is executed, output will be displayed to the terminal screen, from which you can debug the program by the usual techniques. After the program is running well, remove the comment indicators from the redirection commands and test to ensure that everything is written properly to the output file.

A sample run of the program, with the appropriate procedures included, displays to the screen during execution only

```
How many of this item were purchased? 5
What is the cost of each? 23.95

What is the discount rate (e.g., enter 0.10 for 10%)? 0.15

Enter the name of the output file: DAT> OUTDATA
```

To view the output you would issue your operating system's command to TYPE, PRINT, or otherwise show the contents of a file. Instructing your computer to display the output file produced in the test run should show the contents of the file to be

```
Purchase   = $    101.79
Tax        = $      6.36
Amount Due = $    108.15
```

Complete the documentation   Complete documentation for this program is shown in Figure 3–9.

Questions 3.5

1. In the OpenOutput(Extension) and OpenInput(Extension) commands, how does *your* compiler treat "Extension"?
2. Outline, by a fragment of code, how you would use OpenOutput and CloseOutput to write the values of several output variables to a file *and also to your terminal screen*. Be careful not to lose the first values written to the file by writing over them.
3. What disaster occurs if you use the name of the file in which your program is stored as the name of the output file to which data is to be written by the program?
4. Where will the messages "Enter name of output file" and "Enter name of input file" be written by the following fragment of code?

```
BEGIN
  WriteString(''Enter name of output file'');
  OpenOutput(''OUT '');
  WriteString(''Enter name of input file'');
  OpenInput('' IN'');
    ReadCard(Data1);
    ReadReal(Data2);
  CloseInput;
  . . .
  . . .
```

How would you correct the problem, so that both messages are displayed to the terminal screen?
5. Why can it be frustrating to debug a program that redirects all output to a file? What can you do to facilitate the debugging process?

3.6 *Focus on Problem Solving*

There are other valuable tools to assist you in developing computer solutions to difficult problems. In this section, some of those tools—stepwise refinement and logical diagrams in the form of structure charts and flowcharts—are applied to the problem of painting your company logo on the side of a building.

Structure Charts

One effective way to design a program from the top down is to use a diagram of the problem called a structure chart.

Program Description   MakeASale

  This program asks for the number of items sold, cost per item, and
discount rate. It calculates and sends to an output file the total cost,
tax due, and amount due.

Algorithm Development

            Pseudocode for main module

Begin MakeASale
    EnterSalesData(NumberOfItems, CostPerItem)
    CalculateCosts(NumberOfItems, CostPerItem, TotalCost,
           TaxDue, AmountDue)
    open the output file
    DisplayCosts(TotalCost, TaxDue, AmountDue)
    close the output file
End MakeASale

            Pseudocode for procedures

Begin EnterSalesData ((HowMany, UnitCost)
    ask how many of this item were purchased, HowMany
    ask what
END EnterSale

CalculateCost(N
    set TAXRE
    declare
    begin Calcu
        ask wri
        calculat
        calculat
        calcula
        calcula
    end Calcula

Begin Display
    display
    display
    display
End Display

Program Listing

```
MODULE  MakeASale;
   (* Defines and invokes procedures to Calculate and Display Costs
      and Taxes.  OUTPUT REDIRECTED.
      CODE INCOMPLETE.  PROCEDURES MUST BE SUPPLIED FROM FILE CH3E.
      FileName:CH3F2     Modula-2    RKW    Jan. 1991   *)

(* NOTE IMPORT OF OpenOutput, CloseOutput *)
FROM InOut IMPORT WriteString, WriteLn, ReadCard,
                OpenOutput, CloseOutput;

FROM RealInOut IMPORT ReadReal, FWriteReal;

VAR  CostPerItem, TotalCost, TaxDue, AmountDue : REAL;
     NumberOfItems : CARDINAL;
```

Sample Run

```
Displayed to Screen

    How many of this item were purchased? 5
    What is the cost of each? 23.95

    What is the discount rate (e.g., enter 0.10 for 10%)? 0.15

    Enter the name of the output file:  DAT> OUTDATA

Contents of the output file

    Purchase    = $      101.79
    Tax         = $        6.36
    Amount Due  = $      108.15
```

Users' Manual   MakeASale

  The Modula-2 Source Code file is named CH3F2. Procedures
EnterSalesData, CalculateCosts, and DisplayCosts must be incorporated
into the program from file CH3E before it can be compiled, linked, and
executed.
  The program will ask you "How many of this item were purchased?",
"What is the cost of each?", and "What is the discount rate?". The
values NumberOfItems(CARDINAL), CostPerItem(REAL), and DiscountRate
(REAL) should be entered from the keyboard in answer to these questions.
Note that the DiscountRate is entered as a fraction (e.g., 0.15, rather
than 15%) and will be 0.0 if there is no discount. The final results are
displayed only after execution of the program by issuing an operating
system command to display the contents of the output file.

Figure 3–9
Documentation for MakeASale (Example 3.5.1)

Figure 3–10
PaintLogoOnBarn
Illustration
(Example 3.6.1)

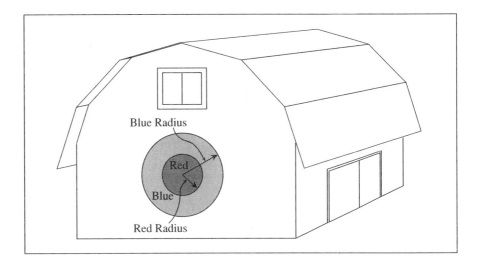

Suppose, for example, that you want to make your company logo—a red circle surrounded by a concentric blue ring—a well-recognized symbol. You decide to pay farmers throughout the country to allow you to paint it on their barns, as illustrated in Figure 3–10. The problem is to determine, for a given-size barn, how much red paint and how much blue paint will be required. Figure 3–11 shows how a structure chart for this problem might look.

A **structure chart** uses a collection of boxes to illustrate and clarify hierarchical aspects of a problem's solution. It always is read from top to bottom. Each level of the chart displays subproblems of the problem to which they are connected in the level above. The order of execution for subproblems on a given level is assumed generally to occur from left to right, although this is an informal convention, not a requirement of the chart. Just as pseudocode often requires modification as the problem is refined, so a structure chart also may encounter revisions as the problem solution develops. The chart and the pseudocode provide effective methods for putting the initial solution on paper so that it can be developed and refined until it meets the user's needs. They also provide documentation to those who need to modify or maintain the solution later. Just as different people's pseudocodes may look different, your structure charts may differ from those in this book; and that's fine, provided they represent good, alternate solutions to the problem.

Stepwise Refinement

Drawing a structure chart and extending it to as many levels as necessary to represent solvable subtasks are steps toward refining the solution of a problem. Writing pseudocode and modifying it until it matches the sequence, selection, iteration, and invocation control structures further refines the solution. This process of proceeding step-by-step from an initial rough idea of how the problem is to be solved to structured, accurate, well-documented code is called **stepwise refinement.**

Flowcharts

In addition to pseudocode, the **flowchart** is another tool programmers have used extensively to refine problem solutions. In recent years, pseudocode almost entirely replaced flowcharts, primarily because flowchart diagrams have been messy to

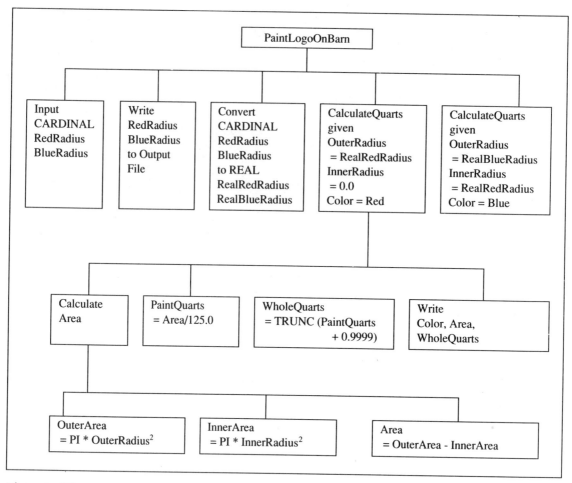

Figure 3–11
Structure Chart for PaintLogoOnBarn (Example 3.6.1)

change, whereas pseudocode is easily modified using a text editor. Nonetheless, many computer professionals still recognize flowcharting as a good way to diagram the logic of a program, which is especially important for developing test data and procedures. Many people who engineer large software projects encourage the use of flowcharts in addition to pseudocode; and Computer-Aided Software Engineering (CASE) tools now available make it easier to create and modify flowcharts. Flowchart symbols are used occasionally in examples throughout this book to help you develop some skill with this technique.

Figure 3–12 illustrates some commonly accepted flowchart symbols, and Figure 3–13 shows flowcharts with matching pseudocode for the selection, iteration, and invocation structures.

Now apply these techniques to the problem of painting your company logo on the barn.

Example 3.6.1

Two concentric circles are drawn on the side of a barn, as shown in Figure 3–10. Determine how much paint is needed to paint inside the smaller circle red and the area between the circles blue.

Figure 3–12
Flowchart Symbols

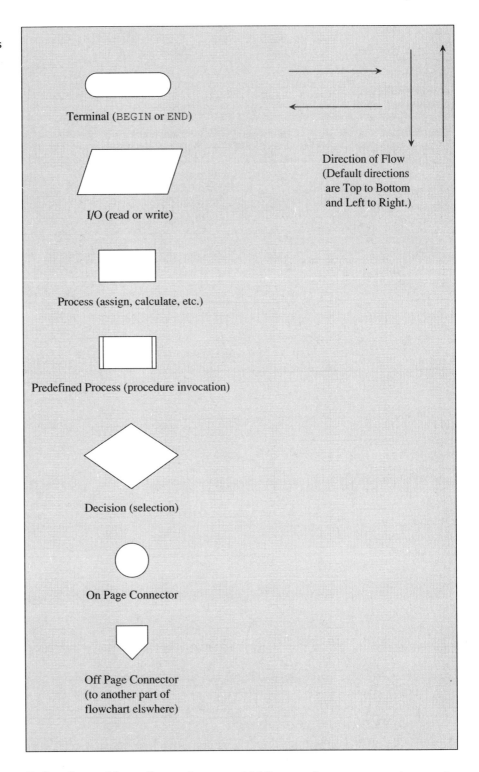

Define the problem   Barn paint covers 125.0 square feet per quart and cannot be purchased in quantities smaller than a quart. CARDINAL values for RedRadius and BlueRadius will be entered by the user at the keyboard. Find the area in square feet within the inner circle, divide by 125 square feet per quart, round the result up to the next-higher cardinal value, and display the minimum number of quarts of red

Figure 3–13
Flowcharts and
Pseudocodes for
Selection, Iteration,
and Invocation
a. Flowchart and
Pseudocode for
Selection
b. Flowchart and
Pseudocode for
Iteration
c. Flowchart and
Pseudocode for
Invocation

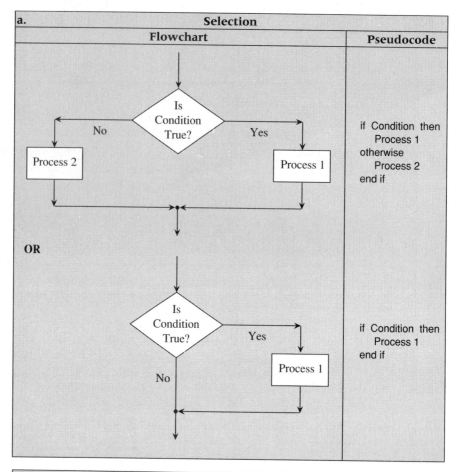

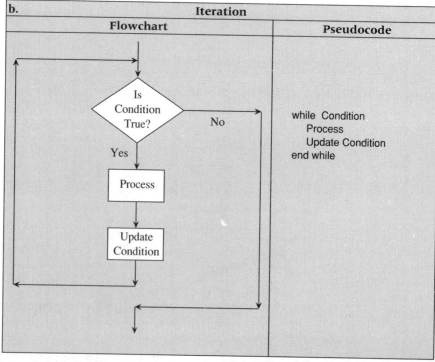

Figure 3–13
(continued)

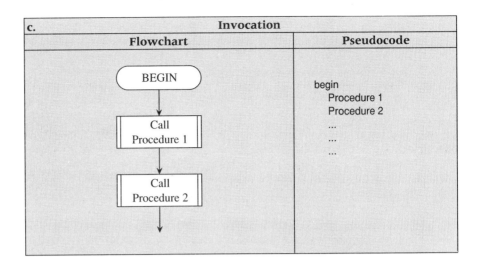

c.	Invocation	
Flowchart		**Pseudocode**

paint needed to cover inside the smaller circle. Perform the same operations to determine the minimum number of quarts of blue paint needed to paint the area between the circles. An editor will be used to create file INFILE; and the two radii, such as 10 and 25, will be read from that file. Output results will be directed to file OUTFILE.

Develop a solution   The area inside the inner circle is given by the formula

$$AreaInner = PI * RedRadius^2.$$

The total red and blue area inside the outer circle is

$$AreaOuter = PI * BlueRadius^2.$$

The area between the circles (to be painted blue) is

$$Area = AreaOuter - AreaInner.$$

CARDINAL RedRadius and BlueRadius will be converted to REAL RealRed-Radius and RealBlueRadius. The formula for finding the amount of Red paint needed is

$$RedPaintQuarts = AreaInner/125.0.$$

RedPaintQuarts will be rounded up to the next CARDINAL value by using the built-in conversion function TRUNC( ), namely,

$$WholeRedQuarts := TRUNC(RedPaintQuarts + 0.9999).$$

(Note that TRUNC(RedPaintQuarts + 1.0) could cause you to buy an extra quart if RedPaintQuarts were integral, such as 4.0. Why? How does adding 0.9999 solve this problem?) WholeBlueQuarts will be determined in the same manner. One procedure can be called twice; once to determine and write WholeRedQuarts, and again to calculate and write WholeBlueQuarts. Create INFILE, and enter the two cardinal numbers 10 and 25; separate the numbers by Enter, space, or comma. Open INFILE immediately after BEGIN and open OUTFILE just before printing the radii and other results.

The structure chart in Figure 3–11 shows graphically how the problem is divided into the steps just described.

Refine the solution   The flowcharts and pseudocode for the main module and PROCEDURE CalculateQuarts are shown in parallel in Figure 3–14.

Modula-2 code

```
MODULE PaintLogoOnBarn;
    (* Calculates Paint Needed to Fill Concentric Circles
       Accepts input from INFILE, directs output to OUTFILE.
       File Name:CH3G     Modula-2     RKW        Jan. 1991    *)

FROM InOut IMPORT WriteString, WriteLn, ReadCard, WriteCard,
                    OpenInput, CloseInput, OpenOutput, CloseOutput;
FROM RealInOut IMPORT FWriteReal;

CONST  MAXCHARSLESS1 = 3;
TYPE COLORTYPE = ARRAY [0..MAXCHARSLESS1] OF CHAR;
VAR  RealRedRadius, RealBlueRadius : REAL;
     RedRadius, BlueRadius : CARDINAL;
     Color : COLORTYPE;

PROCEDURE CalculateQuarts(OuterRadius,InnerRadius:REAL; Color:COLORTYPE);
   CONST  COVERS = 125.0;    PI = 3.14159;
   VAR  OuterArea, InnerArea, Area, PaintQuarts : REAL;
        WholeQuarts  : CARDINAL;
   BEGIN
       OuterArea := PI * OuterRadius * OuterRadius;
       InnerArea := PI * InnerRadius * InnerRadius;
       Area := OuterArea - InnerArea;

       PaintQuarts := Area / COVERS;
       WholeQuarts := TRUNC(PaintQuarts + 0.9999);

       WriteString("Color: "); WriteString(Color); WriteLn;
        WriteString("Area(sq.feet): "); FWriteReal(Area,10,2); WriteLn;
        WriteString("Quarts of Paint Needed: "); WriteCard(WholeQuarts,5);
        WriteLn;
    END CalculateQuarts;

BEGIN  (* PaintLogoOnBarn *)
   (* Open INFILE and Read the Radii *)
   WriteString("Enter input file name (INFILE recommended): ");
    OpenInput("DAT");
   ReadCard(RedRadius); ReadCard(BlueRadius);
   CloseInput;

   (* Open OUTFILE, display radii, call CalculateQuarts *)
   WriteString("Enter output file name (OUTFILE recommended): ");
    OpenOutput("DAT");
   WriteLn; WriteString("The radii are: ");
    WriteCard(RedRadius,5); WriteCard(BlueRadius,5);
    WriteString(" feet."); WriteLn; WriteLn;

   RealRedRadius := FLOAT(RedRadius);   RealBlueRadius := FLOAT(BlueRadius);

   Color := "Red";
   CalculateQuarts(RealRedRadius, 0.0, Color); WriteLn; WriteLn;
```

```
Color := "Blue";
CalculateQuarts(RealBlueRadius, RealRedRadius, Color); WriteLn;
CloseOutput;
END PaintLogoOnBarn.
```

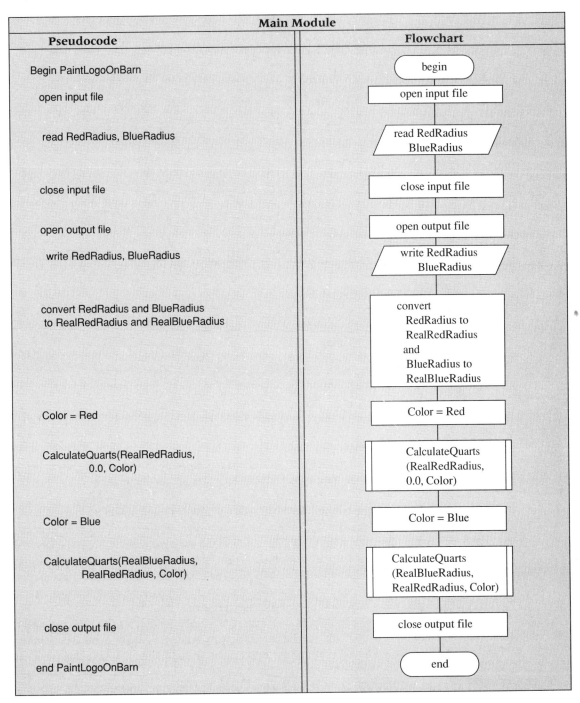

Figure 3–14
Pseudocode and Flowcharts for PaintLogoOnBarn (Example 3.6.1)   *(continued)*

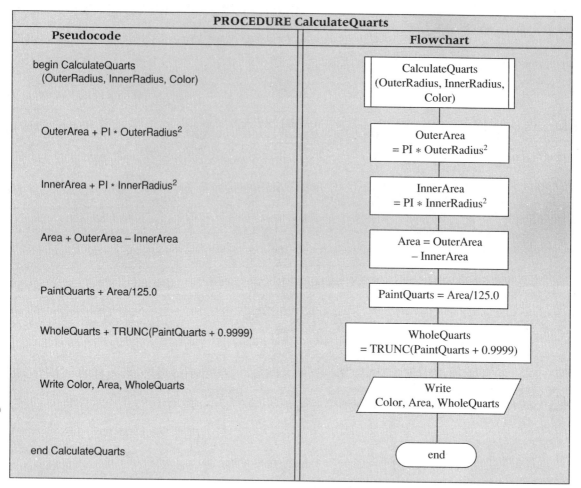

Figure 3–14
(*continued*)

A new type COLORTYPE was defined as an ARRAY OF CHAR. It was needed so that it could be used in the CalculateQuarts procedure heading.

Debug and test   It may be difficult to debug this program with the I/O redirected, because results are not visible during execution. Begin with *comment indicators* around the redirection commands, and run the program with I/O from the keyboard and to the screen first. Once the program is working well, remove the comment indicators from the input redirection, and make sure the program reads data properly from the input file. Finally, remove the comment indicators from the output redirection and complete the testing of the program.

Test values should include appropriate values for RedRadius and BlueRadius (such as 10 and 25) that can be checked easily on the calculator. Also check limiting values (RedRadius = 0), and illegal values (BlueRadius < RedRadius, or a negative radius) to see how the program reacts to those conditions. In the next chapter you will learn how to build safeguards into a program to prevent the user from entering nonsense values. Remember that the input data must first be placed into INFILE using an editor. You will want to display OUTFILE after execution to see the results. Upon execution, you see only

```
Enter input file name (INFILE recommended): DAT> INFILE
Enter output file name (OUTFILE recommended): DAT>
OUTFILE
```

The results, when radii are 10 and 25, are

```
The radii are:     10     25 feet.
Color: Red
Area(sq.feet):          314.16
Quarts of Paint Needed:        3

Color: Blue
Area(sq.feet):          1649.34
Quarts of Paint Needed:        14
```

These are displayed only after executing your system command to display OUTFILE.

Complete the documentation The problem definition, structure chart, pseudocode, flowcharts, code, sample run, and listings of the input and output files should be collected. Documentation is completed by a users' manual, which should state the source code location (File CH3G) and the name of the input file. Users should be warned to take precautions against entering negative or incorrect radii.

Questions 3.6	1. Under what circumstances might you wish to use pseudocode instead of flow-charts, and vice versa? When might you wish to use both?

2. How does a structure chart aid in stepwise refinement of a problem? How should information flow in a structure chart?

3. **a.** Why are none of the parameters in the heading

```
PROCEDURE CalculateQuarts(OuterRadius, InnerRadius : REAL;
                          Color : COLORTYPE);
```

in the PaintLogoOnBarn (Example 3.6.1) preceded by a VAR designation?

   b. How would you change the problem so that Color, Area, and WholeQuarts were written by the main module instead of from the CalculateQuarts procedure?

4. **a.** Draw a structure chart for the MakeASale problem (Example 3.5.1).

   b. Rewrite the pseudocode from that problem in flowchart form.

A Bit of Background

What's a Barn?

Scientists *do* have a sensor of humor! An important measurement in nuclear energy is the effective areas that different atoms and nuclei present to the scattering and absorption of particles. Those areas, called cross sections, are very, very small. During the 1940s, it is said, two physicists were comparing cross section measurements when one exclaimed, "Compared with yours, my cross section is as big as a barn!" The size he had measured was 10^{-28} square meters. From that time on, nuclear cross sections have been measured in *barns*, units of 10^{-28} meters^2.

3.7   *Summary*

Identifiers, Constants, Variables   Constants, variables, data types, procedures, etc., are named in Modula-2 by identifiers. Identifiers should begin with a letter of the alphabet and contain only letters and digits, and capital and lowercase letters are recognized as distinct.

Standard Numeric Data Types and Operations   REAL, CARDINAL, and INTEGER are the standard numeric data types built into Modula-2. Each has an associated range of allowed values, a set of arithmetic operations that may be performed, and commands for reading and writing variables and constants of that type. The arithmetic operations add, subtract, multiply, and divide follow strict rules of precedence, which can be superceded by using parentheses.

Mixed Mode   Functions for converting values from one numeric data type to another are provided in Modula-2 so that mixed-mode expressions, which may produce unexpected results, can be avoided. These functions are summarized in Appendix A.

CHARacter and BOOLEAN Data Types   Two additional standard data types are CHARacter and BOOLEAN, used for handling individual characters and logical operations, respectively. You also may define a type describing a string of characters in the form ARRAY [Start..Stop] OF CHAR. You may read and write string values using ReadString and WriteString procedures from module InOut.

Top-down Design, Stepwise Refinement, Invocation   Top-down design and stepwise refinement are important tools for solving difficult problems. They allow you to break a lengthy problem into smaller tasks and to refine those tasks so that they can be implemented by invoking procedures.

Structure Charts, Pseudocode, Flowcharts   A structure chart shows the hierarchial aspects of solving a problem and the subtasks necessary for solving it. Pseudocode is a written outline of the solution, and a flowchart is a diagram of that solution. All three of these tools are valuable aids in developing and maintaining good, workable code.

I/O Redirection   The OpenInput, CloseInput, OpenOutput, and CloseOutput procedures, imported from module InOut, provide a way for a program to redirect input and output. Thus, data can be accepted from an input file, rather than from the keyboard; and output can be stored on secondary storage media for ready access and retrieval.

3.8   *Exercises*

Exercises marked with (FileName:_____) indicate those that ask you to use, modify, or extend the text examples. The numbers in brackets, [ ], indicate the chapter section that contains the material you need for completing the exercise.

1. [3.2] Write a program that declares variables named by the valid identifiers in Figure 3–1. Make some of the variables CARDINAL, some INTEGER, and some REAL. Then read values from the keyboard for these variables, and write them to the terminal screen. What happens when you attempt to declare variables using identifiers that are not valid?

2. [3.2] Given the variable declarations, determine which statements and commands (a–t) are legal and which are illegal. If illegal, explain why.

```
VAR  NumOfApples, NumOfOranges : CARDINAL;
     Vector, DigitalTemp : INTEGER;
     Distance, Average : REAL;
     Letter, Symbol : CHAR;
     Words, Phrase : ARRAY [0..79] OF CHAR;
     Whoops : BOOLEAN;
```

a. Average := 89.4;

b. Distance := 130;

c. NumOfOranges := (5 * NumOfApples) DIV 3;

d. Vector := VAL(CARDINAL, NumOfApples);

e. DigitalTemp := real(Average);

f. Words := ''We did it!'';

g. NumOfApples := NumOfOranges + Letter;

h. Whoops := (NumOfApples − NumOfOranges) > 5 ;

i. Symbol := Letter;

j. Symbol := Phrase;

k. Distance := Distance MOD Average;

l. Vector := Distance / Average;

m. DigitalTemp := VAL(INTEGER, NumOfOranges);

n. NumOfApples := FLOAT(Average);

o. NumOfOranges := TRUNC(Distance);

p. Average := real(Vector);

q. Distance := real(NumOfApples);

r. DigitalTemp := entier(Average);

s. NumOfApples := NumOfOranges − Distance;

t. NumOfOranges := − 17;

3. [3.2] (Optional) Given the declaration

```
VAR A, B, C, D, G, H : CARDINAL;
```

and the assignments A := 23; B := 176B; C := 0A3CH; D := 219; , what value is displayed by each of the following commands? *Hint:* You might want to use the computer to WriteCard, WriteOct, and WriteHex for all A, B, C, D, G, and H.

a. WriteCard(B, 5);

b. WriteOct(D, 5);

c. WriteCard(C, 5);

d. WriteHex(D, 5);

e. G := A + B;
WriteCard(G, 5);

f. H := C − D;
WriteOct(H, 5);

g. G := B MOD A;
WriteCard(G, 5);

h. G := B DIV A;
WriteCard(G, 5);

i. H := B / A;
WriteCard(H, 5);

j. H := 3 * C − 247B;
WriteHex(H, 5);

4. [3.2] Write, test, and document a program to do the following: Given the current time (Hours and Minutes) on a *24-hour* clock, add a whole number of hours and tell what the new clock reading is and how many days later it will be. *Hint:* Use DIV 24 and MOD 24, and designate midnight as 0:00 hours, instead of 24:00 hours. Example: 17:30 + 37 hours is 6:30, 2 days later.

5. [3.2] In a game of Woodenbleevit, 3 players make up a team. At the end of each round, the team score is the total points accumulated by the team, divided by 3, truncated to the next-smaller whole number. For example, if your team received 76 points in a round, the team score for that round would be 25(76/3 = 25.333, truncated). A game consists of 5 rounds.

Write, test, and document a program in which you enter the total points in a round, divide by 3, and truncate to get the team score for the round. Add up the team scores for the 5 rounds to get the team score for the game. Determine how many points your team lost because of the truncation process. *Hint:* Use DIV 3 and MOD 3.

Test the program with the following total points received by your team:

> Round 1: 14 points (still learning)
> Round 2: 292 points (beginners' luck)
> Round 3: 77 points
> Round 4: 82 points
> Round 5: 45 points

6. [3.4] (FileName:CH2A) Expand the FindCircleArea problem (Example 2.5.1) to find the Diameter and Circumference of the circle as well as the Area. Put the calculations for Area, Diameter, and Circumference in a PROCEDURE, which is called by the main module. Pass the radius to the procedure as an In Only (Value) parameter, and have the procedure pass the Area, Diameter, and Circumference back (as In/Out, VARiable parameters) for the main module to display. *Hint:* Circumference = 2.0 * PI * Radius, Diameter = 2.0 * Radius.

7. [3.4] (FileName:CH3E) Add to the MakeASale program (Example 3.4.1) a procedure that asks for the amount paid by the customer and then subtracts the AmountDue and calculates the amount of change owed to the customer. Include commands in the DisplayCosts procedure to display the amount paid and the change owed.

8. [3.6] (FileName:CH3G) **a.** Refine the PaintLogoOnBarn problem (Exercise 3.6.1) so that it calls separate procedures to (1) read the radii and (2) write the Color, Area, and WholeQuarts. Make the output file contents look "prettier" than those in the example.

b. Suppose that you are threatened with a lawsuit because your logo looks like another company's. To avoid this and cut your losses, you decide to add a third outer ring, painted white, to all of your barn paintings. White paint covers only 62.5 square feet per quart. Modify the program PaintLogoOnBarn so that it asks for the three radii and outputs the appropriate information for Red, Blue, and White paint.

9. [3.4] The roads of Kansas are laid out in a rectangular grid at exactly one-mile intervals as shown in Figure 3–15. Lonesome farmer Pete drives his 1939 Ford pickup x miles east and y miles north to get to widow Sally's farm. Both x and y are entered as CARDINAL numbers. Write, test, and document a program that asks for CARDINAL x and y, and then uses the formula

$$\text{distance} = \text{sqrt}(x * y + y * y)$$

to find the shortest walking distance across the fields to Sally's farm. Since Pete does not understand fractions or decimals very well, the answer must be rounded to the nearest CARDINAL value before it is displayed. A procedure should be used to calculate and print the value of distance. IMPORT the function sqrt (which finds the real square root of a real number) from module

MathLib0. The users' manual must be understandable to Pete, but the rest of the documentation can be written for a programmer.

10. [3.6] Hap's Hazard County Phone Company, Inc., charges for phone calls by Distance (miles) and length of Time (minutes). The Cost of a call (in dollars) is computed by 0.30 * (Time + 0.05 * Distance). An input file contains 3 sets of REAL Time and Distance values for 3 different calls. Write, test, and document a program that reads all 6 values and then passes them to a procedure that calculates and prints the Time, Distance, and Cost for each call and the total cost of all 3 calls.

11. [3.6] When a particular rubber ball is dropped from a given Height (meters), its impact Speed (meters/sec) when it hits the ground is given by Speed = sqrt(2 * g * Height). The ball then rebounds to 2/3 the Height from which it last fell. Write, test, and document a program that
    (1) asks for the initial Height from which the ball is dropped,
    (2) calls a procedure that prints the Height and calculates and prints the impact Speed, returns to the main module,
    (3) calculates the ReboundHeight to which the ball rises,
    (4) calls the procedure again to print the new Height and to calculate and print the new impact Speed, returns to the main module,
    (5) again calculates the ReboundHeight,

Figure 3–15
Kansas roads
(Exercise 9)

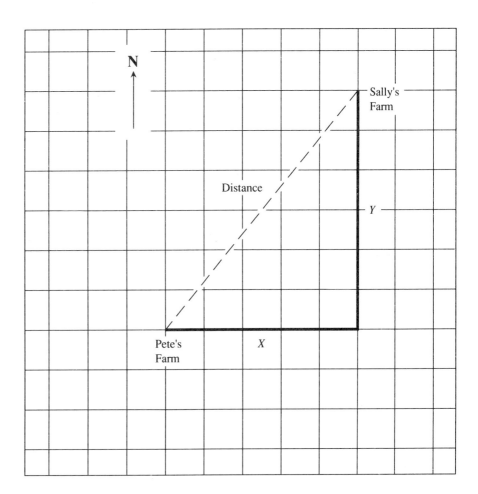

(6) calls the procedure the third time to print the Height and to calculate and print the Speed on the third impact, and then

(7) stops.

The three values of Height and impact Speed should be directed to an output file. Test your program for an initial Height of 2.0 meters. Run the program twice and compare the results for dropping the ball on Earth ($g = 9.81$ meters per sec^2) and on the moon ($g = 1.67$ meters per sec^2).

4

Selection and Iteration

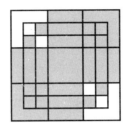

Chapter Outline

Many of the problems presented up to this point could have been solved just as easily with a calculator. Requiring the user to execute an entire program again when the data change can be slow and inefficient. In this chapter, you will learn to apply Modula-2 commands that allow the computer to make and act upon decisions and to repeat tasks with changing values. Extended decision-making and iteration techniques will be discussed in Chapters 7 and 8.

4.1   *IF . . . THEN . . . ELSE*

In the solutions of many problems, different actions must be taken depending upon the values of the data. Examples of simple situations include calculating an area *only if* the measurements are positive, performing a division *only if* the divisor is not zero, printing different messages *depending upon* the value of a grade received, and so on.

The IF . . . THEN . . . ELSE command in Modula-2 is used to implement the **decision structure** in its simplest form—that of choosing between two alternatives. The syntax of this command is either

```
IF Condition THEN
     statements executed if Condition is true;
END; (* IF *)
        (* in this form, no statements are executed
          if the Condition is false. *)
```

or

```
IF Condition THEN
     statements executed if Condition is true;
ELSE
     statements executed if Condition is false;
END; (* IF *)
```

When the running program encounters the IF statement, the Condition is evaluated to determine whether it is true or false. If the Condition is true, the statements following THEN are executed. If the Condition is false, then the statements following the ELSE are executed. In the absence of ELSE, no statements are executed when the Condition is false.

The semicolon (;) separates Modula-2 statements within a program. Semicolons are not required (but are allowed) immediately before an END or an ELSE, since END and ELSE themselves are considered statement delimiters.

Logical Expressions and Operations

The Condition in an IF . . . THEN decision is a logical expression that must evaluate either to TRUE or to FALSE. It may be expressed as a BOOLEAN variable, or it may be written using the **relational operators,** which are

Relational Operator	Meaning
<	less than
<=	less than or equal to
>	greater than

Relational Operator	Meaning
> =	greater than or equal to
=	equal
# or <>	not equal to

and three additional, **logical operators,**

Logical Operator	Explanation
NOT	NOT *P* reverses the truth value of *P* from true to false or vice versa.
AND	*P* AND *Q* means both *P* and *Q* are true.
OR	*P* OR *Q* means either *P* is true, *Q* is true, or both are true.

The Rules of Precedence for treating the relational and logical operators are

Order	Operator
First	(everything in parentheses)
Second	NOT
Third	*, /, DIV, MOD, AND from left to right
Fourth	+, −, OR from left to right
Fifth	<, <=, >, >=, =, # from left to right

It is best to use parentheses, especially when in doubt about the order in which operations will occur. Parentheses are especially important within Boolean conditions when AND and OR are used.

Some valid and invalid logical conditions are shown in Figure 4–1. Study this figure carefully to make certain you understand how each of the values occurs and the reasons for the invalid Conditions. Pay particular attention to those Conditions which repeat identifiers and which compare REAL values. Especially for REAL values, the precision of internal representations almost inevitably prevents two values from being exactly equal. Thus, REAL values should be tested to see if they are acceptably close, rather than equal. For example, test

((RealVal1 − RealVal2) < 0.0001)   AND   ((RealVal2 − RealVal1) < 0.0001))

rather than   RealVal1 = RealVal2.

Use of the Selection structure is illustrated in the following examples.

___

Example 4.1.1

Write and test procedures to read and print the value of a BOOLEAN variable.

Define the problem   There are no built-in procedures in Modula-2 to read or display the value of a BOOLEAN variable. Write a procedure, called ReadBoolean, which reads the CHARacter value T or F and then assigns value TRUE or FALSE respectively to BOOLEAN variable BooleValue. For the WriteBoolean procedure,

```
Assume a program contains the following variable declarations:
VAR   Meters, Feet, HowFar, NumOnHand : INTEGER;
      Balance, BillAmount, DollarsDue : REAL;
      TryIt, ItsOK : BOOLEAN;
```

```
The program BEGINS with assignments:
(* INTEGERs *)
      Meters     := -25;
      Feet       := -7;
      HowFar     := 17;
      NumOnHand := 30;
(* REAL Values *)
      Balance    := 12.6;
      BillAmount := 2.0 * Balance - 12.6;
      DollarsDue := 83.45;
(* BOOLEAN Values *)
      ItsOK := (Meters + Feet) < HowFar;
      TryIt := FALSE;
```

Then the following conditions are TRUE or FALSE as indicated:

Condition	Value
(* BOOLEAN Values *)	
TryIt	FALSE
ItsOK	TRUE
NOT(TryIT)	TRUE
(TryIt) OR (ItsOK)	TRUE
(TryIt) AND (ItsOK)	FALSE
ItsOK / TryIt	Invalid

Condition	Value
(*INTEGERs *)	
Meters >= Feet	FALSE
Meters + Feet	Invalid. Does not evaluate to TRUE or FALSE
Feet + HowFar < NumOnHand	TRUE (+ takes precedence over <)
Meters > 10 AND < 30	Invalid
(Meters > 10) AND (Meters < 30)	FALSE (The parentheses and repeat of Meters are critical.)
HowFar = NumOnHand	FALSE
HowFar + 20 > NumOnHand	TRUE
Feet + 37 <> NumOnHand	FALSE

Condition	Value
(* REAL Values *)	
(BillAmount > 5.2) OR (DollarsDue > 80.0)	TRUE
(Balance < BillAmount + 1.0) AND (DollarsDue < BillAmount + 1.0)	FALSE
DollarsDue # BillAmount	TRUE
BillAmount = Balance	Probably FALSE (because of internal REAL precision)
((BillAmount - Balance)<0.0001) AND ((Balance - BillAmount)<0.0001)	TRUE

Figure 4–1
Valid and Invalid Logical Conditions

let variable BooleValue be the Selection Condition. If BooleValue is TRUE, then print *T*; if BooleValue is FALSE, then print *F*.

Develop a solution In the ReadBoolean procedure heading, the parameter BooleValue will be declared as VAR BooleValue : BOOLEAN. The *VAR* indicates that BooleValue is an In/Out parameter; that is, its value will be passed back to the calling module after the procedure is executed.

Pseudocode for ReadBoolean

```
ReadBoolean(VAR BooleValue : BOOLEAN);
        declare a local CHARacter variable named TFCharacter
        begin
          print "What is the value of the Boolean variable (T or F)?"
          accept TFCharacter from the keyboard
          if TFCharacter = 'T' or 't' then
            assign TRUE to BooleValue
          otherwise
            assign FALSE to BooleValue
        end ReadBoolean
```

In the WriteBoolean procedure heading, BooleValue is an In Only parameter. It is not preceded by a VAR designation, because its value is passed to the procedure but need not be passed back to the calling module after the procedure is executed.

Pseudocode for WriteBoolean

```
WriteBoolean(BooleValue : BOOLEAN);
    begin
      if    BooleValue     then
          print    T
      otherwise
          print    F
      end if
    end WriteBoolean
```

Pseudocode for module TestReadAndWriteBoolean, to test procedures ReadBoolean and WriteBoolean

```
declare BOOLEAN variable TFValue
begin TestReadAndWriteBoolean
  call ReadBoolean(TFValue)
  call WriteBoolean(TFValue)
end     TestReadAndWriteBoolean
```

In the following program, note how the characters *T* and *F* were enclosed within single quotes for the Condition test. The dummy variable Terminator receives the Enter character, used to terminate the response to Read(TFCharacter); if this is not done, the Enter character could be assigned to the next CHARacter variable that is read. Testing the Condition in WriteBoolean is done by

IF   BooleValue   THEN,

not by   IF   BooleValue = TRUE   THEN.

The latter would be accepted; but it is redundant, like asking, ''Is TRUE = TRUE?'' IF . . . THEN . . . ELSE is appropriately used in the WriteBoolean procedure, because there is a decision between only two possibilities. In the ReadBoolean procedure the user is warned that any character other than 'T' is assumed to mean FALSE. Ways of handling decisions between more than two possibilities will be discussed in Chapter 7. Provision has been made in ReadBoolean to allow the user to enter either uppercase or lowercase letters for *T*.

Modula-2 code

```
MODULE TestReadAndWriteBoolean;
    (* Tests procedures ReadBoolean and WriteBoolean to enter and
       display the value of a Boolean variable.
       File Name:CH4A     Modula-2     RKW     Feb. 1991    *)

FROM InOut IMPORT WriteString, WriteLn, Read, Write;

VAR  TFValue : BOOLEAN;

PROCEDURE ReadBoolean(VAR BooleValue : BOOLEAN);
    VAR  TFCharacter, Terminator : CHAR;
    BEGIN
        WriteLn; WriteString("Enter T or F.  ");
        WriteString("Any other character is assumed to mean FALSE:  ");
        Read(TFCharacter); Write(TFCharacter);
        Read(Terminator);WriteLn;

        IF  (TFCharacter = 'T') OR (TFCharacter = 't')   THEN
           BooleValue := TRUE;
        ELSE
           BooleValue := FALSE;
        END; (* IF *)
    END ReadBoolean;

PROCEDURE WriteBoolean(BooleValue : BOOLEAN);
    BEGIN
        IF  BooleValue   THEN
           Write('T'); WriteLn;
        ELSE
           Write('F'); WriteLn;
        END; (* IF *)
    END WriteBoolean;
                                          .
BEGIN (* TestReadAndWriteBoolean *)
    WriteString("What is the value of Boolean variable TFValue? ");
    ReadBoolean(TFValue); WriteLn;

    WriteString("The value of TFValue is  ");
    WriteBoolean(TFValue); WriteLn;
END TestReadAndWriteBoolean.
```

Debug and test   Run and test this program, entering values 'T', 't', 'F', 'f', and other characters, to examine all possibilities. A test run looks like

```
What is the value of Boolean variable TFValue?
Enter T or F. Any other character is assumed to mean FALSE: F
The value of TFValue is FALSE.
```

Complete the documentation   Collect the problem definition, pseudocode, code, and test runs. Write a users' manual.

Example 4.1.2

As a part-time student, you took two courses last term. Calculate and display your grade point average (GPA) for the term.

Define the problem   The student will be asked to enter the course name, grade, and credit hours earned for each course. These will be printed with the lower grade first. The grade point average for the term will be calculated and displayed. A warning message will be printed if the GPA is less than 2.0, and a congratulatory message if the GPA is 3.5 or above.

Develop a solution   Course names will be single word strings, not longer than 12 characters. Grades will be REAL with values between 0.0 and 4.0. Credit hours are cardinal numbers between 1 and 6. The grade point average (GPA) will be calculated from the formula

$$\text{GPA} = [(\text{Credits1} * \text{Grade1}) + (\text{Credits2} * \text{Grade2})]/(\text{Credits1} + \text{Credits2}).$$

In one procedure, called SortTwoGrades, the course name, credits, and grade will be printed for both classes with the lower grade first. Another procedure, CalculateGPA, will calculate and print the GPA. The latter procedure also will print the warning message if GPA < 2.0 or the congratulatory message if GPA >= 3.5.

Refine the solution   *Pseudocode*

```
begin HandleGrades
   call ReadGrade(CourseName1, NumCredits1, Grade1)
   call ReadGrade(CourseName2, NumCredits2, Grade2)
   call SortTwoGrades(CourseName1, CourseName2, NumCredits1, NumCredits2, Grade1,
                   Grade2)
   call CalcGPA(NumCredits1, NumCredits2, Grade1, Grade2)
end HandleGrades

procedure ReadGrade(Name, Credits, Grade)
     begin
        ask for course name, Name
        ask for number of credits, Credits
        ask for course grade, Grade
     end ReadGrade

procedure WriteGrade(Name, Credits, Grade)
     begin
        print Name,     print Credits,     print Grade
     end WriteGrade

procedure SortTwoGrades(Name1, Name2, Credits1, Credits2, Grade1, Grade2)
     begin
        print heading 'Grade          Credits          Course'
        if Grade1 < Grade2 then
           call WriteGrade(Name1, Credits1, Grade1)
           call WriteGrade(Name2, Credits2, Grade2)
        otherwise
           call WriteGrade(Name2, Credits2, Grade2)
           call WriteGrade(Name1, Credits1, Grade1)
        end if
        end SortTwoGrades
```

```
procedure CalculateGPA(Credits1, Credits2, Grade1, Grade2)
     begin
        convert cardinal Credits1 and Credits2 to
                    Credits1Real and Credits2Real
        GPA = ((Credits1Real*Grade1) + (Credits2Real*Grade2)) / (Credits1Real +
                    Credits2Real)
        print GPA
        if    GPA < 2.0
             print warning
        if GPA >= 3.5
           print congratulations
     end CalcGPA
```

Note that the use of procedures in this problem causes the code that follows to be shorter and more readable.

Modula-2 code

```
MODULE HandleGrades;
    (* Finds the GPA for two courses, prints courses in order of
       grade, and prints warning or congratulations message.
       File Name:CH4B      Modula-2      RKW      Feb. 1991      *)

FROM InOut IMPORT WriteString, ReadString, WriteLn,
                             ReadCard, WriteCard;
FROM RealInOut IMPORT ReadReal, FWriteReal;

CONST   LASTCHAR = 11;
TYPE   SHORTSTRING = ARRAY [0..LASTCHAR] OF CHAR;
VAR   CourseName1, CourseName2 : SHORTSTRING;
      NumCredits1, NumCredits2 : CARDINAL;
      Grade1, Grade2 : REAL;

PROCEDURE ReadGrade(VAR Name:SHORTSTRING; VAR Credits:CARDINAL;
                    VAR Grade:REAL);   (* All parameters In/Out *)
   BEGIN
      WriteString("Enter course name (one word, 12 characters or fewer): ");
       ReadString(Name); WriteLn;
      WriteString("Enter course credits (CARDINAL 1 to 6): ");
       ReadCard(Credits); WriteLn;
      WriteString("Enter course grade (REAL 0.0 to 4.0): ");
       ReadReal(Grade); WriteLn;
   END ReadGrade;

PROCEDURE WriteGrade(Name:SHORTSTRING; Credits:CARDINAL; Grade:REAL);
   BEGIN
      FWriteReal(Grade,9,2); WriteCard(Credits,11);
       WriteString("     "); WriteString(Name); WriteLn;
   END WriteGrade;

PROCEDURE SortTwoGrades(Name1, Name2:SHORTSTRING;
                        Credits1, Credits2:CARDINAL; Grade1, Grade2: REAL);
   BEGIN
      WriteString("   Grade     Credits     Course Name"); WriteLn;
      IF  Grade1 < Grade2   THEN
         WriteGrade(Name1, Credits1, Grade1);
         WriteGrade(Name2, Credits2, Grade2);
```

```
       ELSE    (* when Grade2 >= Grade1 *)
          WriteGrade(Name2, Credits2, Grade2);
          WriteGrade(Name1, Credits1, Grade1);
       END; (* IF *)
       WriteLn;
    END SortTwoGrades;

 PROCEDURE CalculateGPA(Credits1,Credits2:CARDINAL; Grade1,Grade2:REAL);
    VAR  GPA, Credits1Real, Credits2Real : REAL;
    BEGIN
       Credits1Real := FLOAT(Credits1);  Credits2Real := FLOAT(Credits2);
       GPA := ((Credits1Real * Grade1) + (Credits2Real * Grade2)) /
                  (Credits1Real + Credits2Real);
       WriteString("Your GPA for the term is:  "); FWriteReal(GPA,6,2);
       WriteLn;

        IF  GPA < 2.0  THEN
           WriteString("Warning.  See your advisor."); WriteLn;
        END; (* IF *)
        IF  GPA >= 3.5  THEN
           WriteString("Congratulations!  You did superb work."); WriteLn;
        END; (* IF *)
     END CalculateGPA;


  BEGIN (* HandleGrades *)
     WriteString("For the first course, "); WriteLn;
      ReadGrade(CourseName1, NumCredits1, Grade1); WriteLn;
     WriteString("For the second course, "); WriteLn;
      ReadGrade(CourseName2, NumCredits2, Grade2); WriteLn;

     SortTwoGrades(CourseName1, CourseName2, NumCredits1, NumCredits2,
                   Grade1, Grade2);

     CalculateGPA(NumCredits1, NumCredits2, Grade1, Grade2);
  END HandleGrades.
```

Debug and test Read the program carefully, and convince yourself that it should produce the following sample run with the input shown.

```
For the first course,
Enter course name (one word, 12 characters or fewer): History
Enter course credits (CARDINAL 1 to 6): 5
Enter course grade (REAL 0.0 to 4.0): 2.3

For the second course,
Enter course name (one word, 12 characters or fewer): French
Enter course credits (CARDINAL 1 to 6): 4
Enter course grade (REAL 0.0 to 4.0): 1.3

        Grade     Credits    Course Name
        1.30         4       French
        2.30         5       History

Your GPA for the term is:        1.86
Warning.  See your advisor.
```

To read code with multiple procedures such as this, start with the BEGIN (* HandleGrades *) of the program module itself. When the module calls a pro-

Figure 4–2
Eighteen Sets of
Test Data for
HandleGrades
(Example 4.1.2)

Credits	Grades	GPA
Credits1 = Credits2	Grade1 = Grade2	Repeat each of
	Grade1 < Grade2	the six cases at
	Grade1 > Grade2	the left for
Credits1 # Credits2	Grade1 = Grade2	GPA >= 3.5 GPA < 2.0, and 2.0 >= GPA < 3.5.
	Grade1 < Grade2	
	Grade1 > Grade2	

cedure (for example, ReadGrade), compare the parameters in the procedure call with those in the procedure heading to determine

1. that the number and types of parameters match,
2. by what names the procedure identifies the parameters, and
3. which parameters are In Only, which are In/Out, and what values will be passed in which direction.

Then trace through the statements in the procedure, starting with BEGIN.

No safeguards are built into this program to prevent illegal entries of credits or grades. You will be able to create those safeguards after you have studied the next section.

If you wish to ensure that this program works for all possible combinations of grades and credits, bear in mind that there are at least eighteen different sets of test data. They are listed in Figure 4–2.

Complete the documentation   Documentation of this program should include a problem description such as

> This program accepts names, credit hours, and grades (on a 4.0 scale) for two courses. It prints courses in order of increasing grade and calculates and prints GPA.

Then the Algorithm Development (pseudocode), Program Listing (code), and Sample Runs should be supplemented by a Users' Manual, such as

> The Modula-2 source code is in file CH4B. The program prompts for the name, credits, and grade for Course 1, then for Course 2. The course Name must be one word with fewer than thirteen characters; Credits should be a whole number between 1 and 6; and Grade is a decimal value between 0.0 and 4.0. *Caution:* the program does nothing to prevent you from entering illegal values and receiving incorrect answers. All entries are echoed to the screen so that you can check them. If an entry is incorrect, rerun the program with new, correct values.

Questions 4.1

1. Given the declarations

                VAR   TimeNow, Deadline : REAL;

what should be displayed by the following fragments of code?

a. TimeNow := 12.36;   Deadline := 8.03;
```
IF  TimeNow > Deadline  THEN
   WriteString("It's later than you think!");
ELSE
   WriteString("Relax.  Time remaining is");
   FWriteReal(Deadline-TimeNow, 10, 2);
END; (* IF *)
WriteLn;
```

b.

```
TimeNow := 2.30; Deadline := TimeNow;
IF TimeNow > Deadline THEN
  FWriteReal(TimeNow, 10, 2);
END; (* IF *)
IF ((TimeNow-Deadline)<0.0001) AND ((Deadline-TimeNow)<0.0001) THEN
    WriteString("The time has come.");
END; (* IF *)
IF Deadline > TimeNow THEN
  FWriteReal(Deadline, 10, 2);
END; (* IF *)
WriteLn;
```

Why are three separate IF statements used here instead of IF . . . THEN . . . ELSE? (In Chapter 7 you will learn other methods of handling decisions when there are more than two options.) Could the middle IF statement be worded IF TimeNow = Deadline THEN . . .? What danger could this pose?

2. Write Modula-2 code fragments to make the following decisions:
   a. Ask for two INTEGER Temperatures. If their values are equal, display the temperature; otherwise do nothing.
   b. Ask for CHARacter values Letter1 and Letter2, representing capital letters of the alphabet, and display them in alphabetical order. (*Hint:* If Letter1 < Letter2, then Letter2 follows Letter1 alphabetically.)
   c. Ask for three CARDINAL values, Num1, Num2, Num3, and display them in decreasing order. (*Hint:* For now, use separate IF statements.)
3. In the program HandleGrades (Example 4.1.1), could the declaration of PROCEDURE WriteGrade just as well have been written *after* the declaration of PROCEDURE SortTwoGrades? Why or why not?

4.2   *WHILE*

Four different commands are available in Modula-2 to implement the **iteration** control structure; namely, WHILE, REPEAT, FOR, and LOOP. Although different situations may be handled most efficiently by making an appropriate choice between these four, right now you will learn how to use WHILE, which can be applied to virtually all iterations. The other iterative structures will be examined, compared, and applied in Chapter 8.

Logically, most iterations have the features shown in Table 4–1.

The WHILE Condition

The WHILE structure tests the Condition *before* any of the instructions within the iterative loop are executed. Thus, if the InitialValue of the Condition is FALSE, no instructions in the loop are executed at all. If no InitialValue for the Condition is defined, most computers act upon whatever values just happen to be in the memory

Table 4–1
Features of Iterations

Order	Iteration Component	Corresponding WHILE-Related Syntax
1	Set an initial Condition.	Condition := InitialValue;
2	Test the Condition. If the Condition is True, execute the instructions in the loop one (more) time; otherwise, exit from the loop.	WHILE Condition DO (* Condition must evaluate to TRUE or FALSE *)
3	Provide executable instructions. Include at least one instruction that changes (updates) the Condition.	executable instructions; (* including at least one instruction to update the Condition *)
4	Define the end of the iterative loop.	END; (* WHILE *) (* Returns to WHILE Condition DO to test the Condition again. *)

locations defining the Condition, and you cannot predict whether the loop will execute or not.

For example, for CARDINAL variable Count,

```
BEGIN
   Count := 5;
   WHILE Count < 10 DO
      WriteCard(Count, 6);
      Count := Count + 2;
   END; (* WHILE *)
   WriteLn; . . . .
```

would display

5   7   9

However,

```
BEGIN
   Count := 12;
   WHILE Count < 10 DO
      WriteCard(Count, 6);
      Count := Count + 2;
   END; (* WHILE *)
   WriteLn; . . . .
```

would display nothing; the first test of the Condition, Count < 10, is FALSE. Also,

```
BEGIN
   WHILE Count < 10 DO
      WriteCard(Count, 6);
      Count := Count + 2;
   END; (* WHILE *)
   WriteLn;  . . . .
```

may or may not do anything—because the initial value of Count is not specified, and the computer bases its decision on whatever value happens to be in memory location Count.

☐ Infinite Loops

Somewhere within the executable instructions, there must be at least one command that changes the Condition. Otherwise, the structure may repeat forever in an infinite loop. For example,

```
BEGIN
   Count := 5;
   WHILE  Count < 10 DO
      WriteCard(Count, 6);
   END; (* WHILE *)
   WriteLn;  . . . .
```

would display

```
5     5     5     5      5 . . . .
```

How many times? Why? The Condition (based on the value of Count) is never updated and is always TRUE.

Everyone, at some time, gets caught in the infinite loop trap. Keyboard control functions, such as pressing a Break key, have been provided by most operating systems to allow execution to be terminated at any time. In extreme situations it may be necessary to turn the computer off and/or reboot the operating system. However, in a well-designed, hand-tested program, such drastic measures never should be required.

Consider the following application of the WHILE structure.

Example 4.2.1

Using the FindSellingPrice algorithm of Example 2.5.2, create a *table* of selling price versus purchase price.

Define the problem   The percent markup will be entered from the keyboard and echoed at the head of the table. The range of purchase prices (from Lowest to Highest) and the Increment between them also will be entered from the keyboard. The table of PurchasePrice versus SellPrice will be displayed to the screen with appropriate headings.

Develop a solution   The formulae for calculating SellPrice from PurchasePrice and percent Markup are still

Fraction Markup = Markup/100.0

Sell Price = Purchase Price + (Fraction Markup * Purchase Price)

However, these now will be included within a WHILE loop to produce a table rather than a single value. Figure 4–3 shows a simple structure chart of this solution.

Refine the solution   Figure 4–4 illustrates the iterative structure of this problem with both pseudocode and a flowchart.

Modula-2 code

```
MODULE CreateSellingPriceTable;
   (* Displays a table of selling price vs purchase price
      given the Lowest and Highest PurchasePrice and percent Markup.
      FileName:CH4C    Modula-2    RKW    Feb. 1991  *)
```

Figure 4–3
Structure Chart for
CreateSelling
PriceTable
(Example 4.2.1)

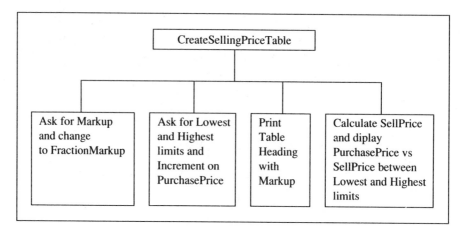

```
FROM InOut IMPORT WriteString, WriteLn;
FROM RealInOut IMPORT ReadReal, FWriteReal;

VAR  PurchasePrice, Markup, FractionMarkup, SellPrice,
     Lowest, Highest, Increment : REAL;

BEGIN  (* CreateSellingPriceTable *)
    (* Ask user for values.  Convert Markup to a fraction. *)
   WriteString("What is the percentage markup? ");
    ReadReal(Markup); WriteLn;
    FractionMarkup := Markup / 100.0;
   WriteString("What is the minimum purchase price? ");
    ReadReal(Lowest); WriteLn;
   WriteString("What is the maximum purchase price? ");
    ReadReal(Highest); WriteLn;
   WriteString("What is the increment between prices? ");
    ReadReal(Increment); WriteLn; WriteLn;

    (* Display Table Heading *)
   WriteString("  When Markup = "); FWriteReal(Markup,6,2);
    WriteString(" percent,"); WriteLn; WriteLn;
   WriteString("Purchase Price     Selling Price"); WriteLn;

    (* Set initial Condition for the iterative WHILE loop. *)
   PurchasePrice := Lowest;

    (* Test and execute while Condition is TRUE *)
   WHILE  PurchasePrice <= Highest  DO
      SellPrice := PurchasePrice  +  (FractionMarkup * PurchasePrice);
      FWriteReal(PurchasePrice,14,2); FWriteReal(SellPrice,17,2); WriteLn;

        (* Update the Condition, so that, after n times through the loop,
           PurchasePrice = Lowest  +  n * Increment  *)
      PurchasePrice := PurchasePrice + Increment
   END; (* WHILE *)
    (* Finally,  PurchasePrice > Highest *)

END CreateSellingPriceTable.
```

Pseudocode	Flowchart

Begin CreateSellingPriceTable
  ask for Markup
 	
convert Markup to FractionMarkup
 	
ask for limits Lowest and Highest
  and Increment on PurchasePrice
 	
print Table Heading with Markup
 	
initialize Condition
  PurchasePrice = Lowest
 	
while PurchasePrice <= Highest
 	
  calculate SellPrice
 	
  print PurchasePrice and SellPrice
 	
  add Increment to PurchasePrice
 	
end while
 	
end CreateSellingPriceTable
	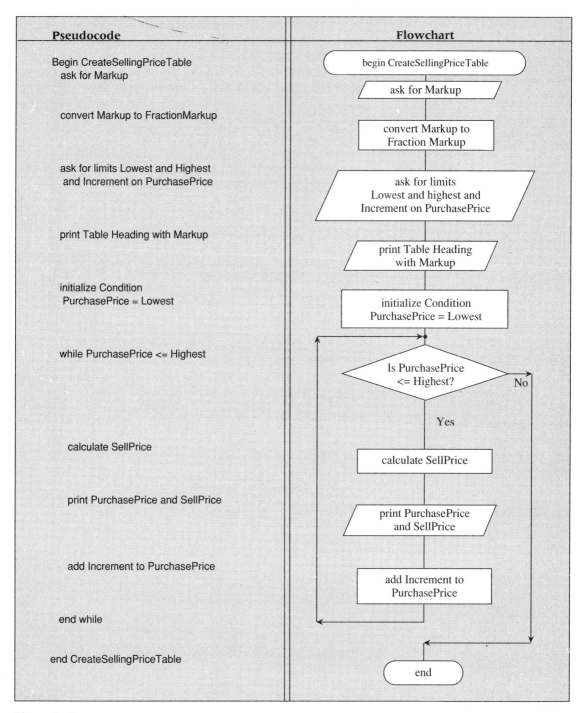

Figure 4–4
Pseudocode and Flowchart for CreateSellingPriceTable (Example 4.2.1)

Debug and test The code for this program contains only three logical steps: (1) ask for input, (2) print the table heading, and (3) initialize the condition and execute the WHILE loop to create the table. Errors may indeed occur if values for Markup, Lowest, Highest, and Increment are entered incorrectly. A common error in developing this code is to forget to initialize PurchasePrice to value Lowest. Another is to neglect to Increment the value of PurchasePrice within the loop, which could give you a first experience with an infinite loop. Here is a sample run.

```
What is the percentage markup? 30.0
What is the minimum purchase price? 2.00
What is the maximum purchase price? 5.00
What is the increment between prices? 0.50

   When Markup =   30.00 percent,

Purchase Price        Selling Price
          2.00                 2.60
          2.50                 3.25
          3.00                 3.90
          3.50                 4.55
          4.00                 5.20
          4.50                 5.85
          5.00                 6.50
```

Complete the documentation Documentation of the problem is left to you. See Exercise 9 at the end of the chapter. You may wish to include both flowchart and pseudocode in the documentation, since both have been developed already.

Questions 4.2

1. Given the declarations

```
VAR Num1, Num2, Step : REAL;
    ItWorks : BOOLEAN;
```

what would be displayed by each of the following fragments of code?

a. BEGIN
```
    Num1 := 3.5;    Num2 := 6.0;
    WHILE  Num1 <= Num2 DO
       FWriteReal(Num1, 10, 2); WriteLn;
       Num1 := Num1 + 0.5;
    END; (* WHILE *)
```

b. BEGIN
```
    Num1 := 10.0;    Num2 := 1.0;    Step := -1.0;
    ItWorks := (Num1 > Num2);
    WHILE ItWorks DO
       FWriteReal(Num2-Num1, 10, 2); WriteLn;
       Num1 := Num1 + Step;
       ItWorks := (Num2 > Num1);
    END; (* WHILE *)
```

2. Given the declarations

```
VAR OldCount, NewCount : CARDINAL;
```

what is wrong with each of the following fragments of code? Correct each so that it does something meaningful.

   a. BEGIN

```
   WHILE OldCount >= 1 DO
      NewCount := OldCount DIV 2;
      WriteCard(OldCount,6); WriteCard(NewCount,6);
       WriteLn;
   END; (* WHILE *)
```

   b. BEGIN

```
   OldCount := 1;    NewCount := 10;
   WHILE (NewCount - OldCount) > 0 DO
      WriteCard(OldCount,6); WriteCard(NewCount,6);
      WriteLn;
   END; (* WHILE *)
```

   c. BEGIN

```
     OldCount := 1;
     WHILE OldCount > 10 DO
        WriteCard(OldCount * 2, 6); WriteLn;
        OldCount := OldCount + 1;
     END; (* WHILE *)
```

3. Using the WHILE structure, write fragments of code to implement each of the following

   a. Display all of the even integers (including 0) from -10 to $+10$, inclusive.

   b. Display a table of Celsius vs. Kelvin temperatures for Celsius = 0.0, 5.0, 10.0, 15.0, . . . , 100.0, where

$$Kelvin = Celsius + 273.15.$$

4.3 *Iterative Applications*

You will discover many valuable applications of iteration structures in problem solving. Three of those—checking that user data entries are acceptable, counting and accumulating running totals, and stopping upon entry of a sentinel value—are illustrated by the examples in this section.

☐ Checking Data Entries

Some programs are allowed to produce meaningless results (or no results at all) when users enter erroneous data. It usually is better to offer users the opportunity to correct their data entry mistakes. The following generic program fragment applies the WHILE structure to allow a user to try repeatedly until he or she enters an acceptable value.

```
Read...(Variable); WriteLn;
WHILE   Condition on Variable is Not Valid DO
   Write...(Variable);
   WriteString('' is invalid because. . . .''); WriteLn;
   WriteString(''Acceptable values are . . . .   Try again. '');
    Read...(Variable); WriteLn;
END; (* WHILE *)
```

Read... and Write... stand for appropriate read and write commands for the type of Variable being displayed.

In the following example the WHILE loop is used to prevent the user from attempting to divide by zero.

Example 4.3.1

Perform long division on cardinal numbers using repeated subtraction.

Define the problem   The quotient in long division is the number of times the divisor can be subtracted from the dividend. The remainder is what is left over after the last subtraction. Perform long division this way. Check your results using DIV and MOD.

Develop a solution   Divisor and Dividend will be entered by the user from the keyboard, with a WHILE loop preventing the program from accepting a Divisor value of zero. A procedure PerformDivision will be called, which uses a WHILE iteration to subtract the Divisor repeatedly from the Dividend, produce a NewDividend on each iteration, CountSubtractions performed, and stop when the NewDividend is less than the Divisor. The final value of CountSubtractions is the quotient, and the last NewDividend is the remainder. The procedure will display quotient and remainder.

Refine the solution   *Pseudocode for module DivideTheHardWay*

```
begin DivideTheHardWay
       ask for Dividend
       ask for Divisor (prevent acceptance of zero)

       PerformDivision(Dividend, Divisor)

       print "for comparison, using DIV, the quotient is",
          Dividend DIV Divisor
          print "and the remainder using MOD is",   Dividend MOD Divisor
end DivideTheHardWay
```

Pseudocode for procedure PerformDivision(Dividend, Divisor)

```
declare local variables NewDividend, CountSubtractions
begin PerformDivision
       initialize NewDividend = Dividend
               CountSubtractions = 0
       while NewDividend >= Divisor
               set NewDividend = NewDividend - Divisor
               add 1 to CountSubtractions
       end while
       print Dividend, "divided by", Divisor, "is", CountSubtractions
          print "with a remainder of", NewDividend
end PerformDivision
```

Note that initializing NewDividend = Dividend in the procedure before the WHILE loop allows you to work with variable NewDividend, while keeping Dividend unchanged for printing later.

Modula-2 code

```
MODULE DivideTheHardWay;
   (* Performs long division by repeated subtraction.
      FileName:CH4D       Modula-2    RKW      Feb. 1991   *)

FROM  InOut IMPORT WriteString, WriteLn, ReadCard, WriteCard;

VAR  Dividend, Divisor : CARDINAL;
```

```
PROCEDURE   PerformDivision(Dividend, Divisor : CARDINAL);
   VAR  NewDividend, CountSubtractions : CARDINAL;
   BEGIN
      NewDividend := Dividend;   CountSubtractions := 0;
      WHILE  NewDividend >= Divisor   DO
         NewDividend := NewDividend - Divisor;
         CountSubtractions := CountSubtractions + 1;
         (* Now,  CountSubtractions = Number of Subtractions Made So Far
            NewDividend = Dividend  -  CountSubtractions * Divisor   *)
      END; (* WHILE *)
      (* Finally, CountSubtractions = Quotient.  NewDividend = Remainder *)

      WriteLn; WriteCard(Dividend,6); WriteString(“  divided by “);
       WriteCard(Divisor,6); WriteString(“  is “);
       WriteCard(CountSubtractions,6); WriteLn;
      WriteString(“       With a remainder of “);
       WriteCard(NewDividend,6); WriteLn; WriteLn;
   END PerformDivision;

BEGIN (* DivideTheHardWay *)
   WriteString(“Dividend = ? “); ReadCard(Dividend); WriteLn;

   WriteString(“Divisor = ? “); ReadCard(Divisor); WriteLn; WriteLn;
   WriteLn;
    WHILE   Divisor = 0  DO    (* Enter new Divisor until Divisor # 0 *)
       WriteCard(Divisor,2);
        WriteString(“ is invalid, because you cannot divide by 0“); WriteLn;
       WriteString(“ Acceptable divisor > 0.  Try again.  Divisor = ? “);
        ReadCard(Divisor); WriteLn; WriteLn;
    END; (* WHILE *)

   PerformDivision(Dividend, Divisor);

   WriteString(“For comparison, using DIV, the quotient is “);
    WriteCard(Dividend DIV Divisor, 6); WriteLn;
   WriteString(“and the remainder using MOD is “);
    WriteCard(Dividend MOD Divisor, 6); WriteLn;
END DivideTheHardWay.
```

Debug and test Logical errors are most likely to occur because of failure to initialize NewDividend and CountSubtractions before entering the WHILE loop or failure to update those variables within the loop. Careful hand checking should eliminate such problems. Test with a variety of Dividends and Divisors. What are the results when the Divisor divides exactly into the Dividend; when the Dividend is zero; when the Divisor is zero? A test run looks like

```
Dividend = ? 23
Divisor = ? 0

0 is invalid, because you cannot divide by 0
Acceptable divisor > 0. Try again. Divisor = ? 7

    23 divided by     7 is     3
      With a remainder of     2

For comparison, using DIV, the quotient is     3
and the remainder using MOD is     2
```

A Bit of Background

Comptometer Arithmetic

In the early 1900s, mechanical calculators, called *Comptometers*, performed only addition. Nonetheless, clever accountants soon discovered that subtraction could be done as well. They wrote the nine's complement on each key. That is, 9 was written on the 0 key, 8 on the 1 key, 7 on the 2 key, and so on. Subtraction was performed by adding the nine's complement, then adding 1. For example, consider the subtraction problem

$$637 - 481 = 156.$$

The nine's complement of 481 is 518, and

$$637 + 518 + 1 = 1\ 156,$$

which gives the answer (156) to the problem when the leftmost carry digit is ignored. It did not take the accountants long to begin multiplying by repeated addition and dividing by repeated subtraction, all on a machine designed to handle only addition.

Many electronic computers perform binary arithmetic in a similar manner, using the two's complement. For example, to subtract

$$111_2\ (= 7_{10}) - 101_2\ (= 5_{10}),$$

find the one's complement of 101 (by changing all ones to zeros and vice versa). Thus, the one's complement of $101_2 = 010_2$. Now add 1 to the one's complement to find the two's complement of 101_2; namely $010_2 + 1 = 011_2$. Then add

$$111_2 + 011_2 = 1\ 010_2.$$

(Binary addition rules are $0 + 0 = 0$, $1 + 0 = 1$, and $1 + 1 = 10$.) When you drop the leftmost carry bit, the correct result of the subtraction is $010_2\ (= 2_{10}.)$

Complete the documentation Collect the problem definition, pseudocode, code, and test run. The users' manual can be short, stating the source code location (CH4D), indicating that Dividend and Divisor are to be entered in response to the prompts, and stating that answers will be displayed on the screen.

Counting and Accumulating Running Totals

Another common task of iteration is to accumulate running totals. In the problem DivideTheHardWay (Example 4.3.1), the values of variables CountSubtractions and NewDividend are both accumulated within the loop; thus, CountSubtractions and NewDividend are called **accumulators.** Accumulators always should be initialized before the loop begins. In this case, the value of CountSubtractions was initialized to 0, and NewDividend was assigned the value of Dividend. Within the loop, the value of CountSubtractions is incremented by 1 in each iteration by the command.

```
CountSubtractions := CountSubtractions + 1,
```

which finds the previous value of CountSubtractions, adds 1, and places the result back into the memory location identified by CountSubtractions. Similarly, New-Dividend is incremented by the value (− Divisor) during each iteration with the replacement command

```
NewDividend := NewDividend - Divisor.
```

A general form of a WHILE-implemented accumulation is

```
Initialize Accumulator;
WHILE Condition DO
    Increment Accumulator;
    Update Condition;
END; (* WHILE *)
```

If the Condition test involves a numerical relationship, such as WHILE Value $<$ TestValue DO, then updating the Condition may itself entail an accumulation, such as incrementing Value in each iteration.

Consider the following example, which uses a counter and an accumulator.

Example 4.3.2

Find the sum of the first N counting numbers, and check the formula for this sum.

Define the problem   Use iteration to accumulate the sum $1 + 2 + \ldots + N$. Then evaluate $N(N + 1)/2$ to verify that this expression gives the same value as the sum of the first N counting numbers.

Develop a solution N will be entered by the user at the keyboard. The sum and the comparison value of $N(N + 1)/2$ will be displayed on the screen. Accumulator Sum will be initialized to 0; counter HowMany will be initialized to 1. A WHILE loop will be used to increment HowMany and accumulate Sum.

Refine the solution   *Pseudocode*

```
begin AccumulateATotal
   ask for N, limit values to 0 < N < 256
   initialize Sum = 0 and HowMany = 1
   while HowMany <= N
      add HowMany to Sum
      add 1 to HowMany
   end while
   print Sum
   calculate and print N(N + 1)/2
end AccumulateATotal
```

Modula-2 code

```
MODULE AccumulateATotal;
   (* Finds the Sum 1 + 2 + ... + N and compares with N(N+1)/2.
      FileName:CH4E      Modula-2      RKW      Feb. 1991    *)

FROM InOut IMPORT WriteString, WriteLn, ReadCard, WriteCard;

VAR   N, Sum, HowMany, TestValue : CARDINAL;

BEGIN
   WriteString("Give me a cardinal number N   (0 > N < 256): ");
   ReadCard(N); WriteLn; WriteLn;
   WHILE   (N <= 0) OR (N >= 256)   DO   (* Enter new N until valid. *)
      WriteCard(N,4); WriteString(" cannot be handled."); WriteLn;
      WriteString("Acceptable N is > 0 and < 256.  Try again.");
      WriteString("  N = ? ");  ReadCard(N); WriteLn; WriteLn;
   END; (* WHILE *)

   Sum := 0;  HowMany := 1;
   WHILE  HowMany <= N  DO
      Sum := Sum + HowMany;
      HowMany := HowMany + 1;
```

```
          (* Now,  Sum = 1 + 2 + ... + HowMany,  where
                    HowMany = number of iterations so far *)
     END; (* WHILE *)
          (* Finally,   Sum = 1 + 2 + ... + N,  and  HowMany = N + 1. *)

     WriteString("The sum 1 + 2 + ... +"); WriteCard(N,4);
      WriteString(" equals "); WriteCard(Sum,6); WriteLn;

     TestValue := N * (N+1) DIV 2 ;
     WriteString("For comparison, for N ="); WriteCard(N,4);
      WriteString(" the value of N(N+1)/2 is "); WriteCard(TestValue,6);
      WriteLn;
END AccumulateATotal.
```

Debug and test   When you perform a test run for $N = 100$, you should see

```
Give me a cardinal number N (0 < N < 256):   280

 280 cannot be handled.
Acceptable N is > 0 and < 256.   Try again.   N = ? 100

The sum  1 + 2 + . . . + 100 equals 5050
For comparison, for N = 100 the value of N(N+1)/2
is 5050
```

The test values for the program should include a range of positive CARDINAL values for *N*. Try 1 (a limit), 3 (a small number that can be checked by hand), 200 (a reasonable number), and 10,000 (which should be rejected by the program because it could cause an overflow error).

Complete the documentation   Complete documentation for this problem is shown in Figure 4–5.

▢ Stopping at a Sentinel Value

A third important application of the iterative structure is to allow the user to perform operations repeatedly on selected values until a final **sentinel** value is entered, which indicates that execution should terminate.

Consider, for example, the following situation, where input data is redirected from an input file, and the program executes until a sentinel value is read from the file.

Example 4.3.3

Given the number of hours worked and the hourly wage, calculate the total pay for each of your employees.

Define the problem   The HoursWorked, HourlyWage, and Names of a number of employees will be found in a previously created input file called EMPLOYEE.IN. The program will read the file and create a table of HoursWorked, HourlyWage, GrossPay, and Name for those employees.

Problem Description

This program accumulates the Sum 1 + 2 + . . . + N and compares the result with N (N + 1) / 2.

Algorithm Development

Pseudocode

Begin AccumulateATotal
    ask for N, limit values to 0 < N < 256
    initialize Sum = 0 and HowMany = 1
    while HowMany <= N
      add HowMany to Sum
      add 1 to HowMany
    end while
    print Sum
    calculate and print N(N+1)/2
end AccumulateATotal

Program Listing

```
MODULE AccumulateATotal;
  (* Finds the Sum 1 + 2 + ... + N and compares with N(N+1)/2.
     FileName:CH4E     Modula-2     RKW     Feb. 1991  *)

FROM InOut IMPORT WriteString, WriteLn, ReadCard, WriteCard;

VAR  N, Sum, HowMany, TestValue : CARDINAL;

BEGIN
  WriteString("Give me a cardinal number N  (0 > N < 256): ");
  ReadCard(N); WriteLn; WriteLn;
  WHILE  (N <= 0) OR (N >= 256)  DO  (* Enter new N until valid. *)
     WriteCard(N,4); WriteString(" cannot be handled."); WriteLn;
        WriteString("Acceptable N is > 0 and < 256.  Try again.");
        WriteString(" N = ? ");  ReadCard(N); WriteLn; WriteLn;
  END; (* WHILE *)

  Sum := 0;  HowMany := 1;
  WHILE  HowMany <= N  DO
     Sum := Sum + HowMany;
     HowMany := HowMany + 1;
     (* Now,  Sum = 1 + 2 + ... + HowMany,  where
              HowMany = number of iterations so far *)
  END; (* WHILE *)
     (* Finally,   Sum = 1 + 2 + ... + N,  and  HowMany = N + 1. *)

  WriteString("The sum 1 + 2 + ... +"); WriteCard(N,4);
  WriteString(" equals "); WriteCard(Sum,6); WriteLn;
```

Sample Run

```
Give me a cardinal number N (0 < N < 256):  280

 280 cannot be handled.
Acceptable N is > 0 and < 256.  Try again.  N = ? 100
```

Users' Manual

Modula-2 source code for the program is in file CH4E. During program execution you will be asked for a cardinal number N, which should be greater than zero (and less than 256 if MAX (CARDINAL) on your

Figure 4–5
Documentation for AccumulateATotal (Example 4.3.2)

A Bit of Background

The Young Gauss

German mathematical genius Johann Carl Friedrich Gauss (1777–1855) professed that he could "reckon" before he could talk. When only two years old, it is said, he discovered an error in his father's business records.

One day in school, young Johann's teacher asked his class to add up the numbers between 1 and 100. To the chagrin of the teacher, who had thought the task would keep the class busy for a while, Gauss almost instantly wrote the answer on his slate and exclaimed, "There it is!" He had reasoned that the series could be written forward and backward and added term-by-term to get 101 one hundred times. Thus the sum was 100(101)/2; and Gauss, at the age of 10, had discovered that

$$1 + 2 + \ldots + N = N(N + 1)/2.$$

Develop a solution   The input file EMPLOYEE.IN can be created using an editor. For illustration, it will be assumed that this file contains the records

10.0	10.35	Adams
25.5	8.15	Jones
40.0	10.50	Lambert
35.25	9.00	Smith
18.4	12.75	Wilson
10000.0		

with each row representing the HoursWorked, HourlyWage, and Name of the particular employee. The last HoursWorked value (10000.0) is patently absurd and is the sentinel indicating that the program should stop.

The program will display the table heading. A WHILE loop will read each employee's name and data and then calculate

$$\text{GrossPay} = \text{HoursWorked} * \text{HourlyWage},$$

and display the results, until a sentinel value $>= 9999.0$ is encountered.

Refine the solution   *Pseudocode*

```
begin MakePayTable
   open the input file
   print the table heading
   read HoursWorked (* initial condition *)
   while HoursWorked < 9999.0 (* sentinel value *)
      read HourlyWage and Name
      calculate GrossPay = HoursWorked * HourlyWage
      print HoursWorked, HourlyWage, GrossPay, Name
      read next value of HoursWorked (* update condition *)
   end while
   close input file
end MakePayTable
```

Modula-2 code

```
MODULE  MakePayTable;
   (* Reads data from an input file and creates a table of employee pay.
      FileName:CH4F     Modula-2     RKW     Feb. 1991  *)
```

```
FROM InOut IMPORT WriteString, ReadString, WriteLn, OpenInput, CloseInput;
FROM RealInOut IMPORT ReadReal, FWriteReal;

CONST  MAXCHARSLESS1 = 19;
TYPE  NAMESTRING = ARRAY [0..MAXCHARSLESS1] OF CHAR;
VAR  Name : NAMESTRING;
     HoursWorked, HourlyWage, GrossPay : REAL;

BEGIN
   WriteString("Name of input file = ? ");  OpenInput("IN");
    WriteLn;
   WriteString("Hours Worked    Hourly Wage    Gross Pay    Name"); WriteLn;

   ReadReal(HoursWorked);               (* initial Condition *)
   WHILE  HoursWorked < 9999.0  DO   (* test for sentinel value *)
      ReadReal(HourlyWage);  ReadString(Name);
      GrossPay := HoursWorked * HourlyWage;
      FWriteReal(HoursWorked,12,2); FWriteReal(HourlyWage,15,2);
       FWriteReal(GrossPay,13,2); WriteString("    "); WriteString(Name);
       WriteLn;
      ReadReal(HoursWorked);               (* update Condition *)
   END; (* WHILE *)

   CloseInput;
END MakePayTable.
```

Debug and test A sample run of this program, with the EMPLOYEE.IN file containing the data shown in *Develop a solution*, displays

```
Name of input file = ? IN> EMPLOYEE.IN

Hours Worked    Hourly Wage    Gross Pay    Name
       10.00          10.35       103.50    Adams
       25.50           8.15       207.83    Jones
       40.00          10.50       420.00    Lambert
       35.25           9.00       317.25    Smith
       18.40          12.75       234.60    Wilson
```

To set the initial condition for the WHILE loop, only HoursWorked is read. HourlyWage and Name are input only after it is determined that HoursWorked is not a sentinel value; and a new value of HoursWorked is read to update the WHILE Condition just before the end of the loop. If HoursWorked, HourlyWage, and Name were read all at once, then dummy values for all three would have to be supplied in the final line of the EMPLOYEE.IN file. (Why?)

Errors in the commands to accept data from an input file often lead to unexpected results. A first debugging step is to insert supplemental write statements that echo the values of HoursWorked, HourlyWage, and Name to the screen immediately after each is read. If this fails, enclose the open and close input file commands within comment indicators, add write commands to prompt you for the values, and test the program with data entered from the keyboard.

Complete the documentation Collect the Problem Description, pseudocode, program listing, and sample run. Remind the users in the users' manual that they should determine the name of the input file before executing the program or that they need to create the input file first.

1. Given the declarations

```
VAR   NumTransactions : CARDINAL;
          Debit, Credit, TotalBill : REAL;
```

what is the effect of each of the following fragments of code? Supply missing arguments to WriteString(" .... ") that will prompt the user with appropriate messages.

a.

```
BEGIN
    ...
    WriteString(". . . .");
    ReadReal(Debit); WriteLn; ReadReal(Credit); WriteLn;
    WHILE  (Debit <0.0) OR (Credit > 0.0) DO
        IF  Debit < 0.0 THEN
            WriteString(" ....");  ReadReal(Debit); WriteLn;
        ELSE
            WriteString(" ....");  ReadReal(Credit); WriteLn;
        END; (* IF *)
    END; (* WHILE *) ...
```

b.

```
BEGIN
    TotalBill := 0.0; NumTransactions := 0;
    WriteString(" ....");  ReadReal(Debit); WriteLn;
    WHILE Debit > 0.0 DO
        NumTransactions := NumTransactions + 1;
        TotalBill := TotalBill + Debit;
        WriteString(" ....");  ReadReal(Debit); WriteLn;
    END; (* WHILE *) . . .
```

2. Write WHILE structure program fragments to handle these situations:
   a. Restrict the user to entering integer temperatures in the range -50 to $+50$ degrees.
   b. Count the number of REAL percentage grades entered, add them up, and stop when 10 grades have been entered. Then print the average of the 10 grades.
   c. Ask for Heights and Surnames of prospective basketball players. Print the Surname, Height, and the message "This is a good prospect." for those 6.0 feet tall or taller. Stop when a Height of less than 3.0 feet is entered.

4.4 *Focus on Problem Solving*

In this section you will develop an amortization table for a loan. The problem of determining the MonthlyPayment amount is addressed first, with emphasis on making programs readable and maintainable. Then the amortization program is developed, with the introduction of loop invariants as a useful debugging tool.

Style

Programs, like people, can have style and class, or they can be messy and difficult to understand. In the 1950s and early 1960s, when a computer was considered large if it had 4 kilobytes of memory and executed one instruction per millisecond, it was critical to write compact, memory-efficient code. Variable names were kept short, blank spaces and lines were kept to a minimum, and few comments were included within the code. Such programs were difficult to read, debug, and maintain. Now that memory is more plentiful and computers operate in the MIPS (Millions of Instructions Per Second) range or faster, structured, readable, well-commented code is a necessity—not just a luxury.

Meaningful Identifiers

Remember from the discussion in Chapter 3, that Modula-2 allows identifier names of virtually unlimited length. Thus, constants and variables can be given meaningful names, such as *NumberOfBoats* instead of *N* or *NB*. In some early versions of languages such as FORTRAN, variable names were limited to six characters. Even worse, BASIC on some old microcomputers allowed identifiers only 1 or 2 characters long. In such circumstances, it was frustrating not only to read the programs, but even to create good variable names in the first place. You should take full advantage of the Modula-2 flexibility that allows for identifiers with meaningful names.

White Space and Indentation

Another important feature of Modula-2 is that white space is ignored. **White space,** which includes spaces, tabulations, and blank lines, is allowed virtually anywhere in the code except within identifier names. This provides the opportunity to separate parts of the program with blank lines and to indent, so that the sets of statements included within a structure are apparent at a glance. Spacing and indentation are used in the examples throughout this book. You should practice doing the same. A good rule of thumb is to indent and align the statements between the start and END of every structure. Figure 4–6 shows one recommended method for a module that contains a WHILE loop, which, in turn, contains an IF . . . THEN . . . ELSE

Figure 4–6
Sample Indentation

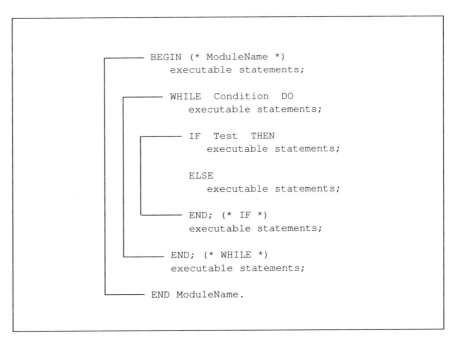

```
BEGIN (* ModuleName *)
    executable statements;

WHILE  Condition  DO
    executable statements;

IF  Test  THEN
    executable statements;

ELSE
    executable statements;

END; (* IF *)
    executable statements;

END; (* WHILE *)
    executable statements;

END ModuleName.
```

decision. Notice that each END statement is commented with the name (IF, WHILE, etc.) of the structure it terminates. With this kind of spacing, brackets can be drawn to assist in debugging. The three structures bracketed in Figure 4–6 are said to be **nested.** Nested structures may not overlap; that is, the brackets may not cross each other. With proper indentation, it is easy to detect and avoid overlapping structures.

Indentation conventions used in this book are

Program Line-Indentation Conventions

1. Indent a line three or more spaces to indicate that it is logically subordinate to (nested within) the previous line.
2. Indent a line only one space to indicate that the line may be considered a logical extension of the line above.

Generally, you cannot go wrong by writing each statement on a separate line. However, in this book, statements that represent a single logical operation (such as printing several values on the same display line) are sometimes placed on the same line of code.

Comments

A third important component of good program style is the insertion of documenting comments within the code. Such comments include those at the head of a module that describe what the module is designed to do, where its source code is found, what language it is written in, who wrote it and when, and who has changed it. Other comments may clarify types, constants, and variables and state what the segments of the program are designed to accomplish. All of these kinds of comments have been used in the examples so far in this book. It should be noted again that comments may be nested. That is,

(* This comment (* which contains another comment *) is legal. *)

To illustrate some differences between readable and not-so-readable code, consider the following example.

Example 4.4.1

Calculate the monthly payments on a loan.

Define the problem Given the MonthlyInterestRate, the Amount of a loan, and the NumberofMonths to pay back the loan, calculate the MonthlyPayment, which is given by the formula

$$\text{MonthlyPayment} = \text{Amount} * \text{MonthlyInterestRate} \\ / [1.0 - (1.0 + \text{MonthlyInterestRate})^{-\text{NumberOfMonths}}]$$

Develop a solution The annual percentage interest rate AnnualInterest (12.0%) will be entered from the keyboard and converted to fractional MonthlyInterestRate by the formula

$$\text{MonthlyInterestRate} = \text{AnnualInterest}/(12.0 * 100.0).$$

The Amount of the loan and the NumberOfYears to pay will be entered from the keyboard as well. NumberOfYears will be converted to NumberOfMonths by multiplying by 12.0 months per year. The MonthlyPayment will be calculated using the formula in the problem definition. An intermediate calculation of

$$(1.0 + \text{MonthlyInterestRate})^{-\text{NumberOfMonths}}$$

will be performed using

$$\exp(-\text{NumberOfMonths} / \ln(1.0 + \text{MonthlyInterestRate})),$$

where exp and ln functions are imported from standard module MathLib0. Finally, Amount, AnnualInterest, NumberofYears, and MonthlyPayment will be displayed to the screen.

Refine the solution   *Pseudocode*

```
begin FindMonthlyPayment
    ask for AnnualInterest rate, Amount, and NumberOfYears
    convert AnnualInterest rate to fractional MonthlyInterestRate
    convert NumberOfYears to NumberOfMonths
    calculate MonthlyPayment
    print Amount, AnnualInterest rate, NumberOfYears, and MonthlyPayment
end FindMonthlyPayment
```

Modula-2 Code

```
MODULE MP; (* FileName:CH4G*)FROM InOut IMPORT WriteString,WriteLn;
FROM RealInOut IMPORT ReadReal,FWriteReal;FROM MathLib0 IMPORT exp,ln;
VAR T,i,AM,M,P,AN,Y:REAL;BEGIN WriteString("Amount AM = ? $");ReadReal(AM);
WriteLn;WriteString("Interest AN = ? ");ReadReal(AN);WriteLn;
WriteString("Years Y = ? ");ReadReal(Y);WriteLn;WriteLn;
i:=AN/(12.0*100.0);M:=Y*12.0;T:=exp(-M*ln(1.0+i));P:=AM*i/(1.0-T);
WriteString("   Amount    Annual%Int    Years    Monthly Payment");
WriteLn;FWriteReal(AM,10,2);  FWriteReal(AN,13,2);FWriteReal(Y,8,0);
FWriteReal(P,19,2);WriteLn;END MP.
```

This code does the job, and it certainly saves space on the page; but it is difficult to read, and nearly impossible to debug. The program appears below in somewhat better form, with two procedures that can be incorporated into the production of an amortization table. See if you like this better.

Modula-2 code

```
MODULE FindMonthlyPayment;
  (* Finds the monthly payment on a loan when the amount, annual
     interest rate, and number of years are given.
     File Name:CH4G2    Modula-2    RKW    Feb. 1991    *)

FROM InOut IMPORT WriteString, WriteLn;
FROM RealInOut IMPORT ReadReal, FWriteReal;
FROM MathLib0 IMPORT exp, ln;

VAR  MonthlyInterestRate, Amount, NumberOfMonths,
     MonthlyPayment, AnnualInterest, NumberOfYears : REAL;


PROCEDURE EnterInitialData(VAR LoanAmount, AnnualInterest, NumYears : REAL);
  BEGIN
     WriteString("What is the amount of the loan?  $ ");
     ReadReal(LoanAmount); WriteLn;
     WriteString("What is the annual percentage interest rate? ");
     ReadReal(AnnualInterest); WriteLn;
```

```
              WriteString("How many years will you take to pay back the loan? ");
                ReadReal(NumYears); WriteLn; WriteLn;
           END EnterInitialData;


   PROCEDURE CalculatePayment(Amount, AnnualInterest, NumYears : REAL;
                        VAR MonthlyPay, NumMonths, MonthlyInterest : REAL);
        VAR  IntermedCalc : REAL;
        BEGIN
              (* Convert annual to monthly values *)
            MonthlyInterest := AnnualInterest / (12.0 * 100.0);
            NumMonths := NumYears * 12.0;

              (* Calculate the MonthlyPayment *)
            IntermedCalc := exp(-NumMonths * ln(1.0 + MonthlyInterest));
            MonthlyPay := Amount * MonthlyInterest / (1.0 - IntermedCalc);

              (* Display the results *)
            WriteString("    Amount    Annual%Int    Years    Monthly Payment");
              WriteLn;
            FWriteReal(Amount,10,2); FWriteReal(AnnualInterest,13,2);
             FWriteReal(NumYears,8,0); FWriteReal(MonthlyPay,19,2); WriteLn;
           END CalculatePayment;


   BEGIN  (* FindMonthlyPayment *)
      EnterInitialData(Amount, AnnualInterest, NumberOfYears);

      CalculatePayment(Amount, AnnualInterest, NumberOfYears,
             MonthlyPayment, NumberOfMonths, MonthlyInterestRate);

   END FindMonthlyPayment.
```

Debug and test To debug, write the program in the second form, not the first. Choose a case that is least difficult to check on the calculator, such as Amount = $10,000, AnnualInterest = 12.0%, and NumberOfYears = 5.0. Then try it for your mortgage or an outstanding loan to see if you get the same results as what the lender told you. Does it check out for special cases, such as when Amount = 0, when AnnualInterest = 0, or when NumberOfMonths = 1? Here is a test run for a particular mortgage:

```
What is the amount of the loan?  $ 62000
What is the annual percentage interest rate? 10.0
How many years will you take to pay back the loan? 30.0

        Amount    Annual%Int    Years    Monthly Payment
      62000.00        10.00        30            544.09
```

Complete the documentation Source code for this program is in file CH4G2. Observe the VAR (In/Out) parameters declared in the procedure headings. These will be needed in the next example. In the users' manual, be sure to warn that the AnnualInterest rate must be expressed in percent; for example, 14.0, not 0.14. Documentation will be completed after the next example, which continues the loan amortization task.

Loop Invariants and Debugging

It can be frustrating to debug an iterative loop. If the statements to update the test condition are left out, the iterations may continue indefinitely, and if the loop contains no write statements, the screen cursor may just blink forever with no apparent response to any keyboard entry, except perhaps a Break key.

Insert Write Statements

One of the most important debugging techniques for iterative techniques is to insert at least one write statement within the loop. Any write statement will help. Even inserting

```
WriteString(''I am here.''); WriteLn;
```

will display "I am here." repeatedly and provide a clue concerning the problem. Even better is to display the values of the variables. For example, this iterative structure, with CARDINAL accumulators Count and Total,

```
Count := 0; Total := 0;
WHILE  Count < 10  DO
   Total := Total + Count;
END; (* WHILE *)
```

is an infinite loop. Why? Inserting write statements

```
WriteString(''I am here.  Count = '');
WriteCard(Count,3);
WriteString(''  Total = ''); WriteCard(Total,6);
WriteLn;
```

just before END; (* WHILE *) would display

```
I am here.  Count = 0  Total = 0
I am here.  Count = 0  Total = 0
I am here.  Count = 0  Total = 0
.  .  .
```

ad infinitum, telling you that the accumulators are not accumulating.

Invariant Assertions

Each time through a WHILE iteration, the variables should have certain, predictable values just before the condition is to be tested again. These predictable values are called **loop invariants.** Comments may be inserted within the loop, usually just before the END; (* WHILE *) command, stating what the values of the invariants should be at that point. Such a comment is called an **assertion** about what the iteration should have accomplished by the time the comment appears. If you examine the WHILE structures in AccumulateATotal (Example 4.3.2), DivideThe-HardWay (Example 4.3.1), and CreateSellingPriceTable (Example 4.2.1), you will see that such assertion comments have been specified in those programs.

Iteration debugging usually is easier if assertions concerning the values of the invariants are included just before the END of the iterative loop. This allows the loop to be checked by following through a few iterations by hand to determine whether the assertions are true. If the assertions are not true, then there is an error in the code, which can be found and corrected. When writing loop structures you should concentrate on what you wish the loop to accomplish in each iteration and remember to specify the invariant assertion in a comment just before the end of the

Figure 4–7
Amortization Table
(Example 4.4.2)

```
What is the amount of the loan?  $ 1500.00
What is the annual percentage interest rate? 14.0
How many years will you take to pay back the loan? 1.0

      Amount    Annual%Int   Years    Monthly Payment
      1500.00       14.00       1             134.68


   Payment  Interest  Principal  Cumulative  Total Paid  New Balance
   Number     Paid       Paid     Interest    to Date         Due
   -----------------------------------------------------------------

      1       17.50     117.18      17.50      134.68      1382.82
      2       16.13     118.55      33.63      269.36      1264.27
      3       14.75     119.93      48.38      404.04      1144.34
      4       13.35     121.33      61.73      538.72      1023.01
      5       11.94     122.75      73.67      673.40       900.27
      6       10.50     124.18      84.17      808.08       776.09
      7        9.05     125.63      93.23      942.76       650.46
      8        7.59     127.09     100.81     1077.45       523.37
      9        6.11     128.57     106.92     1212.13       394.79
     10        4.61     130.07     111.53     1346.81       264.72
     11        3.09     131.59     114.61     1481.49       133.13
     12        1.55     133.13     116.17     1616.17         0.00
```

loop. This will enhance your ability to debug problems in iterative code and to prove that your results are correct.

Example 4.4.2

Amortize a loan.

Define the problem   Produce a loan amortization table like the one in Figure 4–7. The user will enter the Amount of the loan, the AnnualInterest percentage rate, and the NumberOfYears to repay the loan.

Develop a solution   The EnterInitialData procedure from the FindMonthlyPayment module (Example 4.4.1) will be incorporated to ask the user for Amount, AnnualInterest, and NumberOfYears. PROCEDURE CalculatePayment from that module will be used to convert annual to monthly values and to calculate the MonthlyPayment and display the information at the top of the table.

The WHILE iteration necessary to produce the body of the table begins with initialization of

$$
\begin{aligned}
\text{BalanceDue} &= \text{Amount} \\
\text{CumulativeInterest} &= 0.0 \\
\text{PaidToDate} &= 0.0 \\
\text{PaymentNum} &= 0.0
\end{aligned}
$$

Then, the iteration proceeds with these calculations and accumulations:

$$
\begin{aligned}
\text{PaymentNum} &= \text{PaymentNum} + 1.0 \\
\text{InterestPaid} &= \text{BalanceDue} * \text{MonthlyInterestRate} \\
\text{PrincipalPaid} &= \text{MonthlyPayment} - \text{InterestPaid} \\
\text{CumInterest} &= \text{CumInterest} + \text{InterestPaid} \\
\text{PaidToDate} &= \text{PaidToDate} + \text{MonthlyPayment} \\
\text{BalanceDue} &= \text{BalanceDue} - \text{PrincipalPaid}
\end{aligned}
$$

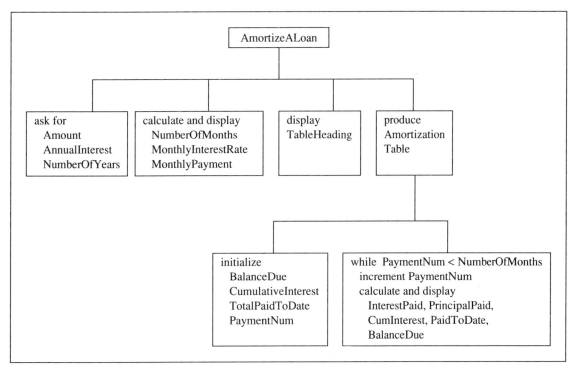

Figure 4-8
Structure Chart for AmortizeALoan (Example 4.4.2)

until PaymentNum equals the NumberOfMonths to repay the loan. The structure chart in Figure 4-8 outlines this solution.

Refine the solution *Pseudocode for Module AmortizeALoan*

```
begin AmortizeALoan
   EnterInitialData(Amount, AnnualInterest, NumberOfYears)
   CalculatePayment(Amount, AnnualInterest, NumberOfYears,
           MonthlyPayment, NumberOfMonths, MonthlyInterestRate)
   DisplayTableHeading
   ProduceAmortizationTable(Amount, MonthlyPayment,
           MonthlyInterestRate, NumberOfMonths)
end AmortizeALoan
```

Pseudocode for procedures

```
EnterInitialData(LoanAmount, AnnualInterest, NumYears)
   begin
      ask for LoanAmount
      ask for AnnualInterest rate
      ask for NumYears to pay back the loan
   end EnterInitialData

CalculatePayment(Amount, AnnualInterest, NumYears, MonthlyPay,
           NumMonths, MonthlyInterest)
   begin
      find MonthlyInterest = AnnualInterest / (12.0 * 100.0)
      NumMonths = NumYears * 12.0
      calculate MonthlyPay
```

```
                    display Amount, AnnualInterest, NumYears, MonthlyPay
                end CalculatePayment

            DisplayTableHeading
                begin
                    print "Payment Number", "Interest Paid", "Principal Paid",
                    "Cumulative Interest", "Total Paid to Date", "New Balance Due"
                    underline heading
                end DisplayTableHeading

            ProduceAmortizationTable(BalanceDue, Payment, MonthlyInterest, NumMonths)
                declare local variables PaymentNum, InterestPaid, PrincipalPaid,
                                CumInterest, PaidToDate
                begin
                    initialize CumInterest = 0.0,     PaidToDate = 0.0,
                            PaymentNum = 0.0
                    while PaymentNum < NumMonths
                        increment PaymentNum
                        calculate and display    InterestPaid, PrincipalPaid,
                                        CumInterest, PaidToDate, BalanceDue
                end while
                end ProduceAmortizationTable
```

Modula-2 Code

```
MODULE AmortizeALoan;
  (* Amortizes a loan when the amount, annual interest rate, and
     number of payback years are given.
     CODE INCOMPLETE.   PROCEDURES EnterInitialData and CalculatePayment
                     must be supplied from FILE CH4G, Example 4.4.1.
     File Name:CH4H2    Modula-2    RKW      Feb. 1991    *)


FROM InOut IMPORT WriteString, WriteLn, Write;
FROM RealInOut IMPORT ReadReal, FWriteReal;
FROM MathLib0 IMPORT exp, ln;


VAR  MonthlyInterestRate, Amount, NumberOfMonths,
     MonthlyPayment, AnnualInterest, NumberOfYears : REAL;


(* Define  PROCEDURES  EnterInitialData and CalculatePayment here.
           See  File  CH4G2,  Example 4.4.1  *)


PROCEDURE DisplayTableHeading;
   VAR CountDashes : CARDINAL;
   BEGIN
      WriteLn; WriteLn;
      WriteString("Payment  Interest  Principal  Cumulative  Total Paid");
       WriteString(" New Balance"); WriteLn;
       WriteString(" Number      Paid      Paid      Interest      to Date");
       WriteString("          Due"); WriteLn;
      CountDashes := 1;
      WHILE  CountDashes <= 65  DO
         Write('-');
         CountDashes := CountDashes + 1;
      END; (* WHILE *)
      WriteLn; WriteLn;
   END DisplayTableHeading;
```

```
PROCEDURE ProduceAmortizationTable(BalanceDue, Payment, MonthlyInterest,
                                   NumMonths : REAL);
    VAR  PaymentNum, InterestPaid, PrincipalPaid, CumInterest,
         PaidToDate : REAL;
  BEGIN
     CumInterest := 0.0;   PaidToDate := 0.0;   PaymentNum := 0.0;
     WHILE  PaymentNum < NumMonths  DO
        PaymentNum    := PaymentNum + 1.0;
        InterestPaid  := BalanceDue * MonthlyInterest;
        PrincipalPaid := Payment - InterestPaid;
        CumInterest   := CumInterest + InterestPaid;
        PaidToDate    := PaidToDate + Payment;
        BalanceDue    := BalanceDue - PrincipalPaid;
        FWriteReal(PaymentNum,7,0); FWriteReal(InterestPaid,10,2);
         FWriteReal(PrincipalPaid,11,2); FWriteReal(CumInterest,12,2);
            FWriteReal(PaidToDate,12,2); FWriteReal(BalanceDue,13,2);
            WriteLn;

           (* Assertions:
               PaymentNum = number of payments made so far
               PaidToDate = PaymentNumber * Payment
               BalanceDue = initial Amount - (PaidToDate - CumInterest)   *)
        END; (* WHILE *)
        WriteLn;
     END ProduceAmortizationTable;


  BEGIN  (* AmortizeALoan *)
     EnterInitialData(Amount, AnnualInterest, NumberOfYears);
     CalculatePayment(Amount, AnnualInterest, NumberOfYears,
             MonthlyPayment, NumberOfMonths, MonthlyInterestRate);
     DisplayTableHeading;
     ProduceAmortizationTable(Amount, MonthlyPayment, MonthlyInterestRate,
                             NumberOfMonths);
  END AmortizeALoan.
```

Debug and test Running the program with Amount = $1500.00, AnnualInterest = 14.0%, and NumberOfYears to pay back the loan = 1.0 should produce the results shown in Figure 4–7. Try some other test data, including limiting values such as Amount = 0.0, NumberOfYears = 0.0, or AnnualInterestRate = 100.00% and see what happens.

Note the invariant assertions before the END of the WHILE loop in PROCEDURE ProduceAmortizationTable. To check the correctness of your results, calculate and display PaidToDate and BalanceDue by the formulae given in those assertions and compare them with the values printed in the table.

Complete the documentation In addition to the usual definition of the problem, structure chart, and pseudocode, it is important to include one or more sample printouts of amortization tables produced by the program.

In the users' manual, warn that the AnnualInterestRate must be entered as a percent (e.g., 14.0, rather than 0.14). Note that NumberOfYears need not be a whole number; for example, you may enter 1.5 years. However, it is left to you to correct the program so that the NumberOfYears printed in the heading is the correct decimal value and that the last payment is considered as a special case so that the final balance is 0.00. The source code file, CH4H2, will require inclusion of procedures EnterInitialData and CalculatePayment from file CH4G2 before the program can be compiled and executed.

Questions 4.4

1. In the AmortizeALoan program (Example 4.4.2) the final BalanceDue may differ from $0.00 if your compiler does not handle many decimal digits of precision for REAL numbers, or if you enter a fractional value (such as 1.7) for the NumberOfYears to pay back the loan. Explain why. What could you do to solve the problem? How would you correct this problem: when you enter 1.7 for NumberOfYears, the table heading shows the Years as 2?

2. The first code, for MODULE MP, in Example 4.4.1, is found in file CH4G. It represents the same problem solution as MODULE FindMonthlyPayment in file CH4G2, except without using procedures. Modify this code with white space and meaningful identifier names to make it more readable; then compile and execute to convince yourself that it produces the same results as FindMonthly-Payment (CH4G2).

3. What would be meaningful assertions before the END; (* WHILE *) statements in these WHILE loops?

   a. AmortizeALoan Example 4.4.2 PROCEDURE DisplayTableHeading

   ```
   WHILE  CountDashes <= 65  DO . . .
   ```
   b. AccumulateATotal Example 4.3.2

   ```
   WHILE  (N <= 0) OR (N >= 256)  DO . . .
   ```
   c. DivideTheHardWay Example 4.3.1

   ```
   WHILE  Divisor = 0  DO
   ```
   d. A loop that counts and displays the CARDINAL multiples of 5 (0, 5, 10, 15, . . .) from 0 to 100.

   e. A loop that begins with initial values Count = 1 and Result = 1, then calculates powers of 3 by accumulating Result := Result * 3 until Count = 10.

4.5 Summary

Selection   The selection structure is implemented in Modula-2 with IF Condition THEN . . ., which executes a collection of commands if the Condition is true. Alternatively, IF Condition THEN . . . ELSE . . . performs one group of operations when the Condition is true and another when the Condition is false.

Logical Operators   The relational operators, =, # or <>, <, >, <=, and >=, and the logical operators, AND, OR, and NOT, allow you to combine values and operations to create meaningful Boolean Conditions for the selection and iteration structures. Rules of precedence govern the order in which these operators are applied. The use of parentheses is encouraged to clarify how a given Boolean expression is to be evaluated.

Iteration   The Modula-2 structure introduced in this chapter for implementing iterations is the WHILE loop, which is applied via the structure

```
Initialize the Condition
WHILE  Condition  DO
   executable instructions;
   (* include an instruction to update the Condition *)
END; (* WHILE *)
```

Debugging a WHILE iteration includes making sure that an initial value of the Condition is defined and avoiding infinite repetitions by updating the Condition with the loop.

Checking Data Entry   One important application of the WHILE loop is to request the user to reenter data until the values are valid.

Accumulating and Counting   Other major tasks performed by iteration are to accumulate running totals and/or to count how many times an operation is performed.

Sentinel Values   A WHILE loop can allow an operation to be repeated until a final (sentinel) value is encountered, which acts as an indicator (or flag) to the program to terminate the iterations.

White Space and Comments   Using indentation, blank spaces, and blank lines (all examples of ''white space'') to indicate and separate logical components of a program can improve the readability and maintainability of your code significantly. Giving meaningful names to identifiers and inserting comments into your code are also critical features of good program style.

Invariant Assertions   When you apply iteration to the solution of problems, you should try to determine exactly what you want to accomplish in each iteration. Then write assertions, in the form of comments, just before

```
END; (* WHILE *),
```

stating what you expect the results to be (including the values of variables within the loop). Such assertions are called *loop invariants*. Defining and checking them carefully can help ensure that your results are correct.

4.6   *Exercises*

Exercises marked with (FileName:_____) indicate those that ask you to use, modify, or extend the text examples. The numbers in brackets, [ ], indicate the chapter section that contains the material you need for completing the exercise.

1. [4.1] **a.** Write, test, and document a program that uses MOD, DIV, and the selection structure to determine whether a CARDINAL number is even or odd. The number will be entered from the keyboard, and then the message ''Even'' or ''Odd'' will be displayed on the screen.

   b. Modify this program to determine whether the number is exactly divisible by any CARDINAL value specified by the user. That is, is it divisible by 3, 7, 13, or any other value you specify?

2. [4.1] Develop, test, and document a program that tests a REAL number to determine whether it is positive or negative. The number will be entered by the user at the keyboard. If it is positive or has a zero value, find and display its square root (using function sqrt from MathLib0). If the number is negative, print a message stating that it does not have a real square root.

3. [4.3] Use the WHILE structure to find the value of 2^n, where n is a cardinal value entered by the user at the keyboard. Code, test, and document. *Hint:* Initialize Result = 1. Accumulate Result := Result * 2.

4. [4.4] (FileName:CH4G2) Modify FindMonthlyPayment (Example 4.4.1) to prevent the user from entering an illegal value for the annual interest rate. That is, write a loop that asks the user repeatedly for the annual interest rate until a value between 1.0 and 25.0 is entered.

Figure 4–9
Savings Table
(Exercise 6)

```
        What is the initial deposit? 200.00
        How much will you deposit each month? 100.00
        What is the annual percentage interest rate? 8.0
        How many years to accumulate savings? 0.5

                Beginning    Interest               New
        Month     Balance        Paid    Deposit    Balance
        -----   ---------    --------    -------    -------
          1       200.00        1.33     100.00     301.33
          2       301.33        2.01     100.00     403.34
          3       403.34        2.69     100.00     506.03
          4       506.03        3.37     100.00     609.40
          5       609.40        4.06     100.00     713.47
          6       713.47        4.76     100.00     818.22
```

5. [4.3] (FileName:CH4F) Modify MakePayTable (Example 4.3.3) to
   a. include an accumulator that adds the total of the GrossPay of all the employees and displays that total at the end of the Gross Pay column of the table.
   b. accept input of data from the keyboard (instead of from an input file) and direct the table to an output file.
6. [4.4] (FileName:CH4H2, CH4G) Using AmortizeALoan (Example 4.4.2) as an analogy, write a program that calculates and displays a table of the Balance in a savings account. The user will enter

   > InitialAmount deposited
   > AnnualInterest rate
   > MonthlyDeposit (fixed amount deposited each month)
   > NumberOfYears (years of deposits made and interest paid)

   Then the program converts AnnualInterest rate to a fractional MonthlyInterestRate and NumberOfYears to NumberOfMonths. It calculates the InterestPaid on the minimum balance during the month, using the algorithm

   > Balance (initial) = InitialAmount
   > InterestPaid   = Balance * MonthlyInterestRate
   > Balance (new)   = Balance (old) + InterestPaid + MonthlyDeposit

   A table is created like that shown in Figure 4–9.
7. [4.3] In the hypothetical Republic of Dwump, the basic unit of currency is the dwork, and the exchange rate at present is 2.57 dworks per U.S. dollar. Develop, test, and document a program that uses the WHILE command to create a table of dollars versus dworks in steps of $0.10 from MinimumDollars to MaximumDollars. MinimumDollars and MaximumDollars will be entered by the user from the keyboard. The exchange rate (2.57 dworks per dollar) and the step value ($0.10) will be declared as CONSTants, so that they can be found and changed easily. Direct the table to an output file, so that it can be displayed, copied, and printed later. The exchange rate should be recorded at the head of the table, and columns Dollars and Dworks should be labeled.
8. [4.3] Use a WHILE loop to determine the smallest cardinal power of 3 that exceeds 30,000. That is, find the smallest n such that $3^n > 30,000$. Develop, test, and document the problem solution. *Hint:* Initialize PowerOfThree = 1. Accumulate PowerOfThree := PowerOfThree * 3, and Count := Count + 1.

9. [4.3] (FileName:CH4C) Modify and document CreateSellingPriceTable (Example 4.2.1) so that:
   a. asking the user for Markup, and Lowest and Highest purchase prices and the Increment between prices is handled in a separate procedure. Include safeguards to ensure that Markup is a percentage number greater than 1.0, that Lowest < Highest, and that Increment <= (Highest − Lowest).
   b. the WHILE loop to calculate and print the table is handled in a separate procedure.
   c. the selling price table is directed to an output file.
10. [4.3] (FileName:CH4E) Modify AccumulateATotal (Example 4.3.2) and update the documentation, to
   a. extend the range of allowable N, by computing $N * [(N + 1) \text{ DIV } 2]$ or $(N \text{ DIV } 2) * (N + 1)$, rather than $N * (N + 1) \text{ DIV } 2$. *Hint:* Use MOD 2 to determine whether N is even or odd. Then to avoid truncation errors, if N is odd, calculate $(N + 1) \text{ DIV } 2$; if N is even, calculate $N \text{ DIV } 2$.
   b. produce a table of Sum and $N(N + 1)/2$ for $N = 1$ to 50.
11. [4.3] A *prime* cardinal number is one that has exactly two different divisors, namely 1 and the number itself. Write, test, and document a program to find and print all the prime numbers less than 100. *Hint:* 2 is prime. For each number from 3 to 99, find Remainder := Number MOD n, where n ranges from 2 to sqrt(Number). (Import sqrt from module MathLib0. If $n >$ sqrt(Number), then the number is not equally divisible by n. Why?) If any Remainder equals 0, then the number is not prime.
12. [4.3] (FileName:CH3E) Modify MakeASale (Chapter 3, Example 3.4.1) so that it repeatedly asks for NumberOfItems, CostPerItem, and DiscountRate for different kinds of items purchased, until the user enters a zero sentinel value for NumberOfItems, which stops the iterations. The program displays the Purchase, Tax, and AmountDue for each type of item and accumulates and displays the total amount due for all of the items purchased.

5

Character Variables

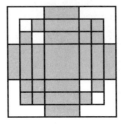

Chapter Outline

Much of the work done in computer science deals directly with data represented in character form. For example, language compilers and interpreters are required to translate program source code represented by characters into machine-executable form. Data stored in files or databases and manipulated by editors or query languages are most often stored as character codes. This chapter extends the CHARacter-type data manipulation, introduced in Chapter 3, with tasks such as finding and using character codes, converting letters between lowercase and uppercase, printing special characters, responding to a menu, and plotting points on a graph. More applications of characters in the form of arrays and strings will be examined in Chapters 10 through 12.

5.1   *CHAR Type*

When a variable is declared to be of type CHAR, sufficient memory space is reserved to store a binary code that represents the character assigned to that variable.

Read, Write, Assignment

Assignment of a single character to a CHARacter variable is done by the Read procedure imported from module InOut or by using the assignment operator (: =) and enclosing the character within single quotes. Display of a character is performed with the Write procedure from module InOut. This program illustrates simple character declaration, assignment, and display:

```
MODULE  DemoCharacters;
   (* Demonstrates character assignment and display.
      FileName:CH5A     Modula-2    RKW     Feb. 1991  *)

FROM InOut IMPORT  Read, Write, WriteString, WriteLn;

CONST  Star = '*';     (* Define character constants '*' and blank space *)
       Blank = ' ';

VAR  Mark, Badge, Token, Sign, EndOfChar : CHAR;

BEGIN
    (* Read characters and terminating key.  Echo to screen with Write  *)
   WriteString("Enter three characters. Press the Enter key after each: ");
    WriteLn;
   Read(Mark); Read(EndOfChar); Write(Mark); WriteLn;
   Read(Sign); Read(EndOfChar); Write(Sign); WriteLn;
   Read(Token); Read(EndOfChar); Write(Token); WriteLn;

    (* Assign a character value *)
   Badge := '+';

    (* Display character constants, variables, and literals *)
   WriteLn;
   Write(Star); Write(Blank); Write(Mark); Write(Blank); Write(Star);
    WriteLn;
   Write('&'); Write(' '); Write(Sign); Write(' '); Write('&'); WriteLn;
   Write(Badge); Write(Badge); Write(Token); Write(Badge); Write(Badge);
    WriteLn;
END DemoCharacters.
```

Executing the program displays these results:

```
Enter three characters. Press the Enter key after each:
S
u
e

*  S  *
&  u  &
++e++
```

EndOfChar represents a CHAR variable that is read and never used. When you Read a character on some systems, the character is stored in a buffer until a terminating key such as Enter is pressed. Then the code for the terminating keys gets assigned as a CHARacter itself. In the program above, if the Read(EndOfChar) after Read(Mark) were omitted, the program may not even wait for you to give it the value of Sign, because Sign already would have been assigned the value of the Enter (or other terminating) key, which was pressed after Mark was entered.

Observe in the code how characters can be handled as literals ('&' or ' '), CONSTants (Star, Blank), or variables (Mark, etc.).

On some systems, the Read(CharacterVariable) command automatically echoes the value of the CharacterVariable to the screen. Then, for example, the combination

```
Read(Mark); Write(Mark);
```

would display the value of Mark twice. If your system does this, you can omit the Write(CharacterVariable) command after each Read(CharacterVariable).

☐ 'Y' or 'N' Decisions

One important application of single characters is that of using 'Y' and 'N' for responses to questions.

The following example shows how this can be accomplished.

Example 5.1.1

Determine the cost of electricity used by an appliance.

Define the problem   Given the appliance rating in Watts and the number of Hours used, calculate the cost of using the appliance and display the results to the screen. After each cost calculation, ask the user to respond with 'Y' or 'N' to the question "Would you like to do it again?"

Develop a solution   Calculate and display

KiloWattHours = (Watts / 1000.0) * Hours
Cost (in cents) = KiloWattHours * CENTSPERKILOWATTHOUR

where CENTSPERKILOWATTHOUR is defined as a CONSTant that can be found and updated readily when electrical rates change.

Refine the solution   Pseudocode and a flowchart of the solution are shown in Figure 5–1.

Pseudocode	Flowchart

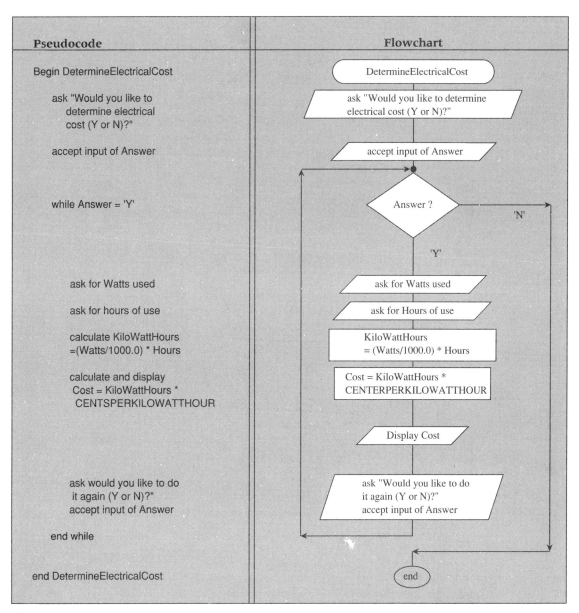

Figure 5–1
Pseudocode and Flowchart for DetermineElectricalCost (Example 5.1.1)

In the Modula-2 code, Answer is initialized before the WHILE loop by asking the user if he or she wants to determine electrical cost. The WHILE Condition is updated by requesting an Answer again before the end of the loop. In this program, only answers 'Y' and 'y' will cause the loop to execute again.

Modula-2 code

```
MODULE DetermineElectricalCost;
  (* Repeatedly determines the cost of running electrical appliances
     until the user answers the question "Do you want to do it again? "
     with a character other than 'Y' or 'y'.
     FileName:CH5B      Modula-2      RKW      Feb. 1991   *)
```

```
FROM InOut IMPORT WriteString, WriteLn, Read, Write;
FROM RealInOut IMPORT ReadReal, FWriteReal;

CONST  CENTSPERKILOWATTHOUR = 9.5;
VAR  Watts, Hours, KiloWattHours, Cost : REAL;
     Answer, ThrowAway : CHAR;

BEGIN
   WriteString("Would you like to determine electrical cost (Y or N)? ");
    Read(Answer); Read(ThrowAway); Write(Answer); WriteLn; WriteLn;
   WHILE    (Answer = 'Y') OR (Answer = 'y')   DO
      WriteString("How many watts does your appliance use? ");
       ReadReal(Watts); WriteLn;
      WriteString("How many hours will you use the appliance? ");
       ReadReal(Hours); WriteLn;

      KiloWattHours := (Watts / 1000.0) * Hours;
      Cost := KiloWattHours * CENTSPERKILOWATTHOUR;

      WriteString("You will use"); FWriteReal(KiloWattHours,10,4);
       WriteString("  kilowatt hours, at");
       FWriteReal(CENTSPERKILOWATTHOUR,6,2);
       WriteString("  cents per kilowatt hour.");  WriteLn;
      WriteString("The total cost is"); FWriteReal(Cost,10,2);
       WriteString("  cents."); WriteLn; WriteLn;

     WriteString("Would you like to do it again (Y or N)? ");
        Read(Answer); Read(ThrowAway); Write(Answer); WriteLn;
   END; (* WHILE *)

   WriteString("O.K. We will stop now."); WriteLn;
END DetermineElectricalCost.
```

Debug and test When the program is executed you should see results similar to the following:

```
Would you like to determine electrical cost (Y or N)? Y

How many watts does your appliance use? 200.0
How many hours will you use the appliance? 10.0
You will use    2.0000  kilowatt hours, at  9.50 cents per kilowatt
hour.
The total cost is     19.0   cents.

Would you like to do it again (Y or N)? N
O.K. We will stop now.
```

A number of problems could cause unexpected or incorrect results. Following through the program by hand with some reasonable test data will help you catch errors in the formulae for calculating KiloWattHours and Cost.

You also should be aware that if the Read command in your system stores characters in a buffer—where they wait for a terminating character—then omitting the Read(ThrowAway) commands can cause the program to execute once and then stop, without waiting for the next Answer. This is because the terminating Enter character would be held in the buffer and assigned to Answer at the next Read(Answer) command.

Complete the documentation   Documentation is simple. Collect the problem definition, pseudocode, flowchart, code, and sample run. The users' manual need not do much more than state where the source code is found (CH5B) and then tell the user to answer the questions posed by the program and watch for results on the screen.

---

1. Determine how the Read(CharacterVariable) command works on your system. Can you discover whether it stores characters entered from the keyboard until a terminating character is entered or assigns each character immediately to the CharacterVariable when its key is pressed? Does it echo the value entered for the CharacterVariable to the screen, or require a Write(CharacterVariable) command to display which key was pressed?

Executing the following code fragments on your machine may help. Pay particular attention in each situation to whether the key pressed appears on the screen once, twice, or not at all. Observe what gets assigned to each CharacterVariable and what is displayed by the program.

Assume the declarations

```
CONST  START = '*';  STOP = '!';
VAR  Ch1, Ch2, Ch3, Dummy : CHAR;
```

then

a.

```
BEGIN
   WriteString("Enter 3 characters; then press the Enter key: ");
   WriteLn;
   Read(Ch1); Read(Ch2); Read(Ch3); Read(Dummy); WriteLn; WriteLn;
   WriteString("Results = "); WriteLn;
   Write(START); Write(Ch1); Write(STOP); WriteLn;
   Write(START); Write(Ch2); Write(STOP); WriteLn;
   Write(START); Write(Ch3); Write(STOP); WriteLn;
   Write(START); Write(Dummy); Write(STOP); WriteLn;
   ....
```

b.

```
BEGIN
   WriteString("Enter 3 characters; press Enter key after each one:");
   WriteLn;
   Read(Ch1); Read(Dummy); Write(Ch1); WriteLn;
   Read(Ch2); Read(Dummy); Write(Ch2); WriteLn;
   Read(Ch3); Read(Dummy); Write(Ch3); WriteLn; WriteLn;
   WriteString("Results = "); WriteLn;
   Write(START); Write(Ch1); Write(STOP); WriteLn;
   Write(START); Write(Ch2); Write(STOP); WriteLn;
   Write(START); Write(Ch3); Write(STOP); WriteLn;
   Write(START); Write(Dummy); Write(STOP); WriteLn;
   ....
```

2. Create two input files, using an editor. The FIRST.IN file contains the following characters:

```
abc <Enter>
```

A Bit of Background

Herman Hollerith

To Herman Hollerith, born in 1860 in Buffalo, New York, goes the credit for creating the original binary character code. After graduating from Columbia University at the age of 19, Hollerith accepted a position with the U.S. Census Office, where he invented a punch-card code and the machine for tabulating the 1890 census. By 1896 his inventions had grown into the Tabulating Machine Company, which became tremendously successful by providing statistical equipment to business and government. He sold the company in 1912 to a conglomerate, which in 1924 became IBM and was headed for the next 30 years by Thomas J. Watson, a former employee of Hollerith's Tabulating Machine Company.

(<Enter> means the Enter key was pressed.) The SECOND.IN file contains these characters:

```
A <Enter>
B <Enter>
C <Enter>
```

Now replace the WriteString command immediately after BEGIN in each program fragment in question 1 above with OpenInput, and add CloseInput at the end of each fragment. Run the two program fragments, first with input coming from FIRST.IN, then with input from SECOND.IN. Try to determine how the Read command acts on your system when input comes from a file, rather than from the keyboard.

3. Write a WHILE loop, to insert into program DetermineElectricalCost (Example 5.1.1) that prevents the program from accepting any value of Answer other than 'y', 'Y', 'n', or 'N'.

5.2 ORD, CHR, and Control Characters

Every character, as well as every number, must be represented internally in a digital computer by binary digits. Numerous codes have been invented in the past century for handling character representations; examples include Hollerith's punched cards, punched paper tape, EBCDIC code used on IBM mainframes, and the currently popular ASCII standard.

ASCII and Other Codes

ASCII (pronounced "as-key") stands for the American Standard Code for Information Interchange. It was developed in the 1960s by a committee of the American National Standards Institute (ANSI). All computer designers who adopt the ASCII standard are assured that their internal character representations are compatible with those of others who adhere to the standard. Most microcomputers and minicomputers, as well as many mainframes, use ASCII either in standard 7-bit form (which provides for $2^7 = 128$ character codes) or in an extended form (which recognizes an 8th bit and allows up to $2^8 = 256$ characters). Appendix E contains a complete table of standard 7-bit ASCII codes, represented in binary, octal, and decimal.

☐ Character-to-Code Conversions and Vice Versa

Two utility functions, ORD and CHR, are built into Modula-2 for converting a character to its code and vice versa. These functions need not be imported; they are part of the Modula-2 system. ORD operates upon a character and returns the CARDINAL decimal value of its code. CHR operates upon a CARDINAL code and returns the character with the given code. If your system uses ASCII, the CARDINAL arguments of the CHR function that represent the printable alphabetic, numeric, or punctuation characters lie in the range 32 to 126. If your computer uses EBCDIC or another code, you should examine a table of the character codes for your system to determine which values between 0 and 255 represent printable characters.

Thus, for example, on an ASCII system, if a constant and variables were declared as

```
CONST  CH = 'q';
VAR    Mark1, Mark2, Mark3 : CHAR;
       Code1, CodeCh : CARDINAL;
```

then the commands

```
Mark1 := 'B'; Code1 := ORD(Mark1);
  Write(Mark1); WriteCard(Code1,5); WriteLn;
Mark2 := CHR(78);
  Write(Mark2); WriteCard(ORD(Mark2),5); WriteLn;
Mark3 := CHR(ORD(97+3));
  Write(Mark3); WriteCard(ORD(Mark3),5); WriteLn;
CodeCh := ORD(CH);
  Write(CH); WriteCard(CodeCh,5); WriteLn;
```

would produce the table

```
B     66
N     78
d    100
q    113
```

The following example shows how you can apply functions ORD and CHR to create a table of the codes used by your machine.

Example 5.2.1

Find the codes for characters 'a' through 'z' and the characters that have codes 33 through 64.

Define the problem   Make a table of decimal, octal, and hexadecimal codes for characters 'a' through 'z'. Given decimal codes 33 through 64, make a table of the characters represented and their codes.

Develop a solution   The user will be asked to enter StartCharacter ('a') and StopCharacter ('z'). Then, a loop in a procedure called PrintCodeTable will print Symbol and its decimal, octal, and hexadecimal codes for all values of Symbol between StartCharacter and StopCharacter.

The user will enter BeginCode (33) and EndCode (64). Then, in a second procedure, called PrintCharTable, a loop will print CHR(Code) and Code for all decimal Codes between BeginCode and EndCode).

Refine the solution
Pseudocode for PrintCodeTable(StartChar, StopChar)

```
begin
    print headings
    initialize Symbol to StartChar
    while Symbol < = StopChar
        assign Code := ORD(Symbol)
        Write(Symbol),WriteCard(Code),WriteOct(Code),WriteHex(Code)
        increment Symbol := CHR( Code + 1 )
    end while
end PrintCodeTable
```

Pseudocode for PrintCharTable(StartCode, StopCode)

```
begin
    print headings
    initialize Code = StartCode
    while Code < = StopCode
      write CHR(Code), Code
      increment Code
    end while
end PrintCharTable
```

Pseudocode for TestCodes

```
begin
    ask for and accept StartCharacter and StopCharacter
    PrintCodeTable(StartCharacter, StopCharacter)
    ask for and accept BeginCode and EndCode
    PrintCharTable(BeginCode, EndCode)
end TestCodes
```

Modula-2 code

```
MODULE TestCodes;
  (* Executes procedures PrintCodeTable and PrintCharTable.
     FileName:CH5C     Modula-2     RKW       Mar. 1991  *)

FROM InOut IMPORT WriteString, WriteLn, Read, Write,
                  ReadCard, WriteCard, WriteOct, WriteHex;

VAR  StartCharacter, StopCharacter, Terminator : CHAR;
     BeginCode, EndCode : CARDINAL;

PROCEDURE PrintCodeTable(StartChar, StopChar : CHAR);
   VAR Symbol : CHAR;  Code : CARDINAL;
   BEGIN
      WriteString("Character  Decimal  Octal      Hex"); WriteLn;
      Symbol := StartChar;
      WHILE  Symbol <= StopChar  DO
         Code := ORD(Symbol);
```

```
            Write(Symbol); WriteCard(Code,14);
             WriteString("        "); WriteOct(Code,3);
             WriteString("        "); WriteHex(Code,3); WriteLn;
            Symbol := CHR(Code + 1);
             (* Assertion: Code = ORD(StartChar) + number of iterations *)
        END; (* WHILE *)
    END PrintCodeTable;

PROCEDURE PrintCharTable(StartCode, StopCode : CARDINAL);
    VAR  Code : CARDINAL;
    BEGIN
        WriteString("Chararacter     Decimal Code"); WriteLn;
        Code := StartCode;
        WHILE  Code <= StopCode  DO
            Write(CHR(Code)); WriteCard(Code,20); WriteLn;
            Code := Code + 1;
             (* Assertion: Code = StartCode + number of iterations  *)
        END; (* WHILE *)
    END PrintCharTable;


BEGIN (* TestCodes *)
    WriteString("Enter the first character for which to find the code.");
     WriteLn; WriteString("Then press Enter: ");
     Read(StartCharacter); Read(Terminator); Write(StartCharacter); WriteLn;
    WriteString("Enter the final character for which to find the code.");
     WriteLn; WriteString("Then press Enter: ");
     Read(StopCharacter); Read(Terminator); Write(StopCharacter); WriteLn;
    PrintCodeTable(StartCharacter, StopCharacter);

    WriteLn; WriteLn;
    WriteString("Enter the first cardinal character code: ");
     ReadCard(BeginCode); WriteLn;
    WriteString("Enter the final cardinal character code: ");
     ReadCard(EndCode); WriteLn;
    PrintCharTable(BeginCode, EndCode);
     WriteLn;
END TestCodes.
```

Debug and test   Run with characters 'a' to 'z' and codes 33 to 64. If your system uses ASCII, you should observe the following:

```
Enter the first character for which to find the code.
Then press Enter: a
Enter the final character for which to find the code.
Then press Enter: z
Character  Decimal  Octal       Hex
a            97     000141      0061
b            98     000142      0062
c            99     000143      0063
d           100     000144      0064

...
...
x           120     000170      0078
y           121     000171      0079
z           122     000172      007A
```

```
Enter the first cardinal character code: 33
Enter the final cardinal character code: 64
Chararacter      Decimal Code
!                    33
"                    34
#                    35
...
...
>                    62
?                    63
@                    64
```

Try some other start and stop characters and codes. What happens if the characters are not printable or the codes are outside the allowable range?

Complete the documentation   Collect the problem definition, pseudocode, code, and sample run. The users' manual will state where the source code is found (CH5C). It should tell users to enter StartCharacter, StopCharacter, BeginCode, and EndCode when requested and warn that these should be in a range representing printable characters.

☐ Control Characters

An examination of the ASCII chart in Appendix E reveals that the characters with decimal codes between 0 and 31 (octal 0 to 37) are called *control characters*. Similar codes with different values are reserved in EBCDIC and other coding schemes. The characters defined by these codes serve to control transmission and storage of data, and many can be implemented from the keyboard by holding the CTRL key down and pressing a letter key. Some of those applied most often to control terminals and printers are shown in Figure 5–2.

Figure 5–2
ASCII Terminal
Control Characters

Function	Octal Code	Decimal Code
Ring Terminal Bell	07C	7
Back Space	10C	8
Tab	11C	9
Line Feed (down)	12C	10
Reverse Line Feed (up)	13C	11
Form Feed (new printer page)	14C	12
Carriage Return	15C	13

To access the control characters from a Modula-2 program, you may either (1) pass the decimal code for the character directly to the CHR function, or (2) define a CHARacter as CONSTant or VARiable. For example, to ring the terminal bell, you could

```
Write(CHR(7));
```

An alternative method to ring the bell is to assign the control value to a CHARacter variable, as in

```
Bell := CHR(7);
```

and then

```
Write(Bell);
```

If you choose to define a CONSTant for the control character, then you should use the octal code with capital letter C appended. For example, the declaration

```
CONST  BELL = O7C;
```

followed by the command

```
Write(BELL);
```

also rings the terminal bell.

The codes for ringing the terminal bell and performing the carriage return work on virtually every modern terminal. However, other control codes—such as those to move the cursor up, down, or backward on the screen—may or may not be implemented in a given system. If your system does not support a particular control character, your attempt to write that character will probably display some strange symbol instead. Also, some systems interpret some control codes differently. For example, in the UNIX operating system, code 12C often causes both a carriage return and line feed. Some experimentation may be valuable to determine how your system interprets control characters.

Incidentally, the two techniques for assigning and using control codes in variables and constants work just as well for the codes of all the printable characters.

A Bit of Background

Old Reliable Shift and Double

On the paper tape used for data storage and transmission through the 1960s and beyond, punched holes or *no* holes in six positions across the tape represented 1s and 0s respectively. Thus there was room for only 2^6 ($= 64$) characters to be represented on the tape. The available characters were 26 uppercase letters, 10 digits, 12 punctuation marks, and some control codes. When new tasks required lowercase letters and more control characters, the means of obtaining twice the character capacity from the same number of bits was discovered on the old reliable typewriter. With shifting, the number of characters available from the typewriter keyboard is doubled. Similarly, reserving two characters in a code for Shift In and Shift Out, creates nearly twice the code capacity. All codes following a Shift In stand for those in an alternate character set, until a Shift Out returns to the primary set. Virtually all common codes since paper tape have shift characters. Some modern machines use the extra set of codes for graphics, others create a different type style (font), while many use them for foreign-language characters. How creative could you be with 128 additional ASCII characters?

A Procedure to Read One Character

The following example develops a procedure you may wish to use in programs whenever you need to read a single character. Later, in Chapter 9, you will see how to save procedures such as this in an external module from which you can import them as needed.

Example 5.2.2

Write a procedure called ReadOneChar that will read a single character and ignore all other characters until a terminating character is detected.

Define the problem   Write a program that reads a key pressed on the keyboard and displays its code on the screen. Use the program to find the code for the Enter or Return key. Then write a procedure called ReadOneChar, which reads a character and ignores any succeeding characters until the Enter or Return key is pressed.

Develop a solution   In the first program, ask the user to press the Enter key, read that character, use ORD to convert to its code, and write the code in decimal and octal form. In the second program, declare a CONSTant called ENTERKEY, and give it the value of the octal code found from the first program. The procedure ReadOneChar will read a character. Then it will enter a WHILE loop that reads and discards subsequent characters until the Enter key is pressed.

Refine the solution
Pseudocode for FindEnterKeyCharacter

```
begin
    ask the user to press the Enter key
    Read the character, EnterKey
    find the code for the character, EnterKeyCode := ORD(EnterKey)
    write the EnterKeyCode in decimal and octal form
end FindEnterKeyCharacter
```

Pseudocode for procedure ReadOneChar(VAR Character)

```
CONST    ENTERKEY = code found from FindEnterKeyCharacter
begin
    read a Character
    read NextCharacter
    while NextCharacter # ENTERKEY
        read NextCharacter
    end while
end ReadOneChar
```

Pseudocode for module to test ReadOneChar

```
begin TestReadChar
    ask for a character Ch
    ReadOneChar(Ch)
    write "The character is ", Ch

    ask for a second character Ch
    ReadOneChar(Ch)
    write "The character is ", Ch
end TestReadChar
```

Modula-2 code

```
MODULE FindEnterKeyCharacter;
   (* Finds the decimal and octal codes for the Enter character.
      FileName:CH5D      Modula-2      RKW      Mar. 1991 *)

FROM InOut IMPORT WriteString, WriteLn, Read, WriteCard, WriteOct;
VAR EnterKey : CHAR;    EnterKeyCode : CARDINAL;

BEGIN
   WriteString("Press the Return or Enter key: ");Read(EnterKey);WriteLn;
   EnterKeyCode := ORD(EnterKey);
   WriteString("The code for the Enter key character is  ");
    WriteCard(EnterKeyCode,4); WriteLn;
   WriteString("In octal, the code for the Enter key character is ");
    WriteOct(EnterKeyCode,4); WriteLn;
END FindEnterKeyCharacter.
```

On some ASCII systems the Enter key is represented by octal code 36 (decimal 30). Using that code, the program would display this result:

```
Press the Return or Enter key:
The code for the Enter key character is  30
In octal, the  code for the Enter key character is  000036
```

```
MODULE TestReadChar;
   (* Tests the Procedure ReadOneChar, to read a character terminated
      by Return or Enter.
      FileName:CH5E      Modula-2      RKW      Mar. 1991 *)

FROM InOut IMPORT Read, Write, WriteString, WriteLn;

VAR Ch : CHAR;

PROCEDURE ReadOneChar(VAR Character : CHAR);
   (* Reads a single character or a list of characters, terminated
      by Return or Enter.  The first character is returned, others
      are ignored.    *)
      CONST  ENTERKEY = 36C;  (* 36C is the ASCII octal code for
                                 Record Separator.  If your computer
                                 uses a different code for Return
                                 or Enter, replace with that code. *)
   VAR NextCh : CHAR;
   BEGIN
      Read(Character); Write(Character); WriteLn;
      Read(NextCh);
      WHILE  NextCh # ENTERKEY  DO
         Read(NextCh);
      END; (* WHILE *)
   END ReadOneChar;

BEGIN (* TestReadChar *)
   WriteLn;WriteString("Enter a character: ");
    ReadOneChar(Ch); WriteLn;
   WriteString("The character is "); Write(Ch); WriteLn;
```

```
    WriteLn;WriteString("Enter a second character: ");
     ReadOneChar(Ch); WriteLn;
    WriteString("The second character is "); Write(Ch); WriteLn;
  END TestReadChar.
```

Remember, *VAR* preceding the parameter *Character* in the procedure heading *ReadOneChar* tells the computer to pass the value of Character back to the module, which invokes ReadOneChar. A test run of this program produced the following:

```
Enter a character: $
The character is $

Enter a second character: J
The second character is J
```

where all other characters pressed between $ and Enter, or between J and Enter, were ignored.

Debug and test   It was necessary to execute the first program to find the EnterKey code before the second program could be completed. Otherwise, debugging and testing follow the pattern used in previous examples.

Complete the documentation   Completing the documentation requires a users' manual, which should state:

1. The Modula-2 source code is in files CH5D and CH5E.
2. The first program must be executed to determine the code for the Enter key. If that is different from the results obtained on the test run, the appropriate value must replace that assigned to CONSTant ENTERKEY in the second program.
3. The first program actually may be used to find the code for any character. Instead of pressing the Enter or Return key, simply press the key for which you wish to find the code.

Questions 5.2

1. For Module TestCodes (Example 5.2.1), write WHILE loops that limit input of
   a. StartCode and StopCode to values representing printable characters.
   b. StartCharacter and StopCharacter so that the code for StartCharacter is less than or equal to the code for StopCharacter.
2. Write a short program to determine the effects on your system of executing Write(CHR(Code)); for the values of Code shown in Figure 5–2 (or their equivalents if your computer uses a different code than ASCII).
3. Given the declarations

   ```
   CONST DASH = '-';  SPACE = 040C;
   VAR CountChars, CountLines : CARDINAL;
   ```

   what would be the result of executing this fragment of code on a system that uses ASCII?

```
BEGIN
   CountChars := 1;
   WHILE  CountChars <= 40  DO
      Write(DASH);
      CountChars := CountChars + 1;
   END; (* WHILE *)
   Write(CHR(7)); WriteLn;

   CountLines := 1;
   WHILE  CountLines <= 10  DO
      Write('*');
      CountChars := 1;
      WHILE  CountChars <= 38  DO
         Write(SPACE);
         CountChars := CountChars + 1;
      END; (* WHILE *)
      Write('*'); Write(CHR(7)); WriteLn;
      CountLines := CountLines + 1;
   END; (* WHILE *)

   CountChars := 1;
   WHILE  CountChars <= 40  DO
      Write(CHR(61));
      CountChars := CountChars + 1;
   END; (* WHILE *)
   WriteLn; WriteLn;
   ....
```

5.3 INC, DEC, and CAP

In the WHILE iterations of some previous examples, counting and accumulating have been accomplished by statements such as

```
Count := Count + 1;
Result := Result + n;
```

or even

```
Symbol := CHR(Code + 1);
```

which increment Count by 1, Result by n, and Symbol to the next character, respectively.

Two standard procedures, INC and DEC, also may be used to increment and decrement values. The general syntax of INC and DEC are

```
INC(Variable, n);    and    DEC(Variable, n);
```

where n is a CARDINAL value specifying how far to increment or decrement the Variable. When n is omitted, its value is 1 by default. The Variable may be of any enumerable (countable) type, which for now means CHAR, CARDINAL, INTEGER, or BOOLEAN, but *not* REAL. For example, the statements above can be replaced by

```
INC(Count);
INC(Result, n);
INC(Symbol);
```

If Number is a CARDINAL variable, then the code fragment

```
Number := 82;
INC(Number,5);
WriteCard(Number,2); WriteLn;
```

would display the value 87. If Letter is a CHAR variable, then

```
Letter := 'q';
DEC(Letter,3);
Write(Letter);
```

display the character 'n'.

INC and DEC are not imported; they are part of the system, just as are functions ORD and CHR.

What Precedes 'A' and Follows 'z'?

The following short program applies INC and DEC to CHARacter variables to find which characters precede 'A' and follow 'z' in the codes used on your machine.

```
MODULE FindPrecedeSucceed;
  (* Finds the predecessor of 'A' and the successor to 'z'.
     FileName:CH5PREC      Modula-2      RKW      Mar. 1991   *)

FROM InOut IMPORT WriteString, WriteLn, Write;

VAR  Letter, Mark : CHAR;

BEGIN
  Letter := 'A';
  DEC(Letter);
  Mark := 'z';
  INC(Mark);
  WriteString("The predecessor of A is "); Write(Letter); WriteLn;
  WriteString("The successor   to z is "); Write(Mark); WriteLn;
END FindPrecedeSucceed.
```

If your computer uses ASCII, the results should be

```
The predecessor of A is @
The successor   to z is {
```

Function CAP

One additional standard function built into the Modula-2 language is CAP(Symbol), with Symbol being a CHARacter variable or constant. CAP(Symbol) returns the capital letter corresponding to a lowercase letter identified by Symbol. If Symbol represents a character other than a lowercase letter of the alphabet, then CAP(Symbol) simply returns that character with no change.

For example, given the declaration

```
VAR  Symbol, Token : CHAR;
```

then

```
Symbol := 'm';
Write(CAP(Symbol)); WriteLn;
```

would display capital letter M. But

```
Symbol := '+';
Token := CAP(Symbol);
Write(Token);
Write(CAP('N')); WriteLn;
```

would display the characters +N without any changes.

The following example applies functions ORD and CAP as well as procedures INC and ReadOneChar (from the previous section) to CHARacter values.

Example 5.3.1

Write a procedure that determines which letter lies halfway between two given letters of the alphabet.

Define the problem   The user will be asked to enter two letters of the alphabet. These will be passed to a procedure that will find the letter midway between them. If there are an even number of letters between the letters entered, then two letters lie midway, and the procedure will determine the first of these.

Develop a solution   It will be assumed that the system uses ASCII or another code in which alphabet letters are represented by 26 contiguous values with no gaps. The CAP function will be applied to the letters so that both letters are tested within the capital-letter range. Half the distance between LeftLetter and RightLetter codes is determined from the formula

$$\text{HalfDistance} = (\ \text{ORD(RightLetter)} - \text{ORD(LeftLetter)}\ )\ \text{DIV } 2$$

Then MidLetter is found by

> Midletter := LeftLetter;
> INC(MidLetter, HalfDistance);

Pseudocode

```
Module TestFindMidCharacter
    begin
        ask for and accept LeftLetter and RightLetter
        DetermineMidCharacter(LeftLetter, RightLetter, MidLetter)
        display MidLetter
    end TestFindMidCharacter

Procedure DetermineMidCharacter(Letter1, Letter2,      VAR MidCharacter)
    begin
        capitalize Letter1, Letter2
        find     HalfDistance = (ORD(Letter2) − ORD(Letter1)) DIV 2
        assign to MidCharacter the character Letter1
        increment MidCharacter by HalfDistance
    end DetermineMidCharacter

Procedure ReadOneChar(VAR Character)
    (* see Example 5.2.2 *)
```

Modula-2 code

```
MODULE  TestFindMidCharacter;
    (* Finds the character midway between two given characters.
       FileName:CH5F      Modula-2      RKW      Mar. 1991 *)

FROM InOut IMPORT WriteLn, WriteString, Read, Write;

VAR  LeftLetter, RightLetter, MidLetter : CHAR;

PROCEDURE  DetermineMidCharacter(Letter1, Letter2 : CHAR;
                                    VAR MidCharacter : CHAR );
    VAR HalfDistance : CARDINAL;
    BEGIN
       Letter1 := CAP(Letter1);  Letter2 := CAP(Letter2);
       HalfDistance := ( ORD(Letter2) - ORD(Letter1) ) DIV 2;
       MidCharacter := Letter1;
       INC(MidCharacter, HalfDistance);
    END DetermineMidCharacter;

PROCEDURE ReadOneChar(VAR Character:CHAR);
    CONST  ENTERKEY = 36C;
    VAR  NextCh : CHAR;
    BEGIN
       Read(Character); Write(Character); WriteLn;
       Read(NextCh);
       WHILE  NextCh # ENTERKEY  DO
          Read(NextCh);
       END; (* WHILE *)
    END ReadOneChar;

BEGIN (* TestFindMidCharacter *)
    WriteString("Enter a letter of the alphabet: ");
     ReadOneChar(LeftLetter);
    WriteString("Enter a subsequent letter of the alphabet: ");
     ReadOneChar(RightLetter);

    DetermineMidCharacter(LeftLetter, RightLetter, MidLetter);
    WriteString("The letter midway between "); Write(LeftLetter);
     WriteString(" and "); Write(RightLetter); WriteString(" is ");
     Write(MidLetter); WriteLn;
END TestFindMidCharacter.
```

Debug and test When the program executes properly you should see something like this:

```
Enter a letter of the alphabet: h
Enter a subsequent letter of the alphabet: r
The letter midway between h and r is M
```

Try it with lowercase letters and uppercase letters. Note that there are no safeguards in the program to ensure that, alphabetically, LeftLetter $<=$ RightLetter *or* that both are alphabetic characters. What happens when you violate these conditions? What happens if you forget the *VAR* preceding parameter *MidCharacter* in procedure DetermineMidCharacter heading? Insert supplemental debugging write commands to display the values of HalfDistance and MidCharacter within the procedure.

Complete the documentation Collect the problem definition, description, pseudocode, code, and sample run. In the users' manual state the source code location (CH5F). Warn users that the letters entered must satisfy the conditions that LeftLetter $<=$ RightLetter and that both must represent characters of the alphabet. Also, make it clear that for this program to give meaningful results, the code used on the system must be ASCII or at least not have numeric gaps between codes for the capital letters. If the octal character code for the Enter key is not 36C on a user's system, the value of CONSTant ENTERKEY in procedure ReadOneChar must be changed to the appropriate value as well.

Consider also the following short example, which illustrates that procedures INC and DEC may be applied to enumerable values other than those of CHARacter type.

Example 5.3.2

Use INC in a program to find the sum of even cardinal numbers from 2 to *N*.

Define the problem In a loop, beginning with Number $= 2$, and using INC to increment by 2 each time, the Sum $2 + 4 + \ldots + N$ will be accumulated.

Develop a solution *N* will be entered from the keyboard. Number will be initialized to 2 and Sum to zero. A WHILE loop will accumulate Sum $:=$ Sum $+$ Number and increment Number by 2 until Number $> N$. The value of Sum will be displayed to the screen.

Refine the solution *Pseudocode*

```
begin FindEvenSum
        ask for N
        initialize    Number = 2,    Sum = 0
        while Number <= N
                accumulate    Sum := Sum + Number
                increment    Number    by    2
        end while
        print Sum
end FindEvenSum
```

Modula-2 code

```
MODULE FindEvenSum;
  (* Finds the Sum of even cardinals up to N.
      File Name:CH5G      Modula-2      RKW      Mar. 1991   *)

FROM InOut IMPORT WriteString, WriteLn, WriteCard, ReadCard;

CONST  STARTAT = 2;
VAR   Number, Sum, HowFar : CARDINAL;

BEGIN
  WriteString("To what value (HowFar) would you like to add? ");
    ReadCard(HowFar); WriteLn;
```

```
   Number := STARTAT;  Sum := 0;
   WHILE  Number <= HowFar   DO
     Sum := Sum + Number;
     INC(Number, 2);
         (* Assertions: Sum = 2 + 4 + ... + Number
                        Number = 2 * (n+1), where n = iterations so far *)
   END; (* WHILE *)

   WriteString("The sum of the even numbers to ");
      WriteCard(HowFar,6); WriteString("  is "); WriteCard(Sum,8); WriteLn;
END FindEvenSum.
```

Debug and test   Test with values of *N* greater than or equal to 2. What happens if *N* < 2 or if *N* < 0? Does it make a difference if you enter an odd number for HowFar?

Complete the documentation   Collect the problem definition, pseudocode, and code. A sample run looks like

```
To what value (HowFar) would you like to add? 22
The sum of the even numbers to     22    is      132
```

The users' manual should warn about overflow. When MAX(CARDINAL) is 65,535, overflow occurs for values of HowFar greater than 510.

Questions 5.3

1. Write a WHILE loop (that uses the DEC procedure to update the WHILE Condition) to display the multiples of 3 backward from 33 to 3, inclusive.

2. Write a WHILE loop (that uses the DEC procedure) to display the capital letters of the alphabet backward from *Z* to *A*.

3. Using ASCII, for CHARacter variables Mark and Letter, what Result is displayed by this fragment of code?

```
BEGIN
    WriteString("Enter a lower case letter: " ); WriteLn;
     Read(Letter); Read(Terminator); Write(Letter); WriteLn;

    Mark := CHR( ( ORD(Letter)  - ORD('a') ) + ORD('A') );
    WriteString("Result =  "); Write(Mark); WriteLn;
    . . . .
```

4. In procedure DetermineMidCharacter of Example 5.3.1, what change (if any) would be caused by replacing the code lines

```
MidCharacter := Letter1;
INC(MidCharacter, HalfDistance);
```

   with

   a. ```
   MidLetterCode := HalfDistance + ORD(Letter1);
   MidCharacter := CHR(MidLetterCode);
   ```

   where MidLetterCode is a CARDINAL variable,

   **b.** ```
   MidCharacter := Letter2;
   DEC(MidCharacter, HalfDistance);
   ```

5. Write a WHILE loop that you could add to the main module TestFindMidCharacter in Example 5.3.1 to ensure that users enter values LeftLetter and Right-

Letter to satisfy the conditions that, alphabetically, LeftLetter $<=$ RightLetter and that LeftLetter and RightLetter are both restricted to letters of the alphabet.

5.4   *The Terminal Module*

What do you do if you want to print alternately to the terminal screen and to an output file? For example, suppose you are directing data to a file; then you display a prompt for the user on the screen, and then you direct more data to the file. If a CloseOutput command is executed to close the file and open the screen, then a subsequent OpenOutput forces the next Write. . . command to write at the beginning of the file, destroying what is already there.

Dr. Wirth's solution to this problem is to provide a standard module Terminal (see Appendix B). The Terminal module contains Read, Write, WriteString, and WriteLn commands that perform the same operations as those with the same names from module InOut, except that commands from the Terminal module always reference the default devices (generally the keyboard and the screen).

IMPORT Terminal

Until now, all IMPORT commands have been of the form

```
FROM ModuleName IMPORT ListOfImportedEntities;
```

However, all of the entities from a given external module may be imported at once by using the command

```
IMPORT ModuleName;
```

When this is done, the programmer must append the module name as a qualifying prefix to any procedure used from that module. If the command

```
IMPORT InOut;
```

is issued at the beginning of a program, then all of the procedures from InOut are available to that program. But to execute WriteString(''Hello!''), for example, it must be qualified by the prefix InOut., as in

```
InOut.WriteString ( " Hello! " );
```

Identifiers qualified by such prefixes are common in computer science. You will see them used again later in the book in conjunction with records and other data structures.

Thus there are two methods of accessing objects with identical names from both InOut and Terminal modules. One of these methods is to import all procedures from both modules, namely,

```
IMPORT Inout;
IMPORT Terminal;
```

and **qualify** each procedure with the appropriate prefix. Then

```
InOut.WriteString ( " Hello! " );  InOut.WriteLn;
```

would direct ''Hello!'' to a file (if an output file has been opened) or to the screen (if no output file has been opened), and

```
Terminal.WriteString(" Goodbye! "); Terminal.WriteLn;
```

would display "Goodbye!" on the screen.

The other method of accessing entities with the same name is to qualify all entities from one module at import time, using the form FROM . . . IMPORT . . . , and then import all of the objects from the other module, using IMPORT . . . (without FROM), and qualify these objects within the program. Hence, you could use

```
FROM InOut IMPORT WriteString, WriteLn;
IMPORT Terminal;
```

and execute

```
WriteString(" Help. "); WriteLn·
Terminal.WriteString(" No help. "); Terminal.WriteLn;
```

Alternatively, you could perform

```
IMPORT InOut;
FROM Terminal IMPORT WriteString, WriteLn;
```

and issue program commands

```
InOut.WriteString("Here it comes. "); InOut.WriteLn;
WriteString(" There it went. "); WriteLn;
```

You may *not* perform both

```
FROM InOut IMPORT WriteString, WriteLn;
FROM Terminal IMPORT WriteString, WriteLn;
```

This would result in a compiler error stating that WriteString and WriteLn are doubly defined identifiers. At any location within a program, identifier names must be unique. Importing commands with the same unqualified names from two different modules results in ambiguity; the computer is unable to determine which procedure you wish to use.

Terminal.Read

The same considerations for using procedures from InOut and Terminal apply if you wish to read from an input file using InOut.Read and from the keyboard using Terminal.Read. On some systems, the Read command from the Terminal module is designed to accept a single character as soon as its key is pressed. When Terminal.Read is used on those systems, it is not required to Read and discard a terminating Enter key character. In the examples in this book it is assumed that Terminal.Read operates in the same manner as InOut.Read. Nonetheless, you may wish to execute the programs in question 1 at the end of Section 5.1, replacing Read with Terminal.Read, to determine if your system treats these two Read commands differently.

☐ Menu-Oriented Programs

One effective technique in designing "user-proof" interactive programs is to present a **menu** on the screen and allow the user to choose only from a limited set of options. This prevents the user from getting lost when the program responds to the entry of an unexpected value. A general menu structure can be built using WHILE and IF, as follows:

```
initialize Selection to a valid choice
WHILE Selection is not Quit    DO
        display menu selections; e.g., A, B, . . . , Q (for QUIT)
        ask for and read Selection (A, B, . . . , Q)
        WHILE Selection is not a valid choice    DO
                ask for and read Selection again
        END WHILE

        IF Selection = 'A' THEN    perform operation A;    END; (* IF *)
        IF Selection = 'B' THEN    perform operation B;    END; (* IF *)
        . . .
        perform no operation if Selection = 'Q'
END WHILE
```

The following example illustrates an application of the Terminal module and a menu.

Example 5.4.1

Write a program that converts a range of Fahrenheit temperatures to Celsius or vice versa.

Define the problem   The program will give the user only 3 choices: Convert from Fahrenheit to Celsius, Convert from Celsius to Fahrenheit, or Quit. Depending upon the choice, the user will enter a range of either Fahrenheit or Celsius temperatures. The table of Fahrenheit versus Celsius temperatures will be directed to an output file.

Develop a solution   A menu will be presented in the form

Here are your choices
       F   Convert Fahrenheit to Celsius
       C   Convert Celsius to Fahrenheit
       Q   Quit
Choose one letter (F, C, or Q)

If F or C is chosen, procedure ConvertFtoC or ConvertCtoF will be called to handle the appropriate conversion. If Q is chosen, the program stops. When any other character is chosen, the menu reappears, along with the message "Try again." The procedures ask the user for a range of temperatures to be converted and apply the conversion equations $F = (9/5) C + 32$ and $C = (5/9) (F - 32)$ as appropriate. The table of results is directed to an output file.

Refine the solution   *Pseudocode*

```
begin module TemperatureConversion
   open output file
   initialize Choice to F
   while Choice # Q (for Quit)
      present the menu (choose from F, C, or Q)
      ask for and read Choice (F, C, or Q)
      while Choice is not F, C, or Q
         ask for and read Choice again
      end while
```

```
                if Choice = F then      ConvertFtoC      end if
                if Choice = C then      ConvertCtoF      end if
              end while
              close output file
            end TemperatureConversion

            procedure ConvertFtoC
                begin
                    write heading ("Fahrenheit Celsius")
                    ask for Lowest and Highest Fahrenheit temperatures
                    initialize Fahrenheit to Lowest
                    while Fahrenheit <= Highest
                      calculate Celsius = (5/9) * (Fahrenheit − 32)
                      display Fahrenheit, Celsius
                      increment Fahrenheit
                    end while
                end ConvertFtoC

            procedure ConvertCtoF
                (* See code below.     Looks like ConvertFtoC with Fahrenheit
                   and Celsius interchanged and the formula
                   Fahrenheit = (9/5) * Celsius      +      32      *)
```

Modula-2 code   Notice that function CAP is applied in this code to accept either capital- or lowercase-letter Choices entered by the user. Also, since an output file is open, Terminal.WriteLn, Terminal.Write, and Terminal.WriteString are used within the menu and whenever a user prompt is to be displayed to the screen.

```
MODULE TemperatureConversion;
    (* Creates Fahrenheit to Celsius conversion table or vice versa.
       FileName:CH5H       Modula-2       RKW       Mar. 1991 *)


FROM InOut IMPORT Read, WriteString, WriteLn, OpenOutput, CloseOutput;
FROM RealInOut IMPORT ReadReal, FWriteReal;
IMPORT Terminal;


VAR  Choice, Terminator : CHAR;

PROCEDURE ConvertFtoC;
    VAR  Lowest, Highest, Fahrenheit, Celsius : REAL;
    BEGIN
        WriteString("Fahrenheit       Celsius"); WriteLn;
        Terminal.WriteString("What is the lowest Fahrenheit to convert? ");
         ReadReal(Lowest); Terminal.WriteLn;
        Terminal.WriteString("What is the highest Fahrenheit? ");
         ReadReal(Highest); Terminal.WriteLn;

        Fahrenheit := Lowest;
        WHILE  Fahrenheit <= Highest  DO
           Celsius := (5.0/9.0) * (Fahrenheit - 32.0);
           FWriteReal(Fahrenheit,10,2); FWriteReal(Celsius,12,2); WriteLn;
           Fahrenheit := Fahrenheit + 1.0;
        END; (* WHILE *)
    END ConvertFtoC;


PROCEDURE ConvertCtoF;
    VAR  Lowest, Highest, Fahrenheit, Celsius : REAL;
```

```
    BEGIN
        WriteString("   Celsius      Fahrenheit"); WriteLn;
        Terminal.WriteString("What is the lowest Celsius to convert? ");
         ReadReal(Lowest); Terminal.WriteLn;
        Terminal.WriteString("What is the highest Celsius? ");
         ReadReal(Highest); Terminal.WriteLn;

        Celsius := Lowest;
        WHILE  Celsius <= Highest  DO
            Fahrenheit := (9.0/5.0) * Celsius  +  32.0;
            FWriteReal(Celsius,10,2); FWriteReal(Fahrenheit,12,2); WriteLn;
            Celsius := Celsius + 1.0;
        END; (* WHILE *)
    END ConvertCtoF;

BEGIN (* TemperatureConversion *)
    Terminal.WriteString("Enter name of output file: ");
     OpenOutput("OUT"); Terminal.WriteLn;

    Choice := 'F';
    WHILE  CAP(Choice) # 'Q' DO
        Terminal.WriteLn; Terminal.WriteLn; Terminal.WriteLn;
        Terminal.WriteString("Here are your choices"); Terminal.WriteLn;
        Terminal.WriteString("    F      Convert Fahrenheit to Celsius");
         Terminal.WriteLn;
        Terminal.WriteString("    C      Convert Celsius to Fahrenheit");
         Terminal.WriteLn;
        Terminal.WriteString("    Q      Quit");
         Terminal.WriteLn; Terminal.WriteLn;

        Terminal.WriteString("What is your choice (F, C, or Q)? ");
         Read(Choice); Read(Terminator); Terminal.Write(Choice);
         Terminal.WriteLn; Terminal.WriteLn;

        WHILE  NOT( (CAP(Choice)='F') OR (CAP(Choice)='C')
                             OR (CAP(Choice)='Q') )  DO
            Terminal.WriteString("Try again.  Please enter only F, C, or Q: ");
             Read(Choice); Read(Terminator); Terminal.Write(Choice);
             Terminal.WriteLn; Terminal.WriteLn;
        END; (* WHILE *)

        IF  CAP(Choice) = 'F'  THEN   ConvertFtoC;  END; (* IF *)
        IF  CAP(Choice) = 'C'  THEN   ConvertCtoF;  END; (* IF *)
        END; (* WHILE *)
        CloseOutput;
    END TemperatureConversion.
```

Debug and test Temporarily commenting out the redirection commands will allow all results to appear on the screen, so that debugging can occur more easily. Test with all choices—F, f, C, c, Q, and q—and at least one other character. To improve the reliability of the program, safeguards could be included in the ConvertFtoC and ConvertCtoF procedures to ensure that Lowest < = Highest. A sample run and printout appears as follows:

A Bit of Background

A Curious Character

If you try to discuss the most exciting character on the keyboard, you will get blank stares and yawns; but a discussion of one of the most interesting characters in modern science might elicit considerable enthusiasm. Dr. Richard Feynman (1918–1988), who received a Nobel Prize in physics in 1965 for his work in quantum electrodynamics, is known not only for his brilliance, but also for his teaching expertise and keen sense of humor. In his last autobiography,* he refers to himself as "a curious character," one who was "interested in all the sciences."

Feynman was one of the first scientists to arrive at Los Alamos Scientific Laboratory in Los Alamos, New Mexico, in 1943. There he became excited about the new computers, which were programmed by manipulating plugs and wires on a patch panel, and became known in Los Alamos social circles for his pranks and his virtuosity on the bongo drums. As a teacher at the California Institute of Technology for more than thirty years, his classroom enthusiasm and genuine concern for students inspired many to greatness. In 1986 he served on the Presidential Commission that investigated the *Challenger* space shuttle accident. His achievements in later years included contributions to the design of the Connection Machine, a massively parallel computer, for the Thinking Machines Company of Cambridge, Massachusetts.

*What Do You Care about What Other People Think? Further Adventures of a Curious Character, Richard P. Feynman as told to Ralph Leighton, W. W. Norton & Company, New York, 1988; pp. 11, 16.

```
Enter name of output file:  Out>CTOF.OUT
Here are your choices
      F     Convert Fahrenheit to Celsius
      C     Convert Celsius to Fahrenheit
      Q     Quit
What is your choice (C, F, or Q)? C
What is the lowest Celsius to convert? 0.0
What is the highest Celsius? 10.0
Here are your choices
      F     Convert Fahrenheit to Celsius
      C     Convert Celsius to Fahrenheit
      Q     Quit
What is your choice (C, F, or Q)? Q
```

After execution, file CTOF.OUT contains

```
   Celsius       Fahrenheit
      0.00          32.00
      1.00          33.80
      2.00          35.60
      3.00          37.40
      4.00          39.20
      5.00          41.00
      6.00          42.80
      7.00          44.60
      8.00          46.40
      9.00          48.20
     10.00          50.00
```

Complete the documentation   Collect the problem definition, pseudocode, code, and sample run. In the users' manual warn the user that the value of the Lowest temperature to be converted must be less than or equal to the Highest.

Questions 5.4	**1.** In the program fragments of question 1 at the end of Section 5.1, replace the Read commands with Terminal.Read. Execute those programs to try to determine how Terminal.Read operates on your system.

2. Refer to the DEFINITION MODULE Terminal in Appendix B. Which of the following could be executed in a program containing IMPORT Terminal;?

a. Terminal.Write

b. Terminal.ReadCard

c. Terminal.Read

d. Terminal.WriteString

e. Terminal.FWriteReal

f. Terminal.WriteInt

g. Terminal.WriteLn

h. Terminal.WriteCard

3. Which of the following are valid and which are invalid combinations of IMPORT commands in a program? In each valid situation, what commands could you use to (1) write the string ''This is a test.'' to the terminal screen and (2) read a value for a CHARacter variable.

a.
```
FROM InOut IMPORT WriteLn, WriteString, Read,
    OpenInput, CloseInput, OpenOutput, CloseOutput;
FROM Terminal IMPORT WriteString, Write;
```

b.
```
IMPORT InOut;
FROM Terminal IMPORT WriteLn, WriteString;
```

c.
```
IMPORT Terminal;
IMPORT InOut;
```

d.
```
FROM InOut IMPORT Read, OpenInput, CloseInput,
    OpenOutput, CloseOutput;
FROM Terminal IMPORT WriteLn, WriteString;
```

4. In the TemperatureConversion program (Example 5.4.1) replace the commands that invoke the CAP function to allow users to enter F, f, C, c, Q, and q as valid choices, but do not use the CAP function.

5.5 *Focus on Problem Solving*

Special graphics terminals and software are available that allow graphing of data with high resolution and in multiple colors. However, handling data with simple CHARacter variables enables you to plot points on a graph using any terminal or printer that displays standard characters. Although such graphs have low resolution, they may be quite adequate to illustrate your point effectively. They do not rely upon special hardware, and they can be implemented by commands from within any Modula-2 program.

In this section you will create a simple character-oriented graph of an equation. More details about graphing are discussed in Chapter 12.

The ABS Function

One standard, built-in, Modula-2 function that will be useful in the program development in this section is ABS, the absolute value function. By definition, for CARDINAL, INTEGER, and REAL values x,

ABS(x)   returns   x if x >= 0,   and
          returns   −x if x < 0.

For example,

when   x = −3.5,   then   ABS(x) = 3.5,
when   x =   0,   then   ABS(x) = 0,
when   x =   7.6,   then   ABS(x) = 7.6,   and
when   x = −137,   then   ABS(x) = 137.

The data type (CARDINAL, INTEGER, or REAL) of ABS(x) always will be the same as the type of the parameter x.

It has been pointed out already that two REAL values rarely are exactly equal because of the limited precision of REAL number representations within the computer. The comparison,

IF   RealA = RealB   THEN . . .

almost always should be stated in terms of whether the values RealA and RealB are acceptably close to each other. The test is written

IF ((RealA − RealB) < 0.0001)   AND   ((RealB − RealA) < 0.0001)   THEN . . .

where both differences RealA − RealB and RealB − RealA are tested, because one of the differences can be negative (that is, less than 0.0001), even though the values may not actually be acceptably close. The ABS function allows you to simplify such a closeness test in the form

IF   ABS(RealA − RealB) < 0.0001   THEN . . .

since ABS(RealA − RealB) always will be positive or zero.

A TabOrFill Procedure

Also needed in plotting points is the ability to perform a relative tab; that is, to skip over a specified number of columns on the page or screen. You may find the following TabOrFill procedure valuable not only in this section but also whenever you need to repeat a specified number of identical characters.

```
PROCEDURE TabOrFill(HowMany:CARDINAL;   FillCharacter:CHAR);
    VAR  CountSpaces : CARDINAL;
    BEGIN
       CountSpaces := 1;
       WHILE  CountSpaces <= HowMany  DO
          Write(FillCharacter);
          INC(CountSpaces);
          (* CountSpaces = no. of FillCharacters written so far + 1*)
       END; (* WHILE *)
    END TabOrFill;
```

You should convince yourself that, when the blank space character (or ASCII character 32_{10} = 040C) is passed to parameter FillCharacter, the procedure performs a relative tab; that is, it writes HowMany number of blank spaces. Whenever any other character is passed to parameter FillCharacter, that character is written HowMany times.

☐ Plotting Points on a Graph

In order to plot points on a given graph, you need to:

1. Define the equation of the curve to be plotted.
2. Determine how the plot should appear, including
   - what characters are to be used for the display,
   - how points and axes will appear, and
   - the limitations on the number of characters that can be displayed across the page or screen.

Each of these tasks will be considered. Then Example 5.5.1 illustrates the steps in plotting a particular curve.

The Equation of a Curve

To keep the plotting procedures as generic as possible, the equation and graph will be written in terms of y as a function of x, $y = f(x)$, such as

$$y = 160.0 + x - 3.0x^2$$

A range of x-values from XMin to XMax, and an increment XStep between x-values, may be requested of the user or defined as CONSTants; and values of y will be calculated from the equation at each value of x. Equations will be limited to single-valued functions—those for which each value of x defines a single y-value.

Appearance of the Plot

The plot will be oriented so that the x-axis points down the page or screen, and the y-axis points across, as shown in Figure 5–3 for a sample plot of $y = 2x + 1$. Then, for each value of x, y is calculated and plotted one line at a time.

   The corresponding values of x and y will be printed at the left of each line, followed by a dotted base line, as shown in Figure 5–3. The base line does not necessarily represent the position of the x-axis; however, if the plot includes a point where $x = 0.0$, the dotted y-axis will be displayed. The PlotCharacter, which will represent the points on the curve, can be defined in the program by a CHARacter CONSTant.

Scaling the y-Values

One more important consideration is the fixed LineWidth; that is, only a limited number of character positions are available across the screen or page. Thus, if the base line represents the minimum value of y (YMin), and values between YMin and the maximum y-value (YMax) are to be plotted, those values must be scaled to fit

Figure 5–3
Orientation of Axes
for a Plot of
$y = 2x + 1$

within the available character positions. This is accomplished by defining a CARDINAL value YPlot for each calculated value of y between YMin and YMax according to the formula:

$$Y\text{Plot} = \text{TRUNC}(\text{LineWidth} * (y - Y\text{Min})/(Y\text{Max} - Y\text{Min}) + 0.5).$$

For each y-value, you will move YPlot number of spaces to the right of the base line and then write the PlotCharacter.

To see how this works, suppose that for a given plot

$$\text{LineWidth} = 60 \text{ character positions,}$$
$$Y\text{Min} = 20, \quad \text{and} \quad Y\text{Max} = 260.$$

Then, substituting into the formula for YPlot,

when y equals		YPlot equals
YMin	20	$\text{TRUNC}(60*(\ 20-20)/(260-20)+0.5) = \text{TRUNC}(\ 0.5) = 0$
midway	140	$\text{TRUNC}(60*(140-20)/(260-20)+0.5) = \text{TRUNC}(30.5) = 30$
YMax	260	$\text{TRUNC}(60*(260-20)/(260-20)+0.5) = \text{TRUNC}(60.5) = 60$

and the values 20 to 260 are scaled linearly onto the 60-position LineWidth. Note that adding 0.5 in the formula before TRUNCating effectively rounds a number to its nearest whole value.

Consider the following example.

Example 5.5.1

Graph the equation $y = 160 + x - 3\,x^2$.

Define the problem   Plot the function $y = 160.0 + x - 3.0\,x^2$ for x values $-7.0 <= x <= +7.0$ in steps of 0.5. Draw the base line and y-axis using dots, and print the values of x and y for each point. Plot once with output directed to the screen. Then plot again with output directed to a file so that it can be printed to hardcopy later.

Develop a solution   The user will be asked to enter the LineWidth, limits on x and y (XMin, XMax, YMin, YMax), and the increment between values of x (XStep). In a procedure called PlotIt, for each line of the plot (for each x-value) the calculated values of y will be scaled to CARDINAL values YPlot. The TabOrFill procedure will be called to print YPlot number of Blank spaces, and then the PlotCharacter will be written. If $x = 0.0$, then TabOrFill will print Dots (representing the y-axis) instead of Blanks. A WHILE loop within procedure PlotIt advances to a new line, increments x, and plots lines until $x = X$Max.

A structure chart for this problem is shown in Figure 5−4.

Refine the solution   *Pseudocode*

```
module PlotACurve
    define PlotCharacter, Dot, and Blank CHARacter CONSTants
    begin
        EnterLimits(MinX, MaxX, StepX, MinY, MaxY, WidthOfLine)
```

Figure 5–4
Structure Chart for
PlotACurve
(Example 5.5.1)

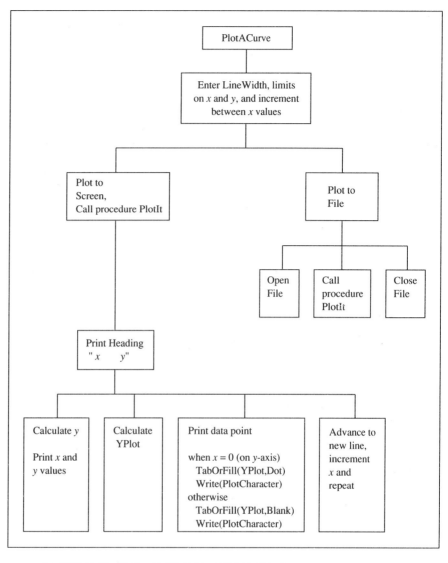

```
PlotIt(MinX, MaxX, StepX, MinY, MaxY, WidthOfLine)

    open output file
    PlotIt(MinX, MaxX, StepX, MinY, MaxY, WidthOfLine)
    close output file
end PlotACurve


procedure EnterLimits(VAR XMin, XMax, XStep, YMin, YMax, LineWidth)
    begin
      ask for and accept LineWidth
      ask for and accept XMin, XMax, XStep
      ask for and accept YMin, YMax
    end EnterLimits


procedure TabOrFill(HowMany, FillCharacter)
    begin
      print Howmany number of FillCharacters
    end TabOrFill


procedure PlotIt(XMin, XMax, XStep, YMin, YMax, LineWidth)
    begin
```

```
                        write heading ("     x              y")
                        initialize   x = XMin
                            while     x < = xMax
                                calculate      y = 160.0 + x − 3.0*x*x
                                print x and y values
                                print base line Dot
                                calculate scaled YPlot value
                                if     x = 0     (* on y-axis *)
                                    TabOrFill(YPlot, Dot)            (* draw y-axis to point   *)
                                    write PlotCharacter             (* plot the point         *)
                                    TabOrFill(LineWidth-YPlot, Dot) (* complete the y-axis     *)
                                otherwise
                                    TabOrFill(Yplot, Blank)         (* tab to point           *)
                                    write PlotCharacter             (* plot the point         *)
                                end if
                                advance to new line,    increment x
                            end while
                        end PlotIt
```

Modula-2 code

```
MODULE PlotACurve;
   (* Plots the curve  y = 160.0 + x − 3*x*x.
      File Name:CH5I      Modula-2      RKW      Mar. 1991  *)


FROM InOut IMPORT WriteString, WriteLn, Write, ReadCard,
                  OpenOutput, CloseOutput;
FROM RealInOut IMPORT FWriteReal, ReadReal;


CONST  PlotCharacter = `*`;  Dot = `.`;  Blank = ` `;
VAR  MinX, MaxX, StepX, MinY, MaxY : REAL;
     WidthOfLine : CARDINAL;


PROCEDURE EnterLimits(VAR XMin, XMax, XStep, YMin, YMax : REAL;
                                      VAR LineWidth : CARDINAL);
   BEGIN
       WriteString("What is the LineWidth in number of character spaces? ");
        ReadCard(LineWidth); WriteLn; WriteLn;

       WriteString("The equation is  y = 160.0  +  x  -  3.0*x*x ");
        WriteLn; WriteLn;

       WriteString("Minimum value of x = ? "); ReadReal(XMin); WriteLn;
       WriteString("Maximum value of x = ? "); ReadReal(XMax); WriteLn;
       WriteString("Increment between x values = ? "); ReadReal(XStep);
        WriteLn; WriteLn;
       WriteString("Your estimated value of YMin = ? "); ReadReal(YMin);
        WriteLn;
       WriteString("Your estimated value of YMax = ? "); ReadReal(YMax);
        WriteLn; WriteLn;
    END EnterLimits;


PROCEDURE TabOrFill(HowMany:CARDINAL;   FillCharacter:CHAR);
   VAR  CountSpaces : CARDINAL;
   BEGIN
       CountSpaces := 1;
       WHILE  CountSpaces <= HowMany  DO
          Write(FillCharacter);
```

```
        INC(CountSpaces);
        (* CountSpaces = number of FillCharacters written so far  +  1 *)
    END; (* WHILE *)
  END TabOrFill;


PROCEDURE PlotIt(XMin, XMax, XStep, YMin, YMax:REAL; LineWidth:CARDINAL);
   VAR  YPlot : CARDINAL;    x, y : REAL;
   BEGIN
      WriteLn; WriteString("     x          y"); WriteLn;
      x := XMin;
      WHILE  x <= XMax   DO

        y := 160.0 + x - 3.0*x*x;

        FWriteReal(x,6,1); FWriteReal(y,8,1);(* values of x and y *)
        WriteString(" "); Write(Dot);        (* write base line dot *)

        YPlot := TRUNC(FLOAT(LineWidth)*(y - YMin) / (YMax - YMin) + 0.5 );

          IF  ABS(x) < 0.0001  THEN                     (* Print Y axis  *)
             TabOrFill(YPlot, Dot);         (* Print Dots to data point *)
             Write(PlotCharacter);              (* Print data on y-axis *)
             TabOrFill(LineWidth-YPlot, Dot);   (* Print rest of axis *)
          ELSE                          (* Just print spaces and data point *)
             TabOrFill(YPlot, Blank);
             Write(PlotCharacter);
          END; (* IF *)
          WriteLn;                                (* Advance to new line *)

          x := x + XStep;                         (* Step to next x *)
          (* x = XMin  +  (number of points plotted) * XStep   *)
      END; (* WHILE *)
   END PlotIt;


BEGIN (* Main Module PlotACurve *)
    EnterLimits(MinX, MaxX, StepX, MinY, MaxY, WidthOfLine);
    PlotIt(MinX, MaxX, StepX, MinY, MaxY, WidthOfLine);

    WriteString("What is the name of the output file? ");
    OpenOutput("OUT");
    PlotIt(MinX, MaxX, StepX, MinY, MaxY, WidthOfLine);;
    CloseOutput;
END PlotACurve.
```

Debug and test   A sample run of the program appears in Figure 5–5. Writing a program of this nature may require considerable debugging. A first test run is likely to produce a display that does not resemble what you expected. As a first step in debugging, you may wish to add supplemental write statements to print values of x, y, and YPlot at appropriate locations to determine that YPlot does not exceed the available LineWidth and that you are not printing more or fewer Dots or Blanks than you intended.

If the calculated values of y fall outside the limits you chose for YMin or YMax, those points may appear at the edges of your graph. To avoid this problem, you can

Figure 5–5
Sample Run of
PlotACurve
(Example 5.5.1)

```
What is the LineWidth in number of character spaces? 50

The equation is  y = 160.0  +  x  -  3.0*x*x

Minimum value of x = ? -9.0
Maximum value of x = ? 6.5
Increment between x values = ? 0.5

Your estimated value of YMin = ? -100.0
Your estimated value of YMax = ? 200.0


      x        y
    -9.0     -92.0 . *
    -8.5     -65.2 .        *
    -8.0     -40.0 .             *
    -7.5     -16.3 .                 *
    -7.0       6.0 .                    *
    -6.5      26.8 .                       *
    -6.0      46.0 .                          *
    -5.5      63.7 .                            *
    -5.0      80.0 .                              *
    -4.5      94.8 .                               *
    -4.0     108.0 .                                 *
    -3.5     119.7 .                                   *
    -3.0     130.0 .                                    *
    -2.5     138.8 .                                     *
    -2.0     146.0 .                                      *
    -1.5     151.8 .                                       *
    -1.0     156.0 .                                        *
    -0.5     158.8 .                                        *
     0.0     160.0 ........................................*.......
     0.5     159.8 .                                        *
     1.0     158.0 .                                        *
     1.5     154.8 .                                       *
     2.0     150.0 .                                      *
     2.5     143.8 .                                       *
     3.0     136.0 .                                    *
     3.5     126.8 .                                   *
     4.0     116.0 .                                 *
     4.5     103.7 .                               *
     5.0      90.0 .                              *
     5.5      74.7 .                           *
     6.0      58.0 .                      *
     6.5      39.7 .                  *
```

have the program calculate *Y*Min and *Y*Max (see Exercise 13 at the end of this chapter). What happens if the value of LineWidth is too large for your screen?

To plot points defined by a different $y = f(x)$ function, you will need to replace the equation immediately after the WHILE statement in procedure PlotIt by the equation for the appropriate function. Try some different equations to obtain plots of other curves. Modula-2 does allow functions to be passed as parameters into procedures such as PlotIt. This advanced topic is discussed in Chapter 17.

Complete the documentation Documentation will include a Problem Description: "Plot the function $y = 160 + x - 3x^2$ for the range XMin $<= x <=$

*X*Max in increments of *X*Step. Draw the base line and *y*-axis, and print the values of *x* and *y* for each point."

Add the structure chart (Figure 5–4) and pseudocode for the Algorithm Development, and a Program Listing of the Modula-2 source code. Complete the documentation with a sample run (Figure 5–5) and a users' manual: "The source code is in file CH5I. Enter the LineWidth, limits, and increment when requested. For meaningful results, enter values such that *X*Min < *X*Max and *X*Step < (*X*Max − *X*Min). LineWidth should not exceed 20 less than the maximum character width of your screen or page. Results will appear on the terminal screen and be directed to an output file as well."

Questions 5.5

1. Explain and/or illustrate how TRUNC(*x*) truncates a positive REAL value *x* to the next-smaller CARDINAL number, whereas TRUNC(*x* + 0.5) *rounds* to the nearest CARDINAL value.

2. Given the equation

   $$Y\text{Plot} = \text{TRUNC(FLOAT(LineWidth))} * (Y - Y\text{Min})/(Y\text{Max} - Y\text{Min}) + 0.5)$$

   make a table that shows the scaled value *Y*plot versus *y* when
   a. LineWidth = 56, *Y*Min = 0.0, and *Y*Max = 300.00 for *y*-values 0.0, 75.0, 150.0, 225.0, and 300.0.
   b. LineWidth = 40, *Y*Min = −20.0, and *Y*Max = 80.0 for *y*-values −20.0, 5.0, 30.0, 55.0, and 80.0.

3. Explain why LineWidth entered in the program PlotACurve (Example 5.5.1) generally should not exceed 20 less than the maximum character width of your screen or page.

4. How would you modify program PlotACurve (Example 5.5.1) so that
   a. the base line and *y*-axis are represented by dashes ('-') instead of dots?
   b. the user is asked to specify the PlotCharacter?
   c. the user is prevented from entering values of *X*Min, *X*Max, and *X*Step that do not satisfy the conditions *X*Min < *X*Max and *X*Step < (*X*Max − *X*Min)?

5. In procedure PlotIt (Example 5.5.1), why is *x* incremented by the command x := x + XStep, rather than by using INC(x, XStep)?

5.6   *Summary*

CHARacter Data Type   Declaration of a CHARacter variable causes sufficient memory to be reserved to store the binary code for the alphanumeric or control character assigned to that variable.

Read and Write   Read and Write procedures imported from standard module InOut (or from module Terminal) read a single character and display its value respectively. Assignment of a character to a variable, using the assignment operator (:=) requires single quotes around the character, as in Character-Variable := 'x'. Response to a Read(CharacterVariable) command requires only the character, without quotes. On many systems Read requires a terminating key (such as Enter) to be pressed after entry of a character, and an additional Read command must be issued to accept the terminating key character. Also, on some systems, Read should be followed by Write if you wish the character that was read to be displayed on the screen.

ORD and CHR Built-in functions ORD(CharacterValue) and CHR(Character-Code) return the decimal code for CharacterValue and the character represented by a given CharacterCode respectively. Codes most commonly used are ASCII and EBCDIC. A Table of ASCII is given in Appendix E.

Control Characters The first 32 characters in ASCII, and corresponding characters in other codes, are control characters used to control data transmission and storage. They, and all other characters, can be accessed by the function CHR(Code), where Code is the appropriate code for that character; or they may be used as CONSTants defined in terms of their octal codes, such as CONST CarriageReturn = 015C; .

ReadOneChar and TabOrFill ReadOneChar(CharacterVariable) reads a single character and ignores all of the others until the Enter key is pressed. TabOrFill(HowMany, FillCharacter) writes the FillCharacter HowMany number of times.

INC and DEC Incrementing or decrementing an INTEGER, CARDINAL, or CHARacter type variable can be done using the procedure INC(EnumerableVariable, N) or DEC(EnumerableVariable, N) where N is the CARDINAL distance by which to increment or decrement. If parameter N is omitted, its default value is 1.

CAP and ABS Two additional built-in functions are CAP(AlphabeticCharacterValue), which changes a lowercase alphabetic character to uppercase, and ABS(NumericValue), which returns the arithmetic absolute value of the NumericValue.

The Terminal Module The standard module Terminal (whose DEFINITION MODULE is shown in Appendix B) contains the procedures Read, Write, WriteString, and WriteLn, which always reference the default I/O devices. These procedures are especially useful when you need to display prompts to the screen when an output file is open or to read characters from the keyboard when an input file is open. You should be careful to IMPORT the entire Terminal module and qualify the procedures (such as Terminal.WriteString) if procedures with the same names are imported from module InOut.

Menus Many programs can be made more "user proof" if they are written so that a menu indicates the only choices that are allowed. CHARacter values are convenient for representing menu choices.

Plotting Points CHARacter variables and values can be useful for displaying information in the form of plotted points on a graph. Although higher-resolution techniques may be available, graphing a curve using characters can be done in Modula-2 on any system with an alphanumeric display and/or printer.

5.7 *Exercises*

Exercises marked with (FileName:_____) indicate those that ask you to use, modify, or extend the text samples. The numbers in brackets, [ ], indicate the chapter section that contains the material you need for completing the exercise.

1. [5.1] (FileName:CH5B) Rewrite the DetermineElectricalCost program (Example 5.1.1) so that the WHILE loop executes again when any character is entered except 'N' or 'n'.

2. [5.1] The surface area A (square inches) and volume V (cubic inches) of a spherical balloon with radius r (inches) are given by the formulae

$$A = 4 * \text{pi} * r^2 \quad \text{and} \quad V = (4/3) * \text{pi} * r^3,$$

where pi $= 3.14159$ approximately. Write a program that asks the user to enter the radius from the keyboard and then returns the area and the volume. The program should then ask for a Y or N answer to the question "Would you like to do it again?" and act accordingly.

3. [5.2] Write a program that prints a table of all of the characters with their decimal, octal, and hexadecimal codes from decimal code 32 through 126. Direct output to a file and print the file to your printer to determine what the printer does with any special characters. Do not try to print the control characters, codes 0 through 31, or code 127.

4. [5.4] Write a program that presents a menu that gives the user the choices

A	Find the code for a character
B	Find the character with a given code
S	Stop

When the choice is A or B, the program asks for the character or the code respectively, uses ORD or CHR to find the answer, prints the character and its code to the screen, and returns to the menu. Make the program as "user proof" as possible; that is, check for choices other than A, B, and S, and do not allow codes less than decimal 32 or greater than decimal 126.

5. [5.2] (FileName:CH5C) Modify TestCodes (Example 5.2.1) so that Start-Character, StopCharacter, BeginCode, and EndCode are requested in a procedure called EnterLimits. In that procedure include safeguards to prevent the user from entering characters or codes for characters that are not printable.

6. [5.3] (FileName:CH5PREC) Expand upon the FindPrecedeSucceed program in Section 5.3 so that the user is asked to specify the starting character, whether a preceding or succeeding character is to be found, and how far away the new character is to be. For example, specifying 'A', succeeding, and 5, would return the fifth character after 'A', namely 'F'.

7. [5.3] **a.** Write a program that converts the codes for alphabet letters to the letters' positions in the alphabet. The program should print a table of the letters and their positions; that is, A 1   B 2   C 3   . . .   Y 25   Z 26. *Hint:* Consider ORD(CAP(Letter)) $-$ ORD('A') $+$ 1.

   b. Use DEC in a program to print a table of the characters Z through A, with their codes and their positions in the alphabet, in reverse alphabetical order.

8. [5.3] (FileName:CH5F) **a.** Write and test a procedure, called *UnCap*, that will change a capital letter to a lowercase letter. *Hint:* Consider

$$(\text{ORD(Letter)} - \text{ORD('A')}) + \text{ORD('a')}.$$

   b. In procedure DetermineMidCharacter (Example 5.3.1), if Letter1 and Letter2 are lowercase, then UnCap MidCharacter before exiting the procedure.

   c. In program TestFindMidCharacter (Example 5.3.1), if there are an even number of letters between LeftLetter and RightLetter, then display *both* of the two letters that lie midway between LeftLetter and RightLetter.

9. [5.3] (FileName:CH5G) Expand the FindEvenSum example (5.3.2) to
   a. ask for the starting and ending numbers to be added, and
   b. allow you to step by any value (not just 2) that is set in a CONSTant declaration. Be sure to use INC to increment the number. For example, if CONST Step $= 5$, StartNum $= 20$, and StopNum $= 100$, the program would find the sum of $20 + 25 + 30 + \ldots + 95 + 100$.

Figure 5–6
A Bar Graph
(Exercise 12)

```
     x            y

    0.0          1.0      .*.............................................

    1.0          3.0      .* * *

    2.0          5.0      .* * * * *

    3.0          7.0      .* * * * * * *

    4.0          9.0      .* * * * * * * * *

    5.0         11.0      .* * * * * * * * * * *

     . . .

     . . .
```

10. [5.4] (FileName:CH5H) Modify module TemperatureConversion (Example 5.4.1) so that a single procedure ConvertTemperatures is used (instead of the two procedures ConvertFtoC and ConvertCtoF) to perform the temperature conversions. *Hint:* Pass Choice to the procedure as a parameter. If CAP(Choice) = 'F', then convert Fahrenheit to Celsius; otherwise, convert the other direction.

11. [5.5] (FileName:CH5I) Draw a graph of $y = x^2$ similar to that in Example 5.5.1. Allow the user to enter the character to be used for the plot of the points as well as the limits on x and the increment between values of x.

12. [5.5] (FileName:CH5I) Draw a bar graph for the function $y = 2x + 1$, where the user enters the limits on x and the increment between values of x. The graph should appear similar to the one in Figure 5–6. *Hint:* For a bar graph, the FillCharacter passed to procedure TabOrFill should be the PlotCharacter rather than Blank. (Why?)

13. [5.5] (FileName:CH5I) Add a procedure to module PlotACurve (Example 5.5.1) that will allow the program to determine YMin and YMax, rather than having the user enter those values. *Hint:* To determine YMin, initialize YMin := 160.0 + XMin − 3.0 * XMin * XMin. Then, in a loop WHILE x <= XMAX, find y for each value of x; and, if $y < Y$Min, replace YMin := y.

14. [5.5] Sales of rubber raincoats for each month of the past year are recorded in a file as:

```
JAN   324   FEB    68   MAR   160   APR   107
MAY   243   JUN    97   JUL   142   AUG    59
SEP   303   OCT   126   NOV     0   DEC    12
```

Write a program that reads the months and numbers from the file, produces a well-labeled bar graph of Rubber Raincoats sold in the year, and directs the graph to a file from where it can be printed. *Hint:* Declare Month as ARRAY [0. .2] OF CHAR, and import ReadString and WriteString from module InOut to read and write Month. Let the values of y be the number sold in a given month.

15. [5.5] Draw a bar graph of $y = x^3 + 1$ in the range $-1.0 <= x <= +5.0$ in steps of 0.5. Allow the user to specify which character will be used for the plot. See the hint in Exercise 12.

16. [5.4] Write a program that presents the user a menu with the choices to print numbers from 0 to 100 counting by 2s, 3s, 5s, or 7s or to Quit. The menu should reappear after the appropriate results are printed. Make the program as "user proof" as possible.

17. [5.3] Write a program that finds the sum of the decimal ASCII codes for all of the characters in your first and last names. Have it print the sum. Then find the remainder obtained when the sum is divided by 23, add 1 to this remainder, and print the result. This is a simple "hashing" technique that can be used to convert your name to a value between 1 and 23 — in order to determine something like which of 23 mailboxes you might be assigned or which of 23 prizes you might receive.

6

Procedures, Functions, and Parameters

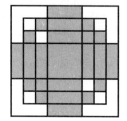

Chapter Outline

This chapter expands upon the methods of writing and calling procedures you have used. You will learn more about using parameters to pass values into and out of procedures, the differences between functions and procedures, and how to write your own functions. An introduction to drivers, stubs, and bottom-up and top-down design will enable you to use procedures for solving problems more effectively.

6.1   *Procedure Structure and Procedure Calls*

A procedure is a program unit that can be invoked from a module or another procedure to perform one action or a few logically related operations. A procedure should be able to stand completely independent, use values passed to it by the program, and/or pass values back to the main program.

Procedure Syntax

A procedure in Modula-2 looks very much like a program module. The sample definition in Figure 6–1 shows the syntax for modules and procedures.

There are four significant differences between the syntax of modules and the syntax of procedures:

1. A procedure heading begins with the word *PROCEDURE,* rather than the word *MODULE.*
2. The procedure heading may contain a list, within parentheses, of names and types of formal *parameters* that define values to be passed into and/or out of the procedure.
3. A semicolon (;), rather than a period (.), follows *END ProcedureName.*
4. All external modules must be IMPORTed through the main program; procedures may not contain the IMPORT statement. However, a procedure may contain nested declarations and definitions of other procedures.

Within a program module, procedure definitions are part of the declarations, as shown in Figure 6–1. Declarations often are written in the order

```
CONSTants;
TYPEs;
VARiables;
PROCEDUREs;
```

In Modula-2, however, the declaration of CONSTants, VARiables, and TYPEs may come in any order, either before or after the procedure declarations. The only restriction is that each entity should be defined before it is used. (Exceptions to this restriction, in the case of pointers and recursion, are discussed later as special situations.)

Program Flow

A procedure may be invoked (or called) by a program, or from another procedure, by stating its name followed by a list of parameters enclosed within parentheses, such as

```
ProcedureName(list of actual parameters);
```

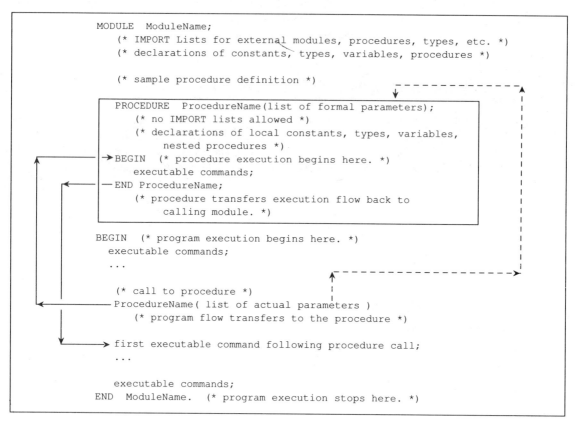

Flow of Program Execution

Passing Parameter Values

```
MODULE  ModuleName;
    (* IMPORT Lists for external modules, procedures, types, etc. *)
    (* declarations of constants, types, variables, procedures *)

    (* sample procedure definition *)

    PROCEDURE  ProcedureName(list of formal parameters);
        (* no IMPORT lists allowed *)
        (* declarations of local constants, types, variables,
            nested procedures *)
    BEGIN  (* procedure execution begins here. *)
        executable commands;
    END ProcedureName;
        (* procedure transfers execution flow back to
            calling module. *)

BEGIN  (* program execution begins here. *)
    executable commands;
    ...

    (* call to procedure *)
    ProcedureName( list of actual parameters )
        (* program flow transfers to the procedure *)

    first executable command following procedure call;
    ...

    executable commands;
END  ModuleName.  (* program execution stops here. *)
```

Figure 6–1
Defining and Calling a Procedure

When a procedure is called, control transfers to the procedure, and the commands following BEGIN are executed in order. When

```
END ProcedureName;
```

is encountered, control is returned to the calling program; and execution proceeds from the command following the command that called the procedure. Defining and calling a procedure, the flow of execution in a program module, and parameter passing are illustrated in Figure 6–1.

A Bit of Background

Procedures

Although the concepts are similar, user-defined subprograms are called by different names in different languages. In Modula-2 they are named *PROCEDURES* (even though some of them are actually functions). Pascal names them *procedures* and *functions*. C language subprograms all are referred to as *functions*, while users of COBOL tend to call them *paragraphs*. Those devoted to FORTRAN and BASIC are partial to the terms *subroutines* and *functions*.

Actual and Formal Parameters

The parameters listed in the command that invokes a procedure,

```
ProcedureName(list of actual parameters);
```

are called **actual parameters.** They are identifiers of values, variables, or expressions in the calling unit. The parameters listed in the procedure heading,

```
PROCEDURE ProcedureName(list of formal parameters);
```

are called **formal parameters.** They are the identifiers of the corresponding variables as they are known within the procedure itself. Formal parameter names may be the same as or different from the identifiers of the actual parameters. Thus a procedure to perform a particular task can be written independently, without requiring that every programmer agree upon variable names or even know in advance which programs may invoke the procedure in the future.

Each procedure reserves its own separate memory locations for its formal parameters. Values of actual parameters are copied to (or referenced from) the procedure's reserved memory locations. For example, assume that a program module contains these declarations:

```
VAR Count:CARDINAL;  Pay:REAL;
PROCEDURE FindTheAnswer(Number:CARDINAL; Amount:REAL);
   ....
```

Then the sequence of instructions

```
Count := 5;
Pay := 39.95;
FindTheAnswer(Count, Pay);  (* procedure call *)
```

copies values from the actual to the formal value (In Only) parameter memory locations, as shown in Figure 6–2. The method of handling formal VARiable (In/Out) parameters is somewhat different and is discussed in Section 6.3.

Questions 6.1

1. In a diagram similar to Figure 6–1, outline how a procedure named BuildATable would be defined in and called from a module named TableTester. Assume that the procedure needs access to commands WriteString, WriteLn, ReadCard, and WriteCard.
2. What are the errors in this procedure definition?

   ```
   PROCEDURE  NowsTheTime(A, B : CARDINAL);
     FROM MathLib0 IMPORT sqrt;
     BEGIN
       FWriteReal(sqrt(A), 12, 4);
     END.
   ```

3. Assume that a procedure with the heading

   ```
   PROCEDURE  NowsTheTime(A, B : CARDINAL);
   ```

   is called from a module by the command

   ```
   NowsTheTime(Hours, Minutes);
   ```

   a. List the actual parameters. List the formal parameters.
   b. What else do you know about Hours and Minutes?
4. Diagram the memory locations for the code on the next page, as in Figure 6–2.

Figure 6–2
Actual and Formal
Value **(In Only)**
Parameter
Relationships

```
(* procedure call *)
FindTheAnswer(Count,              PROCEDURE FindTheAnswer(Number:CARDINAL;
              Pay)                                        Amount:REAL);
```

```
Memory Locations of         Memory Locations of
Actual Parameters           Formal Value (in only)
Accessed from the           Parameters Accessed from
Program Module              Procedure FindTheAnswer
```

```
        Count       is copied to        Number

       ┌───────┐                       ┌───────┐
       │   5   │  ──────────────────▶  │   5   │
       └───────┘                       └───────┘


         Pay        is copied to        Amount

       ┌───────┐                       ┌───────┐
       │ 39.95 │  ──────────────────▶  │ 39.95 │
       └───────┘                       └───────┘
```

```
MODULE Question4;
    (* FileName:S6P1Q4     Modula-2     RKW      Mar. 1991 *)

FROM InOut IMPORT WriteInt, WriteLn, WriteCard;

VAR FirstValue, SecondValue : INTEGER;   OtherNumber : CARDINAL;

PROCEDURE  DisplayResults(Mine, Yours : INTEGER;   Ours : CARDINAL);
    BEGIN
        Mine := 2 * Mine;   Yours := -3 * Yours;
        WriteInt(Mine, 6); WriteLn;
        WriteInt(Yours, 6); WriteLn;
        WriteCard(Ours, 6); WriteLn;
    END DisplayResults;

BEGIN (* Question4 *)
    FirstValue := -17;   SecondValue := -31;   OtherNumber := 4;
    DisplayResults(SecondValue, FirstValue, OtherNumber);
END Question4.
```

6.2   *Value Parameters and Local Variables*

Some procedures require no values to be passed. These do not need a parameter list either in the heading or in the calling command.

A Parameterless Procedure

The following program illustrates a procedure that does not need parameters.

```
MODULE TestPrintTitle;
    (* Tests a parameterless procedure to print a two line title.
       FileName:CH6A      Modula-2      RKW      Mar. 1991 *)

FROM InOut IMPORT WriteString, WriteLn;

PROCEDURE  PrintTitle;
    BEGIN
        WriteString("              Current Inventory"); WriteLn;
        WriteString("Number    Description               Unit Cost");
        WriteLn;
    END PrintTitle;

BEGIN (* TestPrintTitle *)
    WriteString("The procedure PrintTitle is being called now.");
     WriteLn; WriteLn;
    PrintTitle;
END TestPrintTitle.
```

When the program is executed you should see this display:

```
The procedure PrintTitle is being called now.
                        Current Inventory
          Number    Description               Unit Cost
```

When a procedure does not need parameters, the parameter list may either be omitted or left empty in the procedure heading and in the calling command. For example, you may specify

```
PROCEDURE PrintTitle;    or    PROCEDURE PrintTitle( );
```

and

```
PrintTitle;    or    PrintTitle ( );
```

☐ Local Variables

Constants and variables declared within a procedure are **local** to that procedure, which means they are defined only within the procedure. Memory locations are assigned to local entities when the procedure is called and may be used during execution of the commands within the procedure. However, upon exit from the procedure—at the END ProcedureName statement—local memory locations are released, and the values of the local entities are lost.

Local variables are different from the variables in the program that call the procedure, even if particular variables have the same identifier names. Therefore, declaring local variables accomplishes two very important goals:

1. Local variables make it absolutely clear which values the procedure is using.
2. Changing the value of a local variable cannot accidently change any variable defined in the program that invokes the procedure.

☐ Value Parameters

When a value is to be passed only into a procedure, and that value does *not* need to be passed back out of the procedure to the calling unit, the formal parameter to which it is passed is called a **value** (or **In Only**) **parameter.** Formal value parameters are listed in the procedure heading by name and data type.

Memory locations are reserved for formal value parameters when a procedure is called, and the corresponding values of the actual parameters are copied to those memory locations, as illustrated in Figure 6–2. Value-parameter memory locations are released upon exiting from the procedure; the values are lost and are not copied back to the actual parameters in the calling unit.

A TimeDelay Procedure

To illustrate value parameters and local entities, here is a procedure for inserting a delay between commands in a program.

```
PROCEDURE TimeDelay(HowLong : CARDINAL);
   (* Counts off a time delay by displaying periods (.)    *)

   CONST COUNTSPERSECOND = 10000;  BELL = 07C;
   VAR  Counter, Seconds : CARDINAL;

   BEGIN
      WriteLn; WriteLn; WriteString("Counting, please be patient."); WriteLn;
      Seconds := 0;
      WHILE  Seconds < HowLong  DO
         Counter := 0;
         WHILE  Counter < COUNTSPERSECOND  DO
            INC(Counter);
         END; (* WHILE *)
         Write('.');  INC(Seconds);
           (* Assertion: Seconds = number of periods (.) displayed. *)
      END; (* WHILE *)
      Write(BELL);  WriteLn; WriteLn;
   END TimeDelay;
```

Execution of procedure TimeDelay produces the following display:

```
Counting, please be patient.
. . . . . . . . . .
```

If you wish HowLong to represent actual clock seconds you will need to experiment and adjust the CONSTant COUNTSPERSECOND for your machine.

When procedure TimeDelay is called, memory locations are reserved for values of formal value parameter HowLong, CONSTants BELL and COUNTSPERSEC-OND, and local VARiables Counter and Seconds. When procedure execution terminates at END TimeDelay; these locations all are released; and the values of HowLong, COUNTSPERSECOND, BELL, Counter, and Seconds are lost (hence unavailable) to the calling unit.

Actual parameters, passed to formal *value* parameters by a call to a procedure, may be

> variables,
> constants,
> expressions, or
> results of functions.

The *formal* value parameters defined in the procedure heading must be specified by variable identifiers.

Consider, for example, a program module with declarations

```
CONST  TENSEC = 10;
VAR  ElapsedTime : CARDINAL;
PROCEDURE TimeDelay(HowLong : CARDINAL);
     . . . .
```

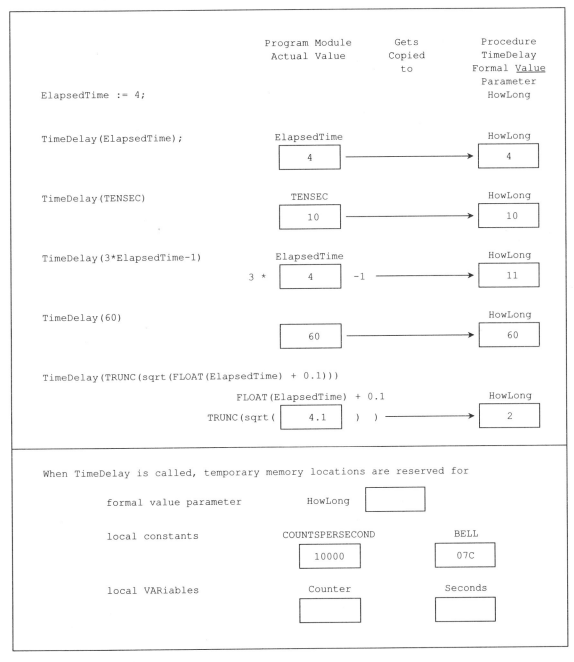

Figure 6–3
Valid Passing of Values to *Value* (In Only) Parameters

All of the calls to TimeDelay in Figure 6–3 would be appropriate. Attempting to display HowLong, Seconds, Count, or COUNTSPERSECOND either before calling or after exiting from procedure TimeDelay would cause an error message, such as "Undefined Variable," because the formal parameters and local variables are defined only within the procedure.

Side Effects

If the procedure modifies the values of formal value parameters, there is no effect on the value of any corresponding entities in the main program, because *value parameters are local* to the procedure. For example, had you decided in the main program, which invokes the procedure TimeDelay, to declare

```
VAR HowLong, ElapsedTime : CARDINAL;
```

and then execute

```
BEGIN   (* main program *)
   . . .
   HowLong := 20;
   Elapsed Time := 4;
   TimeDelay(HowLong);
   TimeDelay(ElapsedTime);
   WriteCard(HowLong,6);   WriteCard(ElapsedTime,6);
   . . .
```

the values displayed by the program would be 20 and 4, even if commands to change HowLong had been executed within the procedure. Formal value parameter HowLong in procedure TimeDelay is only a copy, in a different memory location, of actual parameter HowLong in the main program. Values are copied in only one direction, from main program variables HowLong and ElapsedTime to formal value parameter HowLong, but not back again.

Using value parameters protects actual entities in the calling unit from unintentional, unwanted changes, which are called **side effects.** Problem solvers should give as much attention to preventing them as physicians give to preventing unpleasant side effects from medication.

Matching Parameters

The type of the formal parameter declared in the procedure heading must match the type of the actual parameter passed from the calling unit. In the examples with procedure TimeDelay, both the value parameter HowLong and the values copied to it were declared in their respective units to be CARDINAL.

More than one value parameter may be declared and used if one important rule is followed:

Rule for Using More than One Value Parameter

The number, order, and type of the actual parameters in the calling command must be identical to the number, order, and type of formal parameters in the procedure heading.

For example, suppose that a main module contains the declarations

```
VAR   Roses, Tulips : INTEGER;
      Price, Cost : REAL;
      Letter : CHAR;
```

If the values of all of these were to be passed as actual value parameters to a procedure TryItOut, and if the procedure call were

```
TryItOut( 2*Roses, Tulips, Letter, Cost, Price-0.95 );
```

then the formal value parameters in the procedure header must appear in the same order, namely

```
PROCEDURE TryItOut( Blooms, Bulbs : INTEGER;
                Symbol : CHAR; Money, Charges : REAL);
```

This would create the following correspondence between variables:

Actual Parameter (in main module)	is copied to	Formal Value Parameter (local to TryItOut)
2 * Roses	→	Blooms
Tulips	→	Bulbs
Letter	→	Symbol
Cost	→	Money
Price − 0.95	→	Charges

The following example incorporates the concepts of local variables, value parameters, and procedures with and without parameters.

Example 6.2.1

Write and test a procedure that produces a table of monthly salary for three to five years, given the initial salary and a fixed-percentage annual raise.

Define the problem The president of a growing company offers new hires a guaranteed fixed-percentage raise each year for a specified number of years, usually three to five years. To help potential employees of this company evaluate their offers, you decide to create a procedure that will display a table of Year, MonthlyPay, TotalAnnualSalary, and CumulativeEarnings for the number of years given.

The procedure needs to know REAL StartingSalary, CARDINAL NumberOfYears, and REAL PercentRaise, which will be passed as value (In Only) parameters. A loop calculates the AmountOfRaise, the TotalAnnualSalary, and

```
new MonthlyPay = old MonthlyPay + AmountOfRaise
```

for each year and displays the results for each Year.

Develop a solution Since the procedure requires the three value parameters StartingSalary, NumberOfYears, and AnnualPercentRaise, its heading could be written

```
PROCEDURE  MakeSalaryTable(BeginSalary : REAL;
                NumYears : CARDINAL; RaiseRate : REAL);
```

The formulae required are

```
TotalAnnualSalary  = old MonthlyPay       * 12.0
CumulativeEarnings = CumulativeEarnings + TotalAnnualSalary
AmountOfRaise      = old MonthlyPay       * RaiseRate/100.0
new MonthlyPay     = old MonthlyPay       + AmountOfRaise
```

Parameterless procedure PrintUnacceptableSalary helps prevent the user from entering a StartingSalary less than $1000.00 per month.

Refine the solution   *Pseudocode*

```
main module FollowSalaryChanges
        begin
            ask for and accept StartingSalary
            while StartingSalary < 1000.00
                call procedure PrintUnacceptableSalary( );
                accept new StartingSalary
            end while
            ask for and accept NumberOfYears
            ask for and accept PercentRaise
            call procedure MakeSalaryTable(StartingSalary, NumberOfYears, PercentRaise)
        end FollowSalaryChanges

procedure PrintUnacceptableSalary( )
        begin
            write "Monthly salary must be >= " MINIMUMSALARY
            write "Enter another starting salary: "
        end PrintUnacceptableSalary

procedure PrintTableHeading(IncreaseRate)
        begin
            write "Salary at", IncreaseRate, 'Percent Increase Each Year'
            write "Year     Monthly Salary     This Year's Earnings Cumulative. . ."
        end PrintTableHeading

procedure MakeSalaryTable(BeginSalary, NumYears, RaiseRate)
        declare local variables TotalAnnualSalary, CumulativeEarnings,
                            MonthlyPay, AmountOfRaise, Year

        begin
            call procedure PrintTableHeading(RaiseRate)
            initialize Year = 1,     MonthlyPay = BeginSalary,
                    CumulativeEarnings = 0.00
            while     Year <= NumYears
              TotalAnnualSalary = MonthlyPay * 12.0
              CumulativeEarnings = CumulativeEarnings + TotalAnnualSalary
              display Year, MonthlyPay, TotalAnnualSalary, CumulativeEarnings
              increment Year
                AmountOfRaise = MonthlyPay * RaiseRate/100.0
                MonthlyPay = MonthlyPay + AmountOfRaise
            end while
        end Make Salary Table
```

Modula-2 code

```
MODULE  FollowSalaryChanges;
    (* Produces a table of monthly, annual, and cumulative salaries.
        FileName:CH6B       Modula-2       RKW       Mar. 1991  *)

FROM InOut IMPORT WriteString, WriteLn, ReadCard, WriteCard;
FROM RealInOut IMPORT ReadReal, FWriteReal;

CONST  MINIMUMSALARY = 1000.00;
VAR  StartingSalary, PercentRaise : REAL;
     NumberOfYears : CARDINAL;

PROCEDURE  PrintUnacceptableSalary( );
    BEGIN
        WriteString("Monthly salary must be >= $");
```

```
        FWriteReal(MINIMUMSALARY,10,2); WriteLn;
      WriteString("Enter another starting salary: ");
   END PrintUnacceptableSalary;

PROCEDURE  PrintTableHeading(IncreaseRate : REAL);
   BEGIN
      WriteLn; WriteLn;
      WriteString("Your Salary at"); FWriteReal(IncreaseRate,6,2);
       WriteString(" Percent Increase Each Year"); WriteLn; WriteLn;
      WriteString("Year   Monthly Salary   This Year's Earnings");
       WriteString("   Cumulative Total Paid"); WriteLn; WriteLn;
   END PrintTableHeading;

PROCEDURE MakeSalaryTable(BeginSalary:REAL; NumYears:CARDINAL;
                                             RaiseRate:REAL);
   VAR  TotalAnnualSalary,CumulativeEarnings,MonthlyPay,AmountOfRaise : REAL;
       Year : CARDINAL;
   BEGIN
      PrintTableHeading(RaiseRate);

      Year := 1;   MonthlyPay := BeginSalary;   CumulativeEarnings := 0.00;
      WHILE  Year <= NumYears  DO
         TotalAnnualSalary := MonthlyPay * 12.0;
         CumulativeEarnings := CumulativeEarnings + TotalAnnualSalary;

         WriteCard(Year,4); FWriteReal(MonthlyPay,17,2);
          FWriteReal(TotalAnnualSalary,23,2);
          FWriteReal(CumulativeEarnings,25,2); WriteLn;

             AmountOfRaise := MonthlyPay * RaiseRate/100.0;
             MonthlyPay := MonthlyPay + AmountOfRaise;
             INC(Year);
             (* Assertions:  Year = number of years displayed + 1
                    MonthlyPay = monthly salary for the next year
                    Cumulative Earnings = sum of TotalAnnualSalary's *)
         END; (* WHILE *)
      END MakeSalaryTable;
      BEGIN  (* FollowSalaryChanges *)
         WriteString("What is the monthly starting salary?  $");
          ReadReal(StartingSalary); WriteLn;
          WHILE  StartingSalary < MINIMUMSALARY  DO
             PrintUnacceptableSalary( ); ReadReal(StartingSalary); WriteLn;
          END; (* WHILE *)
          WriteLn;

         WriteString("For how many years do you wish to see salaries? ");
          ReadCard(NumberOfYears); WriteLn;
          WriteString("What is the annual PERCENTAGE salary increase? ");
          ReadReal(PercentRaise); WriteLn;

         MakeSalaryTable(StartingSalary, NumberOfYears, PercentRaise);
      END FollowSalaryChanges.
```

Debug and test Running this program with sample data should give results similar to these:

```
What is the monthly starting salary?   $1210.00

For how many years do you wish to see salaries? 4
What is the annual PERCENTAGE salary increase? 5.5

Your Salary at  5.50  Percent Increase Each Year
```

Year	Monthly Salary	This Year's Earnings	Cumulative Total Paid
1	1210.00	14520.00	14520.00
2	1276.55	15318.60	29838.60
3	1346.76	16161.12	45999.72
4	1420.83	17049.98	63049.71

Check a few results with your calculator. Since most values are displayed, it should not be difficult to find and correct any errors.

Complete the documentation Collect the problem definition, pseudocode, code, and sample test runs. A users' manual for this program should contain at least the following information:

> The Modula-2 source code file is named CH6B. The program asks for starting salary, number of years, and annual percent raise. The raise should be entered in percentage form; e.g., 4.3 percent, rather than 0.043.

Questions 6.2

1. Give at least three examples of useful parameterless procedures.
2. Write a program to test the procedure defined by

```
PROCEDURE  InstallALight;
  VAR  NumCars : CARDINAL;
  BEGIN
    WriteString("How many cars have passed?");
    ReadCard(NumCars);
    IF  NumCars > 5000 THEN
      WriteString("Install a Stop Signal!");
      WriteLn;
    END; (* IF *)
  END InstallALight;
```

3. Give at least three examples of useful procedures that accept copies of actual parameters but do not need to pass values back to the calling units.
4. In a program you have the following declarations:

```
VAR  Roses, Tulips : INTEGER;
     Price, Cost : REAL;    Letter : CHAR;

PROCEDURE TryItOut(Blooms, Bulbs : INTEGER;
            Symbol : CHAR;  Money, Charges : REAL);

PROCEDURE DoItNow(Credit : REAL;    Posies : INTEGER;
            Debit : REAL;   Bouquet : INTEGER);
    . . .
```

Which of the following procedure calls are valid and which are invalid? Why?

a. TryItOut(Tulips, Cost);

b. TryItOut(Tulips, Roses, Letter, Price, 2.0*Price);

c. `TryItOut(-5, Tulips+2, 'W', 3.00, Cost);`

d. `TryItOut(Roses, Cost, Price, Letter, Tulips);`

e. `DoItNow(Letter, Roses, Cost, Tulips);`

f. `DoItNow(Cost, Roses, Price);`

g. `DoItNow(18.75, 800, Cost+1.99, Roses);`

h. `DoItNow(Price, Roses, Price, Roses);`

i.

`TryItOut(6, Tulips, Letter, Cost, Price, Cost+10.00);`

j. `DoItNow;`

5. Procedure BuyItNow is defined by

```
PROCEDURE BuyItNow(Price, Discount : REAL; Days : CARDINAL);
  CONST  GOESUP = 0.10;
  VAR  Cost : REAL;
  BEGIN
    Price := Price - Discount;
    Cost := Price  +  FLOAT(Days)*GOESUP*Price;
    FWriteReal(Price,8,2); WriteLn;
    WriteCard(Days,3);  FWriteReal(Cost,10,2); WriteLn;
  END BuyItNow;
```

The module that calls this procedure contains the statements

```
. . .
Price := 10.00;
Reduction := 0.05 * Price;
DaysFromNow := 5;
BuyItNow(Price,  2.0*Reduction,  DaysFromNow);
FWriteReal(Price,8,2);
. . .
```

For the call to procedure BuyItNow,

a. Show how the IMPORT lists and the variable declarations for Price, Reduction, and DaysFromNow must appear in the calling module.

b. Draw a chart, similar to that of Figure 6–3, that shows the relationship between the actual parameters in the calling module and the formal value parameters in procedure BuyItNow.

c. What values are displayed by the procedure?

d. What value is displayed by the command FWriteReal(Price,8,2) after exiting from the procedure?

e. What would happen if the module called

`BuyItNow(DaysFromNow, Reduction, Price) ?`

6.3 *Variable Parameters*

The procedures discussed in the previous section either have used local variables exclusively or have allowed values to be passed only into the procedure from the calling unit. Often however, you need to pass values from the procedure back to the main program. This can be accomplished by using VARiable parameters.

☐ VAR Parameters

A **formal VARiable (In/Out) parameter** is indicated in a procedure heading by preceding the parameter name with *VAR*. The syntax is

```
PROCEDURE  ProcedureName(VAR ParameterName : ParameterType);
```

In contrast with value parameters, any change the procedure makes in the value of a formal VARiable parameter also occurs in the corresponding actual parameter in the calling unit.

In fact, rather than creating a new memory location and copying a value to it (as occurs with a formal value parameter), a formal VARiable parameter is regarded as another name for the memory location of the corresponding actual parameter.

Value and VARiable parameters of all types may be mixed in a procedure heading and corresponding procedure call, according to the following rule:

Rule for Mixed-Value and Variable Parameters

Multiple actual parameters in the calling command must agree in number, order, and type with the formal parameters in the procedure heading.

For example, suppose that a program module contains the declarations

```
VAR  People, Houses : CARDINAL;    Values : REAL;    Orientation : CHAR;

PROCEDURE HandleDemographics(Census:CARDINAL; VAR MarketValue:REAL;
                             Politics : CHAR; VAR NumHomes:CARDINAL);
  . . . .
```

The effect of the sequence of instructions

```
Orientation := 'R';
People := 5025;
Houses := 1256;
Values := 1.0E+06;
HandleDemograhics(People, Values, Orientation, Houses);
   (* procedure call *)
```

is shown in Figure 6–4. Note that in

```
PROCEDURE HandleDemographics(Census:CARDINAL; VAR MarketValue:REAL;
                             Politics : CHAR; VAR NumHomes:CARDINAL);
```

Census and Politics are formal *value* parameters. The calling command

```
HandleDemographics(People, Values, Orientation, Houses);
```

copies the values of People and Orientation to the *new memory locations* defined by Census and Politics. On the other hand, MarketValue and NumHomes are formal *VARiable* parameters; they are temporary aliases for the *same memory locations* defined by Values and Houses.

Although it is possible to define all formal parameters as VARiable (In/Out) parameters, it would not be a good practice to do so. If the formal parameter value is not needed by the program after exiting from the procedure, then to avoid side effects you should use a value (In Only) parameter, rather than a variable (In/Out) parameter.

When using VARiable parameters, the *actual parameter must be a variable;* it may not be represented by a literal value, an expression, or the result of a function call. Because anything that happens to NumHomes within this procedure also hap-

Figure 6–4
**Actual and Formal
Value and VARiable
Parameter
Relationships**

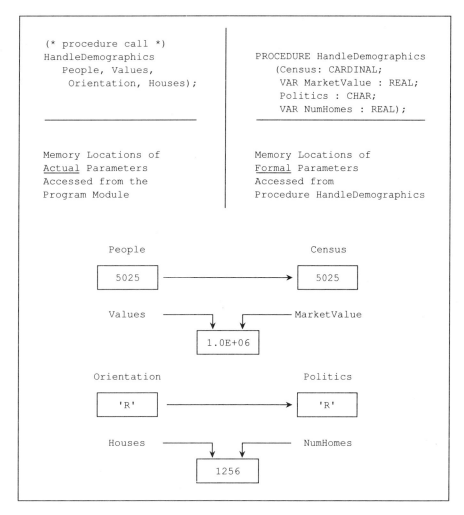

pens to Houses in the program module, it would not make sense to allow Houses to be a constant or an expression to which a value cannot be assigned.

Unlike value parameters, it is not necessary to initialize the actual value of a formal VARiable parameter. For example, if the actual parameter Houses does have a value before calling HandleDemographics, then that becomes the initial value of NumHomes. If variable Houses has not been assigned a value, the memory location it defines is simply available for use by NumHomes in the procedure.

Pointers and Indirect Addressing
(Optional material; may be omitted without loss of continuity.)

In practice, each formal VARiable parameter is designated by its address, which is called a **pointer** to the location of the variable. When variables are declared in a program they are allocated memory locations with specific addresses. When the command

```
HandleDemographics(People, Values, Orientation, Houses);
```

calls

```
PROCEDURE HandleDemographics(Census:CARDINAL;
                   VAR Market Value:REAL; Politics : CHAR;
                             VAR NumHomes:CARDINAL);
```

the memory locations for VARiable parameters MarketValue and NumHomes allocated in the procedure actually contain pointers to the addresses of Values and Houses, respectively. Thus, for example, any operations performed upon NumHomes in the procedure are actually performed upon the contents of the address pointed to by NumHomes; that is, the memory location defined by the program variable Houses. This technique, by which a memory location contains the address of (a pointer to) the actual location of the data, is called **indirect addressing.** Everything that happens to NumHomes also happens to Houses. Even though the memory location containing the pointer NumHomes is released when procedure execution ends, the location and value of Houses remain intact. In Chapter 16 you will learn how to create and access pointers as powerful problem-solving tools.

The following example illustrates the use of value and VARiable parameters.

Example 6.3.1

Write and test a procedure that can be incorporated into programs designed to calculate statistics. The procedure will calculate the Sum, Average, and Sum of Squares of a list of numbers read from a file.

Define the problem The user will specify in the main program HowMany real numbers are to be read from a file. The procedure will read the numbers; calculate their Sum, the sum of their squares (SumSq), and the Average; and pass results back to the program for display on the screen.

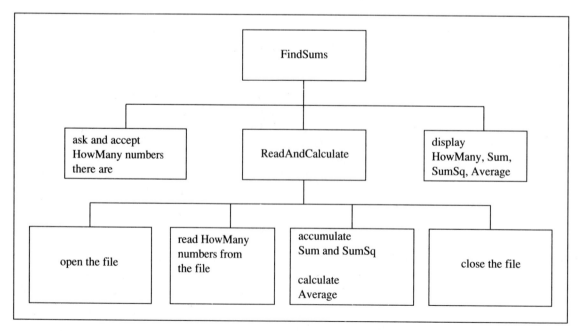

Figure 6–5
Structure Chart for FindSums (Example 6.3.1)

Develop a solution Input will come from a file named by the user. Output will be to the terminal screen. A diagram of the solution is shown in Figure 6–5.

Refine the solution *Pseudocode*

```
Main Module FindSums
    begin FindSums
        ask for and accept HowMany
        ReadAndCalculate(HowMany, Sum, SumSq, Average)
        print HowMany, Sum, SumSq, and Average
    end

Procedure ReadAndCalculate(NumCount, VAR Total,TotalOfSquares,Mean)
    begin ReadAndCalculate
        open Input file
        set ReadSoFar = 0
        initialize Total and TotalOfSquares to 0
        while ReadSoFar < NumCount
            increment ReadSoFar
            read Number
            add Number to Total
            add Number * Number to TotalOfSquares
        end while
        set Mean = Total/NumCount
        close Input file
    end ReadAndCalculate
```

A number of important concepts concerning the passing of parameters are illustrated by this program. HowMany is passed to formal value NumCount, since NumCount will not be changed by the procedure. Sum, SumSq, and Average are referred to in procedure ReadAndCalculate by VARiable parameters Total, TotalOfSquares, and Mean, respectively. The relationships between these parameters are shown in Figure 6–6.

Before the procedure is called, HowMany must have a value that can be passed to value parameter NumCount. Sum, SumSq, and Average need not have initial values before the procedure is called. They are assigned values in the procedure by the commands that initialize and calculate Total, TotalOfSquares, and Mean. Variables ReadSoFar and Number, needed only within the procedure, are declared locally. The input file is opened and closed within the procedure to help avoid unintentional access to the file elsewhere. Since it is easy to encounter difficulties when reading from a file, the debugging write commands—to echo the Numbers to the screen—have been included in the program from the start.

Modula-2 code

```
MODULE FindSums;
    (* Finds Sum, Sum of Squares, and Average of a list of numbers.
        File Name:CH6C    Modula-2    RKW    Mar. 1991   *)

FROM InOut IMPORT WriteLn, WriteString, ReadCard, WriteCard,
                OpenInput, CloseInput;
FROM RealInOut IMPORT ReadReal, FWriteReal;

VAR  HowMany : CARDINAL;   Sum, SumSq, Average : REAL;

PROCEDURE ReadAndCalculate(NumCount : CARDINAL;
                    VAR Total, TotalOfSquares, Mean : REAL);
    (* Reads NumCount real numbers from a file, accumulates sums, finds mean *)
```

```
    VAR  ReadSoFar : CARDINAL;    Number : REAL;
    BEGIN
        WriteString("Name of input file? "); OpenInput ("DAT");
        ReadSoFar := 0;
        Total := 0.0;  TotalOfSquares := 0.0; WriteLn; WriteLn;
        WHILE  ReadSoFar < NumCount  DO
            INC (ReadSoFar);
            ReadReal (Number);
            WriteString("Number "); WriteCard (ReadSoFar, 3);
            WriteString(" is "); FWriteReal (Number, 12, 4); WriteLn;
            Total   :=  Total + Number;
            TotalOfSquares  :=  TotalOfSquares  +  Number * Number;
            (* Assertions:
                Total = Number(1) + Number(2) + ... + Number(ReadSoFar)
```

Figure 6–6
Parameter
Relationships in
FindSums
(Example 6.3.1)

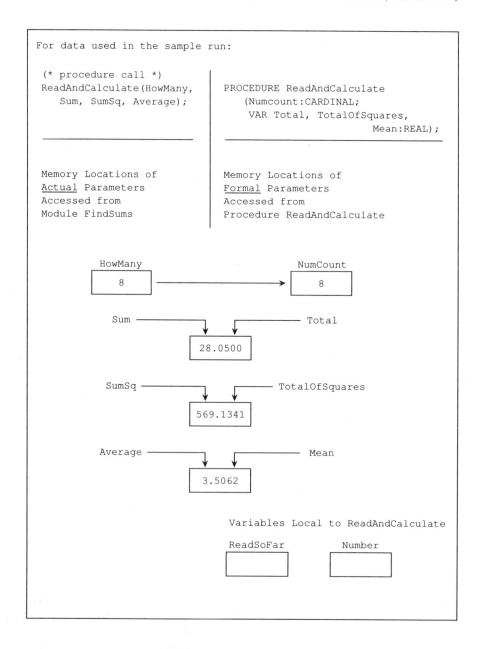

```
              TotalOfSquares = Number(1)*Number(1) + ... +
                              Number(ReadSoFar)*Number(ReadSoFar) *)
     END; (* WHILE *)
     Mean  :=  Total / FLOAT(NumCount);
     CloseInput;  WriteLn; WriteLn;
  END ReadAndCalculate;

BEGIN (* FindSums *)
  WriteString("How many numbers to read from the file? ");
   ReadCard(HowMany); WriteLn;

  ReadAndCalculate(HowMany, Sum, SumSq, Average);

  WriteString("    n         Sum      Sum of Squares     Average"); WriteLn;
  WriteCard(HowMany,4); FWriteReal(Sum,12,4); WriteString("        ");
  FWriteReal(SumSq,13,4); FWriteReal(Average,11,4); WriteLn;
END FindSums.
```

Debug and test   Using your system editor, create a short input file containing the numbers to be read. Most systems allow REAL numbers to be separated by blank spaces or Returns. For example,

```
12.5    -6.2     7.8     2.1     5.4
9.27     8.34   -11.16   4.98   -3.0
```

Run with HowMany = 4, 8, 10, and 12 and check the answers with your calculator. The output, with the data for HowMany = 8, should look like

```
How many numbers to read from the file? 8
Name of input file? DAT> NUMBERS.DAT

Number   1 is       12.5000
Number   2 is       -6.2000
Number   3 is        7.8000
Number   4 is        2.1000
Number   5 is        5.4000
Number   6 is        9.2700
Number   7 is        8.3400
Number   8 is      -11.1600

  n         Sum      Sum of Squares      Average

  8      28.0500          569.1341        3.5062
```

A Bit of Background

Statistics

The Sum, Sum of Squares, and Average of a list of numbers calculated in Example 6.3.1 are commonly used quantities in statistics!

By all means take a course in statistics! Some of the most important applications of mathematics and computing to the real world are in the area of statistics. Whether you are in business, engineering, politics, government, weather forecasting, sports, education, or virtually any other field you can name, being able to handle statistics will give you a decided advantage. It has been claimed that "statistics don't lie, but some statisticians do," and this is true. Statistical methods and data are sometimes misused by people to convince others—people who do not understand statistics—of something the statistics really do not support.

When HowMany = 12, your compiler may cause the last two numbers to be assigned the value 0.0, or it may give you a runtime error such as "Attempt to Read Past End of File." In either case, the answer is incorrect, and the user should be warned that HowMany must not be greater than the number of entries in the file.

Complete the documentation Documentation should include the problem description, pseudocode, code, a sample run, and a listing of the input file. The users' manual should state the location of the source code (CH6C), and a warning regarding the size of HowMany.

Global Variables

Another method for the main program to recognize the variables used in a procedure is to declare all constants and variables in the main program and to use them in the procedures, without passing them as parameters. All entities declared in the calling program are defined to be **global**; that is, their memory locations are accessible automatically to any procedure called by that program. As long as a new memory location is not designated locally (by declaring a local entity or parameter of the same name within the procedure), any change a procedure makes to a global variable is recognized also by the calling program. Although using global entities is simple, it is very poor programming practice.

Why Global Variables Usually Should Not Be Used

1. Unwanted side effects occur when the values of the global variables within the procedures are changed.
2. Global variables require that the names used to designate variables in the procedure be identical to those in the calling program. The procedure loses its portability because every new program that calls it must use the same variable names.
3. The language loses its modularity. Writing independent procedures now requires considerable correlation among programmers.
4. The principle of *information hiding* — the intentional hiding of information from users about how a procedure works or how it defines the data — is defeated.

Nested Procedures

When a procedure contains in its declaration section the declaration of other procedures, the inner procedures are said to be *nested* within the outer one. The entire nested procedure is local to the procedure within which it is declared. For example, in Figure 6–7, Inner1 and Inner2 may be invoked from OuterProcedure but not directly from module DemoNesting nor from NeighborProcedure.

Procedures may be nested within procedures, which themselves are nested. However, programs in which procedures are nested more than two or three levels deep are difficult to read, debug, and maintain. Top-down design and stepwise refinement lend themselves to nesting of procedures. On a structure chart each succeeding level can be considered to represent procedures nested within the level above, as shown in Figure 6–8.

The relationships between identifiers in procedures are discussed here, and the examples in the next section, illustrate some nested procedures.

Define and Declare

In the declaration section of a module or procedure, the names of identifiers for constants, types, variables, and procedures are *declared*; that is, the computer is informed that these entities will be used within that unit and that memory space should be reserved for them.

```
MODULE DemoNesting;
    (* DemoNesting declarations *)

    PROCEDURE OuterProcedure(* list of OuterProcedure formal parameters *)
        (* OuterProcedure local declarations *)

        PROCEDURE  Inner 1 (* list of Inner1 formal parameters *)
            (* Inner1 local declarations *)
            BEGIN  (* Inner1 *)
              . . .
            END Inner1;

        PROCEDURE Inner2 (* list of Inner2 formal parameters *)
            (* Inner2 local declarations *)
            BEGIN (* Inner2 *)
              . . .
              (* may invoke Inner1 *)
              . . .
            END Inner2;

        BEGIN  (* OuterProcedure *)
          . . .
            (* may invoke Inner1 and Inner2 *)
          . . .
        END OuterProcedure;


    PROCEDURE NeighborProcedure (* list of NeighborProcedure formal parameters *)
        (* NeighborProcedure local declarations *)

        BEGIN  (* NeighborProcedure *)
          . . .
            (* may invoke OuterProcedure *)
          . . .
            (* neither Inner1 nor Inner2 may be invoked directly
              from NeighborProcedure *)
          . . .
        END NeighborProcedure;

    BEGIN (* DemoNesting *)
      . . .
        OuterProcedure(* list of actual parameters *)
      . . .
        NeighborProcedure(* list of actual parameters *)
      . . .
        (* neither Inner1 nor Inner2 may be invoked directly from here *)
      . . .
    END DemoNesting;
```

Figure 6–7
Nested Procedures

Figure 6–8
Structure Chart
Showing Possible
Nested Procedures

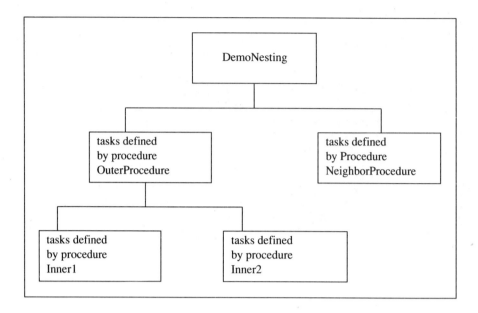

The entities also must be *defined*. Additional information must be given so that the computer knows what to do when identifiers are recognized by the program. The definitions of some of the entities include the following information:

Entity	Definition Information Required
CONSTant	Value of the CONSTant (e.g., −3.4, 'X', TRUE, etc.)
Data TYPE	Values allowed to be assigned to a variable of that type (e.g., ARRAY [0..19] OF CHAR)
VARiable	Data type of the VARiable (e.g., REAL, BOOLEAN, etc.)
PROCEDURE	Local parameters, variables, constants, to be used; commands to be executed when the procedure is invoked.

Scope of Identifiers

Not every constant, variable, parameter, type, and procedure name declared in a program is accessible everywhere within that program. Each of these entities has a *scope* or region of the program where it is said to be *visible* and can be used.

Here are some rules for the scope of identifiers related to procedures. Additional rules will be considered later in the discussion of local modules.

Rules for the Scope of Identifiers

1. The scope of a *global identifier* (an entity imported into or declared in the main program) extends to every procedure in the program with one exception: A global identifier is not visible within any procedure where an identifier with the same name has been declared locally (as a local variable, constant, parameter, type, procedure name, etc.).

2. An entity declared locally within a procedure is not visible outside that procedure. Parameters listed in the heading, and variables, constants, types, and nested procedure names declared within a procedure, are local to that procedure.

3. Any entity declared within a procedure is visible in any procedure nested within it, unless an identifier with the same name has been declared locally within the nested procedure.

4. The position of the declaration of an entity within the procedure or module where it is defined does not change its scope. Declaring entities in a different order does not affect their visibility.

5. Standard identifiers are visible everywhere within a program. The standard identifiers are the reserved words and built-in procedure and function names listed in Appendix A, such as CARDINAL, DEC, TRUNC, etc. Exceptions to this can be forced by declaring local entities with the standard identifier names, but doing so introduces confusion and thus should be avoided.

Figure 6–9 illustrates the rules of scope with lists of "Visible Entities within . . ." each program unit. Study the lists of visible entities and the parameters lists in the procedure calls and headings to convince yourself that they are valid.

In practice, you can determine the scope of an entity and how it is defined by this algorithm:

Determining the Scope and Meaning of an Entity

1. Search the declarations in the procedure or module in which the entity is located.
2. If the entity is not found in the local declarations, search the declarations in the procedure or module that encloses the most recent procedure or module searched. Continue the search outwards until the declaration is found.

For example, in NestedProc of Figure 6–9,

- VblOne *is* a local CARDINAL variable.
- PrmOne is not found in the local declarations of NestedProc.

  is not found in the formal parameter list of NestedProc.

  is not found in the local declarations of OuterProc.

  is a CARDINAL formal parameter of OuterProc.
- CnstOne is not found in the local declarations of NestedProc.

  is not found in the formal parameter list of NestedProc.

  is not found in the local declarations of OuterProc.

  is not found in the formal parameter list of OuterProc.

  is a constant with REAL value 5.4 in module DemoScope.

Questions 6.3

1. Suppose a program module contains the declarations

   ```
   VAR  M1, M2 : CHAR;  M3, M4 : REAL;  M5 : INTEGER;
   ```

   and that the module calls procedure WhatNow with the command

   WhatNow(M1, M2, M3, M4, M5);

   Changes made by procedure WhatNow to M2 and M4 are to be available to the program upon exiting from the procedure.

   a. What should the procedure heading look like?

   b. In a diagram similar to Figure 6–6, show the relationships among variables M1, M2, M3, M4, M5 and parameters listed in your procedure heading.

2. A program declares

   ```
   VAR  Robes, Ties, Underwear : INTEGER;
        Price, Cost, SalesTax : REAL;
        Mark  : CHAR;

   PROCEDURE WhoDoneIt(Dusters,Shorts:INTEGER; VAR Cravats:INTEGER;
              Symbol:CHAR;  VAR Debit,Tax:REAL; Credit:REAL);
        ...
   ```

   and invokes the procedure with the command

```
MODULE DemoScope;
   CONST  CnstOne = 5.4;
   VAR  VblOne:CARDINAL;   VblTwo, VblThree:REAL;

   PROCEDURE  OuterProc(PrmOne:CARDINAL;   VAR PrmTwo,PrmThree:REAL);
   VAR  VblOne:CHAR;   VblFour:REAL:   VblFive:INTEGER;

   PROCEDURE  NestedProc(VblFour:INTEGER; VAR PrmThree:CARDINAL);
      CONST  CnstTwo = 8;
      VAR  VblOne:CARDINAL;   VblFive:CHAR;   VblSix:BOOLEAN;

      BEGIN (* NestedProc *)
         (* Visible Entities within NestedProc
             from NestedProc: CnstTwo, VblOne, VblFive, VblSix,
                         VblFour (a parameter), PrmThree
             from OuterProc: PrmOne, PrmTwo
             from DemoScope: CnstOne, VblTwo, Vblthree    *)
         ...
      END NestedProc;

   BEGIN (* OuterProc *)
      (* Visible Entities within Outerproc
          from OuterProc: VblOne, VblFour, VblFive, PrmOne,
                        PrmTwo, PrmThree, NestedProc
          from DemoScope: CnstOne, VblTwo, VblThree    *)
      ...
      NestedProc(VblFive, PrmOne);
      ...
   END OuterProc;

   PROCEDURE NeighborProc(VAR PrmFour:REAL;   VblOne:REAL);
   CONST  CnstOne = 'T';   CnstThree = -9;
   VAR  VblSeven:REAL;   VblTwo:CHAR;

   BEGIN (* NeighborProc *)
      (* Visible Entities within NeighborProc
          from NeighborProc: CnstOne, CnstThree, VblSeven, VblTwo
                           PrmFour, VblOne (a parameter)
          from DemoScope: VblThree, OuterProc    *)
      ...
   END NeighborProc;

   BEGIN (* DemoScope *)
   (* Visible Entities within DemoScope
       from DemoScope: CnstOne, VblOne, VblTwo, VblThree, OuterProc,
                     NeighborProc    *)
   ...
   OuterProc(VblOne, VblThree, VblTwo);
   ...
   NeighborProc(VblTwo, VblThree);
   . . .
   END DemoScope;
```

Figure 6–9
Scope of Identifiers

```
WhoDoneIt( Robes, Underwear, Ties, Mark, Cost, SalesTax, Price);.
```

In a diagram similar to Figure 6–4, show the relationships between the actual parameters in this procedure call and the formal parameters in the procedure heading.

3. Consider this structure:

```
MODULE  ThisProgram;
   VAR  A, B : REAL;      C, D : INTEGER;

   PROCEDURE  One(P1 : REAL;   VAR P2 : REAL);
      VAR  M, N : CHAR;
      BEGIN  (* One *)
        . . .
      END One;

   PROCEDURE  Two;
      VAR  P, D : INTEGER;      Q, R : REAL;
      BEGIN  (* Two *)
        . . .
        One(Q, R);
        . . .
      END Two;
   BEGIN  (* ThisProgram *)
     . . .
   END ThisProgram.
```

Define the scope of variables and parameters A, B, C, D, M, N, P, Q, R, P1, P2.

4. Examine the ''Visible Entities. . .'' lists in the module and the procedures of Figure 6–9. In each list, for each entity, tell:

a. its data type (CARDINAL, REAL, CHAR, INTEGER); the constant value or procedure name it represents; and

b. the path it takes to get to the location of the ''Visible Entities . . .'' list. (For example, within NestedProc, PrmOne from OuterProc is type CARDINAL. The value of VblOne from DemoScope is passed to formal value parameter PrmOne in OuterProc. PrmOne has an alias in the form of VAR formal parameter PrmThree in NestedProc.)

6.4 *Intrinsic Functions*

Functions are specially defined procedures whose major purpose is to return a single, simple value to the calling unit. Twelve intrinsic (standard, built-in) functions are part of the Modula-2 language. These functions, shown and described in Appendix A, are ABS, CAP, CHR, FLOAT, HIGH, MAX, MIN, ODD, ORD, SIZE, TRUNC, and VAL. Also, five standard procedures, which are not functions, are built into Modula-2 (also shown in Appendix A). These are identified by DEC, EXCL, HALT, INC, and INCL. The intrinsic functions and procedures are always available and need not be imported.

Eight additional mathematical functions can be imported from standard module MathLib0. These functions—real, entier, sqrt, ln, exp, sin, cos, and arctan—are described in Appendix B.

☐   ### Invoking a Function

A "normal" procedure, like the ones you have written so far, is invoked by using its name as a command. In contrast, since a function is designed to return a single value, it is called by using its name wherever a variable or a value would appear. For example, for an INTEGER variable x, using the normal *procedure* INC(x), the program fragment

```
x := -17;
WriteInt(x, 4);
INC(x);        (* use the procedure name as an action *)
WriteInt(x, 4); WriteLn;
```

displays the results

-17 -16

To use the *function* ABS(x), which finds the absolute value of a number x, you would write

```
x := -17;
WriteInt(x, 4);
x := ABS(x);   (* use the function name in place of the
                      value it represents *)
WriteInt(x, 4);
```

which displays the results -17 17

Observe carefully that procedure INC(x) was called by using its name as an action to be performed, while function ABS(x) is used in place of the value or variable it represents.

Those intrinsic functions and procedures in Appendix A that can be used for character handling (CAP, CHR, ORD, INC, and DEC) were discussed in Chapter 5. Some of the functions used for handling and converting between numeric data types (FLOAT, MAX, MIN, TRUNC, VAL, real, entier) were treated in Chapter 3. Now two examples will be presented to illustrate and extend the use of some of the mathematics functions. Those dealing with arrays, types, and sets will be considered later in the book.

Using the sqrt Function and a Nested Procedure

Examine the applications of function sqrt and the use of a nested procedure in the following problem from mathematics.

Example 6.4.1

Solve the quadratic equation.

Define the problem   The roots of the quadratic equations

$$ax^2 + bx + c = 0$$

are the values for which the equation is valid; that is, the values of x for which the expression $ax^2 + bx + c$ has a value of 0. The two roots can be found from the formula

Root1 $= -b/2a + $ sqrt(D)/2a   and   Root2 $= -b/2a - $ sqrt(D)/2a

where $D = b^2 - 4ac$ is called the Discriminant.

Given the values of a, b, and c, find Root1 and Root2.

Develop a solution The user will be asked to enter values *a*, *b*, and *c*. The program will call a procedure FindRoots, which calls a nested procedure CalculateDiscriminant to calculate the value

$$D = b^2 - 4\,ac.$$

If the Discriminant, *D*, is positive or zero, the two real roots

Root1 $= -b/2a + $ sqrt(D)/2a   and   Root2 $= -b/2a - $ sqrt(D)/2a

will be calculated and displayed. If the value of D is negative, the two roots are complex and will be displayed in the form

Root1 $= -b/2a + $ (sqrt($-$D)/2a)i   and   Root2 $= -b/2a - $ (sqrt($-$D)/2a)i

where *i* represents the imaginary number defined by sqrt($-$1).

Strictly speaking, procedure CalculateDiscriminant would be appropriately written as a function, since its purpose is to return a single value, *D*. In the next section you will change normal procedure CalculateDiscriminant to a function.

Refine the solution Part of the pseudocode is shown as part of the documentation in Figure 6–10.

Modula-2 code

```
MODULE  SolveQuadraticEquation;
   (* Find the roots of the quadratic equation.
      FileName:CH6D      Modula-2      RKW      Mar. 1991  *)

FROM InOut IMPORT WriteString, WriteLn;
FROM RealInOut IMPORT FWriteReal, ReadReal;
FROM MathLib0 IMPORT sqrt;

VAR  a, b, c : REAL;

PROCEDURE  EnterAndDisplayValues(VAR A, B, C : REAL);
   BEGIN
      WriteString("What are the quadratic equation coefficients? ");
      WriteLn; WriteString(" a = "); ReadReal(A);
      WriteLn; WriteString(" b = "); ReadReal(B);
      WriteLn; WriteString(" c = "); ReadReal(C); WriteLn; WriteLn;
      WriteString("The equation is: ");
      FWriteReal(A,8,2); WriteString(" x^2  +  ");
      FWriteReal(B,8,2); WriteString(" x  +  ");
      FWriteReal(C,8,2); WriteString("  =  0.00"); WriteLn; WriteLn;
   END EnterAndDisplayValues;

PROCEDURE  FindRoots(A, B, C : REAL);
   VAR  Discriminant, Root1, Root2, RealRootPart, ImagRootPart : REAL;

   PROCEDURE  CalculateDiscriminant(ACoef,BCoef,CCoef:REAL;  VAR D:REAL);
      BEGIN
         D  :=  BCoef * BCoef  -  4.0 * ACoef * CCoef;
      END CalculateDiscriminant;

   BEGIN (* FindRoots *)
      CalculateDiscriminant(A, B, C, Discriminant);
      IF  Discriminant >= 0.0  THEN
         Root1 := -B/(2.0*A) + sqrt(Discriminant)/(2.0*A);
         Root2 := -B/(2.0*A) - sqrt(Discriminant)/(2.0*A);
```

This program asks for coefficients a, b, and c and finds the
real or complex roots of the quadratic equation $ax^2 + bx + c = 0$.

Algorithm Development   Pseudocode

```
module SolveQuadraticEquation
   begin
       EnterAndDisplayValues(a, b, c)
       FindRoots(a, b, c)
   end SolveQuadraticEquation

procedure EnterAndDisplayValues(A, B, C)
   begin
       ask for and accept A, B, C
       print the equation Ax² + Bx + C = 0
   end EnterAndDisplayValues

procedure FindRoots(A, B, C)
   declare procedure CalculateDiscriminant(ACoef, BCoef, CCoef, D)
   begin (* FindRoots *)
       CalculateDiscriminant(A, B, C, Discriminant)
       if Discriminant >= 0
           Root1 = -B/2A + sqrt(Discriminant)/2A
           Root2 = -B/2A - sqrt(Discriminant)/2A
           print "the real roots are" Root1, Root2
       otherwise
           RealRootPart = -B/2A
           ImagRootPart = sqrt(-D)/2A
           print "the complex roots are"
   RealRootPart + ImagRootPart "i"
           RealRootPart - ImagRootPart "i"
       end if
   en
proced
```

Program Listing

```
MODULE  SolveQuadraticEquation;
    (* Find the roots of the quadratic equation.
        FileName:CH6D      Modula-2      RKW      Mar. 1991  *)

FROM InOut IMPORT WriteString, WriteLn;
FROM RealInOut IMPORT FWriteReal, ReadReal;
FROM MathLib0 IMPORT sqrt;

VAR  a, b, c : REAL;

PROCEDURE  EnterAndDisplayValues(VAR A, B, C : REAL);
    BEGIN
        Write
        Writ
        Writ
        Writ
        Write
        FWre
        FWre
        FWre
    END Ente

PROCEDURE
    VAR  Dir

    PROCEDUR
        BEGIN
           D
        END

    BEGIN (
        Calc
        IF
           Ru
           Ru
           Wr
```

Sample Run

```
What are the quadratic equation coefficients?
   a = 2.4
   b = 3.5
   c = 1.6

The equation is: 2.40 x^2 +  3.50 x +  1.60 = 0.00

The complex roots are
  -0.73 +      0.37 i and
  -0.73 -      0.37 i
```

Users' Manual   SolveQuadraticEquation

Modula-2 source code is in file CH6D. Enter the coefficients a, b,
and c from the keyboard when asked; then wait for the roots to be
displayed on the screen.
    Cautions:
    - a cannot be 0.0
    - Modifications will have to be made to the algorithm for finding
      the roots if the coefficients are very large or require more
      digits of accuracy than the internal precision of REAL numbers
      on your system.

Figure 6–10
Documentation for SolveQuadraticEquation (Example 6.4.1)

```
            WriteString("The real roots are "); WriteLn;
             FWriteReal(Root1,8,2); WriteString(" and ");
             FWriteReal(Root2,8,2);
        ELSE
            RealRootPart := -B/(2.0*A);
            ImagRootPart := sqrt(-Discriminant)/(2.0*A);
            WriteString("The complex roots are "); WriteLn;
             FWriteReal(RealRootPart,8,2); WriteString(" + ");
             FWriteReal(ImagRootPart,8,2); WriteString(" i   and"); WriteLn;
             FWriteReal(RealRootPart,8,2); WriteString(" - ");
             FWriteReal(ImagRootPart,8,2); WriteString(" i");
        END; (* IF *)
        WriteLn; WriteLn;
    END FindRoots;

BEGIN (* SolveQuadraticEquation *)
    EnterAndDisplayValues(a, b, c);
    FindRoots(a, b, c);
END SolveQuadraticEquation.
```

Debug and test It is important, especially in a program with nested procedures, that formal parameters are declared appropriately as value or VARiable. Supplemental write statements to display the values of *a, b, c,* and the Discriminant will help in debugging. Test the program with a variety of positive and negative values for *a, b,* and *c.* One simple case, which gives whole, real roots is $a = 1.0$, $b = -5.0$, and $c = 6.0$. A sample run with complex roots is shown in the documentation in Figure 6–10. What happens when $a = 0$? How would you handle this problem? (See Exercise 6 at the end of the chapter.)

Complete the documentation Complete documentation is shown in Figure 6–10. Note the cautions in the users' manual.

Using the exp Function and Adapting Procedures
The following example also illustrates a nested procedure and demonstrates a financial application of the exp function. Observe how procedures you have developed earlier can be adapted to a new situation.

Example 6.4.2

Tabulate and plot the value of an original investment during the first few years given the annual interest rate compounded continuously.

Define the problem An InitialAmount of dollars will be invested at AnnualInterest percentage interest rate for NumYears number of years. Interest will be compounded continuously, so that the Value at the end of a given Year is given by the formula

Value = InitialAmount * exp((AnnualInterest/100.0) * Year).

Function exp is imported from module MathLib0; exp(*x*) means e^x, where e (= approximately 2.71828) is the base of natural logarithms.

The program will produce a bar graph of Value versus Year for Years 0 (time of initial investment) to NumYears.

Develop a solution The main program will call a procedure EnterData to ask for
InitialAmount, AnnualInterest, and NumYears. Then it will call procedure PlotIt
(adapted from Example 5.5.1) to calculate, tabulate, and plot the Values. The
relative tab procedure, TabOrFill, from Example 5.5.1 will be nested within procedure PlotIt.

Refine the solution *Pseudocode*

```
module CalculateFutureValue
    begin
            EnterData(InitialAmount, AnnualInterest, NumYears)
            PlotIt(InitialAmount, AnnualInterest, NumYears)
        end CalculateFutureValue

procedure EnterData(BeginAmt, AnnualRate, NoYrs)
    begin
            ask for and accept BeginAmt, AnnualRate, NoYrs
        end EnterData

procedure PlotIt(StartAmt, InterestRate, NumYr)
    declare nested procedure TabOrFill
    begin
            write StartAmt, InterestRate
            write headings "Year   Value $"
            initialize Year = 0, MinValue = StartAmt
            calculate  MaxValue = StartAmt*exp((InterestRate/100.0) * NumYr)
            while  Year <= NumYr
                calculate  Value = StartAmt*exp((InterestRate/100.0)*Year)
                print Year, Value, and baseline Dot
                calculate scaled ValuePlot = TRUNC(LineWidth*(Value-MinValue)/
                                                   (MaxValue-MinValue) + 0.5)
                TabOrFill(ValuePlot + 1, PlotCharacter), advance to new line
                increment Year
            end while
        end PlotIt

procedure TabOrFill(HowMany, FillCharacter)
    (* see Example 5.5.1 *)
```

Note that, in procedure PlotIt, Value increases with Year, so MinValue and
MaxValue are the Values at Year 0 and at NumYr respectively.

Modula-2 code

```
MODULE CalculateFutureValue;
   (* Plots the future value of an investment compounded continuously.
      FileName:CH6E      Modula-2      RKW       Mar. 1991  *)

FROM MathLib0 IMPORT exp;
FROM InOut IMPORT WriteString, WriteLn, Write, ReadCard, WriteCard;
FROM RealInOut IMPORT FWriteReal, ReadReal;

VAR  InitialAmount, AnnualInterest : REAL;   NumYears : CARDINAL;

PROCEDURE EnterData(VAR BeginAmt, AnnualRate : REAL;   VAR NoYrs : CARDINAL);
   BEGIN
       WriteString("What is the inital amount invested?  $ ");
        ReadReal(BeginAmt); WriteLn; WriteLn;
```

```
      WriteString("What is the annual PERCENTAGE interest rate? ");
       ReadReal(AnnualInterest); WriteLn; WriteLn;
      WriteString("For how many years will you invest? ");
       ReadCard(NoYrs); WriteLn; WriteLn;
   END EnterData;


PROCEDURE PlotIt(StartAmt, InterestRate : REAL;    NumYr : CARDINAL);
   CONST  LineWidth = 50;  PlotCharacter = '$';  Dot = '.';
   VAR  ValuePlot, Year : CARDINAL;
        Value, MinValue, MaxValue : REAL;

   PROCEDURE TabOrFill(HowMany:CARDINAL;   FillCharacter:CHAR);
      VAR  CountSpaces : CARDINAL;
      BEGIN
         CountSpaces := 1;
         WHILE  CountSpaces <= HowMany  DO
            Write(FillCharacter);
            INC(CountSpaces);
            (* CountSpaces = no. FillCharacters written so far  +  1 *)
         END; (* WHILE *)
      END TabOrFill;

   BEGIN  (* PlotIt *)
      WriteLn; WriteString("Initial Investment =  $");
       FWriteReal(StartAmt,12,2); WriteLn;
      WriteString("Annual percentage interest rate =  ");
       FWriteReal(InterestRate,6,2); WriteLn; WriteLn;
      WriteLn; WriteString(" Year    Value $"); WriteLn;
      Year := 0;    MinValue := StartAmt;
      MaxValue := StartAmt * exp( (InterestRate/100.0) * FLOAT(NumYr) );

         WHILE  Year <= NumYr  DO
            Value := StartAmt * exp( (InterestRate/100.0) * FLOAT(Year) );

            WriteCard(Year,5); FWriteReal(Value,11,2);
            WriteString(" "); Write(Dot);        (* write base line dot *)

            ValuePlot := TRUNC(FLOAT(LineWidth)*(Value - MinValue) /
                                       (MaxValue - MinValue) + 0.5 );
            TabOrFill(ValuePlot + 1, PlotCharacter); WriteLn;
            INC(Year);                            (* Step to next Year *)
         END; (* WHILE *)
      END PlotIt;

   BEGIN (* CalculateFutureValue *)
      EnterData(InitialAmount, AnnualInterest, NumYears);
      PlotIt(InitialAmount, AnnualInterest, NumYears);
   END CalculateFutureValue.
```

Debug and test Check that parameters are passed properly to and from the procedures and that equations are typed correctly. The parameters passed to PlotIt are echoed to the screen, which should help in debugging.

Test with a variety of initial investments and interest rates. A sample run appears as follows

```
What is the inital amount invested?  $ 5000.00

What is the annual PERCENTAGE interest rate? 8.5

For how many years will you invest? 10


Initial Investment =  $      5000.00
Annual percentage interest rate =      8.50


    Year    Value $
     0      5000.00 .$
     1      5443.59 .$$$$
     2      5926.52 .$$$$$$$$
     3      6452.31 .$$$$$$$$$$$$
     4      7024.74 .$$$$$$$$$$$$$$$$
     5      7647.95 .$$$$$$$$$$$$$$$$$$$$$
     6      8326.46 .$$$$$$$$$$$$$$$$$$$$$$$$$$$
     7      9065.15 .$$$$$$$$$$$$$$$$$$$$$$$$$$$$$$$$$
     8      9869.39 .$$$$$$$$$$$$$$$$$$$$$$$$$$$$$$$$$$$$$$$$
     9     10744.97 .$$$$$$$$$$$$$$$$$$$$$$$$$$$$$$$$$$$$$$$$$$$$$$$$$$
    10     11698.23 .$$$$$$$$$$$$$$$$$$$$$$$$$$$$$$$$$$$$$$$$$$$$$$$$$$$$$$$$$$$$$
```

Complete the documentation   The equations and problem description are especially important in the documentation for this problem. A short description of how the PlotIt procedure works would help future programmers who wish to adapt the procedure to plot other functions. In the users' manual state the source code location (CH6E) and caution that the annual interest rate should be entered as a percentage; as 8.5 percent, rather than 0.085, for example.

A Bit of Background

Napier's Bones

Scottish mathematician John Napier, born near Edinburgh in 1550, spent most of his life creating methods and devices to make mathematical calculations easier. One of his early inventions was a set of square rods, made of bone, that were used for multiplying whole numbers. Napier is also credited with the discovery that the weight of any object can be found by balancing the object on a scale against weights of relative size 1, 2, 4, 8, ... His most valuable invention, however, was the natural logarithm, which replaced multiplication and division problems with the addition and subtraction of logarithms. For 25 years beginning in 1590, Napier devoted himself almost entirely to generating tables of logarithms.

The contributions of the logarithmic technique to science and technology are immeasurable. Until the advent of electronic calculators and computers, logarithms were *the* approach to lengthy calculations. The logarithmic slide rule, invented by William Oughtred early in the seventeenth century, was the only reasonably affordable computing tool for engineers, scientists, and students until the mid 1970s.

In most modern, high-level programming languages, including Modula-2, you will find a function, such as ln(x), for calculating logarithms.

Questions 6.4	**1.** In SolveQuadraticEquation (Example 6.4.1) write ''Visible Entities within . . .'' lists for module SolveQuadraticEquation and procedures EnterAndDisplayValues, FindRoots, and CalculateDiscriminant, like those in Figure 6–9.

2. In CalculateFutureValue (Example 6.4.2) write ''Visible Entities within . . .'' lists for module CalculateFutureValue and procedures EnterData, PlotIt, and TabOrFill, like those in Figure 6–9.

3. Suppose you have a *function* Disc(A, B, C,) for the program SolveQuadraticEquation (Example 6.4.1) that returns the value of the Discriminant. What changes would you make in the program commands to use this function instead of the procedure CalculateDiscriminant?

4. In MathLib0, functions *sin(x)* and *cos(x)* return the trigonometric sine and cosine, respectively, of an angle *x*. Write a short procedure to calculate the trigonometric tangent (*tan(x)*) and cotangent (*ctn(x)*) of angle *x,* when, by definition,

$$tan(x) = sin(x)/cos(x) \quad and \quad ctn(x) = cos(x)/sin(x).$$

Angle *x* should be accepted by the procedure as a formal value parameter, and the resulting tangent and cotangent should be handled as formal VARiable parameters.

5. Write a short procedure that accepts minimum and maximum positive REAL values LowestX and HighestX and an increment between them and creates a table of *x, sqrt(x), ln(x),* and *exp(x)* for values between Lowest X and Highest X with the given increment.

6.5   *Defining Your Own Functions*

The value returned by a function may be of any simple type (such as REAL, CHAR, CARDINAL, INTEGER, or BOOLEAN). Now you will learn how to define your own functions.

In Modula-2, function procedure definitions differ from the definitions of normal procedures in two ways:

> *Differences between Function Procedures and Normal Procedures*
>
> 1. The function heading differs from a normal procedure heading in that the type of value to be returned by a function procedure is added to the procedure heading after the parameter list and is preceded by a colon (**:**).
> 2. Values are returned by normal procedures through VAR parameters. In a function procedure, a RETURN ValueExpression command is used to specify a value to be returned.

The general syntax of a function is shown in Figure 6–11.

A formal parameter list, indicated by parentheses, must be included in every function heading and call command. However, if no parameters are passed to the function, the parameter list may be empty, as in

```
PROCEDURE  FunctionName( ) : TypeOfValueToReturn;
```

A user-defined function is invoked in the same manner as any intrinsic function, by using its name wherever a variable or constant value of that type would be used.

Function CardPower

As an example, the following function raises a REAL Base number to a CARDINAL Power by multiplying the Base by itself Power number of times.

Figure 6–11
Syntax of a
Function Procedure

```
PROCEDURE FunctionName( formal parameters ) : TypeOfValueToReturn;
    (* no IMPORT lists allowed *)

    (* declarations of local constants, types, variables, nested
        procedures *)

    BEGIN

       executable commands;

       RETURN ValueExpression;
           (* RETURN ValueExpression must appear at least once. *)
           (* ValueExpression may be any expression that evaluates
               to the appropriate TypeOfValueToReturn. *)
       executable commands;

    END FunctionName;
```

```
PROCEDURE  CardPower(Base : REAL;  Power : CARDINAL) : REAL;
    (* Returns  Base raised to Power.
        FileName: CH6CDPWR       Modula-2      RKW       Mar. 1991 *)
    VAR  Count : CARDINAL;  Result : REAL;

   BEGIN
      Count := 1;   Result := 1.0;
      WHILE  Count <= Power  DO
         Result := Result * Base;
         INC(Count);
      END; (* WHILE *)
      RETURN Result;
   END CardPower;
```

This function would be called by using it wherever a REAL value would appear, such as assigning it to a REAL variable Answer as in

```
Answer := CardPower(RealBase, CrdPower);
```

in an Output command, such as

```
FWriteReal( CardPower(RealBase, CrdPower), 10, 4 );
```

or in an expression, such as

```
Answer := 3.0 * CardPower(RealBase, CrdPower) / 2.0;.
```

The RETURN Statement

When a function is invoked, parameters are accepted as in a normal procedure; and execution transfers to the first executable command after the function's BEGIN statement. At the first encounter with a RETURN command in the function, control returns to the point from which the function was invoked within the calling unit.

If more than one RETURN is specified in a function, control returns to the calling unit when the first RETURN is encountered. For example, you could have a structure such as

```
IF  Condition  THEN
   RETURN  Value1;
ELSE
   RETURN  Value2;
END;  (* IF *)
```

which returns Value1 or Value2 depending upon the Condition. However, good structure encourages you to write units that have a single entry and a single exit point. Thus, functions ideally should have only a single RETURN just before END FunctionName; . The IF . . . THEN . . . ELSE structure above can be written with a single exit by declaring a local variable, such as Result, and then writing

```
IF  Condition  THEN
   Result := Value1;
ELSE
   Result := Value2;
END;  (* IF *)
RETURN Result;
```

The command RETURN (not followed by a ValueExpression) may appear in normal procedures to indicate places where control should return to the calling unit. However, such a RETURN command, other than just before END (where it is implied anyway), would violate the single-exit structure and should be used with caution, if at all.

Function Discriminant
Now the procedure CalculateDiscriminant from Example 6.4.1 can be rewritten as a function. Since its purpose is to calculate and return a single REAL value, that function could appear as

```
PROCEDURE  Disc(ACoef, BCoef, CCoef, : REAL) : REAL;
   BEGIN
      RETURN  BCoef * BCoef − 4.0 * ACoef * CCoef;
   END Disc;
```

Then, instead of calling the procedure with

```
CalculateDiscriminant(A, B, C, Discriminant);
```

you would issue the command

```
Discriminant := Disc(A, B, C);
```

Function Procedure or Normal Procedure?

Here are some suggestions to help you decide when to use a function procedure and when to use a normal procedure.

When to Use a Function Procedure
Use a function procedure when the sole purpose is to calculate and return a value of a simple data type (REAL, CARDINAL, CHAR, INTEGER, or BOOLEAN). A function procedure can perform any operation a normal procedure can perform, including passing values through VAR parameters. However, if you wish to pass more than one value, you should consider using a normal procedure instead.

The rules for scope of identifiers and procedures in Section 6.3 apply to function procedures, which may be nested just as normal procedures.

When to Use a Normal Procedure

Use a normal procedure when the type of quantity to be returned is *not* a simple data type. Arrays, records, and other quantities that represent an organized collection of values are called *structured* data types, and as such may be accessed through formal parameters but may not be RETURNed by a function.

When the major purpose is to perform an action or logically related actions instead of, or in addition to, returning a simple value, a normal procedure is a better choice than a function procedure.

The following example illustrates an appropriate use of a function that returns a CHARacter value as well as some normal procedures.

Example 6.5.1

Reject a batch of machine parts if the average tolerance is greater than 1.0%.

Define the problem A collection of machine parts is measured and compared with the DesignMeasure specified by the manufacturer. The percent Tolerance of each part is defined by the formula

Tolerance = 100.0 * ABS(ActualMeasure − DesignMeasure)/DesignMeasure.

Tolerances will be entered into the computer, the MeanTolerance calculated, and the batch of parts accepted if MeanTolerance is less than 1.0%.

Develop a solution A procedure ReadAndAccumulate(VAR Count:CARDINAL; VAR Sum:REAL); will read the Tolerances, count and add them, and stop when a negative value indicates no more parts. This is appropriately a procedure, rather than a function, since it performs logically related actions and returns more than one value to the program.

A function AcceptOrReject(HowMany:CARDINAL; Total:REAL) : CHAR; calculates the MeanTolerance, where MeanTolerance = Total/HowMany. The function then RETURNs 'A' or 'R' for Accept or Reject, depending upon whether Mean-Tolerance < 1.0 or not. This task is handled appropriately by a function, because its purpose is to RETURN one CHARacter value.

Finally, the program prints a message indicating whether the batch of parts is to be accepted or rejected.

Refine the solution *Pseudocode*

```
module RejectTheParts
    begin
        ReadAndAccumulate(NumOfParts, ToleranceSum)
        WhatToDo = AcceptOrReject(NumOfParts, ToleranceSum)
        if    WhatToDo = 'A'
            print "Accept the parts"
        otherwise
            print "Reject the parts"
        end if
    end RejectTheParts

procedure ReadAndAccumulate(Count, Sum)
    begin
        initialize Count = 0, Sum = 0.0
        ask for and accept the first Tolerance
            insure that first Tolerance >= 0.0
        while  tolerance >= 0.0
```

```
                        increment Count
                        Sum = Sum + Tolerance
                        ask for and accept next Tolerance
                   end while
                 end ReadAndAccumulate

           function AcceptOrReject(HowMany, Total)     (* returns a CHAR value *)
                 begin
                      MeanTolerance = Total / HowMany
                      if MeanTolerance < 1.0
                        AorRChar = 'A'
                      otherwise
                        AorRChar = 'R'
                      end if
                      RETURN AorRChar
                 end AcceptOrReject
```

Modula-2 code

```
MODULE   RejectTheParts;
   (* Rejects a batch of parts unless mean Tolerance < 1.0 %
        FileName:CH6F        Module-2      RKW       Mar. 1991  *)


FROM InOut IMPORT  WriteString, WriteLn;
FROM RealInOut IMPORT ReadReal, FWriteReal;


VAR  WhatToDo:CHAR;    NumOfParts:CARDINAL;    ToleranceSum:REAL;


PROCEDURE  ReadAndAccumulate(VAR Count:CARDINAL;  VAR Sum:REAL);
   (* Reads, counts, and adds Tolerances until negative Tolerance entered *)
   VAR  Tolerance : REAL;

   BEGIN
     Count := 0;   Sum := 0.0;

     WriteString("Enter the first PERCENTAGE Tolerance: ");
      ReadReal(Tolerance); WriteLn;
     WHILE  Tolerance < 0.0  DO
        WriteString("First Tolerance must be >= 0.0.");
         WriteString(" Enter first Tolerance again: ");
         ReadReal(Tolerance); WriteLn;
     END; (* WHILE *)

       WHILE  Tolerance >= 0.0  DO
          INC(Count);
          Sum := Sum + Tolerance;
          WriteString("Enter next Tolerance (Stop with negative value): ");
           ReadReal(Tolerance); WriteLn;
       END; (* WHILE *)
     END ReadAndAccumulate;


  PROCEDURE AcceptOrReject(HowMany:CARDINAL;  Total:REAL) : CHAR;
     (* Calculates mean Tolerance and returns 'A' or 'R' *)
     CONST  ACCEPTLEVEL = 1.0;
     VAR  MeanTolerance : REAL;   AorRChar : CHAR;
```

```
    BEGIN
       MeanTolerance := Total / FLOAT(HowMany);
       IF  MeanTolerance < ACCEPTLEVEL  THEN
          AorRChar := 'A';
       ELSE
          AorRChar := 'R';
       END; (* IF *)
       RETURN  AorRChar;
    END AcceptOrReject;

 BEGIN (* Module RejectTheParts *)
    ReadAndAccumulate(NumOfParts, ToleranceSum); WriteLn;

    WhatToDo := AcceptOrReject(NumOfParts, ToleranceSum);
    IF  WhatToDo = 'A'  THEN
       WriteString("Tolerances are acceptable.  Accept the parts.");
    ELSE
       WriteString("Tolerances are unacceptable.  Reject the parts.");
    END; (* IF *)
    WriteLn;
 END RejectTheParts.
```

Debug and test   Note how the structure of function AcceptOrReject was designed with one final RETURN command. The screen display during a sample run appears as:

```
Enter the first PERCENTAGE tolerance: -1.0
First Tolerance must be >= 0.0. Enter first Tolerance again: 1.0
Enter next Tolerance (Stop with negative value):  0.95
Enter next Tolerance (Stop with negative value):  0.38
Enter next Tolerance (Stop with negative value):  1.21
Enter next Tolerance (Stop with negative value):  -1.0

Tolerances are acceptable.  Accept the parts.
```

For debugging, you may wish to insert appropriate write statements that display the values of NumOfParts, ToleranceSum, MeanTolerance, and WhatToDo.

Complete the documentation   In the problem definition it would be valuable to explain that this code, which finds the average of a list of real numbers, could be modified easily to handle exam scores with a 'P'ass or 'F'ail grade, or any similar problem.

Source code is in file CH6F. The program requires the user to enter at least one non-negative tolerance.

Questions 6.5

1. A formula to raise REAL base *a* to REAL power *b* is

```
a^b = exp(b * ln(a))
```

where exp and ln are imported from MathLib0, *a* must be positive, and *b* must be positive or zero. Write a function procedure that accepts REAL *a* and *b* values and returns a^b.

2. Change the function AcceptOrReject in module RejectTheParts (Example 6.5.1) so that it returns BOOLEAN value TRUE if MeanTolerance < 1.0 and FALSE otherwise. Rewrite the module commands, which invoke the function and display the results, to handle the change.

3. a. What does the following function do?

```
PROCEDURE   UnCap(Letter : CHAR) : CHAR;
   BEGIN
      IF  (Letter >= 'A') AND (Letter <= 'Z')  THEN
         RETURN  CHR( ORD(Letter) - ORD('A') + ORD('a') );
      ELSE
         RETURN  Letter;
      END; (* IF *)
   END UnCap;
```

b. Rewrite the function UnCap in part a so that there is only one exit point; that is, only one RETURN just before END UnCap.

4. For each of the following tasks, would it be more appropriate to write a normal procedure or a function procedure? Why?

	Input Parameters	Procedure Task
a.	x and y	Calculate and supply to the program the value of $2x + 3y$.
b.	x and y	Calculate and supply to the program the values of $2x + 3y$ and $3x + 2y$.
c.	none	Read a list of characters and print them in alphabetical order.
d.	none	Find and supply to the program the 10th letter of the alphabet.
e.	HowManyNums SumOfNums SumSqOfNums	Calculate $\text{Mean} = \text{SumOfNums}/\text{HowManyNums}$ $\text{Variance} = (\text{SumSqOfNums} - \text{HowManyNums} * \text{Mean}^2)/(\text{HowManyNums} - 1)$ $\text{StdDev} = \text{sqrt(Variance)}$ Return only StdDev to the program.
f.	HowManyNums SumOfNums SumSqOfNums	Calculate Mean, Variance, StdDev (as in 4e above), and supply all three values to the program.
g.	none	Print the message "Your input is unacceptable. Try again."

6.6 *Local Modules*

(Optional section; may be omitted or covered later without loss of continuity.)

The rules of scope regarding procedures help prevent most side effects, but they do not guarantee absolute protection if global variables or VARiable formal parameters are used carelessly.

Closed Scope

Modula-2 can provide added protection from unwanted side effects. That protection is achieved by enclosing procedures and commands within a **local module.** A local module is said to have **closed scope.** No entities are passed across the module boundaries unless they are imported or exported intentionally.

Local modules may be nested within each other or within procedures. Procedures may be nested within local modules. The unit in which a module is declared is called a **client.** Here are additional rules of scope for identifiers and local modules.

Rules of Scope for Identifiers and Local Modules

1. Entities declared *outside* of a given local module are visible *within* the module only if they are IMPORTed explicitly by the module.
2. Entities declared *within* a given local module are visible *outside* the module only if they are EXPORTed explicitly by the module.
3. Memory locations for local identifiers and parameters in a procedure are established when the procedure is called; the memory is released and the entities vanish when execution of the procedure ends. Memory is allocated for the entities in a module as soon as the surrounding client is created, and the memory is not released until the client vanishes.

Therefore, except in the rare situation when a local module might be nested within a procedure, entities within a local module remain available for repeated use whenever the program reenters the local module.

☐ Local Module Syntax

The syntax of a local module is shown in Figure 6–12. The

```
BEGIN
    executable commands;
    . . .
```

part of the local module is optional. These commands, if present, are executed whenever the program invokes a local module (such as calling a procedure from the module). The commands often are used for assigning initial values to variables.

☐ Importing and Exporting

Features of importing into and exporting from a local module are outlined in Figure 6–13. As shown there, entities that are imported into a local module first must be imported in a client module. If the client imports the entire external module, such as

```
IMPORT InOut;
```

then the local module may import and use individual entities from the module, such as

```
FROM InOut IMPORT WriteLn;
```

If the client imports individual entities from the external module, such as

```
FROM MathLib0 IMPORT sqrt;
```

then the local module may import and use that entity by name, such as

```
IMPORT sqrt;
```

If no ambiguity is likely to occur, then entities may be exported from the local module to be used without qualification by the client, such as are PI, cLight, PROCA, and PROCB in Figure 6–13. *Only one EXPORT list is allowed in a* module, however, and it must follow the import lists directly. If even one entity

Figure 6–12
Syntax of a Local
Module

```
MODULE LocalModuleName;

    IMPORT lists;
       (* This optional feature must be present if there are
          entities used by this module that, in turn, must be
          imported from other modules. *)
       (* These may take the form
               IMPORT ModuleName; or
               FROM ModuleName IMPORT ListOfIdentifiers;
                   where ListOfIdentifiers may contain names of
                   variables, procedures, local modules, or any
                   entity exportable from the specified module. *)

    EXPORT list;
       (* This optional feature must be present if this is a local
          module, and there are entities in this module that are
          to be made available to the client block that contains
          this module. *)
       (* This may take the form
               EXPORT list;
                   for items exported where there will be no
                   duplication of identifiers in the client, or
               EXPORT QUALIFIED list;
                   for items that should be qualified in the
                   client by a prefix consisting of this
                   LocalModuleName.  *)

    (* Declarations and Definitions of Entities in this Module;
       e.g.,Constants, Types, Variables, Procedures, Local
       Modules *)

    BEGIN

       executable commands;

          (* BEGIN executable statements; are required in a main
             program module, but are optional in other modules
             and often are used to initialize variables each time
             the module is invoked.  *)

    END LocalModuleName;

          (* END LocalModuleName will be terminated by a period
             if this is a main program module or an independent,
             external module.  *)
```

needs to be qualified to avoid ambiguity in the client, then all entities will have to
be exported through EXPORT QUALIFIED, and all must be used in qualified form

```
ModuleName.EntityName
```

in the client.

Even if entities are not QUALIFIED on export, programmers may qualify them
in the client module if they choose to do so. Some programmers like to qualify all
entities exported from local modules so that the origin of those entities is explicit.

Figure 6–13
Importing and
Exporting in Local
Module "Science"

```
MODULE  ClientName;
    FROM  MathLib0  IMPORT  sqrt;
    IMPORT InOut;
        ...

    VAR  p, q, r, s, e : REAL;

    MODULE Science;
        FROM InOut IMPORT WriteString, WriteLn;
        IMPORT  sqrt;
        IMPORT  p, q;
        EXPORT PI, cLight, PROCA, PROCB;

        CONST  PI = 3.14159;
        VAR  cLight, e : REAL;

        PROCEDURE  PROCA ...
          BEGIN
              ...
            WriteString("..."); WriteLn;
              ...
          END PROCA;

        PROCEDURE  PROCB. . .
          BEGIN
              ...
            ... := sqrt(p);
            ... := 3.5 * q;
              ...
          END PROCB;

    BEGIN (* optional in a local module *)
        executable commands;
          ...
    END Science;

    BEGIN (* Module ClientName *)
      InOut.WriteString("This is a test.");
        ...
      PROCA...
        ...
      r := PI * sqrt(2.0);
        ...
      PROCB...
        ...
      s := cLight * cLight;
        ...
      Inout.WriteLn;
        ...
    END ClientName.
```

Suppose, for example, that it had been necessary to export the variable *e* from local module Science in Figure 6–13. *e* is defined already as a different variable in the client module. Therefore, the export list in Science would have to appear as

```
EXPORT QUALIFIED e, PI, cLight, PROCA, PROCB
```

and every occurrence of these entities in the client module would have to appear in qualified form as Science.e, Science.PI, Science.cLight, Science.PROCA, or Science.PROCB.

As a working illustration of local modules, consider again the SolveQuadraticEquation code from Example 6.4.2. In the following version, the procedures have been enclosed within local modules. To show the EXPORT feature, the commands to display the roots have been moved to the main module. Study the local module structures and IMPORT and EXPORT lists carefully. Although procedure name EnterAndDisplayValues is not ambiguous, it was decided to qualify it in order to demonstrate EXPORT QUALIFIED. Also observe the statements

```
BEGIN
    Multiplier := 4.0;
```

in MODULE RootFinder, which show how optional initialization commands may be included within a module.

```
MODULE  SolveQuadraticEquation;
   (* LOCAL MODULES VERSION: Find the roots of the quadratic equation.
      FileName:CH6G       Modula-2       RKW       Mar. 1991  *)
FROM InOut IMPORT WriteString, WriteLn;
FROM RealInOut IMPORT FWriteReal, ReadReal;
FROM MathLib0 IMPORT sqrt;
VAR  a, b, c : REAL;

   MODULE  DataEnterer;
      IMPORT WriteString, WriteLn, ReadReal, FWriteReal;
      EXPORT QUALIFIED EnterAndDisplayValues;

      PROCEDURE  EnterAndDisplayValues(VAR A, B, C : REAL);
         BEGIN
            WriteString("What are the quadratic equation coefficients? ");
            WriteLn; WriteString(" a = "); ReadReal(A);
            WriteLn; WriteString(" b = "); ReadReal(B);
            WriteLn; WriteString(" c = "); ReadReal(C); WriteLn; WriteLn;
           WriteString("The equation is: ");
            FWriteReal(A,8,2); WriteString(" x^2  +  ");
            FWriteReal(B,8,2); WriteString(" x  +  ");
            FWriteReal(C,8,2); WriteString("  =  0.00"); WriteLn; WriteLn;
         END EnterAndDisplayValues;
   END DataEnterer; (* local module *)

   MODULE  RootFinder;
      IMPORT sqrt;
      EXPORT Discriminant,Root1,Root2,RealRootPart,ImagRootPart,FindRoots;
      VAR Discriminant,Root1,Root2,RealRootPart,ImagRootPart,Multiplier:REAL;

      PROCEDURE  FindRoots(A, B, C : REAL);
```

```
              PROCEDURE  Disc(ACoef, BCoef, CCoef : REAL) : REAL;
                  BEGIN
                      RETURN  BCoef * BCoef  -  Multiplier * ACoef * CCoef;
                  END  Disc;

          BEGIN (* FindRoots *)
              Discriminant := Disc(A, B, C);
              IF  Discriminant >= 0.0  THEN
                  Root1 := -B/(2.0*A) + sqrt(Discriminant)/(2.0*A);
                  Root2 := -B/(2.0*A) - sqrt(Discriminant)/(2.0*A);
              ELSE
                  RealRootPart := -B/(2.0*A);
                  ImagRootPart := sqrt(-Discriminant)/(2.0*A);
              END; (* IF *)
          END FindRoots;

      BEGIN   (* RootFinder -> Initialize Multiplier *)
          Multiplier := 4.0;
      END  RootFinder;   (* local module *)

    BEGIN (* SolveQuadraticEquation *)
        DataEnterer.EnterAndDisplayValues(a, b, c);
        FindRoots(a, b, c);
         IF  Discriminant >= 0.0  THEN
            WriteString("The real roots are "); WriteLn;
             FWriteReal(Root1,8,2); WriteString(" and "); FWriteReal(Root2,8,2);
        ELSE
            WriteString("The complex roots are "); WriteLn;
            FWriteReal(RealRootPart,8,2); WriteString("  + ");
            FWriteReal(ImagRootPart,8,2); WriteString(" i   and"); WriteLn;
            FWriteReal(RealRootPart,8,2); WriteString("  - ");
            FWriteReal(ImagRootPart,8,2); WriteString(" i");
        END; (* IF *)
      WriteLn; WriteLn;
    END SolveQuadraticEquation.
```

Run the program to convince yourself that it produces the same results as the earlier version.

Questions 6.6

1. In program SolveQuadraticEquation (FileName:CH6G) of this section, which variables, procedures, and functions are visible in
   a. main module SolveQuadraticEquation
   b. local module DataEnterer
   c. local module RootFinder
   d. function Disc?
2. Supply IMPORT and EXPORT lists to make the following program display the message,

A dozen eggs is 12
But a baker's dozen is 13

```
MODULE WhatsADozen;
   CONST Dozen = 12;

MODULE TheStory;
   PROCEDURE TalkItOut(EggsADozen:CARDINAL);
      BEGIN
         WriteString("A dozen eggs is"); WriteCard(EggsADozen,4); WriteLn;
      END TalkItOut;
END TheStory;

MODULE RestOfTheStory;
   VAR BakerDozen : CARDINAL;
   PROCEDURE TalkItOut(RegularDozen:CARDINAL);
      BEGIN
         BakerDozen:=RegularDozen+1; WriteString("But a baker's dozen is");
      END TalkItOut;
END RestOfTheStory;

BEGIN  (* WhatsADozen *)
   TheStory.TalkItOut(Dozen); TalkItOut(Dozen);
   WriteCard(BakerDozen,4); WriteLn;
END WhatsADozen.
```

6.7 *Focus on Problem Solving*

Many of the programs you have written so far have been short enough that the entire code could be written and debugged at once. With programs of increasing length, however, it becomes more difficult to understand long sections of code. An advantage of top-down design is that the general structure of the program can be written as a sequence of procedure calls, and you can concentrate on implementing, testing, and debugging one subtask at a time.

The Driver

To test a procedure by itself, embed it within a program with the fewest commands absolutely necessary to provide values for the parameters and to display the values of the VARiable parameters after the procedure has executed. Such a test program is called a **driver** program.

This pseudocode illustrates the important components of a generic program.

DECLARE
  - Import the Read, Write, and function calls you need.
  - Define variables to match each of the parameters in the procedure heading. Give the variables names that are slightly different from the formal parameters.
  - Include the procedure declaration and definition.

BEGIN
  - Assign or read values to be passed to formal value and/or VARiable parameters.
  - Call the procedure.
  - Write the values of the variables corresponding to the formal VARiable parameters.
END

In Modula-2, a driver would have the form shown in Figure 6–14, and Example 6.7.1 illustrates the use of a driver program.

Figure 6–14
A Modula-2 Driver
Program

```
MODULE ProcedureDriver;
    (* Generic Driver Program-Edit to test a specific procedure. *)

FROM InOut IMPORT WriteString, WriteLn (* and others as needed *);
(* IMPORT from other modules as needed *)

(* CONST Declare constants you wish to pass to the procedure. *)
(* TYPE  Declare any special types needed by the procedure.   *)
(* VAR   Declare variables to match all parameters in the
          procedure heading.   Modify names slightly.          *)

(* Include the PROCEDURE declaration and definition here. *)

BEGIN
    (* Assign or Read values to be passed to formal value and/or
        VARiable parameters. *)

    (* Call the Procedure *)

    (* Display values of all VARiable parameters from the
        procedure.   *)
END ProcedureDriver.
```

Example 6.7.1

Sum and SumSq were calculated in Example 6.3.1. Write and test a procedure to find Sum^2 and the difference between Sum^2 and SumSq.

Define the problem   Assume that you have written this procedure:

```
PROCEDURE CompareSumAndSq(SUM,SUMSQ:REAL;
                            VAR SquareOfSum, Difference:REAL);
    BEGIN
        SquareOfSum := SUM * SUM;
        Difference := ABS(SquareOfSum  -  SUMSQ);
    END CompareSumAndSq;
```

which is to be tested with a driver program and then added to Example 6.3.1.

Develop and refine the solution   The pseudocode for a testing driver program could appear as follows:

declare variables corresponding to SUM, SUMSQ, Difference, SquareOfSum
define procedure CompareSumAndSq
begin
    ask for values to be passed to SUM and SUMSQ
    call CompareSumAndSq
    display value of SquareOfSum and Difference
end

Modula-2 code

```
MODULE DriveCompare;
    (* Driver program to test procedure CompareSumAndSq.
        FileName:CH6H     Modula-2     RKW      Mar. 1991 *)
```

```
FROM InOut IMPORT WriteString, WriteLn;
FROM RealInOut IMPORT ReadReal, FWriteReal;

VAR SUM0, SUMSQ0, SquareOfSum0, Difference0 : REAL;

PROCEDURE CompareSumAndSq(SUM,SUMSQ:REAL; VAR SquareOfSum,Difference:REAL);
   BEGIN
      SquareOfSum := SUM * SUM;
      Difference := ABS(SquareOfSum  -  SUMSQ);
   END CompareSumAndSq;

BEGIN (* DriveCompare *)
   WriteString("Enter value for SUM  : "); ReadReal(SUM0);   WriteLn;
   WriteString("Enter value for SUMSQ: "); ReadReal(SUMSQ0); WriteLn;

   CompareSumAndSq(SUM0, SUMSQ0, SquareOfSum0, Difference0);

   WriteLn;
   WriteString("The square of the Sum and the difference are");
    FWriteReal(SquareOfSum0,12,4); FWriteReal(Difference0,12,4);
   WriteLn;
END DriveCompare.
```

Debug and test Run it and see what happens. Variables in the driver module have been given slightly different names from the formal parameters to make certain they are not used accidentally within the procedure as global variables.

Complete the documentation Collect pseudocode, code, and a sample run. The users' manual would be the content of this section, describing the purpose and implementation of a driver program.

☐ Stubs

Suppose now that you wish to write a new program to handle your company's payroll. It is not unusual to feel overwhelmed by the magnitude of a task such as this. The first step you take is to define the problem by consulting with the payroll office. You discover that your program needs to accomplish these things:

- Data is entered.
  Today's date, employee's last name, and number of hours worked this week will be entered from the keyboard.
- The pay is calculated.
  For 40 hours per week or fewer, the payrate is $8.00 per hour. For hours beyond 40 per week, the payrate is $12.00 per hour.
- Taxes take exactly 30% of everybody's pay.
  The only other deduction is $15 per week for insurance benefits (or 20% of total pay if the total pay is less than $75.00).
- A pay check is printed. Checks are written weekly.
- A report is generated for the employee and the accountants.
  The report must show the employee's name, hours worked, total pay, tax and insurance deductions, and net pay.

These tasks begin a top-down approach to the solution, which you write as pseudocode in the form

```
begin
   EnterData
   CalculatePay
   PrintCheck
   GenerateReport
end
```

Although the logic here is simpler than most problems would require, you would like to test it without all the details of the procedures. So you write this code:

```
MODULE Payroll;
   (* Payroll program with minimal stub procedures
      FileName:CH6J     Modula-2     RKW        Mar. 1991  *)

FROM InOut IMPORT WriteString, WriteLn;

PROCEDURE EnterData;
   BEGIN
      WriteString("You have entered procedure EnterData"); WriteLn;
   END EnterData;

PROCEDURE CalculatePay;
   BEGIN
      WriteString("You have entered procedure CalculatePay"); WriteLn;
   END CalculatePay;

PROCEDURE PrintCheck;
   BEGIN
      WriteString("You have entered procedure PrintCheck"); WriteLn;
   END PrintCheck;

PROCEDURE GenerateReport;
   BEGIN
      WriteString("You have entered procedure GenerateReport"); WriteLn;
   END GenerateReport;

BEGIN (* Payroll *)
   EnterData;
   CalculatePay;
   PrintCheck;
   GenerateReport;
END Payroll.
```

The four procedures declared and called in this module are referred to as **stub procedures.** In its minimal form a stub procedure simply prints a message stating that the procedure has been called. If you execute the program above you will see only an abbreviated stub of each procedure:

```
You have entered procedure EnterData
You have entered procedure CalculatePay
You have entered procedure PrintCheck
You have entered procedure GenerateReport
```

Although in its shortest form a stub procedure simply indicates that the procedure has been entered, as your solution develops you will decide which parameters each

Figure 6–15
A Modula-2 Stub
Procedure

```
PROCEDURE  StubProcedureName(* list of formal parameters *);
   (* Generic Stub Procedure - Edit as necessary. *)

   (* VAR  Declare local DummyVariable(s) as needed. *)

   BEGIN
      WritrString("You have entered procedure StubProcedureName");
      WriteLn;

      (* Display values of formal value parameters. *)
      (* Set temporary values for VARiable parameters. *)
      (* Display temporary values for VARiable parameters. *)

      (* If a function, assign a Value to DummyVariable to be
         returned.
         Display DummyVariable to be returned.
         RETURN DummyVariable *)
   END StubProcedureName;
```

procedure needs. Then it becomes important to include commands in the stub to display value parameters and/or to set dummy values of VARiable parameters that can be displayed by the program after exiting the stub procedure.

In a more complete form, Modula-2 code for a generic stub procedure is shown in Figure 6–15.

☐ Bottom–Up Development

Part of the process just described — that of writing procedures first, testing them with drivers, then building a working module around them — is called **bottom-up development.** Bottom-up development should be used only in conjunction with the top-down design of a problem solution.

In practice, both bottom-up and top-down designs are used. For example, it is not unusual to start with a short code that does something, then start to make it more general, and then begin to discover what the top-down design should be. At each step the program should be kept well structured and well commented, so that when you resume work on it after an absence you will know exactly what you have accomplished so far. In fact, individual members of program development teams are sometimes assigned tasks of writing specific procedures without knowing what the overall top-down design is. Obviously, they are expected to test their procedures with driver programs.

Suppose you decide now to continue the development of your Payroll problem from the bottom up, by first writing the details of procedure CalculatePay. You determine that the parameters and processes needed in that procedure are described by this pseudocode:

```
PROCEDURE CalculatePay(Hrs: REAL; VAR Pay,Tax,Insure,Net:REAL);
     begin
          if Hours <= 40.0
            Pay = Hours * 8.00
          otherwise
            Pay = 40.0 * 8.00 + (Hours − 40.0) * 12.00
          end if
          Tax = 0.30 * Pay
```

```
                      if Pay >= 75.00
                         Insure = 15.00
                      otherwise
                         Insure = 0.20 * Pay
                      end if
                      Net = Pay - Tax - Insure
                   end CalculatePay
```

Now, to test the procedure CalculatePay, you include driver commands in the program to ask for Hours worked and to display Pay, Tax, Insure, and Net. The following code illustrates this step.

```
MODULE Payroll;
   (* Payroll program with driver commands to test CalculatePay and
      minimal stub procedures for EnterData, PrintCheck, GenerateReport.
      FileName:CH6K        Modula-2        RKW         Mar. 1991  *)

FROM InOut IMPORT WriteString, WriteLn;
FROM RealInOut IMPORT ReadReal, FWriteReal;

VAR  Hours, TotalPay, Taxes, Insurance, NetPay : REAL;

PROCEDURE EnterData;
   BEGIN
      WriteString("You have entered procedure EnterData"); WriteLn;
   END EnterData;

   PROCEDURE CalculatePay(Hrs:REAL; VAR Pay, Tax, Insure, Net : REAL);
      CONST  PAYRATE=8.00; OVERTIMERATE=12.00; REGULARHRS=40.0; TAXRATE=0.30;
             FLATINSURE=15.00; INSURERATE=0.20; INSURECUTOFF=75.00;
      BEGIN
         IF  Hrs > REGULARHRS  THEN
            Pay := REGULARHRS * PAYRATE + (Hrs-REGULARHRS) * OVERTIMERATE;
         ELSE
            Pay := Hrs * PAYRATE;
         END; (* IF *)
         Tax := TAXRATE * Pay;
         IF  Pay >= INSURECUTOFF  THEN
            Insure := FLATINSURE;
         ELSE
            Insure := INSURERATE * Pay;
         END; (* IF *)
         Net := Pay - Tax - Insure;
      END CalculatePay;

PROCEDURE PrintCheck;
   BEGIN
      WriteString("You have entered procedure PrintCheck"); WriteLn;
   END PrintCheck;

PROCEDURE GenerateReport;
   BEGIN
      WriteString("You have entered procedure GenerateReport"); WriteLn;
   END GenerateReport;

BEGIN (* Payroll *)
   EnterData;
```

```
   WriteString("Enter Hours worked for CalculatePay procedure: ");
    ReadReal(Hours); WriteLn;
   CalculatePay(Hours, TotalPay, Taxes, Insurance, NetPay); WriteLn;
   WriteString("After executing CalculatePay"); WriteLn;
    WriteString("Total Pay = $"); FWriteReal(TotalPay,6,2); WriteLn;
    WriteString("Taxes     = $"); FWriteReal(Taxes,6,2); WriteLn;
    WriteString("Insurance = $"); FWriteReal(Insurance,6,2); WriteLn;
    WriteString("Net Pay   = $"); FWriteReal(NetPay,6,2); WriteLn; WriteLn;

   PrintCheck;
   GenerateReport;
END Payroll.
```

When 48.5 is entered for hours worked, you should see

```
You have entered procedure EnterData
Enter Hours worked for CalculatePay procedure: 48.5

After executing CalculatePay
Total Pay = $ 422.00
Taxes     = $ 126.60
Insurance = $  15.00
Net Pay   = $ 280.40

You have entered procedure PrintCheck
You have entered procedure GenerateReport
```

Now you can complete the job by replacing the other stub procedures one at a time. Your first replacements still may be stubs that test the parameters you decide need to be passed, such as

```
PROCEDURE PrintCheck(NetPay : REAL);   (* still a stub *)
   BEGIN
       WriteString("You have entered procedure PrintCheck");
WriteLn;
       WriteString("The value of parameter NetPay =");
        FWriteReal(NetPay, 8, 2); WriteLn;
   END PrintCheck;
```

Finally, each stub is replaced by the fully developed procedure and tested separately, and the completed program emerges. (See Exercise 15 at the end of the chapter.)

Questions 6.7

1. A procedure is defined by the code

```
PROCEDURE  FractionToDecimal(Top, Bottom : CARDINAL;
                            VAR Result, Inverse : REAL);
   BEGIN
      Result := FLOAT(Top) / FLOAT(Bottom);
      Inverse := 1.0 / Result;
   END FractionToDecimal;
```

Write the shortest driver program module you can to test this procedure and check the passing of parameters.

2. A FractionHandler program contains this menu:

```
A    Add two fractions
C    Convert a fraction to decimal
M    Multiply two fractions
Q    Quit
```

a. Write pseudocode for the program.

b. Write Modula-2 code for the program with stub procedures for the 4 choices.

c. Insert procedure FractionToDecimal from question 1 into the code with appropriate commands to pass and display the parameters.

3. Pseudocode to calculate the net income from an athletic event is

Determine ticket sales
Find refreshment revenues
Calculate expenses
 for facilities
 for employees
Calculate net income

a. Write a module to test this design with stub procedures for the operations.

b. If

NetIncome = TicketSales + RefreshmentRevenues − FacilitiesExpenses − EmployeeExpenses,

begin the bottom-up development of the solution by writing the procedure CalculateIncome, which computes the NetIncome. Include this procedure in your test module, along with appropriate driver commands.

6.8 *Summary*

Procedures   Procedures are independent units that define subtasks in a code. Procedure syntax looks like module syntax, except that (1) a procedure heading begins with *PROCEDURE* (instead of *MODULE*) and contains a parameter list, (2) no IMPORT lists are allowed within procedures, and (3) END ProcedureName is followed by a semicolon rather than a period.

Flow of Execution   A procedure is invoked by using its name. Program control transfers to the first command following BEGIN in the procedure. When END ProcedureName; is reached, program flow continues from the program command that invoked the procedure.

Actual and Formal Parameters   The parameters specified in the procedure call command are identical to the identifiers in the calling unit and are called *actual* parameters. The parameters in the procedure heading are called *formal* parameters. The number, order, and type of actual parameters must agree with the formal parameters but do not need to have the same identifying names.

Parameters and Local Variables   When a procedure is invoked it reserves separate memory locations for its parameters and any constants and variables declared within the procedure. These are *local* entities, and the reserved memory is released when execution of the procedure terminates. Formal *value* parameters are called ''In Only'' because the procedure receives a copy, but does not change the value, of the corresponding actual parameter. Formal *VARiable* parameters are called ''In/Out'' because the formal parameter name points to (becomes an alias for) the actual parameter, and any changes to one affect the other.

Side Effects and Scope   Modula-2 has strict rules that govern the *scope* of identifiers. Generally, an identifier is *visible* within all procedures that are declared in the unit where the identifier is declared. However, a local identifier or formal value parameter is not visible outside of the procedure where it is declared. The rules of scope help the programmer to avoid such unwanted *side effects* as unintentional value changes.

Functions   Functions are specially defined procedures whose major purpose is to return a single, simple value to the calling unit. *Intrinsic* functions built into

Modula-2 are listed in Appendix A, and some additional standard mathematical functions are found in module *Mathlib0* (Appendix B). A function is called by using its name in place of a variable of the type of value it returns. When you write your own functions, function headings look like procedure headings followed by the data type of the value to be returned. A RETURN ValueExpression; command must appear at least once within the function. This RETURNs the value of ValueExpression to the calling command and transfers control back to the calling unit.

Local Modules Modules can be declared and defined locally within a program module. One major purpose of a *local module* is to protect your program from side effects. A local module acts as if it has a wall around it; no entities are passed across its boundaries unless they are imported or exported explicitly.

Drivers and Stubs The minimal amount of executable code required to test a procedure is called a *driver* program. A driver must handle IMPORT commands, define variables, include the procedure to be tested, assign values, call the procedure, and display values after procedure execution. The minimal procedures needed to test the logic of the program that calls them are called *stub* procedures. A stub procedure should declare parameters and local variables, indicate that the procedure has been called, assign values to VARiable parameters and local variables, and display values of parameters and variables.

Bottom-up Design *Bottom-up* design allows you to write individual procedures and test them using driver programs. *Top-down* design allows you to develop your program logic, and test the structure using stubs. Top-down design, bottom-up design, driver programs, and stub procedures are very powerful tools that enable you to begin with a concept of a problem solution and then build and test code for one subtask at a time.

6.9 *Exercises*

Exercises marked with (FileName:_____) indicate those that ask you to use, modify, or extend the text examples. The numbers in brackets, [ ], indicate the chapter section that contains the material you need for completing the exercise.

1. [6.2] Write a program that asks for a number of Cups of liquid to be used in a recipe. The number of Cups is passed to a procedure that converts it to Tablespoons and Milliliters. (One cup is equal to 16 tablespoons and to 236.58 milliliters).

2. [6.2]
   a. Write and test a procedure MakeMilesKmTable to display a table of Miles converted to Kilometers, given the limits LowMiles and HighMiles and the increment between Miles values.
   b. Have your program call MakeMilesKmTable twice, first with output directed to the screen and again with output directed to a file. Add a parameterless procedure to print the table heading.
   c. Modify the code in MakeMilesKmTable so that two columns are printed. For example, if the limits where LowMiles = 1 to HighMiles = 20, and the increment were 1, the display might look like

```
    Miles = Kilometers  Miles = Kilometers
      1         1.61      11        17.70
      2         3.22      12        19.31
    .  .        .  .    .  .        .  .
    .  .        .  .    .  .        .  .
     10        16.09      20        32.18
```

Hint: Find Split = (HighMiles + LowMiles) DIV 2, let the loop execute from Miles = LowMiles to Split, and calculate and print across one line the values of Miles and Kilometers for Miles and for (Miles − LowMiles + Split + 1).

3. [6.3] (FileName:CH6C)
   a. Add a feature to the FindSums program of Example 6.3.1 to prevent the user from trying to read more numbers than there are in the input file. Assume either
      (1) that the length of the input file is already known and is declared as a constant in the program, or
      (2) that the first number in the input file is not statistical data, but rather the number of statistical data in the file.
   b. Write a users' manual and collect complete documentation for your modified program.

4. [6.3] (FileName:CH6C) Add to FindSums (Example 6.3.1) a procedure CalcStats that accepts the values of HowMany, Sum, SumSq, and Average from the program and calculates

   Variance = (SumSq − HowMany $*$ Average^2)/(HowMany − 1)

   and

   StdDev = sqrt(Variance)

   Have the main program module display the values of HowMany, Sum, SumSq, Average, Variance, and StdDev.

5. [6.3] The height h (meters) and speed v(meters/sec) of an object thrown vertically upward with initial speed $v0$ and gravitational acceleration g (meters/sec^2) are given by

   h = v0 $*$ t − 0.5 $*$ g $*$ t $*$ t   and   v = v0 − g $*$ t.

   Write, test, and document a procedure that accepts $v0$, g, and t from a calling module, and then calculates and makes h and v available to be printed by the main module. Have your program compare h and v for given $v0$ and t on

   ```
   the moon, where g =   1.67 meters/sec²
      Earth, where g =   9.81 meters/sec²
   Jupiter, where g =  25.9  meters/sec².
   ```

6. [6.4] (FileName:CH6D) To the SolveQuadraticEquation program (Example 6.4.1) add the capability of handling the situation where $a = 0$. *Hint:* When $a = 0$, the equation becomes $bx + c = 0$, which has only one root, namely $x = -c/b$. Consider the situations in which $b = 0$ and in which $b <> 0$.

7. [6.5] Heron's formula for the area A of a triangle with sides of lengths a, b, and c is $A = $ sqrt$[s(s − a)(s − b)(s − c)]$, where $s = (a + b + c)/2$. Write, test, and document a function that accepts the values of a, b, and c as value parameters from a calling module, then calculates the values of s and $s(s − a)(s − b)(s − c)$. If $s(s − a)(s − b)(s − c)$ is positive, the procedure calculates A. If $s(s − a)(s − b)(s − c)$ is negative, a, b, and c do not form a triangle, and the procedure sets $A = -1.0$. The value of A is returned by the function, and the program either prints the area or indicates that a, b, and c cannot form a triangle.

8. [6.5] Write a function to find secant$(x) = 1.0 / cos(x)$, where cos is imported from module MathLib0. Write a program that creates a table of secant(*Angle*) for Angles in degrees. *Note:* the parameter x accepted by cos(x) must be in radians. For the table, let *Angle* range between 0 and 89.9 degrees, calculate x radians = *Angle* $*$ PI / 180.0, then cos(x), then secant (x). PI = 3.14159 approximately.

9. [6.5] Function ln*(x)* from module MathLib0 returns logarithms to base *e* (*e* = 2.72828 approximately). Log10*(x)* (logarithm to base 10) is given by the formula log10*(x)* = ln*(x)*/ ln(10.0).
   a. Write a procedure that returns log10*(x)*, given any value *x* > 0.0.
   b. Log*b(x)* (logarithm to base *b*) is given by the formula log*b(x)* = ln*(x)*/ln*(b)*. Write a procedure that returns log*b(x)*, given any values *b* > 0.0 and *x* > 0.0.

10. [6.5] Write and test a function that accepts a character and a distance *n*, then returns the character whose code is *n* units away from the code of the original character. Use INC if *n* is positive and DEC if *n* is negative. Have the function return only printable characters or the Bell character when the character is not printable. For example, passing the character 'F' and distance −3 to the function would return the character 'C'.

11. [6.5] Write and test a function, called ROUND, that accepts any REAL number *x* and returns the closest integer. *Hint:* Use TRUNC and consider positive and negative values of *x* separately.

12. [6.5] (FileName:CH6F) Modify program RejectTheParts (Example 6.5.1) so that it accepts percentage exam scores for a student, the function returns 'P' or 'F' depending upon whether the average of the scores is >= 60% or not, and the program displays a message indicating whether the student passed or failed.

13. [6.5] Figure 6−16 shows a mass *m* kilograms oscillating on a spring. The displacement *y* meters of the object from its equilibrium position is given by the formula

$$y = A * \exp(-bt/2m) * \cos(wt),$$

where *A* = initial displacement at time *t* = 0 seconds, *b* = friction damping coefficient, *w* = angular frequency of oscillation = sqrt(*k*/*m* − (*b*/2*m*)²), and *k* = the spring constant. In a typical physical situation *A* < 1.0 meter, *m* < 5.0 kilograms, *k* < 5.0 newtons per meter, and *b* < 0.5.
   a. Write a function that returns the value of *y*, given *A*, *b*, *m*, *k*, and *t*.
   b. Write a program incorporating the function from part a and the PlotIt and TabOrFill procedures (adapted from Examples 5.5.1 and 6.4.2) to produce a graph of the position *y* of the oscillating mass as a function of time. *Hint:* *Y*Max = approximately *A*, and *Y*Min = approximately −*A*.

14. [6.7] Complete the FractionHandler program of Question 2 at the end of Section 6.7 by replacing the stub procedures with procedures that perform appropriate operations.

15. [6.7] (FileName:CH6K) Write and test procedures EnterData, PrintCheck, and GenerateReport to complete the Payroll task in Section 6.7. Test and document the entire Payroll package. All of the information shown in Figure 6−17 should

Figure 6−16
A Mass on a Spring
(Exercise 13)

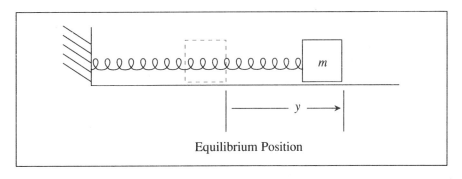

Equilibrium Position

Figure 6–17
Sample Pay Check
(Exercise 15)

```
 ┌─────────────────────────────────────────────────────────┐
 │ Zzyzx Corp.                                       10399   │
 │ 1164 Sunrise Avenue           Date: January 19, 1995     │
 │ Kalispell, Montana                                       │
 │                                                          │
 │ Pay to the Order of  James Dobinson      $      462.50   │
 │                                                          │
 │ UnderSecurity Bank                                       │
 │ Missoula, Mt                                             │
 │                                                          │
 │   680019   15643   72   10399      Authorized Signature  │
 └─────────────────────────────────────────────────────────┘
```

be printed on a blank check form. Print only the check number in the upper right corner and the bank name and account number in the lower left corner. The reports should be in a form that anybody can read and understand. (Do not just print numbers without printing what they represent.) The checks and reports should be written to files so that they can be copied to a printer later. *Hint:* Declare LastName and FirstName as ARRAY [0..19] OF CHAR, then use ReadString and WriteString to enter and display the names.

16. [6.7] Your company soon will open a new office in Germany. So that they can do business there, they have asked you to prepare a comprehensive package that will perform the following conversions on demand:

Measure	**American**	**to**	**Metric**	**by**	**Formula**
distance	inch		centimeter		2.54 cm/in
	foot		meter		0.305 m/ft
	yard		meter		0.9144 m/yd
	mile		kilometer		1.609 km/mi
temperature	Fahrenheit		Celsius		$C = (5/9)(F - 32)$
weight	pound		kilograms		0.454 kg/lb
	ounce		gram		28.35 gm/oz
currency	Dollar		Mark		entered by the user (about 2.5 Mark/$)
capacity	quart		liter		0.946 liter/qt
	teaspoon		milliliter		4.9 ml/tsp
math	degree(angle)		radian		$rad = (PI/180)*(deg)$
	degree		grad		$grad = (200/180)*(deg)$

You may be asked to add more types of conversions later. Do it, and document it. *Suggestions:* Draw a structure chart in which a menu specifies the choice of separate procedures for each type of measure. Write the pseudocode and code with stub procedures for the overall problem. Write and test the individual procedures and replace the stubs one by one.

17. [6.6] Protect the procedures in the following programs by enclosing those procedures within local modules complete with appropriate IMPORT and EXPORT lists to make them work.
   a. (FileName:CH3E) MakeASale (Example 3.4.1)
   b. (FileName:CH3G) PaintLogoOnBarn (Example 3.6.1).
   c. (FileName:CH4B) HandleGrades (Example 4.1.2)
   d. (FileName:CH4H2) AmortizeALoan (Example 4.4.2)
   e. (FileName:CH5F) TestFindMidCharacter (Example 5.3.1)
   f. (FileName:CH5H) TemperatureConversion (Example 5.4.1)
   g. (FileName:CH6C) FindSums (Example 6.3.1)

7

Multiple Selection

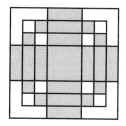

Chapter Outline

Selection among more than two choices has been made so far by repeating IF...END for each possibility. This is acceptable and simple, but it is inefficient and can lead to lengthy code. Other methods of handling multiple selection include nesting IF commands, using ELSIF, and invoking the CASE structure. These methods are discussed in this chapter, as are some more details about using BOOLEAN variables. Decision trees and decision tables are introduced as additional tools for problem solving.

7.1 *Nested IF Structures*

IF commands may be nested within each other and within other structures. The fundamental rule for nesting structures of any type is that inner structures must be contained completely within outer ones; that is, structures may not overlap. The depth to which structures may be nested — structure within structure within structure, etc. — will be determined by the particular compiler and the available memory space. Nesting more than a few levels deep, however, can become confusing and difficult to debug, and other techniques may be preferred in such circumstances.

Figure 7–1 shows legal and illegal nesting. An easy way to determine whether you have nested properly is to ask if the indentation makes sense. Then bracket the beginning and ending commands of each structure to make certain that the structures do not overlap.

Applying Nested IF

To illustrate the application of nested IF commands, consider the following problem from geometry.

Example 7.1.1

Given three numbers, determine whether they form the sides of a triangle. If so, calculate the Area and the Altitude to the triangle's longest base. Determine which type of triangle is formed:

- Right triangle (has 90-degree angle)
  1. isosceles (two sides same length)
  2. scalene (all sides different lengths)
- Not a right triangle
  3. equilateral (all sides same length)
  4. isosceles
  5. scalene

Define the problem   The three sides will be required in increasing order, so that the triangle will appear as in Figure 7–2. h is the altitude to the longest base c.

If the figure is not a triangle, print an appropriate message and stop. Otherwise, calculate the Area and find the Altitude to the longest base, c. Then determine whether it is a right triangle or not. If it is a right triangle, is it isosceles or scalene? If it is not a right triangle, is it equilateral, isosceles, or scalene? Display the triangle type.

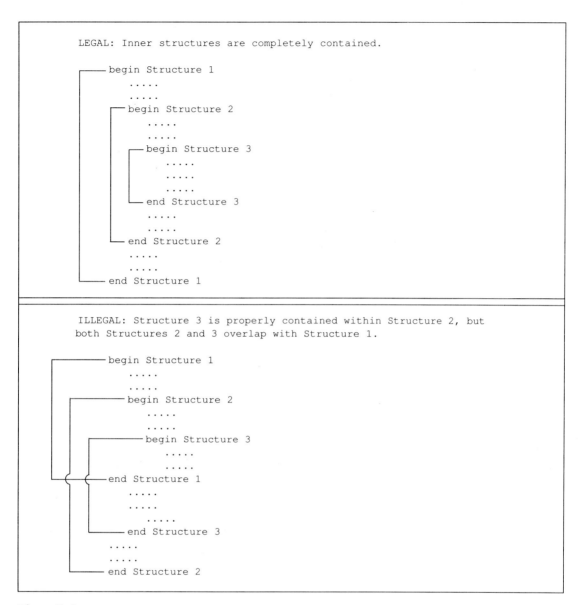

Figure 7–1
Legal and Illegal Nesting of Structures

Figure 7–2
A Triangle with Longest Side *c* (Example 7.1.1)

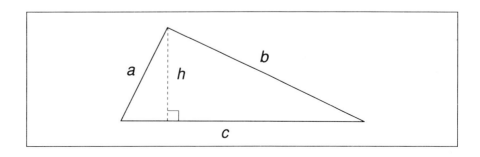

Develop a solution Enter *a, b,* and *c* in increasing order from the keyboard. The logic can be expressed as nested IF structures:

```
if    c < a + b    then
      the figure is a triangle
      Area is given by Heron's formula:
      Area = sqrt[ s*(s − a)*(s − b)*(s − c) ]
      where     s = (a + b + c) / 2.
   Area equals    (1/2)*(base)*(Altitude)
      therefore the Altitude = 2 Area / c

   if c = sqrt(a² + b²)    then
      it is a right triangle

      if    a = b    then
         it is isosceles
      otherwise
         it is scalene
      end if

   otherwise
         it is not a right triangle

   if    a = b = c    then
      it is equilateral
   otherwise
      it is not equilateral

      if    a = b    or    b = c    then
         it is isosceles
      otherwise
         it is scalene
      end if
   end if
   end if
end if
```

Refine the solution Three procedures—EnterSides, FindAreaAndAltitude, and FindTriangleType—will be invoked. Figure 7–3 shows the logic of the solution in a flowchart incorporating these procedures. The flowchart will be helpful later in determining test data.

   Because of the possibility of finite precision truncation errors, the statements to check for equality of real *a, b,* and *c* will be to determine if those values are acceptably close to each other, instead of using *a = b,* and so on. Pay careful attention to the implementation of the nested IF statements in procedure FindTriangleType and their representations by the decision structures in the flowchart.

Modula-2 code

```
MODULE  Triangles;
   (* From 3 sides, finds area, altitude, and triangle type.
      FileName:CH7A      Modula-2      RKW      Apr. 1991 *)

FROM InOut IMPORT WriteString, WriteLn;
FROM RealInOut IMPORT ReadReal, FWriteReal;
FROM MathLib0 IMPORT sqrt;

CONST  Epsilon = 0.0001;  (* to test near equality of REAL values *)
VAR  a, b, c : REAL;    ItsATriangle : BOOLEAN;
```

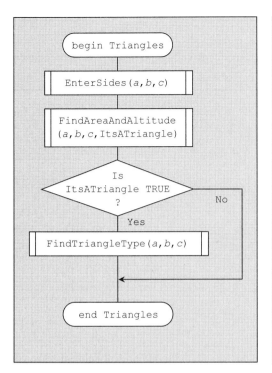

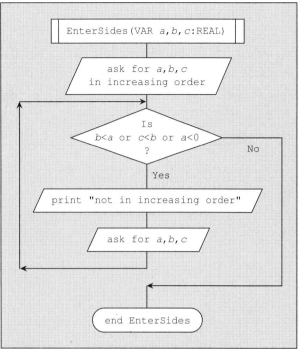

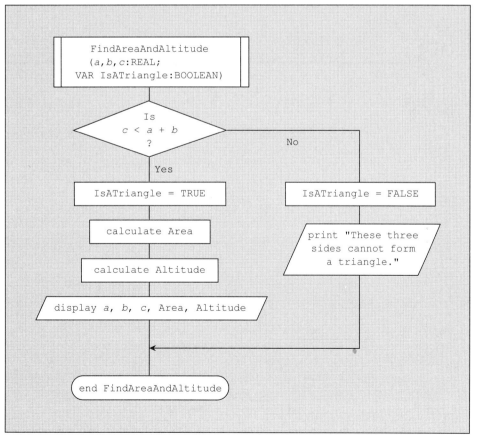

Figure 7–3
Flowchart for Triangles (Example 7.1.1)

(continued)

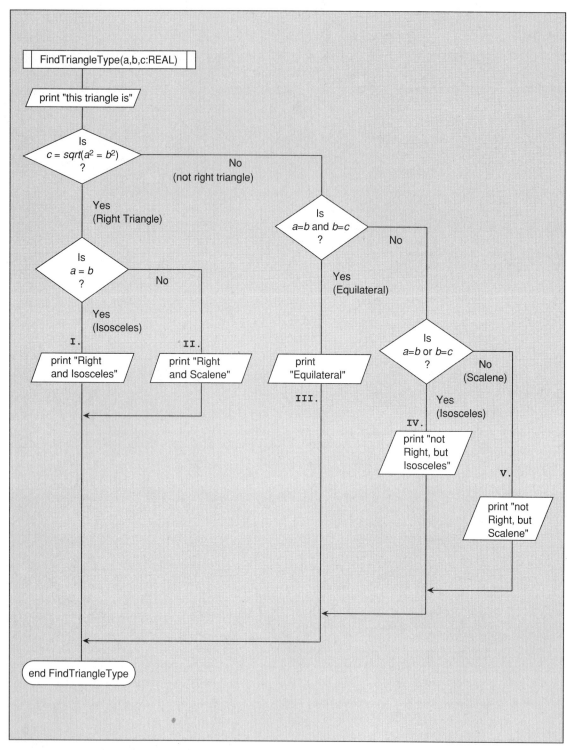

Figure 7–3
(continued)

```
PROCEDURE  EnterSides(VAR a, b, c : REAL);
   BEGIN
      WriteString("Enter sides in increasing order:"); WriteLn;
       WriteString(" a = "); ReadReal(a); WriteLn;
       WriteString(" b = "); ReadReal(b); WriteLn;
       WriteString(" c = "); ReadReal(c); WriteLn; WriteLn;
      WHILE  (b < a) OR (c < b) OR (a < 0.0)  (* not in order *)  DO
         WriteString("Not in increasing order. Try again:"); WriteLn;
          WriteString(" a = "); ReadReal(a); WriteLn;
          WriteString(" b = "); ReadReal(b); WriteLn;
          WriteString(" c = "); ReadReal(c); WriteLn; WriteLn;
      END; (* WHILE *)
   END EnterSides;

PROCEDURE  FindAreaAndAltitude(a,b,c:REAL; VAR IsATriangle:BOOLEAN);
   VAR  s, Area, Altitude : REAL;
   BEGIN
      IF  (a + b) - c > Epsilon  THEN  (* forms a triangle if c < a + b *)
         IsATriangle := TRUE;
         s := (a + b + c)/2.0;   Area := sqrt(s*(s-a)*(s-b)*(s-c));
         Altitude := 2.0 * Area / c;

         WriteLn; WriteString("A triangle with sides");
         FWriteReal(a,12,4); FWriteReal(b,12,4); FWriteReal(c,12,4); WriteLn;
         WriteString(" has an Area      ="); FWriteReal(Area,12,4); WriteLn;
         WriteString(" and an Altitude ="); FWriteReal(Altitude,12,4);
         WriteLn;
      ELSE
         IsATriangle := FALSE;
         WriteString("These three sides cannot form a triangle."); WriteLn;
      END; (* IF *)
   END FindAreaAndAltitude;

PROCEDURE  FindTriangleType(a, b, c : REAL);
   BEGIN
      WriteLn; WriteString("This triangle is");

      IF  ABS(c - sqrt(a*a + b*b)) < Epsilon  THEN (* right triangle *)
         IF  ABS(a - b) < Epsilon  THEN
            WriteString(" Right and Isosceles.");
         ELSE
          WriteString(" Right and Scalene.");
         END; (* IF *)
      ELSE   (* not a right triangle *)
         IF  (ABS(a-b) < Epsilon) AND (ABS(b-c) < Epsilon)  THEN
            WriteString(" Equilateral.");
         ELSE
            IF  (ABS(a-b) < Epsilon) OR (ABS(b-c) < Epsilon)  THEN
               WriteString(" not Right, but Isosceles.");
            ELSE
               WriteString(" not Right, but Scalene.");
            END; (*IF *)
         END; (* IF *)
      END; (* IF *)
      WriteLn;
   END FindTriangleType;
```

```
BEGIN   (* main module Triangles *)
   EnterSides(a, b, c);
   FindAreaAndAltitude(a, b, c, ItsATriangle);
   IF  ItsATriangle  THEN
      FindTriangleType(a, b, c);
   END; (* IF *)
END Triangles.
```

Debug and test   Try some REAL number triplets for *a, b,* and *c*. A sample run looks like

```
Enter sides in increasing order:
  a = 13.2
  b = 14.5
  c = 16.8

A triangle with sides       13.20000        14.5000      16.8000
  has an Area      =       92.2228
  and an Altitude =       10.9789

This triangle is not Right, but Scalene.
```

Complete the documentation   Include the problem definition, the equations defining Area and Altitude, the flowchart, code, a list of values for which the program was tested, and a sample run. The users' manual can be quite short, stating the location of the source code (File CH7A), and instructing users to answer the questions posed by the program.

☐ **Path Testing**

(Optional material; may be skipped or covered later without loss of continuity.)

A flowchart is helpful for determining all possible paths through a program. Developing test data for all of those paths, called *path testing,* ensures that every possible combination of decisions has been considered.

For example, consider the flowchart in Figure 7–3 for the Triangles problem (Example 7.1.1). Examining the main module reveals two paths: the one where ItsATriangle is TRUE and the one where ItsATriangle is FALSE. Procedure FindAreaAndAltitude has the same two paths, which are determined by the conditions $c < a + b$ and NOT$(c < a + b)$, respectively. The test data in lines 1, 2, and 3 of Figure 7–4 pertain to these possibilities.

Look at procedure EnterSides next. The two paths here reflect whether the values *a, b,* and *c* are entered in increasing order ($b < a$ or $c < b$) or whether one or more the values is negative ($a < 0$). Sample test data for these conditions are shown in lines 4 through 8 of Figure 7–4.

Finally, consider the flowchart for FindTriangleType. There are five different paths through the chart, labeled Roman numerals I through V. The requirements here are

7.1 Nested IF Structures **245**

Figure 7–4
Test Values for
Triangles
(Example 7.1.1)

	a	*b*	*c*	**Path Tested**
1.	2.0	3.0	4.0	ItsATriangle = TRUE ($c < a + b$)
2.	2.0	3.0	5.0	ItsATriangle = FALSE ($c = a + b$)
3.	2.0	3.0	12.0	ItsATriangle = FALSE ($c > a + b$)
4.	1.5	2.3	3.4	$a < b < c$ increasing order
5.	1.5	3.4	2.3	$c < b$ not increasing
6.	2.3	1.5	3.4	$b < a$ not increasing
7.	3.4	2.3	1.5	$b < a$ and $c < b$ not increasing
8.	-1.0	3.2	5.4	$a < 0$ not a triangle
9.	2.0	2.0	2.828427	$c = sqrt(a^2 + b^2)$ and $a = b$
10.	2.0	3.0	3.605551	$c = sqrt(a^2 + b^2)$ and $a <> b$
11.	3.5	3.5	3.5	$a = b = c$
12.	13.2	13.2	15.9	$a = b$
13.	13.2	15.9	15.9	$b = c$
14.	13.2	14.5	16.8	$a <> b$ and $b <> c$

Path Number	**Condition**
I	$c = sqrt(a^2 + b^2)$ and $a = b$
II	$c = sqrt(a^2 + b^2)$ and $a <> b$
III	$c <> sqrt(a^2 + b^2)$ and $a = b$ and $b = c$
IV	$c <> sqrt(a^2 + b^2)$ and $a = b$ or $b = c$
V	$c <> sqrt(a^2 + b^2)$ and $a <> b$ and $b <> c$

Test data for these paths appear in lines 9 through 14 of Figure 7–4.

If you run the program with this collection of data you can be sure that every possible decision has been tested.

Questions 7.1

1. **a.** Correct the errors in the following nested IF structure.
    b. Once the errors are corrected, what is displayed by the structure after each of these assignments?
    (1) FirstLetter := 'W'; **(2)** FirstLetter := 'L';
    (3) FirstLetter := 'Z'; **(4)** FirstLetter := 'K'

```
WriteString(''This station is '');
IF  FirstLetter = 'W'  THEN
   WriteString(''eastern.'');
END;
ELSE
   IF  FirstLetter = 'K'  THEN
      WriteString('' western.'');
   END;
   ELSE
      IF  FirstLetter = 'Z'  THEN
         WriteString(''a ham radio.'');
      END;
      ELSE
         WriteString(''of unknown origin.'');
      END;
   END;
END;
```

2. **a.** Convert the flowchart for procedure MakeTheDecision in Figure 7–5 to pseudocode with nested IF statements.
   Hint: For each decision "Is...?" place everything on the "Yes" path between IF and ELSE, and place everything on the "No" path between ELSE and END.
   b. Choose different test values of Grade to display each of the five messages.
3. In program Triangles (Example 7.1.1), *explain why:*
   a. the values *a*, *b*, and *c* are not in increasing order if $b < a$ or $c < b$. Why not test $c < a$ also?
   b. testing for $b < a$ or $c < b$ or $a < 0$ ensures that none of the sides is negative. Why not test $b < 0$ or $c < 0$?
   c. the figure is a triangle only if $c < a + b$. *Hint:* draw pictures for the first three sets of test data in Figure 7–4.
   d. the triangle is equilateral when $a = b$ and $b = c$. Why not test $a = c$ as well?
   e. the triangle is isosceles when $a = b$ or $b = c$. Why not add "or $a = c$" to the test?
4. Write a nested IF structure that will: print "There is a surplus." if expenditures are less than revenues; print "There is a deficit." if expenditures are greater than revenues; otherwise, print "The budget is balanced."

7.2 ELSIF

Another method of handling multiple decisions in Modula-2 is to incorporate the ELSIF command. The general form of the IF statement with ELSIF clauses is shown in Figure 7–6. The notes in the figure are especially important.

Conditions that Are Not Mutually Exclusive

When only one IF...ELSIF condition can be TRUE, those conditions are said to be **mutually exclusive.** For example, when testing the Roll of a die (one of a pair of dice), the Roll condition has only one value (1, 2, 3, 4, 5, or 6); the conditions are mutually exclusive. In the example in Figure 7–6, the conditions are *not* mutually exclusive. In fact, when Apples = 2, Bananas = 3, and Cherries = 4, both conditions Apples < Bananas and Apples < Cherries are TRUE.

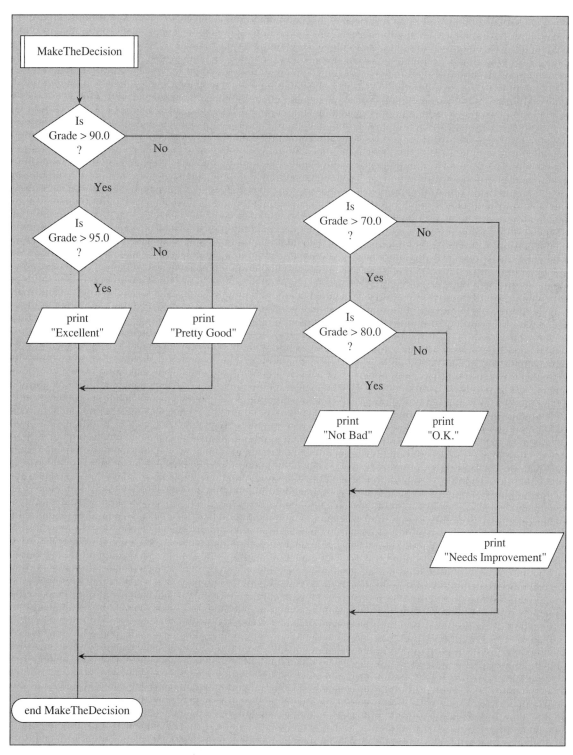

Figure 7–5
MakeTheDecision Flowchart (Section 7.1, Question 2)

```
General Format:

    IF  Condition1  THEN
        statements executed if Condition1 is TRUE;
    ELSIF  Condition2  THEN
        statements executed if Condition2 is TRUE
    ELSIF  Condition3  THEN
        statements executed if Condition3 is TRUE;
    ELSIF ...
        ...
    ELSE  (* optional *)
        statements executed if none of the Conditions is TRUE;
    END; (* IF *)
```

```
Example:

    ...
    VAR  Apples, Bananas, Cherries : CARDINAL;
    ...
    BEGIN
        ...
        Apples := 2;  Bananas := 3;  Cherries: = 4;
        ...
        If  Apples > Bananas THEN
           WriteString("There are more Apples than Bananas.");
        ELSIF Apples < Bananas THEN
           WriteString("There are fewer Apples than Bananas.");
        ELSIF Apples < Cherries THEN
           WriteString("There are fewer Apples than Cherries.");
        ELSE
           WriteString("The relationship between Apples, Bananas, ");
            WriteString("and Cherries is not listed.");
        END; (* IF *)
        ....
```

```
Notes:
   -  There is no "E" in the middle of "ELSIF."
   -  There is only one END in the entire IF...ELSIF...END structure.
   -  ELSE is optional.
```

Figure 7–6
ELSIF Syntax

If the conditions in an ELSIF structure are not mutually exclusive, the statements following the first encountered TRUE condition are executed—and all others are ignored. Decision structures are said to be **short-circuit** evaluated; that is, once a TRUE condition is found, its tasks are performed, and the program exits from the structure. For example, in Figure 7–6, the message

```
There are fewer Apples than Bananas.
```

would be displayed, and the message

```
There are fewer Apples than Cherries.
```

would not be displayed. Even though Apples < Cherries is a TRUE condition, it is ignored because the structure has accomplished its task already.

Applying ELSIF

As an application of ELSIF, consider the following problem:

Example 7.2.1

For a savings account where no deposits or withdrawals have been made during the month, calculate the interest for the month and the end-of-month balance.

Define the problem   The BeginBalance at the beginning of the month will be entered by the user at the keyboard. The annual InterestRate varies, depending upon BeginBalance, according to the following table:

if	$0 < BeginBalance < $5,000	InterestRate = 5.00% ;	
if	$5,000 <= BeginBalance < $10,000	InterestRate = 6.25% ;	
if	$10,000 <= BeginBalance < $20,000	InterestRate = 8.00% ;	and
if	BeginBalance >= $20,000	InterestRate = 9.75% .	

Interest is compounded only at the end of the month, and the interest and new balance are displayed to the screen.

Develop a solution   The required formulae are

$$\text{MonthlyInterestRate} = \text{Annual InterestRate}/(12.0 * 100.0)$$
$$\text{InterestAmount} = \text{MonthlyInterestRate} * \text{BeginBalance}$$

At the end of the month,

$$\text{EndBalance} = \text{BeginBalance} + \text{InterestAmount}$$

Refine the solution   *Pseudocode*

```
begin Savings
   ask for BeginBalance
   if      BeginBalance <  5000.00   then   InterestRate = 5.00
   elsif   BeginBalance < 10000.00   then   InterestRate = 6.25
   elsif   BeginBalance < 20000.00   then   InterestRate = 8.00
   else                                     InterestRate = 9.75

   Calculate MonthlyInterestRate
             InterestAmount
             EndBalance

   print    BeginBalance, InterestRate, InterestAmount, EndBalance
end Savings
```

Modula-2 code

```
MODULE Savings;
   (* Finds the interest and end of month balance on savings.
      FileName:CH7B      Modula-2     RKW        Apr. 1991   *)

FROM InOut IMPORT WriteString, WriteLn;
FROM RealInOut IMPORT ReadReal, FWriteReal;

CONST  RATE1 = 5.00;  RATE2 = 6.25; RATE3 = 8.00;  RATE4 = 9.75;
       MONTHSPERYEAR = 12.0;  CONVERTFACTOR = MONTHSPERYEAR * 100.0;
VAR  BeginBalance, EndBalance, MonthlyInterestRate,
     InterestRate, InterestAmount : REAL;
```

```
BEGIN
    WriteString("Balance at the beginning of the month? $ ");
     ReadReal(BeginBalance); WriteLn; WriteLn;

    IF  BeginBalance < 5000.0   THEN       (*          BeginBalance < 5000   *)
        InterestRate := RATE1;
    ELSIF  BeginBalance < 10000.0  THEN  (*  5000 <= BeginBalance < 10000 *)
        InterestRate := RATE2;
    ELSIF  BeginBalance < 20000.0  THEN  (* 10000 <= BeginBalance < 20000 *)
        InterestRate := RATE3;
    ELSE                                 (* 20000 <= BeginBalance         *)
        InterestRate := RATE4;
    END; (* if *)

    MonthlyInterestRate := InterestRate / CONVERTFACTOR;
    InterestAmount := MonthlyInterestRate * BeginBalance;
    EndBalance := BeginBalance + InterestAmount;
    WriteString("Old Balance  Interest Rate  Interest  New Balance");
     WriteLn; FWriteReal(BeginBalance,11,2); FWriteReal(InterestRate,15,2);
     FWriteReal(InterestAmount,10,2); FWriteReal(EndBalance,13,2); WriteLn;
END Savings.
```

Debug and test   Note the assertion comments in the IF…ELSIF…END structure. Why does the assertion say that the decision

$$5000 <= BeginBalance < 10000$$

is accomplished by

ELSIF BeginBalance < 10000.0 THEN ?

Note also, for illustration, that the CONSTant CONVERTFACTOR was defined by an expression involving previously defined CONSTant MONTHSPERYEAR.

Test this program with different starting balances, including the limiting balances $5,000, $10,000, and $20,000, something less than $5,000, a value between $5,000 and $10,000, something between $10,000 and $20,000, and a balance greater than $20,000. Running the program with starting balance $7215.64 gave these results:

```
Balance at the beginning of the month? $ 7215.64

Old Balance  Interest Rate  Interest  New Balance
    7215.64           6.25     37.58      7253.22
```

Complete the documentation   The problem definition, pseudocode, code (CH7B), and sample run should be accompanied by a list of values for which the program was tested, so that the bank with whom you contracted to produce this program, has some confidence in its validity.

Interchanging Nested IF with ELSIF

Nested IF and ELSIF structures are interchangeable, though they are not necessarily always equally easy to read, and the conversion is not always simple. One way to begin the conversion process is to expand

ELSIF…   to   ELSE
                          IF …

or to write   ELSE   as   ELSIF....
                  IF...

Then decide what the condition must be at each decision point. For example,

The code	could be written as

IF   A = B   THEN
     (* perform operation 1 *)
ELSE
   IF   A < B   THEN
      (* perform operation 2 *)
   ELSE
      (* perform operation 3 *)
  END;   (* IF *)
END; (* IF *)
	IF A = B THEN
	     (* perform operation 1 *)
	
	ELSIF A < B THEN
	     (* perform operation 2 *)
	ELSIF A > B THEN
	     (* perform operation 3 *)
	
	END; (* IF *)

Decision trees and tables, discussed in Section 7.4, will help you determine whether the structures are equivalent. For now, you may wish to try rewriting program Savings (Example 7.2.1) using nested IF structures instead of ELSIF, and to rewrite the Triangles program (Example 7.1.1) using ELSIF instead of nested IFs. (See Exercise 1 at the end of the chapter.)

Questions 7.2

1. In Figure 7–6, list different combinations of values for Apples, Bananas, and Cherries that would cause each of the four messages to be displayed. *Hint:* The values of Apples, Bananas, or Cherries may be equal.

2. In the Savings program (Example 7.2.1), **a.** explain why

ELSIF   BeginBalance < 10000.0   THEN

achieves the same result as

ELSIF (BeginBalance >= 5000.0) AND (BeginBalance < 10000.0) THEN.

b. How would you write the IF...ELSIF.... conditions if you wished to test BeginBalance in decreasing order beginning with BeginBalance >= 20000.0?

c. How would you write the decision structure if you decided to test BeginBalance in this order?

```
if      BeginBalance < 5000.0
if      BeginBalance >= 20000.0
if      5000.0       <= BeginBalance < 10000.0
if      10000.0      <= BeginBalance < 20000.0
```

3. **a.** Correct the errors in this structure:

```
IF  StartTime > 10.0   THEN
    WriteString('' Relax!'');
END;
    ELSIF  StartTime > 5.0   THEN
        WriteString(''Get Ready!'');
    END;
        ELSIF  StartTime > 1.0   THEN
            WriteString(''It's panic time!'');
        END;
        ELSE
            WriteString(''On your mark...!'');
        END;
```

b. Once the errors are corrected, what is displayed when (1) StartTime = 30.0; (2) StartTime = 2.5; (3) StartTime = 1.0?

4. Rewrite the corrected IF...ELSIF... structure from question 3 in nested IF form.

5. a. Rewrite this nested IF structure in IF...ELSIF... form:

```
WriteString('' It helps if you are '')
IF  Basketball  THEN
    WriteString(''tall.'');
ELSE
    IF  Football  THEN
        WriteString(''big.'');
    ELSE
        IF  Boxing  THEN
            WriteString('' aggressive.'');
        ELSE
            WriteString(''alive.'');
        END;
    END;
END;
```

b. As what data type should variables Basketball, Football, and Boxing be declared in a program containing the decision structure in part a?

7.3 *More about BOOLEAN*

The BOOLEAN data type was introduced in Chapter 3, and procedures were written at the beginning of Chapter 4 (Example 4.1.1, FileName:CH4A) for reading and writing BOOLEAN values. BOOLEAN variables and constants are logical entities that may have only the value TRUE or the value FALSE. To determine whether what you have written is a valid BOOLEAN expression, ask yourself, "Does the question, 'Is it true or false?' make sense?" For example, suppose a module contains the variable declarations

```
VAR  B1, B2, B3 : BOOLEAN;
     A, D, C : CARDINAL;
     Symbol, Mark : CHAR;
```

and the assignments

```
A := 3;  D := 7;  C := 13;
Mark := 'r';  Symbol := 't';
```

Then the following BOOLEAN assignments would all be valid, because the question "Is the value of *B* true or false?" could be answered "Yes."

$B1 := TRUE;$	evaluates to	TRUE
$B2 := CHR(ORD(Mark) - 1) = Symbol;$	evaluates to	FALSE
$B3 := 7 + 2 * A \quad >= \quad C;$	evaluates to	TRUE

These assignments would *not* be valid, because the variables could not be said to be true or false:

$$B1 := D;$$
$$B2 := Mark + 7;$$
$$B3 := C - 3 * A;$$

A Bit of Background

George Boole

George Boole, born in Lincoln, England, in 1815, was a self-taught mathematician with limited formal education. Nonetheless, his contributions have led to unlimited applications. His *Mathematical Analysis of Logic* (1847) and *Laws of Thought* (completed in 1854 while he was professor of mathematics at Queens' College in Cork, Ireland) form the basis of modern mathematical logic. In those works he reduced 2000-year-old formal logic to an algebraic method, which became the foundation of the binary techniques used in virtually all modern digital computers.

Boole was loved and admired by the citizens of Cork. He is known to have invited people he met on the street to his home to eat dinner and "talk science." He was dedicated to his work and showed genuine concern for his students. His walking to the college through the rain — in poor health and in wet clothing — to deliver his lectures is believed to have led to the illness that took his life in 1864.

BOOLEAN Expressions

BOOLEAN expressions are formed using constants, variables, the arithmetic operators (+, −, *, /, DIV, MOD), the relational operators (<, <=, >, >=, =, # or <>), and the three logical operators (AND, OR, and NOT). Suppose P and Q are themselves BOOLEAN constants, variables, or expressions. Then the possibilities for P AND Q, P OR Q, and NOT P would be as shown by the *truth tables* in Figure 7–7.

Truth tables often are used to determine whether two expressions are equivalent. Suppose, for example, that you wish to know whether the statement "It is not true that I will not run and that I will not serve if elected." is equivalent to "Either I will run or I will serve if elected." Let A = "I will run."; let B = "I will serve if elected.", and consider the truth table in Figure 7–8. The values in the column A OR B match the values in the column NOT (NOT A AND NOT B); therefore the two statements are indeed equivalent.

ORD and VAL with BOOLEAN

Intrinsic functions ORD and VAL have some important applications with BOOLEAN data types.

The order of the two BOOLEAN values is defined to be

FALSE, TRUE, or FALSE < TRUE.

The implication of this is that

ORD(BooleanValue) = 0 when BooleanValue = FALSE, and
ORD(BooleanValue) = 1 when BooleanValue = TRUE.

This provides a convenient way of writing BOOLEAN values with the command

```
WriteCard( ORD(BooleanValue), 2 );
```

which displays 0 for FALSE and 1 for TRUE.

Figure 7–7
Truth Tables for
AND, OR, and NOT

Truth Table	Notes:

AND

P	Q	P AND Q
True	True	True
True	False	False
False	True	False
False	False	False

P AND Q = TRUE
only when P and Q
both are TRUE.

OR

P	Q	P OR Q
True	True	True
True	False	True
False	True	True
False	False	False

P OR Q is called an
inclusive OR.

P OR Q = TRUE
either when P is TRUE
or when Q is TRUE or
when **both** P and Q are
TRUE.

NOT

P	NOT P
True	False
False	True

NOT P reverses the
value of P from TRUE
to FALSE and vice versa.

The value of NOT(NOT P)
is the same as the value
of P.

Similarly, if you wish to read BOOLEAN values, you may enter CARDINAL values 0 for FALSE and 1 for TRUE, and apply the VAL function to convert them. For example, given the declarations

```
VAR   Number : CARDINAL;   Boole : BOOLEAN:
```

then

```
WriteString(''Enter cardinal value 0 or 1: '');
ReadCard(Number); WriteLn;
Boole := VAL(BOOLEAN, Number);
```

would cause Boole to have value TRUE if the user entered 1 for Number and FALSE if the user entered 0.

Precedence of Operations

The rules of precedence for the arithmetic, relational, and logical operators can be summarized:

Figure 7–8
Truth Table to
Determine
Equivalence

```
A  =  I will run.


B  =  I will serve if elected.

NOT (NOT A AND NOT B)  =  It is not true that (I will not run and
                              that I will not serve if elected).

A OR B  =  Either I will run or I will serve if elected.
```

A	B	A OR B	NOT A	NOT B	NOT A AND NOT B	NOT (NOT A AND NOT B)
T	T	T	F	F	F	T
T	F	T	F	T	F	T
F	T	T	T	F	F	T
F	F	F	T	T	T	F

- First,   Evaluate everything in parentheses from innermost to outermost.
- Second,   NOT
- Third,   *, /, DIV, MOD, AND   Apply from left to right.
- Fourth,   +, −, OR
- Fifth,   <, <=, >, >=, =, # or <>

Unless these rules are observed carefully, the expression may not evaluate to TRUE or FALSE, and the compiler will present an error message such as "Boolean Expression Expected." At other times you may have constructed a valid BOOLEAN expression, but it is evaluated incorrectly.

For example, if Letters, Magazines, and Newspapers are cardinal variables, then

$$\text{Letters} > \text{Magazines} \quad \text{AND} \quad \text{Magazines} > \text{Newspapers}$$

will cause a syntax error, because Magazines AND Magazines is examined first and does not evaluate to TRUE or FALSE. Instead, you should write

$$(\text{Letters} > \text{Magazines}) \quad \text{AND} \quad (\text{Magazines} > \text{Newspapers}).$$

On the other hand, if Letters = 3 and Magazines = 4, then

$$\text{NOT}(\text{Letters} > \text{Magazines}) \quad \text{OR} \quad (7 > 5)$$

evaluates to TRUE, while

$$\text{NOT}((\text{Letters} > \text{Magazines}) \quad \text{OR} \quad (7 > 5))$$

is FALSE. Even if parentheses are not needed, you should use them to make it absolutely clear how a BOOLEAN expression will be evaluated.

Short-Circuit Evaluations

BOOLEAN expressions containing the conjunctions AND and OR are called **compound expressions.** Compound expressions are evaluated from left to right and short-circuit evaluated. That is, as soon as the value of an expression has been determined, the evaluation process stops, and the rest of the expression is not even examined at all.

Observe that

when   *P* is FALSE,   *P* AND *Q* is FALSE,

and *Q* does not need to be evaluated. Similarly,

when   *P* is TRUE,   *P* OR *Q* is TRUE,

and *Q* is not evaluated.

Figure 7–9 shows some examples in which *P* AND *Q* and *P* OR *Q* lead to short-circuit evaluation.

Precautions to Take with Compound Expressions

Observe these cautions when testing compound expressions:
1. List the most critical component first (before AND or OR) to make sure it gets evaluated.
2. Remember that *P* AND *Q* = FALSE does not necessarily mean that *P* = FALSE and *Q* = FALSE.
3. Remember that *P* OR *Q* = TRUE does not necessarily mean that *P* = TRUE and *Q* = TRUE.

BOOLEAN Values as Conditions

Every expression used as a Condition in IF Condition THEN and WHILE Condition DO structures must be BOOLEAN. It is correct to write

IF   Letters > 5   THEN

or   WHILE   Letters + 3 * Magazines <= 20   DO.

However, neither   IF   17   THEN   nor   WHILE   7 − *S*   DO

is valid, because the Conditions 17 and (7 − *S*) are neither TRUE nor FALSE.

Often it is convenient to assign a lengthy condition expression to a BOOLEAN variable and to use the variable itself as the condition. The expression assigned to a BOOLEAN variable Test could be as complex as you wish, so long as it evaluates to TRUE or FALSE. Thus, for example,

Test := ((7 > 5)   AND   NOT(3 < 1))   OR   (12 = 4 * 5)

is perfectly legal. Then you could write

IF   Test   THEN   or   WHILE   NOT(Test)   DO.

...

It is not considered good style to write

IF   Test = TRUE   THEN   or   WHILE   Test = FALSE   DO.

...

The variable Test itself has either the value TRUE or the value FALSE, and is a TRUE or FALSE condition all by itself. Although the conditions Test = TRUE and Test = FALSE are valid, they are redundant, like writing TRUE = TRUE.

Here is an example that illustrates the use of BOOLEAN variables as conditions.

Figure 7–9
Short-Circuit
Evaluation of
Compound
BOOLEAN
Expressions

P AND *Q*	*P* OR *Q*
FALSE when *P* = FALSE (Short-circuit evaluated, *Q* not evaluated.)	TRUE when *P* = TRUE (Short-circuit evaluated, *Q* not evaluated.)

Assume   A := 3;   B := 9;   C := 0;

Examples

Expression	Value	Reason
AND		
(*A* > 5) AND (*B* DIV *C* > 10)	FALSE	*A* > 5 is FALSE short-circuited
(*A* < 5) AND (*B* DIV *C* > 10)	Error	*A* < 5 is TRUE *B* DIV *C* causes "Division by zero" error
(*A* < 5) AND (*B* + *C* < 10)	TRUE	**both** *A* < 5 and *B* + *C* < 10 are TRUE
OR		
(*A* < 5) OR (*B* DIV *C* > 10)	TRUE	*A* < 5 is TRUE short-circuited
(*A* > 5) OR (*B* DIV *C* > 10)	Error	*A* > 5 is FALSE *B* DIV *C* causes "Division by zero" error
(*A* > 5) OR (*B* + *C* > 10)	FALSE	**both** *A* > 5 and *B* + *C* > 10 are FALSE

Example 7.3.1

Automobile insurance rates are based upon the driver's age, whether the driver has had one or more accidents, and the type and age of the car. Calculate auto insurance premiums.

Define the problem   If the driver's age is less than 22 or greater than 78, then there is a 50% surcharge on the basic premium. If the driver has been in no accidents within the past three years, there is a 20% rate reduction. If the car is more than 10 years or fewer than 2 years old, the rate is increased by 40%. If the automobile is large or compact, there is a 30% rate increase over midsized cars. Write a program that asks for the driver's age and accident status, and the size and age of the automobile. Then calculate the annual insurance premium.

Develop a solution   The basic premium will be set as a CONSTant, so that it can be changed as rates fluctuate. BOOLEAN variables will be used for test conditions, namely,

TestAge   := (DriverAge < 22)   OR   (DriverAge > 78)
TestAccidents := (Accidents = 0)
TestSize   := (CarSize = Large)   OR   (CarSize = Compact)
TestVintage   := (Vintage < 2)   OR   (Vintage > 10)

The problem lends itself to separate IF statements, since the conditions are not mutually exclusive.

Refine the solution   *Pseudocode*

```
CONST     BasicCost = 200.00;
begin Insurance
   ask for DriverAge, Accidents, CarSize, Vintage
   set Boolean variables
      TestAge        := (DriverAge < 22)   OR      (DriverAge > 78)
      TestAccidents := (Accidents = 0)
      TestSize       := (CarSize = 'L')    OR      (CarSize = 'C')
      TestVintage   := (Vintage < 2)       OR      (Vintage > 10)
   initialize RateChange = 0.0
   if TestAge        add      0.50 to RateChange
   if TestAccidents add     -0.20 to RateChange
   if TestSize        add      0.30 to RateChange
   if TestVintage    add      0.40 to RateChange

   calculate    Premium = BasicCost    +    RateChange * BasicCost

   print    DriverAge, Accidents, CarSize, Vintage
   print annual Premium
end Insurance
```

Modula-2 code   Note in the code that it has been possible to write each

```
IF   BooleanVariable   THEN ... END
```

decision on a single line because the condition is short. If you decide to deviate from the accustomed style like this, be careful to keep the code as readable as you can by using white space.

```
MODULE FindInsurancePremium;
   (* Finds annual insurance premium.
      FileName:CH7C      Modula-2      RKW      Apr. 1991   *)

FROM InOut IMPORT WriteString, WriteLn, Read, Write,
               ReadCard, WriteCard;
FROM RealInOut IMPORT ReadReal, FWriteReal;

CONST BASICCOST = 200.0;   YOUNG = 22; ELDERLY = 78;
      LARGECAR = 'L';   COMPACTCAR = 'C';   NEWCAR = 2;   OLDCAR = 10;
      AGERATE = 0.50;   ACCIDENTRATE = -0.20;   SIZERATE = 0.30;
      VINTAGERATE = 0.40;
```

```
VAR   TestAge, TestAccidents, TestSize, TestVintage : BOOLEAN;
      DriverAge, Accidents, Vintage : CARDINAL;
      CarSize, ThrowAway : CHAR;    Premium, RateChange : REAL;

BEGIN
   WriteString("What is the driver's age? "); ReadCard(DriverAge); WriteLn;
   WriteString("How many accidents happened in the past 3 years? ");
    ReadCard(Accidents); WriteLn;
   WriteString("What is the size of the car? "); WriteLn;
    WriteString("Enter L for Large, M for Midsize, C for Compact: ");
    Read(CarSize); Read(ThrowAway); Write(CarSize); WriteLn;
   WriteString("How old is the car (years)? "); ReadCard(Vintage);
   WriteLn; WriteLn;

   TestAge       := (DriverAge < YOUNG)  OR  (DriverAge > ELDERLY) ;
   TestAccidents := (Accidents = 0) ;
   TestSize      := (CAP(CarSize) = LARGECAR) OR (CAP(CarSize) = COMPACTCAR);
   TestVintage   := (Vintage < NEWCAR)  OR  (Vintage > OLDCAR) ;

   RateChange := 0.0;
   IF  TestAge       THEN  RateChange := RateChange + AGERATE;      END;
   IF  TestAccidents THEN  RateChange := RateChange + ACCIDENTRATE; END;
   IF  TestSize      THEN  RateChange := RateChange + SIZERATE;     END;
   IF  TestVintage   THEN  RateChange := RateChange + VINTAGERATE;  END;
   Premium := BASICCOST  +  RateChange * BASICCOST;

   WriteString("Driver's Age is "); WriteCard(DriverAge,3); WriteLn;
   WriteString("Number of Accidents in past three years is ");
    WriteCard(Accidents,3); WriteLn;
   WriteString("The vehicle is a ");
      IF  CAP(CarSize) = 'L'  THEN
        WriteString("large sized car. ");
      ELSIF  CAP(CarSize) = 'C'  THEN
        WriteString("compact car. ");
      ELSE
        WriteString("midsized car. ");
      END; (* IF *)  WriteLn;
   WriteString("The age of the car is "); WriteCard(Vintage,3); WriteLn;

   WriteString("Therefore the annual premium is ");
    FWriteReal(Premium,8,2); WriteLn;
END FindInsurancePremium.
```

Debug and test A sample run of this program produced these results:

```
What is the driver's age? 20
How many accidents happened in the past 3 years? 0
What is the size of the car?
Enter L for Large, M for Midsize, C for Compact: c
How old is the car (years)? 12

Driver's Age is  20
Number of Accidents in past three years is    0
The vehicle is a compact car.
The age of the car is 12
Therefore the annual premium is    400.00
```

A Bit of Background

De Morgan's Laws

Augustus De Morgan was born at Madura, India, in 1806 and died in London in 1871. He became a professor of mathematics in London in 1828 and spent many years performing investigations into a variety of mathematical topics. He was a revered teacher and wrote numerous textbooks containing a wealth of information on mathematics and its history, but which generally were very difficult for his students to understand.

De Morgan's contributions to modern computing include two laws by which AND statements can be converted to OR and vice versa. They are

1. NOT (*A* and *B*) = (NOT *A*) OR (NOT *B*), and
2. NOT (*A* OR *B*) = (NOT *A*) AND (NOT *B*).

Thus, from De Morgan's First Law, the statement "Either it is not raining or I am not getting wet" says the same thing as "It is not true that it is raining and I am getting wet." Similarly, from the second law "It is not true that politicians always lie or that teachers always know the facts" becomes "Politicians do not always lie and teachers do not always know the facts."

Figure 7−8 illustrates the proof, using a truth table, of De Morgan's second law in the slightly different form

$$A \text{ OR } B = \text{NOT}((\text{NOT } A) \text{ AND } (\text{NOT } B)).$$

For complete testing of the code, there would be at least 54 different sets of test values—that is, 3 age ranges (less than 22, 22 to 78, greater than 78) *times* 2 accident conditions (zero and nonzero) *times* 3 car sizes (Large, Medium, Compact) *times* 3 vintages (less than 2, between 2 and 10, greater than 10). If you also multiply by the number of limiting conditions (Age = 22, Age = 78, Vintage = 2, Vintage = 10), *the number of test cases grows to 216.* It is not unusual, as in this situation, for complete testing to become as great a task as developing and coding the solution. In fact, in such circumstances it may be valuable to embed the entire program within a test module, which chooses representative values for the variables and runs the program repeatedly.

Complete the documentation In the users' manual warn about entering illegal values for the variables. In practice, you should build in safeguards (see Exercise 3 at the end of the chapter). The problem definition, pseudocode, code (CH7C), and sample run complete the documentation.

☐ BOOLEAN CONSTants as Switches

Until now, after supplemental write statements were used, they were enclosed within comment indicators or removed completely. Such statements can be enclosed within an

IF Condition THEN

structure, where the Condition is a BOOLEAN CONSTant the value of which can be changed easily between TRUE and FALSE. Then supplemental write statements can be written into the code and switched on and off by changing the value of the BOOLEAN CONSTant.

As a simple example, consider the ComputeCircles program, which calculates the Area, Diameter, and Circumference of a circle. BOOLEAN CONSTant switches are incorporated into this code for DEBUGging and for turning REDIRECTion on and off.

```
MODULE ComputeCircles;
   (* Finds the area, diameter, and circumference of a circle.
      Supplemental write and redirection are turned on and off by
      BOOLEAN CONSTant SWITCHES.
      FileName:CH7D      Modula-2      RKW      Apr. 1991  *)

FROM InOut IMPORT WriteString, WriteLn, OpenOutput, CloseOutput;
FROM RealInOut IMPORT ReadReal, FWriteReal;

CONST  PI = 3.14159;
       DEBUG = TRUE;
       REDIRECTOUT = FALSE;

VAR  radius, Area, Diameter, Circumference : REAL;

BEGIN
   WriteString("What is the radius? "); ReadReal(radius); WriteLn;
    IF DEBUG THEN
       WriteString("The value of radius just read is ");
        FWriteReal(radius,12,2); WriteLn; WriteLn;
    END; (* IF *)

   IF REDIRECTOUT THEN
       WriteString("Enter output file name (OUTDATA recommended).");
       OpenOutput("DAT");
   END; (* IF *)

   WriteString("When the radius is "); FWriteReal(radius,12,2); WriteLn;
   Area := PI * radius * radius;
    WriteString("The area is "); FWriteReal(Area,12,2); WriteLn;
   Diameter := 2.0 * radius;
    WriteString("The diameter is "); FWriteReal(Diameter,12,2); WriteLn;
   Circumference := 2.0 * PI * radius;
    WriteString("The circumference is "); FWriteReal(Circumference,12,2);
    WriteLn;

   IF REDIRECTOUT THEN
      CloseOutput;
   END; (* IF *)
END ComputeCircles.
```

A sample run with DEBUG = TRUE, REDIRECTOUT = FALSE, and entering 3.5 for the radius displays:

```
What is the radius? 3.5
The value of radius just read is        3.50

When the radius is        3.50
The area is        38.48
The diameter is        7.00
The circumference is        21.99
```

You will want to test the program with the 4 combinations of TRUE and FALSE values for DEBUG and REDIRECTOUT to convince yourself that changing the values of these CONSTants does indeed switch the echo write and the redirection on and off.

☐ Done, Imported from InOut

Examination of the definition module InOut in Appendix B reveals that a BOOL-EAN variable called *Done* is defined as part of that standard module. "Done" can be imported from InOut. Anytime a call to an InOut procedure succeeds, Done is assigned the value TRUE; whenever an InOut procedure fails to perform its task, the value of Done becomes FALSE.

Done is particularly useful when reading data from a file, to determine whether the Read... command has made an unsuccessful attempt to read past the end of the file.

For example, consider again the procedure ReadAndCalculate from Chapter 6 (Example 6.3.1, FileName:CH6C), which accumulates the Sum and Sum of Squares (SumSq) and finds the Average of a list of Numbers read from an input file. Make the following changes in the ReadAndCalculate code:

1. No variable or parameter HowMany is needed. The WHILE Done DO... structure reads Numbers from the file until ReadInt(Number) fails, at which time Done becomes FALSE. The user does not need to specify HowMany Numbers there are.
2. The Numbers are INTEGERS instead of REAL numbers. Done, from InOut, checks only InOut procedures (such as ReadInt)—and not procedures (such as ReadReal) from other modules. Not all versions of Modula-2 include a "Done" variable in module RealInOut.
3. An initial ReadInt(Number), before WHILE, assigns TRUE to Done, assuming there is at least one Number in the file to be read.
4. The command ReadInt(Number), to read the next Number, has been moved to the end of the loop so that the next action, WHILE Done DO..., is to test whether the ReadInt was successful.
5. The Mean (Average) is calculated using the accumulator ReadSoFar, which counts how many Numbers have been read.

And a new code, ModifiedFindSums, is produced.

```
MODULE ModifiedFindSums;
  (* Finds Sum, Sum of Squares, and Average of a list of integers.  Uses
     BOOLEAN variable Done  to terminate reading from the file.
     FileName:CH7E    Modula-2    RKW    Apr. 1991    *)

FROM InOut IMPORT WriteLn, WriteString, ReadInt, WriteInt,
                  OpenInput, CloseInput, Done;
FROM RealInOut IMPORT FWriteReal;
FROM MathLib0 IMPORT real;
VAR  Sum, SumSq : INTEGER;   Average : REAL;

PROCEDURE ReadAndCalculate(VAR Total,TotalOfSquares:INTEGER;  VAR Mean:REAL);
    (* Reads real numbers from a file, accumulates sums, finds mean *)
    VAR  ReadSoFar, Number : INTEGER;
    BEGIN
        WriteString("Name of input file? "); OpenInput("DAT");
        ReadSoFar := 0;  Total := 0;  TotalOfSquares := 0; WriteLn; WriteLn;
```

```
      ReadInt(Number);
      WHILE  Done  DO
         INC(ReadSoFar);
         WriteString("Number "); WriteInt(ReadSoFar,3);
          WriteString(" is "); WriteInt(Number,12); WriteLn;
         Total   :=  Total + Number;
         TotalOfSquares  :=  TotalOfSquares  +  Number * Number;
         ReadInt(Number);
      END; (* WHILE *)
      Mean   :=  real(Total) / real(ReadSoFar);
      CloseInput;  WriteLn; WriteLn;
   END ReadAndCalculate;

BEGIN (* ModifiedFindSums *)
   ReadAndCalculate(Sum, SumSq, Average);

   WriteString("          Sum       Sum of Squares     Average"); WriteLn;
   WriteInt(Sum,12); WriteString("          ");
   WriteInt(SumSq,13); FWriteReal(Average,11,4);  WriteLn;
END ModifiedFindSums.
```

For a file CH7E.IN containing the INTEGERS

```
12    -6     7    2     5
 9     8   -11    4    -3
```

a sample run appears as follows.

```
Name of input file? CH7E.IN

Number   1 is          12
Number   2 is          -6
Number   3 is           7
Number   4 is           2
Number   5 is           5
Number   6 is           9
Number   7 is           8
Number   8 is         -11
Number   9 is           4
Number  10 is          -3


          Sum      Sum of Squares    Average
           27                 549     2.7000
```

Questions 7.3

1. Given declarations and initial assignments

```
VAR  Boole1, Boole2 : BOOLEAN;   Num2, Num2 : CARDINAL;
     Mark1, Mark2 : CHAR;
...
Num1 := 1;  Num2 := 2;  Mark1 := 'A';   Mark2 := 'C';
Boole1 := TRUE;   Boole2 := FALSE;
```

which of these BOOLEAN assignments are valid and which are invalid? Which are TRUE and which are FALSE?

    a. Boole1 := Boole1 AND (Num1 = 5);
    b. Boole1 := (Num1 + Num2) < 5;
    c. Boole2 := (Num1 + Num2) > 5;
    d. Boole1 := Num1 OR Num2;
    e. Boole2 := Num1 AND Num2;
    f. Boole1 := ORD(Mark1) < ORD('M');
    g. Boole2 := CHR(ORD(Mark2) + 3);
    h. Num1 := ORD(Boole1) + 5;
    i. Boole1 := Num1 > Num2 AND Num2 < Num1;
    j. Boole2 := (Num2 DIV Num1 > Num1) OR FALSE;

2. Use a truth table to determine whether these two statements are equivalent:

    I. They are schoolteachers, and they are not rich.
    II. It is not true that (either they are not schoolteachers or they are rich).

Hint: let A = they are schoolteachers, and let B = they are rich. Label your truth-table columns A, B, NOTA, NOTB, A AND NOT B, NOT A OR B, and NOT(NOT A OR B).

3. Given the declarations and initial assignments in question 1, what is the value of each of these expressions?
    a. ORD(FALSE)
    b. ORD(TRUE)
    c. ORD((Num1 < 5) AND (Num2 > 10))
    d. ORD ((Mark1 = 'A') OR (Num2 < 3))
    e. Val (BOOLEAN, Num1);
    f. VAL(BOOLEAN, Num2 − 2 * Num1)

4. Given the declaration and initial assignments in question 1, for which of the following conditions would Modula-2 short-circuit and not evaluate the expression following AND or OR. For which conditions would the evaluations not short-circuit? Which conditions are TRUE and which are FALSE?
    a. If   (Num1 < 2) OR (Num1 = 6)   THEN ...
    b. WHILE   (Num1 > 2) OR (Mark2 = 'A')   DO ...
    c. WHILE   (Mark1 > Mark2) AND Boole1   DO ...
    d. If ((Num1 + Num2) > Num2) AND (ORD(Mark1) < 1000) THEN ...

5. a. In the program FindInsurancePremium (Example 7.3.1), why not write the four IF...THEN... structures as

```
IF      TestAge        THEN   RateChange := AGERATE;
ELSIF TestAccidents THEN   RateChange := ACCIDENTRATE;
ELSIF TestSize       THEN   RateChange := SIZERATE;
ELSIF TestVintage    THEN   RateChange := VINTAGERATE;
END; (* IF *)
Premium := BASICCOST * (1.0 + RateChange);
```

    b. Given the values DriverAge = 20, Accidents = 0, CarSize = 'C', and Vintage = 12 from the sample run, what would be the Premium calculated with the ELSIF structure in part a?

6. What would be displayed by this program fragment when BOOLEAN switch INSURE is **a.** TRUE; **b.** FALSE?

```
...
CONST INSURE = TRUE;
VAR  NetPay : REAL;
```

```
...
BEGIN
   NetPay := 1000.00;
   IF  INSURE  THEN
      NetPay := NetPay - 0.15 * NetPay;
   END; (* IF *)
   FWriteReal(NetPay, 12, 2);
   ...
```

7. a. Use truth tables to prove De Morgan's laws:

$$\text{NOT}(A \text{ AND } B) = (\text{NOT } A) \text{ OR } (\text{NOT } B)$$
$$\text{NOT}(A \text{ OR } B) = (\text{NOT } A) \text{ AND } (\text{NOT } B)$$

b. Show that another form of De Morgan's laws is

$$P \text{ AND } (\text{NOT } Q) = \text{NOT}((\text{NOT } P) \text{ OR } Q)$$
$$P \text{ OR } (\text{NOT } Q) = \text{NOT}((\text{NOT } P) \text{ AND } Q)$$

Hint: First apply NOT to both sides of the laws in part a, remembering that NOT(NOT M) = M. This gives another form of the laws. (What is it?) Then replace A with P and replace B with (NOT Q).

c. Use De Morgan's laws to rewrite

NOT(Num1 < 5) AND NOT(Num2 > 10)   in a form using OR,   *and*
NOT((Mark1 = 'A') OR (Mark1 = 'C'))   in a form using AND.

7.4 *Decision Trees and Tables*

It may be difficult to tell if a multiple-selection structure will produce the desired results or not. As with any problem, it often helps to draw a picture. Two pictorial representations of selection structures are the decision tree and the decision table.

Consider these two situations:

```
I.    IF    P AND Q    THEN
          WriteString("Action 1"); WriteLn;
      ELSE
          IF    NOT P    AND    NOT Q    THEN
                  WriteString("Action 2"); WriteLn;
          ELSE
                  WriteString("Action 3"); WriteLn;
          END; (* IF *)
      END; (* IF *)

II.   IF    P    THEN
              IF    Q    THEN
                      WriteString("Action 1"); WriteLn;
              ELSE
                      WriteString("Action 2"); WriteLn;
              END; (* IF *)
      ELSE
              WriteString("Action 3"); WriteLn;
      END; (* IF *)
```

Trees

To determine whether structures I and II produce the same results, draw a **Decision Tree** for each one as shown in Figure 7–10.

Figure 7–10
Decision Trees
(Structures I and II)

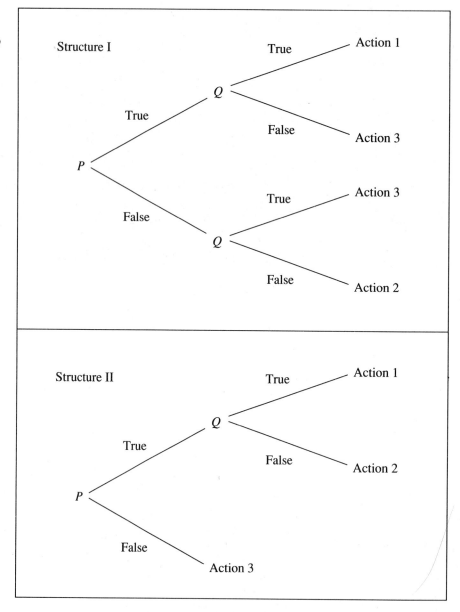

First look at the construction of the tree for Structure II. Beginning with root *P*, draw branches for True and False. On the True branch from *P*, show *Q*, because when *P* is True, *Q* is tested. On the False branch from *P* show Action 3, because when *P* is False "Action 3" is written. From *Q* draw branches for True and False. On the True branch from *Q* show Action 1, because "Action 1" is written when *Q* is True. On the False branch from *Q* show Action 2, which is the message written when *Q* is False.

For Structure I, begin again with root *P* and Draw True and False branches. This time both *P* and *Q* are tested first, so both branches from *P* will go to a *Q* node. Then follow through; if *P* is True and *Q* is True, "Action 1" is printed; if *P* is True and *Q* is False (or vice versa), "Action 3" is printed; and if *P* and *Q* are both False, "Action 2" is printed.

Figure 7−11
Decision Tree
(Structure III)

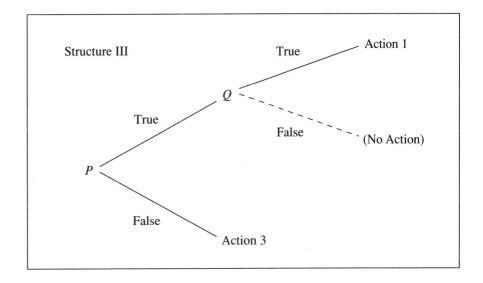

From these two trees it is apparent that structures I and II do not produce the same results. It is possible to have a situation where nothing occurs. For example, a new structure III is

```
III. IF    P    THEN
         IF    Q    THEN
               WriteString("Action 1"); WriteLn;
         END; (* IF *)
     ELSE
         WriteString("Action 3"); WriteLn;
     END; (* IF *)
```

The decision tree would appear as in Figure 7−11. When *Q* is False, the structure does not provide for any action to occur. Therefore, either no False branch from *Q* is drawn at all; or if you prefer, a branch is drawn that terminates in No Action.

Tables

A different kind of diagram for testing selection structures is the **decision table.** A decision table is similar to a truth table. The major difference is that decision tables are used to analyze structures, while truth tables generally are used to analyze single logical expressions. In either case, begin by creating a column for each entity, *P* and *Q* in this case, and listing all possible combinations of truth values for these entities. Then create columns for each possible resulting action and one for No Action, and write "Yes" (or a check mark or X) in the appropriate places in the table where the actions occur.

Figure 7−12 shows the decision tables for each of the three structures. It should be apparent from the tables that Structures I, II, and III produce different results.

You may choose to use decision trees or decision tables, whichever you prefer; but you should practice using both. In some situations it may be easier to construct one than the other. At times you may wish to draw both to make certain that the results agree.

Figure 7–12
Decision Tables
(Structures I, II,
and III)

Structure I

P	Q	Action1	Action2	Action3	No Action
True	True	Yes			
True	False			Yes	
False	True			Yes	
False	False		Yes		

Structure II

P	Q	Action1	Action2	Action3	No Action
True	True	Yes			
True	False		Yes		
False	True			Yes	
False	False			Yes	

Structure III

P	Q	Action1	Action2	Action3	No Action
True	True	Yes			
True	False				Yes
False	True			Yes	
False	False			Yes	

Example 7.4.1

Draw a decision tree and a decision table for the FindTriangleType procedure
(Example 7.1.1).

Define the problem: In pseudocode, the structure of procedure FindTriangle-
Type looks like

```
if    c = sqrt(a² + b²)    then
   if    a = b    then
      right and isosceles
   otherwise
      right and scalene
otherwise
   if    a = b    and    b = c    then
      equilateral
```

```
otherwise
  if    a = b    or    b = c    then
    not right, but isosceles
  otherwise
    not right, but scalene
  end if
end if
end if
```

Draw a decision tree and a decision table for this structure.

Develop and refine the solution The logical entities are $c = \text{sqrt}(a^2 + b^2)$, $(a = b)$, $[(a = b)$ and $(a = c)]$, and $[(a = b)$ or $(a = c)]$. The actions are isosceles right triangle, scalene right triangle, equilateral, isosceles, and scalene. Figure 7–13 shows the decision tree and the decision table. In the decision table—with 4 logical entities—there are $2^4 \, (= 16)$ possible truth combinations. An easy way to make sure you find them all is to begin in the rightmost column alternating T F T F . . . ; then, in the next column to the left, alternate every 2 T T F F T T F F . . . ; in the next column alternate every 4 T T T T F F F F . . . ; then every 8, every 16, and so forth, until all columns are filled. Another way to represent all possibilities is to count in binary from 0000 to 1111; then let 0 represent FALSE, and 1 represent TRUE (shown from bottom up in Figure 7–13).

You may observe that there are several impossible combinations in the decision table. For example, you cannot have $a = b$ TRUE while $[(a = b)$ OR $(b = c)]$ is FALSE; and you cannot have a right triangle where $b = c$. This decision table could be shortened by drawing two tables, one for right triangles and only the logical

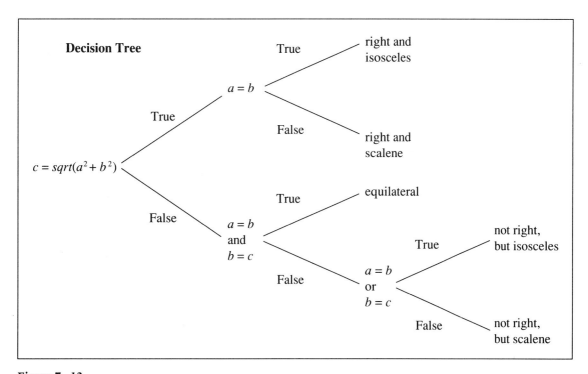

Figure 7–13
Decision Tree and Decision Table for FindTriangleType (Example 7.4.1) *(continued)*

Decision Table

$c = sqrt$ $(a^2 + b^2)$	$a = b$	$a = b$ and $a = c$	$a = b$ or $b = c$	right and isos- celes	right and sca- lene	equi- lateral	not right, but isos- celes	not right, but sca- lene	no action
T 1	T 1	T 1	T 1						Yes*
T 1	T 1	T 1	F 0						Yes*
T 1	T 1	F 0	T 1	Yes					
T 1	T 1	F 0	F 0						Yes*
T 1	F 0	T 1	T 1						Yes*
T 1	F 0	T 1	F 0						Yes*
T 1	F 0	F 0	T 1						Yes*
T 1	F 0	F 0	F 0		Yes				
F 0	T 1	T 1	T 1			Yes			
F 0	T 1	T 1	F 0						Yes*
F 0	T 1	F 0	T 1				Yes		
F 0	T 1	F 0	F 0						Yes*
F 0	F 0	T 1	T 1						Yes*
F 0	F 0	T 1	F 0						Yes*
F 0	F 0	F 0	T 1				Yes		
F 0	F 0	F 0	F 0					Yes	

*These truth combinations are not possible for actual triangles.

Figure 7–13
(continued)

entity $a = b$, and a second table for entities $[(a = b)$ and $(b = c)]$ combined with $[(a = b)$ or $(b = c)]$.

Code, debug, and test   The code was written and tested in Example 7.1.1.

Complete the documentation   Add Figure 7–13 to the documentation in Example 7.1.1.

Questions 7.4

1. a. Redraw the decision table in Figure 7–13 by drawing *two* tables. One table will have the heading ''Right Triangle'' and will show the single condition $a = b$, with actions isosceles, scalene, and no action.

A Bit of Background

Deductive and Inductive Reasoning

Since Aristotle (384–322 B.C.), a fundamental method of thought has been the syllogism with a general proposition, a specific proposition, and a specific conclusion, such as

specific proposition:	My pet is a cat.
general proposition:	All cats have hair.
specific conclusion:	My pet has hair.

This is an example of *deductive logic*, in which general rules lead to specific conclusions. Mathematics and binary logic are based upon deductive reasoning.

On the other hand, the scientific method attempts to draw general conclusions from specific experimental results. For example, a billion objects have been thrown into the air and they all have come back down. Therefore, everything that goes up must come down. This is *inductive logic.* Inductive conclusions can be verified repeatedly but never proved for certain unless the number of possible situations is finite. It takes only one contradictory experiment to disprove an inductive conclusion. For example, a *Voyager* spacecraft was thrown into the air and it did not come down.

The other table will be headed "Not a Right Triangle" and will show conditions [$(a = b)$ and $(b = c)$] and [$(a = b)$ or $(a = c)$], with actions equilateral, isosceles, scalene, and no action.

   b. Write pseudocode for each of the tables in part a.

2. Given the structures

```
I.    IF    (Apples > 5) AND (Oranges > 10)    THEN
          WriteString("You have enough.");
      ELSE
          WriteString("Buy some more.");
      END; (* IF *)


II.   IF    (Apples > 5)    THEN
          IF    (Oranges > 10)    THEN
              WriteString("You have enough.");
          ELSE
              WriteString("Buy some more.");
          END; (* IF *)
      END; (* IF *)
```

   a. Draw decision trees for the two structures.
   b. Draw decision tables for the two structures.
   c. Are the two structures equivalent?

3. Given the decision tree in Figure 7–14,
   a. write Modula-2 code in nested IF form.
   b. write Modula-2 code in ELSIF form. *Hint:* the branch that writes "$A = B = C$" could be represented by

```
ELSIF (A = B) AND (B = C) AND NOT(C = D) THEN (* write '' A = B = C '' *).
```

   c. draw an equivalent decision table.

7.5 CASE

A different selection method may be applied when the choices can be represented by enumerable types (CARDINAL, INTEGER, CHAR, BOOLEAN). This method

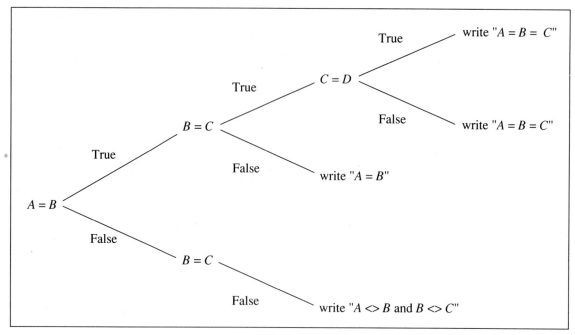

Figure 7–14
Decision Tree (Section 7.4, Question 3)

is the CASE structure, and it allows you to list all possibilities. CASE cannot be used directly with REAL numbers because, for example, you cannot list all of the real numbers between 1.0 and 5.0; there are an infinite number of them. But you can list all CARDINAL and INTEGER values between 1 and 5, and all alphabet CHARacters between *A* and *E*.

The general syntax for a CASE structure is shown in Figure 7–15. Please read the Notes in the figure carefully. They are important.

☐ CASE, Nested IFs, ELSIF, or Separate IFs?

CASE, nested IF statements, ELSIF, and independent IF commands are interchangeable in many, but not all, situations. However, even when several structures *can* be used, one may be more convenient, effective, or efficient than the others.

Here are some considerations that may help you decide which multiple-selection technique to use.

1. When there are more than two choices and the choices can be represented by enumerable data types (CARDINAL, INTEGER, CHAR, BOOLEAN) and can be listed easily, the CASE structure may be most effective.
2. When the choices can be stated as simple, readable compound BOOLEAN expressions, such as *A* OR NOT *B,* then ELSIF structures are relatively easy to employ.
3. When the statements of choices in terms of compound BOOLEAN expressions become difficult to read and understand, such as (*A* OR *B*) AND NOT(*C* OR NOT *D*), nested IF structures with simply stated conditions may create more readable code.

```
    General Format:

        CASE EnumerableExpression OF
            Value1 or List1ofValues : Actions1    |
            Value2 or List2ofValues : Actions2    |
            ...
            ...
            ValueN or ListNofValues : ActionsN;
        ELSE (* optional *)
            ElseActions;
        END; (* CASE *)
```

```
    Example:
...
VAR  Books, ShelfLength : CARDINAL;
...
BEGIN
    ...
    WriteString("How many books do you have? "); ReadCard(Books); WriteLn;
    CASE   Books   OF
        1                : WriteString("Only one book?")                |
        2..5             : WriteString("Will fit on a table.")          |
                                (* Books = 2 or 3 or 4 or 5 *)
        8                : | (* No action when Books = 8; order not critical *)
        6,7              : WriteString("Could fit on a table,");
                              WriteString(" or build a short shelf.")   |
                                (*More than one action, Books = 6 or 7 *)
        9..20, 50..100 : WriteString("Build a bookcase (inches =)");
                            ShelfLength := Books*2; WriteCard(ShelfLength, 6);
                                (* Books between 9 and 20, or 50 and 100 *)
                                (* No vertical bar (|) before ELSE       *)
        ELSE
            WriteString("Sell some of your books."); WriteLn;
            WriteString("I might be interested.");
                        (* For all values of Books not listed above. *)
                        (* No vertical bar (|) before END; (* CASE *) *)
    END; (* CASE *)
    ....
```

NOTES:

-   The vertical bar (|) separates the actions of one case from the
    list of values for the next case.
-   There is no vertical bar (|) before ELSE or before END;(*CASE*)
-   Empty actions are allowed. To make it explicit which values
    require no action, follow the colon by the vertical bar (:|).
-   If the EnumberableExpression has a value that is not listed, then
    in the absence of ELSE no action is performed, or when ELSE is
    present ElseActions are performed.
-   The CASE alternatives usually are listed in order, but they do not
    need to be.

Figure 7–15
CASE Syntax

4. When the choices are not mutually exclusive—that is, when more than one task needs to be accomplished at a given time—independent IF commands may be most efficient. The decisions in FindInsurancePremium (Example 7.3.1, FileName:CH7C) illustrate this situation.

The two examples that follow illustrate the use of CASE for numeric and CHARacter values.

CASE with Numbers

After 1991, the summer Olympic games will be held in those calendar years that are evenly divisible by four; and winter Olympic games will be held in the other even-numbered years. The following program uses CASE with CARDINAL numbers to print out the appropriate message stating whether summer, winter, or no games will be held during a year entered by the user. Note how the value of Year MOD 4 is the deciding condition.

```
MODULE Olympics;
   (* Determines whether Summer, Winter, or no Olympics.
      FileName:CH7F      Modula-2      RKW      Apr. 1991   *)

FROM InOut IMPORT ReadCard, WriteCard, WriteString, WriteLn;

VAR  Year : CARDINAL;

BEGIN
   WriteString("What is the year (after 1991)? ");
    ReadCard(Year); WriteLn;
   WHILE  Year <= 1991  DO
       WriteString("The year must be after 1991. Enter year again: ");
        ReadCard(Year); WriteLn;
   END; (* WHILE *)

   WriteString("In the year "); WriteCard(Year,5);
   CASE  Year MOD 4  OF
      0 : WriteString(" Summer Olympics will be held."); WriteLn |
      2 : WriteString(" Winter Olympics will be held."); WriteLn;
      ELSE
          WriteString(" no Olympics will be held."); WriteLn;
   END; (* CASE *)
END Olympics.
```

In this code you could have used the choices

```
   1,3 : WriteString("no Olympics will be held."); WriteLn;
```

instead of the ELSE option.

Nested CASE with Characters and Done

The following example illustrates the use of CASE with CHARacter variables and nesting of CASE structures. The BOOLEAN variable ''Done'' from module InOut is used to detect the end of data from an input file.

An input file contains a list of last names, first names, and letter grades for students, each on a separate line to ensure that the file can be handled by all versions of Modula-2. (Return is always accepted as a character or string terminator.)

The program reads the complete name and corresponding grade. Report cards are generated with first name, last name, and grade and the teacher's choice from three comments for each grade.

In the procedure ChooseAndReport and nested function SelectIt, pay particularly close attention to these features:

1. The valid values of WhichOne are CHARacters '1', '2', and '3' rather than CARDINAL 1, 2, and 3, since there is a CHARacter Read procedure but no ReadCard in the Terminal module. Also, using CHARacters for menu choices allows the program to check for any key pressed (numeric, alphabetic, punctuation) and makes the program more foolproof. You may wish to add a WHILE loop in function SelectIt to limit selection of WhichOne to '1', '2', or '3'. (See Exercise 14 at the end of the chapter.)
2. Only the message CONSTants MESG4, MESG5, and MESG6 for a 'B' grade have been defined in the program. WriteReportCard is used as a stub procedure for other grades, by passing a generic message for a parameter. The program can be completed by defining MESG1, MESG2, MESG3 for an 'A' grade; MESG7, MESG8, MESG9 for a 'C' grade; and so on. (See Exercise 14 at the end of the chapter.) Also observe the definition of TYPE MSGSTR, which is used in the procedure headings to accept formal value parameter messages.
3. Study carefully the nested CASE structure

```
CASE  Score  OF
     'B'  :  ...
               CASE  Choice  OF
                  . . . .
```

especially where semicolons (;) and vertical bars (|) are used.

```
MODULE  MakeReportCards;
    (* Reads names and grades from a file and generates report cards.
        FileName:CH7G      Modula-2      RKW      Apr. 1991  *)

FROM InOut IMPORT ReadString, WriteString, WriteLn, Read, Write, Done,
                  OpenInput, CloseInput, OpenOutput, CloseOutput;
IMPORT Terminal;

CONST LASTNAMECHAR = 19; LASTMSGCHAR = 49; MESG4 = "Not bad work.";
      MESG5 = "Pretty good.";  MESG6 = "You could do 'A' work.";
TYPE  NAME = ARRAY [0..LASTNAMECHAR] OF CHAR;
      MSGSTR = ARRAY [0..LASTMSGCHAR] OF CHAR;
VAR  LastName, FirstName : NAME;   Grade, GradeTerminator : CHAR;

PROCEDURE WriteReportCard(LName,FName:NAME; LetrGr:CHAR; Message:MSGSTR)
    BEGIN
       WriteLn; WriteString(FName); WriteString("   "); WriteString(LName
       WriteLn; Write(LetrGr); WriteString("   ");
       WriteString(Message); WriteLn; WriteLn;
    END WriteReportCard;

PROCEDURE ChooseAndReport(Last, First : NAME;   Score : CHAR);
    VAR  Choice : CHAR;
```

```
    PROCEDURE SelectIt(Message1, Message2, Message3 : MSGSTR) : CHAR;
      VAR  WhichOne, Discard : CHAR;
      BEGIN  (* SelectIt *)
        Terminal.WriteString("Comment choices are:");Terminal.WriteLn;
         Terminal.WriteString("   1.   ");
          Terminal.WriteString(MESG4); Terminal.WriteLn;
         Terminal.WriteString("   2.   ");
          Terminal.WriteString(MESG5); Terminal.WriteLn;
         Terminal.WriteString("   3.   ");
          Terminal.WriteString(MESG6); Terminal.WriteLn;
        Terminal.WriteString("Choose one (1, 2, 3): ");
         Terminal.Read(WhichOne); Terminal.Read(Discard);
          Terminal.Write(WhichOne); Terminal.WriteLn;
        RETURN WhichOne;
      END SelectIt;

  BEGIN  (* ChooseAndReport *)
         (* ECHO NAME AND GRADE TO SCREEN *)
    Terminal.WriteLn; Terminal.WriteString("Student:   ");
    Terminal.WriteString(First); Terminal.WriteString("   ");
    Terminal.WriteString(Last);  Terminal.WriteString("   ");
    Terminal.WriteString(Score); Terminal.WriteLn;
         (* CHOOSE COMMENT, WRITE REPORT CARD *)
    CASE  Score  OF
       'B' : Choice := SelectIt(MESG4, MESG5, MESG6);
             CASE  Choice  OF
                 '1' : WriteReportCard(Last, First, Score, MESG4) |
                 '2' : WriteReportCard(Last, First, Score, MESG5) |
                 '3' : WriteReportCard(Last, First, Score, MESG6) ;
             END  (* CASE *)   |
       'A', 'C', 'D', 'F' : WriteReportCard(Last,First,Score,"Good Kid!") |
       ELSE
           WriteReportCard(Last,First,Score,"Not a Valid Grade") ;
    END; (* CASE *)
  END ChooseAndReport;

BEGIN (* main module MakeReportCards *)
   WriteString("Input file name? "); OpenInput("IN");
   WriteString("Output file name? "); OpenOutput("OUT");

   ReadString(LastName);
   WHILE  Done  DO
      ReadString(FirstName); Read(Grade); Read(GradeTerminator);
      ChooseAndReport(LastName, FirstName, Grade);
      ReadString(LastName);
   END; (* WHILE *)
   CloseInput;  CloseOutput;
END MakeReportCards.
```

Running the program with an input file CH7G.IN, containing

> Adams
> Tom
> C
> Burns
> Sally
> B

                              Smith
                              Judy
                              L

produces the display

```
Input file name? >IN  CH7G.IN
Output file name? >OUT CH7G.OUT

Student:   Tom    Adams    C

Student:   Sally    Burns    B
Comment choices are:
   1.    Not bad work.
   2.    Pretty good.
   3.    You could do 'A' work.
Choose one (1, 2, 3): 3

Student:   Judy    Smith    L
```

and the output file

```
Tom    Adams
C    Good Kid!

Sally    Burns
B    You could do 'A' work.

Judy    Smith
L    Not a Valid Grade
```

Questions 7.5

1. Write a CASE structure for INTEGER Temperatures that displays the given messages:

Temperature	Message
−20 to −1 and 1 to 30	Mighty cold, check your antifreeze.
0	Exactly zero.
30, 31	Cover your tomato plants.
33 to 67	Below room temperature.
68	Comfortable.
69 to 110	Getting warm.
everything else	Beyond the thermometer range.

2. Given the declaration VAR Letter, Discard : CHAR;
   a. Correct the punctuation in the following program fragment.
   b. After corrections are made what is displayed when the user presses the key (1) 'M'; (2) 'm'; (3) the space bar; (4) '!'; (5) '7'; (6) CTRL/G?

```
Read(Letter); Read(Discard); WriteLn;
Write(Letter); WriteString(" is ");
CASE  ORD(Letter)  OF
   33..126 : CASE  Letter  OF
              'a'..'z' : WriteString("lower case.");
              'A'..'Z' : WriteString("upper case.");
              '0'..'9' : WriteString("a digit.");
           ELSE
              WriteString("a punctuation character.");
           END; (* CASE *)
```

```
      32        : WriteString("the space character.");
   ELSE
       WriteString("Not a printable character.");
END; (* CASE *)
```

7.6 *Focus on Problem Solving*

Even though IF...THEN...ELSE is generally the easiest structure to use when there are only two choices, the CASE structure also can be applied with BOOLEAN (FALSE, TRUE) values and may make the condition being tested more visible and explicit in some circumstances.

In this section, a program is developed to determine the slope, intercepts, and point of intersection of two lines in a plane. For illustration, CASE will be applied to BOOLEAN variables Parallel and Perpendicular.

Lines in the Plane

The equations for two straight lines in the x,y-plane can be written as

$$\text{Line1: } a_1x + b_1y = c_1$$
$$\text{Line2: } a_2x + b_2y = c_2$$

If the coefficients a_1, b_1, c_1 and a_2, b_2, c_2 are known, the x- and y-intercepts, slopes, and point of intersection of the lines can be determined, as shown in Figure 7–16.

If two lines have the same slope, either they are parallel and do not intersect, or (if they have the same intercepts) their equations represent the same line.

One-Dimensional Number Arrays

In some previous examples you have used one-dimensional arrays (lists) of CHARacters, which have been referred to as *character strings*. Arrays can be extended easily to handle one-dimensional lists of numbers. Arrays of other entities and with two, three, or more dimensions are discussed in Chapter 10.

For the problem at hand, consider these declarations:

```
CONST  ARRAYLENGTH = 2;
TYPE  LISTOFREAL = ARRAY [1..ARRAYLENGTH] OF REAL;
VAR a, b, c, Slope, XIntercept, YIntercept : LISTOFREAL;
```

These declarations reserve memory locations, as shown in Figure 7–17.

The **index** or **subscript** (indicated by [1] or [2] for ARRAY [1..2] OF REAL declared above) designates which element of the array is being referenced. In this problem, the index refers to the line being considered. For example, Slope[1] represents the slope of Line1; Slope[2], the slope of Line2.

One major advantage of arrays is that the index may be represented by a variable, so that

$$\text{Slope}[K] = \text{slope of Line1, when } K = 1, \quad \text{and}$$
$$\text{Slope}[K] = \text{slope of Line2, when } K = 2.$$

An individual element of an array may be passed as a parameter to a procedure just as any other single variable. For example, the procedure heading and call

```
PROCEDURE AGivenProcedure(SlopOfLine1 : REAL);  (* procedure heading *)
...
AGivenProcedure(Slope[1]); (* call to AGivenProcedure *)
```

Figure 7–16
Intersecting Lines
in the *x,y*-plane

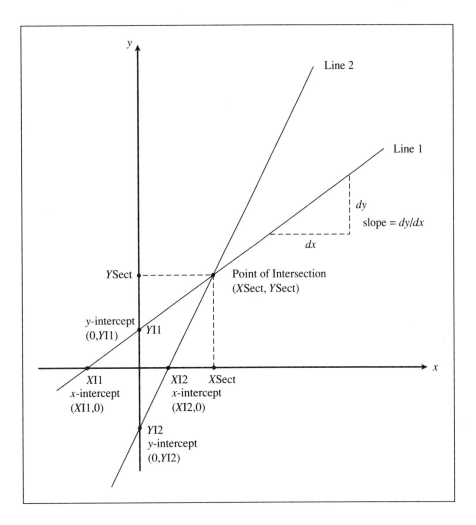

Figure 7–17
One-Dimensional
Arrays of Length
= 2 for Determine
LineFeatures
(Example 7.6.1)

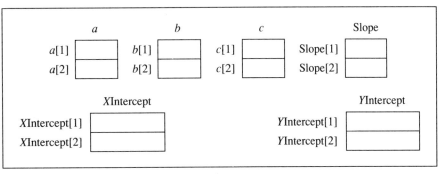

pass REAL value Slope[1] to AGivenProcedure, where it will be known as variable SlopeOfLine1.

Also, in one of the few situations where an array name may be used without an index, an entire array may be passed as a parameter to a procedure. For example, the heading and call

```
PROCEDURE AnotherProcedure(Inclination : LISTOFREAL); (* heading *)
...
AnotherProcedure(Slope);  (* call to AnotherProcedure *)
```

pass	Array Slope	to	Array Inclination
that is,	Slope[1]	is copied to	Inclination[1],
and	Slope[2]	is copied to	Inclination[2].

☐ Solving the Line Equations

Now determine the features of the two lines in the x,y-plane.

Example 7.6.1

Given the equations of two lines in the x,y-plane, determine their slopes, intercepts, and point of intersection.

Define the problem   The equations for the lines can be written as

$$\text{Line1: } a[1]x + b[1]y = c[1]$$
$$\text{Line2: } a[2]x + b[2]y = c[2]$$

Write a program that asks for arrays a, b, and c and prints the equations of the lines. Find the slopes and intercepts shown in Figure 7–16. Then determine whether the lines are parallel to each other, perpendicular, or neither. If the lines have the same slope, determine whether they are parallel or the same line; otherwise, find the point of intersection.

Develop a solution   CASE cannot be used directly with REAL variables. BOOLEAN test conditions, on the other hand, *can* be written using REAL values. For illustration, CASE will be used with BOOLEAN test values Parallel and Perpendicular, though IF…THEN…ELSE would also work.

The Slope of a line defined by $ax + by = c$ is given by Slope $= -a/b$. The x-intercept and y-intercept are given by c/a and c/b, respectively. In this example, the lines will not be horizontal or vertical; that is, neither a nor b will be zero. (In Exercise 15 at the end of the chapter you are invited to extend the solution to handle horizontal and vertical lines.) When the slopes for two lines are equal, either there is no point of intersection or they are the same line. If the slopes are not equal, then the point of intersection is at (XSect, YSect), where

$$X\text{Sect} = (c[2]b[1] - b[2]c[1]) / (a[2]b[1] - a[1]b[2])$$
$$Y\text{Sect} = (a[2]c[1] - c[2]a[1]) / (a[2]b[1] - a[1]b[2])$$

If Slope[2] $= -1.0/$Slope[1], then the lines are perpendicular.

Figure 7–18 shows a decision tree for a procedure PrintIt, to display the results. A structure chart for the solution is illustrated in Figure 7–19.

Refine the solution   *Pseudocode*

```
main module DetermineLineFeatures
begin
    EnterEquations(a, b, c)
    Calculate(a, b, c, Slope, XIntercept, YIntercept, Parallel, Perpendicular, XSect, YSect)
    PrintIt(Parallel, Perpendicular, Slope, XIntercept, YIntercept, XSect, YSect)
end DetermineLineFeatures

procedure EnterEquations(VAR a, b, c : LISTOFREAL)
begin
    ask for a[1], b[1], c[1], a[2], b[2], c[2],
    print equations for Line1 and Line2
end EnterEquations
```

Figure 7–18
Decision Tree for
DetermineLine
Features
(Example 7.6.1)

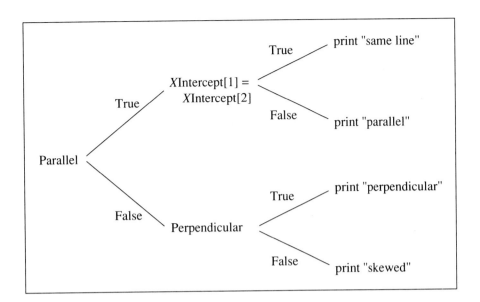

Figure 7–19
Structure Chart for
DetermineLine
Features
(Example 7.6.1)

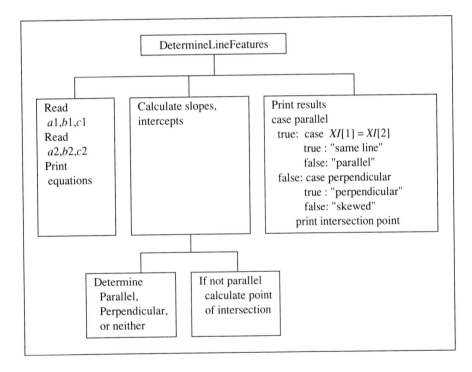

```
procedure Calculate(a,b,c:LISTOFREAL;      VAR m,XI,YI:LISTOFREAL;
         VAR Parallel,Perpendicular:BOOLEAN;      VAR XSect,YSect:REAL)
begin
        calculate slopes        m[K], and intercepts XI[K], YI[K]
        initialize      Parallel and Perpendicular to FALSE
        if              m[2] = m[1]         then Parallel      = TRUE
        else if         m[2] = − 1 / m[1]   then Perpendicular = TRUE

        if NOT(Parallel) then calculate      XSect and YSect
        end Calculate
```

```
procedure     PrintIt(Parallel, Perpendicular : BOOLEAN;     m, XI, YI : LISTOFREAL;
    XSect, YSect : REAL)
begin
   print x and y intercepts and slopes
   case     Parallel
        TRUE : case     XI[1] = XI[2]     (* same intercepts *)
                   TRUE  : print "same line"
                   FALSE : print "parallel"
                end case
        FALSE : case     Perpendicular
                   TRUE  : print "perpendicular"
                   FALSE : print "skewed"
                end case
                print point of intersection (XSect, YSect)
   end case
end PrintIt
```

Observe carefully, in the following code, the placement of vertical lines (|) versus semicolons (;) in the nested CASE structures. The value of the index is important; its name is not. Three different index identifiers—*K*, WhichLine, and Line—were used in the procedures, but it would have been equally acceptable to use the same index name in all three procedures. Note also the illustration of two different ways to increment the indices; that is, as INC(*K*) and as Line := Line + 1.

Modula-2 code

```
MODULE DetermineLineFeatures;
   (* Finds slopes, intercepts, and intersection of two lines.
      FileName:CH7H      Modula-2      RKW      Apr. 1991  *)


FROM InOut IMPORT WriteString, WriteLn, WriteCard;
FROM RealInOut IMPORT ReadReal, FWriteReal;

CONST ARRAYLENGTH = 2;    EPSILON = 0.001;
TYPE LISTOFREAL = ARRAY [1..ARRAYLENGTH] OF REAL;
VAR  Parallel, Perpendicular : BOOLEAN; XSect, YSect : REAL;
     Slope, XIntercept, YIntercept, a, b, c : LISTOFREAL;

PROCEDURE EnterEquations(VAR a, b, c : LISTOFREAL);
   VAR  K : CARDINAL;
   BEGIN
      WriteString("A line equation is  ax + by = c. "); WriteLn;
      WriteString("Enter coefficients a, b, and c. "); WriteLn;
      WriteString("Caution: Make a and b both nonzero. "); WriteLn;
      K := 1;
      WHILE  K <= 2  DO
         WriteString("For Line "); WriteCard(K,1); WriteLn;
          WriteString("   a = "); ReadReal(a[K]);
          WriteString("   b = "); ReadReal(b[K]);
          WriteString("   c = "); ReadReal(c[K]); WriteLn;
         WriteString("The equation is "); WriteLn;
          FWriteReal(a[K],8,3); WriteString("  x  +  ");
          FWriteReal(b[K],8,3); WriteString("  y  =  ");
          FWriteReal(c[K],8,3); WriteLn; WriteLn;
         INC(K);
      END; (* WHILE *)
   END EnterEquations;
```

```
PROCEDURE Calculate(a, b, c : LISTOFREAL;  VAR m, XI, YI : LISTOFREAL;
           VAR Parallel,Perpendicular:BOOLEAN;  VAR XSect, YSect : REAL);
    VAR  WhichLine : CARDINAL;    Divisor : REAL;
    BEGIN
       WhichLine := 1;
       WHILE  WhichLine <= 2  DO
          m[WhichLine] := -a[WhichLine] / b[WhichLine];
          XI[WhichLine] := c[WhichLine] / a[WhichLine];
          YI[WhichLine] := c[WhichLine] / b[WhichLine];
          INC(WhichLine);
       END; (* WHILE *)

       Parallel := FALSE;  Perpendicular := FALSE;
       IF  ABS( m[1] - m[2] ) < EPSILON  THEN
          Parallel := TRUE;
       ELSIF  ABS( m[2] - (-1.0/m[1]) ) < EPSILON  THEN
          Perpendicular := TRUE;
       END;

       IF  NOT(Parallel)  THEN
          Divisor := (a[2]*b[1] - a[1]*b[2]);
          XSect := (c[2]*b[1] - b[2]*c[1]) / Divisor;
          YSect := (a[2]*c[1] - c[2]*a[1]) / Divisor;
       END; (* IF *)
    END Calculate;


PROCEDURE PrintIt(Parallel, Perpendicular : BOOLEAN;
            m, XI, YI : LISTOFREAL;   XSect, YSect : REAL);
    VAR Line : CARDINAL;
    BEGIN
       Line := 1;
       WHILE  Line <= 2  DO
          WriteString("For Line "); WriteCard(Line,1); WriteLn;
          WriteString("   x-intercept, y-intercept: ");
          FWriteReal(XI[Line],8,3); FWriteReal(YI[Line],8,3); WriteLn;
          WriteString("   slope: ");
          FWriteReal(m[Line],8,3); WriteLn; WriteLn;
          Line := Line + 1;
       END; (* WHILE *)

       CASE  Parallel  OF
          TRUE : CASE  ABS(XI[1] - XI[2]) < EPSILON  OF
                 TRUE : WriteString("Equations represent the same line.") |
                 FALSE: WriteString("The lines are parallel.");
               END (* CASE *)  |
          FALSE: CASE  Perpendicular  OF
                 TRUE : WriteString("The lines are perpendicular.") |
                 FALSE: WriteString("The lines are skewed. ");
               END; (* CASE *)
               WriteLn; WriteString("They intersect at (x,y) =");
                FWriteReal(XSect,8,3); FWriteReal(YSect,8,3); WriteLn |
       END; (* CASE *)
    END PrintIt;


BEGIN  (* DetermineLineFeatures *)
    EnterEquations(a, b, c);
```

```
      Calculate(a, b, c, Slope, XIntercept, YIntercept,
                        Parallel, Perpendicular, XSect, YSect);
      PrintIt(Parallel, Perpendicular, Slope, XIntercept, YIntercept,
                                              XSect, YSect);
   END DetermineLineFeatures.
```

Debug and test Check the equations carefully by hand. Compare the order of parameters in the procedure calls with the order in the procedure headings.

Test with at least one parallel case, such as

$$3.0x + 4.0y = 5.0$$
$$6.0x + 8.0y = 20.0 \quad \text{(or} = 10.0 \text{ for ''the same line''),}$$

at least one perpendicular case, such as

$$4.0x + 3.0y = 5.0$$
$$6.0x - 8.0y = 20.0,$$

and at least one skewed case (choose your own values). A test run looks like:

```
A line equation is   ax + by = c
Enter coefficients a, b, and c.
Caution: Make a and b both nonzero.
For Line 1
    a = 2.6    b = -3.4    c = 24.3
The equation is
    2.600 x  +  -3.400 y  =  24.300

For Line 2
    a = -8.5    b = -5.3    c = 35.7
The equation is
    -8.500 x  +  -5.300 y  =  35.700

For Line 1
    x-intercept, y-intercept: 9.346 -7.147
    slope:     0.765

For Line 2
    x-intercept, y-intercept: -4.200 -6.736
    slope:    -1.604
The lines are skewed.
They intersect at (x, y); 0.174 -7.014
```

Complete the documentation The documentation should include the line equations, decision tree, structure chart, and pseudocode. Complete the documentation with the problem definition, code (CH7H), sample run, and a users' manual. In the users' manual, be sure to caution that the program does not handle horizontal or vertical lines, so neither *a* nor *b* should be entered as zero.

Questions 7.6

1. Redraw Figure 7–18, Decision Tree for DetermineLineFeatures (Example 7.6.1) as a Decision *Table*.
2. Show how you would declare the following VARiables.
   a. IntList, as an array of 21 INTEGERs, with index values ranging from 1 to 21.

> **b.** HowManyOfEach, as an array of 10 CARDINAL values, with index values ranging from 0 to 9.
>
> **c.** Sentence, as an array (string) of 80 CHARacters, with index values ranging from 0 to 79.

3. Given the arrays in question 2, write WHILE loops that would:

> **a.** fill IntList with the numbers $-10, -9, \ldots 0, \ldots 9, 10$. *Hint:* Begin with Value $= -10$ and Index $= 1$. In the loop, assign IntList[Index] := Value, and increment Value and Index.
>
> **b.** fill HowManyOfEach with values 10, 9, $\ldots$, 1 (that is, HowManyOfEach[0] = 10, HowManyOfEach[1] = 9, etc.).
>
> **c.** fill Sentence with the first 80 printable characters. In ASCII begin with '!' (ORD('!') = 33).

4. With arrays IntList and HowManyOfEach from question 2, a procedure call appears as:

```
DoSomethingNow(IntList[5], HowManyOfEach[3], IntList, HowManyOfEach);
```

What should the procedure heading for DoSomethingNow look like, if the actual parameters IntList[5] and IntList are to be passed to formal *value* parameters and the others are to be passed to formal *VARiable* parameters?

7.7 *Summary*

Multiple-Selection Structures   The four basic structures for selection among more than two choices are

> repeated IF commands,
> nested IF,
> ELSIF, and
> CASE.

Although these structures often are interchangeable, one may be more readable and efficient than the others in particular cases.

Nested IF   When nesting any structures, the inner structures must be contained completely within the outer ones; their boundaries may not overlap. The BOOLEAN conditions used with nested IF commands tend to be shorter and easier to understand than those needed in most ELSIF structures. However, nesting more than a few levels deep may create code that is difficult to read, debug, and maintain.

ELSIF   When the choices can be stated as relatively simple compound BOOLEAN expressions, the structure IF...ELSIF...ELSE...END may be easiest to employ.

Repeated IF   Repeating IF...END allows you to handle choices that are *not mutually exclusive;* that is, when more than one task must be accomplished.

CASE   The CASE structure is especially valuable when there are more than two choices and they can be listed in terms of simple values of enumerable type.

Path Testing   Complete testing of any program with multiple decisions involves choosing data that will test every possible path through the program. A flowchart can help identify all of the paths.

BOOLEAN Expressions The conditions in decision and iteration structures are BOOLEAN expressions. ORD(BooleanValue) evaluates to 0 when the BooleanValue is FALSE and to 1 when the value is TRUE. VAL(BOOLEAN, CardinalValue) evaluates to FALSE and TRUE for CardinalValue 0 and 1, respectively. These functions can be helpful for output and input of BOOLEAN data.

Evaluation of BOOLEAN expressions is governed by *rules of operator precedence,* and parentheses are used to make the expressions clear. With the expression, "If *P* is TRUE, then *P* OR *Q* is TRUE," the evaluation of *P* OR *Q* is *short-circuited,* and *Q* is not evaluated. Similarly, "When *P* is FALSE, *P* AND *Q* is FALSE," is short-circuit evaluated.

BOOLEAN CONSTants as Switches BOOLEAN CONSTants, such as DEBUG = TRUE, are helpful for switching debugging, redirection, and other features on and off.

Done The BOOLEAN variable "Done," in module InOut, is set to TRUE if a call to an InOut procedure is successful and is set to FALSE if the operation fails. "Done" may be imported and tested. It is especially useful when reading data from an input file.

Decision Trees and Tables Decision trees and decision tables allow you to diagram and check the operation of multiple-selection structures.

Arrays One-dimensional arrays provide a method for representing lists of variables by a single name. Although reference usually is made to a single array element by specifying its *index* or subscript, entire arrays may be passed as parameters to procedures.

7.8 Exercises

Exercises marked with (FileName: _____) indicate those that ask you to use, modify, or extend the text examples. The numbers in brackets, [ ], indicate the section that contains the material you need for completing the exercise.

1. **a.** [7.2] (FileName:CH7A) Rewrite the procedure FindTriangleType (Example 7.1.1) using ELSIF instead of nested IF statements.
   b. [7.4] Draw a decision tree and a decision table for Savings (Example 7.2.1).
   c. [7.2] (FileName:CH7B) Rewrite Savings (Example 7.2.1) using nested IF statements instead of ELSIF.

2. You have inherited a large bag of coins. The date on each coin will determine what you should do with it. If its age is

   less than 5 years, spend it;
   between 5 and 20 years, put it in a drawer;
   between 20 and 50 years, put it in the safe;
   more than 50 years, have it appraised.

   a. [7.4] Draw a decision tree and a decision table for the problem. Write a program—with the current year as a predefined constant—that asks you for the date on the coin and tells you what to do with it, using
   b. [7.1] nested IF structures;

    c. [7.2] ELSIF;

    d. [7.5] CASE.

3. [7.3] (FileName:CH7C) Modify FindInsurancePremium (Example 7.3.1) to safeguard against incorrect entry of values for DriverAge, Accidents, CarSize, and Vintage. To do this, set and test BOOLEAN variables AgeOK, AccidentsOK, SizeOK, and VintageOK. For example, let AgeOK = (Age > 15) AND (Age < = 120).

4. [7.3] **a.** Write a program that reads a list of INTEGER values from an input file and displays how many of the values are negative, how many are zero, and how many are positive. Import ''Done'' from module InOut to terminate reading from the file.

    b. Add a BOOLEAN CONSTant switch to the program to give you the option of accepting INTEGERS from either the file or the keyboard. If the values come from the keyboard, stop when a sentinel value greater than 9999 is entered.

5. [7.3] **a.** Write a program that reads CHARacters from an input file one at a time and writes each one (with lowercase alphabetic characters capitalized) to an output file. Use ''Done'' imported from module InOut to terminate reading from the input file.

    b. Add BOOLEAN CONSTant switches to the program to allow you to turn redirection of input or output on and off. If input redirection is turned off, terminate acceptance of input characters from the keyboard when the sentinel value '&' is entered.

6. [7.3] Use a truth table to tell:

    a. which of the expressions I, II, and III below are logically equivalent;

    b. which expression (I, II, or III) is always true;

    c. which expressions are True when Down is True and Out is False.

      I.   (Down AND NOT Out)   OR   (Out AND NOT Down)

      II.   (Down OR Out)   OR   NOT(Down AND Out)

      III.   NOT((NOT Out OR Down)   AND   (NOT Down OR Out))

7. [7.3] Use a truth table to tell:

    a. which of the expressions I, II, and III below are logically equivalent,

    b. which one is false when T < 100 and H > 90 and C <> 50.

      I.   (T < 100)   AND   ((H > 90)   OR   (C = 50))

      II.   ((T < 100)   AND   (H > 90))   OR   ((T < 100)   AND   (C = 50))

      III.   NOT(T > 100)   OR   (NOT(H > 90)   AND   (C = 50))

8. [7.5] Decimal codes from 0 to 255 convert to hexadecimal codes from 00 to FF. The algorithm for converting these codes from decimal to hex is

$$\text{Hexdigit2} = \text{DecimalCode MOD } 16$$
$$\text{Hexdigit1} = (\text{DecimalCode DIV } 16) \text{ MOD } 16$$

where Hexdigit1 is the leftmost digit and Hexdigit2 is the rightmost digit. Write a program to convert codes between 0 and 255 to hex. Use CASE to convert Hexdigits 10 through 15 to characters 'A' through 'F' and Hexdigits 0 through 9 to characters '0' through '9'. Then write the characters.

9. [7.5] Write a program, using CASE, that converts phone numbers expressed in letters to digits. (You may need to look at your telephone to find the conversions.) The program should be able to handle mixed letters and digits. For example, phone DIG-ITUP would become 344-4887, and ISB4YOU would

Figure 7–20
XOR and Binary
Addition (Exercise
11)

Truth Table	Notes

XOR	eXclusive OR	
P	*Q*	*P* XOR *Q*
True 1	True 1	False 0
True 1	False 0	True 1
False 0	True 1	True 1
False 0	False 0	False 0

P XOR *Q* = TRUE
when *P* is TRUE or
Q is TRUE, but
not when both *P* and
Q are TRUE.

Half-Adder			
A + *B*		Carry	Sum
1 True	1 True	1	0
1 True	0 False	0	1
0 False	1 True	0	1
0 False	0 False	0	0

When 0 represents FALSE
and 1 represents TRUE,
then, for *A* + *B*,
   Sum is *A* XOR *B*
   Carry is *A* AND *B*.

become 472-4968. A procedure to do this could be useful in a communications program that dials telephone numbers you type into it.

10. [7.3] Write a program that will produce the truth tables in Figure 7–7, displaying True and False as 1 and 0, respectively. *Hint:* For example, for all 4 TRUE and FALSE combinations write values of *P, Q,* and *P* AND *Q* using the ORD function.

11. [7.3] The Modula-2 OR operator illustrated in Figure 7–7 is an inclusive OR; *P* OR *Q* is True when *P* is True or *Q* is True or *both* are True. Another valuable "or" operation is the "exclusive or," written *XOR*, whose truth table is shown in Figure 7–20.

  a. Show, using a truth table, that

$$P \text{ XOR } Q = (P \text{ OR } Q) \text{ AND } \text{NOT}(P \text{ AND } Q)$$

  b. Write a function PROCEDURE XOR(P, Q: BOOLEAN): BOOLEAN: that RETURNs the value of *P* XOR *Q*, given the values of *P* and *Q*.

   c. Adding two binary digits $A + B$ can be accomplished by the Half-Adder represented in the table in Figure 7–20, where Sum = A XOR B and Carry = A AND B. Write a program that accepts 0 or 1 as CARDINAL values for Num$A$ and Num$B$, converts them to BOOLEAN values using VAL, finds the Carry and Sum for $A + B$ using AND and the XOR function you wrote in part b, and displays the result using ORD. For example, given Num$A$ = 1 and Num$B$ = 1, the final display should look like $1 + 1 = 10$.

12. [7.5] Write a program that will tell you whether any year is a leap year or not. Every calendar year evenly divisible by 4 is a leap year, except century years not evenly divisible by 400. Thus, 2000 and 2400 will be leap years, but 2100, 2200, and 2300 will not be.

13. [7.5] (FileName:CH7F) Expand the Olympics example to handle years before 1991, when both winter and summer games were held in calendar years evenly divisible by 4.

14. [7.5] (FileName:CH7G) Complete the MakeReportCards program by writing the messages and CASE choices for grades A, C, D, and F. Test with an input file that contains at least one student with each grade (including an invalid grade). Add an appropriate WHILE loop in function SelectIt to limit selection of WhichOne to '1', '2', or '3'.

15. [7.5] (FileName:CH7H)

   a. Rewrite procedure PrintIt in Example 7.6.1 using nested IF structures rather than CASE.

   b. Modify the program DetermineLineFeatures (Example 7.6.1) so that it handles horizontal ($a = 0$) and vertical ($b = 0$) lines. *Hints:* If a line is horizontal its slope is 0, and it has no x-intercept (unless the line is the x-axis; equation $y = 0$). If a line is vertical its slope is infinite (undefined), and it has no y-intercept (unless it is the y-axis; equation $x = 0$).

16. [7.6] Here is a challenge! The Roman numerals are

    I = 1 V = 5 X = 10 L = 50 C = 100 D = 500 M = 1000

An input file contains a list of numbers in Roman-numeral form, such as MCDXCII. Write a program that reads each number, one character at a time, displays the Roman numerals, then converts it to decimal form and displays the result. *Hint:* To make things easier, you may wish to end all Roman numerals in the file with a sentinel (*), and read characters to the *. The decimal equivalent of a Roman number is the sum of all the values represented by the characters. However, you need to save and examine two characters at a time, since a lesser value preceding a larger value (allowed only for IV = 4, IX = 9, XC = 90, CD = 400, and CM = 900) indicates subtraction of the lesser from the larger (for example, XC = 100 − 10 = 90). Thus,

$$\begin{aligned}
MCDXCII &= M + CD + XC + I + I \\
&= 1000 + (-100 + 500) + (-10 + 100) + 1 + 1 \\
&= 1492.
\end{aligned}$$

17. [7.6] Write a program with a main menu that asks if you want to handle squares, circles, or triangles.

If you choose *squares,* the program will ask you for the length of a side S and present a submenu of choices to find the area (S^2), the perimeter ($4 * S$), or the diagonal length ($S * $ sqrt(2)).

If you choose *circles,* the program will ask you for the radius; then a submenu will ask you to choose to find the area, the circumference, or the diameter. See the ComputeCircles (FileName:CH7D) program in Section 7.3 for the formulae.

If you choose *triangles,* the program will ask you for the lengths of the three sides (a, b, c). The submenu will offer choices of determining the perimeter $(a + b + c)$, the area, or the altitude to the longest side. See Triangles (Example 7.1.1; CH7A) for the formulae.

8

More Iteration Structures

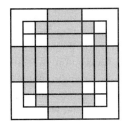

Chapter Outline

This chapter expands upon the concept of iteration, which was introduced in Chapter 4 and has been implemented so far with the WHILE structure. WHILE Condition DO. . . loops—which test at the beginning whether to terminate or to iterate again—are reviewed in this chapter and compared with a REPEAT. . .UNTIL Condition structure, which tests the Condition at the end. You will learn how to implement counting loops with the FOR. . .DO. . . structure. Also, you will examine the LOOP command for handling iterative solutions.

8.1 *WHILE Revisited*

By now, you should be comfortable with the WHILE loop used in examples and exercises in this book.

WHILE Syntax

The syntax of the WHILE Condition DO. . . structure is shown in Figure 8–1. The example in Figure 8–1 produces a table with entries in the form

```
...
2.50 yards = 7.50 feet.
...
```

A Pretest Loop

WHILE is a **pretest** loop; it tests the Condition at the beginning of the program. The Condition must be initialized before encountering the WHILE statement. Iteration continues as long as the Condition is TRUE. If the initial value of the Condition is FALSE, the executable commands within the WHILE loop are never executed at all. To avoid infinite repetitions, the Condition must be updated within the loop.

Conditions involving REAL Values

Tests for equality or inequality of a Condition represented by an expression containing REAL values must be written carefully. Limits on REAL number precision in the computer make it unlikely that two REAL values, such as RealA and RealB, will be exactly equal; and it is questionable whether testing for inequality will produce desired results.

Therefore, you should test

$$ABS(RealA - RealB) < epsilon \quad instead of \quad RealA = RealB$$

where epsilon is a small value (such as 0.0001). This determines whether the values of RealA and RealB are acceptably close to each other. Similarly, test

$$ABS(RealA - RealB) > epsilon \quad instead of \quad RealA <> RealB$$

to determine whether RealA and RealB differ sufficiently.

Questions 8.1

1. In the example code in Figure 8–1, what would be displayed for the following initial values of Yards if the command Yards := Yards + 0.5 were replaced by the given commands?

Figure 8-1
WHILE Syntax

General Format:

```
Condition := InitialValue;
WHILE Condition DO
    executable commands;
END; (* WHILE *)
```

Example:

```
...
VAR  Yards, Feet : REAL;
...
BEGIN
   ...
   Yards := 1.0;              (*initialize the Condition *)
   WHILE  Yards <= 10.0  DO  (* test the Condition *)
      FWriteReal(Yards,7,2); WriteString(" yards = ");
      FWriteReal(3.0*Yards,8,2); WriteString(" feet.");
         WriteLn;
      Yards := Yards + 0.5;(* update the Condition *)
   END; (* WHILE *)
   ....
```

Notes:

* WHILE is a *pretest* loop. The iteration executes while the Condition is TRUE.
* Condition is a BOOLEAN expression, which evaluates to TRUE or FALSE.
* The executable commands should include at least one instruction to update the Condition.

	Initial Yards	Replace Yards := Yards + 0.5; with
a.	10.0	Yards := Yards + 1.0;
b.	12.0	Yards := Yards − 1.0;
c.	0.0	Yards := Yards + 2.0;
d.	5.0	Yards := Yards − 1.0;

e. How would you change the code to display the table in decreasing order for Yards = 10.0 down to Yards = 1.0?

2. Write a fragment of code, with a WHILE loop, that asks for integers one at a time and accumulates their sum until a negative integer is entered as a sentinel "stop" indicator. Then display the sum (not including the sentinel value).

3. Rewrite the code of question 2 to make it read integers from a file and stop when ReadInt fails because it has reached the end of the file. *Hint:* Remember "Done," which is imported from InOut.

4. What Condition determines whether iteration continues or terminates in each of these code fragments? How is the Condition initialized? How is the Condition updated? What happens on execution? Fix it, if necessary, so that it works as you think it should.

a. ```
Count := 100;
WHILE Count <= 10   DO
   WriteCard(Count, 4);
END; (* WHILE *)
```

**b.**  ```
WriteString( "How many? " ); ReadInt(HowMany);
WHILE HowMany > 0   THEN
    WriteString( "Log(HowMany) =" );
    FWriteReal(ln(real(HowMany)),12,4); WriteLn;
END; (* WHILE *)
```

c. ```
Bill := 0.00;
WHILE Bill < 20.00 DO
 FWriteReal(Bill,6,2); FWriteReal(1.05*Bill,8,2);
 WriteLn;
 Bill := Bill + 0.50;
END; (* WHILE *)
```

## 8.2   *REPEAT*

The **posttest** form of iteration — which forces the test of the exit Condition at the end of the loop — is the REPEAT structure.

### REPEAT Syntax

The REPEAT syntax in Modula-2 is shown in Figure 8–2. The example in the figure presents a menu and asks for your Choice repeatedly until you enter a correct Choice ('S', 'D', or 'H').

The REPEAT structure is a rare exception in Modula-2, in that it requires no END command. This is because the end of the structure is clearly defined by the UNTIL statement. This loop continues to iterate until the exit Condition (such as Choice = S or D or H) becomes TRUE. Because the test of the Condition is made at the end, the instructions in the REPEAT loop always will be executed at least once. The Condition must have a value before UNTIL Condition is reached. To avoid infinite repetitions, at least one of the instructions (such as Read(Choice)) must update the exit Condition.

### When to Use REPEAT

The REPEAT structure is especially valuable when

**1.** the instructions must be executed at least once, or
**2.** initializing the Condition before entering the iterative structure is cumbersome.

*Caution:* REPEAT is **unguarded;** that is, whether you want it to or not, the commands between REPEAT and UNTIL will be executed the first time before any testing is done to determine whether that is what you intend.

The example in Figure 8–2 illustrates a situation in which REPEAT is more appropriate than WHILE, because it is not necessary to display the menu and read an initial value of Choice before entering the REPEAT structure; and the entire
```

Figure 8–2
REPEAT Syntax

General Format:

```
REPEAT
    executable commands;
UNTIL  Condition;
```

Example:

```
...
VAR  Choice, Discard : CHAR;
...
BEGIN
   ...
   REPEAT
     WriteString("Here are your choices:"); WriteLn;
     WriteString("  S   Find the Sum"); WriteLn;
     WriteString("  D   Find the Difference"); WriteLn;
     WriteString("  H   Halt the Program"); WriteLn;
     WriteString("Choose one (S, D, or H: "): WriteLn;
      Read(Choice); Read(Discard); Write(Choice); WriteLn;
   UNTIL  CAP(Choice)='S' OR CAP(Choice)='D' OR
          CAP(Choice)='H';
   ....
```

Notes:

- REPEAT defines a *posttest* loop. The iteration executes so long as the Condition is FALSE.
- Condition is a BOOLEAN expression, which evaluates to TRUE or FALSE.
- The executable commands should include at least one instruction to set and/or update the Condition.
- The end of REPEAT...UNTIL is defined by UNTIL rather than END.
- Caution: REPEAT is unguarded. The commands between REPEAT and UNTIL will be executed at least once before any testing is done.

---

menu can be displayed repeatedly without additional code. Compare the pseudocode for this type of presentation using REPEAT and using WHILE:

REPEAT Structure	WHILE Structure
	present the Menu
	ask for Choice
REPEAT	WHILE Choice is not valid DO
present the Menu	present the Menu
ask for Choice	ask for Choice
UNTIL Choice is valid;	END; (* WHILE *)

Obviously, if ''present the Menu'' and ''ask for Choice'' require much code, the REPEAT structure will be considerably more readable.

Another place REPEAT is appropriate is when the user is asked whether to execute again or not. In pseudocode, such a structure appears as

REPEAT Structure	WHILE Structure
	initialize Again Condition to TRUE
REPEAT	WHILE Again Condition is TRUE DO
perform actions;	perform actions;
ask Again?	ask Again?
UNTIL Again Condition is FALSE;	END; (* WHILE *)

The rather artificial step of setting the Again Condition to TRUE before encountering WHILE is not necessary with the REPEAT structure.

Applying REPEAT

Iteration and decision structures may be nested within each other, subject to the condition that the boundaries of nested structures may not overlap (as was shown in Figure 7–1). The following example illustrates nested REPEAT structures that give the user the choice of repeating a calculation to ensure that valid values are entered.

Example 8.2.1

Write a program that uses Newton's method to approximate the rth root of a number.

Define the problem   One way to determine the CARDINAL rth root of a positive REAL number is to iterate repeatedly using Newton's method, which states that a New approximation to the rth root of a Number is given in terms of an Old approximation by the formula

$$\text{New} = (1/r) * ((r - 1) * \text{Old} + \text{Number/Old}^{r-1})$$

Write a program that asks for the Number and which root r you wish to find. The program assigns an initial approximation, Old root $= 1.0$, and enters a loop where it calculates a New root, compares the New root with the Old, and iterates until the difference between Old and New are within 0.0001 of each other.

Develop a solution   The user will be asked to enter the Number and the root r ($>= 2$) from the keyboard. In a function Root, the initial approximation to the root will be 1.0. New will be calculated, displayed, and compared with Old. If the value ABS(New $-$ Old) $>= 0.0001,$ then the value of New will be assigned to Old, and another New will be calculated, displayed, and compared. Otherwise, the value of New will be RETURNed as an approximation to the rth root of Number. Finally, the user will be given the opportunity to calculate the root of another Number.

Refine the solution   The solution is illustrated in Figure 8–3 with a flowchart and pseudocode to show how the REPEAT. . .UNTIL structure is represented in both. REPEAT. . .UNTIL is used as the iterative structure in the main program NewtonRoots, because it does not require the condition Again to be initialized artificially, nor does it require an initial read of Number or r outside the loop. In function Root, REPEAT does not require initialization of Old outside of the loop. To find the $(r - 1)$st power of Old, the program invokes function CardPower(Old, $r - 1$) developed in Section 6.5.

Flowchart	Pseudocode

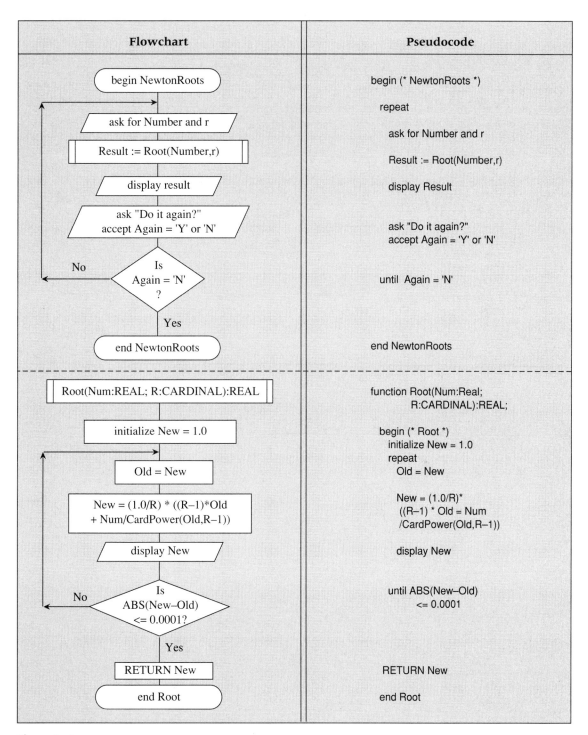

Flowchart side:

begin NewtonRoots

ask for Number and r

Result := Root(Number,r)

display result

ask "Do it again?"
accept Again = 'Y' or 'N'

Is
Again = 'N'
?

No

Yes

end NewtonRoots

Root(Num:REAL; R:CARDINAL):REAL

initialize New = 1.0

Old = New

New = (1.0/R) * ((R–1)*Old
+ Num/CardPower(Old,R–1))

display New

Is
ABS(New–Old)
<= 0.0001?

No

Yes

RETURN New

end Root

Pseudocode side:

```
begin (* NewtonRoots *)

  repeat

    ask for Number and r

    Result := Root(Number,r)

    display Result


    ask "Do it again?"
    accept Again = 'Y' or 'N'


  until  Again = 'N'


end NewtonRoots


function Root(Num:Real;
             R:CARDINAL):REAL;

  begin (* Root *)
    initialize New = 1.0
    repeat
      Old = New

      New = (1.0/R)*
      ((R–1) * Old = Num
      /CardPower(Old,R–1))

      display New


    until ABS(New–Old)
           <= 0.0001



    RETURN New

  end Root
```

Figure 8–3
Flowchart and Pseudocode for NewtonRoots (Example 8.2.1)

Modula-2 code

```
MODULE NewtonRoots;
    (* Finds the rth root of a real Number using Newton's method.
       FileName:CH8A      Modula-2      RKW      Apr. 1991  *)

FROM InOut IMPORT WriteString, WriteLn, ReadCard, WriteCard, Read, Write;
FROM RealInOut IMPORT ReadReal, FWriteReal;

VAR  Number, Result : REAL;   r : CARDINAL;   Again, Discard : CHAR;

PROCEDURE CardPower(Base:REAL;  Power:CARDINAL) : REAL;
    VAR  Count : CARDINAL;   BaseToPower : REAL;
    BEGIN (* CardPower *)
       Count := 1;   BaseToPower := 1.0;
       WHILE  Count <= Power  DO
          BaseToPower := BaseToPower * Base;   INC(Count);
       END; (* WHILE *)
       RETURN BaseToPower;
    END CardPower;


PROCEDURE  Root(Num : REAL;  R : CARDINAL) : REAL;
    CONST Epsilon = 0.0001;
    VAR  New, Old, rReal : REAL;
    BEGIN (* Root *)
       New := 1.0;   rReal := FLOAT(R);   (* First root approximation = 1.0 *)
       REPEAT                          (* Calculate the next approximation. *)
          Old := New;
          New := (1.0/rReal)*( (rReal-1.0)*Old + Num/CardPower(Old,R-1) );
          FWriteReal(New,12,4); WriteLn;
       UNTIL  ABS(New - Old) <= Epsilon;
       RETURN New;
    END Root;


BEGIN (* main module NewtonRoots *)
    REPEAT         (* Iterate as long as user wants to calcualte new roots. *)
       REPEAT  (* ask for Number until Number > 0.0 *)
          WriteString("Of which positive number do you want the root? ");
           ReadReal(Number); WriteLn;
       UNTIL  Number > 0.0;
       REPEAT  (* ask for root until r >= 2 *)
          WriteString("Which cardinal root ( >= 2 ) would you like? ");
           ReadCard(r); WriteLn;
       UNTIL  r >= 2;
       Result := Root(Number, r); WriteLn;
       WriteString("Number          Root(r)       rth root of Number"); WriteLn;
        FWriteReal(Number,9,2);WriteCard(r,13);FWriteReal(Result,23,4);
        WriteLn; WriteLn;

       WriteString("Would you like to do it again? ");
        Read(Again); Read(Discard); Write(Again); WriteLn;
    UNTIL  CAP(Again) = 'N';
END NewtonRoots.
```

Of course, exp(ln(Number) * (1.0/*r*)) could have been used to find the root; but Newton's method does not rely upon the accuracy of exp and ln. The iterative method illustrated in this problem — the method of calculating successive approximations until the results converge — is a practical technique for solving otherwise intractable problems.

Debug and test The successive values of New are displayed by the program so that you can watch the program converge on the correct root. Check carefully to make sure that the formula to calculate New has been typed correctly. Test the program with a variety of CARDINAL roots and REAL Numbers. Here is a sample run.

```
Of which positive number do you want the root? 5.0
Which cardinal root ( >= 2 ) would you like? 3
        2.3333
        1.8617
        1.7220
        1.7101
        1.7100

Number            Root(r)        rth root of Number
      5.00              3                    1.7100

Would you like to do it again? n
```

You should note here that this type of problem lends itself well to **recursion,** a problem-solving method in which a procedure calls itself repeatedly with new actual parameters. Recursion is discussed in detail in Chapter 9. To obtain a recursive solution of this problem, replace the function call

```
Result := Root(Number, r);
```

with a procedure call

```
Root(Number, 1.0, r, Result);
        (* 1.0 is the initial approximation to the root. *)
```

and replace the function Root with the recursive procedure

```
PROCEDURE  Root(Num, Old : REAL;   r : CARDINAL;    VAR New : REAL);
   CONST Epsilon = 0.0001;
   VAR  R : REAL;
   BEGIN (* Root *)
      R := FLOAT(r);
     New := (1.0/R)*( (R-1.0)*Old + Number / CardPower(Old, r-1) );
      FWriteReal(New,12,4); WriteLn;
     IF  ABS(New - Old) > Epsilon   THEN
        Old := New;
         Root(Num, Old, r, New); (* Recursive call to Root procedure *)
     END; (* IF *)
   END Root;
```

(See Exercise 7 at the end of the chapter.)

Complete the documentation Collect the problem definition, equations, pseudocode, code (CH8A), and the sample run. In the users' manual, explain that the CARDINAL root *r* must be 2 or greater and that the REAL Number, of which the root is to be taken, should be positive.

A Bit of Background

Playing on the Seashore

Isaac Newton (1642–1727) invented differential calculus in 1666 at his home, Woolsthorpe, in Lincolnshire, England. The plague had closed Cambridge University, which forced him to take a break from his graduate studies. Newton's method of finding roots, discussed in this chapter, is one of the minor applications of the calculus he created.

By 1669, Newton had been appointed professor of mathematics at Cambridge, where, it is reported, his teaching duties consisted only of lecturing on a topic of his choice once a week during one term each year and of counseling his students occasionally. Newton's major work at Cambridge was research, and his discoveries in gravitation, optics, mechanics, mathematics, as-

tronomy, and many related areas have made him one of our greatest scientists.

He was knighted by Queen Anne in 1705, served as president of the prestigious Royal Society for many years, was twice elected to Parliament, and straightened out England's currency system as Warden of the Mint.

Of his own achievements he said, "I do not know what I may appear to the world; but to myself I seem to have been only like a boy playing on the seashore, and diverting myself in now and then finding a smoother pebble or a prettier shell than ordinary, whilst the great ocean of truth lay all undiscovered before me."

(Adapted from Vera Sanford, *A Short History of Mathematics*, Houghton Mifflin Co., Boston, 1930; p. 55)

Questions 8.2

1. What would be displayed by the following? How would you fix it to do what you think it should do?

```
Hats := 12;
REPEAT
  WriteString( "No. of Hats = " ); WriteCard(Hats,4);
  WriteLn;
  DEC(Hats);
END; (* REPEAT *)
```

2. Write code to verify input data, using REPEAT. For example, write code that asks the user to enter numbers repeatedly until he or she has entered a positive number. Compare your code with a WHILE structure that does the same thing. Which is shorter?

3. **a.** How many times does a WHILE loop execute if the test Condition is FALSE when the WHILE statement is first encountered. Why?

   b. How many times does a REPEAT loop execute if the test Condition begins FALSE and remains FALSE? Why?

4. **a.** Write a Modula-2 REPEAT structure that presents this menu repeatedly until the user enters an appropriate Selection:

```
Your options are:
  R  Read a list of numbers into an array.
  C  Calculate statistics for the array of numbers.
  M  Modify one of the numbers in the array.
  S  Stop.
Select one (R, C, M, or S):
```

   b. Write a WHILE structure to perform the same task. Which appears shorter, the REPEAT structure or the WHILE structure?

5. In program NewtonRoots (Example 8.2.1) rewrite the REPEAT. . .UNTIL structures in the main module as WHILE. . .DO. . . structures. Which appears to be the better structure to use in this program? Why?

8.3 *FOR*

The FOR structure defines a "counting" loop. If the number of iterations, or an expression for calculating the number of iterations, is known in advance, then FOR is a convenient alternative to the other iterative structures. The syntax of the FOR structure is shown in Figure 8–4.

The FOR structure begins by assigning the value of the Initial constant, variable, or expression to the Control variable. After that, the instructions within the body of the loop are executed. The value of Control is incremented automatically by $+1$ (or by the value of ConstantIncrement if present). If Control exceeds the value of Limit, then the FOR loop is exited; otherwise, the instructions within the loop are performed again. If ConstantIncrement is negative, Limit should have a smaller value than Initial, and the process repeats until the value of Control is less than Limit.

Compare the pseudocode of a FOR loop with that for a WHILE structure that performs the same operation:

FOR Structure
```
FOR     Control := Initial TO Limit BY ConstantIncrement     DO
    executable commands;
END; (* FOR *)
```

WHILE Structure
```
initialize Control := Initial;
WHILE     Control <= Limit     DO
    executable commands;
    Control := Control + ConstantIncrement;
END; (* WHILE *)
```

Observe that the Control variable does not need to be initialized before entering the FOR loop; it is assigned automatically to the value of Initial in the first encounter with FOR. Also, Control is not updated by an explicit command within the FOR structure; $+1$ or the value of ConstantIncrement is added automatically by the structure.

Control, Initial, Limit, ConstantIncrement

Compare the example that converts yards to feet using FOR in Figure 8–4 with the same example using WHILE in Figure 8–1.

In FOR syntax, there are some restrictions on Control, Initial, Limit, and ConstantIncrement. These are:

1. Control, Initial, and Limit must be of compatible enumerable types. They may be CARDINAL, INTEGER, CHAR, BOOLEAN, or a user-defined enumeration type (see Chapter 11), but *not* REAL. Control must be a variable; Initial and Limit may be constants, variables, or expressions.

2. The optional ConstantIncrement must be a constant (or an expression containing constants and/or literal values, but not variables) of CARDINAL or INTEGER type, even if the Control variable is of some other enumerable type. (See the example FOR Letter := 'Z' to 'A' . . . in Figure 8–4.) A declared CONSTant may be used for ConstantIncrement, but a variable may not.

3. If the increment is positive (or $+1$ by default) and Initial is greater than Limit, then the statements within the FOR loop will not be executed at all. Similarly, the loop should perform no action if ConstantIncrement is negative and Limit is greater than Initial. For example, neither

Figure 8–4
FOR Syntax

General Format:

```
      FOR  Control := Initial TO Limit  DO
         executable commands;
      END; (* FOR *)
```

or

```
      FOR  Control := Initial TO Limit  BY ConstantIncrement  DO
         executable commands;
      END; (* FOR *)
```

Examples:

```
      . . .
      CONST INITIALYDS = 1;
      VAR  Yards, Count : CARDINAL;   Letter : CHAR;
      . . .
      BEGIN
         . . .
         FOR  Yards := INITIALYDS TO INITIALYDS+10  DO
            WriteCard(Yards,3); WriteString(" yards = ");
            WriteCard(3*Yards,4); WriteString(" feet."); WriteLn;
         END; (* FOR *)
         . . .
         FOR  Letter := 'Z' TO 'A'  BY -1  DO
            Write(Letter);
         END; (* FOR *)
         . . . .
```

Notes:

• Control, Initial, and Limit must be compatible enumerable types.

• Control must be a variable. Initial and Limit may be constants, variables, or expressions.

• BY ConstantIncrement is optional. If absent, the default value is +1. ConstantIncrement must be a constant or an arithmetic expression of CARDINAL or INTEGER type.

• The value of the Control variable should not be changed by commands within the body of the FOR loop.

• The value of the Control variable is undefined after the FOR loop has been exited.

```
      FOR Count := 10 TO 1 BY 2 DO
         WriteCard(Count, 4);
      END; (* FOR *)
```

nor

```
      FOR Count := 1 TO 10 BY -2 DO
         WriteCard(Count, 4);
      END; (* FOR *)
```

will do anything at all.

4. Although not enforced by Modula-2, the value of the Control variable should not be changed (by assignment or otherwise) within the body of the FOR loop. The FOR statement itself increments the value of the Control variable, and any other changes to that variable only invite confusion.

   The values of Initial and Limit, if defined in terms of variables, may be changed within the loop. However, changing these values during execution does not modify the boundaries, determined when the FOR loop was entered, and will not affect the number of iterations initially intended.

5. The value of the Control variable is considered to be undefined (unpredictable) once the FOR loop has been exited. If you need to know its latest value, assign it within the loop to another variable, such as RememberControl := Control;. Then RememberControl can be displayed during or after the iteration process.

When to Use FOR

The FOR loop may be used most appropriately when the number of iterations is known or can be counted easily by the programmer. If the number of iterations is not easily countable, then WHILE or REPEAT is a more appropriate structure.

   For example, given the declarations

```
CONST HIGHCOUNT = 10;  LOWCOUNT = 1;
VAR  Seconds : CARDINAL;
```

a countdown timer could be written as:

```
Seconds := HIGHCOUNT;
WHILE  Seconds >= LOWCOUNT-1  DO
   WriteCard(Seconds, 3); WriteLn;
   DEC(Seconds);
END; (* WHILE *)
```

However, since the number of iterations can be counted easily, a better structure would be

```
FOR  Seconds := HIGHCOUNT  TO  LOWCOUNT-1  BY-1   DO
   WriteCard(Seconds,  3); WriteLn;
END; (* FOR *)
```

To make this loop count actual clock seconds, you would need to insert a call to a properly adjusted procedure such as TimeDelay from Section 6.2.

   Structures where menu selections are made or the user is asked ''Do you want to do it again?'' would not be good candidates for FOR structures, since the number of repetitions cannot be predicted.

   Some code involving REAL variables, such as the yards-to-feet example in Figure 8–1, can be manipulated into FOR loop form by assigning a CARDINAL Counter as a function of the REAL values. In most such situations, however, it is much simpler to leave it as a WHILE loop.

Tracing a FOR Loop

The body of function CardPower in Section 6.5 can be written appropriately as a FOR structure as follows:

```
PROCEDURE  CardPower(Base : REAL;  Power : CARDINAL) : REAL;
   VAR  Count : CARDINAL;  Result : REAL;
BEGIN
   Result := 1.0;
   FOR  Count := 1 TO Power  DO
      Result := Result * Base;
   END; (* FOR *)
   RETURN  Result;
END CardPower;
```

Figure 8–5 traces the values of Count and Result during each iteration of the FOR loop when Base = 2.0 and Power = 3.

☐ Applying FOR

Here is a classic, fun problem that lends itself nicely to solution with the FOR structure.

Figure 8–5
Trace of FOR Loop
for Function Call
Answer :=
CardPower (2.0, 3);

```
BEGIN
   Result := 1.0;

   FOR  Count := 1 TO Power  DO
      Result := Result * Base;
   END; (* FOR *)

   RETURN Result;
END CardPower;
```

Base = 2.0	Power = 3		

Action	Count	Result	Test Condition
before FOR	undetermined	1.0	(Count<=3) = TRUE
Initialize Count:=1	1	1.0 * 2.0 = 2.0	(Count<=3) = TRUE
Increment Count	2	2.0 * 2.0 = 4.0	(Count<=3) = TRUE
Increment Count	3	4.0 * 2.0 = 8.0	(Count<=3) = TRUE
Increment Count END (*FOR*)	undetermined	8.0	(Count<=3) = FALSE
RETURN Result			

Example 8.3.1

A blacksmith's fee for shoeing a horse is one cent for the first nail, two cents for the second nail, four cents for the third nail, and so forth, doubling the cost of each nail. What would it cost you to have him shoe your horse?

Define the problem Assume that each of the 4 horseshoes requires 8 nails, so that there are a total of 32 nails. Write a program that adds $1 + 2 + 2^2 + 2^3 + \ldots + 2^{32-1}$ and divides the result by 100 to find the cost of shoeing the horse in Dollars.

Develop a solution No input will be required. For the sake of interest, the cost of each nail as well as the total cost in cents after each nail will be displayed to the screen. The CentsCost and NailCost (cost per nail in cents) should be REAL values, because they will exceed MAX(CARDINAL) on most machines. NailCost will be initialized to 1.00 cent. Since the number of iterations, NUMBEROFNAILS, is easily counted, a FOR loop is appropriate for calculating and printing NailCost and for accumulating CentsCost. Finally the total cost in Dollars will be displayed.

Refine the solution Figure 8–6 shows how the FOR loop appears in a flowchart and pseudocode for the solution to this problem.

The Control variable NailCount does not need to be initialized; the first encounter with the FOR statement assigns it the Initial value 1. Also, NailCount is not incremented within the loop; the FOR statement performs that task automatically.

Modula-2 code

```
MODULE FindHorseshoeCost;
    (* Finds cost of shoeing a horse at one cent for the first nail,
       then doubling the cost for each of the next 31 nails.
       FileName:CH8B        Modula-2        RKW        Apr. 1991  *)

FROM InOut IMPORT WriteString, WriteLn, WriteCard;
FROM RealInOut IMPORT FWriteReal;

CONST  NUMBEROFNAILS = 32;  COSTMULTIPLIER = 2.0;
VAR  NailCost, CentsCost, DollarsCost : REAL;   NailCount : CARDINAL;

BEGIN
    WriteString("Nail Number     Nail Cost (cents)");
     WriteString("   Total So Far (cents)"); WriteLn;

    NailCost := 1.00;  CentsCost := 0.00;
    FOR  NailCount := 1  TO  NUMBEROFNAILS  DO
       CentsCost := CentsCost + NailCost;
       WriteCard(NailCount,11); FWriteReal(NailCost,22,0);
        FWriteReal(CentsCost,21,0); WriteLn;
       NailCost := NailCost *COSTMULTIPLIER;
    END; (* FOR *)

    DollarsCost := CentsCost / 100.0;
    WriteLn; WriteString("Total Cost = $");
     FWriteReal(DollarsCost,12,2); WriteLn;
END FindHorseshoeCost.
```

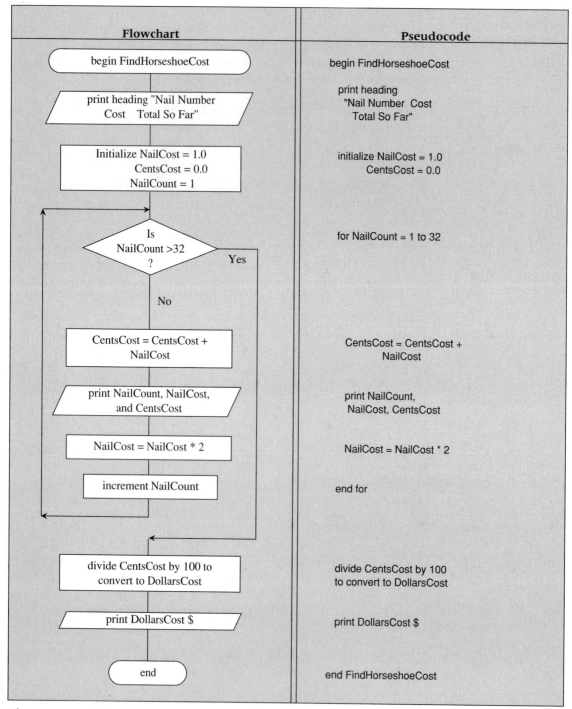

Figure 8–6
Flowchart and Pseudocode for FindHorseshoeCost (Example 8.3.1)

Debug and test   NailCost, NailCount, and CentsCost are displayed within each iteration, so it should not be difficult to determine where errors occur. Since no input is required, testing the program is simply a matter of running it.

The following is an excerpt from a sample run:

```
Nail Number      Nail Cost (cents)     Total So Far (cents)
          1                    1.                         1.
          2                    2.                         3.
          3                    4.                         7.
          4                    8.                        15.
          5                   16.                        31.
        ...                  ...                       ...
        ...                  ...                       ...
         30            536870912.                1073741823.
         31           1073741824.                2147483647.
         32           2147483648.                4294967295.

Total Cost = $ 42949672.95
```

If REAL numbers in your version of Modula-2 have fewer than 10 digits of accuracy, the results will be only approximately correct. See Chapter 17 for a discussion of type LONGREAL, which can help you achieve a greater number of significant digits.

Complete the documentation   Collect the problem definition, pseudocode, code, and sample run. The users' manual should state the source code location, file CH8B. No input is required; run the program and wait for results to be displayed on the screen.

Questions 8.3

1. What is displayed by executing each of these FOR loops? How many iterations does each loop execute? Trace the execution of each in a diagram similar to Figure 8–5.

   a.
   ```
   FOR  Count := 1 TO 1  DO
       Double := 2 * Count;
       WriteCard(Count,5); WriteCard(Double,5);
        WriteLn;
   END; (* FOR *)
   ```

   b.
   ```
   FOR  Count := 1 TO 12  BY  3  DO
       Square := Count * Count;
       WriteCard(Count,5); WriteCard(Square,5);
        WriteLn;
   END; (* FOR *)
   ```

   c.
   ```
   FOR  Count := 10 TO 20  BY  -1  DO
       Cube := Count * Count * Count;
        WriteCard(Count,5); WriteCard(Cube,5); WriteLn;
   END; (* FOR *)
   ```

   d.
   ```
   FOR  Count := 5 TO 2  BY  -2  DO
       Triple := 3 * Count;
       WriteCard(Count,5); WriteCard(Triple,5);
        WriteLn;
   END; (* FOR *)
   ```

   e.
   ```
   FOR  Count := 20 TO 20  BY 5  DO
       Inverse := 1.0 / FLOAT(Count);
   ```

```
            WriteCard(Count,5); FWriteReal(Inverse,10,4);
            WriteLn;
      END; (* FOR *)
```

2. a. In Figure 8–4, what is displayed by the loop

```
FOR  Letter := 'Z' TO 'A' by -1  DO...?
```

b. Write a FOR loop that displays all of the lowercase letters and their positions in the alphabet; that is,

a   1   b   2   c   3   d   4   ...   y   25   z   26.

Hint: Display Letter and ORD(Letter) − ORD('a') + 1. (Why?)

3. What is wrong with this?

```
FOR  Amount := 0.25 TO 10.00  BY  0.25  DO
    FWriteReal(Amount,8,2);
END; (* FOR *)
```

How would you make it work, **a.** using a different iteration structure; **b.** using FOR? *Hint:* Count how many values are displayed.

4. Using FOR loops, rewrite
   a. procedure TabOrFill, Chapter 5, Section 5.5; and
   b. procedure TimeDelay, Chapter 6, Section 6.2.

8.4 *LOOP*

A fourth iterative structure is implemented by the LOOP command. Its syntax is shown in Figure 8–7. The LOOP structure always requires a nested IF of the form

```
IF   Condition   THEN
    EXIT;
END; (* IF *)
```

which sometimes is written on a single line as

```
IF   Condition   THEN   EXIT   END;
```

EXIT is a reserved word (a command built into Modula-2, operable only within a LOOP structure), which terminates the LOOP and directs execution to the command following the END of the LOOP.

When and Why Use LOOP?

The LOOP structure is included in Modula-2 to allow iteration termination when there must be executable statements before and after the command to test whether to EXIT. When the IF. . .THEN EXIT. . . test is the first or last command inside the LOOP, you have a pretest or posttest iteration and you should use WHILE or REPEAT, respectively.

In some rare situations, exiting from the middle might be a simpler structure than WHILE or REPEAT. The example in Figure 8–7 shows a possible application. IF. . .THEN EXIT. . . also may appear more than once throughout the LOOP structure, which allows multiple tests for termination. However, you should use a midtest LOOP structure with caution, since any commands after the EXIT test will not have been executed during the last iteration, and it is easy to obtain unexpected results. Also, as pointed out earlier in the book, good structured programming requires structures with only a single entry and a single exit point.

Figure 8–7
LOOP Syntax

General Format:

```
LOOP
    executable commands;
    IF Condition THEN
        EXIT;
    END; (* IF *)
    executable commands;
END; (* LOOP *)
```

Example:

```
    ...
    VAR  Number, Sum, MeanSoFar : REAL;   HowMany : CARDINAL;
    ...
    BEGIN
        ...
        Sum := 0.0;   HowMany := 0;

    LOOP
        WriteString("Enter a positive REAL Number: ");
        ReadReal(Number); WriteLn;

        IF  Number < 0.0  THEN
            EXIT;
        END;  (* IF *)

        INC(HowMany);
        Sum := Sum + Number;
        MeanSoFar := Sum / FLOAT(HowMany);
    END;  (* LOOP *)
    ....
```

Notes:
- LOOP defines a *midtest* iteration. The iteration executes so long as the Condition is FALSE.
- Condition is a BOOLEAN expression, which evaluates to TRUE or FALSE.
- The executable commands should include at least one instruction to set and/or update the Condition.
- Multiple EXIT statements may appear in a LOOP structure.
- In nested LOOPs, an EXIT statement in the inner LOOP terminates only the inner LOOP.

☐ Applying LOOP

Consider the following example, where LOOP might be applied more simply than WHILE or REPEAT, although one of the latter could produce better structured code.

Example 8.4.1

Read all of the grades from an input file and find their average.

Define the problem   A file contains a list of INTEGER percentage grades that are to be averaged. The first number in the file is a count of the number of grades to follow. Read the number of grades indicated by the first value. Then find and display the average of that number of grades.

Develop a solution The first value in the file (NumOfGrades) is read. In a LOOP, NumofValues number of Grades will be read, a SumOfGrades and GradeCount accumulated, and AverageSoFar calculated. When the appropriate number of Grades have been read, the program EXITs from the LOOP and displays the NumOfGrades and final AverageSoFar. These safeguards will be built in:

- If the file contains no values or NumOfGrades $<=0$, the program will HALT with an error message.
- If there are fewer than NumOfGrades in the file, or if any Grade < 0 or Grade > 100, the program will print a message and EXIT from the LOOP.

Refine the solution *Pseudocode*

```
begin AverageGrades
  open input file
  read NumOfGrades
    if    NumOfGrades <= 0    or    not(Done)
      print "There are no grades in the file"    and    close input file
      HALT
    end if

    initialize    GradeCount = 0,    SumOfGrades = 0,    Aborted = FALSE
    loop
      read Grade
      if    not(Done)    or    Grade < 0    or    Grade > 100
        print "Illegal grade or not enough grades in file"
          set Aborted = TRUE    and    exit from loop
      end if
      increment GradeCount    and    add Grade to SumOfGrades
      calculate    AverageSoFar = SumOfGrades / GradeCount
      if    GradeCount = NumOfGrades    then    EXIT from loop    end if
    end loop

    if    not(Aborted)
      print NumOfGrades    and    AverageSoFar
    end if
    close input file
end AverageGrades
```

Modula-2 code

```
MODULE  AverageGrades;
    (* Finds the average of a list of grades from a file.  The first
    value in the file is the number of grades.
       FileName:CH8C       Modula-2       RKW       Apr. 1991   *)

FROM InOut IMPORT WriteString, WriteLn, ReadInt, WriteInt,
                  Done, OpenInput, CloseInput;
FROM RealInOut IMPORT FWriteReal;
FROM MathLib0 IMPORT real;

VAR  AverageSoFar : REAL;  Aborted : BOOLEAN;
     Grade, SumOfGrades, GradeCount, NumOfGrades : INTEGER;

BEGIN
    WriteString("Name of Input file? "); OpenInput("IN");

    ReadInt(NumOfGrades);
    IF  NOT(Done) OR (NumOfGrades <= 0)   THEN
```

```
      WriteString("There are no grades in the file."); WriteLn;
      CloseInput; HALT;
   END; (* IF *)

   GradeCount := 0;  SumOfGrades := 0;  Aborted := FALSE;
   LOOP
      ReadInt(Grade);
      IF  NOT(Done) OR (Grade < 0) OR (Grade > 100)  THEN
         WriteString("Illegal grade or not enough grades in file.");
         WriteLn;  Aborted := TRUE;
         EXIT;
      END; (* IF *)

      INC(GradeCount);
      SumOfGrades := SumOfGrades + Grade;
      AverageSoFar := real(SumOfGrades) / real(GradeCount);
      IF  GradeCount = NumOfGrades  THEN
         EXIT;
      END; (* IF *)
   END; (* LOOP *)

   IF  NOT(Aborted)  THEN
      WriteString("Average of"); WriteInt(NumOfGrades,4);
       WriteString(" grades equals"); FWriteReal(AverageSoFar,8,2); WriteLn;
   END; (* IF *)

   CloseInput;
END AverageGrades.
```

Note the use of the HALT command, which stops execution of the program when NumOfGrades is incorrect. The use of HALT is simple but not generally good programming practice. Using LOOP is also a reasonably simple way to solve this problem, though not the best of structured programming techniques. (See Exercise 13 at the end of the chapter.)

Debug and test   With an input file CH8C.IN containing the values

5   83   96   76   95   92

a sample run produces this display:

```
Name of Input file? IN> CH8C.IN
Average of   5 grades equals   88.40
```

Complete the documentation   Include the problem definition and list of safeguards with the pseudocode, code, listing of the input file, and sample run. In the users' manual, remind the users that the code (CH8C) must be supplemented by an input file containing the number of Grades to be read, followed by a sufficient number of INTEGER Grades with values between 0 and 100.

Questions 8.4

1. Rewrite the following using the LOOP structure. Which do you consider better code, the original or the LOOP form? Why?
   a. the example in Figure 8–1
   b. the example in Figure 8–2
   c. the examples in Figure 8–4

2. What is displayed after exiting from this LOOP? Is what the display says correct? If not, how would you change the loop to make it correct?

```
Count := 0;   Sum := 0;
LOOP
    INC(Count);
    Sum := Sum + Count;
    IF Count = 10  THEN  EXIT  END;
    Average := FLOAT(Sum) / FLOAT(Count);
END; (* LOOP *)
WriteCard(Sum,6); WriteString( ''divided by'' );
 WriteCard(Count,6);
 WriteString( '' equals '' ); FWriteReal(Average,10,4);
 WriteLn;
```

3. What do each of these LOOP structures display? Why?

   a.
   ```
   LOOP
       WriteString( ''My Name'' ); WriteLn;
   END; (* LOOP *)
   ```

   b.
   ```
   HowMany := 10;
   LOOP
       IF  HowMany > 5  THEN  EXIT  END;
       WriteInt(HowMany,3);   DEC(HowMany);
   END; (* LOOP *)
   ```

   c.
   ```
   HowMany := 10;
   LOOP
       WriteInt(HowMany,3); DEC(HowMany);
       IF  HowMany >= 10  THEN  EXIT  END;
   END; (* LOOP *)
   ```

   d.
   ```
   HowMany := 10;
   LOOP
       WriteInt(HowMany,3);   DEC(HowMany);
       Count := HowMany;
       LOOP
           WriteInt(Count,3);   DEC(Count);
           IF  Count < 0  THEN  EXIT  END;
       END; (* LOOP *)  WriteLn;
       IF  HowMany = 0  THEN  EXIT  END;
   END; (* LOOP *)
   ```

8.5 *Which Iterative Structure to Use*

The examples in previous chapters have shown that the WHILE loop can be applied to virtually every iterative situation. REPEAT, FOR, or LOOP structures, however, may be more convenient or efficient in certain circumstances. Some of the exercises at the end of the chapter ask you to practice replacing one type of loop with others in order to build your confidence and expertise with all four structures and to allow you to observe which ones work best in given situations. The four structures are compared in Figure 8–8. Study the figure carefully. Pay particularly close attention to the Condition, Use When, and Example sections of the figure.

Questions 8.5

1. For each example in Figure 8–8, explain why the indicated structure probably would be the best to use. Write each example using one of the other three iterative structures.

WHILE	REPEAT	FOR	LOOP

General Format:
 	
initialize Condition
WHILE Condition DO
  executable commands;
  (* update Condition *)
END; (* WHILE *)
	General Format:
	
	REPEAT
	  executable commands;
	  (* initialize and/or
	    update Condition *)
	UNTIL Condition;
		General Format:
		
		FOR Control := Initial TO Limit DO
		  executable commands;
		END; (* FOR *)
			General Format:
			
			LOOP
			  executable commands;
			  IF Condition THEN EXIT;
			  END; (* IF *)
			  executable commands;
			END; (* LOOP *)

Test: pretest (top)	**Test:** posttest (bottom)	**Test:** pretest (top)	**Test:** midtest (middle)

Condition:
 	
initialize before WHILE
executes while TRUE
update before END
	Condition:
	
	initialize or set before UNTIL
	executes while FALSE
	update before UNTIL
		Condition:
		
		automatically initialized
		  Control := Initial
		executes while Control <= Limit
		updated automatically
		  FOR increments Control
			Condition:
			
			initialize or set before
			  IF..THEN EXIT...
			executes while FALSE
			update before
			  IF..THEN EXIT...

Use When: unknown number of iterations or Condition involves nonenumerable values protection is needed so that commands are not executed at all when initial Condition is FALSE commands are to be executed when Condition is TRUE	**Use When:** unknown number of iterations or Condition involves nonenumerable values commands are to be executed at least once before the Condition is tested commands are to be executed when Condition is FALSE	**Use When:** iterations can be counted or their number is known by the programmer	**Use When:** execution must be terminated in midloop different Conditions should cause termination at different points in the loop commands are to be executed when Condition is FALSE

Example:
 	
Number := 5.5
WHILE Number <= 10.5 DO
  FWriteReal(Number,10,4);
  FWriteReal(Sqrt(Number),10,4);
  WriteLn;
  Number := Number + 0.25;
END; (* WHILE *)
	Example:
	
	REPEAT
	  WriteString("Enter a posi");
	  WriteString("tive value: ");
	  ReadReal(Number); WriteLn;
	UNTIL Number > 0.0;
		Example:
		
		FOR Counter := 5 TO 10 DO
		  WriteCard(Counter, 6);
		  WriteCard(Counter*Counter, 6);
		  WriteLn;
		END; (* FOR *)
			Example:
			
			LOOP
			  ReadCard(WholeNum);
			  IF MAX(CARDINAL)
			    - WholeNum < Sum THEN
			    EXIT;
			  END; (* IF *)
			  Sum := Sum + WholeNum;
			END; (* LOOP *)

Figure 8–8
Comparison of Iterative Structures

2. Which iterative structure (WHILE, REPEAT, LOOP, FOR) would you use in each of these situations? Write Modula-2 code for the structure.

   a. The computer should display a countdown list such as

   $$10 \quad 9 \quad 8 \quad 7 \quad . \quad . \quad . \quad 1$$

   to allow you to check off the number of disk drives in your inventory as they are sold. However, the list will not be printed unless you have 10 or fewer disk drives left.

   b. You wish to print a list of successively decreasing integers and their square roots. When the first negative integer appears, you will print only the integer (not its square root) and stop.

   c. You wish to insert a time delay into your program by having the computer perform some calculation 1000 times without displaying the results of the calculation.

   d. You wish to read sides a, b, and c of a triangle. Calculate $s = (a + b + c)/2$ and either terminate if $s(s - a)(s - b)(s - c)$ is negative, or find the Area ($= \mathrm{sqrt}(s(s - a)(s - b)(s - c))$) and iterate again for a new triangle.

   e. You wish to print a table of equivalent U.S. dollars and Japanese yen currency values from $0.25 to $10.00 in steps of $0.25.

8.6 *Focus on Problem Solving*

Many problems that involve creating tables of data can be solved effectively by using nested loop structures. This section presents two such problems.

Nested Loops

Iterative structures may be nested within each other, or within other structures, subject to the rule that the boundaries of nested structures may not overlap.

Nested iterations may be the same structures or different structures. For example, FOR could be nested within WHILE, which is nested within LOOP, which occurs between REPEAT and UNTIL, and so on. When loops are nested, execution of the outer loop proceeds more slowly than the inner loop. The total number of iterations equals the number of iterations performed by the outer loop multiplied by the number of iterations performed by the inner loop.

Applying Nested FOR Loops

Consider the following application of nested FOR loops.

Example 8.6.1

Print a multiplication table for values from $1 * 1$ to $12 * 12$.

Define the problem A table of all possible products of CARDINAL numbers from 1 to 12 is to be directed to an output file. Each column and each row of the table will be labeled to indicate which numbers are being multiplied.

Develop a solution The column headings will be printed first. Then a loop will print the row number and call an inner loop to calculate and print the 12 individual products in the row. Since the number of iterations can be counted easily, the FOR structure will be used for both loops. A structure chart of the solution is shown in Figure 8–9.

Refine the solution   *Pseudocode*

```
begin MultTable
    open output file
    print column headings
    for    row = 1 to 12
        print row number
        for column = 1 to 12
            calculate product = row * column
            print product
        end for
        advance to new row
    end for
    close output file
end MultTable
```

In nested FOR loops, it is easy to see that the outer-loop counter variables change more slowly than the inner-loop counters. In this example,

when	row =	1,	column advances through 1 to 12,
then	row =	2,	and column advances through 1 to 12 again,
....			
until	row =	12,	and column advances through 1 to 12.

Study the nested FOR loops in the Modula-2 code carefully.

Modula-2 code

```
MODULE MultTable;
    (* Calculates and prints a multiplication table.
        FileName:CH8D      Modula-2      RKW      Apr. 1991   *)
```

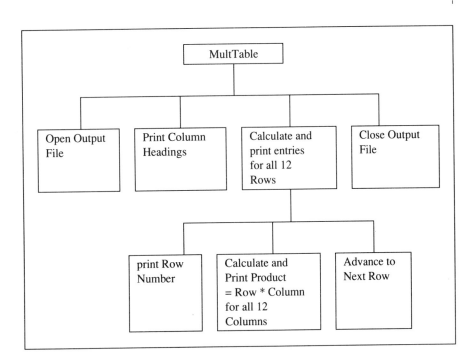

Figure 8–9
Structure Chart for MultTable (Example 8.6.1)

```
FROM InOut IMPORT WriteString, WriteLn, WriteCard, Write,
                  OpenOutput, CloseOutput;

CONST  REDIRECTOUT = TRUE;  HOWHIGH = 12;
VAR  Row, Column, Product : CARDINAL;

BEGIN
   IF  REDIRECTOUT  THEN
      WriteString("What is the output file name? "); OpenOutput("DAT");
   END; (* IF *)

   WriteString("  * |");        (* Write Column Headings *)
   FOR Column := 1 TO HOWHIGH  DO
      WriteCard(Column,5);
   END; (* FOR *)  WriteLn;

   WriteString("----|");    (* Underline Column Headings *)
   FOR Column := 1 TO 5*HOWHIGH  DO
      Write('-');
   END; (* FOR *)    WriteLn;

   FOR  Row := 1 TO HOWHIGH  DO  (* Nested FOR to create Table *)
      WriteCard(Row,3); WriteString(" |");
      FOR  Column := 1 TO HOWHIGH  DO
         Product := Row * Column;
         WriteCard(Product,5);
            (* Assertions: Product  =  Current Row  *  Current Column
                           Column = Current Column                    *)
      END; (* FOR *)
      WriteLn;
         (* Assertion: Row = Current Row *)
   END; (* FOR *)

   IF REDIRECTOUT THEN  CloseOutput; END; (* IF *)
END MultTable.
```

Debug and test Set REDIRECTOUT = FALSE and run with output displayed to the screen. A common error in nested loops like this is to place the WriteLn command inside the inner loop; this would cause all 144 products to be displayed down the length of the screen. In this program, nearly all values are displayed during each iteration. It could be valuable, if results are incorrect, to insert a temporary write statement to display the value of Column during each iteration.

After debugging, set REDIRECTOUT = TRUE and execute the program. Only the output file name is required as input, so testing is a matter of running the program and verifying that the results are correct. The output table is shown in Figure 8–10.

Complete the documentation The users' manual should state where the source code is found (CH8D) and instruct the users to enter an output file name when requested, wait for program execution, and then display the output file. The problem definition, structure chart, pseudocode, and hardcopy of the output file complete the documentation.

Figure 8−10
Multiplication Table
(Output File of
Example 8.6.1)

```
*  |   1    2    3    4    5    6    7    8    9   10   11   12
 --+--------------------------------------------------------
 1 |   1    2    3    4    5    6    7    8    9   10   11   12
 2 |   2    4    6    8   10   12   14   16   18   20   22   24
 3 |   3    6    9   12   15   18   21   24   27   30   33   36
 4 |   4    8   12   16   20   24   28   32   36   40   44   48
 5 |   5   10   15   20   25   30   35   40   45   50   55   60
 6 |   6   12   18   24   30   36   42   48   54   60   66   72
 7 |   7   14   21   28   35   42   49   56   63   70   77   84
 8 |   8   16   24   32   40   48   56   64   72   80   88   96
 9 |   9   18   27   36   45   54   63   72   81   90   99  108
10 |  10   20   30   40   50   60   70   80   90  100  110  120
11 |  11   22   33   44   55   66   77   88   99  110  121  132
12 |  12   24   36   48   60   72   84   96  108  120  132  144
```

Applying Nested WHILE

In nested WHILE loops initialization is best performed just before the beginning of each loop. Thus, for nested loops, the general pattern is

perform initialization for *outer* loop
while still something for outer loop to do
   ...
   perform initialization for *inner* loop
   while still something for inner loop to do
      perform one step
      get ready for the next inner loop step
   end inner loop
   ...
   get ready for the next outer loop step
end outer loop

The following example illustrates nested WHILE iterations.

Example 8.6.2

Print a table of monthly payments for a loan at different interest rates and with different payback periods.

Define the problem   The loan amount is $1000. Calculate and display a table of the monthly payments at 8.0%, 8.5%, 9.0%, 9.5%, and 10.0% interest and for payback periods of 1.0, 1.5, 2.0, 2.5, and 3.0 years. The output should appear as in Figure 8−11.

Develop a solution   The MonthlyPayment on a loan of Amount dollars, at a given AnnualInterest rate, with a number of Years payback period is given by

$$\text{MonthlyPayment} = \text{Amount} * \text{MonthlyInterest}/[1 - (1 + \text{MonthlyInterest})^{-\text{Months}}]$$

where
$$\text{MonthlyInterest} = \text{monthly fractional rate}$$
$$= \text{AnnualInterest}/(12 * 100) \quad \text{and}$$
$$\textit{Months} = 12 * \text{Years.}$$

An outer loop will step through the payback Years (rows of the table). An inner loop will calculate and print the MonthlyPayment (columns) at each of the Annu-

Figure 8–11
Output of Find
PaymentAmounts
(Example 8.6.2)

```
Loan Amount = $          1000.00

                    MONTHLY PAYMENTS  (Dollars)

                    Annual Interest Rate (percent)
Pay (yrs)  |   8.00       8.50       9.00       9.50      10.00
_ _ _ _ _ _|_ _ _ _ _ _ _ _ _ _ _ _ _ _ _ _ _ _ _ _ _ _ _ _ _ _ _
    1.00   |  86.99      87.22      87.45      87.68      87.92
    1.50   |  59.14      59.37      59.60      59.83      60.06
    2.00   |  45.23      45.46      45.68      45.91      46.14
    2.50   |  36.89      37.12      37.35      37.58      37.81
    3.00   |  31.34      31.57      31.80      32.03      32.27
```

alInterest rates. The payback Years, Amount, and AnnualInterest rate will be passed to a function that calculates the MonthlyPayment. A structure chart is shown in Figure 8–12.

Refine the solution   *Pseudocode*

begin FindPaymentAmounts
  print loan amount and table headings
  initialize payback Years to 1.0
  while Years <= 3.0
      print Years
      convert payback Years to Months,
      initialize AnnualInterest rate to 8.0%
      while AnnualInterest <= 10.0%

Figure 8–12
Structure Chart for
FindPayment
Amounts (Example
8.6.2)

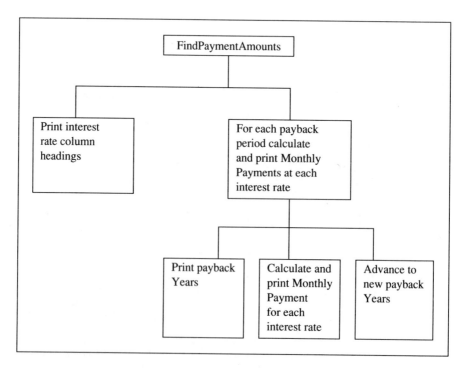

```
        convert AnnualInterest to fractional MonthlyInterest
        MonthlyPayment = Payment(Amount, Months, MonthlyInterest)
        print MonthlyPayment
        increment interest rate to next value
    end while            (* interest rate loop *)
    advance to new line
    increment payback Years to next value
  end while              (* payback Years loop *)
end FindPaymentAmounts

begin function Payment(Amount, Period, Rate : REAL) : REAL
    LastTerm = exp(-Period * ln(1.0 + Rate))
    RETURN    Amount * Rate / (1.0 − LastTerm)
end Payment
```

Pay close attention to the nested WHILE structures in the main module. Observe how the inner loop AnnualInterest condition (the column) advances through values 8.0 to 10.0 for each value of the outer loop payback Years (the row).

Modula-2 code

```
MODULE FindPaymentAmounts;
   (* Prints a table of monthly payments as a function of
      payback Years and AnnualInterest rate.
      FileName:CH8E       Modula-2      RKW       Apr. 1991   *)

FROM InOut IMPORT WriteString, WriteLn, Write;
FROM RealInOut IMPORT FWriteReal;
FROM MathLib0 IMPORT ln, exp;

CONST  STARTINTEREST = 8.0;  STOPINTEREST = 10.0;  STEPINTEREST = 0.5;
       AMOUNT = 1000.0; STARTYEARS = 1.0; STOPYEARS = 3.0; STEPYEARS = 0.5;
VAR Years, AnnualInterest, Months, MonthlyPayment, MonthlyInterest:REAL;

PROCEDURE PrintTableHeading();
   VAR  DashCount : CARDINAL;
   BEGIN
      WriteString("Loan Amount = $"); FWriteReal(AMOUNT,10,2); WriteLn;
      WriteLn; WriteString("              MONTHLY PAYMENTS (Dollars)");
       WriteLn; WriteLn;
      WriteString("              Annual Interest Rate (percent)");
      WriteLn; WriteString("Pay (yrs) |"); AnnualInterest := STARTINTEREST;
      WHILE  AnnualInterest <= STOPINTEREST  DO  (* Column Headings *)
         FWriteReal(AnnualInterest,12,2);
         AnnualInterest := AnnualInterest + STEPINTEREST;
      END; (* WHILE *)  WriteLn;
      WriteString("----------|"); AnnualInterest := STARTINTEREST;
      WHILE  AnnualInterest <= STOPINTEREST  DO  (* Underline Heading *)
         FOR  DashCount := 1 TO 12  DO  Write('-'); END; (* FOR *)
         AnnualInterest := AnnualInterest + STEPINTEREST;
      END; (* WHILE *)  WriteLn;
   END PrintTableHeading;

PROCEDURE Payment(Amount, Period, Rate : REAL) : REAL;
   VAR LastTerm : REAL;
   BEGIN
      LastTerm := exp(-Period * ln(1.0 + Rate));
```

```
      RETURN  Amount * Rate / (1.0 - LastTerm);
   END Payment;

BEGIN (* Module FindPaymentAmounts *)
   PrintTableHeading();

   Years := STARTYEARS;
   WHILE  Years <= STOPYEARS  DO
      FWriteReal(Years,8,2); WriteString("  |");
      Months := Years * 12.0;
      AnnualInterest := STARTINTEREST;

      WHILE  AnnualInterest <= STOPINTEREST  DO
         MonthlyInterest := AnnualInterest / (12.0 * 100.0);
         MonthlyPayment := Payment(AMOUNT, Months, MonthlyInterest);
         FWriteReal(MonthlyPayment,12,2);
         AnnualInterest := AnnualInterest + STEPINTEREST;
      END; (* WHILE AnnualInterest *)
```

Debug and test Execute the program and check at least some of the answers on your calculator. If there are errors, insert supplemental write statements to print intermediate values of the variables during each iteration. A common mistake is improper initialization of the loop. The initialization of the inner loop Condition should occur just before execution of the inner loop (not before the outer loop or elsewhere). Check the equations carefully to make certain they have been entered correctly. Since the program requires no input, testing is done by executing it. Output is shown in Figure 8–11.

Complete the documentation The problem definition, equations, structure chart, pseudocode, code (CH8E), and Figure 8–11 should be supplemented with a short users' manual indicating that the program will run without user input. Tables for different AnnualInterest rates, payback Years, and loan Amounts may be generated by changing the values of the CONSTants at the beginning of the program.

Questions 8.6

1. What is displayed by the following?
   a.
```
   FOR  i := 1 TO 10  DO
        FOR  j := 1 TO 5  DO
             WriteString(" (");  WriteCard(i,2);
               WriteString(",");
             WriteCard(j,1); WriteString(")    ");
        END; (* FOR j *)
        WriteLn;
   END; (* FOR i *)
```

   b.
```
   Amount := 0.0;
   WHILE  Amount < 12.50  DO
        Amount := Amount + 2.50;
        FWriteReal (Amount,7,2);
        FOR  Mult := 2 TO 10  BY  2  DO
             FWriteReal(FLOAT(Mult) * Amount, 7,2);
        END; (* FOR *)
        WriteLn;
   END; (* WHILE *)
```

 c. `CostPerBox := 0.50;`

```
     REPEAT
        WriteString("Maximum No. of Boxes = ");
         ReadCard(MaxBoxes);
        FOR  Boxes := MaxBoxes TO 1  BY  -1  DO
           WriteCard(Boxes,5);
           FWriteReal(CostPerBox * FLOAT(Boxes),10,2);
            WriteLn;
        END;(* FOR *)
        WriteString("Do it again (Y/N)? ");
        Read(Answer); Read(ThrowAway);
     UNTIL  Answer # 'Y' ;
```

2. What is wrong with this? Can you correct it, so that it does something? Would indentation help?

```
Building := 'A';  REPEAT
Write(Building);
FOR  Floor := 1 TO 5  DO
WriteCard(Floor,6); INC(Building);
UNTIL  Building = 'D';  WriteLn;
END; (* FOR *)
```

8.7 *Summary*

Four Iteration Structures The four iterative structures in Modula-2 are

 WHILE Condition DO. . .
 REPEAT. . .UNTIL Condition;
 FOR. . .DO. . .
 LOOP. . .

Their syntax is shown in Figures 8–1, 8–2, 8–4, and 8–7, respectively. With all of the structures except FOR, the programmer is responsible for updating the condition by commands within the body of iterations.

WHILE WHILE Condition DO. . . is a pretest loop. Because the Condition is tested at the beginning of the loop, the commands within the loop may never be executed at all if the initial value of the Condition is FALSE. The WHILE iteration continues as long as the Condition is TRUE. The Condition must be initialized before the WHILE statement.

REPEAT The end of the REPEAT. . .UNTIL Condition structure is defined by UNTIL rather than END. This iteration structure is a posttest loop; the Condition is not tested until the commands within the loop have been executed. This makes the structure valuable for handling situations such as menus or validation of data, where the variables that set the Condition are read within the loop and tested at the end. REPEAT iteration continues as long as the Condition is FALSE.

FOR FOR Control := Initial TO Limit BY ConstantIncrement DO. . . is a counting loop. Control must be a variable of an enumerable data type. Initial and Limit are variables, constants, or expressions of a type compatible with Control. BY ConstantIncrement is optional; if absent, the default increment is +1; if present, ConstantIncrement must be a CARDINAL or INTEGER value. The FOR statement performs the initialization Control := Initial upon entering the loop and automatically increments the Control value with each iteration. Iteration terminates when the value of Control is incremented past the value of Limit. The FOR structure is particularly effective when the number of iterations is known or can be counted easily by the programmer.

LOOP   LOOP is a midtest structure. Exit from the loop can occur from any point within the structure where

$$\text{IF}\quad \text{Condition}\quad \text{THEN}\quad \text{EXIT;}\quad \text{END; (* IF *)}$$

occurs, if the Condition is TRUE at that point. The programmer must set and/or update the Condition before it is tested in the LOOP. The LOOP structure should be used with caution; commands that follow the EXIT test are not executed during the final iteration. However, the structure is useful when the Condition must be tested in midloop or when it is necessary to have multiple possible exit points.

Nested Iterations   When iterative structures are nested, execution of the outer loop proceeds more slowly than execution of the inner loop. When initialization of the Condition is necessary, it should occur just before the beginning of each loop.

8.8 *Exercises*

Exercises marked with (FileName:_____) indicate those that ask you to use, modify, or extend the text examples. The numbers in brackets, [ ], indicate the section that contains the material you need for completing the exercise.

1. [8.5] Decide which iteration structure would be best, and write a program to find the sum, sum of squares, and sum of cubes of the first n cardinal numbers, beginning with 1. Verify that

$$1 + 2 + 3 + \ldots + n = n(n + 1)/2,$$
$$1^2 + 2^2 + 3^2 + \ldots + n^2 = n(n + 1)(2n + 1)/6,$$
$$1^3 + 2^3 + 3^3 + \ldots + n^3 = n^2 * (n + 1)^2/4.$$

2. [8.5] Decide which iteration structure would be best, and write a program to find the sum of the series

$$1/(1 * 2) + 1/(2 * 3) + 1/(3 * 4) + \ldots + 1/(n * (n + 1))$$

Show that the sum equals $n/(n + 1)$. What value does this sum approach as n gets infinitely large?

3. [8.5] Plot a bar graph of the partial sums of

$$100 * (1/(1 * 3) + 1/(3 * 5) + 1/(5 * 7) + \ldots + 1/((2n - 1) * (2n + 1))).$$

Show that the sum equals $100 * n/(2n + 1)$. What value does this sum approach as n gets infinitely large? Partial sums are the sequence of sums through each term, that is,

$$100 * 1/(1 * 3),\quad 100 * (1/(1 * 3) + 1/(3 * 5)),$$
$$100 * (1/(1 * 3) + 1/(3 * 5) + 1/(5 * 7)),\quad \text{etc.}$$

Provide the option of directing the output to a file. Use the iteration structure you consider best, and justify your choice.

 4. [8.5] Plot a bar graph of the partial sums of the alternating harmonic series

$$100 * (1 - 1/2 + 1/3 - 1/4 + \ldots + (-1)^n * (1/n)).$$

What value does this sum approach as n gets infinitely large? Partial sums are $100 * 1$, $100 * (1 - 1/2)$, $100 * (1 - 1/2 + 1/3)$, etc. Provide the option of directing the output to a file. Use the iteration structure you consider best, and justify your choice.

 5. [8.2] (FileName:CH8A) Build safeguards into the NewtonRoots program (Example 8.2.1) to prevent the user from entering a root value $r < 2$ and from requesting a root of a negative Number. Also display the initial guess for Old, and show the values of CardPower(Old, $R - 1$) and ABS(New $-$ Old) in each iteration.

 6. (FileName:CH8A) Rewrite the NewtonRoots program (Example 8.2.1) using **a.** [8.1] WHILE; **b.** [8.3] FOR; **c.** [8.4] LOOP.

 7. [8.2] (FileName:CH8A) In NewtonRoots (Example 8.2.1), make the modifications indicated at the end of *Debug and Test* to change the structure from iteration to recursion, and test the recursive program. Can you outline how the recursion works? *Hint:* New memory locations are reserved and used for formal value parameters each time the procedure is called. Make a chart of the memory locations and their contents for the sample run.

 8. (FileName:CH8B) Rewrite the FindHorseshoeCost program (Example 8.3.1) using **a.** [8.2] REPEAT; **b.** [8.4] LOOP; **c.** [8.1] WHILE. Which is most readable? Why?

 9. [8.5] An arithmetic series is defined by

$$a + (a + d) + (a + 2d) + (a + 3d) + \ldots + (a + (n - 1)d)$$

where a is the first term, d is the "common difference," and n is the number of terms to be added. Write and test a procedure that accepts REAL a and d and CARDINAL n as parameters. Then the procedure displays the terms of the arithmetic series and accumulates and displays the sum of the series. Use the iteration structure you consider best, and justify your choice.

 10. [8.5] Write and test a procedure that prints the first n terms of a geometric series and returns the Sum of the n terms to the calling module. The first n terms of a geometric series, with first term a and common ratio r, are given by

$$a + ar + ar^2 + ar^3 + \ldots + ar^{n-1}.$$

If a and r are REAL and n is CARDINAL, which is the best iteration structure to use? Why?

 11. [8.6] Some parents give their daughter $10.00 on her 12th birthday and promise her they will double the amount of the gift on every birthday till her 21st. That is, the daughter will receive $20 on her 13th birthday, $40 on her 14th, and so on. The question is, can the parents really afford this? What if the parents were to extend the offer to her 30th birthday? Write a program that tells how much the daughter will receive on each birthday and the cumulative amount of money she will receive. *Hint:* This is a geometric series (see Exercise 10).

 12. [8.6] An engineer starts with a salary of $25,000 and receives a $1500 raise each year.
 a. Write a program to print the engineer's salary for each of the first 10 years and the total amount of money the engineer would receive over the 10-year period. *Hint:* This is an arithmetic series (see Exercise 9).

b. Write a program to print annual salaries and the total for 10 years if the engineer begins at $25,000 and receives a 5% raise each year. *Hint:* This is a geometric series (see Exercise 10).

c. Which would be the better contract for the engineer?

13. [8.4] (FileName:CH8C) Change program AverageGrades (Example 8.4.1) so that it uses the most appropriate WHILE, REPEAT, and/or FOR structures, instead of LOOP. Also modify the program so that it does not use the HALT command.

14. [8.6] Use a FOR loop with a nested IF to:

a. write the first 100 CARDINAL numbers that are evenly divisible by 3, in descending order, with 10 across the page; that is,

```
300    297    294    291    288    285    282    279    276    273
270    267    ...    ...
```

Hint: The nested IF will perform WriteLn after 10 numbers have been written.

b. Write the first *N* CARDINAL numbers, evenly divisible by any specified CARDINAL Divisor, with a specified NumberAcross across the page. The user will enter *N*, Divisor, and NumberAcross and specify whether the numbers are to be written in ascending or descending order. *Hint:* You may wish to consider N DIV NumberAcross and N Mod NumberAcross and count the lines, so that the last line can be handled as a special situation.

15. [8.6] (FileName:CH8D) **a.** Use nested iterations to create an addition table similar to the multiplication table in Example 8.6.1. Allow the user to specify the minimum and maximum values for the columns and the minimum and maximum values for the rows.

b. Realizing that the numbers above the diagonal are the same as those below the diagonal, and that they only need to be printed once, modify the programs in Example 8.6.1 and in part a of this exercise to print only those numbers on and below the diagonal. For example, the multiplication table would appear as the triangle shown in Figure 8–13. *Hint:* In the inner loop print values only until Column > Row.

16. [8.6] In the Duchy of Upenchuck, the fundamental unit of currency is the Upenchuck Dragon (UD). Income-tax deductions are based on Salary in units

Figure 8–13
Triangular
Multiplication Table
(Exercise 15b)

*		1	2	3	4	5	6	7	8	9	10	11	12
1		1											
2		2	4										
3		3	6	9									
4		4	8	12	16								
5		5	10	15	20	25							
6		6	12	18	24	30	36						
7		7	14	21	28	35	42	49					
8		8	16	24	32	40	48	56	64				
9		9	18	27	36	45	54	63	72	81			
10		10	20	30	40	50	60	70	80	90	100		
11		11	22	33	44	55	66	77	88	99	110	121	
12		12	24	36	48	60	72	84	96	108	120	132	144

of 10,000 UD and on the number of Dependents the employee has. The formula, designed to favor low-income families, is

Deduction (UD) = Dependents * 500 + 0.05 * (50,000 − Salary).

Beyond 5 dependents and beyond 50,000 UD, the Deduction does not change. There is no tax, hence no deduction, on incomes less than 10,000 UD.

Use nested loops to create a table of Upenchuck income tax Deductions, with Dependents 0 to 5 as the column headings and Salary 10000, 20000, 30000, 40000, 50000 as the rows.

17. [8.6] (FileName:CH8E) Expand the solution of FindPaymentAmounts (Example 8.6.2) to print amortization tables like the one in Figure 8–14 for a given loan amount, each of several different payback periods, and each of several different interest rates specified by the user. *Hints:* Add an amortization table procedure that is called immediately after the monthly payment procedure. Reformat the output to handle printing the amortization tables right after each other. To create an amortization table

```
initialize Balance = Initial Amount of the loan
                Cumulative Interest = 0, Total Paid to Date = 0
                Payment Number = 0
then iterate until Payment Number = Years to Pay * 12
```

The formulae are

Interest   = Balance * Interest Rate / (12.0 * 100.0)
Principal = Monthly Payment − Interest
Balance   = Balance − Principal

Accumulate Cumulative Interest, Total Paid to Date (Cum.Paid), and Payment Number.

18. [8.5] The Fibonacci sequence is 0, 1, 1, 2, 3, 5, 8, 13, . . . where the first two terms are 0 and 1, and each term thereafter is the sum of the two preceding terms; that is, Fib[n] = Fib[$n − 1$] + Fib[$n − 2$].

Figure 8–14
Amortization Table
(Exercise 17)

```
    Initial Amount = $   1500.00
    Annual Interest Rate =  14.00
    Years to Pay =   1.
    Monthly Payment = $   134.68

Pymt.No.  Interest  Principal    Cum.Int.   Cum.Paid   Balance
———— ———— ———— ———— ———— ———— ———— ———— ———— ————
    1     17.50     117.18        17.50     134.68    1382.82
    2     16.13     118.55        33.63     269.36    1264.27
    3     14.75     119.93        48.38     404.04    1144.34
    4     13.35     121.33        61.73     538.72    1023.01
    5     11.94     122.75        73.67     673.40     900.27
    6     10.50     124.18        84.17     808.08     776.09
    7      9.05     125.63        93.23     942.76     650.46
    8      7.59     127.09       100.81    1077.45     523.37
    9      6.11     128.57       106.92    1212.13     394.79
   10      4.61     130.07       111.53    1346.81     264.72
   11      3.09     131.59       114.61    1481.49     133.13
   12      1.55     133.13       116.17    1616.17       0.00
```

A Bit of Background

The Blockhead

One mathematician of the Middle Ages who has had a profound influence on modern science is Leonardo of Pisa (1170–1250). In his youth he was called *Filius Bonacci,* meaning "son of (Guglielmo) Bonacci," and the name "stuck." Hence, he is commonly known today as Fibonacci. He traveled widely, met with scholars throughout the Mediterranean area, and produced four very significant works on arithmetic, algebra, and geometry. One of his discoveries is the sequence of numbers that bears his name: 0, 1, 1, 2, 3, 5, 8, 13, ... After the first two values, 0 and 1, each number of the Fibonacci sequence is obtained from the sum of the preceding two numbers.

Fibonacci often referred to himself as Leonardo Bigollo, probably because *bigollo* is Italian for "traveler." However, another meaning of *bigollo* in Italian is "blockhead." Some people suspect he may have adopted this name to show the professors of his time what a blockhead—a person who had not been educated in their schools—could accomplish.

Some blockhead! The Fibonacci sequence alone describes such natural phenomena as the spiraling patterns of nautilus shells, elephant tusks, sheep horns, birds' claws, pine cones, pineapples, and branching pattern of plants *and* the proliferation of rabbits. The ratio of successively higher adjacent terms in the sequence also approaches the "golden section," a ratio that describes an esthetically pleasing proportion used in the visual arts.

---

a. Write an iterative function that returns the *n*th number in the Fibonacci sequence when *n* is passed to the function as a parameter. For example, when $n = 6$, the function returns the value 5.

b. The "golden section" is considered an esthetically pleasing ratio of length to width and is applied in paintings, architecture, and so on. The ratio of successive numbers in the Fibonacci sequence (5/3, 8/5, 13/8, . . .) approaches the golden ratio more and more closely as the numbers increase. Write a program to print successive approximations to the golden ratio until you know the ratio accurately to 3 decimal places.

19. [8.6] Here is a challenging problem for those who know a little calculus. Newton's method can be used to find the roots of any equation $y(x) = 0$. The $(i + 1)$st approximation $x[i + 1]$ to a root of $y(x) = 0$ is given in terms of the (i)th approximation $x[i]$ by the formula

$$x[i + 1] = x[i] - y(x[i])/y'(x[i]),$$

where $y'(x)$ is the derivative of the function $y(x)$. In the notation of the NewtonRoots example (8.2.1),

$$New = Old - y(Old)/y'(Old).$$

For example, if $y(x) = 3x^2 + 2x - 2$, then $y'/(x) = 6x + 2$, and the roots are found by making a reasonable guess for a first value of Old and iterating with the equation

$$New = Old - (3 * Old^2 + 2 * Old - 2)/(6 * Old + 2).$$

a. Using the development of Example 8.2.1 as a guide, find the two roots of $3x^2 + 2x - 2 = 0$. *Hint:* There is one positive root and one negative root.

b. Extend the solution so that it will find the roots of any function $y(x) = 0$, when functions for $y(x)$ and the derivative of $y(x)$ are placed in the code.

Figure 8–15
Numerical
Integration
(Exercise 20)

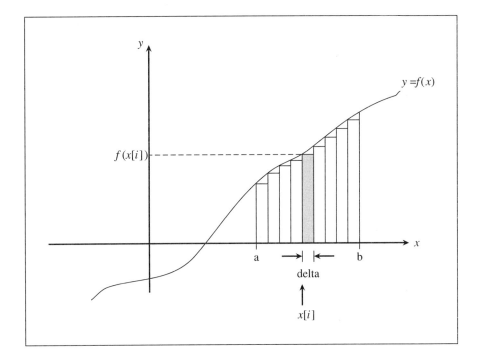

20. [8.6] Here is another challenging problem, based on numerical integration. Refer to the general curve $y = f(x)$ shown in Figure 8–15. The area under the curve between $x = a$ and $x = b$ can be approximated by dividing the interval from a to b into n small rectangles of width delta, where delta $= (b - a)/n$. The area of the rectangle of width delta at position $x[i]$ is AreaRect = delta * $f(x[i])$. The approximate total area under the curve is the sum of the areas of the rectangles,

TotalArea = delta * $(f(a) + f(a + delta) + f(a + 2 * delta)$
$+ f(a + 3 * delta) + \ldots + f(a + (n - 1) * delta))$

The larger the number n of intervals, the better will be the approximation to the TotalArea. For example, suppose you wish to find the area under the curve $y = 3x^2 + 2$ from $x = 1$ to $x = 5$. Then, for 8 rectangles, $n = 8$ and delta $= (5 - 1)/8 = 0.5$, so TotalArea is approximately

TotalArea $= 0.5 * ((3 * (1)^2 + 2) + (3 * (1 + .5)^2 + 2) + (3 * (1 + 2 * .5)^2 + 2)$
$+ \ldots + (3 * (1 + (8 - 1) * .5)^2 + 2)).$

a. Write a program that uses this numerical integration process to calculate the area under a curve between limits $x = a$ and $x = b$, entered by the user. The equation for the curve will be written in the source code for a function PROCEDURE Y(x:REAL):REAL which, when passed a value of x, calculates and returns the value of $y = f(x)$.

   An outer loop will begin with $n = 10$, calculate delta, and call an inner loop. The inner loop will step through x values of a, $a +$ delta, $a + 2 *$ delta, $\ldots$, $a + (n - 1) *$ delta; will call function $Y(x)$ for each x; and will accumulate TotalArea. The outer loop doubles the number of intervals *n,* calculates a new delta, and proceeds until the percentage difference,

$$100.00 * ABS((TotalArea2 - TotalArea1)/TotalArea1)$$

between two successive values of TotalArea is less than 0.1. The number of intervals *n* and the TotalArea are displayed at the end of each iteration of the outer loop.

b. If you are familiar with the trapezoidal rule or Simpson's rule, implement the numerical integration program with those rules and compare the efficiency (the number of intervals required to obtain the same accuracy) with the rectangle method of part a.

9

Problem-Solving Techniques

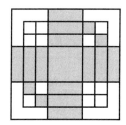

Chapter Outline

In this chapter you will learn to apply the Modula-2 programming concepts explained in the earlier chapters to four additional techniques for solving particular types of problems.

The first technique allows you to place procedures you've developed into an external module from which you can import them into your programs when you need them again. Generating nearly random numbers is the second topic. Random numbers are valuable for creating game-playing programs and they are needed for certain other kinds of programs. The third technique is that of generalizing and adapting previous problem solutions to new, analogous problems. Finally, you will get some practice with the powerful process of recursion.

9.1 *External Modules*

You have learned the importation of procedures and functions from standard external modules beginning with Chapter 2. Now you will create your own external modules and begin to build a library of procedures that you can import into future programs.

Each external module consists of a DEFINITION MODULE and an IMPLEMENTATION MODULE. The DEFINITION module contains the declarations of data types, CONSTants, VARiables, procedures, functions, and other entities that are available to be imported from that module. In Appendix B you can find the standard DEFINITION MODULEs InOut, RealInOut, Terminal, MathLib0, and others, that are part of every Modula-2 compiler. What you do not see in Appendix B are the IMPLEMENTATION modules, which contain the code and details of the entities declared in the DEFINITION modules.

The general syntax of a DEFINITION MODULE and an IMPLEMENTATION MODULE are shown in Figure 9–1.

The DEFINITION Module

The DEFINITION module heading begins with the word *DEFINITION,* which prepares the compiler to accept declarations of entities rather than an executable program. Only the declarations are expressed in the DEFINITION module. Details about how each entity works are hidden from the user in the IMPLEMENTATION module. This enforces the information hiding principle, which is that the user or programmer does not need access to details that are not essential to the task at hand.

Early versions of Modula-2 required a list—in an EXPORT QUALIFIED command—of all entities that were available for export. Current versions of Modula-2 assume that all entities declared in the definition module are exportable, and the EXPORT QUALIFIED statement is not allowed. The EXPORT list will not be used in this book for external modules.

The IMPLEMENTATION Module

The IMPLEMENTATION module begins with the reserved word *IMPLEMENTA- TION* to distinguish it from a normal program module.

The full code definitions for all entities are written in the IMPLEMENTATION module. Those entities required from other modules must be imported, just as for any module. Optional executable statements, which are executed exactly once when the module is imported, may be included at the end of the module, following a

---

Definition Module
```
DEFINITION MODULE ModuleName;
  (* Comments about the module in general *)
  (* EXPORT QUALIFIED
     List of entities that may be exported from the module;
     Required only in old versions of Modula-2 *)
  Declarations of Entities in the Module;
      (* In the form of TYPE, CONST, VAR, PROCEDURE headings with
         complete parameter lists, etc. *)
      (* Comments as desired about each entity *)
END ModuleName.
```

Implementation Module
```
IMPLEMENTATION MODULE ModuleName;
  (* Comments about the module in general *)
IMPORT lists;
      (* Entities used by the procedures in this module, which in turn must
         be imported from other modules *)
Definitions of Entities in the Module;
BEGIN
   executable statements;
END ModuleName.
```

Figure 9–1
DEFINITION MODULE and IMPLEMENTATION MODULE Syntax

BEGIN command. Occasionally, this is a useful option for performing operations such as initialization of variables or execution of a procedure in the module before the execution of the importing program.

Compiling Modules

To prepare an external module for use, perform these operations in order:

1. Use an editor to write the source code for the DEFINITION and IMPLEMEN-TATION modules in separate files (perhaps with file-name extensions .DEF and .MOD, respectively).
2. Compile the DEFINITION module first. This creates a **symbol table file,** which is used to identify the entities that have been declared. DO NOT LINK the DEFINITION module.
3. Compile the IMPLEMENTATION module. This creates an **object code file,** from which the executable code can be imported. DO NOT LINK the IMPLE-MENTATION module.

   Keep the source code files so that you can read, maintain, and upgrade them when necessary. The symbol table file and the object code for the IMPLEMENTA-TION module must be available when entities are to be imported from the module.

Library Utilities

The files for standard modules have been collected in libraries to which your Modula-2 compiler has access. A library utility program may be available. It allows you to inspect, add to, delete from, and update DEFINITION, IMPLEMENTA-

---

TION, symbol table, and object code modules in the libraries. With a library utility you are able to put your own external modules into the libraries. This may be a good idea once you have developed them to a relatively permanent form. However, you can have access to external modules without placing them in the libraries. In fact, that is the way they will be handled while you are developing them with the help of this book. Your system manual should explain how to use the library utility. However, be sure that you have at least one backup copy of the compiler, including all libraries, before attempting to use a library utility program. This will avert disaster in case modules are accidentally changed or deleted.

☐ Module MyMath

Now it is time to create and use an external module.

Example 9.1.1

Create an external module into which you can collect mathematical functions that you develop. Begin with functions that raise a number to a power. Write a program that imports and tests those functions.

Define the problem An external module called MyMath will be created to contain the function CardPower from Section 8.3 and a function RealPower, designed to raise a positive REAL number to a REAL power.

Develop a solution RealPower will apply the formula

$$a^b = \exp(b * \ln(a))$$

where a and b are REAL values, and a is positive. ln and exp will be imported into IMPLEMENTATION MODULE MyMath, but not into the testing program, since the user does not even need to know that RealPower uses those functions.

Refine the solution See the code for RealPower in the IMPLEMENTATION module MyMath below. Remember, the DEFINITION-module source code normally would be edited into a file called MYMATH.DEF, and the IMPLEMENTATION module source code would be in MYMATH.MOD. Compile MYMATH.DEF first. Then compile MYMATH.MOD. *Do not link* either file. Keep the symbol table file and the object code file for MYMATH.MOD, which are created by the compilation process. Here are the modules.

```
DEFINITION MODULE MyMath;
    (* Module MyMath contains user defined mathematics
       functions and procedures.  File Name:MYMATH.DEF      *)

    PROCEDURE CardPower(Base : REAL;  Power : CARDINAL) : REAL;
       (* Raises a Real number Base to a Cardinal Power
          by multiplying Base by itself Power number of times. *)

    PROCEDURE RealPower(RealBase, RealPower : REAL) : REAL;
       (* Raises a Real number Base to a Real Power
          using exp and ln.  Returns 0.0 and an error warning message
          if RealBase <= 0.0 *)

    END MyMath.


IMPLEMENTATION MODULE MyMath;
    (* Module MyMath contains user defined mathematical
       functions and procedures.  File Name:MYMATH.MOD    *)

FROM MathLib0 IMPORT exp, ln;
FROM InOut IMPORT WriteString, WriteLn;

PROCEDURE CardPower(Base:REAL; Power:CARDINAL) : REAL;
    (* Raises a Real number Base to a Cardinal Power
       by multiplying Base by itself Power number of times. *)
    VAR  Count : CARDINAL;  Result : REAL;
    BEGIN
       Result := 1.0;
       FOR  Count := 1 TO Power  DO
          Result := Result * Base;
       END; (* FOR *)
       RETURN Result;
    END CardPower;

PROCEDURE RealPower(RealBase, RealPower : REAL) : REAL;
    (* Raises a Real number Base to a Real Power
       using exp and ln.  Returns 0.0 and an error warning message
       if RealBase <= 0.0  *)
    VAR  Result : REAL;
    BEGIN
       IF  RealBase > 0.0  THEN
          Result := exp(RealPower * ln(RealBase));
       ELSE
          Result := 0.0;
          WriteLn; WriteString("!!!!! ERROR - WARNING !!!!!"); WriteLn;
           WriteString("Base must be > 0.0.  ");
           WriteString("INCORRECT Answer = 0.0 returned.");WriteLn;WriteLn;
       END; (* IF *)
```

```
            RETURN  Result;
        END RealPower;


END MyMath.
```

Pseudocode for the test program is

```
module FindPowers
  import CardPower and RealPower from MyMath
  begin
      repeat
        ask for a real Base number
        display menu    What would you like to do?
                        C       Find a CARDINAL power of the number.
                        R       Find a REAL power of the number.
                        S       Stop.
        ask for Choice (C, R, or S)
        if    Choice is C
          ask for CARDINAL Power, write CardPower(Base, CrdPwr)
        elsif    Choice is R
          ask for REAL Power, write RealPower(Base, RealPwr)
        end if
      until    Choice is not C or R
  end FindPowers
```

Modula-2 code

```
MODULE  FindPowers;
   (* Tests importing of CardPower and RealPower from MyMath.
      FileName:CH9A        Modula-2        RKW        Apr.1991   *)


FROM InOut      IMPORT WriteString, WriteLn, ReadCard, WriteCard, Read, Write;
FROM RealInOut  IMPORT ReadReal, FWriteReal;
FROM MyMath     IMPORT CardPower, RealPower;

VAR  BaseNum,RealPwr:REAL;   CardPwr:CARDINAL;   Choice,Discard:CHAR;

BEGIN
   REPEAT
      WriteString("Enter a REAL Base number: ");ReadReal(BaseNum); WriteLn;

      (* DISPLAY MENU *)
      WriteLn; WriteString("What would you like to do?"); WriteLn;
       WriteString("   C    Find a CARDINAL power of the number."); WriteLn;
       WriteString("   R    Find a REAL power of the number."); WriteLn;
       WriteString("   S    Stop."); WriteLn;
      WriteString("What is your Choice (C, R, or S)?  ");
       Read(Choice); Read(Discard); Write(Choice); WriteLn; WriteLn;

      IF  CAP(Choice) = 'C'  THEN
         WriteString("Enter CARDINAL power: "); ReadCard(CardPwr); WriteLn;
          WriteString("The number raised to that power is");
      (* INVOKE CARDPOWER *)
          FWriteReal( CardPower(BaseNum,CardPwr), 10, 4);
      ELSIF  CAP(Choice) = 'R'  THEN
         WriteString("Enter REAL power: "); ReadReal(RealPwr); WriteLn;
          WriteString("The number raised to that power is");
      (* INVOKE REALPOWER *)
          FWriteReal( RealPower(BaseNum,RealPwr), 10, 4);
```

```
    END; (* IF *)
    WriteLn; WriteLn;

  UNTIL  (CAP(Choice) <> `C`)  AND  (CAP(Choice) <> `R`) ;
END FindPowers.
```

Debug and test First compile the DEFINITION and IMPLEMENTATION modules MYMATH.DEF and MYMATH.MOD. Then work on the program FindPowers. Test with positive values for BaseNum and CardPwr or RealPwr. What happens if BaseNum is negative or zero? Why? Part of a sample run appears as follows:

```
Enter a REAL Base number: 5.5

What would you like to do?
   C    Find a CARDINAL power of the number.
   R    Find a REAL power of the number.
   S    Stop.
What is your Choice (C, R, or S)?  R

Enter REAL power: 2.5
The number raised to that power is   70.9425
....
```

Complete the documentation Documentation includes the problem description, pseudocode for FindPowers, code (CH9A), sample run, and users' guide. Warn the users that the symbol table file and object code file of external module MyMath, with functions CardPower and RealPower, must be available. A listing of DEFINITION MODULE MyMath could be a valuable part of the documentation. A listing of IMPLEMENTATION MODULE MyMath would be included only if there were a need for the user to know the details of how the CardPower and RealPower functions work.

Questions 9.1

1. Suppose in procedure CardPower that Result were assigned initial value 0.0, rather than 1.0. What would happen when you try to find 2.0^3 with the FindPowers program in Example 9.1.1?
2. Suppose in program FindPowers (Example 9.1.1) that you issue the command IMPORT MyMath; rather than FROM MyMath IMPORT CardPower, Real-Power;. What changes would you have to make to the program?
3. An IMPLEMENTATION MODULE OhMy appears as follows:

```
IMPLEMENTATION MODULE OhMy;
   (* Question 3, Section 9.1 *)

FROM InOut IMPORT WriteString;

PROCEDURE  WriteTheMessage();
   BEGIN
      WriteString("The value of ToBe is");
   END WriteTheMessage;

BEGIN
   ToBe := 3;
END OhMy.
```

a. What should the DEFINITION MODULE OhMy look like?

b. What is displayed when the following code is executed?

```
MODULE  TestOhMy;

FROM InOut IMPORT WriteString, WriteLn, WriteCard;
FROM OhMy IMPORT ToBe, WriteTheMessage;

BEGIN
   WriteTheMessage(); WriteCard(ToBe,6); WriteLn;
   ToBe := ToBe + 5;
   WriteTheMessage(); WriteCard(ToBe,6); WriteLn;
END TestOhMy.
```

4. a. The "common" logarithm (to base 10) can be written $\log 10(x)$ and can be calculated from the formula

$$\log 10(x) = \ln(x)/\ln(10.0)$$

Write a function that calculates and returns the "common" logarithm of a positive REAL number x.

b. The trigonometric tangent of an angle x, $\tan(x)$, is given by the formula

$$\tan(x) = \sin(x)/\cos(x).$$

$\text{Tan}(x)$ would cause an "attempt to divide by zero" error when $\cos(x)$ is very close to 0.0. Write a function that calculates and returns $\tan(x)$. If $\cos(x)$ is very close to 0.0, have the function display a warning error message and return the value -99999.99.

c. Incorporate both $\log 10(x)$ and $\tan(x)$ into module MyMath, and write a driver program to import and test these functions.

9.2 *Random Numbers*

In order to perform some types of simulation and to facilitate game playing, you will need to generate **random numbers;** that is, a series of numbers whose order cannot be predicted. In practice, there are no truly random numbers. Dice are never perfect; cards are never shuffled completely randomly; the supposedly random motions of molecules are influenced by the environment, and digital computers can handle numbers only within a finite range and with limited precision. The best one can do is generate *pseudorandom* numbers, which are sufficiently unpredictable for the task at hand.

Generating Pseudorandom Numbers

Modula-2 contains no standard random-number generator. However, many algorithms have been developed for generating pseudorandom numbers. Some of these algorithms utilize enumeration, such as counting bits beginning at some arbitrary location in a changing memory. Another method, used here, creates numbers by performing a calculation.

Consider the following algorithm:

Begin with any CARDINAL number; call it *Seed*.

1. Multiply Seed by a large CARDINAL Multiplier.

2. Add a large CARDINAL Addend. You have created a new CARDINAL Value, which may overflow; but that is all right, you really do not want to know the actual Value.

3. Find the Remainder (Value MOD MAX(CARDINAL)), which can be used as a new Seed to generate the next in a sequence of pseudorandom numbers. If MAX(CARDINAL) = 65535, then Remainder is a number between 0 and 65534.

4. Divide the Remainder by MAX(CARDINAL) to obtain a REAL pseudorandom Result between 0.0 and almost 1.0. (If MAX(CARDINAL) = 65535, the Result lies between 0.0 and 65534.0/65535.0 = 0.99998474.)

The sequence of Results produced by applying this algorithm repeatedly is a set of pseudorandom numbers, between 0.0 and almost 1.0, which is adequate for most applications. A given starting Seed always produces the same sequence. Some systems allow access to the time on the system clock, which could be used as a changing starting Seed. Most often, the user is asked simply to choose a number for the initial Seed. The sequence inevitably will repeat after some number of terms. Research (and trial and error) have determined that Multiplier = 25173 and Addend = 13849 tend to lengthen the distance between repetitions on a system where MAX(CARDINAL) = 65535.

☐ Function Random and Module RandGen

Here is Modula-2 code for a function that, when called repeatedly, generates a pseudorandom sequence of REAL numbers between 0.0 and almost 1.0.

```
PROCEDURE  Random(VAR Seed : CARDINAL) : REAL;
    (* Returns a real pseudorandom number between 0.0 and 0.99998474 *)
    CONST  DIVISOR = 65535;   MULTIPLIER = 25173;   ADDEND = 13849;
    BEGIN
        Seed := (Seed * MULTIPLIER + ADDEND) MOD DIVISOR;
        RETURN  FLOAT(Seed) / FLOAT(DIVISOR);
    END Random;
```

Range checking is a feature of Modula-2 that produces an error message if a value falls outside the prescribed range designed for a given data type. Most versions of the language give you the option of deciding at compile time whether or not range checking will be performed. Modules containing the Random function must be compiled with range checking turned *off*. Otherwise, when Seed overflows its CARDINAL memory space, the program will terminate with an "out of range" error. A solution is to place the procedure in an external module compiled with range checking turned off and import it from there. Figure 9–2 shows such a module, called RandGen. Your system manual should have instructions on how to turn range checking on and off. If you cannot turn range checking off, you can create a less random sequence by setting the constants to much smaller numbers such as DIVISOR = 64, MULTIPLIER = 25, and ADDEND = 13.

☐ Random Values between Low and High

Often you will need a CARDINAL Number between Low and High. To accomplish this, use the formula

Number := TRUNC(FLOAT(High − Low + 1) * Random(Seed) + FLOAT(Low)),

which produces pseudorandom CARDINAL Numbers between Low and High inclusively.

Figure 9–2
Module RandGen
with Function
Random

```
DEFINITION MODULE RandGen;
   (* Contains a pseudorandom number generator.
      MUST BE COMPILED WITH RANGE CHECKING TURNED OFF. *)
PROCEDURE  Random(VAR Seed : CARDINAL) : REAL;
   (* Returns a real pseudorandom number between 0.0 and
      0.99998474 *)
END RandGen.
```

```
IMPLEMENTATION MODULE RandGen;
   (* Contains a pseudorandom number generator.
      MUST BE COMPILED WITH RANGE CHECKING TURNED OFF. *)
PROCEDURE  Random(VAR Seed : CARDINAL) : REAL;
   (* Returns a real pseudorandom number between 0.0 and
      0.99998474 *)
   CONST DIVISOR = 65535; MULTIPLIER = 25173; ADDEND = 13849;
   BEGIN
      Seed := (Seed * MULTIPLIER + ADDEND) MOD DIVISOR;
      RETURN  FLOAT(Seed) / FLOAT(DIVISOR);
   END Random;
END RandGen.
```

☐ A Simple Game

This example is a simple game that illustrates the use of the Random function.

Example 9.2.1

Write a program that plays a HiLo game.

Define the problem The computer chooses a random CARDINAL number between 1 and 100 and asks the user/player to guess its value. Guesses will be counted. The player will be told after each incorrect guess whether the guess was too high or too low, and will be asked for another guess. When the player has found the number, he or she will be told how many guesses it took.

Develop a solution The player will be asked for a Seed, and the computer will choose its random Number by the formula

$$Number := TRUNC(100.0 * Random(Seed) + 1.0).$$

A loop will begin with Count = 0, ask for the Guess, increment Count, compare the Guess with Number, and repeat until Number = Guess. A REPEAT...UNTIL structure ensures that the player gets to guess at least once.

Refine the solution *Pseudocode*

```
begin HiLo
  ask for Seed
  repeat
    find random Number
    initialize    Count = 0
    repeat
      ask for Guess
      increment Count
```

```
            if    Guess < Number    print "Too Low"
            elsif    Guess > Number    print "Too High"
            until    Guess = Number
            write Count
            ask "would you like to do it again?", accept Again
       until    Again is not 'Y'
  end HiLo
```

Modula-2 code

```
MODULE HiLo;
   (* This program plays a mean game of HiLo.
      FileName:CH9B       Modula-2      RKW       Apr. 1991   *)

FROM InOut IMPORT WriteString, WriteLn, ReadCard, WriteCard, Read, Write;
FROM RandGen IMPORT Random;

CONST DEBUG = FALSE;
VAR  Number, Seed, Guess, Count : CARDINAL;
     Answer, ThrowAway : CHAR;

BEGIN
   WriteString("Enter a Seed number between 0 and 65535: ");
   ReadCard(Seed); WriteLn; WriteLn;

   REPEAT
      Number := TRUNC(100.0 * Random(Seed) + 1.0);  (* INVOKE RANDOM *)
      IF  DEBUG  THEN
         WriteString("The number is"); WriteCard(Number,4); WriteLn;
      END; (* IF *)

      Count := 0;
      REPEAT
         WriteString("What is your guess? "); ReadCard(Guess); WriteLn;
         INC(Count);
         IF  Guess < Number  THEN
            WriteString("That is too low."); WriteLn; WriteLn;
         ELSIF  Guess > Number  THEN
            WriteString("That is too high."); WriteLn; WriteLn;
         END; (* IF *)
      UNTIL  Guess = Number;

      WriteString("Congratulations! You did it in ");
       WriteCard(Count,3); WriteString(" guesses."); WriteLn;

      WriteLn; WriteString("Would you like to play again (Y/N)? ");
       Read(Answer); Read(ThrowAway); Write(Answer); WriteLn; WriteLn;
   UNTIL  CAP(Answer) <> 'Y';
END HiLo.
```

Debug and test: CONSTant DEBUG allows the display of Number during debugging. Obviously unless DEBUG is FALSE, the game presents no challenge at all. If the value of Seed overflows, remember to turn range checking off when compiling module RandGen, or to change MULTIPLIER, DIVISOR, and ADDEND to much smaller numbers. Here is a sample run.

```
Enter a Seed number between 0 and 65535: 235

What is your guess? 50
That is too high.

What is your guess? 25
That is too low.

What is your guess? 45
That is too low.

What is your guess? 48
Congratulations!  You did it in   4 guesses.

Would you like to play again (Y/N)?  N
```

Complete the documentation   Including the pseudocode, problem description, and algorithm development in the documentation will help you to expand upon the program. For example, you might wish to allow the player to wager on the number of guesses, to stop play when a user is broke, to have two users play against each other, or any other game-enhancing refinement. The source code is in file CH9B.

☐ Monte Carlo Techniques

Here is a more serious application of random numbers. It uses a technique called a Monte Carlo method, by which large numbers of experiments involving random outcomes are performed to find the approximate solution to a problem.

Example 9.2.2

Use a Monte Carlo method to estimate the area under a curve.

Define the problem   Suppose you have drawn the curve $y = x^2$ on a tile floor, where the length of each tile is 1 unit. Then you build a shallow rectangular box bounded by the x-axis, the lines $x = 1$ and $x = 3$, and the line defined by the height of the curve at $x = 3$, namely $y = 3^2 = 9$. This curve is shown in Figure 9–3a. Now toss $10.00 worth of pennies at random into the box. Find the ratio

$$\frac{\text{Number of pennies between the curve and the } x\text{-axis}}{\text{Total number of pennies in the box}}$$

This ratio will be approximately equal to the ratio of the shaded area under the curve to the total area of the box.

The area of the rectangular box is found by multiplying the length by the width; it is $9 * 2 = 18$ units in this situation. Therefore, approximately

$$(\text{Area under } y = x^2 \text{ between } x = 1 \text{ and } x = 3)/18$$
$$= \frac{\text{Number of pennies under the curve}}{\text{Total number of pennies}}$$

or

$$\text{Area under } y = x^2 \ (for\ 1 <= x <= 3)$$
$$= 18 * \frac{\text{Number of pennies under the curve}}{\text{Total number of pennies}}$$

and you will have approximated the area under the curve by a Monte Carlo method.

Figure 9–3
Curves for Example
9.2.2
a. Curve $y = x^2$
b. A General Curve
$y = f(x)$

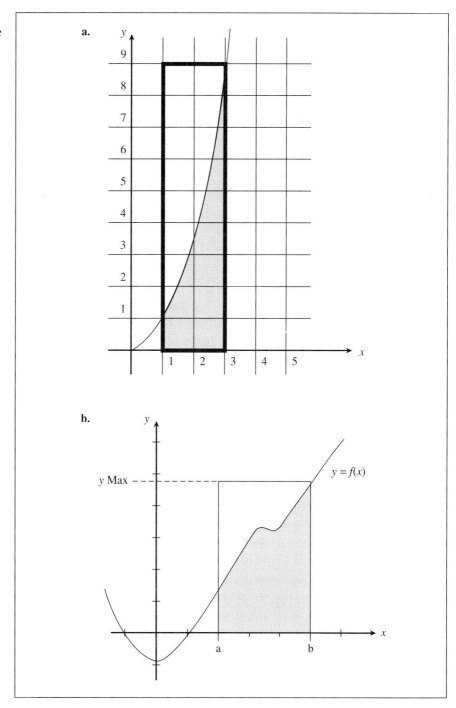

The problem is to write a computer program that effectively tosses pennies and determines the area under any curve $y = f(x)$ between limits $x = a$ and $x = b$.

Develop a solution   An arbitrary curve $y = f(x)$ is shown in Figure 9–3b. For now, restrict yourself to functions and ranges in which the curve is generally ascending (yMax $= f(b)$) or descending (yMax $= f(a)$) and in which the curve lies entirely above the x-axis. The method can be applied to any continuous curve, but without these restrictions, finding yMax and considering parts of the curve below the x-axis are whole new problems.

The equation $y = f(x)$ for the curve will be written in a function that finds y for a given parameter x. For example, let $y = 3 x^2 + 2 x + 1$. Then the function is simply

```
PROCEDURE     f(x : REAL) : REAL;
    BEGIN
            RETURN     3.0 * x * x     +     2.0 * x     +     1.0;
    END f;
```

For any other function $y = f(x)$, just replace the content of the RETURN statement with the expression that defines $f(x)$.

The formula for determining BoxArea for an ascending curve is width * length $= (b - a) * f(b)$. (For a descending curve, yMax occurs at $x = a$ instead of at $x = b$, so the BoxArea would be $(b - a) * f(a)$). Use PROCEDURE f to find yMax $= f(b)$, and calculate the BoxArea $= (b - a) * f(b)$.

Now choose a pair of REAL random numbers xRnd, yRnd, such that $a <= xRnd < b$ and $0 <= yRnd < yMax$, to simulate coordinates (xRnd, yRnd) where a penny would land in the box. A random REAL number between a and almost b is found from the function Random by $(b - a) * Random(Seed) + a$. Using yCalc $= f(xRnd)$, find the value of y on the curve, yCalc, when $x = xRnd$. Then determine whether the penny lies under the curve; that is, whether yRnd $<=$ yCalc. If so, increment UnderCount of pennies under the curve. Increment the PennyCount total number of points chosen. Repeat this process for a large number of points. Then calculate and display the Area under the curve; Area $=$ BoxArea * UnderCount/PennyCount. A structure chart for the solution is shown in Figure 9–4.

Refine the solution   *Pseudocode*

```
module MonteCarlo
    define function f(x), and CONSTant ASCENDING
    begin
        ask for Seed for Random(Seed)
        ask for limits     a     and     b
        if     ASCENDING     yMax = f(b)     otherwise yMax = f(a)
        BoxArea = (b − a) * yMax
        initialize   UnderCount = 0,     PennyCount = 0
        while PennyCount <= 1000
            find     xRnd,     yRnd
            find     yCalc = f(xRnd)
            if     yRnd <= yCalc     increment UnderCount
            increment PennyCount
        end while
        calculate     Area = BoxArea * UnderCount / PennyCount
        print     a, b, Area
    end MonteCarlo
```

Modula-2 code

```
MODULE MonteCarlo;
    (* This program uses the Monte Carlo technique to find
        the area under the curve defined in PROCEDURE f(x).
        FileName:CH9C     Modula-2     RKW     Apr.1991     *)
```

Figure 9–4
Structure Chart for
MonteCarlo
(Example 9.2.2)

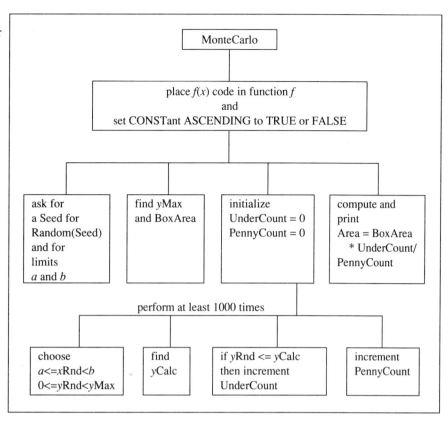

```
FROM InOut IMPORT WriteString, WriteLn, ReadCard, WriteCard;
FROM RealInOut IMPORT ReadReal, FWriteReal;
FROM RandGen IMPORT Random;

CONST  MAXIMUMCOUNT = 1000;
VAR  Seed, UnderCount, PennyCount : CARDINAL;
     xRnd, yRnd, yMax, yCalc, a, b, BoxArea, Area : REAL;

CONST  ASCENDING = TRUE;  (* Curve in function f(x) is ascending. *)
PROCEDURE  f(x : REAL) : REAL;
   BEGIN
      RETURN  3.0 * x * x  + 2.0 * x  + 1.0;
   END f;

BEGIN  (* MonteCarlo *)
   WriteString("Enter a cardinal Seed for Random generator. ");
    ReadCard(Seed); WriteLn;
   WriteString("What is lower limit on x? "); ReadReal(a); WriteLn;
   WriteString("What is upper limit on x? "); ReadReal(b); WriteLn;

   IF  ASCENDING  THEN  yMax := f(b); ELSE  yMax := f(a);  END; (* IF *)
   BoxArea := (b - a) * yMax;

   UnderCount := 0;  PennyCount := 0;
   WHILE  PennyCount < MAXIMUMCOUNT  DO
```

```
      xRnd := (b - a) * Random(Seed)  +  a;
      yRnd := yMax * Random(Seed);
      yCalc := f(xRnd);
      IF  yRnd <= yCalc  THEN  INC(UnderCount);  END; (* IF *)
      INC(PennyCount);
        (* Assertions: PennyCount = Total pennies tossed so far.
              UnderCount = Number of pennies under the curve so far.
              (xRnd,yRnd) = coordinates of latest tossed penny.
              yCalc = height of curve at latest xRnd penny coordinate. *)
    END; (* WHILE *)

    Area := BoxArea * FLOAT(UnderCount) / FLOAT(PennyCount);
    WriteLn; WriteString("For the curve defined in PROCEDURE f(x), ");
     WriteLn; WriteString("between x values a and b = ");
     FWriteReal(a,8,2); FWriteReal(b,8,2); WriteLn;
     WriteString("The area is approximately"); FWriteReal(Area,10,3);
  END MonteCarlo.
```

Debug and test It could be interesting to insert statements to display the values of PennyCount, UnderCount, xRnd, yRnd, and yCalc during each iteration. If you assign a very large value to MAXIMUMCOUNT, you may want to print something during each iteration so the user can see that the program is executing. Test the program for various values of *a* and *b*. Increase MAXIMUMCOUNT for greater accuracy. Alter the function $f(x)$ to find the area under a different curve. If you are comfortable with calculus, compare your answers with the integral of the function; otherwise, sketch the curve on graph paper and estimate the area to see if you are getting reasonable results. A sample run looks like

```
Enter a cardinal Seed for Random generator. 537
What is lower limit on x?  2.0
What is upper limit on x?  4.0

For the curve defined in PROCEDURE f(x),
between x values a and b =       2.00        4.00
The area is approximately     69.996
```

The true area under this curve between $x = 2.0$ and $x = 4.0$ is 70.0.

Complete the documentation Complete documentation for this problem is shown in Figure 9–5. Pay close attention to the users' manual.

Questions 9.2

1. What is the effect of this fragment of code?

```
...
FROM RandGen IMPORT Random;
VAR  Roll1, Roll2, Sum, Seed : CARDINAL;
...
BEGIN
...
    Roll1 := TRUNC(6.0*Random(Seed) + 1.0);
    Roll2 := TRUNC(6.0*Random(Seed) + 1.0);
    Sum := Roll1 + Roll2;
    WriteCard(Roll1,3); WriteCard(Roll2,3); WriteLn;
    IF  (Sum=7) OR (Sum=11)  THEN
        WriteString("We have a winner!"); WriteLn;
    END; (* IF *)
....
```

Problem Description   MonteCarlo

This program uses a Monte Carlo method to estimate the area under a curve $y = f(x)$ between $x = a$ and $x = b$, where the curve is generally ascending (yMax = $f(b)$) or descending (yMax = $f(a)$) in that range. The function $f(x)$ must be entered into the source code for the function. See PROCEDURE $f(x$:REAL) : REAL in the program listing.

The Monte Carlo method for finding the area under a curve is described in detail in Example 9.2.2.

Algorithm Development

y

For a general curve like that shown below, you wish to find the shaded area under $y = f(x)$.

$y = f(x)$

y Max

Structure Chart

MonteCarlo

place $f(x)$ code in function f
and
set CONSTant ASCENDING to TRUE or FALSE

Pseudocode

module MonteCarlo
  define function $f(x)$, and CONSTant ASCENDING
  begin

Program Listing

```
MODULE MonteCarlo;
   (* This program uses the Monte Carlo technique to find
      the area under the curve defined in PROCEDURE f(x).
      FileName:CH9C    Modula-2    RKW    Apr.1991  *)

FROM InOut IMPORT WriteString, WriteLn, ReadCard, WriteCard;
FROM RealInOut IMPORT ReadReal, FWriteReal;
FROM RandGen IMPORT Random;

CONST  MAXIMUMCOUNT = 1000;
VAR  Seed, UnderCount, PennyCount : CARDINAL;
     xRnd, yRnd, yMax, yCalc, a, b, BoxArea, Area : REAL;

CONST  ASCENDING = TRUE; (* Curve in function f(x) is ascending. *)
PROCEDURE  f(x : REAL) : REAL;
   BEGIN
      RETURN  3.0 * x * x  + 2.0 * x  + 1.0;
   END  f;
```

Sample Run

```
      Enter a cardinal Seed for Random generator. 537
      What is lower limit on x? 2.0
      What is upper limit on x? 4.0

      For the curve defined in PROCEDURE f(x),
      between x values a and b =      2.00        4.00
```

Users' Manual   MonteCarlo

You will need to work with the source code(CH9C), because the expression for the curve $y = f(x)$, under which to find the area, must be coded in the RETURN expression in PROCEDURE $f(x$:REAL):REAL. In this documentation the function is $y = 3*x*x + 2*x + 1$.

Sketch the curve between the limits a and b to determine whether it is generally Ascending (yMax = $f(b)$) or Descending (yMax = $f(a)$). Then set CONSTant ASCENDING to TRUE or FALSE accordingly. Execute the program, entering values for a and b when requested. The value of a should be smaller than b.

The approximate area under the curve will be displayed. Be patient; the program takes some time to execute, and nothing is displayed while calculations proceed. To change the number of iterations for more accurate results, increase the value of CONSTant MAXIMUMCOUNT.

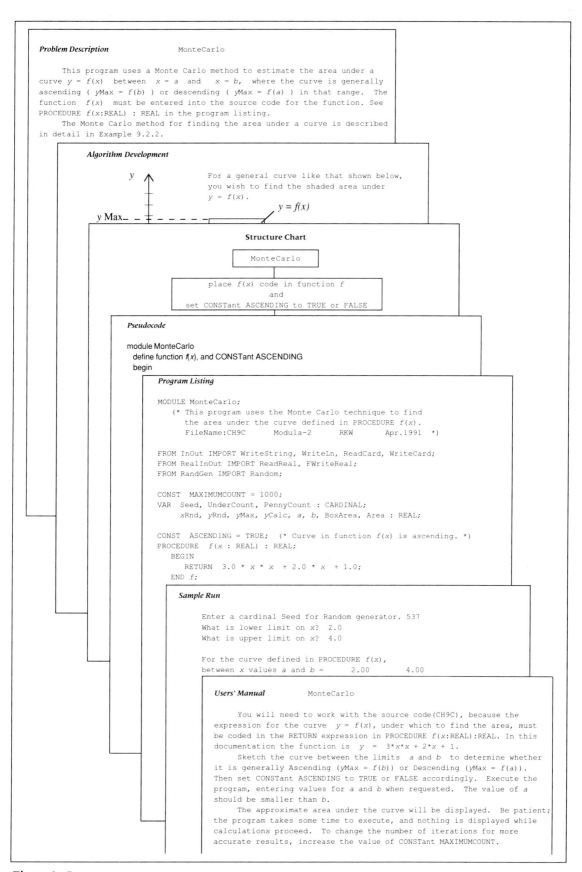

Figure 9–5
Documentation for MonteCarlo (Example 9.2.2)

2. Write a FOR loop that invokes function Random and prints 100 pseudorandom CARDINAL values in the range 2 to 12, on 10 lines with 10 numbers across the screen on each line.

3. What is the effect of this code fragment?

```
...
FROM RandGen IMPORT Random;
VAR  Suit, Number, Seed : CARDINAL;
...
BEGIN
...
    Suit := TRUNC(4.0*Random(Seed) + 1.0);
    CASE  Suit  OF
       1 : WriteString("Heart   ") |
       2 : WriteString("Club    ") |
       3 : WriteString("Diamond") |
       4 : WriteString("Spade   ");
    END; (* CASE *)
    Number := TRUNC(13.0*Random(Seed) + 1.0);
    CASE  Number  OF
       2..10 : WriteCard(Number,6)   |
           1 : WriteString("   Ace") |
          11 : WriteString("  Jack") |
          12 : WriteString(" Queen") |
          13 : WriteString("  King");
    END; (* CASE *)
....
```

4. How would you modify procedure Random to generate REAL numbers from RealLow to almost RealHigh, instead of from 0.0 to almost 1.0?

9.3 *Analogy and Generalization*

Once you have written procedures to solve a particular problem, little effort may be required to rewrite those procedures in a generalized form and then to apply simple modifications to them when you need to solve similar problems. In such circumstances, one problem is said to be an **analog** of the other. (*Analog* is derived from a Greek word meaning "proportionate.") You can build a valuable library by saving programs and procedures for solving analogous problems later.

General Problem Solving

You have applied analogy and generalization already by using features of Modula-2 to solve particular types of problems. For example, you may have discovered that generally

- menus, ask-again, and data-validation algorithms are best handled by using post-test, REPEAT... UNTIL structures,
- FOR loops should be used when the iterations can be counted,
- tables of data can be created using nested iterations,
- the plotting procedures, developed in Section 5.5, can be used to create a variety of point and bar graphs, and so forth.

However, there are many particular types of analogous problems for which the solutions are nearly the same. When confronted with a new task, one question you

---

> ⌐┐
> └┘ *A Bit of Background*
>
> ### Monte Carlo
>
> Monte Carlo is a community within the principality of Monaco on the Mediterranean coast of France. Monte Carlo's fame as a gambling resort is responsible for its name being adopted for mathematical methods involving random numbers.
>
> Monte Carlo techniques involve creating random numbers within given limits and determining what percentage of those numbers meet certain criteria. They can be used to calculate the area between curves (as in this chapter), to estimate the arrival of airplanes at an airport, to predict the percentage of manufactured parts that will be defective, to project the growth and decline of populations with fixed resources, to specify the needed thickness of nuclear-reactor shielding, and so forth.
>
> Monte Carlo calculations were hardly feasible before the development of high-speed computers. In many cases, billions of random numbers must be generated in order to achieve statistically accurate results. If, on a mainframe computer, one choice and test calculation required a microsecond, then a billion calculations would take about 1000 seconds (roughly 17 minutes). On a microcomputer, where a calculation could take a millisecond, a billion calculations would require a million seconds (or eleven and a half days).
>
> Clearly the speed and capacity of a computer are critical for effective application of Monte Carlo techniques. It has not been unusual for a single highly accurate computation of this nature to monopolize a ten-million-dollar supercomputer for hours. However, new machines, which can handle many operations concurrently within parallel processors, are reducing the time required for Monte Carlo calculations with large data samples.

should ask yourself is "Have I solved a similar problem before?" Often it is easier to adapt a previously used, well-documented solution to an analogous problem than to begin all over again. If you have built a wheelbarrow, you should not have to "reinvent the wheel" to build a trailer.

Exponential Growth and Decay

Consider this example, which applies analogy and generalization to a specific type of problem.

Example 9.3.1

Given an algorithm for calculating Bacterial Growth, find a general algorithm for handling any type of exponential growth or decay and apply it to calculate the rate of radioactive decay.

Define the problem   The number N of a population of bacteria at time t is given by the exponential equation

$$N = N0\, e^{kt}$$

where $N0$ is the beginning population (at time 0) and $e = 2.71828$ approximately. The proportionality constant k can be expressed in terms of the amount of time T it takes for the population to double, as

$$k = \ln2/T,$$

where $\ln2 = $ logarithm to the base e of 2. e^x is implemented in Modula-2 by the math function $\exp(x)$. $\ln x$ is implemented by $\ln(x)$.

Assume that procedures called AskForData and Growth have been written already. These procedures find the number N of bacteria at a specified time t, given the number $N0$ at time zero and the doubling time T. Here are the pseudocode and the procedures with a driver program.

Pseudocode

```
BacterialGrowthTestDriver
begin
  loop
    write "Enter negative time t to stop"
    AskForData(TDbl, NumAt0, time)
    if    time < 0    then    exit the loop
    Growth(TDbl, NumAt0, time)
  end loop
end BacterialGrowthTest Driver

procedure AskForData(VAR T, N0, t : REAL)
  begin
    ask for T, N0, and time t
  end AskForData

procedure Growth(T, N0, t : REAL)
  begin
    calculate    k = ln2 / T
    calculate    N = N0 * exp(k * t)
    display t and N
  end Growth
```

Modula-2 code

```
MODULE BacterialGrowthTestDriver;
    (* Finds the number of bacteria at any time t, given the number
       at time 0 and the doubling time.
       FileName:CH9D        Modula-2        RKW        Apr. 1991    *)

FROM InOut IMPORT WriteString, WriteLn;
FROM RealInOut IMPORT ReadReal, FWriteReal;
FROM MathLib0 IMPORT exp, ln;

VAR  TDbl, NumAt0, time : REAL;

PROCEDURE AskForData(VAR T, N0, t : REAL);
   BEGIN
      WriteString("Doubling Time (hours) = ? "); ReadReal(T); WriteLn;
      WriteString("Number of bacteria at time 0 = ? ");ReadReal(N0);WriteLn;
      WriteString("Future time (t, hours) to know number of bacteria = ? ");
       ReadReal(t); WriteLn; WriteLn;
   END AskForData;

PROCEDURE Growth(T, N0, t : REAL);
   VAR  k, N : REAL;
   BEGIN
      k := ln(2.0) / T;   N := N0 * exp(k * t);

      WriteLn; WriteString("At time "); FWriteReal(t,6,2);
       WriteString(" hours the number of bacteria will be ");
       FWriteReal(N,12,2); WriteLn;
   END Growth;
```

```
BEGIN (* BacterialGrowthTestDriver *)
   LOOP
      WriteString("ENTER NEGATIVE TIME t TO STOP"); WriteLn;
      AskForData(TDbl, NumAt0, time);

      IF time < 0.0 THEN EXIT END; (* IF *)

      Growth(TDbl, NumAt0, time);
   END; (* LOOP *)
END BacterialGrowthTestDriver.
```

The problem to be solved is to generalize the solution of the Bacterial Growth procedures to handle any type of exponential growth *or decay*. Then a program that will tell how many radioactive nuclei are left after some time *t*, given the initial number *n*0 and the amount of time for half of the sample to decay (called the *half-life, T*), must be written and tested.

Develop a solution With the formula in the form $N = N0 * \exp(k * t)$, it is easy to handle both exponential growth and decay. The value of k is positive for growth and negative for decay. When the user enters doubling-time T for growth, or half-life T (time it takes for the number N to reach half its initial value $N0$) for decay, k is calculated from $k = \ln(2.0)/T$. T and t may be any units of time (minutes, hours, years, etc.) as long as both are entered in the same units.

Refine the solution Read the following generalized form of the program carefully. In this form, procedure AskForData allows the user to choose Growth and enter doubling time *or* to choose Decay and enter half-life. The positive or negative value of k, rather than T, is passed between procedures.

```
MODULE ChangeTestDriver;
   (* Finds a sample population at any time t, given the number
      at time 0 and the doubling time or half life.
      FileName:CH9E      Modula-2      RKW      Apr. 1991  *)

FROM InOut IMPORT WriteString, WriteLn, Read, Write;
FROM RealInOut IMPORT ReadReal, FWriteReal;
FROM MathLib0 IMPORT exp, ln;

VAR  kValue, NumAt0, time : REAL;

PROCEDURE AskForData(VAR k, N0, t : REAL);
   VAR  T : REAL;    Selection, Dummy : CHAR;
   BEGIN
      REPEAT
         WriteLn; WriteString("Choose one of the following:"); WriteLn;
            WriteString("   G    Solve a Growth problem."); WriteLn;
            WriteString("   D    Solve a Decay problem. "); WriteLn;
         WriteString("Choose one (G, or D): ");
            Read(Selection); Read(Dummy); Write(Selection); WriteLn;WriteLn;
      UNTIL  (CAP(Selection)='G') OR (CAP(Selection)='D');

      IF  CAP(Selection) = 'G' THEN    (* GROWTH Conditions *)
         WriteString("Doubling Time, T  = ? "); ReadReal(T); WriteLn;
         k := ln(2.0) / T;
      ELSE                             (* DECAY  Conditions *)
```

```
            WriteString("Half Life, T  = ? "); ReadReal(T); WriteLn;
            k := -ln(2.0) / T;
         END; (* IF *)

         WriteString("Population at time 0  = ? "); ReadReal(N0); WriteLn;
         WriteString("Future time (t, in same units as T) to know");
          WriteString(" population = ? "); ReadReal(t); WriteLn; WriteLn;
      END AskForData;

PROCEDURE Change(k, N0, t : REAL);
   VAR  N : REAL;
   BEGIN
      N := N0 * exp(k * t);

      WriteLn; WriteString("At time "); FWriteReal(t,6,2);
       WriteString(" the population will be ");
       FWriteReal(N,12,2); WriteLn;
   END Change;

BEGIN (* ChangeTestDriver *)
   LOOP
      WriteString("ENTER NEGATIVE TIME t TO STOP"); WriteLn;
      AskForData(kValue, NumAt0, time);

      IF  time < 0.0  THEN  EXIT  END; (* IF *)

      Change(kValue, NumAt0, time);
   END; (* LOOP *)
END ChangeTestDriver.
```

Now the generalized solution can be modified to handle radioactive decay. The number n of nuclei present at time t is given by

$$n = n0\ e^{-kt}$$

where $n0 =$ number at time 0, $k = \ln 2/T$, and $T =$ half-life.

Modula-2 code

```
MODULE RadioactiveDecay;
   (* Finds the number of nuclei at any time t, given the number
      at time 0 and the half life.
      FileName:CH9F       Modula-2      RKW       Apr. 1991   *)

FROM InOut IMPORT WriteString, WriteLn;
FROM RealInOut IMPORT ReadReal, FWriteReal;
FROM MathLib0 IMPORT exp, ln;

VAR  kValue, NumAt0, time : REAL;

PROCEDURE AskForData(VAR k, N0, t : REAL);
   VAR  T : REAL;
   BEGIN
      WriteString("Half Life, T  = ? "); ReadReal(T); WriteLn;
      k := -ln(2.0) / T;

      WriteString("Nuclei at time 0  = ? "); ReadReal(N0); WriteLn;
```

```
        WriteString("Future time (t, same units as T) to know nuclei = ? ");
        ReadReal(t); WriteLn; WriteLn;
     END AskForData;

PROCEDURE Decay(k, N0, t : REAL);
   VAR  N : REAL;
   BEGIN
      N := N0 * exp(k * t);

      WriteLn; WriteString("At time "); FWriteReal(t,6,2);
      WriteString(" the number of nuclei will be ");
      FWriteReal(N,12,2); WriteLn;
   END Decay;

BEGIN (* RadioactiveDecay *)
   AskForData(kValue, NumAt0, time);
   Decay(kValue, NumAt0, time);
END RadioactiveDecay.
```

Debug and test Run the Bacterial Growth program for sample values such as
$N0 = 2500$, $T = 16$ hours, and $t = 48$ hours. Run the generalized Growth and
Decay program with the same data. You should see the same results from both. Now
run the RadioactiveDecay program with the values for tritium, which has a half-life
$T = 12.4$ years. Suppose you have a very small sample of 9500 tritium nuclei and
you wish to know how many will be left one year from now. A test run of the
program with this data should look like

```
Half-life, T  = ? 12.4
Nuclei at time 0  = ? 9500.0
Future time (t, same units as T) to know nuclei = ? 1.0

At time   1.00 the number of nuclei will be    8983.53
```

Run the generalized Growth and Decay program with the same data. Do you get the
same results?

Complete the documentation To document the RadioactiveDecay program, include the equation for exponential decay, and rewrite the pseudocode for the Bacterial Growth problem to reflect radioactive decay. Include the problem description,
code, and sample run. The users' manual could contain additional information about
the various uses of the program:

> Procedure AskForData and Decay and a short driver program are found in file
> CH9F. You will be asked to enter the half-life and time, which must be expressed in
> the same units (for example, seconds, hours, years, etc.). If the initial number of
> nuclei the program requests is very large, it may be entered in exponential form, such
> as $1.5E + 23$.
>
> The same procedures may be modified to handle any exponential growth or decay
> problem. (See the generalized code file CH9E.)

Questions 9.3

1. Run the Bacterial Growth (CH9D) and generalized Growth and Decay (CH9E)
programs with the data $N0 = 2500.0$, $T = 16.0$ hours, and $t = 48.0$ hours.
Show your results.

A Bit of Background

Radioactivity

Wilhelm Roentgen (1845–1923) discovered X rays in 1895, which led quickly to Henri Becquerel's discovery of natural radioactivity in 1896. Soon the Curies, Rutherford, and others began to study the properties of radioactive materials. One of the great surprises was the "half-life." Instead of finding the expected equal number of nuclear decays during successive equal time intervals, the same *fraction* of the remaining nuclei in a sample was discovered to decay during equal time periods. Thus, if the half-life of a substance containing 10,000 radioactive nuclei were exactly one hour, then, 5000 would remain at the end of the first hour. During the second hour, half of the remaining 5000 would decay, leaving 2500. After the third hour, half of the 2500, or 1250, would be left; and so on.

---

2. Run the RadioactiveDecay (CH9F) and generalized Growth and Decay (CH9E) programs with the following data, and show what results you get.
   a. Tritium decays to helium: half-life = 12.4 years, $n0$ = 9500, t = 2.0 years.
   b. Carbon 14 decays to carbon 12 (used in archeological dating): half-life = 5580 years, $n0$ = 1000, t = 2000 years.
   c. Oxygen 14 decays to nitrogen 14: half-life = 71.1 seconds, $n0$ = 1.0E+06, t = 24 hours. (Don't forget to express T and t in the same units of time.)
3. Suppose you have a population of 100,000 bacteria that are dying off exponentially in a closed dish with no nutrients. The time it takes for half of the bacteria to die is 6 hours. Modify the Bacterial Growth program (CH9D) to handle this situation and determine how many bacteria remain after two days.
4. What happens if Half-life or Doubling time, T, is entered as 0.0 in the programs used in questions 1–3? Would this make sense in any actual physical situation? How would you prevent the user from entering 0.0 for T in these programs?

9.4 Recursion

Because Modula-2 allocates new memory locations for parameters and local variables each time a procedure is called, it is possible for a procedure to invoke itself, a process called **direct recursion.** Similarly, procedure A can invoke procedure B, which in turn invokes procedure A, and this is called **indirect** or **mutual recursion.**

In 1936 Alan Turing showed that, although not every possible problem can be solved by computer, those problems that have recursive solutions also have computer solutions, at least in theory.

Mathematical Recursion

The recursive concept is that the solution to a problem can be stated in terms of "simpler" versions of itself. Some problems can be solved using an algebraic formula that shows recursion explicitly. Such algorithms are expressed by answering the questions

1. What is the first case?
2. How is the $(n + 1)$st case related to the nth case?
3. Where does it stop?

A Bit of Background

The "Universal Algorithm Machine"

In the 1930s and 1940s, Alan Mathison Turing (1912–1954) and others studied in considerable depth the theory of what a computing machine should be able to do. Turing invented a theoretical, pencil-and-paper computer—now appropriately called a Turing machine—that he hoped would be a "universal algorithm machine." That is, he hoped to prove theoretically that all problems could be solved by a set of instructions to a hypothetical computer. What he succeeded in proving was that some problems cannot be solved by *any* machine, just as some problems cannot be solved by any person. However, he did show that algorithms that can be defined recursively can indeed be solved by machine, though it may not be possible to predict how long it will take the machine to find the solution.

Alan Turing's work formed the foundation of computer theory before the first electronic computer was built. His contributions to the team that developed the critical code-breaking computers during World War II led directly to the practical implementation of his theories.

For example, a recursive formula for generating the CARDINAL numbers between 1 and 4 is

1. Begin with $x_1 = 4$.
2. $x_{n+1} = x_n - 1$.
3. Stop when $x_{n+1} = 1$.

To see how to implement this recursive solution on the computer, consider the following program.

```
MODULE  GenerateCardinals;
    (* Generates and displays cardinal values 1 to 4 recursively.
        FileName:CH9G        Modula-2        RKW        Apr. 1991  *)

FROM InOut IMPORT WriteCard, WriteLn;
VAR  EndNumber : CARDINAL;

PROCEDURE   CreateNextNumber(OldNumber:CARDINAL);
    VAR  NewNumber : CARDINAL;
    BEGIN
        IF  OldNumber > 1  THEN              (* Test STOP Condition *)
            NewNumber := OldNumber - 1;
            CreateNextNumber(NewNumber);     (* RECURSIVE CALL *)
        END; (* IF *)

        WriteCard(OldNumber,3);
        WriteLn;
    END CreateNextNumber;

BEGIN  (* GenerateCardinals *)
    EndNumber := 4;
    CreateNextNumber(EndNumber);             (* FIRST CALL *)
    WriteLn;
END GenerateCardinals.
```

Figure 9–6 shows a trace of the memory contents and screen display with each recursive call of the procedure CreateNextNumber. Observe how, when OldNumber > 1, a new call is made to CreateNextNumber(NewNumber), which interrupts the

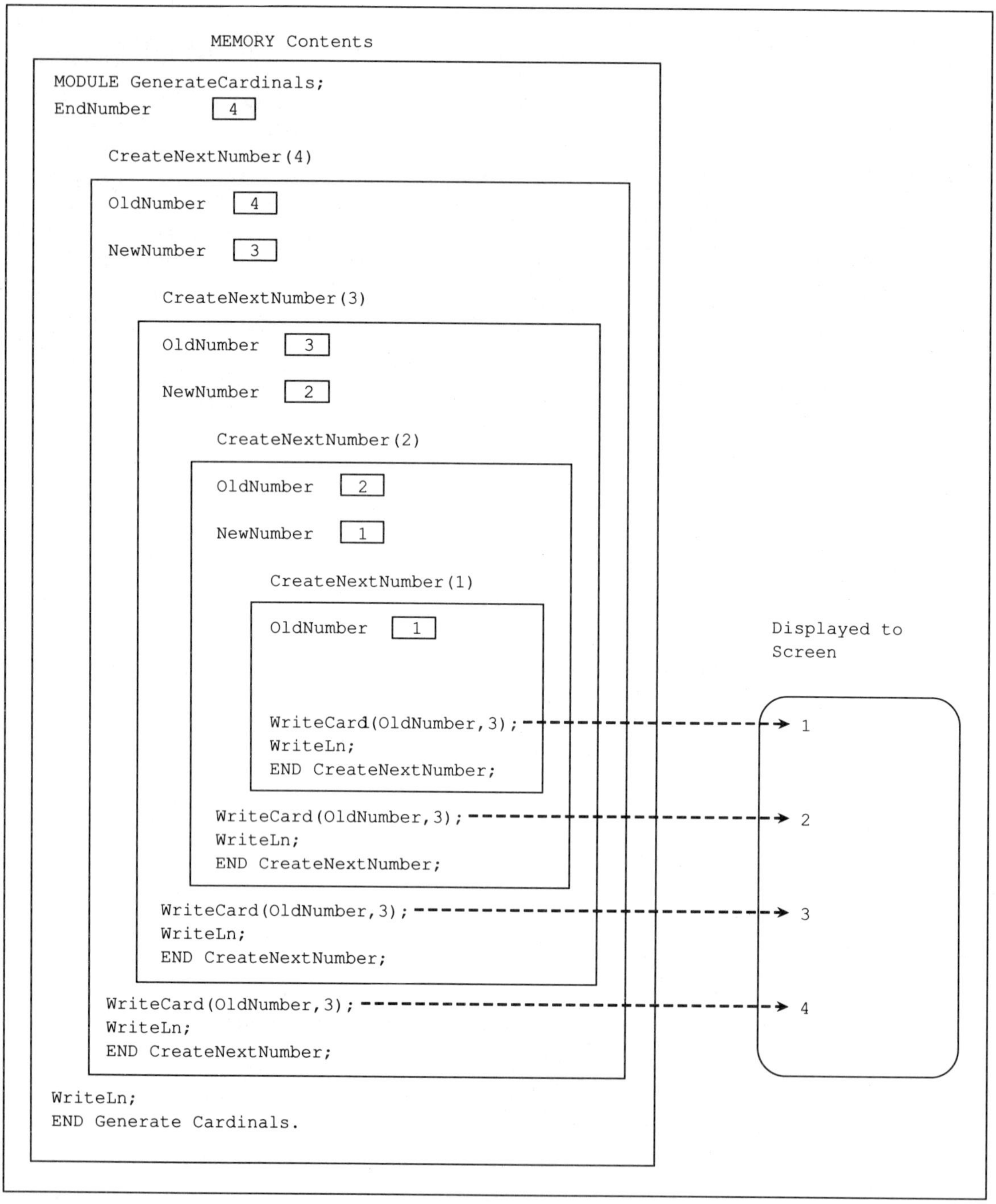

```
MEMORY Contents

MODULE GenerateCardinals;
EndNumber        4

    CreateNextNumber(4)

    OldNumber        4

    NewNumber        3

        CreateNextNumber(3)

        OldNumber        3

        NewNumber        2

            CreateNextNumber(2)

            OldNumber        2

            NewNumber        1

                CreateNextNumber(1)

                OldNumber        1                          Displayed to
                                                            Screen


                WriteCard(OldNumber,3); ------------------> 1
                WriteLn;
                END CreateNextNumber;

            WriteCard(OldNumber,3); ----------------------> 2
            WriteLn;
            END CreateNextNumber;

        WriteCard(OldNumber,3); --------------------------> 3
        WriteLn;
        END CreateNextNumber;

    WriteCard(OldNumber,3); ------------------------------> 4
    WriteLn;
    END CreateNextNumber;

WriteLn;
END Generate Cardinals.
```

Figure 9–6
Trace of Recursion for GenerateCardinals

current execution of the procedure. The test that determines when the recursion stops is IF OldNumber > 1 THEN…. A test for a stop Condition must be included in every recursive algorithm; otherwise, you will continue until available memory overflows. When the stop Condition NOT(OldNumber > 1) is reached, the current procedure proceeds to completion, executing WriteCard(OldNumber,3) and WriteLn and terminating at END CreateNextNumber. Then execution continues where it left off in the previous invocation of the procedure. The program "backs out" of the procedure calls until it reaches module GenerateCardinals, which completes its execution and stops as well.

☐ Defining Recursive Solutions

The recursive method can be applied to any problem in which the solution is represented in terms of solutions to simpler versions of the same problem.

The most difficult tasks in implementing recursion are deciding how to create the process and visualizing what happens at each successive invocation of the procedure. In computer applications, you try to think in terms of the question "If I construct a 'shorter' version (with 'simpler' values of the parameters) of the problem and get an answer, what would I do to get the answer to my original problem?"

To assist you in learning these tasks, another recursive procedure is implemented in the next example.

Example 9.4.1

Convert a decimal number to octal.

Define the problem   Write a program that uses recursive procedure calls to print a CARDINAL number in octal.

Develop a solution   An algorithm for converting a decimal Number to any Base is

    1. Begin
       Divide Number by Base
             RightMostAnswerDigit = Remainder, Number MOD Base
             NewNumber = Quotient, Number DIV Base

    2. Solve the resulting "simpler" problem
       Divide NewNumber by Base
             NextAnswerDigit = Remainder, NewNumber MOD Base
             NewNumber = Quotient, NewNumber DIV Base

    3. Stop when NewNumber = 0.

Observe the recursive nature of this solution; that is, the same steps are to be performed for smaller values of NewNumber until the test Condition, NewNumber = 0, causes termination of the recursion. For example, to convert decimal Number 497 to Base 8, perform these steps:

        RightMostAnswerDigit = 497 MOD 8 = 1
        NewNumber = 497 DIV 8 = 62

          NextAnswerDigit = 62 MOD 8 = 6
          NewNumber = 62 DIV 8 = 7

          NextAnswerDigit = 7 MOD 8 = 7
          NewNumber = 7 DIV 8 = 0

       Stop.

The result is $497_{10} = 761_8$.

To convert this to a computer solution, you need a recursive procedure that

receives Number as a parameter
finds the NextAnswerDigit
finds the NewNumber
if   NewNumber > 0   then
        the procedure calls itself,
            passing NewNumber to the parameter
ends if
prints the NextAnswerDigit

Refine the solution *Pseudocode*

```
begin ConvertDecToOct
  ask for a decimal Number
  write    "the octal equivalent is"
  call    FindADigit(Number)   (* The FIRST CALL to FindADigit *)
end ConvertDecToOct

procedure FindADigit(CardNumber : CARDINAL)
  begin
    NextAnswerDigit = CardNumber MOD 8
    NewNumber       = CardNumber DIV 8
    if    NewNumber > 0    then   (* Test the stop Condition *)
        FindADigit(NewNumber)   (* The RECURSIVE CALL *)
    end if
    print NextAnswerDigit   (* Continue after recursion *)
end FindADigit
```

Modula-2 code

```
MODULE ConvertDecToOct;
   (* Converts a decimal number to octal, using recursion.
      FileName:CH9H        Modula-2        RKW        Apr. 1991   *)

FROM InOut IMPORT WriteString, WriteLn, ReadCard, WriteCard;
VAR   Number : CARDINAL;

PROCEDURE FindADigit( CardNumber : CARDINAL);
   VAR  NextAnswerDigit, NewNumber : CARDINAL;
   BEGIN
      NextAnswerDigit := CardNumber MOD 8;
      NewNumber := CardNumber DIV 8;
      IF NewNumber > 0 THEN              (* Condition for recursive call *)
         FindADigit(NewNumber);          (* THE RECURSIVE CALL *)
      END; (* IF *)

      WriteCard(NextAnswerDigit,1);    (* After recursion, print digit. *)
   END FindADigit;

BEGIN (* ConvertDecToOct *)
   WriteString("Enter a cardinal number: ");
    ReadCard(Number); WriteLn;
   WriteString("The octal equivalent is ");
   FindADigit(Number);                   (* THE FIRST CALL *)
   WriteLn;                              (* All recursion has ended. *)
END ConvertDecToOct.
```

Debug and test Here is the result of a test run:

```
Enter a cardinal number: 497
The octal equivalent is 761
```

To keep track of where you are, try adding extra write statements to display the values of NextAnswerDigit and NewNumber immediately after they are calculated in FindADigit. Also try initializing a variable RecursionCount to 0 in the main module and pass it to FindADigit. Then in

```
PROCEDURE  FindADigit(CardNumber, RecursionCount : CARDINAL);
```

after BEGIN

```
INC(RecursionCount);
WriteString("ENTERing call "); WriteCard(RecursionCount,3); WriteLn;
```

and after END; (* IF *) add

```
WriteString("EXITing call "); WriteCard(RecursionCount,3); WriteLn;
```

To trace this recursive process by hand, you might like to create a diagram like Figure 9–7.

Observe carefully how each procedure is entered and then "backed out of" in reverse order. What would happen if the command WriteCard(NextAnswerDigit,1); were entered immediately after the calculation NextAnswerDigit := CardNumber MOD 8? Can you convince yourself that the digits would be written in the order in which they were calculated instead of in reverse order?

The code for this problem was written with a recursive procedure, since the algorithm was developed in that manner. Many recursive solutions, such as this one, can be written in *iterative* (nonrecursive) form.

For example, you would write an iterative solution to this problem as

```
CardNumber := Number;  DigitCount := 0;
WHILE  CardNumber > 0 DO
   INC(DigitCount);
   NextAnswerDigit[DigitCount] := CardNumber MOD 8;
   NewNumber := CardNumber DIV 8;
   CardNumber := NewNumber;
END; (* WHILE *)

FOR  WhichDigit := DigitCount TO 1  BY −1  DO
   WriteCard(NextAnswerDigit[WhichDigit], 1);
END; (* FOR *)
WriteLn;
```

NextAnswerDigit would be declared as an array,

```
VAR  NextAnswerDigit = ARRAY [1..10] OF CARDINAL;
```

because, in this solution, it is necessary to remember the NextAnswerDigits so that you can write them in reverse order after iteration terminates.

If a problem solution can be expressed iteratively or recursively with equal ease, the iterative solution usually is preferable because it executes faster and uses less memory. For this problem it was easy to write a recursive algorithm, since the problem was stated that way.

```
                    MEMORY Contents

MODULE ConvertDecToOct

Number     [ 497 ]

     FindADigit(497)

     CardNumber          [ 497 ]

     NextAnswerDigit       [ 1 ]

     NewNumber            [ 62 ]

          FindADigit(62)

          CardNumber          [ 62 ]

          NextAnswerDigit      [ 6 ]

          NewNumber            [ 7 ]

               FindADigit(7)

               CardNumber          [ 7 ]

               NextAnswerDigit     [ 7 ]

               NewNumber           [ 0 ]
                                                    Displayed to
                                                    Screen

               WriteCard(NextAnswerDigit,1); ------------->  7    6    1
               END FindADigit;

          WriteCard(NextAnswerDigit,1); ----------------------
          END FindADigit;

     WriteCard(NextAnswerDigit,1); -----------------------------
     END FindADigit;

WriteLn;
END ConvertDecToOct.
```

Figure 9–7
Tracing Recursive Calls of FindADigit (497) (Example 9.4.1)

Complete the documentation   Supplement the problem description with the recursion algorithm used to solve the problem. Pseudocode, code (CH9H), and a sample run show how the program works. If the desire is to demonstrate the recursive technique, it would be a good idea to include Figure 9–7, which illustrates how to trace the process by hand.

In the users' manual state that a CARDINAL decimal value is to be entered when requested by the program. The octal value is then calculated and displayed without further user intervention.

---

1. What would be displayed by this recursive procedure if it is called with the command ShowEm(10, 20)?

```
PROCEDURE  ShowEm(Able, Baker : CARDINAL);
   BEGIN
      IF  Able < Baker  THEN
         WriteCard(Able, 3);  WriteLn;
         INC(Able);
         ShowEm(Able, Baker);
      END; (* IF *)
   END ShowEm;
```

2. What would be displayed by this recursive procedure if it is called with the command NowShowEm(10, 20)?

```
PROCEDURE  NowShowEm(Charlie, Dog : CARDINAL);
   BEGIN
      IF  Charlie < Dog  THEN
         DEC(Dog);
         NowShowEm(Charlie, Dog);
      END; (* IF *)
      WriteCard(Dog, 3);  WriteLn;
   END NowShowEm;
```

3. Write a recursive algorithm for generating all even CARDINAL numbers beginning with 2 and ending at 50. Then write a recursive Modula-2 procedure PROCEDURE Evens(Number, StopValue : CARDINAL); that displays all even CARDINAL numbers from 2 to StopValue.

4. What is wrong with these two recursive processes? What would you do to correct them?

   a. The call is CreateNextNumber(0); and you wish to display CARDINAL numbers from 1 to 4.

   ```
   PROCEDURE  CreateNextNumber(Number : CARDINAL);
      BEGIN
         INC(Number);
         WriteCard(Number, 3);  WriteLn;
         CreateNextNumber(Number);
      END CreateNextNumber;
   ```

   b. The call is FindADigit(497); and you wish to display the octal digits of the answer in reverse order.

   ```
   PROCEDURE  FindADigit(Number : CARDINAL);
      VAR  NextAnswerDigit : CARDINAL;
      BEGIN
         NextAnswerDigit := Number MOD 8;
         WriteCard(NextAnswerDigit, 2);
         Number := Number DIV 8;
         IF  Number < 1000  THEN
            FindADigit(Number);
         END; (* IF *)  WriteLn;
      END FindADigit;
   ```

5. Implement the version of program ConvertDecToOct (Example 9.4.1) with the commands to display NextAnswerDigit, NewNumber, and RecursionCount described in *Debug and Test* of that example.

9.5 *Focus on Problem Solving*

Many problem solutions that can be defined recursively can also be handled by straight iteration, without recursive procedures; and all iterative problems can be written recursively. In this section you will write a *function* in both recursive and iterative form.

Recursion or Iteration?

Generally, an iterative solution will run faster and use memory more efficiently than a recursive solution, but the recursive solution source code may be more compact and easier to write and read. Many problems designed to handle data structures (organized collections of data) are defined in a recursive manner, which makes them easier to program with recursive algorithms. For these problems, if iteration ultimately is required, it may be better to write the program recursively and get it to work, and then rewrite it in iterative form. A useful rule of thumb is

If the problem is stated recursively, or if a solution algorithm is written in recursive form, then the recursive solution may be easier to write and more clear for the user than the iterative solution. If the problem is stated in iterative form, write the iterative solution.

Tail Recursion

Whenever the recursive call is the last executable statement in a procedure, the process is called **tail recursion.** Tail-recursive procedures are easy to rewrite in iterative form, as shown by the comparison of the pseudocode and examples in Figure 9−8. In fact, a well-written compiler can often convert recursion in tail form to iteration.

The Factorial Function

In this example a function is developed in both recursive and iterative forms.

Example 9.5.1

Write a recursive function to calculate *n*-factorial. Then rewrite the function without recursion.

Define the problem   *n*-factorial ($n!$) can be defined recursively by

$$0! = 1$$
$$n! = n * (n - 1)!$$

so that, for example,

$$3! = 3 * 2! = 3 * 2 * 1! = 3 * 2 * 1 * 0! = 3 * 2 * 1 * 1 = 6$$

Take advantage of this recursive property and write a function that finds and returns $n!$ when passed a CARDINAL value.

Figure 9–8
Converting Tail
Recursion to
Iterative Form

General Pseudocode **TAIL RECURSION**
PROCEDURE Recursive(formal parameter list);
    BEGIN
        perform operations;
        update Condition and new parameter Values;
        IF Condition is not Stop THEN
         Recursive(new parameter Values);
        END; (* IF *)
    END Recursive;
BEGIN (* Calling Unit *)
    ...
    Recursive(initial actual parameters);
    ....

Example
```
PROCEDURE  CreateCardNums(OldNum : CARDINAL);
    VAR  NewNum : CARDINAL;
    BEGIN
        WriteCard(OldNum, 3); WriteLn;
        NewNum := OldNum + 1;
        IF  NewNum <=4  THEN
            CreateCardNums(NewNum);
        END;  (* IF *)
    END CreateCardNums;
BEGIN  (* calling unit *)
    . . .
    CreateCardNums(1);
    . . . .
```

General Pseudocode **ITERATION**
BEGIN
    ...
    set initial Conditions and Values
    WHILE Condition is not Stop DO
        perform operations;
        update Condition and Values;
    END; (* WHILE *)
    ....

Example
```
BEGIN
    . . .
    OldNum := 1;  NewNum := OldNum + 1;
    WHILE  NewNum <= 4  DO
        WriteCard(OldNum, 3); WriteLn;
        NewNum := OldNum + 1;
        OldNum := NewNum;
    END;  (* WHILE *)
    . . . .
```

Develop a solution   A recursive function

$$\text{PROCEDURE RecurFact}(n : \text{CARDINAL}) : \text{CARDINAL}$$

will be written that returns $n * \text{RecurFact}(n - 1)$
until $n = 0$, at which time it returns the value 1. A second, purely iterative, function

$$\text{PROCEDURE IterateFact}(n : \text{CARDINAL}) : \text{CARDINAL}$$

will accumulate a product equivalent to $n * (n - 1)!$.

Refine the solution   *Pseudocode*

```
PROCEDURE RecurFact(n : CARDINAL) : CARDINAL
    begin
      if    n = 0
          Factorial = 1
      else
          Factorial = n * RecurFact(n – 1)
      end if
      RETURN Factorial
    end RecurFact

PROCEDURE IterateFact(n : CARDINAL) : CARDINAL
    begin
      Factorial = 1
      for    Count = n to 1 by –1
          Factorial = Count * Factorial
      end for
      RETURN Factorial
    end IterateFact

begin      (* Driver Module TestFactorial *)
  ask for Number    (*    < 9    to avoid CARDINAL overflow    *)
  FactByRecursion = RecurFact(Number)
  FactByIteration = IterateFact(Number)
  print Number, FactByRecursion, FactByIteration
end TestFactorial
```

Modula-2 code

```
MODULE TestFactorial;
    (* Tests recursive and iterative solutions of factorial.
       FileName:CH9J       Modula-2       RKW      Apr. 1991    *)

FROM InOut IMPORT WriteString, WriteLn, ReadCard, WriteCard;
VAR Number, FactByRecursion, FactByIteration : CARDINAL;

PROCEDURE RecurFact(n : CARDINAL): CARDINAL;
    VAR  Factorial : CARDINAL;
    BEGIN
        IF  n = 0  THEN
            Factorial := 1;
        ELSE
            Factorial := n * RecurFact(n-1);
        END; (* IF *)
        RETURN Factorial;
    END RecurFact;
```

```
PROCEDURE IterateFact(n : CARDINAL): CARDINAL;
   VAR  Count, Factorial : CARDINAL;
   BEGIN
      Factorial := 1;
      FOR  Count := n TO 1 BY -1  DO
         Factorial := Count * Factorial;
      END; (* FOR *)
      RETURN Factorial;
   END IterateFact;

BEGIN (* Driver Module TestFactorial *)
   REPEAT
      WriteString("Of what number (less than 9) to find the factorial? ");
       ReadCard(Number); WriteLn; WriteLn;
   UNTIL  Number < 9;

   FactByRecursion := RecurFact(Number);
   FactByIteration := IterateFact(Number);

   WriteString("By recursion the factorial of ");WriteCard(Number,1);
    WriteString(" is ");WriteCard(FactByRecursion,6); WriteLn;
   WriteString("By iteration the factorial of ");WriteCard(Number,1);
    WriteString(" is ");WriteCard(FactByIteration,6); WriteLn;
END TestFactorial.
```

Debug and test   You may wish to add write statements to print the value of Factorial in IterateFact and in RecurFact, so that you can see the progress of the program. Unfortunately, the results here are limited to $n! <=$ MAX(CARDINAL), which means that n must be less than 9 on most small machines. In Chapter 10, a method will be developed for handling factorials of numbers almost as large as you wish. Test the program with $n = 0$, $n = 8$, something in between those, and a value greater than 8. A sample run produces this:

```
Of what number (less than 9) to find the factorial? 8

By recursion the factorial of 8 is   40320
By iteration the factorial of 8 is   40320
```

Complete the documentation   In the documentation, the user should be told that the source code is in file CH9J. It also might be pointed out that the functions RecurFact and/or IterateFact could be included in an external module such as My-Math and imported from there.

Questions 9.5	**1.** Rewrite the procedure ShowEm in question 1 at the end of Section 9.4 using iteration instead of recursion.

2. Rewrite the procedure NowShowEm in question 2 at the end of Section 9.4 using iteration instead of recursion.

3. a. What is accomplished by this recursive procedure if it is called by the command DivideAndConquer(20.0);?

```
PROCEDURE  DivideAndConquer(Value : REAL);
  BEGIN
    Value := Value / 2.0;
```

```
      IF  Value > 1.0  THEN
        DivideAndConquer(Value);
      END;  (* IF *)
      FWriteReal(Value, 8, 3); WriteLn;
   END DivideAndConquer;
```

b. Write an iterative procedure that produces the same result.

4. Draw a diagram similar to Figures 9–6 and 9–7 to trace the memory contents for function RecurFact when the initial value of *n* is 4. Draw a similar diagram for IterateFact. Which solution, RecurFact or IterateFact, do you think is better? Why?

9.6 *Summary*

Four Problem-Solving Techniques   The four techniques for problem solving investigated in this chapter are

Using external modules
Generating pseudorandom numbers
Analogy and generalization
Recursion

External Modules   You can place procedures and functions in external modules so that you can import and use them in future programs. The DEFINITION module contains declarations of CONSTants, data types, VARiables, procedures, and functions that are available for export. The IMPLEMENTATION module contains the code that defines the procedures and functions. Compiling the DEFINITION module first produces a *symbol table file*. Then, compiling the IMPLEMENTATION module produces an *object code* file. Neither module should be linked. The symbol table file and object code file must be available when you try to import entities from the external module.

Modules MyMath and RandGen   A module MyMath was created with functions CardPower and RealPower. It is suggested that you develop and add functions $\log 10(x)$ and $\tan(x)$ to this module. RandGen was created to contain function Random(Seed), which must be compiled with range checking turned off.

Function Random   A function *Random* for generating pseudorandom REAL numbers between 0.0 and almost 1.0 is useful in game-playing programs and for algorithms such as Monte Carlo calculations. Random requires a CARDINAL starting Seed value. A pseudorandom CARDINAL Number in the range Low to High is generated from the formula

Number := TRUNC(FLOAT(High − Low + 1) ∗ Random(Seed) + FLOAT(Low)).

Analogy and Generalization   The first question you should ask when confronted with a new problem is ''Have I solved a similar problem before?'' Considerable effort can be saved by adapting solutions to analogous problems rather than starting all over again. If the problem solutions you have developed are well-documented, you will be able to generalize them and use them repeatedly for new tasks.

Recursion   Many problems are expressed recursively; that is, as repeated, progressively simpler versions of themselves. Recursion exists when a procedure calls itself repeatedly with new parameters until some stop Condition is reached. Iterative algorithms without recursion usually make more efficient use of the computer, but recursive algorithms are often easier to write and read.

Tail-recursive algorithms, in which the recursive call is the last statement executed in a procedure, are particularly easy to convert to iterative form.

9.7   *Exercises*

Exercises marked with (FileName: _____) indicate those that ask you to use, modify, or extend the text examples. The numbers in brackets, [ ], indicate the chapter section that contains the material you need for completing the exercises.

1. [9.1] (FileName:MyMath) Incorporate functions to calculate and return $\log 10(x)$ and $\tan(x)$ — described in Question 2 at the end of Section 9.1 — into module MyMath, and write a driver program to import and test these functions.

2. [9.1] (FileName:MyMath) Write a program that performs multiplication and division of positive REAL numbers using "common" logarithms, $\log 10(x)$. Use these rules:

$$\log 10(A * B) = \log 10(A) + \log 10(B)$$
$$\log 10(A / B) = \log 10(A) - \log 10(B)$$
$$x = \text{antilog}(\log 10(x)) = 10.0^{\log 10(x)} = \text{RealPower}(10.0, \log 10(x))$$

Import common $\log 10(x)$ and RealPower functions from MyMath. (See Exercise 1.) How accurate is this technique?

3. [9.1] (FileName:MyMath) Import $\tan(x)$ from module MyMath (see Exercise 1) and make a table of Angle, $\sin(\text{Angle})$, $\cos(\text{Angle})$, and $\tan(\text{Angle})$ for Angles between 0.0 and 180.0 degrees. Note that the parameter x passed to $\sin(x)$ and $\cos(x)$ must be in radians. The conversion formulae are

$$x \text{ (radians)} = \text{Angle (degrees)} * \pi/180.0$$
$$\text{Angle (degrees)} = x \text{ (radians)} * 180.0/\pi$$

where $\pi = 3.14159$ approximately.

4. [9.1] (FileName:MyMath)
   a. Write a function ROUND that rounds a REAL value to the nearest whole REAL number. For example ROUND(x) would return 38.0, -38.0, 37.0, and -37.0 for values of $x = 37.9$, -37.9, 37.2, and -37.2, respectively. *Hint:* Consider negative and positive values separately.
   b. Add function ROUND to module MyMath and write a driver program that imports and tests ROUND.

5. [9.2] (FileName:RandGen) Write code to test the formula

   Number := TRUNC(FLOAT(High $-$ Low $+$ 1) $*$ Random(Seed) $+$ FLOAT(Low))

   which produces pseudorandom CARDINAL values between Low and High. Try different values of Low and High, and during each run display 300 values on 20 lines, with 15 values on each line.

6. [9.2] (FileName:RandGen) Write a program that tests the effectiveness of Random. Start by initializing 10 counters, such as ZeroCount, OneCount, TwoCount, . . . NineCount to 0. Then generate a large number of pseudorandom CARDINAL numbers between 0 and 9. Each time a 0 occurs increment ZeroCount, when a 1 occurs increment OneCount, etc. Finally, print out the numbers of 0s, 1s, 2s, etc., that occurred.

7. [9.2] (FileName:RandGen) Deal and display a hand of 4 different cards from 4 Suits (Heart, Club, Diamond, Spade) of 13 cards each (named Ace $= 1, 2, 3$, $4, 5, 6, 7, 8, 9, 10$, Jack $= 11$, Queen $= 12$, King $= 13$). *Hints:* See question

3 at the end of Section 9.2. To make sure each card is different, initialize all card Suits and Numbers to a dummy value such as 0; then as Random picks a Suit and a Number, check to make sure the new card does not match any other card.

8. [9.2] It is said that a monkey punching letters at random on a typewriter, could produce the works of Shakespeare, given sufficient time. Put a monkey at a typewriter (in simulation by computer, of course) and have it type letters at random. Count the number of letters typed until the monkey types one of the two-letter words *at, is, he, me, we, up,* or *on.* When one of these words is produced, stop the monkey and display the total number of letters typed. *Hint:* Choose a letter by selecting a random CARDINAL Number between 1 and 26 and using CHR(Number + ORD('*a*') − 1). Why? Remember the previous letter selected each time a letter appears. If the previous letter is *a, i, h, m, w, u,* or *o,* check to see if the new letter creates one of the given words.

9. [9.2] Write a program to play dice. If the total of the two dice is 7 or 11 you win; otherwise, you lose. Embellish this program as much as you like, with betting, different odds, different combinations for win or lose, stopping play when you are broke or reach the house limit, displaying the dice, etc. *Hint:* See Question 1 at the end of Section 9.2.

10. [9.2] (FileName:CH9C) Use the Monte Carlo algorithm, developed in Example 9.2.2 to find an approximate value for π (3.14159 . . .). In Figure 9–9, the shaded area represents one quarter of a circle of radius $r = 1$ unit. The area of the box bounded by the axes and by lines $x = 1$ and $y = 1$ is 1 square unit. The area of the quarter-circle = 1/4 * (area of the circle) = 1/4 * π * r * r = π/4 square units. Therefore, π/4 = Area of Quarter Circle/BoxArea or π = 4 * (Points that fall under the circle)/(Total points chosen). Generate random points inside the box (xRnd, yRnd) such that $0 <= x$Rnd < 1 and $0 <= y$Rnd < 1, and test to see if yRnd $<= y$Calc, where yCalc = $f(x$Rnd), and $f(x)$ is the curve defined by the circle

$$y = f(x) = \text{sqrt}(1 - x^2).$$

Figure 9–9
Calculation of π
(Exercise 10)

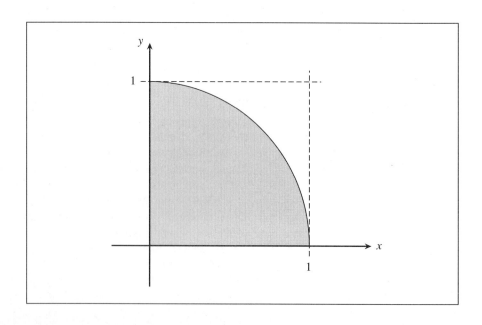

11. [9.2] Here is a version of a problem called ''the random walk.'' It can be extended to two or three dimensions and used to simulate molecular motion, to determine the effectiveness of reactor shielding, or to calculate a variety of other probabilities.

Assume that your very tired and sleepy pet dog leaves his favorite lamp post on warm summer evenings and staggers randomly either 2 steps in the direction toward home or 1 step in the opposite direction. After the first step the dog again staggers randomly two steps toward home or one step backward, and does this again, and again. If the pet reaches a total distance of 10 steps from the lamp post in the direction toward home, you find him and take him home. If the dog arrives back at the lamp post before reaching 10 steps in the direction toward home, he lies down and spends the night at the foot of the lamp post.

Write a program that simulates 500 summer evenings, and calculate and print the percentage of the time your pet sleeps at home in the summer. *Hint:* In a loop choose forward(2) or backward(1) at random. Accumulate the (positive or negative) integer distance the dog has reached toward home. If that distance reaches 10, stop and increment HomeCount by 1. If the distance reaches 0 before it reaches 10, stop but do not increment HomeCount. Repeat this loop 500 times and find the ratio HomeCount/500.

12. [9.3] (FileName:CH9D) Using analogy, write a program that sends to an output file a table of projected population growth in the tiny, prolific country of Humania for every year from 1992 to 2112. The population in 1991 was 17,000. The population doubling time is 24 years.

13. [9.3] (FileName:CH9F) The X-ray intensity I as a function of penetration distance x is given by $I = I0 * \exp(-b * x)$, where $I0$ is the intensity at the surface $(x = 0)$ and b is a proportionality constant measuring the rate of change of I with penetration distance. By analogy, write a program to calculate intensity I as a function of x. Some interesting test values would be estimates for human soft tissue (where $b =$ approximately 0.046 per centimeter) and for human bone (where $b =$ approximately 2.30 per centimeter).

14. [9.3] (FileName:CH9D)
   a. Modify the Bacterial Growth procedure (Example 9.3.1) to print a *chart* of values of N from time 0 to the specified time t in intervals to be chosen by the user. The chart should have titles and column headings as shown in Figure 9–10a. The initial population $N0$ is chosen by the user.
   b. Produce a bar graph similar to that shown in Figure 9–10b. *Hint:* After producing the chart in part a, you should be able to find a reasonable scale factor (such as $N/100$ in Figure 9–10b) to make the graph look ''pretty.''

15. [9.3] (FileName:CH9F) Modify the Radioactive Decay procedures (Example 9.3.1) to produce a chart similar to that shown in Figure 9–10a and a graph similar to that shown in Figure 9–10b.

16. [9.3] (FileName:CH3G) You wish to manufacture dartboards with three concentric circles. You will specify their radii from the keyboard. Using PaintLogoOnBarn (Example 3.6.1) as an analogy, calculate and display the area of the innermost circle and the areas of the rings between the circles on your dartboard.

17. [9.3] (FileName:CH6F) Bids have been submitted for construction of a new building, including separate costs from subcontractors for masonry, plumbing, electrical, and finishing work. Using RejectTheParts (Example 6.5.1) as an analogy, find the total of the subcontractor costs for each bid and reject all bids whose total is greater than the budget allows. Accept the other bids for further study.

18. [9.5] Write a recursive procedure to accept REAL first term a, REAL common difference d or common ratio r, and the CARDINAL number of terms n; and

Figure 9–10
Examples for
Exercise 14
a. Example of Table
to Be Produced
b. Example of
Graph to Be
Produced

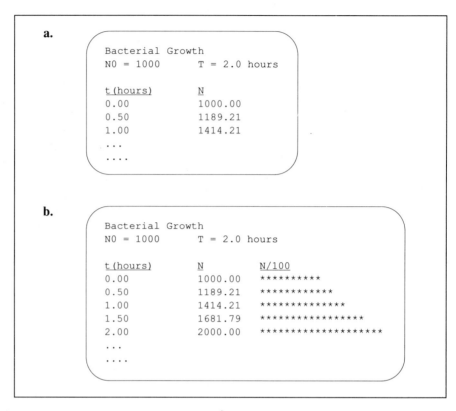

calculate the sum of **a.** an arithmetic series (see Exercise 9, Chapter 8); **b.** a geometric series (see Exercise 10, Chapter 8).

19. [9.5] The Fibonacci sequence is 0, 1, 1, 2, 3, 5, 8, 13, . . . such that the first two terms are 0 and 1, and each nth term thereafter is defined recursively as the sum of the preceding two terms; that is,

$$\text{Fib}(n) = \text{Fib}(n - 1) + \text{Fib}(n - 2).$$

Write a *recursive* function that returns the nth number in a Fibonacci sequence when n is passed to the function as a parameter. For example, when $n = 8$, the function returns the 8th number in the sequence, which is 13.

20. [9.5] (FileName:CH9H) Implement the iterative solution to ConvertDecToOct, which is presented in Example 9.4.1.

21. [9.4] (FileName:CH9H) In ConvertDecToOct (Example 9.4.1),

    a. change the recursive procedure FindADigit to print the octal number backward.

    b. change the program so that it allows you to convert a positive CARDINAL decimal Number to any Base between 2 and 9 (which you enter from the keyboard).

    c. change the program so that it allows you to convert to hexadecimal (Base = 16), in which digits 10 through 15 are displayed as characters 'A' through 'F'.

22. [9.5] **a.** Write iterative and recursive procedures that convert a number in any Base (2 through 9) to decimal. (See Appendix E for the algorithm.)

    b. Draw diagrams similar to Figures 9–6 and 9–7 to show your procedures.

    c. Extend the procedures of part a to handle converting from hexadecimal to decimal. *Hint:* Read the digits in as characters and convert to the appropriate value.

10

Arrays

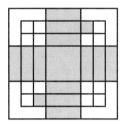

Chapter Outline

Most of the variables used so far in this book have been of **scalar** data types; that is, when a variable is declared, memory space is reserved for a single value of that type. Now you will begin to use **structured** data types; types in which a variable name refers to a group of memory locations, each containing an organized collection of data. This chapter introduces a data structure called the **array**, which represents a collection of items of the same data type.

10.1 *One-Dimensional Arrays*

A one-dimensional array represents a list of items. For example, a student's grades on four assignments could be represented as a list of CHARacters or a list of REAL numbers, as shown in Figure 10–1. The **name** of the array in Figure 10–1a is *LetterGrades*; the **elements** are the individual grades, which are referred to as

```
LetterGrades[1], (element 1, value = A),
LetterGrades[2], (element 2, value = D),
```

etc.

The expression within brackets (**[ ]**) is called an **index** or a **subscript.** An array element is always referred to by the array name and the index that targets that particular element.

All of the elements in an array must have the same data type. The indices or subscripts are defined over a range of values of any enumerable type (such as CHARacter, CARDINAL, or INTEGER).

Figure 10–1
Grades Arrays
a. One-Dimensional Array of CHARacters
b. One-Dimensional Array of REAL Numbers

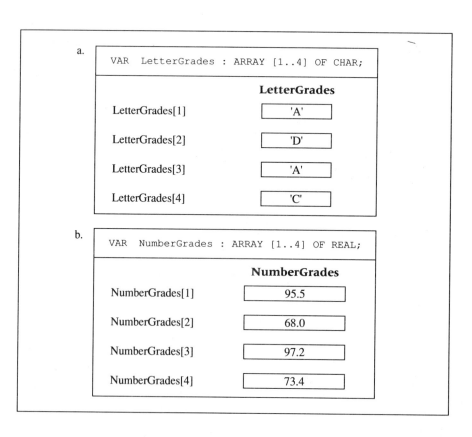

Declaring Arrays

In an array declaration, the lowest and highest index values must be literal values or previously declared CONSTant expressions. This means that the maximum number of elements in the array must be decided in advance. The array should be large enough to contain the greatest number of elements you would expect to use, but it should not be so large that it reserves excessive memory that never will be used.

Figure 10–2 shows some alternative ways of declaring arrays. Observe that any range of enumerable-type variables may be chosen for the indices.

Arrays can be defined completely within a VARiable declaration, as illustrated by the array Temperature in Figure 10–2. Usually, however, it is best to write array declarations like those for Numbers and AlphStart in the figure, with the highest index value (and sometimes the smallest, especially if it is not 0 or 1) defined as a CONSTant, and with the array type declared and defined in a TYPE statement. This will allow you to change the index range easily by redefining the CONSTants.

Figure 10–2
Declaring Arrays

Declarations

```
CONST  SMALLINDEX = 1;  BIGINDEX = 3;
       LOWLIMIT = 'a';  LASTLIMIT = 'c';
TYPE  CARDARRAY = ARRAY [SMALLINDEX..BIGINDEX] OF CARDINAL;
      KINDOFVALUES = ARRAY [LOWLIMIT..LASTLIMIT] OF INTEGER;
VAR  Numbers, WholeValues : CARDARRAY;
     AlphStart : KINDOFVALUES;
     Grades : ARRAY [SMALLINDEX..BIGINDEX] OF CHAR;
     Temperature, HeatMeasure : ARRAY [-2..1] OF REAL;
     CardNums : ARRAY [1..3] of CARDINAL;

     Counter:CARDINAL;  When:INTEGER;  Mark:CHAR;
     (* Scalars referenced in the text. *)
```

Typical Memory Allocations

	Numbers		AlphStart
Numbers[1]	12	AlphStart['a']	−7
Numbers[2]	0	AlphStart['b']	16
Numbers[3]	9621	AlphStart['c']	−1234

	Grades		Temperature
Grades[1]	'D'	Temperature[−2]	98.6
Grades[2]	'F'	Temperature[−1]	212.0
Grades[3]	'A'	Temperature[0]	−40.0
		Temperature[1]	-459.69

Furthermore, it gives you a data TYPE that can be used in procedure headings when passing arrays as parameters. Thus, a preferred generic format for declaring one-dimensional arrays is

```
CONST   SmallIndex   = LiteralEnumerableValue1;
        LargeIndex   = LiteralEnumerableValue2;
TYPE    NameOfArrayType = ARRAY [SmallIndex..LargeIndex] of ElementType;
VAR     ArrayName : NameOfArrayType;
```

Storing and Accessing Array Elements

When array elements are accessed, indices may be represented as variables, constants, or expressions.

Assigning Values

When assigning a value to an array element, the value must be of the appropriate type, and the element to which the value is assigned must be specified. For example, the following assignments result in values shown in "Typical Memory Allocations" in Figure 10–2:

```
Counter := 2;  When := 1;  Mark := 'e';

Numbers[3] := 3 * 3207;
Numbers[Counter - 1] := Counter + 10;
AlphStart['b'] := 20 * When - 4;
AlphStart[CHR(ORD(Mark)-4)] := -7;
Grades[Counter] := CHR(ORD('A') + 5);
Grades[2*Counter - 1] := 'A';
Temperature[When - 3] := 98.6;
```

When the computer recognizes an array variable with an index, such as Grades[2*Counter − 1], the value of the index is calculated first (2 * Counter − 1 = 2 * 2 − 1 = 3). Then that value is substituted for the index (Grades[3]), and the array element at that location is accessed (Grades[3] := 'A'). If *J*, *L*, and *M* all were CARDINAL variables whose value was 3, then Grades[*J*], Grades[*L*], and Grades[*M*] would all represent the same array element, namely, Grades[3].

Index Out of Range

When reference is made to an array element, the index must be of the appropriate type and lie within the declared range. Specifying an index outside of that range causes a "range error." Remember, an index that is too small can be out of range as well as an index that is too large. It is especially easy to fall into a range-error trap when indices are calculated or represented by an expression.

For example, for the arrays declared in Figure 10–2, the following would be invalid assignments:

Invalid Assignment	Reason
Numbers[5] := 93;	index too large
Counter := 2;	
Numbers[Counter − 2] := 18;	index too small
Numbers['a'] := 12;	invalid index type
Numbers[2] := 32.5;	invalid data type

Assigning a Complete Array

There are only two situations when an entire array can be referenced within the body of a program by using the array name without an index. One of these instances (discussed later in this section) is when you want to pass an entire array as a parameter to a procedure. The other occasion is when all of the element values of one array are to be assigned to another array of an identical type.

Two array types are *identical* when both have been declared with the same type definition. Thus, in Figure 10–2, Temperature and HeatMeasure have identical types, as do Numbers and WholeValues. However, many Modula-2 compilers do not recognize separately declared arrays to be identical, even if they appear to be the same.

For example, the compiler may not treat CardNums in Figure 10–2 as an array of identical type as Numbers. Therefore, you may assign

```
WholeValues := Numbers;
```

which would accomplish the same as

```
WholeValues[1] := Numbers[1];
WholeValues[2] := Numbers[2];
WholeValues[3] := Numbers[3];
```

However, an attempt to assign

```
CardNums := Numbers;
```

could cause an "Incompatible Types" error.

Reading and Writing Arrays

Array values are read and written one element at a time, using the read or write command for the appropriate type of scalar value, and you can read or write a single value. Two examples of this are

```
WriteString("First temperature = ? "); ReadReal(Temperature[1]);

Mark := 'c';
WriteInt(AlphStart[Mark],b); WriteLn;
```

Iteration structures, especially FOR loops, are convenient tools for reading and writing all or part of an array. For example,

```
FOR Mark := LOWLIMIT TO 'b'  DO
   WriteString("AlphStart["); Write(Mark); WriteString("] = ? ");
   ReadInt(AlphStart[Mark]); WriteLn;
END; (* FOR *)
```

asks for values   AlphStart[a] = ?   and   AlphStart[b] = ? . Similarly,

```
FOR Counter := 1 TO 3  DO
  Write(Grades[Counter]); WriteLn;
END; (* FOR *)
```

displays all three values of Grades. Because ReadInt and Write commands "expect" single parameters, not entire arrays, it does *not* work to ReadInt(AlphStart) or Write(Grades).

Using and Testing Arrays

Individual array elements, defined by the array name and an index, are variables that can be used where a variable of that scalar type is used. For example, given the declarations in Figure 10–2, these are valid statements:

```
HeatMeasure[1] := 3.0 * Temperature[0] + 100.0;
IF  HeatMeasure[1] < 0.0  THEN
    ...

Counter := 2;
WHILE  Grades[Counter - 1] <> Grades[3]  DO
    ....
```

However, expressions such as

```
IF  Numbers < 5  THEN....
```

are meaningless. The entire array of Numbers is not a single value comparable to scalar value 5.

Passing Arrays as Parameters

Modula-2 is a *strongly typed* language; that is, every VARiable must be declared with a particular type, and every CONSTant has a fixed type. Each value or variable in an expression must be of the same type, and formal parameters in a procedure heading must be of the same type as corresponding actual parameters in the command that invokes the procedure.

Just as any other scalar variable, an individual element of an array may be passed as an actual parameter to a formal parameter of the same type in a procedure. For example, the procedure heading and call

```
PROCEDURE KnockEmDead(Hotness:REAL;  VAR HowMany:CARDINAL);
    ...
  Counter := 2;
  KnockEmDead(Temperature[0], Numbers[Counter-1]);
    ....
```

relates parameters as shown:

Actual Parameter		**Formal Parameter**
Temperature[0]	→	value parameter Hotness
Numbers[1]	↔	VARiable parameter HowMany

Similarly, the function and call

```
PROCEDURE  BreakALeg(Score : CHAR) : INTEGER;
    ...
AlphStart['c'] := BreakALeg(Grades[2]);
```

would pass the value of Grades[2] to parameter Score and assign the INTEGER result RETURNed by the function to AlphStart['c'].

Also, an entire array can be passed as an actual parameter to a formal array parameter in a procedure, provided the actual and formal arrays are the same type. For example, the heading and call

```
PROCEDURE  DoItUpRight(WholeNums:CARDARRAY;
                       VAR PosAndNegs:KINDOFVALUES);
    ...
DoItUpRight(Numbers, AlphStart);
    ....
```

copy the entire array Numbers to the entire value array parameter WholeNums and make the entire array AlphStart a synonym of VARiable parameter PosAndNegs. That is,

Values	are copied to	Value Parameter
Numbers[1]	→	WholeNums[1];
Numbers[2]	→	WholeNums[2];
Numbers[3]	→	WholeNums[3];

and

Actual Parameters	are synonyms of	Formal VARiable Parameters
AlphStart['a']	↔	PosAndNegs['a']
AlphStart['b']	↔	PosAndNegs['b']
AlphStart['c']	↔	PosAndNegs['c']

In the procedure heading, the array parameters must be defined by the same TYPE as the corresponding actual parameters in the procedure call. Therefore, if an array is to be passed to a parameter in a procedure, that array should be declared in terms of a defined TYPE (such as CARDARRAY or KINDOFVALUES) that can be used in the procedure heading.

Big Factorial

Here is a program illustrating the use of arrays to find factorials almost as large as you wish. It incorporates an array in which the elements and the indices both are CARDINAL values.

Example 10.1.1

Write a procedure that calculates the factorial of arbitrarily large numbers.

Define the problem Calculate factorials up to

$$41! = (41 * 40 * 39 * \ldots * 3 * 2 * 1),$$

which contains fifty digits.

Develop a solution Each digit in the factorial will be represented by a single-digit CARDINAL element in an array Answer, which is defined in Figure 10–3. Most compilers allow a *function* to RETURN only a single scalar value, so the program will use a *procedure* BigFactorial, with a VARiable array parameter.
  To calculate $n!$ from $(n - 1)!$, use a loop,

```
Carry = 0
for  Digit   =   1    to   LARGESTINDEX
   Product   =    n * Answer[Digit] + Carry
   Answer[Digit]   =     Product MOD 10
   Carry   =     Product DIV 10
end for
```

To see how this works, assume for the moment that 6! (= 720) is stored in the Answer array, as shown in Figure 10–3. To obtain 7!, use the definition 7! = 7 * 6!, and multiply each of the digits of 6! by 7. Thus, for 7!,

Figure 10–3
Factorial Array
(Example 10.1.1)

```
CONST  LARGESTINDEX = 50;
TYPE   NUMARY = ARRAY [1..LARGESTINDEX] OF CARDINAL;
VAR    Answer : NUMARY;
```

Answer	. . . .	[9]	[8]	[7]	[6]	[5]	[4]	[3]	[2]	[1]
6! =		0	0	0	0	0	0	7	2	0

	. . . .	[9]	[8]	[7]	[6]	[5]	[4]	[3]	[2]	[1]
7! =		0	0	0	0	0	5	0	4	0

start with Carry $= 0$, then
Answer[1] $= 7 * 0 +$ Carry $= 0 + 0 = 0$ Carry 0,
Answer[2] $= 7 * 2 +$ Carry $= 14 + 0 = 4$ Carry 1,
Answer[3] $= 7 * 7 +$ Carry $= 49 + 1 = 0$ Carry 5,
Answer[4] $= 7 * 0 +$ Carry $= 0 + 5 = 5$ Carry 0,
Answer[5] $= 7 * 0 +$ Carry $= 0 + 0 = 0$ Carry 0,
and all of the rest of the digits are zero.

The answer 7! $= 5040$ is shown in Figure 10–3.

Now place this loop within another loop, which begins with 0! $= 1$, and calculates factorials from 1! to n!. The final Answer will be displayed by writing Answer[LARGESTINDEX] to Answer[1].

Refine the solution   *Pseudocode*

```
begin module    TestBigFact
  ask for N (<= 41)
  BigFactorial(N, Result)
  write    N, "factorial = "     WriteBigFactorial(Result)
end TestBigFact

procedure WriteBigFactorial(nFact:NUMARY)
    for      Digit = LARGESTINDEX to 1 by −1       write nFact[Digit]

procedure BigFactorial(n:CARDINAL;    VAR Answer:NUMARY)
    initialize Answer to 0! = 00000...000001
    for     Number = 1 to n
       initialize Carry = 0
       for     Digit = 1 to LARGESTINDEX
            calculate     Product, Answer[Digit], and Carry
```

Modula-2 code

```
MODULE TestBigFact;
   (* Finds factorials numbers up to 41!
      FileName:CH10A     Modula-2     RKW     May 1991   *)

FROM InOut IMPORT WriteString, WriteLn, ReadCard, WriteCard;
```

```
CONST   LARGESTINDEX = 50;
TYPE   NUMARY = ARRAY [1..LARGESTINDEX] OF CARDINAL;
VAR    Result : NUMARY;     N : CARDINAL;

PROCEDURE BigFactorial(n:CARDINAL;   VAR Answer:NUMARY);
    VAR   Number, Digit, Product, Carry : CARDINAL;
    BEGIN   (* BigFactorial *)
       FOR   Digit := 2   TO   LARGESTINDEX   DO
          Answer[Digit] := 0;
       END; (* FOR *)
       Answer[1] := 1;   (*  Initialize Answer to 0! = 000...001   *)

       FOR   Number := 1 TO n   DO
          Carry := 0;
          FOR   Digit := 1 TO LARGESTINDEX   DO
             Product := Number * Answer[Digit] + Carry;
             Answer[Digit] := Product MOD 10;
             Carry := Product DIV 10;
             (* Assertions:  Product = previous digit * Number
                             Answer[Digit] = newest digit
                             Carry = carry to the next digit   *)
          END; (* FOR *)
             (* Assertion:   Answer array = Number factorial *)
       END; (* FOR *)        (* Answer = n factorial *)
    END BigFactorial;

PROCEDURE WriteBigFactorial(nFact:NUMARY);
    VAR   Digit : CARDINAL;
    BEGIN
       FOR Digit := LARGESTINDEX TO 1 BY -1   DO
          WriteCard(nFact[Digit],1);
       END; (* FOR *)   WriteLn;
    END WriteBigFactorial;

BEGIN   (* module TestBigFact *)
    WriteString("Find factorial of which number (<= 41)? ");
    ReadCard(N); WriteLn;
    BigFactorial(N, Result);

    WriteLn; WriteCard(N,3); WriteString(" factorial = ");
    WriteBigFactorial(Result); WriteLn;
END TestBigFact.
```

Debug and test You may find it helpful, when using arrays, to insert supplemental write statements that display the values of the index (Digit in this problem) and the array element (Answer[Digit]) immediately after each calculation. In this problem, it also may be informative to print each value of the Product and Carry. Here is a sample run:

```
Find factorial of which number (<= 41)? 12

 12 Factorial = 000000000000000000000000000000000000000479001600
```

You can remove those leading zeros in Exercise 4 at the end of the chapter.

Complete the documentation   The data representation and solution algorithm would assist a programmer to adapt the solution to similar problems or extend beyond 50 digits and 41!. Source code is in file CH10A. To handle factorials greater than 41! you would need to increase the value of LARGESTINDEX.

Non-CARDINAL Indices

Indices can be enumerable values other than CARDINAL. Consider this example.

Example 10.1.2

Write a procedure that counts CHARacters and displays how often each letter occurs.

Define the problem   An input file contains text that the procedure will read and echo to the screen. Counts of individual alphabet characters *a* to *z* will be accumulated in an array and divided by the total number of letters to obtain an array of frequencies.

Develop a solution   The two arrays used by the procedure are illustrated in Figure 10–4. The indices are CHARacters 'A' to 'Z'.

Figure 10–4
Arrays for
LetterCount and
Frequencies
(Example 10.1.2)

```
CONST  FIRST = 'A';  LAST = 'Z';
TYPE   FREQARRAY  = ARRAY [FIRST..LAST] OF REAL;
       COUNTARRAY = ARRAY [FIRST..LAST] OF CARDINAL;
VAR  Frequencies : FREQARRAY;
     LetterCount : COUNTARRAY;
```

If the input file contents are

The quick red fox jumps over the lazy brown dog.

the final value of the array elements will be

	LetterCount		**Frequencies**
LetterCount['A']	1	Frequencies['A']	0.026
LetterCount['B']	1	Frequencies['B']	0.026
LetterCount['C']	1	Frequencies['C']	0.026
LetterCount['D']	2	Frequencies['D']	0.053
LetterCount['E']	4	Frequencies['E']	0.105
. . .		. . .	
LetterCount['Z']	1	Frequencies['Z']	0.026

A procedure will initialize TotalCount of letters and all elements LetterCount[Index] to 0. For each Letter read from the file, set Index = CAP(Letter). If Index lies in the range 'A' to 'Z', TotalCount and LetterCount[Index] are incremented. LetterFreq[Index] is calculated from LetterCount[Index]/TotalCount. A separate procedure displays TotalCount and the LetterFreq array.

Refine the solution   Pseudocode

```
begin module ReadText
    open input file
    FindFrequencies(Frequencies, LetterTotal)
    WriteFrequencies(Frequencies, LetterTotal)
    close input file
end ReadText

procedure FindFrequencies(VAR LetterFreq:FREQARRAY;
                                       VAR TotalCount:CARDINAL);
    initialize TotalCount and all LetterCount[Index] to 0
    read first Letter
    while Done
        echo Letter to screen
        increment     LetterCount[Letter] and TotalCount
        read next Letter
    end while
    for all Index, LetterFreq[Index] = LetterCount[Index]/TotalCount
procedure     WriteFrequencies(LetterFreq:FREQARRAY;     TotalCount:CARDINAL)
    write TotalCount
    for all Index, write Index and LetterFreq[Index] (* 4 per line *)
```

Modula-2 code

```
MODULE  ReadText;
    (* Reads text from a file and determines letter frequencies.
       FileName:CH10B      Modula-2      RKW      May 1991  *)

FROM InOut IMPORT WriteString, WriteLn, Read, Write, Done, WriteCard,
                OpenInput, CloseInput;
FROM RealInOut IMPORT FWriteReal;

CONST  FIRST = 'A';  LAST = 'Z';
TYPE   FREQARRAY = ARRAY [FIRST..LAST] OF REAL;
VAR  Frequencies : FREQARRAY;   LetterTotal : CARDINAL;

PROCEDURE FindFrequencies(VAR LetterFreq:FREQARRAY; VAR TotalCount:CARDINAL);
    TYPE   COUNTARRAY = ARRAY [FIRST..LAST] OF CARDINAL;
    VAR  LetterCount : COUNTARRAY;   Letter, Index : CHAR;
    BEGIN
        TotalCount := 0;                 (* Initialize all counts to 0. *)
        FOR  Index := FIRST TO LAST  DO
          LetterCount[Index] := 0;
        END; (* FOR *)

        Read(Letter);          (* Read and echo letters, add to counts. *)
        WHILE  Done  DO
          Write(Letter);   Index := CAP(Letter);
          IF  (Index >= FIRST) AND (Index <= LAST)  THEN
            INC(LetterCount[Index]);  INC(TotalCount);
```

```
            END;  (* IF *)
            Read(Letter);
        END;  (* WHILE *)

        FOR  Index := FIRST TO LAST  DO     (* Convert to frequencies. *)
            LetterFreq[Index] := FLOAT(LetterCount[Index])/FLOAT(TotalCount);
        END;  (* FOR *)
    END FindFrequencies;

PROCEDURE WriteFrequencies(LetterFreq:FREQARRAY;   TotalCount:CARDINAL);
    VAR  Index : CHAR;     NumOnLine : CARDINAL;
    BEGIN
        WriteLn; WriteString("Total Number of Letters = ");
         WriteCard(TotalCount,6); WriteLn; WriteLn;
        WriteString("Frequencies of letters in the file:"); WriteLn;
        NumOnLine := 0;
        FOR  Index := FIRST TO LAST  DO
            WriteString("          "); Write(Index);
             FWriteReal(LetterFreq[Index],6,3);
            INC(NumOnLine);      (* Count number on the current line. *)
            IF  NumOnLine = 4  THEN  WriteLn; NumOnLine := 0; END; (* IF *)
        END; (* FOR *)    WriteLn; WriteLn;
    END WriteFrequencies;

BEGIN  (* module ReadText *)
    WriteString("Enter name of input file: "); OpenInput("IN"); WriteLn;
    FindFrequencies(Frequencies, LetterTotal);
    WriteFrequencies(Frequencies, LetterTotal);
    CloseInput;
END ReadText.
```

Debug and test   A sample run appears as follows:

```
Enter name of input file: CH10B.IN

The power of dealing with numbers is a kind of "detached lever"
arrangement, which may be put into a mighty poor watch.  I suppose
it is about as common as the power of moving ones ears voluntarily,
which is a moderately rare endowment.      Oliver Wendell Holmes

Total Number of Letters =    206

Frequencies of letters in the file:
          A 0.078          B 0.015          C 0.024          D 0.034
          E 0.121          F 0.015          G 0.019          H 0.053
          I 0.073          J 0.000          K 0.005          L 0.044
          M 0.049          N 0.063          O 0.092          P 0.029
          Q 0.000          R 0.063          S 0.053          T 0.068
          U 0.024          V 0.019          W 0.039          X 0.000
          Y 0.019          Z 0.000
```

You may wish to display the LetterCount array as well as the Frequencies array. Since the characters from the file are echoed to the screen, it should not be difficult to determine whether the file is being read correctly. All characters (including spaces, punctuation, carriage returns, etc.) are shown on the screen, but only alphabetic letters are counted.

Complete the documentation Since this program is designed to illustrate arrays, Figure 10–4 would be a valuable part of the documentation. For the users who want to use the program to analyze written text, the problem definition and solution algorithm are critical. Include the code (CH10B) and, in the users' manual, indicate that the program asks for the name of an input file, which should have been created previously.

Questions 10.1

1. Suppose that *I, J,* and *K* are CARDINAL variables and that *I* := 1, *J* := 2, and *K* := 3. Referring to Figure 10–1,
   a. what would be displayed by

   ```
   Write(LetterGrades[J]);
   Write(LetterGrades[K-I+J-1]);
   FWriteReal(NumberGrades[I+1], 5, 1);
   ```

   b. What are the errors in

   ```
   Write(LetterGrades[2*K]);
   FWriteReal(NumberGrades[0], 5, 1);
   FWriteReal(NumberGrades, 5, 1);
   ```

2. Refer to Figure 10–2. What would be displayed by the following?
   a.
   ```
   FOR  When := -1 TO +1  DO
       FWriteReal(Temperature[When], 10, 2);
   END; (* FOR *)
   ```

   b. `WriteCard(ORD(Grades[2]) - ORD(Grades[3]), 3);`

   c.
   ```
   FOR  Mark := 'c' TO 'a' BY -1  DO
       WriteInt(AlphStart[Mark], 6);
   END; (* FOR *)
   ```

3. Given Figure 10–2, what would be accomplished by each of the following? If there are syntax errors, identify and correct them.

   a.
   ```
   FOR  Counter := BIGINDEX TO SMALLINDEX  DO
       WholeValuesCounter := 2 × Counter;
   END; ( FOR )
   ```

   b.
   ```
   FOR  Mark := FIRSTLIMIT TO LASTLIMIT  DO
       AlphStart[Mark] := -2 * (ORD(Mark)
                               - ORD(FIRSTLIMIT) + 1);
   END; (* FOR *)
   ```

   c.
   ```
   FOR  Counter := 1  TO 3
       Numbers[Counter]  = 3 - Counter + 1;
   END; (* FOR *)
   ```

   d.
   ```
   FOR  When := -3 TO 0  DO
       HeatMeasure[When] := Temperature[When] + 459.69;
   END; (* FOR *)
   ```

4. Referring to Figure 10–2, write commands to
   a. assign value 32 to AlphStart['b']
   b. declare array variable NewInts to be the same type as AlphStart. Then assign all of the elements of NewInts the same values as corresponding elements of AlphStart.
   c. prompt you for each of the values of array Grades and accept those values from the keyboard.

d. display all of the indices and corresponding elements of array Temperature in reverse order. For example,

$$
\begin{array}{rr}
1 & -459.69 \\
0 & - 40.00 \\
\end{array}
$$
....

5. Modify program TestBigFact (CH10A, Example 10.1.1) so that
   a. no number $N > 41$ will be accepted.
   b. all of the values of Number and Number! from 1 to N are displayed instead of just $N!$.

10.2 Open Arrays

Array index brackets, [ ], are not allowed within procedure headings. For example, you cannot have a procedure containing formal array parameters defined within the heading, as shown here:

```
PROCEDURE  CannotDoIt(Effect : ARRAY [Start..Stop] OF
   CARDINAL; VAR  Ciphers: ARRAY ['a'..'d'] OF CARDINAL);
```

Actual array variables that are to be passed to formal parameters in a procedure must be declared with separate TYPE definitions. That is, if you define ThisArray and ThatArray as follows

```
CONST  LARGEONE = 5; LARGETWO = 'd';
TYPE   ARRAYONE = ARRAY  [1..LARGEONE]  OF CARDINAL;
       ARRAYTWO = ARRAY ['a'..LARGETWO] OF CARDINAL;
VAR  ThisArray : ARRAYONE; ThatArray : ARRAYTWO;
```

then ThisArray and ThatArray can be passed to a procedure via a heading such as

```
PROCEDURE    HereWeGo(Result:ARRAYONE;  VAR Numerals:ARRAYTWO);
```

Once the actual array parameters have been defined there is also another powerful method (called open arrays) of declaring formal array parameters.

Declaring an Open Array

To display arrays ThisArray and ThatArray, you could write two separate procedures—one that accepts parameters of type ARRAYONE, and the other accepting parameters of type ARRAYTWO. However, the bodies of the two procedures would look nearly identical, because the purpose of both procedures would be to display a list of CARDINAL values. Modula-2 provides for situations in which arrays with differing index ranges contain elements of the same type by allowing the declaration of an **open array** in procedure headings. In an open array the index range and index type of the formal array are left open and are determined by the definition of the actual array. For example, you could write the single procedure DisplayArray—shown in Figure 10–5—in which the index range does not appear in the open ARRAY OF CARDINAL specified in the procedure heading.

Inherent in the definition of an open array is that the indices are CARDINAL values *beginning with zero* and that they are matched one-for-one with the indices of the actual array parameter, regardless of the actual parameter index type. Therefore, both procedure calls DisplayArray(ThisArray); and DisplayArray(ThatArray); would work well, because the index ranges of ThisArray and ThatArray are matched to the index range of TestNum, as shown in Figure 10–5.

Figure 10–5
Matching Index
Ranges in Open
Array Parameters

```
. . .
CONST  LARGEONE = 5;   LARGETWO = 'd';
TYPE  ARRAYONE = ARRAY [ 1  .. LARGEONE] OF CARDINAL;
      ARRAYTWO = ARRAY ['a' .. LARGETWO] OF CARDINAL;
VAR  ThisArray : ARRAYONE;    ThatArray : ARRAYTWO;

PROCEDURE  DisplayArray(TestNum:ARRAY OF CARDINAL);
   VAR  Index : CARDINAL;
   BEGIN
      FOR  Index := 0  TO  HIGH(TestNum)  DO
         WriteCard(TestNum[Index], 4); WriteLn;
      END; (* FOR *)
   END DisplayArray;

BEGIN
   ThisArray[1]:=2420;ThisArray[2]:=1835;ThisArray[3]:=5152;
   ThisArray[4]:=1981;ThisArray[5]:=6394;

   ThatArray['a']:=12;ThatArray['b']:= 7;ThatArray['c']:= 8;
   ThatArray['d']:= 5;

   . . .
   DisplayArray(ThisArray);
```

Actual Parameter		copies to	Formal Parameter	
ThisArray[1]	2420	⟶	TestNum[0]	2420
ThisArray[2]	1835	⟶	TestNum[1]	1835
ThisArray[3]	5152	⟶	TestNum[2]	5152
ThisArray[4]	1981	⟶	TestNum[3]	1981
ThisArray[5]	6394	⟶	TestNum[4]	6394

```
   . . .
   DisplayArray(ThatArray);
```

Actual Parameter		copies to	Formal Parameter	
ThatArray['a']	12	⟶	TestNum[0]	12
ThatArray['b']	7	⟶	TestNum[1]	7
ThatArray['c']	8	⟶	TestNum[2]	8
ThatArray['d']	5	⟶	TestNum[3]	5

```
   . . . .
```

The HIGH Function

Modula-2 also provides a standard, built-in function, HIGH(ArrayName), that
RETURNs the upper-index bound of an array, so that you do not need to pass the
size (or largest index) to an open array. HIGH(TestNum) is used in procedure
DisplayArray of Figure 10–5 to determine the upper limit of the Index in the FOR
loop. Because the lower-index bound for array TestNum is 0, the actual number of
elements in TestNum is HIGH(TestNum) + 1.

To see more examples of open arrays, examine closely the procedures Read-String and WriteString in module InOut (Appendix B). Those procedures use an open ARRAY OF CHAR so that they can handle character strings of any length.

Example 10.2.1

Write procedures that generate and display an array of random numbers.

Define the problem Write two procedures, ProduceArray and WriteArray, which use an open ARRAY OF CARDINAL to create and display an array of pseudorandom values between 1 and 10. Then include these procedures in module RandGen along with the function Random developed in Chapter 9.

Develop a solution Procedure WriteArray will display each array element's name and index, as well as its value.
   Procedure ProduceArray calls Random(Seed) repeatedly in the command (TestNum[Index] := TRUNC(10.0 * Random(Seed) + 1.0) to generate the elements of array TestNum.

Refine the solution   *Pseudocode*

```
begin module GenerateTestArray
   ask for a CARDINAL Seed value
   ProduceArray(Seed, TestNum)
   WriteArray(TestNum)
end GenerateTestArray

procedure    ProduceArray(Seed:CARDINAL;    VAR TestNum:ARRAY OF CARDINAL)
   for Index = 0 to HIGH(TestNum)
      TestNum[Index] = TRUNC(10.0 * Random(Seed) + 1.0)

procedure    WriteArray(TestNum : ARRAY OF CARDINAL)
   (* adds 1 to the value of Index to correspond to indices of an
      actual array parameter that begins with index = 1. *)
   for    Index = 0 to HIGH(TestNum)
      write "TestNum[", Index + 1, "] = ", TestNum[Index]
```

Modula-2 code   The program that imports and invokes ProduceArray and Write-Array is

```
MODULE  GenerateTestArray;
   (* Generates and displays an array of CARDINAL values between 1 and 10.
      FileName:CH10C      Modula-2      RKW      May 1991 *)

FROM InOut IMPORT  WriteString, WriteLn, ReadCard;
FROM RandGen IMPORT ProduceArray, WriteArray;

CONST  MAXLISTLENGTH = 6;
TYPE  CARDARRAY = ARRAY [1..MAXLISTLENGTH] OF CARDINAL;
VAR  TestNum : CARDARRAY;    Seed : CARDINAL;

BEGIN
   WriteString("Enter a CARDINAL Seed Value: "); ReadCard(Seed); WriteLn;
   ProduceArray(Seed, TestNum);
   WriteArray(TestNum);
END GenerateTestArray.
```

Figure 10–6
**Module RandGen
with Procedures
ProduceArray and
WriteArray**

```
DEFINITION MODULE RandGen;
    (* Contains a pseudorandom number generator.
       MUST BE COMPILED WITH RANGE CHECKING TURNED OFF. *)

PROCEDURE  Random(VAR Seed : CARDINAL) : REAL;
    (* Returns a real pseudorandom number between 0.0 and
       0.99998474 *)

PROCEDURE  ProduceArray(Seed:CARDINAL;
                          VAR TestNum:ARRAY OF CARDINAL);
    (* Generates an array of CARDINAL values between 1 and 10.  *)

PROCEDURE  WriteArray(TestNum:ARRAY OF CARDINAL);
    (* Displays CARDINAL array with Indices from 1 to ListLength *)

END RandGen.
```

```
IMPLEMENTATION MODULE RandGen;
    (* Contains a pseudorandom number generator.
       MUST BE COMPILED WITH RANGE CHECKING TURNED OFF. *)

FROM InOut IMPORT  WriteString, WriteLn, WriteCard;

PROCEDURE  Random(VAR Seed : CARDINAL) : REAL;
    (* Returns a real pseudorandom number between 0.0 and
       0.99998474 *)
    CONST DIVISOR = 65535;   MULTIPLIER = 25173;   ADDEND = 13849;
    BEGIN
        Seed := (Seed * MULTIPLIER + ADDEND) MOD DIVISOR;
        RETURN  FLOAT(Seed) / FLOAT(DIVISOR);
    END Random;

PROCEDURE  ProduceArray(Seed:CARDINAL;
                          VAR TestNum:ARRAY OF CARDINAL);
    (* Generates an array of CARDINAL values between 1 and 10. *)
    VAR  Index : CARDINAL;
    BEGIN
        FOR  Index := 0 TO HIGH(TestNum)  DO
            TestNum[Index] := TRUNC(10.0 * Random(Seed) + 1.0);
        END; (* FOR *)
    END ProduceArray;

PROCEDURE  WriteArray(TestNum:ARRAY OF CARDINAL);
    (* Displays a CARDINAL array with Indices from 1 to
       HIGH(TestNum)+1. *)
    VAR  Index : CARDINAL;
    BEGIN
        FOR  Index := 0 to HIGH(TestNum)  DO
            WriteString("TestNum["); WriteCard(Index+1, 2);
             WriteString("] ="); WriteCard(TestNum[Index],4); WriteLn;
        END; (* FOR *)
    END WriteArray;

END RandGen.
```

Figure 10–7
TestNum Array for
Searching

```
┌─────────────────────────────────────────────────────────────┐
│                                                               │
│              Enter a CARDINAL Seed value: 183                 │
│                                                               │
├─────────────────────────────────────────────────────────────┤
│                                                               │
│                  TestNum[1]  =       6                        │
│                  TestNum[2]  =       3                        │
│                  TestNum[3]  =       7                        │
│                  TestNum[4]  =      10                        │
│                  TestNum[5]  =       2                        │
│                  TestNum[6]  =      10                        │
│                                                               │
└─────────────────────────────────────────────────────────────┘
```

Module RandGen, with the procedures Random, ProduceArray, and WriteArray, is shown in Figure 10–6.

Debug and test   Remember, module RANDGEN.DEF must be compiled first. Then compile RANDGEN.MOD. with range testing turned off, so that the overflow created by procedure Random is ignored. Finally, compile, link, and execute program GenerateTestArray (CH10C).

When the program was executed with Seed = 183, the array in Figure 10–7 was generated.

Complete the documentation   Critical parts of the documentation for this program are the code (CH10C), a listing of procedures imported from module Rand-Gen, and a description of how those procedures work. It may be valuable to describe open array parameters and the correspondence of indices 0 to HIGH(Test-Num) in the procedures with indices 1 to MAXLISTLENGTH in the Generate TestArray program.

Questions 10.2

Write procedures to perform these four tasks. If you can declare an open array, show the procedure heading and a procedure call command, the value of HIGH(ArrayName), and the relationships between actual array and formal array indices. If it is not appropriate to declare an open array, explain why it is not.

1. Find the average of REAL grades in lists defined by

```
CONST  CLASSONE = 15;   CLASSTWO = 9;
VAR  FourPoint  : ARRAY [1..CLASSONE] OF REAL;
     Percentage : ARRAY [0..CLASSTWO] OF REAL;
```

2. Display, in reverse order, arrays (strings) of CHARacters defined by

```
TYPE  STR1 = ARRAY [0..59] OF CHAR;
VAR   Sentence : STR1;   Name : ARRAY [1..20] OF CHAR;
```

3. Find the Name of the middle child in family arrays defined by

```
CONST NAMELENGTH = 12; MINAGE = 4;   MAXAGE = 19;
TYPE  NAME = ARRAY [1..NAMELENGTH] OF CHAR;
VAR   Jones : ARRAY [MINAGE..MAXAGE] OF NAME;
      Smith : ARRAY [7..11] OF NAME;
```

4. In order of increasing index, write the ItemName, InventoryNo, and Cost arrays defined by

```
TYPE  STR = ARRAY [1..20] OF CHAR;
VAR   ItemName    : ARRAY [1..100] OF STR;
      InventoryNo : ARRAY [1..100] OF INTEGER;
      Cost        : ARRAY [1..100] OF REAL;
```

10.3 *Searching*

Two widespread applications of computers have always been searching and sorting data. Many early business computer systems consisted of machines that performed only searching and sorting operations. In this section, a simple search algorithm is developed and applied to an array.

The Linear Search

In a **linear search** each item of a list is examined in the order it occurs in the list until the desired item is found or the end of the list is reached. This would be analogous to looking at every name in the phone directory, beginning with *Aardvark, Aaron,* until you find the one you want or until you reach *Zzygy, Zora.*

Obviously, this is not the most efficient way to search a long alphabetized list. However, the *advantages* of the linear search are that

1. the algorithm is simple, and
2. the list need not be in any particular order.

Big O Notation

On the average, over a large number of linear searches, if there are N items on a list, you would examine half ($N/2$) of the items before finding the one you want.

A common way to express the length of time for a linear search of a list of length N is to say, "The order of magnitude (within a power of ten) of the number of items examined is N," or "A linear search is an $O(N)$ search." $O(N)$ is **big O notation** for Order of Magnitude $= N$. The binary search (discussed in Chapter 12) is a faster $O(\log N)$ search, but its algorithm is more complex and requires the search list

---

A Bit of Background

Handling Lists with LISP

Methods of handling one-dimensional arrays, or lists, have been especially important in the development of computer science and applications. In fact, in 1958 John McCarthy developed a language at the Massachusetts Institute of Technology specifically for manipulating symbolic strings, or lists, of data defined recursively. This language is called *LISP,* the acronym for *LISt Processing.* It has proved valuable not only for working with symbolic lists, but also for handling problems based on mathematical logic, and it is used extensively in artificial intelligence development projects.

One simple language related to LISP is named *Logo* and has been made particularly user-friendly. It incorporates a technique called "turtle graphics," by which a pointer is moved around the screen to plot geometric figures. Logo has been used widely to teach programming fundamentals to children.

to be in sorted order.

Pseudocode for a *linear search* is

```
begin with the first item
repeat
        compare the item with the desired search item
        advance to next item
until     (search item is found) OR (end of the list is reached)
```

If the list happens to be sorted in ascending order, the search algorithm can be shortened by stopping when an item larger than the search item is encountered. In the pseudocode this would be accomplished at the until statement by adding the test

```
OR (an item larger than the search item is encountered)
```

The following program incorporates the procedures ProduceArray and WriteArray—developed in the previous section and imported from module RandGen—to generate the array in Figure 10–7 and perform a linear search for a SearchValue specified by the user.

```
MODULE  SearchTestArray;
   (* Generates TestNum array in Figure 10-7 and performs a
      LINEAR SEARCH for a value specified by the user.
      FileName:CH10D      Modula-2      RKW      May 1991 *)

FROM InOut IMPORT  WriteString, WriteLn, WriteCard, ReadCard;
FROM RandGen IMPORT ProduceArray, WriteArray;

CONST  MAXLISTLENGTH = 6;   SEED = 183;
TYPE  CARDARRAY = ARRAY [1..MAXLISTLENGTH] OF CARDINAL;
VAR  TestNum : CARDARRAY;   FindIt : CARDINAL;

PROCEDURE  SearchLinear(TestNum:CARDARRAY;   SearchValue:CARDINAL);
   (* Performs a Linear Search of array TestNum for SearchValue *)
   VAR  WhichElement:CARDINAL;   Found:BOOLEAN;
   BEGIN
      WhichElement := 1;   Found := FALSE;
      REPEAT
         IF  TestNum[WhichElement] = SearchValue   THEN
            Found := TRUE;  WriteCard(SearchValue,3);
             WriteString(" is array element"); WriteCard(WhichElement,4);
         END; (* IF *)
         INC(WhichElement);
      UNTIL  Found  OR   (WhichElement > MAXLISTLENGTH);

      IF NOT(Found) THEN
         WriteCard(SearchValue,3); WriteString(" is not in this array.");
      END; (* IF *)
      WriteLn;
   END SearchLinear;

BEGIN   (* module SearchTestArray *)
   ProduceArray(SEED, TestNum);
   WriteArray(TestNum); WriteLn; WriteLn;

   WriteString("For which value to search? ");ReadCard(FindIt);WriteLn;
```

```
    SearchLinear(TestNum, FindIt);    (* Search TestNum array for FindIt. *)
END SearchTestArray.
```

A sample run appears as follows:

```
TestNum[ 1]  =    6
TestNum[ 2]  =    3
TestNum[ 3]  =    7
TestNum[ 4]  =   10
TestNum[ 5]  =    2
TestNum[ 6]  =   10

For which value to search? 10
  10 is array element    4
```

Note that the array does not need to be sorted in any particular order, and that the search stops at the first occurrence of the SearchValue.

Questions 10.3

1. a. Describe the array generated by this code:

```
FROM RandGen IMPORT Random;
CONST  MAXLIST = 'z';
TYPE   SOMEFANCYTYPE = ARRAY ['a'..MAXLIST] OF CHAR;
VAR  NewArray:SOMEFANCYTYPE;    Index:CHAR;    StartItAll,SomeNum:CARDINAL;
BEGIN
    StartItAll := 37;
    FOR  Index := 'a' TO MAXLIST  DO
       SomeNum := TRUNC(26.0 * Random(StartItAll)  +  1.0);
       NewArray[Index] := CHR(ORD('A') + SomeNum - 1);
    END; (* FOR *)

    FOR  Index := 'a' TO MAXLIST  DO
       Write(Index); WriteString("    "); Write(NewArray[Index]); WriteLn;
    END; (* FOR *)
```

    b. Write code that will display NewArray.

    c. How would you change program SearchTestArray (CH10D) so that it allows you to search for a particular value in NewArray?

2. Modify SearchTestArray (CH10D) so that

    a. it finds and displays *all* occurrences of the value of FindIt? *Hint:* Consider the condition tested at the UNTIL... statement.

    b. you can specify from the keyboard the length of the array to be created and searched and the initial Seed value for the random-number generator.

3. a. For program SearchTestArray (CH10D), draw a chart similar to the ones in Figure 10–5 that shows how the TestNum[Index] values in Figure 10–7 relate to TestNum[Index] values as they are recognized by procedures ProduceArray and WriteArray.

    b. Explain how, in the procedures, the two commands

```
FOR  Index := 0 TO HIGH(TestNum)  DO...

WriteCard(Index+1, 2);
```

establish the relationship you illustrated in part a.

4. Modify procedure SearchLinear (CH10D) by changing UNTIL... so that it handles a sorted list more efficiently.

10.4 *Sorting Algorithms*

Numerous algorithms have been developed for sorting and searching, each of them in response to a particular need. As with search algorithms, sort algorithms range from simple and slow to complex and faster.

The Selection Sort

One of the simplest sorting techniques is called the Selection sort. It involves searching a list to find the largest element and interchanging that element with the one at the end of the list. The same operation then is performed repeatedly on sublists from which the last element has been excluded until only two elements are left in the sublist.

In pseudocode,

```
procedure SelectionSort
   begin
     for     LastSubListIndex = MAXLISTLENGTH to 2 by −1
          find the position of the largest element in the sublist
          exchange (Swap) the largest element with the last element
     end for
   end SelectionSort
```

The pseudocode to "find the position of the largest element in the sublist" is

```
begin with index of LargestYet found = 1
   (* the first element is the LargestYet found *)
   for     SubListIndex = 2 to EndOfSubList
      if     LargestYet < CurrentElement     then
      (* if Element[LargestYet] < Element[SubListIndex] *)
      replace LargestYet by current SubListIndex
      end if
   end for
```

Finally, for an array declared by

```
TYPE     SOMEARRAY = ARRAY [1..MAXLISTLENGTH] OF SomeType;
VAR     Datum : SOMEARRAY;
```

the SelectionSort algorithm becomes

```
procedure SelectionSort(VAR Datum:SOMEARRAY)
   begin
     for LastSubListIndex = MAXLISTLENGTH to 2 by −1
       find largest in sublist:
       LargestYet = 1
       for SubListIndex = 2 to LastSubListIndex
          if     Datum[LargestYet] < Datum[SubListIndex]
               LargestYet = SubListIndex
          end if
          end for
        Swap     Datum[LargestYet] with     Datum[LastSubListIndex]
     end SelectionSort
```

A Selection sort on an array of CARDINAL values is illustrated in Figure 10–8.

Figure 10–8
A Selection Sort on
an Array of
CARDINAL Values

The array is produced by Procedure ProduceArray in module RandGen when Seed = 587 and ListLength = 5. Arrows indicate interchange of the largest element with the end of the list.

LastSubListIndex = 5

Original List		After Interchange	
TestNum[1]	7	TestNum[1]	7
TestNum[2]	4	TestNum[2]	4
TestNum[3]	8	TestNum[3]	3
TestNum[4]	5	TestNum[4]	5
TestNum[5]	3	TestNum[5]	8

LastSubListIndex = 4

Before Interchange		After Interchange	
TestNum[1]	7	TestNum[1]	5
TestNum[2]	4	TestNum[2]	4
TestNum[3]	3	TestNum[3]	3
TestNum[4]	5	TestNum[4]	7
TestNum[5]	8	TestNum[5]	8

LastSubListIndex = 3

Before Interchange		After Interchange	
TestNum[1]	5	TestNum[1]	3
TestNum[2]	4	TestNum[2]	4
TestNum[3]	3	TestNum[3]	5
TestNum[4]	7	TestNum[4]	7
TestNum[5]	8	TestNum[5]	8

LastSubListIndex = 2

(No interchange necessary)		Sorted list	
TestNum[1]	3	TestNum[1]	3
TestNum[2]	4	TestNum[2]	4
TestNum[3]	5	TestNum[3]	5
TestNum[4]	7	TestNum[4]	7
TestNum[5]	8	TestNum[5]	8

A Swap Algorithm

The Swap algorithm needed in the Selection sort of an array takes the form

```
procedure Swap(VAR ElementA, ElementB : SomeType);
  declare local variable Temporary : SomeType
  begin
    Temporary = ElementA
    ElementA  = ElementB
    ElementB  = Temporary
  end Swap
```

This Swap algorithm is illustrated in Figure 10–9.

The following program creates an array such as that shown in Figure 10–8 and performs the Selection sort.

Figure 10–9
The Swap
Algorithm

Swap(7, 3)

Command	Memory		
	Element A	**Element B**	**Temporary**
BEGIN (* Swap *)	7	3	
Temporary := ElementA;	7	3	7
ElementA := ElementB;	3	3	7
ElementB := Temporary;	3	7	7
END; (* Swap *)			

```
MODULE  PerformSelectionSort;
   (* Generates an array of CARDINAL values between 1 and 10 and
      performs a Selection Sort on the array.
      FileName:CH10E      Modula-2      RKW      May 1991 *)

FROM InOut IMPORT  WriteString, WriteLn, ReadCard;
FROM RandGen IMPORT ProduceArray, WriteArray;

CONST  MAXLISTLENGTH = 5;    SEED = 587;
TYPE  CARDARRAY = ARRAY [1..MAXLISTLENGTH] OF CARDINAL;
VAR  TestNum : CARDARRAY;

PROCEDURE Swap(VAR  ElementA, ElementB : CARDINAL);
   VAR  Temporary : CARDINAL;
   BEGIN
      Temporary := ElementA;  ElementA := ElementB;  ElementB := Temporary;
   END Swap;

PROCEDURE  SelectionSort(VAR TestNum:CARDARRAY;  MaxListLength:CARDINAL);
   VAR  LastSubListIndex, LargestYet, SubListIndex : CARDINAL;
   BEGIN
      FOR LastSubListIndex := MaxListLength TO 2 BY -1  DO
         LargestYet := 1;
         FOR  SubListIndex := 2 TO LastSubListIndex  DO
            IF  TestNum[LargestYet] < TestNum[SubListIndex]  THEN
               LargestYet := SubListIndex;
            END; (* IF *)
         END; (* FOR *)
         Swap(TestNum[LargestYet], TestNum[LastSubListIndex]);
      END; (* FOR *)
   END SelectionSort;

BEGIN  (* PerformSelectionSort *)
   ProduceArray(SEED, TestNum);
   WriteString("Unsorted, the array is"); WriteLn;
   WriteArray(TestNum); WriteLn; WriteLn;
```

```
    SelectionSort(TestNum, MAXLISTLENGTH);
    WriteString("The Sorted Array is"); WriteLn;
    WriteArray(TestNum); WriteLn; WriteLn;
END PerformSelectionSort.
```

Running this program displays the Original List and the Sorted List in Figure 10–8.

Number of Compares and Interchanges

For a list of N elements, during the $N - 1$ passes through the list, the Selection sort requires

$$(N - 1) + (N - 2) + \ldots + 3 + 2 = (N^2 - N - 2)/2$$

comparisons. Since N^2 is the fastest-growing term, it dominates the other terms for large values of N, and the number of compares is said to be of order N^2; that is, $O(N^2)$. At worst, each pass would require one interchange, when the number of interchanges is $(N - 1)$, or $O(N)$.

For large N, the comparisons can be very time-consuming. (See question 3 at the end of this section.) Therefore, the Selection sort (or the Bubble and Insertion sorts discussed next) can be used for lists of 10 to 20 elements, but faster algorithms (such as the Quick sort discussed in Chapter 12) should be used for longer lists.

☐ The Bubble Sort

The simplest and perhaps most popular sorting algorithm is the Bubble sort. The number of interchanges and the number of compares in this sort both are $O(N^2)$, so it could take roughly twice as long to perform as the Selection sort, where the number of interchanges is only $O(N)$.

The Bubble sort allows the smallest or ''lightest'' element to ''float'' to the top of the list, or the largest, ''heaviest'' element to ''sink'' to the bottom. In the latter case, successive elements are compared and are interchanged when the first is larger than the second. Then the length of the list is reduced by excluding the largest, bottom element, and the comparisons resume.

In pseudocode

```
procedure BubbleSort(VAR Datum : SOMEARRAY)
    for    LastSubListIndex = MAXLISTLENGTH to 2 by -1
        for    CurrentIndex = 1 to LastSubListIndex-1
            if    Datum[CurrentIndex] > Datum[CurrentIndex + 1]
                Swap Datum[CurrentIndex] with Datum[CurrentIndex+1]
            end if
        end for
    end for
end BubbleSort
```

Figure 10–10 illustrates a Bubble sort on the same CARDINAL array that was sorted with the Selection sort. You will want to replace the SelectionSort procedure and the procedure call in the previous program (CH10E) with the following *BubbleSort* procedure and procedure call. Run the program to observe the same results, now created by a Bubble sort.

```
PROCEDURE BubbleSort(VAR TestNum:CARDARRAY;  MaxListLength:CARDINAL);
    VAR  LastSubListIndex, CurrentIndex, SubListIndex : CARDINAL;
    BEGIN
        FOR  LastSubListIndex := MaxListLength TO 2 BY -1  DO
            FOR  CurrentIndex := 1 TO (LastSubListIndex - 1)  DO
```

Figure 10–10
A Bubble Sort on a
CARDINAL Array

The array is produced by Procedure ProduceArray in module RandGen when
Seed = 587 and ListLength = 5. Arrows indicate the elements compared.

LastSubListIndex = 5

Original List

TestNum[1]	7 ←	4	4	4	4
TestNum[2]	4 ←	7 ←	7	7	7
TestNum[3]	8	8 ←	8 ←	5	5
TestNum[4]	5	5	5 ←	8 ←	3
TestNum[5]	3	3	3	3 ←	8
CurrentIndex =	1	2	3	4	

LastSubListIndex = 4

TestNum[1]	4 ←	4	4	4
TestNum[2]	7 ←	7 ←	5	5
TestNum[3]	5	5 ←	7 ←	3
TestNum[4]	3	3	3 ←	7
TestNum[5]	8	8	8	8
CurrentIndex =	1	2	3	

LastSubListIndex = 3

TestNum[1]	4 ←	4	4
TestNum[2]	5 ←	5 ←	3
TestNum[3]	3	3 ←	5
TestNum[4]	7	7	7
TestNum[5]	8	8	8
CurrentIndex =	1	2	

LastSubListIndex = 2   **Sorted List**

TestNum[1]	4 ←	3
TestNum[2]	3 ←	4
TestNum[3]	5	5
TestNum[4]	7	7
TestNum[5]	8	8
CurrentIndex =	1	

```
        IF  TestNum[CurrentIndex] > TestNum[CurrentIndex + 1]  THEN
            Swap(TestNum[CurrentIndex], TestNum[CurrentIndex+1]);
          END; (* IF *)
        END; (* FOR *)
      END; (* FOR *)
    END BubbleSort;
...
...
    BubbleSort(TestNum, MAXLISTLENGTH);
....
```

The Insertion Sort

Still another O(N^2) sorting algorithm is the Insertion sort. The Insertion sort may be somewhat faster than the previous two algorithms if the lists already are partially sorted. Most people apply an Insertion sort when they sort a pile of papers or cards by hand; that is, they insert each successive item into its proper place among those already sorted.

An algorithm for implementing the Insertion sort is

1. Begin with the first element.
2. Compare the second element with the first element, and place it in proper order before or after the first element.
3. Move each succeeding element up in the list until it is inserted in its proper position.

Pseudocode for the insertion sort is

```
procedure InsertionSort(VAR Datum : SOMEARRAY)
  for LastSubListIndex = 2 to MAXLISTLENGTH
    move    Datum[LastSubListIndex] to its proper position within
              the Sublist Datum[1] to Datum[LastSubListIndex – 1]
```

To move Datum[LastSubListIndex] to its proper position, compare with previous elements one-by-one, and interchange as long as it is greater than the previous element; that is,

```
CurrentIndex = LastSubListIndex
while (CurrentIndex>1) and (Datum[CurrentIndex]<Datum[CurrentIndex – 1])
  Swap Datum[CurrentIndex] with Datum[CurrentIndex – 1]
  decrement CurrentIndex
end while
```

Then the final pseudocode is

```
procedure InsertionSort(VAR Datum : SOMEARRAY)
  for LastSubListIndex = 2 to MAXLISTLENGTH
    CurrentIndex = LastSubListIndex
    while    (CurrentIndex > 1) and
                  (Datum[CurrentIndex] < Datum[CurrentIndex – 1])
      Swap    Datum[CurrentIndex] with Datum[CurrentIndex – 1]
      decrement CurrentIndex
    end while
  end for
end InsertionSort
```

Figure 10–11 illustrates an Insertion sort on the same array of 5 CARDINAL numbers. Replace the sort procedure and procedure call in the previous programs (CH10E) with the following *InsertionSort* procedure and procedure call. Run the program to observe the same results, created now by an Insertion sort.

The array is produced by procedure ProduceArray in module RandGen when Seed = 587 and ListLength = 5. Arrows indicate the interchange of elements as the element at the LastSubListIndex is moved to its proper place in the list.

LastSubListIndex = 1

Original List

TestNum[1]	7
TestNum[2]	4
TestNum[3]	8
TestNum[4]	5
TestNum[5]	3

LastSubListIndex = 2

TestNum[1]	7	4
TestNum[2]	4	7
TestNum[3]	8	8
TestNum[4]	5	5
TestNum[5]	3	3
CurrentIndex	2	

LastSubListIndex = 3

(No interchange necessary)

TestNum[1]	4	4
TestNum[2]	7	7
TestNum[3]	8	8
TestNum[4]	5	5
TestNum[5]	3	3
CurrentIndex	3	

LastSubListIndex = 4

TestNum[1]	4	4	4
TestNum[2]	7	7	5
TestNum[3]	8	5	7
TestNum[4]	5	8	8
TestNum[5]	3	3	3
CurrentIndex	4	3	

LastSubListIndex = 4

Sorted List

TestNum[1]	4	4	4	4	3
TestNum[2]	5	5	5	3	4
TestNum[3]	7	7	3	5	5
TestNum[4]	8	3	7	7	7
TestNum[5]	3	8	8	8	8
CurrentIndex	5	4	3	2	

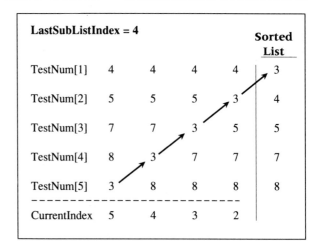

Figure 10–11
An Insertion Sort on a CARDINAL Array

```
PROCEDURE InsertionSort(VAR TestNum:CARDARRAY;  MAXLISTLENGTH:CARDINAL);
   VAR  LastSubListIndex, CurrentIndex, SubListIndex : CARDINAL;
   BEGIN
      FOR  LastSubListIndex := 2 TO MAXLISTLENGTH  DO
         CurrentIndex := LastSubListIndex;
         WHILE  (CurrentIndex > 1) AND
                   (TestNum[CurrentIndex] < TestNum[CurrentIndex-1])  DO
            Swap(TestNum[CurrentIndex], TestNum[CurrentIndex-1]);
            DEC(CurrentIndex);
         END; (* WHILE *)
      END; (* FOR *)
```

Figure 10–12
A File of Accounts
(Example 10.4.1)

The Input File

Smith	1083	21.98
Jones	0968	105.34
Adams	0662	10.50
Fredrich	2240 ·	240.85
Brown	1742	85.49
Nelson	1104	66.22
Cramer	0543	154.23

Declaration of Parallel Arrays

```
TYPE  NAMESTR = ARRAY [0..19] OF CHAR;
      NAMEARY = ARRAY [1..7] OF NAMESTR;
      NUMLIST = ARRAY [1..7] OF CARDINAL;
      AMTLIST = ARRAY [1..7] OF REAL;

VAR   Name:NAMEARY;  AccountNum:NUMLIST;  AmountDue:AMTLIST;
```

Parallel Array Representation

```
              Name              AccountNum                AmountDue

Name[1]       Smith      AccountNum[1]  1083       AmountDue[1]   21.98
Name[2]       Jones      AccountNum[2]  0968       AmountDue[2]  105.34
Name[3]       Adams      AccountNum[3]  0662       AmountDue[3]   10.50
Name[4]    Fredrich      AccountNum[4]  2240       AmountDue[4]  240.85
Name[5]       Brown      AccountNum[5]  1742       AmountDue[5]   85.49
Name[6]      Nelson      AccountNum[6]  1104       AmountDue[6]   66.22
Name[7]      Cramer      AccountNum[7]  0543       AmountDue[7]  154.23
```

```
    END InsertionSort;
...
...
    InsertionSort(TestNum, MAXLISTLENGTH);
....
```

Searching and Sorting Parallel Arrays

Suppose you have a file containing a list of names, CARDINAL account numbers, and REAL amounts due, as shown in Figure 10–12. One way of storing this data in the computer so that it can be searched and sorted is to store the names, account numbers, and amounts in three separate parallel arrays, as shown in the figure. Then, when values are to be interchanged or accessed, values in all of the arrays are considered in order to keep the elements in corresponding positions.

The following example illustrates how parallel arrays can be handled.

Example 10.4.1

Read names, account numbers, and amounts due from a file. Search and sort the accounts.

Define the problem   The accounts shown in the file of Figure 10–12 are to be read into parallel Name, AccountNum, and AmountDue arrays. Those accounts with AmountDue >= 100.00 are to be displayed; and the accounts are to be sorted and displayed in order of increasing AmountDue.

Develop a solution   Procedures will be created to ReadTheFile, SearchFor-Amount, and SortByAmount.

In ReadTheFile, ReadString and WriteString procedures from module InOut will be used to read and display the names. ReadString terminates when a space is encountered; thus ReadString(Name[*i*]), followed by ReadCard(AccountNum[*i*]), and ReadReal(AmountDue[*i*]) will read each line of the file appropriately.

The SearchForAmount procedure will apply a linear search to find the appropriate amounts due. Then the corresponding elements of all three arrays will be displayed when an AmountDue >= 100.00 is found.

SortByAmount could incorporate any of the sorting algorithms. The implementation here will apply the Insertion sort, where an interchange of AmountDue[*i*] with AmountDue[*j*] will be accompanied by interchanges of Name[*i*] with Name[*j*] and AccountNum[*i*] with AccountNum[*j*] in order to keep the three arrays parallel.

Refine the solution   *Pseudocode*

```
begin module SearchAndSort
    ReadTheFile(Name, AccountNum, AmountDue)
    SearchForAmount(Name, AccountNum, AmountDue)
    SortByAmount(Name, AccountNum, AmountDue)
end SearchAndSort

procedure ReadTheFile(VAR Name:NAMEARY; VAR Acct:NUMLIST;
                            VAR Due:AMTLIST)
    open input file
    for     Index = 1 to 7     read     Name[Index], Acct[Index], Due[Index]
    close input file

procedure SearchForAmount(Name:NAMEARY; AcctNum:NUMLIST; Due:AMTLIST)
    (* performs a linear search *)
    for     Index = 1 to 7
        if     Due[Index] >= 100.00
            write     Due[Index], AcctNum[Index], Name[Index]

procedure SortByAmount(Name:NAMEARY;     Acct:NUMLIST;     Due:AMTLIST)
    (* performs an Insertion sort *)
    for     ListLength = 2 to 7
        I = ListLength
        while (I > 1) and (Due[I] < Due[I – 1])
            swap Due[I]    with Due[I – 1],     swap Acct[I] with Acct[I – 1],
            swap Name[I] with Name[I – 1]
            decrement I
        end while
    end for
    for     I = 1 to 7     display     Acct[I], Due[I], Name[I]
```

Modula-2 code

```
MODULE SearchAndSort;
    (* Reads a file into parallel arrays.  Performs a linear search
       and an Insertion sort on the parallel arrays.
```

```
            FileName:CH10H       Modula-2      RKW       May 1991   *)

FROM InOut IMPORT WriteString, WriteLn, ReadString, ReadCard, WriteCard,
                  OpenInput, CloseInput;
FROM RealInOut IMPORT ReadReal, FWriteReal;


CONST  MAXLISTLENGTH = 7;
TYPE   NAMESTR = ARRAY [0..19] OF CHAR;   (* to hold names 20 chars long *)
       NAMEARY = ARRAY [1..MAXLISTLENGTH] OF NAMESTR;
       NUMLIST = ARRAY [1..MAXLISTLENGTH] OF CARDINAL;
       AMTLIST = ARRAY [1..MAXLISTLENGTH] OF REAL;
VAR  Name:NAMEARY;   AccountNum:NUMLIST;    AmountDue:AMTLIST;

PROCEDURE ReadTheFile(VAR Name:NAMEARY; VAR Acct:NUMLIST; VAR Due:AMTLIST);
   VAR  Index : CARDINAL;
   BEGIN
      WriteString("Name of input file? "); OpenInput("IN"); WriteLn;
      FOR  Index := 1 TO MAXLISTLENGTH  DO
         ReadString(Name[Index]); ReadCard(Acct[Index]); ReadReal(Due[Index]);
      END; (* FOR *)
      CloseInput;
   END ReadTheFile;


PROCEDURE SearchForAmount(Name:NAMEARY; AcctNum:NUMLIST; Due:AMTLIST);
   VAR  Index : CARDINAL;       (* performs a linear search *)
   BEGIN
      WriteLn; WriteString("Accounts with $100.00 or more due:"); WriteLn;
      FOR  Index := 1 TO MAXLISTLENGTH  DO
         IF  Due[Index] >= 100.00  THEN
            FWriteReal(Due[Index],10,2);  WriteCard(AcctNum[Index],10);
             WriteString("      ");  WriteString(Name[Index]); WriteLn;
         END; (* IF *)
      END; (* FOR *) WriteLn; WriteLn;
   END SearchForAmount;


PROCEDURE SortByAmount(Name:NAMEARY; Acct:NUMLIST; Due:AMTLIST);
     (* performs an Insertion sort on parallel arrays *)
   VAR  I,ListLength,TempNum:CARDINAL;   TempName:NAMESTR;   TempDue:REAL;
   BEGIN
      FOR  ListLength := 2 TO MAXLISTLENGTH  DO
         I := ListLength;
         WHILE (I > 1) AND (Due[I] < Due[I-1])  DO
            (* Swap corresponding array elements *)
            TempDue := Due[I];   Due[I] := Due[I-1];  Due[I-1] := TempDue;
            TempNum := Acct[I]; Acct[I] := Acct[I-1]; Acct[I-1] := TempNum;
            TempName:= Name[I]; Name[I] := Name[I-1]; Name[I-1] := TempName;
            DEC(I);
         END; (* WHILE *)
      END; (* FOR *)
      WriteLn; WriteString("In order of increasing amount due:"); WriteLn;
      FOR  I := 1 TO MAXLISTLENGTH  DO
         WriteCard(Acct[I],10); FWriteReal(Due[I],10,2);
          WriteString("      "); WriteString(Name[I]); WriteLn;
      END; (* FOR *)
   END SortByAmount;
```

```
BEGIN   (* module SearchAndSort *)
   ReadTheFile(Name, AccountNum, AmountDue);
   SearchForAmount(Name, AccountNum, AmountDue);
   SortByAmount(Name, AccountNum, AmountDue);
END SearchAndSort.
```

Debug and test   A sample run, with a file containing the data shown in Figure 10–12, appears as:

```
Name of input file? CH10H.IN

Accounts with $100.00 or more due:
      105.34         968      Jones
      240.85        2240      Fredrich
      154.23         543      Cramer

In order of increasing amount due:
       662          10.50     Adams
      1083          21.98     Smith
      1104          66.22     Nelson
      1742          85.49     Brown
       968         105.34     Jones
       543         154.23     Cramer
      2240         240.85     Fredrich
```

Test with different input files and varying numbers of customers. To trace the sort process, you may wish to add commands to display the arrays immediately after the data has been read from the file and after each END; (* WHILE *) in the sort procedure.

Complete the documentation   The problem description should discuss parallel arrays and interchanging corresponding elements when sorting. Because WriteString(Name[I]) displays only the number of characters in the Name, if names are not displayed last on the line, some string handling (discussed later in the chapter) will be necessary to align the columns.

The users' manual should state the source code location (CH10H) and indicate that an input file with appropriate data—Figure 10–12 provides an example—must be available before executing the program.

Questions 10.4

1. For procedures SelectionSort, BubbleSort, and InsertionSort, the sorting can be done in *decreasing* order by modifying only one line in each procedure. Show that modification for each procedure, and explain how it changes the sort from increasing to decreasing order.
2. Given a Freq array with data

   $$Freq['a'] = 0.105 \qquad Freq['b'] = 0.893 \qquad Freq['c'] = 0.491$$

   a. show a declaration of the Freq array that would allow the array to be passed as a parameter to a sort procedure.
   b. write a procedure to display the Freq array.
   c. what changes would have to be made to procedures SelectionSort, Bubble-Sort, and InsertionSort to sort the Freq array in increasing order.

A Bit of Background

Matrices

A sophisticated theory for handling matrices was invented in 1858 by Arthur Cayley (1821–1895). Matrix theory is a comprehensive algebra for adding, multiplying, manipulating, and otherwise transforming two-dimensional arrays. One of its major applications has been for solving simultaneous linear equations.

Arthur Cayley's teachers considered him a "born mathematician" at an early age. He easily garnered top honors in mathematics at Cambridge University, but by the age of 25 he was studying law, a profession that would put bread on the table. After enduring 14 agonizing years of legal practice, Cayley was offered the Sadlerian professorship of mathematics at Cambridge. He eagerly accepted the offer, even though it meant a significant reduction in income. Thereafter he spent his life in pursuit of mathematics.

In 1925, sixty-seven years after Cayley invented matrix algebra, Werner Heisenberg recognized its value as the exact tool he needed for developing the theory of quantum mechanics.

---

3. For Selection, Bubble, and Insertion sorts on lists of N items, the number of comparisons is $O(N^2)$. Approximately how much time would it take those procedures to sort 10,000 items on

   a. a microcomputer that takes about 1.0 millisecond (1/1000 second) for one compare;

   b. a mainframe that takes about 1.0 microsecond (1/1,000,000 second) for one compare?

4. Complete this code to make it perform a Selection sort on array People.

```
VAR  ListLength, Biggest, J : _____;       Temp : _____;
     People : ARRAY [_____] OF _____;

BEGIN
   People[-2] := 483;  People[-1] := 121;  People[0] := 5286;
   People[ 1] :=  42;  People[ 2] := 967;  People[3] :=  604;

   FOR  ListLength := ____ TO ____ BY -1  DO
      Biggest := ____;
      FOR  J := ____    TO ListLength  DO
         IF  People[Biggest] < People[ListLength]  THEN
            Biggest := ____;
         END; (* IF *)
      END; (* FOR *)

      Temp := People[Biggest];  People[Biggest] := People[_____];
      People[_____] := Temp;
   END; (* FOR *)
....
```

5. In program SearchAndSort (Example 10.4.1, CH10H),

   a. add commands to display the arrays immediately after the file has been read.

   b. add commands to trace the sort process; that is, to display the arrays between END; (*WHILE *) and END; (* FOR *) in procedure SortByAmount.

   c. what happens to the column alignment if you try to use WriteString to display Names first in each line?

10.5 *Multidimensional Arrays*

The arrays considered so far have represented lists of quantities, such as numbers or characters. Often, however, you will want to work with a table of data or with more complex structures, which need to be handled as arrays of two or more dimensions.

Arrays of Two Dimensions

When the data in a problem can be organized within a single table, where all data values are of the same type, it can be handled as a two-dimensional array.

For example, suppose you need to tabulate the number of sports cars of three different models sold by two different dealers and the amount of revenue generated by each model at each dealership. The data can be represented by the tables shown in Figure 10–13.

Declaring and Accessing Two-Dimensional Arrays

Two-dimensional arrays can be declared in several different ways in Modula-2. First, you can define each array as a type and use the type names in order. For example,

```
TYPE  SHOP = ARRAY [1..2] OF CARDINAL;
      CARANDSHOP = ARRAY ['a'..'c'] OF SHOP;
VAR  HowManySold : CARANDSHOP;
```

Figure 10–13
Arrays for
CarsAndDealers
(Example 10.5.1)

HowManySold

Car	Dealer	
	1	2
'a'	10	7
'b'	5	12
'c'	3	1

DollarTable

Car	Dealer	
	1	2
'a'	111990.00	78393.00
'b'	112850.00	270840.00
'c'	135822.00	45274.00

Price

Car	Dollars
'a'	11199.00
'b'	22570.00
'c'	45274.00

Second, you can declare the type to be an array of arrays. For example,

```
TYPE  CARANDSHOP = ARRAY ['a'..'c'] OF ARRAY [1..2] OF CARDINAL;
VAR   HowManySold : CARANDSHOP;
```

Third, the index-range brackets can be collected in a list. For example,

```
TYPE  CARANDSHOP = ARRAY ['a'..'c'], [1..2] OF CARDINAL;
VAR   HowManySold : CARANDSHOP;
```

Reference to a single element in a two-dimensional array also can be made in different ways. First, the Row and Column designators may be specified in separate brackets ([Row][Column]). Thus, for example,

```
HowManySold['b'][1]  is  5
HowManySold['a'][2]  is  7, etc.
```

Second, the Row and Column designators may be specified as a list within a single set of brackets ([Row, Column]). For example,

```
HowManySold['c', 1] is 3
HowManySold['b', 2] is 12, etc.
```

Nested FOR Loops to Manipulate Arrays

Because indices are enumerable, nested FOR loops provide a convenient way of handling multidimensional arrays.

For example, to read the data into the array HowManySold of Figure 10–13, you could write

```
FOR  Row := 'a' TO 'c'  DO
  FOR  Column := 1 TO 2  DO
    ReadCard(HowManySold[Row, Column]);
  END; (* FOR Column *)
END; (* FOR Row *)
```

This is called **row-order processing** because, for each Row, the inner loop steps through all of the columns, and the values are read in the order:

```
(Row 'a') 10, 7;  (Row 'b') 5, 12;  (Row 'c') 3, 1.
```

Should you decide to display the HowManySold array in **column order**—that is, display all of the elements in column 1, then those in column 2, and so on—you would reverse the order of the FOR loops. For example,

```
FOR  Column := 1 TO 2 DO
  FOR  Row := 'a' TO 'c'  DO
    WriteCard(HowManySold[Row, Column],  6);
  END; (* FOR Row *)
  WriteLn;
END; (* FOR Column *);
```

would display the elements in the order:

```
(Column 1) 10, 5, 3;  (Column 2) 7, 12, 1.
```

The WriteLn command between END;(*FOR Row*) and END;(*FOR Column*) advances to a new line with each successive execution of the outer loop.

Nested loops are also valuable for manipulating arrays. For example, to obtain each element in array DollarTable of Figure 10–13, each element of array How-

ManySold should be multiplied by the appropriate Price. Thus, DollarTable can be created by the structure

```
FOR  Row := 'a' TO 'c'  DO
  FOR  Column := 1 TO 2  DO
    DollarTable[Row,Column] :=
        FLOAT(HowManySold[Row,Column]) * Price[Row];
  END; (* FOR Column *)
END; (* FOR Row *)
```

The following example illustrates the manipulation of two-dimensional arrays.

Example 10.5.1

Find the revenues from the sale of three different sports car models sold by two dealers.

Define the problem   Three different sports car models have prices fixed by the manufacturer at $11,199.00, $22,570.00, and $45,274.00. Write a procedure that asks how many of each model were sold by each dealer. A second procedure displays a table of HowManySold and a table of Revenues (in Dollars). Finally, a third procedure calculates and displays the total number of sports cars sold and the total revenues for each dealer from each model. The arrays appear in Figure 10–13.

Develop a solution   Label the dealers *1* and *2* and the sports car models *a*, *b*, and *c*. Then define two-dimensional arrays as follows:

```
CONST LASTDEALER = 2;  LASTMODEL = 'c';
TYPE  CARANDSHOP = ARRAY ['a'..LASTMODEL],[1..LASTDEALER] OF
                        CARDINAL;
      REVENUES   = ARRAY ['a'..LASTMODEL],[1..LASTDEALER] OF
                        REAL;
VAR   HowManySold : CARANDSHOP;  Dollars : REVENUES;
```

The solution algorithm can be written in pseudocode for each procedure and for the driver program.

Refine the solution   *Pseudocode*

```
begin module CarsAndDealers
  AskForSales(HowManySold)
  DisplaySales(HowManySold, Dollars)
  CalculateTotals(HowManySold, Dollars)
end CarsAndDealers

procedure AskForSales(VAR WhoNum : CARANDSHOP)
  use nested FOR loops to read WhoNum[Car, Dealer] in row order

procedure DisplaySales(Sales:CARANDSHOP;    VAR Dollars:REVENUES)
      set values into array Price
      use nested FOR loops to generate Dollars table in row order,
                          Dollars[Car][Dealer] = Sales[Car][Dealer] * Price[Car]
      display Sales and Dollars tables, both in row order

procedure CalculateTotals(Sale:CARANDSHOP;    Income:REVENUES);
      for Dealer = 1 to 2    (* add values in each column *)
          display Dealer,    initialize TotalCars and TotalDollars to 0
          for Car = 'a' to 'c'
```

$$\text{TotalCars} \quad = \text{TotalCars} + \text{Sales[Car, Dealer]}$$
$$\text{TotalDollars} = \text{TotalDollars} + \text{Income[Car, Dealer]}$$
end for Car
display TotalCars and TotalDollars, and advance to new line

In the following code, entire arrays HowManySold and Dollars are passed as parameters to the procedures. Also, two ways of specifying multiple indices are illustrated; namely, as

Sales[Car][Dealer]   and   Sales[Car, Dealer].

Modula-2 code

```
MODULE CarsAndDealers;
    (* Handles two dimensional arrays of CARDINAL and REAL values.
       FileName:CH10I        Modula-2        RKW        May 1991   *)

FROM InOut IMPORT WriteString, WriteLn, ReadCard, WriteCard, Write;
FROM RealInOut IMPORT FWriteReal;

CONST LASTDEALER = 2;  LASTMODEL = 'c';
TYPE  CARANDSHOP = ARRAY ['a'..LASTMODEL], [1..LASTDEALER] OF CARDINAL;
      REVENUES   = ARRAY ['a'..LASTMODEL], [1..LASTDEALER] OF REAL;
VAR  HowManySold : CARANDSHOP;       Dollars : REVENUES;

PROCEDURE  AskForSales(VAR WhoNum : CARANDSHOP);
   VAR  Dealer : CARDINAL;   Car : CHAR;
   BEGIN
      WriteLn; WriteString("Enter how many of each model for each dealer");
      WriteLn; WriteString("Model  Dealer    HowMany?"); WriteLn;
      FOR  Car := 'a' TO LASTMODEL  DO
         FOR  Dealer := 1 TO LASTDEALER  DO
            Write(Car); WriteCard(Dealer,7); WriteString("    = ?  ");
            ReadCard(WhoNum[Car,Dealer]); WriteLn;
         END; (* FOR Dealer *)
      END; (* FOR Car *)
   END AskForSales;

PROCEDURE DisplaySales(Sales:CARANDSHOP; VAR Dollars:REVENUES);
   VAR  Price : ARRAY ['a'..LASTMODEL] OF REAL;
        Dealer : CARDINAL;  Car : CHAR;
   BEGIN
         (* Generate Dollars Table *)
      Price['a']:=11199.00;  Price['b']:=22570.0;  Price['c']:=45274.0;
      FOR  Car := 'a' TO LASTMODEL  DO
         FOR  Dealer := 1 TO LASTDEALER  DO
            Dollars[Car][Dealer] := FLOAT(Sales[Car][Dealer]) * Price[Car];
         END; (* FOR Dealer *)
      END; (* FOR Car *)

         (* Display Both Tables *)
      WriteLn; WriteLn; WriteString("     HowManySold"); WriteLn;
       WriteString("               Dealers"); WriteLn;
       WriteString("Cars         1         2"); WriteLn; WriteLn;
      FOR  Car := 'a' TO LASTMODEL  DO
         Write(Car);
         FOR  Dealer := 1 TO 2  DO
            WriteCard(Sales[Car,Dealer],13);
```

```
            END; (* FOR Dealer *)
            WriteLn;
        END; (* FOR Car *)


    WriteLn; WriteLn; WriteString("     DollarTable"); WriteLn;
        WriteString("              Dealers"); WriteLn;
        WriteString("Cars          1                2"); WriteLn; WriteLn;
    FOR  Car := 'a' TO LASTMODEL  DO
        Write(Car);
        FOR  Dealer := 1 TO 2  DO
            FWriteReal(Dollars[Car,Dealer],13,2);
        END; (* FOR Dealer *)
        WriteLn;
    END; (* FOR Car *) WriteLn;
END DisplaySales;

PROCEDURE  CalculateTotals(Sales:CARANDSHOP; Income:REVENUES);
    VAR  Dealer,TotalCars:CARDINAL;  Car:CHAR;  TotalDollars:REAL;
    BEGIN
        WriteLn; WriteString("Dealer  CarsSold   TotalRevenue"); WriteLn;
        FOR  Dealer := 1 TO LASTDEALER  DO
            WriteCard(Dealer,6);
            TotalCars := 0;   TotalDollars := 0.0;
            FOR  Car := 'a' TO LASTMODEL  DO
                TotalCars    := TotalCars    + Sales[Car,Dealer];
                TotalDollars := TotalDollars + Income[Car,Dealer];
            END; (* FOR Car *)
            WriteCard(TotalCars,10); FWriteReal(TotalDollars,15,2); WriteLn;
        END; (* FOR Dealer *)
    END CalculateTotals;

BEGIN  (* module CarsAndDealers *)
    AskForSales(HowManySold);
    DisplaySales(HowManySold, Dollars);
    CalculateTotals(HowManySold, Dollars);
END CarsAndDealers.
```

A Bit of Background

To See Things Differently

By 1905, Albert Einstein had developed the *special* theory of relativity, which intimately relates the three dimensions of space with the fourth dimension, time. Although classical mechanics had dealt with both space and time, it took very special insight—the ability to see things differently—to view space-time as a four-dimensional continuum.

By the time Dr. Einstein had formulated the *general* theory of relativity a few years later, mathematical techniques were being developed for expressing space-time in terms of four-dimensional arrays called "tensors." Seeing the universe in four dimensions led to the postulates that there can be no absolute reference frame; that matter and energy are different manifestations of the same entity; and that the speed of light is constant, regardless of how it is measured. Albert Einstein had reconciled many of the apparent conflicts between the theories of gravitation, mechanics, and electromagnetism; and he spent much of the rest of his life searching for the elusive insight that would unify all of the forces of nature.

Debug and test For debugging purposes it could be valuable to insert write statements into the procedures to display the values of the indices and of the results during each iteration. In addition to arrays HowManySold and DollarTable, in Figure 10–13, a sample run displays the following:

```
Enter how many of each model for each dealer
Model  Dealer     HowMany?
a       1     = ?  10
a       2     = ?  7
b       1     = ?  5
b       2     = ?  12
c       1     = ?  3
c       2     = ?  1
```

```
        HowManySold
                 Dealers
Cars          1              2

a            10              7
b             5             12
c             3              1
```

```
        DollarTable
                 Dealers
Cars          1              2

a     111990.00      78393.00
b     112850.00     270840.00
c     135822.00      45274.00
```

```
Dealer  CarsSold    TotalRevenue
   1         18        360662.00
   2         20        394507.00
```

Complete the documentation The source code is in file CH10I. Users enter the appropriate sales data when requested, then wait for the display of results. The problem definition, pseudocode, code, and sample run supplement the documentation.

Arrays of Three or More Dimensions

The concept of a two-dimensional table can be extended to an array of tables or a block of values, and then to an array of blocks, and so forth. Implementing such concepts in Modula-2 becomes a matter of extending the two-dimensional array definition to include three or more sets of indices. Such structures are called **multidimensional arrays.**

Suppose, for example, that you want to express the number of airliners, small planes, and helicopters that landed at airports LAX and SFO on June 4, 5, 6, and 7. Figure 10–14 shows how you might represent such a structure on paper and in Modula-2.

Figure 10–14
A Three-
Dimensional Array
of Air Traffic at
LAX and SFO

```
TYPE LANDINGS = ARRAY [4..7],[1..3],['A'..'B'] OF CARDINAL;
(* [4..7] represents Row: June 4 to June 7
   [1..3] represents Columns: Airliners(1), SmallPlanes(2),
                                              Helicopters(3)
   ['A'..'B'] represents Levels: LAX('A') to SFO('B')    *)

VAR   Traffic : LANDINGS;
```

LAX('A')	1 Airliners	2 SmallPlanes	3 Helicopters
June 4	720	196	65
June 5	648	105	48
June 6	342	52	12
June 7	818	240	81

SFO('B')	1 Airliners	2 SmallPlanes	3 Helicopters
June 4	640	102	55
June 5	542	91	31
June 6	221	35	6
June 7	722	137	72

You can follow the same variety of patterns for declaring multidimensional arrays as for arrays in two dimensions. For example, another way (different from that in the figure) the Traffic array could be declared is

```
TYPE LANDINGS = ARRAY [4..7] OF ARRAY [1..3] OF ARRAY ['A'..'B'] OF CARDINAL;

VAR   Traffic : LANDINGS;
```

Theoretically, there is no limit to the number of dimensions an array can have in Modula-2; however, some implementations of the language may limit the number of dimensions you can use. The total number of elements is the product of the number of allowed indices in each dimension, such as

$$(4 \text{ dates}) * (3 \text{ aircraft types}) * (2 \text{ airports}) = 24$$

elements. This number can outgrow available memory rapidly if multiple index ranges are large; and the processing time to determine the addresses and locate elements grows longer with the number of dimensions and the size of the array.

Accessing Multidimensional Array Elements

You may assign entire compatible multidimensional arrays to each other and pass them to formal parameters, just as with one-dimensional arrays. Otherwise, you

Figure 10–15
Structure Chart for
AirTraffic (Example
10.5.2)

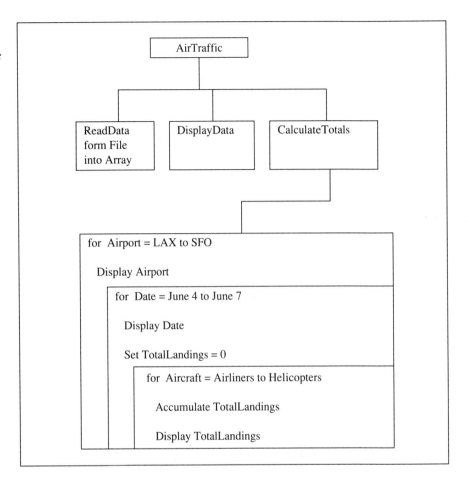

must always refer to single elements in the array by listing specific index values in the appropriate order. For example,   Traffic[5, 3, 'A']   has the CARDINAL value 48, shown in Figure 10–14. Indices used to access a particular array element can be expressed as constants, variables, expressions, or functions. For example, Traffic[7 − 2, 3, CHR(ORD('A'))]   also refers to CARDINAL value 48.

Example 10.5.2

Write a program to display aircraft traffic and calculate the total daily traffic at two airports.

Define the problem   From an input file, read the traffic data shown in Figure 10–14 into a three-dimensional array. Display the traffic tables as shown. Then calculate and display the total number of aircraft landing at each airport each day.

Develop a solution   The three-dimensional array has already been represented graphically and in Modula-2 in Figure 10–14. Figure 10–15 shows the structure of the problem solution desired. A different way of illustrating nested iterations is presented in this figure.

Refine the solution Pseudocode

```
begin module AirTraffic
   ReadData(Traffic)
   DisplayData(Traffic)
   CalculateTotals(Traffic)
end AirTraffic

procedure ReadData(VAR Airports : LANDINGS)
   use nested FOR loops to read the Airports array in order by
      Level(Airport), Rows(Date), and Columns(Aircraft)

procedure DisplayData(Arrivals : LANDINGS)
   use nested FOR loops in order of Level(Airport), Rows(Date),
      and Columns(Aircraft) to display the two tables of landing data.

procedure CalculateTotals(Arrivals : LANDINGS)
   for Airport = LAX TO SFO
      display Airport
      for Date = 4 to 7
         set      TotalLandings = 0,      display Date and headings
         for Aircraft = Airliners to Helicopters
            accumulate TotalLandings
         end for Aircraft
         display TotalLandings and advance to new line
      end for Date,      advance two lines
   end for Airport
```

Modula-2 code

```
MODULE AirTraffic;
   (* Handles a three dimensional array of landings as a function
      of airport, date, and type of aircraft.
      File Name:CH10J     Modula-2     RKW     May 1991   *)

FROM InOut IMPORT WriteLn, WriteString, ReadCard, WriteCard,
                  OpenInput, CloseInput;

TYPE  LANDINGS = ARRAY [4..7],[1..3],['A'..'B'] OF CARDINAL;
VAR   Traffic : LANDINGS;

PROCEDURE ReadData(VAR Airports : LANDINGS);
   VAR  Level : CHAR;   Row, Column : CARDINAL;
   BEGIN
      WriteString("Name of input file? "); OpenInput("IN");
      FOR  Level := 'A' TO 'B'  DO
         FOR  Row := 4 TO 7 DO
            FOR  Column := 1 TO 3 DO
               ReadCard(Airports[Row, Column, Level]);
            END; (* FOR Column *)
         END; (* FOR Row *)
      END; (* FOR Level *)
      CloseInput;
   END ReadData;

PROCEDURE DisplayData(Arrivals : LANDINGS);
   VAR  Airport : CHAR;   Date, Aircraft : CARDINAL;
   BEGIN
      FOR  Airport := 'A' TO 'B'  DO
```

```
      CASE  Airport  OF
         'A' : WriteString("LAX('A')")  |  'B' : WriteString("SFO('B')");
      END; (* CASE *);
      WriteString("              1                 2                 3"); WriteLn;
      WriteString("                    Airliners    SmallPlanes   Helicopters");
       WriteLn; WriteLn;
      FOR  Date := 4 TO 7  DO
         WriteString(" June"); WriteCard(Date,3);
         FOR  Aircraft := 1 TO 3  DO
            WriteCard(Arrivals[Date, Aircraft, Airport], 14);
         END; (* FOR Aircraft *)  WriteLn; WriteLn;
      END; (* FOR Date *)  WriteLn; WriteLn; WriteLn;
   END; (* FOR Airport *)
 END DisplayData;

PROCEDURE CalculateTotals(Arrivals : LANDINGS);
   VAR  Airport : CHAR;   Date, Aircraft, TotalLandings : CARDINAL;
   BEGIN
      FOR  Airport := 'A' TO 'B'  DO
         CASE  Airport  OF
            'A' : WriteString("LAX")  |  'B' : WriteString("SFO");
         END; (* CASE *)  WriteLn;
         FOR  Date := 4 TO 7  DO
            WriteString("June"); WriteCard(Date,3);
            WriteString("       Total Landings = ");  TotalLandings := 0;
            FOR  Aircraft := 1 TO 3  DO
               TotalLandings:=TotalLandings+Arrivals[Date,Aircraft,Airport];
            END; (* FOR Aircraft *)
            WriteCard(TotalLandings,5);   WriteLn;
         END; (* FOR Date *)  WriteLn;
      END; (* FOR Airport *)
   END CalculateTotals;

 BEGIN (* AirTraffic *)
    ReadData(Traffic);  WriteLn;
    DisplayData(Traffic);  WriteLn;
    CalculateTotals(Traffic);
 END AirTraffic.
```

Debug and test Check the triply nested FOR loops carefully to make certain that the order of indices is correct and that WriteLn commands are placed properly for appropriate display of the arrays.

A sample run produces the tables shown in Figure 10–14 and these totals:

. . .

```
    LAX
    June   4       Total Landings =   981
    June   5       Total Landings =   801
    June   6       Total Landings =   406
    June   7       Total Landings =  1139


    SFO
    June   4       Total Landings =   797
    June   5       Total Landings =   664
    June   6       Total Landings =   262
    June   7       Total Landings =   931
```

Complete the documentation   Since the problem is designed to illustrate multi-dimensional arrays, the problem definition should include the description (and Figure 10–14) of the three-dimensional Traffic array. Collect the structure chart, pseudocode, code, and sample run. In the users' manual state the source code location (CH10J). The input file must be prepared in advance in order for the array to be filled properly.

Questions 10.5

1. Show at least two valid ways of defining each of the following arrays in Modula-2. How many elements are in each array?

    a. a table of the maximum REAL temperature at sites *A*, *B*, and *C* on each of the first ten days of the month.

    b. a chart showing whether it rained (TRUE or FALSE) at sites *A*, *B*, and *C* on each of the first ten days of the month.

    c. the number of times patients Johnson, Kennedy, and Larson awoke during the nights of May 28, 29, 30, and 31.

    d. the total inches of rainfall at four locations during each month June through August, in each year 1987 through 1992.

2. Given the code,

```
VAR  Data : ARRAY [1..5],[1..10] OF INTEGER;   i, j : INTEGER;
BEGIN
   FOR  i := 1 TO 5  DO
      FOR  j := 6 TO 10  DO
         Data[i, j] := i * j;   WriteInt(Data[i, j], 7);
      END; (* FOR j *)   WriteLn;
   END; (* FOR i *)
 . . . .
```

    a. what would be displayed by executing the code?

    b. what would be displayed if the order of the FOR statements were reversed?

    c. what would be displayed if the FOR *j* . . . statement were changed to

```
         FOR  j :=  i+1  TO  10  DO ?
```

3. What would be displayed if a program containing this code is executed?

```
VAR  Box : ARRAY [1..2],[1..5],[1..10] OF CARDINAL;
     i, j, k : CARDINAL;
BEGIN
   FOR  i := 1 TO 2  DO
      WriteString(''Table'');  WriteCard(i,3);
       WriteLn;
      FOR  j := 1 TO 5  DO
         FOR  k := 6 TO 10  DO
            Box[i, j, k] = i + j + k;
            WriteCard(Box[i][j][k],  7);
         END; (* FOR k *)   WriteLn;
      END; (* FOR j *)   WriteLn; WriteLn;
   END; (* FOR k *)
 . . . .
```

4. Given this code to display the data in array DollarTable of Figure 10–13,

```
FOR Row := 'a' TO 'c'  DO
   FOR  Column := 1 TO 2  DO
      FWriteReal(DollarTable[Row, Column], 10, 2);
   END; (* FOR Column *)
END; (* FOR Row *)
```

how would the display appear
a. with the code as written?
b. if WriteLn; were inserted between the two END; statements?
c. if WriteLn; followed the FWriteReal( ); command (but not between the END; statements)?

10.6   *Recursion and Arrays   (Optional)*

As discussed in Chapter 9, the recursive process reduces a problem to successively simpler versions of itself. The prospect of diminishing the length of an array with recursive calls to a procedure — until there may be only one or two elements left to consider — makes recursion a very attractive alternative technique for solving many problems involving arrays.

Reversing an Array

Although reversing the order of elements in an array is not difficult to accomplish with the use of iteration (see exercise 20 at the end of the chapter), this task can also be performed with recursion.

Example 10.6.1

Reverse the order of elements in an array by applying recursion.

Define the problem   Given an array, create and display a new array that contains the elements of the original array in reverse order.

Develop a solution   For purposes of illustration, assume INTEGER arrays defined by

```
CONST    LASTINDEX = 3;
TYPE     NUMLIST = ARRAY [0..LASTINDEX] OF INTEGER;
VAR      Original, Final : NUMLIST;
```

Read a list of four values into array Original. Assign Original to Final. Then reverse Final with a recursive procedure. FirstToLast, which picks off the LeftMost element of the array, shifts all of the other elements to the left one position, places the LeftMost element at the rightmost end of the array, and then calls itself with the length of the array reduced by one. Then display the Original and Final arrays.

Refine the solution   *Pseudocode*

```
begin module ReverseIt
    enter elements of Original array
    assign Original to Final
    call FirstToLast(Final, LASTINDEX)      (* FIRST CALL *)
    display Original and Final
end ReverseIt

procedure FirstToLast(VAR List:NUMLIST;    N:CARDINAL)
    if    N > 0         (* N is the current highest array index *)
       assign     List[0] to LeftMost
       shift all elements    List[1] to List[N] one position left
```

assign LeftMost to List[N]
call   FirstToLast(List, N − 1)   (* RECURSIVE CALL *)

Figure 10–16 traces the execution of this program and shows how the recursion works.

Modula-2 code   The recursive procedure FirstToLast repeatedly reduces the List to a shorter List and calls itself until only the 0th element remains.

```
MODULE ReverseIt;
   (* Uses recursion to reverse an array.
      FileName:CH10K    Modula-2    RKW    May 1991   *)

FROM InOut IMPORT WriteString, WriteLn, ReadInt, WriteInt, WriteCard;

CONST  LASTINDEX = 3;
TYPE   NUMLIST = ARRAY [0..LASTINDEX] OF INTEGER;
VAR  Original, Final : NUMLIST;     Count : CARDINAL;

PROCEDURE  WriteList(List : NUMLIST);
   VAR  Index : CARDINAL;
   BEGIN
      FOR  Index := 0 TO LASTINDEX  DO
         WriteInt(List[Index], 6); WriteLn;
      END; (* FOR *) WriteLn;
   END WriteList;

PROCEDURE FirstToLast(VAR List : NUMLIST;  N : CARDINAL);
   (* N = Largest Index to be considered in the List. *)
   VAR  LeftMost : INTEGER;   I : CARDINAL;
   BEGIN
      IF  N > 0  THEN
         LeftMost := List[0];
         FOR I := 0 TO N-1 DO  List[I] := List[I+1]; END;(*FOR*)
         List[N] := LeftMost;
         FirstToLast(List, N-1);    (* RECURSIVE CALL WITH SHORTER ARRAY *)
      END; (* IF *)
   END FirstToLast;

BEGIN   (* main module ReverseIt *)
   WriteString("Enter"); WriteCard(LASTINDEX+1, 5);
    WriteString(" integer values: ");  WriteLn;
   FOR Count := 0 TO LASTINDEX DO
      ReadInt(Original[Count]); WriteLn;
   END; (* FOR *)

   Final := Original;
   FirstToLast(Final, LASTINDEX);          (* FIRST CALL WITH INITIAL ARRAY *)
   WriteLn;
   WriteString("The original list is "); WriteLn; WriteList(Original);
   WriteString("The list reversed is "); WriteLn; WriteList(Final);
END ReverseIt.
```

Debug and test   It is easy to misplace commands in the recursive procedure so that the results achieved are not what you expected. Inserting supplemental write commands into the procedure that will display the List array and the value of

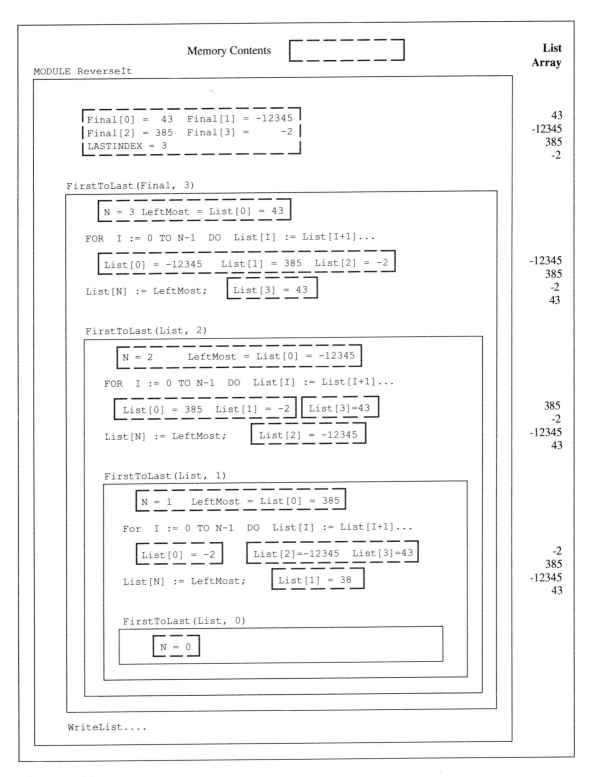

Figure 10–16
Trace of Recursion for ReverseIt (Example 10.6.1)

LeftMost immediately after they are produced will help you determine where any problems exist and what you need to do to correct them. Here are sample results:

```
Enter     4 integer values:
43
-12345
385
-2

The original list is
    43
-12345
   385
    -2

The list reversed is
    -2
   385
-12345
    43
```

Complete the documentation   In the algorithm development, describe the recursive technique used in procedure FirstToLast and include the pseudocode and trace of execution (Figure 10–16). A program listing (CH10K) and the sample run are important to include for prospective users who may wish to modify the program to handle CHARacter strings or other types of arrays.

Questions 10.6

1. Why are recursive techniques especially useful for manipulating arrays?
2. In Example 10.6.1, what modifications must be made to the code to reverse the characters in an array of CHARacters?
3. What Answer would be produced by this code? *Hint:* Try tracing execution in a diagram similar to Figure 10–16.

```
MODULE WhatNow;
   FROM RealInOut IMPORT FWriteReal;
   CONST  HOWFAR = 10;
   TYPE  NUMARY = ARRAY [1..HOWFAR] OF REAL;
   VAR  Count:CARDINAL;  Nums:NUMARY;   Answer:REAL;

PROCEDURE DoesIt(Array:NUMARY; HowManyNow:CARDINAL; VAR Result:REAL);
   BEGIN
      IF  HowManyNow > 0  THEN
         Result := Result + Array[HowManyNow];
         DoesIt(Array, HowManyNow-1, Result);
      END; (* IF *)
   END DoesIt;

BEGIN  (* WhatNow *)
   FOR Count := 1 TO HOWFAR DO  Nums[Count]:=FLOAT(Count*Count); END; (*FOR*)
   DoesIt(Nums, HOWFAR, Answer);
   FWriteReal(Answer,12,2);
END WhatNow.
```

10.7 *Focus on Problem Solving*

Arrays of CHARacters called *strings* are encountered so often that it is a good idea to create special procedures for handling them. In this section you will develop procedures to read and compare CHARacter strings. Then you will use these procedures to search and sort a list of names.

Definition of a String

A string is a one-dimensional array of CHARacters. Zero is almost always chosen as the first index in a string so that the string indices in a calling unit will correspond to those in procedures with formal open ARRAY OF CHAR parameters. For example, a declaration of strings of 80 characters could be written

```
CONST   LASTINDEX = 79;
TYPE    STRING = ARRAY [0..LASTINDEX] OF CHAR;
VAR     NameOne, NameTwo, NameThree, NameFour : STRING;
```

ReadString

You have already used procedure ReadString from the InOut module. For example, ReadString(NameThree) accepts characters from the keyboard or from a file into array NameThree. In most versions of Modula-2, ReadString terminates the read with any character whose code is less than or equal to the Space code. If you wanted NameThree to contain   Sly Old Fox,   you would have to respond to ReadString-(NameThree); with something like   Sly-Old-Fox,   replacing spaces with a printable character such as a hyphen (**-**).

A ReadLine procedure will be developed in this section to accept Spaces as valid characters in a string.

Assignment of Strings

A sequence of characters is assigned to a string variable simply by using double quotes (or single quotes if you prefer; see Section 3.3), as in

```
NameThree := ''Sly Old Fox'';
```

Every character or space between the quotes becomes part of the string. The result of such an assignment is shown in Figure 10–17.

String arrays of CHARacters obey the same rules as other arrays, and an entire array can be assigned to another array of the same type. For example, in Figure 10–17,

```
NameFour := NameThree;
```

would assign   Sly Old Fox   to array NameFour as well.

Individual characters in a string may be accessed by the appropriate index. Thus, for example,

```
Write(NameThree[0]); Write(NameThree[9]); Write(NameThree[5]);
  Write(NameThree[6]); WriteLn;
```

should display the characters

```
Sold.
```

```
CONST  LASTINDEX = 79;

TYPE  STRING = ARRAY [0..LASTINDEX] OF CHAR;

VAR  NameThree, NameFour : STRING;
```

```
NameThree := "Sly Old Fox";

NameFour  := NameThree;
```

	[0]	[1]	[2]	[3]	[4]	[5]	[6]	[7]	[8]	[9]	[10]	[11]	[12]	...	[79]
NameThree	S	l	y	sp	O	l	d	sp	F	o	x	0C			

	[0]	[1]	[2]	[3]	[4]	[5]	[6]	[7]	[8]	[9]	[10]	[11]	[12]	...	[79]
NameFour	S	l	y	sp	O	l	d	sp	F	o	x	0C			

The NULL CHARacter

In most implementations of Modula-2, the ReadString command or assignment of CHARacters to a string variable apply these two rules:

1. If the number of characters read or assigned is fewer than the number allowed by the string array definition, then a Null character (**0C,** ASCII 0) is assigned to the position following the last character entered into the array.
2. If the number of characters read or assigned is greater than or equal to the allowed length of the string, no Null character is assigned, and any additional characters beyond the largest string array index are ignored.

WriteString

The standard procedure WriteString, from module InOut, prints all characters until the end of the string or the Null character is encountered. For example, in Figure 10−17,

```
WriteString(NameThree); WriteLn;
```

would display   Sly Old Fox   , terminating at the Null character (0C) and ignoring whatever happened to be in character positions 12 through 79.

☐ A Strings Module

Most implementations of Modula-2 include a module of procedures for handling Strings. There is no standard for these modules, however, and Strings modules in different versions contain somewhat different procedures.

In this section, you will begin to develop a Strings module of your own, with a TYPE definition,

```
TYPE  STRING = ARRAY [0..79] OF CHAR;
```

corresponding to the 80-character width of a terminal screen. Also included will be

```
PROCEDURE  ReadLine(VAR Destination : ARRAY OF CHAR)
   (* Accepts Space as part of a String *)
```

and a function

```
PROCEDURE  CompareStrings(Source1,Source2:ARRAY OF CHAR):INTEGER;
   (* Allows you to determine the alphabetical order of Strings
   Source1 and Source2. *)
```

In addition, for convenience, your Strings module will contain a version of

```
PROCEDURE TabOrFill(HowMany : CARDINAL; FillCharacter : CHAR);
```

developed in Chapter 5, which writes the FillCharacter HowMany times. Also, a function

```
PROCEDURE Length(Source : ARRAY OF CHAR) : CARDINAL;
```

will be added, which RETURNs the total length of the Source string area or (when Null is present) the number of characters that precede Null.

This Strings module will be expanded with additional procedures in the next chapter. The complete Strings DEFINITION and IMPLEMENTATION modules are presented in Appendix C.

You have two choices for handling strings. Either you can apply the Strings procedures implemented in your system's Modula-2, or you can use the Strings procedures presented in Appendix C, which are developed here and used henceforth in this book.

The ReadLine Procedure

The procedure to read a string array, including all characters with code greater than or equal to the Space character (ASCII 32_{10}), is described by this pseudocode:

```
procedure ReadLine(VAR Destination : ARRAY OF CHAR)
begin with Index = 0     and     read Destination [0]
while     the character read > = Space character and
                              Index < allowed length of the string
   increment Index and read the next character
end while
assign the last character read (Destination[Index]) to
   a variable called Discard     and continue reading characters
   into variable Discard until an end of line (defined by a
   character such as Enter, with code < Space) is reached
if the allowed string length has not been reached and the last
   character not ignored is the end of line, then set that last
   character to Null
end ReadLine
```

The Modula-2 code for this procedure is shown in IMPLEMENTATION MODULE Strings in Figure 10–18. You can either import type STRING from module Strings or define your own arrays of CHARacters, such as

```
FROM Strings IMPORT STRING, ReadLine;
...
TYPE  STR1 := ARRAY [0..19] OF CHAR;
VAR   ShortString : STR1;  LongString : STRING;
      Again : ARRAY [0..2] OF CHAR;
```

In each situation,

```
ReadLine(ShortString); ReadLine(LongString); ReadLine(Again);
```

Figure 10–18
The Beginning of a
Strings Module
with TYPE
STRING,
PROCEDURE
ReadLine, and
Functions
CompareStrings
and Length
(continued)

```
DEFINITION MODULE Strings;
    (*  String handling functions and procedures. Strings are
        terminated by the Null chararacter or when the array
        is filled. *)

CONST  LASTINDEX = 79;  SPACE = ' ';  NULL = 0C;
TYPE   STRING = ARRAY [0..LASTINDEX] OF CHAR;
    (* STRING type may be imported and used when it is desired to
       handle 80-character strings as an abstract data type. *)

PROCEDURE  TabOrFill(HowMany:CARDINAL; FillCharacter:CHAR);
    (* Writes FillCharacter HowMany times. *)

PROCEDURE ReadLine(VAR Destination:ARRAY OF CHAR);
    (* Reads a string of characters, including spaces, until
       a character, such as Return, with ASCII less than 32 is read.
       A Null character marks the end of the string. If the number
       of characters exceeds the length of the string, the
       additional characters are discarded. ReadLine uses Read from
       the InOut module,so ReadLine is redirected when InOut is
       redirected. *)

PROCEDURE Length(Source:ARRAY OF CHAR): CARDINAL;
    (* Returns the CARDINAL number of characters in Source that
       precede the Null character, or the total length of the
       string space if the Null character is not present. *)

PROCEDURE CompareStrings(Source1,Source2:ARRAY OF CHAR):INTEGER;
    (* RETURNs -1 if Source1 comes alphabetically before Source2,
                0 if Source1 = Source2,
               +1 if Source1 comes alphabetically after Source2.*)

END Strings.
```

```
IMPLEMENTATION MODULE Strings;
    (* String-handling functions and procedures. Strings are
       terminated by the Null character or when the array is
       filled. *)

FROM InOut IMPORT Read, Write;

PROCEDURE TabOrFill(HowMany:CARDINAL;  FillCharacter:CHAR);
    VAR  Count : CARDINAL; (* Writes FillCharacter HowMany times. *)
    BEGIN
       For Count := 1 TO HowMany DO Write(FillCharacter);END; (*FOR*)
    END TabOrFIll;
```

the ReadLine procedure works equally well, because it handles an open ARRAY OF CHAR.

The CompareStrings Function
You may have tried unsuccessfully to compare two strings directly with relational operators, as in asking   IF Again >= ''Yes'' THEN... . A Statement like   IF Again >= ''Yes'' THEN...   is an attempt to compare CHARacter array Again with CHARacter array ''Yes.'' You really need to compare Again[0] with 'Y',

Figure 10 — 18
(*continued*)

```
PROCEDURE ReadLine(VAR Destination:ARRAY OF CHAR);
    (* Reads characters, including spaces, until end of line is
       encountered.
       YOU MAY WISH TO REMOVE
       Write(Destination[Index]) COMMANDS IF YOUR SYSTEM READ
       COMMAND ECHOES CHARACTERS TO THE SCREEN. *)
    VAR  Discard : CHAR;  Index : CARDINAL;
    BEGIN
        Index:=0; Read(Destination[Index]);Write(Destination[Index]);
        WHILE (Destination[Index] >= SPACE) AND
              (Index < HIGH(Destination)) DO
          INC(Index);  Read(Destination[Index]);
          Write(Destination[Index]);
        END; (* WHILE *)
        Discard := Destination[Index]; (* Discard additional
        characters. *)
        WHILE  Discard >= SPACE  DO  Read(Discard);  END; (*WHILE *)
        IF (Index <= HIGH(Destination)) AND
           ((Destination[Index])< SPACE) THEN
           Destination[Index] := Null; (*Insert Null if necessary.*)
        END; (* IF *)
    End ReadLine;

PROCEDURE Length(Source:ARRAY OF CHAR):CARDINAL;
    (* Returns the CARDINAL number of characters in Source that
       precede the Null character, or the total length of the
       string space if the Null character is not present. *)
    VAR Index : CARDINAL;
    BEGIN
        Index := 0;
        WHILE (Index <= HIGH(Source)) AND (Source[Index] <> NULL) DO
            INC(Index);
        END; (* WHILE *)
        RETURN Index;
    END Length;

PROCEDURE CompareStrings(Source1,Source2:ARRAY OF CHAR):INTEGER;
    (* RETURNs  -1 if Source1 comes alphabetically before Source2,
                 0 if Source1 = Source2,
                +1 if Source1 comes alphabetically after Source2. *)
    VAR  Index, MaxIndex : CARDINAL;  Result : INTEGER;
    BEGIN
        IF Length(Source1)<=Length(Source2)THEN
           MaxIndex:=Length (Source1)-1;
        ELSE MaxIndex:=Length(Source2)-1;
        END; (* IF *)
        Index := 0;  Result := 0;
        REPEAT
            IF       Source1[Index]>Source2[Index] THEN Result:=+1;
              ELSIF Source1[Index]<Source2[Index] THEN Result:=-1;
            END; (* IF *)  INC(Index);
        UNTIL  (Index > MaxIndex) OR (Result <> 0);
        IF (Result = 0) AND (Length(Source1)<>Length(Source2)) THEN
            IF       Length(Source1)>Length(Source2) THEN Result:=+1;
              ELSE  Result := -1;
            END; (* IF *)
        END; (* IF *)
        RETURN Result;
    END CompareStrings;

END Strings.
```

Again[1] with 'e', and Again[2] with 's'. In fact, the algorithm used to create a CompareStrings function compares the corresponding characters in two strings.

A CompareStrings function will need to obtain the Length of each string—the number of characters preceding the Null character, or the total length of the allowed string space if the Null character is not present. Because an open ARRAY OF CHAR begins with Index = 0, if Null is not present,

```
Length(Source) = HIGH(Source) + 1;
```

otherwise,

```
Length(Source) = position of the Null character.
```

The function

```
PROCEDURE CompareStrings(Source1, Source2 : ARRAY OF CHAR) : INTEGER;
```

will be defined to RETURN

```
-1  if  Source1 comes alphabetically before Source2,
 0  if  Source1 and Source2 are identical strings,  or
+1  if  Source1 comes alphabetically after Source2.
```

The first encounter with different corresponding characters in two strings determines their alphabetical order. For example, if

```
NameOne := ''Hurley'';  and
NameTwo := ''Humphrey'';
```

then CompareStrings(NameOne, NameTwo) should RETURN +1 because the *r* in *Hurley* follows the *m* in *Humphrey* alphabetically.

If the characters in two strings of different length are identical up to the end of the shorter string, then the longer string follows the shorter one alphabetically. For example, if

```
NameOne := ''Hurley'';  and
NameTwo := ''Hurleyson'';
```

then CompareStrings(NameOne, NameTwo) should RETURN −1, because *Hurley* precedes *Hurleyson* alphabetically.

Another important fact to remember when you are comparing strings containing lowercase and uppercase letters is that in ASCII, lowercase letters have larger codes than (and thus follow alphabetically) capital letters; in EBCDIC, the situation is reversed.

The pseudocode for a CompareStrings procedure appears as follows:

```
procedure CompareStrings(Source1,Source2:ARRAY OF CHAR):INTEGER;
    MaxIndex = length of shorter of Source1 or Source2 minus 1
    initialize    Index and Result to 0
    repeat (* compare character by character up to MaxIndex *)
        if    Source1[Index] > Source2[Index], then set    Result = +1
        else if    Source1[Index] < Source2[Index], then Result = -1
        increment Index
    until    Index > MaxIndex    or    Result <> 0
    if the strings are the same up to MaxIndex
                but Length(Source1) <> Length(Source2), then
            set Result = +1    if    Length(Source1) > Length(Source2)
            set Result = -1    if    Length(Source1) < Length(Source2)
    RETURN    Result
end CompareStrings
```

The Modula-2 code for CompareStrings is shown in IMPLEMENTATION MODULE Strings in Figure 10–18.

Searching and Sorting Arrays of Strings

Now that you can read and compare character strings, you are ready to search and sort them.

A Two-Dimensional Array of CHARacters

An array of strings representing a list of names is shown in Figure 10–19. Observe that an array of strings is actually a two-dimensional array of CHARacters, with each row representing a string. For example, in Figure 10–19,

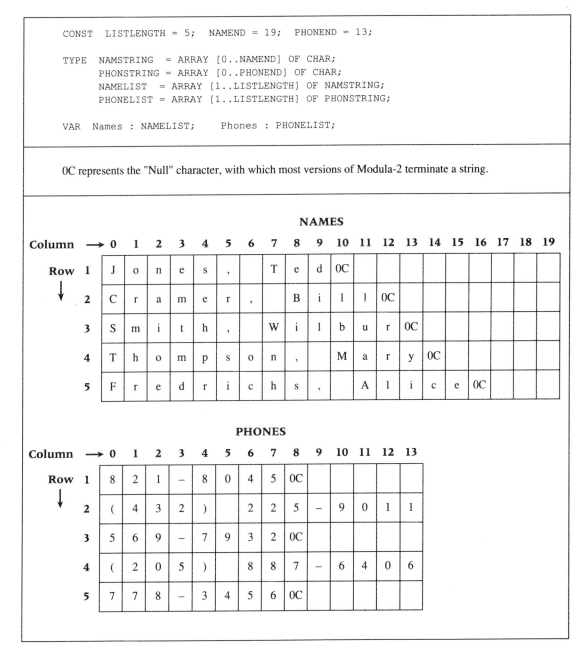

```
CONST  LISTLENGTH = 5;  NAMEND = 19;  PHONEND = 13;

TYPE  NAMSTRING  = ARRAY [0..NAMEND] OF CHAR;
      PHONSTRING = ARRAY [0..PHONEND] OF CHAR;
      NAMELIST   = ARRAY [1..LISTLENGTH] OF NAMSTRING;
      PHONELIST  = ARRAY [1..LISTLENGTH] OF PHONSTRING;

VAR  Names : NAMELIST;    Phones : PHONELIST;
```

0C represents the "Null" character, with which most versions of Modula-2 terminate a string.

NAMES

Column →	0	1	2	3	4	5	6	7	8	9	10	11	12	13	14	15	16	17	18	19
Row 1	J	o	n	e	s	,		T	e	d	0C									
2	C	r	a	m	e	r	,		B	i	l	l	0C							
3	S	m	i	t	h	,		W	i	l	b	u	r	0C						
4	T	h	o	m	p	s	o	n	,		M	a	r	y	0C					
5	F	r	e	d	r	i	c	h	s	,		A	l	i	c	e	0C			

PHONES

Column →	0	1	2	3	4	5	6	7	8	9	10	11	12	13
Row 1	8	2	1	–	8	0	4	5	0C					
2	(	4	3	2	)		2	2	5	–	9	0	1	1
3	5	6	9	–	7	9	3	2	0C					
4	(	2	0	5	)		8	8	7	–	6	4	0	6
5	7	7	8	–	3	4	5	6	0C					

Figure 10–19
Lists of Strings as Two-Dimensional Arrays of CHARacters

```
WriteString(Names[3]);   would display   Smith, Wilbur
WriteString(Phones[2]);   would display   (432) 225-9011, etc.
```

However, each character can be accessed by its position in the array. Thus, for example,

```
Write(Names[4,11]);   would display   a
Write(Names[2, 3]);   would display   m
Write(Phones[4, 0]);   would display   (, etc.
```

Example 10.7.1

Search and sort your "little black book" of names and phone numbers.

Define the problem   Names and phone numbers of your acquaintances are listed in haphazard order in a file:

```
Jones, Ted
821-8045
Cramer, Bill
(432) 225-9011
Smith, Wilbur
569-7932
Thompson, Mary
(205) 887-6406
Fredrichs, Alice
778-3456
```

Read these into the parallel string arrays shown in Figure 10–19. Present a menu that allows you to

- display the arrays
- find a phone number (given the name)
- sort by name
- quit

and perform the appropriate operations.

Develop the solution   Procedures ReadCharStrings and WriteCharStrings will incorporate FOR loops and commands ReadLine and WriteString to fill and display the arrays. The TabOrFill procedure will be invoked to write blanks from the end of a Name to the maximum Name length plus one, so that the Phone numbers can be aligned and displayed on the same line.

Procedure SearchForName will ask for a search Name and perform a linear search, and then display the Name and Phone number if found.

Procedure SortByName will perform an Insertion sort and write the sorted Names and Phone numbers to an output file.

Refine the solution   Declare the Names and Phones arrays shown in Figure 10–19. The pseudocode looks like

```
begin module SearchAndSortBlackBook
  ReadCharStrings(Names, Phones)
  repeat
```

```
        present menu  D        Display the Arrays
                      F        Find a Phone Number
                      S        Sort by Name
                      Q        Quit
        choose    D, F, S, or Q
        case    Choice    of
              D       WriteCharStrings(Names, Phones)
              F       SearchForNames(Names, Phones)
              S       SortByName(Names, Phones)
        until    Choice = Q
     end SearchAndSortBlackBook

     procedure ReadCharStrings(VAR Who:NAMELIST; VAR Number:PHONELIST)
        open input file
        use FOR loop to read names Who and phones Number
        close input file

     procedure WriteCharStrings(Who:NAMELIST;    Number:PHONELIST)
        use FOR loop to write names Who and phones Number
           use TabOrFill to align phone numbers

     procedure SearchForName(Who:NAMELIST;    Number:PHONELIST)
        ask for SearchName
        initialize    Index = 1    and    Found = FALSE
        repeat
           if    Who[Index] = SearchName
             set Found = TRUE, display Name and Number
           increment index
        until    Found    or    Index > ListLength
        if not Found,    print SearchName "is not on the list"

     procedure    SortByName(VAR Who:NAMELIST;    VAR Num:PHONELIST)
        adapt Insertion sort algorithm to sort by Who and interchange
           Who    as well as    Num    to keep arrays parallel
        open output file,    WriteCharStrings(Who, Num), close file
```

Modula-2 code Although the code appears lengthy, it consists of only four short procedures (to read, write, search, and sort parallel arrays of CHARacters), plus a menu-oriented driver program. Observe how CompareStrings, Length, and TabOrFill are used in procedures SearchForName and SortByName.

```
MODULE  SearchAndSortBlackBook;
   (* Reads names and numbers from a file, searches by name, and
      performs an insertion sort by name to a new file.
      FileName:CH10L    Modula-2    RKW    May 1991 *)

FROM InOut IMPORT WriteString, WriteLn, Read, Write,
                  OpenInput, CloseInput, OpenOutput, CloseOutput;
FROM Strings IMPORT ReadLine, Length, CompareStrings, TabOrFill;

CONST  LISTLENGTH = 5;  NAMEND = 19;  PHONEND = 13;  BLANK = ' ';
TYPE  NAMSTRING  = ARRAY [0..NAMEND]   OF CHAR;
      PHONSTRING = ARRAY [0..PHONEND]  OF CHAR;
      NAMELIST   = ARRAY [1..LISTLENGTH] OF NAMSTRING;
      PHONELIST  = ARRAY [1..LISTLENGTH] OF PHONSTRING;
VAR  Names : NAMELIST;  Phones : PHONELIST;
     Choice, Chose, Terminator : CHAR;
```

```
PROCEDURE   ReadCharStrings(VAR Who:NAMELIST;   VAR Number:PHONELIST);
   VAR   Count : CARDINAL;
   BEGIN
      WriteString("Name of Input file: "); OpenInput("IN"); WriteLn;
      FOR   Count := 1 TO LISTLENGTH   DO
         ReadLine(Who[Count]); ReadLine(Number[Count]); WriteLn;
      END; (* FOR *)
      CloseInput;
   END ReadCharStrings;

PROCEDURE   WriteCharStrings(Who:NAMELIST;   Number:PHONELIST);
   VAR   Count : CARDINAL;
   BEGIN
      FOR   Count := 1 TO LISTLENGTH   DO
         WriteString(Who[Count]);   (* Write Name and Blanks past NAMEND *)
          TabOrFill( NAMEND + 2 - Length(Who[Count]), BLANK );
         WriteString(Number[Count]); WriteLn;
      END; (* FOR *)
   END WriteCharStrings;

PROCEDURE   SearchForName(Who:NAMELIST; Number:PHONELIST);
   VAR   SearchName : NAMSTRING;   Index : CARDINAL;   Found : BOOLEAN;
   BEGIN
      WriteString("For which name (Last, First) are you searching? ");
       ReadLine(SearchName); WriteLn;
      Index := 1;  Found := FALSE;
      REPEAT
         IF   CompareStrings(Who[Index], SearchName) = 0   THEN
            Found := TRUE;  WriteString("Name and Phone Number:   ");
            WriteString(Who[Index]); WriteString("   ");
            WriteString(Number[Index]); WriteLn;
         END; (* IF *)
         INC(Index);
      UNTIL   Found OR (Index > LISTLENGTH);

      IF   NOT(Found)   THEN
         WriteString(SearchName); WriteString(" was not found."); WriteLn;
      END; (* IF *)
   END SearchForName;

PROCEDURE   SortByName(VAR Who:NAMELIST;   VAR Num:PHONELIST);
   VAR   LastSubListIndex,Indx:CARDINAL; NStr:NAMSTRING; PStr:PHONSTRING;
   BEGIN
      FOR   LastSubListIndex := 2 TO LISTLENGTH   DO
         Indx := LastSubListIndex;
         WHILE (Indx>1) AND (CompareStrings(Who[Indx],Who[Indx-1]) = -1) DO
            NStr:=Who[Indx]; Who[Indx]:=Who[Indx-1]; Who[Indx-1]:=NStr;
            PStr:=Num[Indx]; Num[Indx]:=Num[Indx-1]; Num[Indx-1]:=PStr;
            DEC(Indx);
         END; (* WHILE *)
      END; (* FOR *)
      WriteString("Name of Output File: "); OpenOutput("OUT"); WriteLn;
       WriteCharStrings(Who, Num); WriteLn;
      CloseOutput;
   END SortByName;
```

```
BEGIN
    ReadCharStrings(Names, Phones);
    REPEAT
        WriteLn; WriteString("Here are your choices:"); WriteLn;
            WriteString("   D    Display the Arrays.");       WriteLn;
            WriteString("   F    Find a Phone Number.");      WriteLn;
            WriteString("   S    Sort the Arrays by Name."); WriteLn;
            WriteString("   Q    Quit.");
        REPEAT
            WriteLn; WriteString("Choose one (D, F, S, or Q): ");
             Read(Choice); Read(Terminator); Write(Choice); WriteLn;
             Chose := CAP(Choice);
        UNTIL  (Chose='D') OR (Chose='F') OR (Chose='S') OR (Chose='Q');

        CASE   Chose  OF
            'D' : WriteCharStrings(Names, Phones); WriteLn |
            'F' : SearchForName(Names, Phones);    WriteLn |
            'S' : SortByName(Names, Phones);       WriteLn |
            'Q' : ;
        END; (* CASE *)
    UNTIL  Chose = 'Q';
END SearchAndSortBlackBook.
```

Debug and test With input from the file shown in *Define the Problem* at the beginning of this example, a sample run displays the data as it is read, then the menu. For a menu-choice *F*, you should see something like

```
Here are your choices:
    D   Display the Arrays.
    F   Find a Phone Number.
    S   Sort the Arays by Name.
    Q   Quit.
Choose the (D, F, S, or Q) : F
For which name (Last, First) are you searching? Thompson, Mary

Name and Phone Number: Thompson, Mary (205) 887-6406
```

Choosing *S* and then *D*, you should see

```
Cramer, Bill          (432) 225-9011
Fredrichs, Alice      778-3456
Jones, Ted            821-8045
Smith, Wilbur         569-7932
Thompson, Mary        (205) 887-6406
```

Test with uppercase and lowercase letters and valid and invalid menu choices. Search for names that are in the file and some that are not.

Complete the documentation In addition to the usual documentation, users should be warned that the SearchName must be entered exactly as it appears in the file, including capital letters, spaces, and commas. The source code (CH10L) must be accompanied by an input file.

Questions 10.7

1. Determine what functions and procedures are available with your computer's implementation of Modula-2 for reading CHARacter strings including Spaces, finding the Length of a string, and Comparing strings.

2. Suppose you declare

```
CONST  LASTINDEX = 9;
TYPE   STR = ARRAY [0..LASTINDEX] OF CHAR;
VAR    Phrase, WhatSaid : STR;
```

and assign Phrase := "Not so old";

a. What is the value of CompareStrings(Phrase, "Not too old")?

b. What happens on your system when you enter, in response to ReadString(WhatSaid), (1) Not so old; (2) Not-so-very-old?

c. What happens when you make the assignment WhatSaid := "Not so very old";?

3. Draw a diagram similar to Figure 10–19 to show what is in arrays WhatsIt[1] and WhatsIt[2] after executing this program. What is displayed by the program?

```
MODULE WhatsItDo;
   FROM InOut IMPORT WriteString, WriteLn, Write, WriteCard, WriteInt;
   FROM Strings IMPORT CompareStrings, Length;
   TYPE  WHAT = ARRAY ['a'..'z'] OF CHAR;  WHATLIST = ARRAY [1..2] OF WHAT;
   VAR   WhatsIt : WHATLIST;    Index : CHAR;   Count : CARDINAL;
BEGIN
   FOR  Index := 'a' TO 'm'  DO
      WhatsIt[1, Index]  :=  CAP(Index);
      WhatsIt[2, Index]  :=  CAP(CHR(ORD('z') - ORD(Index) + ORD('a')));
   END; (* FOR *)  WhatsIt[1,'n'] := 0C;  WhatsIt[2,'n'] := 0C; WriteLn;
   FOR  Count := 1 TO 2  DO
      FOR Index := 'a' TO 'm' DO Write(WhatsIt[Count][Index]); END; WriteLn;
   END; (* FOR *)  WriteLn;
   FOR Count := 1 TO 2 DO WriteString(WhatsIt[Count]); WriteLn; END; WriteLn;
   WriteCard(Length(WhatsIt[1]),6); WriteCard(Length(WhatsIt[2]),6); WriteLn;
   WriteInt(CompareStrings(WhatsIt[1], WhatsIt[2]), 6); WriteLn;
END WhatsItDo.
```

10.8 *Summary*

Arrays Arrays are structures containing ordered lists, tables, or larger collections of data, all of which are the same type.

One-Dimensional Arrays Arrays of one dimension are declared by specifying the name of the array, a range of enumerable *index* values, and the type of elements in the array, such as

```
TYPE   ARYONE = ARRAY [1..10] OF REAL;
VAR    Grades, OtherReals : ARYONE;
```

Individual elements of an array are accessed by the array name and index value — such as Grades[2] — and may be used where a variable of that type would be used.

Accessing a Complete Array An array can be accessed by its name without an index in only two situations:

- when an entire array is assigned to another array of identical type; for example OtherReals := Grades;
- when an entire array is passed as an actual parameter to a formal parameter of an identical array type or similar open type in a procedure.

Otherwise, all references must be to individual array elements.

Open Arrays   Formal array parameters in procedure headings may be *open,* in which case the index type and range chosen by the computer correspond to the actual array parameter. For example,

```
PROCEDURE SomeProcedure(VAR FormalValues : ARRAY OF REAL)
```

could accept array Grades, defined in the summary of one-dimensional arrays above, through a call

```
SomeProcedure(Grades)
```

The indices of an open array always begin with 0, so the call SomeProcedure(Grades) would create the correspondence

$$\begin{array}{rcl}
\text{Grades}[1] & \leftrightarrow & \text{FormalValues}[0] \\
\text{Grades}[2] & \leftrightarrow & \text{FormalValues}[1] \\
& \cdots & \\
\text{Grades}[10] & \leftrightarrow & \text{FormalValues}[\text{HIGH}(\text{FormalValues})]
\end{array}$$

where *HIGH* is a built-in standard function that RETURNs the largest index in an array.

Open arrays are especially valuable when you want to design a single procedure that handles single-dimension arrays with different index ranges, such as those found in standard module InOut, ProduceArray and WriteArray in your module RandGen, and those in the module Strings developed in Section 10.7.

Searching   The linear search algorithm is an $O(N)$ search. It examines each item in a list until the searched item is found or until it is determined that the item is not in the list.

Sorting   The Selection sort, Bubble sort, and Insertion sort are all $O(N^2)$ algorithms, which require an order of magnitude N^2 comparisons of items while sorting a list of N items. If the list is already partially sorted, the Insertion sort may be slightly more efficient than the other two.

Arrays with Two, Three, or More Dimensions   An array can be extended to tables or blocks of data by specifying multiple index ranges. You may visualize a two-dimensional array with rows and columns. Elements are often handled with nested FOR loops.

Recursion with Arrays   Many problems involving arrays lend themselves well to recursive solutions, where each successive recursive procedure call handles a smaller version of the array until there are only one or two elements left to consider.

Strings   A one-dimensional array of CHARacters is called a *String*. String handling is such a common task that most versions of Modula-2 include a Strings-handling module. However, such modules have not been standardized. In this chapter you began to develop your own Strings module with procedures TabOrFill and ReadLine and functions Length and CompareStrings. These procedures can be used to manipulate arrays of CHARacter strings.

10.9   *Exercises*

Exercises marked with (FileName: _____) indicate those that ask you to use, modify, or extend the text examples. The numbers in brackets, [ ], indicate the section that contains the material you need in order to complete the exercise.

1. [10.1] **a.** Write a program that reads a list of REAL percentage grades from the keyboard into an array. The grades are counted as they are read, and entry is terminated by entering a negative value. Then find and display the sum and average of the grades, and list the grades, printing an asterisk (*) in front of each one that falls below the average.

   b. Extend the program to display each grade and its letter equivalent and the letter equivalent of the average. Assume that 90–100 = A, 80–89 = B, 70–79 = C, 60–69 = D, and less than 60 = F.

2. [10.1] (FileName:CH10B) Modify program ReadText so that

   a. both the LetterCount and Frequency arrays are displayed.

   b. the Frequency array is displayed in terms of percentages, (100.0 * Frequency[Index]).

   c. the total number of characters (including spaces, punctuation, etc.) is counted; not just letters. A single Frequency for all nonletter characters is accumulated and displayed along with the Frequency array of the letters.

3. [10.1] Define an array PeopleCount of CARDINAL values for the numbers of Infants, Children, Youths, and Adults.

   As people enter a sports arena, the gatekeeper pushes the appropriately marked keys on a hand-held terminal. When she presses the "Child" key, for example, a *C* is recorded, the "Adult" key records an *A*, etc., and a data file is produced that looks like

   ```
   ACIYYYAACIY....
   ```

   Given such a file (which you can create artificially using an editor), read the characters and accumulate the count of each type of person into the array PeopleCount. Then write to an output file a table of the number of people of each category that were admitted. You may designate the end of the input file either by using Done (imported from InOut) or by placing *X* at the end of the file as a sentinel. Have the program ignore all characters in the file except *I, C, Y,* and *A*.

4. [10.1] (FileName:CH10A) In TestBigFact (Example 10.1.1),

   a. print the results without all of the leading zeros. *Hint:* check the digits and print the remaining number, beginning with the first nonzero digit.

   b. allow factorials up to 69! (which contains 100 digits), and print all of the factorials from 1! to *n*! instead of just the final factorial answer.

   c. add procedure BigFactorial (with 100 digits) to module MyMath.

5. [10.1] Write a program that reads two numbers, each up to 20 digits long; adds them; and displays the result.

6. [10.3] Read a sentence with a maximum of 100 characters, one character at a time, from the keyboard into an array of CHARacters. Entry will terminate with a period (.). Search the array to determine how many times a particular character, specified by the user at the keyboard, occurs in the sentence.

7. [10.4] Read numerical grades into an array from the keyboard. Terminate with a negative entry. Sort and print the grades in *descending* order.

8. [10.4] Read a file containing the last name and age of each child in a group into a Name array and a parallel Age array. Sort and display a list of the children and their ages in order of increasing age.

9. [10.4] Write and test a procedure that returns the positions of the largest and smallest values in any array of REAL numbers, regardless of the range of indices. *Hint:* See the algorithm in the Selection sort for finding the largest value.

10. [10.3] Write and test a function that uses an open array of CHARacters and RETURNs the position of the first occurrence of a user-specified letter in the array or RETURNs -1 if the letter does not occur.

11. Given a one-dimensional array of REAL numbers, find the sum of the numbers
   a. [10.1] using iteration.
   b. [10.6] using recursion. *Hint:* for VAR Num:ARRAY[1..n] OF REAL, if $n = 1$, then the sum is Num[1]; otherwise the sum is Num[n] plus the sum of the first $(n - 1)$ elements.

12. Given a one-dimensional array, print it backward
   a. [10.1] using a simple FOR loop with decreasing indices;
   b. [10.6] using recursion. *Hint:* for VAR LIST:ARRAY [1..n] OF SomeType, if $n = 1$ then print list[1]; otherwise, print List[n] and print the array from 1 to $(n - 1)$ backward.

13. [10.5] Read a list of numbers from a file and insert in row order

```
FOR   ROW  : =  ...
   FOR   Column  : =  ...
```

into a two-dimensional CARDINAL array with the size (Rows, Columns) specified by the user. Then print the array as a two-dimensional table and find and display the sum of all the elements in the array.

14. [10.5] Write one procedure that generates a multiplication table and a second procedure that displays the table. Allow the user to specify the maximum Size—so the table goes from 1 * 1 to Size * Size—and print only those values below the diagonal (see exercise 15 at the end of Chapter 8).

15. [10.5] A matrix is a two-dimensional array of numbers. The sum of two matrices A and B of the same size is a matrix of that size, and each of its elements is the sum of the corresponding elements in A and B. That is, Sum[i,j] = $A[i,j]$ + $B[i,j]$, as illustrated in Figure 10–20. Write a program that adds matrices. *Hint:* Write procedures to read elements into a matrix, to display a matrix in appropriate form, and to accept two matrices and find their sum.

Figure 10–20
The Sum of Matrices (Exercise 15)

$$\begin{pmatrix} 2 & 3 & -1 \\ 5 & 6 & 4 \end{pmatrix} + \begin{pmatrix} 7 & 13 & 9 \\ -8 & 11 & 0 \end{pmatrix}$$

$$= \begin{pmatrix} 2+7 & 3+13 & -1+9 \\ 5+(-8) & 6+11 & 4+0 \end{pmatrix}$$

$$= \begin{pmatrix} 9 & 16 & 8 \\ -3 & 17 & 4 \end{pmatrix}$$

16. [10.5] A magic square is a square array of numbers with N rows and N columns, in which each of the CARDINAL values from 1 to $(N * N)$ appears exactly once, and in which the sum of each column, each row, and each principal diagonal is the same value. For example, Figure 10–21 shows a magic square in which $N = 3$ and the sum of the rows, columns, and diagonals is 15. Write a program that constructs and displays a magic square for any given odd number N. The algorithm is

Insert 1 in the middle of the first row, [Row, Column] = [1, $(N+1)$ DIV 2]
After a number x has been placed, move up one row and to the right one column. Place the next number, $x + 1$, there, *unless*:
    (1) you move off the top (to Row 0) in a Column. Then move to the bottom row and place the next number, $x + 1$, in the bottom row of that Column.
    (2) you move off the right end (to Column = $N + 1$) of a row. Then place $x + 1$ in the first column of that row.
    (3) you move to a position that is already filled or out of the upper-right corner (to Row = 0, Column = $N + 1$). Then place $(x + 1)$ immediately below x.

17. [10.5] Among other applications, "Pascal's triangle" (see Figure 10–22) provides a means of determining the number of possible combinations $C(n,r)$ of n things taken r at a time. For example, the number of possible combinations of five things taken two at a time — that is, $C(5,2)$ — is 10.

Each row begins and ends with 1. Each other element in the row is the sum of the element directly above it and the element to the left of the one above. That is,

Element [n, r] = Element [n - 1, r] + Element [n - 1, r - 1]

Write a program to create and display the first 11 rows of an array representing Pascal's triangle, such that when the user specifies values of $n(< 11)$ and $r(<= n)$, the program displays the value of $C(n,r)$.

18. [10.5] Some prisoners of war devised a system for communicating with each other through the walls of their solitary-confinement cells that is based on arranging the letters of the alphabet in 5 rows:

a	b	c	d	e
f	g	h	i	j
l	m	n	o	p
q	r	s	t	u
v	w	x	y	z

The prisoners spelled messages to each other by tapping the row and column numbers of the letters on the wall, substituting c for the omitted k. For example, h would be 2 taps (row 2), a short pause, and then 3 taps (column 3); and *help* would be "2,3 1,5 3,1 3,5," the digit pairs representing the number of taps for row and column.

Figure 10–21
A Magic Square
(Exercise 16)

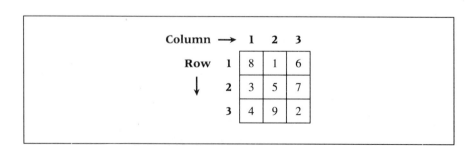

Figure 10–22
Pascal's Triangle
(Exercise 17)

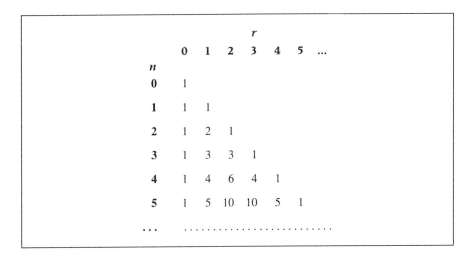

Write a program that loads a two-dimensional array with the letters in the table. Then write a procedure to search the array for the letters in a given string and to convert the string to taps representing the row, column number pairs. Then write a procedure to reverse the process; that is, to convert a sequence of digit pairs to a message string.

19. [10.5] A three-dimensional weather array for the months of July and August of 1991 has planes labeled by the month numbers [7..8]. In each plane there are rows numbered [1..31] representing days, and two columns labeled *A* and *B* representing the day's REAL high and low temperatures, respectively.

Write a program that asks for or assigns the high and low temperatures to the array. Then allow the user to request

- which month and day had the highest temperature, and which had the lowest,
- what were the low and high temperatures for any given day, and
- what was the average high and average low temperature for a given month.

20. [10.6] (FileName:CH10K) Rewrite Example 10.6.1 using iteration rather than recursion to reverse an array.

21. [10.7] **a.** As an employee of the power company, your job is to sit at a keyboard and enter customers' names and number of kilowatt-hours of electricity each used during the preceding month. These names and numbers are placed into parallel arrays of strings and of REAL numbers. Entries are counted as they are entered, and entry terminates when customer name *ZZZZZZ* is entered. Multiply each of the kilowatt-hour array elements by 8.7 cents per kilowatt-hour to produce an array of costs. Calculate and display the total number of kilowatt-hours used, the total cost of electricity used by all customers, and the average cost per customer.

b. Sort the arrays alphabetically by customer name, and display a table of

```
Customer Name    Kilowatt-hours    Cost(Dollars)
```

for all customers. Flag the entry of each customer who is using more than the average by printing an asterisk (*) before the customer name.

22. [10.7] (FileName:CH10L) Extend SearchAndSortBlackBook (Example 10.7.1) to

a. include addresses.

b. put names in alphabetical order by first name when the last names are the same. *Hint:* Use ReadString to read LastName and FirstName into separate arrays. If LastNames are the same, compare FirstNames.

c. have procedure SearchForName ask for a LastName as a SearchName. Then display the names, addresses, and phone numbers of all people in the list who have that last name.

11

Strings and Enumeration Data Types

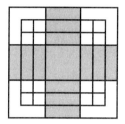

Chapter Outline

In Chapter 10, you began developing a Strings module containing procedures and functions for manipulating CHARacter arrays. This chapter begins by expanding that module and extending your expertise in handling character strings.

Four of the standard data types—CARDINAL, INTEGER, CHAR, BOOLEAN—are **enumerable;** their possible values can be counted. These four types, and the fifth standard type REAL, are *scalar* types, as opposed to composite, *structured* types such as arrays. The standard data types are also **ordered;** that is, when two values are specified, it is clear which one comes first. For numeric types this order is specified by each number's position on the number line; for BOOLEAN data, the order is defined as FALSE and then TRUE.

The BOOLEAN data type is unique among the five standard data types, in that its two values (FALSE and TRUE) constitute a short list. Thus, it can also be regarded as an **enumeration type,** since it can be specified easily by listing every possible value. This chapter will extend the scalar types available to you. One method of doing this is to limit an existing enumerable type to a subrange of its values; another method is to list all possible values for new enumeration types.

11.1 *The Strings Module*

As discussed in Section 10.7, your version of Modula-2 probably will be accompanied by a module that contains procedures for manipulating character strings. However, opinions differ about how strings should be handled, so the procedures and functions contained by your module may differ from those of other versions of Modula-2.

String-Handling Functions and Procedures

The minimum string-handling capabilities provided by most compilers are listed in Figure 11–1. Both the DEFINITION and IMPLEMENTATION modules containing these procedures are presented in Appendix C so that you can readily locate them when you need them. You can invoke the Strings module incorporated in your compiler, but you will need to examine the module carefully to determine any differences in procedure names and parameters. Examples and exercises in this book incorporate the functions and procedures described in Figure 11–1 and Appendix C. Function Position and procedures Concatenate, Assign, Copy, Delete, and Insert have been added to TabOrFill, Length, and CompareStrings, which were developed in Section 10.7. Learning how these work will strengthen your ability to manipulate arrays.

Using the Definition of a String

Strings can be manipulated either by considering one character at a time or by invoking string-handling procedures. The example here illustrates string handling using the definition of a string as an array of CHARacters and ReadLine, Compare-Strings, and Length from the Strings module.

Figure 11−1
Common
String-Handling
Functions and
Procedures (See
also DEFINITION
and
IMPLEMENTATION
MODULE Strings
in Appendix C.)

Assume definitions

```
VAR   Source, Source1, Source2, Destination : ARRAY OF CHAR;
      Symbol, FillCharacter : CHAR;
      HowMany, Index, StartIndex, CopyHowMany, DeleteHowMany,
                                  InsertPosn : CARDINAL;
```

Built-In Standard Functions

```
HIGH(Source)
   (* Returns the CARDINAL value of the largest index in the open
      array of characters representing the string source. *)
SIZE(Source)
   (* Returns the number of storage units, i.e., array locations,
      allocated for the storage of Source. In some versions of
      Modula-2, SIZE must be imported from SYSTEM or another
      module. *)
Symbol  :=  Source[Index]
   (* Assigns the character from Source at position Index, where
      indices in an array of length n range from 0 through n-1,
      to the character variable Symbol. *)
Source[Index]  :=  Symbol
   (* Replaces the character at position Index in string Source
      with the character represented by Symbol. *)
```

Procedures Imported from Standard Module InOut

```
ReadString(Destination)
   (* Reads a character string into array Destination. Input is
      terminated by a blank or Enter. Leading blanks are ignored.
      The Null character, 0C, indicates the end of the string. *)
WriteString(Source)
   (* Writes the characters from Source until the Null character,
      0C, or the end of the string is encountered. *)
```

(*continued*)

Example 11.1.1

Determine whether or not a string is a palindrome.

Define the problem Accept a string of characters entered from the keyboard into an array. Determine whether the string is a palindrome; that is, does it read the same backward and forward?

Develop a solution An original string with 80 or fewer characters is entered using the ReadLine procedure. Then the string array will be copied, one character at a time, into a second array. Each letter will be capitalized, and all nonalphabetic characters will be ignored. This capitalized array will be reversed, and both arrays will be displayed. CompareStrings will determine whether the capitalized string and its reverse are equivalent.

Refine the solution *Pseudocode*

begin module PalindromeTest
  ReadLine(OriginalString) from the keyboard

Figure 11–1
(continued)

Functions from a Strings Module

```
Length(Source)
    (* Returns the CARDINAL number of characters in Source that
        precede the Null character, 0C, or the total length of the
        string space if the Null character is not present. *)
Position(Source, Destination)
    (* Returns the index position of the first character in the
        first occurrence of substring Source within string
        Destination. If Source is not found in Destination, then
        Position returns the Length of the Destination string. *)
CompareStrings(Source1, Source2)
    (* Returns INTEGER
            -1  if Source1 comes alphabetically before Source2,
             0  if Source1 = Source2,
            +1  if Source1 comes alphabetically after Source2. *)
```

Procedures from a Strings Module

```
TabOrFill(HowMany, FillCharacter)
    (* writes FillCharacter  HowMany times *)
ReadLine(Destination)
    (* Reads a string of characters, including spaces, until a
        character, such as Enter, with ASCII less than decimal 32
        is read. *)
Concatenate(Source1, Source2, Destination)
    (* Appends the string Source2 to the end of string Source1
        and stores the result in string location Destination.
        If the concatenated strings will not fit into Destination,
        then the leftmost characters up to the Length of the
        Destination space are stored. *)
Assign(Source, Destination)
    (* Copies string Source to string Destination. If Length
        (Source) > HIGH(Destination), then the leftmost characters
        from Source are copied until Destination is filled. *)
Copy(Source, StartIndex, CopyHowMany, Destination)
    (* Characters from Source, beginning at position StartIndex,
        and continuing for CopyHowMany number of characters, are
        copied to string location Destination. If CopyHowMany >
        SIZE(Destination), then the leftmost characters from Source
        are copied until Destination is filled. *)
Delete(Source, StartIndex, DeleteHowMany)
    (* DeleteHowMany number of characters are deleted from Source,
        beginning with the character at position StartIndex;
        the remaining characters in Source are shifted left to fill
        in the spaces left by the deletions. *)
Insert(Source, Destination, InsertPosn)
    (* Inserts string Source into Destination beginning at position
        InsertPosn in Destination. If inserting all of Source would
        result in a string that exceeds the memory allocated for
        Destination, then Source is inserted and the result is
        truncated, so that Destination is filled. *)
```

```
CopyAndCap(OriginalString, CapitalString)
ReverseIt(CapitalString, ReverseString)
display CapitalString and ReverseString
CompareStrings(CapitalString, ReverseString)
   and state whether a palindrome or not
end PalindromeTest

CopyAndCap(OrigString;   VAR CapString)
  begin with OrigIndex and CapIndex both zero
  repeat
     if   OrigString[OrigIndex] is a letter
        capitalize and assign to CapString[CapIndex],
          increment CapIndex
       end if
       increment OrigIndex
     until OrigIndex exceeds HIGH(OrigString) or Null encountered
     if   CapIndex <= HIGH(CapString) terminate with Null

ReverseIt(CapString, VAR RevString)
  set   LastIndex = Length(CapString) − 1
  for   Index = 0 to LastIndex
     RevString[Index] = CapString[LastIndex − Index]
  end for
  if   LastIndex < HIGH(CapString) terminate with Null
```

Modula-2 code

```modula2
MODULE  PalindromeTest;
   (* Accepts a String and determines whether it is a palindrome.
      FileName:CH11A      Modula-2      RKW      June 1991 *)

FROM InOut IMPORT WriteString, WriteLn;
FROM Strings IMPORT ReadLine, Length, CompareStrings;

CONST  NULL = 0C;
TYPE STRING = ARRAY [0..79] OF CHAR;
VAR  OriginalString, CapitalString, ReverseString : STRING;

PROCEDURE CopyAndCap(OrigString:STRING;   VAR CapString:STRING);
   VAR  OrigIndex, CapIndex : CARDINAL;    Letter : CHAR;
   BEGIN
      OrigIndex := 0;   CapIndex := 0;
      REPEAT
         Letter := CAP(OrigString[OrigIndex]);
         IF   (Letter >= 'A') AND (Letter <= 'Z') THEN
            CapString[CapIndex] := Letter;   INC(CapIndex);
         END; (* IF *)   INC(OrigIndex);
      UNTIL (OrigIndex > HIGH(OrigString)) OR (OrigString[OrigIndex] = NULL);
      IF CapIndex <= HIGH(CapString) THEN CapString[CapIndex] := NULL; END;
   END CopyAndCap;

PROCEDURE  ReverseIt(CapString:STRING;   VAR RevString:STRING);
   VAR Index, LastIndex : CARDINAL;
   BEGIN
      LastIndex := Length(CapString) - 1;
      FOR  Index := 0  TO  LastIndex  DO
         RevString[Index] := CapString[LastIndex - Index];
      END; (* FOR *)
```

```
      IF LastIndex < HIGH(CapString) THEN RevString[LastIndex+1]:=NULL; END;
   END ReverseIt;

BEGIN (* module PalindromeTest *)
   WriteString("Enter a string, 1 to 80 characters."); WriteLn;
    WriteString("At least one character must be a letter."); WriteLn;
    ReadLine(OriginalString); WriteLn; WriteLn;

   CopyAndCap(OriginalString, CapitalString);
   ReverseIt(CapitalString, ReverseString);

   WriteString("The capitalized and reversed strings are:"); WriteLn;
    WriteString(CapitalString); WriteLn;
    WriteString(ReverseString); WriteLn; WriteLn;

   IF  CompareStrings(CapitalString, ReverseString) = 0  THEN
      WriteString("The string is a PALINDROME!"); WriteLn;
   END; (* IF *)
END PalindromeTest.
```

Debug and test   It is easy to commit range errors in this program by exceeding the array index limits or using an empty string. Supplemental write statements to display indices will help you find and correct such errors. The order of the UNTIL conditions in procedure CopyAndCap takes advantage of short-circuit evaluation to prevent a range error in the absence of Null. A sample run with a palindrome appears as

```
Enter a string, 1 to 80 characters.
At least one character must be a letter.
Stop, pots!

The capitalized and reversed strings are:
STOPPOTS
STOPPOTS

The string is a PALINDROME!
```

Complete the documentation   Explain what a palindrome is and how this program detects them. Include pseudocode, code (CH11A), and sample runs. Warn the users that the string entered must contain at least one alphabetic character.

STRING as an Abstract Data Type

A declaration

```
TYPE  STRING = ARRAY [0..79] OF CHAR;
```

is included in the DEFINITION MODULE Strings in Appendix C. This STRING type, together with the operations defined for it by the procedures in the Strings module, constitute an **abstract data type.** A user can import STRING and manipulate variables of that type, using the operations defined for it, without ever having to know that its underlying definition is an array of CHARacters with indices beginning at 0.

User-defined strings whose indices begin with values other than 0 would not be abstract. The user would have to understand how the Strings module functions and procedures operate in order to adjust the index values RETURNed and/or passed as parameters.

The following example illustrates the use of STRING as an abstract data type.

Example 11.1.2

Censor a text by replacing selected words.

Define the problem The user will specify which words are to be replaced in a block of text and with what they will be replaced. The text will be read from an input file. The censored text will be written to the screen and finally to an output file. Multiple replacements of a repeated word will occur, and additional words may be specified for replacement.

Develop a solution Text will be defined as an array of STRINGs. The lines will be read using ReadLine and terminated by pressing Enter. The text will be terminated at the end of a maximum number of lines or by a blank line of length zero (press Enter twice). Figure 11–2 illustrates how Position, Delete, and Insert are used to censor each line.

Refine the solution *Pseudocode*

```
begin module Censor
    ReadText from the input file and WriteText
    repeat
        ask for OldWord to Delete, ask for NewWord replacement,
        CensorIt, then ask if the user would like to censor more
    until no more
```

```
OldWord to censor   : the;          Length("the") = 3
NewWord replacement : my
```

Line to be censored:

0	1	2	3	4	5	6	7	8	9	10	11	12	13	14	15	16	17	18	19	20	21	22	23
T	h	e		t	h	e	m	e		i	s		t	h	e		b	e	s	t	.	0C	

First Pass*

Position("the", Line) = 4   Delete(Line, 4, 3);

0	1	2	3	4	5	6	7	8	9	10	11	12	13	14	15	16	17	18	19	20	21	22	23
T	h	e		m	e		i	s		t	h	e		b	e	s	t	.	0C				

Insert("my", Line, 4);

0	1	2	3	4	5	6	7	8	9	10	11	12	13	14	15	16	17	18	19	20	21	22	23
T	h	e		m	y	m	e		i	s		t	h	e		b	e	s	t	.	0C		

Second Pass

Position("the", Line) = 12   Delete(Line, 12, 3);

0	1	2	3	4	5	6	7	8	9	10	11	12	13	14	15	16	17	18	19	20	21	22	23
T	h	e		m	y	m	e		i	s		b	e	s	t	.	0C						

Insert("my", Line, 12);

0	1	2	3	4	5	6	7	8	9	10	11	12	13	14	15	16	17	18	19	20	21	22	23
T	h	e		m	y	m	e		i	s		m	y		b	e	s	t	.	0C			

Third Pass
Stop   Position("the", Line) = 20 = Length(Line)

* Note: *The* differs from *the* and is not replaced.

Figure 11–2
Censoring a Line (Example 11.1.2)

```
        WriteText to screen and output file
        end Censor

        procedure ReadText
            open input file,      initialize line count to 0
            repeat
                increment line number, ReadLine of text
            until a line of length 0 or maximum number of lines is reached
            if length of last line is 0
                decrement line count to ignore last empty line

        procedure CensorIt
            for all lines
                repeat
                    find Position of Oldword, Delete OldWord, Insert NewWord
                until Position becomes end of line
```

        procedure WriteText
          for all lines   WriteString(line of text),   WriteLn

Modula-2 code Observe the use of abstract data type STRING and its defined operations ReadLine, Position, Length, Delete, Insert, and CompareStrings. Nowhere in this code does the programmer need to know or use the underlying definition of STRING as an array of characters.

```modula-2
MODULE Censor;
  (* Replaces censored words in a block of text.
     File Name:CH11B    Modula-2    RKW    June 1991  *)

FROM InOut   IMPORT WriteString, WriteLn, ReadString, OpenInput,
                    CloseInput, OpenOutput, CloseOutput;
FROM Strings IMPORT STRING, Position, Length, ReadLine,
                    Insert, Delete, CompareStrings;

CONST  MAXLINES = 10;
TYPE   LINES = ARRAY [1..MAXLINES] OF STRING;
VAR  Text : LINES;    NumLines : CARDINAL;    OldWord, NewWord : STRING;
     Again : ARRAY [0..2] OF CHAR;

PROCEDURE ReadText(VAR Text:LINES; VAR LineCount:CARDINAL);
   BEGIN
      WriteString("Name of input file?"); OpenInput("IN");
      LineCount := 0;
      REPEAT
        INC(LineCount);  ReadLine(Text[LineCount])
      UNTIL  (Length(Text[LineCount]) = 0)  OR  (LineCount = MAXLINES);
      IF  Length(Text[LineCount]) = 0   THEN
         DEC (LineCount);   (* Ignore an empty last line. *)
      END; (* IF *)
      CloseInput;
   END ReadText;

PROCEDURE CensorIt(VAR Text:LINES; NumLines:CARDINAL; LoseIt,FindIt:STRING);
   VAR  Where, LineNo : CARDINAL;
   BEGIN
      FOR  LineNo := 1 TO NumLines  DO
         REPEAT
            Where := Position(LoseIt, Text[LineNo]);
            IF  Where < Length(Text[LineNo])   THEN
               Delete(Text[LineNo], Where, Length(LoseIt));
               Insert(FindIt, Text[LineNo], Where);
            END; (* IF *)
         UNTIL  Where = Length(Text[LineNo]);
      END; (* FOR *)
   END CensorIt;

PROCEDURE WriteText(Text:LINES; NumLines:CARDINAL);
   VAR  LineNo : CARDINAL;
   BEGIN
      FOR  LineNo := 1 TO NumLines  DO
         WriteString(Text[LineNo]); WriteLn;
      END; (* FOR *)
   END WriteText;
```

```
BEGIN   (* Module Censor *)
    ReadText(Text, NumLines);    WriteLn;
     WriteString("Original:"); WriteLn; WriteText(Text, NumLines);
     WriteLn; WriteLn;

    REPEAT
        WriteString("Word to censor:    "); ReadString(OldWord); WriteLn;
        WriteString("Replacement word: "); ReadString(NewWord);
        CensorIt(Text, NumLines, OldWord, NewWord); WriteLn; WriteLn;
        WriteString("Censor more (yes or no)? "); ReadString(Again); WriteLn;
    UNTIL  CompareStrings(Again,"yes") <> 0;

    WriteLn;
    WriteString("Censored:"); WriteLn; WriteText(Text, NumLines); WriteLn;
    WriteLn; WriteString("To what file to write censored text? ");
     OpenOutput("OUT");  WriteText(Text, NumLines); CloseOutput;
END Censor.
```

Debug and test Problems in this program can be attacked by examining one procedure at a time. Adding a WriteString(Text[LineCount]) command immediately after ReadLine(Text[LineCount]) in Procedure ReadText will assure you that each line is read correctly. Next concentrate on WriteText, which is short enough that most problems should be syntax errors caught by the compiler. In CensorIt, displaying the value of Where, and adding diagnostic WriteString(Text[LineNo]) commands after each call to Delete and Insert, will produce a trace of the censor process similar to Figure 11–2.

After removing all of the diagnostic commands, a sample run appears as

```
Name of input file? CH11B.IN

Original:
Our time is marked by the prominence of the sciences.
It is marked by very rapid changes and very great growth -
growth in science, growth in productivity, growth in population,
growth in travel, growth in communication.
              J. Robert Oppenheimer, The Flying Trapeze, 1964

Word to censor:   growth
Replacement word: expansion

Censor more (yes or no)? yes
Word to censor:   n
Replacement word: x

Censor more (yes or no)? no

Censored:
Our time is marked by the promixexce of the sciexces.
It is marked by very rapid chaxges axd very great expaxsiox -
expaxsiox ix sciexce, expaxsiox ix productivity, expaxsiox ix populatiox,
expaxsiox ix travel, expaxsiox ix commuxicatiox.
              J. Robert Oppexheimer, The Flyixg Trapeze, 1964


To what file to write censored text? CH11B.OUT
```

Complete the documentation Documentation includes the usual problem description, pseudocode, code, and sample run. Explain what it means that STRING is used as an abstract data type. In the users' manual state the source code (CH11B) and that users will be asked to enter the following information:

1. Name of the input file. The input file must contain text of 80 or fewer characters per line and must be terminated by pressing Enter. The file should end with a blank line (an extra Enter) if it contains fewer lines than specified by MAX-LINES.
2. Words to censor and replacement words. Answer "Censor more (yes or no)?" with *no* or *yes* (not *Yes* or *YES*).
3. Name of the output file for the final censored text.

Questions 11.1

1. Given

```
VAR   Locution: ARRAY [0..39] OF CHAR;
      Which : CARDINAL;
...
Assign  (''Hot dogs and mustard!'', Locution);
```

   a. What is displayed by

```
FOR  Which := 4 TO 6  DO  Write(Locution[Which]); END;
```

   b. What value is returned by Position("and", Locution)?
   c. Write the code to replace *mustard* with *ketchup*.

2. Given STRING imported from Strings, and this code:

```
VAR  S1, S2, S3 : ARRAY [0..9] OF CHAR;
     T1, T2 : STRING;
...
ReadLine(S1); (* Answer with   ''Nobody knows''  *)
Assign (''Go for it!'', S2);
Assign ('' Sometimes all good people must make it happen. '', T1);
```

   a. What is displayed by

```
WriteString(S1); WriteLn; WriteString(S2); WriteLn;
WriteCard(Position(''body'', S1), 3); WriteLn;
WriteCard(Position(S2, T1), 3); WriteLn;
```

   b. What is displayed by

```
Assign(T1, S3);  WriteString(S3);  WriteLn;
Assign(T1, T2);  Copy(S1, 0, 7, S3);
Concatenate(S3, S2, S3); WriteString(S3); WriteLn;
Delete(T2, 14, 4);  Insert(S2, T2, 14);
WriteString(T2);  WriteLn;
```

3. Modify program Censor (Example 11.1.2, CH11B) so that it recognizes
   a. only free-stranding OldWords to be censored. *Hint:* precede and follow Old-Word with space.
   b. *yes*, *Yes*, and *YES* in response to "Censor more?".

11.2 *Subrange Types*

One simple method of building a new data type is to limit the number of values you use from an enumerable type, such as by declaring

```
TYPE  AGE = [0..120];  UPPERCASE = ['A'..'Z'];
VAR  HowOld : AGE;  Symbol : UPPERCASE;
```

This way, variable HowOld is limited to CARDINAL values from 0 to 120, and Symbol is restricted to the alphabet CHARacters from *A* to *Z*. Assigning a value less than 0 or larger than 120 to HowOld or any character other than a capital letter to Symbol should result in a runtime range error, which will terminate program execution.

You can define subranges of the enumerable data types, but not of REAL. Four syntaxes for defining variables with subrange types are illustrated in Figure 11–3. Syntax II, in which the TYPE is declared explicitly and the base type is not specified, is the most commonly used. A type that is not declared explicitly in a TYPE statement is said to be "anonymous." InitialConstant and FinalConstant are literal values of the same enumerable type. These constants define the limits of values of that type that can be assigned to variables within the particular subrange. If left anonymous, the *base type* is determined by the type of InitialConstant and FinalConstant. Thus, in Figure 11–3, the base types of variables HowOld, Symbol, and HowHot are CARDINAL, CHAR, and INTEGER, respectively.

Order of Declarations

Modula-2 allows considerable flexibility in the order in which CONSTants, TYPEs, and VARiables are declared. An important rule is that a TYPE definition must precede the declaration of any VARiable of that type. Normally, if constants, types, variables, and procedures are all declared, they are declared in the order shown in Figure 11–4. However, the order of declarations between the IMPORT lists and BEGIN can be changed and mixed, as long as each identifier is defined before it is used.

Generally, the executable instructions in a program work only with variables, not with type names. For example, you can assign values to variables HowOld and Symbol, but not to types AGE or UPPERCASE; you can increment HowOld, but not AGE; and so on.

Writing and Reading Subrange Type Variables

Procedures in module InOut allow you to write the values of variables of a given subrange type by using the appropriate Write . . . command for the base type of that subrange. For example, you may

```
WriteCard(HowOld, 5);
Write(Symbol);
WriteInt(HowHot, 6);
```

Many implementations of Modula-2 allow you to read a variable of a subrange type by using the InOut module Read . . . command of the appropriate base type. However, some will not allow you to read subrange variables this way; and many will not check to determine that the value is in the proper range when the InOut Read . . . commands are used.

Figure 11–3
Declaring Variables
of Subrange Type

Syntax I (Declare a TYPE and Base Type explicitly.)

  TYPE TypeName = BaseTypeName[InitialConstant . . FinalConstant];
  VAR VariableName : TypeName;

Example: ```
TYPE AGE=CARDINAL[0..120]; UPPERCASE=CHAR['A'..'Z'];
VAR HowOld : AGE;   Symbol : UPPERCASE;
```

---

**SyntaxII**  (Declare a TYPE explicitly; leave Base Type anonymous.)

  TYPE TypeName = [InitialConstant . . FinalConstant];
  VAR  VariableName : TypeName;

*Example:*  ```
TYPE TEMPERATURE = [-40..212];  AGE = [0..120];
     LOWERCASE = ['a'..'z'];
VAR  HowHot : TEMPERATURE;  HowOld : AGE;
     Letter : LOWERCASE;
  (* HowHot is a subrange of INTEGER. HowOld is a
     subrange of CARDINAL. Letter is a subrange of
     CHAR. *)
```

Syntax III (Make TYPE anonymous; Base Type explicit.)

  VAR VariableName : BaseTypeName[InitialConstant . . FinalConstant];

Example: ```
VAR HowHot:INTEGER[-40..212]; Symbol:CHAR['A'..'Z'];
```

---

**Syntax IV**  (Leave both TYPE and Base Type anonymous.)

  VAR  VariableName : [InitialConstant . . FinalConstant];

*Example:*  ```
VAR  HowOld : [0..120]  HowHot : [-40..212];
     Letter : ['a'..'z'];
  (* HowHot is a subrange of INTEGER. HowOld is a
     subrange of CARDINAL. Letter is a subrange of
     CHAR. *)
```

To ensure readability and range checking,

1. declare a variable of the appropriate base type,
2. use the corresponding InOut Read . . . command, and
3. assign the value read to the subrange type variable.

Range checking is performed when the assignment occurs. For example, the instructions

```
...
TYPE  TEMPERATURE : [-40..212];
VAR  HowHot : TEMPERATURE:    EnterTemp : INTEGER;
...
BEGIN
  WriteString(''Enter temperature: '');
    ReadInt(EnterTemp); WriteLn; HowHot := EnterTemp;
```

Figure 11-4
Common Order of
Declarations

```
MODULE  Name;

    IMPORT  lists;

    CONSTant  definitions;

    TYPE  definitions;

    VARiable  declarations;

    PROCEDURE  definitions;


    BEGIN  (* module Name *)

        ...
```

```
    WriteString("The temperature is ");
        WriteInt(HowHot, 10); WriteLn;
    ....
```

will read an INTEGER value EnterTemp, assign its value to HowHot (or produce a range error message if EnterTemp lies outside the -40 to 212 range), and display the value of HowHot.

☐ Reasons for Using Subranges

So why use subranges at all? Although they may strike you as only a nuisance, they *do* prevent users from entering values outside the desired range. Any attempt to assign a value outside the allowed subrange of a variable should cause a runtime error. Such errors, which usually terminate program execution, should be prevented in a finished program; but subrange checking can be especially valuable in debugging a program. It helps detect where calculations are producing incorrect results and where safeguards should be inserted to prevent users from entering incorrect values. Another reason for declaring subranges is that subrange variables may need less memory. Variable HowOld, for example, is restricted to CARDINAL values less than 121, which can be stored in 7 bits rather than the 16 required on most small systems for storing unrestricted CARDINAL numbers. Finally, and perhaps most important, anyone who reads a program with declared subranges can discover immediately the expected range of values for a given variable.

☐ Range Checking

Ideally, the computer should always check variables to determine whether they lie within the proper range, unless you specify that you do not want such range checking to occur. Unfortunately, checking for range errors expands the size of the object code. Therefore, many Modula-2 compilers will not require the computer to check whether subrange conditions are met unless you specifically turn on subrange checking by specifying a parameter or flag—such as **/R, .R,** or **$R**—when you compile. Refer to your compiler manual for the convention used on your system.

Consider the following example, which illustrates how variables of subrange type may be passed as parameters to and from procedures.

A Bit of Background

Whoops!

In the "old days" of computing, the physicists at a large international laboratory in Europe used Control Data Corporation (CDC) computers. It is rumored that when CDC sent them a new ver- sion of their language compiler that included range checking, the physicists demanded to have the old version back because their programs would no longer run.

Example 11.2.1

Add time in hours, minutes, and seconds.

Define the problem Given the current time on a 24-hour (military) clock, mea- sured in hours, minutes, and seconds, determine what time it will be, including the number of days later, when some number of hours, minutes, and seconds are added to that time.

Develop a solution Users will enter the initial time in Hours, Minutes, and Sec- onds. Then the amount of time to be added—AddHours, AddMinutes, AddSeconds—will be requested, and the new time will be calculated by the algorithm

```
TempSeconds : = Seconds + Addseconds;
NewSeconds  : = TempSeconds MOD 60;
TempMinutes : = Minutes + Add Minutes + TempSeconds DIV 60;
NewMinutes  : = TempMinutes MOD 60;
TempHours   : = Hours + AddHours + TempMinutes DIV 60;
NewHours    : = TempHours MOD 24;
Days        : = TempHours DIV 24;
```

Days, NewHours, NewMinutes, and NewSeconds will be displayed to the screen as well as the initial time and the amount of time added. Minutes and Seconds vari- ables will be declared as a subrange [0..59] of base type CARDINAL. Hours will be limited to [0..23], and Days will simply be CARDINAL. The number of minutes and seconds to be added will be limited to values between 0 and 59, but the number of hours to be added will not be limited.

Refine the solution *Pseudocode*

```
begin module AddTime
  ask for initial Hr, Min, and Sec (procedure EnterTime)
  ask for AddHr, AddMin, and AddSec (procedure EnterTime)
  calculate Days, NewHr, NewMin, and NewSec (procedure CalcNewTime)
    (* see algorithm above *)
  echo initial time, added time, and new time (procedure WriteTime)
```

Modula-2 code

```
MODULE AddTime;
    (* Adds military time in hr, min, and sec, with range checking.
     FileName:CH11C.MOD     Modula-2     RKW     June 1991  *)

FROM InOut IMPORT WriteString, WriteLn, ReadCard, WriteCard;
```

```
TYPE M60CARD = [0..59];   M24CARD = [0..23];
VAR Sec, AddSec, NewSec, Min, AddMin, NewMin : M60CARD;
    Hr, NewHr : M24CARD;      AddHr, Days : CARDINAL;

PROCEDURE  EnterTime(VAR Hr : CARDINAL;   VAR Min, Sec : M60CARD);
    VAR  InHr, InMin, InSec : CARDINAL;
    BEGIN
        WriteString("Hours              : "); ReadCard(InHr);   WriteLn;
        WriteString("Minutes (0 to 59): "); ReadCard(InMin); WriteLn;
        WriteString("Seconds (0 to 59): "); ReadCard(InSec); WriteLn; WriteLn;
        Hr := InHr; Min := InMin; Sec := InSec;
    END EnterTime;

PROCEDURE  CalcNewTime(Sec,AddSec,Min,AddMin:M60CARD;  Hr:M24CARD;
                       AddHr:CARDINAL;   VAR NewSec,NewMin:M60CARD;
                       VAR NewHr:M24CARD;  VAR Days:CARDINAL);
    VAR  TempSec, TempMin, TempHr : CARDINAL;
    BEGIN
        TempSec := Sec + AddSec;                      NewSec := TempSec MOD 60;
        TempMin := Min + AddMin + TempSec DIV 60;  NewMin := TempMin MOD 60;
        TempHr  := Hr  + AddHr  + TempMin DIV 60;  NewHr  := TempHr  MOD 24;
        Days    := TempHr DIV 24;
    END CalcNewTime;

PROCEDURE  WriteTime(Hr:CARDINAL; Min,Sec:M60CARD);
    BEGIN
        WriteCard(Hr,5); WriteCard(Min,10); WriteCard(Sec,10);
    END WriteTime;

BEGIN (* module AddTime *)
    WriteString("Enter current time (hours between 0 and 23):"); WriteLn;
    EnterTime(Hr, Min, Sec); WriteLn;
    WriteString("Enter time to add  (hours >= 0):"); WriteLn;
    EnterTime(AddHr, AddMin, AddSec); WriteLn;


    CalcNewTime(Sec,AddSec,Min,AddMin,Hr,AddHr,NewSec,NewMin,NewHr,Days);

    WriteLn; WriteString("           Hours    Minutes    Seconds"); WriteLn;
    WriteString("Begin Time: "); WriteTime(Hr, Min, Sec); WriteLn;
    WriteString("Add Time:   "); WriteTime(AddHr, AddMin, AddSec); WriteLn;
    WriteString("Final Time: "); WriteTime(NewHr, NewMin, NewSec);
    WriteCard(Days,7); WriteString(" days later."); WriteLn;
END AddTime.
```

Debug and test In procedure EnterTime, the times are read as CARDINAL values InHr, InMin, and InSec, and assigned to Hr, Min, and Sec for range checking. Because AddHr can be any CARDINAL value, parameter Hr in EnterTime and WriteTime is declared as CARDINAL, rather than as type M24CARD. Hand-check the code carefully to make certain that the equations have been entered correctly. InHr, InMin, InSec, and TempHr, TempMin, TempSec are the only variables whose values are not echoed to the screen. You may wish to display these variables and check that assignments and calculations are being performed as you expected.

Test the program with variables within and outside the acceptable ranges. Do not forget to specify the range-checking option when you compile, if your system

---

MOD 60

Before 1700 B.C. the Mesopotamians developed a calendar with 360 days per year, which had to be adjusted periodically to make up for the extra 5¼ days it takes the earth to complete its yearly revolution around the sun. However, 360 days is very close to 12 complete cycles of lunar phases (months), and certainly, 360 was expressed nicely in the Mesopotamian base-60 number system. In fact, in modern symbols, 360 (base 10) = 6 (base 60). Thus it was natural that the circle should be divided into 360 units (now called *degrees*), which in turn were divided into 60 sub-units (minutes), and further divided into 60 parts (seconds).

By the peak of Greek civilization the stars had been grouped into constellations. Twelve of these, which the Greeks called the *zodiac*, lie along the ecliptic path traced by the sun in its apparent annual trek around the earth. Each constellation of the zodiac rises over the eastern horizon and sets in the west during a daily apparent revolution of the stars about the earth. Hence, there are 12 risings and 12 settings, or 24 periods (now called *hours*), in a day.

---

requires it. Try values that give zero answers for hours, minutes, or seconds. Try values that result in carries to each time unit. What happens if you enter negative values for any of the variables? Here is a sample run:

```
Enter current time (hours between 0 and 23):
Hours          : 13
Minutes (0 to 59): 05
Seconds (0 to 59): 49

Enter time to add  (hours >= 0):
Hours          : 182
Minutes (0 to 59): 58
Seconds (0 to 59): 47


             Hours   Minutes   Seconds
Begin Time:    13        5        49
Add Time:     182       58        47
Final Time:     4        4        36      8 days later.
```

Complete the documentation   The pseudocode indicates that the equations from the "Develop a Solution" phase are to be incorporated. Therefore, those equations, and the problem definition, should be included in the documentation, along with the pseudocode, code, and sample run. Source code is in file CH11C. Users should be warned about the range of values allowed when entering times.

Questions 11.2

1. In general, to whom is it more important to specify subrange types in a program, the programmer or the user? Why?
2. Given the declarations,

   ```
   TYPE  SKYSCRAPER = [-6..30];
   VAR  Floor : SKYSCRAPER;   PushButton : INTEGER;
   ```

   a. what is the anonymous base type of Floor?

b. what commands would you issue to accept a value from the keyboard that could be assigned to variable Floor, and that would be checked for the appropriate range?

3. What is wrong with this code? Correct it so that it works, with range checking.

```
...
TYPE  PEOPLE = CHAR ['A'..'C'];
VAR  Who : PEOPLE;
...
BEGIN
   WriteString("What type of person are you (A, B, or C)? ");
    Read(PEOPLE); WriteLn; WriteLn;
   Write(Who); Write(PEOPLE); WriteString(" are supposed to be ");
   CASE  Who  OF
      'A' : WriteString("aggressive.")   |
      'B' : WriteString("moderate.  ")   |
      'C' : WriteString("laid back. ");
   END; (* CASE *)  WriteLn;
....
```

4. In program AddTime (Example 11.2.1, CH11C) if users enter hours, minutes, or seconds outside of the appropriate ranges, the program terminates with a range-error message. Make the program user-proof; that is, make it ask again, instead of terminating, when a user enters an incorrect value.

11.3   *User-Defined Types*

Other types can be defined by the programmer in Modula-2. These are called *enumeration* types, because all possible values for variables of these types must be enumerated—that is, listed. The primary purpose of using enumeration types is to make a program easier to read by listing the specific values that can be assigned to the variables and limiting those values to meaningful names. Syntaxes for defining an enumeration-type variable in Modula-2 are shown in Figure 11–5. The constants in the list of identifiers are scalar values. They are ordered by their appearance in the list and are treated throughout a module—and in all included procedures—as constants. The rules for the scope of the type, variables, and constant identifiers are the same as for any other identifier. Suppose, for example, that you declare variables Color and Beans as in Figure 11–5. Then you could assign Color := Orange and Beans := Pinto, but *not* Color := 3, Color := 'R', Beans := 5, and so on.

Operations on Enumeration Types

The built-in operations available for enumeration types are defined by the

- assignment operator   :=
- relational operators   <, <=, >, >=, =, and # or <>
- ordinal functions   ORD, VAL,
- ordinal procedures   INC, DEC.

You can assign appropriate values to an enumeration-type variable and compare values of the variable, such as

```
Color := Green;
IF Color > Orange THEN
```

Figure 11–5
Syntaxes for
Defining an
Enumeration-Type
Variable

Syntax I (Enumeration Type is explicit.)

TYPE   EnumerationTypeName = (list of constant identifiers);
VAR   VariableName : EnumerationTypeName;

Example: ```
TYPE RAINBOW=(Red, Orange, Yellow, Green, Blue, Violet);
VAR Color : RAINBOW;
```

---

**Syntax II** (Enumeration Type is anonymous.)

VAR   VariableName : (list of constant identifiers);

*Example:*   ```
VAR  Beans : (Lima, Pinto, Snap, Black, Chili);
```

```
(* Color > Orange is TRUE, since Green follows Orange
   in the type definition of Figure 11-5. *)
...
```

You can find the position of a scalar value in the type identifier list. For example, the statements

```
Color := Green;
WriteCard(Ord(Color), 4); (* ORD(Green) = 3 *) WriteLn;
```

display the position 3. Observe that counting begins with 0, so

```
when  Color := Red,     ORD(Color) is 0,
when  Color := Orange,  ORD(Color) is 1,
...
when  Color := Violet,  ORD(Color) is 5.
```

To find which constant value occupies a given position in the list, use VAL with the type name; so

```
VAL(RAINBOW, 0)  is  Red,
VAL(RAINBOW, 2)  is  Yellow,  etc.
```

Finally, you can increment and decrement the values of enumeration-type variables. For example,

```
Color := Green;
INC(Color, 2) (* changes the value of Color to Violet. *)
Color := Green;
DEC(Color, 2) (* changes the value of Color to Orange. *)
```

Of course, if you try to increment or decrement past the end of the list in either direction, such as in

```
Color := Orange; DEC(Color, 3);
```

you probably will encounter a range error.

Rules for Enumeration Types

Mutual Exclusivity
The same constant value may not be used in two types. These definitions would be invalid:

```
TYPE RAINBOW = (Red, Orange, Yellow, Green, Blue, Violet);
     PRIMARY = (Red, Yellow, Blue);
VAR  Color : RAINBOW;  Paint : PRIMARY;
     NoBeans : (Lima, Pinto, Green, Black, Chili);
```

You would get an error message such as "doubly defined identifier" because type PRIMARY uses the same identifiers as type RAINBOW. Also, the anonymous type for NoBeans contains Green, which duplicates an identifier in RAINBOW.

However, subranges of enumeration types may be declared and defined. Thus, these declarations would be valid:

```
TYPE  RAINBOW = (Red, Orange, Yellow, Green, Blue, Violet);
      YELLOWISH = [Orange..Green];
      BLUISH = [Blue..Violet];
      VERYRED = [Red..Red];  (* short, but legal *)
VAR   Color : RAINBOW;
      MidColor : YELLOWISH;  HighFrequencyColor : BLUISH;
      RedColor : VERYRED;
```

Then, of course, the values that could be assigned to variable HighFrequencyColor would be limited to Blue and Violet; the values allowed for MidColor would be Orange, Yellow, and Green; and the variable RedColor could accept only the value Red.

No Standard Enumerable Type Values

Enumeration-type constants must be mutually exclusive with the standard enumerable types (CARDINAL, INTEGER, CHAR, or BOOLEAN) as well as with each other. Therefore, these declarations would not be valid:

Invalid Type	Reason
TYPE BLOOD = ('A', 'B', 'O');	'A', 'B', 'O' are constants of CHAR type.
TYPE ROWS = (5, 15, 26);	5, 15, 26 are constants of CARDINAL type.
TYPE WHETHER = (TRUE, FALSE);	TRUE, FALSE are constants of BOOLEAN type.

Of course, you can declare types to be subranges of the standard enumerable types or with literals other than CHARacters, such as

Valid Type
TYPE BLOOD = (A, B, O, AB);
TYPE LINES = [5..26];
TYPE WHICH = [FALSE..TRUE];

☐ Reading and Writing Enumeration Types

Since the values in enumeration types are defined in the program that uses them, there can be no standard utility procedures in Modula-2 for reading and writing these values. You will need to write your own procedures to handle reading and writing the values of the variables of the enumeration types you define. However, ORD and WriteCard may be useful in debugging. For example, the commands

```
Color := Blue;
IF Color = Blue THEN WriteCard(ORD(Color), 1); END; (* IF *)
```

would display the position 4, which tells you that the value of Color is the fifth (remember, Counting begins at Red with 0) constant in the list, or the value Blue.

Procedures ReadRainbow and WriteRainbow in the following program allow you to read and write values of type RAINBOW. CASE is applied to the enumerable values Red..Violet in procedure WriteRainbow. In procedure ReadRainbow, however, CASE could not be used because the tested values are strings (such as ''Yellow''), not enumerable values.

```
MODULE TestReadAndWriteRainbow;
   (* Tests procedures to read and write colors.
      FileName:CH11D      Modula-2      RKW        June 1991  *)

FROM InOut IMPORT WriteString, WriteLn, ReadString;
FROM Strings IMPORT CompareStrings;

TYPE  RAINBOW = (Red, Orange, Yellow, Green, Blue, Violet);
VAR   Color : RAINBOW;

PROCEDURE WriteRainbow(Shade:RAINBOW);
   (* Accepts a value of type RAINBOW and displays a corresponding string. *)
   BEGIN
      CASE   Shade   OF
         Red   : WriteString("Red")    |   Orange: WriteString("Orange") |
         Yellow: WriteString("Yellow") |   Green : WriteString("Green")  |
         Blue  : WriteString("Blue");  |   Violet: WriteString("Violet");
      END; (* CASE *)
   END WriteRainbow;

PROCEDURE ReadRainbow(VAR Shade:RAINBOW);
   (* Asks for a color in the form of a string, and assigns the
      equivalent value from TYPE RAINBOW to the variable Shade  *)
   VAR  Hue : ARRAY [0..5] OF CHAR;   Accepted : BOOLEAN;
   BEGIN
      REPEAT
         WriteString("Enter one of the following colors"); WriteLn;
         WriteString("Red, Orange, Yellow, Green, Blue, or Violet:  ");
         ReadString(Hue);  Accepted := TRUE;  WriteLn;

         IF     CompareStrings(Hue,  "Red")    = 0   THEN   Shade := Red;
         ELSIF  CompareStrings(Hue,  "Orange") = 0   THEN   Shade := Orange;
         ELSIF  CompareStrings(Hue,  "Yellow") = 0   THEN   Shade := Yellow;
         ELSIF  CompareStrings(Hue,  "Green")  = 0   THEN   Shade := Green;
         ELSIF  CompareStrings(Hue,  "Blue")   = 0   THEN   Shade := Blue;
         ELSIF  CompareStrings(Hue,  "Violet") = 0   THEN   Shade := Violet;
         ELSE
            Accepted := FALSE; WriteLn; WriteString("Try again! "); WriteLn;
         END; (* IF *)
      UNTIL  Accepted;
   END ReadRainbow;

BEGIN   (* module TestReadAndWriteRainbow *)
   ReadRainbow(Color);
   WriteLn; WriteString("The value of variable Color is ");
   WriteRainbow(Color); WriteLn;
END TestReadAndWriteRainbow.
```

☐ A Beginner's Expert System

This example suggests some practical uses for enumeration types.

Example 11.3.1

Write a simple expert system program that will help a customer select the microcomputer best-suited to him or her.

Define the problem Your store sells three models of microcomputers:

- the Amarti, priced at $1500, which handles color graphics well
- the Jonathan, priced at $2500, which is extremely user-friendly
- the JCN, priced at $5000, which has lots of memory and hard-disk space; designed for computer professionals, it does a reasonable job with color graphics.

Write a program that gives the user these choices:

- How much Money can you spend? $2000, $3000, $6000
- What is the most important Application: Color graphics, user Friendly, Professional work?

If the Money and the Application match one of your machines, suggest the appropriate computer; otherwise, recommend another store.

Develop a solution Enumeration types will be used for the Money and Application choices. Also an enumeration type MICROS will be defined with the names of the three computers plus None and AnotherStore. Since MICROS will be used only within procedure MakeRecommendation (and nested procedure WriteComputerChoice), type MICROS will be declared and defined there. The structure chart in Figure 11–6 is a diagram of the rules for making the decisions.

Refine the solution *Pseudocode*

```
begin module ComputerChoices
   PresentMoneyMenu
      ask for Money: TwoThousand, ThreeThousand, SixThousand
   PresentApplicationMenu
      ask for Application: Color, Friendly, Professional
   MakeRecommendation
      Computer2 = None
      case Money
         TwoThousand :   case Application
                           Color      : Computer = Amarti
                           else         Computer = Another Store
         ThreeThousand: case Application
                           Color      : Computer = Amarti
                           Friendly   : Computer = Jonathan
                           else         Computer = Another Store
         SixThousand :   case Application
                           Color        : Computer = Amarti
                                           Computer2 = JCN
                           Friendly     : Computer = Jonathan
                           Professional : Computer = JCN
      write Computer Choice
         if Computer2 <> None, write Computer2
end ComputerChoices
```

Figure 11–6
Structure Chart for ComputerChoices (Example 11.3.1)

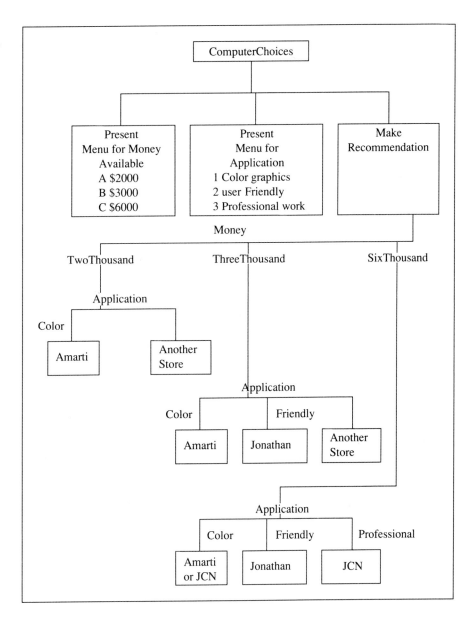

Modula-2 code

```
MODULE ComputerChoices;
   (* Simple expert system to choose between three computers.
      FileName:CH11E       Modula-2       RKW       June 1991 *)

FROM InOut IMPORT Read, Write, WriteString, WriteLn;

TYPE  COST = (TwoThousand, ThreeThousand, SixThousand);
      USES = (Color, Friendly, Professional);
VAR  Money:COST;  Application:USES;

PROCEDURE PresentMoneyMenu(VAR Amount:COST);
   VAR MoneyChoice, CapMoney, Discard : CHAR;
```

```
BEGIN
   REPEAT
      WriteLn; WriteString("How much money do you have? "); WriteLn;
      WriteString("      A      $2000.00"); WriteLn;
      WriteString("      B      $3000.00"); WriteLn;
      WriteString("      C      $6000.00"); WriteLn;
       WriteString("Choose one (A, B, or C): ");
       Read(MoneyChoice); Read(Discard);
       CapMoney :=  CAP(MoneyChoice); Write(CapMoney); WriteLn;
   UNTIL  (CapMoney >= 'A') AND (CapMoney <= 'C');
   CASE  CapMoney  OF
      'A' : Amount := TwoThousand |   'B' : Amount := ThreeThousand |
      'C' : Amount := SixThousand;
   END; (* CASE *)
END PresentMoneyMenu;

PROCEDURE PresentApplicationMenu(VAR IWant:USES);
   VAR ApplChoice, Discard : CHAR;
   BEGIN
      REPEAT
         WriteLn; WriteString("What should the computer do? "); WriteLn;
         WriteString("      1      Handle Color Graphics"); WriteLn;
         WriteString("      2      Be Very User Friendly"); WriteLn;
         WriteString("      3      Handle Professional Work"); WriteLn;
          WriteString("Choose one (1, 2, or 3): ");
          Read(ApplChoice); Read(Discard); Write(ApplChoice); WriteLn;
      UNTIL  (ApplChoice >= '1') AND (ApplChoice <= '3');
      CASE  ApplChoice  OF
         '1' : IWant := Color |    '2' : IWant := Friendly |
         '3' : IWant := Professional ;
      END; (* CASE *)
   END PresentApplicationMenu;

PROCEDURE MakeRecommendation(Money:COST; Application:USES);
   TYPE  MICROS = (Amarti, Jonathan, JCN, None, AnotherStore);
   VAR Computer, Computer2 :MICROS;
   PROCEDURE WriteComputerChoice(Machine:MICROS);
      BEGIN
         CASE  Machine  OF
            Amarti        : WriteString("Amarti")                |
            Jonathan      : WriteString("Jonathan")              |
            JCN           : WriteString("JCN")                   |
            None          : WriteString("no computer at all") |
            AnotherStore  : WriteString("another store")         ;
         END; (* CASE *)
      END WriteComputerChoice;

   BEGIN (* MakeRecommendation *)
      Computer2 := None;
      CASE  Money  OF
         TwoThousand   : CASE  Application  OF
                            Color    : Computer := Amarti   ;
                            ELSE        Computer := AnotherStore ;
                         END | (* CASE *)
         ThreeThousand : CASE  Application  OF
                            Color    : Computer := Amarti    |
```

```
                                 Friendly : Computer := Jonathan ;
                                 ELSE        Computer := AnotherStore ;
                           END | (* CASE *)
          SixThousand    :   CASE  Application  OF
                                 Color    : Computer := Amarti;
                                           Computer2:= JCN        |
                                 Friendly : Computer := Jonathan |
                                 Professional : Computer := JCN;
                           END ; (* CASE *)
      END; (* CASE *)  WriteLn;
      WriteString("You probably would be happiest with ");
       WriteComputerChoice(Computer);
      IF  Computer2 <> None  THEN
          WriteString(" or perhaps "); WriteComputerChoice(Computer2);
      END; (* IF *) WriteString("."); WriteLn;
   END MakeRecommendation;

BEGIN  (* module ComputerChoices *)
   WriteString("This program will help you choose a computer."); WriteLn;
   PresentMoneyMenu(Money); WriteLn;
   PresentApplicationMenu(Application); WriteLn;
   MakeRecommendation(Money, Application); WriteLn;
END ComputerChoices.
```

Debug and test   When enumeration types are used in a problem, a common error is to try to read or write the values using standard procedures. It may be helpful to test the PresentMoneyMenu and PresentApplicationMenu procedures first, with a short driver program. If the MakeRecommendation procedure does not work properly, test the outer case structure by replacing the innermost CASE structures with diagnostic WriteString commands. Complete testing involves trying all nine cases, plus some invalid choices. Here is a sample run with valid choices:

```
This program will help you choose a computer.

How much money do you have?
         A      $2000.00
         B      $3000.00
         C      $6000.00
Choose one (A, B, or C): C

What should the computer do?
         1       Handle Color Graphics
         2       Be Very User Friendly
         3       Handle Professional Work
Choose one (1, 2, or 3): 1

You probably would be happiest with Amarti or perhaps JCN.
```

Obviously, the size of the program increases dramatically as the number of choices in your inventory increases. However, the problem need not become much more complex, since the solution algorithm remains similar, regardless of the number of choice combinations.

Complete the documentation   Collect the problem definition, structure chart, pseudocode, code, and sample run. Since the users' choices are limited to those

---

---

defined by the menus, there should be no need for cautions or warnings in the users' manual. In fact, you want the customer to be able to walk into the store, sit down at the computer, and obtain the necessary information without having to refer to a manual at all. However, store employees will need to know the source code (CH11E) and object code locations so that they can load the program for the customer.

☐ Importing Types from an External Module

The scope of a data type follows the same rules as the scope of variables, namely,

Rules for the Scope of Data Types

1. The scope of a *global data type* (a type imported into or declared in the main program) extends to every procedure in the program, with one exception:
   A global type is not visible in any procedure in which a type with the same name has been declared locally.
2. A data type declared locally within a procedure is not visible outside that procedure.
3. A data type declared within a procedure is visible in any procedure nested within it, unless a type with the same name has been declared locally within the nested procedure.

A type can be declared in an external DEFINITION module and imported by name. Importing an enumeration type also causes its constant identifiers to be imported.

To illustrate, consider a version of the ComputerChoices program from Example 11.3.1. The procedures and types have been included in an external module ComStore, shown in Figure 11–7. The program itself is very short.

```
MODULE ComputerChoices2;
    (* Simple expert system to choose between three computers.
       Types and Procedures imported from module ComStore.
       FileName:CH11F    Modula-2    RKW    June 1991   *)
```

Figure 11–7
**External Module
ComStore
Containing Types
and Procedures for
ComputerChoices2.**

```
DEFINATION MODULE ComStore;

TYPE  COST = (TwoThousand, ThreeThousand, SixThousand);
      USES = (Color, Friendly, Professional);

PROCEDURE PresentMoneyMenu(VAR Amount:COST);
PROCEDURE PresentApplicationMenu(VAR IWant:USES);
PROCEDURE MakeRecommendation(Money:COST; Application:USES);

END ComStore.
```

```
IMPLEMENTATION MODULE ComStore;

FROM InOut IMPORT Read, Write, WriteString, WriteLn;

PROCEDURE PresentMoneyMenu(Var Amount:COST);
   VAR MoneyChoice, CapMoney, Discard : CHAR;
   BEGIN
      REPEAT
         WriteLn; WriteString("How much money do you have?");
          WriteLn;
         WriteString("     A      $2000.00"); WriteLn;
         WriteString("     B      $3000.00"); WriteLn;
         WriteString("     C      $6000.00"); WriteLn;
          WriteString("Choose one (A, B, or C): ");
          Read(MoneyChoice); Read(Discard);
          CapMoney := CAP(MoneyChoice); Write(CapMoney); WriteLn;
      UNTIL  (CapMoney >= 'A') AND (CapMoney <= 'C');
      CASE  CapMoney  OF
         'A' : Amount := TwoThousand |
         'B' : Amount := ThreeThousand |
         'C'; : Amount := SixThousand;
      END; (* CASE *)
   END PresentMoneyMenu;

PROCEDURE PresentApplicationMenu(VAR IWant:USES);
   VAR ApplChoice, Discard : CHAR;
   BEGIN
      REPEAT
         WriteLn; WriteString("What should the computer do? ");
          WriteLn;
         WriteString("     1      Handle Color Graphics"); WriteLn;
         WriteString("     2      Be Very User Friendly"); WriteLn;
         WriteString("     3      Handle Professional Work");
          WriteLn;
          WriteString("Choose one (1, 2, or 3): ");
          Read(ApplChoice); Read(Discard); Write(ApplChoice);
           WriteLn;
      UNTIL  (ApplChoice >= '1') AND (ApplChoice <= '3');
      CASE  ApplChoice  OF
         '1' : IWant := Color |    '2' : I Want := Friendly |
         '3' : IWant := Professional;
      END; (* CASE *)
   END PresentApplicationMenu;
```

(*continued*)

Figure 11 — 7
(continued)

```
PROCEDURE MakeRecommendation(Money:COST; Application:USES);
    TYPE  MICROS = (Amarti, Jonathan, JCN, None, AnotherStore);
    VAR Computer, Computer2 :MICROS;
    PROCEDURE WriteComputerChoice(Machine:MICROS);
        BEGIN
            CASE  Machine  OF
                Amarti       : WriteString("Amarti")              |
                Jonathan     : WriteString("Jonathan")           |
                JCN          : WriteString("JCN")                |
                None         : WriteString("no computer at all")  |
                AnotherStore : WriteString("another store")        ;
            END; (* CASE *)
        END WriteComputerChoice;

    BEGIN
        Computer2 := None;
        CASE  Money  OF
            TwoThousand   : CASE  Application  OF
                                Color   : Computer  := Amarti   ;
                                ELSE       Computer  := AnotherStore ;
                            END | (* CASE *)
            ThreeThousand : CASE  Application  OF
                                Color   : Computer  := Amarti   |
                                Friendly : Computer := Jonathon ;
                                ELSE       Computer  := AnotherStore ;
                            END | (* CASE *)
            SixThousand   : CASE  Application  OF
                                Color   : Computer  := Amarti;
                                          Computer2 := JCN      |
                                Friendly : Computer := Jonathan |
                                Professional : Computer  := JCN;
                            END ; (* CASE *)
        END; (* CASE *)  WriteLn;
        WriteString("You probably would be happiest with ");
         WriteComputerChoice(Computer);
        IF  Computer2 <> None  THEN
            WriteString(" or perhaps ");
            WriteComputerChoice(Computer2);
        END; (* IF *) WriteString(".");WriteLn;
    END MakeRecommendation;

END ComStore.
```

```
FROM InOut IMPORT WriteString, WriteLn;
FROM ComStore IMPORT  COST, USES, PresentMoneyMenu,
            PresentApplicationMenu, MakeRecommendation;

VAR  Money:COST;  Application:USES;

BEGIN
    WriteString("This program will help you choose a computer."); WriteLn;
    PresentMoneyMenu(Money); WriteLn;
    PresentApplicationMenu(Application); WriteLn;
    MakeRecommendation(Money, Application); WriteLn;
END ComputerChoices2.
```

Note how data types COST and USES are defined in the DEFINITION MOD-ULE ComStore and IMPORTed from there. These types and the constants Two-Thousand, ThreeThousand, SixThousand, Color, Friendly, and Professional are all available within program ComputerChoices2.

Type MICROS could have been defined in the DEFINITION module but it has been left within procedure MakeRecommendation, since it is used only there. Thus, MICROS and its constants are not directly available within program Computer-Choice2.

Remember, compile DEFINITION MODULE ComStore first. Then compile IMPLEMENTATION MODULE ComStore and then compile, link, and execute the program in file CH11F.

☐ Compatible Types

Mixing variables of different types in an expression is generally not allowed. For example, you would *not* define *A* and *B* to be CARDINAL and *P* to be REAL and try to assign *A* := *B* + *P*. In some situations, however, types that are not exactly the same are *compatible* and thus may be used together.

Individual variables are said to be *assignment compatible* if they can be assigned to one another and no operators except assignment operators are involved. That is, you may write *L* := *M*, if *L* and *M* are assignment compatible. Figure 11–8 summarizes the rules for compatibility of data types.

When variables do not meet any of the criteria for compatibility described in Figure 11–8, those variable types are *incompatible*.

Questions 11.3

1. Given TYPE RAINBOW in Figure 11–5,
   a. Can you define *overlapping* subranges types, such as

   ```
   TYPE  EARLY = [Red..Green]; LATE = [Yellow..Violet];
   VAR   OneColor : EARLY; TwoColor : LATE;
   ```

   Try it!
   b. What values could be assigned to OneColor; to TwoColor?
   c. What would be VAL(LATE,2)? Are you sure? Try it!
   d. If TwoColor := Green; what is ORD(TwoColor)? Are you sure? Try it!
2. Modify procedure ReadRainbow (CH11D) so that it accepts leading CHARac-ters 'R', 'O', 'Y', 'G', 'B', and 'V' of the color names and uses a CASE structure to assign the colors to parameter Shade.
3. Given the declarations,

   ```
   TYPE  FLOWERS = (Petunia, Rose, Tulip, Iris);
   VAR   Plant, What : FLOWERS; Number : CARDINAL;
   ```

   What is displayed by each of the following?
   a. FOR Plant := Petunia TO Iris DO
       WriteCard (3 - ORD(Plant), 6); END;

   b. Plant := Iris; DEC(Plant,2);
       IF Plant < Rose THEN WriteString (''Petunia'',
       ELSE WriteString(''Rose or more ''); END;

Figure 11–8
Assignment-
Compatible Types

Identical Types   Variables of identical type, which are declared with
the same type identifier, are always compatible.

Example: ```
TYPE   SMALLCARD = [0..10];
VAR Num1 : SMALLCARD;   Num2 : SMALLCARD;
    (* Num1 and Num2 are identical, hence compatible. *)
```

**Equal Types**  When two types are declared equal to each other, variables of
those types are compatible.

*Example:*     ```
TYPE  POSANDNEG = INTEGER;
VAR  A : POSANDNEG;    B : INTEGER;
    (* A and B are compatible. *)
```

Subrange When one type is a subrange of another, variables of those types are
compatible as long as values outside the subrange are not used.

Example: ```
TYPE STORM = (Thunder, Lightning, Rain, Hail, Snow);
          WETTEST = [Thunder..Rain];
VAR Weather : STORM;   WetDay : WETTEST;
    (* Weather and WetDay are compatible when values are
          restricted to Thunder, Lightning, Rain. *)
```

**Overlapping Subranges**  When two types are subranges of the same base type,
variables of those types are compatible as long as values are limited to those for
which the subranges overlap.

*Example:*     ```
TYPE  SMALLINT = [-10..10];   SMALLPOS = INTEGER[0..5];
VAR  Tiny : SMALLINT;   Tinier : SMALLPOS;
    (* Tiny and Tinier are compatible as long as values
          are restricted to 0, 1, 2, 3, 4, and 5. *)
```

CARDINAL ⟶ INTEGER When one variable is compatible with INTEGER and
another is compatible with CARDINAL, the two variables are assignment compatible
as long as values are restricted to the range in which CARDINAL and INTEGER
overlap.

Example: ```
VAR CardNum : CARDINAL;   IntNum : INTEGER;
    (* CardNum and IntNum are assignment compatible as
          long as values are limited to the range 0 to
          MAX(INTEGER). *)
```

```
c.  Plant := VAL(FLOWERS,0);
    WHILE Plant < Iris DO
     CASE Plant OF
       Petunia : WriteString(''Petunia '') |
       Rose : WriteString(''Rose '') |
       Tulip : WriteString(''Tulip '') |
       Iris : WriteString(''Iris '');
     END; (* CASE *) INC(Plant);
    END; (* WHILE *)
```

What is wrong with each of the following? Correct the code so that valid
operations are performed.
```

    d. FLOWERS := '' Tulip '';

    e. FOR Number := 3 TO 0 DO
        WriteCard(VAL(Plant, Number), 5); END;

    f. Read(What);
        CASE What OF
         Petunia : Plant := '' Petunia '' |
         Rose : Plant := ''Rose'' |
         Tulip : Plant := ''Tulip'' |
         Iris : Plant := ''Iris;
        END; (* CASE *)

4. For program ComputerChoices (Example 11.3.1, CH11E),
    a. there are 9 valid test cases. What are they? What is displayed for each case?
    b. modify the program, so that when you have $6000.00 and the Application is Color, if you need lots of memory the recommendation is JCN; otherwise, the recommendation is Amarti.

5. Given the declarations in the examples of Figure 11–8, which of these assignments are valid and which are invalid? If invalid, explain why.
    a. Num2 := 61273; Num1 := Num2;

    b. Num1 := 7; Num2 := Num1;

    c. A := 5; Num2 := A;

    d. WetDay := Rain; A := -ORD(WetDay);

    e. Weather := VAL(STORM,4); WetDay := Weather;

    f. IntNum := -32000; Tiny := IntNum;

    g. Tinier := 3; Num2 := Tinier;

    h. CardNum := 2 * 21816; B := CardNum;

    i. WetDay := Lightning;
        Weather := VAL(STORM, ORD(WetDay)+2);

    j. Tiny := -2 * 5; Num1 := -Tiny;

11.4 *Focus on Problem Solving*

Enumeration types can be valuable in arrays. Array elements and array indices can become especially descriptive when users define them in terms of their own enumeration types. In this section, you will examine some arrays that incorporate enumeration types and then develop a program for displaying a multidimensional array of distances between towns.

Declaring Arrays with User-Defined Types

Figure 11–9 illustrates some one dimensional arrays with elements and/or indices declared in terms of user defined types. The figure shows that the array indices can be defined by a type name or by a range of values of that type, such as

```
VAR  PeopleCount : ARRAY PEOPLEINDICES OF CARDINAL;
```

or

```
VAR  PeopleCount : ARRAY [Infant..Adult] OF CARDINAL;
```

Figure 11−9
Arrays with
User-Defined Types

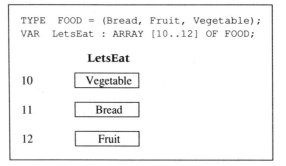

```
TYPE  PEOPLEINDICES = (Infant, Child, Youth, Adult);
VAR  PeopleCount : ARRAY PEOPLEINDICES OF CARDINAL;
```

PeopleCount

Infant	5
Child	8
Youth	15
Adult	13

```
TYPE  FOOD = (Bread, Fruit, Vegetable);
VAR  LetsEat : ARRAY [10..12] OF FOOD;
```

LetsEat

10	Vegetable
11	Bread
12	Fruit

```
TYPE  PTS = (x, y);
VAR  Point : ARRAY [x..y] OF REAL;
```

Point

| *x* | 7.5 |
| *y* | 0.76 |

```
TYPE  VOWELS = (a, e, i, o, u, y);
VAR  VowelCount : ARRAY [a..u] OF CARDINAL;
```

VowelCount

a	15
e	35
i	12
o	8
u	5

Note that for VARiable VowelCount, the indices are a subrange [a..u] of the type VOWELS.

Possible applications of the arrays in the figure could be the number of Infants, Children, Youth, and Adults entering a sports arena (PeopleCount), ''of the day'' restaurant items numbered 10 through 12 on a menu (LetsEat), the *x* and *y* coordinates of points in a plane (Point), or the count of each vowel in a book (VowelCount).

A Three-Dimensional Distance Array

Now apply enumerable type indices to an array of three dimensions.

Example 11.4.1

Write a program to display a three-dimensional array of distances in miles and kilometers between Elko, Fallon, and Ely.

Define the problem For charts on a map, you want to display the distances between the three towns. The distances are shown in Figure 11–10. Write a program that assigns the mileage values to the Miles table of the array, converts all of the values to kilometers, and assigns the values to the Kilometer table of the array.

Develop a solution The three-dimensional array can be represented graphically as the two tables shown in Figure 11–10. Each cell in the tables contains a REAL value representing a Kilometers or Miles distance between corresponding cities. The array will be declared as

    TYPE   TOWNS = (Elko, Fallon, Ely);   MEASURE = (Miles, Kilom);
    VAR   Dist : ARRAY [Miles..Kilom], [Elko..Ely], [Elko..Ely] OF REAL;

Figure 11–10
Distance Tables
(Examples 11.4.1)

Miles	Elko	Fallon	Ely
Elko	0	253	187
Fallon	253	0	257
Ely	187	257	0

Kilometers	Elko	Fallon	Ely
Elko	0	407	301
Fallon	407	0	414
Ely	301	414	0

For Row = Elko to Ely and Col = Elko to Ely, the known values will be assigned to Dist[Miles, Row, Col]. These values will be multiplied by 1.609 to obtain the entries in the plane Dist[Kilom, Row, Col]. Then the Miles and Kilometers planes of the array will be displayed separately.

Refine the solution   *Pseudocode*

```
begin module BoxOfDistances
    assign values to Dist[Miles, Row, Col]
    for   Row = Elko to Ely
        for   Col = Elko to Ely
            set   Dist[Kilom, Row, Col] =   1.609 * Dist[Miles, Row, Col]
    for   Plane = Miles to Kilom
        if   Plane = Miles print "Miles"; otherwise, print "Kilometers"
        print headings "Elko      Fallon      Ely"
        for   Row = Elko to Ely
            print name of Row
            for   Col = Elko to Ely
                print   Dist[Plane, Row, Col]
            end for Col   and      advance to next row
        end for Row
        separate tables by a few lines
    end for Plane
end BoxOfDistances
```

Note the use of CASE in the Modula-2 code to write the names of the Row towns.

Modula-2 code

```
MODULE BoxOfDistances;
    (* Three dimensional distance table, enumeration type indices
        FileName:CH11G      Modula-2      RKW      June 1991   *)

FROM InOut IMPORT WriteString, WriteLn;
FROM RealInOut IMPORT FWriteReal;

TYPE   TOWNS = (Elko, Fallon, Ely);   MEASURE = (Miles, Kilom);
VAR   Dist : ARRAY [Miles..Kilom],[Elko..Ely],[Elko..Ely] OF REAL;
      Row, Col: TOWNS;   Plane: MEASURE;

BEGIN (* BoxOfDistances *)
    Dist[Miles,Elko,Elko]    :=    0.0;   Dist[Miles,Elko,Fallon]   := 253.0;
    Dist[Miles,Elko,Ely]     := 187.0;   Dist[Miles,Fallon,Elko]   := 253.0;
    Dist[Miles,Fallon,Fallon] :=   0.0;   Dist[Miles,Fallon,Ely]    := 257.0;
    Dist[Miles,Ely,Elko]     := 187.0;   Dist[Miles,Ely,Fallon]    := 257.0;
    Dist[Miles,Ely,Ely]      :=    0.0;

    FOR   Row := Elko   TO   Ely   DO
        FOR   Col := Elko   TO   Ely   DO
            Dist[Kilom,Row,Col] := 1.609 * Dist[Miles,Row,Col];
        END; (* FOR Col *)
    END; (* FOR Row *)

    FOR Plane := Miles   TO   Kilom   DO
        WriteLn;
        IF   Plane = Miles   THEN   WriteString("          MILES");
            ELSE   WriteString("          KILOMETERS");
        END; (* IF *)   WriteLn; WriteLn;
```

```
      WriteString("          |     Elko    Fallon      Ely"); WriteLn;
      WriteString("——|——————————"); WriteLn;
      FOR  Row :=  Elko  TO  Ely  DO
         CASE  Row  OF
            Elko    :  WriteString("Elko    |")   |
            Fallon  :  WriteString("Fallon  |")   |
            Ely     :  WriteString("Ely     |");
         END; (* CASE *)
         FOR  Col := Elko  TO  Ely  DO
            FWriteReal(Dist[Plane, Row, Col], 10, 1);
            (* Assertion:  Dist = Miles or Kilometers, as defined by
                           Plane, between Row town and Col town.    *)
         END; (* FOR Col *)  WriteLn;
      END; (* FOR Row *)  WriteLn; WriteLn; WriteLn; WriteLn;
   END; (* FOR Plane *)
END BoxOfDistances.
```

Debug and test Make sure that the names are spelled consistently. Check the triply nested FOR loops carefully for placement of WriteLn commands to display the tables properly. A sample run produced the following output:

MILES

		Elko	Fallon	Ely
	|			
Elko	|	0.0	253.0	187.0
Fallon	|	253.0	0.0	257.0
Ely	|	187.0	257.0	0.0

KILOMETERS

		Elko	Fallon	Ely
	|			
Elko	|	0.0	407.1	300.9
Fallon	|	407.1	0.0	413.5
Ely	|	300.9	413.5	0.0

Complete the documentation Since the problem is designed to illustrate multidimensional arrays with enumeration-type indices, the problem definition should include the description of the three-dimensional Dist array. Collect the pseudocode, code, and sample run. In the users' manual state the source code location (CH11G). Instruct users how to change entries in type TOWNS and assignments at the beginning of the program to display tables for other towns.

Questions 11.4

1. Why should types PTS and VOWELS shown in Figure 11–9 not both be defined in the same program?

2. Assume that you have these declarations:

```
TYPE  GAME = (Soccer, Football, Baseball, Swimming, Tennis, Others);
      ACTIVITIES = ARRAY [Soccer..Tennis] OF CARDINAL;
VAR  Index : GAME;   Sport : ACTIVITIES;
```

    a. Draw a diagram that shows the contents of array Sport after executing this command line:

```
FOR Index := Soccer TO Tennis DO Sport[Index] := ORD(Index); END;
```

     b. Write code to display array Sport in reverse order, showing the index and value of each element.

     c. What would be displayed by executing this code?

```
Index := VAL(GAME,0);
WHILE  Index < Others DO
  Sport[Index] := 10 * (ORD(Index) + 1);
  WriteCard(Sport[Index], 6); WriteLn; INC(Index);
END; (* WHILE *)
```

3. a. Show the declaration of a two-dimensional array for a game card on which columns are labeled *B, I, N, G,* and *O;* five rows are labeled *4, 5, 6, 7,* and *8;* and each cell on the card will be filled (TRUE) or empty (FALSE).

     b. Why would it be difficult to declare an enumeration type if the five rows were to be labeled, *4, 12, 15, 26, 35?*

     c. Write code that asks for a row number or a column number on the game card and determines if all of the elements in that row or column are filled.

11.5 *Summary*

Strings   Modules containing functions and procedures for handling character arrays accompany most versions of Modula-2. Consult your compiler manual to determine which functions and procedures are available. The Strings module developed in this book contains type STRING; functions Length, Position, and CompareStrings; and procedures ReadLine, Concatenate, Assign, Copy, Delete, and Insert. Details of this module are in Appendix C.

Abstract Data Type   Strings can be handled by considering the arrays one CHARacter at a time, or they can be handled by importing type STRING and limiting operations to its string-handling functions and procedures. In that case, STRING is an *abstract* data type; that is, a data type the programmer can use without even needing to know its underlying definition.

Subrange Types   For debugging the program and enhancing the program's readability, it is useful to limit values to *subranges* of the enumerable types. A subrange is defined by specifying the base type and the starting and ending constants; for example,

```
TYPE  AGE = CARDINAL [0..120];
VAR   HowOld : AGE;
```

The base type (CARDINAL for type AGE) can be left *anonymous* if it can be discerned from the range limits.

Range Checking   To implement range checking you may need to specify, when the program is compiled, that range checking is to be enabled. In many cases, values should be read into a variable that is not subrange-limited, in which case the range is checked upon assignment of a value to the subrange variable.

User-Defined Types   Programmers can define *enumeration types* by listing all possible values that can be assigned to a variable. For example,

```
TYPE  LEGUMES = (Lima, Pinto, Snap, Black, Chili);
VAR   Beans : LEGUMES;
```

The list of contants in type LEGUMES defines the values that variable Beans can have.

     Subranges of enumeration types are allowed, but no two user-defined types within the same program may use the same enumeration constants. For example, Black may not be defined as a value in type LEGUMES and also in another type such as TINT. Enumeration types may not include values of the standard (CARDINAL, INTEGER, CHAR, BOOLEAN) enumerable types.

Standard operations on enumeration types are assignment, comparison (using relational operators), ORD, VAL, INC, and DEC. Special procedures and functions must be written to handle other operations such as read and write.

Importing Types   User-defined types can be defined in an external DEFINITION module and IMPORTed from there. If a type and all of its supporting functions and procedures can be imported from an external module without the programmer needing to know the underlying definition, then it is said to be an *abstract* data type.

Compatible Types   Two enumerable types are *assignment-compatible* when values of one type can be assigned to variables of the other type. Such compatibility is limited to identical types, equal types, overlapping ranges, and subranges such as those described in Figure 11–8. Otherwise, types are incompatible and should not be mixed within an expression or statement unless a type-conversion function (see Appendix A) is applied.

Arrays with User-Defined Types   Enumeration types and subranges can be used for array elements and array indices. Such types may make the program more readable and meaningful.

11.6 *Exercises*

Exercises marked with (FileName:_____) indicate those that ask you to use, modify, or extend the text examples. The numbers in brackets, [ ], indicate the section that contains the material you need in order to complete the exercise.

1. [11.1] Your typewriter has a broken *e* key. Replace each occurrence of *e* in a string with *x*.

2. [11.1] **a.** Count the number of times each of the pronouns *I* and *me* appear in a paragraph in which each sentence (terminated by a period) is a separate string of 80 or fewer characters.

   b. Replace all occurrences of *I* and *me* with *we* and *us*, respectively.

3. [11.1] Given a phone number with letters and digits, convert it to all digits. For example, *MA5–3871* would become *625–3871*. *Hint:* Read all numbers and digits into a string, replace the letters, and display the resulting string. Refer to your telephone dial for the conversion table. *Q* and *Z* do not appear on the dial.

4. [11.1] **a.** Write and test a procedure that encrypts a string by replacing each character with the character a specified distance away. Thus, if the specified distance is 5, then *a* becomes *f*, *b* becomes *g*, c becomes *h*, and so on. Assume wraparound at the end of the alphabet, so that if the distance is 5, then *v* becomes *a*, *w* becomes *b*, *x* becomes *c*, etc. Replace all nonalphabetic characters, such as spaces and punctuation marks, with nonalphabetic characters of your choice.

   b. Write an inverse procedure that decrypts the string. Translate each nonalphabetic character back to a space.

5. [11.1] Draw a box of characters of your choice around a Title string. For example, if the Title is ''This Is It,'' and you choose the ' + ' character, the printed result should look something like

```
+ + + + + + + + + + + + + + +
+    This   Is  It     +
+ + + + + + + + + + + + + + +
```

Your program should allow you to choose the box character and the number of spaces, *N*, to place before and after the Title string within the box. (*N* = 2 in the example shown.) *Hint:* Use Length(Title). Create top and bottom lines separately from the middle line.

6. [11.1] A form letter begins

```
Dear Mr. Jones,
Enclosed is a prize number that may win ONE MILLION
DOLLARS for the Jones family of Bozeman, Montana.
This is your chance to . . . .
```

Write a program that concatenates the names, cities, and states from a list in an input file to the appropriate strings. Produce ''personalized'' form letters for all the names on the list. For example, to produce the above and similar letters to Mr. Wilson of Eureka, California, and to Mr. Occupant of 87544, NewMexico, the first entries in the input file would be

```
          Jones     Bozeman    Montana
          Wilson    Eureka     California
          Occupant  87544      NewMexico
```

7. [11.1] (FileName:CH11A) In program PalindromeTest (Example 11.1.1),
   a. add safeguards so that the string entered contains at least one alphabetic character.
   b. modify the program so that palindromes can contain digits, for example *SKI2321KS*.

8. [11.1] Here is a problem for which developing an algorithm may be a challenge. Anagrams are found by shuffling the letters of a string. Write a program that finds the anagrams of a word. For example, an anagram of *The Nudist Colony* is *No Untidy Clothes*. *Hint:* Begin with a short example word, perhaps with 4 characters, to develop an algorithm. Print out all possible permutations of the characters in the string array representing the word. *Caution:* The total number of anagrams of a string of *N* characters is the number of permutations of *N* things taken all at once, which is *N*!. Thus, the total number of anagrams of the 15-character phrase *The Nudist Colony* is 15!, or approximately 1.3 trillion—which would take your computer some time to generate and a lot of paper to print it out. The human brain as yet may be the only efficient tool for generating meaningful anagrams of strings longer than 6 or 7 characters.

9. [11.2] The billing department of the hospital is checking patient accounts. Write a program that will read from an input file the name, age, number of days spent in the hospital, and the amount of the bill for 10 patients. Age should be limited to values between 0 and 120, and days of hospital stay will be from 1 to 180. If the patient's age is less than 65, print the bill. If the age is between 65 and 71, calculate a 20% discount, print the bill with the discount, and tell how many years are left to collect before the patient turns 72. If the patient is older than 72, then print ''It is too late to collect.'' In every case, print the name, age, and length of stay in the hospital.

10. [11.2] (FileName:CH11C) Modify program AddTime (Example 11.2.1) to
   a. add an appropriate subrange type for degrees and a procedure to add in MOD 360. Then extend the solution to handle the addition of degrees, minutes, and seconds, as well as hours, minutes, and seconds.
   b. to handle a 12-hour clock with A.M. and P.M. instead of 24-hour (military) time. *Hint:* For Hours use MOD 12 arithmetic and a subrange. If the number of half-days (12-hour periods) later is odd, reverse the A.M./P.M. designa-

tion. State the number of half-days later. *Caution:* When initial hours = 12 or final hours = 0, you have situations that must be handled specially.

11. [11.3] Write a program, using an enumeration type with scalar values that are the names of the days of the week, and with subrange types for workdays (Monday through Friday), weekends (Saturday and Sunday), and "blue" workdays (Monday through Wednesday). Ask the user what day it is, and then tell whether it is a weekend or a workday. If it is a workday, tell whether it is a "blue" workday or not. *Hint:* Begin the week with Monday and end it with Sunday to make the subranges work.

12. [11.3] (FileName:CH11D) In program TestReadAndWriteRainbow, rearrange the colors in type RAINBOW so that a subrange type for primary pigments (Red, Yellow, Blue) can be defined as well. Then use the procedures defined in the program to ask for two colors. The program will determine and print whether both colors entered are primary pigments or not. If they are both primary pigments, mix them and display the resulting color (Red + Yellow = Orange, Red + Blue = Violet, Yellow + Blue = Green).

13. [11.3] (FileName:CH11E) Using program ComputerChoices (Example 11.3.1) as a guide, write a simple expert system using enumeration types that will help the user decide whether the outcome is

- I mow the lawn (IMow)
- I hire somebody to mow the lawn (YouMow).
- The lawn does not get mowed (NoMow).

The input types are

- The grass is (Tall, Short).
- The mower is (Working, Broken).

The rules are

- If the grass is tall, it gets mowed by someone.
- If the grass is short, it does not get mowed.
- If the mower is working, I mow the lawn.
- If the mower is broken, I hire someone to mow the lawn.

14. [11.3] (FileName:CH11E) Using program ComputerChoices (Example 11.3.1) as a guide, write a simple expert system using enumeration types that will help the user decide whether the outcome is

- I cook fish for dinner (Fish).
- I make stew for dinner (Stew).
- We go out for dinner (GoOut).
- We have no dinner (NoFood).

The input types are

- My spouse (Hates, Likes) fish.
- I feel (Tired, Ambitious).
- I am (Mad, NotMad).

The rules are

- If I am tired and not mad, we go out.
- If I am ambitious and mad, and my spouse hates fish, we have fish.
- If I am tired and mad, we have no dinner.
- In all other cases we have stew.

15. [11.3] A large company hires employees whose job classifications are administrator, engineer, physician, accountant, secretary, custodian, and dockworker. In this particular company, the first three of these are considered "salaried" employees; the others are termed "hourly." In an external DEFINITION module, define an enumeration type whose scalar values are the seven job classifications, and define a subrange type of the three salaried categories. Write a program that imports these types and reads from an input file the employee number and classification for at least twenty employees. The program will accumulate, and print to an output file, a meaningful report of the total number of employees in each of the seven job classifications and the total number of salaried employees.

16. [11.4] A file contains the names of blood donors with their blood type (A, B, O, or AB) and the number of pints they have donated to date.
   a. Read the file into parallel arrays for name, blood type, and number of pints donated.
   b. Search the arrays and print out the name and number of pints donated for all those who have a particular blood type specified by a user at the keyboard.
   c. Use the information in the arrays to fill a one-dimensional array of total NumPints of each type donated, with the array indices being A, B, O, and AB.

17. [11.4] Count the vowels in a text string of 80 or fewer CHARacters. Accumulate the counts in an array with indices a, e, i, o, u, and y, and display the string and the vowel-count array.

18. [11.4] a. Define two-dimensional arrays of MyCollection and YourCollection, where the column indices are the media (tape, CD, record), the row indices are the kind of music (Classical, Rock, Religious, Rap, Jazz, Other), and the elements of the arrays are CARDINAL values indicating how many of each media and kind are in the collection.
   b. Write a procedure to fill the arrays with random CARDINAL values between 0 and 50, and display the arrays.
   c. Write a program that
      (1) asks for the kind of music and displays how many of that kind are in MyCollection and in YourCollection,
      (2) determines separately who has the most tapes, the most CDs, and the most records,
      (3) allows you to buy or discard music and then update and display the arrays.

19. [11.4] (FileName:CH11G) Modify program BoxOfDistances (Example 11.4.1) to
   a. read the initial Miles values from a file,
   b. calculate and display only the elements below the diagonal of each distance table,
   c. add Pioche, with the Miles from Pioche to Elko, Fallon, and Ely being 294, 366, and 109, respectively.

20. [11.4] Modify each of the following as indicated:
   a. program CarsAndDealers (CH10I, Example 10.5.1) so that the array indices are enumeration types DEALERS = (JonesAuto, FreewaySales), and MODELS = (Sunray, Porka, Miserate);
   b. program AirTraffic (CH10J, Example 10.5.2) so that the array indices are the airports (LAX, SFO), the Aircraft (Airliners, SmallPlanes, Helicopters), and the dates [4..7].
   c. Exercise 3, Chapter 10, so that the PeopleCount array indices are (Infant, Child, Youth, Adult)
   d. Exercise 19, Chapter 10, so that the array indices are the month abbreviations (JUL, AUG), the days [1..31], and the temperature descriptions (High, Low).

12

More Graphs, Types, Search, and Sort

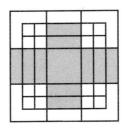

Chapter Outline

In earlier chapters we have plotted points on a graph (Section 5.5), performed a linear search (Section 10.3), and investigated some $O(N^2)$ sorting algorithms (Section 10.4.).

In this chapter we examine graphing techniques in more detail. A graphics module is presented that contains procedures for producing character-oriented point and bar graphs. Procedure types are introduced and used to pass functions to the graphics module. Faster methods of searching and sorting are implemented with recursive versions of the binary search and Quicksort algorithms.

Although the material presented in this chapter will extend your problem-solving skills, the remainder of the book does not rely heavily upon the details of the topics discussed here.

12.1 A Graphics Module

Although there are no Modula-2 standards for graphics, some systems may have graphics-handling modules. There are two fundamental types of graphics. One is **character-oriented graphics,** which can be managed on any terminal or printer. The other is **extended graphics,** which requires special graphics circuitry—usually in the form of a plug-in board, a special terminal and printer, and software designed for that particular hardware.

Character-Oriented Graphics

Character graphics techniques draw figures with very low resolution, using alphanumeric characters. In Section 5.5 you developed and applied procedures TabOrFill and PlotIt to create graphs using characters. Though not as exciting as extended graphics, routines to handle characters are machine independent and can be written in Modula-2 code. Appendix C contains a graphics module that includes procedures for handling the display of two-dimensional data either in point (line) form or as a bar graph. Since both the DEFINITION and IMPLEMENTATION modules for graphics are included in the appendix, they can be implemented on any system regardless of what other graphics capabilities may be available.

The procedures in module Graphics extend the earlier methods to handle any data that can be represented by parallel X and Y arrays. Axes are drawn, the values are displayed, and the data can be sorted in order of increasing x values before plotting.

Plotting Parallel Arrays of *x, y* Data

Figure 12–1 lists the procedures in module Graphics. Normally, PlotIt and SortXY would be called directly from a program to graph discrete x and y data. Procedure PlotIt has some restrictions: (1) there must be at least two data points; (2) for line graphs, no two points may have the same x value; (3) data for line graphs must be sorted in order of ascending x; and (4) the graphs are most meaningful when the y values are scaled to lie in a range between 1 and 1000. Scaling is usually accomplished by multiplying all y values by the same factor. For example, consider multiplying millions of dollars by 1/10000, or fractions of an inch by 100, to place those values into an appropriate range.

Examine IMPLEMENTATION MODULE Graphics carefully to see how the procedures work. You can copy, extend, and modify these procedures to meet your needs. The following example shows an application of procedures SortXY and PlotIt. Experiment with this example to see what you can do by giving different

Figure 12−1
Character Graphics
Handling
Procedures

```
PlotIt(X, Y : ARRAY OF REAL)
 (* Calls either LinePlot or BarPlot for X, Y, as requested by
    the user. Allows the user to specify the graph width and finds
    the minimum and maximum Y values for scaling purposes. *)

SortXY(VAR X, Y : ARRAY OF REAL)
 (* Performs a Selection sort to arrange parallel arrays X and
    Y in order of increasing X values. *)

FindMinAndMax(Z : ARRAY OF REAL;   VAR ZMin, ZMax: REAL)
 (* Finds min & max values in array Z. *)

ConvertToArray(YCalc : FunctionType;   VAR X, Y : ARRAY OF REAL)
 (* Converts a function, y = f(x),  of type PROCEDURE(REAL):REAL;
    passed from the calling module as YCalc, to a corresponding
    set of points, defined by arrays X and Y. *)

TabOrFill(HowMany : CARDINAL;   FillCharacter : CHAR)
 (* Writes FillCharacter  HowMany times. *)

SwapReals(VAR ElementA, ElementB : REAL)
 (* Interchanges REAL Elements A and B. *)

FindXInterval(X : ARRAY OF REAL;   VAR dx : REAL)
 (* Finds dx interval for line graph such that
    dx >= minimum x separation between points. *)

PrintYScale(YMin, YMax : REAL;   Width, YPlot0 : CARDINAL)
 (* Prints the Y Scale along leading edge of the graph. *)

LinePLot(X, Y : ARRAY OF REAL;   Width, YPlot0 : CARDINAL;
                                 Symbol : CHAR; YMin, YMax : REAL)

 (* Produces a scaled, point plot of Y vs X with constant
    intervals along the x-axis. *)

BarPlot(X, Y: ARRAY OF REAL;   Width, YPlot0 : CARDINAL;
                               Symbol : CHAR;  YMin, YMax : REAL)
 (* Produces a bar graph of Y vs X.   *)
```

answers to the questions posed by the Graphics procedures regarding plot symbol, bar or line graph, plot width, and number of plot lines.

Example 12.1.1

Illustrate the revenue, expenditures, and excess of revenue over expenditures for the BachRock Society during the years 1983 through 1992.

Define the problem   The society's treasurer has supplied file BACHROCK.DAT containing revenues and expenditures for the years 1983 to 1992 in order of decreasing revenue, as shown in Figure 12−2. For your presentation to the board of directors you need three graphs:

- total revenue versus year,
- total expenditures versus year, and
- the excess of total revenue over total expenditures versus year.

Figure 12–2
Revenues and
Expenditures of the
BachRock Society
(Example 12.1.1)

Year	Total Revenue (thousands of dollars)	Total Expenditures (thousands of dollars)
1992.0	60.3	61.5
1991.0	59.8	56.3
1989.0	51.1	50.8
1990.0	48.2	50.9
1988.0	45.9	44.9
1985.0	42.1	41.8
1987.0	40.7	39.9
1984.0	34.2	30.8
1986.0	27.5	30.4
1983.0	26.3	31.4

BachRock Society Financial Summary
1983–1992

Develop a solution   Observe that the values in Figure 12–2 have already been scaled in terms of thousands of dollars. This constitutes a first step in making the graph meaningful. Arrays will be declared as follows:

```
CONST NUMYEARS = 10;
TYPE   REALLIST = ARRAY [1..NUMYEARS] OF REAL;
VAR    Temporary, Year, Revenue, Expenditure : REALLIST;
```

These operations will be performed in order:

1. Read the file into parallel arrays Year, Revenue, Expenditure.
2. Sort Revenue by Year.
3. Sort Expenditure by Year.
4. Plot Revenue vs. Year.
5. Plot Expenditure vs. Year.
6. Plot Revenue minus Expenditure vs. Year.

Refine the solution   *Pseudocode*

```
begin module BachRockFinances
      open file BACHROCK.DAT, read data into arrays, close file
      echo Year, Revenue, Expenditure arrays to the screen

      copy Year to Temporary,      (* sort arrays *)
      SortXY(Temporary,Revenue), SortXY(Year,Expenditure)

      (* plot revenues and expenditures *)
      Print "X = Year",   "Y = Revenue x $1000"
      PlotIt(Year,Revenue)         (* line graph, symbol R, width 50 *)
      Print "X = Year",   "Y = Expenditures x $1000"
      PlotIt(Year,Expenditure)         (* line graph, symbol E, width 50 *)

      for all Years,      (* plot excess of revenue over expenditures *)
          Temporary[YearCount] = Revenue[YearCount] – Expenditure[YearCount]
```

Print "X = Year", "Y = Excess (Revenue − Expenditures) x 1000"
PlotIt(Year,Temporary)   (* bar graph, symbol +, width 30 *)
end BachRockFinances

Modula-2 code

```
MODULE BachRockFinances;
   (* Plots the revenues, expenditures, and excess revenues over
      expenditures for BachRock Society for 1983 through 1992.
      FileName:CH12A      Modula-2     RKW     June 1991  *)

FROM InOut IMPORT WriteString, WriteLn, OpenInput, CloseInput;
FROM RealInOut IMPORT ReadReal, FWriteReal;
FROM Graphics IMPORT PlotIt, SortXY;

CONST  NUMYEARS = 10;   TYPE  REALLIST = ARRAY [1..NUMYEARS] OF REAL;
VAR   Temporary,Year,Revenue,Expenditure:REALLIST;   YearCount:CARDINAL;

BEGIN
    (* Read the file into arrays  Year, Revenue, and Expenditure *)
   WriteString("Input file name (BACHROCK.DAT)? "); OpenInput("DAT");
   FOR  YearCount := 1 TO NUMYEARS  DO
      ReadReal(Year[YearCount]);
      ReadReal(Revenue[YearCount]); ReadReal(Expenditure[YearCount]);
   END; (* FOR *)  CloseInput; WriteLn; WriteLn;

    (* Echo  Year, Revenue, and Expenditure to screen *)
   WriteString("          BachRock Society Financial Summary");
    WriteLn; WriteLn;
    WriteString("       Total Revenue      Total Expenditures"); WriteLn;
    WriteString(" Year     ($ x 1000)          ($ x 1000)"); WriteLn;
   FOR  YearCount := 1 TO NUMYEARS  DO
      FWriteReal(Year[YearCount],5,0);   FWriteReal(Revenue[YearCount],11,2);
      FWriteReal(Expenditure[YearCount],22,2); WriteLn;
   END; (* FOR *)  WriteLn; WriteLn;

    (* Sort by Year *)
   Temporary:=Year; SortXY(Temporary, Revenue); SortXY(Year, Expenditure);

    (* Plot Revenues and Expenditures *)
   WriteString("X = Year,  Y = Revenue x $1000");
    PlotIt(Year, Revenue);  WriteLn; WriteLn;
   WriteString("X = Year,  Y = Expenditures x $1000");
    PlotIt(Year, Expenditure); WriteLn; WriteLn;

    (* Plot Excess of Revenues over Expenditures *)
   FOR  YearCount :=  1 TO NUMYEARS  DO
      Temporary[YearCount] := Revenue[YearCount] - Expenditure[YearCount];
   END; (* FOR *)
   WriteString("X = Year,  Y = Excess Revenue - Expenditures x $1000");
    PlotIt(Year, Temporary); WriteLn;
END BachRockFinances.
```

Debug and test In addition to echoing the data in Figure 12–2, a sample run produces the display shown in Figure 12–3. The PlotIt procedure prompts for the plot symbol, the type of graph (bar or line), and the width of the graph (number of spaces to assign between minimum and maximum values of *y*). For a line graph, the

Figure 12-3
Sample Run of
BachRockFinances
(Example 12.1.1)

```
Input file name (BACHROCK.DAT)? BACHROCK.DAT
...
X = Year,  Y = Revenue x $1000
What character to use for plot symbol? R
Would you like a
      B     Bar Graph?
      L     Line Graph?
Choose one, B or L:     L
What is plot width in print spaces?
   Width must be > 6 and <= 60: 50
The minimum number of Lines for Graph will be      10
Would you like more lines than   10 (Y/N)? N

                      26                                          60
    X         Y      ===============================================
  1983.0     26.3  R
  1984.0     34.2  .        R
  1985.0     42.1  .               R
  1986.0     27.5  .R
  1987.0     40.7  .                   R
  1988.0     45.9  .                       R
  1989.0     51.1  .                           R
  1990.0     48.2  .                         R
  1991.0     59.8  .                              R
  1992.0     60.3  .                               R
                   X

X = Year,  Y = Expenditures x $1000

What character to use for plot symbol? E
Would you like a
      B     Bar Graph?
      L     Line Graph?
Choose one,  B or L:   L
What is plot width in print spaces?
   Width must be > 6 and <= 60: 50
The minimum number of Lines for Graph will be      10
Would you like more lines than   10 (Y/N)? N
```

approximate number of lines (graph length in the *x* direction) is also shown, and you have the opportunity to request more lines (larger spacing). Because the LinePlot procedure sorts the data if it is not already sorted, the *line plots* would have been ordered by increasing Year even if the calls to SortXY had been omitted, but the program would *not* have sorted the data for a bar graph.

Complete the documentation   The definition of the problem, list of operations to be performed, pseudocode, code, sample run, and users' manual comprise the documentation for this problem. Warn users about the prompts for input file name, plot symbol, type of graph, and width and length of graph. The source code file is CH12A. The size and content of the input data can be changed by modifying the input file and CONSTant NUMYEARS.

Figure 12–3
(continued)

```
                          30                                                  62
      X         Y       =================================================
   1983.0     31.4     .E
   1984.0     30.8     E
   1985.0     41.8     .                  E
   1986.0     30.4     E
   1987.0     39.9     .           E
   1988.8     44.9     .                      E
   1989.0     50.8     .                              E
   1990.0     50.9     .                              E
   1991.0     56.3     .                                    E
   1992.0     61.5     .                                          E
                          X


   X = Year,   Y = Excess (Revenue - Expenditures) x $1000

   What character to use for plot symbol? +
   Would you like a
          B      Bar Graph?
          L      Line Graph?
   Choose one,  B or L:      B
   What is plot width in print spaces?
      Width must be > 6  and  <=  60: 30


                          -5              0             4
      X         Y       ================================
   1983.0     -5.1     ++++++++++++++++.
   1984.0      3.4                    .++++++++++++
   1985.0      0.3                    .+
   1986.0     -2.9            ++++++++++.
   1987.0      0.8                    .+++
   1988.0      1.0                    .++++
   1989.0      0.3                    .+
   1990.0     -2.7             +++++++++.
   1991.0      3.5                    .+++++++++++++
   1992.0     -1.2                ++++.
```

Questions 12.1

1. Examine the documentation for your Modula-2 compiler. Are graphics modules included? What commands are available?
2. Using the procedures from the Graphics module in Appendix C, what would be produced by the following code?

```
FROM Graphics IMPORT SortXY, PlotIt;
...
VAR  S, T : ARRAY [0..19] OF REAL;    I : CARDINAL;
...
BEGIN
   FOR  I := 0 TO 19  DO
      T[I] := FLOAT(I);   S[I] := T[I] * T[I];
      IF  I MOD 2 = 0  THEN  T[I] := -T[I];  END; (* IF *)
   END; (* FOR *)
   SortXY(T, S);   PlotIt(T, S);
....
```

3. What are the purposes of procedures FindXInterval and PrintYScale in module Graphics (Appendix C)? Were they used in Example 12.1.1? Why were they not IMPORTed into the BachRockFinances code?

4. Given parallel arrays *X* and *Y*,

Index	x	y	Index	x	y
1	−5.2	−34.4	5	−5.2	−30.6
2	6.3	22.7	6	2.0	−5.1
3	−4.1	−20.0	7	3.6	0.8
4	3.8	1.4	8	−2.8	−10.5

What would be the result of executing this code:

```
. . .
FROM Graphics IMPORT SortXY, PlotIt;
. . .
VAR X, Y : ARRAY [1..8] OF REAL;
. . .
BEGIN
   . . .
   SortXY(X, Y);  PlotIt(X, Y);
   . . . .
```

a. if you decided to do a bar graph?

b. if you decided to do a line graph? Why? *Hint:* Examine the data and procedure FindXInterval in IMPLEMENTATION MODULE Graphics.

c. What would happen if *x*[5] were changed from −5.2 to −528.0 and you chose to do a bar graph?

d. a line graph? Why?

e. Change *x*[5] to −6.3 and *x*[7] to +1.0; now try a line graph. Observe the display of *x* and *y* axes.

5. Show which procedures you would import from Graphics and what the commands would look like (for the arrays described in question 4) to

a. find the minimum and maximum values of *Y*;

b. sort the parallel arrays *X* and *Y* in order of increasing *y* values;

c. interchange the values *y*[2] and *y*[7];

d. display the arrays *X* and *Y* with 25 dashes ('−') between the *x* and *y* values on each line.

12.2   *Procedure Types*

Modula-2 provides for procedure types that permit you to pass procedures and functions to and from modules and other procedures. The definition of a procedure type looks much like a procedure heading and relays information about the number and types of parameters used by a procedure of that type. The syntax for declaring procedure types and variables is shown in Figure 12−4. General guidelines for using procedure types are summarized in Figure 12−5.

Type PROC

One standard procedure type in Modula-2, PROC, can be used without declaring or importing it. It is predefined within the language as

```
TYPE  PROC = PROCEDURE;
```

Figure 12–4
Syntax for
Procedure Types
and Variables

Syntax

TYPE ProcedureTypeName = PROCEDURE(List of Formal Value and/or
                                      Variable Parameter Types);
TYPE FunctionTypeName = PROCEDURE(List of Formal Value and/or
                                      Variable Parameter Types) : Type of
                                      Value Returned by Function;
VAR ProcedureVariableName : ProcedureTypeName;
      FunctionVariableName : FunctionTypeName;

Example:

```
TYPE  ARITHMPROC = PROCEDURE(REAL, REAL) : REAL;
VAR  DoIt, FindSlope : ARITHMPROC;

(* The functions Add and FindSlope are both of type ARITHMPROC. *)

PROCEDURE  Add(a, b : REAL) : REAL;
   BEGIN
      RETURN  a + b;
   END Add;

PROCEDURE  FindSlope(deltaX, deltaY : REAL) : REAL;
   VAR  Slope : REAL;
   BEGIN
      Slope := deltaY / deltaX;
      RETURN Slope;
   END FindSlope;
```

Procedures of type PROC have no parameters. For example, you could define
VAR WhatNow : PROC; and

```
PROCEDURE PrintAMessage; (* or PROCEDURE PrintAMessage( ); *)
   BEGIN
    WriteString(''This is a generic message.''); WriteLn;
   END PrintAMessage;
```

Then PrintAMessage is a procedure with an empty parameter list and could be
assigned as a value to WhatNow,

```
WhatNow := PrintAMessage;
```

or passed directly to another procedure as a parameter of type PROC.

Passing Procedures as Parameters

The following example illustrates passing procedures as parameters.

Example 12.2.1

Read a string of characters, such as $3+5$ or $5-6$, and perform the operation
indicated.

Define the problem A string of three characters consisting of a single digit, the
symbol ' + ' or ' − ', and another single digit will be read into a CHARacter array.

Figure 12–5
Guidelines for
Using Procedure
Types

Assume:

```
TYPE  ARITHMPROC = PROCEDURE(REAL, REAL) : REAL;
VAR  DoIt, AnotherTask : ARITHMPROC;
     x, y, Result : REAL;   Upshot : INTEGER;

PROCEDURE  Calculate(Operation:ARITHMPROC;   p,q:REAL;
                     VAR Answer: REAL;  VAR ChopAnswer:INTEGER);
   BEGIN
      Answer := Operation(p, q);  ChopAnswer := entier(Answer);
   END Calculate;

     (  plus functions Add and FindSlope of type ARITHMPROC, as
     * shown in Figure 12-4 *)
```

Guidelines

1. Values of procedure types refer to entire blocks of code
    that contain the procedures.

2. A procedure value can be assigned to a procedure variable.
        Example: DoIt := Add;

3. Values of identical procedure variables can be assigned to
    each other.
        Example: AnotherTask := DoIt;

4. Some (but not all) implementations of Modula-2 allow
    comparison of procedure variables for equality.
        Example: If AnotherTask = DoIt THEN. . .

5. Procedure values or variables can be used as parameters
    in a procedure call.
        Examples: Calculate(DoIt, x, y, Result, Upshot);
                     Calculate(FindSlope, x, y, Result, Upshot);

6. A procedure variable can be called by a program.
        Example: WriteReal(DoIt(x,y), 8, 2);

7. A procedure value can be RETURNed by a function.

8. As procedure values, you may NOT use built-in, standard
    procedures (such as ABS, DEC, ORD, etc.) or procedures
    that are local to other procedures.

The digits will be converted to REAL values LeftNum and RightNum, and the ' + '
or ' − ' will be assigned to a CHARacter variable Op.

If Op = ' + ', then procedure Add (from Figure 12–4) and the two REAL values
will be passed to PROCEDURE Calculate (of Figure 12–5). If Op = ' − ', a
procedure Subtract (similar to Add) will be passed to Calculate. REAL and INTE-
GER results will be displayed.

Develop a solution Read the string, checking to make certain Op is ' + ' or ' − '
and that the digits lie between '0' and '9'. Convert the digits to REAL values.

- If Op = ' + ', then Calculate(Add, LeftNum, RightNum, Result, Upshot).
- If Op = ' − ', then Calculate(Subtract, LeftNum, RightNum, Result, Upshot).
- Display Result and Upshot.

Refine the solution   *Pseudocode*

```
begin module AddOrSubtract
    AskForString(LeftNum, RightNum, Op)
    case      Op
        '+' : Calculate(Add, LeftNum, RightNum, Result, Upshot)
        '−' : Calculate(Subtract, LeftNum, RightNum, Result, Upshot)
    display      Result and Upshot
end AddOrSubtract

procedure Calculate (* see Figure 12−5 *)

procedure Add (* see Figure 12−4 *)

procedure Subtract (a, b, : REAL) : REAL;
    begin    RETURN    a − b;        END Subtract

procedure AskForString(VAR a, b : REAL; VAR WhatToDo : CHAR)
    repeat
        ask for string      Calc[0],      Calc[1],      Calc[2]
    until    Calc[0] and Calc[2] are digits    and    Calc[1] is '+' or '−'
                  (* Determine numeric values of Calc[0] and Calc[2] *)
    set    a = ORD(Calc[0]) − ORD('0')      set    b = ORD(Calc[2]) − ORD('0')
    set    WhatToDo = Calc[1]
```

Modula-2 code

```
MODULE   AddOrSubtract;
    (* Illustrates procedure types and passing procedures.
       FileName:CH12B      Modula-2      RKW      June 1991 *)

FROM InOut IMPORT WriteString, WriteLn, WriteInt, Write, ReadString;
FROM RealInOut IMPORT FWriteReal;    FROM MathLib0 IMPORT entier, real;

TYPE   ARITHMPROC = PROCEDURE(REAL, REAL) : REAL;
VAR   LeftNum,RightNum,Result:REAL;  Op:CHAR;  Upshot:INTEGER;

PROCEDURE  Add(a, b : REAL) : REAL;            (* of type ARITHMPROC *)
    BEGIN     RETURN  a + b;     END Add;

PROCEDURE  Subtract(a, b : REAL) : REAL;       (* of type ARITHMPROC *)
    BEGIN     RETURN  a - b;     END Subtract;

PROCEDURE Calculate(Operation : ARITHMPROC;    x, y : REAL;
                    VAR Answer : REAL;    VAR ChopAnswer : INTEGER);
    BEGIN
        Answer := Operation(x,y);    ChopAnswer := entier(Answer);
    END Calculate;

PROCEDURE AskForString(VAR a, b : REAL;    VAR WhatToDo : CHAR);
    VAR  Calc : ARRAY [0..2] OF CHAR;
    BEGIN
        REPEAT
            WriteString("Enter digit, + or -, digit (no spaces): ");
            ReadString(Calc); WriteLn;
```

```
        UNTIL  (Calc[0] >= '0') AND (Calc[0] <= '9')    AND
                  ( (Calc[1]='+') OR (Calc[1]='-') )    AND
                      (Calc[2] >= '0') AND (Calc[2] <= '9');
        a := real(ORD(Calc[0]) - ORD('0'));  WhatToDo := Calc[1];
        b := real(ORD(Calc[2]) - ORD('0'));
    END AskForString;

BEGIN (* module AddOrSubtract *)
    AskForString(LeftNum, RightNum, Op);
    CASE  Op  OF
        '+' : Calculate(Add,      LeftNum, RightNum, Result, Upshot) |
        '-' : Calculate(Subtract, LeftNum, RightNum, Result, Upshot);
    END; (* CASE *)

    FWriteReal(LeftNum,3,1); Write(Op); FWriteReal(RightNum,3,1);
     WriteString(" = "); FWriteReal(Result,4,1); WriteLn;
    WriteString("Truncated, the result is "); WriteInt(Upshot,3); WriteLn;
END AddOrSubtract.
```

Debug and test   There are simpler and shorter ways to add and subtract without declaring a procedure type, but those ways do not illustrate procedures as parameters. Observe how functions Add and Subtract are passed to procedure Calculate. Test with all possible characters '0' through '9', with operations ' + ' and ' − ', and with an invalid string.

Complete the documentation   Because the program is designed to illustrate passing procedures as parameters, the documentation should include at least the following:

- *Problem Description:* The program accepts a string of form 'a + b' or 'a − b' and performs the indicated operation.
- *Algorithm Development:* Discuss procedure types and passing procedures as parameters. Include pseudocode.
- *Program Listing:* Source file CH12B.
- *Sample Run:*   Enter digit, + or −, digit (no spaces): $5-8$
                          $5.0 - 8.0 = -3.0$
                          Truncated, the result is -3.
  It might also be a good idea to enter an invalid string.
- *Users' Manual:* Source code is in file CH12B. Enter a string in the form requested and wait for results to be displayed.

☐ Passing Function $y = f(x)$ as an Abstract Data Type

The ability to pass a function as a procedure type can be valuable in graphing equations. If you examine DEFINITION MODULE Graphics in Appendix C, you will discover that it contains a type declaration

```
TYPE  FunctionType = PROCEDURE(REAL):REAL;
```

and a procedure definition

```
    PROCEDURE ConvertToArray(YCalc:FunctionType; VAR X,Y:ARRAY OF REAL);
```

These declarations allow users to treat any function of the form $y = f(x)$ (which returns a REAL y value, given a REAL x value) as a variable of type FunctionType. The function can be passed as a parameter to procedure ConvertToArray.

For purposes of character graphics, any function $y = f(x)$ can be considered to be an abstract data type as defined by FunctionType and the operations performed by the procedures in the Graphics module. When the procedure defining $y = f(x)$ is passed to ConvertToArray, discrete x, y values defined by the function are calculated and assigned to parallel X and Y arrays. A subsequent call to PlotIt produces a graph of the function.

For example, to obtain a plot of $(y = x^2 - x - 2)$, you could define in your program

```
PROCEDURE  YPoly(x :REAL) : REAL;
  BEGIN
    RETURN  x * x - x - 2.0;
  END  YPoly;
```

Then call ConvertToArray(YPoly, X, Y); which requests lower and upper bounds for x and produces arrays X and Y of points on the curve between these bounds. Finally, a call to PlotIt(X, Y) creates a graph of those values.

In the next example, the computer does some serious work for you by plotting a curve that is not easy to draw by hand.

Example 12.2.2

Plot the Gaussian distribution curve, given the standard deviation and the mean value.

Define the problem The height, y, of Gaussian (Normal) distribution curve for values of x distributed about mean, m, with standard deviation, s, is given by

$$y = (1/(s * \text{sqrt}(2\pi))) * \exp(-(x - m)^2/2s^2)$$

The program should ask users for the values of m and s and then draw a point graph of the curve. To see a meaningful plot, users will be advised by the program to choose lower and upper limits on x to be approximately $m - 3s$ and $m + 3s$, respectively.

Develop a solution Users will be asked for values of the mean, m, and the standard deviation, s. A function procedure YCurve(x) will be defined to return

$$y = (1.0/(s * \text{sqrt}(2.0 * \pi))) * \exp(-(x - m) * (x - m)/(2.0 * s * s))$$

with π equal to approximately 3.14159. YCurve will be passed into the procedure ConvertToArray, which will be imported from the graphics module, and which will convert the curve to arrays of corresponding x and y values. The size of the array, CONSTant NUMBEROFPOINTS, will be set arbitrarily to 19. The program also will calculate $m - 3s$ and $m + 3s$ and suggest to users that these be assigned as the lower and upper bounds on x, which will be requested by procedure ConvertToArray. Since the values of y for the normal distribution are positive fractions, less than 1.0, they will be scaled by a factor of 100 so that the graph is more readable. Finally, procedure PlotIt will be invoked to plot the graph.

A structure chart for the solution is shown in Figure 12–6.

Refine the solution *Pseudocode*

```
NormalCurve
    define PROCEDURE YCurve(x:REAL) : REAL
    begin
```

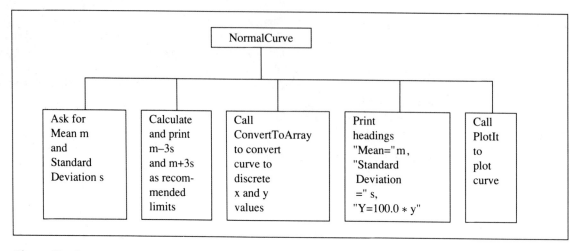

Figure 12–6
Structure Chart for NormalCurve (Example 12.2.2)

```
ask for global values m and s
calculate and print recommended bounds on x
   lower: m – 3s      upper: m + 3s
ConvertToArray(YCurve,X,Y)
print headings
   "Mean = ", m      "Standard Deviation = ", s
   "Y = 100.0 * Height of Normal Curve"
PlotIt(X,Y)
end NormalCurve
```

```
PROCEDURE YCurve(x:REAL) : REAL
   y = 100.00 / (s * sqrt(2.0 * PI)) * exp( –(x–m)*(x–m) / (2.0*s*s))
   return y
```

Modula-2 code

```
MODULE NormalCurve;
   (* Plots the Normal (Gaussian) distribution curve, given
      the mean value, m,  and the standard deviation, s.
      FileName:CH12C     Modula-2     RKW       June 1991  *)

FROM InOut IMPORT WriteString, WriteLn;
FROM RealInOut IMPORT FWriteReal, ReadReal;  FROM MathLib0 IMPORT sqrt, exp;
FROM Graphics IMPORT ConvertToArray, PlotIt;

CONST  NUMBEROFPOINTS = 19;   SCALEFACTOR = 100.0;
VAR  X,Y:ARRAY [1..NUMBEROFPOINTS] OF REAL;  m,s,x:REAL;  I:CARDINAL;

PROCEDURE  YCurve(x : REAL): REAL;
   CONST  PI = 3.14159;    VAR  y : REAL;
   BEGIN
      y := SCALEFACTOR*1.0/(s*sqrt(2.0*PI))* exp(-(x-m)*(x-m)/(2.0*s*s));
      (* m and s are global.  y = Normal curve times SCALEFACTOR.*)
      RETURN y;
   END YCurve;

BEGIN  (* main module NormalCurve *)
   WriteString("What is the mean value? "); ReadReal(m); WriteLn;
   WriteString("What is the standard deviation? "); ReadReal(s); WriteLn;
```

```
        WriteString("Recommended upper and lower bounds on x"); WriteLn;
          WriteString("   Lower = m - 3s = "); FWriteReal(m-3.0*s,8,2); WriteLn;
          WriteString("   Upper = m + 3s = "); FWriteReal(m+3.0*s,8,2); WriteLn;
        ConvertToArray(YCurve, X, Y);      WriteLn;

        WriteString("Mean = "); FWriteReal(m,8,2); WriteLn;
        WriteString("Standard Deviation = "); FWriteReal(s,8,2); WriteLn;WriteLn;
        WriteString("Y = 100 * Height of Normal Curve"); WriteLn;

        PlotIt(X, Y);
END NormalCurve.
```

Debug and test: It is important to make certain that the function in the procedure YCurve is entered correctly so that the appropriate function is plotted. Constant NUMBEROFPOINTS can be increased or decreased to make the plot more or less precise.

A sample run is shown in Figure 12–7.

Complete the documentation   Documentation should include the problem definition and algorithm development, which in turn should encompass the structure chart, pseudocode, and Modula-2 code. Warn users that there may be a short delay after specifying the lower and upper limits on *x*, while the program generates the *X* and *Y* arrays. The source code is in file CH12C. The Graphics module must be available when this program is compiled.

Questions 12.2

1. For module AddOrSubtract (Example 12.2.1, CH12B) show the changes in the program to declare VAR DoIt : ARITHMPROC; then assign DoIt := Add; or DoIt := Subtract; and pass DoIt to procedure Calculate. Will the program still work?
2. Complete the code to graph the function $y = x^2 - x - 2$, described by PROCEDURE YPoly in this section.
3. Complete this code by supplying missing declarations, IMPORTs, and commands. What does it do? How and why?

```
(* FileName:CH12F *)
...
PROCEDURE  DoWhat(Proc1, Proc2: ARITHMPROC) : ARITHMPROC;
   VAR  ReturnIt : ARITHMPROC;    Choice, Discard : CHAR;
   BEGIN
      ReturnIt:=Proc2;  WriteString("What would you like to do?"); WriteLn;
       WriteString("   A  Add");       WriteLn;
       WriteString("   S  Subtract"); WriteLn;
      WriteString("Choose one (A or S): ");
       Read(Choice); Read(Discard); Write(Choice); WriteLn;
      IF  CAP(Choice) = 'A' THEN  ReturnIt:=Proc1;  END;(*IF*)
      RETURN  ReturnIt;
   END  DoWhat;

BEGIN
   ReadReal(x); WriteLn; ReadReal(y); WriteLn;
   LetsDoIt := DoWhat(Add, Subtract);   FWriteReal(LetsDoIt(x,y),8,2);
   ....
```

Figure 12-7
Sample Run of
NormalCurve
(Example 12.2.2)

```
What is the mean value? 5.5
What is the standard deviation? 2.3
Recommended upper and lower bounds on x
    Lower = m - 3s =    -1.40
    Upper = m + 3s =    12.40

Lower bound on x = ?  -1.40
Upper bound on x = ?  12.40
    -1.4     0.2
    -0.6     0.5
     0.1     1.1
     ...
     5.5    17.3
     6.3    16.4
     ...
    11.6     0.5
    12.4     0.2

Mean =      5.50
Standard Deviation =      2.30

Y = 100 * Height of Normal Curve

What character to use for plot symbol? *

Would you like a
      B      Bar Graph?
      L      Line Graph?
Choose one,  B or L:      L

What is plot width in print spaces?
   Width must be > 6  and  <=  60: 50

The minimum number of Lines for Graph will be      19
Would you like more lines than   19 (Y/N)? N


                        0                                                17
        X       Y       ===============================================
      -1.4     0.2      *
      -0.6     0.5      *
       0.1     1.1      ..*........................................Y
       0.9     2.3      .      *
       1.7     4.3      .           *
       2.4     7.1      .                *
       3.2    10.5      .                     *
       4.0    13.9      .                          *
       4.7    16.4      .                             *
       5.5    17.3      .                               *
       6.3    16.4      .                             *
       7.0    13.9      .                          *
       7.8    10.5      .                     *
       8.6     7.1      .                *
                        .
       9.3     4.3      .           *
      10.1     2.3      .      *
      10.9     1.1      . *
      11.6     0.5      *
      12.4     0.2      *
                        X
```

12.3   *Other Graphics Techniques*

Extended, high-resolution graphics modules are available with some versions of Modula-2. Development of these modules generally involves assembly or machine language, and their application requires special graphics circuitry, display terminals, and printers. This section provides a very short introduction to some extended graphics concepts you may encounter.

Turtlegraphics

One common extended graphics module you may see is called **Turtlegraphics.** In Turtlegraphics the (0, 0) position is often assumed to be at the center of the screen, and the horizontal *(x)* and vertical *(y)* coordinates of points can have positive and negative values up to a few hundred in magnitude. Commands are used to move a cursor—an arrow or other pointer—around the screen. Typical Turtlegraphics commands specify the distance and direction the turtle is to be moved. Figure 12−8 lists some of those commands.

The following simple program shows how Turtlegraphics might be used to draw a rectangle 30 units wide and 20 units high with a starting vertex of (−5, 5), as shown in Figure 12−9. If the commands in Figure 12−8 could be imported from a Turtlegraphics module, then a program to draw this rectangle could appear as

```
MODULE TurtleDraw;
   (* Draws a 30 x 20-unit rectangle, beginning at (-5, 5).
   Assume that the initial direction of the turtle points
   horizontally to the right, and that angles are specified
   in degrees. *)
   FROM Turtlegraphics IMPORT Forward, Right, SetPosition, Clear,
                                                        HideTurtle;


   BEGIN
      Clear;
```

A Bit of Background

Graphics on Your Machine

For graphics purposes, a screen is divided into small rectangular areas called *picture elements*, or *pixels*. An image is created by manipulating the intensity and color of the individual pixels. The resolution or sharpness of the image is established by the number of available pixels, which in turn is determined by the graphics hardware in your computer.

The earliest graphics adapters for IBM personal computers and clones were "Hercules cards" (developed by Hercules Computer Technology Corporation for monochrome graphics) and "CGA cards" (Color/Graphics Adapter cards, created by IBM). A CGA graphics plug-in card divided the screen into 320 pixels horizontally by 200 pixels vertically, each of which could display one of four colors. Now PCs have progressed through EGA (Enhanced Graphics Adapter) to VGA (Video Graphics Array) and super VGA, which can handle in excess of 1024 × 768 pixels in 256 or more colors. Other computer manufacturers, such as NeXT, Apple Computer, Sun Microsystems, Digital Equipment Corporation, and many others, have developed their own hardware and software for handling high-resolution graphics. Some of these systems are designed specifically with graphics in mind.

Before you purchase a computer for graphics, you should determine your needs and how much you are willing to spend. If your goal is to extend the capability of your current machine, check carefully whether your system will support new graphics hardware and software before you invest in circuit cards and peripherals.

Figure 12–8
Typical
Turtlegraphics
Commands

```
Forward(x)   Moves the turtle x units in the direction in which
             it points.

Backward(x)  Moves the turtle x units in the direction opposite
             from which it points.

Right(angle) Turns the turtle clockwise through the specified
             angle.

Left(angle)  Turns the turtle counterclockwise through the
             specified angle.

SetPosition(x,y)  Place the turtle at coordinate position (x,y).

ShowTurtle   Displays the character that represents the turtle.

HideTurtle   Hides the turtle character so that it is not
             displayed on the screen.

Clear   Erases all lines from the screen.
```

Figure 12–9
A 30 × 20-Unit
Rectangle
Beginning at
(−5, 5)

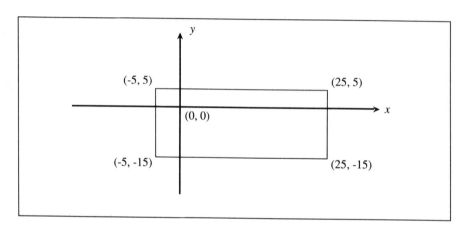

```
SetPosition(-5, 5);
Forward(30);
Right(90);
Forward(20);
Right(90);
Forward(30);
Right(90);
Forward(20);
Right(90);
HideTurtle;
END TurtleDraw.
```

☐ Draw-and-Paint

In another type of graphics called **Draw-and-Paint graphics,** lines can be drawn, and closed elliptical and polygonal areas can be drawn and shaded by specifying points, endpoints, patterns, and colors. With this technique the origin (0, 0) of the *x, y*-coordinate system often is assumed to be at the upper left corner of the screen. Typical commands in Draw-and-Paint type graphics are shown in Figure 12–10.

Now draw the same 30 × 20 rectangle as before but beginning at position (315, 195), as shown in Figure 12–11. Assume that the graphics commands of Figure 12–10 can be imported from a module called DrawAndPaint. A program to perform this operation could appear as

```
MODULE DAPDraw;
  (* Draws a 30 x 20-unit rectangle, beginning at (315, 195). *)
  FROM DrawAndPaint IMPORT Line, Clear;

BEGIN
  Clear;
  Line(315, 195,   345, 195);
  Line(345, 195,   345, 215);
  Line(345, 215,   315, 215);
  Line(315, 215,   315, 195);
END DAPDraw.
```

Drawing rectangles with these graphics modules may seem trivial, but it will get you started if your system supports extended graphics. With some research in your graphics manual, you should be able to expand your talent to produce some interesting work.

Figure 12–10
Typical
Draw-and-Paint
Graphics
Commands

Plot(*x*, *y*) Lights a minimum-size rectangle called a pixel at coordinates *x*, *y*.

Line(*x1*, *y1*, *x2*, *y2*) Draws a straight line between points (*x1*, *y1*) and (*x2*, *y2*).

Circle(*x*, *y*, *r*) Draws a circle with radius *r* and center at (*x*, *y*).

Clear Erases all figures from screen.

Shade(*x*, *y*, Color, Pattern) Shades the closed area within which point (*x*, *y*) is found, using the color and pattern (such as cross-hatched) specified. The graphics manual should present tables of cardinal numbers for Color and Pattern and their effects.

Figure 12–11
A 30 × 20-Unit
Rectangle
Beginning at (315, 195)

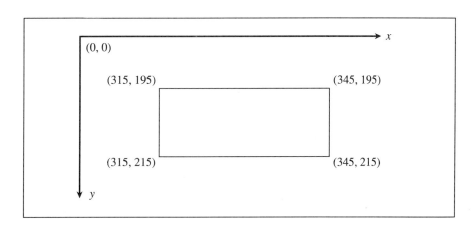

A Bit of Background

Planets and Pixels

One of the major contributions of scientists at the Jet Propulsion Laboratory in Pasadena, California, to the space effort has been the development of techniques for taking pictures in space and transmitting them back to Earth. It was JPL's concept to divide the camera field of view into pixels, to measure the intensity of light at each pixel, and then to digitally transmit the intensity measurements to the lab's computers, which are able to reconstruct an image from this data. Colors are determined by measuring the light intensities passed through various filters.

Not only has this technique produced spectacular pictures of the planets and of Jupiter's red spot as seen by *Voyager* and other spacecraft, but a major spin-off of this method is the bit-mapped graphics capability developed for today's personal computers. Much of the microcomputer technology upon which society now depends had its beginnings in space-race research to produce ever-smaller, better, more reliable instruments and the techniques for making them work.

Questions 12.3

1. Determine whether your system has software modules to support extended, high-resolution graphics. What commands are available?
2. If your system does support extended graphics, implement a program to draw the rectangle in Figure 12–9 or 12–11, and (if available) shade and/or color the inside of the rectangle.
3. **a.** Using extended graphics commands, cap the rectangle in Figure 12–9 or 12–11 with a triangle of the same width and height as the rectangle.
   b. If the commands are available, inscribe a circle at the center of the rectangle.

12.4 The Binary Search

The linear search of an array of N elements to find a desired element requires an average of $N/2$ probes, which is very slow if you are searching a long list such as a telephone directory. If the list has been sorted, however, you can use a faster technique called a **binary search.**

In a binary search, you examine first an item near the middle of the list; then, an item at the center of the appropriate half; then, an item at the center of the proper quarter, and so on, until the search item is found. In the average situation, the list length is halved each time until only one item is left. If this takes x probes for a list of N items, then you search until

$$N * (1/2) * (1/2) * \ldots * (1/2) \quad = \quad N * (1/2)^x \quad = \quad 1 \text{ item.}$$

Then $N/2^x = 1$, or $2^x = N$, or $x = \log_2 N$. Thus the number of probes for a binary search averages $\log_2 N$, which equals approximately $3.3 * \log_{10} N$ or roughly $1.44 * \ln(N)$.

For example, finding a particular name in an alphabetical directory with $N = 1000$ names would require an average of 500 (= $N/2$) probes with a linear search. With a binary search, only about 10 (= $3.3 * \log_{10} N$) probes would be required.

A Recursive Binary-Search Algorithm

Although it is not difficult to write an iterative algorithm for a binary search, the nature of the search makes recursion particularly appropriate. A recursive algorithm for a binary search for a Target element in an Array sorted in ascending order, with indices 1 to N, is

```
Set Low = 1 and High = NumOfElements
    (* Initialize the search range to encompass the entire Array. *)
BinarySearch(Array, Target, Low, High)
            (* Array, Target, Low, and High are all Value parameters. *)
        Position = (Low + High) DIV 2     (* Find the position of the middle element. *)

    If   Low > High     then
            indicate that the Target element is not in the Array

        else   if the element at Position equals the Target element
                return the Position of the Target element

        else   if the element at Position is greater than Target
                    (* then the Target is in the first half of the array. *)
                set High = Position − 1,    do not change Low
                    (* Define the new search range to be the lower half of the previous search range. *)
                BinarySearch(Array, Target, Low, High) (* recursive call *)

        else       (* if the element at Position is less than Target *)
                    (* then the Target is in the last half of the array. *)
                set Low = Position + 1,    do not change High
                    (* Define the new search range to be the upper half of the previous search range. *)
                BinarySearch(Array, Target, Low, High) (* recursive call *)
        end if
end BinarySearch
```

Figure 12–12 illustrates the recursive binary search of an array of Cities for Target city Omaha. This algorithm also allows you to determine when the Target is not in the list at all, because in that situation the value of Low eventually becomes greater than High. You can convince yourself of this by following through the search process in Figure 12–12 for a Target (such as Detroit) that is not in the array.

Recursion works especially well for the binary search, since the same search occurs repeatedly for smaller subranges of the array until the desired Target is found or until it is determined that the Target is not there. The following example illustrates a Modula-2 implementation of the binary search technique.

Example 12.4.1

Implement a binary search in Modula-2 and use it to search a two-dimensional array of Cities and States to determine the State in which a given City is located.

Define the problem   The recursive binary-search algorithm just outlined is to be coded in Modula-2. An input file CITIES.DAT contains this data in alphabetical order

```
Boise           Idaho
Cincinnati      Ohio
Dallas          Texas
Indianapolis    Indiana
KansasCity      Missouri
Milwaukee       Wisconsin
NewYork         NewYork
Phoenix         Arizona
SaltLakeCity    Utah
Tulsa           Oklahoma
```

Search List

Cities

[1]	Albuquerque	[6]	Miami
[2]	Chicago	[7]	Omaha
[3]	Denver	[8]	Seattle
[4]	Honolulu	[9]	Toledo
[5]	LosAngeles	[10]	Wichita

Search for Target Element Omaha

```
Low = 1   High = 10

BinarySearch(Cities, Omaha, 1, 10)

   Position = (1 + 10) DIV 2 = 5
     (* First element examined is Cities[5], LosAngeles * )
   LosAngeles < Omaha, so set Low = Position + 1 = 5 + 1 = 6

   BinarySearch(Cities, Omaha, 6, 10)

      Position = (6 + 10) DIV 2 = 8
         (* Next element examined is Cities[8], Seattle *)
      Seattle > Omaha, so set High = Position -1 = 8 - 1 = 7

      BinarySearch(Cities, Omaha, 6, 7)

         Position = (6 + 7) DIV 2 = 6
            (* Next element examined is Cities[6], Miami *)
         Miami < Omaha, so set Low = Position + 1 = 6 + 1 = 7

         BinarySearch(Cities, Omaha, 7, 7)

            Position = (7 + 7) DIV 2 = 7
               (* Next element examined is Cities[7], Omaha *)
            Omaha = Omaha, so display Omaha and Position 7

         end BinarySearch

      end BinarySearch

   end BinarySearch

end BinarySearch
```

Figure 12–12
Binary Search Illustration

The file will be read into a two-dimensional City, State array. The program will instruct users to enter a City name. Then the BinarySearch procedure will search for the City, and the Position of the City and State in the array will be returned.

Develop a solution The algorithm for the binary search procedure has been developed already. For this problem, BinarySearch will be implemented as a function that returns an INTEGER value. When the Target is found, the function will return the Target Position index; when Low > High, the function will return a value of − 1 to indicate that the Target City was not found.

Refine the solution   *Pseudocode*

```
begin module CitySearch
   ReadAndDisplayCities(Cities)
   SearchForCity(Cities, WhereIsCity)
   if     WhereIsCity = − 1       indicate that City is not in the array
          otherwise display target City, State, and position in the array
   end CitySearch

procedure ReadAndDisplayCities(VAR Towns)
   open input file,    read Cities and States into array,    close file
   display array    (row number,    City,    State)

procedure    SearchForCity(Towns, VAR CityPosn)
   ask for TargetCity
   set    Low = 1   and   High = Number of rows in the array
   CityPos := BinarySearch(Towns, TargetCity, Low, High)
              (* first call to recursive function BinarySearch *)

procedure BinarySearch(Array, Target, Low, High) : INTEGER
   set    Posn = (Low + High) DIV 2
   set    AlphOrder = CompareStrings(Array[Posn,City], Target)
   if    AlphOrder <> 0        and     Low <= High
         if    AlphOrder > 0        set  High = Posn − 1    (* go to lower half *)
         else                       set  Low = Posn + 1    (* go to upper half *)
         RETURN BinarySearch(Towns,TargetCity,Low,High)       (* recursive call *)
   else
         if    AlphOrder = 0       set    ReturnIt = Posn    (* target found *)
         else    ReturnIt = − 1           (* Low > High, target not found *)
         RETURN    ReturnIt         (* Return Posn or − 1 and exit recursion *)
```

Modula-2 code   The BinarySearch function corresponds to the algorithm described earlier, except that the order of testing has been altered so that there is only one RETURN final exit from the function. The IF DEMO . . . structures display the binary search process. Note the use of TabOrFill in procedure ReadAndDisplay-Cities to align the State names.

```
MODULE CitySearch;
   (* Reads Cities and States into a two dimensional array.
      Performs a binary search on the array for the Target city.
      FileName:CH12D     Modula-2     RKW     June 1991   *)

FROM InOut IMPORT WriteString, ReadString, WriteCard, WriteLn, WriteInt,
                OpenInput, CloseInput;
FROM Strings IMPORT Length, CompareStrings, TabOrFill;

CONST MAXROWS = 10;  DEMO = TRUE;  MAXSTRINDEX = 14;  Blank = ' ';
TYPE  STR = ARRAY [0..MAXSTRINDEX] OF CHAR;   CITYST = (City, State);
      WHERE = ARRAY [1..MAXROWS],[City..State] OF STR;
VAR  Cities : WHERE;  WhereIsCity : INTEGER;

PROCEDURE ReadAndDisplayCities(VAR Towns:WHERE);
   VAR  WhichRow : CARDINAL;
   BEGIN
      WriteString("Input file name (CITIES.DAT) = ? "); OpenInput("DAT");
      WhichRow := 1;
      REPEAT
```

```
            ReadString(Towns[WhichRow,City]);
            ReadString(Towns[WhichRow,State]); INC(WhichRow);
        UNTIL  WhichRow > MAXROWS;                      CloseInput;

        WriteLn; WriteString("The array is: City            State"); WriteLn;
        FOR  WhichRow := 1 TO MAXROWS  DO
            WriteCard(WhichRow,12); TabOrFill(2, Blank);
            WriteString(Towns[WhichRow, City]);
             TabOrFill(17 - Length(Towns[WhichRow, City]), Blank);
            WriteString(Towns[WhichRow, State]); WriteLn;
        END; (* FOR *)  WriteLn;
    END ReadAndDisplayCities;


PROCEDURE BinarySearch(Array:WHERE; Target:STR; Low,High:CARDINAL):INTEGER;
    (* Performs a binary search on Array for Target element.
       Low and High are the limits of the indices for the search.
       Returns Position of the Target, or -1 if Target is not found. *)
    VAR  Posn : CARDINAL;   AlphOrder, ReturnIt : INTEGER;
    BEGIN
        Posn   := (Low + High) DIV 2;   (* Position of middle element *)
            IF  DEMO  THEN
                WriteCard(Low,5); WriteCard(High,6); WriteCard(Posn,10);
                WriteString("  "); WriteString(Cities[Posn,City]); WriteLn;
            END; (* IF DEMO *)
        AlphOrder :=  CompareStrings(Array[Posn,City], Target);
        IF  (AlphOrder <> 0)  AND  (Low <= High) THEN
            IF AlphOrder>0 THEN High := Posn - 1;  (* New range = lower half *)
                ELSE  Low := Posn + 1;            (* New range = upper half *)
            END; (* IF *)
            RETURN BinarySearch(Array, Target, Low, High); (* Recursive call *)
        ELSE
            IF  AlphOrder = 0  THEN  ReturnIt := Posn;       (* Target found *)
                ELSE  ReturnIt := -1;       (* Low > High, Target not present *)
            END; (* IF *)
            RETURN  ReturnIt;               (* Return Posn and Exit Recursion *)
        END; (* IF *)
    END BinarySearch;


PROCEDURE SearchForCity(Towns:WHERE; VAR CityPosn:INTEGER);
    VAR  TargetCity : STR;   Low, High : CARDINAL;
    BEGIN
        WriteString("For what city are you searching? ");
         ReadString(TargetCity); WriteLn;   Low := 1;  High := MAXROWS;
            IF  DEMO  THEN
                WriteString("Binary Search Process: "); WriteLn;
                WriteString(" Low  High  Position   City"); WriteLn;
            END; (* IF DEMO *)
        CityPosn := BinarySearch(Towns, TargetCity, Low, High); WriteLn;
    END SearchForCity;


BEGIN  (* module CitySearch *)
    ReadAndDisplayCities(Cities);
    SearchForCity(Cities, WhereIsCity);

    IF  WhereIsCity = -1   THEN
        WriteString("That city is not in the array.");
```

```
    ELSE
       WriteString(Cities[WhereIsCity,City]); WriteString(" is at position");
       WriteInt(WhereIsCity,5); WriteString(" in the array, and is in ");
       WriteString(Cities[WhereIsCity,State]);
    END; (* IF *)  WriteLn;
END CitySearch.
```

Debug and test: If the array is not in alphabetical order, a sort procedure would have to be invoked before BinarySearch would work. On the other hand, if you create the input file with an editor, sorting could be done at that time by inserting each new entry into its proper place in the list.

A number of precautions need to be taken with this program:

1. It is a good idea to insert WriteString(Towns[WhichRow,City]) and WriteString-(Towns[WhichRow,State]) immediately after the corresponding ReadString commands in procedure ReadAndDisplayCities in order to ensure that the file is being read correctly.
2. TargetCity must be spelled exactly as it appears in the file, including the use of uppercase and lowercase, and spaces must be avoided in City and State names.
3. Low and/or High must be initialized before calling BinarySearch. Neglecting to do this will cause the program to fail, as will using the REAL divide (/) rather than DIV in calculating Posn.
4. In the BinarySearch function, it is tempting to try to compare Array[Posn,City] with Target using relational operators, as in

```
IF  Array[Posn,City] > Target  THEN . . .
```

rather than

```
IF CompareStrings(Array[Posn,City], Target) > 0  THEN . . .
```

Some versions of Modula-2 may allow this, but many will not.
5. Be certain to call BinarySearch as a function, rather than as a procedure. Because BinarySearch returns a value, the recursive call must RETURN Binary-Search(   ).

Here is a sample run:

```
Input file name (CITIES.DAT) = ? CITIES.DAT
The array is: City           State
            1  Boise          Idaho
            2  Cincinnati     Ohio
            3  Dallas         Texas
            4  Indianapolis   Indiana
            5  KansasCity     Missouri
            6  Milwaukee      Wisconsin
            7  NewYork        NewYork
            8  Phoenix        Arizona
            9  SaltLakeCity   Utah
           10  Tulsa          Oklahoma

For what city are you searching? Dallas
Binary Search Process:
   Low  High  Position  City
     1   10          5  KansasCity
     1    4          2  Cincinnati
     3    4          3  Dallas

Dallas is at position    3 in the array, and is in Texas
```

Complete the documentation The problem definition, pseudocode, code, and sample run are all important in the documentation for this problem. Since the problem is designed to implement the binary search, it would be helpful to include the binary-search algorithm and the illustration from Figure 12–12. The source code is in file CH12D. CompareStrings, Length, and TabOrFill are imported from a Strings module. Warn users that the program does not allow spaces in City and State names, and that TargetCity names must be spelled exactly as they are in the input file. When CONSTant DEMO is set to FALSE, the program displays only the final result—rather than the entire search process.

Questions 12.4

1. For program CitySearch (Example 12.4.1, CH12D) and the CITIES.DAT input file, illustrate on paper a search for SanFrancisco (which is not in the file). Show that eventually Low > High.
2. Assume that a given probe for an item on a list requires 1 millisecond (1/1000 sec) on a particular microcomputer and 1 microsecond (1/1,000,000 sec) on a mainframe. Compare the approximate times required to perform a linear search and a binary search on both machines when the number of items on the list is **a.** 100, **b.** 10,000, and **c.** 1,000,000.
3. Show how you would modify the BinarySearch function (Example 12.4.1, CH12D) to find the position of a particular CARDINAL number in an array of TYPE WHERE = ARRAY [1..MAXROWS] OF CARDINAL;
4. How would you change the BinarySearch algorithm to find an item in a list that has been sorted in order from highest to lowest?

12.5 The Quicksort

The sorting algorithms discussed in Chapter 10 require $O(N^2)$ comparisons, which makes them very slow for long lists of length N. In 1962, C. A. R. Hoare published an article called "QuickSort" in *Computer Journal* (vol. 5, pp. 10–15), in which he described a new sorting algorithm he had developed, which was so much faster than previous algorithms that it became known as *the* **Quicksort.**

Hoare's Quicksort algorithm, which is also called a "partition sort," divides a list into two smaller sublists and sorts each sublist by partitioning it into two smaller sublists, and so forth. Ideally each partition divides the lists into equal parts. Lists may need to be subdivided x times until there is only one item in each sublist, so that

$$N * (1/2) * (1/2) * \ldots * (1/2) = N/2^x = 1;$$

then $x = \log_2 N$. Each time a partition is made, all of the items in the list being divided are examined; so in the aggregate, each division represents N comparisons. Therefore, the total number of compares for an ideal Quicksort is $O(N * \log_2 N)$, approximately $3.3 * N * \log_{10} N$ or $1.44 * N * \ln(N)$.

Given $N = 1000$ items, for example, the average number of comparisons for the Selection sort would be roughly $1,000,000 \ (= 1000^2)$, whereas the average comparisons for the Quicksort could be approximately $10,000 \ (= 3.3 * 1000 * \log_{10} 1000)$.

It should be noted that in the worst possible situation only one item would be separated from the list in each partition. Then the number of sublist divisions, x, would be N; and the number of Quicksort comparisons could be as many as $O(N^2)$.

Figure 12–13 illustrates the first few steps of a Quicksort on an array of names. When two names are compared, the one that comes first alphabetically will be said to have a value ''less than'' the other. Then the Quicksort algorithm for the examples illustrated in Figure 12–13 is

1. Two CARDINAL values Left and Right are assigned to the indices at the limits of the list to be sorted. In this example, Left = 0 and Right = 9.

2. Partition the list. Assign movable counters to Left and Right. Call them Up and Down (to describe which direction they will move), so that initially Up = Left = 0 and Down = Right = 9.

3. Choose a Pivot value, which can be any element in the list. If it is assumed that the list may be partially sorted already, a reasonable guess for Pivot is close to the middle of the list. However, common variations of the Quicksort are to set the pivot at the leftmost element, in the middle, or randomly. In this example, try Pivot point = (Up + Down) DIV 2 = 4; the name at the Pivot point is *Gail.*

4. Repeat until Up and Down pass each other; that is, until Up > Down.
   a. Move Up until a value greater than or equal to Pivot *(Gail)* is found, namely *Tim;* and move Down until a value less than or equal to Pivot *(Gail)* is found, namely *Abby.*
   b. Interchange these two values at Up and Down. Then increment Up and decrement Down, as shown in Figure 12–13b. Note in the figure that Up will not move anymore, but that Down will move to *Babs.* Then *Babs* will be interchanged with *Gail,* Up will be incremented, and Down will be decremented—as shown in Figure 12–13c. (Now that Up > Down, the list has been partitioned; that is, all elements between Left and Down are smaller than any element between Up and Right.)

5. Now execute the Quicksort again to sort the list between Left and Down; also execute Quicksort to sort the list between Up and Right. (If your machine had multiple CPUs, these two sorts could be performed concurrently by different CPUs to speed up the process; a single-processor computer must perform one sort at a time. Concurrent processes are discussed in a later chapter.)

The whole process is repeated with ever-smaller parts of the list until the sort is completed.

A Recursive Quicksort Algorithm

Although an iterative algorithm can be devised for Quicksort with the use of ''stack structures'' (which are discussed in Chapter 16), recursion makes it a simpler process. Here is recursive pseudocode for the Quicksort on the list of names.

```
QuickSort(VAR List:PEOPLE;    Left,Right:CARDINAL)
    VAR    Up, Down : CARDINAL
    begin
        if Left < Right
            Up = Left, Down = Right
            Partition(List, Up, Down)
            QuickSort(List, Left, Down)
            QuickSort(List, Up, Right)
        end if
    end QuickSort
```

```
Partition(VAR List:PEOPLE;  VAR Up,Down:CARDINAL)
    VAR Pivot : CARDINAL
```

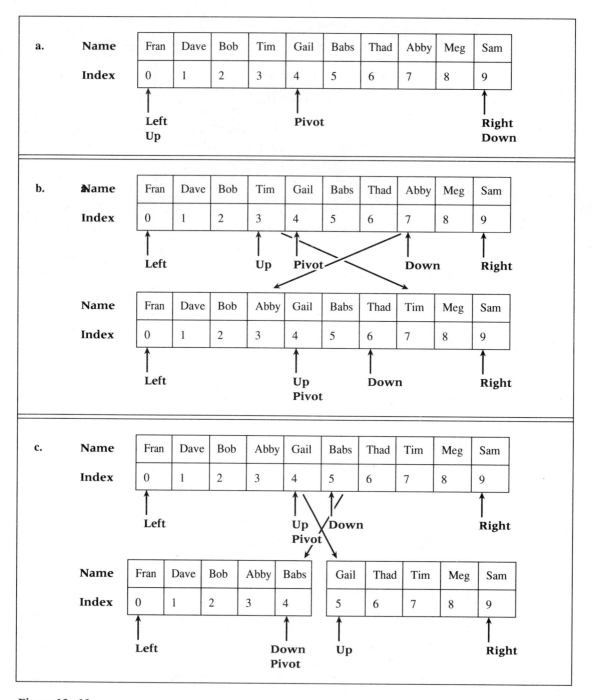

Figure 12–13
Quicksort Partitions **a.** Array of Names to Be Sorted **b.** The First Steps of Partitioning **c.** Partitioning
Continued

```
begin
    Pivot = (Up + Down) DIV 2
    repeat
        while List[Up] < List[Pivot]
            increment Up    (* Move Up to the right. *)
        end while
        while List[Down] > List[Pivot]
            decrement Down        (* Move Down to the left. *)
        end while

        if Up <= Down
            swap List[Up] with List[Down]
            increment Up
            if Down > 0      then decrement Down end if
        end if
    until Up > Down
            (* Assertions: Up will be greater than Down.
                           List[Left..Up] <= Pivot.
                           List[Down..Right] >= Pivot.   *)
    end Partition
```

This example implements Quicksort in Modula-2.

Example 12.5.1

Perform a Quicksort on the array of names shown in Figure 12–13.

Define the problem   Read the names in the figure from an input file into an array. Quicksort the array. Display the array before and after sorting.

Develop a solution   Perform these operations in order:

1. Read the names from the file into the array.
2. Display the array.
3. Quicksort the array.
4. Display the array.

Refine the solution   *Pseudocode*

```
begin module DemoQuickSort
    ReadNames(NameList)
    DisplayNames(NameList)
    QuickSort(NameList, LowIndex, HighIndex)
    DisplayNames(NameList)
end DemoQuickSort

procedure ReadNames(VAR List)
    open input file,     read Names into array List,     close file

procedure DisplayNames(List)
    for    NameCount = LowIndex to HighIndex     WriteString(List[NameCount])

procedure QuickSort(VAR List;    Left, Right)
    (* See QuickSort and Partition procedures above. *)
```

Modula-2 code   Read the QuickSort and Partition procedures carefully to convince yourself that they do perform the sort as described in the pseudocode. By hand, follow through the QuickSort and Partition procedures on the NameList array, recording the values of Up, Down, Left, Right, and Pivot, and drawing the array after each interchange. You may wish to insert write statements into the program to display these values and the array at each step of the process.

```
MODULE DemoQuickSort;
    (* Demonstrates QuickSort on an array of Names.
       FileName:CH12E        Modula-2      RKW      June 1991  *)

FROM InOut IMPORT ReadString, WriteCard, WriteString, WriteLn,
                  OpenInput, CloseInput;
FROM Strings IMPORT CompareStrings;

CONST  LOWINDEX = 0;  HIGHINDEX = 9;  HIGHSTRINDEX = 3;
TYPE  STR = ARRAY [0..HIGHSTRINDEX] OF CHAR;
      PEOPLE = ARRAY [LOWINDEX..HIGHINDEX] OF STR;
VAR  NameList : PEOPLE;

PROCEDURE Partition(VAR List:PEOPLE;  VAR Up,Down:CARDINAL);
    VAR  Pivot:CARDINAL;  TempName : STR;
    BEGIN
        Pivot := (Up + Down) DIV 2;
        REPEAT
            WHILE  CompareStrings(List[Up], List[Pivot]) < 0  DO
                INC(Up);    (* Move Up to the right *)
            END; (* WHILE *)
            WHILE  CompareStrings(List[Down], List[Pivot]) > 0  DO
                DEC(Down);  (*Move Down to the left.*)
            END; (* WHILE *)
            IF  Up <= Down  THEN (* Interchange records Up and Down *)
                TempName:=List[Down]; List[Down]:=List[Up]; List[Up]:=TempName;
                INC(Up);                (* Move Up and Down *)
                IF  Down > 0  THEN  DEC(Down); END; (* IF *)
            END; (* IF *)
        UNTIL  Up > Down;
        (*Assertions:List[Left..Up]<=Pivot, Up>Down, List[Down..Right]>=Pivot*)
    END Partition;

PROCEDURE QuickSort(VAR List:PEOPLE;  Left,Right:CARDINAL);
    VAR  Up, Down : CARDINAL;
    BEGIN
        IF  Left < Right  THEN
            Up := Left; Down := Right;
            Partition(List, Up, Down);
            QuickSort(List, Left, Down);
            QuickSort(List, Up, Right);
        END; (* IF *)
    END QuickSort;

PROCEDURE ReadNames(VAR List:PEOPLE);
    VAR  NameCount : CARDINAL;
    BEGIN
        WriteString("Input file (NAMES.IN) = ? ");  OpenInput("IN");
        FOR  NameCount := LOWINDEX  TO  HIGHINDEX  DO
            ReadString(List[NameCount]);
        END; (* FOR *)                          CloseInput;
    END ReadNames;
```

```
PROCEDURE DisplayNames(List:PEOPLE);
   VAR  NameCount : CARDINAL;
   BEGIN
      FOR  NameCount := LOWINDEX  TO  HIGHINDEX  DO
         WriteString(List[NameCount]);  WriteString("     ");
      END; (* FOR *)
   END DisplayNames;

BEGIN  (* module DemoQuickSort *)
   ReadNames(NameList);
   WriteLn; WriteString("The unsorted list is:"); WriteLn;
   DisplayNames(NameList); WriteLn;
   QuickSort(NameList, LOWINDEX, HIGHINDEX);
   WriteLn; WriteString("The sorted list is:"); WriteLn;
   DisplayNames(NameList); WriteLn;
END DemoQuickSort.
```

Debug and test The errors most likely to cause disaster in this program are

- not declaring List, Up, and Down as VAR parameters,
- reversing > or < in the Partition procedure, and
- comparing Up or Down with Pivot instead of comparing the array elements List[Up] and List[Down] with List[Pivot].

Here is a sample run:

```
Input file (NAMES.IN)  = ? NAMES.IN
The unsorted list is:
Fran    Dave    Bob    Tim    Gail    Babs    Thad    Abby    Meg    Sam


The sorted list is:
Abby    Babs    Bob    Dave    Fran    Gail    Meg    Sam    Thad    Tim
```

Complete the documentation Because the program is designed to illustrate the QuickSort, include in the documentation a discussion of how Quicksort works, as well as the problem description, development, pseudocode, and code (CH12E). Include a listing of the input file with the sample run.

The input file NAMES.IN must be created before the program is executed. A CompareStrings procedure must be available from a Strings module. The size of the array and length of the Names can be modified by changing the CONSTant values and the contents of the input file.

Questions 12.5

1. For program DemoQuickSort (Example 12.5.1, CH12E)
   a. take the NameList array from Figure 12–13 and follow through the Quick-Sort and Partition procedures by hand, on paper, recording the values of Up, Down, Left, Right, and Pivot, and drawing the array after each interchange.
   b. insert statements and structures similar to the IF DEMO THEN . . . structures in program CitySearch (Example 12.4.1, CH12D) to trace the values of Up, Down, Left, Right, and Pivot, and display the array at each step of the Quicksort process.
2. Assume that an item-compare operation requires 1 millisecond on a particular microcomputer and 1 microsecond on a mainframe. Calculate the approximate times needed to perform a Selection sort and an ideal Quicksort on both ma-

chines when the number of items on the list is **a.** 100, **b.** 10,000, and **c.** 1,000,000.

3. Show how you would modify the Quicksort and Partition procedures (Example 12.5.1, CH12E) to sort an array of REAL numbers.

4. How would you modify the Quicksort and Partition procedures to sort a list in reverse order, from Highest to Lowest values?

12.6   *Summary*

Character-Oriented Graphics   The graphics-handling capability of a computer is hardware and software dependent. However, low-resolution graphs can be created on any system. Appendix C contains a graphics module with procedures for sorting parallel arrays of REAL values that uses characters to construct line and bar plots of the data.

Procedure Types   Modula-2 allows you to use procedure types, which declare the parameter types and the type of value to be returned by a function. You can pass entire procedures and functions as parameters between modules and other procedures.

Plotting y = f(x)   An important application of procedure types is to pass functions of the form $y = f(x)$ to procedure ConvertToArray in the Graphics module in order to produce line and bar plots for those functions.

Extended Graphics   Some systems include modules for high-resolution, pixel-oriented Turtlegraphics, "draw-and-paint" graphics, or other graphing techniques. The development of such modules generally involves code oriented to a particular machine, and implementation depends upon the availability of special hardware.

Binary Search   Searching a long list of N items can be tedious if you are using a linear search, which requires $O(N)$ probes. In a binary search, you first examine an item near the middle of the list, then at the center of the appropriate half, then at the middle of the proper quarter, and so forth. The binary search, with $O(\log_2 N)$ probes, is faster.

The Quicksort   In the early 1960s, C. A. R. Hoare devised a Quicksort (or *partition* sort), which partitions a list of N items into two sublists, applies the partition process to each sublist, and so on, until the list is sorted. This process is easily implemented with recursion. In the ideal situation, the Quicksort can require as few as $O(N * \log_2 N)$ compares.

12.7   *Exercises*

Exercises marked with (FileName:_____) indicate those that ask you to use, modify, or extend the text examples. The numbers in brackets, [ ], indicate the section that contains the material you need in order to complete the exercise.

1. [12.1] During a ten-day period, the stock-market industrials average fluctuated as follows:

Day	Industrials Average
1	2839
2	2876
3	2907
4	2892

Day	Industrials Average
5	2933
6	2948
7	2957
8	2917
9	2882
10	2902

Draw a bar graph showing the amount by which the market fluctuated above and below the 2900 level during the ten days.

2. [12.1] Seasonally adjusted total monthly retail sales for the United States during a twelve-month period were

Month	Sales ($ billions)	Month	Sales ($ billions)
June	$134.8	December	139.0
July	135.5	January	140.0
August	136.0	February	139.2
September	135.8	March	139.4
October	137.7	April	140.9
November	139.6	May	141.1

Draw a meaningful bar graph comparing monthly sales for the period.

3. [12.1] During a given experiment, particle detectors measured the following numbers of protons scattered at selected angles (with respect to the initial particle beam direction) from a target sample:

Angle (degrees)	Particles Detected
0.0	25,400
+ 10.0	13,290
− 10.0	12,842
+ 35.0	7,640
− 35.0	6,418
+ 90.0	5,040
− 90.0	4,997
+ 135.0	3,742
− 135.0	3,681
+ 170.0	2,894
− 170.0	2,502

Read the data in the order given, then plot a point (line) graph of the number of particles versus angle. Don't forget to sort the data and scale it so that the graph is meaningful.

4. [12.1] Draw a bar chart showing the number of times the vowels *a, e, i, o,* and *u* appear in a string of text. *Hint:* examine the characters in the string and accumulate the vowel counts. Let array X values 1.0 to 5.0 represent the vowels, and array Y equal the corresponding vowel counts. Print a header that relates the letters *a, e, i, o,* and *u* to the REAL X values.

5. [12.2] (FileName:CH12B)
   a. Extend program AddOrSubtract (Example 12.2.1) to include multiplication (Op = '∗'), division (Op = '/'), and exponentiation (Op = '∧'). $a \wedge b$ raises positive REAL a to the REAL b power using $a^b = \exp(b * \ln a)$.
   b. Extend program AddOrSubtract to accept any positive REAL number (which must include a decimal point), followed by an operator, followed by another

positive REAL number. Spaces and any other characters should be ignored, and division by zero should be prevented. For example, the program should be able to handle such strings as $41.765 - 0.71$ and $5.0 * 6.24$.

6. [12.2] Write a program that tabulates values of any function of

```
TYPE   FUNKY  =  PROCEDURE(REAL)  :  REAL;
```

between limits *a* and *b* specified by the user. For example,

```
PROCEDURE CubeLessOne(x : REAL)  :  REAL;
    BEGIN
        RETURN x * x * x  -   1.0;
    END CubeLessOne;
```

would be one such function that could be passed as a parameter to PROCE-DURE MakeATable(f:FUNKY; a, b:REAL). Test your program with at least three different functions of type FUNKY.

7. [12.2] If you are comfortable with calculus, write a program that integrates any function of TYPE TOINTEGRATE = PROCEDURE(REAL):REAL between limits *a* and *b* specified by the user. The integral should be found using the trapezoidal rule:

$$\int_a^b f(x)dx = (1/2) * \Delta x * [f(x_0) + 2f(x_1) + 2f(x_2) + \ldots + 2f(x_{n-1}) + f(x_n)]$$

where

$$\Delta x = (b - a)/n \quad \text{and} \quad x_0 = a, \quad x_n = b, \quad x_i = x_0 + i(\Delta x).$$

Begin with $n = 10$ and keep doubling n until two consecutive answers are within 0.0005 of each other.

Test your program with at least three different functions of type TOINTE-GRATE. (*Hint:* Choose at least one simple function, such as a polynomial, that you can integrate by hand to see if the answer is correct.)

8. [12.2] Develop a program that defines a procedure type and variable

```
TYPE WORDHANDLER  =  PROCEDURE(ARRAY OF CHAR)
VAR DisplayIt : WORDHANDLER;
```

Write two procedures, ReverseLastWord and DisplayFirstWord, which accept a parameter Phrase (ARRAY OF CHAR) and display the last word of the Phrase in reverse order or the first word in normal order, respectively. A menu will assign DisplayFirstWord or ReverseLastWord to DisplayIt, and DisplayIt will

---

A Bit of Background

Computing on the Range

The projectile range problem provided a major impetus to the development of early electronic computers. During World War II approximately 15 minutes were required to calculate by hand the trajectory of a single artillery shell. Based in part upon previous work by others, Dr. John Mauchley and student J. Presper Eckert at the University of Pennsylvania created the ENIAC, a computer that could perform trajectory calculations in fewer than 30 seconds. The ENIAC, which was not operational until after the war in 1946, covered 15,000 square feet of floor space, weighed 30 tons, incorporated 18,000 vacuum tubes, consumed 140 kilowatts of power, cost nearly half a million 1946 dollars, and had to be rewired for every new program. It was hardly a portable machine to use at the front. Now, of course, more computing power is available in a laptop computer.

Figure 12–14
Projectile Motion
(Exercise 10)

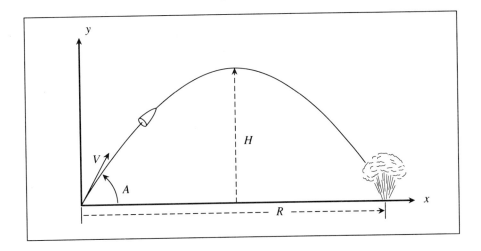

be called to perform the appropriate operation.

9. [12.2] Plot the curve $y = x \cos(x)$, with x measured in radians and the function cos imported from module MathLib0. Try x in the range -8 to $+8$ to see a significant part of the curve. Plot at least 25 points.

10. [12.2] The path of a projectile fired from the ground is shown in Figure 12–14. The equation relating height (y meters) and distance (x meters) of the projectile trajectory is

$$y = (\sin A/\cos A) * x - g * x^2/(2 * v^2 * (\cos A)^2)$$

with v = initial speed (meters/sec) and g = 9.8 meters/sec^2. Sin and cos can be imported from MathLib0, and angle A must be expressed in radians between 0 and 1.57 (= 90 degrees).

   a. For a given angle A and speed v, create a point (line) graph of height y versus distance x. Plot at least 25 points.

   b. Estimate the range R where the object strikes the ground.

   c. Determine the maximum height H reached by the projectile.

11. [12.2] On the surface of a liquid at a given instant in time, the height h (meters) of a wave radiating from a source at $x = 0$ is given as a function of distance x (meters) from the source by

$$h = h0 * \exp(-k * x) * \cos(2 * \pi * x/L).$$

π = approximately 3.14159, L is the wavelength of the wave (in meters), and k is a damping coefficient (typically a small number between 0.1 and 0.9). Use the procedures from the Graphics module to create plots of the height (h) of the wave versus distance (x) from the source for various values of initial height $h0$, L, and k. Let x range at least from 0 to $2L$. Plot at least 25 points for each graph. *Hint:* You may choose either to repeat the calls to ConvertArray and PlotIt for different functions with different $h0$, k, and L values, or to change the ConvertToArray procedure so that $h0$, k, and L can be passed from your main module clear through to the calculation of y.

12. [12.3] If your system supports extended graphics, implement the program of question 3 at the end of Section 12.3.

13. [12.3] If your system supports extended graphics, draw the sawtooth pattern shown in Figure 12–15. The length of the sides of each succeeding equilateral

Figure 12–15
Sawtooth Pattern
(Exercise 13)

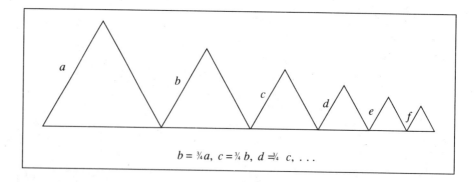

$b = \frac{3}{4}a,\ c = \frac{3}{4}b,\ d = \frac{3}{4}c, \ldots$

triangle is 3/4 the length in the preceding triangle. If possible, shade each triangle with a different color and/or pattern.

14. **a.** [12.4] (FileName:CH12D) Modify the BinarySearch procedure of Example 12.4.1 to produce a procedure that can be applied to CARDINAL numbers.

  b. [12.5] (FileName:CH12E) Create an array of random CARDINAL numbers between 1 and 100. Quicksort this array and perform a binary search for a number specified by the user. Can you create an interesting game from this?

15. **a.** [12.4] (FileName:CH12D) Modify program CitySearch (Example 12.4.1) so that it asks for and searches for cities repeatedly—without exiting and losing the sorted array—until a city named *ZZZZZZ* is requested.

  b. [12.5] (FileName:CH12D) Add a Quicksort procedure to program City-Search to sort the array in alphabetical order by City before performing the binary search.

16. [12.4] (FileName:CH12D) Rewrite the binary search algorithm using iteration structures instead of recursion.

17. [12.4] Create parallel arrays of Occupant names and their home addresses (between 1299 and 100) on a particular street in descending Address order. Perform a binary search of the Address array for an address in a particular range (such as between 960 and 951) specified from the keyboard, and display the Name and address of the Occupant who lives there.

18. [12.5] Read REAL percentage grades into an array from the keyboard. Terminate with a negative entry. Quicksort and display the grades in descending order.

19. [12.5] Read a file that contains the first name, last name, and age of each child in a group into parallel arrays.

  a. Before sorting, perform a linear search and display the names and ages of all the children under the age of 12. Why is a linear search more appropriate than a binary search here?

  b. Quicksort and display a list of the children and their ages in order of increasing age.

20. [12.2] (FileName:CH12F) Using the program fragment in question 3, Section 12.2, as a guide, write a function that accepts procedures

```
ReadNumbersFromFile(VAR Numbers: ARRAY OF REAL)
FindAndDisplayTheSum(Numbers : ARRAY OF REAL)
FindAndDisplayTheAverage(Numbers : ARRAY OF REAL)
DisplayTheArray(Numbers : ARRAY OF REAL)
QuickSortNumbers(VAR Numbers : ARRAY OF REAL)
```

as parameters. The function displays a menu asking which operation you want to perform and returns the appropriate procedure to the program, which then performs that operation. The program will invoke the menu function repeatedly to allow you to perform different operations until you tell it to stop.

13

Records

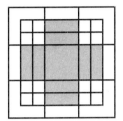

Chapter Outline

An array allows access to a list or a table of data of the same type under one identifier. At times however, you may want to store information of varying types—such as a name String, a CARDINAL number of items, a REAL amount of a bill, a BOOLEAN flag, and so forth—all in one structure. A structure that stores different types of data under a single identifier is called a *data record,* or simply a *record.*

13.1 *Introducing Records*

A **record** is a collection of data under one heading, where the data need not be all of the same type. For example, consider the following printed information about two of your company's valued customers:

Name	Phone	Number of Bicycles Purchased	Kind of Bicycles Purchased	Total Bill	Good Credit Risk?
Ann Smith	312-3542	6	Street	897.00	TRUE
Al Williams	415-0093	9	Racing	3239.55	FALSE

Each line of this printout can be considered a data record for a customer. Each record consists of a number of **data fields,** each containing particular information about the customer. In this example, there are six fields for each customer: the Name and Phone number fields (represented by CHARacter Strings), the CARDINAL Number of Bicycles purchased, the kind of Bicycle in terms of a user-defined type (Mountain, Street, Racing), the REAL Total Bill, and a field containing BOOLEAN value TRUE or FALSE that records your judgement of the customer's credit worthiness.

☐ A Record Data Type

In Modula-2 you define a record by specifying a type and a variable. The syntax for a record declaration appears in Figure 13–1. If more than one field is of one type, or if more than one variable is of the same record type, the names of those fields or records can be collected in a list, separated by commas. Field types can be simple (INTEGER, BOOLEAN, REAL, and so on), user-defined enumeration, or other structured types (arrays, records, and so on). If the field type is user-defined, it must be declared before the record definition. The same field names can be used in different record type declarations.

Customer and Patron record variables containing six fields illustrated above could be defined as shown in the Example in Figure 13–1.

☐ Record Fields

When any operation involving records is to be carried out, you specify a qualifying record *variable* name (not the record type name) followed by a period and then the field name. For example, if the values for Ann Smith were to be assigned to the record variable Customer, you would write

```
Customer.Name    := ''Ann Smith'';
Customer.Phone   := ''312-3542'';
```

Figure 13–1
Syntax for Record
Definition

Syntax

```
TYPE RecordName = RECORD
                    FieldOneName : FIELDONETYPE;
                    FieldTwoName : FIELDTWOTYPE;
                        . . .
                    FieldNName   : FIELDNTYPE;
                END;  (* RECORD *)
```

Example:

```
CONST  MAXSTRLEN = 50;
TYPE   STR = ARRAY[1..MAXSTRLEN] OF CHAR;
       KIND = (Mountain, Street, Racing);
       CLIENT = RECORD
                   Name, Phone : STR;
                   NumBikes    : CARDINAL;
                   BikeKind    : KIND;
                   Bill        : REAL;
                   GoodRisk    : BOOLEAN;
                END; (* RECORD *)
VAR  Customer, Patron : CLIENT;
```

```
Customer.NumBikes  := 6;
Customer.BikeKind  := Street;
Customer.Bill      := 897.00;
Customer.GoodRisk  := TRUE;
```

Any comparison, read, write, or other operation must be executed upon the field name qualified by the record name. To write the phone number, number of Bicycles purchased, total bill, and credit risk, for example, would require these transactions:

```
WriteString(Customer.Phone);
WriteCard(Customer.NumBikes, 5);
FWriteReal(Customer.Bill, 8, 2);
IF  Customer.GoodRisk  THEN
  WriteString("   Good Credit Risk" );
ELSE
  WriteString("   Poor Risk, Send C.O.D. ");
END; (* IF *)  WriteLn;
```

For the values previously assigned to record Ann Smith, this would display

```
312-3542   6  897.00   Good Credit Risk
```

Records may be assigned to records of an identical type by using the record names. For example, the command

```
Patron := Customer;
```

would cause the values in all of the Customer fields to be assigned to the equivalent Patron fields, such as

```
Patron.Name := Customer.Name;
```

```
Patron.Phone := Customer.Phone;
and so forth.
```

Records can be declared locally within procedures. Furthermore, an entire record can be passed as a parameter to a procedure by specifying the record variable name in the procedure call *and* a formal record parameter name and type in the procedure heading. For example, the call ShipSlip(Customer) passes all fields of record Customer at once to the formal record parameter Buyer in

```
PROCEDURE ShipSlip(Buyer : CLIENT);
```

Remember, CLIENT is a record *type;* and Buyer is a record *variable.*

Individual fields also may be passed as parameters. For example, a call TryItOut(Customer.NumBikes); would pass the single CARDINAL field value Customer.NumBikes to parameter HowMany in a

```
PROCEDURE TryItOut(HowMany : CARDINAL);
```

The following example illustrates how individual records might be handled in a simplified mail order system.

Example 13.1.1

Accept a telephone order for Bicycles. Determine the total cost of the order and whether to bill the customer or send the order C.O.D.

Define the problem   A customer will call in an order for Bicycles, giving his or her name, address, phone number, number of Bicycles desired, and kind of Bicycles. For now, all Bicycles on one order must be the same kind (a restriction removed in Exercise 3 at the end of the chapter). Mountain bikes cost $269.95 each; Street bikes, $149.50; and Racing bikes, $359.95. The total bill will be calculated. Based upon the user's knowledge of the customer, the computer will prepare instructions to ship the Bicycles and either send a bill to the customer or require (C.O.D.) payment on delivery.

Develop a solution   A record type is defined similar to the one described in Figure 13–1, and record variable Customer is declared. The program calls a procedure that asks for Name, Address, Phone, Number of Bicycles, and Kind of Bicycles. Then the user is asked whether the customer is a good credit risk, and the total bill is calculated. A second procedure prints shipping instructions. Figure 13–2 is a structure chart for the solution.

Refine the solution   *Pseudocode*

```
begin module BicycleOrders
        RecvOrder(Customer)
        ShipSlip(Customer)
end BicycleOrders

PROCEDURE RecvOrder
        initialize Costs of Mountain, Street, and Racing bikes
        ask for Patron's Name, Address, Phone, NumBikes, BikeKind
        calculate Patron's Bill given the BikeKind
        determine whether Patron is a good risk
```

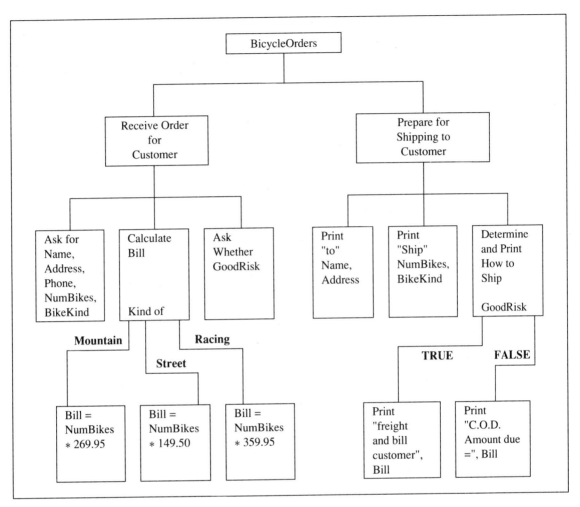

Figure 13–2
Structure Chart for BicycleOrders (Example 13.1.1)

```
PROCEDURE ShipSlip
        print Buyer's name and address and NumBikes, BikeKind,
        freight or C.O.D.,    and Bill amount
```

Modula-2 code Note the definitions of the CLIENT record type and variable
Customer. Observe that just the Customer record name is passed to the procedures
(to Patron in RecvOrder, and to Buyer in ShipSlip).

Assignments, reading, writing, and comparing are performed for the *individual
values* in the fields, not for entire records. The record TYPE identifier names are
used only to define variables and parameters.

```
MODULE BicycleOrders;
    (* Processes phone orders for a customer.  Illustrates records.
      File Name:CH13A     Modula-2     RKW      June 1991 *)

FROM InOut IMPORT WriteString, WriteLn, ReadCard, WriteCard, Read, Write;
FROM RealInOut IMPORT FWriteReal;    FROM Strings IMPORT ReadLine;
```

```
CONST  MAXSTRLEN = 50;
TYPE   STR = ARRAY [1..MAXSTRLEN]OF CHAR;
       KIND = (Mountain, Street, Racing);
       CLIENT = RECORD
                    Name, Address, Phone : STR;
                    NumBikes             : CARDINAL;
                    BikeKind             : KIND;
                    Bill                 : REAL;
                    GoodRisk             : BOOLEAN;
                END; (* RECORD *)
VAR  Customer : CLIENT;

PROCEDURE RecvOrder(VAR Patron : CLIENT);
    VAR  TakeARisk,CapRisk,Use,CapUse,Discard:CHAR;  Cost:ARRAY KIND OF REAL;
    BEGIN
        Cost[Mountain]:=269.95; Cost[Street]:=149.50; Cost[Racing]:=359.95;

        WriteLn; WriteString("Customer information? "); WriteLn;
        WriteString(" Name:        "); ReadLine(Patron.Name);
        WriteString(" Address:   "); ReadLine(Patron.Address);
        WriteString(" Phone No.: "); ReadLine(Patron.Phone); WriteLn;
        WriteString("How many Bicycles are ordered? ");
         ReadCard(Patron.NumBikes); WriteLn;

        REPEAT
           WriteString("Kind of Bicycle ordered:"); WriteLn;
            WriteString("   M    Mountain"); WriteLn;
            WriteString("   S    Street"); WriteLn;
            WriteString("   R    Racing"); WriteLn;
           WriteString("Choose one (M, S, or R): "); Read(Use); Read(Discard);
            CapUse:=CAP(Use); Write(CapUse); WriteLn; WriteLn;
        UNTIL  (CapUse='M') OR (CapUse='S') OR (CapUse='R');
         CASE  CapUse  OF
            'M' :  Patron.BikeKind := Mountain |
            'S' :  Patron.BikeKind := Street   |
            'R' :  Patron.BikeKind := Racing;
          END; (* CASE *)

        Patron.Bill := FLOAT(Patron.NumBikes) * Cost[Patron.BikeKind];

        REPEAT
           WriteString("Is this customer a good risk (Y/N)? ");
            Read(TakeARisk); Read(Discard);
             CapRisk := CAP(TakeARisk); Write(CapRisk); WriteLn;
        UNTIL  (CapRisk='Y') OR (CapRisk='N');
         Patron.GoodRisk := (CapRisk = 'Y');
    END RecvOrder;

PROCEDURE ShipSlip(Buyer : CLIENT);
    BEGIN
        WriteLn; WriteLn;
        WriteString("           Shipping Instructions: "); WriteLn; WriteLn;
        WriteString("To: ");  WriteString(Buyer.Name); WriteLn;
         WriteString("    "); WriteString(Buyer.Address); WriteLn;
        WriteString("Ship "); WriteCard(Buyer.NumBikes,5); WriteString("   ");
        CASE  Buyer.BikeKind  OF
```

```
      Mountain : WriteString(" Mountain Bikes  ")  |
      Street   : WriteString(" Street Bikes    ")  |
      Racing   : WriteString(" Racing Bikes    ");
   END; (* CASE *)  WriteLn;

   IF  Buyer.GoodRisk  THEN
      WriteString("by freight, and bill the customer $");
   ELSE
      WriteString("C.O.D.   Amount due on delivery = $");
   END; (* IF *)  FWriteReal(Buyer.Bill, 8, 2);  WriteLn;
 END ShipSlip;

BEGIN  (* module BicycleOrders *)
   RecvOrder(Customer);
   ShipSlip(Customer);
END BicycleOrders.
```

Debug and test The errors most likely to be encountered in a program that uses records are those related to undefined or incompatible variables. Such errors occur when the user attempts to use a field name alone (such as *Bill*), without specifying the record to which it belongs (as in *Patron.Bill*). Also, it is a common mistake to attempt to use a record name without specifying the field (such as writing *Buyer* instead of *Buyer.Name*). Of course, you need to develop your own code for writing the values of user-defined BikeKind or BOOLEAN GoodRisk fields.

Testing should include valid data as well as illegal values for Kind and GoodRisk, and perhaps addresses that exceed 50 characters. Check some results to make sure that the Bill is calculated correctly. Here is a sample run.

```
Customer information?
 Name:      Ann Smith
 Address:   1234 Wilson Lane, Hooper NV  86123
 Phone No.: 312-3542

How many Bicycles are ordered? 6
Kind of Bicycle ordered:
    M      Mountain
    S      Street
    R      Racing
Choose one (M, S, or R): S

Is this customer a good risk (Y/N)? Y


            Shipping Instructions:

To: Ann Smith
    1234 Wilson Lane, Hooper NV  86123
Ship    6     Street Bikes
by freight, and bill the customer $  897.00
```

Complete the documentation In the algorithm development, be sure to discuss how the records are defined. The code itself is very important here; users need to see the structure declarations and record-handling commands. Pseudocode and sample runs help the users understand how the program is designed and how it works. The users' manual should contain at least the following information:

The source code file is CH13A. A Strings module containing a ReadLine procedure must be available. The cost of Bicycles can be changed by assigning different values to the Cost array at the beginning of the procedure RecvOrder. A customer may not mix kinds of Bicycles in one order.

☐ A Record-Based Abstract Data Type

A technical application of records is illustrated by vector analysis. In two dimensions, vectors are pairs of numbers that represent directed arrows in a plane. The definitions of vectors and operations of vector arithmetic, developed here as an abstract data type, can also be applied to complex numbers and points in a plane. Two-dimensional vectors can be written in the form

$$v1 = (a, b) \quad \text{and} \quad v2 = (c, d),$$

where a and b are called the x and y *components* of $v1$, and c and d are the components of $v2$. These operational definitions apply:

addition: $v1 + v2 = (a, b) + (c, d) = (a + c, b + d)$

negation: $-v1 = -(a, b) = (-a, -b)$

subtraction: $v1 - v2 = v1 + (-v2) = (a - c, b - d)$

Figure 13–3
Addition of Vectors,
$v = (9, 4)$ and
$w = (3, 5)$

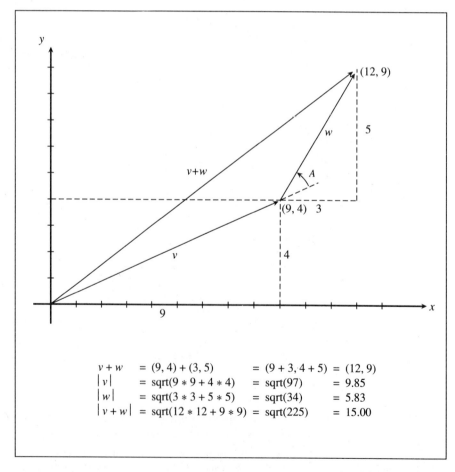

$$
\begin{aligned}
v + w &= (9, 4) + (3, 5) & &= (9 + 3, 4 + 5) = (12, 9) \\
|v| &= \text{sqrt}(9 * 9 + 4 * 4) & &= \text{sqrt}(97) & &= 9.85 \\
|w| &= \text{sqrt}(3 * 3 + 5 * 5) & &= \text{sqrt}(34) & &= 5.83 \\
|v + w| &= \text{sqrt}(12 * 12 + 9 * 9) & &= \text{sqrt}(225) & &= 15.00
\end{aligned}
$$

magnitude: Length of vector v1, or distance of point (a, b) from (0, 0)

$$= |v1| = |(a, b)| = sqrt(a^2 + b^2).$$

scalar product: v1 · v2 = (a, b) · (c, d) = ac + bd

Magnitude and scalar product are single, *scalar* values, not vectors. For example, the sum of vectors $v = (9, 4)$ and $w = (3, 5)$ is shown graphically in Figure 13–3.

Although a vector could be defined as an array of REAL values x and y, it is convenient to represent vectors with records, such as

```
TYPE  VECTOR = RECORD
            x, y : REAL;
          END; (* RECORD *)
VAR  v1, v2 : VECTOR;
```

Then the components of vector $v1$ are the REAL values stored in fields $v1.x$ and $v1.y$. Remember, ultimately it is the values in the x and y fields that must be read, written, and manipulated.

Example 13.1.2

Incorporate two-dimensional vector arithmetic into external module MyMath, and write a program that will ask for two vectors and then find their sum, difference, magnitudes, and scalar product.

Define the problem   In Chapter 9, a module called MyMath was created. Now add procedures to that module for finding the sum and negation, as well as functions for the magnitude and scalar product of two vectors.

A program asks the user for two vectors v and w and finds the sum, difference, magnitudes, and scalar product.

A Bit of Background

Gibbs's Vectors

By 1880, American mathematician and physicist Josiah Willard Gibbs (1839–1903) had created the modern system of vector analysis—almost simultaneously with, but independently of, self-taught British physicist Oliver Heaviside. In 1863 Gibbs had received from Yale the first doctorate degree in engineering awarded in the United States, and by 1871 he was professor of mathematical physics at his alma mater, where he remained the rest of his life.

Gibbs was long intrigued by Sir William Hamilton's theory of quaternions,* and the system he created was a modification of it. By the 1890s Professor Gibbs was teaching his new vector-analysis technique every year in a course consisting of up to 90 lectures.

Gibbs's vector notation allows complex formulae to be written and manipulated in abbreviated forms. Consequently, he has been a major contributor to science in the twentieth century. He created a major branch of physics called statistical mechanics and is responsible for ideas that form the basis of physical chemistry and thermodynamics. He is one of the greatest native-born American scientists but has remained almost totally unknown to the general public.

Quaternions: the calculus of a generalized complex number composed of a real number and a vector and depending on one real and three imaginary units, according to Webster's dictionary.

Develop a solution TYPE VECTOR is declared in the DEFINITION module. The new vector procedures in DEFINITION and IMPLEMENTATION MODULEs MyMath are shown in Figure 13–4. Module MyMath is shown in its entirety in Appendix C. Operations VectorSum and VectorNegate are defined as procedures

Figure 13–4
Vector Procedures
in DEFINITION
and
IMPLEMENTATION
MODULEs
MyMath

```
DEFINITION MODULE MyMath;
    (* Module MyMath contains user-defined mathematics functions
        and procedures. File Name:MYMATH.DEF *)

TYPE  VECTOR = RECORD   (* Defines a two-dimensional vector. *)
                  x, y : REAL;
                END; (* RECORD *)

PROCEDURE  VectorSum(V1, V2 : VECTOR;  VAR Result : VECTOR);
    (* Finds the Sum of two-dimensional vectors V1, V2. *)

PROCEDURE  VectorNegate(V : VECTOR;  VAR Result : VECTOR);
    (* Finds the Negative of a two-dimensional vector. *)

PROCEDURE VectorMagnitude(V : VECTOR) : REAL;
    (* Finds real scalar magnitude of a two-dimensional vector. *)

PROCEDURE ScalarProduct(V1, V2 : VECTOR) : REAL;
    (* Finds real scalar product of two-dimensional vectors V1,V2. *)
END MyMath.
```

```
IMPLEMENTATION MODULE MyMath;
    (* Module MyMath contains user-defined mathematical functions
        and procedures. File Name: MYMATH.MOD *)

FROM MathLib0 IMPORT sqrt;

PROCEDURE  VectorSum(V1, V2 : VECTOR;  VAR Result : VECTOR);
    (* Finds the Sum of two-dimensional vectors V1, V2. *)
    BEGIN
        Result.x := V1.x + V2.x;  Result.y := V1.y + V2.y;
    END VectorSum;

PROCEDURE  VectorNegate(V : VECTOR;  VAR Result : VECTOR);
    (* Finds the Negative of a two-dimensional vector. *)
    BEGIN
        Result.x := -V.x;  Result.y := -V.y;
    END VectorNegate;

PROCEDURE  VectorMagnitude(V : VECTOR) : REAL;
    (* Finds the real scalar magnitude of two-dimensional vector. *)
    BEGIN
        RETURN  sqrt(V.x * V.x + V.y * V.y);
    END VectorMagnitude;

PROCEDURE  ScalarProduct(V1, V2 : VECTOR) : REAL;
    (* Finds real scalar product of two-dimensional vectors V1,V2.*)
    BEGIN
        RETURN V1.x * V2.x + V1.y * V2.y;
    END ScalarProduct;
END MyMath.
```

with a VAR parameter Result:VECTOR, because functions in standard Modula-2 cannot RETURN structured data, such as a VECTOR record.

In the program,

- Ask for two vectors, *v* and *w*, and echo them to the screen.
- Let Total = VectorSum(*v, w,* Total), and display Total.*x* and Total.*y*.
- Let Diff = VectorSum(*v*, VectorNegate(*w*), Diff), and display Diff.*x* and Diff.*y*.
- Let Product = ScalarProduct (*v, w*), and display Product.
- Let *v*Mag = VectorMagnitude(*v*) and *w*Mag = VectorMagnitude(*w*), and display *v*Mag and *w*Mag.

Refine the solution   *Pseudocode*

```
begin module VectorOperations
        ReadVector(v),      ReadVector(w)
        WriteVector(v),        WriteVector(w)
        call     VectorSum(v, w, Total),      WriteVector(Total)
        call     VectorNegate(w, wNeg),      call VectorSum(v, wNeg, Diff),
          WriteVector(Diff)
        Product = ScalarProduct(v, w),      write Product
          vMag = VectorMagnitude(v), wMag = VectorMagnitude(w),
          write vMag and wMag
end VectorOperations

PROCEDURE WriteVector(V)
        write     ( V.x , V.y )

PROCEDURE ReadVector(VAR V)
        ReadReal(V.x),      ReadReal(V.y)
```

Modula-2 code   Type VECTOR and procedures VectorSum, VectorNegate, VectorMagnitude, and ScalarProduct are imported from MyMath. Even though you can pass entire records as parameters to the procedures, you should remember that all of the other operations on the vectors must be performed upon the individual REAL fields. The Difference, *v* − *w*, is calculated from *v* + (−*w*). Procedure WriteVector is defined within the program itself, rather than in the MyMath module, since people write vectors a variety of ways, such as

```
(a, b),   ai + bj,   and   a + bi.
```

By now, you realize that whenever you define a data structure, you must also define a procedure to display it. To make the VECTOR data type truly abstract (so that the programmer does not need to know that it is a record with REAL *x* and *y* fields), the ReadVector and WriteVector procedures should also be part of module MyMath.

```
MODULE VectorOperations;
    (* Shows vector operations from module MyMath and passing a vector record
       as a parameter.  Vectors are manipulated with individual REAL fields.
       FileName:CH13B      Modula-2      RKW      June 1991   *)

FROM InOut IMPORT WriteString, WriteLn;
FROM RealInOut IMPORT ReadReal, FWriteReal;
FROM MyMath IMPORT VECTOR, VectorSum, VectorNegate,
                    VectorMagnitude, ScalarProduct;
```

```
VAR  v, w, wNeg, Total, Diff : VECTOR;    vMag, wMag, Product : REAL;

PROCEDURE  ReadVector(VAR V : VECTOR);
   BEGIN
       WriteString("  What is the x component? "); ReadReal(V.x); WriteLn;
       WriteString("  What is the y component? "); ReadReal(V.y); WriteLn;
   END ReadVector;

PROCEDURE WriteVector(V : VECTOR);
   (* Writes Vector V in the form (a, b). *)
   BEGIN
       WriteString("( "); FWriteReal(V.x,7,2); WriteString(" ,");
       FWriteReal(V.y,7,2); WriteString(" )");
   END WriteVector;

BEGIN  (* VectorOperations *)
   WriteString("For vector  v: "); WriteLn; ReadVector(v);
   WriteString("For vector  w: "); WriteLn; ReadVector(w); WriteLn;

   WriteString("Vectors v and w are: "); WriteLn;
     WriteVector(v); WriteLn;  WriteVector(w); WriteLn; WriteLn;

   VectorSum(v, w, Total);
     WriteString("Sum:             v + w  = ");WriteVector(Total);WriteLn;

   VectorNegate(w, wNeg);   VectorSum(v, wNeg, Diff);
     WriteString("Difference:      v - w  = ");WriteVector(Diff);WriteLn;

   Product := ScalarProduct(v,w);
     WriteString("Scalar product: v dot w = "); FWriteReal(Product,7,2);
     WriteLn;

   vMag := VectorMagnitude(v);     wMag := VectorMagnitude(w);
     WriteString("Magnitudes of v and w respectively =");
     FWriteReal(vMag,7,2); WriteString(" and"); FWriteReal(wMag,9,2);
     WriteLn;

END VectorOperations.
```

Debug and test   To belabor a very important point, remember that nearly all manipulations of records must be performed on individual fields within those records. Trying to ReadReal(v) or ReadReal(VECTOR), instead of ReadReal(v.x) or ReadReal(v.y), is a sure way to encounter errors.

Test the program with vectors that have positive and negative components and with a zero vector (0, 0). Check your results by sketching the vectors on graph paper.

A sample run with two arbitrary vectors looks like

```
For vector  v:
  What is the x component? 4.32
  What is the y component? 5.97
For vector  w:
  What is the x component? 6.01
  What is the y component? 3.00

Vectors v and w are:
(    4.32 ,    5.97 )
(    6.01 ,    3.00 )

Sum:            v + w   = (   10.33 ,    8.97 )
Difference:     v - w   = (   -1.69 ,    2.97 )
Scalar product: v dot w =    43.87
Magnitudes of v and w respectively =    7.37 and    6.72
```

Complete the documentation   This problem is designed to demonstrate operations for a vector data type as well as record handling. Include the vector TYPE definition and vector handling procedures from DEFINITION MODULE MyMath in the algorithm development part of your documentation. In the users' manual, give the source code location (CH13B) and state that module MyMath must be present when the program is compiled.

Questions 13.1

1. Explain the differences between the fields in a record and parallel arrays of related items.
2. Define a record data type and variable for a business, including fields for the business name, description of the product or service, address, number of employees, and annual revenue.
3. Define a record data type and variable for a single kind of screw in your parts inventory, with fields for inventory number, screw length, diameter, number of threads per inch, kind of head (hex, Phillips, standard slot), material (steel, brass, other), and cost.
4. In Example 13.1.2, if ReadVector and WriteVector were included in module MyMath, then VECTOR would truly be an abstract data type, because the programmer would not need to know the underlying definition of VECTOR in order to perform the operations defined for it. Write only a DEFINITION module for a truly abstract data type defining a record for United States coins (penny, nickel, dime, quarter, half-dollar, dollar) and the operations of reading and writing the coin names, adding their values, and making change for a purchase.

13.2 *Arrays of Records*

Although there are some applications for individual records, collections of records in arrays or files can be more useful. Record arrays are the subject of this section. In Chapter 14 you will learn more about handling records in data files.

Arrays of records allow you to handle lists of data containing fields of different types. So far, this has required parallel arrays, with each array corresponding to a different type of field.

Arrays of Records Replacing Parallel Arrays

Suppose you want to keep better track of the friends in your address book by storing the following information about each person:

```
Name (First, Last)  Phone Number  Age  Height  Hair Color
```

Previously, you would have stored this information in six separate, parallel arrays. Now declare a record type MORTAL, an array TYPE PEOPLE, and an array VARiable Friends to produce the six fields shown in Figure 13–5. Then you have the array of records illustrated in the lower portion of the figure.

Manipulation of the records still occurs within the individual fields. If you wanted to assign a Name and Age to Friends[5], you could execute

```
Friends[5].FirstName := ''Robert'';
Friends[5].LastName := ''Ferguson'';
Friends[5].Age := 26;
```

To compare the Height of Friends[3] with the Height of Friends[1], you could use

```
IF  Friends[3].Height > Friends[1].Height  THEN ...
```

and so on.

The array index qualifies the record name, Friends[Index]. Index specifies which record to access. The field name is appended to specify which field within the record you wish to use.

Arrays of records can be searched and sorted just as arrays of any type of data. An entire record can be assigned at once to another record variable of the same type, and when that is done all of the fields within it are moved with it. You need not interchange each field separately, as you do with corresponding arrays, but the same amount of data is moved.

Record Keys

Usually, when you are searching or sorting an array of records you are interested in a particular field in each record. For example, you may want to sort in order of increasing Age or alphabetically by LastName. The field sorted on is called the **key field,** and searching and sorting are said to be performed "by record key." Different fields can be designated as keys at different times for different purposes. Searching is facilitated when the key is *unique* in each record; that is, when no other record has the same key. Therefore, it is common for unique values, such as social security number, employee number, or account number to be designated as the **primary key** of a record. If the primary search key (such as a Name) may not be unique, then another field (such as an account number) is often designated as the **secondary key,** and searching and sorting occur first in order by the primary key, and then by the secondary key.

```
CONST  NAMLEN = 12;  PHONLEN = 16;  NUMMORTALS = 20;
TYPE   HAIR     = (Blond, Red, Brown, Black, Other);
       NAME     = ARRAY [1..NAMLEN] OF CHAR;
       PHONESTR = ARRAY [1..PHONLEN] OF CHAR;
       MORTAL   = RECORD
                     FirstName, LastName : NAME;
                     Phone               : PHONESTR;
                     Age                 : CARDINAL;
                     Height              : REAL;
                     HairColor           : HAIR;
                  END; (* RECORD *)
       PEOPLE = ARRAY [1..NUMMORTALS] OF MORTAL;
VAR    Friends : PEOPLE;
```

Friends

	FirstName	LastName	Phone	Age	Height	HairColor
Friends[1]	Tom	Smith	302-4178	23	73.5	Blond
Friends[2]	Mary	Adams	(826)-417-0185	19	69.0	Black
Friends[3]	Sue	Jones	421-0569	21	62.8	Brown
Friends[4]	Will	Anderson	(709)-618-4193	28	67.2	Red
...						
Friends[20]						

Figure 13–5
Friends Array of PEOPLE Records

Example 13.2.1

Read records of information about your friends into your address-book array from an input file. Sort them into alphabetical order by LastName. Search for and display the records of those who have Red hair.

Define the problem Assume that you have created an input file called PALS haphazardly, and that it appears as

```
23   Tom Smith  302-4178  73.5  Blond
19   Mary Adams  (826)-417-0185  69.0  Black
21   Sue Jones  421-0569  62.8  Brown
28   Will Anderson  (709)-618-4193  67.2  Red
26   Robert Ferguson  722-2347  69.0  Brown
22   Anita Rincon  (215)-441-9375  65.0  Red
24   Ed Jones  (314)-221-8788  70.5  Other
20   Buddy Brady  880-6345  71.8  Blond
```

```
25   Jill Holmes   (710)-123-9823   67.6   Red
29   Dave Williamsen   192-3820   66.5   Black
28   Sally Cherry   (622)-317-4441   68.2   Blond
```

This data is to be read into the array of records defined by type PEOPLE and variable Friends as in Figure 13–5. A Selection sort will be used to sort the records into alphabetical order by last name; thus, LastName is the primary key field. The sorted array of records will be displayed to the screen and directed to an output file called SORTPALS.

A linear search will be performed, using HairColor as the key field, to find and display the records of all of the Friends who have Red hair.

Develop a solution The CARDINAL Age appears first for each record in file PALS. This is because Done will be used to detect the end of the file; and though all versions of Modula-2 set Done to FALSE when ReadCard fails, not all versions do the same for ReadString. The program will do following:

- Define the array of Friends.
- Open file PALS, read the records into Friends, and close the file.
- Sort array Friends, display sorted array, and write to output file.
- Search for and display the redheads.

Refine the solution *Pseudocode*

```
begin module RecordArrayHandler
        ReadRecords(Friends, NumFriends) from the file
        SelectionSort(Friends, NumFriends)
        WriteArray(Friends, NumFriends) to the screen and the output file
        LinearSearch(Red, Friends, NumFriends) for redheads
end RecordArrayHandler

PROCEDURE ReadRecords(VAR Persons,     VAR HowMany)
        open input file
        read all fields of each Persons record from the file until NOT(Done)
                accumulate the record count in variable HowMany
        close input file

PROCEDURE WriteRecord(Human)
        write the fields of a single record, Human

PROCEDURE WriteTheArrays(Persons, HowMany)
        for FriendCount = 1 to HowMany   WriteRecord(Persons[FriendCount])

PROCEDURE SelectionSort(VAR Persons: HowMany)
        (* See Section 10.3, CH10E *)

PROCEDURE LinearSearch(FindIt, Persons, HowMany)
        for FriendCount = 1 to HowMany
                if   Persons[FriendCount].HairColor = Red then
                WriteRecord(Persons[FriendCount])
```

Modula-2 code Examine carefully the definitions of record MORTAL, array of records PEOPLE, and variable Friends. The entire Friends array is passed to procedures ReadRecords, SelectionSort, and LinearSearch as array Persons. Each of those procedures works with individual fields of a particular record Persons[Friend-Count]. On the other hand, a single record Persons[FriendCount] is passed to parameter Human in procedure WriteRecord. Remember, the array index qualifies the *record* name, not the field name.

```
MODULE RecordArrayHandler;
   (* Illustrates definition and handling of an array of records,
      including reading, writing, sorting, and searching.
      FileName:CH13C       Modula-2     RKW       June 1991  *)

FROM InOut IMPORT WriteString, WriteLn, ReadCard, WriteCard, WriteInt,
        ReadString, OpenInput, CloseInput, OpenOutput, CloseOutput, Done;
FROM RealInOut IMPORT ReadReal, FWriteReal;
FROM Strings IMPORT Length, CompareStrings, TabOrFill;

CONST  NAMLEN = 12;  PHONLEN = 16;  NUMMORTALS = 20;
TYPE   HAIR = (Blond, Red, Brown, Black, Other);
       NAME = ARRAY [1..NAMLEN] OF CHAR;
       PHONESTR = ARRAY[1..PHONLEN] OF CHAR;
       MORTAL = RECORD
                   FirstName, LastName : NAME;
                   Phone               : PHONESTR;
                   Age                 : CARDINAL;
                   Height              : REAL;
                   HairColor           : HAIR;
                END; (* RECORD *)
       PEOPLE = ARRAY [1..NUMMORTALS] OF MORTAL;
VAR    Friends : PEOPLE;    NumFriends : CARDINAL;

PROCEDURE ReadRecords(VAR Persons:PEOPLE;  VAR HowMany:CARDINAL);
   VAR  TempColor:ARRAY [1..5] OF CHAR;  TempAge:CARDINAL;  Compare:INTEGER;
   BEGIN
      WriteString("Name of input file(PALS.IN)=?"); OpenInput("IN");
      HowMany := 0;
      REPEAT
         ReadCard(TempAge);
         IF  Done  THEN
            INC(HowMany);  Persons[HowMany].Age := TempAge;
            ReadString(Persons[HowMany].FirstName);
            ReadString(Persons[HowMany].LastName);
            ReadString(Persons[HowMany].Phone);
            ReadReal(Persons[HowMany].Height);
            ReadString(TempColor);
            IF   CompareStrings(TempColor, "Blond") = 0   THEN
                Persons[HowMany].HairColor := Blond;
            ELSIF CompareStrings(TempColor, "Black") = 0   THEN
                Persons[HowMany].HairColor := Black;
            ELSIF CompareStrings(TempColor, "Brown") = 0   THEN
                Persons[HowMany].HairColor := Brown;
            ELSIF CompareStrings(TempColor, "Red"  ) = 0   THEN
                Persons[HowMany].HairColor := Red;
            ELSE Persons[HowMany].HairColor :=Other;
            END; (* IF TempColor *)
         END; (* IF Done *)
      UNTIL  NOT(Done) OR (HowMany = NUMMORTALS);
      CloseInput;
   END ReadRecords;
```

```
PROCEDURE  WriteRecord(Human:MORTAL);
   VAR  TabHowFar : CARDINAL;
   BEGIN
      WriteString(Human.FirstName);WriteString(" ");
      WriteString(Human.LastName);
      TabHowFar := 2*NAMLEN-Length(Human.LastName)-Length(Human.FirstName)+2;
      TabOrFill(TabHowFar, ' ');  WriteCard(Human.Age, 4);
      FWriteReal(Human.Height, 6, 1);
      CASE  Human.HairColor  OF
         Blond:WriteString(" Blond  ") | Black:WriteString(" Black  ") |
         Brown:WriteString(" Brown  ") | Red  :WriteString(" Red    ") |
         Other:WriteString(" Other  ");
      END; (* CASE *)
      WriteString(Human.Phone);
   END WriteRecord;

PROCEDURE  WriteTheArray(Persons : PEOPLE;   HowMany : CARDINAL);
   VAR  FriendCount : CARDINAL;
   BEGIN
      FOR  FriendCount := 1 TO HowMany  DO
         WriteRecord(Persons[FriendCount]); WriteLn;
      END; (* FOR *)
   END WriteTheArray;

PROCEDURE  Swap(VAR RecordA, RecordB : MORTAL);
   VAR  TempPerson : MORTAL;
   BEGIN
      TempPerson := RecordA;  RecordA := RecordB;  RecordB := TempPerson;
   END Swap;

PROCEDURE  SelectionSort(VAR Persons:PEOPLE;   HowMany:CARDINAL);
   VAR  ListLength, LargestYet, FriendCount : CARDINAL;
   BEGIN
      FOR  ListLength := HowMany  TO  2  BY  -1 DO
         LargestYet := 1;
         FOR  FriendCount := 2  TO  ListLength  DO
            IF CompareStrings(Persons[FriendCount].LastName,
                              Persons[LargestYet].LastName) > 0 THEN
               LargestYet := FriendCount;
            END; (* IF *)
         END; (* FOR  *)
         Swap(Persons[LargestYet], Persons[ListLength]);
      END; (* FOR *)
   END SelectionSort;

PROCEDURE  LinearSearch(FindIt:HAIR; Persons:PEOPLE; HowMany:CARDINAL);
   VAR  FriendCount:CARDINAL;
   BEGIN
      FOR  FriendCount := 1 TO HowMany DO
         IF  Persons[FriendCount].HairColor = Red  THEN
            WriteRecord(Persons[FriendCount]); WriteLn;
         END; (* IF *)
      END; (* FOR *)  WriteLn;
   END LinearSearch;
```

```
BEGIN (* main module RecordArrayHandler *)
   ReadRecords(Friends, NumFriends);
   SelectionSort(Friends, NumFriends); WriteLn;
   WriteString("The sorted array is: "); WriteLn;
    WriteTheArray(Friends, NumFriends); WriteLn;
    WriteString("Name of output file(SORTPALS.OUT)=? "); OpenOutput("OUT");
    WriteTheArray(Friends, NumFriends); WriteLn;        CloseOutput;


   WriteLn; WriteString("The redheads are: "); WriteLn;
    LinearSearch(Red, Friends, NumFriends);  WriteLn;
END RecordArrayHandler.
```

Debug and test The sort and search procedures are modifications of those in Chapter 10. Compare these to see what changes have been made to accommodate record arrays.

This is a lengthy program, but debugging can be straightforward if you begin with the main module procedure calls and then follow through each procedure. Substituting stub procedures (or just inserting WriteString commands to indicate when you enter and exit the procedures) will help you locate errors.

Remember to distinguish between passing the entire record array (Friends) of type PEOPLE and a single record (Persons[FriendCount]) of type MORTAL to and from procedures.

Adding WriteRecord(Persons[HowMany]) in procedure ReadRecords will help you determine whether the records are being read correctly from the file. Adding a supplemental WriteCard(FriendCount,3) in procedure WriteArrays also will help trace the process.

Here is a sample run.

```
Name of input file(PALS.IN)=? PALS.IN
The sorted array is:
Mary   Adams              19   69.0 Black   (826)-417-0185
Will   Anderson           28   67.2 Red     (709)-618-4193
Buddy  Brady              20   71.8 Blond   880-6345
Sally  Cherry             28   68.2 Blond   (622)-317-4441
Robert  Ferguson          26   69.0 Brown   722-2347
Jill  Holmes              25   67.6 Red     (710)-123-9823
Ed   Jones                24   70.5 Other   (314)-221-8788
Sue  Jones                21   62.8 Brown   421-0569
Anita  Rincon             22   65.0 Red     (215)-441-9375
Tom  Smith                23   73.5 Blond   302-4178
Dave  Williamsen          29   66.5 Black   192-3820


Name of output file(SORTPALS.OUT)=? SORTPALS.OUT


The redheads are:
Will   Anderson           28   67.2 Red     (709)-618-4193
Jill  Holmes              25   67.6 Red     (710)-123-9823
Anita  Rincon             22   65.0 Red     (215)-441-9375
```

The output file SORTPALS will contain the sorted array shown in the sample run.

Complete the documentation   Since the point of this problem is to illustrate the use of record arrays, the documentation should include notes similar to those that appear throughout the example, as well as the problem definition, pseudocode, code, and sample run with input and output files. The users' manual should state the source code location (CH13C) and caution that a Strings module is called upon to provide functions Length, CompareStrings, and TabOrFill. The input file, PALS, also must be present before program execution.

Questions 13.2

1. A record type is defined by

```
TYPE   STR = ARRAY [1..20] OF CHAR;
       INVENTORY = RECORD
                      Description, InventoryNumber : STR;
                      Price : REAL;
                   END; (* RECORD *)
```

Write the following
a. a declaration for an array of 100-Item records of type INVENTORY.
b. a statement that reads the Price of the 15th Item.
c. an assignment of inventory number A0355 to Item 83.
2. Define an array of records for up to 50 factory employees, in which each record contains fields for name, age, social security number, hourly wage, and years with the company. Write the following
a. statements that display the name and number of years with the company for the 25th employee in the array.
b. a loop that, for every employee, adds 1 to the number of years with the company and adds 50 cents to the hourly wage.

13.3   *The WITH Statement*

Where access is required to many fields of the same record, it is convenient to be able to refer only to the field names without having to qualify each field with the record name.

WITH Statement Shorthand

The WITH statement allows a shorthand method of accessing record fields. For example, given the record definition for a bicycle Customer defined earlier in Figure 13–1, and

```
VAR  Use, Answer : ARRAY [1..8] OF CHAR;
```

you could read the fields for record Customer with the statements

```
ReadString(Customer.Name); ReadString(Customer.Address);
ReadString(Customer.Phone); ReadCard(Customer.NumBikes);
ReadString(Use);
```

Observe how many times the qualifier *Customer.* has been required. The WITH statement allows you to write these commands in the form

```
WITH   Customer   DO
   ReadString(Name);   ReadString(Address);
   ReadString(Phone); ReadCard(NumBikes);
   ReadString(Use);
END: (* WITH *)
```

Whenever reference is made to a field name between

```
WITH Customer DO...   and   END; (* WITH *),
```

that field is part of record Customer. WITH-statement syntax is shown in Figure 13–6.

WITH statements can be nested when reference is made to more than one record or to a record within a record. Be careful, however, that the field name refers to the most recently specified record name.

For example, given record variables Customer and record array Friends (from Figure 13–5), you could create a structure such as

```
WITH Customer DO
   WriteString(Name); WriteCard(NumBikes,6); WriteLn;
   FOR  Index := 1 TO HowMany  DO
      WITH  Friends[Index]  DO
         WriteString(LastName); WriteCard(Age,4);
         WriteLn;
      END; (* WITH Friends *)
   END; (* FOR *)
   FWriteReal(Bill,8,2); WriteLn;
END; (* WITH Customer *)
```

Name, NumBikes, and Bill are fields of the Customer record, whereas LastName and Age are fields of record Friends[Index].

In record arrays, the WITH statement must refer to a single record—such as, WITH Friends[Index]—not to the entire array.

☐ Nested Records

Any field within a record can be defined as a record itself. For example, you could declare field Count of type HOWMANY to be a record within RECORD type COLLECTIONS, as follows:

```
TYPE   STR = ARRAY [1..20] OF CHAR;
       HOWMANY = RECORD
                      Dollars : REAL;
                      Days  : CARDINAL;
                 END;
```

Figure 13–6
WITH-Statement
Syntax

WITH   RecordName   DO

      statements in which field names may be used alone,
without qualifying prefix   RecordName.

END;   (* WITH *)

```
COLLECTION = RECORD
                  Name          : STR;
                  Temperature   : INTEGER;
                  Count         : HOWMANY;
             END;
VAR  Item : COLLECTION;
```

An Item record is shown in graphic form in Figure 13–7. To assign a value to the Temperature field in record Item, you would write

```
Item.Temperature := -10;  or  WITH Item DO
                                   Temperature := -10;
                               END; (* WITH *)
```

To assign a value to the subfield Days in the Count field of Item, you would specify

```
Item.Count.Days := 30;  or  WITH Item DO
                                Count.Days  := 30;
                            END; (* WITH *)
```

or

```
WITH  Item.Count  DO
   Days := 30;
END; (* WITH *)
```

or even

```
WITH  Item  DO
   WITH  Count  DO
      Days := 30;
   END; (* WITH Count *)
END; (* WITH Item *)
```

The following example demonstrates WITH and shows the structure of an array of nested records.

Example 13.3.1

Create a data structure for representing hospital patients, and calculate patient bills.

Define the problem Representative information about a group of medical patients is shown in Figure 13–8. Define a data structure that will record this information for five patients. Read this data into the structure from input file, MEDICAL:

```
Robert  Sorensen  61  217.90  84.25  63.44  2  6
1182 25th St
JohnDay  OR  98762
```

Figure 13–7
A Record Nested
within a Record

Item			
		Count	
Name	**Temperature**	**Dollars**	**Days**
IceRink	−10	537.00	30

Name First Last	Address Street City State Zipcode	Age	Debt Hospital Doctor Pharmacy	DaysOfCare InPatient OutPatient
Robert Sorensen	1182 25th Street JohnDay OR 98762	61	217.90 84.25 63.44	2 6
Rita Martinez	815 Buchanan Ave Williams AZ 82173	27	582.96 479.63 84.90	29 0

```
Rita Martinez  27   582.96   479.63   84.90   29   0
815 Buchanan Ave
Williams   AZ   82173

Francine Appleton  68   2123.23   654.00   228.21   32   5
513 Peringrin Blvd
StFrancis    MN   21394-3005

George Thomas  53   105.49   486.88   241.56   2   45
10865 Doughboy St
LosAngeles   CA   90413-8273

Gary Allred  78   409.54   441.32   142.09   31   0
226 Mountain Road
Hoover   NB   70014-1275
```

Display the Name, Address, total days of care (Inpatient + Outpatient), and total debt (Hospital + Doctor + Pharmacy) for all patients. Print bills for all patients Age 65 or older, with their Name, Address, and a listing of their Hospital, Doctor, and Pharmacy debts. Then calculate and print on the bill a display of the total bill less a 20% senior-citizen discount.

Develop a solution   See the beginning of the Modula-2 BillingPatients code that follows for the array of nested records structure for record Patient of TYPE MOR-TALS. Elements of array Patient contain all of the information fields needed for each Patient. To assign a value to the Age of Patient[2], for example, you would write

```
Patient[2].Age := 27;   or   WITH   Patient[2]   DO
                                  Age := 27;
                              END; (* WITH *)
```

To assign an amount for the Pharmacy bill of Patient[2], you would specify the subfield Pharmacy within the Debt field of Patient[2], namely

```
Patient[2].Debt.Pharmacy := 84.90;
```

Alternatively you could write

WITH   Patient[2].Debt   DO   or   WITH   Patient[2]   DO
    Pharmacy := 84.90;   Debt.Pharmacy   :=   84.90
END; (* WITH *)   END; (* WITH *)

or even

        WITH   Patient[2]   DO
           WITH   Debt   DO
              Pharmacy := 84.90;
           END; (* WITH Debt *)
        END; (* WITH Patient[2] *)

To illustrate the variety of methods that can be used, the file is read into the array of records without using the WITH statement. Writing and searching the file invokes WITH commands. For Patient[Which Patient], the

$$\begin{aligned} \text{TotalBill} = \ &\text{Patient[WhichPatient].Debt.Hospital} \\ &+ \ \text{Patient[WhichPatient].Debt.Doctor} \\ &\quad + \ \text{Patient[WhichPatient].Debt.Pharmacy} \end{aligned}$$

which will be written

    WITH   Patient[WhichPatient].Debt   DO
      TotalBill := Hospital + Doctor + Pharmacy;
    END; (* WITH *)

Similar calculations will be used to calculate TotalDaysOfCare.

Figure 13–9 shows a structure chart of the solution.

Refine the solution.   *Pseudocode*

```
begin module BillingPatients
      ReadRecords(Patient) for patients from file MEDICAL
      for all patient records      DisplayPatient(Patient[WhichPatient])
      WriteSeniorBills(Patient)      for senior citizens
end BillingPatients

PROCEDURE ReadRecords(VAR SickOne)
      open file, read records from the file in array SickOne, close file

PROCEDURE DisplayPatient(WhoWasIll)
      display all fields of a single WhoWasIll record

PROCEDURE WriteSeniorBills(Seniors)
      for all array records Senior[Count]
            WITH    Seniors[Count]
                  if    Age >= 65
                     display Patient record
                     calculate and display discounted bill
```

Modula-2 code   The most important features to examine in this code are the definition and application of the array of nested records. In the ReadRecords procedure, the fields are defined within records of records by the double qualifiers and periods. ReadLine is used to read the Street address, which is likely to contain blank spaces. Study carefully the uses of WITH in the other procedures.

```
MODULE BillingPatients;
  (* Illustrates an array of nested records and the use of WITH.
     File Name:CH13D     Modula-2     RKW     June 1991   *)
```

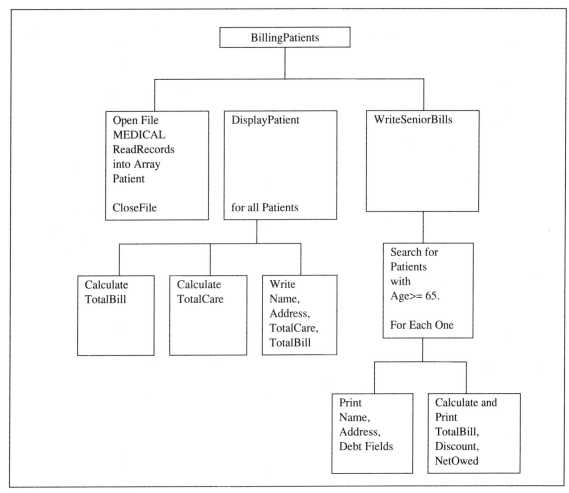

Figure 13-9
Structure Chart for BillingPatients (Example 13.3.1)

```
FROM InOut IMPORT ReadString, WriteString, WriteLn, ReadCard,
                 WriteCard, OpenInput, CloseInput;
FROM RealInOut IMPORT ReadReal, FWriteReal;   FROM Strings IMPORT ReadLine;

CONST  MAXPATIENTS = 5;  MAXGENERIC = 20;  MAXSTATE = 2;  MAXZIP = 10;
TYPE   GENERICSTR = ARRAY [1..MAXGENERIC] OF CHAR;
       STATESTR = ARRAY [1..MAXSTATE] OF CHAR;
       ZIPSTR = ARRAY [1..MAXZIP] OF CHAR;
       NAMEREC  = RECORD
                     First, Last : GENERICSTR;
                  END;
       PLACEREC = RECORD
                     Street, City : GENERICSTR;
                     State        : STATESTR;
                     Zipcode      : ZIPSTR;
                  END;
       BILLREC  = RECORD
                     Hospital, Doctor, Pharmacy : REAL;
                  END;
```

```
        DAYSREC   = RECORD
                        InPatient, OutPatient : CARDINAL;
                  END;
        PERSON    = RECORD
                        Name        : NAMEREC;
                        Address     : PLACEREC;
                        Age         : CARDINAL;
                        Debt        : BILLREC;
                        DaysOfCare  : DAYSREC;
                  END;
      MORTALS = ARRAY [1..MAXPATIENTS] OF PERSON;
VAR   Patient : MORTALS;    WhichPatient : CARDINAL;

PROCEDURE ReadRecords(VAR SickOne : MORTALS);
   VAR   Count : CARDINAL;
   BEGIN
      WriteString("Input file name (MEDICAL.IN) = ? "); OpenInput("IN");
      FOR  Count := 1 TO MAXPATIENTS  DO
         ReadString(SickOne[Count].Name.First);
         ReadString(SickOne[Count].Name.Last);
         ReadCard(SickOne[Count].Age);
         ReadReal(SickOne[Count].Debt.Hospital);
         ReadReal(SickOne[Count].Debt.Doctor);
         ReadReal(SickOne[Count].Debt.Pharmacy);
         ReadCard(SickOne[Count].DaysOfCare.InPatient);
         ReadCard(SickOne[Count].DaysOfCare.OutPatient);
         ReadLine(SickOne[Count].Address.Street);
         ReadString(SickOne[Count].Address.City);
         ReadString(SickOne[Count].Address.State);
         ReadString(SickOne[Count].Address.Zipcode);
      END; (* FOR *)                              CloseInput;
   END ReadRecords;

PROCEDURE DisplayPatient(WhoWasIll : PERSON);
   VAR  TotalBill : REAL;    TotalCare : CARDINAL;
   BEGIN
      WITH  WhoWasIll  DO
         WITH  Debt  DO
            TotalBill := Hospital + Doctor + Pharmacy;
         END; (* WITH Debt *)
         WITH  DaysOfCare  DO
            TotalCare := InPatient + OutPatient;
         END; (* WITH DaysOfCare *);
         WITH  Name  DO
            WriteString(First); WriteString("  "); WriteString(Last);
         END; (* WITH Name *)  WriteLn;
         WITH  Address  DO
            WriteString("     "); WriteString(Street); WriteLn;
            WriteString("     "); WriteString(City); WriteString(", ");
            WriteString(State);WriteString("  ");WriteString(Zipcode);
         END; (* WITH Address *)  WriteLn;
         WriteString("Total Days of Care = ");WriteCard(TotalCare,5);
         WriteLn;  WriteString("Total Bill =      $");
         FWriteReal(TotalBill,8,2); WriteLn;
      END; (* WITH WhoWasIll *)
   END DisplayPatient;
```

```
PROCEDURE WriteSeniorBills(Seniors : MORTALS);
   VAR  Count : CARDINAL;   TotalBill, Discount, NetOwed : REAL;
   BEGIN
      FOR  Count := 1 TO MAXPATIENTS  DO
         WITH  Seniors[Count]  DO
            IF  Age >= 65  THEN
               WriteLn; WriteLn;
               WITH  Name  DO
                  WriteString(First); WriteString(" "); WriteString(Last);
               END; (* WITH Name *)  WriteLn;
               WITH  Address  DO
                  WriteString("     "); WriteString(Street); WriteLn;
                  WriteString("     "); WriteString(City);
                  WriteString(", "); WriteString(State); WriteString("  ");
                  WriteString(Zipcode); WriteLn;
               END; (* WITH Address *)
               WITH  Debt  DO
                  WriteString("Hospital Bill = $");
                  FWriteReal(Hospital,8,2); WriteLn;
                  WriteString("Doctor Bill =   $");
                  FWriteReal(Doctor,8,2); WriteLn;
                  WriteString("Pharmacy Bill = $");
                  FWriteReal(Pharmacy,8,2); WriteLn;
                  TotalBill := Hospital + Doctor + Pharmacy;
               END; (* WITH Debt *)

               Discount := 0.20 * TotalBill;
               NetOwed := TotalBill - Discount;
               WriteString("Total Bill =              $");
               FWriteReal(TotalBill,10,2); WriteLn;
               WriteString("Senior Citizen Discount = $ -");
               FWriteReal(Discount,8,2); WriteLn;
               WriteString("Net Amount Owed =         $");
               FWriteReal(NetOwed,10,2); WriteLn;
            END; (* IF *)
         END; (* WITH Seniors[Count] *)
      END; (* FOR *)
   END WriteSeniorBills;

BEGIN (* module BillingPatients *)
   ReadRecords(Patient);  WriteLn;

   FOR  WhichPatient := 1  TO  MAXPATIENTS  DO
      DisplayPatient(Patient[WhichPatient]); WriteLn; WriteLn;
   END; (* FOR *)

   WriteSeniorBills(Patient);
END BillingPatients.
```

Debug and test   If you do not obtain correct results, add a procedure that writes each field of the record as soon as it has been read from the file. Be careful with parameters. The array of records is passed to ReadRecords and WriteSeniorBills. Only a single record is passed to DisplayPatient. When nesting WITH (as when nesting any other structures) inner structures must be contained completely within outer structures.

For testing, file MEDICAL should include a variety of data for senior and younger citizens. Here is a sample run. For brevity, ellipses (...) indicate output not shown. The initial ellipses indicate a list of the addresses, which are displayed because the ReadLine procedure echoes characters to the screen.

```
Input file name (MEDICAL.IN) = ? MEDICAL>IN
...
Robert   Sorensen
    1182 25th St
    JohnDay, OR  98762
Total Days of Care =      8
Total Bill =        $   365.59
...


Francine  Appleton
    513 Peringrin Blvd
    StFrancis, MN  21394-3005
Hospital Bill = $ 2123.23
Doctor Bill =   $  654.00
Pharmacy Bill = $  228.21
Total Bill =                 $   3005.44
Senior Citizen Discount = $ -  601.09
Net Amount Owed =            $   2404.35
....
```

Complete the documentation Documentation for this program is shown in Figure 13–10

Questions 13.3

Consider the following nested structure for daily production at the Indemnado Silver Mining Company.

```
CONST  NUMDAYS = 31;  STRLEN = 10;
TYPE   STR = ARRAY [1..STRLEN] OF CHAR;
       INCOME = RECORD
                    OuncesMined, DollarsIncome : REAL;
                END;
       COST  = RECORD
                   MinersPay, MillExpense : REAL;
               END;

       DAYSTAKE = RECORD
                      SupervisorName : STR;
                      DayOfMonth     : CARDINAL;
                      Earnings       : INCOME;
                      Expenses       : COST;
                  END;
```

1. Show the declaration of an array of Today records of type DAYSTAKE, which register what happened at the mine for each day in a 31 day month.
2. Show how you would read the DayOfMonth field and the SupervisorName field into the 23rd Today record **a.** without using WITH; **b.** using WITH.
3. Show how you would assign 3500 ounces mined, $87,500 income, $9000 miners' pay, and $12,000 mill expense to the 23rd Today record.
4. Correct the mistakes, so that the following fragment of code assigns the SupervisorName and the operating costs for the 13th.

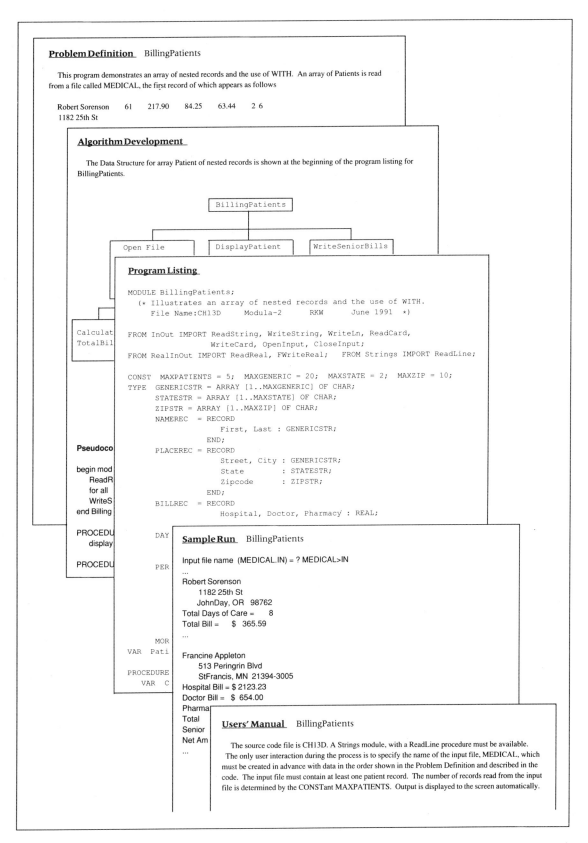

Problem Definition BillingPatients

This program demonstrates an array of nested records and the use of WITH. An array of Patients is read from a file called MEDICAL, the first record of which appears as follows

Robert Sorenson   61   217.90   84.25   63.44   2 6
1182 25th St

Algorithm Development

The Data Structure for array Patient of nested records is shown at the beginning of the program listing for BillingPatients.

BillingPatients

Open File   DisplayPatient   WriteSeniorBills

Calculat
TotalBil

Pseudoco

begin mod
   ReadR
   for all
   WriteS
end Billing

PROCEDU
   display

PROCEDU

Program Listing

```
MODULE BillingPatients;
   (* Illustrates an array of nested records and the use of WITH.
      File Name:CH13D    Modula-2    RKW    June 1991  *)

FROM InOut IMPORT ReadString, WriteString, WriteLn, ReadCard,
               WriteCard, OpenInput, CloseInput;
FROM RealInOut IMPORT ReadReal, FWriteReal;   FROM Strings IMPORT ReadLine;

CONST  MAXPATIENTS = 5;  MAXGENERIC = 20;  MAXSTATE = 2;  MAXZIP = 10;
TYPE  GENERICSTR = ARRAY [1..MAXGENERIC] OF CHAR;
      STATESTR = ARRAY [1..MAXSTATE] OF CHAR;
      ZIPSTR = ARRAY [1..MAXZIP] OF CHAR;
      NAMEREC  = RECORD
                     First, Last : GENERICSTR;
                 END;
      PLACEREC = RECORD
                     Street, City : GENERICSTR;
                     State         : STATESTR;
                     Zipcode       : ZIPSTR;
                 END;
      BILLREC  = RECORD
                     Hospital, Doctor, Pharmacy : REAL;
```

DAY

PER

MOR
VAR Pati

PROCEDURE
VAR C

Sample Run BillingPatients

Input file name (MEDICAL.IN) = ? MEDICAL>IN
...
Robert Sorenson
    1182 25th St
    JohnDay, OR 98762
Total Days of Care =   8
Total Bill = $ 365.59
...

Francine Appleton
    513 Peringrin Blvd
    StFrancis, MN 21394-3005
Hospital Bill = $ 2123.23
Doctor Bill = $ 654.00
Pharma
Total
Senior
Net Am
...

Users' Manual BillingPatients

The source code file is CH13D. A Strings module, with a ReadLine procedure must be available.
The only user interaction during the process is to specify the name of the input file, MEDICAL, which must be created in advance with data in the order shown in the Problem Definition and described in the code. The input file must contain at least one patient record. The number of records read from the input file is determined by the CONSTant MAXPATIENTS. Output is displayed to the screen automatically.

Figure 13–10
Documentation for BillingPatients (Example 13.3.1)

```
WITH  COST  DO
  MinersPay[13] := 8350.0;
  WITH  Today[13]  DO
    MillExpense := 10482.75;
END; (* WITH COST *)
  SupervisorName := ''John'';
  END; (* WITH Today[13] *);
```

13.4 *Focus on Problem Solving*

In this section, you will see how to define records so that users may choose different combinations of data to be stored. A program for handling commercial and residential real estate listings will be developed.

Variant Records

A **variant record** is a record structure containing fields that can be defined differently to serve the needs of different users. Suppose, for example, that you are a

Record Type PROPERTY

Record Name	YearBuilt	Address	Cost	Class	Business		SquareFeet	
Building1	1987	350 Main	315000.	Commercial	Warehouse		32000	
					Num Rooms	Num Baths	Num Floors	
Building2	1956	1287 Park	196000.	House	10	4	2	

```
CONST  MAXSTRINDEX = 59;
TYPE  STR = ARRAY [0..MAXSTRINDEX] OF CHAR;
      BuildingType = (Commercial, House);
            Use = (Warehouse, Office);
      PROPERTY = RECORD
                YearBuilt : CARDINAL;
                Address   : STR;
                Cost      : REAL;
                CASE  Class : BuildingType  OF
                    Commercial : Business             :Use;
                                 SquareFeet           :REAL |
                    House      : NumRooms,NumBaths,NumFloors:CARDINAL;
                END; (* CASE Class *)
                END; (* RECORD PROPERTY *)
VAR  Building1, Building2, OtherBuilding : PROPERTY;
```

Figure 13–11
Real Estate Records with Variant Parts

realtor with a number of properties to sell. The descriptions of the properties are to be stored in an array of records. For each property you designate whether it is a commercial building or a house, and you store its address, year of construction, and listing price. If it is a commercial building, you must specify whether it is a warehouse or an office building and the total square feet of floor space. For a home you need to store the number of baths, rooms (excluding baths), and floors. Since the descriptions differ, you could consider establishing separate arrays for houses and commercial buildings. However, you need to record all property descriptions together, and the records will be defined with variant parts as illustrated for two particular buildings in Figure 13–11. The declaration of the structure for these records is also shown in the figure.

The YearBuilt, Address, Cost, and Class fields are common to all records of type PROPERTY. The Class field is called a **tag field** because it "tags" or describes which other fields will be included in the record. The tag field may have any valid identifier name, such as Class, WhatKind, WhichOne, or the like.

If the Class tag field has a value of Commercial, the record includes variant fields Business and SquareFeet. If the value in the Class tag field is House, the variant fields are NumRooms, NumBaths, and NumFloors. The fields Business, SquareFeet, NumRooms, NumBaths, and NumFloors form the **variant part** of the record, because what is stored in that part depends upon the Class tag field.

For example, if BldgChar and Discard are CHARacter variables, then code to ask for the values for record OtherBuilding could be

```
WITH  OtherBuilding  DO
   (* Determine YearBuilt, Address, Cost *)
   WriteString("Enter YearBuilt: "); ReadCard(YearBuilt);WriteLn;
   WriteString("Enter Address  : "); ReadString(Address);WriteLn;
   WriteString("Enter Cost     : "); RealReal(Cost);      WriteLn;WriteLn;

   (* Determine Class *)
   REPEAT
      WriteString("What type of building, Commercial(C) or House(H)? ");
       Read(BldgChar); Read(Discard); Write(BldgChar); WriteLn;
   UNTIL  (BldgChar = 'C') OR (BldgChar = 'H');
   IF  BldgChar = 'C'  THEN  Class := Commercial;
    ELSE  Class := House;
   END; (* IF *)

   (* Fill Variant Parts *)
   IF  Class = Commercial  THEN
      REPEAT
         WriteString("Building Use, Warehouse(W) or Office(O)? ");
          Read(BldgChar); Read(Discard); Write(BldgChar); WriteLn;
      UNTIL  (BldgChar = 'W') OR (BldgChar = 'O');
      IF  BldgChar = 'W'  THEN  Business := Warehouse;
       ELSE  Business := Office;
      END; (* IF *)
      WriteString("Enter square feet: ");  ReadReal(SquareFeet); WriteLn;
   ELSE
      WriteString("Enter Number of Rooms : ");ReadCard(NumRooms); WriteLn;
      WriteString("Enter Number of Baths : ");ReadCard(NumBaths); WriteLn;
      WriteString("Enter Number of Floors: ");ReadCard(NumFloors);WriteLn;
   END; (* IF *)
END; (* WITH *)
```

Figure 13–12
Record Syntax with
Variant Parts

```
RECORD
        List 1 of Fields;
        List 2 of Fields;
            ...
        List n of Fields;
END;    (* RECORD *)

A List of Fields contains either

        List of Field Names  :  Type of Field
    or
        CASE  TagFieldName  ;  TagFieldType  OF
            Variant 1 |
            Variant 2 |
                ...
            Variant i |
                ...
            Variant n ;
        ELSE
            List of Fields;
        END; (* CASE *)

where the ELSE clause is optional.

Variant i takes the form
    List of Case Label Names  :  Type of Field
```

Figure 13–12 shows general record structure syntax, expanded to include variant parts.

☐ Guidelines for Using Variant Records

Here are some facts and rules to keep in mind when you are using variant records.

1. The CASE structure in the record declaration is used to define the values that can be accepted by the TagFieldName and Case Labels, rather than to offer choices between executable commands. For example, before you refer to Building1.NumBaths, the tag field must have been set as Building1.Class := House;. The current value of the tag field is in effect until it is changed to another value.

2. Nonvariant and variant parts can be mixed within a record, and a record can have multiple variant parts. For example, you could add other variant parts to the PROPERTY record in Figure 13–11, such as

```
CASE  Location   : WhereItIs  OF
  Local          : Street, Zip
  National       : Street, City, State, Zip                  : STR |
  International : Street, City, State, Zip, Country : STR;
END; (* CASE Location *)
```

Usually, a compiler assigns sufficient memory to variant records to store the longest possible record. Therefore, when the tag field assignment is Other-Building.Location := National; then space allocated for OtherBuilding.Country is inaccessible and unused.

3. In recent versions of Modula-2 the variant part of a record can be empty. The programmer has the option of specifying that there will be no fields for a given value of the tag. For example, you could declare

```
CASE Class : BuildingType OF
  Recreational : |
  Commercial    : Business:Use;  SquareFeet:REAL |
  House         : NumRooms, NumBaths, NumFloors : CARDINAL ;
END; (* CASE *)
```

if you wished no fields to be defined as part of the variant when the value of Class is Recreational.

4. An ELSE clause can be included within a variant record CASE structure. For example, if BuildingType included values other than Commercial and House, you might specify

```
CASE  Class : BuildingType  OF
   Commercial : Business : Use;  SquareFeet:REAL |
   House : NumRooms, NumBaths, NumFloors : CARDINAL;
ELSE
   Description : ARRAY [0..79] OF CHAR;
END; (* CASE *)
```

which would allow you to have a string description field for any other type of property.

5. WITH can be used for records with variant parts. Any field that is itself declared to be a nested record can be specified in the WITH structure heading.

6. If a nonvariant record structure will solve the problem just as well, use it! Just as with excessive nesting of other structures, variant records can be more difficult to read and use than simpler nonvariant structures. However, in certain situations variant records are needed and should be employed.

☐ An Array of Variant Records

This example shows the implementation of an array of variant records.

Example 13.4.1

Store your real estate listings in an array of records, distinguishing between commercial and residential properties. Calculate and display the cost per square foot of each commercial building and the cost per room of each house.

Define the problem   Your real estate information will be defined as an array of records with a variant part as shown in Figure 13–11. The data for five records will be read from an input file into the array. All of the records for commercial properties will be displayed along with the cost per square foot. Then all of the records for homes will be displayed along with the cost per room.

Develop a solution   The input file, called REALTY.IN, contains at least five records in this form:

```
1987
350 Main Street
315000.00
Commercial  Warehouse  32000
```

```
1956
1287 Park Avenue
196000.00
House   10   4   2
...
```

An array of records will be defined by

```
CONST    NUMPROPS = 5;
TYPE     REALESTATE = ARRAY [1..NUMPROPS] OF PROPERTY;
VAR      Building : REALESTATE;
```

where type PROPERTY is defined as in Figure 13–11. Three procedures will

- Read the data from the input file into the array.
- Search the array for Class = Commercial, calculate the Cost per Square Foot, and display those records.
- Search the array for Class = House, calculate the Cost per Room, and display those records.

Refine the solution   *Pseudocode*

```
begin module RealProperty
      ReadFile(Building)
      DisplayCommercial(Building)
      DisplayHouse(Building)
end RealProperty

procedure ReadFile(VAR Bldg)
      open file REALTY.IN
      for Count = 1 to NUMPROPS
            WITH Bldg[Count]
                  read YearBuilt, Address, Cost, Class
                  if Class = Commercial
                        read Business, SquareFeet
                  else
                        read NumRooms, NumBaths, NumFloors
      close file

procedure DisplayCommercial(Bldg)
      print headings
      for Count = 1 to NUMPROPS
            WITH Bldg[Count]
                  if Class = Commercial
                  CostPerSqFt = Cost/SquareFeet
                  print fields of Bldg[Count],    print CostPerSqFt

procedure DisplayHouse(Bldg : REALESTATE)
      print headings
      for Count = 1 to NUMPROPS
            WITH Bldg[Count]
                  if Class = House
                        CostPerRoom = Cost/NumRooms
                        print fields of Bldg[Count],    print CostPerRoom
```

Modula-2 code   Study the variant record declaration carefully.

```
MODULE RealProperty;
  (* Illustrates an array of variant Real Estate records.
```

```
            FileName:CH13E      Modula-2      RKW      July 1991 *)

FROM InOut IMPORT ReadString, WriteString, ReadCard, WriteCard,
                 WriteLn, OpenInput, CloseInput;
FROM RealInOut IMPORT ReadReal, FWriteReal;
FROM Strings IMPORT ReadLine, TabOrFill, CompareStrings;

CONST  NUMPROPS = 5;  MAXSTRINDEX = 59;
TYPE   STR = ARRAY [0..MAXSTRINDEX] OF CHAR;
       BuildingType = (Commercial, House);
               Use = (Warehouse, Office);
       PROPERTY = RECORD
                     YearBuilt : CARDINAL;
                     Address   : STR;
                     Cost      : REAL;
                     CASE  Class : BuildingType  OF
                        Commercial : Business                    : Use;
                                     SquareFeet                  : REAL |
                           House        : NumRooms,NumBaths,NumFloors: CARDINAL;
                     END; (* CASE Class *)
                  END; (* RECORD PROPERTY *)
       REALESTATE = ARRAY [1..NUMPROPS] OF PROPERTY;
VAR  Building : REALESTATE;

PROCEDURE ReadFile(VAR Bldg : REALESTATE);
   VAR  Count : CARDINAL;   TempString : ARRAY [0..9] OF CHAR;
   BEGIN
      WriteString("Input file name (REALTY.IN) = ? ");  OpenInput("IN");
      FOR  Count := 1 TO NUMPROPS  DO
         WITH  Bldg[Count]  DO   (* Read fields for each Bldg record. *)
            ReadCard(YearBuilt);  ReadLine(Address);  ReadReal(Cost);
            ReadString(TempString);
            IF  CompareStrings(TempString, "Commercial") = 0  THEN
               Class := Commercial;
               ReadString(TempString);
               IF CompareStrings(TempString, "Warehouse") = 0  THEN
                  Business := Warehouse;  ELSE Business := Office;
               END; (* IF *)
               ReadReal(SquareFeet);
            ELSE
               Class := House;
                ReadCard(NumRooms);ReadCard(NumBaths);ReadCard(NumFloors);
            END; (* IF *)
         END; (* WITH *)
      END; (* FOR *)
      CloseInput;
   END ReadFile;

 PROCEDURE DisplayCommercial(Bldg : REALESTATE);
    VAR  Count : CARDINAL;  CostPerSqFt : REAL;
    BEGIN
       WriteLn; WriteLn; WriteLn;                          (* Write Headings *)
       WriteString("Commercial Properties:"); WriteLn;
       WriteString("YearBuilt   Address"); WriteLn;
       WriteString(" Cost        Business   SquareFeet    Cost/Sq.Ft");
       WriteLn;  TabOrFill(49, '-');  WriteLn;
```

```
        FOR  Count := 1 TO NUMPROPS  DO
            WITH  Bldg[Count]  DO
                IF  Class = Commercial THEN (*Write Commercial record fields.*)
                    CostPerSqFt := Cost / SquareFeet;
                    WriteCard(YearBuilt,4); TabOrFill(8, ' ');
                    WriteString(Address); WriteLn;  FWriteReal(Cost,11,2);
                    IF Business = Warehouse THEN WriteString("  Warehouse");
                     ELSE WriteString("  Office    ");
                    END; (* IF *)
                    FWriteReal(SquareFeet,13,2);  FWriteReal(CostPerSqFt,14,2);
                    WriteLn; WriteLn;
                END; (* IF *)
            END; (* WITH *)
        END; (* FOR *)
    END DisplayCommercial;


PROCEDURE DisplayHouse(Bldg : REALESTATE);
    VAR  Count : CARDINAL;   CostPerRoom : REAL;
    BEGIN
        WriteLn; WriteLn; WriteLn;                      (* Write Headings *)
        WriteString("Residential Homes:"); WriteLn;
        WriteString("YearBuilt   Address"); WriteLn;
        WriteString("  Cost        Rooms(excl.Baths)  Baths  Floors");
        WriteString("    Cost/Room"); WriteLn; TabOrFill(56, '-'); WriteLn;
        FOR  Count := 1 TO NUMPROPS  DO
            WITH  Bldg[Count]  DO
                IF  Class = House  THEN   (* Write House record fields. *)
                    CostPerRoom := Cost / FLOAT(NumRooms);
                    WriteCard(YearBuilt,4); TabOrFill(8, ' ');
                    WriteString(Address); WriteLn; FWriteReal(Cost,11,2);
                    WriteCard(NumRooms,18); WriteCard(NumBaths, 7);
                    WriteCard(NumFloors,8); FWriteReal(CostPerRoom,12,2);
                    WriteLn; WriteLn;
                END; (* IF *)
            END; (* WITH *)
        END; (* FOR *)
    END DisplayHouse;

BEGIN (* module RealProperty *)
    ReadFile(Building);
    DisplayCommercial(Building);
    DisplayHouse(Building);
END RealProperty.
```

Debug and test: Top-down design suggests that procedures ReadFile, Display-Commercial, and DisplayHouse could be written as stub procedures and the logic of the main module tested first. Then ReadFile could be written and debugged; and finally the other two procedures would be written and debugged. Add supplemental write statements to display each field immediately after it is read. If the Display . . . procedures do not seem to be revealing the correct properties, write the Address and Class fields for each building immediately after the WITH Bldg[Count] DO... command, to identify which record and which Class the program has encountered.

Here is a sample run.

A Bit of Background

Some Things Never Change

Although records may have variant parts, the way records are handled in Modula-2 as well as the type of quantities calculated by a given set of commands within a program generally remain invariant. Similarly, though perceived differently by various observers, a fundamental physical phenomenon remains the same. Many times the difficult task in algorithm development—as in life—is to separate the critical invariant concepts from the superficial variables.

Arthur Cayley (1821–1895) and James Joseph Sylvester (1814–1897) worked together for years to develop a method of distinguishing between invariants and variants. Both men were recognized for their mathematical genius at an early age, and both graduated near the top of their classes in the Cambridge colleges. The two were admitted to the bar and endured the legal profession in England for some time as a means of earning their livelihood while pursuing their love of mathematics.

Cayley was a gentle man who rarely lost his temper. His collected works comprise thirteen volumes with over 960 papers. Sylvester's life, on the other hand, was stormy, interrupted by only one relatively tranquil period between 1876 and 1883 as a professor at the new Johns Hopkins University in the United States. Sylvester contrasted their lives by stating that, after they spent some time as bachelors in London, Cayley had settled down to a quiet, peaceful, married life at Cambridge, whereas he had never married and had been "fighting the world all his days."

```
Input file name (REALTY.IN) = ? REALTY.IN
```

Commercial Properties:

YearBuilt Cost	Address Business	SquareFeet	Cost/Sq.Ft
1987 315000.00	350 Main Street Warehouse	32000.00	9.84
1985 250000.00	182 Commerce Street Office	12000.00	20.83

Residential Homes:

YearBuilt Cost	Address Rooms(excl.Baths)	Baths	Floors	Cost/Room
1956 196000.00	1287 Park Avenue 10	4	2	19600.00
1980 81000.00	18321 25th Street 6	2	1	13500.00
1937 57500.00	902 Brinkman Place 5	1	1	11500.00

Complete the documentation The narrative describing the use of records with variant parts would be important in the documentation for this program—which is designed to illustrate variant records. Also include the problem description, algorithm development (including the variant record declaration), pseudocode, code, and sample run. In the users' manual, state the source code location (CH13E). Remind users that the input file, REALTY.IN, must be created in advance. Read-Line, TabOrFill, and CompareStrings procedures must be available for import from a Strings module. The number of records read into the array from the input file can be modified by changing CONST NUMPROPS.

Questions 13.4

1. For program RealProperty (Example 13.4.1, CH13E), in addition to what is shown in the example, the sample run displays all of the addresses immediately after the input file name is entered. Why? (*Hint:* Note how Addresses are read.) How would you correct this?
2. In the Guidelines for Using Variant Records, items 2, 3, and 4 suggest additions to the PROPERTY record defined in Figure 13-11.
   a. Show the entire PROPERTY record declaration with these additions.
   b. All Locations need Street and Zip fields. Show how you would change the record PROPERTY declaration to make these fields nonvariant. How would you handle Case Location of Local?
3. Create a variant record structure to record the employees for your company. For each employee you will have nonvariant fields for the first and last names, address, gender, social security number, and date of birth. There will be two tag fields, with the accompanying variant fields described as

```
tag field marital status:
      married   : name of spouse, number of declared dependents
      widowed   : number of declared dependents
      divorced  : number of declared dependents
      single    : no additional information

tag field type of salary:
      hourly : hourly pay rate, overtime pay rate
      weekly : weekly salary, hourly rate for over 40 hr%week
      annual : annual salary
```

13.5 *Summary*

Records A record is a collection of data under one heading, whose fields may contain different TYPEs of data. For example, a record for a given Pupil could contain fields Name(String), Age(CARDINAL), GPA(REAL), and Year(enumeration Frosh, Soph, Jr, Sr).

Accessing Records Except for passing an entire record or array of records as a parameter or assigning a record to an identical record, records are manipulated and accessed one field at a time. For example, you could

```
WriteString(Pupil.Name);
WriteCard(Pupil.Age, 4);
```

and so on, but you could not Write...(Pupil) unless you had defined an appropriate WriteRecord procedure for displaying individual fields.

Arrays of Records Arrays of records are common applications of records. An example is an array of Students in a particular course. An array index defines the record (not the field), and a reference to a field would be written in the form

```
RecordArrayName[Index].FieldName
```

so that a reference should be Students[5].Age, *not* Students.Age[5].

When invoking procedures with record arrays, you must be careful in specifying your wish to pass a single field (Students[5].Age), a record (Student[5]), or the entire array (Students) to the procedure, and then list the parameters in the procedure heading with the appropriate type.

WITH   The structure WITH RecordName DO... END; (* WITH *) helps reduce repetition of the record name. Thus,

```
WITH  Pupil  DO
   WriteString(Name);  WriteCard(Age, 4);
END; (* WITH *)
```

displays the Name and Age fields of record Pupil. Nested WITH statements should be used with caution when referring to different records or nested records; an unqualified field belongs to the record specified in the most recent WITH statement.

Variant Records   Records can have variant parts; that is, the kinds of data stored may differ within a record structure, as specified by a tag field. The variant parts are declared using a CASE structure, as shown in Figure 13-12. Variants add a level of complexity to records and should be used when and only when they are necessary.

13.6 *Exercises*

Exercises marked with (FileName:_____) indicate those that ask you to use, modify, or extend the text examples. The numbers in brackets, [ ], indicate the section that contains the material you need in order to complete the exercise.

1. [13.1] Write a program that defines a record for an item inventory in a store. The record will contain fields for the Description, Inventory Number, Storage Bin Location, Number on Hand, and Wholesale Cost of the Item. A procedure should allow you to change the wholesale cost and update the number on hand as the item is ordered or sold. If the number on hand becomes less than 10, display a warning message that the stock is low.

2. [13.1] Everybody says you can't add apples and oranges. To prove them wrong develop a program that handles a record describing the produce in your store including apples, oranges, and bananas. Each type of produce in the record will have fields for the produce name, amount on hand, and retail price. As you order or sell each type, the amount on hand will change. If the amount on hand of any type gets to be less than 30, print a message suggesting that more be ordered. If the amount on hand gets to be over 200, print a sign that advertises them for sale at 25% off the regular retail price.

3. [13.1] (FileName:CH13A) Modify the program of Example 13.1.1 so that a customer may order a variety of kinds of Bicycles. *Hint:* Change the record so that there is a number field for each Bicycle kind containing how many of that kind were ordered. You might name these fields NumMtnBikes, NumStBikes, and so on, and eliminate the current BikeKind field.

4. [13.1] Construct a record that contains all of the short biographical information about yourself that you think is important, such as name, age, height, hair color, eye color, monthly salary, address, and so on. Write a program that will allow you to enter data into the record and to change the contents of the fields when necessary.

5. [13.1] (FileName:CH13B)

    a. The cross product $v1 \times v2$ of two vectors in (x, y) is a vector that points perpendicular to the x, y-plane. If $v1 = (a, b)$ and $v2 = (c, d)$, then the magnitude of the cross product $v1 \times v2$ is a single, scalar value defined by $(a * d) - (b * c)$. Add a function for finding the magnitude of the cross product to module MyMath, and add calculation of this value to the program of Example 13.1.2.

    b. For vectors v and w shown in Figure 13–3, angle A between the vectors is given by the equation

$$A(\text{degrees}) = (180/\pi) * \arctan(\text{sqrt}(1 - (\cos A)^2)/\cos A)$$

    with $\cos A = \text{ScalarProduct}(v, w)/(\text{VectorMagnitude}(v) * \text{VectorMagnitude}(w))$ and $\pi = $ approximately 3.14159. Cos and arctan are imported from MathLib0. Add a calculation to the program for finding angle A between vectors v and w.

6. [13.1] (FileName:CH13B) If you are familiar with complex numbers, use Example 13.1.2 as an analog and develop a program to add, subtract, multiply, complement, and find the magnitudes of two complex numbers.

7. [13.2] Expand the inventory problem of exercise 1 to handle an array of up to 20 item records. Load the inventory array initially from an input file you have created using an editor. Have the program then give you a report of all of the inventory items and make up order forms for those whose quantity is less than 10.

8. [13.2] (FileName:CH13A) Modify the problem of Example 13.1.1 to handle an array of records so that you can take up to 50 orders for Bicycles during the day and prepare shipping orders for all of them at once at the end of the day.

9. [13.2] (FileName:CH13B) Starting with Example 13.1.2 as a guide, create an array of records representing points in the x, y-plane. Enter a set of points into the array, either from the keyboard or from a file. Have your program transform the record data to parallel X and Y arrays and use the procedures from module Graphics (Appendix C) to sort the points in order of increasing x, and plot them.

10. [13.3] (FileName:CH13C) Modify the address book Example (13.2.1) to

    a. use WITH in procedures ReadRecords and WriteRecord.

    b. search repeatedly for names without losing the array. For example, without exiting the program users could ask to find Sue Jones and then Tom Smith, then Will Anderson, and so on, until Stop Stop or a similar flag is entered.

    c. add, modify, and delete records. *Hint:* A common way to delete a record is to perform a logical deletion; for example, you might change the last name to ZZZZZZ, which will flag the record as deleted. Then a sort puts all of those records at the end, and an add becomes a search for a ZZZZZZ record, which is then modified to hold the added data.

11. [13.3] A catalog for a small specialty company contains up to 30 items.

a. Create a nested record array data structure for these items whereby each item will have

```
Item Name
Catalog
  Description
  Catalog Number
  Catalog Page
Cost
  Wholesale
  Retail Member Cost
  Retail NonMember Cost
```

Catalog and Cost are nested records within the Item record. Write a program that allows you to read (from the keyboard or a file) the item name, catalog description, catalog number, page number, and wholesale prices for at least ten items. Then the program fills in the member and nonmember costs, where Cost.Member = 1.1 * Cost.Wholesale, and the nonmember cost is 30% above Wholesale cost. Display the completed array of records.

b. Sort the array by catalog page, display, and store the sorted array in a file.

c. Search the array to determine those items whose nonmember prices are less than $25.00.

12. [13.3] a. Create an array of nested records for recording when events on the local police blotter occurred. The records should have the form

```
Event
  Description
  Officer in Charge
Date
  Month (3-letter abbreviation JAN, FEB, etc.)
  Day
  Year
Time
  Hour (24-hour clock)
  Minute
```

with Event, Date, and Time being nested records within each blotter record. Read at least ten events either from the keyboard or a file, and display the array of records with dates converted to MO/DAY/YR form, such as 12/26/89, and times converted to AM/PM form, such as 3:25 PM.

b. Sort the array alphabetically by the last name of the officer in charge, display the sorted array, and store the sorted array in a file.

c. Search the array and display all records for a given officer in charge.

d. Search the array and display all events that occurred in DEC 1989.

13. [13.3] The first 18 elements in the periodic table, their atomic numbers, and the weight of a common isotope of each are shown in Figure 13–13.

The atomic number represents the number of protons in the nucleus as well as the number of electrons surrounding the nucleus. The number of neutrons in the nucleus equals the atomic weight minus the atomic number. The electrons fill shells surrounding the nucleus with a maximum of 2 electrons in the innermost shell, 8 in the next shell, and 8 in the third shell. For example, as shown in the partial table of Figure 13–13, phosphorus (number 15, with 15

Figure 13–13
The Periodic Table
(Exercise 13)

Symbol	Name	Atomic Number	Atomic Weight	Neutrons	Electrons in OuterShell
H	Hydrogen	1	1	0	1
He	Helium	2	4		
Li	Lithium	3	7		
Be	Beryllium	4	9		
B	Boron	5	11		
C	Carbon	6	12		
N	Nitrogen	7	14		
O	Oxygen	8	16	8	6
F	Fluorine	9	19	10	7
Ne	Neon	10	20		
Na	Sodium	11	23		
Mg	Magnesium	12	24	12	2
Al	Aluminum	13	27		
Si	Silicon	14	28		
P	Phosphorus	15	31	16	5
S	Sulfur	16	32		
Cl	Chlorine	17	35		
A	Argon	18	40		

electrons) would have 2 electrons in the inner shell, 8 in the second shell, and the remaining 5 in the outer shell. Similarly, magnesium (number 12) has shells of 2, 8, and 2 electrons. Generally, the elements that combine most easily are those whose outer-shell electrons combine to fill a shell, which happens here when the sum of the elements' outer-shell electrons equals 8. Thus hydrogen (1 outer-shell electron) would be expected to combine with fluorine (7 outer-shell electrons); magnesium (2 in outer shell) with oxygen (6 in outer shell); and so on.

a. Create an array of records for the first 18 chemical elements. Each record should have fields for the element name, symbol, number, weight, number of neutrons, and number of electrons in the outer shell.

Read the symbols, names, numbers, and weights from an input file that you have created using an editor. Have the program complete filling the fields of the records by performing the calculations described. Then display the entire array and write it to a file.

b. Sort the elements alphabetically by name and display the sorted array of records.

c. Have the program search for and display the elements that are likely to be inert (those with a full outer shell of 2 or 8 electrons). Then list those pairs of elements most likely to combine. *Hint:* For each number N, 1 through 7, find the elements with N electrons in the outer shell, and those with $8 - N$ electrons in the outer shell.

14. [13.4] (FileName:CH13E) Extend the RealProperty (Example 13.4.1) to

a. display the Address, Cost, and YearBuilt for all houses built before 1980;

b. display the records and cost per square foot for all commercial properties whose cost per square foot is less than $20.00;

c. display the total cost, address, and number of rooms for homes with more than five rooms (which might be used for offices).

15. Create a variant record structure to hold the information for your most prized possessions. Your collection includes U.S. coins, U.S. stamps, rocks, and other items. For each record, fields will be included for the date acquired and the estimated value. The tag field will be the type of item, and the variant fields will be

● for coins: the coin date, the denomination (face value in cents), the mint (P, D, or S for Philadelphia, Denver, or San Francisco);

● for stamps: the date printed, the denomination (face value in cents), a BOOLEAN field indicating whether the stamp has been cancelled or not;

● for rocks: the name or type or rock, the mass in grams;

● for other items: a string field describing the item.

a. Write a program that allows you to fill an array of records describing your collection. Then display the records for all items.

b. Have the program find and display the records for items whose estimated value is greater than a value specified by the user.

c. Display the records for the coins and stamps in the collection, along with the ratio of estimated value divided by the denomination of each coin and stamp.

16. Create an array of variant records to accept the dimensions of three geometric figures. Each record will contain a field for the area and perimeter of the figure. The variant fields for the three figures will be as follows:

```
Rectangle: width, height;
Circle: radius;
Square: length of a side;
```

a. Write a program to fill the variant fields of the array with dimensions of ten figures. The program should present a menu listing the three types of figures and ask for the respective dimension(s) for each type of figure. After all ten figures and their dimensions have been entered, the program will calculate the area and perimeter of each figure. Finally, display the entire contents of all ten records.

b. Add a feature that will allow users to choose which type of figure, display all of the records for that type of figure, and allow users to change the dimensions of any figure displayed. A change will cause the program automatically to recalculate and update the area and perimeter fields and display the results.

14

Data Files

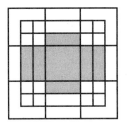

Chapter Outline

This chapter will help you to better manage sequential streams of text data and explain the concepts of binary and random-access files. Module InOut procedures for redirecting data from input files and to output files are discussed. The advantages and disadvantages of using these procedures—OpenInput, CloseInput, OpenOutput, and CloseOutput—are examined and weighed. A technique for handling files by using procedures from a FileSystem module is illustrated and compared with redirection.

14.1 *Streams Handled by InOut*

All input and output (I/O) operations handled by procedures from the module InOut are performed with characters. Module RealInOut supplements the character I/O procedures of InOut. CHARacter strings representing numbers are converted to their numeric values by procedures ReadCard, ReadInt, and ReadReal, and numbers are converted to their CHARacter representations by the corresponding write procedures. These modules consider data as a sequential *stream* of characters into or out of the storage area.

InOut procedures assume that I/O refers to a terminal unless directed otherwise by the program. *Redirection* of I/O is performed by using the OpenInput, CloseInput, OpenOutput, and CloseOutput commands. You will remember that OpenInput ("Extension") opens an area on the disk from which all read commands extract data until CloseInput closes the disk area and reopens the terminal keyboard for input. Similarly, OpenOutput("Extension") opens an area on the disk to which all write commands send data until CloseOutput closes the disk area and reopens the terminal screen for output.

Data can be stored more permanently on disks than in the computer memory, and disks provide greater storage capacity. The data stored in a particular disk area compose a **data file,** or simply a *file*. A file can be considered to be an array or list of records stored on disk (or on some other medium external to the volatile computer memory). The files handled by procedures from module InOut are **text files.** They are readable — that is, legible to humans — because everything in them is represented in character-code form. Text files can be printed or displayed with operating-system commands such as PRINT or TYPE.

Features of InOut Redirection

By now, you are familiar with some of the limitations of InOut redirection.

Limitations of InOut Files

1. Only one input stream and one output stream can be open at any one time.
2. The user must specify the file names interactively during program execution; the InOut procedures do not open a file without user intervention.
3. Only sequential text files, by which data is written or read in CHARacter form, one character after another in a stream, are allowed.
4. A file defined by InOut procedures is configured either for reading data or writing data; not for both.

Updating a particular record involves reading all of the records from one file and copying them to another, writing updates to the new file where they are to replace old data.

Done

The BOOLEAN variable **Done,** imported from InOut, determines whether or not the operation of an InOut procedure has been successful. If a call to an InOut procedure succeeds, Done is assigned the value TRUE; if an InOut procedure fails to perform its task, the value of Done becomes FALSE. In previous examples, testing variable Done has proved particularly useful in determining whether a Read-Card or other read command has made an attempt to read past the end of the file. (Some implementations of Modula-2 do not set Done to FALSE for a failed Read-String command.) Testing the value of Done is beneficial with other operations as well. For example, if a disk is full, Done will be set to FALSE when an unsuccessful OpenOutput or Write command is issued.

End of Line

For records defined by InOut procedures, a Record Separator character is used to mark the end of a line. This character is referred to as **EOL** (for *End-Of-Line*). It can be created from the keyboard by pressing the Enter (or Return) key. In code, most versions of the language recognize a Carriage Return, a Line Feed, or a Carriage Return–Line Feed combination as End-Of-Line.

☐ The FilePosition Indicator

Whenever a file is open, a **FilePosition** indicator is maintained. For sequential streams, like those controlled by InOut procedures, FilePosition is handled as follows: OpenInput places FilePosition at the beginning of the file. Then FilePosition moves forward as data are read, so that it always points to the location from which the next character will be read.

OpenOutput also places the FilePosition indicator at the beginning of the file, and FilePosition moves forward as data are written so that it always points to the location where the next character will be written. In a file that has been opened for output, however, FilePosition also defines the location of the end of the file. Consequently, once a file has been opened for output, the entire stream of data must be written to the file before CloseOutput occurs. If this is not done, a new OpenOutput sets FilePosition at the beginning of the file, which places all data previously in the file past the end of the file—and they are lost.

Since InOut procedures handle only one input and one output stream at once, the Terminal module (introduced in Chapter 5) allows characters to be written to and read from the terminal without redirection being terminated. Remember, a Close-Output followed by OpenOutput of the same file effectively erases all previous contents of the file; and CloseInput followed by OpenInput of the same file resets FilePosition so that the next read is at the beginning of the file.

The following example demonstrates how the InOut streams-handling procedures can be used to delete, add, and modify records in a file.

Example 14.1.1

Use procedures from the InOut module to create and manipulate sequential data files.

Define the problem Create a data file by entering these ten records from the keyboard and writing them to an output file.

Month	Day	Year	Month	Day	Year
JUL	4	1776	JAN	1	2000
APR	1	1976	OCT	12	1492
DEC	6	1941	OCT	4	1957
JUL	20	1969	APR	12	1961
NOV	23	1989	DEC	25	1968

Month will be represented by a string of CHARacters, whereas Day and Year are treated as CARDINAL values.

Read the contents of the original file, now reopened for input, one record at a time. Display each record to the screen as it is read. Decide whether to modify, add, or delete; and write the appropriate record or records to a new output file. The new file contains the updated data, and the original file is kept for backup.

To test the program, (1) change record APR 1 1976 to APR 10 1996, (2) add a record JUN 6 1944 between records DEC 6 1941 and JUL 20 1969, and (3) delete record APR 12 1961.

Develop a solution The structure chart in Figure 14–1 represents a solution of the problem. Except for a WriteString command, many Terminal modules handle only one character at a time. Therefore, procedures are written in this program to read a string from the terminal and convert a CARDINAL value to a string. A new function converts a string of CHARacters to a CARDINAL value.

Refine the solution *Pseudocode*

```
begin module StreamHandler
      display instructions
      CreateFirst(NumRecords)
      Modify(NumRecords)
end StreamHandler

procedure CreateFirst(VAR HowMany)
      open FIRST for output
      enter first Month
      while Month <> "Stop"
            enter Month, Day, and Year from terminal
            write Month, Day, and Year to file
            enter next Month
      end while, close FIRST

procedure Modify(HowMany)
      open FIRST for input       open SECOND for output
      for all records
            read ThisRecord from FIRST and display ThisRecord
            choose (C)opy, (M)odify, (D)elete, or (A)dd
            when choice is
                  Add or Modify : read NewRecord from terminal
                                      write NewRecord to file SECOND
                  Add or No Change : write ThisRecord to file SECOND
                  Delete : do nothing
      end for,    Close FIRST and SECOND

procedure ReadStrFromTerm(VAR Value)
      read a string of CHARacters from the terminal

procedure CardToString(Num)
```

Figure 14–1
Structure Chart for
StreamHandler
(Example 14.1.1)

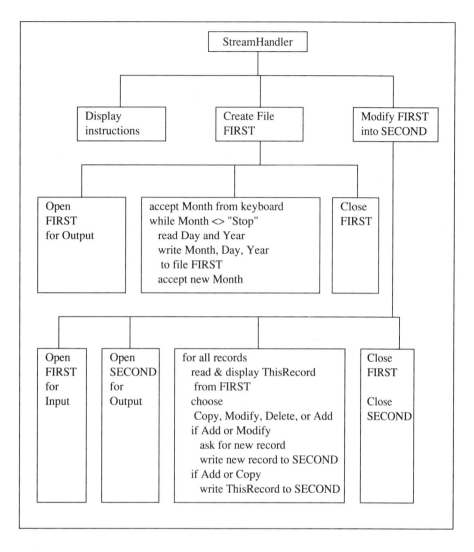

convert CARDINAL Num to CHARacters representing its digits
display the characters to the terminal screen

procedure StringToCard(In) : CARDINAL
return CARDINAL value of string of digit CHARacters IN

Modula-2 code Concentrate on the Modify procedure first. Each record is read from the input file, examined, and then (1) copied to the new file, (2) not written if it is to be deleted, (3) written with modifications, or (4) written after an added record. All of the records are read and written in order. Due to the nature of sequential files, there can be no stopping, skipping, or backing up until all of the input file data have been considered and the entire output file has been written.

Although record type HAPPEN is defined in the main module, the record variables are defined locally within the procedures, since the main module neither uses the records nor passes them as parameters. It is not necessary to define an array of records, because the procedures act upon one record at a time, and the collection of records is stored in the files rather than in a memory array.

Because the Terminal module does not contain ReadCard, WriteCard, or Read-String procedures, CARDINAL and string values must be displayed and read using only Terminal.WriteString, Terminal.Read, and Terminal.Write procedures. These problems provide the means of illustrating the development of procedures and functions for handling strings and numbers in text files.

Procedures ReadStrFromTerm and recursive CardToString, as well as function StringToCard, are nested within procedure Modify. Examine these subprograms to build your repertory of problem-solving algorithms.

```
MODULE StreamHandler;
  (* Copies files with editing, using InOut sequential file procedures.
     FileName:CH14A        Modula-2      RKW        July 1991  *)

FROM InOut IMPORT ReadString, WriteString, WriteLn, ReadCard, WriteCard,
            OpenInput, CloseInput, Read, Write, OpenOutput, CloseOutput;
IMPORT Terminal;  FROM Strings IMPORT Length, CompareStrings;

CONST  Space = ' ';  Comma = ',';  Null = 0C;
TYPE   STR = ARRAY [0..4] OF CHAR;
       HAPPEN = RECORD  Month:STR;  Day,Year:CARDINAL;   END; (* RECORD *)
VAR   NumRecords : CARDINAL;

PROCEDURE CreateFirst(VAR HowMany : CARDINAL);
   VAR   Event : HAPPEN;
   BEGIN
      WriteString("Name of first file(FIRST.DAT) = ? ");OpenOutput("DAT");
      HowMany := 0;    Terminal.WriteLn;
      WITH   Event   DO
         Terminal.WriteString("Month: "); ReadString(Month);
         WHILE  (CompareStrings(Month, "Stop") <> 0) AND
                   (CompareStrings(Month, "stop") <> 0)     DO
            INC(HowMany); Terminal.WriteString("  Day  : ");ReadCard(Day);
            Terminal.WriteString("  Year : "); ReadCard(Year);
             Terminal.WriteLn;                  (* Write record to file *)
             WriteString(Month);WriteCard(Day,4);WriteCard(Year,6);WriteLn;
             Terminal.WriteString("Month: "); ReadString(Month);
         END; (* WHILE *) Terminal.WriteLn;
      END; (* WITH *)                              CloseOutput;
   END CreateFirst;

PROCEDURE Modify(HowMany : CARDINAL);
   VAR ThisRecord, NewRecord : HAPPEN;    WhichRec : CARDINAL;
      Choose, Chose, Discard : CHAR;   DayStr, YearStr : STR;

   PROCEDURE ReadStrFromTerm(VAR Value : ARRAY OF CHAR);
      VAR  Count : CARDINAL;
      BEGIN
         Count := 0;  (* Read while >Space, not comma, & still room *)
         Terminal.Read(Value[Count]); Terminal.Write(Value[Count]);
         WHILE  (Value[Count] > Space) AND (Value[Count] # Comma)
                                    AND (Count < HIGH(Value))    DO
             INC(Count);
             Terminal.Read(Value[Count]); Terminal.Write(Value[Count]);
         END; (* WHILE *)
         IF  (Count < HIGH(Value)) OR (Value[Count] <= Space)
               OR (Value[Count] = Comma)  THEN  Value[Count] := Null;
```

```
        END;  (* IF *)
    END ReadStrFromTerm;

PROCEDURE CardToString(Num : CARDINAL);
    VAR DigitRep : CHAR;
    BEGIN
        DigitRep := CHR( Num MOD 10  + ORD('0') ); Num := Num DIV 10;
        IF  Num > 0  THEN  CardToString(Num); END; (* IF *)
        Terminal.Write(DigitRep);
    END CardToString;

PROCEDURE StringToCard(In : ARRAY OF CHAR) : CARDINAL;
    VAR  WhichChar, Out : CARDINAL;
    BEGIN
        Out := 0;
        FOR  WhichChar :=  0  TO  Length(In)-1  DO
           Out  :=  10 * Out  +  ORD(In[WhichChar]) - ORD('0');
        END; (* FOR *)  RETURN Out;
    END StringToCard;

BEGIN  (* procedure Modify *)
    WriteString("Name of first file(FIRST.DAT)= ? ");OpenInput("DAT");
    WriteString("Name of new file(SECOND.DAT) = ? ");OpenOutput("DAT");
    FOR  WhichRec := 1  TO  HowMany  DO
        WITH  ThisRecord  DO
            ReadString(Month);ReadCard(Day);ReadCard(Year);
            Terminal.WriteLn;
            Terminal.WriteString("The record just read is  ");
            Terminal.WriteString(Month); Terminal.WriteString("  ");
            CardToString(Day); Terminal.WriteString(",  ");
            CardToString(Year); Terminal.WriteLn; Terminal.WriteLn;
        END; (* WITH ThisRecord *)
        REPEAT
            Terminal.WriteString("Choose (C)opy, (M)odify, (D)elete,");
            Terminal.WriteString(" (A)dd:  "); Terminal.Read(Choose);
            Terminal.Read(Discard); Chose := CAP(Choose);
            Terminal.Write(Chose); Terminal.WriteLn;
        UNTIL (Chose='C') OR (Chose='M') OR (Chose='D') OR (Chose='A');
        IF  (Chose = 'M') OR (Chose = 'A')  THEN
            Terminal.WriteString("Specify new record: ");Terminal.WriteLn;
            WITH  NewRecord  DO
                Terminal.WriteString(" Month: "); ReadStrFromTerm(Month);
                Terminal.WriteString(" Day  : "); ReadStrFromTerm(DayStr);
                Terminal.WriteString(" Year : "); ReadStrFromTerm(YearStr);
                Terminal.WriteLn;
                WriteString(Month); WriteCard(StringToCard(DayStr),4);
                WriteCard(StringToCard(YearStr),6);WriteLn;
            END; (* WITH NewRecord *)
        END; (* IF *)
        IF  (Chose = 'A') OR (Chose = 'C')  THEN
            WITH  ThisRecord  DO
                WriteString(Month); WriteCard(Day,4); WriteCard(Year,6);
            END; (* WITH ThisRecord *) WriteLn;
        END; (* IF *)
    END; (* FOR *)                           CloseInput; CloseOutput;
END Modify;
```

```
BEGIN (* module StreamHandler *)
    WriteString("When entering Month, use 3 letters (e.g. SEP),");
     WriteString(" and end with Stop."); WriteLn; WriteLn;
    CreateFirst(NumRecords);
    Modify(NumRecords);
END StreamHandler.
```

Debug and test Numerous procedures and functions need to be debugged and tested. If you encounter difficulties, begin by writing driver modules and testing the procedures and functions nested within Modify. To determine whether the Create-First and Modify procedures work, use your operating system commands to display FIRST and SECOND after execution of the program. Try deleting the CreateFirst-(NumRecords) call from the main module, set NumRecords = number of records in SECOND, and run the program again, using SECOND as the input file and some new file (such as THIRD) for output. This will convince you that SECOND is a text file that can be read in the same manner as FIRST.

In procedure ReadStrFromTerm, if your Terminal.Read echoes characters to the screen, delete each Terminal.Write(Value[Count]) to avoid double character display.

Here is part of a sample run. Ellipses (. . .) represent additional output not shown.

```
When entering Month, use 3 letters (e.g. SEP), and end with Stop.

Name of first file(FIRST.DAT) = ? FIRST.DAT

Month: JUL  Day  : 4  Year : 1776
Month: APR  Day  : 1  Year : 1976
...
Month: Stop
Name of first file(FIRST.DAT)= ? FIRST.DAT
Name of new file(SECOND.DAT) = ? SECOND.DAT

The record just read is  JUL  4,  1776

Choose (C)opy, (M)odify, (D)elete, (A)dd:  C

The record just read is  APR  1,  1976

Choose (C)opy, (M)odify, (D)elete, (A)dd:  M
Specify new record:
 Month: APR  Day  : 10  Year : 1996
....
```

When you ask your system command to display files FIRST and SECOND, you should see

```
        FIRST                SECOND
    JUL   4  1776       JUL   4  1776
    APR   1  1976       APR  10  1996
    DEC   6  1941       DEC   6  1941
    JUL  20  1969       JUN   6  1944
    NOV  23  1989       JUL  20  1969
    JAN   1  2000       NOV  23  1989
    OCT  12  1492       JAN   1  2000
    OCT   4  1957       OCT  12  1492
    APR  12  1961       OCT   4  1957
    DEC  25  1968       DEC  25  1968
```

A Bit of Background

Privacy, Security, and Files

Data files have been around a long time, mainly on paper stored in filing cabinets. Terms such as *open, close,* and *lookup* that we use in handling computer files are reminders of older techniques for accessing paper files in drawers.

Today most files are stored electronically, and the amount of information that is collected and stored proliferates wildly. Because it is easier to transmit bits and bytes than to ship paper folders, increasingly serious problems of security have arisen and many people's privacy has been invaded. Whenever an individual fills out a government form or a credit application, submits a mail order, applies for a job, writes a check, or uses a credit card, "the data monster" is fed. Each

time those files are shared among government agencies or private enterprises, the individual loses more of his or her privacy.

In order to help protect U.S. citizens' Constitutional rights, the Fair Credit Reporting Act was passed in 1970, followed by the Federal Privacy Act in 1974. These Acts specify that it is illegal for a business to keep secret files, that you are entitled to examine and correct any data collected about you, and that government agencies and contractors must show justification for accessing your records. Efforts continue to create mechanisms that will serve to preserve the individual's security and privacy.

Complete the documentation The problem definition, structure chart, pseudocode, and sample run should be supplemented in the documentation by hardcopy of files FIRST and SECOND. In the users' manual, state the source code location (CH14A), and remind users that procedures Length and CompareStrings are imported from a Strings module. Since the prompts given by the program are brief, explain what (C)opy, (M)odify, (D)elete, and (A)dd do. The function String-ToCard returns strange results if the In string contains CHARacters other than digits. Safeguards can be built into the program to prevent this.

Questions 14.1

1. Explain when and why it is a disadvantage that InOut procedures can handle only one input stream and one output stream at a time.
2. Why are procedures ReadStrFromTerm and CardToString and function String-ToCard used in Example 14.1.1? Why not use ReadString, ReadCard, and WriteCard instead?
3. Consider function StringToCard in Example 14.1.1.
   a. Outline step-by-step how the function would convert CHARacter string "3185" to CARDINAL value 3185.
   b. What would be the CARDINAL value of Out if In were the string "R2D2"?
   c. What could you do to prevent In from containing CHARacters other than digits 0 through 9?
4. Consider procedure CardToString in Example 14.1.1. Outline step-by-step the process that would be performed by the procedure when the value of Num is 3185.

14.2 *Streams Handled by FileSystem*

Complications encountered in Example 14.1.1 were due primarily to limitations of the InOut procedures. With InOut, only one input and one output stream can be open at once; file names must be specified interactively, and only sequential text files are accessible. Fortunately, other file-handling procedures are available.

☐ The FileSystem Module

Procedures for manipulating files without the limitations of InOut differ in the various versions of Modula-2. Niklaus Wirth included a low-level module called **FileSystem** in his development of the language that extends file-handling capabilities. **Low-level** features are machine-dependent; that is, their implementation may depend upon the design of the particular computer system. Most Modula-2 packages include modules with the features of FileSystem, but the procedure names and methods of operation differ. (Consult your compiler manual for details.) The low-level FileSystem or other file-handling modules are necessary when InOut procedures will not handle a task satisfactorily.

The FileSystem features for handling sequential text streams are listed in Figure 14–2. The features of direct (random) access and binary file handling are discussed in the following sections of this chapter. Appendix C contains a more complete DEFINITION module for FileSystem, which includes all of the features used in this book.

Advantages and Disadvantages of FileSystem
The advantages of using FileSystem are that

1. you still can use convenient InOut procedures for terminal I/O,
2. you can have as many files open for input and output as you wish, and
3. the Read or Write mode of a FileSystem file can be changed without moving the FilePosition indicator.

It is a disadvantage that FileSystem procedures read and write only single characters of a text file. WriteString, WriteLn, and other read and write operations must be created by you, the programmer; the procedures developed in Example 14.1.1 and in IMPLEMENTATION MODULE Strings (Appendix C) provide some guidelines for you.

☐ FileSystem Procedures

Here is a summary of the FileSystem procedures listed in Figure 14–2.

ReadChar, WriteChar
ReadChar and WriteChar read and write a single character at the current FilePosition in an appropriately opened file.

File, eof, res, done
File is defined in FileSystem as a RECORD type, containing two important user-accessible fields named *eof* and *res*. For example, if files have been declared in the program by

```
VAR   MyFile, YourFile : File;
```

then   MyFile.eof   becomes TRUE when the FilePosition indicator points past the end of the file (such as when an attempt has been made to read past the end of file). Field   MyFile.res   has the value *done* whenever a call to a FileSystem procedure is successful and the value *notdone* when a call is unsuccessful.

```
TYPE   Response = (done, notdone);
          (* Response is used to return error messages. Only
             done/notdone will be used here. Others are system
             dependent, used primarily for system development. *)

TYPE   File = RECORD
                  eof : BOOLEAN;
                  (* This field becomes TRUE when FilePosition
                     pointer progresses past the end of file. *)

                  res : Response;
                  (* This field will contain the word done if a
                     call to a procedure is successful, and
                     notdone or some other error indicator if not
                     successful. *)
              END   (* RECORD *)

PROCEDURE   Lookup(VAR f:File;FileName:ARRAY OF CHAR;New:BOOLEAN);
   (* Associates FileName with file f, opens file f for use, and
      sets the FilePosition pointer to the beginning of the file.
      If New is TRUE and file f does not already exist, then
      Lookup creates and opens a new file. *)

PROCEDURE   Close(VAR f:File);
   (* Closes file associated with variable name f. *)

PROCEDURE   Rename(VAR f:FILE;   NewName:ARRAY OF CHAR);
   (* Renames file referred to by variable f to a file with the
      name specified by NewName. *)

PROCEDURE SetRead(VAR f:File);
   (* Sets file referred to by variable f to Read only mode. *)

PROCEDURE SetWrite(VAR f:File);
   (* Sets file referred to by variable f to Write only mode. *)

PROCEDURE SetModify(VAR f:File);
   (* Sets file referred to by variable f to allow both Read and
      Write operations. *)

PROCEDURE   Reset(VAR f:File);
   (* Resets FilePosition pointer to the beginning of the file
      and sets field eof to FALSE. The mode, Read/Write/Modify,
      becomes undefined until a Set command is issued or until
      the next read or write occurs. *)

PROCEDURE   ReadChar(VAR f:File; VAR Ch:CHAR);
   (* Reads a single character from open file f and moves the
      FilePosition pointer forward. If the FilePosition moves
      past the end of the file, then field eof is set to TRUE. *)

PROCEDURE   WriteChar(VAR f:File; VAR Ch:CHAR);
   (* Writes a single character to open file f and moves the
      FilePosition pointer and the end of file forward.
      If the FilePosition pointer already happens to be past the
      end of the file, then WriteChar inserts the character
      before the end of file. *)
```

Lookup

Procedure Lookup(VAR f:File; FileName:ARRAY OF CHAR; New:BOOLEAN); opens a file for use, sets the FilePosition indicator to the beginning of the file, and associates the FileName with record variable *f*.

New = TRUE

If a named file does not exist and parameter New is TRUE, then Lookup creates and opens a new file of that name. For example, the call

```
Lookup(MyFile,  " FIRST " ,  TRUE);
```

would associate the file name FIRST with variable MyFile and open the file if it exists or create and open a new file called FIRST.

New = FALSE

When parameter New is FALSE, such as in

```
Lookup(YourFile,  " ORIGINAL " ,  FALSE);
```

then the call of Lookup causes a search for already-existing file ORIGINAL, associates it with record variable YourFile, and opens it. If the system cannot find ORIGINAL, the procedure will not open a file, and the field YourFile.res will contain notdone.

Users can be prompted for the file names, if desired, by defining variables and executing commands such as

```
CONST  MAXFNLEN = 12;
VAR  NameofFile : ARRAY [1..MAXFNLEN] OF CHAR;
     IsItNew : BOOLEAN;  Answer, Discard : CHAR;
     ...
     WriteString("Enter file name: ");
       ReadString(NameofFile); WriteLn;
     WriteString("Will it be a new file (Y/N)? ");
       Read(Answer); Read(Discard); WriteLn;
     IF  Answer = 'Y'  THEN
       IsItNew := TRUE;
     ELSE
       IsItNew := FALSE;
     END; (* IF *)
     Lookup(FirstFile, NameofFile, IsItNew);
```

Close

Procedure call Close(MyFile), referring to MyFile that was opened in ''Lookup'' in subsection New = TRUE, closes the file FIRST.

Mode, SetRead, SetWrite, SetModify

When a file is opened, its mode (Read, Write, or Modify) is undefined. The mode is defined in one of two ways:

1. The mode is set automatically to Read only or Write only by the first ReadChar or WriteChar command, respectively.

2. The mode is set or reset explicitly by

```
SetRead(f),  SetWrite(f),  or  SetModify(f).
```

Once the mode of a file is set, it can be changed without closing the file by calling one of the three Set . . . procedures. When the mode is changed in this manner, FilePosition remains at its current location. A read command, in Read-only mode, reads from the position indicated by FilePosition. In Write-only mode, a write command writes to the position pointed to by FilePosition. When the file is set to Modify mode, you can read from or write to the file, in which case a write command writes over the latest data preceding the FilePosition indicator. SetModify permits you to replace data, which is done by moving FilePosition to the appropriate location using ReadChar or SetPos (discussed in Section 14.4).

Reset

The Reset(f) procedure moves the FilePosition indicator back to the beginning of the file. If the eof field contains TRUE, it is reset to FALSE unless the file is empty, in which case the mode of the file is again undefined until a Set . . . procedure is called or until a ReadChar of WriteChar command is executed.

☐ Handling Sequential Files with FileSystem

To illustrate sequential file handling with FileSystem commands, this example repeats the process of Example 14.1.1 using FileSystem rather than InOut procedures for the files, and reserves InOut for terminal I/O.

Example 14.2.1

Use procedures from the FileSystem module to create and manipulate sequential data files.

Define the problem   Create a data file by reading records of ten dates of the form AUG 23 1986 from the keyboard into a file that has been opened and set to Write-only mode. Now close and reopen the file, and set the mode to Read-only. Open a second file in Write-only mode, read the contents of the first file one record at a time, display each record to the screen, and decide whether to modify, add, delete, or copy each record to the second file.

Develop a solution   The structure chart of the solution is shown in Figure 14–1.

Refine the solution   The pseudocode is the same as that for StreamHandler in Example 14.1.1, except that the procedures and functions previously nested within Modify have been moved to the main module to make them available globally. The procedures have been changed and supplemented to reflect the necessary tasks of reading and writing strings and CARDINAL numbers using ReadChar and Write-Char.

   The newly written or rewritten string-handling procedures are

ReadStringFromFile (* Reads a string from the file, ignoring leading characters with code
                    < = Space and terminating with any character whose code
                    < = Space. *)
WriteStringToFile (* Writes a string to the file. *)
WriteLnToFile (* Writes a carriage return followed by a line feed. *)
WriteCardToFile (* Converts a CARDINAL number to characters, which it writes to the file.*)

Since ReadChar and WriteChar used by the procedures requires the file designator, each of these procedures receives the file designator *f* as a VARiable parameter.

Modula-2 code This code follows the pattern of the one in Example 14.1.1. InOut procedures are used now to handle the terminal, and special procedures have been written to perform string and CARDINAL read and write operations on the files using the FileSystem ReadChar and WriteChar commands. Procedure Read-StringFromFile uses essentially the same algorithm as ReadStrFromTerm in Example 14.1.1. WriteCardToFile uses the same recursive algorithm as the previous CardToString. Function StringToCard has not changed. WriteStringToFile and WriteLnToFile are new. Lookup and Close open and close the files, respectively.

```
MODULE FileHandler;
    (* Copies files with editing, using FileSystem seq. file procedures.
        FileName:CH14B     Modula-2     RKW     July 1991  *)

FROM InOut IMPORT WriteString, ReadString, WriteLn, ReadCard, WriteCard,
                  Read, Write;
FROM FileSystem IMPORT File, Lookup, Close, ReadChar, WriteChar
                       (* optional: , SetRead, SetWrite *);
FROM Strings IMPORT Length, CompareStrings;

CONST  Space = ' '; Null = 0C;  CrgReturn = 15C;  LineFeed = 12C;
TYPE   STR = ARRAY [0..4] OF CHAR;
TYPE HAPPEN = RECORD  Month:STR;  Day,Year:CARDINAL;  END; (* RECORD *)
VAR  NumRecords : CARDINAL;

PROCEDURE WriteLnToFile(VAR f : File);
    (* New line indicator will be CR then LF.  If your system does not
       use ASCII, change CONSTants CrgReturn and LineFeed for your code. *)
    BEGIN
       WriteChar(f, CrgReturn);  WriteChar(f, LineFeed);
    END WriteLnToFile;

PROCEDURE WriteStringToFile(VAR f : File;  Value : ARRAY OF CHAR);
    VAR  NumChars, WhichChar : CARDINAL;
    BEGIN
       NumChars := Length(Value) - 1;
       FOR WhichChar:=0 TO NumChars DO
          WriteChar(f, Value[WhichChar]);
       END; (* FOR *)
    END WriteStringToFile;

PROCEDURE ReadStringFromFile(VAR f:File;  VAR Value:ARRAY OF CHAR);
    (* Leading code <= Space is ignored.  Then characters are read
       until code <= Space is encountered. *)
    VAR  Count : CARDINAL;  TempChar : CHAR;
    BEGIN
       REPEAT
          ReadChar(f, TempChar);
       UNTIL  (TempChar > Space) OR (f.eof);      Count := 0;
       IF  f.eof  THEN  Value[Count] := Null;
        ELSE  Value[Count] := TempChar;
       END; (* IF *)
       WHILE  (Value[Count] > Space) AND (Count < HIGH(Value))  DO
```

```
            INC(Count);   ReadChar(f, Value[Count]);
        END; (* WHILE *)
        IF  (Count < HIGH(Value)) OR (Value[Count] <= Space)   THEN
            Value[Count]:=Null;
        END;(*IF*)
    END ReadStringFromFile;

PROCEDURE WriteCardToFile(VAR f : File;   Num : CARDINAL);
    VAR  DigitRep : CHAR;
    BEGIN
        DigitRep := CHR( Num MOD 10  +  ORD('0') );   Num := Num DIV 10;
        IF  Num > 0  THEN  WriteCardToFile(f, Num);  END;(*IF*)
        WriteChar(f, DigitRep);
    END WriteCardToFile;

PROCEDURE StringToCard(In:ARRAY OF CHAR) : CARDINAL;
    VAR  WhichChar, Out : CARDINAL;
    BEGIN
        Out := 0;
        FOR  WhichChar := 0  TO  Length(In) - 1   DO
            Out  :=  10 * Out  +  ORD(In[WhichChar]) - ORD('0');
        END; (* FOR *)   RETURN Out;
    END StringToCard;

PROCEDURE CreateFirst(VAR HowMany : CARDINAL);
    VAR  FirstFile : File;   Event : HAPPEN;
    BEGIN
        Lookup(FirstFile, "FIRST", TRUE);
        (* SetWrite(FirstFile) optional, WriteChar(FirstFile, ) sets mode *)
        HowMany := 0;  WriteLn;
        WITH  Event  DO
            WriteString("Month: "); ReadString(Month);
            WHILE  (CompareStrings(Month, "Stop") <> 0)  AND
                    (CompareStrings(Month, "stop") <> 0)   DO
                INC(HowMany);  WriteString(" Day  : "); ReadCard(Day);
                WriteString("  Year : "); ReadCard(Year); WriteLn;
                                            (* Write record to file *)
                WriteStringToFile(FirstFile, Month);
                 WriteStringToFile(FirstFile, "  ");
                WriteCardToFile(FirstFile, Day);
                 WriteStringToFile(FirstFile, "  ");
                WriteCardToFile(FirstFile, Year); WriteLnToFile(FirstFile);

                WriteString("Month: "); ReadString(Month);
            END; (* WHILE *) WriteLn;
        END; (* WITH *)       Close(FirstFile);
    END CreateFirst;

PROCEDURE Modify(HowMany : CARDINAL);
    VAR  ThisRecord, NewRecord : HAPPEN;   WhichRec : CARDINAL;
         Choose, Chose, Discard : CHAR;   DayStr, YearStr : STR;
         FirstFile, SecFile : File;
    BEGIN
        Lookup(FirstFile, "FIRST", FALSE);
        (* SetRead(FirstFile) optional, ReadChar(FirstFile, ) sets mode *)
        Lookup(SecFile, "SECOND", TRUE);
```

```
            (* SetWrite(SecFile) optional, WriteChar(SecFile, ) sets mode *)
        FOR  WhichRec := 1  TO  HowMany  DO
            WITH  ThisRecord  DO
                ReadStringFromFile(FirstFile, Month);
                ReadStringFromFile(FirstFile, DayStr);
                ReadStringFromFile(FirstFile, YearStr);  WriteLn;
                WriteString("The record just read is  "); WriteString(Month);
                Day := StringToCard(DayStr);  WriteCard(Day,4);
                Year := StringToCard(YearStr);  WriteCard(Year,6);
            END; (* WITH ThisRecord *) WriteLn; WriteLn;
            REPEAT
                WriteString("Choose (C)opy, (M)odify, (D)elete, (A)dd: ");
                 Read(Choose); Read(Discard); Chose := CAP(Choose);
                 Write(Chose); WriteLn;
            UNTIL (Chose='C') OR (Chose='M') OR (Chose='D') OR (Chose='A');
            IF  (Chose = 'M') OR (Chose = 'A')  THEN
                WriteString("Specify new record: "); WriteLn;
                WITH  NewRecord  DO
                    WriteString("Month: "); ReadString(Month);
                    WriteString(" Day  : "); ReadCard(Day);
                    WriteString(" Year : "); ReadCard(Year); WriteLn;
                    WriteStringToFile(SecFile, Month);
                     WriteStringToFile(SecFile, "  ");
                    WriteCardToFile(SecFile, Day);
                     WriteStringToFile(SecFile, "  ");
                    WriteCardToFile(SecFile, Year); WriteLnToFile(SecFile);
                END; (* WITH NewRecord *)
            END; (* IF *)
            IF  (Chose = 'A') OR (Chose = 'C')  THEN
                WITH  ThisRecord  DO
                    WriteStringToFile(SecFile, Month);
                     WriteStringToFile(SecFile, "  ");
                    WriteCardToFile(SecFile, Day);
                     WriteStringToFile(SecFile, "  ");
                    WriteCardToFile(SecFile, Year);  WriteLnToFile(SecFile);
                END (* WITH ThisRecord *)
            END; (* IF *)
        END; (* FOR *)
        Close(FirstFile);  Close(SecFile);
    END Modify;

BEGIN (* main module FileHandler *)
    WriteString("When entering Month, use 3 letters (e.g. SEP),");
     WriteString(" and end with Stop."); WriteLn; WriteLn;
    CreateFirst(NumRecords);
    Modify(NumRecords);
END FileHandler.
```

Debug and test The program has not changed drastically from the one in Example 14.1.1. Commands that may need debugging are those that handle the files. Most procedures require the file designator (VAR f:File) to be a VARiable parameter. For each new file-handling procedure you may want to write a separate driver program (similar to those described in Section 6.7) that opens a file and passes the file designator to the procedure.

The sample run appears the same as the one for Example 14.1.1, except that in this version you do not enter the file names interactively.

Complete the documentation   Documentation will be similar to that for Exercise 14.1.1, except that the source code (file CH14B) illustrates using the FileSystem procedures.

Questions 14.2

1. Examine the FileSystem module (or the equivalent) for your system, and describe the differences (if any) between the sequential stream-handling procedures in your system and those described in Figure 14–2.
2. Explain how the Done variable defined in module InOut differs from the done value defined in module FileSystem.
3. Rewrite the first few lines of procedures CreateFirst and Modify in example 14.2.1 so that they prompt the user for the names of the files to be opened, instead of including those names explicitly in the Lookup parameters.
4. Referring again to Example 14.2.1,
   a. modify procedure StringToCard so that it recognizes a leading ' + ' or ' − ' and converts the string to an INTEGER value.
   b. Modify procedure WriteCardToFile so that it writes an INTEGER value to the file.

14.3   *Binary Files*

(The material presented in this section will be useful to you in the future, but total mastery of it is not necessary for understanding the remainder of the book.)

Data can be stored in files in the form of binary WORDs. The WORD data type usually is imported from SYSTEM and represents the small number of bytes (2, 4, etc.) that your computer is designed to handle in one operation. Files of binary WORDs are called **binary files.** The bytes in binary files do not necessarily represent CHARacter codes expected by operating system commands designed to display text. Therefore, an attempt to TYPE or PRINT a binary file usually results in a meaningless display. Binary files are used for storing data that will be read and interpreted by a program.

Advantages of Binary Files

The advantages of using binary files, as opposed to text files, are twofold.

1. Numbers are stored more compactly, and the file requires less space on the storage medium. For example, in a text file the CARDINAL value 30429 is converted to the codes for characters *3, 0, 4, 2,* and *9* and stored as 5 bytes of code. The same number in binary is 0111 0110 1101 1101, which can be stored in only 2 bytes.
2. Conversion of values, such as REAL numbers, into CHARacter form for storage and back again upon retrieval, may reduce the accuracy of those numbers and is wasteful of computer time. Storage in a binary file requires no such conversions.

☐ ReadWord, WriteWord

Dr. Wirth's FileSystem module contains two procedures that facilitate reading and writing binary files. These are

```
PROCEDURE ReadWord(VAR f:File; VAR W:WORD);
```

and

```
PROCEDURE WriteWord(VAR f:File; W:Word);
```

ReadWord retrieves a word from the file and advances FilePosition to the next word. WriteWord writes a word to the file and moves FilePosition so that it points to the location where the next word will be written.

Like text files, data in binary files may be accessed sequentially or with the random-access techniques illustrated in the next section. The following example illustrates sequential access to a binary file.

Example 14.3.1

Write a string of characters to a binary file and then retrieve and interpret them.

Define the problem   A CHARacter string will be entered from the keyboard into an array. The array will be written to a binary file. Then the file will be read and the characters displayed.

Develop a solution   After the characters are read, they will be packed, two at a time, into WORDs. The *WORDs* will be written to a binary file, using the Write-Word procedure. Then the binary file will be read one *CHARacter* at a time, using ReadChar, and displayed to the screen. Figure 14–3 is a structure chart of the solution.

Refine the solution   *Pseudocode*

It is assumed that a WORD is two bytes and that a CHARacter is one byte. If these have different lengths on your system, you will need to modify procedure Pack-TheChars.

```
begin module BinStoreChars
       ReadAString(CharList, NumChars)
       PackTheChars(CharList, WordList, NumChars)
       WriteToFile(WordList, NumChars)
       ReadAndDisplay(NumChars)
end BinStoreChars

procedure ReadAString(VAR CharList,    VAR HowManyChars)
```

Figure 14–3
Structure Chart for
BinStoreChars
(Example 14.3.1)

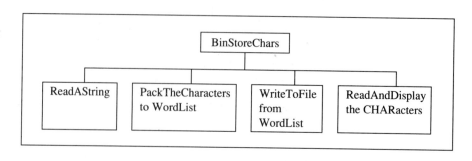

```
          ask for string CharList
          concatenate a Blank if necessary to make Length even
          set    HowManyChars = Length(CharList)

     procedure PackTheChars(CharList,    VAR WordList,    HowManyChars)
          initialize CharCount = 0
          while    CharCount < HowManyChars − 1
                pack CharList[CharCount] and CharList[CharCount + 1]
                    into    WordList[CharCount DIV 2]
                increment    CharCount    by    2
          end while

     procedure    WriteToFile(WordList,    HowManyChars)
          open file,    write all WordList words to file,    close file

     procedure    ReadAndDisplay(HowManyChars)
          open file,    read all CHARacters from file and display,    close file
```

Modula-2 code   Observe the import lists that are necessary for handling the files, WORDs, and strings. In procedure PackTheChars, successive characters are moved to a CHARacter string called TwoChar and then assigned to a WordList WORD. WORD(TwoChar) may or may not be necessary on your system for converting array TwoChar to a WORD compatible with a WordList element. In ReadAndDisplay, ReadChar retrieves bytes from the file one CHARacter at a time.

```
MODULE BinStoreChars;
   (* Stores characters in a binary file of WORDs, retrieves them
      as CHARacters and displays the characters.
      FileName:CH14C      Modula-2      RKW      July 1991 *)

FROM InOut IMPORT WriteString, WriteLn, Write, OpenInput, CloseInput;
FROM FileSystem IMPORT File, Lookup, Close, WriteWord, ReadChar;
FROM SYSTEM IMPORT WORD;
FROM Strings IMPORT STRING, Length, Concatenate, ReadLine;

CONST  Null = 0C; Blank = ' ';  LASTWORD = 39;
TYPE   WRDLST = ARRAY [0..LASTWORD] OF WORD;
VAR   CharList,SecondList:STRING;   WordList:WRDLST;   NumChars:CARDINAL;

PROCEDURE ReadAString(VAR CharList:STRING;   VAR HowManyChars:CARDINAL);
   BEGIN
      REPEAT
         WriteString("Enter a string (at least one character):");WriteLn;
          ReadLine(CharList); WriteLn;
      UNTIL (Length(CharList) >= 1);
      IF  ODD(Length(CharList))   THEN            (* make Length even *)
         Concatenate(CharList, Blank, CharList);
      END; (* IF *)   HowManyChars := Length(CharList);
   END ReadAString;

PROCEDURE PackTheChars(CharList : STRING;   VAR WordList : WRDLST;
                                            HowManyChars : CARDINAL);
   VAR TwoChars:ARRAY [0..1] OF CHAR; ThisWord:WORD; CharCount:CARDINAL;
   BEGIN
      CharCount := 0;
      WHILE  CharCount < HowManyChars - 1  DO
         TwoChars[0]:=CharList[CharCount];
         TwoChars[1]:=CharList[CharCount+1];
```

```
            WordList[CharCount DIV 2] := WORD(TwoChars);
              (* Assertion: WordList[i] = CharList[2i] + CharList[2i+1] *)
            INC(CharCount, 2);
        END; (* WHILE *)
    END PackTheChars;

    PROCEDURE WriteToFile(WordList : WRDLST;  HowManyChars : CARDINAL);
        VAR  MaxWordIndex, WordCount : CARDINAL;  BinFile : File;
        BEGIN
            Lookup(BinFile, "CHARTERS.BIN", TRUE);   (* Open new file *)
            MaxWordIndex := HowManyChars DIV 2  - 1;
            FOR  WordCount := 0  TO  MaxWordIndex  DO
                WriteWord(BinFile, WordList[WordCount]);
            END; (* FOR *)    Close(BinFile);
        END WriteToFile;

    PROCEDURE ReadAndDisplay(HowManyChars : CARDINAL);
        (* Reads BinFile WORDS back as CHARacters. *)
        VAR  BinFile : File;  WhichChar : CARDINAL;  ThisChar : CHAR;
        BEGIN
            Lookup(BinFile, "CHARTERS.BIN", FALSE);   (* Open existing file *)
            FOR  WhichChar := 0  TO  HowManyChars-1  DO
                ReadChar(BinFile, ThisChar);  Write(ThisChar);
            END; (* FOR *)     WriteLn;  Close(BinFile);
        END ReadAndDisplay;

BEGIN (* module BinStoreChars *)
    ReadAString(CharList, NumChars);
    PackTheChars(CharList, WordList, NumChars);
    WriteToFile(WordList, NumChars);
    ReadAndDisplay(NumChars);
END BinStoreChars.
```

Debug and test   *Caution:* Procedures for handling WORDs and binary files are considered *low-level* code. Few safeguards are built into the language for low-level procedures, and various versions implement them quite differently. See your system manual for file-handling procedures if you are having trouble. Handling REAL values (or other data types longer than a WORD) in binary files can require pointers and ADDRESSes, which are discussed in Chapters 16 and 17. A sample run asks for a string and echoes that string while reading it from the file.

Complete the documentation   Some discussion of binary files and the differences between ReadWord, WriteWord and ReadChar, WriteChar would be an asset to serious users of this program. Warn the programmer that versions of Modula-2 differ in their implementation of low-level features such as binary files and WORDs. The source code file is CH14C. Length, Concatenate and ReadLine are imported from a Strings module. When a string is requested, users can enter from 1 to 80 characters, terminated by Enter (or Return).

Questions 14.3

1. **a.** What do you see if you use an operating-system command such as TYPE or PRINT to display the binary file CHARTERS.BIN produced in Example 14.3.1? Why?
   b. Is it possible that you would see a meaningful display of CHARTERS.BIN on some systems and not on others? Why?

2. Under what circumstances might you want to use a binary file rather than a text file?

3. Assuming that an INTEGER just fills a WORD, supply appropriate IMPORT lists and VARiable declarations to make this program fragment work. What does the program do? What happens if you try to use an operating system command to display file TRYIT.BIN?

```
BEGIN
    Nums[1]:=-1; Nums[2]:=2; Nums[3]:=-3; Nums[4]:=-1234; Nums[5]:=12345;

    Lookup(BFile, "TRYIT.BIN", TRUE);
    FOR  Count := 1 TO 5  DO
        ThisWord := WORD(Nums[Count]);   WriteWord(BinFile, ThisWord);
    END; (* FOR *)   Close(BFile);

    Lookup(BFile, "TRYIT.BIN", FALSE);
    FOR  Count := 1 TO 5  DO
        ReadWord(BFile, ThisWord);
        ThisNum := INTEGER(ThisWord);   WriteInt(ThisNum,6); WriteLn;
    END; (* FOR *)   Close(BFile);
    . . . .
```

14.4 *Focus on Problem Solving*

Up to this point in this book, access to files has been sequential. This is adequate when files are small or when activity is high — that is, when most of the records are to be accessed at once. However, if you have several thousand records and want to see just one or just a few records, searching the entire file sequentially would probably be unacceptably slow. In this section you will look at **direct-access** (also called **random-access**) techniques for finding a single record and develop a program that gives you direct access to text file records.

Direct-Access Files

Each record's position in an array is indicated by an index. If you know exactly which array location is occupied by the record you seek, you can retrieve that record directly.

If every data file could be read from secondary storage into a memory array, all you would need would be techniques for handling files sequentially and procedures for manipulating arrays. However, primary memory is expensive, the amount of memory that can be addressed is limited, and it is often unrealistic to store an entire file in memory.

The trend in computer development is toward **virtual memory,** which allows parts of a file to be moved to and from memory so rapidly that it appears that the file resides there, even though the actual memory is not large enough to accommodate the entire file at once. Eventually, virtual memory techniques may make direct file access unnecessary, but for the near future it is important to know how to retrieve and replace a single file record quickly.

For direct access, special file-handling commands beyond those designed to handle sequential streams are needed.

Direct-Access Procedures in FileSystem

Three procedures in FileSystem provide direct (random) access to records. All three procedures refer to the byte location of FilePosition by using two CARDINAL values, high and low. The bits of low are concatenated to the bits of high to represent a nonnegative integer. For example, if CARDINAL numbers are represented by 16 bits, the FilePosition indicator will be represented by 32 bits and will have values ranging from 0 (the address of the first byte of the file) to $2^{32} - 1 = 4,294,967,295$, which provides for files with a sizable number of bytes. FilePosition in such a system would be calculated in decimal notation by

$$\text{FilePosition} = (\text{high} * 2^{16}) + \text{low} = (\text{high} * 65,536) + \text{low}.$$

(Some systems use a type LONGCARD, with 4 or more bytes, instead of high and low to describe FilePosition.)

The three direct-access procedures are

```
PROCEDURE Length(VAR f:File; VAR high,low:CARDINAL);
   (* After executing this procedure, high,low represents
   the total length in bytes of the file. *)

PROCEDURE GetPos(VAR f:File; VAR high,low:CARDINAL);
   (* After executing this procedure, high,low represents
   the current value of FilePosition. *)

PROCEDURE SetPos(VAR f:File; high,low:CARDINAL);
   (* Modifies FilePosition to point to the
   indicated high,low byte position. *)
```

For example, a call

```
SetPos(FileVariable, 0, 0)
```

would set the FilePointer to the beginning of the file, and the calls

```
Length(FileVariable, Upper, Lower)
SetPos(FileVariable, Upper, Lower)
```

would set the FilePointer to the end of the file.

The Byte Count

It is the user/programmer's responsibility to know or calculate the byte-count position of the record of interest for random access to the file. Thus to retrieve a record from a file that has been opened in Read mode, the program must provide the high, low byte count to the call

```
SetPos(FileVariable, high, low)
```

and then read the number of characters in the record, using the ReadChar command.

SIZE and TSIZE

Two functions help determine the byte count. SIZE(VariableName) returns the length in bytes of a variable. TSIZE(DataTypeIdentifier) returns the byte length of the specified data type. In recent versions of Modula-2, SIZE accepts either a VariableName or a DataTypeIdentifier parameter. SIZE may always be available or it may need to be imported from SYSTEM. TSIZE almost always must be imported.

The byte length of a record can be determined by displaying SIZE(RecordVariableName); and if record counts begin at 0, then record N should begin at byte position $N * \text{SIZE(RecordVariableName)}$.

Now it is time to make it work.

☐   **A Banking Program**

> **Example 14.4.1**

A bank's customer records are to be stored in a file so that an individual's records can be accessed randomly by account number.

Define the problem   To keep the illustration as simple as possible, retrieve five records from a file. CARDINAL account numbers will be 0 through 4. Display and update the account balance.

Develop a solution
The solution involves three operations:

1. Create the file by entering five customer records, such as

> AcctNum = 2   FirstName = May   LastName = French   Balance = $5.00

Customer will be defined as a record with four fields. To take advantage of ReadChar and WriteChar procedures and minimize conversions, all of the fields will be entered and stored as text strings.

2. The byte location of the beginning of the record with a particular AcctNum is BeginAcct = AcctNum * SIZE(Customer). Individual field locations are calculated from SIZE(Customer.AcctNum), SIZE(Customer.FirstName), and so on. Record fields are read and written starting at FilePositions set by SetPos(CustFile, high, low). For this short file, high = 0, and low equals the beginning byte location of the field.

3. To update a Customer.Balance field, a new balance will be written in the old Balance field of the appropriate record.

Refine the solution   *Pseudocode*

```
begin module DirectBanking
        determine the sizes of the customer record and each field
        CreateFile(CustFile)
        RetrieveAndUpdate(CustFile)
end module DirectBanking

procedure CreateFile(VAR CustFile)
        open a new file
        for all customers
                ask for names and balance
                write acctnum, names, and balance to file using
                    WriteField(CustFile, field name, beginning byte count of field)
        close file

procedure RetrieveAndUpdate(VAR CustFile)
        open the file,    set to Modify mode
        repeat
                ask which customer (0..4) AcctNo
                if a valid customer
                        set WhichAcct = StringToCard(AcctNo)
                        ReadAndDisplay(CustFile, AcctNo)
                        if balance is to be updated
                                ask for new balance, WriteField(CustFile,NewBal,BeginBal)
        until not a valid customer
```

```
procedure WriteField(VAR CustFile, Field, Where)
        SetPos(CustFile, 0, Where)
        WriteChar    all field characters until Null or end of field
        fill remainder of field with Blanks

procedure ReadField(VAR CustFile,    VAR Field,    Where)
        SetPos(CustFile, 0, Where)
        ReadChar    field characters until Null or end of field

procedure ReadAndDisplay(VAR CustFile,    AcctNo)
        ReadField    all fields, given the field name and byte count for
          the beginning of the field
        WriteString    fields to the screen

procedure    StringToCard(In):CARDINAL    (* see Example 14.1.1. *)
```

Modula-2 code Pay close attention to the calculation of the beginning byte count for each record and field, which is used in SetPos. Note that the Customer record and Size... variables are used globally.

```
MODULE DirectBanking;
   (* Illustrates direct access to text files.
        FileName:CH14D       Modula-2       RKW        July 1991   *)

FROM InOut IMPORT WriteString,WriteLn,ReadString,WriteCard,Read,Write;
FROM FileSystem IMPORT File,Lookup,Close,ReadChar,WriteChar,SetPos,
                                               SetModify, SetWrite;
FROM Strings IMPORT Length;   FROM SYSTEM IMPORT SIZE;

CONST  MAXGNRSTR=11;  MAXACTSTR=5;  HIGHREC=4;  Blank=' ';  Null=0C;
TYPE GNRSTR=ARRAY[0..MAXGNRSTR]OF CHAR; ACTSTR=ARRAY[0..MAXACTSTR]OF CHAR;
     WHO = RECORD
                AcctNum : ACTSTR;   (* 0 <= AcctNum <= HIGHREC *)
                FirstName, LastName, Balance : GNRSTR;
           END; (* RECORD *)
VAR  Customer : WHO; CustFile : File; (* Customer & Sizes used globally *)
     SizeCust, SizeAcct, SizeName, SizeBal : CARDINAL;

PROCEDURE WrtBlnk;  BEGIN  WriteString("   "); END WrtBlnk;

PROCEDURE StringToCard(In: ARRAY OF CHAR) : CARDINAL;
   VAR WhichChar, Out : CARDINAL;
   BEGIN    Out := 0;
      FOR  WhichChar := 0 TO Length(In) -1  DO
         Out := 10 * Out  +  ORD(In[WhichChar]) - ORD('0');
      END; (* FOR *)    RETURN Out;
   END StringToCard;

PROCEDURE WriteField(VAR CustFile:File; Field:ARRAY OF CHAR;
                                                Where:CARDINAL);
   VAR  Count, Index : CARDINAL;
   BEGIN
      Index := 0;  SetPos(CustFile, 0, Where);
      REPEAT
         WriteChar(CustFile, Field[Index]);  INC(Index);
      UNTIL  (Field[Index-1] = Null) OR (Index > HIGH(Field));
      FOR Count:=Index TO HIGH(Field) DO WriteChar(CustFile,Blank);END;
   END WriteField;
```

```
PROCEDURE ReadField(VAR CustFile:File; VAR Field:ARRAY OF CHAR;
                                             Where:CARDINAL);
    VAR  Index : CARDINAL;
    BEGIN    Index := 0;  SetPos(CustFile, 0, Where);
        REPEAT
            ReadChar(CustFile, Field[Index]);  INC(Index);
        UNTIL  (Field[Index-1] = Null) OR (Index > HIGH(Field));
    END ReadField;

PROCEDURE ReadAndDisplay(VAR CustFile : File;  AcctNo : ARRAY OF CHAR);
    VAR  BeginAcct : CARDINAL;
    BEGIN
        BeginAcct  := StringToCard(AcctNo) * SizeCust;
        WITH  Customer  DO
            ReadField(CustFile, AcctNum, BeginAcct);
            ReadField(CustFile, FirstName, BeginAcct+SizeAcct);
            ReadField(CustFile, LastName, BeginAcct+SizeAcct+SizeName);
            ReadField(CustFile, Balance, BeginAcct+SizeAcct+2*SizeName);
            WriteString("Customer:  ");
             WriteString(AcctNum); WrtBlnk; WriteString(FirstName); WrtBlnk;
             WriteString(LastName); WrtBlnk; WriteString(Balance); WriteLn;
        END; (* WITH *)
    END ReadAndDisplay;


PROCEDURE CreateFile(VAR CustFile : File);
    VAR  WhichCust, BeginAcct : CARDINAL;
    BEGIN
        Lookup(CustFile, "CUSTOMER.DAT", TRUE);   SetWrite(CustFile);
        FOR  WhichCust := 0 TO HIGHREC  DO
            WriteString("Enter customer");WriteCard(WhichCust,6);WriteLn;
            WITH  Customer  DO
                AcctNum[0] := CHR(WhichCust + ORD('0'));  AcctNum[1] := Null;
                WriteString("FirstName: "); ReadString(FirstName);
                WriteString("  LastName: "); ReadString(LastName);
                WriteString("  CurrentBalance: $");ReadString(Balance);
                BeginAcct:= WhichCust*SizeCust;
                WriteField(CustFile, AcctNum, BeginAcct);
                WriteField(CustFile, FirstName, BeginAcct+SizeAcct);
                WriteField(CustFile, LastName, BeginAcct+SizeAcct+SizeName);
                WriteField(CustFile, Balance, BeginAcct+SizeAcct+2*SizeName);
            END; (* WITH *)  WriteLn;
        END; (* FOR *)            Close(CustFile);
    END CreateFile;

PROCEDURE  RetrieveAndUpdate(VAR CustFile : File);
    VAR Answer, CapAnsw, Discard : CHAR;  NewBal : GNRSTR;
        AcctNo : ACTSTR;   WhichAcct, BeginBal : CARDINAL;
    BEGIN
        Lookup(CustFile, "CUSTOMER.DAT", FALSE);   SetModify(CustFile);
        REPEAT
            WriteLn; WriteString("Which customer (0,1,...)? ");
             WriteString(" (Stop with number >"); WriteCard(HIGHREC,6);
             WriteString("): "); ReadString(AcctNo); WriteLn;
            WhichAcct := StringToCard(AcctNo);
            IF  WhichAcct <= HIGHREC  THEN
                ReadAndDisplay(CustFile, AcctNo); WriteLn;
                WriteString("UpdateBalance (Y/N)? "); Read(Answer);
```

```
            Read(Discard);CapAnsw:=CAP(Answer);Write(CapAnsw);WriteLn;
         IF  CapAnsw = 'Y'  THEN
            WriteString("New Balance = $ "); ReadString(NewBal);
             BeginBal:=StringToCard(AcctNo)*SizeCust+SizeAcct+2*SizeName;
             WriteField(CustFile, NewBal, BeginBal);
          END; (* IF *)
        END; (* IF *)
      UNTIL   WhichAcct > HIGHREC;
      Close(CustFile);
   END RetrieveAndUpdate;

BEGIN (* module DirectBanking *)
   SizeCust := SIZE(Customer);  SizeName := SIZE(Customer.LastName);
   SizeAcct := SIZE(Customer.AcctNum); SizeBal := SIZE(Customer.Balance);
   CreateFile(CustFile);
   RetrieveAndUpdate(CustFile);
END DirectBanking.
```

Debug and test   It is easy to forget to SetPos before reading and writing fields. SetModify is required after the file is opened in procedure RetrieveAndUpdate so that you can both read and write. It may be helpful to add statements after each SetPos to GetPos(CustFile, high, low) and then display low to determine that the FilePosition is where it should be. You also may wish to display the total Length of the file, using the FileSystem Length function. Consider inserting a HALT command temporarily after CreateFile in the main module. When the program stops you can use an operating system command to display CUSTOMER.DAT to determine whether it has been filed correctly.

Here is a sample run:

```
Enter customer      0
FirstName: Adam    LastName: Wilson    CurrentBalance: $54.32
Enter customer      1
FirstName: Susan   LastName: Johnson    CurrentBalance: $25.67
Enter customer      2
FirstName: May    LastName: French    CurrentBalance: $5.00
Enter customer      3
FirstName: Jim    LastName: Burns    CurrentBalance: $1234.56
Enter customer      4
FirstName: Wilma    LastName: Richardstown    CurrentBalance: $102536.78

Which customer (0,1,...)?  (Stop with number >    4):  4
Customer:  4   Wilma   Richardstown   102536.78

UpdateBalance (Y/N)? Y
New Balance = $ 1025367.84
Which customer (0,1,...)?  (Stop with number >    4):  4
Customer:  4   Wilma   Richardstown   1025367.84
```

```
UpdateBalance (Y/N)? N

Which customer (0,1,...)?  (Stop with number >    4):  8
```

Complete the documentation   Important elements of the documentation would be the problem definition, pseudocode, code, sample run, and a printout of the direct-access file CUSTOMER.DAT with a description of why the latter appears the way it does.

The source code file is CH14D. A Strings module with function Length and a module such as FileSystem with the appropriate file-handling procedures must be available. The name of the direct-access file can be changed within the Lookup commands, or the program may be changed so that users are prompted for the file name. The direct-access file is created as a new file in CreateTheFile and opened subsequently as an existing file within RetrieveAndUpdate.

☐ Buffering, Doio

Many systems use a buffer in conjunction with FileSystem to reduce the time the CPU spends waiting for slow I/O. A **buffer** is a special part of main memory, typically a few kilobytes in length, that acts as a window on the file. Access to the buffer is much faster than direct access to a disk.

A Bit of Background

Nature's Random Nature

Although computer users choose to access particular single records intentionally, to the *computer*, the choices would seem to be random. Thus the terms *random access* and *direct access* are used interchangeably. Random events are used in certain calculations—such as Monte Carlo techniques—to simulate distinct physical phenomena. This is because most humans have tended to regard Nature as random and unpredictable.

Others, however, have argued that Nature is fundamentally deterministic. Pierre Simon de Laplace wrote in "A Philosophical Essay on Probability" (1814) that the world is determined: "Given for one instant an intelligence which could comprehend all the forces by which nature is animated and the respective situation of the beings who compose it—an intelligence sufficiently vast to submit these data to analysis—it would embrace in the same formula the movements of the greatest bodies of the universe and those of the lightest atom; for it, nothing would be uncertain, and the future, as the past, would be present to its eyes."

On the other hand, Werner Heisenberg, in a lecture on the uncertainty principle at the University of Chicago in 1929, pointed out that ". . . the resolution of the paradoxes of atomic physics can be accomplished only by further renunciation of old and cherished ideas. Most important of these is the idea that natural phenomena obey exact laws—the principle of causality."

As they have for centuries, philosophers continue to argue about whether Nature is determinate and predictable or random. What do *you* think?

In *Write* mode, WriteChar operations write to the memory buffer. When the buffer is full, it is copied (or ''flushed'') automatically to the appropriate location in the file.

In *Read* mode, the buffer contains some portion of the file, and ReadChar actually reads from the buffer. When the buffer has been read completely, or when a read is requested from a portion of the file not in the buffer, the buffer is reloaded automatically from the appropriate portion of the file.

In *Modify* mode, both reading and writing access the buffer until FilePosition points to an area outside the buffer. Then the buffer content is copied to the file, and the buffer is reloaded from the new FilePosition.

Usually, buffering is transparent to the user/programmer; the system takes care of buffer operations. The Close command automatically flushes anything in the Write buffer to the file. Should the programmer need control of the buffer, Dr. Wirth's FileSystem module contains

```
PROCEDURE Doio(VAR f:File).
```

In *Read* mode, **Doio** causes the buffer to be filled, starting at the current FilePosition. In *Write* mode, Doio copies the buffer content to the old FilePosition and sets the indicator to the new FilePosition without changing the buffer contents. In *Modify* mode, Doio copies the buffer content to the old FilePosition and loads the buffer from the new FilePosition.

☐ Hashing

Often there is no convenient list of customers or account numbers to serve directly as record numbers. In such situations an **external key** (such as a name) must be converted to an **internal key** (the array index or byte-count record address). Storing a record at the internal address derived from the external key—and using the same key-conversion process when searching for the record—ensures that the information can be retrieved in direct-access mode.

The process of converting external to internal keys is called **hashing.** There is no perfect hash function: in various situations some hash codes work better than others. However, a class of hashing techniques that often works well is the Division/Remainder method, an algorithm of which is described and illustrated in Figure 14-4.

The number of probes required to find a given record depends upon the number of **synonyms** (records that ''hash'' to the same address). If the number of collisions between synonym addresses is excessive, increase the space by at least 30% over the expected number of records. Otherwise, modify the hash procedure or try a completely different hash function. Other methods of handling collisions—such as linking synonyms in a list, each one pointing to the next—may be more complex but more efficient.

Questions 14.4

1. **a.** For debugging program DirectBanking (Example 14.4.1, CH14D) it was suggested that Length (from module FileSystem) be used to display the total length of the file. However, Length has been imported from Strings. Why does this present a problem? How would you solve the problem?

Figure 14−4
Division/Remainder
Algorithm

Algorithm

1. Determine the number of spaces, N, needed to store the data. Choose a prime number for N at least 20% larger than the maximum number of records.

 The prime number helps reduce the number of synonyms (different record keys that convert to the same address), and the extra 20% space facilitates handling address collisions between synonyms.

2. If the record key is not a number, convert it to a numeric Key.

3. Calculate the remainder Key MOD N, which is a value between 0 and N-1 and can be used as the index or address of the record.

4. Store the record at the address determined by Key MOD N. If a collision occurs (a synonym is already stored at this address), store the record at the next-higher unfilled address.

 Assume that record 0 logically follows space N-1 if the search for empty space runs past the end of the allocated area.

5. To retrieve the data, convert the key with the same hash formula to determine where the record is stored. If the desired record does not appear there, search successively higher addresses until it is found.

 If the search extends past record N-1, continue the search at record 0.

Example: Store the record whose key is Brown.

1. You anticipate having 100 records, so you increase this value by 20% and choose the next larger prime number, $N = 127$. If you choose N not prime, internal keys tend to be clustered in periodically spaced bunches, rather than spread out evenly.

2. Convert Brown to a number. One way of doing this is to add the decimal ASCII codes for the characters. Then ORD('B') + ORD('r') + ORD('o') + ORD('w') + ORD('n') = $66 + 114 + 111 + 119 + 110 = 520$

3. Find 520 MOD 127 = 12.

4. Store the record at address 12. If address 12 is already occupied by a synonym and a "collision" occurs, then try addresses 13, 14, 15, . . .   until an empty space is found where the record can be stored. If this search extends beyond space 126, continue the search at 0.

5. To retrieve Brown, convert it to address 12, with exactly the same technique used to store the record. Begin your search for the record at address 12.

  b. It was suggested also that you display file CUSTOMER.DAT. Will you see anything meaningful if you use operating-system commands such as TYPE or PRINT to do this? Why or why not? Will the display be "pretty"?

  c. If you made the AcctNum field 4 characters (bytes) long instead of 6, what would the record length be? And how would a display of CUSTOMER.DAT look on an 80-column screen?

2. a. Convert the LastNames in the sample run of Example 14.4.1 to record numbers by the hashing algorithm illustrated in Figure 14–4. How many synonyms are created? Where would each record actually be stored?

  b. Write Modula-2 code to perform this hash conversion.

14.5   *Summary*

Data File   Data stored on a permanent medium, such as tape, CD, or magnetic disk, constitute a data file. Typically, the organization of data files is similar to arrays of records.

InOut Streams   Redirection procedures in standard module InOut are designed to handle data in sequential streams. Only one input stream and one output stream can be open and accessible at one time. The Terminal module allows you to read and write CHARacters at the terminal while I/O is redirected to a file.

Text Files   All data stored in files by InOut procedures are in text (CHARacter) form, and these text files can be displayed by operating-system commands. The Terminal module contains only procedures for reading and writing CHARacters; the user must provide procedures for converting numeric data and handling strings.

FilePosition   File-handling procedures keep track of where to read or write by a FilePosition pointer. FilePosition is set at the beginning of the file when the file is opened and moves forward with each read or write command. When writing to a sequential stream, FilePosition also marks the end of the file.

The FileSystem Module   Most implementations of Modula-2 contain some version of Dr. Wirth's FileSystem module, with procedures for handling several files at once. With FileSystem you can set the mode of access to read only, write only, or read and write (modify). Reading and writing numeric data and strings requires you to create your own procedures and conversion functions.

Binary Files   The FileSystem module contains procedures that read and write computer WORDs of data in binary form, without converting them to CHARacter codes. Data are stored more efficiently in binary files than in text files, but operating-system commands designed to display text files do not produce meaningful displays of binary data. Binary file procedures are low-level code. Because of this, data must be packed or split into WORDs, and there are few safeguards to ensure that your program will work on another machine.

Direct Access/Random Access   An array of records in memory is a direct- or random-access data structure; that is, any record can be found quickly by entering its index number. In Modula-2, direct access to records in a file is handled by calculating the starting byte count of each field. Before reading or writing, FilePosition can be moved to the appropriate position with the SetPos procedure.

Hashing   For direct access, it may be necessary to convert external keys to internal addresses or index values before storing or retrieving records. This conversion process is called *hashing*. A Division/Remainder hash algorithm is illustrated in Figure 14–4.

14.6   *Exercises*

Exercises marked with (FileName: _____) indicate those that ask you to use, modify, or extend the text examples. The numbers in brackets, [ ], indicate the section that contains the material you need in order to complete the exercise.

1. Work this problem using both (1) [14.1] InOut module file-handling procedures and (2) [14.2] FileSystem module file-handling procedures.
   a. You want to have a program that allows you to enter the following information from the keyboard for each one of up to 20 students in a class:

   ```
   Name    Exam 1    Exam 2    Homework    Final Exam
           Score     Score     Average     Score
   ```

   with the students' scores and averages being in a 0 to 100 percent format. The program then calculates the final grade, using the formula

   $$\text{Final Grade} = (0.20 * \text{Exam1}) + (0.20 * \text{Exam2}) + (0.35 * \text{Homework}) + (0.25 * \text{Final Exam})$$

   and assigns a letter grade on the basis of 90–100 = A, 80–89 = B, 70–79 = C, 60–69 = D, less than 60 = F. All of the information, including Final Grade and Letter Grade, are then displayed and stored to a file.
   b. Write a procedure to read the file, change the relative weights of the grades, recalculate new Final Grades and Letter Grades, and write the new data to a file.

2. Work this problem using both (1) [14.1] InOut module file-handling procedures and (2) [14.2] FileSystem module file-handling procedures.

Figure 14–5
Files to be Merged
(Exercise 2)

File 1		File 2	
Aardvark	0.69	Camel	0.65
Bear	0.33	Goat	1.29
Donkey	2.85	Kangaroo	1.89
Lion	0.86	Monkey	4.25
Pig	0.79	Otter	0.45
Raccoon	3.50	Quetzal	6.82
Tiger	0.59	Seal	1.50
Wolf	0.14		

Two files contain the data shown in Figure 14–5. Each file is in sorted alphabetical order. Read the data from the two files and merge them into a single, sorted file. *Hint:* Read the first record from both lists. Determine which one comes first and store it in the new file. Then read the next record from the list whose record was just stored. Compare it with the record remaining after the earlier comparison. Write the one that comes first alphabetically, and so on. When one list has been exhausted, write the remaining records from the other list to the new file.

3. Work this problem using both (1) [14.1] (FileName:CH14A) InOut procedures and (2) [14.2] (FileName:CH14B) FileSystem procedures.

   a. Enter from the keyboard the following information about your small company's ten employees, and sort this information into a file.

   Name Social Security   Sex   Hourly   Years with
          Number   (M/F)   Wage   the Company

   b. Write a procedure that allows you to read the file, change the HourlyWage for any employee, and create a new, updated file. This procedure also should allow you to add or delete employees.

   c. Write a procedure that reads the file one record at a time, asks for the number of hours worked by that employee this month, and calculates and displays each employee's total pay for the month.

   d. Write a procedure that you call once a year, which for every employee increments YearsWithTheCompany by one year, increases the hourly wage by 5%, and creates a new file with the new data.

4. Work this problem using both (1) [14.1] InOut procedures and (2) [14.2] FileSystem procedures.

   a. Write a program that allows you to enter from the keyboard the number of water balloon launchers sold by your company each month of the past two years and the selling price of the launchers during each of those months. (The cost fluctuates wildly from month to month, depending upon the season and demand.) The program then calculates the revenue for each month and stores the number of launchers, price per launcher, and revenue for each of the months in a file.

   b. Read the file and plot a bar graph of launchers sold versus month. Then plot a second bar graph of revenue versus month.

5. [14.3] (FileName:CH14C) Implement program BinStoreChars (Example 14.3.1) on your system.

6. [14.3] (FileName:CH14C) a. Determine the number of bytes required for a CARDINAL value and a WORD on your system, using SIZE and/or TSIZE procedures.

   b. Write a program similar to BinStoreChars (Example 14.3.1), that writes an array of CARDINAL values to a binary file and then retrieves them, sorts them in ascending order, and displays them in sorted order. What do you see when you command the operating system to display the file?

7. [14.3] (FileName:CH14C) a. Using Example 14.3.1 as a guide, write weather-bank data records to a binary file. The records should contain a date field (an array of CHARacters in the form MO/DA/YR) and the maximum and minimum Fahrenheit INTEGER temperatures for that date. *Hint:* Determine how many bytes are in each field by using SIZE or TSIZE. Then write each field separately.

    b. Retrieve the records from the file, and display those for which the maximum temperature was greater than 90 degrees.

8. [14.4] (FileName:CH14D) To Example 14.4.1:

    a. Add the capability to delete a record logically from the file by replacing the LastName with *ZZZZZZ*.

    b. Add the capability to change the LastName in a record in the file.

9. [14.4] Write a program that uses both (1) an array and (2) a text file to store an organization's membership records in direct-access mode. The small organization will have as many as 50 members. It is decided to use the last two digits of the social security number for each member

```
DIV 2
```

as a storage address and to reserve 61 spaces to store the records. (Is this a reasonable hash function? Why or why not?) The membership record should include the member's name, CARDINAL age, the year he or she joined the organization, social security number (SSN), and address. For a text file, procedures need to be written for converting the Age and the last two digits of SSN between CARDINAL and CHARacter values.

    a. Read at least 10 members into the organization from an input file created previously using an editor.

    b. Provide the capability to display, delete, add, and change a member's record. (Note that the key used for hashing should never change for this set of records. Why not?)

    c. Write procedures to determine how many years each person has been a member, the average age of the members, and the average length of membership for the current members. Display each member's name, age, and length of membership. Finally, display the two averages.

10. [14.4] Write a program to perform the following, using both (1) an array and (2) a text file.

You have collected information about cities in your state. Rather than hashing, you decide to store each city's name, population, and elevation above sea level, and the name of its mayor or city manager in some arbitrary order (perhaps alphabetically, by size, or as you think of the city; your choice).

    a. Write a program to accept the data for a number of cities (either from the keyboard or from a file). Store the data in the array or file in the order they are read. Then print a "tickler list" of array index or file record number (and/or byte location if you choose) with each city name. For example,

```
1. Cheyenne
2. Casper
3. RockSprings
   . . .
```

    b. Post the tickler list from part a, on paper, next to your desk. Write a procedure that will display the entire contents of the record for a city when you enter the city's name and record address (which you have found on the tickler list).

    c. Store the tickler list in part a in a separate temporary array. Sort the array alphabetically by city name, and print it alphabetically. For example,

```
Casper        2.
Cheyenne      1.
RockSprings   3.
    . . .
```

Posting this list next to your desk will make it easier for you to find the cities quickly and apply the look-up procedure of part b.

15

Sets

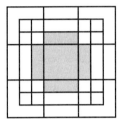

Chapter Outline

This chapter is concerned with data structures called **sets,** which represent collections of related objects. Sets are especially useful for defining lists of valid selections and for solving problems to which logical operations such as AND, OR, and NOT are applied.

15.1 *Defining Set*

A set is a collection of objects, or **elements,** none of which are duplicates and the order of which is unimportant. If an attempt is made to place into a set an element that duplicates an existing element of the set, the duplicate element is ignored and the set is not changed. In Modula-2, sets must contain only constants whose values are of an enumeration or subrange type. Sets are defined by listing their elements within braces, { }.

For example, sets could be defined as

```
A = {act, book, copy}    B = {act, book, act, copy}
    (* enumeration type *)
NumS1 = {1, 3, 2}    NumS2 = {3, 2, 3, 1}
    (* subrange of CARDINAL *)
```

Since duplicate elements and order are ignored, *A* and *B* are considered to be the same set, and *NumS*1 is equivalent to *NumS*2.

Set List and Rule Definitions

Mathematically, sets are specified either by listing their elements or by a rule from which all of the elements of the set can be generated. These sets are also equivalent:

```
P = {2, 4, 6, 8, 10}
Q = {x|x = even cardinal number and 0 < x <= 10}.
```

The mathematical definition of set *Q* reads "the set of values *x*, such that *x* is an even cardinal number greater than zero and less than or equal to ten."

The Base Type

Except for the double-dot notation that defines subranges, Modula-2 requires that sets of elements be listed—rather than defined in code by a mathematical rule. There are some additional restrictions.

A **set type** must be defined in terms of an enumeration or subrange **base type,** such as

```
TYPE PETTYPE = (dog, cat, bird, fish); (* base types *)
     CHANNELTYPE = [2..13];

     ThePetSet = SET OF PETTYPE;         (* set types *)
     SetOfVHF = SET OF CHANNELTYPE;
     UnderTenSet = SET OF [0..9];
```

Set types ThePetSet, SetOfVHF, and UnderTenSet are defined in terms of the base types, which in this case are the enumeration type PETTYPE and two CARDINAL subranges, [2..13] and [0..9], respectively.

Original versions of Modula-2 limited the base types to

- user-defined enumeration types, and
- a subrange of the CARDINAL numbers.

Each system had a maximum number, NumElements, of values the base type could contain. Typically, NumElements would be the number of bits in a memory word, so that sets could be represented internally using only one word of memory. Thus, on a system where word size is 16 bits,

- NumElements = 16,
- an enumeration base type could include up to 16 elements, and
- the largest value in a CARDINAL subrange type would be NumElements − 1 = 15.

Some new compilers allow sets of other enumerable types, such as a subrange of CHAR or INTEGER. If your system is reasonably new, it may allow sets to use two, three, or more words, in which case the value of NumElements is two, three, or more times the number of bits in a word. The examples in this book assume the original, limited situation, in which NumElements = 16 and base types are restricted to user-defined enumeration types and CARDINAL subranges with values less than 16.

☐ Set Variables and Values

Set variables are defined in terms of set types. For the set types just discussed you could declare

```
VAR  Animals, Pets : ThePetSet;
        (* can accept values dog, cat, bird, fish *)
     Television, Watch : SetOfVHF;
        (* can accept CARDINAL values 2 through 13 *)
     Numbers, Interesting, Blah, OfNoInterest : UnderTenSet;
        (* can accept CARDINAL values 0 through 9 *)
```

Set values are the sets assigned to set variables or used as set constants or within set expressions. Set values for a particular set may be

- the empty set, { }, the set containing no elements at all,
- the set containing all of the values defined by the base type, or
- a proper subset containing some (but not all) of the values in the base type.

In Modula-2, set values are defined by an expression consisting of the set type followed by a beginning brace, a list of the elements to be included in the value (or valid descriptions of them), and an ending brace. For example, these are all valid set values constructed from type ThePetSet:

```
ThePetSet{dog..bird}      (* subset containing dog, cat, bird *)
ThePetSet{cat, bird, fish}(* subset containing cat, bird, fish *)
ThePetSet{dog, cat..fish} (* the entire set of all pets in base *)
ThePetSet{ }              (* the empty set *)
ThePetSet{cat}            (* set containing the single element cat *)
```

Set elements are **unordered,** even though set base types (such as PETTYPE) are ordered. Thus the set value ThePetSet{cat, bird, fish} is equivalent to the set value ThePetSet{bird, fish, cat}.

Once a set value has been defined it can be *assigned* to a compatible set variable or used in expressions involving set operators. Assignment is performed using the familiar assignment operator (:=). These are valid set assignments:

```
Animals       := ThePetSet{dog, cat};
Television    := SetOfVHF{2, 4, 5, 7, 11, 13};
OfNoInterest  := UnderTenSet{0};
Interesting   := UnderTenSet{2, 4, 6, 8};
Blah          := UnderTenSet{1..5, 7};
Numbers       := Interesting;    (* assignment of an entire set *)
```

Set Constants

Although there is no such thing as a record constant, and the only array constants are character strings, you can define *set* CONSTants when the base type is anonymous if it is a valid subrange type for sets (such as CARDINAL).

For example, some CONSTant definitions are

```
CONST   OddNums = {1, 3, 5, 7, 9};
          Three = {3};
```

Of course, declarations

```
CONST   TWOPETS = ThePetSet{dog, fish};
          NoTV = SetOfVHF{ };    (* the empty set *)
```

should follow the declaration of TYPEs ThePetSet and SetOfVHF.

Operations that can be performed on sets are shown and described in Figure 15-1.

Using Sets for Menu Selection

One important application of sets is validity checking of selections from a menu. Instead of using a complicated CASE or IF structure, you determine whether the selection is a member of the set of allowed values. Here is an example.

Example 15.1.1   Use a set to restrict the selections from a library collection.

Define the problem   In a small branch library, you find a listing of categories of books that gives the beginning catalog number for each category and the number of the aisle where the category is shelved.

Category	Reference No.	Aisle
Science	500.0	3
Art	700.0	4
History	300.0	2
People	100.0	1
Miscellaneous	1200.0	5

Write a program that presents a menu from which library users select the type of material they want to find. After a user has made a choice, the program tells him or her the first reference number for that category and which aisle to search.

Definitions and Assignments

```
TYPE  PETTYPE   = (dog, cat, bird, fish);
      ThePetSet = SET OF PETTYPE;
VAR  NoPets, PetSet1, PetSet2, PetSet3, PetSet4, PetSet5 : ThePetSet;

     NoPets  := ThePetSet{ };
     PetSet1 := ThePetSet{dog, cat, bird};
     PetSet2 := ThePetSet{cat, fish};
     PetSet3 := ThePetSet{dog, bird, fish};
     PetSet4 := ThePetSet{cat, bird, dog};
     PetSet5 := ThePetSet{dog, cat, fish};
```

Binary Operations

The circles represent sets P and Q, and the shaded areas represent the sets created by the binary operations.

+ Union   (∗ The union P + Q is the set of elements in P or in Q or in both. ∗)

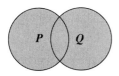

PetSet1 + PetSet2 has the value { dog, cat, bird, fish }

$P + Q$

– Difference   (∗ The difference P – Q is the set of elements in P but not in Q. ∗)

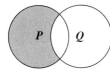

PetSet1 – PetSet2 has the value { dog, bird, }

$P - Q$

∗ Intersection   (∗ The intersection P ∗ Q is the set of elements in both P and Q. ∗)

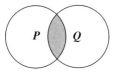

PetSet1 ∗ PetSet2 has the value { cat }

$P * Q$

/ Symmetric Difference (∗ The symmetric difference P / Q is the set of elements in P or in Q but not in both. ∗)

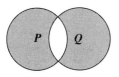

PetSet1 / PetSet2 has the value { dog, bird, fish }

P / Q

Relational Operators

Each relational operation produces a BOOLEAN result.

=	**equal**	(* Set P = Set Q if both have the same base type and contain exactly the same elements. *)

        PetSet1=PetSet4   has the value TRUE.
        PetSet1=PetSet2   has the value FALSE.

# or <>	**not equal**	(* Set P # Set Q if one contains at least one element that is not in the other. *)

        PetSet1#PetSet4   has the value FALSE.
        PetSet1#PetSet3   has the value TRUE.

<=	**subset of**	(* Set P <= Set Q if every element in P is also found in Q; that is, if P is a subset of Q. *)

If Q also contains at least one element that is not in P, then P is said to be a proper subset of Q. The empty set is a subset of every set.

        PetSet2<=PetSet5   has the value TRUE.
        NoPets<=PetSet2   has the value TRUE.
        PetSet2<=PetSet1   has the value FALSE.

>=	**superset of**	(* Set P >= Set Q if every element of Q is also found in P; that is, if P is a superset of Q. *)

        PetSet5>=PetSet2   has the value TRUE.
        PetSet3>=PetSet1   has the value FALSE.
        PetSet4>=NoPets   has the value TRUE.

IN	**member of**	(* For element t and set P, t IN P is TRUE if element t is one of the members of set P; then it is said "t is in P." *)

        birdINPetSet1   has the value TRUE.
        birdINPetSet2   has the value FALSE.

Built-in Standard Procedures

INCL	**include**	(* INCL(P, t) adds element t to set P. *)

        INCL(PetSet2, dog)   adds element dog to PetSet2, which is now the set
                      { cat, fish, dog }

This performs the same operation as
PetSet2 := PetSet2 +ThePetSet{dog}.

EXCL	**exclude**	(* EXCL(P, t) removes element t from set P.*)

        EXCL(PetSet3, bird)   removes element bird from PetSet3, which is now the set
                      { dog, fish }.

This performs the same operation as
PetSet3 :=PetSet3 -ThePetSet{bird}

Figure 15-1
(continued)

Figure 15–2
**Structure Chart for
SelectABook
(Example 15.1.1)**

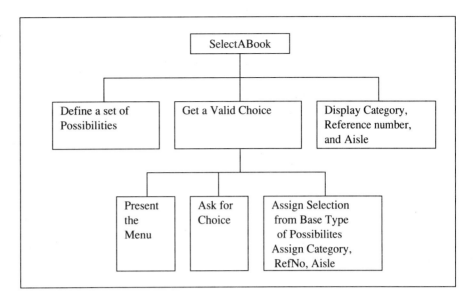

Develop a solution   One way of building in a validity check for menu choices is
to define a set of Possibilities that contains all of the categories *and* a Wrong choice.
For example,

```
TYPE   BOOKS = (Science, Art, People, History, Miscellaneous, Wrong);
       BookSet = SET OF BOOKS;
VAR    Possibilities : BookSet;
```

Then assign

```
Possibilities := BookSet{Science, Art, People, History, Miscellaneous};
```

Present the users with a menu from which they are to select character *S, A, P, H,*
or *M* to indicate their Choice. Assign Selection from the base type (BOOKS) of
Possibilities; and assign Category, Reference number, and Aisle. Using the IN
operator, check whether the selection is valid. Display Category, Reference number,
and Aisle. Figure 15–2 is a structure chart of the solution.

Refine the solution   *Pseudocode*

```
begin module SelectABook
      assign Possibilities
      present Menu
        S Science,    A Art,    P People,    H History,    M Miscellaneous
      repeat
        ask Choice, convert Choice to Selection
        Category, Reference No., and Aisle are assigned
      until Selection IN Possibilities
      display Category, Reference number, Aisle
end SelectABook
```

Modula-2 code   Critical parts of this code are the set definitions and assignment
of Possibilities. Observe the use of IN in the expression

```
UNTIL   Selection   IN   Possibilities;
```

for determining whether the selection is correct.

A less preferable alternative that does not use sets would be

```
UNTIL   (Selection = Science) OR (Selection = Art)
        OR (Selection = People) OR (Selection = History)
        OR (Selection = Miscellaneous);
```

This alternative requires more code, it would be more susceptible to logic and syntax errors, and it could require more processing time.

Of course, you could also test

```
UNTIL Selection IN BookSet{Science, Art, People, History, Miscellaneous};
```

```
MODULE SelectABook;
    (* Illustrates use of Sets in making Menu choices.
          FileName:CH15A      Modula-2      RKW      July 1991  *)
FROM InOut IMPORT WriteString, WriteLn, WriteCard, Read, Write;
FROM RealInOut IMPORT FWriteReal;

TYPE  BOOKS = (Science, Art, People, History, Miscellaneous, Wrong);
       BookSet = SET OF BOOKS;
VAR   Possibilities : BookSet;     Selection : BOOKS;
      Choice, Discard : CHAR;      Category : ARRAY [0..14] OF CHAR;
      Aisle : CARDINAL;            RefNo : REAL;

BEGIN
   Possibilities
          := BookSet{ Science, Art, People, History, Miscellaneous };
   WriteString("Here are the books available: "); WriteLn;
    WriteString("     S    Science"); WriteLn;
    WriteString("     A    Art"); WriteLn;
    WriteString("     P    People"); WriteLn;
    WriteString("     H    History"); WriteLn;
    WriteString("     M    Miscellaneous"); WriteLn;
   REPEAT
      WriteString("What is your choice (S, A, P, H, M) ? ");
       Read(Choice); Read(Discard); Write(Choice); WriteLn;
      CASE  Choice  OF
          'S','s': Selection := Science; Category := "Science       ";
                 RefNo := 500.0;  Aisle := 3  |
           'A','a': Selection := Art;       Category := "Art           ";
                 RefNo := 700.0;  Aisle := 4  |
           'P','p': Selection := People;  Category := "People        ";
                 RefNo := 100.0;  Aisle := 1  |
          'H','h': Selection := History; Category := "History       ";
                 RefNo := 300.0;  Aisle := 2  |
         'M','m': Selection := Miscellaneous;
                  Category := "Miscellaneous ";
                  RefNo := 1200.0; Aisle := 5;
          ELSE  Selection := Wrong;
       END; (* CASE *)
    UNTIL  Selection  IN  Possibilities;

   WriteLn; WriteString("You chose "); WriteString(Category); WriteLn;
    WriteString("The reference numbers begin at"); FWriteReal(RefNo,8,1);
    WriteString("   on aisle"); WriteCard(Aisle,3); WriteLn;
END SelectABook.
```

┌───┐
│ *A Bit of Background* │
├───┤

Cantor's Infinitely Troublesome Sets

George Cantor, one of Germany's greatest mathematicians in the late nineteenth century, was born in Petrograd, Russia, in 1845, the son of a Danish merchant. He studied in Zurich, Switzerland, and then in Goettingen and Berlin, Germany, before being appointed professor of mathematics in Halle, Germany, in 1872.

When he was about 30 he refined the age-old intuitive concept of collections of objects into a mathematical theory of sets. His proofs regarding sets with an infinite number of members made him one of the founders of a logically consistent theory of infinity and the continuum. This work was so controversial and it raised so much opposition that he was denied an appointment at the University of Berlin. It was not until shortly before his death in Halle in 1918 that Cantor was vindicated by the acceptance of his work by mathematicians around the world.

Elementary and secondary school students in the 1960s and 1970s plagued bewildered parents for help with their homework in the "new math" based primarily on Cantor's sets.

Debug and test Any errors in this problem are most likely to occur in the definition and assignment of set values. Study carefully how the sets are defined and created. Data entered by the user are characters corresponding to the categories of books. The set data with which the program is tested should include all of the valid choices and some representative invalid choices. Here is a sample run

```
Here are the books available:
     S    Science
     A    Art
     P    People
     H    History
     M    Miscellaneous
What is your choice (S, A, P, H, M) ? H

You chose History
The reference numbers begin at   300.0   on aisle   2
```

Complete the documentation The problem definition, structure chart, pseudocode, code, and a sample run would provide a short, clear description of the problem and its solution. Since the problem is designed to illustrate sets, the users' manual should give the set definitions and explain that the valid selections can be changed by changing the base type BOOKS and the assignment to Possibilities. The source code is in file CH15A.

Questions 15.1

1. In Example 15.1.1 (CH15A), expand BookSet, the set of Possibilities, and the menu choices to include HomeAndGarden, Reference number 600.0, Aisle 6.
2. Refer to Figure 15–1.
   a. Define a set type of the light chemical elements, H, He, Li, Be, B, C, N, O, F, Ne, Na, and Mg, whose atomic numbers are 1 through 12, respectively.
   b. Define set variables of this type called *Inert, HighlyActive, Abundant,* and *AllLight*.

c. Include in each set only these elements:

Set	Elements
Inert	He, Ne
HighlyActive	H, Li, Na
Abundant	H, He, C, N, O
AllLight	(all twelve)

d. List the elements contained in each of these sets: Inert + Abundant, Abundant * HighlyActive, Abundant − Inert, Abundant/HighlyActive.
e. Is Inert <= Abundant a TRUE expression?
f. Write a fragment of code that asks for a choice of one of the light elements and tests the choice's validity. Then the code determines to which set or sets (Inert, HighlyActive, Abundant, AllLight) the choice belongs.

15.2 *Set Operations*

Many applications of sets are related to mathematics and require the use of the set operations defined in Figure 15–1.

Here is an example that illustrates the application of set operations INCL, IN, =, <=, and *. INCL allows you to add an element to—that is, to include an element in—a set. IN provides a means of testing whether an element belongs to a set. The relational operator <= determines whether one set is a **subset** of another, and the equality operator, =, determines whether the sets contain exactly the same elements. Binary operation *P* * *Q* creates the **intersection** set, which contains the elements that are in both set *P* and set *Q*. Though not illustrated in the example, binary operation *P* + *Q* creates the **union** set of all elements found in either *P* or *Q* or in both; operation *P* − *Q* removes any elements that are in set *Q* from set *P;* and EXCL removes a single element from a set.

Example 15.2.1

Generate a set containing the prime factors of a CARDINAL number specified by the user. Then display the members of the set; determine whether the values 1, 2, 3, and 5 are all prime factors of the number; and find the set of small prime factors with values less than 11.

Define the problem The user will be asked to enter a CARDINAL Number of which the program will find the prime factors. A prime factor, *P,* is a nonzero CARDINAL number that divides evenly into Number and has no factors other than 1 and *P.* A set will be created that contains the prime factors of Number. Then the Number and its prime factors will be displayed. To illustrate subset and intersection operations, it will be determined whether the set {1, 2, 3, 5} is a subset of the prime factors of Number, and the intersection of the set of prime factors with the set {1..10} will be the set of prime factors with values less than 11.

Develop a solution If your compiler limits CARDINAL set elements to values less than 16, users will be restricted to values of Number less than 256.

After having divided a number by all of the prime factors less than its square root, there will be at most one prime factor left. For example, the square root of 66

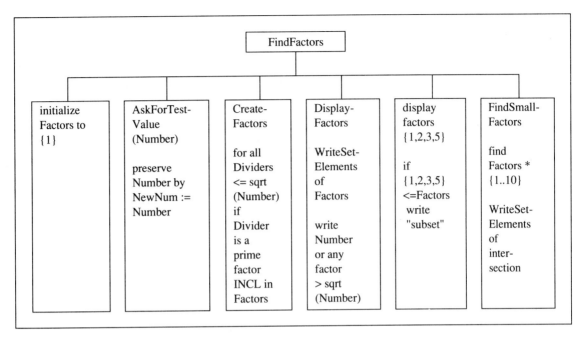

Figure 15–3
Structure Chart for FindFactors (Example 15.2.1)

is about 8.12. Dividing 66 by prime factors 2 and 3 leaves one last prime factor, namely 11. If such a factor greater than the square root exists, it will be treated as a special case.

Although there is disagreement about whether 1 is prime, in this example 1 will be considered a prime factor of every number, so set Factors will be initialized to {1}. Then the other small prime factors will be INCLuded in Factors as they are determined in a procedure CreateFactors.

CreateFactors will invoke BOOLEAN function DetermineIfPrime to decide if a factor is prime. Variables Factors and SmallFactors will have subrange base type [1..15], and both sets will be initialized to the empty set.

A procedure DisplayFactors will invoke WriteSetElements, which extracts and displays all elements of set Factors. Then DisplayFactors will display any additional factor that is greater than sqrt(Number).

Procedures DisplayOneToFive and FindSmallFactors will determine whether {1, 2, 3, 5} is a subset of factors and use the intersection operation (*) to find and display all factors between 1 and 10.

The solution structure is shown in Figure 15–3.

Refine the solution   *Pseudocode*

```
begin module FindFactors
        initialize Factors to {1}
        AskForTestValue(Number),
        preserve Number for later use, NewNum = Number
        CreateFactors(Factors, NewNum)
        DisplayFactors(Number, NewNum, Factors)
        DisplayOneToFive(Factors)     (* Illustrate subset operation *)
        FindSmallFactors(Factors)     (* Show intersection operation *)
end FindFactors
```

```
procedure AskForTestValue(VAR Num)
        ask for Num until    0 < Num <= MAXVALUE

procedure WriteSetElements(ThisSet, LowLimit, HighLimit)
        for all PossibleElements between LowLimit and HighLimit
                if PossibleElement IN ThisSet, write PossibleElement

procedure DisplayFactors(Number, NewNum, Factors)
        WriteSetElements(Factors, 1, MAXVALUE)
        if     Factors contains only element 1
            write Number                (* 1 and Number are the only prime factors *)
        else if NewNum > sqrt(Number)
            write NewNum                (* NewNum is a prime factor > sqrt(Number) *)

function DetermineIfPrime(ThisFactor) : BOOLEAN
        assume    IsPrime = TRUE
        for    FactorDivider = 2 to sqrt(ThisFactor)
               IsPrime = IsPrime AND (ThisFactor MOD FactorDivider <> 0)
        return IsPrime

procedure CreateFactors(VAR PrimeDividers,    VAR Num)
        initialize Divider = 2
        while Divider < sqrt(Num)
            if    Num MOD Divider = 0    (* Divider is a factor *)
                  find new Num = Num DIV Divider
                  if    DetermineIfPrime(Divider)    (* Divider is a prime factor *)
                        INCL(PrimeDividers, Divider)
            else increment Divider        (* Divider not prime factor, try next *)
        end while

procedure DisplayOneToFive(Factors)
        if    {1,2,3,5} <= Factors
              if    not({1,2,3,5} = Factors), write "proper subset"
              else    write "improper subset"
        else    write "not subset"

procedure FindSmallFactors(Factors)
        SmallFactors = Factors * {1..10}
        WriteSetElements(SmallFactors, 1, 7)
```

Modula-2 code Observe closely how sets are handled in this code. Note the definition of the set CONSTants FACTORSONEFIVE and SETONETEN in terms of the same type as VARiable Factors, which enables you to compare FACTORS-ONEFIVE with Factors and find Factors * SETONETEN. Study the use of < = and = in procedure DisplayOneToFive. Note the initialization of Factors to {1}. Observe the operation INCL(PrimeDividers, Divider) in CreateFactors, which adds element Divider to the set PrimeDividers. Note how sets are passed as parameters to and from procedures and how set SmallFactors is declared locally within procedure FindSmallFactors.

The situation in which another prime factor NewNum > sqrt(Number) exists is treated without adding NewNum to the Factors set, which would cause a range error when NewNum > 15.

```
MODULE FindFactors;
    (* Uses sets to find the prime factors of a number N <= 255,
    to determine whether {1, 2, 3, 5} is a subset of those
    factors, and to pick out prime factors < 11.
        FileName:CH15B     Modula-2     RKW     July 1991   *)
```

```
FROM InOut IMPORT WriteString, WriteLn, ReadCard, WriteCard;
FROM MathLib0 IMPORT sqrt;

CONST  MAXVALUE = 15;    MAXNUM = MAXVALUE * MAXVALUE;
TYPE   NUMBERS = CARDINAL[1..MAXVALUE];   SMALLNUMSET = SET OF NUMBERS;
CONST FACTORSONEFIVE = SMALLNUMSET{1,2,3,5};
       SETONETEN = SMALLNUMSET{1..10};
VAR  Factors : SMALLNUMSET;  Number, NewNum : CARDINAL;

PROCEDURE AskForTestValue(VAR Num : CARDINAL);
   BEGIN
     REPEAT
        WriteString("Find factors of what cardinal number (<=");
         WriteCard(MAXNUM,4);WriteString(") ? "); ReadCard(Num);WriteLn;
       UNTIL  (Num > 0) AND (Num <= MAXNUM);
     END AskForTestValue;

PROCEDURE WriteSetElements(ThisSet : SMALLNUMSET;
                                   LowLimit, HighLimit : NUMBERS);
   VAR  PossibleElements : NUMBERS;
   BEGIN
      FOR  PossibleElements := LowLimit TO HighLimit  DO
         IF  PossibleElements IN ThisSet  THEN
            WriteCard(PossibleElements, 4);
         END; (* IF *)
      END; (* FOR *)
   END WriteSetElements;

PROCEDURE DisplayFactors(Number,NewNum:CARDINAL; Factors:SMALLNUMSET);
   BEGIN
      WriteLn; WriteString("Prime factors of ");
       WriteCard(Number,4); WriteString(" are:    ");

      WriteSetElements(Factors, 1, MAXVALUE);

      IF  Factors = SMALLNUMSET{1}  THEN     (* Prime factors are 1 and *)
         WriteCard(Number,4);                   (* the Number itself *)
      ELSIF  NewNum > TRUNC(sqrt(FLOAT(Number))) THEN
         WriteCard(NewNum,4); (* NewNum is prime factor > sqrt(Number) *)
      END; (* IF *)  WriteLn;
   END DisplayFactors;

PROCEDURE DetermineIfPrime(ThisFactor:NUMBERS) : BOOLEAN;
   VAR  FactorLimit, FactorDivider : NUMBERS;  IsPrime : BOOLEAN;
   BEGIN
      IsPrime := TRUE; (* initial assumption *)
      FactorLimit := TRUNC(sqrt(FLOAT(ThisFactor)));
      FOR  FactorDivider := 2  TO  FactorLimit  DO
         IsPrime := IsPrime AND (ThisFactor MOD FactorDivider <> 0);
      END; (* FOR FactorDivider *)   RETURN IsPrime;
   END DetermineIfPrime;

PROCEDURE CreateFactors(VAR PrimeDividers:SMALLNUMSET; VAR Num:CARDINAL);
   VAR  Divider, Limit : NUMBERS;
   BEGIN
      Limit  :=  TRUNC(sqrt(FLOAT(Num)));   Divider := 2;
      WHILE  Divider <= Limit  DO
```

```
                (* Determine whether Divider is a factor of Num *)
        IF   Num MOD Divider = 0   THEN              (* Divider is a factor *)
            Num := Num DIV Divider;              (* Num left after dividing *)

            IF  DetermineIfPrime(Divider)  THEN    (* Include Divider in *)
                INCL(PrimeDividers, Divider);          (* set PrimeDividers *)
            END; (* IF *)

            ELSE  INC(Divider); (* Divider not a factor, try next Divider *)
          END; (* IF *)
        (* Assertion: Divider included in set Dividers if a prime factor *)
      END; (* WHILE *);
    END CreateFactors;

PROCEDURE DisplayOneToFive(Factors : SMALLNUMSET);
    (* Determine whether {1, 2, 3, 5} is a subset of Factors. *)
    BEGIN
      WriteLn;  WriteString("Set {1, 2, 3, 5} ");
      IF  FACTORSONEFIVE <= Factors  THEN                    (* if a subset *)
          IF  NOT(FACTORSONEFIVE = Factors)  THEN  (* if proper subset *)
            WriteString("is a proper subset of these factors.");
          ELSE                (* if a subset, but not a proper subset *)
            WriteString("is an improper subset of these factors.");
          END; (* IF *)
      ELSE                                        (* if not a subset *)
          WriteString("is NOT a subset of these factors.");
      END; (* IF *)  WriteLn;
    END DisplayOneToFive;

PROCEDURE FindSmallFactors(Factors : SMALLNUMSET);
    (* use intersection ( * ) to find SmallFactors < 11 *)
    VAR  PossibleFactors : NUMBERS;  SmallFactors : SMALLNUMSET;
    BEGIN
      SmallFactors := Factors * SETONETEN;
      WriteString("The small prime factors ( <11 ) are:  ");
       WriteSetElements(SmallFactors, 1, 7);  WriteLn;
    END FindSmallFactors;

BEGIN  (* module FindFactors *)
    Factors := SMALLNUMSET{1};              (* Initialize Factors to {1} *)

    AskForTestValue(Number);
    NewNum := Number;                  (* preserve Number for future use *)
    CreateFactors(Factors, NewNum);
    DisplayFactors(Number, NewNum, Factors);

    DisplayOneToFive(Factors); (* Is {1,2,3,5} a subset of Factors? *)
    FindSmallFactors(Factors);
END FindFactors.
```

Debug and test   It is most important that base types for all sets to be compared
are the same. For example, on many systems, defining CONST FACTORSONE-

FIVE = {1, 2, 3, 5} directly and VAR Factors : SMALLNUMSET would lead to an incompatibility error when FACTORSONEFIVE is compared with Factors.

Test data should include numbers such as 30 (FACTORSONEFIVE is an improper subset), 210 (FACTORSONEFIVE is a proper subset), 165 (all its prime factors are less than sqrt(Number)), 213 (has a prime factor greater than sqrt(Number)), 83 (a prime number), and so on. In fact, a test program could be created by enclosing the main module within the loop

```
FOR Number := 1 TO MAXNUM DO ... END; (* FOR *)
```

and removing the call to AskForTestValue. Then the program would test all valid values of Number and allow you to make absolutely certain that it works for any value the user might enter. You also will want to test the program for values outside the range 0 < Number <= MAXNUM to make sure those are properly rejected.

Here are two sample runs.

```
Find factors of what cardinal number (<= 225) ? 210
Prime factors of  210 are:       1   2   3   5   7
Set {1, 2, 3, 5} is a proper subset of these factors.
The small prime factors ( <11 ) are:       1   2   3   5   7


Find factors of what cardinal number (<= 225) ? 213
Prime factors of  213 are:       1   3  71
Set {1, 2, 3, 5} is NOT a subset of these factors.
The small prime factors ( <11 ) are:       1   3
```

Complete the documentation In the users' manual, indicate that the range of Numbers for which the program will find prime factors is 0 < Number <= 255. If your system handles larger sets, then this range can be expanded by redefining CONSTant MAXVALUE. The program only lists prime factors; it does not indicate how many times those factors appear. This limitation could be removed by changing the CreateFactors procedure, but then a structure other than sets would probably be used, since sets do not contain repeated values. The source code for the program is CH15B. The only interaction of the user with the process is to enter the value of Number. The documentation is completed with the problem description, structure chart, pseudocode, code, and sample runs.

Questions 15.2

1. **a.** Using a FOR loop and INCL, show how you would create a set containing the even CARDINAL values between 1 and 15.
   b. Starting with the set in part a, use a FOR loop and EXCL to create a set containing even CARDINAL numbers between 1 and 15 that are not multiples of 3.
2. **a.** Write declarations for sets named *Minnesota, Wisconsin, Illinois, Indiana, Michigan, Ohio, Pennsylvania,* and *NewYork* that may contain the names of the Great Lakes *(Superior, Michigan, Huron, Erie, Ontario).* *Be careful:* defining *Michigan* as a set name and as an element name will cause a "doubly defined identifier" error.
   b. Write a short fragment of code that will fill the sets named for states bordering the Great Lakes with the lakes they border, namely

State	Bordering Lakes
Minnesota	Superior
Wisconsin	Superior, Michigan
Illinois	Michigan
Indiana	Michigan
Michigan	Michigan, Superior, Huron, Erie
Ohio	Erie
Pennsylvania	Erie
New York	Erie, Ontario

    c. Write short fragments of code to create these sets from those in part b:
- the lakes bordered by both Illinois and Wisconsin
- the lakes bordered by either Minnesota or Ohio or by both
- the subset of lakes bordered by Michigan that also are bordered by Wisconsin
- the lakes bordered by Michigan, but not by Wisconsin

    d. Write a short code fragment to determine which of the sets in part b are equivalent.

15.3 *Bitset*

One of the easiest ways to work with single bits in Modula-2 is through the BITSET type. BITSET is the only predefined, standard set type in Modula-2. It is defined as

```
TYPE BITSET = SET OF [0..W-1];
```

where *W* usually equals the length of a computer word — often 16 or 32 bits — on your machine. It is assumed here that $W = 16$ bits, but be aware that your system may differ from this.

    Thus, without declaring type BITSET, you can declare variables such as

```
CONST  SETSIZE = 10;
VAR  B1, B2 : BITSET;
     Words : ARRAY [1..SETSIZE] OF BITSET;
```

    Values of type BITSET can be defined with or without using the term *BITSET*. For example, you could assign

```
B1 := BITSET {0, 1, 5};
B2 := {1, 5..9}
Words[10] := BITSET {0..3, 8..11, 15};
Words[4]  := {0, 1, 5};
Words[1]  := B2;
```

Then Words[1] and *B2* represent the same set. Similarly, Words[4] and *B1* have the same value.

    The meaning of a BITSET value is that in a word, with bits numbered from 0 through $W - 1$, the bits in the word specified by elements of the set are binary 1s, and the other bits are 0s. Figure 15-4 shows the words defined by the assignments. It should be noted that some systems number bits from left to right and/or beginning with one instead of zero. Most small computers, and many larger ones, use the

Figure 15–4
Words Defined by
BITSET

```
B1 := BITSET{0, 1, 5}
Words[4] := {0, 1, 5}
```

15	14	13	12	11	10	9	8	7	6	5	4	3	2	1	0
0	0	0	0	0	0	0	0	0	0	1	0	0	0	1	1

```
B2 := {1, 5..9}
Words[1] := B2
```

15	14	13	12	11	10	9	8	7	6	5	4	3	2	1	0
0	0	0	0	0	0	1	1	1	1	1	0	0	0	1	0

```
Words[10] := BITSET{0..3, 8..11, 15}
```

15	14	13	12	11	10	9	8	7	6	5	4	3	2	1	0
1	0	0	0	1	1	1	1	0	0	0	0	1	1	1	1

Figure 15–5
BITSET Operations

Operation		Example
$B1 + B2$	OR	$\{0,1,5\} + \{1,5..9\} = \{0,1,5..9\}$
$B1 * B2$	AND	$\{0,1,5\} * \{1,5..9\} = \{1,5\}$
$B1 - B2$ $= B1 * NOT(B2)$	Difference	$\{0,1,5\} - \{1,5..9\}$ $= \{0,1,5\} * NOT\{1,5..9\}$ $= \{0,1,5\} * \{0,2..4, 10..15\} = \{0\}$
$B1/B2$	XOR Exclusive OR	$\{0,1,5\}/\{1,5..9\} = \{0,6..9\}$
INCL($B1, i$)	Set bit i in $B1$	INCL($B1, 2$) = INCL($\{0,1,5\}, 2$) $= \{0, 1, 2, 5\}$
EXCL($B1, i$)	Clear bit i in $B1$	EXCL($B1, 1$) = EXCL($\{0,1,5\}, 1$) $= \{0, 5\}$
$\{0..15\} - B1$	Complement $B1$	$\{0..15\} - \{0,1,5\} = \{2..4, 6..15\}$

convention shown in Figure 15–4. Reference to BITSET in your compiler manual should show if and how your system differs from this convention.

Boolean logic can be performed on words that are handled as BITSET values. Some of these operations are defined in Figure 15–5.

This example illustrates the use of BITSET for handling binary numbers.

Example 15.3.1

Convert a decimal number to binary and represent it in BITSET form. Then calculate and display the binary two's complement of the number.

Define the problem   Users will enter a CARDINAL number whose value is less than 32768 from the keyboard. The number will be converted to binary in BITSET form and displayed in binary. Then the two's complement of the number will be calculated in BITSET form and displayed.

Develop a solution   To obtain the two's complement, complement the number (change all 0s to 1s and vice versa), and then add 1. Every number has a two's complement. However, binary arithmetic becomes particularly convenient if two's complements are used to represent negative values.

For example, in four bits, $5_{10} = 0101_2$. To represent -5_{10}, take $5_{10} = 0101$, complement to 1010, and add 1; so in four-bit two's complement, $-5_{10} = 1011_2$.

This problem solution contains four procedures:

1. Convert a CARDINAL number to binary in BITSET form.
2. Display the binary number represented by a BITSET.
3. Display a BITSET.
4. Compute the two's complement of a BITSET number.
   a. Complement the number.
   b. Add 1.

A structure chart of the solution is shown in Figure 15–6.

Refine the solution   *Pseudocode*

```
begin module TwosComplement
        ask for Number (< 32768),    write Number
        ConvertToBits(Number, NumSet)
        DisplayBits(NumSet)
        write    " – ",    Number, "in twos complement form: "
        Find2sComplement(NumSet, TwoComplSet)
        DisplayBits(TwoComplSet)
end TwosComplement

procedure ConvertToBits(Num, VAR Binary)
        Binary = BITSET{ }       (* Initialize Binary to empty set. *)
        initialize Bit = 0
        while    Bit <= 15    and    Num > 0
                if    Num MOD 2 = 1        (* Divide Num by 2. If remainder = 1, *)
                        INCL(Binary, Bit)        (* set Bit in Binary BITSET.            *)
                end if
                Num = Num DIV 2,    increment Bit
        end while
        if    SHOWBITSET,    DisplayBitSet(Binary)

procedure DisplayBits(Binary)
        for    Bit = 15 to 0 by  – 1
                if    Bit IN Binary    then    write '1'    else    write '0'

procedure Find2sComplement(Binary, VAR ComplSet)
        set    ComplSet = BITSET{0..15} – Binary;    (* Complement Binary *)
        (* Add 1 *)                    initialize    Carry = 1,    Bit = 0
```

Figure 15-6
Structure Chart for TwosComplement (Example 15.3.1)

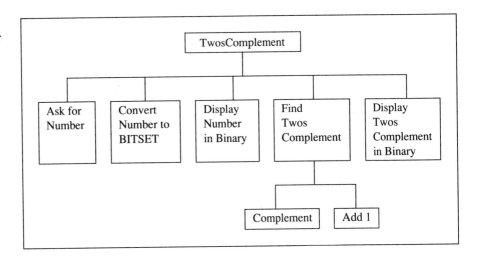

```
while    Bit <= 15    and Carry = 1
    if    Bit IN ComplSet    then    EXCL(ComplSet, Bit)
                                        (* 1 + 1 =0, Carry = 1 *)
        else INCL(ComplSet, Bit),    Carry = 0    (*    0 + 1 = 1, Carry = 0 *)
        end if,    increment Bit
    end while
    if    SHOWBITSET,    DisplayBitSet(ComplSet)

procedure DisplayBitSet(ThisSet)
    for    Bit = 0 to 15
        if    Bit IN ThisSet, write Bit
```

Modula-2 code Carefully observe the use of BITSET in the code. Binary is initialized to an empty BITSET at the beginning of procedure ConvertToBits. Convince yourself—by doing an example on paper if needed—that the IN, EXCL, and INCL features in the while loop in Find2sComplement actually do add the initial Carry = 1 value to the binary number represented by ComplSet.

```
MODULE TwosComplement;
    (* Illustrates the use of BITSET by finding the bitset representation
       CARDINAL number, displaying the binary value, then finding and
       displaying the two's complement of the number.
       FileName:CH15C      Modula-2      RKW      July 1991   *)

FROM InOut IMPORT WriteString, WriteLn, WriteCard, ReadCard;

CONST  SHOWBITSET = TRUE;
VAR  Number : CARDINAL;  NumSet, TwoComplSet : BITSET;

PROCEDURE DisplayBits(Binary : BITSET);
    VAR  Bit : [0..15];
    BEGIN
        FOR  Bit := 15 TO 0 BY -1  DO
            IF  Bit IN Binary  THEN  WriteString("1 ");
            ELSE  WriteString("0 ");
            END; (* IF *)
        END (* FOR *)
    END DisplayBits;
```

```
    PROCEDURE DisplayBitSet( ThisSet: BITSET);
       VAR  Bit : [0..15];
       BEGIN
          WriteString("The bitset representation is {");
          FOR  Bit := 0 TO 15  DO
             IF  Bit IN ThisSet  THEN  WriteCard(Bit,3);  END; (* IF *)
          END; (* FOR *)  WriteString(" }");
       END DisplayBitSet;

    PROCEDURE ConvertToBits(Num : CARDINAL;  VAR Binary : BITSET);
       VAR  Bit : [0..15];
       BEGIN
          Binary := BITSET{};           (* Initialize Binary to empty set. *)
          Bit := 0;
          WHILE  (Bit <= 15) AND (Num > 0)  DO
             IF  Num MOD 2 = 1  THEN
                INCL(Binary, Bit);        (* If remainder = 1, set bit i. *)
             END; (* IF *)
             Num := Num DIV 2;     (* Set conditions to find next digit. *)
             INC(Bit);
          END; (* WHILE *)
          IF  SHOWBITSET  THEN  DisplayBitSet(Binary); END; (*IF*)
       END ConvertToBits;

    PROCEDURE Find2sComplement(Binary:BITSET;  VAR ComplSet:BITSET);
       VAR  Carry : [0..1];  Bit : [0..15];
       BEGIN
          ComplSet := BITSET{0..15} - Binary;      (* Complement Binary. *)
          (* Add 1. *)
          Carry := 1;   Bit := 0;
          WHILE  (Bit <= 15) AND (Carry = 1)  DO
             IF  Bit IN ComplSet  THEN
                EXCL(ComplSet, Bit);   (* 1 + 1 = 0,  Carry = 1 *)
             ELSE
                INCL(ComplSet, Bit);   (* 0 + 1 = 1,  Carry = 0 *)
                Carry := 0;
             END; (* IF *)   INC(Bit);
          END; (* WHILE *)
          IF  SHOWBITSET  THEN  DisplayBitSet(ComplSet); END;(*IF*)
       END Find2sComplement;

BEGIN (* module TwosComplement *)
    REPEAT                                          (* Enter Number *)
       WriteString("Enter a cardinal number < 32768: ");
       ReadCard(Number); WriteLn;
    UNTIL  Number < 32768;
                                     (* Convert to Binary and Display *)
    WriteLn; WriteCard(Number,6); WriteString(" : "); WriteLn;
    ConvertToBits(Number, NumSet);  WriteLn;
    DisplayBits(NumSet);  WriteLn;
                                  (* Find Twos Complement and Display *)
    WriteLn; WriteString(" - "); WriteCard(Number,6);
     WriteString(" in twos complement form : "); WriteLn;
    Find2sComplement(NumSet, TwoComplSet);  WriteLn;
    DisplayBits(TwoComplSet);  WriteLn;
END TwosComplement.
```

Debug and test   For top-down design, you would write stub procedures for DisplayBits, ConvertToBits, and Find2sComplement first, and then test the logic of the main module. Had the calls to DisplayBitSet not been included to display the Binary and ComplSet BITSETs, you probably would want to insert them for debugging purposes. Test the program with small values for the number (such as 5), with large values (such as 32767), and with illegal values (>32767). Check a few answers by hand. Here is a sample run

```
Enter a cardinal number < 32768: 5280

  5280 :
The bitset representation is {   5   7 10 12 }
0 0 0 1 0 1 0 0 1 0 1 0 0 0 0 0

  -    5280 in twos complement form :
The bitset representation is {   5   6   8   9 11 13 14 15 }
1 1 1 0 1 0 1 1 0 1 1 0 0 0 0 0
```

Complete the documentation   Complete documentation of this problem is illustrated in Figure 15–7.

***

Questions 15.3

1. Could you have used BITSET to define any of the sets FACTORSONEFIVE, SETONETEN, or Factors in module FindFactors (Example 15.2.1, CH15B)? Why or why not?
2. **a.** What is the content of the four sets after executing this code fragment? Are the commands in the first line after BEGIN necessary? Why?

```
...
VAR  Set1, Set2, Set3, Set4 : BITSET;
...
BEGIN
   Set1 := {};  Set2 := {};  Set3 := {};  Set4 := {};
   FOR  Value := 2 TO MAXVALUE  DO
      IF  Value MOD 2 = 0  THEN  INCL(Set1, Value);  END;(*IF*)
   END; (* FOR *)
   Set2 := Set1;
   FOR  Value := 0 TO MAXVALUE  DO
      IF  Value MOD 3 = 0  THEN  EXCL(Set2, Value); END;(*IF*)
   END; (*FOR *)
   Set3 := Set1/Set2;
   Set4 := {0..15} - Set3;   Set4 := Set1 * Set4;
....
```

     b. Complete the code fragment with appropriate imports and declarations; add a procedure to display the sets, and run the program to confirm your answers in part a.

Problem Description TwosComplement

This program asks for a CARDINAL value less than 32768 and displays its BITSET and 16-bit binary representation. Then the program finds the two's complement form of the negative of the number and displays the representation both as a BITSET and in binary form.

Algorithm Development TwosComplement

Conversion from decimal to binary is accomplished by repeated division by 2 and recording the remainders. The two's complement is obtained by complementing the number (changing all 0's to 1's and vice versa) and then adding 1. The set operations IN, INCL, and EXCL are employed to perform these operations.

Structure Chart

```
                    TwosComplement
   ┌──────────┬──────────┬────────┬──────────┬─────────┐
 Ask for   Convert    Display    Find      Display
 Number    Number to  Number     Twos      Twos
```

Pseudoc

begin m
  ask f
    Con
    Displ
    write
    Find
    Displ
end Tw

procedu
  Bina
  initia
  whil
    if

Program Listing TwosComplement

```modula2
MODULE TwosComplement;
   (* Illustrates the use of BITSET by finding the bitset representation
      CARDINAL number, displaying the binary value, then finding and
      displaying the two's complement of the number.
      FileName:CH15C      Modula-2      RKW      July 1991  *)

FROM InOut IMPORT WriteString, WriteLn, WriteCard, ReadCard;

CONST  SHOWBITSET = TRUE;
VAR  Number : CARDINAL; NumSet, TwoComplSet : BITSET;

PROCEDURE DisplayBits(Binary : BITSET);
   VAR  Bit : [0..15];
   BEGIN
      FOR  Bit := 15 TO 0 BY -1  DO
         IF  Bit IN Binary  THEN  WriteString("1 ");
         ELSE  WriteString("0 ");
         END; (* IF *)
      END (* FOR *)
   END DisplayBits;

PROCEDURE DisplayBitSet( ThisSet: BITSET);
   VAR  Bit : [0..15];
   BEGIN
      WriteString("The bitset representation is {");
      FOR  Bit := 0 TO 15  DO
         IF  Bit IN ThisSet  THEN  WriteCard(Bit,3);  END; (* IF *)
      END; (* FOR *)  WriteString(" }");
   END DisplayBitSet;

PROCEDURE ConvertToBits(Num : CARDINAL;  VAR Binary : BITSET);
   VAR  Bit : [0..15];
   BEGIN
      Bi
      Bi
      WH
```

Sample Run TwosComplement

```
Enter a cardinal number < 32768: 5280

   5280 :
The bitset representation is {  5  7  10  12 }
0 0 0 1 0 1 0 0 1 0 1 0 0 0 0 0

   -  5280 in twos complement form :
The bitset representation is {  5  6  8  9 11 13 14 15 }
1 1 1 0 1 0 1 1 0 1 1 0 0 0 0 0
```

Users' Manual TwosComplement

The source code for this program is in file CH15C. No special external modules are required for compilation, other than InOut. The program asks for an appropriate CARDINAL value. Entry of too large a value will cause the program to request another value. Entry of a negative value for the CARDINAL number will cause termination of the program or a disply of erroneous results, depending upon the system. If the entry is correct, results are displayed without further input from the user.

Figure 15−7
Documentation of TwosComplement (Example 15.3.1)

15.4 *Summary*

Sets Sets are collections of items, in which duplicates are ignored and the order is unimportant. In Modula-2, sets are defined by listing their elements in terms of a base type. Some versions of the language limit sets to 16 elements, which are either CARDINAL values in the subrange [0..15] or enumeration-type values.

Set Operations Binary operations that can be performed on sets include Union (+), Difference (−), Intersection (*), and Symmetric Difference (/). Logical operations allow you to determine equality (=), subset (<=), or superset (>=) relationships between sets and whether a particular value is an element of (IN) a set. A single element can be added to or removed from a set using the INCL and EXCL procedures.

Applications of Sets Checking menu choices for validity is made simpler by determining whether the choice is IN the set of valid choices. Sets are also useful for collecting and comparing lists of values and solving problems in mathematics.

BITSET One set type in Modula-2 is predefined over a subrange of CARDINAL values as

```
TYPE BITSET = SET OF [0..W-1]   (where often W = 16 or 32).
```

BITSET-type variables can be declared without importing or defining BIT-SET, and set values can be assigned without the BITSET preface. BITSET is convenient to use for collections of CARDINAL values and for handling binary number operations.

15.5 *Exercises*

Exercises marked with (FileName:_____) indicate those that ask you to use, modify, or extend the text examples. The numbers in brackets, [ ], indicate the section that contains the material you need in order to complete the exercise.

1. [15.1] Use a set, with base type a subrange of CARDINAL numbers, to ensure that users enter appropriate choices when presented with this menu:

```
How big do you want your triangle to be?
            2      Two Rows
            4      Four Rows
            6      Six Rows
Choose one (2, 4, or 6):
```

Depending upon the choice, the computer will display one of the triangles shown in Figure 15–8.

2. [15.1] Use a set, with base type (Red, Orange, Yellow, Green, Blue, Violet), to ensure that users enter appropriate choices when presented with this menu:

```
In what part of the spectrum are you working?
            R      Red, low frequency range
            Y      Yellow, mid frequency range
            B      Blue, high frequency range
Choose one (R, Y, or B):
```

The computer will print different messages, depending upon the choice. If the choice is *R*, the message is "You may use Red or Orange." If the choice is *Y*,

Figure 15–8
Triangles
(Exercise 1)

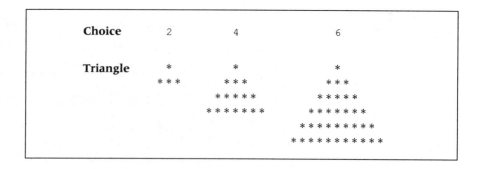

the message is "You may use Orange, Yellow, or Green." If the choice is *B,* the message is "You may use Green, Blue, or Violet."

3. [15.1] (FileName:CH15A) Write a program using sets, similar to the program of Example 15.1.1, that asks which TV channel (channels 2–13) the user wants to watch. Assume that VHF broadcasts are on channels 2, 4, 5, 7, 11, and 13 in your area. The program then determines and displays whether the user will get a signal when tuned to the channel that she or he selected arbitrarily.

4. [15.2] The only two salespersons in the shoe store you own are Michael and Stephanie. Each works three or four days a week. Your store is open Monday through Saturday, and you need at least one salesperson each day, except Saturday when you must have both salespersons. Each Saturday Michael and Stephanie hand you their schedules for the coming week, which are separate sets containing values from base type (Mon, Tue, Wed, Thu, Fri, Sat). Write a program that checks their schedules to see if every day is covered by at least one salesperson and if both employees plan to show up for work on Saturday. *Hint:* Check the union of Michael and Stephanie's schedules to determine whether every day is included. Check the intersection of the schedules for Saturday.

5. [15.2] Write a program that creates the set of CARDINAL values, *x,* that satisfy the inequality $(3x + 5) < (32 + x)$. Then the program should ask the user for an arbitrary small CARDINAL value (< 16) and determine whether the value is a solution to the inequality.

6. [15.2] Create a set type and set variables whose base is a list of the names of 10 magazines to which you might like to subscribe. Beginning with the empty set, create the set of the 4 magazines to which you *will* subscribe. (Use INCL or the union operator.) Write a procedure to display the members of the set. (*Hint:* If a value is a member of the set of all possible values in the base type, print it.) Create a set (using the difference operator) of the 6 magazines to which you will not subscribe right now, and display the members of that set.

   Six months from now, you begin receiving letters randomly from the ten publishers, asking you to subscribe. As you receive a letter, check to see if that magazine is already in the set of magazines to which you subscribe. If not, decide whether you wish to add that to your subscription set or not. If you already subscribe, decide whether to renew or to delete that magazine from your subscription set. After each change to the subscription set, update the nonsubscription set, and display the members of both sets.

7. [15.2] (FileName:CH15B) Modify FindFactors (Example 15.2.1) so that repeated factors are remembered and displayed. For example, the factors of 180 would be listed as 1 2 2 3 3 5. *Hint:* You probably will want to store the factors

in some structure other than a set, since a set does not recognize duplicate values.

8. [15.2] The animal control office needs to keep a record of which animals are kept at which addresses. For convenience, on a particular street the homes are numbered in the animal control records as Home[1], Home [2], Home[3], and so on. The structure for each Home[*i*] will be a set containing elements from the base type (dog, cat, fish, bird, otherpet, horse, otherfarmanimal). Thus the data structure will be an array of sets.

   a. Write a program that allows you to take a census and enter, home by home, which types of animal are at each home for all of the homes on the street. *Hint:* If ANIMALS is the base type and PetSet = SET OF ANIMALS is the set type, then variable operations could take the form Home[1] := PetSet{cat, dog} or INCL(Home[2], Horse), and so on. Of course, if no pet is at Home[5], then Home[5] = PetSet { }, the empty set.

   b. Now assume that a second parallel array of strings contains the addresses of the homes. Search the census and print out the addresses of all homes that (1) have horses or other farm animals or (2) should have dog licenses.

9. [15.3] (FileName:CH15C) Write a program that asks for two 16-bit words in BITSET form.

   a. Display the binary-number representation of each word.

   b. Find the complement of each word. Find the union (OR), the intersection (AND), and the exclusive union (XOR) of the two words. Display the binary-number representation of each result.

   c. Assume that the leftmost bit is a sign bit, where 0 represents positive and 1 represents negative. Also, the rightmost bit will be 0 for even numbers and 1 for odd numbers. Determine and display whether each original word and each result in part b is positive or negative *and* whether each is even or odd.

10. [15.3] Assume that a 16-bit word represents a machine-language instruction as shown in Figure 15–9. In this instruction, the leftmost 4 bits represent the Opcode, which indicates the operation to be performed. The next 6 bits are Operand1, and the rightmost 6 bits are Operand2, the addresses upon which the instruction is to operate. For example, if 1101 represented ADD, then the instruction in Figure 15–9 might be written in assembly language as *ADD 52 57* or (where the Opcode is written in its hexadecimal equivalent) *D 52 57*. This could mean ''add the content of memory location 57 to the content of memory location 52.''

   a. Ask for a machine-language code to be entered from the keyboard in binary form, as a string of 0s and 1s. Convert the code to a BITSET value.

   b. Display the hexadecimal equivalent of the Opcode (a value between 0 and F) and the Operands in decimal form (decimal values between 0 and 63). *Hint:* One way to proceed would be to separate out the Opcode by performing an AND operation between the BITSET form of the instruction and of

Figure 15–9
A 16-bit Machine
Language
Instruction
(Exercise 10)

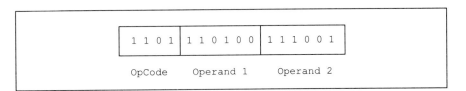

a pattern 1111 000000 000000, which is called a *mask*. An AND of this mask with the instruction in Figure 15–9 would give the result

1101 000000 000000

Why? Dividing the CARDINAL decimal value of this result by 4096 produces the decimal value of Opcode 1101, which can be displayed in hex.

11. [15.3] **a.** Multiply a CARDINAL value less than 32768 by two. Accomplish this by representing the number in BITSET form, shifting all of the bits to the left one place and converting the new BITSET back to CARDINAL form.

    b. Divide a CARDINAL number (NUM) by two by shifting its BITSET representation one bit to the right. Determine whether the remainder (NUM MOD 2) will be 0 or 1 by checking the rightmost bit before shifting.

12. [15.3] Given two CARDINAL numbers, convert them to binary, display, and use BITSET to determine which is larger. *Hint:* One way to proceed is to begin with $i = 15$, compare bits i in both numbers, and then decrement i until you find a value of i that is in the BITSET representation of one of the numbers and not in the other.

16

Pointers and Dynamic Data Structures

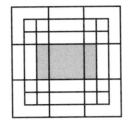

Chapter Outline

The data types we have used so far in this book are **static** data structures, structures for which memory space must be reserved before program execution begins. For example, constant values must be used in the main module to define the size of an array. When a declared array space is filled, it can be extended only by redefining the array size and recompiling the program.

A **dynamic** data structure, on the other hand, is one for which memory space grows or diminishes under process control. It is not necessary to reserve a fixed amount of memory for the structure in advance. In Modula-2, dynamic data structures often are implemented using *pointers* that refer to the addresses where the data are stored.

16.1   *Pointers*

A **pointer** identifies a memory location where the address of a variable is stored. The pointer's name is declared within the module. The variable to which it points does not have a name; it is an **anonymous** variable. An anonymous variable's type can be a simple type, a user-defined enumeration type, or a structured type.

For example, suppose that you wish to use the INTEGER value − 17, which somehow has been stored in memory location 12304, as shown in Figure 16−1. A variable, Pntr1, declared in the module as a pointer, can contain the address of the anonymous variable, location 12304. The value of Pntr1 in this hypothetical situation would be address 12304. Of course, the pointer itself is stored at some address, which, for the illustration, is assumed arbitrarily to be at location 19763. Since the location 12304 itself has no name, it can be found only by its pointer reference. In fact, the anonymous variable is called the **referent** of the pointer, and it is indicated by appending the caret symbol (∧) to the pointer name, Pntr1∧. Thus, if you could display Pntr1, you would discover its value to be 12304 in this example. If you were to display the value of the referent of the pointer, Pntr1∧, you would see − 17.

A pointer referent variable is *accessed indirectly*. First you find the location that contains the address of the variable; then you access the address to find the value of the variable. Space for pointers and their referents can be allocated and deallocated under program control, so this indirect access provides a way to create dynamic data structures.

Figure 16−1
An Anonymous
INTEGER Variable
with a Pointer

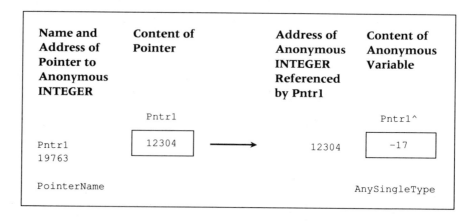

Name and Address of Pointer to Anonymous INTEGER	Content of Pointer	Address of Anonymous INTEGER Referenced by Pntr1	Content of Anonymous Variable
	Pntr1		Pntr1^
Pntr1 19763	12304 ⟶	12304	−17
PointerName			AnySingleType

☐ ### Pointer Variables

Modula-2 syntax for defining and declaring a pointer is shown in Figure 16–2.

In the figure example, type NUMBER has been declared *after* it was used in the declaration of type POINTSTONUMBER. This exception to the general rule that every identifier must be declared before it is used allows you to assign pointers to pointers. This example declaration could have been written

```
VAR  PntrValue1, PntrValue2  :  POINTER TO INTEGER;
```

or

```
TYPE POINTSTONUMBER = POINTER TO INTEGER;
VAR  PntrValue1, PntrValue2  :  POINTSTONUMBER;
```

which creates a TYPE (POINTSTONUMBER) that can be used in parameter lists and elsewhere. Any of these declarations defines the two variables to be pointers to memory locations that contain INTEGER values.

Figure 16–2
Pointer Declaration
Syntax

```
General Syntax

    TYPE  PointerTypeName  =  POINTER TO AnySingleType;

          AnySingleType  =  type definition
                            (* may be simple, enumeration,
                               array,record, set, etc. *)

    VAR  PointerName : PointerTypeName;
```

Example:

```
    TYPE  POINTSTONUMBER = POINTER TO NUMBER;

              NUMBER = INTEGER;

    VAR  PntrValue1, PntrValue2 : POINTSTONUMBER;
```

Notes

1. *POINTER TO* are reserved words used to define the pointer referent type.

2. A referent type (to which a pointer points) can be declared *after* it has been used in the pointer TYPE declaration.

3. A list of PointerName variables, separated by commas, can be declared to be of type POINTER TO PointerTypeName.

4. AnySingleType defines the type of values to be stored in the location pointed to by the PointerName variable.

☐ ALLOCATE, DEALLOCATE, SIZE, TSIZE

Two procedures and two functions are used by a program to create and release space for anonymous variables during execution. They are

- Functions

  SIZE(*V*) or SIZE(*T*)
  > (* Returns the CARDINAL number of bytes required to store variable *V* or data of type *T*. *)

  TSIZE (*T*)
  > (* Returns the CARDINAL number of bytes required to store data of type *T*. *)

- Procedures

  ALLOCATE(PointerName, SIZE(AnySingleType))
  > (* Reserves space for a pointer and an anonymous referent variable of type Any-SingleType, and assigns variable PointerName to point to that variable. *)

  DEALLOCATE(PointerName, SIZE(AnySingleType))
  > (* Releases the storage space allocated to PointerName and its anonymous referent. *)

ALLOCATE and DEALLOCATE must be imported from a standard module called Storage. SIZE(*T*) is a built-in standard function that is available in most versions of Modula-2. So

```
ALLOCATE(PntrValue1, SIZE(INTEGER));
```

would reserve sufficient memory space to hold the INTEGER value to which PntrValue1 refers.

The space reserved by ALLOCATE(PointerName, SIZE(AnySingleType)); is released and made available for other use by the command

```
DEALLOCATE(PointerName, SIZE(AnySingleType)).
```

The value in that space is lost when space is deallocated, so this command should be used with caution.

Some versions of Modula-2 allow you to abbreviate ALLOCATE(PointerName, SIZE(*T*)) by the command NEW(PointerName) and to abbreviate DEALLO-CATE(PointerName, SIZE(*T*)) by DISPOSE(PointerName), importing NEW and DISPOSE from Storage.

Function SIZE(*T*) can be used to discover how much space is required to store a variable *V* or a type *T*. In some implementations of Modula-2, two separate functions, SIZE(*V*) and TSIZE(*T*), must be imported from SYSTEM to return the memory space required by a variable *V* and a type *T*, respectively. If your system requires TSIZE to find the size of a type, then the second argument in ALLOCATE and DEALLOCATE must be TSIZE(*T*), rather than SIZE(*T*).

☐ The Value of a Pointer

The ALLOCATE procedure assigns to the pointer variable the address reserved for a value of the specified type.

NIL

The only value that can be assigned to a pointer directly is NIL. **NIL** is a predefined constant that means ''point to nowhere'' and is assigned when the pointer is not to have a referent. For example, you can

```
ALLOCATE(PntrValue4, SIZE(AnySingleType));
```

and then assign

```
PntrValue4 := NIL;
```

regardless of what AnySingleType represents. With the exception of NIL, you (the programmer) do not assign a constant value to a pointer variable with the assignment operator (:=), because *you* do not choose the address; the computer does.

Assigning Pointer to Pointer

You can make a pointer point to the same address as another pointer of an identical type by assigning the value of the first pointer to the second pointer. The difference between assigning referents and assigning pointer values is illustrated in Figure 16–3. After the assignments of referents, PntrValue2∧ := PntrValue1∧, the separate locations referenced by the pointers contain the same value. After the assignment PntrValue2 := PntrValue1 both pointers contain the same address and point to the same anonymous variable location. After a pointer, such as PntrValue4, has been assigned a NIL value, you can cause it to point to a valid memory location by assigning it another pointer value, such as PntrValue4 := PntrValue2.

Displaying a Pointer Value

Since the computer chooses the address to which a pointer refers, it is not necessary for you to know the actual address value of a pointer. Consequently, there is no standard procedure in Modula-2 for displaying the address value of a pointer. However, some systems allow you to display a pointer value by a command such as

```
WriteCard(VAL(CARDINAL, PointerName), 6).
```

Examples in this chapter that use such a command to display pointer values contain comments to remind you that this feature may not be available to you.

What you really want to know is the value of the anonymous variable referenced by the pointer. This can be displayed by the appropriate Write . . . command. For example, in Figure 16–3,

```
WriteInt(PntrValue1∧, 6);
```

would display the value -17.

Operations on Pointer Variables

Only three operations are allowed on pointer variables:

1. ALLOCATE or DEALLOCATE memory space for the pointer and its referent. (An attempt to deallocate a pointer that has the value NIL may cause a runtime error.)
2. Assign the value NIL to a pointer or assign a pointer value to another pointer of an identical type.
3. Compare pointers for equality—that is, determine if they refer to the same address.

Arithmetic or logical operations (other than = , <>, or **#**) can be performed upon the anonymous *referents* of the pointers, but not upon the pointer variables themselves.

☐ Addition with Pointers

This program illustrates how pointers work, by using pointers to add two numbers and store and display the result.

Figure 16–3
Assignment of One
Pointer Value to
Another

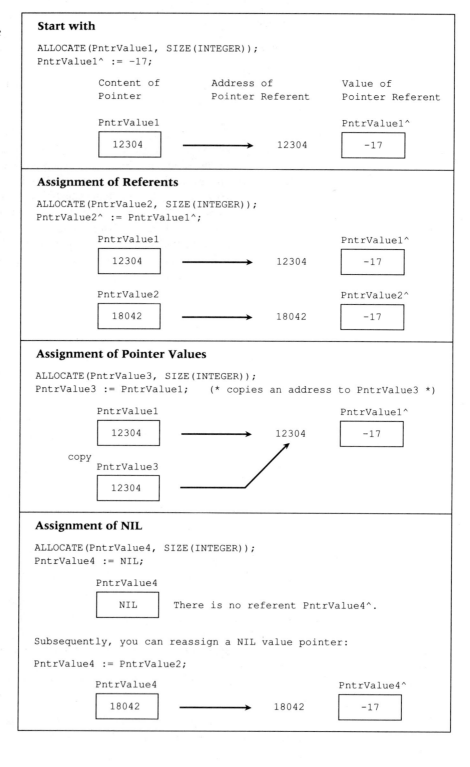

```
MODULE AddWithPointers;
    (* Adds two numbers.  Numbers and Sum are pointer referents..
       FileName:CH16A     Modula-2    RKW      July 1991  *)

FROM InOut IMPORT WriteString, WriteLn, WriteCard;
FROM RealInOut IMPORT ReadReal, FWriteReal;
FROM Storage IMPORT ALLOCATE;
    (* FROM SYSTEM IMPORT SIZE, TSIZE;  if necessary.
       Use TSIZE in all ALLOCATE commands if your system requires it. *)

TYPE  NUMPTR = POINTER TO REAL;
VAR   Num1Ptr, Num2Ptr, SumPtr : NUMPTR;

BEGIN
    ALLOCATE(Num1Ptr, SIZE(REAL));  (* Allocate memory spaces to hold *)
    ALLOCATE(Num2Ptr, SIZE(REAL));  (* REAL numbers pointed to by      *)
    ALLOCATE(SumPtr,  SIZE(REAL));  (* Num1Ptr, Num2Ptr, SumPtr.       *)

    WriteString("What are the REAL addends? "); WriteLn;
     WriteString("Num1Ptr^ = "); ReadReal( Num1Ptr^ ); WriteLn;
     WriteString("Num2Ptr^ = "); ReadReal( Num2Ptr^ ); WriteLn;
        (* Read real values into referents of Num1Ptr and Num2Ptr. *)

    SumPtr^  :=  Num1Ptr^ + Num2Ptr^ ;
        (* Referent SumPtr^ =  sum of referents Num1Ptr^ and Num2Ptr^ *)

    (* Display results *)
    WriteString("The sum of "); FWriteReal(Num1Ptr^, 8, 2);
     WriteString(" and ");       FWriteReal(Num2Ptr^, 8, 2);
     WriteString(" is ");        FWriteReal(SumPtr^, 8, 2);WriteLn;WriteLn;

    (* If pointer display is not supported, DELETE commands to END. *)
     WriteString("The addresses of Num1Ptr^, Num2Ptr^, and SumPtr^");
    WriteLn; WriteString("during this particular run on this  ");
    WriteLn; WriteString("computer system were: ");
    WriteCard(VAL(CARDINAL, Num1Ptr), 6);
    WriteCard(VAL(CARDINAL, Num2Ptr), 6);
    WriteCard(VAL(CARDINAL, SumPtr), 6); WriteLn;
END AddWithPointers.
```

If your system supports the display of pointers, a sample run would appear as follows:

```
What are the REAL addends?
NumPtr1∧ = 13.4
NumPtr2∧ = -5.7
The sum of     13.40 and     -5.70 is     7.70

The addresses of Num1Ptr∧, Num2Ptr∧, and SumPtr∧
during this particular run on this
computer system were,     639   647   655
```

Figure 16–4 illustrates the memory contents for this run. In the code, observe the difference between the pointers (Num1Ptr, Num2Ptr, SumPtr) and the referents or memory locations to which they point (Num1Ptr∧, Num2Ptr∧, SumPtr∧). The values of both are displayed. If your system does not support pointer display, you will need to remove the code lines that do that.

Figure 16–4
Adding with
Pointers

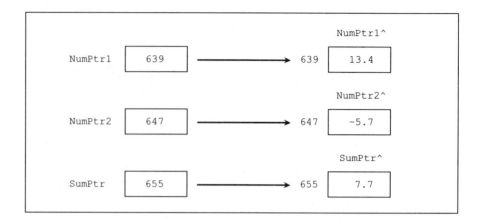

ALLOCATE and DEALLOCATE were imported from the Storage module. Some systems require you to import SIZE from SYSTEM as well. If your system requires you to use TSIZE in the ALLOCATE command, then import TSIZE from SYSTEM and replace all occurrences of SIZE.

Be careful! Confusing pointers with their referents can be disastrous.

☐ Available

A dynamic data structure can grow so large that the ALLOCATE command will fail because no more memory is available for allocating. When a call to ALLOCATE fails, the program terminates with an error message. A BOOLEAN function,

```
PROCEDURE Available(Size: CARDINAL) : BOOLEAN
```

can be imported from the Storage module and used to prevent such an occurrence. For example, if you were allocating INTEGER size space to pointer variable Pntr-Value1, you could execute

```
IF  Available(SIZE(INTEGER))   THEN
  ALLOCATE(PntrValue1, SIZE(INTEGER));
ELSE
  WriteString('' WARNING: Space not available; did not allocate '');
  WriteLn;
END; (* IF *)
```

This would ensure that ALLOCATE is executed only if space is available.

☐ Records with Pointers

A pointer can point to a record, which in turn can have a field that contains a pointer of the same type.

For example, suppose you want to allocate space dynamically to records containing a Name field, an Age field, and a field that points to another Name and Age record. You could create the data structure shown in Figure 16–5. POINTSTO-SOMEONE defines the type of a pointer that points to a record of type WHO. In turn, WHO contains field PointToAnother of type POINTSTOSOMEONE. To provide this capability it is necessary to allow a pointer type to be defined *before* the type of variable to which it points.

Figure 16–5
Two Name and Age
Records,
PersonPtrl∧ and
PersonPtr2∧

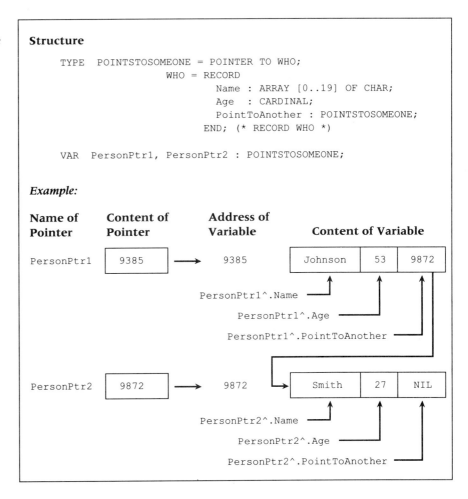

To illustrate, suppose that two of these records were stored at memory locations 9385 and 9872, as shown in Figure 16–5. This situation could be generated by the command sequence:

```
ALLOCATE(PersonPtrl, SIZE(WHO));
PersonPtrl∧.Name := ''Johnson''; PersonPtrl∧.Age := 53;
PersonPtrl∧.PointToAnother := NIL;
ALLOCATE(PersonPtr2, SIZE(WHO));
PersonPtrl∧.PointToAnother := PersonPtr2;
WITH PersonPtr2∧ DO
   Name := ''Smith''; Age := 27;
   PointToAnother := NIL;
END; (* WITH *)
```

Observe how sufficient space was allocated to PersonPtr1 for a record of type WHO. Then values for the Name and Age were assigned to the appropriate fields in the record location referred to by PersonPtr1, and NIL was assigned temporarily to field PointToAnother. Similarly, space had to be allocated to PersonPtr2 before values could be assigned to its referent record fields. Then the pointer field PersonPtrl∧.PointToAnother was assigned the newly allocated address of the second record.

For illustration, all three fields of variable PersonPtr2/\ were assigned values using the WITH structure. Assigning NIL to the PointToAnother field in PersonPtr2/\ indicates that there are no more records to which to point.

1. **a.** Determine whether your system supports WriteCard(VAL(CARDINAL, PointerName), 6). If not, does your Modula-2 compiler manual suggest another method of displaying pointer values?

   b. Which does your system require, SIZE or TSIZE, in ALLOCATE and DEALLOCATE commands? Must SIZE be imported from SYSTEM?

2. Implement AddWithPointers (CH16A) on your system.

3. Given the declaration VAR Where : POINTER TO CARDINAL; what is the difference between WriteCard(Where/\, 6); and WriteCard(VAL(CARDINAL, Where), 6);?

4. Write declarations and code that will allocate space and assign the REAL value 3.14159 to the referent location of a pointer named PointsToPI.

5. What would be displayed by this fragment of code if properly supported by import commands and other missing statements?

```
...
CONST  e = 2.71828;
TYPE   LOCATE = POINTER TO REAL;
VAR    PtToValue : LOCATE;

BEGIN
    ALLOCATE(PtToValue, SIZE(REAL));
    ReadReal(PtToValue^);   (* Respond with 2.0 *)
    PtToValue^ := e * PtToValue^;
    FWriteReal(PtToValue^, 12, 6);
    ....
```

6. To the following fragment of code, add import lists and missing statements, and correct the errors, so that it displays

   A
   Z
   AZ

   (and the addresses where these values are stored, if your system supports pointer display.)

```
...
TYPE  SHORTSTR = ARRAY [0..1] OF CHAR;    SHORTPTR = POINTER TO SHORTSTR;
VAR   P1, P2, P3 : POINTER TO SHORTPTR;

BEGIN
    ALLOCATE(P1,SIZE(CHAR));ALLOCATE(P2,SIZE(CHAR));ALLOCATE(P3,SIZE(CHAR));
    P1^ := "A";   P2^ := "Z";
    WriteString(P1^); WriteLn; WriteString(P2^); WriteLn;
    P3 := P1 + P2;
    WriteString(P3^);WriteLn;
    WriteCard(VAL(CARDINAL,P1),6);  WriteCard(VAL(CARDINAL,P2),6);
    WriteCard(VAL(CARDINAL,P3), 6); WriteLn;
    ....
```

7. Create a pointer to a Customer record data type. The Customer records contain Name and Date(Strings), BillAmount(REAL), and GoodRisk(BOOLEAN) fields, as well as a field that can be used to point to the next Customer.

    Declare three variables of this pointer type and write code to assign values to the fields of the three records, so that the first record points to the second, the second points to the third, and the third "points to nowhere." Check whether space is available before trying to allocate space for each record.

16.2 *Stacks*

Now that you are acquainted with pointer notation and how pointers work, it is time to introduce some dynamic data structures that can be implemented with pointers. In this section, the *stack* structure is defined. In the next few sections you will look at queues, linked lists, and binary trees.

Creating a Stack

A **stack** is a Last In, First Out (**LIFO**) data structure—a structure in which the item added to the stack last is the first to be removed. Common experiences with stacks include the "in basket" on your desk, where the item on top is likely to be the first one you remove and process. A stack of books on a table and trays in a cafeteria are other examples of this situation. Stacks provide a simple reversal capability.

    In computing, the return addresses from procedure calls often are stored on stacks, so that when a module calls procedure *A,* which calls procedure *B,* which calls procedure *C,* a return from *C* returns first to *B,* which eventually returns to *A* and then to the module.

PUSH and POP
The operation of placing a new item on top of the stack is called a **PUSH.** Removal of an item from a stack is called a **POP** operation. A variable called the **TopOfStack (TOS)** pointer always points to the address of the element added to the stack most recently.

    Figure 16–6a illustrates storing CHARacters on a stack and then removing them one by one to display them in reverse order. In Figure 16–6b you see a representation of storing return addresses from procedure calls.

Stack Operations
Stacks can be handled with three operations, namely

- CreateStack
  (* Define an empty stack space and an indicator that denotes the top of the stack, where the last addition to the stack is stored. *)
- PUSH
  (* Add an item to the top of the stack and move the top-of-stack indicator to the new item *)
- POP
  (* Remove the top item from the stack and move the top-of-stack indicator to the next item in the stack. *)

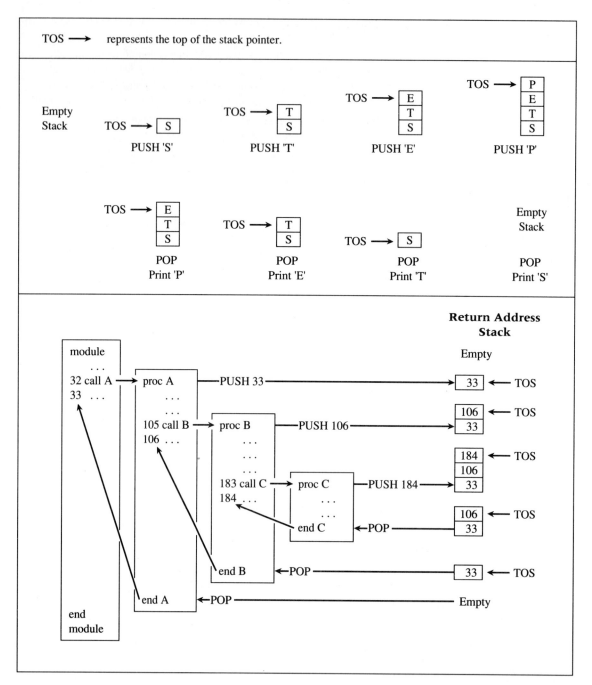

Figure 16–6
Use of Stacks to Store and Retrieve Items in Reverse Order **a.** A Stack of CHARacters **b.** A Stack of Return Addresses from Procedure Calls

Pointer Implementation of a Stack

Although stacks can be represented with arrays, implementation of truly dynamic stacks is managed with pointers.

Assume that the record type of data to be stored on the stack is declared as

```
TYPE  WHATSONSTACK = RECORD
                 Characters : CHRARY;
                 (* ARRAY [0..MAXCHS] OF CHAR *)
                 Number : REAL;
                 PreviousRecPtr : POINTTOSTACK;
               END; (* RECORD WHATSONSTACK *)
```

and that the pointer type is

```
TYPE  POINTTOSTACK = POINTER TO WHATSONSTACK;
```

Then the three stack operations can be described in terms of pointers as follows

```
PROCEDURE CreateStack(VAR TopOfStack : POINTTOSTACK)
 (* Initialize a TopOfStack pointer by setting its value to NIL, which
    indicates that the stack is empty. *)


PROCEDURE PUSH(VAR TopOfStack:POINTTOSTACK; WhatToPush:WHATSONSTACK)
 (* Allocate a new record space, if available, and assign values to the
    fields in that space. A pointer in the new record accepts the
    previous value of TopOfStack, and TopOfStack becomes the address of
    the newly allocated space. Thus, each record contains a pointer
    that points to the previous stack location.*)


PROCEDURE POP(VAR TopOfStack:POINTTOSTACK;
                         VAR WhatIsPopped:WHATSONSTACK)
 (* If TopOfStack = NIL, print a message that the stack is empty.
    Otherwise, assign the field values referenced by TopOfStack to
    record WhatIsPopped. Deallocate the record space on the top of the
    stack. Assign TopOfStack the value of pointer
    WhatIsPopped^.PreviousRecPtr so that TopOfStack now points to the
    record previous to the one just removed. *)
```

These three operations are illustrated in Figure 16–7.

An additional procedure, for displaying stack contents, will be useful. Its definition is

```
PROCEDURE PrintStack(TopOfStack : POINTTOSTACK)
 (* Print headings, set a Counter = 1, and call nested recursive
    procedure PrintNextRecord(TopOfStack, Counter). *)


PROCEDURE PrintNextRecord(WhereOnStack:POINTTOSTACK; Count:CARDINAL)
 (* If WhereOnStack = NIL, write ''End of Stack  .
  Otherwise
    display fields of record at WhereOnStack if Count = 1,  display
    '' <--- Top Of Stack'') set pointer WhereOnStack = WhereOnStack^.
    PreviousRecPtr increment Count recursive call PrintNextRecord
    (WhereOnStack, Count)  *)
```

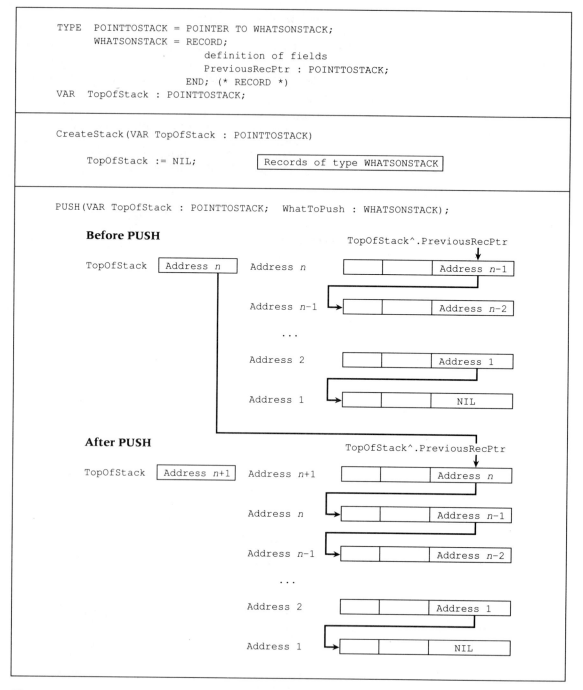

Figure 16–7   *(continued)*
Pointer Implementation of CreateStack, PUSH, and POP

These declarations and procedures are written in DEFINITION and IMPLEMEN-TATION MODULE Dynamic in Appendix C. Study them carefully to discern how they work.

In order to debug these stack-handling procedures you must have a thorough understanding of the data structure, how the pointers work, and how the procedures

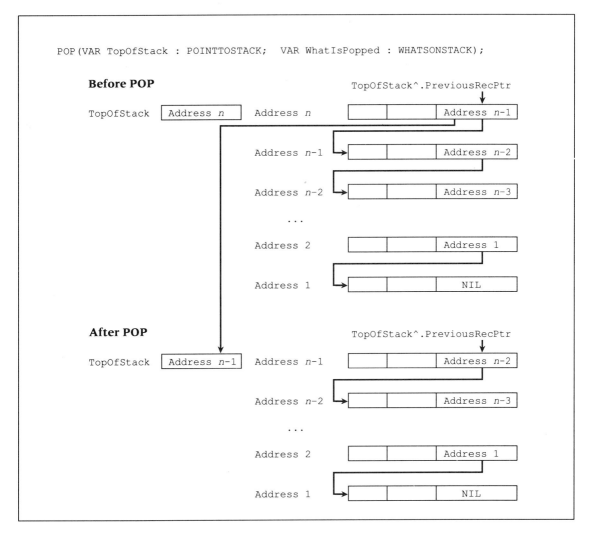

```
POP(VAR TopOfStack : POINTTOSTACK;  VAR WhatIsPopped : WHATSONSTACK);
```

Before POP

After POP

Figure 16-7
(*continued*)

are to operate before you begin coding. Make certain that variable and parameter types agree. Procedures CreateStack, PUSH, POP, and PrintStack must be debugged as a package, since a stack must be created and have something in it before it can be printed; and PrintStack must work before it can be determined whether the other procedures have worked properly.

The following program invokes the stack-handling procedures from module Dynamic. It PUSHes CHARacters entered from the keyboard (until an asterisk, ***,** is entered) and then POPs and displays them in reverse order.

```
MODULE StackCharacterHandler;
   (* Receives a list of characters into a stack, then removes
      and displays them in reverse order.
      FileName:CH16B    Modula-2    RKW      July 1991  *)

FROM InOut IMPORT WriteString, WriteLn, ReadString;
FROM Dynamic IMPORT CreateStack, PrintStack, PUSH, POP,
                    POINTTOSTACK, WHATSONSTACK;
```

```
CONST   SHOWSTACK = TRUE;
VAR  ThisStack : POINTTOSTACK;        RecordContent : WHATSONSTACK;

PROCEDURE ReadAndStore(VAR StackTop : POINTTOSTACK);
   VAR  ThisRecord : WHATSONSTACK;
   BEGIN     (* Read and store the characters. *)
      WriteString("Enter single characters ");
      WriteString(" (separated by Space or Return);");
      WriteString(" stop with *. "); WriteLn;
      REPEAT
         ReadString(ThisRecord.Characters);
         ThisRecord.Number := 0.0;   (* unused dummy value *)
         PUSH(StackTop, ThisRecord);

         IF  SHOWSTACK  THEN
            WriteLn; PrintStack(StackTop); WriteLn; WriteLn;
         END; (* IF *)
      UNTIL  ThisRecord.Characters[0] = '*';   WriteLn;
   END ReadAndStore;

PROCEDURE RetrieveAndDisplay(StackTop : POINTTOSTACK);
   VAR  ThisRecord : WHATSONSTACK;
   BEGIN     (* Retrieve and display the characters. *)
      WHILE  StackTop # NIL  DO  (* While the stack is not empty. *)
         POP(StackTop, ThisRecord);
         WriteString(ThisRecord.Characters);
         IF  SHOWSTACK  THEN
            WriteLn; PrintStack(StackTop); WriteLn; WriteLn;
         END; (* IF *)
      END; (* WHILE *)
   END RetrieveAndDisplay;

BEGIN  (* module StackCharacterHandler *)
   CreateStack(ThisStack);
   ReadAndStore(ThisStack);
   RetrieveAndDisplay(ThisStack);
END StackCharacterHandler.
```

Note that the stack is created in module StackCharacterHandler. Then procedure ReadAndStore PUSHes the characters onto the stack; finally procedure Retrieve-AndDisplay POPs the characters one at a time and displays them. One parameter passed to each stack-handling procedure is the name of the stack; it is actually the name of the top-of-stack pointer. In PUSH and POP you also specify the name of the record that contains the data to be pushed onto the stack or the name of the record that will contain the data popped from the stack. SHOWSTACK is a BOOL-EAN CONSTant, which if TRUE causes the stack contents to be displayed. The single characters entered are read as strings, because module Dynamic provides for a string field (ARRAY [0..MAXCHS] OF CHAR) in record type WHATSON-STACK.

This program is straightforward if you remember which variables are pointers to records and which are records.

If you run the program with SHOWSTACK = FALSE, the program displays something like

```
Enter single characters (separated by Space or Return); stop with *.
LAP*
*PAL
```

If your system supports pointer display, and CONSTant SHOWSTACK = TRUE, you should see a display like that in Figure 16–8.

RPN Arithmetic

One important application of stacks is for calculations by the method called **Reverse Polish Notation (RPN),** *postfix,* or stack arithmetic.

In RPN (postfix) notation, arithmetic operations between two values are written on paper in the form

$$4 \quad 5 \quad + \qquad \text{or} \qquad 12 \quad 4 \quad /,$$

rather than in the familiar direct, algebraic (*infix*) form

$$4 + 5 \qquad \text{or} \qquad 12/4.$$

RPN arithmetic can be performed easily using a stack. For example, the infix calculations 12/4 and $(9 * 2) - 7$ can be written in the postfix forms, 12 4 / and 9 2 * 7 − , and performed as shown in Figure 16–9.

You can implement RPN yourself by using the procedures already developed in module Dynamic.

Example 16.2.1

Perform the calculation 3 + (4 * 5) using stack arithmetic.

Define the problem New procedures StackMultiply(StackName) and Stack-Add(StackName) will perform multiplication and addition, using the PUSH and POP procedures from module Dynamic. The program will ask for the appropriate values and perform 3 + (4 * 5), which is written in RPN as 3 4 5 * +.

To interpret this postfix notation, read from the left until you come to an operator (*); perform the indicated operation on the preceding two values (4 5 * = 20). This gives you a new postfix expression (3 20 +). Search for the next operator (+), and perform that operation (3 20 + = 23).

Develop a solution The REAL Number field of the WHATSONSTACK record defined in module Dynamic will be used. The Characters field will be assigned a dummy value and ignored. StackMultiply and StackAdd assume that the two values are already on the stack. The procedures POP the values, multiply or add them, and PUSH the Product or Sum back onto the stack.

When the program is executed, the user will PUSH values 3, 4, and 5 to the stack first. Then StackMultiply and StackAdd will be called, and the result will be displayed. Two menus determine which operation is to be performed next. From one menu the user chooses to display the stack, to PUSH, to POP, to perform arithmetic, or to stop the program. If the choice is to perform arithmetic, the second menu presents the choice Multiply or Add.

Refine the solution *Pseudocode*

```
begin module StackArithmetic
     CreateStack(StackName)
     repeat
          PresentMenu
             ask for Selection ( 1 Display top of stack) (2 PUSH) (3 POP)
                              (4 Perform Arithmetic) (5 STOP)
```

Figure 16-8
Sample Run of
StackCharacterHandler
(CH16B) with
SHOWSTACK =
TRUE on a System
that Supports
Pointer Display

```
Enter single characters separated by Space or Return; stop with *.

L
Address   Characters   Number   PrevRecPtr
   643    L              0.00        NIL  ← - - Top Of Stack
End of Stack

A
Address   Characters   Number   PrevRecPtr
   663    A              0.00        643  ← - - Top Of Stack
   643    L              0.00        NIL
End of Stack

P
Address   Characters   Number   PrevRecPtr
   683    P              0.00        663  ← - - Top Of Stack
   663    A              0.00        643
   643    L              0.00        NIL
End of Stack

*
Address   Characters   Number   PrevRecPtr
   703    *              0.00        683  ← - - Top Of Stack
   683    P              0.00        663
   663    A              0.00        643
   643    L              0.00        NIL
End of Stack


*
Address   Characters   Number   PrevRecPtr
   683    P              0.00        663  ← - - Top Of Stack
   663    A              0.00        643
   643    L              0.00        NIL
End of Stack

P
Address   Characters   Number   PrevRecPtr
   663    A              0.00        643  ← - - Top Of Stack
   643    L              0.00        NIL
End of Stack

A
Address   Characters   Number   PrevRecPtr
   643    L              0.00        NIL  ← - - Top Of Stack
End of Stack

L
Address   Characters   Number   PrevRecPtr
End of Stack
```

```
            case Choice of
                1 : DisplayTop(StackName)    2: AskPush(StackName)
                3 : if StackName = NIL, write "Empty"
                       else    POP(StackName, Value), display Value
                4 : PresentArithmeticMenu(StackName)
           until Selection = 5
        end StackArithmetic
```

```
procedure DisplayTop(ThisStack)
    if    ThisStack = NIL, write "Stack is Empty"
    else   write record fields for ThisStack∧

procedure AskPush(VAR ThisStack)
    ask for record WhatToPush fields, and PUSH(ThisStack, WhatToPush)

procedure StackAdd(VAR ThisStack)
    POP(ThisStack, Addend1),    POP(ThisStack, Addend2))
    Sum = Addend1 + Addend2
    PUSH(ThisStack, Sum),    display Sum

procedure StackMultiply(VAR ThisStack)
    POP(ThisStack, Multiplicand),    POP(ThisStack, Multiplier)
    Product = Multiplicand * Multiplier
    PUSH(ThisStack, Product),    display Product

procedure PresentArithmeticMenu(VAR ThisStack)
    if    ThisStack or ThisStack∧.PreviousRecPtr = NIL
            write "too few items on stack"
    else
            ask for Choice (A Add), (M Multiply), (N None of these)
    end if
    if    Choice = 'A',    StackAdd(ThisStack)
    else if   Choice = 'M',    StackMultiply(ThisStack)
```

Modula-2 code   To help users keep track of which menu is active, one menu asks for a numeric selection, whereas the other asks for a character. The main menu Selection is checked for membership IN BITSET{1..5}.

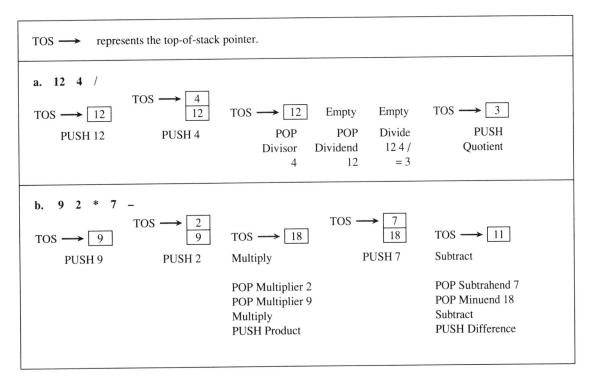

Figure 16-9
RPN Calculates with Stack Arithmetic a. 12 4 /   b. 9 2 * 7 −

The main module repeats the primary menu and calls the appropriate procedures until the user chooses to Stop. The StackName pointer is passed as a parameter through all procedures and back again by those procedures that change the stack. The choice to POP the top of the stack displays to the user the values that were popped and where they can be found. Product.Character and Sum.Character are assigned dummy values only to ensure that PUSH command receives valid parameter fields.

```
MODULE StackArithmetic;
  (* Performs stack add and multiply.
     FileName:CH16C      Modula-2      RKW       July 1991  *)

FROM InOut IMPORT WriteString, ReadString, WriteLn, ReadCard, Read, Write;
FROM RealInOut IMPORT FWriteReal, ReadReal;
FROM Dynamic IMPORT POINTTOSTACK, WHATSONSTACK, CreateStack, PUSH, POP;

VAR StackName: POINTTOSTACK;  Value : WHATSONSTACK;    Selection : CARDINAL;

PROCEDURE DisplayTop(ThisStack: POINTTOSTACK);
   VAR  Value : WHATSONSTACK;
   BEGIN
      IF  ThisStack = NIL  THEN
         WriteString("The stack is EMPTY."); WriteLn;
      ELSE
         WriteString("On the top of the stack: "); WriteLn;
         WriteString(ThisStack^.Characters);
         FWriteReal(ThisStack^.Number, 8, 2); WriteLn;
      END; (* IF *)
   END DisplayTop;

PROCEDURE AskPush(VAR ThisStack: POINTTOSTACK);
   VAR  WhatToPush : WHATSONSTACK;
   BEGIN
      WriteString("What values to push onto the stack? "); WriteLn;
      WriteString("      Characters: "); ReadString(WhatToPush.Characters);
      WriteString("      Number: ");     ReadReal(WhatToPush.Number);
      PUSH(ThisStack, WhatToPush);  WriteLn;
   END AskPush;

PROCEDURE StackAdd(VAR ThisStack: POINTTOSTACK);
   VAR  Addend1, Addend2, Sum : WHATSONSTACK;
   BEGIN
      POP(ThisStack, Addend1);  POP(ThisStack, Addend2);
      Sum.Characters := Addend1.Characters;
      Sum.Number := Addend1.Number + Addend2.Number;
      PUSH(ThisStack, Sum);
      WriteString("After addition, result on top of stack = ");
       FWriteReal(ThisStack^.Number, 8, 2); WriteLn;
   END StackAdd;

PROCEDURE StackMultiply(VAR ThisStack: POINTTOSTACK);
  VAR  Multiplicand, Multiplier, Product : WHATSONSTACK;
  BEGIN
      POP(ThisStack, Multiplicand); POP(ThisStack, Multiplier);
      Product.Characters := Multiplicand.Characters;
```

```
        Product.Number := Multiplicand.Number * Multiplier.Number;
        PUSH(ThisStack, Product);
        WriteString("After multiplication, result on top of stack = ");
         FWriteReal(ThisStack^.Number, 8, 2); WriteLn;
    END StackMultiply;

PROCEDURE PresentArithmeticMenu(VAR ThisStack: POINTTOSTACK);
    VAR  Choice, CapChoice, Discard : CHAR;
    BEGIN      WriteLn;
        IF  (ThisStack = NIL) OR (ThisStack^.PreviousRecPtr = NIL) THEN
           WriteString("Too few items on stack.");
           WriteString(" Operation not performed.");  WriteLn;
        ELSE
           WriteString("Which arithmetic operation? "); WriteLn;
              WriteString("     A    Add"); WriteLn;
              WriteString("     M    Multiply"); WriteLn;
              WriteString("     N    None of these"); WriteLn;
           REPEAT
              WriteString("Choose one (A, M, N): "); Read(Choice);
               Read(Discard); Write(Choice); CapChoice:=CAP(Choice); WriteLn;
           UNTIL (CapChoice='A') OR (CapChoice='M') OR (CapChoice='N');
           IF      CapChoice = 'A' THEN  StackAdd(ThisStack);
            ELSIF  CapChoice = 'M' THEN  StackMultiply(ThisStack);
           END; (* IF *)
        END; (* IF *)
    END PresentArithmeticMenu;

BEGIN (* module StackArithmetic *)
    CreateStack(StackName);
    REPEAT   WriteLn;
      WriteString("What would you like to do? "); WriteLn;
       WriteString("     1     Display top of stack"); WriteLn;
       WriteString("     2     PUSH a value to the stack"); WriteLn;
       WriteString("     3     POP a value from the stack"); WriteLn;
       WriteString("     4     Perform arithmetic operation"); WriteLn;
       WriteString("     5     Stop"); WriteLn;
      REPEAT
         WriteString("Choose one (1, 2, 3, 4, 5): ");
         ReadCard(Selection); WriteLn;
      UNTIL  Selection IN BITSET{1..5};
      CASE  Selection  OF
         1 : DisplayTop(StackName) |   2 : AskPush(StackName)      |
         3 : IF  StackName = NIL THEN
                WriteString("The stack is EMPTY.  Cannot POP."); WriteLn;
             ELSE
                POP(StackName, Value); WriteLn;
                WriteString("Just popped");  WriteLn;
                WriteString(" Value.Characters = ");
                 WriteString(Value.Characters); WriteLn;
                WriteString(" Value.Number    = ");
                 FWriteReal(Value.Number, 8, 2); WriteLn;
             END | (* IF *)
         4 : PresentArithmeticMenu(StackName) ;
      END (* CASE *)
    UNTIL  Selection = 5;
END StackArithmetic.
```

Debug and test The process of solving one simple problem has led to a comprehensive stack-handling program. Make sure that each procedure that POPs from or displays the stack checks first to see that the stack is not empty. Before performing arithmetic operations on two values, check to make sure that at least two items are on the stack; namely, that (ThisStack # NIL) and that (ThisStack/\.PreviousRecPtr # NIL).

It may be wise to test the logic of the main module first by writing stub procedures for all choices (except PUSH, and POP, which you know work already). Then procedure PresentArithmeticMenu could be tested with stub procedures in the same manner.

Figure 16–10 shows a sample run that performs 3 + (4 * 5) = 3 4 5 * +, where 3, 4, and 5 are all pushed onto the stack; then the multiplication is performed, followed by the addition.

Figure 16–10
Sample Run of StackArithmetic (Example 16.2.1, CH16C)

```
Ellipses (...) indicate where the menus would appear again.

What would you like to do?
     1      Display top of stack
     2      PUSH a value to the stack
     3      POP a value from the stack
     4      Perform arithmetic operation
     5      Stop
Choose one (1, 2, 3, 4, 5): 2
What values to push onto the stack?
     Characters: A      Number: 3
...

Choose one (1, 2, 3, 4, 5): 2
What values to push onto the stack?
     Characters: B      Number: 4
...

Choose one (1, 2, 3, 4, 5): 2
What values to push onto the stack?
     Characters: C      Number: 5
...

Choose one (1, 2, 3, 4, 5): 4

Which arithmetic operation?
     A      Add
     M      Multiply
     N      None of these
Choose one (A, M, N): M
After multiplication, result on top of stack =    20.00

What would you like to do?
...

Choose one (1, 2, 3, 4, 5): 4

Which arithmetic operation?
...

Choose one (A, M, N): A
After addition, result on top of stack =    23.00


...

Choose one (1, 2, 3, 4, 5): 5
```

Complete the documentation   Complete documentation of this program is shown in Figure 16–11

---

1. **a.** Draw a diagram similar to Figure 16–6a of the job folders arriving and leaving the ''in basket'' on your desk. Each job is designated by a name and the number of minutes needed to handle it.

   b. How would you modify the StackCharacterHandler program (CH16B) to keep track of these jobs?

2. To program StackArithmetic (CH16C) add a main menu Selection to display the entire stack, and show how displaying the entire stack could be implemented by calling PrintStack from module Dynamic.

3. Show step-by-step how procedures PUSH and POP (IMPLEMENTATION MODULE Dynamic) perform their operations on a stack of at least three records of type WHATSONSTACK filled with Character and Number values of your choice at hypothetical addresses. Illustrate the stack and indicate the values of the variables at all important steps in the procedures.

4. State whether a stack structure would be appropriate for each of these tasks. Indicate why or why not.

   a. A word processor must remember a line of up to 80 characters. Pressing the Backspace key deletes the previous character, and pressing CTRL/Backspace deletes the entire line.

   b. Customers must wait one to three months for delivery of their new automobiles. The dealer creates a list that will determine the ''fair'' order in which customers should get their cars; that is, the order in which they placed their orders.

   c. Search downward in a pile of magazines until you find the issue for last January. Each magazine was placed on the pile as soon as it was read.

   d. A programming team accepts jobs and prioritizes them on the basis of urgency.

   e. People have formed a line at a bus stop. When the bus arrives, those at the end of the line enter the bus first.

A Bit of Background

Lukasiewicz and RPN

Postfix algebraic notation was created in 1951 by Polish mathematician and logician Jan Lukasiewicz. Hence it often is called *Reverse Polish Notation,* or *RPN.*

   Dr. Lukasiewicz, born in 1878, studied and taught mathematics at the University of Lvov before becoming a respected professor at the University of Warsaw. He received an appointment in 1919 to the post of Minister of Education in Poland and, with Stanislaw Lesniewski, founded the Warsaw School of Logic.

   After World War II, Jan and his wife, Regina, found themselves exiled in Belgium. When he was offered a professorship at the Royal Academy in Dublin, they moved to Ireland, where they remained until his death in 1956.

   RPN was critical in the design of early microprocessors in the 1960s and 1970s. Stack arithmetic, based on the work of Dr. Lukasiewicz, allows computations to be performed quickly with short machine-language instructions. Stack-handling instructions require no address operands and have made it possible for very small computers to handle large tasks effectively. Pocket calculators developed by the Hewlett-Packard Corporation are especially notable for their use of RPN and have made stack arithmetic the favorite of many scientists and engineers.

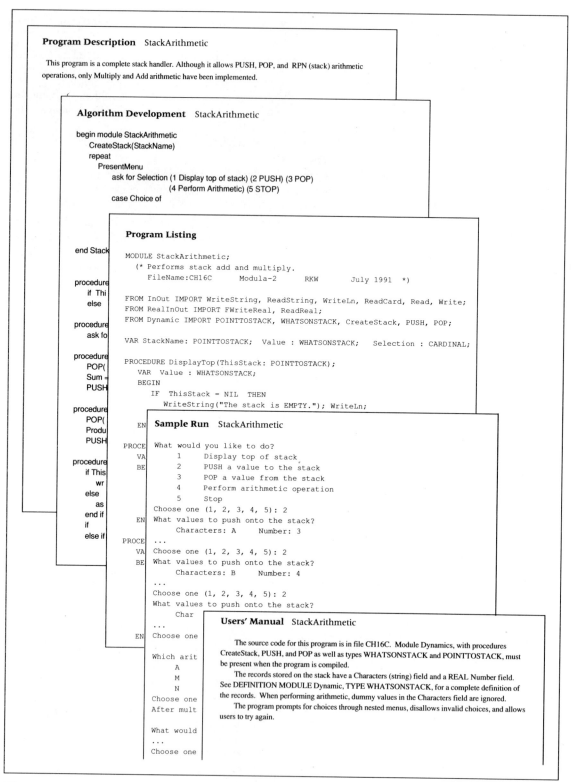

Program Description StackArithmetic

This program is a complete stack handler. Although it allows PUSH, POP, and RPN (stack) arithmetic operations, only Multiply and Add arithmetic have been implemented.

Algorithm Development StackArithmetic

```
begin module StackArithmetic
    CreateStack(StackName)
    repeat
        PresentMenu
            ask for Selection (1 Display top of stack) (2 PUSH) (3 POP)
                              (4 Perform Arithmetic) (5 STOP)
            case Choice of
```

end Stack

procedure
    if Thi
    else

procedure
    ask fo

procedure
    POP(
    Sum =
    PUSH

procedure
    POP(
    Produ
    PUSH

procedure
    if This
        wr
    else
        as
    end if
    if
    else if

Program Listing

```
MODULE StackArithmetic;
  (* Performs stack add and multiply.
     FileName:CH16C    Modula-2    RKW    July 1991  *)

FROM InOut IMPORT WriteString, ReadString, WriteLn, ReadCard, Read, Write;
FROM RealInOut IMPORT FWriteReal, ReadReal;
FROM Dynamic IMPORT POINTTOSTACK, WHATSONSTACK, CreateStack, PUSH, POP;

VAR StackName: POINTTOSTACK;  Value : WHATSONSTACK;   Selection : CARDINAL;

PROCEDURE DisplayTop(ThisStack: POINTTOSTACK);
    VAR  Value : WHATSONSTACK;
    BEGIN
        IF  ThisStack = NIL  THEN
            WriteString("The stack is EMPTY."); WriteLn;
```

Sample Run StackArithmetic

```
What would you like to do?
     1      Display top of stack
     2      PUSH a value to the stack
     3      POP a value from the stack
     4      Perform arithmetic operation
     5      Stop
Choose one (1, 2, 3, 4, 5): 2
What values to push onto the stack?
     Characters: A      Number: 3
...
Choose one (1, 2, 3, 4, 5): 2
What values to push onto the stack?
     Characters: B      Number: 4
...
Choose one (1, 2, 3, 4, 5): 2
What values to push onto the stack?
     Char
...
Choose one

Which arit
     A
     M
     N
Choose one
After mult

What would
...
Choose one
```

Users' Manual StackArithmetic

The source code for this program is in file CH16C. Module Dynamics, with procedures CreateStack, PUSH, and POP as well as types WHATSONSTACK and POINTTOSTACK, must be present when the program is compiled.

The records stored on the stack have a Characters (string) field and a REAL Number field. See DEFINITION MODULE Dynamic, TYPE WHATSONSTACK, for a complete definition of the records. When performing arithmetic, dummy values in the Characters field are ignored.

The program prompts for choices through nested menus, disallows invalid choices, and allows users to try again.

Figure 16–11
Documentation of StackArithmetic (Example 16.2.1)

16.3   *Queues*

A second important data structure that can be made dynamic with pointers is called a **queue** (pronounced "cue"). Items are removed from a queue in the order in which they are entered. Thus, the queue is a First In, First Out (**FIFO**) structure.

An example of a queue could be the waiting list of customers for rare handmade automobiles. The first customer on the list would receive the first car; the second customer would receive the second, and so on. Suppose, for example, that the customers are

```
1     Burns
2     Smith
3     Wilson
4     Carson
```

A pointer, called *QueueOut*, points to the customer who is next in line to be taken out of the queue and receive his or her car. Let's say that Burns is this customer. Another pointer, called *QueueIn*, points to the location in the queue where the name of the next person to order a car will be placed. If Burns were removed from the queue and Jones and Thomas were added, the queue and pointers would appear as in Figure 16–12. If Smith, Wilson, Carson, Jones, and Thomas were all supplied with automobiles without adding anyone else to the queue, then QueueOut and QueueIn would both point to the same location (location 7 in this instance), and the queue would be empty. Thus when QueueIn = QueueOut the queue is empty, and a new queue is created by allocating a location to which both QueueIn and QueueOut point.

Creating a Queue

Queues are handled with three operations. They are

- CreateQueue
  (* Define a new, empty Queue and pointers QueueIn and QueueOut to keep track of next item to be removed and where next item will be added. *)
- AddToQueue
  (* Add an item to the queue and advance the QueueIn indicator. *)
- RemoveFromQueue
  (* Remove an item at QueueOut and advance the QueueOut indicator. *)

Figure 16–12
A Queue with Pointers

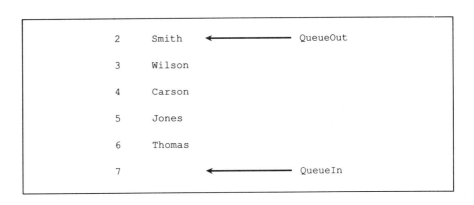

Pointer Implementation of a Queue

Queues can also be simulated using arrays; however, queues implemented with pointers—with space allocated and deallocated under program control—are dynamic.

Assume that the record type of data to be stored in the queue is declared to be

```
TYPE WHATSINQUEUE = RECORD
                      Characters : CHRARY; Number : REAL;
                      NextRecPtr : POINTTOQUEUE;
                      END; (* RECORD WHATSINQUEUE *)
```

and that the pointer type is

```
TYPE POINTTOQUEUE = POINTER TO WHATSINQUEUE;
```

Then the three queue operations can be described in pointer notation as

```
PROCEDURE CreateQueue(VAR QueueIn, QueueOut : POINTTOQUEUE)
 (* Define QueueIn and QueueOut pointers, to both of which is allocated
    the same memory space. The pointers in the record at location
    QueueIn/QueueOut will be assigned the value NIL. *)

PROCEDURE AddToQueue(VAR QueueIn:POINTTOQUEUE;
        QueueOut:POINTTOQUEUE; WhatToAdd:WHATSINQUEUE)
 (* Allocate a new space, if available, at NewSpacePtr. Assign What-
    ToAdd values to the fields at location QueueIn. QueueIn∧.NextRecPtr
    will be assigned the NewSpacePtr value, so that each record points
    to the next one in the queue. Assign NewSpacePtr to QueueIn, then
    assign QueueIn∧.NextRecPtr the value NIL. *)

PROCEDURE RemoveFromQueue(QueueIn:POINTTOQUEUE;
        VAR QueueOut:POINTTOQUEUE; VAR WhatsRemoved:WHATSINQUEUE)
 (* If QueueOut = QueueIn, a message is printed indicating that the
    queue is empty. Otherwise, the field values referenced by QueueOut,
    including the NextRecPtr, are assigned to record WhatsRemoved. The
    space QueueOut is deallocated. QueueOut is assigned the value of
    WhatsRemoved.NextRecPtr, so that QueueOut then points to the next
    record after the one just removed. *)
```

These three operations are illustrated in Figure 16–13.

An additional procedure, to display the queue, is useful. Its definition is

```
PROCEDURE PrintQueue(QueueIn, QueueOut : POINTTOQUEUE)
 (* Print headings and call nested recursive procedure PrintQRecord-
    (QueueOut, QueueIn, QueueOut). Then print an empty record for
    location QueueIn. *)

    PROCEDURE PrintQRecord(WhereInQueue,QueueIn,QueueOut:POINTTOQUEUE)
      (* If WhereInQueue∧.NextRecPtr <> NIL, you are not past the
         last queue record; display fields of record at WhereInQueue.
         If WhereInQueue = QueueOut, display ''<-- QueueOut'' set
         pointer WhereInQueue = WhereInQueue∧.NextRecPtr recursive
         call PrintQRecord(WhereInQueue,QueueIn, QueueOut) *)
```

These declarations and procedures appear in DEFINITION and IMPLEMENTATION MODULE Dynamic in Appendix C. Study them carefully to discern how they work.

```
TYPE  POINTTOQUEUE = POINTER TO WHATSINQUEUE;
      WHATSINQUEUE = RECORD
                        definition of fields
                        NextRecPtr : POINTTOQUEUE;
                     END; (* RECORD *)
VAR  QueueIn, QueueOut : POINTTOQUEUE;
```

```
CreateQueue(VAR QueueIn, QueueOut : POINTTOQUEUE)
     ALLOCATE(QueueIn, SIZE(WHATSINQUEUE));
     QueueIn^.NextRecPtr := NIL;
     QueueOut := QueueIn;
```

Records of type WHATSINQUEUE

QueueIn and QueueOut   Address 1

QueueIn^.NextRecPtr
QueueOut^.NextRecPtr
$\downarrow$

Address 1 | no data here yet | NIL

(*continued*)

Figure 16–13
Illustration of CreateQueue

A Customer-Waiting Queue

This example illustrates the use of a queue to handle a list of waiting customers.

Example 16.3.1

Use a queue to keep track of waiting customers and to keep a running total of customers you have served.

Define the problem   Procedures CreateQueue, AddToQueue, RemoveFrom-Queue, and PrintQueue will be imported from module Dynamic to handle the customer records.

Develop a solution   To make the queue-handling procedures somewhat generic, the records to be stored in the queue will be defined with the character string field, REAL number field, and next record pointer field declared in DEFINITION MOD-ULE Dynamic (Appendix C). Examine the queue-handling procedures in module Dynamic carefully to convince yourself that they accomplish the tasks discussed in this section and illustrated in Figure 16–13. In PrintQueue, observe how the empty QueueIn/\ record is handled separately. Remove the indicated statements if your system does not support the display of pointers. Note how this code follows very closely that of the stack-handling procedures in Section 16.2.

Now you are ready to add and remove names to and from the queue and service your customers. As names are added in the Characters field, consecutive numbers—beginning with 0—will be recorded in the Number field to give you a running total of customers served.

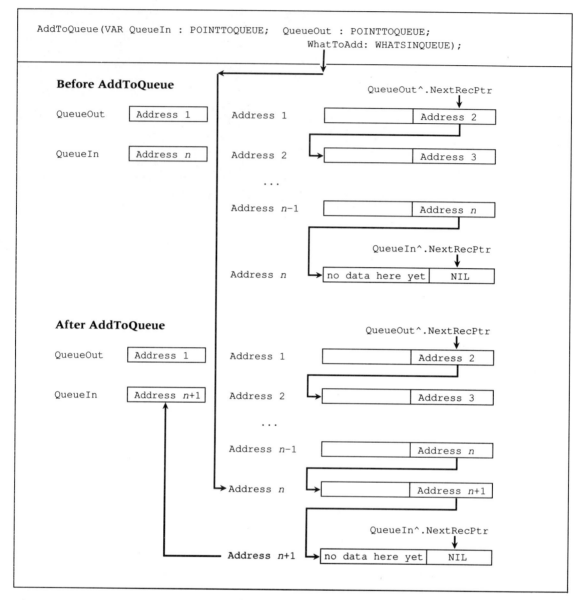

Figure 16–13 (continued)
Illustration of **RemoveFromQueue**

Refine the solution   *Pseudocode*

```
begin module CustomerQueue
    CreateQueue(ThisQIn, ThisQOut)
    repeat
        PresentMenu(Choice)
        case Choice of
            A : ask for name to add, AddToQueue(ThisQIn,ThisQOut,QRecord)
            R : if queue is not empty
                    RemoveFromQueue(ThisQIn, ThisQOut, QRecord)
                    print data removed
```

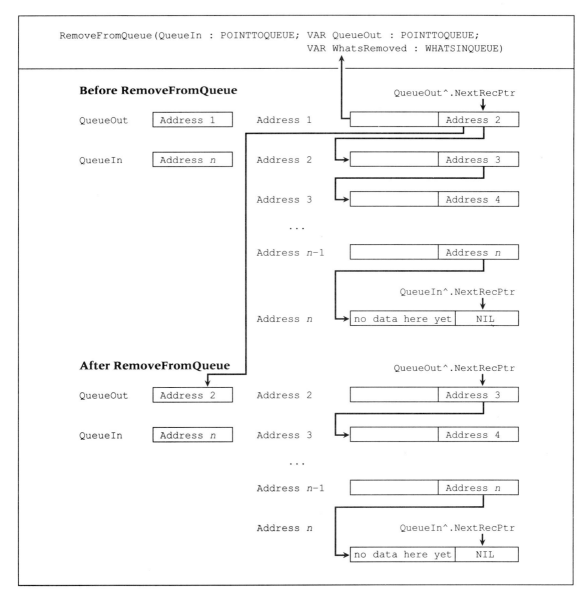

```
RemoveFromQueue(QueueIn : POINTTOQUEUE; VAR QueueOut : POINTTOQUEUE;
                          VAR WhatsRemoved : WHATSINQUEUE)
```

Figure 16–13 (continued)
Illustration of AddToQueue

```
        P : PrintQueue(ThisQIn, ThisQOut)
        S : no action
      until Choice IN {S}
end CustomerQueue

procedure PresentMenu(VAR Choose)
      present selections:   Add to Queue, Remove from Queue
                            Print the Queue, Stop
      repeat
        ask for Choice character
        convert to Choose in BASESET{A, R, P, S, Wrong}
      until Choose in {A, R, P, S}
```

Modula-2 code The queue is created first. Then a loop presents a menu that allows the user to select the operation he or she wants to perform, with the computer asking for data to be added to the queue and displaying the data removed. Sets are used to check for valid choices. The counting Number field is maintained by adding 1 to the current QueueIn/\.Number to get the next QueueIn/\.Number. A running variable OldNumber is used to accomplish this.

```
MODULE CustomerQueue;
  (* Stores customer names in a queue waiting list and keeps
     a running total of customers served.
     FileName:CH16D      Modula-2      RKW       July 1991  *)

FROM InOut IMPORT WriteString, WriteLn, Read, Write, ReadString;
FROM RealInOut IMPORT FWriteReal;
FROM Dynamic IMPORT POINTTOQUEUE, WHATSINQUEUE, CreateQueue,
                    AddToQueue, RemoveFromQueue, PrintQueue;

TYPE  BASESET = (A, R, P, S, Wrong);  CHOICESET = SET OF BASESET;
VAR  ThisQIn, ThisQOut : POINTTOQUEUE;
     QRecord : WHATSINQUEUE;   OldNumber : REAL;   Choice : BASESET;

PROCEDURE PresentMenu(VAR Choose : BASESET);
  VAR  Choice, Discard : CHAR;
  BEGIN
    WriteLn; WriteString("Would you like to"); WriteLn;
     WriteString("     A     Add to Queue"); WriteLn;
     WriteString("     R     Remove from Queue"); WriteLn;
     WriteString("     P     Print the Queue"); WriteLn;
     WriteString("     S     Stop"); WriteLn;
    REPEAT
       WriteString("Choose one (A, R, P, S): "); Read(Choice);
        Read(Discard); Write(Choice); WriteLn;
       CASE  CAP(Choice)  OF
            'A' : Choose := A |   'R' : Choose := R |
            'P' : Choose := P |   'S' : Choose := S;
           ELSE  Choose := Wrong; WriteString("Wrong Choice"); WriteLn;
        END; (* CASE *)
     UNTIL  Choose  IN  CHOICESET{A, R, P, S}; WriteLn;
  END PresentMenu;

BEGIN (* module CustomerQueue *)
   CreateQueue(ThisQIn, ThisQOut);    OldNumber := -1.0;

   REPEAT
     PresentMenu(Choice);

     CASE  Choice  OF
       A : WriteLn; WriteString("What name to add to queue? ");
            ReadString(QRecord.Characters);
            QRecord.Number := OldNumber+1.0;
            OldNumber := QRecord.Number;
            AddToQueue(ThisQIn, ThisQOut, QRecord)  |
        R : IF  ThisQIn = ThisQOut  THEN
              WriteString("EMPTY Queue.  No record to remove."); WriteLn;
```

```
        ELSE
            RemoveFromQueue(ThisQIn, ThisQOut, QRecord);
            WriteString("The data just removed is "); WriteLn;
             WriteString("QRecord.Characters: ");
             WriteString(QRecord.Characters);
             WriteString("      QRecord.Number:");
             FWriteReal(QRecord.Number, 8, 1); WriteLn;
         END  |  (* IF *)
      P : PrintQueue(ThisQIn, ThisQOut);
    END; (* CASE *)
  UNTIL  Choice  IN  CHOICESET{S};
END CustomerQueue.
```

Debug and test   Procedures CreateQueue, AddToQueue, RemoveFromQueue, and PrintQueue in module Dynamic will need to be debugged as a package so that each one can be used to test the others. Analyze and handcheck the algorithms carefully. Don't forget to increment and assign the running OldNumber count to the record Number field when calling AddToQueue. A sample run is shown in Figure 16–14.

Complete the documentation   Along with the problem definition, pseudocode, and code, the appropriate declarations and procedures from DEFINITION MODULE Dynamic should be included in the documentation. This will allow users to see the record and pointer declarations and the required parameters. The source code file is CH16D. Warn users that module Dynamic must be available when this program is compiled.

Questions 16.3

1. a. Draw a diagram illustrating a line of people waiting to buy theater tickets, where each person has a name and an amount of money for tickets.
   b. How would you modify the CustomerQueue program (CH16D) to keep track of these people?

⌐¬ A Bit of Background

Stacking the Deque

Stacks and queues are two special forms of a more general data structure called a *dequeue* or *deque* (pronounced "deck"). *DEQueue* stands for *Double-Ended Queue.*

In a deque structure, data is handled in one of four ways:

1. Insert at the end and remove from the beginning. This is the First In, First Out (FIFO) queue structure.
2. Insert at the beginning and remove from the end, which represents a type of inverted FIFO queue.
3. Insert at the end and remove from the end. This is the familiar Last In, First Out (LIFO) stack.

4. Insert at the beginning and remove from the beginning, also a LIFO technique.

Structures 1 and 3 are treated in this chapter; structures 2 and 4 sometimes are used for keeping track of memory addresses—such as when programming is done in machine language or when records are handled in a file. When a high-level language, such as Modula-2, manages the data area automatically, users may not be aware of where the data are being stored or of which type of deque is being applied.

Figure 16–14
A Sample Run of
CustomerQueue
(Example 16.3.1,
CH16D)

```
Ellipses (...) indicate where the menu would appear again.


Would you like to
     A       Add to Queue
     R       Remove from Queue
     P       Print to Queue
     S       Stop
Choose one (A, R, P, S): R

EMPTY Queue.  No record to remove.
     ...
Choose one (A, R, P, S): A
What name to add to queue? Williams
     ...
Choose one (A, R, P, S): A
What name to add to queue? Jones
     ...
Choose one (A, R, P, S): A
What name to add to queue? Smith
     ...
Choose one (A, R, P, S): P
Address   Characters        Number    NextRecPtr
   1007   Williams           0.00        1039    ←-- QueueOut
   1039   Jones              1.00        1071
   1071   Smith              2.00        1103
   1103                                   NIL    ←-- QueueIn

     ...
Choose one (A, R, P, S): R
The data just removed is
QRecord.Characters: Williams  QRecord.Number:      0.0

     ...
Choose one (A, R, P, S): P
Address   Characters        Number    NextRecPtr
   1039   Jones              1.00        1071    ←-- QueueOut
   1071   Smith              2.00        1103
   1103                                   NIL    ←-- QueueIn

     ...
Chose one (A, R, P, S): S
```

2. Add to program CustomerQueue (CH16D) a menu Choice to display only the records at QueueIn and QueueOut, and show how it could be implemented.

3. Show step-by-step how procedures AddToQueue and RemoveFromQueue (IMPLEMENTATION MODULE Dynamic) perform their operations on the queue displayed in Figure 16–14. Illustrate the queue and indicate the values of the variables at each important step in the procedures.

4. State whether a queue, a stack, or neither, would be appropriate for each of these lists. Indicate the reasons for your choice.

  a. A waiting list of customers to be seated in a restaurant.

  b. Names of students on a pile of papers to be graded. Each paper submitted goes on top of the pile, and papers are graded from the top down.

    c. Your address book, which you organize alphabetically by persons' last names and businesses' names.

    d. Patients admitted to a clinic and assigned to physicians on a first come, first served basis.

16.4 *Linked Lists*

Linked lists are data structures that encompass stacks and queues as special cases. A list of item records is often created and maintained in sorted order by some key field. In a linked list, a Start of List pointer keeps track of where the list begins, and a pointer in each record contains the address of the next record. This allows the records to be read in sequential order. The pointer in the last record has the value NIL.

When a record is added to a linked list, it is allocated a new space, and the pointers in the list are updated so that—when they are followed from record to record—the new record appears to be in a position determined by a prescribed order (such as alphabetically).

A deletion deallocates a space and changes the pointers so that the deleted record is no longer referenced. Figure 16–15 illustrates a list that is linked in alphabetical order by a Characters field. It shows the addition of one record to the list and deletion of another record.

The concept of a linked list can be extended to make a list readable in more than one order by linking different fields with multiple pointers. Also, more sophisticated operations on linked lists can be handled by adding dummy header and/or trailer records to the lists.

☐ Pointer Implementation of a Linked List

Assume that the linked list data structure looks like

```
TYPE   POINTTOLIST = POINTER TO WHATSINLIST;
       WHATSINLIST = RECORD
                        Characters : CHRARY;
                        Number : CARDINAL;
                        NextRecPtr : POINTTOLIST;
                END; (* RECORD WHATSINLIST *)
VAR   StartOfList, NewRecordPtr : POINTTOLIST;
```

Then the operations for handling a linked list are

```
PROCEDURE CreateLinkList(VAR StartOfList : POINTTOLIST)
 (* Define pointer StartOfList and assign it a value NIL. *)



PROCEDURE AddToLinkList(VAR StartOfList, AfterWhereToAdd : POINTTOLIST;
                             WhatToAdd : WHATSINLIST)
 (* If available, allocate a new location to a pointer NewSpacePtr.
    Insert new record into NewSpacePtr∧. Assign the pointer from the
    record that logically precedes NewSpacePtr∧ to NewSpacePtr∧.
    NextRecPtr. Assign the value NewSpacePtr to AfterWhereToAdd∧.
    NextRecPtr (the pointer field in the preceding record). *)

PROCEDURE DeleteFromLinkList(VAR StartOfList, AfterWhereToDelete,
                             WhereToDelete : POINTTOLIST)
```

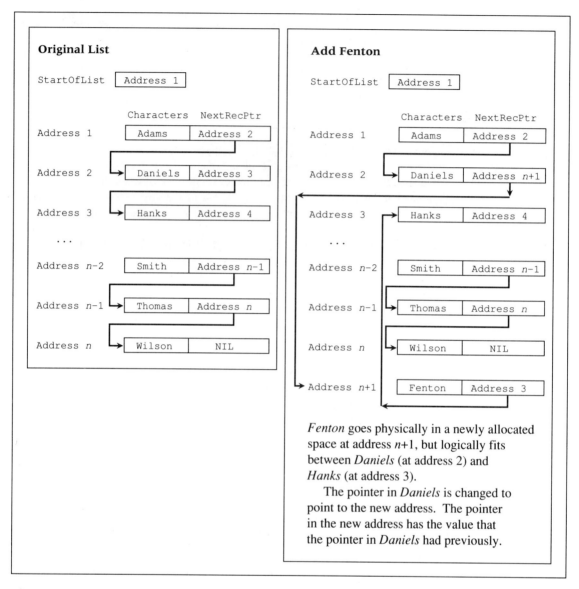

Fenton goes physically in a newly allocated space at address *n+1*, but logically fits between *Daniels* (at address 2) and *Hanks* (at address 3).

The pointer in *Daniels* is changed to point to the new address. The pointer in the new address has the value that the pointer in *Daniels* had previously.

Figure 16–15
A Linked List with Addition and Deletion *(continued)*

```
(* Assign the pointer from the record to be deleted to the pointer
   field in the logically preceding record (AfterWhereToDelete∧.
   NextRecPtr := WhereToDelete∧.NextRecPtr). Deallocate the space
   held by record WhereToDelete∧. If the first record is to be de-
   leted, then the StartOfList pointer is assigned the pointer value
   of the record that previously followed StartOfList. *)


PROCEDUREPrintLinkList(StartOfList : POINTTOLIST)
  (* Print headings and call nested procedure PrintLink-
     Record(StartOfList). *)

    PROCEDURE PrintLinkRecord(WhereInList : POINTTOLIST)
      (* If WhereInList = NIL, write ''End of Linked List''
```

Figure 16–15
(continued)

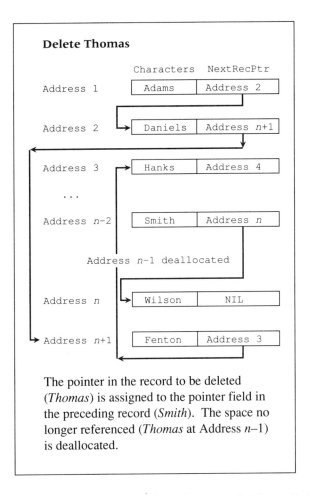

Delete Thomas

```
              Characters   NextRecPtr
Address 1      Adams       Address 2
Address 2      Daniels     Address n+1
Address 3      Hanks       Address 4
   ...
Address n-2    Smith       Address n

        Address n-1 deallocated

Address n      Wilson      NIL
Address n+1    Fenton      Address 3
```

The pointer in the record to be deleted
(*Thomas*) is assigned to the pointer field in
the preceding record (*Smith*). The space no
longer referenced (*Thomas* at Address *n*–1)
is deallocated.

```
else display fields of record WhereInList∧
if WhereInList = StartOfList, write ''StartOfList''
set pointer WhereInList = WhereInList∧.NextRecPtr
recursive call PrintLinkRecord(WhereInList) *)
```

These declarations and procedures appear in DEFINITION and IMPLEMENTA-
TION MODULE Dynamic in Appendix C. Study them carefully. Note their resem-
blance to the procedures developed for stacks and queues. Procedure AddToLink-
List wants an AfterWhereToAdd value of NIL if the new record is to be added at the
beginning of the list. Procedure DeleteFromLinkList wants an AfterWhereToDelete
value of NIL if the first record is to be deleted, and a WhereToDelete value of NIL
if the record is not in the list.

A Linked Inventory List

Here is an example that illustrates the use of a linked list to maintain inventory
records.

Example 16.4.1

Create a list of inventory items — each with an item name and a part number — that
is sorted by part number. Then add one item in the middle of the list, one at the
beginning, and one at the end. Remove an item from someplace in the list.

Define the problem A list of items is

Name	Part Number
Nut	102
Bolt	114
Screw	243
Pliers	483

Create a linked list of these items that is sorted in order of the given part numbers. Then add Hammer 198, Washer 97, and Clamp 502, linking them by pointers in order of part number. Finally, remove Bolt 114. Show the linked list.

Develop a solution The problem solution will be structured in terms of a menu that allows you to add to, delete from, or print a linked list or to stop. When adding to the list, the record to be added will be requested, and then a linear search on the Number field will find the position where the record should be added. Deleting from the list performs a search for the record to be deleted and then deletes the record. Adding and deleting records at the beginning of the list are treated as special situations.

Refine the solution *Pseudocode*

```
begin module LinkInventory
  CreateLinkList(ThisList)
  repeat
    PresentMenu(Choice)
    case Choice of
      A : ask for record to add(TempContent)
          AddItNow(ThisList, TempContent)
      D : ask which record to delete(TempContent)
          DeleteItNow(ThisList, TempContent)
      P : PrintLinkList(ThisList)
    end case
  until Choice IN {S}
end LinkInventory

procedure AddItNow(VAR StartOfList; WhatToAdd)
  if StartOfList = NIL (list empty)
  or    StartOfList∧.Number > number to add
  then the record goes at the beginning of the list,
    set Previous = NIL
  else
    initialize    LookAt to StartOfList
    repeat
      Previous = LookAt,    LookAt = Previous∧.NextRecPtr
    until    LookAt∧.Number > number to add
    or    end of list (LookAt = NIL)
  end if
  AddToLinkList(StartOfList, Previous, WhatToAdd)

procedure DeleteItNow(VAR StartOfList; WhatToDelete)
  if list is empty (StartOfList = NIL) or
  StartOfList∧.Number (contains WhatToDelete.Number) then
    delete first record, set Previous = NIL, LookAt = StartOfList
  else
    initialize LookAt to StartOfList
    repeat
```

```
                    Previous = LookAt, LookAt = Previous/\.NextRecPrt
                  until number is found or at end of the list
                  end if
                  DeleteFromLinkList(StartOfList, Previous, LookAt)

          procedure PresentMenu(VAR Choose)    (* see Example 16.3.1 *)
```

Modula-2 code In this code you search for the position at which to add or from which to delete, based upon the search key (the Number field). Examine the AddItNow and DeleteItNow procedures to see how they handle the special situations of adding and deleting at the beginning of the list.

```
MODULE LinkInventory;
    (* allows the user to create a linked list sorted by Number
       field and to add to and delete from the list.
       FileName:CH16E     Modula-2      RKW       July 1991   *)

FROM InOut IMPORT WriteString, WriteLn, ReadString, Read, Write;
FROM RealInOut IMPORT ReadReal;
FROM Dynamic IMPORT CreateLinkList, PrintLinkList, AddToLinkList,
                    DeleteFromLinkList, POINTTOLIST, WHATSINLIST;

TYPE  BASESET = (A, D, P, S, Wrong); CHOICESET = SET OF BASESET;
VAR   ThisList : POINTTOLIST;   TempContent : WHATSINLIST;
      Choice : BASESET;

PROCEDURE  AddItNow(VAR StartOfList:POINTTOLIST;  WhatToAdd:WHATSINLIST);
    VAR  Previous, LookAt : POINTTOLIST;
    BEGIN
        (* Linear search for Previous, after which new record will come. *)
        IF  (StartOfList = NIL)  OR ( (StartOfList # NIL) AND
                      (StartOfList^.Number > WhatToAdd.Number) )   THEN
             (* List is empty or new record goes at beginning. *)
            Previous := NIL;
        ELSE  (* New record goes somewhere other than at beginning. *)
            LookAt := StartOfList;
            REPEAT
                Previous := LookAt;  LookAt := Previous^.NextRecPtr;
                UNTIL (LookAt^.Number>WhatToAdd.Number) (*Nextrecord>WhatToAdd*)
                    OR (LookAt = NIL); (* New record goes at end of list. *)
        END; (* IF *)

        AddToLinkList(StartOfList, Previous, WhatToAdd);
    END AddItNow;

PROCEDURE DeleteItNow(VAR StartOfList : POINTTOLIST;
                                        WhatToDelete : WHATSINLIST);
    VAR  Previous, LookAt : POINTTOLIST;
    BEGIN
        IF (StartOfList = NIL) (* List is empty. *)  OR
           (ABS(StartOfList^.Number - WhatToDelete.Number) < 0.5)   THEN
           (*Delete 1st Rec>*)
            Previous := NIL;  LookAt := StartOfList;
        ELSE  (* Delete from somewhere other than first record. *)
            LookAt := StartOfList;
```

```
        REPEAT
            Previous := LookAt;  LookAt := Previous^.NextRecPtr;
        UNTIL (LookAt = NIL) (* End of list found. *) OR
            (ABS(LookAt^.Number - WhatToDelete.Number) < 0.5); (* found *)
    END;  (* IF *)

    DeleteFromLinkList(StartOfList, Previous, LookAt);
END DeleteItNow;

PROCEDURE PresentMenu(VAR Choose : BASESET);
  VAR  Choice, Discard: CHAR;
  BEGIN
    WriteLn; WriteString("What would you like to do?"); WriteLn;
      WriteString("     A      Add a Record to the List"); WriteLn;
      WriteString("     D      Delete a Record from the List");WriteLn;
      WriteString("     P      Print the Linked List"); WriteLn;
      WriteString("     S      Stop"); WriteLn;
    REPEAT
      WriteString("Choose one (A, D, P, S): "); Read(Choice);
       Read(Discard); Write(Choice); WriteLn;
      CASE  CAP(Choice)  OF
          'A' : Choose := A |    'D' : Choose := D |
          'P' : Choose := P |    'S' : Choose := S;
          ELSE  Choose := Wrong; WriteString("Wrong Choice"); WriteLn;
      END; (* CASE *)
    UNTIL  Choose IN CHOICESET{A, D, P, S};  WriteLn;
  END PresentMenu;


BEGIN  (* Module TestLink *)
   CreateLinkList(ThisList);

   REPEAT
     PresentMenu(Choice);

     CASE  Choice  OF
        A : WriteString("What record to add?"); WriteLn;
             WriteString("Item Name      : ");
             ReadString(TempContent.Characters); WriteLn;
             WriteString("Inventory Number: ");
             ReadReal(TempContent.Number); WriteLn;
             AddItNow(ThisList, TempContent)       |
        D : WriteString("What record to delete?");WriteLn;
             WriteString("Item Name      : ");
             ReadString(TempContent.Characters); WriteLn;
             WriteString("Inventory Number: ");
             ReadReal(TempContent.Number); WriteLn;
             DeleteItNow(ThisList, TempContent)     |
        P : PrintLinkList(ThisList);
     END; (* CASE *)
   UNTIL  Choice  IN  CHOICESET{S};
END LinkInventory.
```

Debug and test   Some of the Linked List handling procedures in the Dynamic
module are interdependent and would have to be debugged together so that each one
can be used to test the others. The logic of the AddItNow and DeleteItNow procedures should be checked carefully to make certain that the appropriate parameter

values are passed to procedures AddToLinkList and DeleteFromLinkList, especially when one (or more) of those parameters is (are) to have a NIL value.

The sample run requested in the problem definition is shown in Figure 16–16.

Complete the documentation   Include the stack-handling type and procedure declarations from DEFINITION MODULE Dynamic with the code, pseudocode, problem definition, and sample run. The users' manual should state the source code

Figure 16–16
A Sample Run of LinkInventory (Example 16.4.1, CH16E)
(*continued*)

```
Ellipses (...) indicate where the menu would appear again.

What would you like to do?
    A       Add a Record to the List
    D       Delete a Record from the List
    P       Print the Linked List
    S       Stop
Choose one (A, D, P, S): A

What record to add?
Item Name       : Nut
Inventory Number : 102
    ...
Choose one (A, D, P, S): A
What record to add?
Item Name       :Bolt
Inventory Number :114
    ...
Choose one (A, D, P, S): A
What record to add?
Item Name       : Screw
Inventory Number : 243
    ...
Choose one (A, D, P, S): A
What record to add?
Item Name       : Pliers
Inventory Number : 483
    ...
Choose one (A, D, P, S): P
Address   Characters          Number     NextRecPtr
    1090   Nut                 102            1114      StartOfList
    1114   Bolt                114            1138
    1138   Screw               243            1162
    1162   Pliers              483            NIL
End of Linked List

    ...
Choose one (A, D, P, S): A
What record to add?
Item Name       : Hammer
Inventory Number : 198
    ...
Choose one (A, D, P, S): A
What record to add?
Item Name       : Washer
Inventory Number : 97
```

Figure 16–16
(continued)

```
   ...
Choose one (A, D, P, S): A
What record to add?
Item Name       : Clamp
Inventory Number: 502
   ...
Choose one (A, D, P, S): P
Address   Characters          Number      NextRecPtr
   1210   Washer                  97            1090          StartOfList
   1090   Nut                    102            1114
   1114   Bolt                   114            1186
   1186   Hammer                 198            1138
   1138   Screw                  243            1162
   1162   Pliers                 483            1234
   1234   Clamp                  502             NIL
End of Linked List


   ...
Choose one (A, D, P, S): D
What record to delete?
Item Name       : Bolt
Inventory Number: 114
   ...
Choose one (A, D, P, S): P
Address  Characters           Number      NextRecPtr
   1210   Washer                  97            1090          StartOfList
   1090   Nut                    102            1186
   1186   Hammer                 198            1138
   1138   Screw                  243            1162
   1162   Pliers                 483            1234
   1234   Clamp                  502             NIL
End of Linked List


   ...
Choose one (A, D, P, S): S
```

A Bit of Background

Artificial Intelligence

One of the major steps toward creating dynamic machines that "learn" as they work is the development of dynamic data structures.

In 1950, Alan Turing proposed a test in which an expert enters questions at an isolated terminal. Presumably, artificial intelligence (AI) is achieved when the expert cannot discern whether the answers returned to the screen have been produced by a human or by a machine. Although there are problems with the Turing test, its concepts have spawned numerous research efforts.

By the mid 1960s, many AI researchers believed the efforts to create "thinking machines" were futile. Today, however, much lively research and development is focused on such topics as dynamic problem solving, computer vision, robotics, natural language processing, speech and pattern recognition, and neural networks—all of which are encompassed within the field of artificial intelligence.

Development of techniques that allow machines to emulate humans have proliferated in recent years with the development of computers that are smaller, faster, more powerful, and less expensive. Most people agree that computers could never replace all human decision making. There is also general agreement that society must remain alert and remain in control of important decisions that require human compassion, ethics, and understanding.

location (CH16E). Warn users that the Dynamic module must be available when the program is compiled. When adding or deleting a record, this program checks only the Number field.

---

1. **a.** Draw a diagram illustrating a linked alphabetized list of credit union customers. Each customer has a name and a savings account balance.
   b. How would you modify the LinkInventory program (CH16E) to keep track of these customers?
2. Add to program LinkInventory (CH16E) a menu Choice to find and display a single record in the list, given either the Item Name or the Inventory Number.
3. Show step-by-step how procedures AddToLinkList and DeleteFromLinkList (IMPLEMENTATION MODULE Dynamic) perform their operations on the longest list displayed in Figure 16–16. Consider situations of adding and deleting at the beginning, the middle, and the end of the list. Illustrate the list and indicate the values of the variables at each important step in the procedures.
4. State whether a linked list, a queue, or a stack would be the best structure for each of the following. Give reasons for your choice.
   a. An alphabetized list of skis, by brand name, and how many are on hand each morning at a ski rental shop.
   b. The color and diameter of plastic rings on a vertical peg set in concrete.
   c. The names of passengers waiting in line to board an airplane.
   d. A program that builds an index for a book. The indexer adds topics and page numbers as they are encountered while reading the book, and the index is printed in alphabetical order.

16.5   *Information Hiding and Opaque Data Types*

The principle of **information hiding** declares that information not necessary for users to know may be hidden from their view. For example, when you use a REAL variable you need not know how REAL numbers are represented and handled internally by the computer.

In Modula-2, information with which users need not be concerned may be hidden in external modules. In some previous examples, details of procedures have been concealed in IMPLEMENTATION modules, but data type declarations have not been quite so well hidden in the DEFINITION module.

Opaque Pointer Types

When an exportable pointer type is defined in an IMPLEMENTATION module, it is said to be **opaque.** In the DEFINITION module, only the name of an opaque data type is declared. Generally, Modula-2 limits opaque types to pointers. A program module may import opaque types and declare variables of those types.

Operations on Opaque Types

The only operations that can be performed by a program on variables of an imported opaque type are assignment, tests for equality, and those defined by the procedures in the IMPLEMENTATION module from which the type was imported.

Figure 16–17 shows the syntax for declaring an opaque type. A module may contain definitions of many opaque pointer types.

▢ Opaque Type SPACEPT

This problem allows users to add points in three-dimensional space without having to know the details about how those points are defined or manipulated.

Example 16.5.1

Write a program to read points in space, add them, and display the sum.

Define the problem   Users will be asked to enter x, y, and z coordinates of two points. The points will be added and the coordinates of the sum will be displayed. The SPACEPT data type and the procedures to operate on variables of that type will be opaque.

Develop a solution   Figure 16–18 reveals DEFINITION and IMPLEMENTATION MODULE Threes. In the DEFINITION module, only the name of TYPE SPACEPT is declared, along with the headings of the PROCEDUREs. This information should be all that a programmer needs to know to solve the problem.

The program will

- allocate space for two points and the sum
- ask for the two points to be entered from the keyboard
- calculate the sum
- display the two points and their sum.

Figure 16–17
DEFINITION and IMPLEMENTATION Module Syntax for Declaring an Opaque Pointer Type

```
DEFINITION MODULE ModuleName;

    TYPE  OpaquePointerTypeIdentifier;

    (* headings of PROCEDURES defined in IMPLEMENTATION module *)
    ...
END ModuleName.
```

```
IMPLEMENTATION MODULE ModuleName;
    (* IMPORT lists *)

    TYPE  OpaquePointerTypeIdentifier = POINTER TO ...
            (* Ellipses (...) indicate another TYPE definition,
               such as a RECORD, to which
               OpaquePointerTypeIdentifier points. *)

    (* PROCEDURE definitions *)
    ...
END ModuleName.
```

```
DEFINITION MODULE Threes;

TYPE  SPACEPT; (*A pointer TYPE describing 3-D space coordinates.*)

PROCEDURE AllocateSpace(VAR Where : SPACEPT);
   (* Allocates space for a SPACEPT type variable. *)

PROCEDURE ReadSpacePt(VAR Coords : SPACEPT);
   (* Reads x, y, and z coordinates of a point in space. *)

PROCEDURE SpaceAdd(Coords1, Coords2 : SPACEPT; VAR Sum : SPACEPT);
   (* Adds:  Sum = Coords1 + Coords 2 *)

PROCEDURE DisplaySpace(Coords : SPACEPT);
   (* Display x, y, and z coordinates of a point in space. *)

END Threes.
```

```
IMPLEMENTATION MODULE Threes;

FROM InOut IMPORT WriteString, WriteLn;
FROM RealInOut IMPORT ReadReal, FWriteReal;
FROM Storage IMPORT ALLOCATE;
(* Import SIZE or TSIZE from SYSTEM if necessary. *)

TYPE  SPACEREC = RECORD
                    x, y, z : REAL;
                 END; (* RECORD *)
      SPACEPT = POINTER TO SPACEREC;

PROCEDURE AllocateSpace(VAR Where : SPACEPT);
   (* Allocates space for a SPACEPT type variable. *)
   BEGIN
      ALLOCATE(Where, SIZE(SPACEREC));
   END AllocateSpace;

PROCEDURE ReadSpacePt(VAR Coords : SPACEPT);
   (* Reads x, y, and z coordinates of a point in space. *)
   BEGIN
      WriteString("Enter coordinates of a point in space:");
      WriteLn;
      WriteString("x = "); ReadReal(Coords^.x);
      WriteString("    y = "); ReadReal(Coords^.y);
      WriteString("    z = "); ReadReal(Coords^.z); WriteLn;
   END ReadSpacePt;

PROCEDURE SpaceAdd(Coords1, Coords2 : SPACEPT;  VAR Sum : SPACEPT);
   (* Adds:  Sum = Coords1 + Coords2 *)
   BEGIN
      Sum^.x := Coords1^.x + Coords2^.x;
      Sum^.y := Coords1^.y + Coords2^.y;
      Sum^.z := Coords1^.z + Coords2^.z;
   END SpaceAdd;

PROCEDURE DisplaySpace(Coords : SPACEPT);
   (* Display x, y, and z coordinates of a point in space. *)
   BEGIN
      WriteString("("); FWriteReal(Coords^.x, 8, 2);
      FWriteReal(Coords^.y, 8, 2);
      FWriteReal(Coords^.z, 8, 2); WriteString(" )");
   END DisplaySpace;

END Threes.
```

Refine the solution *Pseudocode*

```
begin module AddInSpace
     AllocateSpace for Place1, Place2, and Total
     ReadSpace for Place1 and Place2
     SpaceAdd(Place1, Place2, Total)
     DisplaySpace for Place1, Place2, and Total
end AddInSpace
```

Modula-2 code

```
MODULE  AddInSpace;
   (* Uses opaque type SPACEPT and adds points in space.
      FileName:CH16G      Modula-2     RKW       July 1991  *)

FROM InOut IMPORT WriteString, WriteLn;
FROM Threes IMPORT SPACEPT, ReadSpacePt, SpaceAdd,
                   DisplaySpace, AllocateSpace;

VAR  Place1, Place2, Total : SPACEPT;

BEGIN
   AllocateSpace(Place1); AllocateSpace(Place2); AllocateSpace(Total);

   WriteString("For Point 1:"); WriteLn;
    ReadSpacePt(Place1); WriteLn; WriteLn;
   WriteString("For Point 2:"); WriteLn;
    ReadSpacePt(Place2); WriteLn; WriteLn;

   SpaceAdd(Place1, Place2, Total);

   WriteString("Place 1 = "); DisplaySpace(Place1); WriteLn;
   WriteString("Place 2 = "); DisplaySpace(Place2); WriteLn;
   WriteString("Sum     = "); DisplaySpace(Total);  WriteLn;
END AddInSpace.
```

Debug and test Note that *all* operations on variables of opaque type SPACEPT are performed by procedures imported from module Threes. The *only* other operations the program module could perform on those variables would be assignment, such as

```
Place2 := Place1;
```

or tests for equality, such as

```
IF  Place1 = Place2  THEN. . . .
```

Here is a sample run:

```
For Point 1:
Enter coordinates of a point in space:
x = -34.5      y = 8.25      z = 163.68


For Point 2:
Enter coordinates of a point in space:
x = 4.08      y = 37.12      z = -9.08
```

```
Place 1 = (  -34.50     8.25   163.68 )
Place 2 = (    4.08    37.12    -9.08 )
Sum     = (  -30.42    45.37   154.60 )
```

Complete the documentation Documentation should include the problem definition, pseudocode, code, sample run, and DEFINITION MODULE Threes, but probably *not* IMPLEMENTATION MODULE Threes. In the users' manual, source code location (CH16G) should be followed by instructions to enter *x, y,* and *z* coordinates of two points when requested and wait for results to be displayed.

Questions 16.5

1. Regarding program AddInSpace (Example 16.5.1, CH16G),
   a. what would happen if you tried to execute

   `ALLOCATE(Place1, SIZE(SPACEPT))?`

   b. What would happen if you did not execute AllocateSpace(Place1)?
   c. Could you execute the command Place2∧.y := Place1∧.x? Why or why not?
   d. Add the capability of finding the difference $(x1 - x2, y1 - y2, z1 - z2)$ between points $(x1, y1, z1)$ and $(x2, y2, z2)$.
   e. Add the capability of finding the scalar product $(x1 * x2) + (y1 * y2) + (z1 * z2)$. *Hint:* You may want to define a new type, since the scalar product is a single REAL value.

2. **a.** In a DEFINITION and IMPLEMENTATION module, define an opaque data type that points to SOCKS = (Brown, Black, Blue, Argyle) and a procedure for choosing two socks at random.
   b. Write a program to choose two socks from a drawer in the dark and tell whether they match or not.
   c. Create and examine numerous lists of at least ten socks chosen at random from the drawer. Determine the minimum number of socks you would need to take from the drawer to be absolutely certain that two of them will match.

16.6 *Focus on Problem Solving*

In some dynamic data structures each record has multiple pointers. One of these is the tree structure, in which any record can point to any number of records at another level. This section centers on the special class of **binary trees,** in which no record has more than two pointers. You will develop procedures to create and search an ordered binary tree.

Binary Trees

A common example of a binary tree is a notification structure — sometimes called a *telephone tree* — by which the head of an organization assigns each member to telephone two others when a message must be spread quickly. Such a tree is shown in Figure 16–19.

All binary trees have a **root node** to which no other records point; the root is Jean Kent in Figure 16–19. In computer science, structure trees are usually shown growing downward from the root.

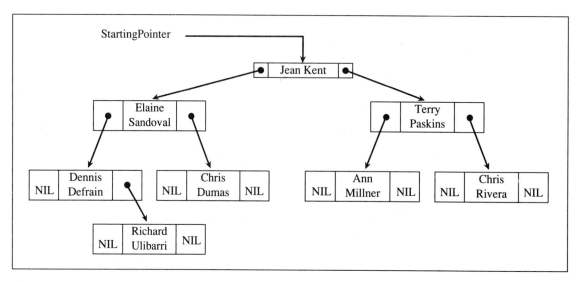

Figure 16–19
A Notification Tree

A "starting pointer" points to the root record space. Other than the root, every entry in the tree is called an **internal node** and is pointed to by its **parent node.** Each node record has two pointer fields—which we will call *LeftPtr* and *RightPtr*— that point to the node's **descendants.** Some pointer fields contain the value NIL to indicate that these branches of the tree extend no further.

Each internal node in a binary tree defines a subtree consisting of that node and all of its descendants. If a node has no descendants, its left and right pointers are both NIL, and it is called a **leaf node;** its subtree is said to be empty.

Creating an Ordered Binary Tree

One critical application of the binary tree structure is creating and searching an ordered tree. The following example places items on a binary tree and retrieves them in sorted order.

Example 16.6.1

Use a binary tree to sort records from an input file. Then write them in sorted order to an output file.

Define the problem An input file contains the names of subatomic particles and their masses at rest.

```
Photon          0
Electron        0.511
Pion+         139.6
Neutrino        0
Proton        938.3
KMeson+       493.7
EtaMeson      548.8
Muon          105.7
```

```
Neutron        939.6
Lambda         1116
Sigma-         1197
Xi0            1315
Xi-            1321
Omega          1672
```

Read the records one by one and store them on a binary tree in sorted order alphabetically by particle name. That is, if a name is greater than (comes alphabetically after) the previous name, store it on the right branch; if it is alphabetically smaller, store it on the left. Read these records from the tree in order from smallest to largest, and write the records into a new, sorted file.

For example, referring to the input file list, begin by storing *Photon* as the root of the tree. Then store *Electron* (< *Photon*) pointed to by the LeftPtr of the *Photon* record. Store *Pion+* (> *Photon*) pointed to by the RightPtr of *Photon*, as shown in Figure 16–20. Now read *Neutrino* from the file. *Neutrino* is less than *Photon*, so it should be stored to *Photon*'s left, but that pointer is already assigned to *Electron*; so a recursive call to the procedure to store the record looks at *Photon*'s left descendent, *Electron*. *Neutrino* is greater than *Electron*, so *Electron*'s RightPtr will point to *Neutrino*. As each record is added as a node to the tree, its own pointers are assigned the value NIL as a signal that, as yet, that branch extends no further.

To read the tree and write to disk, begin with the root and follow left pointers until a LeftPtr value NIL is reached. Read this record and write to the file. In the partial tree of Figure 16–20, this would be the record *Electron*. Examine the RightPtr of *Electron*, follow to *Neutrino*, then left to *KMeson+*, which has a NIL LeftPtr; so *KMeson+* is next written to the file. *KMeson+* has a NIL RightPtr as well, so *Neutrino* becomes the next record written, and then *Photon*, then *Pion+*, and *Proton*.

For a list of *N* items, this search requires $O(\log_2 N)$ reads if there are equal numbers of nodes on left and right branches; that is, if the tree is "balanced." If the order of the input file happened to be alphabetical to start with, you would get a one-sided tree, and the search would become an $O(N)$ linear search. There are algorithms for balancing trees to restore the efficiency.

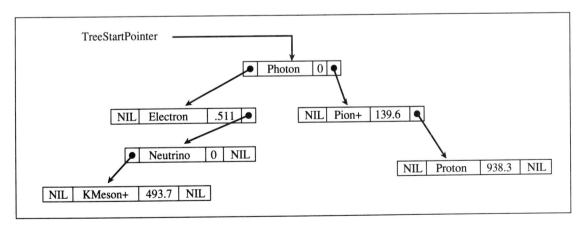

Figure 16–20
Sorted Particle Tree (Example 16.6.1)

Develop a solution The particle record data structure will appear as

```
TYPE    TREEPOINTER       = POINTER TO PARTICLERECORD;
        PARTICLERECORD    = RECORD
                                Name : ARRAY [0..9] OF CHAR;
                                Mass : REAL;
                                LeftPtr, RightPtr : TREEPOINTER;
                                END; (* RECORD PARTICLERECORD *)
VAR     TreeStartPointer : TREEPOINTER;
```

Three procedures are needed:

- FillTheTree(VAR TreeStartPointer : TREEPOINTER)
    (* Reads records from the file and builds a sorted binary tree. *)
- AddToTree(VAR WhereOnTree:TREEPOINTER; Particle:PARTICLERECORD)
    (* A recursive procedure that adds a single particle record to the tree. *)
- ReadTheTree(WhereOnTree:TREEPOINTER)
    (* A recursive procedure that reads records in order from the tree and writes them to a file. *)

Figure 16–21 is a structure chart of the problem solution.

Figure 16–21
Structure Chart for TreeSortParticle (Example 16.6.1)

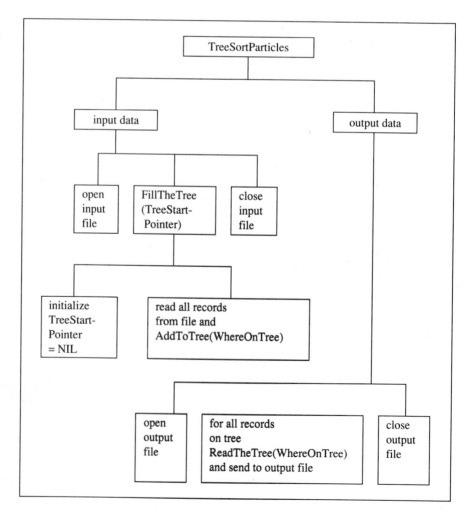

Refine the solution   *Pseudocode*

```
begin module TreeSortParticles
    open input file,    FillTheTree(TreeStartPointer), close input file
    open output file, ReadTheTree(TreeStartPointer), close output file
end TreeSortParticles


procedure AddToTree(VAR WhereOnTree; Particle)
    if WhereOnTree # NIL (* Pointer not NIL, try next location. *)
        if    Particle.Name < WhereOnTree∧.Name then
            (* recursive call to the left subtree *) AddToTree(WhereOnTree∧.LeftPtr, Particle)
        else    (* recursive call to the right subtree *) AddToTree(WhereOnTree∧.RightPtr, Particle)
        end if
    else    (* Extend branch, assign values to new space. *)
        ALLOCATE ParticleRecord space
        assign values to the space, set Left and Right pointers to NIL


procedure FillTheTree(VAR TreeStartPointer)
    initialize    TreeStartPointer = NIL
        (* Create tree by defining TreeStartPointer. *)
    for all records
        read a record from file
        AddToTree(TreeStartPointer, Particle)
            (* For each record, begin search again at root node. *)


procedure ReadTheTree(WhereOnTree)
    (* If WhereOnTree = NIL, do nothing; search has ended on that branch. *)
    if    WhereOnTree # NIL    (* Search the left subtree first. *)
        ReadTheTree(WhereOnTree∧.LeftPtr)
        write record Particle to the output file
            (* Keep moving through left subtrees until LeftPtr = NIL, then write the latest record value
                and back out of recursion to previous value. *)
        ReadTheTree(WhereOnTree∧.RightPtr)
            (* Search the right subtree.   Remember at each call of ReadTheTree, at each level, the
                left subtree gets searched before you reach here.   Eventually the right pointer will be
                NIL, so you will back out recursively and write previous values. *)
```

Modula-2 code   The apparently simple recursive structure of this program (Fill-TheTree, then ReadTheTree) is designed to accomplish a sophisticated task. This is because tree operations to "do something" to each node on a tree are defined recursively as

`DoSomething(LeftSubtree); Process(Root); DoSomething(RightSubtree);`

You can accomplish this nonrecursively, but you would have to work hard to get the code right.

Procedure FillTheTree reads the records from the file and adds them to the tree by calling recursive procedure AddToTree. AddToTree checks to see whether a record is at the end of a branch (pointer WhereOnTree = NIL). If not, the left or right subtree is called, depending upon where the new record should be stored. Otherwise, the branch is extended, and the record is stored.

Similarly, ReadTheTree searches the left branch until the end of a branch is reached and then writes that record to the file. After a left branch has been exhausted (at each recursive level), the corresponding right branch is examined.

```
MODULE TreeSortParticles;
   (* Performs a binary tree sort of records of data on elementary
      particles read from an input file.  Writes the data to an output
      file sorted alphabetically by particle name.
      FileName:CH16F        Modula-2      RKW        July 1991   *)

FROM InOut IMPORT WriteString, ReadString, WriteLn,
                  OpenInput, CloseInput, OpenOutput, CloseOutput;
FROM RealInOut IMPORT ReadReal, FWriteReal;
FROM Strings IMPORT CompareStrings, Length, TabOrFill;
FROM Storage IMPORT ALLOCATE, DEALLOCATE;
(* If your system requires the use of TSIZE rather than SIZE
   to determine size of a type, then   FROM SYSTEM IMPORT TSIZE;
   and replace SIZE by TSIZE in the ALLOCATE instruction below. *)

CONST  NUMPARTICLES = 14;  NAMLEN = 9;  Blank = ' ';
TYPE   NAMARY = ARRAY [0..NAMLEN] OF CHAR;
       TREEPOINTER = POINTER TO PARTICLERECORD;
       PARTICLERECORD = RECORD
                             Name : NAMARY;  Mass : REAL;
                             LeftPtr, RightPtr : TREEPOINTER;
                        END; (* RECORD *)
VAR   TreeStartPointer : TREEPOINTER;

PROCEDURE  AddToTree(VAR WhereOnTree:TREEPOINTER; Particle:PARTICLERECORD);
   BEGIN
      IF  WhereOnTree # NIL  THEN  (* Try appropriate branch. *)
         IF CompareStrings(Particle.Name, WhereOnTree^.Name)<0 THEN
            (* Recursive call to left subtree. *)
            AddToTree(WhereOnTree^.LeftPtr, Particle);
         ELSE
            (* Recursive call to right subtree. *)
            AddToTree(WhereOnTree^.RightPtr, Particle);
         END; (* IF *)

      ELSE  (* Extend branch, assign values & NIL pointers. *)
         ALLOCATE(WhereOnTree, SIZE(PARTICLERECORD));
         WhereOnTree^.Name := Particle.Name;
         WhereOnTree^.Mass := Particle.Mass;
         WhereOnTree^.LeftPtr := NIL;  WhereOnTree^.RightPtr := NIL;
      END; (* IF *)
   END AddToTree;

PROCEDURE FillTheTree(VAR TreeStartPointer: TREEPOINTER);
   VAR  Particle : PARTICLERECORD;  WhichParticle : CARDINAL;
   BEGIN
      TreeStartPointer := NIL;  (* Create tree. *)

      (* Read records from the file. *)
      FOR  WhichParticle := 1 TO NUMPARTICLES  DO
         ReadString(Particle.Name);  ReadReal(Particle.Mass);
         (* Insert record into the tree. *)
         AddToTree(TreeStartPointer, Particle);
      END; (* FOR *)
   END FillTheTree;
```

```
PROCEDURE  ReadTheTree(WhereOnTree:  TREEPOINTER);
   BEGIN
      IF   WhereOnTree # NIL   THEN    (* Search subtree. *)
         (* Recursive call to left subtree. *)
         ReadTheTree(WhereOnTree^.LeftPtr);
         (* When pointer = NIL, at a subtree root, write root record.*)
         WriteString(WhereOnTree^.Name);
          TabOrFill(NAMLEN+2-Length(WhereOnTree^.Name), Blank);
         FWriteReal(WhereOnTree^.Mass, 10, 3); WriteLn;

         (* After left subtree, read the right subtree. *)
         ReadTheTree(WhereOnTree^.RightPtr);
      END; (* IF *)
   END ReadTheTree;

BEGIN (* module TreeSortParticles *)
   WriteString("Input file name(PARTICLE.IN) = ? ");   OpenInput("IN");
    FillTheTree(TreeStartPointer);                      CloseInput;

   WriteString("Output file name(PARTICLE.OUT) = ? "); OpenOutput("OUT");
    ReadTheTree(TreeStartPointer);                      CloseOutput;
END TreeSortParticles.
```

Debug and test   To see that records are read correctly from the input file, it could be helpful to IMPORT Terminal and perform a Terminal.WriteString(Particle.Name) in procedure FillTheTree just before the AddToTree call. Similarly, inserting commands to display the records and pointers at each recursive call of AddToTree in the procedure AddToTree, *and* at each recursive call of ReadTheTree in procedure ReadTheTree, would allow you to see each step of the insert and recover processes. However, you would need to create a procedure (similar to those in Example 14.1.1) to write REAL masses to the terminal.

For the PARTICLE.IN input file that appears in the ''Define the Problem'' subsection, a sample run of the program looks like

```
Input file name(PARTICLE.IN) = ? PARTICLE.IN
Output file name(PARTICLE.OUT = ? PARTICLE.OUT
```

and a display of the output file PARTICLE.OUT is

```
Input file name(PARTICLE.IN) = ? PARTICLE.IN
Output file name(PARTICLE.OUT = ? PARTICLE.OUT
```

and a display of the output file PARTICLE.OUT is

```
Electron       0.511
EtaMeson     548.800
KMeson+      493.700
Lambda      1116.000
Muon         105.700
Neutrino       0.000
Neutron      939.600
Omega       1672.000
```

```
Photon          0.000
Pion+         139.600
Proton        938.300
Sigma-       1197.000
Xi-          1321.000
Xi0          1315.000
```

which shows that the program has produced the desired results.

Complete the documentation Since this problem is designed to illustrate creation of an ordered binary tree, the problem definition should be supplemented with the explanation of binary trees from the beginning of this section or one that you write. The structure chart, pseudocode, code, and sample run will complete the illustration of how the program works. The users' manual should specify the source code location, CH16F. Warn users that the CompareStrings, TabOrFill, and Length from Strings, ALLOCATE AND DEALLOCATE from Storage, and possibly SIZE or TSIZE from SYSTEM should be available when the program is compiled. Interaction of the user with the program requires only that the input and output file names be specified at runtime. Of course, the input file should have been created in advance. Results are seen in the output file.

Questions 16.6

1. On paper, by hand, complete the binary tree of Figure 16–20 by adding the remaining records one at a time from the PARTICLE.IN file.
2. Draw a diagram to trace the operation of procedure ReadTheTree (Example 16.6.1, CH16F) on the tree you completed in question 1.
3. Algebraic expressions can be represented on a binary tree where each operator node points left and right to its operands. The values become leaves on the tree. Such a tree for $(9 * 2) - 3$ is shown in Figure 16–22. Show how you could construct such a tree for the calculation $(21/7 + 6) * (4 - 8)$. Then illustrate how you would traverse the tree to perform the calculation. *Hint:* Draw the tree from the bottom up.

16.7 *Summary*

Pointers A pointer, such as PointerName, identifies a memory location that contains the address of an anonymous variable. The anonymous variable is accessed as the *referent* of the pointer, indicated by PointerName$\wedge$.

Allocate Pointers are dynamic. A program can ALLOCATE and DEALLOCATE space for a pointer and its referent so that the memory used can grow or diminish as needed during program execution.

Pointer Values Although you may assign values to a pointer *referent* (such as Pntr1$\wedge := -17$), the only values you may assign to a pointer itself are NIL and the value of another pointer (Pntr2 := Pntr1). You can display *referent values* with the appropriate Write... command, but only some versions of Modula-2 allow you to display the pointer-address value with a command such as WriteCard(VAL(CARDINAL, Pntr1), 6).

Stacks A stack is a Last In, First Out (LIFO) list of items. A new item is PUSHed onto a stack, and the item at the top of the stack is POPped from the stack.

Figure 16–22
A Tree for
Algebraic
Expression
(9 * 2) − 3 (Section
16.6, Question 3)

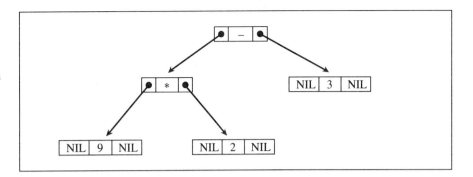

An implementation of stacks with pointers creates a dynamic data structure. Procedures to CreateStack, PUSH, POP, and PrintStack are found in external module Dynamic in Appendix C.

Queues   A queue is a First In, First Out (FIFO) list of items. Queues are useful for maintaining first-come, first-served lists. Implementation of a queue involves maintaining QueueIn, which points to where the next item will be added, and QueueOut, which points to the next item to be removed. Queue-handling procedures CreateQueue, AddToQueue, RemoveFromQueue, and PrintQueue are found in module Dynamic in Appendix C.

Linked Lists   In a linked list, each item points to the next item, thus defining a logical order in which the items are accessed. Adding and deleting items to and from a linked list is accomplished by reassigning pointers, as implemented in Example 16.4.1.

Opaque Data Types   The details of a pointer type can be made *opaque* to the programmer by defining the type within an external IMPLEMENTATION module and only naming it in the corresponding DEFINITION module. The only operations available on an opaque pointer-type variable are assignment, tests for equality, and those defined by the procedures in the IMPLEMEN-TATION module.

Binary Trees   Pointers and recursion are especially effective for implementing sophisticated tree structures in a reasonably noncomplicated manner. Binary trees, in which each node has at most two descendants, are useful for creating and searching ordered lists.

16.8   *Exercises*

Exercises marked with (FileName:_____) indicate those that ask you to use, modify or extend the text examples. The numbers in brackets, [ ], indicate the section that contains the material you need in order to complete the exercise.

1. [16.1] (FileName:CH16A) Extend program AddWithPointers to perform subtraction, multiplication, and division operations, storing the difference, product, and quotient in separate pointer-referenced locations.

2. [16.1] Write a program that asks for two lowercase characters and stores them in separate pointer-referenced locations. Then capitalize the characters and store the capital letters in pointer-referenced locations. Concatenate all four

characters into a string that is stored in a fifth pointer-referenced location. Display the contents of all five locations.

3. [16.1] Define an array of pointers

```
TYPE  PointToIt = POINTER TO CARDINAL;
VAR  ListOfPointers : ARRAY [1..10] OF PointToIt;
```

Read ten numbers into the individual locations referenced by the pointers. That is,

```
ListOfPointers[1]∧  contains the first number,
ListOfPointers[2]∧  contains the second number, etc.
```

Now add all of the numbers and store the result in a pointer-referenced location. Display the contents of all of the locations. *Hint:* Remember to ALLOCATE space for the values.

4. [16.2] Write a program that includes PUSH and POP procedures to simulate a stack of REAL numbers using an array. *Hint:* Let the array type be [1..HOW-MANYMAX] OF REAL, and let the TopOfStack indicator be the index of the item placed in the array last. TopOfStack = 0 when the array is empty.

5. [16.2] (FileName:CH16B) Using program StackCharacterHandler as your guide, implement a stack that represents an "in box" on your desk, where the Characters field is used to describe the task to be done. The Number field contains a time stamp of when the job arrived; for example, 820 and 1315 would represent 8:20 A.M. and 1:15 P.M., respectively. Your secretary fills the box with a number of tasks when the mail arrives in the morning and adds work periodically. You work continuously, all day long, to POP the tasks from the stack and take care of them. When the stack is empty you may go home.

6. A group of people have arrived at a bus stop and are lined up in the order indicated:

1. Chaplin	4. Laurel	7. Olivier	10. Garland
2. West	5. Hardy	8. Wayne	
3. Taylor	6. Burton	9. Stewart	

a. [16.2] Read the names from an input file into a stack and display the order in which they board the bus when the bus stops at the end of the line.

b. [16.3] Read the names into a queue and display the order in which they board the bus when the bus stops at the front of the line.

7. [16.2] Write a single-line word processor. As characters are typed they are PUSHed onto a stack. Some characters have special meanings:

#	Erase the previous character. (POP it from the stack.)
@	Kill the entire line. (Empty the stack.)
?!. or Enter	Terminate line entry. (Move the stack characters to an array, and write the array in appropriate order to an output file.)

8. [16.2] (FileName:CH9J) In recursive procedures, the parameters usually are stored on a stack. The recursive procedure in the factorial program developed in Example 9.5.1 was written

```
PROCEDURE RecurFact(n : CARDINAL): CARDINAL;
  VAR  Factorial : CARDINAL;
  BEGIN
    IF  n = 0  THEN
      Factorial := 1;
```

```
    ELSE
        Factorial := n * RecurFact(n-1);
    END; (* IF *)
    RETURN Factorial;
END RecurFact;
```

The successive values of parameter *n* are stored on a stack. For example, if the initial call were Value := RecurFact(5), then 5 would be PUSHed onto the stack for *n*. Then the first call to RecurFact($n-1$) would PUSH 4, the next call would PUSH 3, and so on, until the value of the parameter equals 0. Then the values would be popped one at a time and multiplied by the previous Product until the stack is empty.

Write a program, using a stack, that performs the same operation as the RecurFact procedure for a given value of *n*, entered by the user at the keyboard. After each PUSH, the contents of the stack should be displayed. After each POP, the contents of the stack and the value of Factorial should be displayed.

9. [16.2] (FileName:CH16C) In the StackArithmetic module (Example 16.2.1),

   a. Implement a StackInterchange procedure. StackInterchange should POP the top two elements from the stack and PUSH them back onto the stack in the opposite order.

   b. Implement a StackDivide procedure. StackDivide should POP the top element *x* from the stack, take its reciprocal, $1/x$, and PUSH the reciprocal back onto the stack. Then StackMultiply is called. That is, $y/x = y * (1/x)$. To avoid trying to perform division by zero, check for $x = 0$. Test your new module by performing the operations $(3 + 5)/2$ and $(2/(3 + 5)) * (20 + 4)$.

   c. Implement a StackSubtract procedure. Perform StackSubtract by negating the top of the stack value (POP, negate, PUSH) and then call StackAdd. That is, $a - b$ is handled as $a + (-b)$. Test your new module by performing the operations $6 * (8 - 3)$ and $-(5 - 2) * (4 - 7 * (11 + 9))$.

10. [16.3] (FileName:CH16D) Write a queue-handling program similar to CustomerQueue (Example 16.3.1), which asks customers for their names as they place orders at a fast food restaurant. Orders are processed in the same sequence as they are placed. The order taker examines the queue and calls the name when the order is ready. Also keep track, in the Number field, of total customers served. If removing a record will empty the queue (when QueueOut/\.NextRecPtr = QueueIn), remember the content of the Number field so that it can be used to continue the count when the next customer arrives. When the queue is empty, print a message telling the staff that they may take a break.

11. [16.3] Descriptions of jobs waiting in a computer for the printer are generally kept in a queue. Write a program to keep track of printing jobs, recorded by user name and anticipated length (in seconds) of the job. Add jobs to the queue as printouts are requested, and remove them from the queue as they are serviced. When a user adds a job to the queue, display a message for him or her giving an estimate of how long it will be before the job is printed. *Hint:* To estimate the time, accumulate lengths of all prior jobs in the queue.

12. [16.3] On your electronic mail terminal you receive notes to call people. Each message contains the Name and Phone number of the caller as well as a date in the form Month/Day/Year and a 24-hour-clock time in the form Hour:Minutes. A Latest Attempt time field is initially set to 0, indicating that no attempt has yet been made to return the call. For example, a particular record may appear as

```
Jan Williamsen  (215)384-9176   8/14/90   17:05   0
```

Write a program to store these records in a queue as they arrive and to feed them to you one at a time, upon request. If you cannot reach a person when you try to call, place that record at the bottom of the queue and fill the Latest Attempt time field with the time you tried to return the call, in the form DaysLater/Hour:Minutes. Thus, if your last unsuccessful attempt to return Jan Williamsen's call was on 8/16/90 at 4:20 P.M., the new record stored at QueueIn would be

```
Jan Williamsen  (215)384-9176   8/14/90   17:05   2/16:20.
```

13. [16.3] (FileName:CH16D) Here is a challenging problem! Add priority to the CustomerQueue of Example 16.3.1. That is, before you remove a customer from the queue, examine the name and ask whether this customer is to be served and removed from the queue. If the answer is yes, proceed as usual. If the answer is no, examine the next record in the queue, ask again, and so forth, until you find a favored customer. Then serve that customer and remove her or his record from the queue.

14. [16.4] (FileName:CH16E) Create a linked list of electrical power customers by name and the number of kilowatt-hours of electricity used last month. Read the data from an input file that contains this information:

Customer Name	Kilowatt-Hours Used
Adams	388
Brown	240
Cramer	591
Edwards	816
Garrett	212
Miller	350
Swenson	425
Taylor	472

Link the records, as they are entered, in order of increasing power usage. After you have entered all of the records you learn that Cramer really used only 391 kilowatt-hours and that Brown used 420. Make these corrections. (*Hint:* The easiest way to correct a record might be to delete it and add a new one.) Furthermore, Edwards has left the state; delete that record. The Thompson family's electricity was connected in the middle of the month, and their use was 180 kilowatt-hours; add this record. Display the contents of the final linked list, in order of increasing electricity used.

15. [16.4] A linked list is used to keep track of the members of an exclusive club. Each record contains the member's name and age. Enter the following members and ages into the list, linked in order of *decreasing* age:

Richardson	42	Swallow	28
Green	27	Merkle	50
Appleton	32	Tingey	32
Pierce	55	Barker	61

Display the list in order of decreasing age. Next month, when you update the list, Tingey and Swallow will have had birthdays, Pierce will have moved away and dropped out of the club, and Flinders (age 43) will have joined the club. Display the contents of the new linked list in order of decreasing age.

16. [16.4] (FileName:CH16E) Modify the DeleteItNow procedure in Example 16.4.1 so that it checks to make sure that both the item name and the inventory number indicated by the user match those of the record in the list before a deletion is made from the linked list. Test your program with appropriate data.

17. [16.4] Here is an ambitious project involving multiply linked lists! Write procedures and a program to store records of customer names and amount due on their bills in a linked list. Each record should contain two pointer fields: one to link in alphabetical order by last name, and the other to link in order of increasing amount due. Test your program with appropriate data, and display the records twice: once alphabetically, and then in order of increasing bill. *Hint:* One algorithm is to pass StartOfNameList and StartOfAmtList pointers to the AddItNow procedure and to find the PreviousName and PreviousAmount record pointers, passing both of those to AddToLinkList to update both NextNamePtr and NextAmountPtr fields each time a record is added.

18. [16.5] Write part of a cryptography program that performs a secretly defined process to accept lowercase characters from the keyboard and display the uppercase letter that is the same distance from the end of the alphabet as the entered letter is from the beginning. That is, *a* becomes *Z*, *b* becomes *Y*, *c* becomes *X,* and so on.

    Since this is a secret code, the opaque data types for letters entered and letters returned, and the procedures used, are to be hidden in the IMPLEMENTATION module.

19. [16.5] (FileName:CH13B) Change module MyMath and program VectorOperations (Example 13.1.2) to make TYPE VECTOR truly opaque.

20. [16.5] (FileName:CH16B, CH16D, CH16E) Here is another challenge! Change module Dynamic and the StackCharacterHandler, CustomerQueue, and LinkInventory example programs in this chapter to make the stack, queue, and linked-list structures truly opaque.

21. [16.6] (FileName:CH16F)
    a. Modify the TreeSortParticles program (Example 16.6.1) to read and sort the club member list in Exercise 15 into decreasing age order. Read the tree and display the sorted list.
    b. If your system supports pointer display, add statements in procedure Read-TheTree, immediately after the Write… command, to display the current

Figure 16–23
A Multiplication Table (Exercise 23)

*	1	2	3	4	5
1	1	2	3	4	5
2	2	4	6	8	10
3	3	6	9	12	15
4	4	8	12	16	20
5	5	10	15	20	25

record address and the LeftPtr and RightPtr field values. By hand, draw the binary tree represented by these records.

22. [16.6] Write a tree sort program that asks for CARDINAL numbers to be entered from the keyboard and places them on a binary tree in sorted order. Then the program should read the tree and display the sorted list of numbers to the screen.

23. [16.6] The multiplication table shown in Figure 16–23 is stored (without row and column headings) in an input file. Read the table into a two-dimensional array. Now read the rows of the array into a binary tree, sorted in order of decreasing row number. Then read the tree in sorted order and display the multiplication table with the rows in reverse order from the original input file. *Hint:* The structure stored on the tree is now an array of the numbers in one row, rather than a record.

17

System, Coroutines, and Special Features

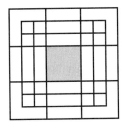

Chapter Outline

As you may have concluded by now, the problems you can solve with Modula-2 are almost limitless. Although this *introduction* to computer science with Modula-2 is drawing to a close, a wealth of material is available for further study and application.

This concluding chapter examines some data types that provide additional numerical accuracy. Then the discussion turns to features of the SYSTEM for addressing memory and to coroutines and concurrent processes. Finally, some special advanced features of Modula-2 are introduced.

17.1 *Data Types for Extended Range and Accuracy*

The largest and smallest values of INTEGER and CARDINAL numbers accepted by your Modula-2 system can be determined by using the built-in functions MAX and MIN. For example, on many microcomputers that use 16 bits for a CARDINAL number and 15 bits plus a sign bit for INTEGERS,

```
WriteCard(MAX(CARDINAL), 12);
WriteInt(MAX(INTEGER), 12);
```

and

```
WriteInt(MIN(INTEGER), 12);
```

would display the results 65535, 32767, and -32768, respectively.

MAX and MIN are not designed for use with REAL numbers, but your system manual should tell you the REAL range and accuracy. For example, a real number could be represented with 32 bits as shown in Figure 17–1. In this case the exponent e in two's complement form could have values between -128 and $+127$, and the binary mantissa f would have 23-digit accuracy (or 24 bits in a common mode of "hiding" the first nonzero bit). These REAL numbers would range in magnitude from $f \times 2^{-128}$ to $f \times 2^{127}$ or approximately $f \times 10^{-38}$ to $f \times 10^{38}$. The accuracy of f is 23 or 24 binary digits, or approximately 7 decimal digits.

In many instances you have discovered that this limits your capability. For example, 9-factorial equals 362,880, which exceeds MAX(CARDINAL) in a 16-bit memory space. Similarly, a 32-bit REAL number representation would be insufficient for expressing such things as the speed of light (299,792,458 meters per second) to the accuracy with which it has been measured and the number of hydrogen atoms in a star (roughly 10^{55}).

In the third and fourth editions of *Programming in Modula-2*, Niklaus Wirth included two number types to help solve such problems. One of these is LONGINT, and the other is LONGREAL. Many Modula-2 compilers have incorporated these types, and some versions include a LONGCARD type. Usually, each of these numeric types utilizes twice as much memory for storage of a variable as the normal INTEGER, REAL, or CARDINAL type.

For example, if INTEGER occupies 15 bits plus a sign bit and can represent whole numbers between $-2^{15}(-32768)$ and $2^{15} - 1$ (32767), then a LONGINT variable would be expected to use 31 bits plus a sign so that

```
MIN(LONGINT) = -2,147,483,648(-2³¹)
```

and

```
MAX(LONGINT)  = 2,147,483,647(2³¹- 1).
```

Figure 17–1
32-bit REAL Number Representation

			Sign			
			Bit	Exponent, *e*		Mantissa, *f*
				8 bits		23 bits

If REAL occupied 32 bits, then LONGREAL typically would require 64 bits, and in one representation could have a sign bit, an 11-bit exponent, and a 52-bit mantissa, representing numbers of magnitude $f \times 2^{-1024}$ to $f \times 2^{1023}$, or roughly $f \times 10^{-307}$ to $f \times 10^{307}$. In this situation, the accuracy of f would be 52 binary digits, or approximately 15 decimal digits. Many versions of the language implement REAL with 8 bytes, and there is no LONGREAL.

Unfortunately, there is no consistent standard on how to use LONG. . . numeric types. On some systems ReadLongInt and WriteLongInt, ReadLongCard and WriteLongCard, and ReadLongReal and WriteLongReal are included in the InOut and RealInOut modules. In other systems some or all of these are included in special I/O modules. In still another version, LONG. . . variables can be read or written using the common ReadInt, ReadCard, ReadReal and WriteInt, WriteCard, WriteReal commands. On some systems a literal LONGINT is written with the trailing *L* (such as in *25431L*), and a LONGREAL is written in exponential form with *E* replaced by *D*, representing Double precision (as in *2.81764936D + 212*). In other compilers it is sufficient to declare a variable to be of LONG. . . type, and then all values assigned to that variable are assumed automatically to be of that type without special *L* or *D* notations. It may even be necessary to convert values using expressions such as *VAL(LONGINT, value)*. It would be worth your time to consult your compiler manual to determine whether and how your system handles LONG. . . numeric values and the range and accuracy that can be achieved.

The following example shows one implementation of LONGINT.

Example 17.1.1

Rewrite the iterative factorial procedure of Example 9.5.1 using LONGINT.

Define the problem   Extend the range of factorials that can be calculated by the function IterateFact in Example 9.5.1 (CH9J) by declaring *n*, Factorial, and the function IterateFact to be of type LONGINT.

Develop a solution   To illustrate a "difficult" implementation, assume that LONGINT is a standard type, that WriteLongInt and ReadLongInt are imported from a special module, that the FOR-loop control variable cannot be LONGINT, and that conversions must be made between LONGINT and CARDINAL. Your system may handle things differently. Now modify the code of Example 9.5.1 to handle LONGINT.

Refine the solution   See the pseudocode for Example 9.5.1.

Modula-2 code

```
MODULE TestLongFactorial;
    (* Iterative solution of factorial, using LONGINT.
        FileName:CH17A      Modula-2      RKW      July 1991  *)
```

```
(* NOTE: For illustration of a "difficult" case, the program assumes
         that LONGINT is a standard type, that ReadLongInt and
         WriteLongInt are imported from a special module, and that
         conversions have to be made using VAL.  If your system handles
         LONGINT differently, make changes to accomodate differences. *)

FROM InOut IMPORT WriteString, WriteLn;
FROM LongIO IMPORT ReadLongInt, WriteLongInt;

VAR  Number, FactByIteration : LONGINT;

PROCEDURE IterateFact(n : LONGINT): LONGINT;
   VAR  Factorial : LONGINT;    Count : CARDINAL;
   BEGIN
      Factorial := VAL(LONGINT, 1);
      FOR  Count := VAL(CARDINAL, n) TO 1 BY -1 DO
         Factorial := VAL(LONGINT, Count) * Factorial;
      END; (* FOR *)
      RETURN Factorial;
   END IterateFact;

BEGIN (* module TestFactorial *)
   WriteString("Of what number (less than 13) to find the factorial? ");
    ReadLongInt(Number); WriteLn;
   WHILE   (Number < VAL(LONGINT,1))  OR  (Number > VAL(LONGINT,12))   DO
      WriteLn; WriteString("Try another  1 <= Number <= 12 : ");
       ReadLongInt(Number);  WriteLn;
   END; (* WHILE *)

   FactByIteration := IterateFact(Number);

   WriteString("The factorial of "); WriteLongInt(Number,10);
    WriteString(" is ");WriteLongInt(FactByIteration,16); WriteLn;
 END TestLongFactorial.
```

Debug and test   If this code does not run on your machine, the assumptions made about the way your compiler handles LONGINT are incorrect. Check your compiler manual to determine how to declare, read, and write LONGINT variables. A sample run should look like

```
Of what number (less than 13) to find the factorial? 12
The factorial of         12 is         479001600
```

Complete the documentation   In the users' manual the source code is stated as CH17A. If MAX(LONGINT) = 2,147,483,647, you are limited by this program to finding factorials of numbers smaller than 13.

| Questions 17.1 | **1. a.** Determine how LONGINT is handled on your computer, and implement TestLongFactorial (Example 17.1.1, CH17A).
b. Consult your compiler manual or use the library utility on your system to determine whether LONGREAL and LONGCARD are implemented. Use MIN and MAX to determine the range of LONGINT and LONGCARD. Determine the range and accuracy of REAL and/or LONGREAL. |

---

2. Write a program that displays all of the powers of ten (1, 10, 100, 1000, . . .) from 1 to MAX(LONGCARD) or to MAX(LONGINT).

17.2   *Using System Pseudomodule Features*

SYSTEM does not reside in an external file as do the other modules in Modula-2. Therefore, it often is called a *pseudomodule*. Nevertheless, Modula-2 programs can import and use certain entities from this module that are unique to the particular computer for which SYSTEM was written. Although not all systems are the same, two types and two functions can always be imported from SYSTEM. They are

Type   WORD
Type   ADDRESS
Function   ADR
Function   TSIZE.

(On some systems, SIZE also must be imported from SYSTEM.)

TSIZE and WORD

Function TSIZE(TypeName) returns a CARDINAL value representing the length, generally in bytes, of memory required to store a quantity of the type specified by the TypeName. Execute this short program:

```
MODULE WriteTypeSizes;
  (* Writes sizes of various types, using TSIZE.
     FileName:CH17B    Modula-2    RKW    July 1991  *)

FROM InOut IMPORT WriteCard, WriteString, WriteLn;
FROM SYSTEM IMPORT TSIZE, WORD;
```

```
TYPE   INTARRAY = ARRAY [1..10] OF INTEGER;
       TESTREC  = RECORD
                     A : CHAR;
                     B : ARRAY [0..1] OF CARDINAL;
                  END;
       USERDEF  = (Bread, Meat, Milk, Cheese);

BEGIN
   WriteString("TSIZE(INTEGER) = ");WriteCard(TSIZE(INTEGER),7); WriteLn;
   WriteString("TSIZE(CARDINAL)= ");WriteCard(TSIZE(CARDINAL),7);WriteLn;
   WriteString("TSIZE(WORD)    = ");WriteCard(TSIZE(WORD),7);    WriteLn;
   WriteString("TSIZE(REAL)    = ");WriteCard(TSIZE(REAL),7);    WriteLn;
   WriteString("TSIZE(BOOLEAN) = ");WriteCard(TSIZE(BOOLEAN),7); WriteLn;
   WriteString("TSIZE(CHAR)    = ");WriteCard(TSIZE(CHAR),7);    WriteLn;
   WriteString("TSIZE(INTARRAY)= ");WriteCard(TSIZE(INTARRAY),7);WriteLn;
   WriteString("TSIZE(TESTREC) = ");WriteCard(TSIZE(TESTREC),7); WriteLn;
   WriteString("TSIZE(USERDEF) = ");WriteCard(TSIZE(USERDEF),7); WriteLn;
END WriteTypeSizes.
```

On a typical microcomputer, the following values, representing the number of bytes reserved on that system for each indicated type, would be shown:

```
TSIZE(INTEGER)  =          2
TSIZE(CARDINAL) =          2
TSIZE(WORD)     =          2
TSIZE(REAL)     =          8
TSIZE(BOOLEAN)  =          1
TSIZE(CHAR)     =          1
TSIZE(INTARRAY) =         20
TSIZE(TESTREC)  =          5
TSIZE(USERDEF)  =          1
```

Type WORD is defined by various systems as the length of a computer word or as two bytes. The length of a word may be 16 or 32 bits or longer. The only operation that is standard upon variables of type WORD is assignment. However, WORD is particularly useful when used as a formal parameter type in a procedure heading, because the actual parameters listed in the procedure call can be of any type that is the same size as WORD. Thus, on a machine for which TSIZEs for WORD, CARDINAL, and INTEGER are the same, a procedure with heading

```
PROCEDURE  WhatEver(Value : WORD);
```

can accept an actual parameter of type INTEGER or CARDINAL. If TSIZE of CHAR is half of that of WORD, then you could define

```
TYPE   TWOCHAR = RECORD
                   Ch1, Ch2 : CHAR;
                 END;
VAR   Symbol : TWOCHAR;
```

and you could call WhatEver(Symbol) as well, because Symbol is a variable that occupies the same space as one WORD.

Generic Procedures using WORD

The property of WORD-type variables that allows them to accept values of any type of the same size is useful in writing generic procedures for performing an operation on different kinds of variables. The following program defines and tests such a generic procedure.

Example 17.2.1

Write a generic function that determines whether a value can be divided some whole number of times by a given divisor.

Define the problem   Write a function WHOLE that returns TRUE only if a given Value can be divided, with zero remainder, by any particular CARDINAL Divisor. It should work for INTEGERs, CARDINAL values, and even for the code of a CHARacter.

Develop a solution   Function WHOLE will accept formal parameters Reckon (a WORD) and Divider (CARDINAL). Reckon and Divider are converted to INTEGER, and the BOOLEAN Answer returned is (Reckon MOD Divider = 0).

The test program asks for a Divisor and then for an INTEGER, a CARDINAL number, and a CHARacter. It invokes WHOLE for each one and displays the result.

INTEGERs and CARDINAL values can be passed directly to the procedure, since their TSIZE is the same as WORD. To handle characters, variable Symbol will be defined to be a record (TWOCHAR) containing two characters. Symbol.Ch2 will be set to null, and the character of interest will be assigned to Symbol.Ch1. Then Symbol will be passed as an actual parameter to procedure Increment.

Refine the solution   *Pseudocode*

```
begin module TestWhole
  ask for Divisor
  ask for an INTEGER, Num1
      set IsItWhole = WHOLE(Num1, Divisor), WriteAnswer(IsItWhole)
  ask for a CARDINAL number, CardNum2
      set IsItWhole = WHOLE(CardNum2, Divisor), WriteAnswer(IsItWhole)
  ask for a CHARacter, Symbol.Ch1
      set Symbol.Ch2 = OC
      set IsItWhole = WHOLE(Symbol, Divisor), WriteAnswer(IsItWhole)
end TestWhole

function WHOLE(Reckon : WORD; Divider : CARDINAL) : BOOLEAN;
  Answer = (Reckon MOD Divider = 0), Return Answer

procedure WriteAnswer(Result)
  if    Result, write "can be divided"
  else    write "has a remainder"
```

Modula-2 code   Observe how variables of types INTEGER, CARDINAL, and TWOCHAR are all handled by passing them to formal parameter Reckon of type WORD. Since the only standard operation on WORD is assignment, Reckon is converted to an INTEGER before dividing.

```
MODULE TestWhole;
  (* A function WHOLE determines whether a value is divisible by a
     CARDINAL divisor, with zero remainder.
       FileName:CH17C      Modula-2      RKW      July 1991  *)
```

```
FROM InOut IMPORT WriteString, WriteLn, ReadCard, WriteCard,
                  Read, Write, ReadInt, WriteInt;
FROM SYSTEM IMPORT WORD;

TYPE  TWOCHAR = RECORD
                    Ch1, Ch2 : CHAR;
                END;
VAR  Symbol : TWOCHAR;  Num1 : INTEGER;  Divisor, CardNum2 : CARDINAL;
     Discard : CHAR;   IsItWhole : BOOLEAN;

PROCEDURE WHOLE(Reckon : WORD;  Divider : CARDINAL) : BOOLEAN;
   VAR  Answer : BOOLEAN;
   BEGIN
      Answer := ( INTEGER(Reckon) MOD INTEGER(Divider) = 0 );
      RETURN Answer;
   END WHOLE;

PROCEDURE WriteAnswer(Result : BOOLEAN);
   BEGIN
      IF  Result THEN  WriteString("  Can be divided with no remainder.");
       ELSE          WriteString("  Has a nonzero remainder when divided.");
      END; (* IF *)  WriteLn;
   END WriteAnswer;

BEGIN (* TestWhole *)
   REPEAT
      WriteString("CARDINAL Divisor(>0) = ? ");ReadCard(Divisor);WriteLn;
   UNTIL Divisor > 0;  WriteLn;

   WriteString("Specify an INTEGER value: "); ReadInt(Num1); WriteLn;
   IsItWhole := WHOLE(Num1, Divisor); WriteAnswer(IsItWhole); WriteLn;

   WriteString("Specify a CARDINAL value: "); ReadCard(CardNum2); WriteLn;
   IsItWhole := WHOLE(CardNum2, Divisor); WriteAnswer(IsItWhole);WriteLn;

   WriteString("Enter a single CHARacter: ");
    Read(Symbol.Ch1); Read(Discard); Write(Symbol.Ch1); WriteLn;
    Symbol.Ch2 := 0C;   (* Set leftmost byte of Symbol to 0's *)
    WriteString("The code for this character"); WriteLn;
   IsItWhole := WHOLE(Symbol, Divisor); WriteAnswer(IsItWhole); WriteLn;
END TestWhole.
```

Debug and test Remember that type WORD must be imported from SYSTEM. If this program does not execute properly on your system, the way WORDs are handled may be different, and you should consult your compiler manual. In type TWOCHAR, the first field, Ch1, is assigned to the rightmost byte, and the second field, Ch2, is assigned to the leftmost byte in Symbol. If your system reverses this convention, the value of Symbol.Ch1 will not be changed by Increment, and you will have to reverse Ch1 and Ch2 in the TWOCHAR type definition.

A sample run appears as:

```
CARDINAL Divisor(>0) = ? 7

Specify an INTEGER value: -5040
   Can be divided with no remainder.
```

```
Specify a CARDINAL value: 12345
  Has a nonzero remainder when divided.

Enter a single CHARacter: i
The code for this character
  Can be divided with no remainder.
```

Complete the documentation Hopefully, by now, you are reciting in your sleep that documentation consists of the problem description, algorithm development (including pseudocode), program listing, sample run, and users' manual. The source code file is CH17C.

Generic Procedures using ARRAY OF WORD

In some versions of Modula-2, you can pass an actual parameter of any type whatsoever to a formal procedure parameter of open type ARRAY OF WORD. Then you can refer to individual words within the procedure with appropriate indices ranging from [0] to [HIGH(FormalParameterName)]. This feature, when available, gives you tremendous capacity to write generic procedures that work with variables of any type you choose.

Compatible Pointer Types

Different types of variables can be made to appear compatible when their locations in memory are accessed through pointers. The ADDRESS type and ADR function facilitate these operations.

ADDRESS Type

ADDRESS is a standard type defined on most systems as

```
TYPE ADDRESS = POINTER TO WORD;
```

However, a few versions of Modula-2 treat it as TYPE ADDRESS = POINTER TO BYTE; in which BYTE refers to 8 bits of memory. The way ADDRESS works internally is dependent upon the architecture of the computer, and there is no guarantee that programs using ADDRESS are portable to a different type of machine. Nevertheless, it can be a powerful tool, if you are careful.

When a variable, such as Location, is declared to be of type ADDRESS — that is, when VAR Location : ADDRESS; — then, just as with any other pointer variable, Location can be assigned or compared with another pointer of the same type. The content of the memory address pointed to by Location is called the *referent* of Location and is designated *Location*∧.

One very important feature unique to pointer variables of type ADDRESS is that they are assignment-compatible with pointers of any other type. In other words, suppose that you declare

```
VAR  Guide : POINTER TO TypeName;
```

where *TypeName* is the name of any type whatsoever (standard, numeric, character, array, record, user-defined, or another). Then it is valid to make the assignments

```
Location := Guide;      and      Guide := Location;
```

Even though Location points to WORDs and Guide points to another type, the site of those variables in memory is the same. Hence, after Guide is assigned to Location or vice versa, Location∧ and Guide∧ are the same data interpreted in different ways. When procedures are being used, an actual parameter of any pointer type can be passed to a formal parameter of type ADDRESS. Typically, variables of type ADDRESS can be incremented (or decremented) to point to the next (or previous) WORD.

Function ADR

The function ADR(VariableName) returns the memory location, as a pointer of type ADDRESS, of the first WORD in the variable defined by VariableName. SIZE(VariableName) or TSIZE(VariableType) can be used to determine the total number of bytes the variable occupies.

Many computers reserve special memory locations for data to be accessed by particular peripheral devices, such as a video display terminal. User access to these locations can be managed with ADDRESS and ADR. Another use of type AD-DRESS and function ADR is for moving and interpreting the data in particular memory locations, as illustrated in the following example.

Example 17.2.2

Move CHARacter data to a buffer, where they are interpreted as CARDINAL values representing CHARacter codes.

Define the problem Usually, when data are moved from memory to an output device, they are first moved to a buffer. The buffer is a collection of memory locations where the data can be held until the output device is ready to receive them, and where they can be transformed to a form acceptable to the receiving medium if necessary.

In this problem, a string of characters will be entered from the keyboard into an ARRAY [ ] OF CHAR. Then the string will be moved to a set of memory locations called *Buffer*. The content of the Buffer will be displayed as an array of CARDINAL values, which will be shown to represent the code for the characters.

Develop a solution An array of CHAR will be declared to contain the string called *Phrase,* and an array of CARDINAL will be defined for the Buffer contents. It will be assumed that TSIZE(CARDINAL) = 2 * TSIZE(CHAR).

The characters of Phrase will be read from the keyboard, using ReadLine. If Phrase contains an odd number of characters, blank will be concatenated so that Length(Phrase) divided by 2 represents a whole number of CARDINAL WORDs. Then a procedure, CopyThem, will accept ADR(Phrase) and ADR(Buffer) as pointers FromSite and ToSite of ADDRESS type, and Length(Phrase) will be accepted as the number of bytes to copy. CopyThem will copy the contents of Phrase to the Buffer one byte at a time, using a loop that assigns ToSite∧ := FromSite∧ and increments the pointers one byte at a time.

Finally, the Phrase and the corresponding CARDINAL Buffer contents will be displayed, and a procedure Interpret will be called to display how the contents of the Buffer are interpreted.

Figure 17–2 is a structure chart of the solution.

Refine the solution *Pseudocode*

```
begin module BufferIt
  ask for Phrase
```

Figure 17-2
Structure Chart for
BufferIt (Example
17.2.2)

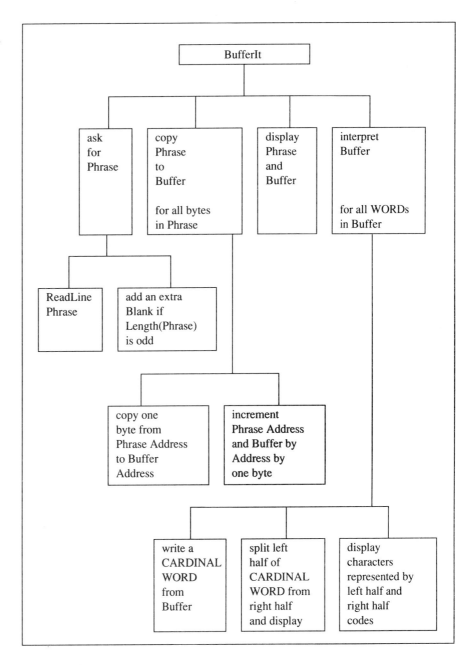

```
        concatenate a blank if Length(Phrase) is odd
        CopyThem(ADR(Phrase), ADR(Buffer), No. of bytes in Phrase)
        for WordCounter = 1 to length of buffer, display Buffer[WordCounter]
        Interpret(Buffer, Phrase)
    end BufferIt

    procedure CopyThem(FromSite,ToSite:ADDRESS;    HowManyBytes:CARDINAL)
        for ByteCount = 1 to HowManyBytes
            copy   FromSite/\  to   ToSite/\   (* copy one byte at a time *)
            increment   FromSite and ToSite    by one byte

    procedure Interpret(Code:CONTENT;    Phrase:STRING)
        for   WordCount = 1 to half of Length(Phrase)
```

FirstCode = Leftmost   8 bits of Code[WordCount]   (Code DIV 256)
SecndCode = Rightmost 8 bits of Code[WordCount]   (Code MOD 256)
display   FirstCode, SecndCode, CHR(FirstCode), CHR(SecndCode)

Modula-2 code   Carefully examine the use of ADR and ADDRESS in this program.

```
MODULE BufferIt;
  (* Accepts a string of characters, moves them to a simulated
     buffer, reads them from the buffer as CARDINAL values,
     and interprets them as the codes of the CHARacters.
     Demonstrates use of ADDRESS type and ADR function.
     FileName:CH17D       Modula-2      RKW       July 1991   *)

FROM InOut IMPORT WriteString, WriteLn, WriteCard, Write;
FROM SYSTEM IMPORT ADR, ADDRESS;
FROM Strings IMPORT Length, ReadLine, Concatenate;

CONST  NUMCHRS = 80;   NUMCARDS = NUMCHRS DIV 2;
TYPE   STRING = ARRAY [1..NUMCHRS] OF CHAR;
       CONTENT = ARRAY [1..NUMCARDS] OF CARDINAL;
VAR  Phrase : STRING;  Buffer : CONTENT;  WordCounter : CARDINAL;

PROCEDURE CopyThem(FromSite,ToSite:ADDRESS; HowManyBytes:CARDINAL);
   VAR  ByteCount : CARDINAL;
   BEGIN
     FOR ByteCount := 1 TO HowManyBytes  DO
        ToSite^ := FromSite^;  (* Copy one byte at a time. *)
        INC(FromSite);  INC(ToSite);
     END; (* FOR *)
   END CopyThem;


PROCEDURE Interpret(Code:CONTENT; Phrase:STRING);
   VAR  WordCount, FirstCode, SecndCode : CARDINAL;
   BEGIN
     WriteLn;WriteString("The interpretation of the buffer is: ");WriteLn;
     FOR  WordCount := 1 TO (Length(Phrase) DIV 2)  DO
        FirstCode := Code[WordCount] DIV 256;
        SecndCode := Code[WordCount] MOD 256;
        WriteCard(Code[WordCount],7); WriteString(" =  256 * ");
        WriteCard(FirstCode, 3); WriteString("  +  ");
        WriteCard(SecndCode, 3); WriteLn;
        WriteString("    which are the codes for characters   ");
        Write(CHR(FirstCode)); WriteString("  and  ");
        Write(CHR(SecndCode)); WriteLn;
     END; (* FOR *)
   END Interpret;


BEGIN (* BufferIt *)
   WriteString("Enter a string of characters:"); WriteLn;
   ReadLine(Phrase); WriteLn;
   IF  Length(Phrase) DIV 2  # 0  THEN    (* Insure that Phrase *)
     Concatenate(Phrase, " ", Phrase);    (* has an even number *)
   END; (* IF *)                          (* of bytes.          *)
```

```
CopyThem(ADR(Phrase), ADR(Buffer), Length(Phrase));

WriteString("The string: "); WriteLn; WriteString(Phrase); WriteLn;
 WriteString("is represented in the buffer as CARDINAL values");
 WriteLn; WriteLn;

FOR WordCounter := 1 TO (Length(Phrase) DIV 2)   DO
    WriteCard(Buffer[WordCounter],7); WriteLn;
END; (* FOR *)

Interpret(Buffer, Phrase);
END BufferIt.
```

Debug and test This program may not run on your computer. Here is a list of some potential problems and suggestions for correcting them:

1. The names and operation of procedures Length, ReadLine, and Concatenate may differ if you use a Strings module other than the one in Appendix C. Check your Strings module and make necessary changes.
2. The lengths of CARDINAL and CHAR could be different from one WORD and half a WORD, respectively, in your system. If so, change how CARDINAL values and CHARacters are stored, read, and interpreted.
3. It may be necessary for INC(FromSite) and INC(ToSite) to increment by WORDs instead of by bytes. If so, try something like INC(FromSite, TSIZE-(WORD)) and INC(ToSite, TSIZE(WORD)).

Watch for seemingly small errors that could cause disaster. Note that the *addresses* of Phrase and Buffer—namely, ADR(Phrase) and ADR(Buffer)—must be passed as variables to the ADDRESS pointers, and that the *contents* of those addresses (indicated by the referent caret, ∧) are copied to between Phrase and Buffer. If the length of the Phrase array STRING is more than twice the length of Buffer array CONTENT, you will run out of Buffer before you have copied all of Phrase. When displaying the Interpret codes, use Write(CHR(FirstCode)), rather than WriteString or WriteCard. Remember that ADR and ADDRESS must be imported from SYSTEM.

Here is a sample run.

```
Enter a string of characters:
Eureka!

The string:
Eureka!
is represented in the buffer as CARDINAL values

   30021
   25970
   24939
    8225

The interpretation of the buffer is:
   30021 =  256 * 117  +    69
      which are the codes for characters    u   and   E
   25970 =  256 * 101  +   114
      which are the codes for characters    e   and   r
```

```
24939 =  256 *  97  +  107
   which are the codes for characters   a  and  k
 8225 =  256 *  32  +  33
   which are the codes for characters      and  !
```

Complete the documentation   It would help programmers who are trying to learn how to use ADR and ADDRESS to include descriptions of those entities and the notes from "Debug and test" about possible differences between machines that address words and machines that address bytes.

The source code file is CH17D. A Strings module with Length, ReadLine, and Concatenate must be present. Users enter a string of characters and then press Enter or Return to terminate.

Questions 17.2

1. Run the WriteTypeSizes program (CH17B) on your computer to determine the relative sizes of CHAR, CARDINAL, INTEGER, WORD, and REAL.
2. **a.** Does ADDRESS point to a WORD or to a byte on your machine?
   b. When you INC(FromSite), where FromSite is an ADDRESS pointer, does it advance one byte or more?
   c. Implement program BufferIt (Example 17.2.2, CH17D) on your computer.
3. Implement program TestWhole (Example 17.2.1, CH17C) on your computer.

17.3   *Coroutines*

Procedures are subordinate entities within a program, whose commands are executed from the beginning each time they are called. Control is maintained by a driving program, a procedure, or a module. Sometimes you would like to have multiple components that participate on equal levels toward the solution of a problem. For example, when simulating a physical phenomenon in which a number of independent operations occur simultaneously, you would want to model the operations with separate routines that progress through time with equal status.

One way of handling such situations is with **coroutines.** A coroutine is a **process** (a subprogram in operation) that transfers control to another operation and then resumes where it left off when control is transferred back to it. As with all processes, a coroutine need *not* begin execution from the beginning each time it is called. The values of all local variables are maintained and are available when execution of a process, such as a coroutine, resumes.

Figure 17–3 illustrates a program that contains two coroutines, *A* and *B,* which transfer control back and forth between them. A program can have many coroutines.

Coroutines are created from procedures. They are processes located at memory ADDRESSes where there is sufficient memory workspace allocated to them for storing variables and other quantities necessary for keeping track of their status.

NEWPROCESS and TRANSFER

Two procedures create coroutines and transfer control in Modula-2. These procedures are NEWPROCESS and TRANSFER, and they are imported from SYSTEM or another low-level module, such as Processes. The definitions of NEWPROCESS and TRANSFER are shown in Figure 17–4.

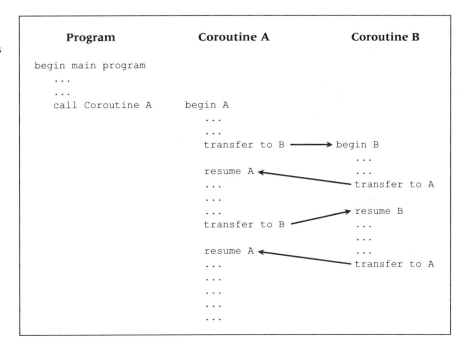

Figure 17–3
Transfer of Control between Coroutines A and B

Program	**Coroutine A**	**Coroutine B**

Restrictions on Coroutines

Some restrictions apply to the procedures from which coroutines are created. Since these procedures must be of standard type PROC, they can have no parameters and they cannot be functions. Nor may they be local to other procedures. However, they can contain their own local procedures, call other procedures, *and* call *themselves* if recursion is necessary.

The workspace size (WkSpSize) allocated to a coroutine in the NEWPROCESS procedure must be sufficiently large to contain (1) the local variables, (2) the state of the coroutine when it is suspended (location of the next command to be executed, and so on), and (3) any stack created when the coroutine calls other procedures. This size will represent a number of WORDs. For the discussion that follows, assume that a workspace size of 1000 is sufficient (and probably wastefully large). The creation and initial execution of a coroutine from a procedure called *TakeIt* are shown in the example in Figure 17–4.

If NEWPROCESS and TRANSFER on your system require MainProg or CoroutineTakeIt to be of type PROCESS, rather than of type ADDRESS, then you should import PROCESS and declare VAR MainProg, CoroutineTakeIt : PROCESS.

Executing Coroutines

NEWPROCESS only *sets up* a coroutine process; execution must be started by a TRANSFER command. In Figure 17–4, TRANSFER finds the current location of the coroutine at the address of CoroutineTakeIt, stores the return location of the main program module in MainProg, and begins execution of the coroutine created from procedure TakeIt.

If an executing coroutine encounters the END of the procedure from which it was created, the entire program stops, because there is no information as to which instructions are to be executed next. Therefore, most procedures for coroutines contain an infinite loop, have a TRANSFER just before END, or specify some condition that will terminate program execution.

Figure 17–4
Definition of
Procedures
NEWPROCESS
and **TRANSFER**

```
PROCEDURE   NEWPROCESS(P:PROC;WkSpAddr:ADDRESS;WkSpSize:CARDINAL;
                                    VAR NewPrcAddr:ADDRESS);
    (* P is a procedure of type PROC from which the process is
       created. WkSpAddr is the address of the workspace for
       the coroutine. WkSpSize is the size of the workspace, in
       bytes or words. NewPrcAddr is the starting address of the
       new process. *)

PROCEDURE   TRANSFER(VAR Srce, Dest : ADDRESS);
    (* Srce and Dest are process addresses. The Source operation
       is suspended, and its address is stored in Srce. Control
       is transferred to the Destination process at address Dest,
       which resumes execution from the point where it was
       suspended previously. *)
```

Example:

```
MODULE WhatEver;
FROM SYSTEM IMPORT WORD, ADDRESS, ADR, NEWPROCESS, TRANSFER;

CONST  SizeWorkSpace = 1000;
VAR  WorkSpace : ARRAY [1..SizeWorkSpace] OF WORD;
     MainProg, CoroutineTakeIt : ADDRESS;

PROCEDURE  TakeIt;  (* Remember, no parameters!  Type is PROC. *)
    VAR...
    BEGIN
       ...
    END TakeIt;

BEGIN   (* module WhatEver *)
    ...
    NEWPROCESS(TakeIt,ADR(WorkSpace),SIZE(WorkSpace),
            CoroutineTakeIt);
    TRANSFER(MainProg, CoroutineTakeIt);
    ...
END WhatEver.
```

Notes

1. NEWPROCESS and TRANSFER must be imported from SYSTEM or another
    library module.

2. In some versions of Modula-2, type PROCESS must be imported from SYSTEM,
    and NewPrcAddr, Srce, and Dest are declared to be of type PROCESS, rather than
    of type ADDRESS.

Allocating and Deallocating Memory

Memory space is allocated to a coroutine through the NEWPROCESS command. If
you want to free that space, you can deallocate the workspace (with DEALLOCATE
CoroutineTakeIt, for example). Of course, once a coroutine workspace has been
deallocated, you cannot transfer control to that coroutine again.

Here is a simple example that illustrates the operation of coroutines.

Example 17.3.1

Use coroutines to calculate and display the partial sums of the series $1 + 2 + 3 + \ldots + N$.

Define the problem   One coroutine will count numbers $1, 2, 3, \ldots N$ and display the Count. A second coroutine will accept the Count and then accumulate and display the Sum. The program will terminate before the Sum exceeds MAX (CARDINAL).

Develop a solution   Two procedures, Increment (which increments the Count), and AddItUp (which determines the partial Sum), will be used to create corresponding coroutines. Because these procedures must be of type PROC (no parameters), Count will be a global variable that can be accessed by either coroutine. Sum will be local to AddItUp. The main program module will create the coroutines at addresses IncrementCoroutine and AddCoroutine and will transfer control to IncrementCoroutine. Thereafter, control will be transferred back and forth between the coroutines with each succeeding Count until the Sum exceeds MAX(CARDINAL).

Refine the solution   *Pseudocode*

```
begin module SumIt
  Newprocess(IncrementCoroutine)
  Newprocess(AddCoroutine)
  print headings
  transfer(MainProg, IncrementCoroutine)
end SumIt

procedure Increment
  Count = 0
  loop    (* forever *)
    increment Count,    print Count
    transfer(IncrementCoroutine, AddCoroutine)

procedure AddItUp
  Sum = 0
  loop
    if   Sum < MAX(CARDINAL) − Count
      add Count to Sum,    print Sum
      transfer(AddCoroutine, IncrementCoroutine)
    else   exit from loop
```

Modula-2 code   The value of local variable Sum is maintained even after control is transferred from AddItUp. The TRANSFER statement in both loops occurs just before the end of the loop so that when the coroutine receives control again, the next command executed is the one at the beginning of the loop. The coroutines are created in the main program, using NEWPROCESS. Then control is transferred from the main program to the first coroutine. The condition

```
IF   Sum < MAX(CARDINAL)  − Count   THEN ... ELSE EXIT ...
```

ensures that coroutine AddCoroutine reaches END AddItUp, which stops the program, before an overflow condition is encountered.

```
MODULE SumIt;
    (* Uses coroutines to find the partial sums of 1 + 2 + ... + N.
        FileName:CH17E      Modula-2      RKW      July 1991  *)

FROM InOut IMPORT WriteString, WriteLn, WriteCard;
FROM SYSTEM IMPORT WORD, ADDRESS, ADR, NEWPROCESS, TRANSFER;

    (* Assumes that NEWPROCESS AND TRANSFER are in SYSTEM, that coroutines
        are defined in terms of ADDRESS (rather than PROCESS), and that SIZE
        is available without importing.  If your system differs, change
        import lists and VARiable declarations accordingly. *)

CONST  SizeWorkSpace = 1000;
VAR  WorkSpIncrement, WorkSpAdd : ARRAY [1..SizeWorkSpace] OF WORD;
        MainProg, IncrementCoroutine, AddCoroutine : ADDRESS;  Count:CARDINAL;

PROCEDURE Increment;
    BEGIN
        Count := 0;
        LOOP
            INC(Count);  WriteCard(Count,6);
            TRANSFER(IncrementCoroutine, AddCoroutine);
        END; (* LOOP *)
    END Increment;

PROCEDURE AddItUp;
    VAR Sum : CARDINAL;
    BEGIN
        Sum := 0;
        LOOP
            IF   Sum < MAX(CARDINAL)-Count   THEN
                Sum := Sum + Count;  WriteCard(Sum, 17); WriteLn;
                TRANSFER(AddCoroutine, IncrementCoroutine);
            ELSE
                EXIT;   (* from loop *)
            END; (* IF *)
        END; (* LOOP *)
    END AddItUp;

BEGIN   (* main module SumIt *)
    NEWPROCESS(Increment, ADR(WorkSpIncrement),
                        SIZE(WorkSpIncrement), IncrementCoroutine);
    NEWPROCESS(AddItUp, ADR(WorkSpAdd), SIZE(WorkSpAdd), AddCoroutine);

    WriteString("Number    Sum to Number"); WriteLn;
    TRANSFER(MainProg, IncrementCoroutine);
END SumIt.
```

Debug and test See the comment notes immediately after the IMPORT lists for changes you might need to make so that this program will compile and run on your system. In calls to NEWPROCESS and TRANSFER, be sure that the actual parameters are listed in proper order and declared as the appropriate type.

Here are the start and end of a sample run.

```
Number     Sum to Number
     1                 1
     2                 3
     3                 6
     4                10
     5                15
   ...               ...
   ...               ...
   359             64620
   360             64980
   361             65341
   362
===>  coroutine end
```

Complete the documentation   Collect the problem definition, pseudocode, code, and sample run. Some discussion of coroutines would be appropriate. The source code is in file CH17E. Warn users that it may be necessary to import NEWPRO-CESS and TRANSFER from a module other than SYSTEM and that MainProg, IncrementCoroutine, and AddCoroutine may need to be defined as type PROCESS rather than ADDRESS. Execution of the program requires no user interaction.

Questions 17.3

1. In the program SumIt (CH17E),
   a. Why is the test condition in AddItUp in the form

$$\text{Sum} \quad < \quad \text{MAX(CARDINAL)} - \text{Count}$$

   instead of $\text{Sum} \quad < \quad \text{MAX(CARDINAL)}$

   or even $\text{Sum} \quad + \quad \text{Count} < \text{MAX(CARDINAL)}$?

   b. What would happen if Count were declared as a local variable in procedure Increment? What would happen if Sum were a global variable, rather than local to AddItUp?

A Bit of Background

Von Neumann Machines

Hungarian-born American mathematician John von Neumann (1903–1957) has been called "the Father of Modern Computing." In part, this is because he implemented Turing's concept of storing the computer program in memory.

Since 1945, digital computers that execute a sequence of programmed instructions have been referred to as *von Neumann machines*. So-called fifth-generation systems are designed with large numbers of parallel processors that split a problem into processes for concurrent execution. These are not von Neumann machines, since they do not operate as a single processor execut-ing a sequence of commands, with data and program instructions moving across a single bus. Nonetheless, without the concept of stored programs, these machines could not have been developed.

Recognized as a professional mathematician from the age of 19, John von Neumann made important contributions in fields ranging from logic, analysis, statistics, and pure and applied mathematics to nuclear energy, computing, and game theory. His genius in science and technology changed the world.

2. Implement program SumIt (Example 17.3.1, CH17E) on your system.
3. Add a third procedure and coroutine to program SumIt to calculate and display the sums of squares, $1^2 + 2^2 + 3^2 + \ldots + N^2$. Where does the test to stop execution need to be now?

17.4   *Concurrent Processes*

Programs that are executing simultaneously in different processors on a multiprocessor machine would be truly **concurrent processes.** Coroutines provide a means of simulating concurrency on a single-processor computer by allowing the processes defined by the coroutines to transfer control to each other. Thus, coroutines can give the appearance that multiple processes are occurring at once.

Module Processes

In his book *Programming in Modula-2,* Dr. Wirth provides a module called *Processes* for manipulating multiple processes. Whether these processes are executed simultaneously in multiple processors or at different times on a single processor depends upon the computer. IMPLEMENTATION MODULE Processes is written to handle the single- or multiple-processor environment for which the particular version of Modula-2 is designed. For single-processor machines, the underlying implementation of Processes generally is in the form of coroutines so that when a new process is created and its execution is begun, execution of the calling process is suspended automatically. In multiprocessor machines, on the other hand, a process might call and start another process without suspending its own execution. In that case, the programmer must tell each process when to stop and wait. DEFINITION MODULE Processes is shown in Figure 17–5.

StartProcess, SEND, WAIT
A call of StartProcess creates a process from the specified parameterless procedure of type PROC, dynamically allocates a workspace of the indicated size to the process, and begins execution of the process. When an executing process executes WAIT(Signal), its operation is suspended; it is resumed only when some other process SENDs the Signal for which the process is WAITing. When several processes have executed a WAIT command for the same Signal, they are placed in a queue and "awakened" by successive SEND commands in a first-come, first-served order. Each SEND(Signal) causes only one process (or none, if no process is awaiting that Signal) to resume execution.

Processes are especially appropriate for handling independent, simultaneous events that interact at times. These include diverse situations such as one process filling a buffer and another process removing and using the data from the buffer, physical events such as moving objects that eventually affect other objects' actions, and so on.

Example 17.4.1

Find the distance between two ships, one of them sailing northward and the other eastward.

Figure 17–5
DEFINITION
MODULE Processes

```
DEFINITION MODULE Processes;
   (* Allows establishment of multiple processes and
      communication between processes. *)

      TYPE SIGNAL;
         (* Provides a method of synchronizing processes. *)

      PROCEDURE StartProcess(P:PROC;  WkSpSize:CARDINAL);
         (* Dynamically creates a process from procedure P,
            allocates workspace for the process, and begins
            execution of the process. *)

      PROCEDURE  SEND(VAR S:SIGNAL);
         (* Sends a signal for another process to resume
            execution. *)

      PROCEDURE  WAIT(VAR S:SIGNAL)
         (* Suspends operation of the currently executing process
            in which WAIT is executed and waits for another
            process to SEND a signal to resume execution. *)

      PROCEDURE  Awaited(VAR S:SIGNAL) : BOOLEAN;
         (* Returns the value TRUE if at least one process is
            waiting for signal S. Returns FALSE otherwise. *)

      PROCEDURE  Init(VAR S:SIGNAL);
         (* Every signal must be initialized, using Init,
            before use. *)
```

Define the problem   Two ships leave the same dock at the same time. One ship sails north at speed $v1$; the other sails east at speed $v2$. $v1$ and $v2$ are specified in knots (nautical miles per hour) by the user at the keyboard. In increments of TIMEINTERVAL = 1 minute, find and tabulate the positions of the ships and the distance between them. Positions y and x and the Distance are shown in Figure 17–6. The tabulation continues until one of the ships falls off the edge of the flat Earth at a distance of 100 nautical miles (100 nm) from the dock.

Develop a solution   Although other means can be used to solve this problem, you will use three particular processes. At intervals of one minute, Process Ship1 calculates and displays the time and the distance of ship 1. It then waits while the program SENDs the signal for Process Ship2 to do the same for ship 2, which then also waits for a signal to resume. The program then SENDs a signal to process DistProcess, which calculates and displays the distance between the ships and then waits for a signal to resume. A LOOP in the main program repeats the sequence of sending signals to the three processes. In Ship1 and Ship2 a check is made to determine whether the ship's position exceeds 100 nm. If so, a HALT is encountered, which terminates the program.

Parameters cannot be passed between processes, because the underlying procedures must be of type PROC. Therefore, ship position variables y and x will be global so that they are available to all processes. $v1$, $v2$, Dist, and time t may be local to their individual procedures.

Figure 17–6
The Distance
between Two Ships
(Example 17.4.1)

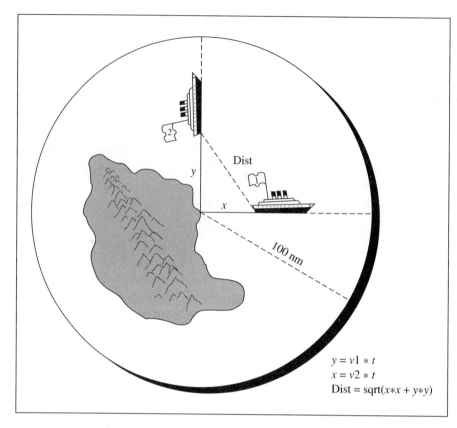

$$y = v1 * t$$
$$x = v2 * t$$
$$Dist = sqrt(x*x + y*y)$$

Refine the solution   *Pseudocode*

```
begin module TwoShips
        initialize signals MoveShip1, MoveShip2, FindDist
        StartProcess(Ship1, SIZE(Wksp1))
        StartProcess(Ship2, SIZE(Wksp2))
        StartProcess(Distance, SIZE(WkspDist))
        loop
          send MoveShip1, send MoveShip2, send FindDist
end TwoShips

procedure Ship1
    ask for v1
    wait for signal MoveShip1,    initialize    y = 0,   t = 0
    while    y < 100
      t = t + TIMEINTERVAL     (* Find time since ship left dock. *)
      y = y  +  v1 * TIMEINTERVAL   (* Find new position. *)
      print t and y,    wait for signal MoveShip1
    end while,    HALT

procedure Ship2
    ask for v2
    wait for signal MoveShip2,    initialize    x = 0
    while x < 100
      x = x  +  v2 * TIMEINTERVAL,    print x
      wait for signal MoveShip2
    end while,    HALT

procedure Distance
    print headings,    wait for signal FindDist
```

```
loop
   Dist  =  sqrt(x * x + y * y),    print Dist
   wait for signal FindDist
```

Modula-2 code StartProcess not only creates a process and allocates space for it; it also begins execution of the process. Thus the three StartProcess calls in the main program cause the three procedures to ask for *v*1 and *v*2 and to print the headings, respectively, and then to wait for signals to resume. Thereafter, the main program repeatedly issues the SEND(MoveShip1), SEND(MoveShip2), and SEND(Find-Dist) commands. In the first cycle, the time and positions are initialized, and the ships make their first moves.

On a single-processor machine, a SEND command suspends execution of the process that issues it; the main program loop is suspended until the called process WAITs, at which time the program loop continues. On multiprocessor machines, a SEND command does not suspend execution; without WAIT commands, all of the processes can run at once.

```
MODULE TwoShips;
   (* Uses three processes to tabulate the positions of and
      distance between two ships at intervals of one minute.
      FileName:CH17F     Modula-2     RKW     July 1991  *)

FROM InOut IMPORT WriteLn, WriteString;
FROM RealInOut IMPORT ReadReal, FWriteReal;
FROM MathLib0 IMPORT sqrt;   FROM SYSTEM IMPORT WORD;
FROM Processes IMPORT SIGNAL, StartProcess, SEND, WAIT, Init;
(* If necessary, import SIZE from SYSTEM *)

CONST  TIMEINTERVAL = 1.0/60.0;   (* 1/60 hour = 1 minute *)
       WorkSpaceSize = 1000;   EARTHRADIUS = 100.0;
VAR  Wksp1, Wksp2, WkspDist : ARRAY [1..WorkSpaceSize] OF WORD;
     MoveShip1, MoveShip2, FindDist : SIGNAL;   x, y : REAL;

PROCEDURE Ship1;
   VAR t, v1 : REAL;
   BEGIN
      WriteString("  What is the northbound ship speed (knots)? ");
       ReadReal(v1); WriteLn;
      WAIT(MoveShip1);       y := 0.0;   t := 0.0;
      WHILE  y < EARTHRADIUS  DO
         t := t + TIMEINTERVAL; (* t = time since ships left dock.*)
         y := y + v1 * TIMEINTERVAL;  (* Calculate new position.  *)
         FWriteReal(t,10,4);  FWriteReal(y,14,4);  WAIT(MoveShip1);
      END; (* WHILE *)    HALT;
   END Ship1;

PROCEDURE Ship2;
   VAR  v2 : REAL;
   BEGIN
      WriteString("  What is the eastbound ship speed (knots)? ");
       ReadReal(v2); WriteLn;
      WAIT(MoveShip2);    x := 0.0;
      WHILE  x < EARTHRADIUS  DO
         x := x + v2 * TIMEINTERVAL;  (* Calculate new position.  *)
         FWriteReal(x,14,4);   WAIT(MoveShip2);
```

```
        END; (* WHILE *)        HALT;
    END Ship2;

PROCEDURE Distance;
  VAR Dist : REAL;
  BEGIN
      WriteLn; WriteString("   Time(hr)       Ship1(nm)       Ship2(nm)");
      WriteString("     Distance(nm)"); WriteLn;
      WAIT(FindDist);
      LOOP
        Dist := sqrt(x*x + y * y); FWriteReal(Dist,16,4); WriteLn;
        WAIT(FindDist);
      END; (* LOOP *)
  END Distance;

BEGIN (* main module TwoShips *)
    Init(MoveShip1);   Init(MoveShip2);   Init(FindDist);

    StartProcess(Ship1, SIZE(Wksp1));
    StartProcess(Ship2, SIZE(Wksp2));
    StartProcess(Distance, SIZE(WkspDist));
    LOOP
      SEND(MoveShip1);      SEND(MoveShip2);      SEND(FindDist);
    END; (* LOOP *)
END TwoShips.
```

Debug and test It is very easy for an inappropriately placed SEND or WAIT command to suspend operation of the entire program while all of the processes wait for signals that never come. This situation is called **deadlock.** You should be able to determine where a deadlock occurs.

Here are the start and end of a sample run.

```
What is the northbound ship speed (knots)? 20.0
What is the eastbound ship speed (knots)? 30.0
```

Time(hr)	Ship1(nm)	Ship2(nm)	Distance(nm)
0.0167	0.3333	0.5000	0.6009
0.0333	0.6667	1.0000	1.2019
0.0500	1.0000	1.5000	1.8028
0.0667	1.3333	2.0000	2.4037
0.0833	1.6667	2.5000	3.0046
...			
...			
3.2667	65.3333	98.0000	117.7813
3.2833	65.6667	98.5000	118.3823
3.3000	66.0000	99.0000	118.9832
3.3167	66.3333	99.5000	119.5841
3.3333	66.6667	100.0000	120.1850
3.3500	67.0000		

```
===>  HALT called
```

Complete the documentation For the *last* time, collect the problem description, the algorithm development, program listing, and sample run. For this problem, include a discussion of processes and the effects of type SIGNAL. Give some information about procedures StartProcess, SEND, and WAIT and explain the differences in how they act on single-processor and multiprocessor systems. Source code is in file CH17F. Users enter the speeds of the ships in knots. A fast ship probably does not exceed 60 knots.

Questions 17.4

1. If a deadlock occurred in program TwoShips (Example 17.4.1, CH17F), how would you attempt to discover its location? *Hint:* Try displaying a local counter in each procedure.
2. **a.** Implement the TwoShips program (CH17F) on your system.
   b. How would you change the program to make the ships travel in the same direction at different speeds?

17.5   *Other Features of Modula-2*

Additional features are provided with some Modula-2 compilers. They are not discussed in depth here, but some of them are mentioned to extend your awareness of the full capability of the language. Consult your system manual and books dealing with advanced topics in computer science to learn if these features are available to you and how they can be implemented.

Interrupts

Most computers have an **interrupt** feature, which causes a signal to be generated automatically by the hardware when some particular event occurs—such as an event

---

A Bit of Background

Rosy or Bleak?

In the twenty years prior to 1970, the computer industry grew as much as 20 percent per year. In that era of large machines, a person who knew anything about computers or programming could expect to be inundated with job offers. By 1971, old systems were being phased out, and new equipment was being introduced at the same time that the U.S. economy entered a major recession. Small computer companies declared bankruptcy, and larger ones instituted cutbacks. The professional Association for Computing Machinery rose to the occasion by teaching unemployed computer professionals job-search skills.

As mini- and microcomputers pervaded small businesses in the late 1970s and the 1980s, the demand for computer personnel again exceeded the supply, and companies competed for computer science graduates with very attractive salaries. University departments of data processing, information systems, and computer science overflowed with students.

By the late 1980s and early 1990s, another economic setback caused job-hunting difficulties for inexperienced new graduates, and enrollments in many university computer science curriculums dropped by 50% or more. Computing students discovered that to be assured of an entry-level position, they must become proficient in systems, maintenance, networking, analysis, electronics, business, or some other area as well as in programming.

So what about the future? Statistics gathered by the National Science Foundation and others continue to predict a critical shortage of computer professionals. Will this predicted shortage be accompanied by an increase in demand for well-trained graduates?

What does *your* crystal ball say?

that makes an input or output operation need the attention of the processor. Some versions of Modula-2 supply a procedure called *IOTRANSFER* that manages interrupts. Typically, IOTRANSFER suspends a NEWPROCESS-generated coroutine, called an **interrupt handler,** until a particular interrupt signal is detected. Upon receipt of that signal, the interrupt handler executes instructions to perform whatever service is needed and then suspends its operation and transfers control back to the process that was interrupted. If procedure IOTRANSFER is present, it is found in SYSTEM or another processes-related module.

☐ Overlays

In some versions of Modula-2 provision is made for a program to call another program module and use it much like a procedure. Such a feature allows program components called **subprograms** to be called into memory only when they are needed. When a number of subprograms use the same memory locations at different times, they are said to **overlay** each other. This allows more programs to be executed than there is room for in memory all at once. In those versions of the language that support it, this feature is often implemented by a procedure named *Call* or *CallOverlay* that is imported from an external module.

☐ Windows

Dr. Wirth's *Programming in Modula-2* describes a module called **Windows,** which allows you to partition the screen into ''windows'' that provide views to multiple operations at once. Windows, with menus that pop up inside other menus and then disappear, are defined by packages of information. The information about the existing window is pushed onto a stack when a new window is called, and is then popped back when the new one disappears.

Many implementations of the language support using multiple windows in one form or another. Consult your manual regarding if, when, where, and how windowing can be handled.

☐ Assembly Language

Finally, like it or not, some tasks simply cannot be programmed, others are too messy to program, and still others execute too slowly when programmed in a high-level language. Those are times when **assembly** or **machine language** must be invoked to produce code for a specific machine. Most Modula-2 systems provide a mechanism for incorporating assembly or machine language procedures into a program. Often this is accomplished by including special terms such as *MODULE* and *IMPORT* in the assembly code and creating a Modula-2 DEFINITION MODULE to refer to the procedures written in the assembly language. Of course, to use this feature you must become familiar with the assembly language for your machine and consult the Modula-2 compiler manual for specific details.

🗗 17.6 *Summary*

LONGINT   Type LONGINT variables usually occupy 4 bytes of memory and extend the maximum value of INTEGER beyond 2 billion. Special procedures to read and write LONGINT values are imported from an external module. Some versions of Modula-2 also define LONGCARD and LONGREAL data types.

SYSTEM   SYSTEM is a pseudomodule that is part of the compiler, not a separate external module. Types WORD and ADDRESS and functions TSIZE and ADR (and sometimes SIZE) are imported from SYSTEM.

Generic Procedures   Procedure parameters of type WORD are compatible with values, variables, and structures with the same type size. On some systems, ARRAY OF WORD parameters are considered compatible with every type. This allows a variety of data to be handled with a single generic procedure.

ADDRESS   Type ADDRESS is a pointer to WORD and is compatible with pointers to other data types. Function ADR(VariableName) returns the memory location, as an ADDRESS pointer, of VariableName. ADDRESS and ADR can be used to store, retrieve, and interpret data differently as needed for particular applications.

Coroutines   Coroutines are processes created by a program from parameterless PROC-type procedures. Coroutines TRANSFER control between each other and the program module, rather than being invoked as procedures.

Concurrent Processes   Processes that operate simultaneously or appear to do so are said to be *concurrent*. Coroutines provide one way of implementing concurrent processes. In addition, processes can be created with the Start-Process procedure from module Processes. Process operation is controlled by SENDing and WAITing for appropriate signals.

Other Features   Other features of Modula-2 include provisions for interrupt management, the handling of overlays, window graphics, and the incorporation of assembly-language routines into programs.

17.7 *Exercises*

Exercises marked with (FileName:_____) indicate those that ask you to use, modify, or extend the text examples. The numbers in brackets, [ ], indicate the section that contains the material you need in order to complete the exercise.

1. [17.1] Einstein's special relativity says that for objects traveling at a speed v relative to observers who consider themselves at rest, as the speed v approaches the speed of light c, the apparent mass m increases, clocks appear to run more slowly (time intervals t increase), and the apparent length L decreases.

   Given the speed of light $c = 299{,}792{,}458$ meters/second, write a program to display tables of the ratios

   $$m/m0 = 1/\text{sqrt}(1 - v^2/c^2)$$
   $$t/t0 = 1/\text{sqrt}(1 - v^2/c^2)$$
   $$L/L0 = \text{sqrt}(1 - v^2/c^2)$$

   to the best accuracy your system allows, for values of v from 0 to $0.999c$. Use LONGREAL variables if your compiler supports them.

2. [17.1] Write a program to accumulate the sum $1 + 2 + 3 + \ldots + N$ and compare the result with $N(N + 1)/2$. Use LONGINT (or LONGCARD if supported by your compiler) variables, and determine the largest value of N for which you can calculate the sum.

3. [17.1] Module MyMath (Appendix C) contains a procedure that raises a REAL number to a CARDINAL power. Rewrite the procedure to raise an INTEGER base to an INTEGER power, and determine the limits on the size of the base and power for which this procedure gives accurate results on your machine if you declare the base and the power to be
   a. INTEGER variables;
   b. LONGINT variables.

4. [17.1] One formula for calculating pi from an infinite series is

$$\pi = \text{sqrt}(6 * (1 + 1/(2 * 2) + 1/(3 * 3) + 1/(4 * 4) + \ldots))$$

Write a program to calculate π from this series as accurately as your system allows. *Hints:* Using LONGINT or LONGCARD may give more or less accuracy than using LONGREAL. You may want to calculate

$$\pi * \pi/6 = 1 + 1/(2 * 2) + 1/(3 * 3) + 1/(4 * 4) + \ldots$$

first, and then multiply by 6 and take sqrt to obtain π.

5. [17.1] A formula for calculating *e* (the base of natural logarithms, ln) is

$$e = 1 + 1/1! + 1/2! + 1/3! + 1/4! + \ldots$$

where *n*! represents *n*-factorial. Write a program to calculate *e* from this series as accurately as your system allows.

6. [17.2] (FileName:CH17C) Using program TestWhole (Example 17.2.1) as a guide, write your own generic procedure Increment to perform the same operations as standard procedure INC(*x*, *n*).

7. [17.2] Write and test a generic Swap procedure that interchanges two values passed to it as actual parameters of type INTEGER or CARDINAL or of any record whose size is equal to TSIZE(WORD).

8. [17.2] (FileName:CH17C) Write a generic procedure that performs a logical delete by setting any INTEGER or CARDINAL number passed to it to zero and setting any CHARacter passed to it to null. *Hints:* See Example 17.2.1 for a way of handling the character. Consider passing the actual parameter to a formal parameter of type WORD. Assign the value of the formal parameter to a value of type BITSET, and change the BITSET value to the empty set.

9. [17.2] (FileName:CH17D) Extend the BufferIt program (Example 17.2.2) to convert the CARDINAL values in Buffer to binary, and display the stream of bits that might be transmitted out through a serial port.

10. [17.2] (FileName:CH17D) Reverse program BufferIt (Example 17.2.2) to ask for character codes to be placed into an input buffer, copy them to a string-type memory block, and display the resulting characters.

11. [17.2] Using the ADDRESS type, write a program to ask for REAL numbers and display the way they are represented in binary and/or hexadecimal representation within your computer's memory.

12. [17.2] Define an array of records, in which each record contains a student name (array of CHARacters), age (CARDINAL), and rank in class (CARDINAL).
    a. Fill the array from the keyboard or an input file. Move the array to a CARDINAL-type output buffer. Display the output buffer.
    b. Convert the CARDINAL values in the output buffer to hexadecimal, and display the stream of hex values that might be transmitted over an 8-line parallel port.

13. [17.3] (FileName:CH17E) To program SumIt (Example 17.3.1), add a coroutine to find and display the products $1 \times 2 \times 3 \ldots \times N$ while counting and

finding the partial sums. Declare Count, Sum, and Product to be of type LONGINT, and stop executing before Product exceeds MAX(LONGINT).

14. [17.3] An arithmetic expression is entered from the keyboard. The expression consists of a string of characters formed by single digits separated by ' + ' or ' − ' and (to make life simple) terminated by the character ' = '. For example,

$$4+3-5= \quad \text{and} \quad 7+9-2+1-5=$$

Calculations are defined from left to right, so that the value of $4+3-5=$ would be $(4+3) - 5 = 7 - 5 = 2$.

   a. Write a program with three coroutines. One coroutine parses the expression; that is, it reads the characters from left to right. It first reads the first digit and saves that as the answer so far. Then it reads until it comes to an Op Digit where Op is ' + ' or ' − '. When it comes to ' = ', it displays the answer and stops.

   When Op Digit is read, control is transferred to an Add coroutine or a Subtract coroutine, as appropriate for the Op character. These coroutines add to or subtract from the answer so far and transfer control back to the parsing coroutine.

   b. Expand part a to handle multiplication and division (Op * and /). Assume that all calculations are still performed from left to right.

15. [17.3] The wholesale prices of items in your inventory are stored in an array. Write a program, using two coroutines, to calculate the retail price of every item and to store the retail prices in a new array. Each item is to be marked up 20%, and a $5.00 handling charge is added. Thus the retail price of each item will be computed by

$$Retail = 1.20 * Wholesale + 5.00.$$

One coroutine will multiply a single element of the Wholesale array by 1.20. The second coroutine will add $5.00 to the result calculated by the first coroutine and transfer control back to the main program, which displays and then stores the result, chooses a new array element, and then transfers control back to the first coroutine.

   If you have multiple processors in your machine, one can be adding $5.00 while another is multiplying the next value by 1.20. This is called a **pipeline** operation.

16. [17.4] (FileName:CH17F) Extend the TwoShips problem (Example 17.4.1) to include a fourth process that finds and displays the speed of separation S (in knots) of the ships, where, for positions y and x, $S = (y * v1 + x * v2)/\text{Dist}$.

17. [17.4] (FileName:CH17F) Two empty, runaway locomotives begin 50 miles apart and head toward each other on a straight track at speeds $v1$ and $v2$ miles per hour, entered by the user from the keyboard. The situation is shown in Figure 17–7.

   Using Example 17.4.1 as a guide, write a program with two processes to calculate and display a table of time, distance $x1$, and distance $x2$, for small time intervals, until the locomotives collide. Determine the point and time of collision. *Hint:* The collision occurs when $50 - x2 = x1$.

Figure 17–7
Two Locomotives on a Collision Course
(Exercise 17)

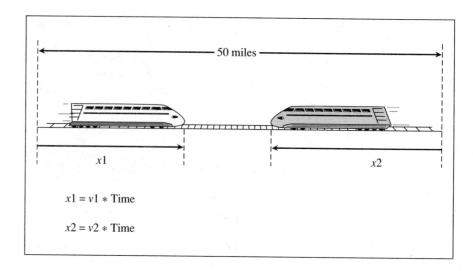

50 miles

$x1$

$x2$

$x1 = v1 * \text{Time}$

$x2 = v2 * \text{Time}$

18. [17.4] (FileName:CH17E) Implement program SumIt (Example 17.3.1) using procedures from the Processes module, rather than NEWPROCESS and TRANSFER.

19. [17.4] Implement Exercise 14 using procedures from the Processes module, rather than NEWPROCESS and TRANSFER.

A

*Standard
Functions and Procedures,
Reserved Identifiers,
Conversions*

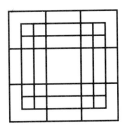

Standard Functions and Procedures

Functions

Function	Operation
ABS(x)	Returns the absolute value of *x*. (*x* can be CARDINAL, INTEGER, or REAL. ABS(*x*) will have the same type as *x*.)
CAP(Symbol)	Returns the capital (uppercase) letter corresponding to CHARacter variable Symbol. (Makes no change if Symbol is not a lowercase letter.)
CHR(m)	Returns the CHARacter with ordinal number *m*.
FLOAT(m)	Converts CARDINAL *m* to a REAL value.
HIGH(array)	Returns a CARDINAL value 1 less than the length of one-dimensional open array.
MAX(TypeName)	Returns the largest value of CARDINAL or INTEGER type.
MIN(TypeName)	Returns the smallest value of CARDINAL or INTEGER type.
ODD(m)	Returns BOOLEAN value TRUE or FALSE depending upon whether CARDINAL or INTEGER *m* is even or odd.
ORD(Enum)	Returns the position of variable Enum within its CARDINAL, INTEGER, CHARacter, or enumeration type list.
SIZE(Name)	Returns the size of variable Name. (In some versions of Modula-2, Name may also be the name of a type, in which case SIZE returns the size of any variable of that type. In some versions, SIZE must be imported from SYSTEM.)
TRUNC(x)	Returns the CARDINAL, truncated, whole-number part of positive REAL number *x*.
VAL(Name,n)	Returns the value of CARDINAL, INTEGER, CHARacter, or enumeration type Name, whose ordinal position in that type is *n*.

Procedures

Procedure	Operation
DEC(m) and DEC(m,n)	Decrements CARDINAL, INTEGER, CHARacter or enumeration variable *m* by 1 and by *n*, respectively.
EXCL(set, i)	Excludes *i* from set.
HALT	Stops program execution.
INC(m) and INC(m,n)	Increments CARDINAL, INTEGER, CHARacter, or enumeration variable *m* by 1 and by *n*, respectively.
INCL(set, i)	Includes *i* in set.

Reserved Identifiers

Reserved Words

AND	DO	IF	OF	SET
ARRAY	ELSE	IMPLEMENTATION	OR	THEN

BEGIN	ELSEIF	IMPORT	POINTER	TO
BY	END	IN	PROCEDURE	TYPE
CASE	EXIT	LOOP	QUALIFIED	UNTIL
CONST	EXPORT	MOD	RECORD	VAR
DEFINITION	FOR	MODULE	REPEAT	WHILE
DIV	FROM	NOT	RETURN	WITH

☐ Reserved Constant Values

FALSE   TRUE   NIL

☐ Reserved Types

BITSET	CARDINAL	INTEGER	LONGINT	PROC
BOOLEAN	CHAR	LONGCARD	LONGREAL	REAL

☐ Operator Symbols

+	addition, set addition
−	arithmetic negation, subtraction, set difference
*	multiplication, set intersection
/	REAL division, set symmetric difference
IN	set membership

=	equal
<> or #	not equal
<	less than
<=	less than or equal
>	greater than
>=	greater than or equal

AND	conjunction
NOT	negation
OR	disjunction

DIV	CARDINAL and INTEGER division
MOD	CARDINAL and INTEGER modulus (remainder)
:=	assignment
ˆ	pointer referent

Summary of Type Conversion Functions

☐ Type Conversion Functions

These type conversion functions are machine-independent; the code in which they are used can be moved to any machine that has a standard Modula-2 compiler. All attempted conversions are checked for validity during run time.

Standard Functions

These standard functions are always available; they do not need to be imported from an external module.

From	To	Function	Example (Assume variables VAR C:CARDINAL; R:REAL; I:INTEGER;)
INTEGER	CARDINAL	VAL ( )	C := VAL(CARDINAL, I);
CARDINAL	INTEGER	VAL ( )	I := VAL(INTEGER, C);
CARDINAL	REAL	FLOAT ( )	R := FLOAT(C);
REAL	CARDINAL	TRUNC( ) (truncates decimals)	C := TRUNC(R); (To *round* a real number use C := TRUNC(R + 0.5).

Standard Utility Functions

These utility functions must be imported from standard external module MathLib0.

From	To	Function	Example
INTEGER	REAL	real ( )	R := real(I);
REAL	INTEGER	entier ( )	I := entier(R);

☐ Type Transfer Functions

These type transfer functions are available without having to be imported from an external module. However, their implementation is machine-dependent. The internal representations of transferred data do not change, and attempted conversions are not checked for validity during run time.

From	To	Function	Example
INTEGER	CARDINAL	CARDINAL ( )	C := CARDINAL(I);
CARDINAL	INTEGER	INTEGER ( )	I := INTEGER(C);

B

Definition Modules, Standard

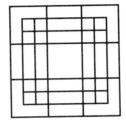

This appendix contains short definition modules for
Modula-2 modules InOut, RealInOut,
Terminal, MathLib0, Storage, and SYSTEM.

InOut

```
DEFINITION MODULE InOut;

    (* Module InOut provides procedures for performing I/O of
CARDINAL, INTEGER, and CHAR data.  Also included are procedures for
redirecting input and output from and to a single sequential file
stream. *)

FROM SYSTEM IMPORT WORD;
FROM FileSystem IMPORT File;

CONST  EOL = 36C;   (* End of Line Character *)

VAR  Done : BOOLEAN;   (* Flag for indicating success or failure of
                          an operation. *)
     termCH : CHAR;    (* termCH is set to the character entered by
                          the user to terminate an input. *)

PROCEDURE OpenInput(Default : ARRAY OF CHAR);
  (* Accepts a file name from the terminal, opens that file, and
     causes all input by InOut procedures to be received from that
     file rather than from the keyboard.  The Default extension is
     added to the file name if the user terminates the file name by
     a period.  The value of Done becomes TRUE if the file could be
     opened, FALSE otherwise. *)

PROCEDURE OpenOutput(Default : ARRAY OF CHAR);
  (* Accepts a file name from the terminal, opens that file, and
     causes all output by InOut procedures to be sent to that file
     rather than to the terminal screen.  The Default extension is
     added to the file name if the user terminates the file name by
     a period.  The value of Done becomes TRUE if the file could be
     opened, FALSE otherwise. *)

PROCEDURE CloseInput;
  (* Closes the file opened by OpenInput and causes input to be
     received from the keyboard again. *)

PROCEDURE CloseOuput;
  (* Closes the file opened by OpenOutput and causes output to be
     directed to the terminal screen again. *)

PROCEDURE Read(VAR Ch: CHAR);
  (* Reads a single character from the input stream into Ch.  The value
     of Done is TRUE unless the end of the input file has been
     reached.*)

PROCEDURE ReadString(VAR S : ARRAY OF CHAR);
  (* Reads a character string, terminated by any character whose code
     is less than or equal to that of the Space character (ASCII 32).
     Appends a NULL character to the end of the string if the number
     of characters is fewer than that allowed in the character array.
     Ignores characters beyond the limits of the character array. *)
```

```
PROCEDURE ReadInt(VAR X : INTEGER);
   (* Reads a string of characters which contains digits and may be
      preceded by a '+' or '-' character, representing an integer.
      Converts the string to an INTEGER value.
      The value of Done is FALSE if the input is invalid. *)

PROCEDURE ReadCard(VAR X : CARDINAL);
   (* Reads a string of characters which contains digits and represents
      a cardinal number.  Converts the string to a CARDINAL value.
      The value of Done is FALSE if the input is invalid. *)

PROCEDURE Write(Ch : CHAR);
   (* Writes a single character to the output stream. *)

PROCEDURE WriteLn;
   (* Writes an End of Line sequence. *)

PROCEDURE WriteString(S : ARRAY OF CHAR);
   (* Writes the string of characters in S.  Terminates at the end
      of the string array or at the NULL character, whichever occurs
      first. *)

PROCEDURE WriteInt(X : INTEGER;  FieldWidth : CARDINAL);
   (* Writes the INTEGER X as a decimal number, right justified in a
      field of width FieldWidth.  If the size of X is greater than
      FieldWidth, then FieldWidth is ignored. *)

PROCEDURE WriteCard(X, FieldWidth : CARDINAL);
   (* Writes the CARDINAL value X as a decimal number, right justified
      in a field of width FieldWidth.  If the size of X is greater than
      FieldWidth, then FieldWidth is ignored. *)

PROCEDURE WriteOct(X, FieldWidth : CARDINAL);
   (* Writes a CARDINAL value X as an octal number.  See WriteCard
      above. *)

PROCEDURE WriteHex(X, FieldWidth : CARDINAL);
   (* Writes a CARDINAL value X as a hexadecimal number.  See WriteCard
      above. *)

END InOut.
```

 ## *RealInOut*

```
DEFINITION MODULE RealInOut;

   (* Provides procedures for the input and output of REAL numbers.
      I/O will be redirected when InOut procedures are redirected using
      OpenInput and OpenOutput.  Read commands convert valid character
      strings to REAL values.  Write commands convert REAL values to
      character strings for output and write them right justified in
      the specified FieldWidth. *)

VAR  Done : BOOLEAN;   (* Flag for indicating the success or failure
                          of a read operation. *)
```

```
PROCEDURE ReadReal(VAR X : REAL);
   (* Reads a REAL number from the input stream or keyboard.  The
      decimal number may be in either fixed point or in exponential
      notation.  Done will be set to FALSE if the characters read
      do not represent a valid REAL number. *)

PROCEDURE WriteReal(X : REAL;  FieldWidth : CARDINAL);
   (* Writes the decimal REAL value of X in exponential notation,
      right justified in a field of width FieldWidth.  If the
      FieldWidth is too small, the number is rounded until it
      fits in the field or until a single digit after the decimal
      point is left.  If the number still will not fit, then
      FieldWidth is ignored, and sufficient space is used. *)

PROCEDURE WriteRealOct(X : REAL);
   (* Writes the REAL value of X in octal form. *)

(* The following procedure is not standard.  However, it appears in
many versions of Modula-2 in module RealInOut in one of its three forms
as indicated. *)

PROCEDURE FWriteReal(X:REAL;  FieldWidth,DecimalDigits:CARDINAL);
   or
PROCEDURE WriteRealFixed(X:REAL;  FieldWidth,DecimalDigits:CARDINAL);
   or
PROCEDURE WriteRealFormat(X:REAL;  FieldWidth,DecimalDigits:CARDINAL);
   (* Writes the decimal REAL value of X in fixed point notation,
      right justified in a field of width FieldWidth, rounded to
      DecimalDigits number of digits after the decimal point. *)

END RealInOut.
```

 ## *Terminal*

```
DEFINITION MODULE Terminal;

   (* Provides for I/O of characters from the keyboard and to the
      terminal screen and for output of a string to the screen.
      These procedures are not redirected by OpenInput or
      OpenOutput.  *)

PROCEDURE Read(VAR Ch : CHAR);
   (* Reads a single character from the keyboard into variable Ch.
      May or may not require a terminating character.
      The character may or may not be displayed. *)

PROCEDURE BusyRead(VAR Ch : CHAR);
   (* Reads a single character from the keyboard into variable Ch.
      If no character has been typed, returns the NULL character, 0C,
      to Ch. *)
```

```
PROCEDURE ReadAgain(VAR Ch : CHAR);
   (* Causes the last character read to be returned again upon the
      next call to Read. *)

PROCEDURE Write(Ch : CHAR);
   (* Writes the single character Ch to the screen. *)

PROCEDURE WriteLn;
   (* Writes the End of Line character to the screen. *)

PROCEDURE WriteString(S : ARRAY OF CHAR);
   (* Writes the characters from string S to the screen, until the
      length of the string array or NULL is encountered, whichever
      occurs first. *)

END Terminal.
```

MathLib0

```
DEFINITION MODULE MathLib0;

   (* Provides functions, in addition to those built into the language
      described in Appendix A, for handling mathematical operations. *)

PROCEDURE real(X : INTEGER) : REAL;
   (* Returns the REAL equivalent value of INTEGER X. *)

PROCEDURE entier(X : REAL) : INTEGER;
   (* Returns the largest INTEGER value less than or equal to REAL X. *)

PROCEDURE sqrt(X : REAL) : REAL;
   (* Returns the REAL square root of REAL argument X. *)

PROCEDURE ln(X : REAL) : REAL;
   (* Returns the natural logarithm (base e) of positive REAL
      value X. *)

PROCEDURE exp(X : REAL) : REAL;
   (* Returns the exponential (base e raised to the X power) of X. *)

PROCEDURE sin(X : REAL) : REAL;
   (* Returns the trigonometric sine of REAL angle X, which must be
      expressed in radians. *)

PROCEDURE cos(X : REAL) : REAL;
   (* Returns the trigonometric cosine of REAL angle X, which must be
      expressed in radians. *)

PROCEDURE arctan(X : REAL) : REAL;
   (* Returns the REAL radian value of the angle whose trigonometric
      tangent is X. *)

END MathLib0.
```

Storage

```
DEFINITION MODULE Storage;

  (* Provides procedures for allocating and deallocating memory
     storage dynamically during program execution.  Note that
     calls to the older procedures NEW and DISPOSE are translated
     by Storage modules in recent versions of Modula-2 to
     ALLOCATE and DEALLOCATE respectively. *)


FROM SYSTEM IMPORT ADDRESS;

PROCEDURE ALLOCATE(VAR Addr : ADDRESS;  Size : CARDINAL);
  (* Allocates an area of the given Size and returns to parameter
     Addr the address of the area reserved.  If memory
     is not available to be allocated, the program terminates
     with an error message. *)

PROCEDURE DEALLOCATE(VAR Addr : ADDRESS;  Size : CARDINAL);
  (* Releases Size number of memory units starting at address
     Addr.  The program terminates with an error message if fewer
     than Size storage units have been allocated at Addr. *)

PROCEDURE Available(Size : CARDINAL) : BOOLEAN;
  (* Returns the value TRUE if there is enough memory available
     to allocate Size number of units.  Returns FALSE if there
     is not sufficient memory available. *)

END Storage.
```

SYSTEM

```
DEFINITION MODULE SYSTEM;

  (* Module SYSTEM is not stored in a separate library file.  It is
     part of the Modula-2 compiler code.  Thus it is called a pseudomodule.
     However, the procedures and types of this module may
     be imported and used to perform system-level operations. *)


TYPE  WORD;      (* A type that is assignment-compatible with all data types
                    that use one word of memory.  The size of a WORD varies
                    from computer to computer. *)
      ADDRESS = POINTER TO WORD;  (* Represents a memory address.  *)


PROCEDURE ADR(X : AnyType) : ADDRESS;
  (* Returns the address of variable X.  X may be of any type. *)
```

PROCEDURE TSIZE(AnyType) : CARDINAL;
   (* Returns the size of a data type, as the number of memory units
      required for storage of a variable of that type. On some
      systems, TSIZE returns the number of bytes; on other systems,
      the number of memory words is returned. *)

(* The following two procedures, for implementing concurrent processes
   and coroutines, are sometimes found in the SYSTEM pseudomodule.
   In other versions of Modula-2, they may be found in the Processes
   module (see Appendix C) or some other module. *)

PROCEDURE NEWPROCESS(P : PROC;   Addr : ADDRESS;   Size : CARDINAL;
                     VAR NewAddr : ADDRESS);
   (* P represents a parameterless procedure from which the new
      process is defined. Addr defines the beginning of the
      workspace reserved for the process. Size is the size of
      the workspace in memory units. The starting address of the
      new process is assigned to NewAddr. *)

PROCEDURE TRANSFER(VAR Source, Destination : ADDRESS);
   (* Suspends operation of the Source process and resumes operation
      of the Destination process from where that Destination process
      was last suspended. *)

END SYSTEM.

C

Definition and Implementation Modules, Nonstandard

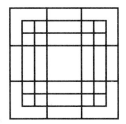

The first two modules presented in this appendix—FileSystem and Processes—are included with most Modula-2 compilers; therefore, only their DEFINITION modules are given here. Since these modules' implementations differ somewhat in the various versions of the language, they are included here rather than in Appendix B.

The third module here is called *Strings*. Nearly every version of Modula-2 includes a strings module, but the names and operations of strings procedures and functions vary with compilers. Because of this, a complete strings module containing the most commonly used commands was developed for the examples and exercises in this book. Both the DEFINITION and IMPLEMENTATION modules for strings used in this book are included here so that you can incorporate them into your system if you should desire to do so.

Other modules in this appendix—Graphics, MyMath, Dynamic, and RandGen—are unique to this book and are used for some of the examples and exercises. Both DEFINITION and IMPLEMENTATION modules are provided so that you can use them freely.

The final module, FRealOut, contains a procedure FWriteReal for displaying REAL numbers in floating point format, which will be especially valuable if no equivalent of this procedure accompanies your Modula-2 compiler.

FileSystem

```
DEFINITION MODULE FileSystem;
  (* The FileSystem module was developed by Niklaus Wirth for
    manipulating files without the limitations of the InOut
    module procedures.  Most Modula-2 compilers are accompanied
    by a module which includes the features of FileSystem, but in
    many versions the implementation will be somewhat different.
    Consult your compiler manual for details.
        The FilePosition pointer refers to the location of the
    next data item to be read or where the next item will be
    written.  This pointer is advanced automatically by each
    read and write procedure.  *)


FROM SYSTEM IMPORT WORD;

TYPE  Response = (done, notdone ... );
                (* Numerous response values are defined to indicate
                  errors in file operations.  Flag done acts similarly
                  to variable Done in the InOut module. *)


      File = RECORD
              res : Response; (* File.res = done indicates that
                                a call to a FileSystem procedure
                                was successful. *)
              eof : BOOLEAN;  (* File.eof = TRUE indicates that
                                end of file has been encountered. *)
              ......          (* Other fields of the File record
                                may be defined for different
                                systems. *)
            END; (* RECORD *)



PROCEDURE Lookup(VAR F:File;  FileName:ARRAY OF CHAR;  New:BOOLEAN);
  (* Opens a file with system name FileName.  If New is TRUE, the
    file is created.  If New is FALSE, an existing file with the
    specified FileName will be sought and opened if found. The
    FilePosition pointer is set to the beginning of the file. *)


PROCEDURE Create(VAR F:File;  DeviceName:ARRAY OF CHAR);
  (* Creates a temporary file on the specified device.
    For example, specifying "A:" for the device name would
    create a scratchpad file on the disk in drive A. *)


PROCEDURE Close(VAR F:File);
  (* Closes file F which has previously been opened by Lookup.  To
    prevent loss of data, each file which has been opened in a
    program should be Closed before program execution terminates. *)


PROCEDURE Rename(VAR F:File;  FileName:ARRAY OF CHAR);
  (* Changes the name of an open file to the new FileName. *)
```

PROCEDURE SetRead(VAR F:File);
    (* Sets file F to read only mode. Read mode also may be set
    implicitly simply by executing a ReadChar` or ReadWord
    command. The FilePosition pointer is not moved by SetRead. *)

PROCEDURE SetWrite(VAR F:File);
    (* Sets file F to write only mode. Write mode also may be set
    implicitly simply by executing a WriteChar or WriteWord
    command. The FilePostion pointer is not moved by SetWrite. *)

PROCEDURE SetModify(VAR F:File);
    (* Sets the mode of file F so that both read and write operations
    may be performed on a the file. The FilePostion pointer is
    not moved by SetModify. *)

PROCEDURE SetOpen(VAR F:File);
    (* Opens the mode of file F, so that the next read, write, or set
    operation will reset the file to a new mode. The FilePosition
    pointer is not moved by this procedure. *)

PROCEDURE Reset(VAR F:File);
    (* Repositions to FilePosition pointer to the beginning of the
    file and puts the file in Open mode, so that the next read,
    write, or set operation will reset the file to a new mode. *)

PROCEDURE ReadChar(VAR F:File; VAR Ch:CHAR);
    (* Reads a single character from file F into variable Ch. If
    the FilePosition pointer is past the end of file, then
    field F.eof becomes TRUE. *)

PROCEDURE ReadWord(VAR F:File; VAR W:WORD);
    (* Reads a word from file F into WORD type variable W. If
    the FilePosition pointer is past the end of file, the
    field F.eof becomes TRUE. *)

PROCEDURE Again(VAR F:File);
    (* Moves the FilePosition indicator so that the next call to
    ReadChar or ReadWord fetches the same character or word as
    the previous call. *)

PROCEDURE WriteChar(VAR F:File; Ch:CHAR);
    (* Writes the single character specified by Ch to file F at the
    position defined by the FilePosition pointer. *)

PROCEDURE WriteWord(VAR F:File: W:WORD);
    (* Writes the single word W to file F at the position defined by
    the FilePosition pointer. *)

PROCEDURE SetPos(VAR F:File; high,low:CARDINAL);
    (* Sets the value of the FilePosition indicator to point to the byte
    at position 2^{16} * high + low. *)

PROCEDURE GetPos(VAR F:File; VAR high,low:CARDINAL);
    (* Returns the byte number in high and low to which the FilePosition
    indicator points, such that byte number = 2^{16} * high + low. *)

```
PROCEDURE Length(VAR F:File;  VAR high,low:CARDINAL);
   (* Returns the total length of the file in bytes in high and low,
      where  length is represented by  2^16 * high  +  low.  *)
```

```
PROCEDURE  Doio(VAR F:File);
   (*      In Read mode, the buffer associated with the file is filled
      starting at the current FilePosition.
           In Write mode, the buffer contents are copied to the file,
      starting at FilePosition.  FilePosition is updated.  The buffer
      contents are not changed.
           In Modify mode, the buffer contents are copied to the file,
      starting at FilePosition.  FilePosition is updated.  The buffer
      is filled starting at the new FilePosition.  *)
```

```
END FileSystem.
```

Processes

```
DEFINITION MODULE Processes;

      (* The Processes module provides procedures and functions
         which provide for execution of concurrent processes. *)


TYPE  SIGNAL;   (* This is a type which is opaque to the user and
                   which provides communication between processes. *)


PROCEDURE StartProcess(P : PROC;   N : CARDINAL);
   (* Starts the process defined by parameterless procedure P.
      N memory units are reserved for the process workspace. *)


PROCEDURE SEND(VAR S : SIGNAL);
   (* Allows the process which is waiting for signal S to resume
      execution. *)


PROCEDURE WAIT(VAR S : SIGNAL);
   (* Suspends execution of the current process until the signal
      S is sent by another process. *)


PROCEDURE Awaited(S : SIGNAL) : BOOLEAN;
   (* Returns the value TRUE if there is a process waiting for
      signal S.  Returns FALSE otherwise. *)


PROCEDURE Init(VAR S : SIGNAL);
   (* Every signal S must be intialized, by calling this procedure,
      before that signal can be used. *)
```

(* In some versions of Modula-2, procedures NEWPROCESS and
TRANSFER, for handling coroutines, may be included in this module
instead of in the SYSTEM module. See the SYSTEM module in Appendix B
for a description of these two procedures. *)

END Processes.

Strings

DEFINITION MODULE Strings;
   (* String handling functions and procedures. Strings are terminated
     by the Null chararacter or when the array is filled. *)

CONST LASTINDEX = 79; SPACE = ' '; NULL = 0C;
TYPE   STRING = ARRAY [0..LASTINDEX] OF CHAR;
   (* STRING type may be imported and used when it is desired to
     handle 80 character strings as an abstract data type. *)

PROCEDURE TabOrFill(HowMany:CARDINAL; FillCharacter:CHAR);
   (* Writes FillCharacter HowMany times. *)

PROCEDURE ReadLine(VAR Destination:ARRAY OF CHAR);
   (* Reads a string of characters, including spaces, until a character,
     such as Return, with ASCII less than 32 is read. A Null character
     marks the end of the string. If the number of characters exceeds
     the length of the string, the additional characters are discarded.
     ReadLine uses Read from the InOut module, so ReadLine is redirected
     when InOut is redirected. *)

PROCEDURE Length(Source:ARRAY OF CHAR):CARDINAL;
   (* Returns the CARDINAL number of characters in Source which
     precede the Null character, or the total length of the
     string space if the Null character is not present. *)

PROCEDURE CompareStrings(Source1,Source2:ARRAY OF CHAR):INTEGER;
   (* RETURNs -1 if Source1 comes alphabetically before Source2,
         0 if Source1 = Source2,
        +1 if Source1 comes alphabetically after Source2. *)

PROCEDURE Position(Source,Destination:ARRAY OF CHAR):CARDINAL;
   (* Returns the index position of the first character in the
     first occurrence of substring Source within string
     Destination. If Source is not found in Destination, then
     Position returns the Length of the Destination string. *)

PROCEDURE Concatenate(Source1,Source2:ARRAY OF CHAR;
                       VAR Destination:ARRAY OF CHAR);
   (* Appends the string Source2 to the end of string Source1
     and stores the result in string location Destination.
     If the concatenated strings will not fit into Destination,
     then the leftmost characters up to the Length of the
     Destination space are stored. *)

```
PROCEDURE Assign(Source:ARRAY OF CHAR;  VAR Destination:ARRAY OF CHAR);
   (* Copies string Source to string Destination.
      If Length(Source) > HIGH(Destination), then the leftmost
      characters from Source are copied until Destination is filled. *)

PROCEDURE Copy(Source:ARRAY OF CHAR; StartIndex, CopyHowMany:CARDINAL;
                                    VAR Destination:ARRAY OF CHAR);
   (* Characters from Source, beginning at position StartIndex, and
      continuing CopyHowMany number of characters, are copied to
      string location Destination.
      If  CopyHowMany > HIGH(Destination)+1, then the characters
      from Source are copied until Destination is filled. *)


PROCEDURE Delete(VAR Source:ARRAY OF CHAR;
                                 StartIndex,DeleteHowMany:CARDINAL);
   (* DeleteHowMany number of characters are deleted from Source,
      beginning with the character at position StartIndex; and the
      remaining characters in Source are shifted left to fill
      in the spaces left by the deletions.  *)

PROCEDURE Insert(Source:ARRAY OF CHAR; VAR Destination:ARRAY OF CHAR;
                                          InsertPosn:CARDINAL);
   (* Inserts string Source into Destination beginning at position
      InsertPosn in Destination.  If  InsertPosn = Length(Destination),
      then Source is concatenated to Destination.  If inserting all
      of Source would result in a string which exceeds the memory
      allocated for Destination, then Source is inserted and the
      result is truncated, so that Destination is just filled. *)

END Strings.
─────────

IMPLEMENTATION MODULE Strings;
   (* String handling functions and procedures.  Strings are terminated
       by the Null character or when the array is filled.  *)

FROM InOut IMPORT Read, Write;

PROCEDURE TabOrFill(HowMany:CARDINAL;  FillCharacter:CHAR);
   VAR  Count : CARDINAL;     (* Writes FillCharacter HowMany times. *)
   BEGIN
      FOR Count := 1 TO HowMany DO  Write(FillCharacter); END; (*FOR*)
   END TabOrFill;

PROCEDURE ReadLine(VAR Destination:ARRAY OF CHAR);
   (* Reads characters, including spaces, until end of line is encountered.
      YOU MAY WISH TO REMOVE Write(Destination[Index]) COMMANDS IF YOUR
      SYSTEM READ COMMAND ECHOES CHARACTERS TO THE SCREEN. *)
   VAR  Discard : CHAR;  Index : CARDINAL;
   BEGIN
      Index := 0;  Read(Destination[Index]); Write(Destination[Index]);
      WHILE (Destination[Index] >= SPACE) AND (Index < HIGH(Destination)) DO
         INC(Index);  Read(Destination[Index]);  Write(Destination[Index]);
      END; (* WHILE *)
```

```
        Discard := Destination[Index];   (* Discard additional characters. *)
        WHILE  Discard >= SPACE  DO  Read(Discard);  END; (* WHILE *)
        IF (Index <= HIGH(Destination)) AND ((Destination[Index]) < SPACE) THEN
           Destination[Index] := NULL;         (* Insert Null if necessary. *)
        END; (* IF *)
    END ReadLine;

PROCEDURE Length(Source:ARRAY OF CHAR):CARDINAL;
    (* Returns the CARDINAL number of characters in Source which
       precede the Null character, or the total length of the
       string space if the Null character is not present. *)
    VAR  Index : CARDINAL;
    BEGIN
        Index := 0;
        WHILE (Index <= HIGH(Source)) AND (Source[Index] <> NULL)  DO
           INC(Index);
        END; (* WHILE *)
        RETURN Index;
    END Length;


PROCEDURE CompareStrings(Source1,Source2:ARRAY OF CHAR):INTEGER;
    (* RETURNs   -1  if Source1 comes alphabetically before Source2,
                  0  if Source1 = Source2,
                 +1  if Source1 comes alphabetically after Source2.  *)
    VAR  Index, MaxIndex : CARDINAL;   Result : INTEGER;
    BEGIN
        IF Length(Source1)<=Length(Source2) THEN MaxIndex:=Length(Source1)-1;
           ELSE  MaxIndex:=Length(Source2)-1;
        END; (* IF *)
        Index := 0;  Result := 0;
        REPEAT
           IF         Source1[Index] > Source2[Index]  THEN  Result := +1;
              ELSIF   Source1[Index] < Source2[Index]  THEN  Result := -1;
           END; (* IF *)  INC(Index);
        UNTIL  (Index > MaxIndex) OR (Result <> 0);
        IF  (Result = 0) AND (Length(Source1) <> Length(Source2))  THEN
           IF         Length(Source1) > Length(Source2)  THEN  Result := +1;
              ELSE  Result := -1;
           END; (* IF *)
        END; (* IF *)
        RETURN Result;
    END CompareStrings;


PROCEDURE Position(Source,Destination:ARRAY OF CHAR):CARDINAL;
    (* Returns the index position of the first character in the
       first occurrence of substring Source within string
       Destination.  If Source is not found in Destination, then
       Position returns the Length of the Destination string. *)
    VAR  PosblPosn, SrcIndex, LastPosblPosn : CARDINAL;
    BEGIN
        IF  Length(Source) <= Length(Destination)  THEN
           LastPosblPosn := Length(Destination) - Length(Source);
           FOR  PosblPosn := 0 TO LastPosblPosn  DO
              SrcIndex := 0;
```

```
            LOOP
              IF (SrcIndex > HIGH(Source)) OR (Source[SrcIndex] = NULL) THEN
                 RETURN  PosblPosn;
              END; (* IF *)
              IF (Source[SrcIndex] # Destination[PosblPosn + SrcIndex]) THEN
                 EXIT;
              END; (* IF *)
              INC(SrcIndex);
            END; (* LOOP *)
       END; (* FOR *)
    END; (* IF *)
    RETURN  Length(Destination);
END Position;

PROCEDURE Concatenate(Source1,Source2:ARRAY OF CHAR;
                                    VAR Destination:ARRAY OF CHAR);
   (* Appends the string Source2 to the end of string Source1
      and stores the result in string location Destination.
      If the concatenated strings will not fit into Destination,
      then the leftmost characters up to the Length of the
      Destination space are stored.  *)
   VAR  DestIndex, MaxIndex, Src2Index : CARDINAL;
   BEGIN
      MaxIndex := HIGH(Destination);
      IF  MaxIndex > HIGH(Source1)   THEN
         MaxIndex := HIGH(Source1);
      END; (* IF *)
      DestIndex := 0;
      WHILE  (DestIndex <= MaxIndex) AND  (Source1[DestIndex] # NULL)  DO
         Destination[DestIndex] := Source1[DestIndex];   INC(DestIndex);
      END; (* WHILE *)
      IF  DestIndex <= HIGH(Destination)  THEN
         MaxIndex := HIGH(Source2);
         IF  MaxIndex > (HIGH(Destination) - DestIndex)  THEN
            MaxIndex := HIGH(Destination) - DestIndex;
         END; (* IF *)
         Src2Index := 0;
         WHILE  (Src2Index <= MaxIndex) AND  (Source2[Src2Index] # NULL)  DO
            Destination[DestIndex] := Source2[Src2Index];
            INC(DestIndex);   INC(Src2Index);
         END; (* WHILE *)
         IF  DestIndex <= HIGH(Destination)  THEN
            Destination[DestIndex] := NULL;
         END; (* IF *)
      END; (* IF *)
   END Concatenate;

PROCEDURE Assign(Source:ARRAY OF CHAR;  VAR Destination:ARRAY OF CHAR);
   (* Copies string Source to string Destination.
      If  Length(Source) > HIGH(Destination), then the leftmost
      characters from Source are copied until Destination is filled.  *)
   VAR  Index : CARDINAL;
   BEGIN
      Index := 0;
      WHILE  (Index <= HIGH(Source)) AND (Index <= HIGH(Destination))
                                    AND (Source[Index] # NULL)  DO
```

```
        Destination[Index] := Source[Index];    INC(Index);
    END; (* WHILE *)
    IF  Index <= HIGH(Destination)   THEN
        Destination[Index] := NULL;
    END; (* IF *)
END Assign;


PROCEDURE Copy(Source:ARRAY OF CHAR; StartIndex, CopyHowMany:CARDINAL;
                                       VAR Destination:ARRAY OF CHAR);
    (* Characters from Source, beginning at position StartIndex, and
       continuing CopyHowMany number of characters, are copied to
       string location Destination.
       If  CopyHowMany > HIGH(Destination)+1, then the characters
       from Source are copied until Destination is filled.  *)
    VAR  MaxIndex, SrcIndex : CARDINAL;
    BEGIN
        IF  CopyHowMany > HIGH(Destination)+1  THEN
            CopyHowMany := HIGH(Destination)+1;
        END; (* IF *)
        MaxIndex  :=  HIGH(Source) + 1;
        IF  (StartIndex >= MaxIndex)  OR  (CopyHowMany = 0)  THEN
            Destination[0] := NULL;
        ELSE
            IF  (StartIndex + CopyHowMany) > MaxIndex  THEN
                CopyHowMany  :=  MaxIndex - StartIndex;
            END; (* IF *)
            FOR  SrcIndex := StartIndex TO StartIndex + CopyHowMany - 1  DO
                Destination[SrcIndex - StartIndex]  :=  Source[SrcIndex];
            END; (* FOR *)
            IF  CopyHowMany <= HIGH(Destination)  THEN
                Destination[CopyHowMany] := NULL;
            END; (* IF *)
        END; (* IF *)
    END Copy;


PROCEDURE Delete(VAR Source:ARRAY OF CHAR;
                                 StartIndex, DeleteHowMany:CARDINAL);
    (* DeleteHowMany number of characters are deleted from Source,
       beginning with the character at position StartIndex; and the
       remaining characters in Source are shifted left to fill
       in the spaces left by the deletions.  *)
    VAR  NumInSource, SrcIndex : CARDINAL;
    BEGIN
        NumInSource := Length(Source);
        IF  StartIndex <= NumInSource  THEN
            IF  (StartIndex + DeleteHowMany) > NumInSource  THEN
                DeleteHowMany  :=  NumInSource - StartIndex;
            END; (* IF *)
                (* Move Source between StartIndex and NumInSource to left *)
            FOR  SrcIndex := StartIndex  TO  NumInSource - DeleteHowMany  DO
                Source[SrcIndex]  :=  Source[SrcIndex + DeleteHowMany];
            END; (* FOR *)
            SrcIndex := NumInSource - DeleteHowMany;
            IF  SrcIndex <= HIGH(Source)  THEN
                Source[SrcIndex] := NULL;
```

```
          END;  (* IF *)
      END;  (* IF *)
END Delete;

PROCEDURE Insert(Source:ARRAY OF CHAR; VAR Destination:ARRAY OF CHAR;
                                          InsertPosn:CARDINAL);
    (* Inserts string Source into Destination beginning at position
       InsertPosn in Destination.  If  InsertPosn = Length(Destination),
       then Source is concatenated to Destination.  If inserting all
       of Source would result in a string which exceeds the memory
       allocated for Destination, then Source is inserted and the
       result is truncated, so that Destination is just filled. *)
    VAR  SrcLngth, DestLngth, DestIndex, SrcIndex : CARDINAL;
    BEGIN
        IF  InsertPosn <= Length(Destination)  THEN
            SrcLngth := Length(Source);  DestLngth := Length(Destination);
            IF  (InsertPosn + SrcLngth)  > (HIGH(Destination) + 1)  THEN
                SrcLngth  :=  HIGH(Destination) + 1  - InsertPosn;
            END;  (* IF *)
            IF  (DestLngth + SrcLngth) > HIGH(Destination)+1  THEN
                DestLngth  :=  HIGH(Destination)+1  - SrcLngth;
            END;  (* IF *)
                (* Shift trailing part of Destination to the right *)
            FOR  DestIndex := DestLngth  TO  InsertPosn  BY  -1  DO
                Destination[DestIndex + SrcLngth] := Destination[DestIndex];
            END;  (* FOR *)
                (* Fill in with Source *)
            FOR  SrcIndex := 0  TO  SrcLngth - 1  DO
                Destination[InsertPosn + SrcIndex] := Source[SrcIndex];
            END;  (* FOR *)
        END;  (* IF *)
    END Insert;

END Strings.
```

Graphics

```
DEFINITION MODULE Graphics;
    (* Contains procedures for producing bar and line character oriented
       graphics of two dimensional data, supplied in the form of parallel
       X and Y arrays of REAL numbers.
    LIMITATIONS:
        1.  There must be at least two X, Y points.
        2.  For Line Plots no two points may have the same X value.
        3.  For Line Plots the range of X values should not be more than
            an order of magnitude greater than the smallest separation
            between any two X values.
        4.  Y values plot best if scaled between O(1) and O(1000).  *)

TYPE  FunctionType = PROCEDURE(REAL):REAL;

PROCEDURE  TabOrFill(HowMany:CARDINAL;  FillCharacter:CHAR);
    (* Writes FillCharacter  HowMany times. *)
```

```
PROCEDURE   SwapReals(VAR ElementA, ElementB : REAL);
    (* Interchanges REAL Elements A and B. *)

PROCEDURE FindMinAndMax(Z:ARRAY OF REAL;  VAR ZMin, ZMax: REAL);
    (* Finds min & max values in array Z. *)

PROCEDURE FindXInterval(X:ARRAY OF REAL; VAR dx:REAL);
    (* Finds  dx  interval for line graph such that
        dx >= minimum  x  separation between points. *)

PROCEDURE PrintYScale(YMin,YMax:REAL;  Width,YPlot0:CARDINAL);
    (* Prints the Y Scale along leading edge of the graph. *)

PROCEDURE SortXY(VAR X, Y : ARRAY OF REAL);
    (* Performs a Selection sort to arrange parallel arrays X and Y
        in order of increasing X values. *)

PROCEDURE ConvertToArray(YCalc:FunctionType; VAR X,Y:ARRAY OF REAL);
    (* Converts a function,  y = f(x),  of type PROCEDURE(REAL):REAL;
        passed from the calling module as YCalc, to a corresponding
        set of points, defined by arrays  X and  Y.  *)

PROCEDURE LinePlot(X, Y: ARRAY OF REAL;  Width, YPlot0 : CARDINAL;
                                    Symbol : CHAR;   YMin, YMax : REAL);
    (* Produces a scaled, point plot of Y vs X with constant intervals
        along the x-axis.  *)

PROCEDURE BarPlot(X, Y: ARRAY OF REAL; Width, YPlot0 : CARDINAL;
    (* Produces a bar graph of Y vs X. *)  Symbol:CHAR;   YMin,YMax:REAL);

PROCEDURE PlotIt(X, Y : ARRAY OF REAL);
    (* Calls either LinePlot or BarPlot for X, Y,  as requested by the
        user.  Allows the user to specify the graph width and finds
        the minimum and maximum Y values for scaling purposes.   *)

END Graphics.
──────────

IMPLEMENTATION MODULE Graphics;
    (* Contains procedures for producing bar and line character oriented
        graphics of two dimensional data, supplied in the form of parallel
        X and Y arrays of REAL numbers.
    LIMITATIONS:
        1.  There must be at least two X, Y points.
        2.  For Line Plots no two points may have the same X value.
        3.  For Line Plots the range of X values should not be more than
                an order of magnitude greater than the smallest separation
                between any two X values.
        4.  Y values plot best if scaled between O(1) and O(1000).  *)

FROM InOut IMPORT WriteString,WriteLn,Read,ReadCard,Write,WriteInt,WriteCard;
FROM RealInOut IMPORT ReadReal, FWriteReal;    FROM MathLib0 IMPORT entier;

CONST XWID = 6; XDEC = 1;  YWID = 8; YDEC = 1;  Blank = ` `;  Dot = `.`;
      MAXWIDTH = 60;  EPSILON = 0.001;  LINEPTRATIO = 10;
```

```
PROCEDURE  TabOrFill(HowMany:CARDINAL;   FillCharacter:CHAR);
   VAR  Count : CARDINAL;     (* Writes FillCharacter  HowMany times. *)
   BEGIN
      FOR  Count := 1 TO HowMany DO  Write(FillCharacter) ; END;(*FOR*)
   END TabOrFill;


PROCEDURE  SwapReals(VAR ElementA, ElementB : REAL);
   VAR  TempElmt : REAL;      (* Interchanges REAL Elements A and B. *)
   BEGIN
      TempElmt := ElementA;  ElementA := ElementB;  ElementB := TempElmt;
   END SwapReals;


PROCEDURE FindMinAndMax(Z:ARRAY OF REAL;  VAR ZMin, ZMax: REAL);
   VAR  WhichPt : CARDINAL;     (* Finds min & max values in array Z. *)
   BEGIN
      ZMin := Z[0];  ZMax := Z[0];
      FOR  WhichPt := 1 TO HIGH(Z)  DO
         IF  ZMin > Z[WhichPt]  THEN  ZMin := Z[WhichPt]; END;(*IF*)
         IF  ZMax < Z[WhichPt]  THEN  ZMax := Z[WhichPt]; END;(*IF*)
      END; (* FOR *)
   END FindMinAndMax;


PROCEDURE FindXInterval(X:ARRAY OF REAL; VAR dx:REAL);
   (* Finds  dx  interval for line graph such that
       dx >= minimum  x  separation between points. *)
   VAR  MinPtSep, XMin, XMax : REAL;   Answer, Discard : CHAR;
       NumPts, WhichPt, NumPlotLines : CARDINAL;
   BEGIN
      NumPts := HIGH(X) + 1;  (* MinPtSep = smallest separation between *)
      MinPtSep := X[1]-X[0];                  (* any adjacent X values. *)
      FOR  WhichPt := 2 TO NumPts-1  DO
         IF  MinPtSep > X[WhichPt] - X[WhichPt-1]  THEN
            MinPtSep :=  X[WhichPt] - X[WhichPt-1];
         END; (* IF *)
      END; (* FOR *)

IF  ABS(MinPtSep) <= EPSILON  THEN
   WriteLn; WriteString("No two points may have the same X value.");
    WriteLn; WriteString("Execution will halt.  Check input data.");
   WriteLn; HALT;
END; (* IF *)
FindMinAndMax(X, XMin, XMax);
NumPlotLines := TRUNC( (XMax-XMin)/ MinPtSep + 1.0 );
WriteString("The minimum number of Lines for Graph will be");
 WriteCard(NumPlotLines,8); WriteLn;
IF  NumPlotLines DIV NumPts >= LINEPTRATIO  THEN
   WriteString("There will be"); WriteCard(NumPlotLines DIV NumPts,8);
    WriteString(" or more lines for each point."); WriteLn;
    WriteString("You must have some points very close and some ");
    WriteString(" spread far apart."); WriteLn;
   REPEAT
      WriteLn; WriteString("Do you still want this plot (Y/N)? ");
       Read(Answer); Read(Discard); Write(Answer); WriteLn;
      IF  CAP(Answer) = 'N' THEN  WriteLn;
         WriteString("Execution will halt.  Check input data.");
          WriteLn; HALT;
```

```
          END;  (* IF *)
       UNTIL  (CAP(Answer)='Y') OR (CAP(Answer)='N');
   END;  (* IF *)
   REPEAT
      WriteString("Would you like more lines than ");
       WriteCard(NumPlotLines,4); WriteString(" (Y/N)? ");
       Read(Answer); Read(Discard); Write(Answer); WriteLn;
      IF  CAP(Answer) = 'Y' THEN
         WriteString("How many lines would you like? ");
         ReadCard(NumPlotLines); WriteLn;
      END; (* IF *)  WriteLn;
   UNTIL  (CAP(Answer) = 'Y') OR (CAP(Answer) = 'N');

      (* Adjust NumPlotLines, if necessary, so that dx <= MinPtSet. *)
   NumPlotLines := NumPlotLines - 1;
   REPEAT
      NumPlotLines := NumPlotLines + 1;
      dx := ( (X[NumPts-1]+0.5) - (X[0]-0.5) ) / FLOAT(NumPlotLines);
                        (* dx = constant spacing along x-axis *)
   UNTIL  dx <= MinPtSep;
END FindXInterval;

PROCEDURE PrintYScale(YMin,YMax:REAL;  Width,YPlot0:CARDINAL);
   (* Prints the Y Scale along leading edge of the graph. *)
   BEGIN
      IF  YMin < -0.05  THEN
         TabOrFill(12, Blank); WriteInt(entier(YMin+0.5),6);
         IF  YMax <= 0.0  THEN
            TabOrFill(Width-6, Blank); WriteInt(entier(YMax+0.5),6);
         ELSE
            IF  (YPlot0 >= 1) AND (YPlot0 <> Width)  THEN
               TabOrFill(YPlot0-2, Blank); WriteInt(0,1);
            END; (* IF *)
            IF  Width >= (YPlot0 + 6)  THEN
               TabOrFill(Width-YPlot0-5,Blank);WriteInt(entier(YMax+0.5),6);
            END; (* IF *)
         END; (* IF *)
      ELSIF  ABS(YMin) <= 0.05  THEN
         TabOrFill(16, Blank);  WriteInt(0,1);
         TabOrFill(Width-5, Blank); WriteInt(entier(YMax+0.5), 6);
      ELSE
         TabOrFill(11, Blank); WriteInt(entier(YMin+0.5),6);
         TabOrFill(Width-5, Blank); WriteInt(entier(YMax+0.5),6);
      END; (* IF *) WriteLn;
      WriteString("   X        Y     "); TabOrFill(Width+2, '='); WriteLn;
   END PrintYScale;

PROCEDURE SortXY(VAR X, Y : ARRAY OF REAL);
   (* Performs a Selection sort to arrange parallel arrays X and Y
      in order of increasing X values. *)
   VAR NumPts, LastSubListIndex, LargestYet, SubListIndex : CARDINAL;
   BEGIN
      NumPts := HIGH(X) + 1;  (* NumPts = length of array X  *)
      FOR  LastSubListIndex := NumPts-1 TO 1 BY -1   DO
         LargestYet := 0;
         FOR  SubListIndex := 1 TO LastSubListIndex   DO
            IF  X[LargestYet] < X[SubListIndex]   THEN
```

```
              LargestYet := SubListIndex;
          END; (* IF *)
        END; (* FOR *)
        SwapReals(X[LargestYet], X[LastSubListIndex]);
        SwapReals(Y[LargestYet], Y[LastSubListIndex]);
    END; (* FOR *)
END SortXY;

PROCEDURE ConvertToArray(YCalc:FunctionType; VAR X,Y:ARRAY OF REAL);
    (* Converts a function,  y = f(x),  of type PROCEDURE(REAL):REAL;
       passed from the calling module as YCalc, to a corresponding
       set of points, defined by arrays  X and  Y.  *)
    VAR  dx, lowbound, upbound : REAL;   WhichPt, NumPts : CARDINAL;
    BEGIN
        NumPts := HIGH(X) + 1;   WriteLn;
        REPEAT
           WriteString("Lower bound on x = ? "); ReadReal(lowbound); WriteLn;
           WriteString("Upper bound on x = ? "); ReadReal(upbound); WriteLn;
        UNTIL  lowbound < upbound;
        dx  :=  (upbound - lowbound) / FLOAT(NumPts-1);

        WhichPt:=0;  X[WhichPt]:=lowbound;  Y[WhichPt]:=YCalc(X[WhichPt]);
        FOR  WhichPt := 1 TO NumPts-1  DO
            X[WhichPt] := X[WhichPt-1] + dx;  Y[WhichPt] := YCalc(X[WhichPt]);
        END; (* FOR *)

        FOR  WhichPt := 0 TO NumPts-1  DO
            FWriteReal(X[WhichPt],XWID,XDEC);
            FWriteReal(Y[WhichPt],YWID,YDEC); WriteLn;
        END; (* FOR *)
    END ConvertToArray;

PROCEDURE LinePlot(X, Y: ARRAY OF REAL;  Width, YPlot0 : CARDINAL;
                                     Symbol : CHAR;    YMin, YMax : REAL);
    (* Produces a scaled, point plot of Y vs X with constant intervals
          along the x-axis.  *)
    VAR  NumPts, WhichPt, YPlot : CARDINAL;   dx, XPlot : REAL;
    BEGIN
        NumPts := HIGH(X)+1;   WhichPt := 0;
        LOOP  (* Sort by increasing X, if not already sorted. *)
           IF  X[WhichPt+1] - X[WhichPt] < 0.0  THEN  SortXY(X,Y); EXIT;
             ELSIF  WhichPt >= NumPts - 2  THEN  EXIT;
           END; (* IF *)  INC(WhichPt);
        END; (* LOOP *)
        FindXInterval(X, dx);  PrintYScale(YMin, YMax, Width, YPlot0);
WhichPt := 0;  XPlot := X[0];    (* Plot the points on the graph. *)
WHILE  XPlot  <=  X[NumPts-1] + dx/2.0   DO
   IF (ABS(XPlot-X[WhichPt])<=dx/2.0) AND (ABS(XPlot)<=dx/2.0) THEN
   (* when near X[WhichPt] & at y-axis(XPlot=0), plot point & y-axis *)
      FWriteReal(X[WhichPt],XWID, XDEC);
       FWriteReal(Y[WhichPt],YWID,YDEC); TabOrFill(2, Blank);
      YPlot := TRUNC(FLOAT(Width)*(Y[WhichPt]-YMin) / (YMax - YMin));
      TabOrFill(YPlot, Dot);  Write(Symbol);
      IF  Width >= (YPlot + 1)  THEN
          TabOrFill(Width-YPlot-1, Dot);
      END; (* IF *)  Write('Y');  INC(WhichPt);
```

```
      ELSIF (ABS(XPlot-X[WhichPt])>dx/2.0) AND (ABS(XPlot)<=dx/2.0) THEN
      (* when not near X[WhichPt] but at y-axis(XPlot=0), plot y-axis *)
         FWriteReal(0.0,XWID,XDEC); TabOrFill(YWID+3,Blank);
          TabOrFill(Width, Dot); Write('Y');
      ELSIF (ABS(XPlot-X[WhichPt])<=dx/2.0) AND (ABS(XPlot)>dx/2.0) THEN
      (* when near X[WhichPt] & not at y-axis, plot point and x-axis *)
         FWriteReal(X[WhichPt],XWID, XDEC);
          FWriteReal(Y[WhichPt],YWID,YDEC); TabOrFill(2, Blank);
         YPlot := TRUNC(FLOAT(Width)*(Y[WhichPt]-YMin) / (YMax - YMin));
         IF   YPlot < YPlot0  THEN        (* y < 0 *)
            TabOrFill(YPlot, Blank); Write(Symbol);
            IF   YPlot0 >= (YPlot + 1)   THEN
               TabOrFill(YPlot0-YPlot-1, Blank);
            END; (* IF *)  Write(Dot);
         ELSIF   YPlot = YPlot0   THEN  (* y = 0 *)
            TabOrFill(YPlot0, Blank); Write(Symbol);
         ELSE                         (* y > 0 *)
            TabOrFill(YPlot0, Blank);
            IF   YPlot >= YPlot0+1   THEN
               Write(Dot); TabOrFill(YPlot-YPlot0-1, Blank);
            END; (* IF *) Write(Symbol);
         END; (* IF *)   INC(WhichPt);
      ELSE   (* when not near point and not at y-axis, plot x-axis *)
         TabOrFill(XWID+YWID+2+YPlot0, Blank);  Write(Dot);
      END; (* IF *)  WriteLn;    XPlot := XPlot + dx;
   END; (* WHILE *)
   TabOrFill(XWID+YWID+2+YPlot0, Blank); Write('X'); WriteLn;
END LinePlot;

PROCEDURE BarPlot(X, Y: ARRAY OF REAL; Width, YPlot0 : CARDINAL;
   (* Produces a bar graph of Y vs X. *)  Symbol:CHAR;   YMin,YMax:REAL);
   VAR  NumPts, WhichPt, YPlot : CARDINAL;
   BEGIN
      NumPts := HIGH(X)+1; PrintYScale(YMin, YMax, Width, YPlot0);
      FOR  WhichPt := 0  TO  NumPts-1  DO  (* Draw the bars and x-axis *)
         FWriteReal(X[WhichPt],XWID, XDEC);
          FWriteReal(Y[WhichPt],YWID,YDEC); TabOrFill(2, Blank);
         YPlot := TRUNC(FLOAT(Width)*(Y[WhichPt]-YMin) / (YMax - YMin));
         IF   YPlot < YPlot0  THEN  (* y < 0, YPlot = scaled value of y *)
            TabOrFill(YPlot, Blank);
            IF   YPlot0 >= YPlot   THEN
               TabOrFill(YPlot0-YPlot, Symbol);
            END; (* IF *)  Write(Dot);
         ELSIF   YPlot = YPlot0   THEN   (* y = 0 *)
            TabOrFill(YPlot0, Blank);  Write(Symbol);
         ELSE      (* y > 0 *)
            TabOrFill(YPlot0, Blank);  Write(Dot);
            IF YPlot>=YPlot0 THEN TabOrFill(YPlot-YPlot0, Symbol); END;(*IF*)
         END; (* IF *)  WriteLn;
      END; (* FOR *)
   END BarPlot;


PROCEDURE PlotIt(X, Y : ARRAY OF REAL);
   (* Calls either LinePlot or BarPlot for X, Y,  as requested by the
       user.  Allows the user to specify the graph width and finds
       the minimum and maximum Y values for scaling purposes.  *)
```

```
VAR  GraphType, CapType, Symbol, Answer, Discard : CHAR;
     Bar:BOOLEAN;   NumPts,Width,YPlot0:CARDINAL;   YMin,YMax:REAL;
BEGIN
   NumPts := HIGH(X) + 1;  WriteLn; WriteLn;
   REPEAT
      WriteString("What character to use for plot symbol? ");
      Read(Symbol); Read(Discard); Write(Symbol); WriteLn; WriteLn;
   UNTIL  (Symbol > Blank);

   REPEAT
      WriteString("Would you like a  "); WriteLn;
      WriteString("     B     Bar Graph?"); WriteLn;
      WriteString("     L     Line Graph?"); WriteLn;
       WriteString("Choose one,  B or L:     ");
       Read(GraphType); Read(Discard);
        CapType := CAP(GraphType); Write(CapType);
   UNTIL  (CapType = 'L') OR (CapType = 'B');
   Bar := (CapType = 'B');  WriteLn; WriteLn;

   REPEAT
      WriteString("What is plot width in print spaces? "); WriteLn;
      WriteString("  Width must be > 6  and  <= ");
      WriteCard(MAXWIDTH,3); WriteString(": ");
      ReadCard(Width); WriteLn; WriteLn;
   UNTIL  (Width > 6) AND (Width <= MAXWIDTH);
      FindMinAndMax(Y, YMin, YMax);   (* Find x-axis position. *)
   IF  (YMax - YMin) < 1.0  THEN  YMax  :=  YMin + 1.0;  END;(*IF*)
   IF  YMin > 0.0  THEN  YPlot0 := 0;
    ELSIF  YMax < 0.0  THEN  YPlot0 := Width;
    ELSE YPlot0 := TRUNC(FLOAT(Width)*(0.0-YMin) / (YMax - YMin));
   END; (* IF *)  WriteLn;

    IF  Bar   THEN  BarPlot(X, Y, Width, YPlot0, Symbol, YMin, YMax);
       ELSE         LinePlot(X, Y, Width, YPlot0, Symbol, YMin, YMax);
    END;(*IF*)
   END PlotIt;

END Graphics.
```

MyMath

```
DEFINITION MODULE MyMath;
   (* Module MyMath contains user defined mathematics
      functions and procedures.  File Name:MYMATH.DEF     *)

TYPE  VECTOR = RECORD   (* Defines a two dimensional vector. *)
                 x, y : REAL;
                 END; (* RECORD *)

PROCEDURE CardPower(Base : REAL;  Power : CARDINAL) : REAL;
   (* Raises a Real number Base to a Cardinal Power
      by multiplying Base by itself Power number of times. *)
```

```
PROCEDURE RealPower(RealBase, RealPower : REAL) : REAL;
    (* Raises a Real number Base to a Real Power
       using exp and ln.  Returns 0.0 and an error warning message
       if RealBase <= 0.0 *)

PROCEDURE Log10( x : REAL ) : REAL;
    (* Finds Log base 10 of number x.  Halts if x <= 0. *)

PROCEDURE  VectorSum(V1, V2 : VECTOR;  VAR Result : VECTOR);
    (* Finds the Sum of two dimensional vectors V1, V2. *)

PROCEDURE  VectorNegate(V : VECTOR;  VAR Result : VECTOR);
    (* Finds the Negative of a two dimensional vector. *)

PROCEDURE  VectorMagnitude(V : VECTOR) : REAL;
    (* Finds the real scalar magnitude of a two dimensional vector. *)

PROCEDURE  ScalarProduct(V1, V2 : VECTOR) : REAL;
    (* Finds the real scalar product of two dimensional vectors V1,V2.*)

END MyMath.
```

```
IMPLEMENTATION MODULE MyMath;
    (* Module MyMath contains user defined mathematical
       functions and procedures.  File Name:MYMATH.MOD    *)

FROM MathLib0 IMPORT exp, ln, sqrt;
FROM InOut IMPORT WriteString, WriteLn;

PROCEDURE CardPower(Base:REAL; Power:CARDINAL) : REAL;
    (* Raises a Real number Base to a Cardinal Power
       by multiplying Base by itself Power number of times. *)
    VAR  Count : CARDINAL;  Result : REAL;
    BEGIN
       Result := 1.0;
       FOR  Count := 1 TO Power  DO
          Result := Result * Base;
       END; (* FOR *)
       RETURN Result;
    END CardPower;

PROCEDURE RealPower(RealBase, RealPower : REAL) : REAL;
    (* Raises a Real number Base to a Real Power
       using exp and ln.  Returns 0.0 and an error warning message
       if RealBase <= 0.0  *)
    VAR  Result : REAL;
    BEGIN
       IF  RealBase > 0.0  THEN
          Result := exp(RealPower * ln(RealBase));
       ELSE
          Result := 0.0;
          WriteLn; WriteString("!!!!! ERROR - WARNING !!!!!"); WriteLn;
           WriteString("Base must be > 0.0.  ");
           WriteString("INCORRECT Answer = 0.0 returned.");WriteLn;WriteLn;
       END; (* IF *)
       RETURN  Result;
    END RealPower;
```

```
PROCEDURE Log10(x : REAL) : REAL;
   (* Returns Log (base 10) of positive x.  Halts if x <= 0. *)
   BEGIN
      IF x <= 0.0 THEN WriteString("There is no log of  x <= 0."); HALT;
         ELSE            RETURN  ln(x) / ln(10.0);
      END; (* IF *)
   END Log10;

PROCEDURE  VectorSum(V1, V2 : VECTOR;  VAR Result : VECTOR);
   (* Finds the Sum of two dimensional vectors V1, V2. *)
   BEGIN
      Result.x  :=  V1.x + V2.x;   Result.y  :=  V1.y + V2.y;
   END VectorSum;

PROCEDURE  VectorNegate(V : VECTOR;  VAR Result : VECTOR);
   (* Finds the Negative of a two dimensional vector. *)
   BEGIN
      Result.x  :=  - V.x;   Result.y  :=  - V.y;
   END VectorNegate;

PROCEDURE  VectorMagnitude(V : VECTOR) : REAL;
   (* Finds the real scalar magnitude of a two dimensional vector. *)
   BEGIN
      RETURN  sqrt(V.x * V.x  +  V.y * V.y);
   END VectorMagnitude;

PROCEDURE  ScalarProduct(V1, V2 : VECTOR) : REAL;
   (* Finds the real scalar product of two dimensional vectors V1,V2.*)
   BEGIN
      RETURN  V1.x * V2.x  +  V1.y * V2.y;
   END ScalarProduct;

END MyMath.
```

Dynamic

```
DEFINITION MODULE Dynamic;
   (* Procedures for handling stacks, queues, and linked lists using
      pointers.  Data record fields are a CHARacter string, a REAL number,
      and a pointer to another record.  The size of the string or the
      record definition may be modified by changing MAXCHS and record
      types WHATSONSTACK, WHATSINQUEUE, OR WHATSINLIST in the DEFINITION
      MODULE, as needed.

      If your system requires the use of TSIZE(TypeName) instead of SIZE,
      then in the IMPLEMENTATION MODULE you should to add
      FROM SYSTEM IMPORT TSIZE and change SIZE to TSIZE wherever
      it appears in the ALLOCATE and DEALLOCATE commands.

      FileName:DYNAMIC.DEF      Modula-2      RKW      July 1991  *)
```

```
CONST  MAXCHS = 19;   Blank = ` `;
TYPE   CHRARY = ARRAY [0..MAXCHS] OF CHAR;
       POINTTOSTACK = POINTER TO WHATSONSTACK;
       WHATSONSTACK = RECORD
                          Characters : CHRARY;    Number : REAL;
                          PreviousRecPtr : POINTTOSTACK;
                      END; (* RECORD WHATSONSTACK *)

       POINTTOQUEUE = POINTER TO WHATSINQUEUE;
       WHATSINQUEUE = RECORD
                          Characters : CHRARY;    Number : REAL;
                          NextRecPtr : POINTTOQUEUE;
                      END; (* RECORD WHATSINQUEUE *)

       POINTTOLIST = POINTER TO WHATSINLIST;
       WHATSINLIST =  RECORD
                          Characters : CHRARY;    Number : REAL;
                          NextRecPtr : POINTTOLIST;
                      END; (* RECORD WHATSINLIST *)

PROCEDURE CreateStack(VAR TopOfStack:POINTTOSTACK);
   (* Initializes a new stack by setting Stack Pointer to NIL. *)

PROCEDURE PrintStack(TopOfStack:POINTTOSTACK);
   (* Displays the contents of a stack. *)

PROCEDURE PUSH(VAR TopOfStack:POINTTOSTACK; WhatToPush:WHATSONSTACK);
   (* PUSH record WhatToPush to the top of the stack. *)

PROCEDURE POP(VAR TopOfStack:POINTTOSTACK;
                                    VAR WhatIsPopped:WHATSONSTACK);
   (* POP record from top of stack into record WhatIsPopped. *)

PROCEDURE CreateQueue(VAR QueueIn, QueueOut: POINTTOQUEUE);
   (* Initializes a new queue by allocating a record space to
      QueueIn and QueueOut and setting pointer field to NIL. *)

PROCEDURE PrintQueue(QueueIn, QueueOut: POINTTOQUEUE);
   (* Displays the contents of a queue. *)

PROCEDURE AddToQueue(VAR QueueIn:POINTTOQUEUE; QueueOut:POINTTOQUEUE;
                        WhatToAdd:WHATSINQUEUE);
   (* Add record WhatToAdd to the QueueIn position. *)

PROCEDURE RemoveFromQueue(QueueIn: POINTTOQUEUE;
                        VAR QueueOut: POINTTOQUEUE;
                        VAR WhatsRemoved: WHATSINQUEUE);
   (* Remove record from QueueOut position to record WhatsRemoved. *)

PROCEDURE CreateLinkList(VAR StartOfList: POINTTOLIST);
   (* Initializes a new linked list setting StartOfList
      pointer field to NIL. *)

PROCEDURE PrintLinkList(StartOfList:POINTTOLIST);
   (* Displays a linked list in link order by Number field. *)
```

```
PROCEDURE AddToLinkList(VAR StartOfList, AfterWhereToAdd:POINTTOLIST;
                                      WhatToAdd:WHATSINLIST);
    (* Add record WhatToAdd logically in the AfterWhereToAdd position.
       If AfterWhereToAdd is NIL, then add the record to the beginning
       of the list. *)

PROCEDURE DeleteFromLinkList(VAR StartOfList, AfterWhereToDelete,
                                WhereToDelete: POINTTOLIST);
    (* Remove record from position WhereToDelete which logically
       follows AfterWhereToDelete. If AfterWhereToDelete is NIL, then
       delete the first record.  If WhereToDelete is NIL, the record
       is not on the list, and nothing is deleted. *)

END Dynamic.


IMPLEMENTATION MODULE Dynamic;
    (* Procedures for handling stacks, queues, and linked lists using
       pointers.  Data record fields are a CHARacter string, a REAL number,
       and a pointer to another record.  The size of the string or the
       record definition may be modified by changing MAXCHS and record
       types WHATSONSTACK, WHATSINQUEUE, OR WHATSINLIST in the DEFINITION
       MODULE, as needed.

       If your system requires the use of TSIZE(TypeName) instead of SIZE,
       then in the IMPLEMENTATION MODULE you should to add
       FROM SYSTEM IMPORT TSIZE and change SIZE to TSIZE wherever
       it appears in the ALLOCATE and DEALLOCATE commands.

       FileName:DYNAMIC.MOD     Modula-2      RKW        July 1991  *)

FROM InOut IMPORT WriteString, WriteLn, WriteCard;
FROM RealInOut IMPORT FWriteReal;
FROM Storage IMPORT ALLOCATE, DEALLOCATE, Available;
FROM Strings IMPORT Length, TabOrFill;
    (* If your system requires the use of TSIZE instead of SIZE
       for determining the size of a type, then add
       FROM SYSTEM IMPORT TSIZE;
       and change every occurrence of SIZE in ALLOCATE AND DEALLOCATE
       to TSIZE. *)

PROCEDURE CreateStack(VAR TopOfStack:POINTTOSTACK);
    (* Initializes a new stack by setting Stack Pointer to NIL. *)
    BEGIN
       TopOfStack := NIL;
    END CreateStack;

PROCEDURE PrintStack(TopOfStack:POINTTOSTACK);
    (* Displays the contents of a stack. *)
    VAR Counter : CARDINAL;

    PROCEDURE PrintNextRecord(WhereOnStack:POINTTOSTACK;
                                         Count : CARDINAL );
       (* Recursive procedure to display individual stack records *)
       BEGIN
          IF  WhereOnStack = NIL  THEN  (* if past stack end *)
             WriteString("End of Stack"); WriteLn;
```

```
        ELSE
            (* Display current address. Omit next statement
               if your system does not support printing pointers. *)
            WriteCard(VAL(CARDINAL,WhereOnStack), 7); WriteString("  ");
            WITH  WhereOnStack^  DO    (* Display record content. *)
                WriteString(Characters);
                 TabOrFill(MAXCHS+1-Length(Characters), Blank);
                FWriteReal(Number,8,2);

                (* Delete the following IF structure if your system
                   does not allow you to display values of pointers. *)
                IF  NextRecPtr # NIL  THEN
                    WriteCard(VAL(CARDINAL,NextRecPtr), 12);
                ELSE
                    WriteString("         NIL");
                    END; (* IF *)
                END; (* WITH *)

            IF  Count = 1  THEN   (* Print TOS indicator if top record. *)
                WriteString(" <-  Top Of Stack");
            END; (* IF *)  WriteLn;

            (* Point to next record. *)
            WhereOnStack := WhereOnStack^.PreviousRecPtr; Count:=Count+1;

            (* RECURSIVE CALL to display the next record. *)
            PrintNextRecord(WhereOnStack, Count);
        END; (* IF WhereOnStack *)
    END PrintNextRecord;

  BEGIN (* PrintStack *)
    (* Display headings. *)
    WriteString("Address  Characters    Number   PrevRecPtr");WriteLn;
    Counter := 1;  (* Begin printing records from top of stack. *)
    PrintNextRecord(TopOfStack, Counter);
  END PrintStack;

PROCEDURE PUSH(VAR TopOfStack:POINTTOSTACK; WhatToPush:WHATSONSTACK);
  (* PUSH record WhatToPush to the top of the stack. *)
  VAR  NewSpacePtr : POINTTOSTACK;
  BEGIN
    (* Set up a new space for incoming date. *)
    IF Available(SIZE(WHATSONSTACK))  THEN
        ALLOCATE(NewSpacePtr, SIZE(WHATSONSTACK));
        WITH  NewSpacePtr^  DO  (* Assign data to the new space. *)
            Characters := WhatToPush.Characters;
            Number := WhatToPush.Number;
            PreviousRecPtr := TopOfStack;(* The pointer in the new data *)
        END; (* WITH *)                  (* points to old top of stack. *)
        TopOfStack := NewSpacePtr; (*Top of stack points to new record.*)
    ELSE
        WriteString("WARNING: No space; nothing was PUSHed."); WriteLn;
    END; (* IF Available *)
  END PUSH;

PROCEDURE POP(VAR TopOfStack:POINTTOSTACK;
                           VAR WhatIsPopped:WHATSONSTACK);
```

```
    (* POP record from top of stack into record WhatIsPopped. *)
    BEGIN
        IF  TopOfStack = NIL  THEN
            WriteString("The Stack Is EMPTY! "); WriteLn;
        ELSE
            WITH  WhatIsPopped  DO      (* Assign values from TopOfStack^ *)
                Characters := TopOfStack^.Characters; (* to WhatIsPopped. *)
                Number := TopOfStack^.Number;
                PreviousRecPtr := TopOfStack^.PreviousRecPtr;
            END; (* WITH *)

            (* Release the space from which WhatIsPopped was just read. *)
            DEALLOCATE(TopOfStack, SIZE(WHATSONSTACK));
            TopOfStack := WhatIsPopped.PreviousRecPtr;
            (* TopOfStack now points to the new topmost record on stack. *)
        END; (* IF *)
    END POP;


PROCEDURE CreateQueue(VAR QueueIn, QueueOut: POINTTOQUEUE);
    (* Initializes a new queue by allocating a record space to
       QueueIn and QueueOut and setting pointer field to NIL. *)
    BEGIN
        IF  Available(SIZE(WHATSINQUEUE))  THEN
            ALLOCATE(QueueIn, SIZE(WHATSINQUEUE));
            QueueIn^.NextRecPtr := NIL;    QueueOut := QueueIn;
        END; (* IF *)
    END CreateQueue;


PROCEDURE PrintQueue(QueueIn, QueueOut: POINTTOQUEUE);
    (* Displays the contents of a queue. *)

    PROCEDURE PrintQRecord(WhereInQueue, QueueIn, QueueOut : POINTTOQUEUE);
        (* Recursive procedure to display individual queue records *)
        BEGIN
        IF  WhereInQueue^.NextRecPtr # NIL  THEN   (* if not past queue end *)

            (* Display current address. Omit next statement
               if your system does not support printing pointers. *)
            WriteCard(VAL(CARDINAL,WhereInQueue), 7); WriteString("  ");

            WITH  WhereInQueue^  DO   (* Display record content. *)
                WriteString(Characters);
                TabOrFill(MAXCHS+1-Length(Characters), Blank);
                FWriteReal(Number,10,2);

                (* Delete the following IF structure if your system
                   does not allow you to display values of pointers. *)
                IF  NextRecPtr # NIL  THEN
                    WriteCard(VAL(CARDINAL,NextRecPtr), 12);
                ELSE
                    WriteString("           NIL");
                END; (* IF *)
            END; (* WITH *)
            IF  WhereInQueue = QueueOut THEN (* Print QueueOut indicator *)
                WriteString(" <- QueueOut   ");   (* if at Out Position. *)
            END; (* IF *)  WriteLn;
```

```
              (* Point to next record. *)
              WhereInQueue := WhereInQueue^.NextRecPtr;

              (* RECURSIVE CALL to display the next record. *)
              PrintQRecord(WhereInQueue, QueueIn, QueueOut);
          END; (* IF WhereInQueue *)
     END PrintQRecord;

   BEGIN (* PrintQueue *)
       (* Display headings. *)
       WriteString("Address  Characters   ");
        WriteString("            Number  NextRecPtr");WriteLn;
       (* Begin printing records at QueueOut. *)
       PrintQRecord(QueueOut, QueueIn, QueueOut);

       (* Print empty QueueIn record. *)
       WriteCard(VAL(CARDINAL,QueueIn), 7); (*Delete for no pointers.*)
        TabOrFill(MAXCHS+1+12, Blank);
       WriteString("          NIL <- QueueIn"); WriteLn;
   END PrintQueue;

PROCEDURE AddToQueue(VAR QueueIn:POINTTOQUEUE; QueueOut:POINTTOQUEUE;
                        WhatToAdd:WHATSINQUEUE);
   (* Add record WhatToAdd to the QueueIn position. *)
   VAR  NewSpacePtr : POINTTOQUEUE;
   BEGIN
       IF  Available(SIZE(WHATSINQUEUE))  THEN
          (* Set up a new space for incoming date. *)
          ALLOCATE(NewSpacePtr, SIZE(WHATSINQUEUE));

          WITH  QueueIn^  DO  (* Assign data to the new space. *)
             Characters := WhatToAdd.Characters;
             Number := WhatToAdd.Number;
             NextRecPtr := NewSpacePtr; (* The pointer in the new data *)
          END; (* WITH *)            (* points to newly allocated space. *)

          QueueIn := NewSpacePtr; (* QueueIn points to new record space *)
          QueueIn^.NextRecPtr := NIL;          (* with a pointer to NIL. *)
       ELSE
          WriteString("WARNING: No space; nothing was added."); WriteLn;
       END; (* IF *)
   END AddToQueue;

PROCEDURE RemoveFromQueue(QueueIn: POINTTOQUEUE;
                          VAR QueueOut: POINTTOQUEUE;
                          VAR WhatsRemoved: WHATSINQUEUE);
   (* Remove record from QueueOut position to record WhatsRemoved. *)
   BEGIN
       IF  QueueIn = QueueOut   THEN
          WriteString("The Queue Is EMPTY! "); WriteLn;
       ELSE
          WITH  WhatsRemoved  DO    (* Assign values from QueueOut^ *)
             Characters := QueueOut^.Characters; (* to WhatsRemoved. *)
             Number := QueueOut^.Number;
             NextRecPtr := QueueOut^.NextRecPtr;
          END; (* WITH *)
```

```
              (* Release the space from which WhatIsPopped was just read. *)
              DEALLOCATE(QueueOut, SIZE(WHATSINQUEUE));

              QueueOut := WhatsRemoved.NextRecPtr;
              (* QueueOut now points to the next record to be removed. *)
        END; (* IF *)
    END RemoveFromQueue;

PROCEDURE CreateLinkList(VAR StartOfList: POINTTOLIST);
    (* Initializes a new linked list setting StartOfList
       pointer field to NIL. *)
    BEGIN
        StartOfList := NIL;
    END CreateLinkList;

PROCEDURE PrintLinkList(StartOfList:POINTTOLIST);
    (* Displays a linked list in link order by Number field. *)

PROCEDURE PrintLinkRecord(WhereInList: POINTTOLIST);
    (* Recursive procedure to display a single link list record *)
    BEGIN
        IF  WhereInList = NIL  THEN  (* past end of list *)
            WriteString("End of Linked List"); WriteLn;
        ELSE
            (* Display current address. Omit next statement
               if your system does not support printing pointers. *)
            WriteCard(VAL(CARDINAL,WhereInList), 7); WriteString("  ");

            WITH  WhereInList^  DO    (* Display record content. *)
               WriteString(Characters);
               TabOrFill(MAXCHS+1-Length(Characters), Blank);
               FWriteReal(Number,10,2);

               (* Delete the following IF structure if your system
                  does not allow you to display values of pointers. *)
               IF  NextRecPtr # NIL   THEN
                  WriteCard(VAL(CARDINAL,NextRecPtr), 12);
               ELSE
                  WriteString("         NIL");
               END; (* IF *)
            END; (* WITH *)

            IF  WhereInList = StartOfList  THEN (* Print Start indicator *)
               WriteString("      StartOfList");
            END; (* IF *)  WriteLn;

            (* Point to next record. *)
            WhereInList := WhereInList^.NextRecPtr;

            (* RECURSIVE CALL to display the next record. *)
            PrintLinkRecord(WhereInList);
        END; (* IF WhereInList *)
    END PrintLinkRecord;

BEGIN (* PrintLinkList *)
    (* Display headings. *)
```

```
        WriteString("Address   Characters   ");
        WriteString("              Number  NextRecPtr");WriteLn;
        (* Begin printing records at StartOfList. *)
      PrintLinkRecord(StartOfList);
  END PrintLinkList;

PROCEDURE AddToLinkList(VAR StartOfList, AfterWhereToAdd:POINTTOLIST;
                                        WhatToAdd:WHATSINLIST);
    (* Add record WhatToAdd logically in the AfterWhereToAdd position.
       If AfterWhereToAdd is NIL, then add the record to the beginning
       of the list. *)
    VAR  NewSpacePtr : POINTTOLIST;
    BEGIN
      IF  Available(SIZE(WHATSINLIST))  THEN
          (* Set up a new space for incoming data. *)
          ALLOCATE(NewSpacePtr, SIZE(WHATSINLIST));

          (* Assign data to the new space. *)
          NewSpacePtr^.Characters := WhatToAdd.Characters;
          NewSpacePtr^.Number := WhatToAdd.Number;
          IF  AfterWhereToAdd = NIL  THEN   (* Add at begin of list. *)
             NewSpacePtr^.NextRecPtr := StartOfList;
             StartOfList := NewSpacePtr; (* New record points to previous
                   start of list, and StartOfList is now the new record. *)
          ELSE    (* Add at a location other than at begin of list. *)
             NewSpacePtr^.NextRecPtr := AfterWhereToAdd^.NextRecPtr;
             (* The pointer in the previous data record is moved to
                the new record. *)
             AfterWhereToAdd^.NextRecPtr := NewSpacePtr;
             (* The pointer in the previous data record now points
                to the newly added record. *)
          END; (* IF *)
      ELSE  WriteString("WARNING: No space, nothing was added.");WriteLn;
      END; (* IF *)
    END AddToLinkList;

PROCEDURE DeleteFromLinkList(VAR StartOfList, AfterWhereToDelete,
                                        WhereToDelete: POINTTOLIST);
    (* Remove record from position WhereToDelete which logically
       follows AfterWhereToDelete. If AfterWhereToDelete is NIL, then
       delete the first record.  If WhereToDelete is NIL, the record
       is not on the list, and nothing is deleted. *)
    VAR TempPointer : POINTTOLIST;
    BEGIN
      IF  StartOfList = NIL  THEN
          WriteString("The list is EMPTY.  No deletion made.");
      ELSIF  WhereToDelete = NIL  THEN
          WriteString("This data is not on the list. No deletion made.");
      ELSIF  AfterWhereToDelete = NIL  THEN   (* Delete first record. *)
          TempPointer := StartOfList^.NextRecPtr;
          DEALLOCATE(StartOfList, SIZE(WHATSINLIST));
          StartOfList := TempPointer;
      ELSE   (* Delete from location other than first record. *)
          AfterWhereToDelete^.NextRecPtr := WhereToDelete^.NextRecPtr;
          (* Previous record now points past record to be deleted. *)
          DEALLOCATE(WhereToDelete, SIZE(WHATSINLIST));
```

```
            END; (* IF *)  WriteLn;
        END DeleteFromLinkList;

    END Dynamic.
```

RandGen

```
DEFINITION MODULE RandGen;
    (* Contains a pseudorandom number generator.
       MUST BE COMPILED WITH RANGE CHECKING TURNED OFF. *)

PROCEDURE  Random(VAR Seed : CARDINAL) : REAL;
    (* Returns a real pseudorandom number between 0.0 and 0.99998474 *)

PROCEDURE  ProduceArray(Seed:CARDINAL;  VAR TestNum:ARRAY OF CARDINAL);
    (* Generates an array of CARDINAL values between 1 and 10.  *)

PROCEDURE  WriteArray(TestNum:ARRAY OF CARDINAL);
    (* Displays a CARDINAL array with Indices from 1 to ListLength. *)

END RandGen.
```

```
IMPLEMENTATION MODULE RandGen;
    (* Contains a pseudorandom number generator.
       MUST BE COMPILED WITH RANGE CHECKING TURNED OFF. *)

FROM InOut IMPORT  WriteString, WriteLn, WriteCard;

PROCEDURE  Random(VAR Seed : CARDINAL) : REAL;
    (* Returns a real pseudorandom number between 0.0 and 0.99998474 *)
    CONST  DIVISOR = 65535;   MULTIPLIER = 25173;   ADDEND = 13849;
    BEGIN
        Seed := (Seed * MULTIPLIER + ADDEND) MOD DIVISOR;
        RETURN  FLOAT(Seed) / FLOAT(DIVISOR);
    END Random;

PROCEDURE  ProduceArray(Seed:CARDINAL;  VAR TestNum:ARRAY OF CARDINAL);
    (* Generates an array of CARDINAL values between 1 and 10. *)
    VAR  Index : CARDINAL;
    BEGIN
        FOR  Index := 0 TO HIGH(TestNum)  DO
            TestNum[Index] := TRUNC(10.0 * Random(Seed) + 1.0);
        END; (* FOR *)
    END ProduceArray;

PROCEDURE  WriteArray(TestNum:ARRAY OF CARDINAL);
    (* Displays a CARDINAL array with Indices from 1 to HIGH(TestNum)+1. *)
    VAR  Index : CARDINAL;
    BEGIN
        FOR  Index := 0 TO HIGH(TestNum)  DO
            WriteString("TestNum["); WriteCard(Index+1, 2);
             WriteString("] ="); WriteCard(TestNum[Index],4); WriteLn;
        END; (* FOR *)
    END WriteArray;

END RandGen.
```

FRealOut

```
DEFINITION MODULE FRealOut;
    (* Contains procedure FWriteReal(Num, Width, Decimals) which displays
       REAL Num, right justified in a field with Width characters,
       including Decimals number of digits after the decimal point.
             Rounds the last decimal digit.  If Width is too small, the
       procedure uses the space necessary to display the number with the
       requested number of decimal characters.
    FileName:FRealOut      Modula-2      RKW        Aug. 1991   *)
    (* TO IMPLEMENT:
        1. Compile (but do not link) DEFINITION MODULE FRealOut.
        2. Compile (but do not link) IMPLEMENTATION MODULE FRealOut.
        3. Copy FRealOut symbol table and object code files to your
             work disk.
        4. In programs, specify    FROM FRealOut IMPORT FWriteReal;
    OR
    Copy FWriteReal and nested CreateDigit procedures to appropriate
    library files (eg. RealInOut), and import FWriteReal from there. *)

PROCEDURE FWriteReal(Num : REAL;    Width, Decimals : CARDINAL);

END FRealOut.




IMPLEMENTATION MODULE FRealOut;
    (* Contains procedure FWriteReal(Num, Width, Decimals) which displays
    REAL Num, right justified in a field with Width characters,
    including Decimals number of digits after the decimal point.
    FileName:FRealOut      Modula-2      RKW        Aug. 1991   *)

FROM InOut IMPORT Write;

PROCEDURE FWriteReal(Num : REAL;    Width, Decimals : CARDINAL);
    CONST  NEG= -';  DOT= .';  BLANK=' ';  ZERO='0';  ONE='1';
           EPSILON = 1.0E-10;
    VAR  PlusVal : REAL;  DecmlCt : CARDINAL;

    PROCEDURE  CreateDigit(NewNum : REAL;  Count, Carry : CARDINAL);
        (* Recursive procedure to separate & display digits, sign, & . *)
        VAR  Ch : CHAR;    CalcNum : REAL;
             Digit, LeadCt, HowManyDivs, CountMults : CARDINAL;
        BEGIN
          IF  Count = Decimals + 1  THEN  (* character=decimal point *)
              CH := DOT; INC(Count); CreateDigit(NewNum, Count, Carry);
          ELSE  (* character is a digit *)
              (* Retrieve last digit without exceeding MAX(CARDINAL) *)
              CalcNum := NewNum;  HowManyDivs := 0;
              WHILE  CalcNum >= 10.0  DO
                 CalcNum := CalcNum/10.0;   INC(HowManyDivs);
              END; (* WHILE *)
              FOR  CountMults := 1 TO HowManyDivs  DO
                 CalcNum := 10.0 * (CalcNum - FLOAT(TRUNC(CalcNum)));
              END; (* FOR *)
              Digit := TRUNC(CalcNum + 0.5) + Carry;  Carry := 0;
              Ch := CHR(Digit + ORD(ZERO));   INC(Count);
              IF  Ch > '9'  THEN  Carry := 1; Ch := ZERO; END; (* IF *)
              NewNum := (NewNum - CalcNum)/10.0;   (* new = old DIV 10 *)
              IF (NewNum)>=1.0-EPSILON) OR (Count<=Decimals) THEN
                  CreateDigit(NewNum, Count, Carry)    (* recursive call *)
```

```
      ELSE      (* end recursion, display leading characters *)
        IF   ABS(Num) >= 1.0   THEN
          FOR LeadCt:=Width TO Count+2BY-1 DO Write(BLANK); END;
          IF   Num < 0.0   THEN
            IF Carry = 0 THEN Write(BLANK); Write(NEG);
             ELSE   Write(NEG); Write(ONE);
            END; (* IF *)
          ELSE   (* when Num >= 0.0 *) Write(BLANK);
            IF Carry=0 THEN Write(BLANK);ELSE Write(ONE); END;
          END; (* IF *)
        ELSE    (* when Num < 1.0 *)
          FOR LeadCt:=Width TO Count+3BY-1 DO Write(BLANK); END;
          IF Num < 0.0 THEN Write(NEG); ELSE Write(BLANK); END;
          IF Carry=0 THEN Write(ZERO); ELSE Write(ONE);  END;
          Write(DOT);
        END; (* IF *)
      END; (* IF *)
    END; (* IF *)
    Write(Ch);        (* writes digits in reverse from calculation *)
  END CreateDigit;

BEGIN (* FWriteReal *)
  PlusVal := ABS(Num); (* initialize Value, Width, and Decimals *)
  IF Width = 0 THEN Width := 1  END;(*IF*)
  IF (PlusVal < 1.0) AND (Decimals = 0) THEN Decimals := 1  END;
  FOR DecmlCt := 1 TO Decimals DO PlusVal := PlusVal * 10.0   END;
  CreateDigit(PlusVal, 1, 0);  (* first call to display digits *)
END FWriteReal;

END FRealOut.
```

D

Syntax Diagrams,
Comparison of Modula-2 and Pascal

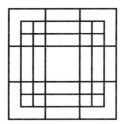

Many people find charts and diagrams useful for clarifying and remembering concepts and ideas. Thus the first purpose of this appendix is to provide diagrams of Modula-2 structures. These syntax diagrams provide an alternate means of presenting the fundamental constructs of the Modula-2 language that have been described in words in Chapters 2 through 17.

Syntax diagrams also provide a convenient, compact matrix for comparing Modula-2 structures with those of standard Pascal. Providing such a comparison is the second purpose of this appendix. You may be familiar with Pascal already and would like to learn Modula-2, or vice versa. The diagrams and text here point out the slight, critical differences that make Modula-2 so powerful and will help you to make the transition from one language to the other.

The diagrams are adapted from those in the fourth edition of Dr. Wirth's *Programming in Modula-2** with permission from the publisher. As much as possible, their presentation reflects the order of narrative in this book.

To read a syntax diagram, simply begin at the upper left of the figure and follow the arrows. Multiple arrows indicate alternative choices; loops indicate possible repetitions.

*From Wirth, Niklaus. *Programming in Modula-2*, 4th ed. (Texts and Monographs in Computer Science). Copyright © 1988. Reprinted by permission of Springer–Verlag, Berlin–Heidelberg.

Program Module

☐ Syntax Diagrams

Program Module

> ──→ MODULE ──→ Module Name Identifier ──→ ... [──→ Constant Priority Expression ──→] ──→ ; ... Import ... ──→ Block ──→ Module Name Identifier ──→ . ──→

On some systems, a CARDINAL-valued Constant Priority Expression is allowed. On such systems, each interrupt has an associated priority; and this feature in the module heading is regarded as a command to disable any interrupt whose priority is equal to or less than the value specified by the Constant Priority Expression.

Block

> ──→ Declarations ... ──→ BEGIN ──→ Statements ──→ END ──→

The block is the heart of any module.

☐ Modula-2 versus Pascal

In standard Pascal the word *Program* is used, rather than the word *Module,* at the beginning of a program unit. There are no import lists, and the program-terminating period immediately follows the END of the block. The program name may be followed by a list of identifiers specifying input and output devices. Thus the **program-unit syntax** in Pascal appears as

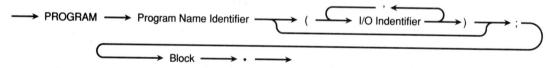

> ──→ PROGRAM ──→ Program Name Identifier ──→ (──→ I/O Indentifier ──→) ──→ ; ──→ Block ──→ . ──→

Declarations

Syntax Diagrams

Declaration

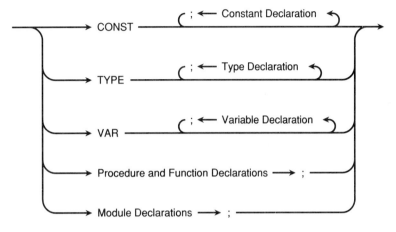

Identifier

Identifier List

Constant Declaration

Constant Expression

Expression

Simple Expression

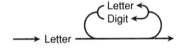

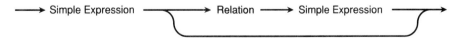

Term

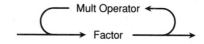

Add Operator

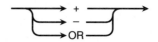

Mult Operator

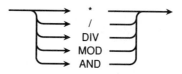

Integer

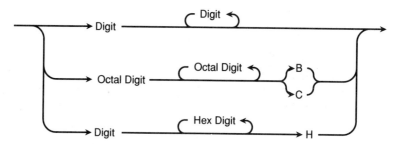

Factor

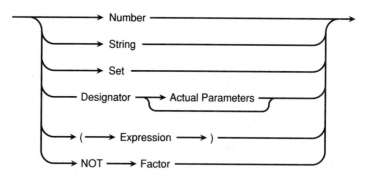

Relation

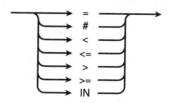

Real

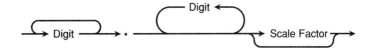

Scale Factor

Number

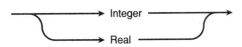

Digit

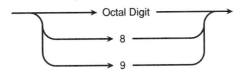

Octal Digit

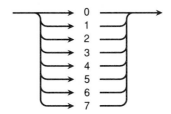

Hex Digit

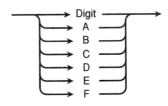

String

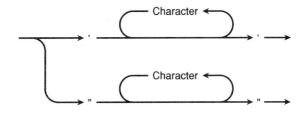

Type

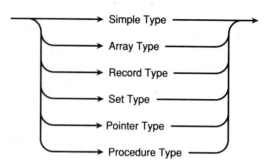

Type Declaration

Variable Declaration

 ## Modula-2 versus Pascal

Declarations

Pascal declarations appear the same as the Modula-2 declarations, with four exceptions:

1. Pascal is not case-sensitive; uppercase and lowercase letters are used interchangeably. Thus, for example, *TAX, Tax,* and *tax* would all represent the same identifier.

2. Pascal allows **Label declarations**—a list of 1- to 4-digit numbers—before constant identifiers:

where *label* is 1 to 4 digits. A **goto label** statement is available in Pascal. The label must be declared in the Block, and any single statement may be prefaced by the **label :** . Thereafter, a goto label within that block will transfer control to the statement. There is no equivalent goto command or label declaration in Modula-2.

3. Octal numbers are not directly accessible in Pascal. Some versions of Pascal allow hexadecimal constants, which are generally preceded by a **$** symbol; for example, $3AF2.

4. In Pascal, **<>** is used as the relational operator for inequality. It and **#** are used interchangeably in Modula-2.

Type Variables and Constants

In Pascal, the Read, ReadLn, Write, and WriteLn commands are used to enter and display every type of variable and constant. The **. . . Ln** suffix indicates that a new line command (typically carriage return, line feed) is to be performed after the Read or Write operation.

There is no CARDINAL variable type in Pascal; INTEGER type must be used instead. When writing an INTEGER value, the field width argument is optional. If specified, it is separated from the value identifier by a colon (:), rather than a comma. A predefined constant, **maxint,** serves the same function in Pascal as MAX(INTEGER) does in Modula-2.

If variable ReCalc specifies a REAL value in PASCAL, then

- WriteLn(ReCalc) displays the value in exponential form,
- WriteLn(ReCalc : 3) would limit the exponential display to 3 digits after the decimal point, and
- WriteLn(ReCalc : 12 : 3) would create the same floating point display as FWrite-Real(ReCalc, 12, 3) in Modula-2.

Write or WriteLn may be used in Pascal to display the TRUE or FALSE value of a BOOLEAN variable; but, as in Modula-2, you may not read a BOOLEAN value using Read or ReadLn.

A Pascal expression that contains all REAL numbers, REAL *and* INTEGER numbers, *or* the REAL division operator (/) always has a REAL value. Truncating and rounding REAL numbers to INTEGER values are accomplished in Pascal by the built-in transfer functions trunc( ) and round ( ), respectively.

File Handling
In standard Pascal redirection of text I/O is accomplished by file-handling routines as follows:

- The name(s) of the input and/or output file(s) are listed in the I/O Identifiers in the program heading. For example, with

```
PROGRAM Circles(input, output, OUTDATA);
```

- input will be taken from the default input device, and the programmer can direct output either to the default output device or to file OUTDATA.
- The files must be declared to be of type TEXT; for example,

```
VAR OUTDATA : TEXT;
```

- A file is opened for output by the command ReWrite(FileName); for example,

```
ReWrite(OUTDATA);
```

- A file is opened for input by the command ReSet(FileName).
- Read and Write commands that address a file must specify the file name as their first argument; for example,

```
WriteLn(OUTDATA, 'The area is ', A:12:2);
```

- Open files should be closed before the end of the program with the command Close(FileName).
- A text file must be passed to a procedure as a VARiable parameter of type TEXT before the procedure can use it.

Some versions of Pascal differ from the standard when handling files and redirection. See your Pascal compiler manual for details.

Statement

Syntax Diagrams

Statement

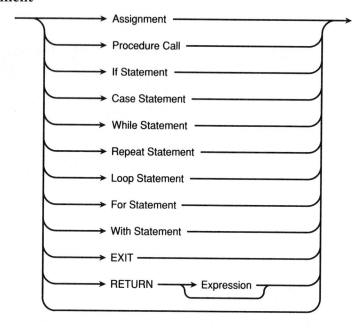

Assignment

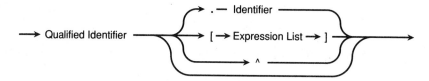

Designator

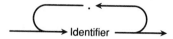

Qualified Identifier

Expression List

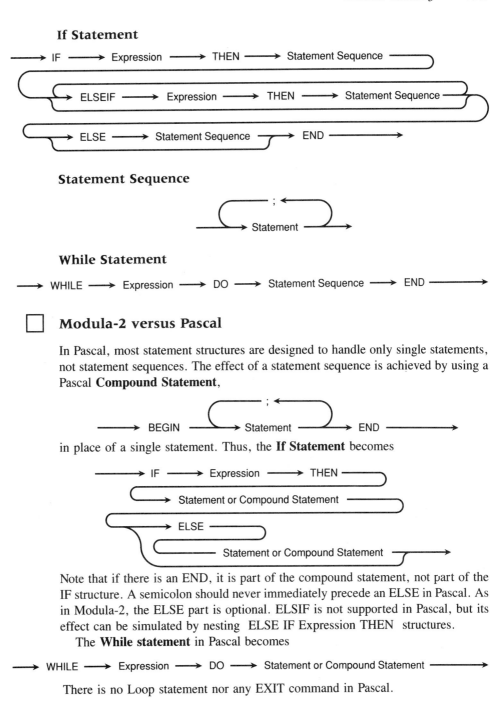

If Statement

Statement Sequence

While Statement

☐ Modula-2 versus Pascal

In Pascal, most statement structures are designed to handle only single statements, not statement sequences. The effect of a statement sequence is achieved by using a Pascal **Compound Statement**,

in place of a single statement. Thus, the **If Statement** becomes

Note that if there is an END, it is part of the compound statement, not part of the IF structure. A semicolon should never immediately precede an ELSE in Pascal. As in Modula-2, the ELSE part is optional. ELSIF is not supported in Pascal, but its effect can be simulated by nesting ELSE IF Expression THEN structures.

The **While statement** in Pascal becomes

There is no Loop statement nor any EXIT command in Pascal.

Character Handling

☐ Modula-2 versus Pascal

In most versions of Pascal, a ReadLn(Character Variable) command automatically discards any terminating character, so the Return or another terminator does not need to be explicit.

The features of the Modula-2 INC(m) and DEC(m) are implemented in Pascal by the functions succ(m) and pred(m), respectively, and the increment or decrement step is always 1.

Pascal has no built-in function comparable to CAP(symbol) in Modula-2.

Procedures and Parameters

Syntax Diagrams

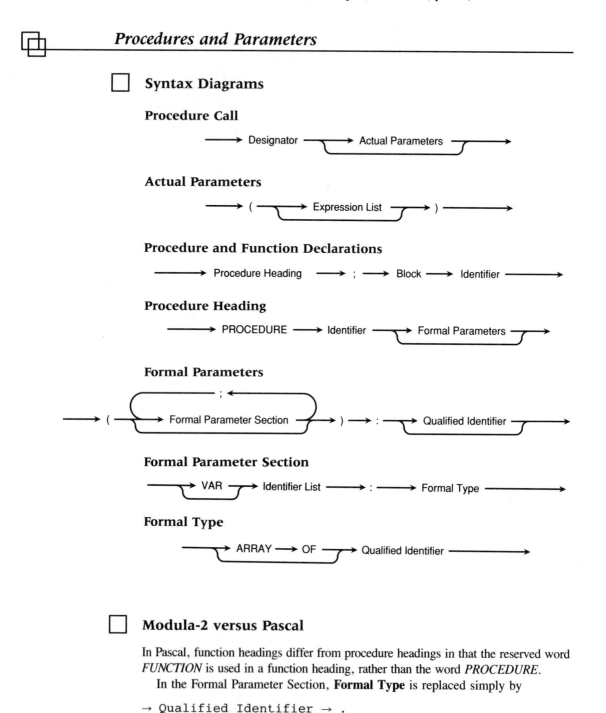

Procedure Call

Actual Parameters

Procedure and Function Declarations

Procedure Heading

Formal Parameters

Formal Parameter Section

Formal Type

Modula-2 versus Pascal

In Pascal, function headings differ from procedure headings in that the reserved word *FUNCTION* is used in a function heading, rather than the word *PROCEDURE*.

In the Formal Parameter Section, **Formal Type** is replaced simply by

$\rightarrow$ Qualified Identifier $\rightarrow$.

There are no open arrays in Pascal, and brackets, [ ], cannot be included in a parameter list. Thus, all array types used in a parameter list must be defined in advance by name.

Case Statement

☐ **Syntax Diagrams**

Case Statement

```
───▶ CASE ───▶ Expression ───▶ OF ───▶ Case
```

```
───▶ ELSE ───▶ Statement Sequence ───▶ END ───▶
```

Case

```
───▶ Case Label List ───▶ : ───▶ Statement Sequence ───▶
```

Case Label List

```
───▶ Constant Expression ───▶ .. ───▶ Constant Expression ───▶
```

☐ **Modula-2 versus Pascal**

In standard Pascal, the **Case** structure operates on single statements or compound statements, does not use the vertical bar (|), does not allow an ELSE clause, and does not recognize ellipses (..). Thus, its syntax is represented by

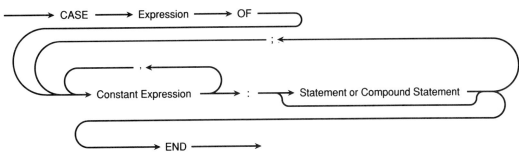

For explicit values that require no action, the colon (:) may be followed immediately by the semicolon (;). Note also that in Pascal there is no equivalent of the BOOLEAN variable Done for checking whether an operation has been accomplished successfully. However, the function eof(FileName) can be used to determine whether an attempt is being made to read past the end of a file.

Intrinsic Functions

☐ **Modula-2 versus Pascal**

Modula-2 procedures INC(m) and DEC(m) correspond to functions succ(m) and pred(m) in Pascal. INC(m,n), DEC(m,n), CAP, EXCL, INCL, FLOAT, HIGH,

HALT, SIZE, and VAL are not implemented in Pascal. Modula-2 MAX(INTEGER) is maxint in Pascal. Pascal has an additional function, round(x), which rounds a real number to the nearest integer value. The functions abs(x), cos(x), odd(m), sqr(x) which squares the value of *x*, arctan(x), ord(Enum), chr(m), sqrt(x), ln(x), sin(x), and exp(x) are built into Pascal, as well as the BOOLEAN functions eoln(f) and eof(f), which determine whether the end of the line and the end of the file have been reached, respectively.

External and Local Modules

Syntax Diagrams

Definition Module

Implementation Module

Definition

Local Module Declaration, Program Module

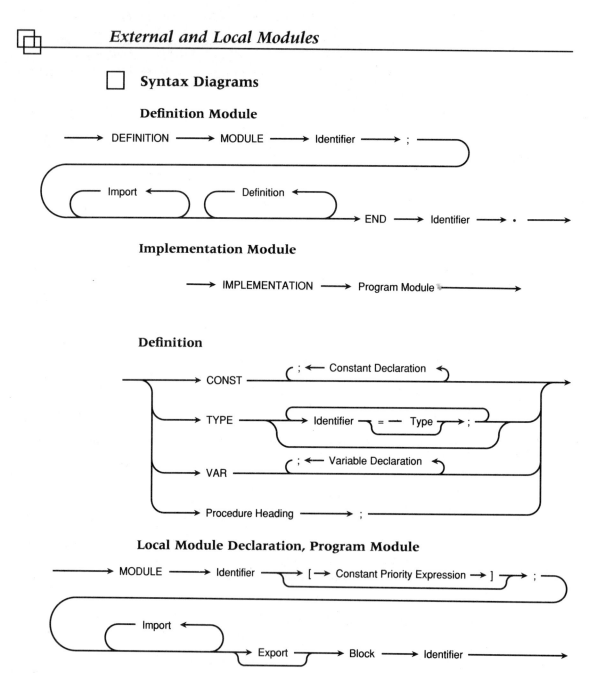

Import

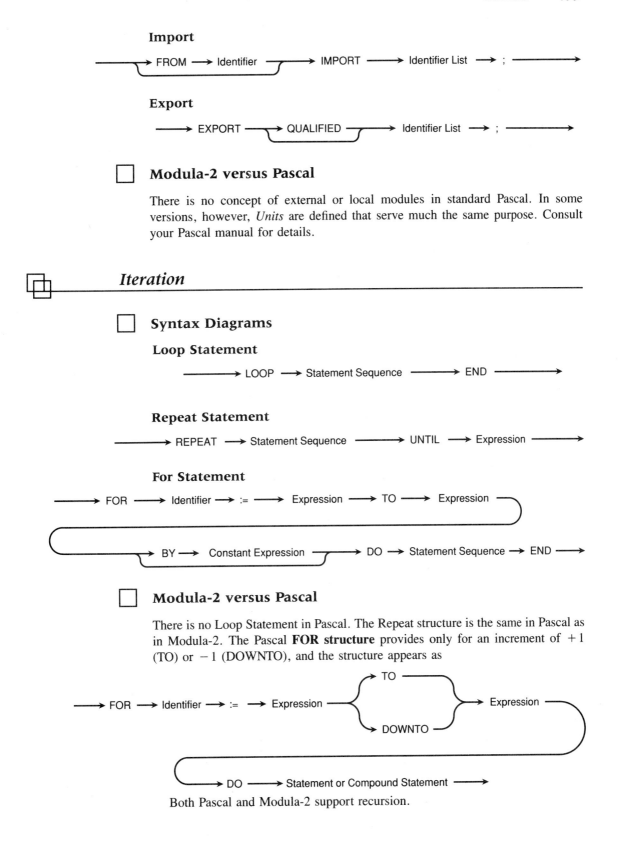

Export

Modula-2 versus Pascal

There is no concept of external or local modules in standard Pascal. In some versions, however, *Units* are defined that serve much the same purpose. Consult your Pascal manual for details.

Iteration

Syntax Diagrams

Loop Statement

Repeat Statement

For Statement

Modula-2 versus Pascal

There is no Loop Statement in Pascal. The Repeat structure is the same in Pascal as in Modula-2. The Pascal **FOR structure** provides only for an increment of $+1$ (TO) or -1 (DOWNTO), and the structure appears as

Both Pascal and Modula-2 support recursion.

Simple Types

Syntax Diagrams

Simple Type

```
                    ┌──────────────→ Qualified Identifier ──────────┐
                    │                                               │
                    ├──────────────→ Enumeration ───────────────────┤
                    │                                               │
                    └──────────────→ Subrange Type ─────────────────┘
```

Subrange Type

```
    ┌──→ Qualified Identifier ─┐
    │                          │
    └──────────────────────────┘
         └────→ [ → Constant Expression → .. → Constant Expression → ] ──→
```

Enumeration

```
    ──────→ ( ──→ Identifier List ──→ ) ──────→
```

Modula-2 versus Pascal

In standard Pascal, subrange types are defined without an Identifier and without brackets. The Pascal **Subrange Type** diagram appears as

```
    ──────→ Constant Expression ──────→ .. ──────→ Constant Expression ──────→
```

Enumeration types are defined the same as in Modula-2.

Type compatibility in Pascal mimics that in Modula-2. Since there are no external modules in standard Pascal, there are no opaque data types.

Arrays

Syntax Diagram

Array Type

```
                          ┌──── , ←───┐
                          │           │
    ──────→ ARRAY ────────→ Simple Type ──→ OF ──→ Type ──────→
```

Modula-2 versus Pascal

In Pascal, the subscript or index name or list is enclosed within brackets, [ ], so that the Pascal **Array Type** diagram is

```
                              ┌──── , ←───┐
                              │           │
    ──────→ ARRAY ──→ [ ──────→ Simple Type ──→ ] ──→ OF ──→ Type ──────→
```

Also in Pascal, array, record, file, and set types can be preceded by the reserved word *PACKED,* which causes variables of such types to be packed more tightly into available memory space. This feature is not implemented in Modula-2.

Single-dimensional arrays of characters are called *strings* in both languages. Characters are generally assigned to individual array elements in a Pascal string, rather than being assigned or read all at once. Some versions of Pascal do, however, allow assignment or reading a list of characters into a *packed* array of characters. String literals in Pascal are enclosed between single quotes ('), not between double quotes (' '). Inclusion of an apostrophe in a Pascal string is accomplished by entering two apostrophes ('').

In contrast with the Modula-2 ReadString command, reading a string in Pascal does not automatically append a null character after the last character. Therefore, writing a string in Pascal displays the entire length of the array of characters.

The use of open array types for parameters is not a feature of standard Pascal.

Note that the differences in the use of brackets in the array and subrange definitions just given would result in the Pascal declaration of a two-dimensional INTEGER array variable, for example, as

```
VAR MDArray : ARRAY [L1..U1, L2..U2] OF INTEGER;
```

in contrast with the Modula-2 form

```
VAR MDArray : ARRAY [L1..U1], [L2..U2] OF INTEGER;
```

Records

Syntax Diagrams

Record Type

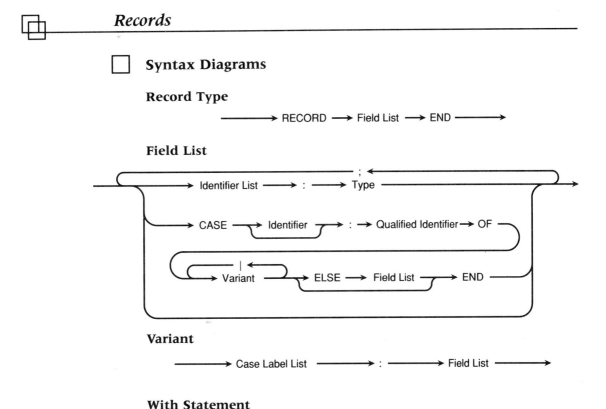

Field List

Variant

With Statement

Modula-2 versus Pascal

In Pascal, records are defined and used in the same manner as in Modula-2. The differences in syntax arise in part from the syntax for CASE whenever records with variant parts are declared. The syntax forms for the field list and variant part of records in Pascal are shown here.

Pascal Field List

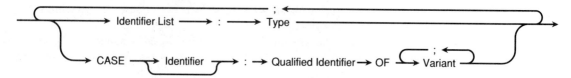

Pascal Variant

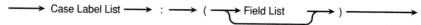

In Pascal the field list in the variant part is enclosed in parentheses. An empty field list indicates that no variant part exists for that particular case label. Also, no END is associated with the WITH structure in Pascal.

Pascal With Statement

Files

Modula-2 versus Pascal

In Pascal, a standard **File Type** is defined by

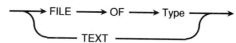

TEXT is a built-in file type representing character strings that allows redirection, as described in the "Declarations" section near the beginning of this appendix. A binary file also may be defined in Pascal to be of any type, such as

```
TYPE   NumFile : FILE OF INTEGER;
VAR   Counters : NumFile;
```

Opening, closing, reading, and writing these files is handled essentially in the same manner as the text files described earlier in this appendix. The variable Done is not provided in Pascal. However, the end of a file F can be detected by the built-in BOOLEAN function eof(F).

In Modula-2, there is no standard file type. Text and binary files are handled with special modules such as InOut and FileSystem, as described in this book.

Sets

☐ Syntax Diagrams

Set Type

$$\longrightarrow \text{SET} \longrightarrow \text{OF} \longrightarrow \text{Simple Type} \longrightarrow$$

Set

$$\longrightarrow \text{Qualified Identifier} \longrightarrow \{ \longrightarrow \text{Element} \longrightarrow \} \longrightarrow$$

Element

$$\longrightarrow \text{Expression} \longrightarrow .. \longrightarrow \text{Expression} \longrightarrow$$

☐ Modula-2 versus Pascal

In Pascal, **Set** values are defined with square brackets and without a preceding identifier; that is, as

$$\longrightarrow [\longrightarrow \text{Element} \longrightarrow] \longrightarrow$$

There is no Pascal equivalent of the Modula-2 BITSET. Set operations in Pascal include $+$, $-$, $*$, IN, $=$, $<>$, $<$, $>$, $<=$, and $>=$, but *not* INCL, EXCL, or $/$.

Pointers

☐ Syntax Diagram

Pointer Type

$$\longrightarrow \text{POINTER} \longrightarrow \text{TO} \longrightarrow \text{TYPE} \longrightarrow$$

☐ Modula-2 versus Pascal

In Pascal the **Pointer Type** definition is

$$\longrightarrow \text{^} \longrightarrow \text{Type} \longrightarrow$$

Storage would be allocated and deallocated for a pointer-type variable P in Pascal by the commands NEW(P) and DISPOSE(P), respectively. No SIZE or TSIZE functions are available in Pascal, so NEW and DISPOSE do not request the size of the referent. The referent of a pointer P is designated in Pascal, as in Modula-2, by **P∧**.

Procedure Passing

Syntax Diagram

Procedures and functions are passed as parameters in Modula-2 by declaring procedure types.

Procedure Type

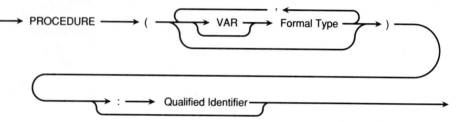

Modula-2 versus Pascal

Although there is no procedure type in Pascal, procedures and functions can be passed as parameters by including the procedure or function heading in its entirety within the parameter list. For example,

```
PROCEDURE  DoItNow( FUNCTION FindOne(x:REAL):INTEGER);
```

Built-in (predefined) procedures and functions cannot be used as actual parameters. Functions cannot return procedure values.

Other Features

Standard Pascal provides no built-in equivalent of LONGINT, LONGREAL, WORD, BYTE, or ADDRESS type, nor does it provide an ADR function. Coroutines and concurrent processes are not supported in standard Pascal. Equivalents of some of these features are found in some versions of Pascal, however.

E

Data Representations

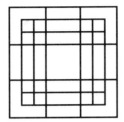

ASCII

Historically, a variety of codes have been used for CHARacter representations, including those for punched cards and paper tape, EBCDIC, ASCII, and many others. One of the currently most popular codes is the American Standard Code for Information Interchange (ASCII), which is presented here. If your system uses a different code, its definition should be available to you in the system manual. *(The first 32 ASCII codes are control characters.)*

Character	Decimal	Octal	Hexadecimal	Implementation on Some Keyboards
NUL (Null)	0	0	0	
SOH (Start of Header)	1	1	1	CTRL/A
STX (Start of Text)	2	2	2	CTRL/B
ETX (End of Text)	3	3	3	CTRL/C
EOT (End of Transmission)	4	4	4	CTRL/D
ENQ (Enquire)	5	5	5	CTRL/E
ACK (Acknowledge)	6	6	6	CTRL/F
BEL (Terminal Bell)	7	7	7	CTRL/G
BS (Backspace)	8	10	8	CTRL/H
HT (Horizontal Tab)	9	11	9	CTRL/I
LF (Line Feed)	10	12	A	CTRL/J
VT (Vertical Tab)	11	13	B	CTRL/K
FF (Form Feed)	12	14	C	CTRL/L
CR (Carriage Return)	13	15	D	CTRL/M
SO (Shift Out)	14	16	E	CTRL/N
SI (Shift In)	15	17	F	CTRL/O
DLE (Data Link Escape)	16	20	10	CTRL/P
DCI (Device Control 1)	17	21	11	CTRL/Q
DC2 (Device Control 2)	18	22	12	CTRL/R
DC3 (Device Control 3)	19	23	13	CTRL/S
DC4 (Device Control 4)	20	24	14	CTRL/T
NAK (Negative Acknowledge)	21	25	15	CTRL/U
SYN (Synchronous Idle)	22	26	16	CTRL/V
ETB (End Transmission Block)	23	27	17	CTRL/W
CAN (Cancel)	24	30	18	CTRL/X
EM (End of Medium)	25	31	19	CTRL/Y
SUB (Substitute)	26	32	1A	CTRL/Z
ESC (Escape)	27	33	1B	
FS (File Separator)	28	34	1C	
GS (Group Separator)	29	35	1D	
RS (Record Separator)	30	36	1E	\<Enter\>
US (Unit Separator)	31	37	1F	
SPACE	32	40	20	\<Space Bar\>
!	33	41	21	
,,	34	42	22	
#	35	43	23	
$	36	44	24	
%	37	45	25	
&	38	46	26	
,	39	47	27	
(	40	50	28	
)	41	51	29	
*	42	52	2A	
+	43	53	2B	
,	44	54	2C	
-	45	55	2D	
.	46	56	2E	
/	47	57	2F	
0	48	60	30	
1	49	61	31	
2	50	62	32	
3	51	63	33	

Character	Decimal	Octal	Hexadecimal	Implementation on Some Keyboards
4	52	64	34	
5	53	65	35	
6	54	66	36	
7	55	67	37	
8	56	70	38	
9	57	71	39	
:	58	72	3A	
;	59	73	3B	
<	60	74	3C	
=	61	75	3D	
>	62	76	3E	
?	63	77	3F	
@	64	100	40	
A	65	101	41	
B	66	102	42	
C	67	103	43	
D	68	104	44	
E	69	105	45	
F	70	106	46	
G	71	107	47	
H	72	110	48	
I	73	111	49	
J	74	112	4A	
K	75	113	4B	
L	76	114	4C	
M	77	115	4D	
N	78	116	4E	
O	79	117	4F	
P	80	120	50	
Q	81	121	51	
R	82	122	52	
S	83	123	53	
T	84	124	54	
U	85	125	55	
V	86	126	56	
W	87	127	57	
X	88	130	58	
Y	89	131	59	
Z	90	132	5A	
[	91	133	5B	
\	92	134	5C	
]	93	135	5D	
^	94	136	5E	
	95	137	5F	
`	96	140	60	
a	97	141	61	
b	98	142	62	
c	99	143	63	
d	100	144	64	
e	101	145	65	
f	102	146	66	
g	103	147	67	

Character	Decimal	Octal	Hexadecimal	Implementation on Some Keyboards
h	104	150	68	
i	105	151	69	
j	106	152	6A	
k	107	153	6B	
l	108	154	6C	
m	109	155	6D	
n	110	156	6E	
o	111	157	6F	
p	112	160	70	
q	113	161	71	
r	114	162	72	
s	115	163	73	
t	116	164	74	
u	117	165	75	
v	118	166	76	
w	119	167	77	
x	120	170	78	
y	121	171	79	
z	122	172	7A	
{	123	173	7B	
|	124	174	7C	
}	125	175	7D	
~	126	176	7E	
del	127	177	7F	

Parity Checking

Usually, a computer reserves one byte (8 bits) of memory space for a 7-bit ASCII character. The 8th bit often is ignored or used to double the number of characters in "extended" ASCII. Sometimes, however, the 8th bit is used for **parity checking.** (*Parity* refers to the odd vs. even correspondence between two integers.) Parity checking is achieved by appending an additional bit to a character code to help detect errors. On paper, the parity bit is usually written as the leftmost bit.

In even parity, the parity bit is assigned either a 0 or a 1, whichever is necessary to make the total number of 1s in the character (including the parity bit) an even number. Thus, the even-parity bit for ASCII K (1 0 0 1 0 1 1) is 0, which gives the code (0 1 0 0 1 0 1 1) an even number of 1s—it has 4. The even-parity bit for ASCII L (1 0 0 1 1 0 0) is 1, making the code 1 1 0 0 1 1 0 0—which also has an even number of bits. An accidental change of any bit in these character codes would make the total number of 1s odd and would be detected as a parity error. Similar, but opposite, considerations hold for odd parity, in which the total number of 1s in the code is an odd number.

Parity checking detects errors only if a single bit (or an odd number of bits) has been changed. This can be useful for checking data stored on a tape or disk. However, when data are moved over "noisy" transmission lines, errors can occur in bursts of many bits at a time. To detect errors in such cases, insertion of multiple parity bits in each character and other schemes, such as Cyclic Redundancy Check (CRC) calculations, have been devised.

Figure E–1
Binary, Decimal,
Octal, Hexadecimal
Equivalents

Binary	Decimal	Octal	Hexidecimal
0 000	0	0	0
0 001	1	1	1
0 010	2	2	2
0 011	3	3	3
0 100	4	4	4
0 101	5	5	5
0 110	6	6	6
0 111	7	7	7
1 000	8	10	8
1 001	9	11	9
1 010	10	12	A
1 011	11	13	B
1 100	12	14	C
1 101	13	15	D
1 110	14	16	E
1 111	15	17	F
00 01 0 000	16	20	10
00 01 0 001	17	21	11
00 01 0 010	18	22	12
00 01 0 011	19	23	13
00 01 0 100	20	24	14
00 01 0 101	21	25	15
00 01 0 110	22	26	16
00 01 0 111	23	27	17
00 01 1 000	24	30	18
00 01 1 001	25	31	19
00 01 1 010	26	32	1A
00 01 1 011	27	33	1B
00 01 1 100	28	34	1C
00 01 1 101	29	35	1D
00 01 1 110	30	36	1E
00 01 1 111	31	37	1F
00 10 0 000	32	40	20

Number Conversions

The first few binary numbers are shown in Figure E–1 with their decimal, octal, and hexadecimal equivalents. The binary numbers can be reproduced easily by noting that the units column alternates between 0 and 1 with successive numbers, the second column (representing $2^1 = 2$) alternates every two numbers, the third column (representing $2^2 = 4$) alternates every four numbers, the fourth column (representing $2^3 = 8$) alternates every eight numbers, and so on. Leading zeros in the binary numbers in the table are insignificant, just as are leading zeros in decimal numbers.

☐ Conversion between Octal, Binary, and Hexadecimal

In octal-to-binary number conversions and vice versa, each group of three binary digits is equivalent to one corresponding octal digit. In hexadecimal-to-binary conversions and vice versa, each group of four binary digits is equivalent to one corresponding hexadecimal digit.

Example E.1

Convert the binary number 1011110 to octal and to hexadecimal. Convert 7635 (octal) and 3F9 (hex) to binary.

Solution Segmenting 1011110 from the right into groups of three and padding the leftmost group with leading zeros yields 001 011 110. According to the chart in figure E-1, these are equivalent to octal digits *1, 3,* and *6,* respectively. Thus, 1011110 = 136 (octal).

Segmenting 1011110 from the right into groups of four and padding the leftmost group with a leading zero yields 0101 1110. Using figure E-1, these are found to be equivalent to hexadecimal digits *5* and *E*. Thus, 1011110 = 5E (hex).

Each digit in 7635 (octal) converts to three binary digits according to the chart. Thus, 7 6 3 5 (octal) = 111 110 011 101 (binary).

For 3F9 (hexadecimal), each hex digit corresponds to four binary digits in the chart. Thus, 3 F 9 (hex) = 0011 1111 1001 (binary).

☐ Conversion from Binary, Octal, and Hexadecimal to Decimal

To convert binary numbers to their decimal equivalents, use the definitions of the columns, as in this example.

Example E.2

Convert the binary number 1011110 to decimal.

Solution Observe first that decimal digits represent powers of 10, depending upon their place values. For example, the decimal number 4675 is really

	5 units	$= 5 \times 10^0$	=	5 ×	1	=	5
plus	7 tens	$= 7 \times 10^1$	=	7 ×	10	=	70
plus	6 hundreds	$= 6 \times 10^2$	=	6 ×	100	=	600
plus	4 thousands	$= 4 \times 10^3$	=	4 ×	1000	=	4000

1000	100	10	1	
10^3	10^2	10^1	10^0	
4	6	7	5	= 4675

Since binary counting is done by 2s, rather than by 10s, each column represents a power of 2. Thus 1 0 1 1 1 1 0 is

64	32	16	8	4	2	1
2^6	2^5	2^4	2^3	2^2	2^1	2^0
1	0	1	1	1	1	0

which equals

$$1 \times 64 \quad + \quad 0 \times 32 \quad + \quad 1 \times 16 \quad + \quad 1 \times 8 \quad + \quad 1 \times 4$$
$$+ \quad 1 \times 2 \quad + \quad 0 \times 1 \quad = \quad 94 \text{ (decimal)}.$$

Note that any number raised to the 0 power equals the value 1.

To convert octal numbers to decimal, consider that each digit represents a power of 8, and add the place values accordingly.

Example E.3

Convert 7635 (octal) to decimal.

Solution

512	64	8	1
8^3	8^2	8^1	8^0
7	6	3	5

equals

$$7 \times 512 \quad + \quad 6 \times 64 \quad + \quad 3 \times 8 \quad + \quad 5 \times 1 \quad = \quad 3997 \text{ (decimal)}.$$

Converting hexadecimal numbers to decimal is performed by the same process, where place values are powers of 16.

Example E.4

Convert 3F9 (hexadecimal) to decimal.

Solution

256	16	1
16^2	16^1	16^0
3	F	9

equals

$$3 \times 256 \quad + \quad F \times 16 \quad + \quad 9 \times 1;$$

but the decimal equivalent of F is 15. Therefore,

$$3 \, F \, 9 \text{ (hex)} \quad = \quad 3 \times 256 \quad + \quad 15 \times 16 \quad + \quad 9 \times 1 \quad = \quad 1017 \text{ (decimal)}.$$

Conversion from Decimal to Binary, Octal, and Hexadecimal

One of the simplest ways to convert a decimal number to binary is to perform repeated division by 2, keep track of the remainders at each step of the process, and then read the remainders from last to first.

Example E.5

Find the binary equivalent of the decimal number 215.

Solution Perform these operations:

	Remainder
215 divided by 2 = 107	1
107 divided by 2 = 53	1
53 divided by 2 = 26	1
26 divided by 2 = 13	0
13 divided by 2 = 6	1
6 divided by 2 = 3	0
3 divided by 2 = 1	1
1 divided by 2 = 0	1

Reading the remainders from the bottom up, we find that

$$215 \text{ (decimal)} = 1\ 1\ 0\ 1\ 0\ 1\ 1\ 1 \text{ (binary)}.$$

Conversions from decimal to octal and hexadecimal are performed by the same process, except that divisions are by 8 and 16, respectively.

Example E.6

Convert the decimal number 60182 to octal and to hexadecimal.

Solution Of course, the number could be converted to binary (by repeated division by 2) and the result converted directly to octal or hex. However, fewer divisions are necessary if you convert directly.

To convert to octal

	Remainder
60182 divided by 8 = 7522	Your calculator shows remainder 0.75, which is 6/8; thus the remainder is 6
7522 divided by 8 = 940	2
940 divided by 8 = 117	4
117 divided by 8 = 14	5
14 divided by 8 = 1	6
1 divided by 8 = 0	1

Reading the remainders from the bottom up gives you

$$60182 \text{ (decimal)} = 1\ 6\ 5\ 4\ 2\ 6 \text{ (octal)}.$$

Similarly,

	Remainder
60182 divided by 16 = 3761	Your calculator shows remainder 0.1375, which is 6/16; thus the remainder is 6
3761 divided by 16 = 235	1
235 divided by 16 = 14	11
14 divided by 16 = 0	14

Reading the remainders from the bottom up gives you 60182 (decimal) = 14 11 1 6 (hexadecimal); but the characters representing 14 and 11 in hexadecimal are *E* and *B*, respectively. Therefore,

$$60182 \text{ (decimal)} = E\ B\ 1\ 6 \text{ (hexadecimal)}.$$

Exercises

1. Convert each of these binary numbers to octal, hexadecimal, and decimal:
  a. 11011   **b.** 1111010   **c.** 10110110   **d.** 10110010111

2. Convert each of these hexadecimal values to binary, octal, and decimal:
  a. 5B   **b.** FACE

3. Convert each of these octal numbers to binary, hexadecimal, and decimal:
  a. 53   **b.** 2741

4. Convert each of these decimal numbers to binary, octal, and hexadecimal:
  a. 23   **b.** 193   **c.** 485   **d.** 5962

F

Solutions to Selected Exercises

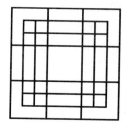

This appendix contains solutions to a few selected end-of-chapter exercises. These solutions are designed to help you learn by illustrating some problem-solving algorithms. Please keep in mind that often there are many ways to approach a problem. You will find here only one solution per exercise, certainly not the only solution, and in many instances it is not the most efficient or elegant solution. You may wish to expand upon these solutions by structuring them better, by making them more efficient or more user-friendly, or by extending their operation.

☐ Chapter 2

Exercise 8

Pseudocode for CH2EX8   JC Gordon   Dec 89

Begin. ThreeResistor
　　initialize values of the three resistors
　　　　for example,   R1 = 5.0,   R2 = 20.0,   R3 = 40.0
　　write question for user to screen
　　　"Are the three resistors connected in series or parallel? (S/P) "
　　　　read answer from keyboard
　　If Ans = S Then R = R1 + R2 + R3
　　Else If Ans = P Then R = 1.0 /((1/R1) + (1/R2) + (1/R3))
　　Else write message to screen "Incorrect answer, S or P"

　　write value of R to screen
　　　"The resistance value for the three resistors is" R
End ThreeResistor.

Exercise 16

```
MODULE PaymentResults;
    (*  Given loan, annual interest rate, and monthly payments calculate
        and print the portion of the first months payment that goes to
        interest and the portion that goes to principle, and the balance
        after the first payment.
        FileName:CH2EX16     Modula-2     JC Gordon     Jan 1990     *)
```

```
FROM InOut IMPORT WriteString, WriteLn;
FROM RealInOut IMPORT FWriteReal;

VAR  Loan, AnnualInt, Payment, MonthlyInt  :  REAL;
         ToPrinciple, ToInterest, Balance  :  REAL;

BEGIN    (* main module *)
   (* initialize variables *)
   Loan := 62000.00;    AnnualInt := 0.1;    Payment := 544.11;

   (* calculations *)
   MonthlyInt := AnnualInt / 12.0;
   ToInterest := Loan * MonthlyInt;  ToPrinciple := Payment - ToInterest;
   Balance := Loan - ToPrinciple;

   (* print header information to monitor *)
   WriteString("For a loan of $");FWriteReal(Loan,8,2);
     WriteString(" with an annual interest rate of ");
     FWriteReal(AnnualInt*100.0,2,0);WriteString("%");WriteLn;
   WriteString("and a monthly payment of $");FWriteReal(Payment,6,2);
     WriteString(" the first months payment");WriteLn;
     WriteString("would be broken out as follows:"); WriteLn;WriteLn;

   (* print calculation results to monitor *)
   WriteString("Amount out of payment to interest =");
     FWriteReal(ToInterest,6,2);WriteLn;
   WriteString("Amount out of payment to principle =");
     FWriteReal(ToPrinciple,6,2);WriteLn;
   WriteString("Balance after the first month =");
     FWriteReal(Balance,8,2); WriteLn;
END PaymentResults.
```

▢ Chapter 3

Exercise 5

```
MODULE Woodenbleevit;
   (* Program to calculate the scores for 5 rounds of the game Woodenbleevit.
      FileName:CH3EX5       Modula-2      JC Gordon      Jan 1990          *)

FROM InOut IMPORT WriteString, WriteLn, ReadCard, WriteCard;

VAR Rnd1Pts, Rnd2Pts, Rnd3Pts, Rnd4Pts, Rnd5Pts, LostPts,
     TrncPts1, TrncPts2, TrncPts3, TrncPts4, TrncPts5, TotalPts : CARDINAL;

BEGIN
   WriteString("Enter team scores for rounds ");WriteLn;
     WriteString(" 1: "); ReadCard(Rnd1Pts); WriteLn;
     WriteString(" 2: "); ReadCard(Rnd2Pts); WriteLn;
     WriteString(" 3: "); ReadCard(Rnd3Pts); WriteLn;
     WriteString(" 4: "); ReadCard(Rnd4Pts); WriteLn;
     WriteString(" 5: "); ReadCard(Rnd5Pts); WriteLn;

   LostPts := Rnd1Pts MOD 3  +  Rnd2Pts MOD 3  +  Rnd3Pts MOD 3
                 + Rnd4Pts MOD 3  +  Rnd5Pts MOD 3;
```

```
     TrncPts1 := Rnd1Pts DIV 3;   TrncPts2 := Rnd2Pts DIV 3;
        TrncPts3 := Rnd3Pts DIV 3;   TrncPts4 := Rnd4Pts DIV 3;
        TrncPts5 := Rnd5Pts DIV 3;
     TotalPts :=  TrncPts1 + TrncPts2 + TrncPts3 + TrncPts4 + TrncPts5;

     WriteString("The truncated team scores for the round are: "); WriteLn;
      WriteString(" 1: "); WriteCard(TrncPts1, 6); WriteLn;
      WriteString(" 2: "); WriteCard(TrncPts2, 6); WriteLn;
      WriteString(" 3: "); WriteCard(TrncPts3, 6); WriteLn;
      WriteString(" 4: "); WriteCard(TrncPts4, 6); WriteLn;
      WriteString(" 5: "); WriteCard(TrncPts5, 6); WriteLn; WriteLn;
     WriteString("For a total of "); WriteCard(TotalPts, 6); WriteLn; WriteLn;
      WriteString("Total points lost by truncating were");
      WriteCard(LostPts, 6); WriteLn;
END Woodenbleevit.
```

Exercise 10

```
MODULE HapHazardPhoneCosts;
    (* Reads time and distance values, from input file, used to calculate
       the cost of phone calls in Hap's Hazard County.
       FileName:CH3EX10   Modula-2    JC Gordon    Mar 1990          *)


FROM InOut IMPORT WriteString, WriteLn, OpenInput, CloseInput;
FROM RealInOut IMPORT ReadReal, FWriteReal;


VAR  TotalSoFar, T1, D1, T2, D2, T3, D3 : REAL;


(* procedure to calculate call costs *)
PROCEDURE CalcCosts(Time, Distance : REAL;  VAR TotalCost : REAL);
    VAR CallCost : REAL;
    BEGIN
       CallCost := 0.30 * (Time + 0.05 * (Distance));
       TotalCost := TotalCost + CallCost;
       FWriteReal(Time,7,2); FWriteReal(Distance,16,2);
       FWriteReal(CallCost,13,2); WriteLn;
    END CalcCosts;


BEGIN   (* main module *)
   WriteString("Enter name of your input file. ");  OpenInput ("DAT");
      (* read from input file *)
   ReadReal(T1); ReadReal(D1); ReadReal(T2); ReadReal(D2);
    ReadReal(T3); ReadReal(D3);
   CloseInput;

   WriteString("    TIME           DISTANCE           COST"); WriteLn;
   WriteString("——————————————————————————"); WriteLn;

   TotalSoFar := 0.0;
    (* call CalcCost procedure, sending it values for Time & Distance *)
    CalcCosts(T1,D1,TotalSoFar);   CalcCosts(T2,D2,TotalSoFar);
     CalcCosts(T3,D3,TotalSoFar);
```

```
    (* print total cost of calls *)
    WriteString("———————————————————"); WriteLn;
    WriteString("           Total Phone Costs = ");
     FWriteReal(TotalSoFar,7,2); WriteLn;
END HapHazardPhoneCosts.
```

▢ Chapter 4

Exercise 1a

```
MODULE CardEvenOdd;
    (*   Program to print, to the screen, either EVEN or ODD given a
         CARDINAL number entered at the keyboard by the user.
         FileName: CH4EX1A.MOD    Modula-2    JC Gordon    Mar 1990  *)

FROM InOut IMPORT WriteString, WriteLn, ReadCard;

VAR  Num, Rem  :  CARDINAL;

BEGIN
    WriteString("Type in your CARDINAL number (>= 0) and press RETURN: ");
     ReadCard(Num);WriteLn;

    Rem := Num MOD 2;
    IF Rem = 0 THEN
        WriteString("Your number is EVEN")
    ELSE
        WriteString("Your number is ODD")
    END;  (* IF *)
END CardEvenOdd.
```

Exercise 7

```
MODULE DollarToDwork;
    (*   Program to create a currency exchange table and write it to an
         output file on disk.
         FileName: CH4EX7    Modula-2    JC Gordon    Mar 1990   *)

FROM InOut IMPORT WriteString, WriteLn, OpenOutput, CloseOutput;
FROM RealInOut IMPORT ReadReal, FWriteReal;

CONST  ExchangeRate = 2.57;    Step = 0.10;
VAR  MinimumDollars, MaximumDollars, Dwork  :  REAL;

BEGIN
    WriteString("Enter low dollars : "); ReadReal(MinimumDollars); WriteLn;
    WriteString("Enter high dollars: "); ReadReal(MaximumDollars); WriteLn;
    WHILE MinimumDollars > MaximumDollars DO
        WriteString("Low must be less than High. Try again."); WriteLn;
        WriteString("Low  = "); ReadReal(MinimumDollars); WriteLn;
        WriteString("High = "); ReadReal(MaximumDollars); WriteLn;
    END;  (* WHILE *)  WriteLn;

    WriteString("What is the output file name: "); OpenOutput("OUT");WriteLn;
```

```
    WriteString("U. S. Dollar versus Dwork Currency Exchange Table ");
     WriteLn;WriteString("            (in steps of ");FWriteReal(Step,4,2);
     WriteString(" )");WriteLn;
     WriteString("  Current exchange rate =");FWriteReal(ExchangeRate,5,2);
     WriteString(" Dworks per Dollar");WriteLn;
     WriteLn;WriteString("    DOLLARS      DWORKS");WriteLn;WriteLn;

    WHILE MinimumDollars <= MaximumDollars DO
        FWriteReal(MinimumDollars,9,2); Dwork:=MinimumDollars/ExchangeRate;
        FWriteReal(Dwork,9,2); WriteLn;
        MinimumDollars := MinimumDollars + Step;
    END;  (* WHILE *)
    CloseOutput;     (*  close output file   *)
    WriteLn;WriteString("Program complete, check your output file.");
END DollarToDwork.
```

☐ Chapter 5

Exercise 2

```
MODULE CH5EX2;
    (* Chapter 5, Exercise 2.  Repeatedly asks the user for the
       radius of a sphere and returns the area and volume. *)

FROM InOut IMPORT WriteLn, WriteString, Read, Write;
FROM RealInOut IMPORT ReadReal, FWriteReal;

CONST  PI = 3.14159;
VAR  Radius : REAL;     Answer, ThrowAway : CHAR;

BEGIN
   Answer := 'Y';
   WHILE  (Answer = 'Y') OR (Answer = 'y')  DO
      WriteLn;  WriteString("What is the radius of the sphere? ");
       ReadReal(Radius); WriteLn;
      WriteString("The Area of the sphere = ");
       FWriteReal(4.0*PI*Radius*Radius, 12,2); WriteLn;
      WriteString("The Volume of the sphere = ");
       FWriteReal((4.0/3.0)*PI*Radius*Radius*Radius, 12,2); WriteLn;
      WriteLn; WriteString("Would you like to do it again (Y or N)?  ");
       Read(Answer);  Read(ThrowAway); Write(Answer); WriteLn;
   END; (* WHILE *)
END CH5EX2.
```

Exercise 16

```
MODULE CH5EX16;
    (* Chapter 5, Exercise 16.  Counts to 100 by 2's, 3's, 5's,
       or 7,s as specified by the user. *)

FROM InOut IMPORT WriteLn, WriteString, WriteCard, Read, Write;

VAR  Choice, ThrowAway : CHAR;     Count, NumOnLine : CARDINAL;

BEGIN
   Choice := 'A';
   WHILE   Choice # 'Q'  DO
```

```
                WriteLn; WriteString("What would you like to do?"); WriteLn;
                WriteString("   A    Count by 2's."); WriteLn;
                WriteString("   B    Count by 3's."); WriteLn;
                WriteString("   C    Count by 5's."); WriteLn;
                WriteString("   D    Count by 7's."); WriteLn;
                WriteString("   Q    Quit."); WriteLn;
                WriteString("Choose one (A, B, C, D, or Q):   ");
                    Read(Choice); Read(ThrowAway); Write(Choice); WriteLn;
                WHILE  NOT((Choice = 'Q') OR (Choice = 'A') OR (Choice = 'B')
                            OR (Choice = 'C') OR (Choice = 'D'))  DO
                    WriteString("Choose one (A, B, C, D, or Q):  ");
                     Read(Choice); Read(ThrowAway); Write(Choice); WriteLn;
                END; (* WHILE *)  WriteLn;
                IF  Choice # 'Q'  THEN
                   NumOnLine := 1;  Count := 0;
                   WHILE  Count <= 100   DO
                       WriteCard(Count, 10);
                       IF  Choice = 'A'  THEN  INC(Count,2);  END; (* IF *)
                       IF  Choice = 'B'  THEN  INC(Count,3);  END; (* IF *)
                       IF  Choice = 'C'  THEN  INC(Count,5);  END; (* IF *)
                       IF  Choice = 'D'  THEN  INC(Count,7);  END; (* IF *)
                       INC(NumOnLine);
                       IF  NumOnLine > 5  THEN  NumOnLine := 1;  WriteLn; END;(*IF*)
                   END; (* WHILE *)
                END; (* IF *)
            END; (* WHILE *)
    END CH5EX16.
```

☐ Chapter 6

Exercise 7

```
MODULE CH6EX7;
    (* Heron's formula for a triangle.  Chapter 6, Exercise 7 *)

FROM InOut IMPORT WriteString, WriteLn;    FROM MathLib0 IMPORT sqrt;
FROM RealInOut IMPORT FWriteReal, ReadReal;

VAR  Side1, Side2, Side3, Area : REAL;

PROCEDURE  CalcArea(a, b, c : REAL) : REAL;
    VAR  AreaSq, s, A : REAL;
    BEGIN
        s := (a + b + c) / 2.0;  AreaSq := s * (s - a) * (s - b) * (s - c);
        IF AreaSq<0.0 THEN  A := -1.0; ELSE  A := sqrt(AreaSq); END;(*IF*)
        RETURN A;
    END CalcArea;

BEGIN
    WriteString("Enter triangle sides: "); WriteLn;
     WriteString("Side1 = "); ReadReal(Side1); WriteLn;
     WriteString("Side2 = "); ReadReal(Side2); WriteLn;
     WriteString("Side3 = "); ReadReal(Side3); WriteLn; WriteLn;
    Area := CalcArea(Side1, Side2, Side3);

    IF  Area >= 0.0  THEN
       WriteString("The area = "); FWriteReal(Area,7,2);
```

```
      ELSE
        WriteString("These three sides cannot form a triangle.");
      END; (* IF *)  WriteLn;
END CH6EX7.
```

☐ Chapter 7

Exercise 8

```
MODULE CH7EX8;
   (* Chapter 7, Exercise8.  Converts decimal 0 - 255 to hex 00 - FF. *)

FROM InOut IMPORT WriteString, WriteLn, Write, ReadCard, WriteCard;

VAR  DecimalCode, HexDigit1, HexDigit2 : CARDINAL;
     HexChar1, HexChar2 : CHAR;

BEGIN
   WriteString("Tell me a Decimal code between 0 and 255: ");
    ReadCard(DecimalCode); WriteLn;
   HexDigit2 := DecimalCode MOD 16;
   HexDigit1 := (DecimalCode DIV 16) MOD 16;

   CASE  HexDigit1  OF
      0..9   : HexChar1 := CHR(ORD('0')+HexDigit1    ) |
      10..15 : HexChar1 := CHR(ORD('A')+HexDigit1-10);
   END; (* CASE *)
   CASE  HexDigit2  OF
      0..9   : HexChar2 := CHR(ORD('0')+HexDigit2)        |
      10..15: HexChar2 := CHR(ORD('A')+HexDigit2-10);
   END; (* CASE *)

   WriteString("Decimal Code "); WriteCard(DecimalCode,4);
    WriteString(" converts to Hex Code ");
    Write(HexChar1); Write(HexChar2); WriteLn;
END CH7EX8.
```

☐ Chapter 8

Exercise 2

```
MODULE CH8EX2;
   (* Chapter 8, Exercise 2.  Finds the sum of 1/1*2 + 1/2*3)+...+
      1/n*(n+1) using REPEAT.  NOT THE MOST EFFICIENT.  WHY?  *)

FROM InOut IMPORT WriteLn, WriteString, ReadCard, WriteCard;
FROM RealInOut IMPORT FWriteReal;

VAR  Sum : REAL;  WhichTerm, NumTerms : CARDINAL;

BEGIN
   WriteLn; WriteString("This program finds the sum"); WriteLn;
    WriteString("1/1*2  +  1/2*3  +  1/3*4  + ...  +  1/n*(n+1)");
    WriteLn; WriteString("Sum how many terms, n?  "); ReadCard(NumTerms);

   WhichTerm := 1;  Sum := 0.0;
   REPEAT
```

```
        Sum := Sum + 1.0/FLOAT(WhichTerm * (WhichTerm+1));
        INC(WhichTerm);
    UNTIL  WhichTerm > NumTerms;
    WriteLn; WriteString("The sums is"); FWriteReal(Sum,10,6); WriteLn;

    WriteLn; WriteString("For comparison, n/(n+1) = ");
     FWriteReal(FLOAT(NumTerms)/FLOAT(NumTerms+1), 10, 6); WriteLn;

    WriteLn; WriteString("So you can determine what the sum ");
     WriteString("approaches as n gets very large: "); WriteLn;
     WriteString("      n         Sum"); WriteLn;
    FOR  NumTerms := 1000 TO 10000 BY 1000  DO
        WriteCard(NumTerms,5);
        FWriteReal(FLOAT(NumTerms)/FLOAT(NumTerms+1),10,6); WriteLn;
    END; (* FOR *)
END CH8EX2.
```

Exercise 20b

```
MODULE CH8EX20B;
    (* Chapter 8, Exercise 20b.  Integrates a function Y(x) from a to b
       Uses Simpson's rule. *)

FROM InOut IMPORT WriteLn, WriteString, WriteCard;
FROM RealInOut IMPORT ReadReal, FWriteReal;   FROM MathLib0 IMPORT exp;

VAR  A, B : REAL;

PROCEDURE  Y(x : REAL) : REAL;
    (* Your function to integrate should be written in the
       RETURN command of this function procedure. *)
    BEGIN
      RETURN  5.0*exp(-x) - 2.0*x + 7.0;
    END Y;

PROCEDURE SimpsonRule(a, b : REAL);
     (* Simpson rule: n must be even,
        (delta/3)*(f(a) + 4f(a+delta) + 2(f(a+2delta) + ...(alternate
              4 then 2) ... + 2f(b-2delta) + 4f(b-delta) + f(b))   *)
    VAR  delta, x, Diff, TotalArea1, TotalArea2 : REAL;
         Count, NumIntervals : CARDINAL;
    BEGIN
       WriteLn; WriteString("PLEASE BE PATIENT.  This make take a while.");
        WriteLn; WriteLn;
       WriteLn; WriteString("Calculating to within 0.1% accuracy, ");
        WriteString("using Simpson's rule:"); WriteLn;
       WriteLn; WriteString("No. of Intervals      Approx. Area"); WriteLn;
       NumIntervals := 5;   TotalArea1 := 0.0;
       REPEAT
          NumIntervals := 2*NumIntervals; delta:=(b-a)/FLOAT(NumIntervals);
          TotalArea2 := (delta/3.0) * (Y(a) + Y(b));  x := a;
          FOR  Count := 1 TO NumIntervals-1  DO
             x := x + delta;
             IF  Count MOD 2 = 1  THEN
                TotalArea2 := TotalArea2 + (delta/3.0) * 4.0 * Y(x);
             ELSE
                TotalArea2 := TotalArea2 + (delta/3.0) * 2.0 * Y(x);
```

```
              END;  (* IF *)
          END;  (* FOR *)
          IF  ABS(TotalArea2) > 0.001   THEN
              Diff := 100.0*ABS(TotalArea2 - TotalArea1)/TotalArea2;
          ELSIF  ABS(TotalArea1) > 0.001   THEN
              Diff := 100.0*ABS(TotalArea2 - TotalArea1)/TotalArea1;
          ELSE
              Diff := 0.0;
          END;  (* IF *)
          TotalArea1 := TotalArea2;
          WriteCard(NumIntervals,16); FWriteReal(TotalArea2,16,4); WriteLn;
      UNTIL  ABS(Diff) < 0.1;
END SimpsonRule;


BEGIN (* main module *)
   WriteLn;  WriteString("Make sure the function Y(x) represents ");
    WriteString("the function to integrate."); WriteLn;
   WriteLn;  WriteString("Enter lower integration limit: ");
    ReadReal(A); WriteLn;
   REPEAT
      WriteString("Enter upper Integration limit:   ");
       ReadReal(B); WriteLn;
      IF  B <= A  THEN
          WriteString("Must have upper > lower.  Try again."); WriteLn;
      END;  (* IF *)
   UNTIL  B > A;

   SimpsonRule(A, B);   WriteLn;
END CH8EX20B.
```

☐ Chapter 9

Exercise 8

```
MODULE CH9EX8;
   (* Chapter 9, Exercise 8.  Counts the number of letters
      typed at random until one of the words  at,  is,  he,  me,
      we,  up,  or on  is produced. *)

FROM InOut IMPORT WriteLn, WriteString, ReadCard, WriteCard, Write;
FROM RandGen IMPORT Random;

VAR  Letter1, Letter2 : CHAR;   Seed, OnLine, Num, Count : CARDINAL;
     Test, WordTyped : BOOLEAN;

BEGIN (* main Module *)
   WriteLn; WriteString("Enter a Seed number between 0 and 65535:   ");
    ReadCard(Seed);   WriteLn;

   WordTyped := FALSE;    Count := 1;  OnLine := 1;
   Num := TRUNC(26.0 * Random(Seed) + 1.0);
   Letter1 := CHR(Num + 96);   Write(Letter1);

   REPEAT
      INC(Count);   INC(OnLine);
      Num := TRUNC(26.0 * Random(Seed) + 1.0);
```

```
      Letter2 := CHR(Num + 96);   Write(Letter2);
      IF  OnLine > 60  THEN  WriteLn; OnLine := 1; END; (* IF *)

      Test :=      ( (Letter1 = `a`)  AND   (Letter2 = `t`) )
               OR ( (Letter1 = `i`)  AND   (Letter2 = `s`) )
               OR ( (Letter2 = `e`)  AND   ( (Letter1 = `m`) OR
                     (Letter1 = `h`) OR (Letter1 = `w`) ) )
               OR ( (Letter1 = `u`)  AND   (Letter2 = `p`) )
               OR ( (Letter1 = `o`)  AND   (Letter2 = `n`) );

      IF  Test  THEN  WordTyped := TRUE;  END; (* IF *)
      Letter1 := Letter2;
   UNTIL  WordTyped;  WriteLn;

   WriteCard(Count, 5); WriteString(" letters were typed before");WriteLn;
   WriteString("at, is, he, me, we, up, or on  was produced."); WriteLn;
END CH9EX8.
```

☐   **Chapter 10**

Exercise 3

```
MODULE CH10EX3;
   (* Chapter 10, Exercise 3.  Reads a file of ACIYYYAACIY...
      and counts number of Adults, Children, Infants, and Youth
      admitted. *)

FROM InOut IMPORT Read, Done, WriteCard, WriteString, WriteLn,
                 OpenInput, OpenOutput, CloseInput, CloseOutput;

VAR  PeopleCount : ARRAY [1..4] OF CARDINAL;
     Entry : CHAR;  Counter : CARDINAL;

BEGIN
   OpenInput("IN");
   FOR Counter := 1 TO 4 DO  (* Initialize array to 0's *)
      PeopleCount[Counter] := 0;
   END; (* FOR *)

   LOOP
      Read(Entry);
      IF  NOT(Done)  THEN  EXIT;  END; (*IF*)
      CASE  Entry  OF
         `I` :   INC(PeopleCount[1]) |  `C` :   INC(PeopleCount[2])   |
         `Y` :   INC(PeopleCount[3]) |  `A` :   INC(PeopleCount[4])   ;
      END; (* CASE *)
   END; (* LOOP *)

   CloseInput; OpenOutput("OUT");
   WriteLn;  WriteString("People admitted:"); WriteLn;
   WriteString("Infants : "); WriteCard(PeopleCount[1], 6);WriteLn;
   WriteString("Children: "); WriteCard(PeopleCount[2], 6); WriteLn;
   WriteString("Youth   : "); WriteCard(PeopleCount[3], 6); WriteLn;
   WriteString("Adults  : "); WriteCard(PeopleCount[4], 6); WriteLn;
   CloseOutput;
END CH10EX3.
```

Exercise 12b

```
MODULE C10EX12b;
   (* Chapter 10, Exercise 12b.  Creates an array of cardinal values,
      then prints them backwards USING RECURSION, PART b ONLY. *)

FROM InOut IMPORT WriteLn, WriteString, WriteCard;

TYPE  CARDARRAY = ARRAY [1..10] OF CARDINAL;
VAR  Numbers : CARDARRAY;   Counter : CARDINAL;

PROCEDURE CreateArrayOfOdds(VAR Num : CARDARRAY);
   VAR  n : CARDINAL;
   BEGIN
      FOR  n := 1 TO 10  DO  Num[n]  := 2 * n + 1; END; (* FOR *)
   END CreateArrayOfOdds;

PROCEDURE RecursivePrint(Num : CARDARRAY;  Which : CARDINAL);
   BEGIN
      IF  Which = 1  THEN WriteCard(Num[1], 6);
       ELSE WriteCard(Num[Which], 6);  RecursivePrint(Num, Which-1);
      END; (* IF *)
   END RecursivePrint;

BEGIN (* main module *)
   CreateArrayOfOdds(Numbers);
   WriteLn; WriteString("An array of odd numbers:"); WriteLn;
   FOR Counter := 1 TO 10 DO  WriteCard(Numbers[Counter], 6); END;(*FOR*)

   WriteLn; WriteLn; WriteString("Backwards, using recursion:"); WriteLn;
   RecursivePrint(Numbers, 10);  WriteLn;
END C10EX12b.
```

☐ Chapter 11

Exercise 9

```
MODULE CH11EX9;
   (* Chapter 11, Exercise 9.  Handles simple hospital patient
      records, using subranges. *)

FROM InOut IMPORT WriteLn, ReadString, WriteString, ReadCard,
                 WriteCard, OpenInput, CloseInput;
FROM RealInOut IMPORT ReadReal, FWriteReal;

TYPE  CARE = CARDINAL [1..180];     AGE = CARDINAL [0..120];
VAR  Name : ARRAY [0..79] OF CHAR;  Age : AGE;  DaysOfCare : CARE;
     Bill : REAL;  Count, EnterAge, EnterDays : CARDINAL;

BEGIN
   WriteLn; WriteString("Name of input file?"); OpenInput ("IN");

   FOR  Count := 1 TO 10  DO
      ReadString(Name); WriteLn; ReadCard(EnterAge); WriteLn;
       Age := EnterAge;
      ReadCard(EnterDays); WriteLn; DaysOfCare := EnterDays;
       ReadReal(Bill); WriteLn; WriteLn;
```

```
      WriteString("Name:              "); WriteString(Name); WriteLn;
      WriteString("Age:               "); WriteCard(Age,4); WriteLn;
      WriteString("Days in Hospital: "); WriteCard(DaysOfCare,4); WriteLn;

      IF  Age < 65  THEN
         WriteString("Bill =  $"); FWriteReal(Bill, 10, 2);
      ELSIF  (Age >= 65) AND (Age < 72)  THEN
         WriteString("Bill with 20 percent senior discount =  $");
         FWriteReal(Bill*0.80, 10, 2); WriteLn;
         WriteString("Years left to collect before patient turns 72 =");
         WriteCard(72 - Age, 3);
      ELSE
         WriteString("It is too late to collect from this patient.");
         WriteLn; WriteString("You will have to take his/her  $");
         FWriteReal(Bill, 10, 2); WriteString("  as a loss.");
      END; (* IF *)  WriteLn;
   END; (* FOR *)                              CloseInput;
END CH11EX9.
```

Exercise 20c

```
MODULE CH11EX20c;
   (* Chapter 11, Exercise 20c.  Reads a file of ACIYYYAACIY...
      and counts number of Adults, Children, Infants, and Youth
      admitted. ARRAY INDICES OF TYPE PERSON.  PART c ONLY. *)

FROM InOut IMPORT Read, Done, WriteCard, WriteString, WriteLn,
                  OpenInput, OpenOutput, CloseInput, CloseOutput;

TYPE  PERSON = (Infant, Child, Youth, Adult);
VAR  PeopleCount : ARRAY PERSON OF CARDINAL;  Entry:CHAR;  Counter:PERSON;

BEGIN
   OpenInput("IN");
   FOR Counter := Infant TO Adult DO   (* Initialize array to 0's *)
      PeopleCount[Counter] := 0;
   END; (* FOR *)

   LOOP
      Read(Entry);
      IF  NOT(Done)  THEN  EXIT;  END;(*IF*)
      CASE  Entry  OF
         'I' :  INC(PeopleCount[Infant])  |
         'C' :  INC(PeopleCount[Child])   |
         'Y' :  INC(PeopleCount[Youth])   |
         'A' :  INC(PeopleCount[Adult])   ;
      END; (* CASE *)
   END; (* LOOP *)

   CloseInput; OpenOutput("OUT");
   WriteLn;  WriteString("People admitted:"); WriteLn;
   WriteString("Infants : "); WriteCard(PeopleCount[Infant], 6);WriteLn;
   WriteString("Children: "); WriteCard(PeopleCount[Child], 6); WriteLn;
   WriteString("Youth   : "); WriteCard(PeopleCount[Youth], 6); WriteLn;
   WriteString("Adults  : "); WriteCard(PeopleCount[Adult], 6); WriteLn;
   CloseOutput;
END CH11EX20c.
```

□ **Chapter 12**

Exercise 3

```
MODULE CH12EX3;
   (* Chapter 12, Exercise 3.  Plot Number of Particles versus angle. *)

FROM InOut IMPORT WriteString, WriteLn, OpenInput, CloseInput;
FROM Graphics IMPORT PlotIt, SortXY;     FROM RealInOut IMPORT ReadReal;

VAR  X, Y : ARRAY [1..11] OF REAL;    Particle : CARDINAL;

BEGIN
   WriteString("What is the input file name? ");  OpenInput("DAT");
     FOR  Particle := 1 TO 11  DO               (* Read the data *)
        ReadReal(X[Particle]);   ReadReal(Y[Particle]);
     END; (* FOR *)
   CloseInput;

   FOR  Particle := 1 TO 11  DO            (* Scale the Y values *)
     Y[Particle] := (Y[Particle] - 2500.0) / 100.0;
   END; (* FOR *)

   SortXY(X, Y);  PlotIt(X, Y);  WriteLn;
   WriteString("           PARTICLES VERSUS ANGLE"); WriteLn;
     WriteString("X ==> Angle (degrees)"); WriteLn;
     WriteString("Y ==> (Number of Particles - 2500) / 100.0"); WriteLn;
END CH12EX3.
```

Exercise 14

```
MODULE CH12EX14;
   (* Chapter 12, Exercise 14.  Generates a random array of 20
      cardinal values.  QuickSorts the array.  Asks for
      a Target cardinal value.  Performs a binary search. *)

FROM InOut IMPORT WriteString, ReadCard, WriteCard, WriteLn, WriteInt;
FROM RandGen IMPORT Random;

CONST  MaxSize = 20;
TYPE   LIST = ARRAY [1..MaxSize] OF CARDINAL;
VAR    Numbers : LIST;    Target : CARDINAL;
       Seed, Low, High, Index, J : CARDINAL;    Value : INTEGER;

PROCEDURE Partition(VAR Array : LIST;  VAR Up, Down : CARDINAL);
   VAR Pivot, TempNum : CARDINAL;
   BEGIN
      Pivot := (Up + Down) DIV 2;
      REPEAT
         WHILE Array[Up] < Array[Pivot]   DO  INC(Up); END; (* WHILE *)
         WHILE Array[Down] > Array[Pivot] DO  DEC(Down); END; (*WHILE*)
         IF  Up <= Down   THEN
            TempNum := Array[Down];  Array[Down] := Array[Up];
             Array[Up]:=TempNum;
            INC(Up);
            IF  Down > 0  THEN  DEC(Down); END; (* IF *)
```

```
         END; (* IF *)
      UNTIL  Up > Down;
   END Partition;

PROCEDURE QuickSort(VAR Array : LIST;  Left, Right : CARDINAL);
   VAR  Up, Down : CARDINAL;
   BEGIN
      IF  Left < Right  THEN
         Up := Left;  Down := Right;    Partition(Array, Up, Down);
         QuickSort(Array, Left, Down);  QuickSort(Array, Up, Right);
      END; (* IF *)
   END QuickSort;

PROCEDURE BinarySearch(VAR Array : LIST;  Target : CARDINAL;
                              Low, High : CARDINAL) : INTEGER;
   VAR  Position : CARDINAL;  ReturnIt : INTEGER;
   BEGIN
      Position  := (Low + High) DIV 2;  (* Position of middle element *)
      IF  (Array[Position] <> Target) AND (Low <= High)  THEN
         IF  Array[Position] > Target  THEN  High := Position - 1;
            ELSE  Low := Position + 1;
         END; (* IF *)
         RETURN BinarySearch(Array, Target, Low, High);
      ELSE
         IF  Array[Position] = Target  THEN  ReturnIt := Position;
            ELSE  ReturnIt := -1;
         END; (* IF *)
         RETURN  ReturnIt;
      END; (* IF *)
   END BinarySearch;

BEGIN  (* main module *)
   WriteString("Enter a Seed number between 0 and 65535: ");
    ReadCard(Seed); WriteLn;

   FOR Index := 1 TO MaxSize  DO  (* generate numbers *)
      Numbers[Index] := TRUNC(100.0 * Random(Seed) + 1.0);
   END; (* FOR *)

   Low := 1;  High := MaxSize;   QuickSort(Numbers, Low, High);
   WriteLn; WriteString("The sorted Numbers are: "); WriteLn;
   FOR  Index := 1 TO MaxSize  DO
      WriteCard(Index,4); WriteCard(Numbers[Index], 11); WriteLn;
   END; (* FOR Index *)  WriteLn;

   WriteString("For what number (1 to 100) were you searching? ");
    ReadCard(Target); WriteLn;   Low := 1;  High := MaxSize;

   Value := BinarySearch(Numbers, Target, Low, High);  WriteLn;
   IF  (Value >= 1)  AND  (Value <= VAL(INTEGER,MaxSize))  THEN
      WriteCard(Numbers[Value], 7);
       WriteString(" is at position "); WriteInt(Value,4);
       WriteString(" in the sorted array."); WriteLn;
   ELSE
      WriteCard(Target,7); WriteString(" is not in this array.");
   END; (* IF *)  WriteLn;
END CH12EX14.
```

☐ **Chapter 13**

Exercise 11

```
MODULE CH13EX11;
   (* Chapter 13, Exercise 11.  Inventory for a small firm. *)

FROM InOut IMPORT ReadString, WriteString, OpenInput, CloseInput,
                  OpenOutput, CloseOutput, ReadCard, WriteCard,
                  WriteLn;
FROM RealInOut IMPORT ReadReal, FWriteReal;
FROM Strings IMPORT CompareStrings, ReadLine;

TYPE   DESCRIP = ARRAY [1..80] OF CHAR;
       NAME = ARRAY [1..20] OF CHAR;
       CATDESCR = RECORD
                     Describe : DESCRIP;  CatNum : NAME;  CatPg : CARDINAL;
                  END;
       COST    = RECORD
                     Wholesale, RetMem, RetNon : REAL;
                  END;
       ITEM    = RECORD
                     ItemName : NAME;  Description : CATDESCR;  Cost : COST;
                  END;
       WHATSITS = ARRAY [1..30] OF ITEM;
VAR   Items : WHATSITS;   Count : CARDINAL;

PROCEDURE ReadRecords(VAR What:WHATSITS; VAR HowMany:CARDINAL);
   BEGIN
      HowMany := 0;   ReadLine(What[HowMany+1].ItemName);
      WHILE  CompareStrings(What[HowMany+1].ItemName, "ZZZZZZ") <> 0   DO
         INC(HowMany);
         ReadLine(What[HowMany].Description.Describe);
         ReadString(What[HowMany].Description.CatNum);
         ReadCard(What[HowMany].Description.CatPg);
         ReadReal(What[HowMany].Cost.Wholesale);
         ReadLine(What[HowMany+1].ItemName);
      END; (* WHILE *)
   END ReadRecords;

PROCEDURE WriteRecords(What:WHATSITS; HowMany:CARDINAL);
   VAR   Which : CARDINAL;
   BEGIN
      FOR  Which := 1 TO HowMany  DO
         WriteString("Item Name: ");
          WriteString(What[Which].ItemName); WriteLn;
         WriteString("Description: ");
          WriteString(What[Which].Description.Describe); WriteLn;
         WriteString("Catalog Page and Catalog Number: ");
          WriteCard(What[Which].Description.CatPg, 4); WriteString("   ");
          WriteString(What[Which].Description.CatNum); WriteLn;
         WriteString("Costs (WholeSale, Member, NonMember): $ ");
          FWriteReal(What[Which].Cost.Wholesale,7,2);
          FWriteReal(What[Which].Cost.RetMem,7,2);
          FWriteReal(What[Which].Cost.RetNon,7,2); WriteLn; WriteLn;
```

```
    END;  (* FOR *)
END WriteRecords;


PROCEDURE CompleteData(VAR What:WHATSITS;  HowMany:CARDINAL);
    VAR  Which : CARDINAL;
    BEGIN
        FOR  Which := 1 TO HowMany  DO
            WITH  What[Which].Cost  DO
                RetMem := Wholesale  +  0.1 * Wholesale;
                RetNon := Wholesale  +  0.3 * Wholesale;
            END; (* WITH *)
        END; (* FOR *)
    END CompleteData;

PROCEDURE SortByPage(VAR Whats:WHATSITS;  N:CARDINAL);
    (* Selection sort on catalog page numbers *)
    VAR  LastIndex, MaxPage, SubListIndex : CARDINAL;   TempWhat : ITEM;
    BEGIN
        FOR  LastIndex := N TO 2 BY -1  DO
            MaxPage := 1;
            FOR  SubListIndex := 2 TO LastIndex  DO
                IF  Whats[MaxPage].Description.CatPg <
                            Whats[SubListIndex].Description.CatPg   THEN
                    MaxPage := SubListIndex;
                END; (* IF *)
            END; (* FOR SubListIndex *)

            TempWhat := Whats[MaxPage];  Whats[MaxPage] := Whats[LastIndex];
            Whats[LastIndex] := TempWhat;
        END; (* FOR LastIndex *)
    END SortByPage;

PROCEDURE SearchNonPrices(Whats:WHATSITS;  N:CARDINAL);
    VAR  Which : CARDINAL;
    BEGIN
        WriteLn; WriteString("NonMember prices for the following ");
        WriteString("items are less than $ 25.00"); WriteLn;
        WriteString("NonMember Price $     Item"); WriteLn;
        FOR  Which := 1 TO N  DO
            IF  Whats[Which].Cost.RetNon < 25.00   THEN
                FWriteReal(Whats[Which].Cost.RetNon,7,2);
                WriteString("                   ");
                WriteString(Whats[Which].ItemName); WriteLn;
            END; (* IF *)
        END; (* FOR *)
    END SearchNonPrices;

BEGIN (* module CH13EX14 *)
    WriteString("What is the name of the input file? ");  OpenInput("DAT");
    ReadRecords(Items, Count);  CloseInput;

    CompleteData(Items, Count);  WriteLn;
    WriteString("The items in the inventory are:"); WriteLn;
    WriteRecords(Items, Count);    WriteLn;
```

```
SortByPage(Items, Count);    WriteLn;
WriteString("Sorted by catalog page number, the items are:"); WriteLn;
WriteRecords(Items, Count);   WriteLn; WriteLn;
WriteString("Store this information in which file?"); OpenOutput("OUT");
WriteRecords(Items, Count);                           CloseOutput;

SearchNonPrices(Items, Count);
END CH13EX11.
```

☐ Chapter 14

Exercise 4b

```
MODULE CH14EX4B;
    (* THIS HAS LOTS OF STRING AND NUMBER FILE HANDLING PROCEDURES
       which you may find useful to put in an external file.
       NO GUARANTEES of absolute accuracy are claimed. *)

    (* Chapter 14, Exercise 4b.  Uses arrays and FileSystem procedures
       to accumulate, store, and plot balloon launcher sales and
       revenues.  *)

FROM InOut IMPORT WriteLn, WriteString, ReadCard, WriteCard, ReadString;
FROM FileSystem IMPORT File, Lookup, Close, ReadChar, WriteChar;
FROM RealInOut IMPORT ReadReal, FWriteReal;
FROM Graphics IMPORT PlotIt, BarPlot, LinePlot;
FROM Strings IMPORT Length, Concatenate;

CONST  MONTHS = 24;
TYPE   LAUNCHREC = RECORD
                      NumSold : CARDINAL;
                      Price, Revenue : REAL;
                   END; (* RECORD *)
       LAUNCHARY = ARRAY [1..MONTHS] OF LAUNCHREC;
VAR   Launchers, Balloons : LAUNCHARY;
      f : File;   FileName : ARRAY [1..14] OF CHAR;

PROCEDURE WriteStringToFile(VAR f : File;  Value : ARRAY OF CHAR);
   VAR  N, i : CARDINAL;
   BEGIN
      N := Length(Value) - 1;
       FOR  i := 0  TO  N  DO  WriteChar(f, Value[i]);  END; (* FOR *)
   END WriteStringToFile;

PROCEDURE ReadStringFromFile(VAR f:File;  VAR Value:ARRAY OF CHAR);
    (* This procedure ignores leading characters with code less than
       or equal to Space, then reads characters until a character with
       code <= Space is encountered.  It concatenates the  characters
       to Value. *)
    VAR  Letter : ARRAY [0..0] OF CHAR;
    BEGIN
       REPEAT
          ReadChar(f, Letter[0]);
       UNTIL  ORD(Letter[0]) > 32;
       Value[0]  := 0C;   (* Initialize to empty string. *)
       WHILE  ORD(Letter[0]) > 32  DO
```

```
            Concatenate(Value, Letter[0], Value);
            ReadChar(f, Letter[0]);
         END; (* WHILE *)
   END ReadStringFromFile;

PROCEDURE WriteCardToFile(VAR f : File;  Num : CARDINAL);
   VAR  DigitRep : CHAR;
   BEGIN
      DigitRep := CHR( Num MOD 10  + ORD('0') );
      Num  :=  Num DIV 10;
      IF  Num > 0  THEN  WriteCardToFile(f, Num);  END; (* IF *)
      WriteChar(f, DigitRep);
   END WriteCardToFile;

PROCEDURE StringToCard(In:ARRAY OF CHAR;  VAR Out:CARDINAL);
   VAR  i, j, N, Power, Mult : CARDINAL;
   BEGIN
      Out := 0;    N := Length(In) - 1;
      FOR  i := 0 TO N  DO
         Power := N - i;  Mult := 1;
         IF  Power > 0  THEN
            FOR j := 1 TO Power  DO  Mult := Mult * 10; END; (* FOR j *)
         END; (* IF *)
         Out  :=  Out  +  (ORD(In[i]) - ORD('0')) * Mult;
      END; (* FOR *)
   END StringToCard;

PROCEDURE StringToReal(In:ARRAY OF CHAR;  VAR Out:REAL);
   (* The string must have at least one digit before and at
      least one digit after the decimal point, even if those
      digits are 0. Total number of digits, including
      decimal point should not exceed 10, and there should be
      no more than 4 digits after the decimal point. *)
   VAR  N, i, DigitsBeforeDec, TenPower, StartOfFrac : CARDINAL;
        Digit : ARRAY [0..10] OF CARDINAL;    Fraction : REAL;
   BEGIN
      N := Length(In) - 1; (* Handle the whole number part *)
      i := 0;
      Digit[i] := ORD(In[i]) - ORD('0');  INC(i);
      WHILE  In[i] # '.'  DO
         Digit[i] := ORD(In[i]) - ORD('0');  INC(i);
      END; (* WHILE *);
      DigitsBeforeDec := i;  Out := FLOAT(Digit[0]);
      IF  DigitsBeforeDec > 1  THEN
         FOR  i := 1  TO  DigitsBeforeDec-1  DO
            Out := Out * 10.0  + FLOAT(Digit[i]);
         END; (* FOR *)
      END; (* IF *)
              (* Handle decimal fraction part *)
      StartOfFrac := DigitsBeforeDec + 1; TenPower := 1; Fraction := 0.0;
      IF  N >= StartOfFrac  THEN
         FOR  i := StartOfFrac TO N  DO
            TenPower := TenPower * 10; Digit[i] := ORD(In[i]) - ORD('0');
            Fraction := Fraction + FLOAT(Digit[i])/FLOAT(TenPower);
         END; (* FOR *)
      END; (* IF *)
```

```
        Out := Out + Fraction;
    END StringToReal;

PROCEDURE WriteRealToFile(VAR f:File;  RNum:REAL;  ND:CARDINAL);
    (* ND = number of digits to be written after the decimal
        point.  Writes a 0 before the decimal point if RNum < 1.0 *)
    VAR  i, Card1, Card2, TenPower : CARDINAL;
    BEGIN
        Card1 := TRUNC(RNum); TenPower := 1;
        FOR  i := 1 TO ND  DO
            TenPower := TenPower * 10;
        END; (* FOR *)
        Card2 := TRUNC( RNum - FLOAT(TRUNC(RNum)*TenPower) + 0.5 );
        IF  Card1 = 0  THEN  WriteChar(f, '0');
          ELSE  WriteCardToFile(f, Card1);
        END; (* IF *)
        WriteChar(f, '.');  WriteCardToFile(f, Card2);
    END WriteRealToFile;


PROCEDURE ReadSales(VAR BL:LAUNCHARY);
    VAR  i : CARDINAL;
    BEGIN
        WriteLn; WriteString("Enter Sales: "); WriteLn;
        FOR  i := 1 TO MONTHS  DO
            WITH  BL[i]  DO
                WriteString("Month"); WriteCard(i,3);
                WriteString("  No. Sold?  "); ReadCard(NumSold);
                WriteString("          Unit Price $ "); ReadReal(Price);
            END; (* WITH *) WriteLn;
        END; (* FOR *)
    END ReadSales;


PROCEDURE CalcRevenues(VAR BL:LAUNCHARY);
    VAR  i : CARDINAL;
    BEGIN
        FOR  i := 1 TO MONTHS  DO
            BL[i].Revenue := FLOAT(BL[i].NumSold) * BL[i].Price;
        END; (* FOR *)
    END CalcRevenues;


PROCEDURE StoreToFile(BL:LAUNCHARY);
    VAR  i : CARDINAL;
    BEGIN
        WriteLn; WriteString("Enter output file name  ");
        ReadString(FileName); Lookup(f, FileName, TRUE);
        FOR  i := 1 TO MONTHS  DO
            WITH  BL[i]  DO
                WriteCardToFile(f,NumSold);  WriteStringToFile(f,"  ");
                WriteRealToFile(f,Price,2); WriteStringToFile(f,"  ");
                WriteRealToFile(f,Revenue,2); WriteStringToFile(f,"  ");
            END; (* WITH *)
        END; (* FOR *)    Close(f);
    END StoreToFile;


PROCEDURE ReadFromFile(VAR BL:LAUNCHARY);
    VAR  i : CARDINAL; TempNum, TempPr, TempRev : ARRAY [1..20] OF CHAR;
```

```
      BEGIN
         WriteLn; WriteString("Enter same file name  ");
         ReadString(FileName); Lookup(f, FileName, FALSE);
         FOR  i := 1 TO MONTHS  DO
            WITH  BL[i]  DO
                ReadStringFromFile(f,TempNum); ReadStringFromFile(f,TempPr);
                ReadStringFromFile(f,TempRev);
                StringToCard(TempNum, NumSold); StringToReal(TempPr,Price);
                StringToReal(TempRev, Revenue);
            END; (* WITH *)
         END; (* FOR *)    Close(f);
      END ReadFromFile;

PROCEDURE  PlotNumbers(BL:LAUNCHARY);
   VAR  X, Y : ARRAY [1..MONTHS] OF REAL;    i : CARDINAL;
   BEGIN
      FOR  i := 1 TO MONTHS  DO
         X[i] := FLOAT(i);    Y[i] := FLOAT(BL[i].NumSold);
      END; (* FOR *)
      PlotIt(X,Y);   WriteLn; WriteLn;
      WriteString("Plot of No. of Balloon Launchers vs. Month"); WriteLn;
      WriteString("   X ==> Month       Y ==> No. Launchers"); WriteLn;
   END PlotNumbers;

PROCEDURE  PlotRevenues(BL:LAUNCHARY);
   VAR  X, Y : ARRAY [1..MONTHS] OF REAL;    i : CARDINAL;
   BEGIN
      FOR  i := 1 TO MONTHS  DO
         X[i] := FLOAT(i);    Y[i] := BL[i].Revenue;
      END; (* FOR *)
      PlotIt(X,Y);   WriteLn; WriteLn;
      WriteString("Plot of Balloon Launch Revenues vs. Month"); WriteLn;
      WriteString("   X ==> Month       Y ==> $ Revenue"); WriteLn;
   END PlotRevenues;

BEGIN (* main module *)
   ReadSales(Launchers);
   CalcRevenues(Launchers);
   StoreToFile(Launchers);
   ReadFromFile(Balloons);
   PlotNumbers(Balloons);
   PlotRevenues(Balloons);
END CH14EX4B.
```

☐ Chapter 15

Exercise 5

```
MODULE CH15EX5;
   (* Chapter 15, Exercise 5.  Finds solution set of (3x + 5) < (32 + x). *)

FROM InOut IMPORT WriteString, WriteLn, ReadCard, WriteCard;

TYPE  SMALLNUMS = [0..15];
      SMALLNUMSET = SET OF SMALLNUMS;
VAR  SolutionSet : SMALLNUMSET;      x : CARDINAL;
```

```
BEGIN
   SolutionSet := SMALLNUMSET{ };
   FOR  x := 0 TO 15   DO
      IF  (3*x  + 5) < (32 + x)   THEN INCL(SolutionSet, x); END;(*IF*)
   END; (* FOR *)  WriteLn;

   WriteString("There are some small cardinal values between 0");
    WriteString(" and 16 which are"); WriteLn;
    WriteString("solutions to the inequality (3x + 5) < (32 + x).");
    WriteLn; WriteLn;
   REPEAT
      WriteLn;
      WriteString(" What is your guess for a solution?");
      WriteString(" Enter a value > 16 to stop: ");ReadCard(x); WriteLn;
      IF  x  IN  SolutionSet  THEN
         WriteString("Correct,"); WriteCard(x,3);
         WriteString(" is a solution. "); WriteLn;
      ELSE
         WriteString("Sorry,"); WriteCard(x,3);
         WriteString(" is not a solution. "); WriteLn;
      END; (* IF *)
   UNTIL  x > 16;
END CH15EX5.
```

☐ Chapter 16

Exercise 15

```
MODULE CH16EX15;
   (* Chapter 16, Exercise 15.  Creates a linked list of people
      sorted by decreasing age in a Number field. *)

FROM InOut IMPORT WriteString, WriteLn, ReadString, Read, Write,
                  OpenOutput, CloseOutput;
FROM RealInOut IMPORT ReadReal, FWriteReal;
FROM DYNLT IMPORT MAXCHS, CreateLinkList, AddToLinkList,
                  DeleteFromLinkList, POINTTOLIST, WHATSINLIST;
FROM Strings IMPORT Length, CompareStrings, TabOrFill;

CONST  Blank = ' ';
VAR  ThisList : POINTTOLIST;    TempContent : WHATSINLIST;
     CapChoice : CHAR;  Deleted : BOOLEAN;

PROCEDURE PresentMenu(VAR Chose : CHAR);
   VAR Choose, Discard : CHAR;
   BEGIN
      WriteLn; WriteString("What would you like to do?"); WriteLn;
      WriteString("      A      Add a Member to the List"); WriteLn;
      WriteString("      D      Delete a Member from the List");WriteLn;
      WriteString("      U      Update a Member record");WriteLn;
      WriteString("      P      Print the Linked List"); WriteLn;
      WriteString("      S      Stop"); WriteLn;
      REPEAT
         WriteString("Choose one (A, D, P, S): ");
         Read(Choose); Read(Discard); Write(Choose); WriteLn; WriteLn;
         Chose := CAP(Choose);
```

```
        UNTIL  (Chose = 'A') OR (Chose = 'D') OR (Chose = 'P')
                            OR (Chose = 'S')  OR (Chose = 'U');
    END PresentMenu;

PROCEDURE  PrintTheList(StartOfList:POINTTOLIST);
    PROCEDURE  PrintLinkRecord(WhereInList: POINTTOLIST);
        BEGIN
            IF  WhereInList # NIL  THEN  (* past end of list *)
                WITH  WhereInList^  DO  (* Display record content. *)
                    WriteString(Characters);
                    TabOrFill(MAXCHS + 1 - Length(Characters), Blank);
                    FWriteReal(Number,10,0); WriteLn;
                END; (* WITH *)
                WhereInList := WhereInList^.NextRecPtr;
                PrintLinkRecord(WhereInList);
            END; (* IF WhereInList *)
        END PrintLinkRecord;
    BEGIN (* PrintTheList *)
        PrintLinkRecord(StartOfList);
    END PrintTheList;

PROCEDURE  AddItNow(VAR StartOfList: POINTTOLIST; WhatToAdd: WHATSINLIST);
    VAR  Previous, LookAt : POINTTOLIST;
    BEGIN
        IF  (StartOfList = NIL)  OR ( (StartOfList # NIL) AND
                        (StartOfList^.Number < WhatToAdd.Number) )   THEN
            Previous := NIL;
        ELSE  (* New record goes somewhere other than at beginning. *)
            LookAt := StartOfList;
            REPEAT
                Previous := LookAt;  LookAt := Previous^.NextRecPtr;
            UNTIL  (LookAt^.Number < WhatToAdd.Number)
                    OR (LookAt = NIL);  (* New record goes at end of list. *)
        END; (* IF *)
        AddToLinkList(StartOfList, Previous, WhatToAdd);
    END AddItNow;

PROCEDURE  DeleteItNow(VAR StartOfList: POINTTOLIST;
                WhatToDelete: WHATSINLIST; VAR Deleted:BOOLEAN);
    VAR  Previous, LookAt : POINTTOLIST;
    BEGIN
        Deleted := FALSE;
        IF (StartOfList = NIL) (* List is empty. *)  OR
            (CompareStrings(StartOfList^.Characters,
                    WhatToDelete.Characters)=0) (*Delete 1st Rec*) THEN
            Previous := NIL;  LookAt := StartOfList;
        ELSE  (* Delete from somewhere other than first record. *)
            LookAt := StartOfList;
            REPEAT
                Previous := LookAt; LookAt := Previous^.NextRecPtr;
            UNTIL (LookAt = NIL) (*End of list found*) OR (*Record Found*)
                (CompareStrings(LookAt^.Characters, WhatToDelete.Characters)=0);
        END; (* IF *)
        IF  LookAt # NIL  THEN  Deleted := TRUE; END;(*IF*)
        DeleteFromLinkList(StartOfList, Previous, LookAt);
    END DeleteItNow;
```

```
PROCEDURE DoWhatNow(Chose : CHAR);
   BEGIN
      CASE   Chose  OF
         'A' : WriteString("What record should I add?"); WriteLn;
                 WriteString("Member's Name: ");
                 ReadString(TempContent.Characters); WriteLn;
                 WriteString("Member's Age : ");
                 ReadReal(TempContent.Number); WriteLn;
                 AddItNow(ThisList, TempContent)        |
         'D' : WriteString("What record should I delete?");WriteLn;
                 WriteString("Member's Name: ");
                 ReadString(TempContent.Characters); WriteLn;
                 DeleteItNow(ThisList, TempContent, Deleted)   |
         'P' : PrintTheList(ThisList)  |
         'U' : WriteString("What record should I update?");WriteLn;
                 WriteString("Member's Name: ");
                 ReadString(TempContent.Characters); WriteLn;
                 WriteString("Member's Previous Age : ");
                 ReadReal(TempContent.Number); WriteLn;
                 DeleteItNow(ThisList, TempContent, Deleted);
                 IF  Deleted  THEN
                    TempContent.Number := TempContent.Number + 1.0;
                    AddItNow(ThisList, TempContent);
                 END; (* IF *)
      END; (* CASE *)
   END DoWhatNow;

BEGIN  (* module TestLink *)
   CreateLinkList(ThisList);
   REPEAT
      PresentMenu(CapChoice);
      DoWhatNow(CapChoice);
   UNTIL  CapChoice = 'S';  WriteLn;

   WriteString("Write results to what file? ");   OpenOutput("DAT");
   PrintTheList(ThisList);                         CloseOutput;
END CH16EX15.
```

☐ Chapter 17

Exercise 14a

```
MODULE CH17EX14A;
   (* Chapter 17, Exercise 14a.  Uses coroutines to parse and
      evaluate expressions such as  3+5-7=. *)

FROM InOut IMPORT WriteString, WriteLn, WriteInt;
FROM SYSTEM IMPORT WORD, NEWPROCESS, TRANSFER, ADDRESS, ADR;
FROM Strings IMPORT Length, ReadLine;

CONST  SizeWorkSpace = 1000;
TYPE  STR = ARRAY [0..49] OF CHAR;
VAR  WorkSpParse,WorkSpAdd,WorkSpSubtr: ARRAY [1..SizeWorkSpace] OF WORD;
     MainProg, ParseCor, AddCor, SubtrCor : ADDRESS;
     Count, Answer : INTEGER;  Num : CARDINAL;
     Expr : STR;       OK : BOOLEAN;       Op : CHAR;
```

```
PROCEDURE EnterString(VAR Expr : STR);
   VAR  WhichChar : CARDINAL;
   BEGIN
      WriteLn; WriteString("Enter a valid arithmetic expression with ");
      WriteString("positive single digit values,"); WriteLn;
      WriteString("separated by + or - operators."); WriteLn;
      WriteString("NO SPACES, TERMINATE WITH = THEN <Enter>."); WriteLn;
      REPEAT
         WriteString("For example: 7+9-2+1-5=<Enter>  "); ReadLine(Expr);
         (* Check for validity *) WriteLn;  Count := 0;  OK := TRUE;
         FOR WhichChar := 0 TO Length(Expr)-1  DO
            IF NOT( ((Expr[WhichChar]>='0') AND (Expr[WhichChar]<='9'))
              OR (Expr[WhichChar]='+') OR (Expr[WhichChar]='-')
              OR (Expr[WhichChar]='=') ) THEN    OK := FALSE;
            END; (* IF *)
             IF (Expr[WhichChar]>='0') AND (Expr[WhichChar]<='9') THEN
               INC(Count);
              ELSE  DEC(Count);
             END; (* IF *)
         END; (* FOR *)
         IF (Count#0) OR (Expr[Length(Expr)-1]#'=') THEN OK := FALSE; END;
         IF NOT(OK) THEN WriteString("Invalid. Try again: "); END;(*IF*)
      UNTIL OK;
   END EnterString;

PROCEDURE Parse;
   BEGIN
      Count := 0;  Answer := VAL(INTEGER, ORD(Expr[Count])-ORD('0'));
      LOOP
         INC(Count);  Op := Expr[Count];
         IF  Op = '='  THEN  EXIT;  END; (* IF *)
            INC(Count);  Num := ORD(Expr[Count]) - ORD('0');
            IF  Op = '+' THEN
               TRANSFER(ParseCor, AddCor);
            ELSIF  Op = '-' THEN
               TRANSFER(ParseCor, SubtrCor);
         END; (* IF *)
      END; (* LOOP *)
      WriteString(Expr); WriteInt(Answer, 8); WriteLn;
   END Parse;

PROCEDURE Add;
   BEGIN
      LOOP
         Answer := Answer+VAL(INTEGER, Num); TRANSFER(AddCor, ParseCor);
      END; (* LOOP *)
   END Add;

PROCEDURE Subtr;
   BEGIN
      LOOP
         Answer := Answer-VAL(INTEGER, Num); TRANSFER(SubtrCor, ParseCor);
      END; (* LOOP *)
   END Subtr;

BEGIN (* MainProg *)
   EnterString(Expr);
```

```
    NEWPROCESS(Parse, ADR(WorkSpParse), SIZE(WorkSpParse), ParseCor);
    NEWPROCESS(Add, ADR(WorkSpAdd), SIZE(WorkSpAdd), AddCor);
    NEWPROCESS(Subtr, ADR(WorkSpSubtr), SIZE(WorkSpSubtr), SubtrCor);
    TRANSFER(MainProg, ParseCor);
END CH17EX14A.
```

Index

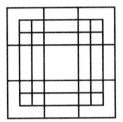